Strategic Management

CUSTOM EDITION

Dess; McNamara

Glasgow Caledonian University

ISBN 13: 9781308891613

McGraw-Hill Custom Publishing

http://create.mheducation.com/uk/

Published by McGraw-Hill Education, 2 Penn Plaza, New York, NY 10121.

Copyright ©2016 by McGraw-Hill Education. All rights reserved. No part of this publication may be reproduced or distributed in any form or by any means, or stored in a database or retrieval system, without prior written permission of the publisher, including, but not limited to, any network or other electronic storage or transmission, or broadcast for distance learning.

This McGraw-Hill Custom text may include materials submitted to McGraw-Hill for publication by the instructor of this course. The instructor is solely responsible for the editorial content of such materials.

Cover image: ©iStock.com

ISBN: **9781308891613**

Strategic Management
CUSTOM EDITION

Contents

i. Dedication 1
ii. About the Authors 2
iii. Preface 4
iv. A Guided Tour 16

Strategic Analysis 19
1. The Strategic Management Process 21
2. Strategic Management: Creating Competitive Advantages 22
3. Analyzing the External Environment of the Firm: Creating Competitive Advantages 56
4. Assessing the Internal Environment of the Firm 94
5. Recognizing a Firm's Intellectual Assets: Moving beyond a Firm's Tangible Resources 128

Strategic Formulation 165
6. Business-Level Strategy: Creating and Sustaining Competitive Advantages 166
7. Corporate-Level Strategy: Creating Value through Diversification 200
8. International Strategy: Creating Value in Global Markets 232
9. Entrepreneurial Strategy and Competitive Dynamics 268

Strategic Implementation 299
10. Strategic Control and Corporate Governance 300
11. Creating Effective Organizational Designs 336
12. Strategic Leadership: Creating a Learning Organization and an Ethical Organization 370
13. Managing Innovation and Fostering Corporate Entrepreneurship 402

Case Analysis 437
14. Analyzing Strategic Management Cases 438

Cases 479
15. Robin Hood 481
16. Edward Marshall Boehm, Inc. 483
17. American International Group and the Bonus Fiasco 484
18. Southwest: is Luv Soaring? 487
19. Jetblue Airlines: Getting Over the "Blues"? 494
20. Backers Beware: Kickstarter Is Not a Store 501
21. Weight Watchers International Inc. 507
22. Dippin Dots: is the Future Frozen? 518

23. Jamba Juice: Feeling the Squeeze or Juicing Up? 528
24. Ann Taylor: Survival in Specialty Retail 537
25. Greenwood Resources: A Global Sustainable Venture in the Making 548
26. Tata Starbucks: How to Brew a Sustainable Blend for India 562
27. Avon: A New Era? 569
28. The Boston Beer Company: Poised for Growth 579
29. Zynga: Room for a Final Round or is the Game Over? 591
30. Apple Inc.: Still Taking a Bite Out of the Competition? 597
31. Campbell: How to Keep the Soup Simmering 610
32. United Way Worldwide 623
33. The Global Casino Industry 632
34. Ebay 636
35. Yahoo! 648
36. World Wrestling Entertainment 653
37. QVC 659
38. Nintendo's Wii U 664
39. Mcdonald's 674
40. Procter & Gamble 680
41. Microfinance: Going Global . . . and Going Public? 686
42. Samsung Electronics 689
43. Heineken 695
44. Freshdirect: is it Really Fresh? 700
45. Johnson & Johnson 713
46. General Motors 719
47. Is One Ford Really Working? 725
48. Emirates Airline 742
49. Cirque Du Soleil 750
50. Pixar 754
51. Rhino Capture in Kruger National Park 759
A. Company Index 771
B. Name Index 781
C. Subject Index 793
D. Clear and Rigorous Concepts Deserve Fresh & Excellent Cases 815
E. Endsheet 822

Credits

i. Dedication: *Chapter from Strategic Management: Text and Cases, Eighth Edition by Dess, McNamara, Eisner, 2016* 1
ii. About the Authors: *Chapter from Strategic Management: Text and Cases, Eighth Edition by Dess, McNamara, Eisner, 2016* 2
iii. Preface: *Chapter from Strategic Management: Text and Cases, Eighth Edition by Dess, McNamara, Eisner, 2016* 4
iv. A Guided Tour: *Chapter from Strategic Management: Text and Cases, Eighth Edition by Dess, McNamara, Eisner, 2016* 16

Strategic Analysis 19
1. The Strategic Management Process: *Chapter from Strategic Management: Text and Cases, Eighth Edition by Dess, McNamara, Eisner, 2016* 21
2. Strategic Management: Creating Competitive Advantages: *Chapter 1 from Strategic Management: Text and Cases, Eighth Edition by Dess, McNamara, Eisner, 2016* 22
3. Analyzing the External Environment of the Firm: Creating Competitive Advantages: *Chapter 2 from Strategic Management: Text and Cases, Eighth Edition by Dess, McNamara, Eisner, 2016* 56
4. Assessing the Internal Environment of the Firm: *Chapter 3 from Strategic Management: Text and Cases, Eighth Edition by Dess, McNamara, Eisner, 2016* 94
5. Recognizing a Firm's Intellectual Assets: Moving beyond a Firm's Tangible Resources: *Chapter 4 from Strategic Management: Text and Cases, Eighth Edition by Dess, McNamara, Eisner, 2016* 128

Strategic Formulation 165
6. Business-Level Strategy: Creating and Sustaining Competitive Advantages: *Chapter 5 from Strategic Management: Text and Cases, Eighth Edition by Dess, McNamara, Eisner, 2016* 166
7. Corporate-Level Strategy: Creating Value through Diversification: *Chapter 6 from Strategic Management: Text and Cases, Eighth Edition by Dess, McNamara, Eisner, 2016* 200
8. International Strategy: Creating Value in Global Markets: *Chapter 7 from Strategic Management: Text and Cases, Eighth Edition by Dess, McNamara, Eisner, 2016* 232
9. Entrepreneurial Strategy and Competitive Dynamics: *Chapter 8 from Strategic Management: Text and Cases, Eighth Edition by Dess, McNamara, Eisner, 2016* 268

Strategic Implementation 299
10. Strategic Control and Corporate Governance: *Chapter 9 from Strategic Management: Text and Cases, Eighth Edition by Dess, McNamara, Eisner, 2016* 300
11. Creating Effective Organizational Designs: *Chapter 10 from Strategic Management: Text and Cases, Eighth Edition by Dess, McNamara, Eisner, 2016* 336
12. Strategic Leadership: Creating a Learning Organization and an Ethical Organization: *Chapter 11 from Strategic Management: Text and Cases, Eighth Edition by Dess, McNamara, Eisner, 2016* 370
13. Managing Innovation and Fostering Corporate Entrepreneurship: *Chapter 12 from Strategic Management: Text and Cases, Eighth Edition by Dess, McNamara, Eisner, 2016* 402

Case Analysis 437
14. Analyzing Strategic Management Cases: *Chapter 13 from Strategic Management: Text and Cases, Eighth Edition by Dess, McNamara, Eisner, 2016* 438

Cases 479
15. Robin Hood: *Strategic Management: Text and Cases, Eighth Edition* 481
16. Edward Marshall Boehm, Inc.: *Strategic Management: Text and Cases, Eighth Edition* 483
17. American International Group and the Bonus Fiasco: *Strategic Management: Text and Cases, Eighth Edition* 484
18. Southwest: is Luv Soaring?: *Strategic Management: Text and Cases, Eighth Edition* 487
19. Jetblue Airlines: Getting Over the "Blues"?: *Strategic Management: Text and Cases, Eighth Edition* 494
20. Backers Beware: Kickstarter Is Not a Store: *Strategic Management: Text and Cases, Eighth Edition* 501
21. Weight Watchers International Inc.: *Strategic Management: Text and Cases, Eighth Edition* 507
22. Dippin Dots: is the Future Frozen?: *Strategic Management: Text and Cases, Eighth Edition* 518
23. Jamba Juice: Feeling the Squeeze or Juicing Up?: *Strategic Management: Text and Cases, Eighth Edition* 528
24. Ann Taylor: Survival in Specialty Retail: *Strategic Management: Text and Cases, Eighth Edition* 537
25. Greenwood Resources: A Global Sustainable Venture in the Making: *Strategic Management: Text and Cases, Eighth Edition* 548
26. Tata Starbucks: How to Brew a Sustainable Blend for India: *Strategic Management: Text and Cases, Eighth Edition* 562
27. Avon: A New Era?: *Strategic Management: Text and Cases, Eighth Edition* 569
28. The Boston Beer Company: Poised for Growth: *Strategic Management: Text and Cases, Eighth Edition* 579
29. Zynga: Room for a Final Round or is the Game Over?: *Strategic Management: Text and Cases, Eighth Edition* 591
30. Apple Inc.: Still Taking a Bite Out of the Competition?: *Strategic Management: Text and Cases, Eighth Edition* 597
31. Campbell: How to Keep the Soup Simmering: *Strategic Management: Text and Cases, Eighth Edition* 610
32. United Way Worldwide: *Strategic Management: Text and Cases, Eighth Edition* 623
33. The Global Casino Industry: *Strategic Management: Text and Cases, Eighth Edition* 632
34. Ebay: *Strategic Management: Text and Cases, Eighth Edition* 636
35. Yahoo!: *Strategic Management: Text and Cases, Eighth Edition* 648
36. World Wrestling Entertainment: *Strategic Management: Text and Cases, Eighth Edition* 653
37. QVC: *Strategic Management: Text and Cases, Eighth Edition* 659
38. Nintendo's Wii U: *Strategic Management: Text and Cases, Eighth Edition* 664
39. Mcdonald's: *Strategic Management: Text and Cases, Eighth Edition* 674
40. Procter & Gamble: *Strategic Management: Text and Cases, Eighth Edition* 680
41. Microfinance: Going Global . . . and Going Public?: *Strategic Management: Text and Cases, Eighth Edition* 686
42. Samsung Electronics: *Strategic Management: Text and Cases, Eighth Edition* 689
43. Heineken: *Strategic Management: Text and Cases, Eighth Edition* 695
44. Freshdirect: is it Really Fresh?: *Strategic Management: Text and Cases, Eighth Edition* 700
45. Johnson & Johnson: *Strategic Management: Text and Cases, Eighth Edition* 713
46. General Motors: *Strategic Management: Text and Cases, Eighth Edition* 719
47. Is One Ford Really Working?: *Strategic Management: Text and Cases, Eighth Edition* 725
48. Emirates Airline: *Strategic Management: Text and Cases, Eighth Edition* 742
49. Cirque Du Soleil: *Strategic Management: Text and Cases, Eighth Edition* 750
50. Pixar: *Strategic Management: Text and Cases, Eighth Edition* 754
51. Rhino Capture in Kruger National Park: *Instructor submitted material* 759
A. Company Index: *Chapter from Strategic Management: Text and Cases, Eighth Edition by Dess, McNamara, Eisner, 2016* 771
B. Name Index: *Chapter from Strategic Management: Text and Cases, Eighth Edition by Dess, McNamara, Eisner, 2016* 781
C. Subject Index: *Chapter from Strategic Management: Text and Cases, Eighth Edition by Dess, McNamara, Eisner, 2016* 793
D. Clear and Rigorous Concepts Deserve Fresh & Excellent Cases: *Chapter from Strategic Management: Text and Cases, Eighth Edition by Dess, McNamara, Eisner, 2016* 815
E. Endsheet: *Chapter from Strategic Management: Text and Cases, Eighth Edition by Dess, McNamara, Eisner, 2016* 822

DEDICATION

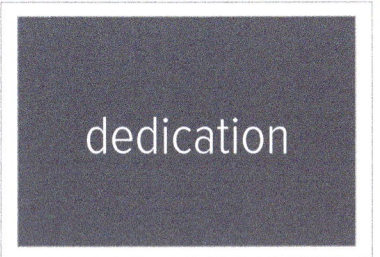

To my family, Margie and Taylor; my parents, Bill and Mary Dess; and Michael Wood

—Greg

To my wonderful wife, Gaelen; my children, Megan and AJ; and my parents, Gene and Jane

—Gerry

To my family, Helaine, Rachel, and Jacob

—Alan

We'd like to thank Tom Lumpkin for his many valuable contributions to previous editions of *Strategic Management.* We certainly wish him the best with his scholarship, work as Co-Editor of *Strategic Entrepreneurship Journal,* and other professional endeavors.

ABOUT THE AUTHORS

Gregory G. Dess

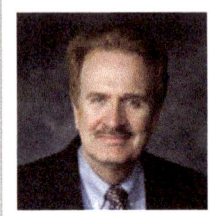

is the Andrew R. Cecil Endowed Chair in Management at the University of Texas at Dallas. His primary research interests are in strategic management, organization–environment relationships, and knowledge management. He has published numerous articles on these subjects in both academic and practitioner-oriented journals. He also serves on the editorial boards of a wide range of practitioner-oriented and academic journals. In August 2000, he was inducted into the *Academy of Management Journal*'s Hall of Fame as one of its charter members. Professor Dess has conducted executive programs in the United States, Europe, Africa, Hong Kong, and Australia. During 1994 he was a Fulbright Scholar in Oporto, Portugal. In 2009, he received an honorary doctorate from the University of Bern (Switzerland). He received his PhD in Business Administration from the University of Washington (Seattle) and a BIE degree from Georgia Tech.

Gerry McNamara

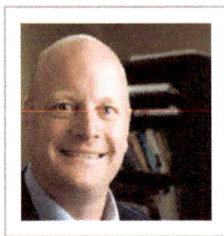

is a Professor of Management at Michigan State University. He received his PhD from the Carlson School of Management at the University of Minnesota. His research focuses on strategic decision making, organizational risk taking, and mergers and acquisitions. His research has been published in numerous journals, including the *Academy of Management Journal, Strategic Management Journal, Organization Science, Organizational Behavior and Human Decision Processes, Journal of Management,* and *Journal of International Business Studies.* Dr. McNamara's research on mergers and acquisitions has been abstracted in *The Wall Street Journal, Harvard Business Review, The New York Times, Bloomberg Businessweek, The Economist,* and *Financial Week.* He served as an Associate Editor for the *Academy of Management Journal* and currently serves on the editorial boards of the *Academy of Management Journal* and the *Strategic Management Journal.*

Alan B. Eisner

is Professor of Management and Department Chair, Management and Management Science Department, at the Lubin School of Business, Pace University. He received his PhD in management from the Stern School of Business, New York University. His primary research interests are in strategic management, technology management, organizational learning, and managerial decision making. He has published research articles and cases in journals such as *Advances in Strategic Management, International Journal of Electronic Commerce, International Journal of Technology Management, American Business Review, Journal of Behavioral and Applied Management,* and *Journal of the International Academy for Case Studies.* He is the former Associate Editor of the Case Association's peer-reviewed journal, *The CASE Journal.*

PREFACE

Welcome to the Eighth Edition of *Strategic Management: Text and Cases!* We are all very pleased with the constructive and positive feedback that we have received on our work. Here's some of the encouraging feedback we have received from our reviewers:

The content is current and my students would find the real-world examples to be extremely interesting. My colleagues would want to know about and I would make extensive use of the following features: "Learning from Mistakes," "Strategy Spotlights," "Issues for Debate," and I especially like the "Reflecting on Career Implications" feature. Bottom line: The authors do a great job of explaining complex material and at the same time their use of up-to-date examples promotes learning.

Jeffrey Richard Nystrom, University of Colorado at Denver

The application of key strategic management concepts to real-world examples throughout the book is superb. They engage the students and provide a way for them to understand the relevance of what can sometimes be abstract and complicated. The cases are engaging and challenging, providing an excellent way for students to perform strategic analysis and gain confidence in doing so.

Krista B. Lewellyn, University of Wyoming

There are many strengths: (1) explanations of concepts are clear and concise, yet comprehensive, (2) covers new developments in the field when new editions are published, and (3) covers the strategic analysis concepts (e.g., industry analysis, resources and capabilities, etc.) very well. Great textbook. I think it is the best in the market, and that is why I have used it for over seven years.

Moses Acquaah, University of North Carolina at Greensboro

The text is thorough and all-inclusive. I don't need to refer to another book as a backup. It addresses all aspects of strategic management from the initial inspiration of a vision to the nuts and bolts of putting the plan to work. It is well structured; it is clear not only how each chapter builds on the previous ones but also how analysis, formulation, and implementation are interrelated.

Lois Shelton, California State University, Northridge

I use *Strategic Management* in a capstone course required of all business majors, and students appreciate the book because it synergizes all their business education into a meaningful and understandable whole. My students enjoy the book's readability and tight organization, as well as the contemporary examples, case studies, discussion questions, and exercises.

William Sannwald, San Diego State University

It is the best-written textbook for the undergraduate course that I have come across. Application materials tie concepts to real-world practice.

Justin L. Davis, Ohio University

The Dess book overcomes many of the limitations of the last book I used in many ways: (a) presents content in a very interesting and engrossing manner without compromising the depth and comprehensiveness, (b) inclusion of timely and interesting illustrative examples, (c) includes an excellent array of long, medium, and short cases that can be used to balance depth and variety, and (d) EOC exercises do an excellent job of complementing the chapter content.

Sucheta Nadkarni, University of Cambridge

We work hard to improve our work and we are most appreciative of the extensive and constructive feedback that many strategy professionals have graciously given us. We strive to incorporate their ideas into the Eighth Edition—and we acknowledge them by name later in the Preface.

We believe we have made valuable improvements throughout our many revised editions of *Strategic Management.* At the same time, we strive to be consistent and "true" to our original overriding objective: a book that satisfies three R's: relevant, rigorous, and readable. That is, our tagline (paraphrasing the well-known Secret deodorant commercial) is "Strong enough for the professor; made for the student." And we are pleased that we have received feedback (such as the comments on the previous page) that is consistent with what we are trying to accomplish.

To continue to earn the support of strategy instructors (and students!), we try to use an engaging writing style that minimizes unnecessary jargon and covers all of the traditional bases. We also integrate some central themes throughout the book—such as globalization, technology, ethics, environmental sustainability, and entrepreneurship—that are vital in understanding strategic management in today's global economy. We draw on short examples from business practice to bring concepts to life by providing 72 Strategy Spotlights (more detailed examples in sidebars).

Unlike other strategy texts, we provide three separate chapters that address timely topics about which business students should have a solid understanding. These are the role of intellectual assets in value creation (Chapter 4), entrepreneurial strategy and competitive dynamics (Chapter 8), and fostering entrepreneurship in established organizations (Chapter 12). We also provide an excellent and thorough chapter on how to analyze strategic management cases.

In developing *Strategic Management: Text and Cases,* we certainly didn't forget the instructors. As we all know, you have a most challenging (but rewarding) job. We did our best to help you. We provide a variety of supplementary materials that should help you in class preparation and delivery. For example, our chapter notes do not simply summarize the material in the text. Rather (and consistent with the concept of strategy), we ask ourselves: "How can we add value?" Thus, for each chapter, we provide numerous questions to pose to help guide class discussion, at least 12 boxed examples to supplement chapter material, and three detailed "teaching tips" to further engage students. For example, we provide several useful insights on strategic leadership from one of Greg's colleagues, Charles Hazzard (formerly Executive Vice President, Occidental Chemical). Also, we completed the chapter notes—along with the entire test bank—ourselves. That is, unlike many of our rivals, we didn't simply farm the work out to others. Instead, we felt that such efforts help to enhance quality and consistency—as well as demonstrate our personal commitment to provide a top-quality total package to strategy instructors. With the Eighth Edition, we also benefited from valued input by our strategy colleagues to further improve our work.

Let's now address some of the key substantive changes in the Eighth Edition. Then we will cover some of the major features that we have had in previous editions.

What's New? Highlights of the Eighth Edition

We have endeavored to add new material to the chapters that reflects the feedback we have received from our reviewers as well as the challenges today's managers face. Thus, we all invested an extensive amount of time carefully reviewing a wide variety of books, academic and practitioner journals, and the business press.

We also worked hard to develop more concise and tightly written chapters. Based on feedback from some of the reviewers, we have tightened our writing style, tried to eliminate redundant examples, and focused more directly on what we feel is the most important content in

PREFACE

each chapter for our audience. The overall result is that we were able to update our material, add valuable new content, and—at the same time—shorten the length of the chapters.

Here are some of the major changes and improvements in the Eighth Edition:

- **A new feature: "Insights from Executives."** We have conducted six interviews with executives from a wide variety of organizations. They have been extremely helpful in addressing issues that are salient to strategic management. We sincerely appreciate their participation, and we acknowledge each of them later in the Preface. For example, in Chapter 3, Lise Saari (Former Director of Global Employee Research, IBM) addresses some of the challenges facing organizations when it comes to recruiting and developing talent, and she considers why some human resource initiatives may fail. In Chapter 7, Terrie Campbell (Vice President of Strategic Marketing at Ricoh Americas Corporation) points out some of the challenges associated with adapting marketing strategies to local tastes and markets, and she explains how she can help ensure that managers and employees throughout Ricoh have a global perspective. And, in Chapter 8, David Drews (Executive Vice President and CFO of Project: WorldWide, a global network of marketing agencies) discusses the common drivers of new venture failures as well as the importance of social networks in creating competitive advantages.

- **A new feature: "Insights from Research."** We include this feature in six chapters of the Eighth Edition. In "Insights from Research," we summarize key research findings on a variety of issues and, more importantly, address their relevance for making organizations (and managers!) more effective. For example, in Chapter 2 we discuss findings from a meta-analysis (research combining many individual studies) to debunk several myths about older workers—a topic of increasing importance, given the changing demographics in many developed countries. In Chapter 4, we address a fascinating study that found that "dormant ties" (people we have not been in contact with for at least three years) can be extremely valuable. And, in Chapter 8, we explore useful research findings to consider when leading virtual teams.

    In each of the first 12 chapters, we include one of the two new Insights features to enrich our text.

- **Most of the 12 opening "Learning from Mistakes" vignettes that lead off each chapter are totally new.** Unique to this text, they are all examples of what can go wrong, and they serve as an excellent vehicle for clarifying and reinforcing strategy concepts. After all, what can be learned if one simply admires perfection?

- **Half of our "Strategy Spotlights" (sidebar examples) are brand new, and many of the others have been thoroughly updated.** Although we have reduced the number of Spotlights from the previous edition to conserve space, we still have a total of 72—by far the most in the strategy market. We focus on bringing the most important strategy concepts to life in a concise and highly readable manner. And we work hard to eliminate unnecessary detail that detracts from the main point we are trying to make. Also, consistent with our previous edition, many of the Spotlights focus on three "hot" issues that are critical in leading today's organizations: ethics, environmental sustainability, and crowdsourcing.

Key content changes for the chapters include:

- **Chapter 1 addresses challenges associated with making a business case for sustainability initiatives.** The ROI on sustainability projects is difficult to quantify for many reasons: Necessary data are often not available, many of the benefits are intangible, and the projects may require a longer payback period. We provide examples from three companies that have endeavored to overcome such challenges by stressing the intangible benefits the firm may attain as well as the importance of taking a broader stakeholder perspective in evaluating such initiatives.

- **Chapter 2 discusses the value of "perceptual acuity" in assessing the environment.** The term *perceptual acuity* was coined by Ram Charan, an adviser to many Fortune 500 CEOs. He defines it as "the ability to sense what is coming before the fog clears." He provides examples of how some executives have enhanced their perceptual acuity by constantly meeting with people and searching out information.
- **Chapter 3 addresses the perils and challenges associated with integrating customers into their firm's value chain.** Clearly, firms can benefit by incorporating their customers into the value creation process. For example, firms can team up with customers to design and build products to satisfy their particular needs. Or firms can leverage the power of crowdsourcing. However, there can be downsides. For example, customers can "hijack" crowdsourcing efforts, and rather than offering constructive feedback, they may address serious concerns—or even ridicule the company!
- **Chapter 4 discusses how a firm's human capital can be enhanced by redefining jobs, as well as the importance of recognizing both inherent and acquired diversity.** Many successful firms are redefining the jobs of their most valuable talent by transferring some of their less critical tasks to lower-skilled employees either inside or outside the company. Hence, by redefining high-value knowledge jobs, organizations can not only successfully address skills shortages but also lower costs and enhance job satisfaction. In this chapter, we also distinguish between two types of diversity—inherent (e.g., race and gender) and acquired (e.g., traits gained by experience). Findings indicate that companies whose leaders exhibited such "two-dimensional diversity" not only enjoyed greater market share gains but also were more likely to capture new markets.
- **Chapter 5 discusses the value of data analytics as a means to achieve an integrated overall low-cost and differentiation strategy.** While it is a challenge to pursue both differentiation and low cost simultaneously, some successful firms are finding that using data analytics allows them to better customize their product and service offerings to customers while more efficiently and fully using the resources of the company. We illustrate the potential power of data analytics with examples from Pepsi and Kaiser Permanente.
- **Chapter 6 addresses research that highlights the importance of the effective allocation of corporate capital in the portfolio management of diversified firms and presents a discussion of the concept of an "acq-hire."** Recent research has supported the contention that the effective allocation of resources is a central and important role of corporate offices in diversified firms. However, studies have also found that many firms do not adjust their capital allocations in response to changes in the performance of units or the attractiveness of the markets in which units of the corporation compete. We discuss when the need to reallocate resources is critical, and we highlight that the effective use of corporate resources can be a source of competitive advantage for diversified firms. We also discuss the concept of an acq-hire, in which a firm purchases another firm primarily to hire key personnel from the target firm. We use Apple's acquisition of Beats as a prime example of this phenomenon.
- **Chapter 7 discusses an additional motive for international expansion—learning—and outlines concerns about how the rule of law has declined in the U.S. in recent years, increasing the political risk of operating in the U.S.** Expanding into new

PREFACE

geographic markets has, at times, been seen as an action that can distract managers from succeeding in the firm's home markets. We discuss how expansion into new markets provides a range of learning opportunities for firms, and we provide research evidence showing that international expansion often leads to improvements in home-market performance. Also, while the U.S. has long been seen as a business-friendly market, we discuss how changes in U.S. laws and regulations in recent years have made it a less attractive market for firms to enter or invest in.

- **Chapter 8 addresses two key issues associated with entrepreneurial firms: ways to deliberately search for entrepreneurial ideas and the personality traits of successful entrepreneurs.** We include a set of structured actions experienced entrepreneurs use to look for new entrepreneurial opportunities, including asking yourself questions about frustrations with current products or processes; having conversations with employees, customers, and suppliers; looking at shifts in other markets that could be translated to your market; and looking for ideas used in the past but forgotten and unexploited now. We also discuss how successful entrepreneurs differ from corporate managers on the Big Five personality traits.

- **Chapter 9 includes an extended discussion of nonmonetary incentive systems and a new discussion on the attentional focus of effective boards.** A number of studies have found that for employees who are satisfied with their base salary, nonfinancial motivators are more effective than cash incentives in building long-term employee motivation. We discuss three key ways firms can motivate their employees beyond the simple use of cash. We have also added a discussion of how the boards of directors of effective companies differ from the boards of ineffective firms in regard to the time they spend on board activities and how they focus their time.

- **Chapter 10 discusses the concept of a holacracy—an extreme version of a boundaryless organization.** To succeed in highly dynamic markets, according to some scholars and managers, firms need to ditch formal hierarchies and become more democratic. We discuss one type of structure that reflects this ideal, the holacracy. Most firms using this type of structure are small start-ups. There are obvious challenges in using a democratic structure in large firms. Zappos, the first large firm to try using a holacracy, is identified as a natural experiment to see if this new type of design has potential in larger firms.

- **Chapter 11 discusses the attributes of a learning organization. In this edition, we discuss how leadership development is a key aspect of a learning organization.** To learn and grow, firms need to continually build the leadership skills of their employees, but these efforts often go wrong. We outline four key attributes of effective leadership development programs.

- **Chapter 12 introduces the idea that firms can draw great value from failed innovations.** Failure is not fun or easy, but it can be very valuable. When firms innovate, they hope that they choose the most promising technological paths, but there is great uncertainty, and they often choose the wrong path. Interestingly, that may be the route to eventual success. We discuss why firms that initially choose the wrong technological path often turn out to be the ultimate winner in the market—if they respond well to the initial failure.

- **Chapter 13 introduces the value of asking heretical questions.** Such an approach can be valuable in case discussions because these questions help to challenge conventional wisdom. Although our discussion draws primarily on its application

to environmental sustainability initiatives, the approach has useful implications for challenges faced by managers in a wide variety of firms and industries.
- **Chapter 13 updates our Appendix: Sources of Company and Industry Information.** Here, we owe a big debt to Ruthie Brock and Carol Byrne, library professionals at the University of Texas at Arlington. These ladies have graciously provided us with comprehensive and updated information for the Eighth Edition that is organized in a range of issues. These include competitive intelligence, annual report collections, company rankings, business websites, and strategic and competitive analysis. Such information is invaluable in analyzing companies and industries.
- **We have worked hard to further enhance our excellent case package with a major focus on fresh and current cases on familiar firms.**
    - More than half of our cases are author-written (much more than the competition).
    - We have updated our users favorite cases, creating fresh stories about familiar companies to minimize instructor preparation time and "maximize freshness" of the content.
    - We have added 5 exciting new cases to the lineup including Avon, Tata, Starbucks, and Greenwood Resources.
    - We have also extensively updated 26 familiar cases including Apple, eBay, JetBlue, Johnson & Johnson, Zynga and many others.
    - Many videos to match the cases.

What Remains the Same: Key Features of Earlier Editions

Let's now briefly address some of the exciting features that remain from the earlier editions.

- **Traditional organizing framework with three other chapters on timely topics.** Crisply written chapters cover all of the strategy bases and address contemporary topics. First, the chapters are divided logically into the traditional sequence: strategy analysis, strategy formulation, and strategy implementation. Second, we include three chapters on such timely topics as intellectual capital/knowledge management, entrepreneurial strategy and competitive dynamics, and fostering corporate entrepreneurship and new ventures.
- **"Learning from Mistakes" chapter-opening cases.** To enhance student interest, we begin each chapter with a case that depicts an organization that has suffered a dramatic performance drop, or outright failure, by failing to adhere to sound strategic management concepts and principles. We believe that this feature serves to underpin the value of the concepts in the course and that it is a preferred teaching approach to merely providing examples of outstanding companies that always seem to get it right. After all, isn't it better (and more challenging) to diagnose problems than admire perfection? As Dartmouth's Sydney Finkelstein, author of *Why Smart Executives Fail,* notes: "We live in a world where success is revered, and failure is quickly pushed to the side. However, some of the greatest opportunities to learn—for both individuals and organizations—come from studying what goes wrong."* For example, we'll see how (and why!) Groupon's stock price went from a high of $26 a share when it debuted on NASDAQ in November 2011 to around $6 near the end of 2014. Clearly, imitation in the "daily deals"

---
*Personal communication, June 20, 2005.

industry was creating havoc. However, CEO Andrew Mason wasn't helping the situation with the questionable accounting practices that took place under his leadership, as well as his "goofball antics" (as noted by CNBC's Herb Greenberg). We'll also explore how Stroh's Brewing Company was undone by Peter Stroh, the fifth generation of the family to lead the firm, who took over as CEO in 1980. Rather than sticking to the tried-and-true business plan of catering to the needs of the Midwest working class, he undertook a disastrous series of acquisitions. And we'll look at the recent problems faced by Tesco, a large global retailer. In addition to its failed entry into the U.S. market and increasing pressure at home from hard-discounting rivals, Tesco has been tarred in the press by accounting irregularities and flawed corporate governance.

- **"Issue for Debate"—at the end of each chapter.** We find that students become very engaged (and often animated!) in discussing an issue that has viable alternate points of view. It is an exciting way to drive home key strategy concepts. For example, in Chapter 1, Seventh Generation is faced with a dilemma that confronts its values, and the firm must decide whether or not to provide its products to some of its largest customers. At issue: While the firm sympathizes (and their values are consistent) with the striking workers at the large grocery chains, should Seventh Generation cross the picket lines? In Chapter 4, some interesting trade-offs must be considered when a firm under financial duress has to make a choice: begin furloughs or lay off employees (David Cote, chairman and CEO of Honeywell, provides an insightful perspective). And, in Chapter 7, we address Medtronic's decision to acquire Covidien, an Irish-based medical equipment manufacturer, for $43 billion. Medtronic's primary motive: lower its taxes by moving its legal home to Ireland—a country that has lower rates of taxation on corporations. Some critics may see such a move as unethical and unpatriotic. Supporters would argue that the move will help the firm save on taxes and benefit its shareholders.

- **Throughout the chapters, we provide many excerpts from interviews with top executives from Adam Bryant's *The Corner Office*.** Such viewpoints provide valuable perspectives from leading executives and help to drive home the value and purpose of key strategy concepts. For example, we include the perspectives of Tim Brown (CEO of IDEO) on employee empowerment, Richard Anderson (CEO of Delta Airlines) on strategy analysis, and Gordon Bethune (former CEO of Continental Airlines) on the importance of incentive systems.

- **"Reflecting on Career Implications . . ."** We provide insights that are closely aligned with and directed to three distinct issues faced by our readers: prepare them for a job interview (e.g., industry analysis), help them with current employers or their career in general, or help them find potential employers and decide where to work. We believe this will be very valuable to students' professional development.

- **"Reflecting on Career Implications" for each chapter.** This feature—at the end of each chapter—will help instructors drive home the immediate relevance/value of strategy concepts. It focuses on how an understanding of key concepts helps business students early in their careers.

- **Consistent chapter format and features to reinforce learning.** We have included several features in each chapter to add value and create an enhanced learning experience. First, each chapter begins with an overview and a list of key learning objectives. Second, as previously noted, the opening case describes a situation in which a company's performance eroded because of a lack of proper application of strategy concepts. Third, at the end of each chapter there are four different types of questions/exercises that should help students assess their understanding and application of material:

1. Summary review questions.
2. Experiential exercises.
3. Application questions and exercises.
4. Ethics questions.

Given the centrality of online systems to business today, each chapter contains at least one exercise that allows students to explore the use of the web in implementing a firm's strategy.

- **Key Terms.** Approximately a dozen key terms for each chapter are identified in the margins of the pages. This addition was made in response to reviewer feedback and improves students' understanding of core strategy concepts.
- **Clear articulation and illustration of key concepts.** Key strategy concepts are introduced in a clear and concise manner and are followed by timely and interesting examples from business practice. Such concepts include value-chain analysis, the resource-based view of the firm, Porter's five-forces model, competitive advantage, boundaryless organizational designs, digital strategies, corporate governance, ethics, and entrepreneurship.
- **Extensive use of sidebars.** We include 72 sidebars (or about six per chapter) called "Strategy Spotlights." The Strategy Spotlights not only illustrate key points but also increase the readability and excitement of new strategy concepts.
- **Integrative themes.** The text provides a solid grounding in ethics, globalization, environmental sustainability, and technology. These topics are central themes throughout the book and form the basis for many of the Strategy Spotlights.
- **Implications of concepts for small businesses.** Many of the key concepts are applied to start-up firms and smaller businesses, which is particularly important since many students have professional plans to work in such firms.
- **Not just a textbook but an entire package.** *Strategic Management* features the best chapter teaching notes available today. Rather than merely summarizing the key points in each chapter, we focus on value-added material to enhance the teaching (and learning) experience. Each chapter includes dozens of questions to spur discussion, teaching tips, in-class group exercises, and about a dozen detailed examples from business practice to provide further illustrations of key concepts.

Teaching Resources

Instructor's Manual (IM)
Prepared by the textbook authors, along with valued input from our strategy colleagues, the accompanying IM contains summary/objectives, lecture/discussion outlines, discussion questions, extra examples not included in the text, teaching tips, reflecting on career implications, experiential exercises, and more.

Test Bank
Revised by Christine Pence of the University of California–Riverside, the test bank contains more than 1,000 true/false, multiple-choice, and essay questions. It has now been tagged with learning objectives as well as Bloom's Taxonomy and AACSB criteria.

PREFACE

- **Assurance of Learning Ready.** Assurance of Learning is an important element of many accreditation standards. Dess 8e is designed specifically to support your Assurance of Learning initiatives. Each chapter in the book begins with a list of numbered learning objectives that appear throughout the chapter. Every test bank question is also linked to one of these objectives, in addition to level of difficulty, topic area, Bloom's Taxonomy level, and AACSB skill area. *EZ Test,* McGraw-Hill's easy-to-use test bank software, can search the test bank by these and other categories, providing an engine for targeted Assurance of Learning analysis and assessment.
- **AACSB Statement.** The McGraw-Hill Companies is a proud corporate member of AACSB International. Understanding the importance and value of AACSB accreditation, Dess 8e has sought to recognize the curricula guidelines detailed in the AACSB standards for business accreditation by connecting selected questions in Dess 8e and the test bank to the general knowledge and skill guidelines found in the AACSB standards. The statements contained in Dess 8e are provided only as a guide for the users of this text. The AACSB leaves content coverage and assessment within the purview of individual schools, the mission of the school, and the faculty. While Dess 8e and the teaching package make no claim of any specific AACSB qualification or evaluation, we have labeled selected questions within Dess 8e according to the six general knowledge and skills areas.
- **Computerized Test Bank Online.** A comprehensive bank of test questions is provided within a computerized test bank powered by McGraw-Hill's flexible electronic testing program, *EZ Test Online* (www.eztestonline.com). *EZ Test Online* allows you to create paper and online tests or quizzes in this easy-to-use program. Imagine being able to create and access your test or quiz anywhere, at any time, without installing the testing software! Now, with *EZ Test Online,* instructors can select questions from multiple McGraw-Hill test banks or author their own and then either print the test for paper distribution or give it online.
- **Test Creation.**
    - Author/edit questions online using the 14 different question-type templates.
    - Create printed tests or deliver online to get instant scoring and feedback.
    - Create question pools to offer multiple versions online—great for practice.
    - Export your tests for use in *WebCT, Blackboard,* and Apple's *iQuiz.*
    - Compatible with *EZ Test Desktop* tests you've already created.
    - Sharing tests with colleagues, adjuncts, TAs is easy.
- **Online Test Management.**
    - Set availability dates and time limits for your quiz or test.
    - Control how your test will be presented.
    - Assign points by question or question type with drop-down menu.
    - Provide immediate feedback to students or delay until all finish the test.
    - Create practice tests online to enable student mastery.
    - Your roster can be uploaded to enable student self-registration.
- **Online Scoring and Reporting.**
    - Automated scoring for most of *EZ Test*'s numerous question types.
    - Allows manual scoring for essay and other open response questions.
    - Manual rescoring and feedback are also available.

- *EZ Test*'s grade book is designed to easily export to your grade book.
- View basic statistical reports.
- **Support and Help.**
  - User's guide and built-in page-specific help.
  - Flash tutorials for getting started on the support site.
  - Support website: *www.mhhe.com/eztest.*
  - Product specialist available at 1-800-331-5094.
  - Online training: *http://auth.mhhe.com/mpss/workshops/.*

PowerPoint Presentation

Prepared by Pauline Assenza of Western Connecticut State University, it consists of more than 400 slides incorporating an outline for the chapters tied to learning objectives. Also included are instructor notes, multiple-choice questions that can be used as Classroom Performance System (CPS) questions, and additional examples outside the text to promote class discussion.

McGraw-Hill Connect™ Management

Less Managing. More Teaching. Greater Learning. McGraw-Hill *Connect Management* is an online assignment and assessment solution that connects students with the tools and resources they'll need to achieve success.

- **McGraw-Hill *Connect Management* Features.** *Connect Management* offers a number of powerful tools and features to make managing assignments easier, so faculty can spend more time teaching. With *Connect Management,* students can engage with their coursework anytime and anywhere, making the learning process more accessible and efficient. *Connect Management* offers you the features described below.
  - There are chapter quizzes for the first 12 chapters, consisting of 15–25 multiple-choice questions, testing students' overall comprehension of concepts presented in the chapter.
  - There are two specially crafted interactives for each of the first 12 chapters that drill students in the use and application of the concepts and tools of strategic analysis.
  - The majority of the *Connect* exercises are automatically graded, thereby simplifying the task of evaluating each class member's performance and monitoring the learning outcomes.
- **Student Progress Tracking.** *Connect Management* keeps instructors informed about how each student, section, and class are performing, allowing for more productive use of lecture and office hours. The progress-tracking function enables you to
  - View scored work immediately and track individual or group performance with assignment and grade reports.
  - Access an instant view of student or class performance relative to learning objectives.
  - Collect data and generate reports required by many accreditation organizations, such as AACSB.

- **Smart Grading.** When it comes to studying, time is precious. *Connect Management* helps students learn more efficiently by providing feedback and practice material when they need it, where they need it. When it comes to teaching, your time also is precious. The grading function enables you to
  - Have assignments scored automatically, giving students immediate feedback on their work and side-by-side comparisons with correct answers.
  - Access and review each response, manually change grades, or leave comments for students to review.
  - Reinforce classroom concepts with practice tests and instant quizzes.
- **Simple Assignment Management.** With *Connect Management,* creating assignments is easier than ever, so you can spend more time teaching and less time managing. The assignment management function enables you to
  - Create and deliver assignments easily with selectable test bank items.
  - Streamline lesson planning, student progress reporting, and assignment grading to make classroom management more efficient than ever.
  - Go paperless with online submission and grading of student assignments.
- **Instructor Library.** The *Connect Management* Instructor Library is your repository for additional resources to improve student engagement in and out of class. You can select and use any asset that enhances your lecture. The *Connect Management* Instructor Library includes
  - Instructor's Manual
  - PowerPoint® Presentations
  - Test Bank
  - Case Support (Teaching Notes, Case PowerPoints, Case financials)
  - Video Library (Video Guide and Video Links related to each chapter)

The Business Strategy Game and GLO-BUS Online Simulations

Both allow teams of students to manage companies in a head-to-head contest for global market leadership. These simulations give students the immediate opportunity to experiment with various strategy options and to gain proficiency in applying the concepts and tools they have been reading about in the chapters. To find out more or to register, please visit *www.mhhe.com/thompsonsims.*

Additional Resources for Course Design and Delivery

Create

Craft your teaching resources to match the way you teach! With McGraw-Hill *Create, www.mcgrawhillcreate.com,* you can easily rearrange chapters, combine material from other content sources, and quickly upload content you have written, like your course syllabus or teaching notes. Find the content you need in *Create* by searching through thousands of leading McGraw-Hill textbooks. Arrange your book to fit your teaching style. *Create* even allows you to personalize your book's appearance by selecting the cover and adding your name, school, and course information. Order a *Create* book and you'll receive a complimentary print review copy in three to five business days or a complimentary electronic review copy (eComp) via email in about one hour. Go to *www.mcgrawhillcreate.com* today and register. Experience how McGraw-Hill *Create* empowers you to teach *your* students *your* way.

E-Book Options

E-books are an innovative way for students to save money and to "go green." McGraw-Hill's e-books are typically 40 percent of bookstore price. Students have the choice between an online and a downloadable *CourseSmart* e-book.

Through *CourseSmart,* students have the flexibility to access an exact replica of their textbook from any computer that has Internet service, without plug-ins or special software via the version, or create a library of books on their hard drive via the downloadable version. Access to *CourseSmart* e-books is one year.

Features: *CourseSmart* e-books allow students to highlight, take notes, organize notes, and share the notes with other *CourseSmart* users. Students can also search terms across all e-books in their purchased *CourseSmart* library. *CourseSmart* e-books can be printed (5 pages at a time).

More info and purchase: Please visit *www.coursesmart.com* for more information and to purchase access to our e-books. *CourseSmart* allows students to try one chapter of the e-book, free of charge, before purchase.

McGraw-Hill Higher Education and Blackboard

McGraw-Hill Higher Education and Blackboard have teamed up. What does this mean for you?

1. **Your life, simplified.** Now you and your students can access McGraw-Hill's *Connect* and *Create* right from within your Blackboard course—all with one single sign-on. Say goodbye to the days of logging in to multiple applications.
2. **Deep integration of content and tools.** Not only do you get single sign-on with *Connect* and *Create,* you also get deep integration of McGraw-Hill content and content engines right in Blackboard. Whether you're choosing a book for your course or building *Connect* assignments, all the tools you need are right where you want them—inside Blackboard.
3. **Seamless gradebooks.** Are you tired of keeping multiple gradebooks and manually synchronizing grades into Blackboard? We thought so. When a student completes an integrated *Connect* assignment, the grade for that assignment automatically (and instantly) feeds into Blackboard grade center.
4. **A solution for everyone.** Whether your institution is already using Blackboard or you just want to try Blackboard on your own, we have a solution for you. McGraw-Hill and Blackboard can now offer you easy access to industry-leading technology and content, whether your campus hosts it or we do. Be sure to ask your local McGraw-Hill representative for details.

McGraw-Hill Customer Care Contact Information

At McGraw-Hill, we understand that getting the most from new technology can be challenging. That's why our services don't stop after you purchase our products. You can email our product specialists 24 hours a day to get product training online. Or you can search our knowledge bank of Frequently Asked Questions on our support website. For customer support, call 800-331-5094, email *hmsupport@mcgraw-hill.com,* or visit *www.mhhe.com/support.* One of our technical support analysts will be able to assist you in a timely fashion.

A GUIDED TOUR

After reading this chapter, you should have a good understanding of the following learning objectives:

- **LO1.1** The definition of strategic management and its four key attributes.
- **LO1.2** The strategic management process and its three interrelated and principal activities.
- **LO1.3** The vital role of corporate governance and stakeholder management, as well as how "symbiosis" can be achieved among an organization's stakeholders.
- **LO1.4** The importance of social responsibility, including environmental sustainability, and how it can enhance a corporation's innovation strategy.
- **LO1.5** The need for greater empowerment throughout the organization.
- **LO1.6** How an awareness of a hierarchy of strategic goals can help an organization achieve coherence in its strategic direction.

Learning Objectives

Learning Objectives numbered LO5.1, LO5.2, LO5.3, etc., with corresponding icons in the margins to indicate where learning objectives are covered in the text.

Learning from Mistakes

Learning from Mistakes vignettes are examples of where things went wrong. Failures are not only interesting but also sometimes easier to learn from. And students realize strategy is not just about "right or wrong" answers, but requires critical thinking.

Strategy Spotlight

These boxes weave themes of ethics, globalization, and technology into every chapter of the text, providing students with a thorough grounding necessary for understanding strategic management. Select boxes incorporate crowdsourcing, environmental sustainability, and ethical themes.

Strategic Management: Text and Cases, Eighth Edition   **17**

INSIGHTS

The "Insights" feature is new to this edition. "Insights from Executives" spotlight interviews with executives from worldwide organizations about current issues salient to strategic management. "Insights from Research" summarize key research findings relevant to maintaining the effectiveness of an organization and its management.

Exhibits

Both new and improved exhibits in every chapter provide visual presentations of the most complex concepts covered to support student comprehension.

Reflecting on Career Implications

This section before the summary of every chapter consists of examples on how understanding of key concepts helps business students early in their careers.

xxvii

A GUIDED TOUR

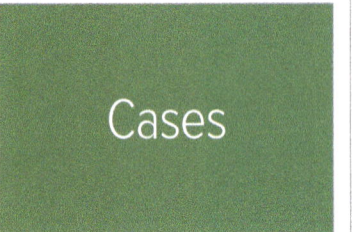

Updated case lineup provides 9 new cases. The majority of the remaining cases have been revised to "maximize freshness" and minimize instructor preparation time. New cases for this edition include well-known companies such as Tata Starbucks, the Casino Industry, and General Motors.

Strategic Analysis

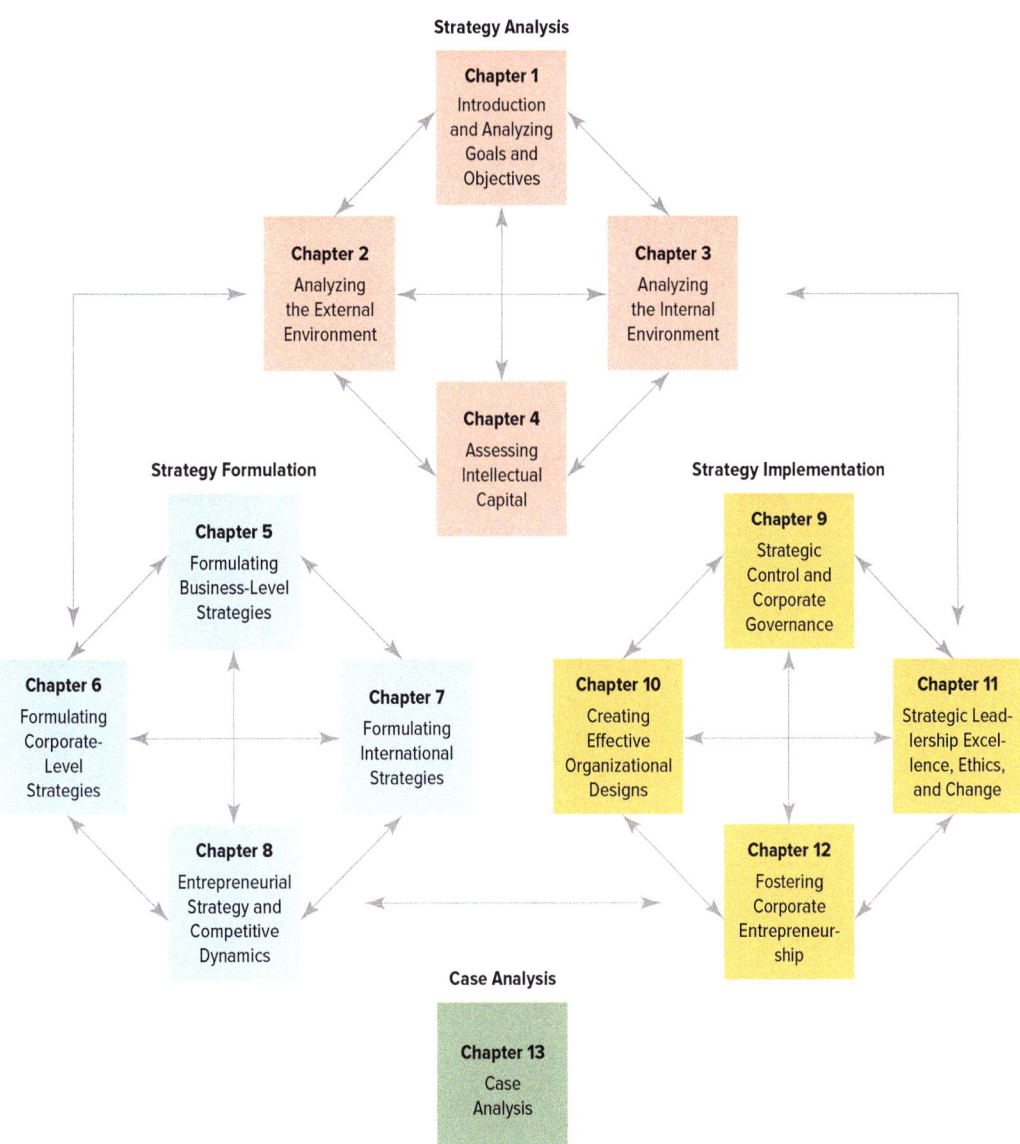

Strategic Management
Creating Competitive Advantages

chapter 1

After reading this chapter, you should have a good understanding of the following learning objectives:

LO1.1 The definition of strategic management and its four key attributes.

LO1.2 The strategic management process and its three interrelated and principal activities.

LO1.3 The vital role of corporate governance and stakeholder management, as well as how "symbiosis" can be achieved among an organization's stakeholders.

LO1.4 The importance of social responsibility, including environmental sustainability, and how it can enhance a corporation's innovation strategy.

LO1.5 The need for greater empowerment throughout the organization.

LO1.6 How an awareness of a hierarchy of strategic goals can help an organization achieve coherence in its strategic direction.

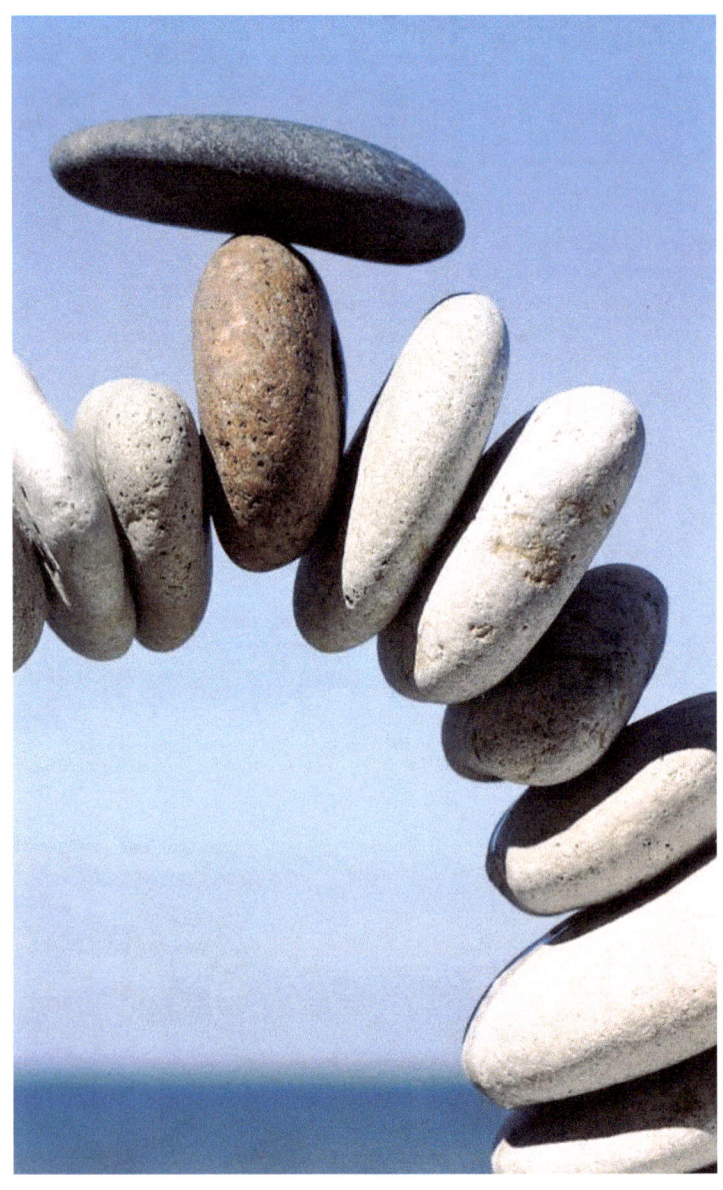

PART 1: STRATEGIC ANALYSIS

Learning from Mistakes

What makes the study of strategic management so interesting? Today, many new start-ups become globally recognized names seemingly overnight. At the same time, we see many of yesteryear's high-flying firms struggling to regain some of their earlier elite status or even to survive. As colorfully noted by Arthur Martinez, Sears's former chairman: "Today's peacock is tomorrow's feather duster."[1]

Consider the following:[2]

- Only 74 of the original 500 companies in the S&P Index were still around 40 years later—a mortality rate of more than 10 per year. In 1935, firms in the S&P 500 would have an average lifetime of 90 years. By 2011, the average lifetime was down to 18 years.
- In March 2000, the top five stocks on the NASDAQ Stock Exchange were Cisco, Microsoft, Intel, Qualcomm, and Oracle. As of mid-2014, the top five were Apple, Google, Microsoft, *Amazon.com*, and Facebook.
- Until a few years ago, many customers were willing to pay more than $200 for a GPS unit. Today, most people use free navigation apps on their smartphones instead. In just 18 months, GPS makers have lost 85 percent of their market value, as noted by *The Economist*.
- Twenty years ago it was almost unimaginable that a South Korean firm would be a global car giant, that an Indian firm would be one of the world's largest technology outfits, or that a Chinese Internet colossus would list on an American stock exchange.

Maintaining competitive success or even surviving over long periods of time is indeed very difficult for companies of any size. As John Donahue, CEO of eBay, notes, "Almost every company has hot moments. But only great companies achieve strong, sustainable performance over time."[3] Next, let's take a look at Groupon, which, after its high-profile initial public offering (IPO) in 2011 that raised over $900 million, has struggled to live up to the initial expectations.

Andrew Mason met his earliest investor, Eric Lefkofsky, in 2003 when he was working as a web designer. Five years later, Lefkofsky provided $1 million to fund Mason's first entrepreneurial effort—a company called The Point—an interactive web platform that was originally intended to bring groups of like-minded people together behind a social cause like hunger or helping the homeless.

This idea didn't pan out; Mason and Lefkofsky pivoted into a more commercially friendly application of the same concept—Groupon. As we all know, Groupon would eventually grow into one of the most talked-about and hyped tech companies in recent history. In fact, *The Wall Street Journal* stated that it had "been called the fastest-growing company in history" before its 2011 IPO.

Today, Groupon has over 10,000 employees worldwide and has sold over 6 million group coupons. The company was so hot that at one point it rejected an all-cash $6 billion buyout offer from Google. The offer would have put $420 million and $1 billion in Mason's and Lefkofsky's pockets, respectively. But investors were confident that a company with as much heat and momentum as Groupon back in 2011 would certainly fetch far more value with an IPO. Unfortunately, by April 2015, Andrew Maron had been fired and the firm had lost over 70 percent of its market value since its highly successful IPO.

So what went wrong? GRPN debuted on the NASDAQ in early November 2011 at $26 a share. Investors and employees rejoiced—and Mason's shares were worth $1.196 billion and Lefkofsky's were worth $2.86 billion. Unfortunately, the opening price of $26 would be the firm's all-time high point. Groupon caught flak for questionable accounting practices that did not include marketing costs, and in the spring of 2012 it had to issue a restatement of earnings after admitting it didn't set aside enough money for refunds. In addition, few of the many acquisitions that were made were successful.

More serious was the unforeseen fact that group daily deals turned out to be much of a fad. Most people who tried Groupon (or one of the dozens of imitators) were typically not impressed. Worse, stories of small businesses losing thousands of dollars offering Groupon became common. For example, according to a recent study by Raymond James, 67 percent of merchants found Groupon users' spending habits were "lower" than those of their typical customers. And another survey indicated that just 3 percent of respondents said that these types of promotions brought them repeat business!

Other huge challenges became fending off the never-ending crop of imitator firms and needing to constantly hunt for new local businesses to offer a deal. To meet such challenges, Groupon had to hire thousands of new employees around the world. The associated costs shrunk margins at a time when revenue was dropping precipitously.

Mason, as CEO, hardly helped his own cause. He was known by many for not taking his role as CEO of a publicly traded company seriously enough. He was named "Worst CEO of the Year" by Herb Greenberg of CNBC, who wrote, in part, "Mason's goofball antics, which can come off more like a big kid than a company leader, almost make a mockery of corporate leadership—especially for a company with a market value of more than $3 billion. It would be excusable, even endearing, if the company were doing well (think Herb Kelleher of Southwest Airlines) but it's not. Sales growth is through the floor." The following would seem to support Greenberg's sentiments:

- Mason annoyed the SEC when he wrote a lengthy, profanity-laden memo that was promptly leaked to the press in the middle of the company's pre-IPO quiet period. In the memo, he touted Groupon's prospects and trashed the financial press for critical coverage of the company. The SEC ultimately forced Groupon to include the document in its IPO filing.
- In April 2012, Mason outlined the firm's corporate strategy at an all-hands meeting, which was observed via webcast by a reporter. At one point, his voice broke. "Sorry, too much beer," he said. Mason then proceeded to tell his employees that Groupon needed to grow up!
- A *Vanity Fair* piece, for which Mason posed with a cat on his head, relates how he had purchased a spotted pony named Spice that he planned to give to New York City Mayor Michael Bloomberg, who was visiting the firm. Disaster was averted only moments before Bloomberg arrived, after a Groupon employee discovered, via Google, that the mayor's daughter, Georgina, had recently suffered a concussion and a fractured spine during a horse-riding incident. Needless to say, Spice did not return to New York City with the mayor.

With mounting losses and a stock price falling through the floor, the Groupon board fired Mason in February 2013. His severance package was not what anyone would expect for a corporate CEO. Given that he had an annual salary of $756.72 (at "his own recommendation"), he walked away with just $378.36—six months' salary! He also received health coverage for 180 days. Of course, he was hardest hit when it came to his personal net worth. The value of his shares had peaked at $1.2 billion at the time of the IPO. But, at the time of his exit, they were worth $230 million—an amount that reflects the company's nearly 80 percent drop in market value from its IPO only a year and a half earlier.

Epilogue: As of April 2015 Groupon shares were hovering around $7, and it had losses of over $200 million for the years 2012-2014. Ayush Singh, an analyst, believes Groupon may again be a realistic acquisition candidate for Google. The stock is fairly cheap, and Singh believes Google would have little trouble integrating the firm into its Google Offers business, Groupon's direct competitor. This could give rise to cost synergies, which the companies would otherwise spend on outdoing each other.

Discussion Questions

1. What actions should Groupon have taken to avoid the steep drop in its stock price?
2. Is this an attactive industry? Why? Why not?

Sources: Cohen, T. 2014. Why (GRPN) stock is lower today. www.thestreet.com, June 2: np; Brownell, M. 2013. CEO Andrew Mason out at Groupon after stock plummets. www.dailyfinance.com, February 28: np; Silverman, R. E., & Gellman, L. 2014. Ice bucket challenge: Too much success? *The Wall Street Journal,* September 17: B8; Singh, A. 2014. Time to buy Groupon's terrific turnaround. *Seekingalpha.com,* July 16: np; Gustin, S. 2013. Groupon fires CEO Andrew Mason: The rise and fall of tech's enfant terrible. *business.time.com,* March 1: np; and *finance.yahoo.com.*

The recent problems faced by Groupon illustrate how even innovative firms can struggle in the marketplace if they do not anticipate and respond proactively to changes in the environment. Today's leaders face a large number of complex challenges in the global marketplace. In considering how much credit (or blame) they deserve, two perspectives of leadership come immediately to mind: the "romantic" and "external control" perspectives.[4] First, let's look at the **romantic view of leadership.** Here, the implicit assumption is that the leader is the key force in determining an organization's success—or lack thereof.[5] This view dominates the popular press in business magazines such as *Fortune, Businessweek,* and *Forbes,* wherein the CEO is either lauded for his or her firm's success or chided for the organization's demise.[6] Consider, for example, the credit that has been bestowed on leaders such as Jack Welch, Andrew Grove, and Herb Kelleher for the tremendous accomplishments when they led their firms, General Electric, Intel, and Southwest Airlines, respectively.

> **romantic view of leadership**
> situations in which the leader is the key force determining the organization's success—or lack thereof.

Similarly, Apple's success in the last decade has been attributed almost entirely to the late Steve Jobs, its former CEO, who died on October 5, 2011.[7] Apple's string of hit products, such as iMac computers, iPods, iPhones, and iPads, is a testament to his genius for developing innovative, user-friendly, and aesthetically pleasing products. In addition to being a perfectionist in product design, Jobs was a master showman with a cult following. During his time as CEO between 1997 and 2011, Apple's market value soared by over $300 billion!

On the other hand, when things don't go well, much of the failure of an organization can also, rightfully, be attributed to the leader.[8] Groupon's leadership clearly failed to respond effectively to important changes taking place in the daily deals industry. In contrast, Apple fully capitalized on emerging technology trends with a variety of products, including sophisticated smartphones.

The contrasting fortunes of Hewlett-Packard under two different CEOs also demonstrate the influence leadership has on firm performance.[9] When Carly Fiorina was fired as CEO of the firm in February 2005, HP enjoyed an immediate increase in its stock price of 7 percent—hardly a strong endorsement of her leadership! Her successor, Mark Hurd, led the firm to five years of outstanding financial results. Interestingly, when he abruptly resigned on August 6, 2010, the firm's stock price dropped 12 percent almost instantly! (To provide some perspective, this represents a decrease in HP's market value of about $12 billion.)

> For a more recent example, consider the announced exit of Dave Barger, chief executive of JetBlue Airways Corp. since 2007.[10] He has been highly criticized in recent years for the discount carrier's lagging performance. There is hope his replacement, Robin Hayes, a former British Airways executive, will make changes to help keep costs in line as well as enhance revenue by such actions as adding seats to aircraft (i.e., decreasing legroom) and imposing baggage fees. Perhaps not too surprising, JetBlue's shares rose nearly 40 percent between May and mid-August 2014, when speculation began circulating that Barger might be preparing to resign. And, when his resignation was announced a month later, shares immediately jumped 4 percent. (To give some perspective, even with the recent run-up, JetBlue's stock was up only 9 percent during Barger's tenure—compared to a gain of more than 140 percent for Southwest Airlines during the same period!)

However, such an emphasis on the leader reflects only part of the picture. Consider another perspective, called the **external control view of leadership.** Here, rather than making the implicit assumption that the leader is the most important factor in determining organizational outcomes, the focus is on external factors that may positively (or negatively) affect a firm's success. We don't have to look far to support this perspective. Developments in the general environment, such as economic downturns, new technologies, governmental legislation, or an outbreak of major internal conflict or war, can greatly restrict the choices that are available to a firm's executives. For example, several book retailers, such as Borders and Waldenbooks, found the consumer shift away from brick-and-mortar bookstores to online book buying (e.g., Amazon) and digital books an overwhelming environmental force against which they had few defenses.

> **external control view of leadership**
> situations in which external forces—where the leader has limited influence—determine the organization's success.

Major unanticipated developments can often have very negative consequences for businesses regardless of how well formulated their strategies are.

Let's look at a few recent examples:[11]

- In the aftermath of BP's disastrous oil well explosion on April 20, 2010, the fishing and tourism industries in the region suffered significant downturns. BP itself was forced to pay a $20 billion fine to the U.S. government.
- On March 11, 2011, a 9.0 earthquake and tsunami devastated Japan and resulted in the loss of more than 20,000 lives. During the next two trading days, the country's stock exchange (Nikkei) suffered its biggest loss in 40 years. The disaster hit nearly every industry hard—especially energy companies. For example, Tokyo Electric Power Co., which operates a nuclear power plant that was severely damaged, fell 24.7 percent, and Toshiba Corp., a maker of nuclear power plants, slid 19.5 percent. Firms as diverse as Toyota, Honda, and Sony were forced to halt production because extensive damage to roads and distribution systems made it nearly impossible to move products.

A major piece of legislation with far-reaching consequences for businesses in the United States is the Affordable Care Act, commonly referred to as Obamacare. The Insights from Executives sidebar 1.1 provides a perspective on this law from Melvin Alexander, CPA, former chief financial officer of Kentucky One Health and other large health care systems.

Before moving on, it is important to point out that successful executives are often able to navigate around the difficult circumstances that they face. At times it can be refreshing to see the optimistic position they take when they encounter seemingly insurmountable odds. Of course, that's not to say that one should be naive or Pollyannaish. Consider, for example, how one CEO, discussed next, is handling trying times.[12]

Name a general economic woe, and chances are that Charles Needham, CEO of Metorex, is dealing with it.

- Market turmoil has knocked 80 percent off the shares of South Africa's Metorex, the mining company that he heads.
- The plunge in global commodities is slamming prices for the copper, cobalt, and other minerals Metorex unearths across Africa. The credit crisis makes it harder to raise money.
- Fighting has again broken out in the Democratic Republic of Congo, where Metorex has a mine and several projects in development.

Such problems might send many executives to the window ledge. Yet Needham appears unruffled as he sits down at a conference table in the company's modest offices in a Johannesburg suburb. The combat in northeast Congo, he notes, is far from Metorex's mine. Commodity prices are still high, in historical terms. And Needham is confident he can raise enough capital, drawing on relationships with South African banks. "These are the kinds of things you deal with, doing business in Africa," he says.

1.1 INSIGHTS FROM EXECUTIVES

MELVIN ALEXANDER, CPA

BIOSKETCH

Melvin Alexander is presently executive director of Principled Solutions Enterprise (PSE), a management consulting firm specializing in health care. PSE's scope of services ranges from operational improvement (e.g., financial turnarounds, workflow redesigns) to strategic services (e.g., plan development and implementation, capital planning, and service line analysis). Alexander previously served as a chief financial officer of Kentucky One Health (Louisville, Kentucky), Norman Regional Health System (Norman, Oklahoma), and North Oaks Health System (Hammond, Louisiana). He also served in the U.S. Air Force as a medical service corps officer.

Alexander is a certified public accountant and a fellow of both the Healthcare Financial Management Association and the American College of Healthcare Executives. He received a bachelor of science degree in business administration (University of Texas at Dallas, 1980) and a master's of business administration (City University of Seattle, 1990), and he completed the Strategy Development for Senior Executives program (Marshall School of Business, University of Southern California, 2011).

1. *Can you explain ways in which the health care industry has responded to the ACA? Is there a difference between small and big firms in the ways in which they respond?*

   The component of the ACA that changes how Medicare pays hospitals and physicians is a major driver for the structural changes in the health care industry. The structural changes have resulted in consolidations of hospitals, increases in physicians employed by hospitals, and expanded service lines (e.g., hospitals offering health insurance). The large hospital systems (owners of multiple hospitals) have responded by acquiring other hospitals, improving quality by standardizing processes, and taking steps to prepare to become Accountable Care Organizations (ACOs) in order to optimize the changes in Medicare. The smaller organizations have not taken the same path because of resource limitations and local environmental issues (e.g., location).

   Under the ACA, Medicare beneficiaries will be assigned to an Accountable Care Organization (ACO) for health care services. The ACO will receive a single payment for each Medicare beneficiary assigned. The single payment will be divided and distributed by the ACO service providers (e.g., hospitals, physicians, ancillary care providers). The ACO essentially has the "risk" and responsibility of managing its beneficiaries' health care needs. Hospital systems are best equipped to become an ACO. The ACO concept demands comprehensive services and a continuum of services, multiple hospitals, and physicians in its network to deliver quality and timely care to assigned Medicare beneficiaries. Additionally, the ACO will need to have a good understanding of its assigned patients' health care statuses and needs, effective preventive care programs, and information technology systems that monitor patient activities. This is necessary because if the cost of care to provide services for the beneficiaries is lower than the "bundled payment" received, the ACO then makes a profit. If the cost of services is higher than payments received, the ACO loses money. The ACO concept absorbs the financial risk from the government, and this, in the long run, should reduce the amount of tax dollars spent on health care. In 2013, 25.4 percent of tax dollars paid for health care for Medicare and Medicaid patients.

2. *Environmental changes typically most often require strategic change by firms in order to survive. What strategic changes do you foresee in the next three to five years?*

   There will be new strategies to ensure success of the new law as well as to achieve projected returns on the large investments made. The new strategies will center on changing the behavior of the health care consumers (e.g., patients, insured beneficiaries). Areas ranging from preventive care to new providers of health care to improved technology will be focal points of the strategies. To ensure success and compliance, there will likely be both "carrot" and "stick" incentives for health consumers to comply.

   Preventive care will have a long-term impact on controlling costs and predictability of future service needs. The level of preventive care includes follow-up and frequent communication after major health procedures. Ensuring the patient has the appropriate medication and is following treatment plans is a form of the new model of preventive care. Health insurers and pharmaceutical companies have vested interests in preventive care as the insurer's long-term expenses could be reduced and pharmaceutical firms benefit by realizing increased revenues from their products.

   Other strategies will focus on the point of care and delivery site of health care services. This means patients may have to change physicians and receive health care services for major procedures in new locations. Health care systems as well as insurers will want their patients treated in "centers of excellence" for major health care procedures. For some patients, this may mean having

continued

continued

procedures done in different states. This strategy will be a challenge; however, patients currently make such decisions in traveling to health care organizations such as the MD Anderson Cancer Center in Houston, Texas, and the Mayo Clinic in Rochester, Minnesota, because they are viewed as centers of excellence.

The major information technology investment encouraged by the government (through incentives to hospitals and physicians' practices in the early 2000s) will have a significant role with both preventive care and service delivery at centers of excellence.

What Is Strategic Management?

Given the many challenges and opportunities in the global marketplace, today's managers must do more than set long-term strategies and hope for the best.[13] They must go beyond what some have called "incremental management," whereby they view their job as making a series of small, minor changes to improve the efficiency of their firm's operations.[14] Rather than seeing their role as merely custodians of the status quo, today's leaders must be proactive, anticipate change, and continually refine and, when necessary, make dramatic changes to their strategies. The strategic management of the organization must become both a process and a way of thinking throughout the organization.

Defining Strategic Management

LO1.1
The definition of strategic management and its four key attributes.

strategic management
the analyses, decisions, and actions an organization undertakes in order to create and sustain competitive advantages.

strategy
the ideas, decisions, and actions that enable a firm to succeed.

competitive advantage
a firm's resources and capabilities that enable it to overcome the competitive forces in its industry(ies).

operational effectiveness
performing similar activities better than rivals.

Strategic management consists of the analyses, decisions, and actions an organization undertakes in order to create and sustain competitive advantages. This definition captures two main elements that go to the heart of the field of strategic management.

First, the strategic management of an organization entails three ongoing processes: *analyses, decisions,* and *actions.* Strategic management is concerned with the *analysis* of strategic goals (vision, mission, and strategic objectives) along with the analysis of the internal and external environments of the organization. Next, leaders must make strategic decisions. These *decisions,* broadly speaking, address two basic questions: What industries should we compete in? How should we compete in those industries? These questions also often involve an organization's domestic and international operations. And last are the *actions* that must be taken. Decisions are of little use, of course, unless they are acted on. Firms must take the necessary actions to implement their **strategies.** This requires leaders to allocate the necessary resources and to design the organization to bring the intended strategies to reality.

Second, the essence of strategic management is the study of why some firms outperform others.[15] Thus, managers need to determine how a firm is to compete so that it can obtain advantages that are sustainable over a lengthy period of time. That means focusing on two fundamental questions:

- *How should we compete in order to create* **competitive advantages** *in the marketplace?* Managers need to determine if the firm should position itself as the low-cost producer or develop products and services that are unique and will enable the firm to charge premium prices. Or should they do some combination of both?
- *How can we create competitive advantages in the marketplace that are unique, valuable, and difficult for rivals to copy or substitute?* That is, managers need to make such advantages sustainable, instead of temporary.

Sustainable competitive advantage cannot be achieved through operational effectiveness alone.[16] The popular management innovations of the last two decades—total quality, just-in-time, benchmarking, business process reengineering, outsourcing—are all about operational effectiveness. **Operational effectiveness** means performing similar activities better than rivals. Each of these innovations is important, but none lead to sustainable competitive advantage because everyone is doing them. Strategy is all about being different. Sustainable competitive advantage is possible only by performing different activities from rivals or performing similar activities in different ways. Companies such as Walmart, Southwest Airlines, and IKEA have developed unique, internally consistent, and difficult-to-imitate activity systems that have provided them with sustained competitive advantages. A company with a good strategy must make clear choices about what it wants to accomplish. Trying to do everything that your rivals do eventually leads to mutually destructive price competition, not long-term advantage.

The Four Key Attributes of Strategic Management

Before discussing the strategic management process, let's briefly talk about four attributes of strategic management.[17] It should become clear how this course differs from other courses that you have had in functional areas, such as accounting, marketing, operations, and finance. Exhibit 1.1 provides a definition and the four attributes of strategic management.

First, strategic management is *directed toward overall organizational goals and objectives.* That is, effort must be directed at what is best for the total organization, not just a single functional area. Some authors have referred to this perspective as "organizational versus individual rationality."[18] That is, what might look "rational" or ideal for one functional area, such as operations, may not be in the best interest of the overall firm. For example, operations may decide to schedule long production runs of similar products to lower unit costs. However, the standardized output may be counter to what the marketing department needs to appeal to a demanding target market. Similarly, research and development may "overengineer" the product to develop a far superior offering, but the design may make the product so expensive that market demand is minimal.

As noted by David Novak, CEO of Yum Brands:[19]

> I tell people that once you get a job you should act like you run the place. Not in terms of ego, but in terms of how you think about the business. Don't just think about your piece of the business. Think about your piece of the business and the total business. This way, you'll always have a broader perspective.

Second, strategic management *includes multiple stakeholders in decision making.*[20] **Stakeholders** are those individuals, groups, and organizations that have a "stake" in the success of the organization, including owners (shareholders in a publicly held corporation), employees, customers, suppliers, the community at large, and so on. (We'll discuss this in more detail later in this chapter.) Managers will not be successful if they focus on a single stakeholder. For example, if the overwhelming emphasis is on generating profits for the owners, employees may become alienated, customer service may suffer, and the suppliers may resent demands for pricing concessions.

Third, strategic management *requires incorporating both short-term and long-term perspectives.*[21] Peter Senge, a leading strategic management author, has referred to this need as a "creative tension."[22] That is, managers must maintain both a vision for the future of the organization and a focus on its present operating needs. However, financial markets can exert significant pressures on executives to meet short-term performance targets. Studies

stakeholders
individuals, groups, and organizations that have a stake in the success of the organization, including owners (shareholders in a publicly held corporation), employees, customers, suppliers, and the community at large.

EXHIBIT 1.1
Strategic Management Concepts

Definition: Strategic management consists of the analyses, decisions, and actions an organization undertakes in order to create and sustain competitive advantages.

Key Attributes of Strategic Management

- Directs the organization toward overall goals and objectives.
- Includes multiple stakeholders in decision making.
- Needs to incorporate short-term and long-term perspectives.
- Recognizes trade-offs between efficiency and effectiveness.

have shown that corporate leaders often take a short-term approach to the detriment of creating long-term shareholder value.

Andrew Winston addresses this issue in his recent book, *The Big Pivot:*[23]

> Consider the following scenario: It's near the end of the quarter and on your desk sits a project that you know will make money—it has a guaranteed positive net present value (NPV)—but it would reduce your earnings this quarter. Do you invest?
>
> In a study that posed this question to 400 CFOs, a majority said they would not do it. In addition, 80 percent of the executives would decrease R&D spending, advertising, and general maintenance. So what happens if you cut back on these things to prop up short-term earnings *every* quarter? Logically, you don't invest in projects with good paybacks and you under spend on initiatives that build longer-term value. Your earnings targets in future quarters actually get harder to hit.

Fourth, strategic management *involves the recognition of trade-offs between effectiveness and efficiency.* Some authors have referred to this as the difference between "doing the right thing" (**effectiveness**) and "doing things right" (**efficiency**).[24] While managers must allocate and use resources wisely, they must still direct their efforts toward the attainment of overall organizational objectives.

Successful managers must make many trade-offs. It is central to the practice of strategic management. At times, managers must focus on the short term and efficiency; at other times, the emphasis is on the long term and expanding a firm's product-market scope in order to anticipate opportunities in the competitive environment. For example, consider Kevin Sharer's perspective. He is CEO of Amgen, the giant $20 billion biotechnology firm:

> A CEO must always be switching between what I call different altitudes—tasks of different levels of abstraction and specificity. At the highest altitude you're asking the big questions: What are the company's mission and strategy? Do people understand and believe in these aims? Are decisions consistent with them? At the lowest altitude, you're looking at on-the-ground operations: Did we make that sale? What was the yield on that last lot in the factory? How many days of inventory do we have for a particular drug? And then there's everything in between: How many chemists do we need to hire this quarter? What should we pay for a small biotech company that has a promising new drug? Is our production capacity adequate to roll out a product in a new market?[25]

Some authors have developed the concept of **"ambidexterity,"** which refers to a manager's challenge to both align resources to take advantage of existing product markets and proactively explore new opportunities.[26] Strategy Spotlight 1.1 discusses ambidextrous behaviors that are required for success in today's challenging marketplace.

effectiveness
tailoring actions to the needs of an organization rather than wasting effort, or "doing the right thing."

efficiency
performing actions at a low cost relative to a benchmark, or "doing things right."

ambidexterity
the challenge managers face of both aligning resources to take advantage of existing product markets and proactively exploring new opportunities.

The Strategic Management Process

LO1.2
The strategic management process and its three interrelated and principal activities.

We've identified three ongoing processes—analyses, decisions, and actions—that are central to strategic management. In practice, these three processes—often referred to as strategy analysis, strategy formulation, and strategy implementation—are highly interdependent and do not take place one after the other in a sequential fashion in most companies.

Intended versus Realized Strategies

strategic management process
strategy analysis, strategy formulation, and strategy implementation.

Henry Mintzberg, a management scholar at McGill University, argues that viewing the strategic management process as one in which analysis is followed by optimal decisions and their subsequent meticulous implementation neither describes the strategic management process accurately nor prescribes ideal practice.[27] He sees the business environment as far from predictable, thus limiting our ability for analysis. Further, decisions are seldom based on optimal rationality alone, given the political processes that occur in all organizations.[28]

STRATEGY SPOTLIGHT 1.1

AMBIDEXTROUS BEHAVIORS: COMBINING ALIGNMENT AND ADAPTABILITY

A recent study involving 41 business units in 10 multinational companies identified four ambidextrous behaviors in individuals. Such behaviors are the essence of ambidexterity, and they illustrate how a dual capacity for alignment and adaptability can be woven into the fabric of an organization at the individual level.

They take time and are alert to opportunities beyond the confines of their own jobs. A large computer company's sales manager became aware of a need for a new software module that nobody currently offered. Instead of selling the customer something else, he worked up a business case for the new module. With management's approval, he began working full time on its development.

They are cooperative and seek out opportunities to combine their efforts with others. A marketing manager for Italy was responsible for supporting a newly acquired subsidiary. When frustrated about the limited amount of contact she had with her peers in other countries, she began discussions with them. This led to the creation of a European marketing forum which meets quarterly to discuss issues, share best practices, and collaborate on marketing plans.

They are brokers, always looking to build internal networks. When visiting the head office in St. Louis, a Canadian plant manager heard about plans for a $10 million investment for a new tape manufacturing plant. After inquiring further about the plans and returning to Canada, he contacted a regional manager in Manitoba, who he knew was looking for ways to build his business. With some generous support from the Manitoba government, the regional manager bid for, and ultimately won, the $10 million investment.

They are multitaskers who are comfortable wearing more than one hat. Although an operations manager for a major coffee and tea distributor was charged with running his plant as efficiently as possible, he took it upon himself to identify value-added services for his clients. By developing a dual role, he was able to manage operations and develop a promising electronic module that automatically reported impending problems inside a coffee vending machine. With corporate funding, he found a subcontractor to develop the software, and he then piloted the module in his own operations. It was so successful that it was eventually adopted by operations managers in several other countries.

A recent *Harvard Business Review* article provides some useful insights on how one can become a more ambidextrous leader. Consider the following questions:

- **Do you meet your numbers?**
- **Do you help others?**
- **What do you do for your peers?** Are you just their in-house competitor?
- **When you manage up, do you bring problems—or problems with possible solutions?**
- **Are you transparent?** Managers who get a reputation for spinning events gradually lose the trust of peers and superiors.
- **Are you developing a group of senior-managers who know you and are willing to back your original ideas with resources?**

Sources: Birkinshaw, J. & Gibson, C. 2004. Building ambidexterity into an organization. *MIT Sloan Management Review*, 45(4): 47–55; and Bower, J. L. 2007. Solve the succession crisis by growing inside-out leaders. *Harvard Business Review*, 85(11): 90–99.

Taking into consideration the limitations discussed above, Mintzberg proposed an alternative model. As depicted in Exhibit 1.2, decisions following from analysis, in this model, constitute the ***intended* strategy** of the firm. For a variety of reasons, the intended strategy rarely survives in its original form. Unforeseen environmental developments, unanticipated resource constraints, or changes in managerial preferences may result in at least some parts of the intended strategy remaining *unrealized*.

Consider an important trend affecting law firms:

> Many of the leading corporations have reduced their need for outside legal services by increasingly expanding their in-house legal departments.[29] For example, companies and financial institutions spent an estimated $41 billion on their internal lawyers in 2014, a 22 percent increase since 2011. And a survey of 1,200 chief legal officers found that 63 percent of respondents are now "in-sourcing" legal work they used to send out to law firms or other service providers. In response, many large law firms have been forced to move away from commodity practices such as basic commercial contracts to more specialized areas like cross-border transactions and global regulatory issues.

Thus, the final **realized strategy** of any firm is a combination of deliberate and emergent strategies.

> **intended strategy**
> strategy in which organizational decisions are determined only by analysis.

> **realized strategy**
> strategy in which organizational decisions are determined by both analysis and unforeseen environmental developments, unanticipated resource constraints, and/or changes in managerial preferences.

EXHIBIT 1.2 Realized Strategy and Intended Strategy: Usually Not the Same

Source: Adapted from Mintzberg, H. & Waters, J. A., "Of Strategies: Deliberate and Emergent," *Strategic Management Journal*, Vol. 6, 1985, pp. 257–272.

Next, we will address each of the three key strategic management processes—strategy analysis, strategy formulation, and strategy implementation—and provide a brief overview of the chapters.

Exhibit 1.3 depicts the strategic management process and indicates how it ties into the chapters in the book. Consistent with our discussion above, we use two-way arrows to convey the interactive nature of the processes.

Strategy Analysis

> *We measure, study, quantify, analyze every single piece of our business. . . . But then you've got to be able to take all that data and information and transform it into change in the organization and improvements in the organization and the formalization of the business strategy.*
>
> —Richard Anderson, CEO of Delta Airlines[30]

strategy analysis
study of firms' external and internal environments, and their fit with organizational vision and goals.

Strategy analysis may be looked upon as the starting point of the strategic management process. It consists of the "advance work" that must be done in order to effectively formulate and implement strategies. Many strategies fail because managers may want to formulate and implement strategies without a careful analysis of the overarching goals of the organization and without a thorough analysis of its external and internal environments.

Analyzing Organizational Goals and Objectives (Chapter 1) A firm's vision, mission, and strategic objectives form a hierarchy of goals that range from broad statements of intent and bases for competitive advantage to specific, measurable strategic objectives.

Analyzing the External Environment of the Firm (Chapter 2) Managers must monitor and scan the environment as well as analyze competitors. Two frameworks are provided: (1) The general environment consists of several elements, such as demographic and economic segments, and (2) the industry environment consists of competitors and other organizations that may threaten the success of a firm's products and services.

Assessing the Internal Environment of the Firm (Chapter 3) Analyzing the strengths and relationships among the activities that constitute a firm's value chain (e.g., operations,

EXHIBIT 1.3 The Strategic Management Process

Strategy Analysis
- Chapter 1: Introduction and Analyzing Goals and Objectives
- Chapter 2: Analyzing the External Environment
- Chapter 3: Analyzing the Internal Environment
- Chapter 4: Assessing Intellectual Capital

Strategy Formulation
- Chapter 5: Formulating Business-Level Strategies
- Chapter 6: Formulating Corporate-Level Strategies
- Chapter 7: Formulating International Strategies
- Chapter 8: Entrepreneurial Strategy and Competitive Dynamics

Strategy Implementation
- Chapter 9: Strategic Control and Corporate Governance
- Chapter 10: Creating Effective Organizational Designs
- Chapter 11: Strategic Leadership Excellence, Ethics, and Change
- Chapter 12: Fostering Corporate Entrepreneurship

Case Analysis
- Chapter 13: Case Analysis

marketing and sales, and human resource management) can be a means of uncovering potential sources of competitive advantage for the firm.[31]

Assessing a Firm's Intellectual Assets (Chapter 4) The knowledge worker and a firm's other intellectual assets (e.g., patents) are important drivers of competitive advantages and wealth creation. We also assess how well the organization creates networks and relationships as well as how technology can enhance collaboration among employees and provide a means of accumulating and storing knowledge.[32]

Strategy Formulation

> "You can have the best operations. You can be the most adept at whatever it is that you're doing. But, if you have a bad strategy, it's all for naught."
>
> —Fred Smith, CEO of FedEx[33]

strategy formulation
decisions made by firms regarding investments, commitments, and other aspects of operations that create and sustain competitive advantage.

Strategy formulation is developed at several levels. First, business-level strategy addresses the issue of how to compete in a given business to attain competitive advantage. Second, corporate-level strategy focuses on two issues: (a) what businesses to compete in and (b) how businesses can be managed to achieve synergy; that is, they create more value by working together than by operating as stand-alone businesses. Third, a firm must develop international strategies as it ventures beyond its national boundaries. Fourth, managers must formulate effective entrepreneurial initiatives.

Formulating Business-Level Strategy (Chapter 5) The question of how firms compete and outperform their rivals and how they achieve and sustain competitive advantages goes to the heart of strategic management. Successful firms strive to develop bases for competitive advantage, which can be achieved through cost leadership and/or differentiation as well as by focusing on a narrow or industrywide market segment.[34]

Formulating Corporate-Level Strategy (Chapter 6) Corporate-level strategy addresses a firm's portfolio (or group) of businesses. It asks: (1) What business (or businesses) should we compete in? and (2) How can we manage this portfolio of businesses to create synergies among the businesses?

Formulating International Strategy (Chapter 7) When firms enter foreign markets, they face both opportunities and pitfalls.[35] Managers must decide not only on the most appropriate entry strategy but also how they will go about attaining competitive advantages in international markets.[36]

Entrepreneurial Strategy and Competitive Dynamics (Chapter 8) Entrepreneurial activity aimed at new value creation is a major engine for economic growth. For entrepreneurial initiatives to succeed, viable opportunities must be recognized and effective strategies must be formulated.

Strategy Implementation

> "We could leave our strategic plan on an airplane, and it wouldn't matter. It's all about execution."
>
> —John Stumpf, CEO of Wells Fargo[37]

strategy implementation
actions made by firms that carry out the formulated strategy, including strategic controls, organizational design, and leadership.

Clearly, sound strategies are of no value if they are not properly implemented.[38] **Strategy implementation** involves ensuring proper strategic controls and organizational designs, which includes establishing effective means to coordinate and integrate activities within the firm as well as with its suppliers, customers, and alliance partners.[39] Leadership plays a central role to ensure that the organization is committed to excellence and ethical behavior. It also promotes learning and continuous improvement and acts entrepreneurially in creating new opportunities.

Strategic Control and Corporate Governance (Chapter 9) Firms must exercise two types of strategic control. First, informational control requires that organizations continually monitor and scan the environment and respond to threats and opportunities. Second, behavioral control involves the proper balance of rewards and incentives as well as cultures and boundaries (or constraints). Further, successful firms (those that are incorporated) practice effective corporate governance.

Creating Effective Organizational Designs (Chapter 10) Firms must have organizational structures and designs that are consistent with their strategy. In today's rapidly changing competitive environments, firms must ensure that their organizational boundaries—those internal to the firm and external—are more flexible and permeable.[40] Often, organizations develop strategic alliances to capitalize on the capabilities of other organizations.

Creating a Learning Organization and an Ethical Organization (Chapter 11) Effective leaders set a direction, design the organization, and develop an organization that is committed to excellence and ethical behavior. In addition, given rapid and unpredictable change, leaders must create a "learning organization" so that the entire organization can benefit from individual and collective talents.

Fostering Corporate Entrepreneurship (Chapter 12) Firms must continually improve and grow as well as find new ways to renew their organizations. Corporate entrepreneurship and innovation provide firms with new opportunities, and strategies should be formulated that enhance a firm's innovative capacity.

Chapter 13, "Analyzing Strategic Management Cases," provides guidelines and suggestions on how to evaluate cases in this course. Thus, the concepts and techniques discussed in the first 12 chapters can be applied to real-world organizations.

Let's now address two concepts—corporate governance and stakeholder management—that are critical to the strategic management process.

The Role of Corporate Governance and Stakeholder Management

Most business enterprises that employ more than a few dozen people are organized as corporations. As you recall from your finance classes, the overall purpose of a corporation is to maximize the long-term return to the owners (shareholders). Thus, we may ask: Who is really responsible for fulfilling this purpose? Robert Monks and Neil Minow provide a useful definition of **corporate governance** as "the relationship among various participants in determining the direction and performance of corporations. The primary participants are (1) the shareholders, (2) the management (led by the chief executive officer), and (3) the board of directors."[41] This relationship is illustrated in Exhibit 1.4.

The board of directors (BOD) are the elected representatives of the shareholders charged with ensuring that the interests and motives of management are aligned with those of the owners (i.e., shareholders). In many cases, the BOD is diligent in fulfilling its purpose. For

LO1.3
The vital role of corporate governance and stakeholder management, as well as how "symbiosis" can be achieved among an organization's stakeholders.

corporate governance
the relationship among various participants in determining the direction and performance of corporations. The primary participants are (1) the shareholders, (2) the management (led by the chief executive officer), and (3) the board of directors.

EXHIBIT 1.4 The Key Elements of Corporate Governance

Management
(Headed by the chief executive officer)

Shareholders
(Owners)

Board of Directors
(Elected by the shareholders to represent their interests)

example, Intel Corporation, the giant $55 billion maker of microprocessor chips, practices sound governance. Its BOD follows guidelines to ensure that its members are independent (i.e., are not members of the executive management team and do not have close personal ties to top executives) so that they can provide proper oversight; it has explicit guidelines on the selection of director candidates (to avoid "cronyism"). It provides detailed procedures for formal evaluations of directors and the firm's top officers.[42] Such guidelines serve to ensure that management is acting in the best interests of shareholders.[43]

Recently, there has been much criticism as well as cynicism by both citizens and the business press about the poor job that management and the BODs of large corporations are doing. We only have to look at the scandals at firms such as Arthur Andersen, Best Buy, Olympus, Enron, Tyco, and ImClone Systems.[44] Such malfeasance has led to an erosion of the public's trust in corporations. For example, according to the 2014 CNBC/Burson-Marsteller Corporation Perception Indicator, a global survey of 25,000 individuals, only 52 percent of the public in developed markets has a favorable view of corporations.[45] Forty-five percent felt corporations have "too much influence over the government." More than half of the U.S. public said "strong and influential" corporations are "bad" even if they are promoting innovation and growth, and only 9 percent of the public in the United States says corporate CEOs are "among the most respected" in society. Perhaps it may be a bit reassuring to big business that a 2013 poll revealed that the public's view of Congress was significantly less positive than its view of root canals, NFL replacement referees, colonoscopies, France, and even cockroaches!

One area in which public anger is most pronounced is the excessive compensation of the top executives of well-known firms. It is now clear that much of the bonus pay awarded to executives on Wall Street in the past few years was richly undeserved.[46] In the three years that led up to the collapse of seven big financial institutions in 2008, the chief executives of those firms collected a total of $80 million in performance bonuses and raked in $210 million in severance pay and earnings from stock sales. The trend continues. 2011 was a poor year for financial stocks: 35 of the 50 largest financial company stocks fell that year. The sector lost 17 percent—compared to flat performance for the Standard & Poor's 500. However, even as the sector struggled, the average pay of finance company CEOs rose 20.4 percent. For example, JPMorgan CEO Jamie Dimon was the highest-paid banker—with $23.1 million in compensation, an 11 percent increase from the previous year. The firm's shareholders didn't do as well—the stock fell 20 percent.[47]

Of course, excessive pay is not restricted to financial institutions. Consider Staples, whose earnings fell by 43 percent in the first quarter of 2014 after a rough 2013 in which operating income fell by double digits. As expected, Staples' earnings weren't high enough for top executives to receive incentive pay. But the board decided to approve a "retention cash award" to motivate and retain the company's already well-paid executives. As a result, CEO Ron Argent was given $300,000 in cash on top of his $10.8 million total compensation package—which had already increased 40 percent in 2013. (Shareholders had lost 25 percent over the past year.) As noted by Will Becker, an analyst with Behind the Numbers, "This is the worst kind of bonus as the compensation committee essentially changed the rules of the game after the game had already been played."[48]

Clearly, there is a strong need for improved corporate governance, and we will address this topic in Chapter 9.[49] We focus on three important mechanisms to ensure effective corporate governance: an effective and engaged board of directors, shareholder activism, and proper managerial rewards and incentives.[50] In addition to these internal controls, a key role is played by various external control mechanisms.[51] These include the auditors, banks, analysts, an active financial press, and the threat of hostile takeovers.

Alternative Perspectives of Stakeholder Management

Generating long-term returns for the shareholders is the primary goal of a publicly held corporation.[52] As noted by former Chrysler vice chairman Robert Lutz, "We are here to

stakeholder management
a firm's strategy for recognizing and responding to the interests of all its salient stakeholders.

serve the shareholder and create shareholder value. I insist that the only person who owns the company is the person who paid good money for it."[53]

Despite the primacy of generating shareholder value, managers who focus solely on the interests of the owners of the business will often make poor decisions that lead to negative, unanticipated outcomes.[54] For example, decisions such as mass layoffs to increase profits, ignoring issues related to conservation of the natural environment to save money, and exerting excessive pressure on suppliers to lower prices can harm the firm in the long run. Such actions would likely lead to negative outcomes such as alienated employees, increased governmental oversight and fines, and disloyal suppliers.

Clearly, in addition to *shareholders*, there are other *stakeholders* (e.g., suppliers, customers) who must be taken into account in the strategic management process.[55] A stakeholder can be defined as an individual or group, inside or outside the company, that has a stake in and can influence an organization's performance. Each stakeholder group makes various claims on the company.[56] Exhibit 1.5 provides a list of major stakeholder groups and the nature of their claims on the company.

Zero Sum or Symbiosis? There are two opposing ways of looking at the role of stakeholder management.[57] The first one can be termed "zero sum." Here, the various stakeholders compete for the organization's resources: the gain of one individual or group is the loss of another individual or group. For example, employees want higher wages (which drive down profits), suppliers want higher prices for their inputs and slower, more flexible delivery times (which drive up costs), customers want fast deliveries and higher quality (which drive up costs), the community at large wants charitable contributions (which take money from company goals), and so on. This zero-sum thinking is rooted, in part, in the traditional conflict between workers and management, leading to the formation of unions and sometimes ending in adversarial union–management negotiations and long, bitter strikes.

Consider, for example, the many stakeholder challenges facing Walmart, the world's largest retailer.

> Walmart strives to ramp up growth while many stakeholders are watching nervously: employees and trade unions; shareholders, investors, and creditors; suppliers and joint venture partners; the governments of the U.S. and other nations where the retailer operates; and customers. In addition many non-governmental organizations (NGOs), particularly in countries where the retailer buys its products, are closely monitoring Walmart. Walmart's stakeholders have different interests, and not all of them share the firm's goals. Each group has the ability, in various degrees, to influence the firm's choices and results. Clearly, this wasn't the case when Sam Walton built his first store in Rogers, Arkansas, in 1962![58]

There will always be conflicting demands on organizations. However, organizations can achieve mutual benefit through stakeholder symbiosis, which recognizes that stakeholders

EXHIBIT 1.5
An Organization's Key Stakeholders and the Nature of Their Claims

Stakeholder Group	Nature of Claim
Stockholders	Dividends, capital appreciation
Employees	Wages, benefits, safe working environment, job security
Suppliers	Payment on time, assurance of continued relationship
Creditors	Payment of interest, repayment of principal
Customers	Value, warranties
Government	Taxes, compliance with regulations
Communities	Good citizenship behavior such as charities, employment, not polluting the environment

are dependent upon each other for their success and well-being.⁵⁹ Consider Procter & Gamble's "laundry detergent compaction," a technique for compressing even more cleaning power into ever smaller concentrations.

P&G perfected a technique that could compact two or three times as much cleaning powder into a liquid concentration. This remarkable breakthrough has led to not only a change in consumer shopping habits but also a revolution in industry supply chain economics. Here's how several key stakeholders are affected:

> *Consumers* love concentrated liquids because they are easier to carry, pour, and store. *Retailers*, meanwhile, prefer them because they take up less floor and shelf space, which leads to higher sales-per-square-foot—a big deal for Walmart, Target, and other big retailers. *Shipping and wholesalers*, meanwhile, prefer reduced-sized products because smaller bottles translate into reduced fuel consumption and improved warehouse space utilization. And, finally, *environmentalists* favor such products because they use less packaging and produce less waste than conventional products.⁶⁰

Although it often appears the interests of stakeholder groups are in conflict with each other, leading companies are increasingly realizing that learning to partner with governments and communities, suppliers and customers—and even longtime rivals—is essential for dealing with big, complex problems. Strategy Spotlight 1.2 discusses how firms like Nike, Walmart, and Patagonia have started working with a number of stakeholder groups through the Sustainable Apparel Coalition in order to improve the environmental impact of their products.

Social Responsibility and Environmental Sustainability: Moving beyond the Immediate Stakeholders

Organizations cannot ignore the interests and demands of stakeholders such as citizens and society in general that are beyond its immediate constituencies—customers, owners, suppliers, and employees. The realization that firms have multiple stakeholders and that evaluating their performance must go beyond analyzing their financial results has led to a new way of thinking about businesses and their relationship to society.

First, *social responsibility* recognizes that businesses must respond to society's expectations regarding their obligations to society. Second, the *triple bottom line approach* evaluates a firm's performance. This perspective takes into account financial, social, and environmental performance. Third, *making the case for sustainability initiatives* addresses some of the challenges managers face in obtaining approvals for such project—and how to overcome them.

> **social responsibility**
> the expectation that businesses or individuals will strive to improve the overall welfare of society.

> **LO1.4**
> The importance of social responsibility, including environmental sustainability, and how it can enhance a corporation's innovation strategy.

Social Responsibility Social responsibility is the expectation that businesses or individuals will strive to improve the overall welfare of society.⁶¹ From the perspective of a business, this means that managers must take active steps to make society better by virtue of the business being in existence.⁶² What constitutes socially responsible behavior changes over time. In the 1970s affirmative action was a high priority; during the 1990s and up to the present time, the public has been concerned about environmental quality. Many firms have responded to this by engaging in recycling and reducing waste. And in the wake of terrorist attacks on New York City and the Pentagon, as well as the continuing threat from terrorists worldwide, a new kind of priority has arisen: the need to be vigilant concerning public safety.

Today, demands for greater corporate responsibility have accelerated.⁶³ These include corporate critics, social investors, activists, and, increasingly, customers who claim to assess corporate responsibility when making purchasing decisions. Such demands go well beyond product and service quality.⁶⁴ They include a focus on issues such as labor standards, environmental sustainability, financial and accounting reporting, procurement, and environmental practices.⁶⁵ At times, a firm's reputation can be tarnished by exceedingly

1.2 STRATEGY SPOTLIGHT — ENVIRONMENTAL SUSTAINABILITY

THE SUSTAINABLE APPAREL COALITION

The story of the Sustainable Apparel Coalition (SAC) began with a letter designed to get the attention of even a busy CEO. At the top: the logos of Walmart and Patagonia. John Fleming, Walmart's chief merchandising officer, and Yvon Chouinard, Patagonia's founder, signed the letter that invited chief executives of some of the world's biggest clothing companies—normally fierce rivals—to join together to develop an index to measure the environmental impact of their products.

Shortly thereafter, Walmart and Patagonia convened a group of 10 apparel companies in the belief that the adoption of a single, standardized index would drive efficiency and innovation across the apparel value chain and reduce environmental impact and supply chain risks. The so-called Higgs Index enabled companies to compare environmental performance outcomes in areas such as energy efficiency, material waste, water use, and sustainable raw materials. It provided benchmarks at the company, product, and factory levels. Drawing on work already done by Nike and the Outdoor Industry Association, the coalition quickly built a prototype of the index and began testing it in the fall of 2011, across more than 50 brands, retailers, and suppliers. The SAC's benchmarks have mobilized a "race to the top," in which companies that score lower than their competitors on the index are motivated to improve their ratings. (The first version of the Higgs Index was released in July 2012, and it was revised in December 2013.)

The Higgs Index has played a key role in not only driving better outcomes but also influencing capital investment decisions and changing operational behaviors. Target and other major retailers have integrated the index into their supplier scorecard, using the measures to select suppliers. Apparel brands have used the index to help reduce fabric waste through improved product design. Also, manufacturers have used it to justify investments in new capabilities such as wastewater recycling and enhanced energy efficiency. The index even improves performance within companies, as departments compare their scores and engage in productive competitions.

The SAC now has approximately 145 members, representing brands, retailers, suppliers, and other organizations that together account for more than one-third of the global apparel and footwear industry. Its vision: "an apparel and footwear industry that produces no unnecessary environmental harm and has a positive impact on the people and communities associated with its activities."

Sources: Guerin, D. (chief of staff, Sustainable Apparel Coalition). 2014. *personal communication:* October 9; Nidumolu, R., Ellison, J., Whalen, J., & Billman, E. 2014. The collaboration imperative. *Harvard Business Review,* 92(4): 76–84; Gunther, M. 2012. Behind the scenes at the Sustainable Apparel Coalition. *www.greenbix.com,* July 26, np; and *www.apparelcoalition.org.*

---

poor judgment on the part of one of its managers. For example, BP CEO Tony Hayward's decision to withhold information from the public about the magnitude of the oil spill in the Gulf of Mexico further damaged the firm's reputation.

A key stakeholder group that appears to be particularly susceptible to corporate social responsibility (CSR) initiatives is customers.[66] Surveys indicate a strong positive relationship between CSR behaviors and consumers' reactions to a firm's products and services.[67] For example:

- Corporate Citizenship's poll conducted by Cone Communications found that "84 percent of Americans say they would be likely to switch brands to one associated with a good cause, if price and quality are similar."[68]
- Hill & Knowlton/Harris's Interactive poll reveals that "79 percent of Americans take corporate citizenship into account when deciding whether to buy a particular company's product and 37 percent consider corporate citizenship an important factor when making purchasing decisions."[69]

Such findings are consistent with a large body of research that confirms the positive influence of CSR on consumers' company evaluations and product purchase intentions across a broad range of product categories.

The Triple Bottom Line: Incorporating Financial as Well as Environmental and Social Costs Many companies are now measuring what has been called a **"triple bottom line."** This involves assessing financial, social, and environmental performance. Shell, NEC, Procter & Gamble, and others have recognized that failing to account for the environmental and social costs of doing business poses risks to the company and its community.[70]

> **triple bottom line**
> assessment of a firm's financial, social, and environmental performance.

The environmental revolution has been almost four decades in the making.[71] In the 1960s and 1970s, companies were in a state of denial regarding their firms' impact on the natural environment. However, a series of visible ecological problems created a groundswell for strict governmental regulation. In the U.S., Lake Erie was "dead," and in Japan, people died of mercury poisoning. More recently, Japan's horrific tsunami that took place on March 11, 2011, and Hurricane Sandy's devastation on the East Coast of the United States in late October 2012 have raised alarms. Clearly, the effects of global warming are being felt throughout the world.

Stuart Hart, writing in the *Harvard Business Review*, addresses the magnitude of problems and challenges associated with the natural environment:

> The challenge is to develop a *sustainable global economy:* an economy that the planet is capable of supporting indefinitely. Although we may be approaching ecological recovery in the developed world, the planet as a whole remains on an unsustainable course. Increasingly, the scourges of the late twentieth century—depleted farmland, fisheries, and forests; choking urban pollution; poverty; infectious disease; and migration—are spilling over geopolitical borders. The simple fact is this: in meeting our needs, we are destroying the ability of future generations to meet theirs . . . corporations are the only organizations with the resources, the technology, the global reach, and, ultimately, the motivation to achieve sustainability.[72]

Environmental sustainability is now a value embraced by the most competitive and successful multinational companies.[73] The McKinsey Corporation's survey of more than 400 senior executives of companies around the world found that 92 percent agreed with former Sony president Akio Morita's contention that the environmental challenge will be one of the central issues in the 21st century.[74] Virtually all executives acknowledged their firms' responsibility to control pollution, and 83 percent agreed that corporations have an environmental responsibility for their products even after they are sold.

For many successful firms, environmental values are now becoming a central part of their cultures and management processes.[75] And, as noted earlier, environmental impacts are being audited and accounted for as the "third bottom line." According to a recent corporate report, "If we aren't good corporate citizens as reflected in a Triple Bottom Line that takes into account social and environmental responsibilities along with financial ones—eventually our stock price, our profits, and our entire business could suffer."[76] Also, a CEO survey on sustainability by Accenture debunks the notion that sustainability and profitability are mutually exclusive corporate goals. The study found that sustainability is being increasingly recognized as a source of cost efficiencies and revenue growth. In many companies, sustainability activities have led to increases in revenue and profits. As Jeff Immelt, the CEO of General Electric, puts it, "Green is green."[77] Strategy Spotlight 1.3 provides examples of how environmental initiatives can really pay off financially, that is, increase revenues and cut costs. We mention such well-known companies as Clorox, GE, DuPont, and IBM that represent a wide range of industries. Clearly, one could argue that the benefits go far beyond "good PR"!

Many firms have profited by investing in socially responsible behavior, including those activities that enhance environmental sustainability. However, how do such "socially responsible" companies fare in terms of shareholder returns compared to benchmarks such as the Standard & Poor's 500 Index? Let's look at some of the evidence.

> SRI (socially responsible investing) is a broad-based approach to investing that now encompasses an estimated $3.7 trillion, or $1 out of every $9 under professional management in the United States.[78] SRI recognizes that corporate responsibility and societal concerns are considerations in investment decisions. With SRI, investors have the opportunity to put their money to work to build a more sustainable world while earning competitive returns both today and over time.

1.3 STRATEGY SPOTLIGHT — ENVIRONMENTAL SUSTAINABILITY

GOING GREEN CAN BOOST REVENUES AND CUT COSTS

Harold Sirkin, senior partner of the Boston Consulting Group (BCG), recently commented: "In days past, many sustainability efforts would have been the result of government prodding or public pressure, or would have been undertaken for PR purposes. Today's executives know better. They realize that 'green,' our convenient euphemism for sustainability, is the color of money." Let's look at how some well-known firms have benefited financially from such initiatives.

Increased Revenues

- Clorox's Green Works line of plant-based cleaning materials captured 42 percent of the natural cleaning products market in its first year.
- GE earns more than $18 billion a year from its "ecomagination" product lines, each of which contributes to solving global sustainability challenges.
- Mitsubishi expects $13.3 billion in annual sales by 2016 from clean technologies, including solar systems, heat pumps, and other energy-efficient power devices.
- DuPont expects an additional $6 billion in annual revenues through product innovation based on sustainability.

Lower Costs

- Northrup Grumman saved $2 million in energy costs at a single facility by installing reflective roofs and fluorescent lighting, replacing old equipment, and making minor temperature and humidity-level adjustments.
- IBM saved $49 million by investing $1 million in a green overhaul of one of its data centers in Kentucky; it also boosted the center's IT capacity eight times, without raising the energy footprint, through energy efficiency improvements.
- Baxter International, over the past decade, has received an average return of approximately $3 for every $1 invested in its environmental initiatives, which it has documented on its annual Environmental Financial Statement of environmental costs and benefits.
- The Fairmont Royal York in Toronto invested $25,000 in an energy conservation program to replace leaky steam traps and fix leaks, which resulted in an annual savings of over $200,000.

Sources: Sirkin, H. L. 2013. A sustainable business model pays off. *www.businessweek.com*, November 26: np; Anonymous. Why go green? The business case for sustainability. *greenhotelscombined.com*, undated, np; and Esty, D. C. & Simmons, P. J. 2011. *The green to gold business playbook*. Hoboken, NJ: Wiley.

And, as the saying goes, nice guys don't have to finish last. The ING SRI Index Fund, which tracks the stocks of 50 companies, enjoyed a 47.4 percent return in a recent year. That easily beat the 2.65 percent gain of the Standard & Poor's 500 stock index. A review of the 145 socially responsible equity mutual and exchange-traded funds tracked by Morningstar also shows that 65 percent of them outperformed the S&P 500.[79]

Making the Business Case for Sustainability Initiatives We mentioned many financial and nonfinancial benefits associated with sustainability initiatives in the previous section. However, in practice, such initiatives often have difficulty making it through the conventional approval process within corporations. This is primarily because, before companies make investments in projects, managers want to know their return on investment.[80]

The ROIs on sustainability projects are often very difficult to quantify for a number of reasons. Among these are:

1. *The data necessary to calculate ROI accurately are often not available when it comes to sustainability projects.* However, sustainability programs may often find their success beyond company boundaries, so internal systems and process metrics can't capture all the relevant numbers.
2. *Many of the benefits from such projects are intangible.* Traditional financial models are built around relatively easy-to-measure, monetized results. Yet many of the benefits of sustainability projects involve fuzzy intangibles, such as the goodwill that can enhance a firm's brand equity.
3. *The payback period is on a different time frame.* Even when their future benefits can be forecast, sustainability projects often require longer-term payback windows.

1.4 STRATEGY SPOTLIGHT

STRATEGY AND THE VALUE OF INEXPERIENCE

Peter Gruber, chairman of Mandalay Entertainment, discovered that great ideas can come from the least expected sources. During the filming of the movie *Gorillas in the Mist*, his production company faced many problems. Rwanda—the site of the filming—was on the verge of revolution, the film needed to use 200 animals, and the screenplay required the gorillas to follow a script, that is, do what the script called for and "act." If that failed, the fallback position was to use dwarfs in gorilla suits on a soundstage—a strategy that usually failed.

Gruber explains how the "day was saved" by someone with very limited experience:

> We called an emergency meeting to solve these problems. In the middle of it, a young intern asked, "What if you let the gorillas write the story?" Everyone laughed and wondered what she was doing in the meeting with experienced filmmakers. Hours later, someone casually asked her what she had meant. She said, "What if you send a really good cinematographer into the jungle with a ton of film to shoot the gorillas, then you could write a story around what the gorillas did on film." It was a brilliant idea. And we did exactly what she suggested: We sent Alan Root, an Academy Award–nominated cinematographer into the jungle for three weeks. He came back with phenomenal footage that practically wrote the story for us.

The upshot? The film cost $20 million to shoot—half the original budget. And it was nominated for five Academy Awards—including Sigourney Weaver for best actress—and it won two Golden Globe Awards.

Source: Gruber, P. 1998. My greatest lesson. *Fast Company,* 14: 88–90; and *imdb.com.*

Clearly, the case for sustainability projects needs to be made on the basis of a more holistic and comprehensive understanding of all the tangible and intangible benefits rather than whether or not they meet existing hurdle rates for traditional investment projects. For example, 3M uses a lower hurdle rate for pollution prevention projects. When it comes to environmental projects, IKEA allows a 10- to 15-year payback period, considerably longer than it allows for other types of investment. And Diversey, a cleaning products company, has employed a portfolio approach. It has established two hurdles for projects in its carbon reduction plan: a three-year payback and a cost per megaton of carbon avoided. Out of 120 possible projects ranging from lighting retrofits to solar photovoltaic systems, only 30 cleared both hurdles. Although about 60 of the other ideas could reach *one,* an expanded 90-project portfolio, all added together, met the double hurdle. Subsequently, Diversey was able to increase its carbon reduction goal from 8 to 25 percent and generated a higher net present value.

Such approaches are the result of the recognition that the intangible benefits of sustainability projects—such as reducing risks, staying ahead of regulations, pleasing communities, and enhancing employee morale—are substantial even when they are difficult to quantify. Just as companies spend large fortunes on launching advertising campaigns or initiating R&D projects without a clear quantification of financial returns, sustainability investments are necessary even when it is difficult to calculate the ROE of such investments. The alternative of not making these investments is often no longer feasible.

The Strategic Management Perspective: An Imperative throughout the Organization

LO1.5
The need for greater empowerment throughout the organization.

Strategic management requires managers to take an integrative view of the organization and assess how all of the functional areas and activities fit together to help an organization achieve its goals and objectives. This cannot be accomplished if only the top managers in the organization take an integrative, strategic perspective of issues facing the firm and everyone else "fends for themselves" in their independent, isolated functional areas. Instead, people throughout the organization must strive toward overall goals.

The need for such a perspective is accelerating in today's increasingly complex, interconnected, ever-changing, global economy. As noted by Peter Senge of MIT, the days when Henry Ford, Alfred Sloan, and Tom Watson (top executives at Ford, General Motors, and IBM, respectively) "learned for the organization are gone."[81]

To develop and mobilize people and other assets, leaders are needed throughout the organization.[82] No longer can organizations be effective if the top "does the thinking" and the rest of the organization "does the work." Everyone must be involved in the strategic management process. There is a critical need for three types of leaders:

- *Local line leaders* who have significant profit-and-loss responsibility.
- *Executive leaders* who champion and guide ideas, create a learning infrastructure, and establish a domain for taking action.
- *Internal networkers* who, although they have little positional power and formal authority, generate their power through the conviction and clarity of their ideas.[83]

Top-level executives are key in setting the tone for the empowerment of employees. Consider Richard Branson, founder of the Virgin Group, whose core businesses include retail operations, hotels, communications, and an airline. He is well known for creating a culture and an informal structure where anybody in the organization can be involved in generating and acting upon new business ideas. In an interview, he stated:

> Speed is something that we are better at than most companies. We don't have formal board meetings, committees, etc. If someone has an idea, they can pick up the phone and talk to me. I can vote "done, let's do it." Or, better still, they can just go ahead and do it. They know that they are not going to get a mouthful from me if they make a mistake. Rules and regulations are not our forte. Analyzing things to death is not our kind of thing. We very rarely sit back and analyze what we do.[84]

To inculcate a strategic management perspective, managers must often make a major effort to effect transformational change. This involves extensive communication, incentives, training, and development. For example, under the direction of Nancy Snyder, a corporate vice president, Whirlpool, the world's largest producer of household appliances, brought about a significant shift in the firm's reputation as an innovator.[85] This five-year initiative included financial investments in capital spending as well as a series of changes in management processes, including training innovation mentors, making innovation a significant portion of leadership development programs, enrolling all salaried employees in online courses in business innovation, and providing employees an innovation portal to access multiple innovation tools and data.

Many successful executives reward honesty and input and show their interest in learning what others are thinking. Methods vary and include holding town-hall meetings, seeking the advice of people at all levels of the firm, and asking employees what they would do if they were in charge. As noted by Tim Brown, CEO of the premier design consulting firm IDEO: "The best can come from anywhere in an organization. So you'd better do a good job of spotting and promoting them when they come, and not let people's positions dictate how influential their ideas are."[86]

We'd like to close with our favorite example of how inexperience can be a virtue. It further reinforces the benefits of having broad involvement throughout the organization in the strategic management process (see Strategy Spotlight 1.4).

Ensuring Coherence in Strategic Direction

Employees and managers must strive toward common goals and objectives.[87] By specifying desired results, it becomes much easier to move forward. Otherwise, when no one knows what the firm is striving to accomplish, individuals have no idea of what to work

LO1.6

How an awareness of a hierarchy of strategic goals can help an organization achieve coherence in its strategic direction.

toward. Alan Mulally, CEO at Ford Motor Company, stresses the importance of perspective in creating a sense of mission:

> I think the most important thing is coming to a shared view about what we're trying to accomplish—whether you're a nonprofit or a for-profit organization. What are we? What is our real purpose? And then, how do you include everybody so you know where you are on that plan, so you can work on areas that need special attention. And then everybody gets a chance to participate and feel that accomplishment of participating and contributing.[88]

Organizations express priorities best through stated goals and objectives that form a **hierarchy of goals,** which includes the firm's vision, mission, and strategic objectives.[89] What visions may lack in specificity, they make up for in their ability to evoke powerful and compelling mental images. On the other hand, strategic objectives tend to be more specific and provide a more direct means of determining if the organization is moving toward broader, overall goals.[90] Visions, as one would expect, also have longer time horizons than either mission statements or strategic objectives. Exhibit 1.6 depicts the hierarchy of goals and its relationship to two attributes: general versus specific and time horizon.

hierarchy of goals organizational goals ranging from, at the top, those that are less specific yet able to evoke powerful and compelling mental images, to, at the bottom, those that are more specific and measurable.

vision organizational goal(s) that evoke(s) powerful and compelling mental images.

Organizational Vision

A **vision** is a goal that is "massively inspiring, overarching, and long term."[91] It represents a destination that is driven by and evokes passion. For example, Wendy Kopp, founder of Teach for America, notes that her vision for the organization, which strives to improve the quality of inner-city schools, draws many applicants:

> We're looking for people who are magnetized to this notion, this vision, that one day all children in our nation should have the opportunity to attain an excellent education. And that magnetizes certain people. And so it's more about them—it's their vision, it's not my vision. It's our collective vision.[92]

Leaders must develop and implement a vision. A vision may or may not succeed; it depends on whether or not everything else happens according to an organization's strategy. As Mark Hurd, Hewlett-Packard's former CEO, humorously points out: "Without execution, vision is just another word for hallucination."[93]

In a survey of executives from 20 different countries, respondents were asked what they believed were a leader's key traits.[94] Ninety-eight percent responded that "a strong sense of vision" was the most important. Similarly, when asked about the critical knowledge skills, the leaders cited "strategy formulation to achieve a vision" as the most important skill. In other words, managers need to have not only a vision but also a plan to implement it. Regretfully, 90 percent reported a lack of confidence in their own skills and ability to conceive a vision. For example, T. J. Rogers, CEO of Cypress Semiconductor, an electronic-chip maker that faced some difficulties in 1992, lamented that his own shortsightedness caused the danger: "I did not have the 50,000-foot view, and got caught."[95]

EXHIBIT 1.6 A Hierarchy of Goals

One of the most famous examples of a vision is Disneyland's: "To be the happiest place on earth." Other examples are:

- "Restoring patients to full life." (Medtronic)
- "We want to satisfy all of our customers' financial needs and help them succeed financially." (Wells Fargo)
- "Our vision is to be the world's best quick service restaurant." (McDonald's)
- "To organize the world's information and make it universally accessible and useful." (Google)
- "Connecting the world through games." (Zynga)

Although such visions cannot be accurately measured by a specific indicator of how well they are being achieved, they do provide a fundamental statement of an organization's values, aspirations, and goals. Such visions go well beyond narrow financial objectives, of course, and strive to capture both the minds and hearts of employees.

The vision statement may also contain a slogan, diagram, or picture—whatever grabs attention.[96] The aim is to capture the essence of the more formal parts of the vision in a few words that are easily remembered, yet that evoke the spirit of the entire vision statement. In its 20-year battle with Xerox, Canon's slogan, or battle cry, was "Beat Xerox." Motorola's slogan is "Total Customer Satisfaction." Outboard Marine Corporation's slogan is "To Take the World Boating."

Clearly, vision statements are not a cure-all. Sometimes they backfire and erode a company's credibility. Visions fail for many reasons, including the following:[97]

The Walk Doesn't Match the Talk   An idealistic vision can arouse employee enthusiasm. However, that same enthusiasm can be quickly dashed if employees find that senior management's behavior is not consistent with the vision. Often, vision is a sloganeering campaign of new buzzwords and empty platitudes like "devotion to the customer," "teamwork," or "total quality" that aren't consistently backed by management's action.

Irrelevance   Visions created in a vacuum—unrelated to environmental threats or opportunities or an organization's resources and capabilities—often ignore the needs of those who are expected to buy into them. Employees reject visions that are not anchored in reality.

Not the Holy Grail   Managers often search continually for the one elusive solution that will solve their firm's problems—that is, the next "holy grail" of management. They may have tried other management fads only to find that they fell short of their expectations. However, they remain convinced that one exists. A vision simply cannot be viewed as a magic cure for an organization's illness.

Too Much Focus Leads to Missed Opportunities   The downside of too much focus is that in directing people and resources toward a grandiose vision, losses can be devastating. Consider Samsung's ambitious venture into automobile manufacturing:

> In 1992, Kun-Hee Lee, chairman of South Korea's Samsung Group, created a bold strategy to become one of the 10 largest car makers by 2010. Seduced by the clarity of the vision, Samsung bypassed staged entry through a joint venture or initial supply contract. Instead, Samsung borrowed heavily to build a state-of-the-art research and design facility and erect a greenfield factory, complete with cutting-edge robotics. Samsung Auto suffered operating losses and crushing interest charges from the beginning. And within a few years the business was divested for a fraction of the initial investment.[98]

An Ideal Future Irreconciled with the Present Although visions are not designed to mirror reality, they must be anchored somehow in it. People have difficulty identifying with a vision that paints a rosy picture of the future but does not account for the often hostile environment in which the firm competes or that ignores some of the firm's weaknesses.

Mission Statements

mission statement
a set of organizational goals that includes the purpose of the organization, its scope of operations, and the basis of its competitive advantage.

A company's **mission statement** differs from its vision in that it encompasses both the purpose of the company and the basis of competition and competitive advantage.

Exhibit 1.7 contains the vision statement and mission statement of WellPoint Health Network, a giant $73 billion managed health care organization. Note that while the vision statement is broad-based, the mission statement is more specific and focused on the means by which the firm will compete.

Effective mission statements incorporate the concept of stakeholder management, suggesting that organizations must respond to multiple constituencies. Customers, employees, suppliers, and owners are the primary stakeholders, but others may also play an important role. Mission statements also have the greatest impact when they reflect an organization's enduring, overarching strategic priorities and competitive positioning. Mission statements also can vary in length and specificity. The three mission statements below illustrate these issues.

- "To produce superior financial returns for our shareholders as we serve our customers with the highest quality transportation, logistics, and e-commerce." (Federal Express)
- "Build the best product, cause no unnecessary harm, use business to inspire and implement solutions to the environmental crisis." (Patagonia)
- "To be the very best in the business. Our game plan is status go . . . we are constantly looking ahead, building on our strengths, and reaching for new goals. In our quest of these goals, we look at the three stars of the Brinker logo and are reminded of the basic values that are the strength of this company . . . People, Quality and Profitability. Everything we do at Brinker must support these core values. We also look at the eight golden flames depicted in our logo, and are reminded of the fire that ignites our mission and makes up the heart and soul of this incredible company. These flames are: Customers, Food, Team, Concepts, Culture, Partners, Community, and Shareholders. As keeper of these flames, we will continue to build on our strengths and work together to be the best in the business." (Brinker International, whose restaurant chains include Chili's and On the Border)[99]

Few mission statements identify profit or any other financial indicator as the sole purpose of the firm. Indeed, many do not even mention profit or shareholder return.[100] Employees of organizations or departments are usually the mission's most important audience. For them, the mission should help to build a common understanding of purpose and commitment to nurture.

EXHIBIT 1.7
Comparing WellPoint Health Network's Vision and Mission

Vision
WellPoint *will redefine our industry:*
Through a new generation of consumer-friendly products that put individuals back in control of their future.

Mission
The WellPoint companies provide health *security* by offering a *choice* of quality branded health and related financial services *designed* to meet the *changing* expectations of individuals, families, and their sponsors throughout a *lifelong* relationship.

Source: WellPoint Health Network company records.

1.5 STRATEGY SPOTLIGHT

HOW THE JAMES IRVINE FOUNDATION REDEFINED ITS MISSION

Several years ago the James Irvine Foundation undertook its first comprehensive strategic planning effort in more than a decade. The foundation's mission is "to expand opportunity for the people of California to participate in a vibrant, successful, and inclusive society." As of 2014, it had about $1.8 billion in assets, and it awarded $69 million in grants in 2013.

Over time, however, this inspirational statement had led to a sprawling portfolio of grants, and the foundation's leaders had come to recognize that it was far too open-ended to be useful in making program and funding decisions. To decide where the foundation could have the most lasting impact, they commissioned research on a broad range of issues facing Californians, including education, health, and the environment. Through its research, the foundation found that changing demographics, technology, and audience expectations would influence dramatically how art museums, symphony orchestras, and theaters would run their establishments.

The senior team was soon flooded in data. Some findings leaped out—the significant challenges facing California's youth, for one. But given the magnitude of the state's needs, the team quickly realized that numbers alone could justify a large variety of funding decisions. So it honed in on three critical organizational values: addressing the root causes rather than crises, enabling Californians to help themselves, and working on problems that might attract like-minded partners or funders. Guided by both values and data, the team redefined its mission and selected youths aged 14 to 24 as the primary beneficiaries of its funding, and education as the primary lever for change. For example, in 2012 the foundation approved seven grants totaling more than $1.75 million to help increase the number of low-income youth who complete high school on time and attain a postsecondary degree by the age of 25.

The Irvine Foundation had to make some hard decisions: What, for instance, should it do about its long-standing commitment to the arts? The arts did not emerge from the data as a critical challenge, but decades of investment there had given Irvine unique assets in the form of reputation and relationships. Furthermore, its exit would have a disproportionately harsh impact on the field. Thus, the foundation's leaders continued arts funding, albeit at a much lower level, and devised a new arts strategy in 2012. This new strategy offers risk capital to encourage and fuel arts engagement by local organizations.

Sources: Perry, S. 2014. James Irvine Foundation taps interim CEO for permanent post. *philanthropy.com*, September 18: np. Ditkoff, S. W. & Colby. S. J. 2009. Galvanizing philanthropy. *Harvard Business Review*, 87(11): 109; A conversation with John Jenks, Irvine's chief investment officer. Undated. *www.irvine.com*, np; Emerling, S. 2009. James Irvine Foundation rewards the innovators. *www.articles.latimes.com*, June 17: np; and Ramirez, J. 2012. Our new arts strategy's first grants. *www.irvine.com*, June 22: np.

A good mission statement, by addressing each principal theme, must communicate why an organization is special and different. Two studies that linked corporate values and mission statements with financial performance found that the most successful firms mentioned values other than profits. The less successful firms focused almost entirely on profitability.[101] In essence, profit is the metaphorical equivalent of oxygen, food, and water that the body requires. They are not the point of life, but without them, there is no life.

Vision statements tend to be quite enduring and seldom change. However, a firm's mission can and should change when competitive conditions dramatically change or the firm is faced with new threats or opportunities.

The transformation of the James Irvine Foundation is described in Strategy Spotlight 1.5. This philanthropic foundation switched from the broad mission "to expand opportunity for the people of California" to a narrow mission that focuses on the education of youths aged 14 to 24.

Strategic Objectives

Strategic objectives are used to operationalize the mission statement.[102] That is, they help to provide guidance on how the organization can fulfill or move toward the "higher goals" in the goal hierarchy—the mission and vision. Thus, they are more specific and cover a more well-defined time frame. Setting objectives demands a yardstick to measure the fulfillment of the objectives.[103]

Exhibit 1.8 lists several firms' strategic objectives—both financial and nonfinancial. While most of them are directed toward generating greater profits and returns for the owners of the business, others are directed at customers or society at large.

> **strategic objectives** a set of organizational goals that are used to operationalize the mission statement and that are specific and cover a well-defined time frame.

EXHIBIT 1.8
Strategic Objectives

Strategic Objectives (Financial)

- Increase sales growth 6 percent to 8 percent and accelerate core net earnings growth from 13 percent to 15 percent per share in each of the next 5 years. (Procter & Gamble)
- Generate Internet-related revenue of $1.5 billion. (AutoNation)
- Increase the contribution of Banking Group earnings from investments, brokerage, and insurance from 16 percent to 25 percent. (Wells Fargo)
- Cut corporate overhead costs by $30 million per year. (Fortune Brands)

Strategic Objectives (Nonfinancial)

- We want a majority of our customers, when surveyed, to say they consider Wells Fargo the best financial institution in the community. (Wells Fargo)
- Reduce volatile air emissions 15 percent by 2015 from 2010 base year, indexed to net sales. (3M)
- Our goal is to help save 100,000 more lives each year. (Varian Medical Systems)
- We want to be the top-ranked supplier to our customers. (PPG)

Sources: Company documents and annual reports.

For objectives to be meaningful, they need to satisfy several criteria. An objective must be:

- *Measurable.* There must be at least one indicator (or yardstick) that measures progress against fulfilling the objective.
- *Specific.* This provides a clear message as to what needs to be accomplished.
- *Appropriate.* It must be consistent with the organization's vision and mission.
- *Realistic.* It must be an achievable target given the organization's capabilities and opportunities in the environment. In essence, it must be challenging but doable.
- *Timely.* There must be a time frame for achieving the objective. As the economist John Maynard Keynes once said, "In the long run, we are all dead!"

When objectives satisfy the above criteria, there are many benefits. First, they help to channel all employees' efforts toward common goals. This helps the organization concentrate and conserve valuable resources and work collectively in a timely manner.

Second, challenging objectives can help to motivate and inspire employees to higher levels of commitment and effort. Much research has supported the notion that people work harder when they are striving toward specific goals instead of being asked simply to "do their best."

Third, as we noted earlier in the chapter, there is always the potential for different parts of an organization to pursue their own goals rather than overall company goals. Although well intentioned, these may work at cross-purposes to the organization as a whole. Meaningful objectives thus help to resolve conflicts when they arise.

Finally, proper objectives provide a yardstick for rewards and incentives. They will ensure a greater sense of equity or fairness when rewards are allocated.

A caveat: When formulating strategic objectives, managers need to remember that too many objectives can result in a lack of focus and diminished results:

> A few years ago CEO Tony Petrucciani and his team at Single Source Systems, a software firm in Fishers, Indiana, set 15 annual objectives, such as automating some of its software functions. However, the firm, which got distracted by having so many items on its objective list, missed its $8.1 million revenue benchmark by 11 percent. "Nobody focused on any one thing," he says. Going forward, Petrucciani decided to set just a few key priorities. This helped the company to meet its goal of $10 million in sales. Sometimes, less is more![104]

In addition to the above, organizations have lower-level objectives that are more specific than strategic objectives. These are often referred to as short-term objectives—essential components of a firm's "action plan" that are critical in implementing the firm's chosen strategy. We discuss these issues in detail in Chapter 9.

ISSUE FOR DEBATE

Seventh Generation's Decision Dilemma

A strike idled 67,300 workers of the United Food and Commercial Workers (UFCW) who worked at Albertsons, Ralphs, and Vons—all large grocery store chains. These stores sold natural home products made by Seventh Generation, a socially conscious company. Interestingly, the inspiration for its name came from the Great Law of the Haudenosaunee. (This Law of Peace of the Iroquois Confederacy in North America has its roots in the 14th century.) The law states that "in our every deliberation we must consider the impact of our decisions on the next seven generations." Accordingly, the company's mission is "To inspire a revolution that nurtures the health of the next seven generations," and its values are to "care wholeheartedly, collaborate deliberately, nurture nature, innovate disruptively, and be a trusted brand."

Clearly, Seventh Generation faced a dilemma: On the one hand, it believed that the strikers had a just cause. However, if it honored the strikers by not crossing the picket lines, the firm would lose the shelf space for its products in the stores it had worked so hard to secure. Honoring the strikers would also erode its trust with the large grocery stores. On the other hand, if Seventh Generation ignored the strikers and proceeded to send its products to the stores, it would be compromising its values and thereby losing trust and credibility with several stakeholders—its customers, distributors, and employees.

Discussion Questions

1. How important should the Seventh Generation values be considered when deciding what to do?
2. How can Seventh Generation solve this dilemma?

Sources: Russo, M. V. 2010. *Companies on a mission: Entrepreneurial strategies for growing sustainably, responsibly, and profitably.* Stanford: Stanford University Press: 94–96; Seventh Generation. 2012. Seventh generation's mission—Corporate social responsibility. *www.seventhgeneration.com*, np; Foster, A. C. 2004. Major work stoppage in 2003. U.S. Bureau of Labor and Statistics. Compensation and Working Conditions. *www.bls.gov*, November 23: np; Fast Company. 2008. 45 social entrepreneurs who are changing the world. Profits with purpose: Seventh Generation. *www.fastcompany*, np; and Ratical. Undated. The six nations: Oldest living participatory democracy on earth. *www.ratical.org*, np.

Reflecting on Career Implications . . .

- **Attributes of Strategic Management:** The attributes of strategic management described in this chapter are applicable to your personal careers as well. What are your overall goals and objectives? Who are the stakeholders you have to consider in making your career decisions (family, community, etc.)? What trade-offs do you see between your long-term and short-term goals?

- **Intended versus Emergent Strategies:** While you may have planned your career trajectory carefully, don't be too tied to it. Strive to take advantage of new opportunities as they arise. Many promising career opportunities may "emerge" that were not part of your intended career strategy or your specific job assignment. Take initiative by pursuing opportunities to get additional training (e.g., learn a software or a statistical package), volunteering for a short-term overseas assignment, etc. You may be in a better position to take advantage of such emergent opportunities if you take the effort to prepare for them. For example, learning a foreign language may position you better for an overseas opportunity.

- **Ambidexterity:** In Strategy Spotlight 1.1, we discussed the four most important traits of ambidextrous individuals. These include looking for opportunities beyond the description of one's job, seeking out opportunities to collaborate with others, building internal networks, and multitasking. Evaluate yourself along each of these criteria. If you score low, think of ways in which you can improve your ambidexterity.

- **Strategic Coherence:** What is the mission of your organization? What are the strategic objectives of the department or unit you are working for? In what ways does your own role contribute to the mission and objectives? What can you do differently in order to help the organization attain its mission and strategic objectives?

- **Strategic Coherence:** Setting strategic objectives is important in your personal career as well. Identify and write down three or four important strategic objectives you want to accomplish in the next few years (finish your degree, find a better-paying job, etc.). Are you allocating your resources (time, money, etc.) to enable you to achieve these objectives? Are your objectives measurable, timely, realistic, specific, and appropriate?

summary

We began this introductory chapter by defining strategic management and articulating some of its key attributes. Strategic management is defined as "consisting of the analyses, decisions, and actions an organization undertakes to create and sustain competitive advantages." The issue of how and why some firms outperform others in the marketplace is central to the study of strategic management. Strategic management has four key attributes: It is directed at overall organizational goals, includes multiple stakeholders, incorporates both short-term and long-term perspectives, and incorporates trade-offs between efficiency and effectiveness.

The second section discussed the strategic management process. Here, we paralleled the above definition of strategic management and focused on three core activities in the strategic management process—strategy analysis, strategy formulation, and strategy implementation. We noted how each of these activities is highly interrelated to and interdependent on the others. We also discussed how each of the first 12 chapters in this text fits into the three core activities.

Next, we introduced two important concepts—corporate governance and stakeholder management—which must be taken into account throughout the strategic management process. Governance mechanisms can be broadly divided into two groups: internal and external. Internal governance mechanisms include shareholders (owners), management (led by the chief executive officer), and the board of directors. External control is exercised by auditors, banks, analysts, and an active business press as well as the threat of takeovers. We identified five key stakeholders in all organizations: owners, customers, suppliers, employees, and society at large. Successful firms go beyond an overriding focus on satisfying solely the interests of owners. Rather, they recognize the inherent conflicts that arise among the demands of the various stakeholders as well as the need to endeavor to attain "symbiosis"—that is, interdependence and mutual benefit—among the various stakeholder groups. Managers must also recognize the need to act in a socially responsible manner which, if done effectively, can enhance a firm's innovativeness. The "shared value" approach represents an innovative perspective on creating value for the firm and society at the same time. The managers also should recognize and incorporate issues related to environmental sustainability in their strategic actions.

In the fourth section, we discussed factors that have accelerated the rate of unpredictable change that managers face today. Such factors, and the combination of them, have increased the need for managers and employees throughout the organization to have a strategic management perspective and to become more empowered.

The final section addressed the need for consistency among a firm's vision, mission, and strategic objectives. Collectively, they form an organization's hierarchy of goals. Visions should evoke powerful and compelling mental images. However, they are not very specific. Strategic objectives, on the other hand, are much more specific and are vital to ensuring that the organization is striving toward fulfilling its vision and mission.

SUMMARY REVIEW QUESTIONS

1. How is "strategic management" defined in the text, and what are its four key attributes?
2. Briefly discuss the three key activities in the strategic management process. Why is it important for managers to recognize the interdependent nature of these activities?
3. Explain the concept of "stakeholder management." Why shouldn't managers be solely interested in stockholder management, that is, maximizing the returns for owners of the firm—its shareholders?
4. What is "corporate governance"? What are its three key elements, and how can it be improved?
5. How can "symbiosis" (interdependence, mutual benefit) be achieved among a firm's stakeholders?
6. Why do firms need to have a greater strategic management perspective and empowerment in the strategic management process throughout the organization?
7. What is meant by a "hierarchy of goals"? What are the main components of it, and why must consistency be achieved among them?

key terms

romantic view of leadership 5
external control view of leadership 6
strategic management 8
strategy 8
competitive advantage 8
operational effectiveness 8
stakeholders 9
effectiveness 10
efficiency 10
ambidexterity 10
strategic management process 10
intended strategy 11
realized strategy 11
strategy analysis 12
strategy formulation 14
strategy implementation 14
corporate governance 15
stakeholder management 16
social responsibility 18
triple bottom line 19
hierarchy of goals 24
vision 24
mission statement 26
strategic objectives 27

experiential exercise

Using the Internet or library sources, select four organizations—two in the private sector and two in the public sector. Find their mission statements. Complete the following exhibit by identifying the stakeholders that are mentioned. Evaluate the differences between firms in the private sector and those in the public sector.

Organization Name			
Mission Statement			
Stakeholders (√ = mentioned)			
1. Customers			
2. Suppliers			
3. Managers/employees			
4. Community-at-large			
5. Owners			
6. Others?			
7. Others?			

application questions & exercises

1. Go to the Internet and look up one of these company sites: *www.walmart.com*, *www.ge.com*, or *www.fordmotor.com*. What are some of the key events that would represent the "romantic" perspective of leadership? What are some of the key events that depict the "external control" perspective of leadership?
2. Select a company that competes in an industry in which you are interested. What are some of the recent demands that stakeholders have placed on this company? Can you find examples of how the company is trying to develop "symbiosis" (interdependence and mutual benefit) among its stakeholders? (Use the Internet and library resources.)
3. Provide examples of companies that are actively trying to increase the amount of empowerment in the strategic management process throughout the organization. Do these companies seem to be having positive outcomes? Why? Why not?
4. Look up the vision statements and/or mission statements for a few companies. Do you feel that they are constructive and useful as a means of motivating employees and providing a strong strategic direction? Why? Why not? (*Note:* Annual reports, along with the Internet, may be good sources of information.)

ethics questions

1. A company focuses solely on short-term profits to provide the greatest return to the owners of the business (i.e., the shareholders in a publicly held firm). What ethical issues could this raise?
2. A firm has spent some time—with input from managers at all levels—on developing a vision statement and a mission statement. Over time, however, the behavior of some executives is contrary to these statements. Could this raise some ethical issues?

references

1. Gunther, M. 2010. Fallen angels. *Fortune,* November 1: 75–78.
2. The four bulleted items are drawn from Karlgaard, R. 2014. *The soft edge.* San Francisco: Jossey-Bass; Lim, P. J. 2014. As Nasdaq rocks, don't get rolled. *CNNmoney.com,* May: 46; Downess, L. & Nunes, P. 2014. *Big bang disruption.* New York: Penguin; Anonymous. 2014. One world. *The Economist,* May 31: 16; and Colvin, G. 2014. Four things that worry business. *Fortune,* October 27: 32.
3. Donahue, J. 2012. What do CEOs admire? *Fortune,* March 19: 143.
4. For a discussion of the "romantic" versus "external control" perspective, refer to Meindl, J. R. 1987. The romance of leadership and the evaluation of organizational performance. *Academy of Management Journal,* 30: 92–109; and Pfeffer, J. & Salancik, G. R. 1978. *The external control of organizations: A resource dependence perspective.* New York: Harper & Row.
5. A recent perspective on the "romantic view" of leadership is provided by Mintzberg, H. 2004. Leadership and management development: An afterword. *Academy of Management Executive,* 18(3): 140–142.
6. For a discussion of the best and worst managers for 2008, read Anonymous. 2009. The best managers. *BusinessWeek,* January 19: 40–41; and The worst managers. On page 42 in the same issue.

7. Burrows, P. 2009. Apple without its core? *BusinessWeek,* January 26/February 2: 31.
8. For a study on the effects of CEOs on firm performance, refer to Kor, Y. Y. & Misangyi, V. F. 2008. *Strategic Management Journal,* 29(11):1357–1368.
9. Charan, R. & Colvin, G. 2010. Directors: A harsh new reality. *money.cnn.com,* October 6: np.
10. Reed, T. 2014. Why JetBlue CEO Dave Barger was chased out by Wall Street. *www.thestreet.com,* September 18: np; and Carey, S. 2014. JetBlue chief to depart; will bag fees arrive? *The Wall Street Journal,* September 10: B1–B2.
11. Dobson, C. 2010. Global airlines lost $1.7 billion due to Iceland ash cloud. *www.theepochtimes.com,* May 23: np; and Pylas, P. 2011. Nikkei slides 11 percent on radiation fears. *www.finance.yahoo.com,* March 14: np.
12. Ewing, J. 2008. South Africa emerges from the shadows. *BusinessWeek,* December 15: 52–56.
13. For an interesting perspective on the need for strategists to maintain a global mind-set, refer to Begley, T. M. & Boyd, D. P. 2003. The need for a global mind-set. *MIT Sloan Management Review,* 44(2): 25–32.
14. Porter, M. E. 1996. What is strategy? *Harvard Business Review,* 74(6): 61–78.
15. See, for example, Barney, J. B. & Arikan, A. M. 2001. The resource-based view: Origins and implications. In Hitt, M. A., Freeman, R. E., & Harrison, J. S. (Eds.), *Handbook of strategic management:* 124–189. Malden, MA: Blackwell.
16. Porter, M. E. 1996. What is strategy? *Harvard Business Review,* 74(6): 61–78; and Hammonds, K. H. 2001. Michael Porter's big ideas. *Fast Company,* March: 55–56.
17. This section draws upon Dess, G. G. & Miller, A. 1993. *Strategic management.* New York: McGraw-Hill.
18. See, for example, Hrebiniak, L. G. & Joyce, W. F. 1986. The strategic importance of managing myopia. *Sloan Management Review,* 28(1): 5–14.
19. Bryant, A. 2011. *The corner office.* New York: Times Books.
20. For an insightful discussion on how to manage diverse stakeholder groups, refer to Rondinelli, D. A. & London, T. 2003. How corporations and environmental groups cooperate: Assessing cross-sector alliances and collaborations. *Academy of Management Executive,* 17(1): 61–76.
21. Some dangers of a short-term perspective are addressed in Van Buren, M. E. & Safferstone, T. 2009. The quick wins paradox. *Harvard Business Review,* 67(1): 54–61.
22. Senge, P. 1996. Leading learning organizations: The bold, the powerful, and the invisible. In Hesselbein, F., Goldsmith, M., & Beckhard, R. (Eds.), *The leader of the future:* 41–58. San Francisco: Jossey-Bass.
23. Winston, A. S. 2014. *The big pivot.* Boston: Harvard Business Review.
24. Loeb, M. 1994. Where leaders come from. *Fortune,* September 19: 241 (quoting Warren Bennis).
25. Hemp, P. 2004. An interview with CEO Kevin Sharer. *Harvard Business Review,* 82(7/8): 66–74.
26. New perspectives on "management models" are addressed in Birkinshaw, J. & Goddard, J. 2009. What is your management model? *MIT Sloan Management Review,* 50(2): 81–90.
27. Mintzberg, H. 1985. Of strategies: Deliberate and emergent. *Strategic Management Journal,* 6: 257–272.
28. Some interesting insights on decision-making processes are found in Nutt, P. C. 2008. Investigating the success of decision making processes. *Journal of Management Studies,* 45(2): 425–455.
29. Smith, J. 2014. Go-to lawyers are in-house. *The Wall Street Journal,* September 15: B6.
30. Bryant, A. 2009. The corner office. *nytimes.com,* April 25: np.
31. A study investigating the sustainability of competitive advantage is Newbert, S. L. 2008. Value, rareness, competitive advantages, and performance: A conceptual-level empirical investigation of the resource-based view of the firm. *Strategic Management Journal,* 29(7): 745–768.
32. Good insights on mentoring are addressed in DeLong, T. J., Gabarro, J. J., & Lees, R. J. 2008. Why mentoring matters in a hypercompetitive world. *Harvard Business Review,* 66(1): 115–121.
33. Karlgaard, R. 2014. *The soft edge.* San Francisco: Jossey-Bass.
34. A unique perspective on differentiation strategies is Austin, R. D. 2008. High margins and the quest for aesthetic coherence. *Harvard Business Review,* 86(1): 18–19.
35. Some insights on partnering in the global area are discussed in MacCormack, A. & Forbath, T. 2008. *Harvard Business Review,* 66(1): 24, 26.
36. For insights on how firms can be successful in entering new markets in emerging economies, refer to Eyring, M. J., Johnson, M. W., & Nair, H. 2011. New business models in emerging markets. *Harvard Business Review,* 89(1/2): 88–95.
37. *Fortune.* 2012. December 3: 6.
38. An interesting discussion of the challenges of strategy implementation is Neilson, G. L., Martin, K. L., & Powers, E. 2008. The secrets of strategy execution. *Harvard Business Review,* 86(6): 61–70.
39. Interesting perspectives on strategy execution involving the link between strategy and operations are addressed in Kaplan, R. S. & Norton, D. P. 2008. Mastering the management system. *Harvard Business Review,* 66(1): 62–77.
40. An innovative perspective on organizational design is found in Garvin, D. A. & Levesque, L. C. 2008. The multiunit enterprise. *Harvard Business Review,* 86(6): 106–117.
41. Monks, R. & Minow, N. 2001. *Corporate governance* (2nd ed.). Malden, MA: Blackwell.
42. Intel Corp. 2007. *Intel corporation board of directors guidelines on significant corporate governance issues.* www.intel.com
43. Jones, T. J., Felps, W., & Bigley, G. A. 2007. Ethical theory and stakeholder-related decisions: The role of stakeholder culture. *Academy of Management Review,* 32(1): 137–155.
44. For example, see: The best (& worst) managers of the year, 2003. *BusinessWeek,* January 13: 58–92; and Lavelle, M. 2003. Rogues of the year. *Time,* January 6: 33–45.
45. Baer, D. A. 2014. The West's bruised confidence in capitalism. *The Wall Street Journal,* September 22: A17; and Miller, D. 2014. Greatness is gone. *Dallas Morning News,* October 26: 1 D.
46. Hessel, E. & Woolley, S. 2008. Your money or your life. *Forbes,* October 27: 52.
47. Task, A. 2012. Finance CEO pay rose 20% in 2011, even as stocks stumbled. *www.finance.yahoo.com,* June 5: np.
48. Matthews, C. 2014. 5 companies that pay CEOs big for a job poorly done. *fortune.com,* June 17: np.

49. Some interesting insights on the role of activist investors can be found in Greenwood, R. & Schol, M. 2008. When (not) to listen to activist investors. *Harvard Business Review,* 66(1): 23–24.

50. For an interesting perspective on the changing role of boards of directors, refer to Lawler, E. & Finegold, D. 2005. Rethinking governance. *MIT Sloan Management Review,* 46(2): 67–70.

51. Benz, M. & Frey, B. S. 2007. Corporate governance: What can we learn from public governance? *Academy of Management Review,* 32(1): 92–104.

52. The salience of shareholder value is addressed in Carrott, G. T. & Jackson, S. E. 2009. Shareholder value must top the CEO's agenda. *Harvard Business Review,* 67(1): 22–24.

53. Stakeholder symbiosis. 1998. *Fortune,* March 30: S2.

54. An excellent review of stakeholder management theory can be found in Laplume, A. O., Sonpar, K., & Litz, R. A. 2008. Stakeholder theory: Reviewing a theory that moves us. *Journal of Management,* 34(6): 1152–1189.

55. For a definitive, recent discussion of the stakeholder concept, refer to Freeman, R. E. & McVae, J. 2001. A stakeholder approach to strategic management. In Hitt, M. A., Freeman, R. E., & Harrison, J. S. (Eds.), *Handbook of strategic management:* 189–207. Malden, MA: Blackwell.

56. Harrison, J. S., Bosse, D. A., & Phillips, R. A. 2010. Managing for stakeholders, stakeholder utility functions, and competitive advantage. *Strategic Management Journal,* 31(1): 58–74.

57. For an insightful discussion on the role of business in society, refer to Handy, op. cit.

58. Camillus, J. 2008. Strategy as a wicked problem. *Harvard Business Review,* 86(5): 100–101.

59. Stakeholder symbiosis. op. cit., p. S3.

60. Sidhu, I. 2010. *Doing both.* Upper Saddle River, NJ: FT Press, 7–8.

61. Thomas, J. G. 2000. Macro-environmetal forces. In Helms, M. M. (Ed.), *Encyclopedia of management* (4th ed.): 516–520. Farmington Hills, MI: Gale Group.

62. For a strong advocacy position on the need for corporate values and social responsibility, read Hollender, J. 2004. What matters most: Corporate values and social responsibility. *California Management Review,* 46(4): 111–119.

63. Waddock, S. & Bodwell, C. 2004. Managing responsibility: What can be learned from the quality movement. *California Management Review,* 47(1): 25–37.

64. For a discussion of the role of alliances and collaboration on corporate social responsibility initiatives, refer to Pearce, J. A. II. & Doh, J. P. 2005. The high impact of collaborative social initiatives. *MIT Sloan Management Review,* 46(3): 30–40.

65. Insights on ethical behavior and performance are addressed in Trudel, R. & Cotte, J. 2009. *MIT Sloan Management Review,* 50(2): 61–68.

66. Bhattacharya, C. B. & Sen, S. 2004, Doing better at doing good: When, why, and how consumers respond to corporate social initiatives. *California Management Review,* 47(1): 9–24.

67. For some findings on the relationship between corporate social responsibility and firm performance, see Margolis, J. D. & Elfenbein, H. A. 2008. *Harvard Business Review,* 86(1): 19–20.

68. Cone Corporate Citizenship Study, 2002, www.coneinc.com.

69. Refer to *www.bsr.org*.

70. For an insightful discussion of the risks and opportunities associated with global warming, refer to Lash, J. & Wellington, F. 2007. Competitive advantage on a warming planet. *Harvard Business Review,* 85(3): 94–102.

71. This section draws on Hart, S. L. 1997. Beyond greening: Strategies for a sustainable world. *Harvard Business Review,* 75(1): 66–76; and Berry, M. A. & Rondinelli, D. A. 1998. Proactive corporate environmental management: A new industrial revolution. *Academy of Management Executive,* 12(2): 38–50.

72. Hart, op. cit., p. 67.

73. For a creative perspective on environmental sustainability and competitive advantage as well as ethical implications, read Ehrenfeld, J. R. 2005. The roots of sustainability. *MIT Sloan Management Review,* 46(2): 23–25.

74. McKinsey & Company. 1991. *The corporate response to the environmental challenge.* Summary Report. Amsterdam: McKinsey & Company.

75. Delmas, M. A. & Montes-Sancho, M. J. 2010. Voluntary agreements to improve environmental quality: Symbolic and substantive cooperation. *Strategic Management Journal,* 31(6): 575–601.

76. Vogel, D. J. 2005. Is there a market for virtue? The business case for corporate social responsibility. *California Management Review,* 47(4): 19–36.

77. Esty, D. C. & Charnovitz, S. 2012. Green rules to drive innovation. *Harvard Business Review,* 90(3): 120–123.

78. Chamberlain, M. 2013. Socially responsible investing: What you need to know. *Forbes.com*, April 24: np.

79. Kaahwarski, T. 2010. It pays to be good. *Bloomberg Businessweek,* February 1 to February 8: 69.

80. This discussion draws on Kuehn, K. & McIntire, L. 2014. Sustainability a CFO can love. *Harvard Business Review,* 92(4): 66–74; and Esty, D. C. & Winston, A. S. 2009. *Green to gold.* Hoboken, NJ: Wiley.

81. Senge, P. M. 1990. The leader's new work: Building learning organizations. *Sloan Management Review,* 32(1): 7–23.

82. For an interesting perspective on the role of middle managers in the strategic management process, refer to Huy, Q. H. 2001. In praise of middle managers. *Harvard Business Review,* 79(8): 72–81.

83. Senge, 1996, op. cit., pp. 41–58.

84. Kets de Vries, M. F. R. 1998. Charisma in action: The transformational abilities of Virgin's Richard Branson and ABB's Percy Barnevik. *Organizational Dynamics,* 26(3): 7–21.

85. Hamel, G. 2006. The why, what, and how of management innovation. *Harvard Business Review,* 84(2): 72–84.

86. Bryant, A. 2011. *The corner office.* New York: St. Martin's/Griffin, 6.

87. An interesting discussion on how to translate top management's goals into concrete actions is found in Bungay, S. 2011. How to make the most of your company's strategy. *Harvard Business Review,* 89(1/2): 132–140.

88. Bryant, A. 2011. *The corner office.* New York: St. Martin's/Griffin, 171.

89. An insightful discussion about the role of vision, mission, and strategic objectives can be found in Collis, D. J. & Rukstad, M. G. 2008. Can you say what your strategy is? *Harvard Business Review,* 66(4): 82–90.

90. Our discussion draws on a variety of sources. These include Lipton, M. 1996. Demystifying the development of an organizational vision. *Sloan Management Review,* 37(4): 83–92; Bart, C. K. 2000. Lasting inspiration. *CA Magazine,* May: 49–50; and Quigley, J. V. 1994. Vision: How leaders develop it, share it, and sustain it. *Business Horizons,* September–October: 37–40.
91. Lipton, op. cit.
92. Bryant, A. 2011. *The corner office.* New York: St. Martin's/Griffin, 34.
93. Hardy, Q. 2007. The uncarly. *Forbes,* March 12: 82–90.
94. Some interesting perspectives on gender differences in organizational vision are discussed in Ibarra, H. & Obodaru, O. 2009. Women and the vision thing. *Harvard Business Review,* 67(1): 62–70.
95. Quigley, op. cit.
96. Ibid.
97. Lipton, op. cit. Additional pitfalls are addressed in this article.
98. Sull, D. N. 2005. Strategy as active waiting. *Harvard Business Review,* 83(9): 120–130.
99. Company records.
100. Lipton, op. cit.
101. Sexton, D. A. & Van Aukun, P. M. 1985. A longitudinal study of small business strategic planning. *Journal of Small Business Management,* January: 8–15, cited in Lipton, op. cit.
102. For an insightful perspective on the use of strategic objectives, refer to Chatterjee, S. 2005. Core objectives: Clarity in designing strategy. *California Management Review,* 47(2): 33–49.
103. Ibid.
104. Harnish, V. 2011. Five ways to get your strategy right. *Fortune,* April 11: 42.

photo credits

Page 2: © Anatoli Styf/Getty Images/RF

Analyzing the External Environment of the Firm
Creating Competitive Advantages

chapter 2

After reading this chapter, you should have a good understanding of the following learning objectives:

LO2.1 The importance of developing forecasts of the business environment.

LO2.2 Why environmental scanning, environmental monitoring, and collecting competitive intelligence are critical inputs to forecasting.

LO2.3 Why scenario planning is a useful technique for firms competing in industries characterized by unpredictability and change.

LO2.4 The impact of the general environment on a firm's strategies and performance.

LO2.5 How forces in the competitive environment can affect profitability, and how a firm can improve its competitive position by increasing its power vis-à-vis these forces.

LO2.6 How the Internet and digitally based capabilities are affecting the five competitive forces and industry profitability.

LO2.7 The concept of strategic groups and their strategy and performance implications.

PART 1: STRATEGIC ANALYSIS

Learning from Mistakes

Analyzing the external environment is a critical step in recognizing and understanding the opportunities and threats that organizations face. And here is where some companies fail to do a good job.

Consider the example of Salemi Industries and the launch of its product, Cell Zone, in 2005. Although it tried to carefully analyze its potential market, it misread the market's demand for the product and paid a steep price for its mistake.[1] Mobile phone usage was sharply increasing, and its founder observed that patrons in places such as restaurants would be annoyed by the chatter of a nearby guest having a private (but loud!) conversation. Salemi Industries interpreted this observation as an opportunity to create the Cell Zone: a "commercial sound resistant cell phone booth that provides a convenient and disturbance-free environment to place and receive phone calls . . . with a design feature to promote product or service on its curvilinear outer shell," according to the firm's website.

Salemi Industries' key error was that it failed to take into consideration an emerging technology—the increasing popularity of text messaging and other nonvoice communication technology applications and how that would affect the sales of its product. In addition to this technology shift, the target locations (restaurants) thought the price ($3,500) was too steep, and they were not interested in or willing to give up productive square footage for patrons to hold private conversations. Not surprisingly, the firm has sold only 300 units (100 of them in college libraries), and Salemi Industries has lost over $650,000 to date.

Discussion Questions

1. What is the biggest stumbling block for Cell Zone?
2. Are there other market segments where Cell Zone might work?

Successful managers must recognize opportunities and threats in their firm's external environment. They must be aware of what's going on outside their company. If they focus exclusively on the efficiency of internal operations, the firm may degenerate into the world's most efficient producer of buggy whips, typewriters, or carbon paper. But if they miscalculate the market, opportunities will be lost—hardly an enviable position for their firm. As we saw from the Cell Zone example, misreading the market can lead to negative consequences.

In *Competing for the Future,* Gary Hamel and C. K. Prahalad suggest that "every manager carries around in his or her head a set of biases, assumptions, and presuppositions about the structure of the relevant 'industry,' about how one makes money in the industry, about who the competition is and isn't, about who the customers are and aren't, and so on."[2] Environmental analysis requires you to continually question such assumptions. Peter Drucker, considered the father of modern management, labeled these interrelated sets of assumptions the "theory of the business."[3] The struggle of Groupon (Chapter 1) clearly illustrates that if a company does not keep pace with changes in the nature of competition, it becomes difficult to sustain competitive advantages and deliver strong financial results.

A firm's strategy may be good at one point in time, but it may go astray when management's frame of reference gets out of touch with the realities of the actual business situation. This results when management's assumptions, premises, or beliefs are incorrect or when internal inconsistencies among them render the overall "theory of the business" invalid.

As Warren Buffett, investor extraordinaire, colorfully notes, "Beware of past performance 'proofs.' If history books were the key to riches, the Forbes 400 would consist of librarians."

In the business world, many once-successful firms have fallen. Today we may wonder who will be the next Blockbuster, Borders, Circuit City, or Radio Shack.

Creating the Environmentally Aware Organization

LO2.1
The importance of developing forecasts of the business environment.

So how do managers become environmentally aware?[4] Ram Charan, an adviser to many Fortune 500 CEOs, provides some useful insights with his concept of **perceptual acuity**.[5] He defines it as "the ability to sense what is coming before the fog clears." He draws on Ted Turner as an example: Turner saw the potential of 24-hour news before anyone else did. All the ingredients were there, but no others connected them until he created CNN. Like Turner, the best CEOs are compulsively tuned to the external environment and seem to have a sixth sense that picks up anomalies and detects early warning signals which may represent key threats or opportunities.

perceptual acuity
the ability to sense what is coming before the fog clears.

How can perceptual acuity be improved? Although many CEOs may complain that the top job is a lonely one, they can't do it effectively by sitting alone in their office. Instead, high-performing CEOs are constantly meeting with people and searching out information. Charan provides three examples:

- One CEO gets together with his critical people for half a day every eight weeks to discuss what's new and what's going on in the world. The setting is informal, and outsiders often attend. The participants look beyond the lens of their industry because some trends that affect one industry may impact others later on.
- Another CEO meets four times a year with about four other CEOS of large, but noncompeting, diverse global companies. Examining the world from multiple perspectives, they share their thinking about how different trends may develop. The CEO then goes back to his own weekly management meeting and throws out "a bunch of hand grenades to shake up people's thinking."
- Two companies ask outsiders to critique strategy during their board's strategy sessions. Such input typically leads to spirited discussions that provide valued input on the hinge assumptions and options that are under consideration. Once, the focus was on pinpointing the risk inherent in a certain strategy. Now, discussions have led to finding that the company was missing a valuable opportunity.

We will now address three important processes—scanning, monitoring, and gathering competitive intelligence—used to develop forecasts.[6] Exhibit 2.1 illustrates relationships among these important activities. We also discuss the importance of scenario planning in anticipating major future changes in the external environment and the role of SWOT analysis.[7]

EXHIBIT 2.1 Inputs to Forecasting

- Environmental scanning → Forecasts
- Environmental monitoring → Forecasts
- Competitive intelligence → Forecasts

The Role of Scanning, Monitoring, Competitive Intelligence, and Forecasting

Environmental Scanning **Environmental scanning** involves surveillance of a firm's external environment to predict environmental changes and detect changes already under way.[8,9] This alerts the organization to critical trends and events before changes develop a discernible pattern and before competitors recognize them.[10] Otherwise, the firm may be forced into a reactive mode.[11]

Experts agree that spotting key trends requires a combination of knowing your business and your customer as well as keeping an eye on what's happening around you. Such a big-picture/small-picture view enables you to better identify the emerging trends that will affect your business.

Leading firms in an industry can also be a key indicator of emerging trends.[12] For example, with its wide range of household goods, Procter & Gamble is a barometer for consumer spending. Any sign that it can sell more of its premium products without cutting prices sharply indicates that shoppers may finally be becoming less price-sensitive with everyday purchases. In particular, investors will examine the performance of beauty products like Olay moisturizers and CoverGirl cosmetics for evidence that spending on small, discretionary pick-me-ups is improving.

Environmental Monitoring **Environmental monitoring** tracks the evolution of environmental trends, sequences of events, or streams of activities. They may be trends that the firm came across by accident or ones that were brought to its attention from outside the organization.[13] Monitoring enables firms to evaluate how dramatically environmental trends are changing the competitive landscape.

One of the authors of this text has conducted on-site interviews with executives from several industries to identify indicators that firms monitor as inputs to their strategy process. Examples of such indicators included:

- *A Motel 6 executive.* The number of rooms in the budget segment of the industry in the United States and the difference between the average daily room rate and the consumer price index (CPI).
- *A Pier 1 Imports executive.* Net disposable income (NDI), consumer confidence index, and housing starts.
- *A Johnson & Johnson medical products executive.* Percentage of gross domestic product (GDP) spent on health care, number of active hospital beds, and the size and power of purchasing agents (indicates the concentration of buyers).

Such indices are critical for managers in determining a firm's strategic direction and resource allocation.

Competitive Intelligence **Competitive intelligence** (CI) helps firms define and understand their industry and identify rivals' strengths and weaknesses.[14] This includes the intelligence gathering associated with collecting data on competitors and interpreting such data. Done properly, competitive intelligence helps a company avoid surprises by anticipating competitors' moves and decreasing response time.[15]

Examples of competitive analysis are evident in daily newspapers and periodicals such as *The Wall Street Journal, Bloomberg Businessweek,* and *Fortune.* For example, banks continually track home loan, auto loan, and certificate of deposit (CD) interest rates charged by rivals. Major airlines change hundreds of fares daily in response to competitors' tactics. Car manufacturers are keenly aware of announced cuts or increases in rivals' production volume, sales, and sales incentives (e.g., rebates and low interest rates on financing). This information is used in their marketing, pricing, and production strategies.

LO2.2
Why environmental scanning, environmental monitoring, and collecting competitive intelligence are critical inputs to forecasting.

environmental scanning
surveillance of a firm's external environment to predict environmental changes and detect changes already under way.

environmental monitoring
a firm's analysis of the external environment that tracks the evolution of environmental trends, sequences of events, or streams of activities.

competitive intelligence
a firm's activities of collecting and interpreting data on competitors, defining and understanding the industry, and identifying competitors' strengths and weaknesses.

Keeping track of competitors has become easier today with the amount of information that is available on the Internet. The following are examples of some websites that companies routinely use for competitive intelligence gathering.[16]

- *Slideshare.* A website for publicly sharing PowerPoint presentations. Marketing teams have embraced the platform and often post detail-rich presentations about their firms and products.
- *Quora.* A question-and-answer site popular among industry insiders who embrace the free flow of information about technical questions.
- *Ispionage.* A site that reveals the ad words that companies are buying, which can often shed light on new campaigns being launched.
- *YouTube.* Great for finding interviews with executives at trade shows.

At times, a firm's aggressive efforts to gather competitive intelligence may lead to unethical or illegal behaviors.[17] Strategy Spotlight 2.1 provides an example of a company, United Technologies, that has set clear guidelines to help prevent unethical behavior.

A word of caution: Executives must be careful to avoid spending so much time and effort tracking the actions of traditional competitors that they ignore new competitors. Further, broad environmental changes and events may have a dramatic impact on a firm's viability. Peter Drucker, wrote:

> Increasingly, a winning strategy will require information about events and conditions outside the institution: noncustomers, technologies other than those currently used by the company and its present competitors, markets not currently served, and so on.[18]

Consider the failure of specialized medical lab Sleep HealthCenters.[19] Until recently, patients suffering from sleep disorders, such as apnea, were forced to undergo expensive overnight visits to sleep clinics, including Sleep HealthCenters, to diagnose their ailments. The firm was launched in 1997 and quickly expanded to over two dozen locations. Revenue soared from nearly $10 million in 1997 to $30 million in 2010.

However, the rapid improvements in the price and performance of wearable monitoring devices changed the business, gradually at first and then suddenly. For one thing, the more comfortable home setting produced more effective measurements. And the quick declines in the cost of wearable monitoring meant patients could get the same results at one-third the price of an overnight stay at a clinic. By 2011, Sleep HealthCenters' revenue began to decline, and the firm closed 20 percent of its locations. In 2012, its death knells sounded: Insurance companies decided to cover the less expensive option. Sleep HealthCenters abruptly closed its doors.

Environmental Forecasting Environmental scanning, monitoring, and competitive intelligence are important inputs for analyzing the external environment. **Environmental forecasting** involves the development of plausible projections about the direction, scope, speed, and intensity of environmental change.[20] Its purpose is to predict change.[21] It asks: How long will it take a new technology to reach the marketplace? Will the present social concern about an issue result in new legislation? Are current lifestyle trends likely to continue?

Some forecasting issues are much more specific to a particular firm and the industry in which it competes. Consider how important it is for Motel 6 to predict future indicators, such as the number of rooms, in the budget segment of the industry. If its predictions are low, it will build too many units, creating a surplus of room capacity that would drive down room rates.

A danger of forecasting is that managers may view uncertainty as black and white and ignore important gray areas.[22] The problem is that underestimating uncertainty can lead to strategies that neither defend against threats nor take advantage of opportunities.

In 1977 one of the colossal underestimations in business history occurred when Kenneth H. Olsen, president of Digital Equipment Corp., announced, "There is no reason

---

environmental forecasting
the development of plausible projections about the direction, scope, speed, and intensity of environmental change.

LO2.3
Why scenario planning is a useful technique for firms competing in industries characterized by unpredictability and change.

2.1 STRATEGY SPOTLIGHT — ETHICS

ETHICAL GUIDELINES ON COMPETITIVE INTELLIGENCE: UNITED TECHNOLOGIES

United Technologies (UT) is a $65 billion global conglomerate composed of world-leading businesses with rich histories of technological pioneering, such as Otis Elevator, Carrier Air Conditioning, and Sikorsky (helicopters). UT believes strongly in a robust code of ethics. One such document is the Code of Ethics Guide on Competitive Intelligence. This encourages managers and workers to ask themselves these five questions whenever they have ethical concerns.

1. Have I done anything that coerced somebody to share this information? Have I, for example, threatened a supplier by indicating that future business opportunities will be influenced by the receipt of information with respect to a competitor?
2. Am I in a place where I should not be? If, for example, I am a field representative with privileges to move around in a customer's facility, have I gone outside the areas permitted? Have I misled anybody in order to gain access?
3. Is the contemplated technique for gathering information evasive, such as sifting through trash or setting up an electronic "snooping" device directed at a competitor's facility from across the street?
4. Have I misled somebody in a way that the person believed sharing information with me was required or would be protected by a confidentiality agreement? Have I, for example, called and misrepresented myself as a government official who was seeking some information for some official purpose?
5. Have I done something to evade or circumvent a system intended to secure or protect information?

Sources: Nelson, B. 2003. The thinker. *Forbes*, March 3: 62–64; The Fuld war room—Survival kit 010. Code of ethics (printed 2/26/01); and *www.yahoo.com*.

---

for individuals to have a computer in their home." The explosion in the personal computer market was not easy to detect in 1977, but it was clearly within the range of possibilities at the time. And, historically, there have been underestimates of the growth potential of new telecommunication services. The electric telegraph was derided by Ralph Waldo Emerson, and the telephone had its skeptics. More recently, an "infamous" McKinsey study in the early 1980s predicted fewer than 1 million cellular users in the United States by 2000. Actually, there were nearly 100 million.[23]

Obviously, poor predictions never go out of vogue. Consider some other "gems"—typically predicted by very knowledgeable people:[24]

- In a January 2014 survey by *The Wall Street Journal*, 49 economists expected oil to end 2014 at about $95 a barrel, up from about $92 at the time of the survey. *(Oil ended the year at about $54 a barrel.)*
- "Freddie Mac and Fannie Mae are fundamentally sound . . . I think they are in good shape going forward." —Barney Frank (D-Mass.), House Financial Services Committee Chairman, July 14, 2008. *(Two months later, the government forced the mortgage giants into conservatorships.)*
- "There is no chance that the iPhone is going to get any significant market share." —Steve Ballmer, former CEO of Microsoft, in 2007. *(The lineup has sold more than 500 million devices.)*
- "I think you guys are just a bunch of hippies selling food to other hippies." —a venture capitalist's response to an invitation to invest in Whole Foods, 1980.

And, going far back in time . . .

- "I don't see how it could possibly be made into a movie." —Margaret Mitchell, author of *Gone with the Wind*, on its potential as a motion picture, after selling the movie rights to producer David O. Selznick in 1936. *("GWTH," as the film would come to be known, became one of the most celebrated movies in history, won 10 Oscars, and broke all box office records.)*
- "The baseball mania has run its course. It has no future as a professional endeavor." —*Cincinnati Gazette* editorial, 1879.

Jason Zweig, an editor at *The Wall Street Journal,* provides an important cautionary note (and rather colorful example!) regarding the need to question the reliability of forecasts: "Humans don't want accuracy; they want assurance . . . people can't stand ignoring all predictions; admitting that the future is unknowable is just too frightening."[25]

> The Nobel laureate and retired Stanford University economist Kenneth Arrow did a tour of duty as a weather forecaster for the U.S. Air Force during World War II. Ordered to evaluate mathematical models for predicting the weather one month ahead, he found that they were worthless. Informed of that, his superiors sent back another order: "The Commanding General is well aware that the forecasts are no good. However, he needs them for planning purposes."

scenario analysis
an in-depth approach to environmental forecasting that involves experts' detailed assessments of societal trends, economics, politics, technology, or other dimensions of the external environment.

Scenario Analysis Scenario analysis is a more in-depth approach to forecasting. It draws on a range of disciplines and interests, among them economics, psychology, sociology, and demographics. It usually begins with a discussion of participants' thoughts on ways in which societal trends, economics, politics, and technology may affect an issue.[26] Scenario analysis involves the projection of future possible events. It does not rely on extrapolation of historical trends. Rather, it seeks to explore possible developments that may only be connected to the past. That is, several scenarios are considered in a scenario analysis in order to envision possible future outcomes. Strategy Spotlight 2.2 provides an example of scenario planning at PPG Industries.

SWOT Analysis

To understand the business environment of a particular firm, you need to analyze both the general environment and the firm's industry and competitive environment. Generally, firms compete with other firms in the same industry. An industry is composed of a set of firms that produce similar products or services, sell to similar customers, and use similar methods of production. Gathering industry information and understanding competitive dynamics among the different companies in your industry is key to successful strategic management.

SWOT analysis
a framework for analyzing a company's internal and external environments and that stands for strengths, weaknesses, opportunities, and threats.

One of the most basic techniques for analyzing firm and industry conditions is **SWOT analysis.** SWOT stands for strengths, weaknesses, opportunities, and threats. It provides "raw material"—a basic listing of conditions both inside and surrounding your company.

The Strengths and Weaknesses refer to the internal conditions of the firm—where your firm excels (strengths) and where it may be lacking relative to competitors (weaknesses). Opportunities and Threats are environmental conditions external to the firm. These could be factors in either the general or the competitive environment. In the general environment, one might experience developments that are beneficial for most companies, such as improving economic conditions that lower borrowing costs, or trends that benefit some companies and harm others. An example is the heightened concern with fitness, which is a threat to some companies (e.g., tobacco) and an opportunity to others (e.g., health clubs). Opportunities and threats are also present in the competitive environment among firms competing for the same customers.

The general idea of SWOT analysis is that a firm's strategy must:

- Build on its strengths.
- Remedy the weaknesses or work around them.
- Take advantage of the opportunities presented by the environment.
- Protect the firm from the threats.

Despite its apparent simplicity, the SWOT approach has been very popular. First, it forces managers to consider both internal and external factors simultaneously. Second, its emphasis on identifying opportunities and threats makes firms act proactively rather than reactively. Third, it raises awareness about the role of strategy in creating a match between

2.2 STRATEGY SPOTLIGHT

SCENARIO PLANNING AT PPG

PPG Industries, the Pittsburgh-based manufacturer of paints, coatings, optical products, specialty materials, chemicals, glass, and fiber glass, has paid dividends every year since 1899 and has maintained or increased dividends every year since 1972. With sales over $13 billion and operations in more than 60 countries, PPG is truly a global player. Although considered a very successful company, PPG has had its share of strategic errors. Realizing that business was slowing down in its core businesses, PPG acquired medical electronics businesses from Honeywell and Litton Industries in 1986 and from Allegheny International in 1987. However, these efforts at diversification proved to be failures, as the firm's competence in low-cost, standardized production in stable, mature industries was of little help in the highly volatile biomedical industry, where customization was vital. Seven years later, PPG exited the medical electronics business by selling off these units. To profit from the construction boom in China, PPG entered the Chinese market with a focus on glass. After years of losses, the company realized that it would have to focus on coatings.

These costly failures led PPG to a new emphasis on strategic planning. One of the key tools it uses today is scenario planning. PPG has developed four alternative futures based on differing assumptions about two key variables: the cost of energy (because its manufacturing operations are energy-intensive) and the extent of opportunity for growth in emerging markets. In the most favorable scenario, cost of energy will stay moderate and stable and opportunities for growth and differentiation will be fast and strong. In this scenario, PPG determined that its success will depend on having the resources to pursue new opportunities. On the other hand, in the worst-case scenario, cost of energy will be high and opportunities for growth will be weak and slow. This scenario would call for a complete change in strategic direction. Between these two extremes lies the possibility of two mixed scenarios. First, opportunity for growth in emerging markets may be high, but cost of energy may be high and volatile. In this scenario, the company's success will depend on coming up with more efficient processes. Second, cost of energy may remain moderate and stable, but opportunities for growth in emerging markets may remain weak and slow. In this situation, the most viable strategy may be one of capturing market share with new products.

Developing strategies based on possible future scenarios seems to be paying off for PPG Industries. The company's net income soared to $3.2 billion in 2013—nearly a 200 percent increase over the prior two-year period.

Sources: Camillus, J. C. 2008. Strategy as a wicked problem. *Harvard Business Review*, 86(5): 98–106; www.ppg.com; and www.finance.yahoo.com.

---

the environmental conditions and the firm's internal strengths and weaknesses. Finally, its conceptual simplicity is achieved without sacrificing analytical rigor. (We will also address some of the limitations of SWOT analysis in Chapter 3.)

While analysis is necessary, it is also equally important to recognize the role played by intuition and judgment. Steve Jobs, the legendary former chairman of Apple, took a very different approach in determining what customers *really* wanted:[27]

> Steve Jobs was convinced market research and focus groups limited one's ability to innovate. When asked how much research was done to guide Apple when he introduced the iPad, Jobs famously quipped: "None. It isn't the consumers' job to know what they want. It's hard for (consumers) to tell you what they want when they've never seen anything remotely like it."
>
> Jobs relied on his own intuition—his radarlike feel for emerging technologies and how they could be brought together to create, in his words "insanely great products, that ultimately made the difference." For Jobs, who died in 2011 at the age of 56, intuition was no mere gut call. It was, as he put it in his often-quoted commencement speech at Stanford, about "connecting the dots, glimpsing the relationships among wildly disparate life experiences and changes in technologies."

general environment
factors external to an industry, and usually beyond a firm's control, that affect a firm's strategy.

The General Environment

The **general environment** is composed of factors that can have dramatic effects on firm strategy.[28] We divide the general environment into six segments: demographic, sociocultural, political/legal, technological, economic, and global. Exhibit 2.2 provides examples of key trends and events in each of the six segments of the general environment.

LO2.4
The impact of the general environment on a firm's strategies and performance.

EXHIBIT 2.2
General Environment: Key Trends and Events

Demographic
- Aging population
- Rising affluence
- Changes in ethnic composition
- Geographic distribution of population
- Greater disparities in income levels

Sociocultural
- More women in the workforce
- Increase in temporary workers
- Greater concern for fitness
- Greater concern for environment
- Postponement of family formation

Political/Legal
- Tort reform
- Americans with Disabilities Act (ADA) of 1990
- Deregulation of utility and other industries
- Increases in federally mandated minimum wages
- Taxation at local, state, federal levels
- Legislation on corporate governance reforms in bookkeeping, stock options, etc. (Sarbanes-Oxley Act of 2002)
- Affordable Care Act (Obamacare)

Technological
- Genetic engineering
- Three-dimensional (3D) printing
- Computer-aided design/computer-aided manufacturing systems (CAD/CAM)
- Research in synthetic and exotic materials
- Pollution/global warming
- Miniaturization of computing technologies
- Wireless communications
- Nanotechnology

Economic
- Interest rates
- Unemployment rates
- Consumer price index
- Trends in GDP
- Changes in stock market valuations

Global
- Increasing global trade
- Currency exchange rates
- Emergence of the Indian and Chinese economies
- Trade agreements among regional blocs (e.g., NAFTA, EU, ASEAN)
- Creation of WTO (leading to decreasing tariffs/free trade in services)
- Increased risks associated with terrorism

Before addressing each of the six segments in turn, consider Dominic Barton's insights in response to a question posed to him by an editor of *Fortune* magazine: *What are your client's worries right now?* (Barton is global managing director of McKinsey, the giant consulting firm.)[29]

> "They're pretty consistent around the world. The big one now is geopolitics. Whether you're in Russia, China, anywhere the assumed stability that was there for the past 20 or so years—it's not there. The second is technology, which is moving two to three times faster than management. Most CEOs I talk to are excited and paranoid at the same time. Related to that is cyber security: the amount of time and effort to protect systems and look at vulnerabilities is big.
>
> "A fourth trend is the shift in economic power, with 2.2 billion new middle-class consumers in the next 15 years, and it's moving to Asia and Africa. Do you have the right type of people in your top 100? Are you in those markets? Those are the four big ones we see everywhere."

The Demographic Segment

Demographics are the most easily understood and quantifiable elements of the general environment. They are at the root of many changes in society. Demographics include elements such as the aging population,[30] rising or declining affluence, changes in ethnic composition, geographic distribution of the population, and disparities in income level.[31]

The impact of a demographic trend, like all segments of the general environment, varies across industries. Rising levels of affluence in many developed countries bode well for brokerage services as well as for upscale pets and supplies. However, this trend may adversely affect fast-food restaurants because people can afford to dine at higher-priced restaurants. Fast-food restaurants depend on minimum-wage employees to operate efficiently, but the competition for labor intensifies as more attractive employment opportunities become prevalent, thus threatening the employment base for restaurants. Let's look at the details of one of these trends.

The aging population in the United States and other developed countries has important implications. Although the percentage of those 65 and over in the U.S. workforce bottomed in the 1990s, it has been rising ever since.[32] According to the Bureau of Labor Statistics, 59 percent of workers 65 and older were putting in full-time hours in 2013, a percentage that has increased steadily over the past decade. And, according to a 2014 study by Merrill Lynch and the Age Wave Consulting firm, 72 percent of preretirees aged 50 and over wanted to work during their retirement. "Older workers are to the first half of the 21st century what women were to the last half of the 20th century," says Eugene Steuerle, an economist at the Urban Institute.

There are a number of misconceptions about the quality and value of older workers. The Insights from Research box on page 46, however, debunks many of these myths.

demographic segment of the general environment genetic and observable characteristics of a population, including the levels and growth of age, density, sex, race, ethnicity, education, geographic region, and income.

The Sociocultural Segment

Sociocultural forces influence the values, beliefs, and lifestyles of a society. Examples include a higher percentage of women in the workforce, dual-income families, increases in the number of temporary workers, greater concern for healthy diets and physical fitness, greater interest in the environment, and postponement of having children. Such forces enhance sales of products and services in many industries but depress sales in others. The increased number of women in the workforce has increased the need for business clothing merchandise but decreased the demand for baking product staples (since people would have less time to cook from scratch). The health and fitness trend has helped industries that manufacture exercise equipment and healthful foods but harmed industries that produce unhealthful foods.

Increased educational attainment by women in the workplace has led to more women in upper-management positions.[33] Given such educational attainment, it is hardly surprising

sociocultural segment of the general environment the values, beliefs, and lifestyles of a society.

INSIGHTS FROM RESEARCH

NEW TRICKS: RESEARCH DEBUNKS MYTHS ABOUT OLDER WORKERS

Overview

People often think that older workers are less motivated and less healthy, resist change and are less trusting, and have more trouble balancing work and family. It turns out these assumptions just aren't true. By challenging these stereotypes in your organization, you can keep your employees working.

What the Research Shows

In a 2012 paper published by *Personnel Psychology,* researchers from the University of Hong Kong and the University of Georgia examined 418 studies of workers' ages and stereotypes. A meta-analysis—a study of studies—was conducted to find out if any of the six following stereotypes about older workers—as compared with younger workers—was actually true:

- They are less motivated.
- They are less willing to participate in training and career development.
- They are more resistant to change.
- They are less trusting.
- They are less healthy.
- They are more vulnerable to work-family imbalance.

After an exhaustive search of studies dealing with these issues, the investigators' meta-analytic techniques turned up some interesting results. Older workers' motivation and job involvement are actually slightly higher than those of younger workers. Older workers are slightly more willing to implement organizational changes, are not less trusting, and are not less healthy than younger workers. Moreover, they're not more likely to have issues with work-family imbalance. Of the six investigated, the only stereotype supported was that older workers are less willing to participate in training and career development.

Why This Matters

Business leaders must pay attention to the circumstances of older workers. According to the U.S. Bureau of Labor Statistics, 19.5 percent of American workers were 55 and older in 2010, but by 2020 25.2 percent will be 55 and older. Workers aged 25–44 should drop from 66.9 to 63.7 percent of the workforce during the same period. These statistics make clear that recruiting and training older workers remain critical.

When the findings of the meta-analysis are considered, the challenge of integrating older workers into the workplace becomes acute. The stereotypes held about older workers don't hold water, but when older workers are subjected to them, they are more likely to retire and experience a lower quality of life. Business leaders should attract, retain, and encourage mature employees' continued involvement in workplaces because they have much to offer in the ways of wisdom, experience, and institutional knowledge. The alternative is to miss out on a growing pool of valuable human capital.

How can you deal with age stereotypes to keep older workers engaged? The authors suggest three effective ways:

- Provide more opportunities for younger and older workers to work together.
- Promote positive attributes of older workers, like experience, carefulness, and punctuality.
- Engage employees in open discussions about stereotypes.

Adam Bradshaw of the DeGarmo Group Inc. has summarized research on addressing age stereotypes in the workplace and offers practical advice. For instance, make sure hiring practices identify factors important to the job other than age. Managers can be trained in how to spot age stereotypes and can point out to employees why the stereotypes are often untrue by using examples of effective older workers. Realize that older workers can offer a competitive advantage because of skills they possess that competitors may overlook.

Professor Tamara Erickson, who was named one of the top 50 global business thinkers in 2011, points out that members of different generations bring different experiences, assumptions, and benefits to the workforce. Companies can gain a great deal from creating a culture that welcomes workers of all ages and in which leaders address biases.

Key Takeaways

- The percentage of American workers 55 years old and older is expected to increase from 19.5 percent in 2010 to 25.2 percent in 2020.
- Many stereotypes exist about older workers. A review of 418 studies reveals these stereotypes are largely unfounded.
- Older workers subjected to negative stereotypes are more likely to retire and more likely to report lower quality of life and poorer health.
- When business leaders accept stereotypes about older workers, they lose out on these workers' wisdom and experience. And by 2020 employers may have a smaller pool of younger workers than they do today.
- Solutions include creating opportunities for younger and older workers to work together and having frank, open discussions about stereotypes.

continued

continued

Apply This Today

The stereotypes people often hold about older workers are largely unfounded. Let's face it: The labor force is aging, and astute companies can gain a great deal by attracting and retaining these valuable employees. Train your employees to accept colleagues of all ages—and the entire organization will benefit.

Research Reviewed

Ng, T. W. H. & Feldman, D. C. 2012. Evaluating six common stereotypes about older workers with meta-analytical data. *Personnel Psychology,* 65: 821–858. We thank Matthew Gilley, Ph.D., of *businessminded.com* for contributing this research brief.

---

that companies owned by women have been one of the driving forces of the U.S. economy; these companies (now more than 9 million in number) account for 40 percent of all U.S. businesses and have generated more than $3.6 trillion in annual revenue. In addition, women have a tremendous impact on consumer spending decisions. Not surprisingly, many companies have focused their advertising and promotion efforts on female consumers. Consider, for example, Lowe's efforts to attract female shoppers:

> Lowe's has found that women prefer to do larger home-improvement projects with a man—be it a boyfriend, husband, or neighbor. As a result, in addition to its "recipe card classes" (that explain various projects that take only one weekend), Lowe's offers co-ed store clinics for projects like sink installation. "Women like to feel they're given the same attention as a male customer," states Lowe's spokesperson Julie Valeant-Yenichek, who points out that most seminar attendees, whether male or female, are inexperienced.[34]

Home Depot recently spent millions of dollars to add softer lighting and brighter signs in 300 stores. Why? It is an effort to match rival Lowe's appeal to women.

The Political/Legal Segment

Political processes and legislation influence environmental regulations with which industries must comply.[35,36] Some important elements of the political/legal arena include tort reform, the Americans with Disabilities Act (ADA) of 1990, the repeal of the Glass-Steagall Act in 1999 (banks may now offer brokerage services), deregulation of utilities and other industries, and increases in the federally mandated minimum wage.[37]

Government legislation can also have a significant impact on the governance of corporations. The U.S. Congress passed the Sarbanes-Oxley Act in 2002, which greatly increases the accountability of auditors, executives, and corporate lawyers. This act responded to the widespread perception that existing governance mechanisms failed to protect the interests of shareholders, employees, and creditors. Clearly, Sarbanes-Oxley has also created a tremendous demand for professional accounting services.

Legislation can also affect firms in the high-tech sector of the economy by expanding the number of temporary visas available for highly skilled foreign professionals.[38] For example, a bill passed by the U.S. Congress in October 2000 allowed 195,000 H-1B visas for each of the following three years—up from a cap of 115,000. However, beginning in 2006 and continuing through 2015, the annual cap on H-1B visas has shrunk to only 65,000—with an additional 20,000 visas available for foreigners with a master's or higher degree from a U.S. institution. Many of the visas are for professionals from India with computer and software expertise. In 2014, companies applied for 172,500 H-1B visas. This means that at least 87,500 engineers, developers, and others couldn't take jobs in the United States.[39] As one would expect, this is a political "hot potato" for industry executives as well as U.S. labor and workers' rights groups. The key arguments against H-1B visas are that H-1B workers drive down wages and take jobs from Americans.

Strategy Spotlight 2.3 provides some facts and points out the important role immigrants have played in innovation and job creation in the United States.

> **political/legal segment of the general environment** how a society creates and exercises power, including rules, laws, and taxation policies.

2.3 STRATEGY SPOTLIGHT

IMMIGRANTS, INNOVATION, AND NEW JOB CREATION

Although there is debate about immigration in terms of the alleged threat to American jobs, the fact is quite the opposite: Those who move to the U.S. are prodigious job creators. The United States may be losing ground as a magnet for global entrepreneurs due to a huge backlog of visas that allow them to start new businesses. Last year, efforts to boost available green cards and create a new visa class for immigrant entrepreneurs failed. Hence, many foreign-born scientists and entrepreneurs are leaving the U.S., while such countries as Canada, Australia, Chile, and Singapore look to reap the benefits.

Consider the following:

- First-generation immigrants or their children had founder roles in more than 40 percent of the Fortune 500, including such marquee companies as AT&T, Procter & Gamble, Goldman Sachs, Pfizer, eBay, Google, Intel, Kraft, Cigna, and Kohl's.

- Immigrants are more than twice as likely to found a company as are native-born citizens. They started 28 percent of all new U.S. businesses in 2011, despite accounting for just 12.9 percent of the total population. And in Silicon Valley, the percentage of new companies started by foreign-born entrepreneurs was a remarkable 43.9 percent during 2006–2012.

- Immigrants contributed to more than half of the international patents filed by giant multinationals such as Qualcomm (72 percent), Merck (65 percent), General Electric (64 percent), and Cisco (60 percent).

- Immigrant-owned companies now generate more than $775 billion in annual revenue and $100 billion in income. They employ 1 of every 10 workers.

Sources: Alsever, J. 2014. Immigrants: America's job creators. *Fortune.com*, June 16: 56; and Malone, M. S. 2014. The self-inflicted U.S. brain drain. *The Wall Street Journal*, October 16: A19.

Over time, government regulations often have a tendency to become increasingly complex. For example, many would likely argue that billing requirements for Medicare reimbursements have become absurd. Consider the following from *The Economist*:[40]

> Doctors and other health professionals say it is becoming harder to stay on the right side of the rules as billing requirements grow more convoluted. In 2015, Medicare will have an astonishing 140,000 codes, including nine for injuries caused by turkeys. (Was the victim struck or pecked? Once or more often? Did he or she suffer negative after-effects? And so on).
>
> Many clinics have fallen under suspicion and had payments suspended, only to win a reprieve when the facts are examined closely. Medicare alone has a backlog of nearly a half million appeals.

The Technological Segment

technological segment of the general environment innovation and state of knowledge in industrial arts, engineering, applied sciences, and pure science; and their interaction with society.

Developments in technology lead to new products and services and improve how they are produced and delivered to the end user.[41] Innovations can create entirely new industries and alter the boundaries of existing industries.[42] Technological developments and trends include genetic engineering, Internet technology, computer-aided design/computer-aided manufacturing (CAD/CAM), research in artificial and exotic materials, and, on the downside, pollution and global warming.[43] Petroleum and primary metals industries spend significantly to reduce their pollution. Engineering and consulting firms that work with polluting industries derive financial benefits from solving such problems.

Nanotechnology is becoming a very promising area of research with many potentially useful applications.[44] Nanotechnology takes place at industry's tiniest stage: one-billionth of a meter. Remarkably, this is the size of 10 hydrogen atoms in a row. Matter at such a tiny scale behaves very differently. Familiar materials—from gold to carbon soot—display startling and useful new properties. Some transmit light or electricity. Others become harder than diamonds or turn into potent chemical catalysts. What's more, researchers have found that a tiny dose of nanoparticles can transform the chemistry and nature of far bigger things.

Another emerging technology is physiolectics, which is the practice of linking wearable computing devices with data analysis and quantified feedback to improve performance.[45]

An example is sensors in shoes (such as Nike+, used by runners to track distance, speed, and other metrics). Another application focuses on people's movements in various work settings. Tesco's employees, for instance, wear armbands at a distribution center in Ireland to track the goods they are gathering. The devices free up time that employees would otherwise spend marking clipboards. The armband also allots tasks to the wearer, forecasts his or her completion time, and quantifies the wearer's precise movements among the facility's 9.6 miles of shelving and 111 loading bays.

The Economic Segment

The economy affects all industries, from suppliers of raw materials to manufacturers of finished goods and services, as well as all organizations in the service, wholesale, retail, government, and nonprofit sectors.[46] Key economic indicators include interest rates, unemployment rates, the consumer price index, the gross domestic product, and net disposable income.[47] Interest rate increases have a negative impact on the residential home construction industry but a negligible (or neutral) effect on industries that produce consumer necessities such as prescription drugs or common grocery items.

Other economic indicators are associated with equity markets. Perhaps the most watched is the Dow Jones Industrial Average (DJIA), which is composed of 30 large industrial firms. When stock market indexes increase, consumers' discretionary income rises and there is often an increased demand for luxury items such as jewelry and automobiles. But when stock valuations decrease, demand for these items shrinks.

economic segment of the general environment characteristics of the economy, including national income and monetary conditions.

The Global Segment

More firms are expanding their operations and market reach beyond the borders of their "home" country. Globalization provides both opportunities to access larger potential markets and a broad base of production factors such as raw materials, labor, skilled managers, and technical professionals. However, such endeavors also carry many political, social, and economic risks.[48]

Examples of key elements include currency exchange rates, increasing global trade, the economic emergence of China, trade agreements among regional blocs (e.g., North American Free Trade Agreement, European Union), and the General Agreement on Tariffs and Trade (GATT) (lowering of tariffs).[49] Increases in trade across national boundaries also provide benefits to air cargo and shipping industries but have a minimal impact on service industries such as bookkeeping and routine medical services.

A key factor in the global economy is the rapid rise of the middle class in emerging countries. The number of consumers in Asia's middle class is rapidly approaching the number in Europe and North America combined. An important implication of this trend is the dramatic change in hiring practices of U.S. multinationals. Consider:

global segment of the general environment influences from foreign countries, including foreign market opportunities, foreign-based competition, and expanded capital markets.

> Thirty-five U.S.-based multinational firms have recently added jobs faster than other U.S. employers, but nearly three-fourths of those jobs were overseas, according to a *Wall Street Journal* analysis. Those companies, which include Wal-Mart Stores Inc., International Paper Co., Honeywell International, Inc., and United Parcel Service, boosted their employment at home by 3.1 percent, or 113,000 jobs, at roughly the same rate of increase as the nation's other employers. However, they also added more than 333,000 jobs in their far-flung—and faster growing—foreign operations.[50]

Relationships among Elements of the General Environment

In our discussion of the general environment, we see many relationships among the various elements.[51] For example, a demographic trend in the United States, the aging of the population, has important implications for the economic segment (in terms of tax policies to provide benefits to increasing numbers of older citizens). Another example is the emergence of information technology as a means to increase the rate of productivity gains in the

United States and other developed countries. Such use of IT results in lower inflation (an important element of the economic segment) and helps offset costs associated with higher labor rates.

The effects of a trend or event in the general environment vary across industries. Governmental legislation (political/legal) to permit the importation of prescription drugs from foreign countries is a very positive development for drugstores but a very negative event for U.S. drug manufacturers. Exhibit 2.3 provides other examples of how the impact of trends or events in the general environment can vary across industries.

Crowdsourcing: A Technology That Affects Multiple Segments of the General Environment Before moving on, let's consider the Internet. The Internet has been a leading and highly visible component of a broader technological phenomenon—the emergence of digital technology. These technologies are altering the way business is conducted and having an effect on nearly every business domain.

One application of digital technology is **crowdsourcing,** which will be a theme throughout the text. It has affected multiple elements of the general environment, such as technology, globalization, and economics. When and where did the term originate?[52] In January 2006, open sourcing was, for most businesspeople, little more than an online curiosity. At that time, Jeff Howe of *Wired* magazine started to write an article about the phenomenon. However, he soon discovered a far more important story to be told: Large—as well as small—companies in a wide variety of industries had begun farming out serious tasks to individuals and groups on the Internet. Together with his editor, Mark Robinson, they coined a new term to describe the phenomenon. In June 2006, the article appeared in which *crowdsourcing* was defined as the tapping of the "latent talent of the (online) crowd." It has become the term of choice for a process that is infiltrating many aspects of business life.

Clearly, crowdsourcing has claimed some well-known successes, particularly on the product development front. Consider:

- The Linux operating system, created as an open-source alternative to Windows and UNIX, can be downloaded for free and altered to suit any user's needs. And with all the firepower brought to bear by the online open-source community, bugs in the system get fixed in a matter of hours.
- One of Amazon's smartest moves was to invite its customers to write online reviews. The customers are neither paid nor controlled by the company, but the content that they create adds enormous value to other customers and, therefore, to Amazon.
- Roughly 5 million users per month swear by Wikipedia. The free online encyclopedia was created and updated by Internet volunteers to the tune of roughly 2 million articles and counting.

Throughout this book, we will introduce examples of crowdsourcing to show its relevance to key strategy concepts. For example, in Chapter 3, we discuss how Procter & Gamble used it to develop social connections through digital media that enable the firm to codesign and coengineer new innovations with buyers. In Chapter 4, we discuss how SAP, the giant software company, uses crowdsourcing to tap knowledge well beyond its firm boundaries via the nearly 3 million participants in its Community Network. In Chapter 5, we explain how Unilever is using crowdsourcing to advance its sustainability initiatives. In Chapter 12, we discuss how NASA is working with Innocentive to overcome some of the technology challenges associated with deep-space missions.

Strategy Spotlight 2.4 explains how Lego has used crowdsourcing to help the toymaker strengthen its ties to customers and increase revenues.

> **crowdsourcing**
> practice wherein the Internet is used to tap a broad range of individuals and groups to generate ideas and solve problems.

EXHIBIT 2.3 The Impact of General Environmental Trends on Various Industries

Segment/Trends and Events	Industry	Positive	Neutral	Negative
Demographic				
Aging population	Health care	✓		
	Baby products			✓
Rising affluence	Brokerage services	✓		
	Fast foods			✓
	Upscale pets and supplies	✓		
Sociocultural				
More women in the workforce	Clothing	✓		
	Baking products (staples)			✓
Greater concern for health and fitness	Home exercise equipment	✓		
	Meat products			✓
Political/legal				
Tort reform	Legal services			✓
	Auto manufacturing	✓		
Americans with Disabilities Act (ADA)	Retail			✓
	Manufacturers of elevators, escalators, and ramps	✓		
Technological				
Genetic engineering	Pharmaceutical	✓		
	Publishing		✓	
Pollution/global warming	Engineering services	✓		
	Petroleum			✓
Economic				
Interest rate decreases	Residential construction	✓		
	Most common grocery products		✓	
Global				
Increasing global trade	Shipping	✓		
	Personal service		✓	
Emergence of China as an economic power	Soft drinks	✓		
	Defense			✓

2.4 STRATEGY SPOTLIGHT — CROWDSOURCING

LEGO'S EFFECTIVE USE OF CROWDSOURCING

Lego runs its crowdsourcing program with Cuusoo System, a Japanese company. "Both children and adults these days are used to being, and expect to be, more involved," says Mads Nipper, chief marketing officer, at Lego's headquarters in Billund, Denmark. The Lego Cuusoo site—which translates roughly to "my Lego wish" in Japanese—helps the company develop ideas that its 180 designers might not come up with on their own.

How does it work? People create a model, take photos, write a project description, and submit their idea on the Lego website (ideas.lego.com). Projects that garner more than 10,000 votes from site visitors are evaluated by designers and executives to ensure they meet such requirements as safety and playability and they fit with the Lego brand. Those whose models are chosen get 1 percent of their toy's net revenue. Plus, the Lego website asserts: "You're featured in the set materials, receive a royalty on sales, and are recognized as the product creator." Projects are reviewed about three times a year. Those scheduled for the next round include a bird, an Apple store, and a train inspired by writer Jules Verne.

A recent winner was Brent Waller, a 35-year old video game developer, who spent his childhood crafting plastic brick versions of characters from such television movies as *Teenage Mutant Turtles* and *Batman*. His miniature version of the Cadillac ambulance from Bill Murray's 1984 comedy *Ghostbusters* went into production in June 2014. Claims Waller: "It's any Lego fan's dream to have an official set they created." Brent's persistence paid off! He had struck out a few times before his big hit: His previous designs of houses, robots, and Batman's Batmobile weren't chosen.

Sources: Gustafsson, K. 2014. Who ya gonna call? Lego dials fans. *Bloomberg Businessweek*, March 19: 27–28; and www.ideas.lego.com.

LO2.5

How forces in the competitive environment can affect profitability, and how a firm can improve its competitive position by increasing its power vis-à-vis these forces.

industry
a group of firms that produce similar goods or services.

competitive environment
factors that pertain to an industry and affect a firm's strategies.

Porter's five forces model of industry competition
a tool for examining the industry-level competitive environment, especially the ability of firms in that industry to set prices and minimize costs.

The Competitive Environment

Managers must consider the competitive environment (also sometimes referred to as the task or industry environment). The nature of competition in an **industry,** as well as the profitability of a firm, is often directly influenced by developments in the competitive environment.

The **competitive environment** consists of many factors that are particularly relevant to a firm's strategy. These include competitors (existing or potential), customers, and suppliers. Potential competitors may include a supplier considering forward integration, such as an automobile manufacturer acquiring a rental car company, or a firm in an entirely new industry introducing a similar product that uses a more efficient technology.

Next, we will discuss key concepts and analytical techniques that managers should use to assess their competitive environments. First, we examine Michael Porter's five-forces model that illustrates how these forces can be used to explain an industry's profitability.[53] Second, we discuss how the five forces are being affected by the capabilities provided by Internet technologies. Third, we address some of the limitations, or "caveats," that managers should be familiar with when conducting industry analysis. Finally, we address the concept of strategic groups, because even within an industry it is often useful to group firms on the basis of similarities of their strategies. As we will see, competition tends to be more intense among firms *within* a strategic group than between strategic groups.

Porter's Five Forces Model of Industry Competition

The **"five forces" model** developed by Michael E. Porter has been the most commonly used analytical tool for examining the competitive environment. It describes the competitive environment in terms of five basic competitive forces:[54]

1. The threat of new entrants.
2. The bargaining power of buyers.
3. The bargaining power of suppliers.
4. The threat of substitute products and services.
5. The intensity of rivalry among competitors in an industry.

Each of these forces affects a firm's ability to compete in a given market. Together, they determine the profit potential for a particular industry. The model is shown in Exhibit 2.4. A manager should be familiar with the five forces model for several reasons. It helps you decide whether your firm should remain in or exit an industry. It provides the rationale for increasing or decreasing resource commitments. The model helps you assess how to improve your firm's competitive position with regard to each of the five forces.[55] For example, you can use insights provided by the five forces model to understand how higher entry barriers that discourage new rivals from competing with you.[56] Or how to develop strong relationships with your distribution channels. You may decide to find suppliers who satisfy the price/performance criteria needed to make your product or service a top performer.

The Threat of New Entrants The **threat of new entrants** refers to the possibility that the profits of established firms in the industry may be eroded by new competitors.[57] The extent of the threat depends on existing barriers to entry and the combined reactions from existing competitors.[58] If entry barriers are high and/or the newcomer can anticipate a sharp retaliation from established competitors, the threat of entry is low. These circumstances discourage new competitors. There are six major sources of entry barriers.

> **threat of new entrants**
> the possibility that the profits of established firms in the industry may be eroded by new competitors.

Economies of Scale **Economies of scale** refers to spreading the costs of production over the number of units produced. The cost of a product per unit declines as the absolute volume per period increases. This deters entry by forcing the entrant to come in at a large scale and risk strong reaction from existing firms or come in at a small scale and accept a cost disadvantage. Both are undesirable options.

> **economies of scale**
> decreases in cost per unit as absolute output per period increases.

Product Differentiation When existing competitors have strong brand identification and customer loyalty, **product differentiation** creates a barrier to entry by forcing entrants to spend heavily to overcome existing customer loyalties.

> **product differentiation**
> the degree to which a product has strong brand loyalty or customer loyalty.

EXHIBIT 2.4 Porter's Five Forces Model of Industry Competition

Sources: From Michael E. Porter, "The Five Competitive Forces That Shape Strategy," Special Issue on HBS Centennial. Harvard Business Review 86, No. 1 (January 2008), 78–93. Reprinted with permission of Michael E. Porter.

Capital Requirements The need to invest large financial resources to compete creates a barrier to entry, especially if the capital is required for risky or unrecoverable up-front advertising or research and development (R&D).

switching costs
one-time costs that a buyer/supplier faces when switching from one supplier/buyer to another.

Switching Costs A barrier to entry is created by the existence of one-time costs that the buyer faces when switching from one supplier's product or service to another.

Access to Distribution Channels The new entrant's need to secure distribution for its product can create a barrier to entry.

Cost Disadvantages Independent of Scale Some existing competitors may have advantages that are independent of size or economies of scale. These derive from:

- Proprietary products
- Favorable access to raw materials
- Government subsidies
- Favorable government policies

Managers often tend to overestimate the barriers of entry in many industries. There are any number of cases where new entrants found innovative ways to enter industries by cleverly mixing and matching existing technologies. For example, companies, medical researchers, governments, and others are creating breakthrough technology products *without having to create any new technology.*[59] Geoff Colvin, a senior editor at *Fortune,* calls this "the era of Lego Innovation," in which significant and valuable advances in technology can be achieved by imaginatively combining components and software available to everyone. Such a trend serves to reduce entry barriers in many industries because state-of-the-art technology does not have to be developed internally—rather, it is widely available and, Colvin asserts, "we all have access to a really big box of plastic bricks."

MIT's Media Lab has created robots powered by Android smartphones. After all, those devices can see, hear, recognize speech, and talk; they know where they are, how they're oriented, and how fast they're moving. And, through apps and an Internet connection, they can do a nearly infinite number of other tasks, such as recognize faces and translate languages. Similarly, teams at the University of South Carolina combined off-the-shelf eye-tracking technology with simple software they wrote to detect whether a driver was getting drowsy; any modern car has enough computing power to handle this job easily.

bargaining power of buyers
the threat that buyers may force down prices, bargain for higher quality or more services, and play competitors against each other.

The Bargaining Power of Buyers Buyers threaten an industry by forcing down prices, bargaining for higher quality or more services, and playing competitors against each other. These actions erode industry profitability.[60] The power of each large buyer group depends on attributes of the market situation and the importance of purchases from that group compared with the industry's overall business. A buyer group is powerful when:

- *It is concentrated or purchases large volumes relative to seller sales.* If a large percentage of a supplier's sales are purchased by a single buyer, the importance of the buyer's business to the supplier increases. Large-volume buyers also are powerful in industries with high fixed costs (e.g., steel manufacturing).
- *The products it purchases from the industry are standard or undifferentiated.* Confident they can always find alternative suppliers, buyers play one company against the other, as in commodity grain products.
- *The buyer faces few switching costs.* Switching costs lock the buyer to particular sellers. Conversely, the buyer's power is enhanced if the seller faces high switching costs.

- *It earns low profits.* Low profits create incentives to lower purchasing costs. On the other hand, highly profitable buyers are generally less price-sensitive.
- *The buyers pose a credible threat of backward integration.* If buyers either are partially integrated or pose a credible threat of backward integration, they are typically able to secure bargaining concessions.
- *The industry's product is unimportant to the quality of the buyer's products or services.* When the quality of the buyer's products is not affected by the industry's product, the buyer is more price-sensitive.

At times, a firm or set of firms in an industry may increase its buyer power by using the services of a third party. FreeMarkets Online is one such third party.[61] Pittsburgh-based FreeMarkets has developed software enabling large industrial buyers to organize online auctions for qualified suppliers of semistandard parts such as fabricated components, packaging materials, metal stampings, and services. By aggregating buyers, FreeMarkets increases the buyers' bargaining power. The results are impressive. In its first 48 auctions, most participating companies saved over 15 percent; some saved as much as 50 percent.

Although a firm may be tempted to take advantage of its suppliers because of high buyer power, it must be aware of the potential long-term backlash from such actions. A recent example is the growing resentment that students have toward state universities in California because of a steep 32 percent increase in tuition. Let's see why they have so little bargaining power.

> Students protested by taking over a classroom building. As noted by *Forbes* writer Asher Hawkins: "It was a futile effort. Students who are already embarked on a four-year program are something of a captive audience, and California's state coffers are empty."[62] After all, students have high exit costs, primarily because of the difficulty in transferring credits to another university. Plus, there are fewer openings at other UC campuses due to budget cuts, and there is increasing demand for them from overseas students. All these factors erode student bargaining power.
>
> After the increase, the tuition and fees for in-state undergraduate students will come to about $10,000 for the academic year (this represents a compound annual increase of nearly 10 percent over the past decade). Although this may still seem like a reasonable price for a high-quality education, there could be more price increases ahead.

The Bargaining Power of Suppliers Suppliers can exert bargaining power by threatening to raise prices or reduce the quality of purchased goods and services. Powerful suppliers can squeeze the profitability of firms so far that they can't recover the costs of raw material inputs.[63] The factors that make suppliers powerful tend to mirror those that make buyers powerful. A supplier group will be powerful when:

- *The supplier group is dominated by a few companies and is more concentrated (few firms dominate the industry) than the industry it sells to.* Suppliers selling to fragmented industries influence prices, quality, and terms.
- *The supplier group is not obliged to contend with substitute products for sale to the industry.* The power of even large, powerful suppliers can be checked if they compete with substitutes.
- *The industry is not an important customer of the supplier group.* When suppliers sell to several industries and a particular industry does not represent a significant fraction of its sales, suppliers are more prone to exert power.
- *The supplier's product is an important input to the buyer's business.* When such inputs are important to the success of the buyer's manufacturing process or product quality, the bargaining power of suppliers is high.

bargaining power of suppliers
the threat that suppliers may raise prices or reduce the quality of purchased goods and services.

- ***The supplier group's products are differentiated, or it has built up switching costs for the buyer.*** Differentiation or switching costs facing the buyers cut off their options to play one supplier against another.
- ***The supplier group poses a credible threat of forward integration.*** This provides a check against the industry's ability to improve the terms by which it purchases.

The formation of Delta Pride Catfish is an example of the power a group of suppliers can attain if they exercise the threat of forward integration.[64] Catfish farmers in Mississippi historically supplied their harvest to processing plants run by large agribusiness firms such as ConAgra and Farm Fresh. When the farmers increased their production of catfish in response to growing demand, they found, much to their chagrin, that processors were holding back on their plans to increase their processing capabilities in hopes of higher retail prices for catfish.

What action did the farmers take? About 120 of them banded together and formed a cooperative, raised $4.5 million, and constructed their own processing plant, which they supplied themselves. ConAgra's market share quickly dropped from 35 percent to 11 percent, and Farm Fresh's market share fell by over 20 percent. Within 10 years, Delta Pride controlled over 40 percent of the U.S. catfish market. Recently, Delta Pride changed its ownership structure and became a closely-held corporation. In 2014, it had revenues of $80 million, employed 600 people, and processed 80 million pounds of catfish.

The Threat of Substitute Products and Services All firms within an industry compete with industries producing **substitute products and services.**[65] Substitutes limit the potential returns of an industry by placing a ceiling on the prices that firms in that industry can profitably charge. The more attractive the price/performance ratio of substitute products, the tighter the lid on an industry's profits.

Identifying substitute products involves searching for other products or services that can perform the same function as the industry's offerings. This may lead a manager into businesses seemingly far removed from the industry. For example, the airline industry might not consider video cameras much of a threat. But as digital technology has improved and wireless and other forms of telecommunication have become more efficient, teleconferencing has become a viable substitute for business travel. That is, the rate of improvement in the price–performance relationship of the substitute product (or service) is high.

Consider the case of hybrid cars as a substitute for gasoline-powered cars.[66] Hybrid cars, such as the Toyota Prius, have seen tremendous success since the first hybrids were introduced in the late 1990s. Yet the market share of hybrid cars has been consistently low—reaching 2.4 percent in 2009, rising to 3.3 percent (the peak) in 2013, and declining to only 3 percent in 2014. Such results are even more surprising given that the number of models almost doubled between 2009 and 2014—24 to 47. That's more choices, but fewer takers. While some may believe the hybrid car industry feels pressure from other novel car segments such as electric cars (e.g., Nissan Leaf), the primary competition comes from an unusual suspect: plain old gas combustion cars.

The primary reason many environmental and cost-conscious consumers prefer gasoline-powered over hybrid cars is rather simple. Engines of gasoline-powered cars have increasingly challenged the key selling attribute of hybrid cars: fuel economy. While hybrid cars still slightly outcompete modern gasoline cars in terms of fuel economy, consumers increasingly don't see the value of paying as much as $6,000 extra for a hybrid car when they can get around 40 mpg in a gasoline car such as the Chevrolet Cruz or Hyundai Elantra.

The Intensity of Rivalry among Competitors in an Industry Firms use tactics like price competition, advertising battles, product introductions, and increased customer service or warranties. Rivalry occurs when competitors sense the pressure or act on an opportunity to improve their position.[67]

Some forms of competition, such as price competition, are typically highly destabilizing and are likely to erode the average level of profitability in an industry.[68] Rivals easily match price cuts, an action that lowers profits for all firms. On the other hand, advertising battles expand overall demand or enhance the level of product differentiation for the benefit of all firms in the industry. Rivalry, of course, differs across industries. In some instances it is characterized as warlike, bitter, or cutthroat, whereas in other industries it is referred to as polite and gentlemanly. Intense rivalry is the result of several interacting factors, including the following:

- *Numerous or equally balanced competitors.* When there are many firms in an industry, the likelihood of mavericks is great. Some firms believe they can make moves without being noticed. Even when there are relatively few firms, and they are nearly equal in size and resources, instability results from fighting among companies having the resources for sustained and vigorous retaliation.
- *Slow industry growth.* Slow industry growth turns competition into a fight for market share, since firms seek to expand their sales.
- *High fixed or storage costs.* High fixed costs create strong pressures for all firms to increase capacity. Excess capacity often leads to escalating price cutting.
- *Lack of differentiation or switching costs.* Where the product or service is perceived as a commodity or near commodity, the buyer's choice is typically based on price and service, resulting in pressures for intense price and service competition. Lack of switching costs, described earlier, has the same effect.
- *Capacity augmented in large increments.* Where economies of scale require that capacity must be added in large increments, capacity additions can be very disruptive to the industry supply/demand balance.
- *High exit barriers.* Exit barriers are economic, strategic, and emotional factors that keep firms competing even though they may be earning low or negative returns on their investments. Some exit barriers are specialized assets, fixed costs of exit, strategic interrelationships (e.g., relationships between the business units and others within a company in terms of image, marketing, shared facilities, and so on), emotional barriers, and government and social pressures (e.g., governmental discouragement of exit out of concern for job loss).

Rivalry between firms is often based solely on price, but it can involve other factors. Consider, for example, the intense competition between Uber Technologies Inc. and Lyft Inc., which are engaged in a fierce, ongoing battle in the taxi industry:[69]

> The bitter war between Uber and Lyft has spilled into dozens of cities where they are racing to provide the default app for summoning a ride within minutes. The two rivals are busy undercutting each other's prices, poaching drivers, and co-opting innovations. These actions have increasingly blurred the lines between the two services.
>
> The potential market for these firms may stretch far beyond rides. Investors who have bid up the value of Uber to over $18.2 billion in June 2014 are betting that it can expand into becoming the backbone of a logistics and delivery network for various services—a type of FedEx for cities.
>
> The recruitment of drivers is the lifeblood for the services as they attempt to build the largest networks with the fastest pickup times. For example, many Uber drivers are motivated to poach Lyft's drivers in order to get a bounty—$500 for referring a Lyft driver and $1,000 for referring a Lyft "mentor," an experienced Lyft contractor who helps train new drivers.
>
> In June 2014, another shot over the bow took place when both companies unveiled similar carpooling services within hours of each other. Lyft Line and Uber Pool let passengers ride with strangers and split the bill—lowering the cost of regular commutes. Lyft claims that it had been developing the carpooling model for several years and acquired

a team to lead the effort months ago, according to John Zimmer, Lyft's president. He adds, "I think it's flattering when other companies look at how we're innovating and want to do similar things."

On the other hand, Lyft has borrowed heavily from Uber, which had originated a real-time map that showed nearby drivers. Lyft's design is quite similar. Further, Lyft's "prime time" prices for peak-demand times are a variation of Uber's surge pricing.

The ease with which both firms can imitate each other's features may lead one to believe that the ride-sharing industry has low barriers to entry. After all, since Uber and Lyft don't own cars or employ chauffeurs, they are basically matchmakers between drivers and passengers. However, investors who have poured $2 billion into the two rivals are betting the apps will have staying power. Millions of people are now used to riding with Uber, and the app is still one of the most popular programs in Apple's App Store. Says Bill Gurley, a partner at Benchmark, a large diversified financial services firm, and a member of Uber's board: "Being installed on someone's iPhone on the home page is a pretty sticky place to be."

Exhibit 2.5 summarizes our discussion of industry five-forces analysis. It points out how various factors, such as economies of scale and capital requirements, affect each "force."

LO2.6
How the Internet and digitally based capabilities are affecting the five competitive forces and industry profitability.

Internet
a global network of linked computers that use a common transmission format, exchange information, and store data.

How the Internet and Digital Technologies Are Affecting the Five Competitive Forces

The **Internet** is having a significant impact on nearly every industry. Internet-based and digital technologies have fundamentally changed the ways businesses interact with each other and with consumers. In most cases, these changes have affected industry forces in ways that have created many new strategic challenges. In this section, we will evaluate Michael Porter's five-forces model in terms of the actual use of the Internet and the new technological capabilities that it makes possible.

The Threat of New Entrants In most industries, the threat of new entrants has increased because digital and Internet-based technologies lower barriers to entry. For example, businesses that reach customers primarily through the Internet may enjoy savings on other traditional expenses such as office rent, sales-force salaries, printing, and postage. This may encourage more entrants who, because of the lower start-up expenses, see an opportunity to capture market share by offering a product or performing a service more efficiently than existing competitors. Thus, a new cyber entrant can use the savings provided by the Internet to charge lower prices and compete on price despite the incumbent's scale advantages.

Alternatively, because digital technologies often make it possible for young firms to provide services that are equivalent or superior to an incumbent, a new entrant may be able to serve a market more effectively, with more personalized services and greater attention to product details. A new firm may be able to build a reputation in its niche and charge premium prices. By so doing, it can capture part of an incumbent's business and erode profitability.

Another potential benefit of web-based business is access to distribution channels. Manufacturers or distributors that can reach potential outlets for their products more efficiently by means of the Internet may enter markets that were previously closed to them. Access is not guaranteed, however, because strong barriers to entry exist in certain industries.[70]

The Bargaining Power of Buyers The Internet and wireless technologies may increase buyer power by providing consumers with more information to make buying decisions and by lowering switching costs. But these technologies may also suppress the power of traditional buyer channels that have concentrated buying power in the hands of a few, giving buyers new ways to access sellers. To sort out these differences, let's first distinguish between two types of buyers: end users and buyer channel intermediaries.

EXHIBIT 2.5 Competitive Analysis Checklist

Threat of New Entrants Is High When:	High	Low
Economies of scale are		X
Product differentiation is		X
Capital requirements are		X
Switching costs are		X
Incumbent's control of distribution channels is		X
Incumbent's proprietary knowledge is		X
Incumbent's access to raw materials is		X
Incumbent's access to government subsidies is		X

Power of Buyers Is High When:	High	Low
Concentration of buyers relative to suppliers is	X	
Switching costs are		X
Product differentiation of suppliers is		X
Threat of backward integration by buyers is	X	
Extent of buyer's profits is		X
Importance of the supplier's input to quality of buyer's final product is		X

Power of Suppliers Is High When:	High	Low
Concentration relative to buyer industry is	X	
Availability of substitute products is		X
Importance of customer to the supplier is		X
Differentiation of the supplier's products and services is	X	
Switching costs of the buyer are	X	
Threat of forward integration by the supplier is	X	

Threat of Substitute Products Is High When:	High	Low
Differentiation of the substitute product is	X	
Rate of improvement in price–performance relationship of substitute product is	X	

Intensity of Competitive Rivalry Is High When:	High	Low
Number of competitors is	X	
Industry growth rate is		X
Fixed costs are	X	
Storage costs are	X	
Product differentiation is		X
Switching costs are		X
Exit barriers are	X	
Strategic stakes are	X	

End users are the final customers in a distribution channel. Internet sales activity that is labeled "B2C"—that is, business-to-consumer—is concerned with end users. The Internet is likely to increase the power of these buyers for several reasons. First, the Internet provides large amounts of consumer information. This gives end users the information they need to shop for quality merchandise and bargain for price concessions. Second, an end user's switching costs are potentially much lower because of the Internet. Switching may involve only a few clicks of the mouse to find and view a competing product or service online.

In contrast, the bargaining power of distribution channel buyers may decrease because of the Internet. *Buyer channel intermediaries* are the wholesalers, distributors, and retailers who serve as intermediaries between manufacturers and end users. In some industries, they are dominated by powerful players that control who gains access to the latest goods or the best merchandise. The Internet and wireless communications, however, make it much easier and less expensive for businesses to reach customers directly. Thus, the Internet may increase the power of incumbent firms relative to that of traditional buyer channels. Strategy Spotlight 2.5 illustrates some of the changes brought on by the Internet that have affected the legal services industry.

The Bargaining Power of Suppliers Use of the Internet and digital technologies to speed up and streamline the process of acquiring supplies is already benefiting many sectors of the economy. But the net effect of the Internet on supplier power will depend on the nature of competition in a given industry. As with buyer power, the extent to which the Internet is a benefit or a detriment also hinges on the supplier's position along the supply chain.

The role of suppliers involves providing products or services to other businesses. The term "B2B"—that is, business-to-business—often refers to businesses that supply or sell to other businesses. The effect of the Internet on the bargaining power of suppliers is a double-edged sword. On the one hand, suppliers may find it difficult to hold on to customers because buyers can do comparative shopping and price negotiations so much faster on the Internet.

On the other hand, several factors may also contribute to stronger supplier power. First, the growth of new web-based business may create more downstream outlets for suppliers to sell to. Second, suppliers may be able to create web-based purchasing arrangements that make purchasing easier and discourage their customers from switching. Online procurement systems directly link suppliers and customers, reducing transaction costs and paperwork.[71] Third, the use of proprietary software that links buyers to a supplier's website may create a rapid, low-cost ordering capability that discourages the buyer from seeking other sources of supply. *Amazon.com*, for example, created and patented One-Click purchasing technology that speeds up the ordering process for customers who enroll in the service.[72]

Finally, suppliers will have greater power to the extent that they can reach end users directly without intermediaries. Previously, suppliers often had to work through intermediaries who brought their products or services to market for a fee. But a process known as *disintermediation* is removing the organizations or business process layers responsible for intermediary steps in the value chain of many industries.[73] Just as the Internet is eliminating some business functions, it is creating an opening for new functions. These new activities are entering the value chain by a process known as *reintermediation*—the introduction of new types of intermediaries. Many of these new functions are affecting traditional supply chains. For example, delivery services are enjoying a boom because of the Internet. Many more consumers are choosing to have products delivered to their door rather than going out to pick them up.

The Threat of Substitutes Along with traditional marketplaces, the Internet has created a new marketplace and a new channel. In general, therefore, the threat of substitutes is heightened because the Internet introduces new ways to accomplish the same tasks.

Consumers will generally choose to use a product or service until a substitute that meets the same need becomes available at a lower cost. The economies created by Internet technologies have led to the development of numerous substitutes for traditional ways of doing business.

Another example of substitution is in the realm of electronic storage. With expanded desktop computing, the need to store information electronically has increased dramatically. Until recently, the trend has been to create increasingly larger desktop storage capabilities and techniques for compressing information that create storage efficiencies. But a viable

2.5 STRATEGY SPOTLIGHT

BUYER POWER IN LEGAL SERVICES: THE ROLE OF THE INTERNET

The $260 billion U.S. legal services industry, which includes about 180,000 firms, historically was a classic example of an industry that leaves buyers at a bargaining disadvantage. One of the key reasons for the strong bargaining position of law firms is high information asymmetry between lawyers and consumers, meaning that highly trained and experienced legal professionals know more about legal matters than the average consumer of legal services.

The Internet provides an excellent example of how unequal bargaining power can be reduced by decreasing information asymmetry. A new class of Internet legal services providers tries to accomplish just that and is challenging traditional law services along the way. For instance, *LawPivot.com*, a recent start-up backed by Google Ventures and cofounded by a former top Apple Inc. lawyer, allows consumers to interact with lawyers on a social networking site. This service allows customers to get a better picture of a lawyer's legal skills before opening their wallets. As a result, information asymmetry between lawyers and consumers is reduced and customers find themselves in a better bargaining position. Another example is *LegalZoom.com*, a service that helps consumers to create legal documents. Customers familiar with *LegalZoom.com* may use their knowledge of the time and effort required to create legal documents to challenge a lawyer's fees for custom-crafted legal documents.

Sources: Jacobs, D. L. 2011. Google takes aim at lawyers. *Forbes*, August 8: np; Anonymous. 2011. Alternative law firms: Bargain briefs. *The Economist*, August 13: 64; and Anonymous. 2014. Legal services industry profile. *First Research*, August 25: np.

---

substitute has emerged: storing information digitally on the Internet. Companies such as Dropbox and Amazon Web Services are providing web-based storage that firms can access simply by leasing space online. Since these storage places are virtual, they can be accessed anywhere the web can be accessed. Travelers can access important documents and files without transporting them physically from place to place.

The Intensity of Competitive Rivalry Because the Internet creates more tools and means for competing, rivalry among competitors is likely to be more intense. Only those competitors that can use digital technologies and the web to give themselves a distinct image, create unique product offerings, or provide "faster, smarter, cheaper" services are likely to capture greater profitability with the new technology.

Rivalry is more intense when switching costs are low and product or service differentiation is minimized. Because the Internet makes it possible to shop around, it has "commoditized" products that might previously have been regarded as rare or unique. Since the Internet reduces the importance of location, products that previously had to be sought out in geographically distant outlets are now readily available online. This makes competitors in cyberspace seem more equally balanced, thus intensifying rivalry.

The problem is made worse for marketers by the presence of shopping robots ("bots") and infomediaries that search the web for the best possible prices. Consumer websites like mySimon seek out all the web locations that sell similar products and provide price comparisons.[74] Obviously, this focuses the consumer exclusively on price. Some shopping infomediaries, such as CNET, not only search for the lowest prices on many different products but also rank the customer service quality of different sites that sell similarly priced items.[75] Such infomediary services are good for consumers because they give them the chance to compare services as well as price. For businesses, however, they increase rivalry by consolidating the marketing message that consumers use to make a purchase decision into a few key pieces of information over which the selling company has little control.

Using Industry Analysis: A Few Caveats

For industry analysis to be valuable, a company must collect and evaluate a wide variety of information. As the trend toward globalization accelerates, information on foreign markets as well as on a wider variety of competitors, suppliers, customers, substitutes, and potential new entrants becomes more critical. Industry analysis helps a firm not only to evaluate the profit potential of an industry but also to consider various ways to strengthen its position vis-à-vis the five forces. However, we'd like to address a few caveats.

First, *managers must not always avoid low-profit industries (or low-profit segments in profitable industries).*[76] Such industries can still yield high returns for some players who pursue sound strategies. As examples, consider Paychex, a payroll-processing company, and WellPoint Health Network, a huge health care insurer:[77]

> Paychex, with $2 billion in revenues, became successful by serving small businesses. Existing firms had ignored them because they assumed that such businesses could not afford the service. When Paychex's founder, Tom Golisano, failed to convince his bosses at Electronic Accounting Systems that they were missing a great opportunity, he launched the firm. It now serves nearly 600,000 clients in the United States and Germany. Paychex's after-tax-return on sales is a stunning 25 percent.
>
> In 1986, WellPoint Health Network (when it was known as Blue Cross of California) suffered a loss of $160 million. That year, Leonard Schaeffer became CEO and challenged the conventional wisdom that individuals and small firms were money losers. (This was certainly "heresy" at the time—the firm was losing $5 million a year insuring 65,000 individuals!) However, by the early 1990s, the health insurer was leading the industry in profitability. The firm has continued to grow and outperform its rivals even during economic downturns. By 2012, its revenues and profits were $61 billion and $2.5 billion, respectively.

zero-sum game
a situation in which multiple players interact, and winners win only by taking from other players.

Second, five-forces analysis implicitly *assumes a* **zero-sum game,** *determining how a firm can enhance its position relative to the forces.* Yet such an approach can often be shortsighted; that is, it can overlook the many potential benefits of developing constructive win–win relationships with suppliers and customers. Establishing long-term mutually beneficial relationships with suppliers improves a firm's ability to implement just-in-time (JIT) inventory systems, which let it manage inventories better and respond quickly to market demands. A recent study found that if a company exploits its powerful position against a supplier, that action may come back to haunt the company.[78] Consider, for example, General Motors' heavy-handed dealings with its suppliers:[79]

> In 2014, GM was already locked in a public relations nightmare as a deadly ignition defect triggered the recall of over 2.5 million vehicles.[80] At the same time, it was faced with another perception problem: poor supplier relations. GM is now considered the worst big automaker to deal with, according to a new survey of top suppliers in the car industry in the United States.
>
> The annual survey, conducted by the automotive consultant group, Planning Perspectives Inc., asks the industry's biggest suppliers to rate the relationships with the six automakers that account for more than 85 percent of all cars and light trucks in the U.S. Those so-called "Tier 1" suppliers say GM is their least favorite big customer—less popular than even Chrysler, the unit of Fiat Chrysler Automobiles that had "earned" the dubious distinction since 2008.
>
> The suppliers gave GM low marks on all kinds of measures, including its overall trustworthiness, its communication skills, and its protection of intellectual property. The suppliers also said that GM was the automaker least likely to allow them to raise prices to recoup unexpected materials cost increases. In return, parts executives have said they tend to bring hot new technology to other carmakers first—certainly something that makes it more difficult for GM to compete in this hotly contested industry.

Third, the five-forces analysis also has been criticized for *being essentially a static analysis.* External forces as well as strategies of individual firms are continually changing the structure of all industries. The search for a dynamic theory of strategy has led to

EXHIBIT 2.6 The Value Net

```
                CUSTOMERS
                    ▲
                    │
                    │
SUBSTITUTORS ── THE COMPANY ── COMPLEMENTORS  ◄── Interactions between
                    │                              players on the
                    │                              horizontal axis
                    ▼
                 SUPPLIERS
                    ▲
                    │
         Transactions between players
             on the vertical axis
```

Sources: Adapted from "The Right Game: Use Game Theory Shape Strategy," by A. Brandenburger and B.J. Nalebuff, July-August 1995 Harvard Business Review.

greater use of game theory in industrial organization economics research and strategy research.

Based on game-theoretic considerations, Brandenburger and Nalebuff recently introduced the concept of the value net,[81] which in many ways is an extension of the five-forces analysis. It is illustrated in Exhibit 2.6. The value net represents all the players in the game and analyzes how their interactions affect a firm's ability to generate and appropriate value. The vertical dimension of the net includes suppliers and customers. The firm has direct transactions with them. On the horizontal dimension are substitutes and complements, players with whom a firm interacts but may not necessarily transact. The concept of complementors is perhaps the single most important contribution of value net analysis and is explained in more detail below.

Complements typically are products or services that have a potential impact on the value of a firm's own products or services. Those who produce complements are usually referred to as complementors.[82] Powerful hardware is of no value to a user unless there is software that runs on it. Similarly, new and better software is possible only if the hardware on which it can be run is available. This is equally true in the video game industry, where the sales of game consoles and video games complement each other. Nintendo's success in the early 1990s was a result of its ability to manage its relationship with its complementors. Nintendo built a security chip into the hardware and then licensed the right to develop games to outside firms. These firms paid a royalty to Nintendo for each copy of the game sold. The royalty revenue enabled Nintendo to sell game consoles at close to their cost, thereby increasing their market share, which, in turn, caused more games to be sold and more royalties to be generated.[83]

Despite efforts to create win–win scenarios, conflict among complementors is inevitable.[84] After all, it is naive to expect that even the closest of partners will do you the favor of abandoning their own interests. And even the most successful partnerships are seldom trouble-free. Power is a factor that comes into play as we see in Strategy Spotlight 2.6 with the example of Apple's iPod—an enormously successful product.

We would like to close this section with some recent insights from Michael Porter, the originator of the five-forces analysis.[85] He addresses two critical issues in conducting a

> **complements**
> products or services that have an impact on the value of a firm's products or services.

2.6 STRATEGY SPOTLIGHT

APPLE'S IPOD: RELATIONSHIPS WITH ITS COMPLEMENTORS

In 2002, Steve Jobs began his campaign to cajole the major music companies into selling tracks to iPod users through the iTunes Music Store, an online retail site. Most industry executives, after being burned by illegal file-sharing services like Napster and Kazaa, just wanted digital music to disappear. However, Jobs's passionate vision persuaded them to climb on board. He promised to reduce the risks that they faced by offering safeguards against piracy, as well as a hip product (iPod and iPad Touch) that would drive sales.

However, Apple had a much stronger bargaining position when its contracts with the music companies came up for renewal in April 2005. By then, iTunes had captured 80 percent of the market for legal downloads. The music companies, which were receiving between 60 and 70 cents per download, wanted more. Their reasoning: If the iTunes Music Store would only charge $1.50 or $2.00 per track, they could double or triple their revenues and profits. Since Jobs knew that he could sell more iPods if the music was cheap, he was determined to keep the price of a download at 99 cents and to maintain Apple's margins. Given iTunes' dominant position, the music companies had little choice but to relent.

Apple's foray into music has been tremendously successful. Since the iPod's introduction in 2001, Apple has sold over 300 million iPod units worldwide. And iTunes software and services are still going strong, increasing to $16 billion in 2013—a 71 percent increase over 2011! Having won the music market, Apple's success elsewhere has come even more quickly. Apple's millions of users create powerful network effects, exerting a strong gravitational pull on content providers to participate in the iTunes ecosystem. By mid-2013, the iTunes store had captured more than 65 percent of the market for digital movies and television programming—a market largely created by Apple.

Sources: Downes, L. & Nunes, P. 2014. *Big bang disruption.* New York: Penguin; Reisinger, D. 2012. Why the iPod (yes, the iPod) still matters. *Fortune,* October 8: 79; Hesseldahl, A. 2008. Now that we all have iPods. *BusinessWeek,* December 15: 36; Apple Computer Inc. 10-K, 2010; 2012 Apple, Inc. Annual Report; and Yoffie, D. B. & Kwak, M. 2006. With friends like these: The art of managing complementors. *Harvard Business Review,* 84(9): 88–98.

---

good industry analysis, which will yield an improved understanding of the root causes of profitability: (1) choosing the appropriate time frame and (2) a rigorous quantification of the five forces.

- *Good industry analysis looks rigorously at the structural underpinnings of profitability. A first step is to understand the time horizon.* One of the essential tasks in industry analysis is to distinguish short-term fluctuations from structural changes. A good guideline for the appropriate time horizon is the full business cycle for the particular industry. For most industries, a three- to five-year horizon is appropriate. However, for some industries with long lead times, such as mining, the appropriate horizon may be a decade or more. It is average profitability over this period, not profitability in any particular year, which should be the focus of analysis.

- *The point of industry analysis is not to declare the industry attractive or unattractive but to understand the underpinnings of competition and the root causes of profitability.* As much as possible, analysts should look at industry structure quantitatively, rather than be satisfied with lists of qualitative factors. Many elements of five forces can be quantified: the percentage of the buyer's total cost accounted for by the industry's product (to understand buyer price sensitivity); the percentage of industry sales required to fill a plant or operate a logistical network to efficient scale (to help assess barriers to entry); and the buyer's switching cost (determining the inducement an entrant or rival must offer customers).

strategic groups
clusters of firms that share similar strategies.

LO2.7
The concept of strategic groups and their strategy and performance implications.

Strategic Groups within Industries

In an industry analysis, two assumptions are unassailable: (1) No two firms are totally different, and (2) no two firms are exactly the same. The issue becomes one of identifying groups of firms that are more similar to each other than firms that are not, otherwise known as **strategic groups**.[86] This is important because rivalry tends to be greater among firms that are alike. Strategic groups are clusters of firms that share similar strategies. After all, is Kmart more concerned about Nordstrom or Walmart? Is Mercedes more concerned about Hyundai or BMW? The answers are straightforward.[87]

These examples are not meant to trivialize the strategic groups concept.[88] Classifying an industry into strategic groups involves judgment. If it is useful as an analytical tool, we must exercise caution in deciding what dimensions to use to map these firms. Dimensions include breadth of product and geographic scope, price/quality, degree of vertical integration, type of distribution (e.g., dealers, mass merchandisers, private label), and so on. Dimensions should also be selected to reflect the variety of strategic combinations in an industry. For example, if all firms in an industry have roughly the same level of product differentiation (or R&D intensity), this would not be a good dimension to select.

What value is the strategic groups concept as an analytical tool? *First, strategic groupings help a firm identify barriers to mobility that protect a group from attacks by other groups.*[89] Mobility barriers are factors that deter the movement of firms from one strategic position to another. For example, in the chainsaw industry, the major barriers protecting the high-quality/dealer-oriented group are technology, brand image, and an established network of servicing dealers.

The second value of strategic grouping is that it *helps a firm identify groups whose competitive position may be marginal or tenuous.* We may anticipate that these competitors may exit the industry or try to move into another group. In recent years in the retail department store industry, firms such as JCPenney and Sears have experienced extremely difficult times because they were stuck in the middle, neither an aggressive discount player like Walmart nor a prestigious upscale player like Neiman Marcus.

Third, strategic groupings *help chart the future directions of firms' strategies.* Arrows emanating from each strategic group can represent the direction in which the group (or a firm within the group) seems to be moving. If all strategic groups are moving in a similar direction, this could indicate a high degree of future volatility and intensity of competition. In the automobile industry, for example, the competition in the minivan and sport utility segments has intensified in recent years as many firms have entered those product segments.

Fourth, strategic groups are *helpful in thinking through the implications of each industry trend for the strategic group as a whole.* Is the trend decreasing the viability of a group? If so, in what direction should the strategic group move? Is the trend increasing or decreasing entry barriers? Will the trend decrease the ability of one group to separate itself from other groups? Such analysis can help in making predictions about industry evolution. A sharp increase in interest rates, for example, tends to have less impact on providers of higher-priced goods (e.g., Porsches) than on providers of lower-priced goods (e.g., Chevrolet Cobalt), whose customer base is much more price-sensitive.

Exhibit 2.7 provides a strategic grouping of the worldwide automobile industry.[90] The firms in each group are representative; not all firms are included in the mapping. We have identified four strategic groups. In the top left-hand corner are high-end luxury automakers that focus on a very narrow product market. Most of the cars produced by the members of this group cost well over $100,000. Some cost over twice that amount. The 2015 Ferrari California T starts at $201,940, and the 2015 Lamborghini Huracan will set you back $237,250 (in case you were wondering how to spend your employment signing bonus). Players in this market have a very exclusive clientele and face little rivalry from other strategic groups. At the other extreme, in the lower left-hand corner is a strategic group that has low-price/quality attributes and targets a narrow market. These players, Hyundai and Kia, limit competition from other strategic groups by pricing their products very low. The third group (near the middle) consists of firms high in product pricing/quality and average in their product-line breadth. The final group (at the far right) consists of firms with a

EXHIBIT 2.7 The World Automobile Industry: Strategic Groups

[Strategic groups chart with axes "Price" (Low to High) and "Breadth of Product Line" (Low to High):
- Ferrari, Lamborghini, Porsche (High price, Low breadth)
- Mercedes, BMW (High price, medium breadth)
- Toyota, Ford, General Motors, Chrysler, Honda, Nissan (medium-high price, High breadth)
- Hyundai, Kia (Low-medium price, medium breadth)
- Chery, Geely, Tata Motors (Low price, Low breadth)]

Note: Members of each strategic group are not exhaustive, only illustrative.

broad range of products and multiple price points. These firms have entries that compete at both the lower end of the market (e.g., the Ford Focus) and the higher end (e.g., Chevrolet Corvette).

The auto market has been very dynamic and competition has intensified in recent years.[91] For example, some players are going more upscale with their product offerings. In 2009, Hyundai introduced its Genesis, starting at $33,000. This brings Hyundai into direct competition with entries from other strategic groups such as Toyota's Camry and Honda's Accord. And, in 2010, Hyundai introduced the Equus model. It was priced at about $60,000 to compete directly with the Lexus 460 on price. To further intensify competition, some upscale brands are increasingly entering lower-priced segments. In 2014, Audi introduced the Q3 SUV at a base price of only $32,500. And BMW, with its 1-series, is another well-known example. Such cars, priced in the low $30,000s, compete more directly with products from broad-line manufacturers like Ford, General Motors, and Toyota. This suggests that members of a strategic group can overcome mobility barriers and migrate to other groups that they find attractive if they are willing to commit time and resources.

Our discussion would not be complete, of course, without paying some attention to recent entries in the automobile industry that will likely lead to the formation of a new strategic group—placed at the bottom left corner of the grid in Exhibit 2.7. Three firms—China's Zhejiang Geely Holding Company, China's Chery Automobile Company, and India's Tata Motors—have introduced models that bring new meaning to the term "subcompact."[92] Let's take a look at these econoboxes.

> Chery's 2013 QQ model sells for between $6,083 and $8,170 in the Chinese market and sports horsepower in the range of only 51 to 74. Geely's best-selling four-door sedan, the Free Cruiser, retails from $5,440 to $7,046. The firm has gone more upscale with some offerings, such as the GX7, a sports utility vehicle with a price starting at $14,910.
>
> For low price-points, India's Tata Motors has everyone beat by the proverbial mile. In January 2008, it introduced the Nano as the "World's Cheapest Car," with an astonishing retail price of only $2,500. It is a four-door, five-seat hatchback that gets 54 miles to the gallon (but this economy originally came with a 30 horsepower motor). Initially, it was

ISSUE FOR DEBATE

Should Large Firms Further Delay Payments to their Suppliers?

In 2013, Mondelez International, the snack and food company recently spun off by Kraft Foods, sent a letter to its suppliers explaining its new policy: 120 days before paying a bill is now standard operating policy. It appears that this is a growing trend—companies withholding payment to suppliers after a service is performed or a product delivered. Procter & Gamble drew complaints when it started negotiating with suppliers to extend the delay in payments to 75 days, up from 45 days. Unilever is considering a similar move, and Merck has broached the subject of waiting 90 days to pay its vendors and suppliers.

One can easily understand why a large company would be tempted to hold off paying its suppliers. Holding onto millions—or even billions—of dollars for an extra month or two (or four) can free up cash to invest or generate whatever interest it can gain. In an environment in which businesses are continually scrambling to boost earnings in an uncertain economic climate, it's an easy way to hike profits.

Bill Dunkelberg, chief economist for the National Federation of Independent Businesses, has a different perspective: "It's mean. It's a pain in the butt and costly for small firms that are having this happen to them." Small companies are often very vulnerable because one large customer may make up the bulk of a small firm's sales, leaving it with little choice but to accede to the demands of a giant company—effectively financing the customer for 120 days.

In response to an inquiry by Becky Quick, a *Fortune* writer, a Mondelez spokesman emailed a statement, reading in part: "Extending our payment terms allows us to better align with industry (norms) and make sure we compete on fair grounds, while simultaneously improving transparency and predictability of payment processes." However, it may appear ironic that the company tailors its terms so that its customers are penalized if they don't pay for confections within 15 days of receipt and for snacks within 25 days, according to an industry insider.

Discussion Questions
1. Should Mondelez and other companies follow the practice of lengthening payment terms with their suppliers? Why? Or why not?
2. Do you feel that this practice can raise ethical issues?
3. What actions can suppliers take to respond to the lengthening of the payment terms?

Source: Quick, B. 2013. A snack maker's unsavory business practices. *Fortune*, September 2: 54.

---

a big hit in India. However, after sales peaked at about 80,000 units in 2011–2012, they crashed to only 21,000 units in 2013–2014. As noted by Girish Wagh, the man behind the Nano, "People started looking at Nano not as a low-cost innovation, but as a cheap car. This, among other factors, also hurt the chances." Needless to say, Tata has made many attempts to make the car more upscale, with a correspondingly higher price.

Not surprisingly, some automakers have recently entered the Indian market with more desirable offerings. Several have offerings that are called compact sedans, but they are actually hatchbacks with a tiny trunk tacked on. These models include Suzuki's Dzire, Honda's Amaze, and Hyundai's Xcent. Prices start at around $8,000, and with the added cachet of a sedan silhouette that adds only a few hundred dollars, these models have become very popular with Indian buyers. This niche is one of the few car segments that soared, while the country's overall car market shrunk.

Reflecting on Career Implications . . .

- **Creating the Environmentally Aware Organization:** Advancing your career requires constant scanning, monitoring, and intelligence gathering not only to find future job opportunities but also to understand how employers' expectations are changing. Consider using websites such as LinkedIn to find opportunities. Merely posting your résumé on a site such as LinkedIn may not be enough. Instead, consider in what ways you can use such sites for scanning, monitoring, and intelligence gathering.

- **SWOT Analysis:** As an analytical method, SWOT analysis is applicable for individuals as it is for firms. It is important for you to periodically evaluate your strengths and weaknesses as well as potential opportunities and threats to your career. Such analysis should be followed by efforts to address your weaknesses by improving your skills and capabilities.

- **General Environment:** The general environment consists of several segments, such as the demographic, sociocultural, political/legal, technological, economic, and global environments. It would be useful to evaluate how each of these segments can affect your career opportunities. Identify two or three specific trends (e.g., rapid technological change, aging of the population, increase in minimum wages) and their impact on your choice of careers. These also provide possibilities for you to add value for your organization.

- **Five-Forces Analysis:** Before you go for a job interview, consider the five forces affecting the industry within which the firm competes. This will help you to appear knowledgeable about the industry and increase your odds of landing the job. It also can help you to decide if you want to work for that organization. If the "forces" are unfavorable, the long-term profit potential of the industry may be unattractive, leading to fewer resources available and—all other things being equal—fewer career opportunities.

summary

Managers must analyze the external environment to minimize or eliminate threats and exploit opportunities. This involves a continuous process of environmental scanning and monitoring as well as obtaining competitive intelligence on present and potential rivals. These activities provide valuable inputs for developing forecasts. In addition, many firms use scenario planning to anticipate and respond to volatile and disruptive environmental changes.

We identified two types of environments: the general environment and the competitive environment. The six segments of the general environment are demographic, sociocultural, political/legal, technological, economic, and global. Trends and events occurring in these segments, such as the aging of the population, higher percentages of women in the workplace, governmental legislation, and increasing (or decreasing) interest rates, can have a dramatic effect on a firm. A given trend or event may have a positive impact on some industries and a negative, a neutral, or no impact on others.

The competitive environment consists of industry-related factors and has a more direct impact than the general environment. Porter's five-forces model of industry analysis includes the threat of new entrants, buyer power, supplier power, threat of substitutes, and rivalry among competitors. The intensity of these factors determines, in large part, the average expected level of profitability in an industry. A sound awareness of such factors, both individually and in combination, is beneficial not only for deciding what industries to enter but also for assessing how a firm can improve its competitive position. We discuss how many of the changes brought about by the digital economy can be understood in the context of five-forces analysis. The limitations of five-forces analysis include its static nature and its inability to acknowledge the role of complementors. Although we addressed the general environment and competitive environment in separate sections, they are quite interdependent. A given environmental trend or event, such as changes in the ethnic composition of a population or a technological innovation, typically has a much greater impact on some industries than on others.

The concept of strategic groups is also important to the external environment of a firm. No two organizations are completely different nor are they exactly the same. The question is how to group firms in an industry on the basis of similarities in their resources and strategies. The strategic groups concept is valuable for determining mobility barriers across groups, identifying groups with marginal competitive positions, charting the future directions of firm strategies, and assessing the implications of industry trends for the strategic group as a whole.

SUMMARY REVIEW QUESTIONS

1. Why must managers be aware of a firm's external environment?
2. What is gathering and analyzing competitive intelligence, and why is it important for firms to engage in it?
3. Discuss and describe the six elements of the external environment.
4. Select one of these elements and describe some changes relating to it in an industry that interests you.
5. Describe how the five forces can be used to determine the average expected profitability in an industry.

6. What are some of the limitations (or caveats) in using five-forces analysis?
7. Explain how the general environment and industry environment are highly related. How can such interrelationships affect the profitability of a firm or industry?
8. Explain the concept of strategic groups. What are the performance implications?

key terms

perceptual acuity 38
environmental scanning 39
environmental monitoring 39
competitive intelligence 39
environmental forecasting 40
scenario analysis 42
SWOT analysis 42
general environment 43
demographic segment of the general environment 45
sociocultural segment of the general environment 45
political/legal segment of the general environment 47
technological segment of the general environment 48
economic segment of the general environment 49
global segment of the general environment 49
crowdsourcing 50
industry 52
competitive environment 52
Porter's five-forces model of industry competition 52
threat of new entrants 53
economies of scale 53
product differentiation 53
switching cost 54
bargaining power of buyers 54
bargaining power of suppliers 55
threat of substitute products and services 56
substitute products and services 56
intensity of rivalry among competitors in an industry 56
Internet 58
zero-sum game 62
complements 63
strategic groups 64

experiential exercise

Select one of the following industries: personal computers, airlines, or automobiles. For this industry, evaluate the strength of each of Porter's five forces as well as complementors.

Industry Force	High? Medium? Low?	Why?
1. Threat of new entrants		
2. Power of buyers		
3. Power of suppliers		
4. Power of substitutes		
5. Rivalry among competitors		
6. Complementors		

application questions & exercises

1. Imagine yourself as the CEO of a large firm in an industry in which you are interested. Please (1) identify major trends in the general environment, (2) analyze their impact on the firm, and (3) identify major sources of information to monitor these trends. (Use Internet and library resources.)
2. Analyze movements across the strategic groups in the U.S. retail industry. How do these movements within this industry change the nature of competition?
3. What are the major trends in the general environment that have impacted the U.S. pharmaceutical industry?
4. Go to the Internet and look up *www.kroger.com*. What are some of the five forces driving industry competition that are affecting the profitability of this firm?

ethics questions

1. What are some of the legal and ethical issues involved in collecting competitor intelligence in the following situations?
    a. Hotel A sends an employee posing as a potential client to Hotel B to find out who Hotel B's major corporate customers are.
    b. A firm hires an MBA student to collect information directly from a competitor while claiming the information is for a course project.
    c. A firm advertises a nonexistent position and interviews a rival's employees with the intention of obtaining competitor information.
2. What are some of the ethical implications that arise when a firm tries to exploit its power over a supplier?

references

1. Schneider, J. & Hall, J. 2011. Can you hear me now? *Harvard Business Review,* 89(4): 23; Hornigan, J. 2009. Wireless Internet use—Mobile access to data and information. *www.pewinternet.org,* July 22: np; and Salemi Industries. 2012. Home page. *www.salemiindustries.com,* December 20: np.
2. Hamel, G. & Prahalad, C. K. 1994. *Competing for the future.* Boston: Harvard Business School Press.
3. Drucker, P. F. 1994. Theory of the business. *Harvard Business Review,* 72: 95–104.
4. For an insightful discussion on managers' assessment of the external environment, refer to Sutcliffe, K. M. & Weber, K. 2003. The high cost of accurate knowledge. *Harvard Business Review,* 81(5): 74–86.
5. Merino, M. 2013. You can't be a wimp: Making the tough calls. *Harvard Business Review,* 91(11): 73–78.
6. For insights on recognizing and acting on environmental opportunities, refer to Alvarez, S. A. & Barney, J. B. 2008. Opportunities, organizations, and entrepreneurship: Theory and debate. *Strategic Entrepreneurship Journal,* 2(3): entire issue.
7. Charitou, C. D. & Markides, C. C. 2003. Responses to disruptive strategic innovation. *MIT Sloan Management Review,* 44(2): 55–64.
8. Our discussion of scanning, monitoring, competitive intelligence, and forecasting concepts draws on several sources. These include Fahey, L. & Narayanan, V. K. 1983. *Macroenvironmental analysis for strategic management.* St. Paul, MN: West; Lorange, P., Scott, F. S., & Ghoshal, S. 1986. *Strategic control.* St. Paul, MN: West; Ansoff, H. I. 1984. *Implementing strategic management.* Englewood Cliffs, NJ: Prentice Hall; and Schreyogg, G. & Stienmann, H. 1987. Strategic control: A new perspective. *Academy of Management Review,* 12: 91–103.
9. An insightful discussion on how leaders can develop "peripheral vision" in environmental scanning is found in Day, G. S. & Schoemaker, P. J. H. 2008. Are you a "vigilant leader"? *MIT Sloan Management Review,* 49(3): 43–51.
10. Elenkov, D. S. 1997. Strategic uncertainty and environmental scanning: The case for institutional influences on scanning behavior. *Strategic Management Journal,* 18: 287–302.
11. For an interesting perspective on environmental scanning in emerging economies, see May, R. C., Stewart, W. H., & Sweo, R. 2000. Environmental scanning behavior in a transitional economy, Evidence from Russia. *Academy of Management Journal,* 43(3): 403–427.
12. Bryon, E. 2010. For insight into P&G, check Olay numbers. *Wall Street Journal,* October 27: C1.
13. Tang, J. 2010. How entrepreneurs discover opportunities in China: An institutional view. *Asia Pacific Journal of Management,* 27(3): 461–480.
14. Walters, B. A. & Priem, R. L. 1999. Business strategy and CEO intelligence acquisition. *Competitive Intelligence Review,* 10(2): 15–22.
15. Prior, V. 1999. The language of competitive intelligence, Part 4. *Competitive Intelligence Review,* 10(1): 84–87.
16. Hill, K. 2011. The spy who liked me. *Forbes,* November 21: 56–57.
17. Wolfenson, J. 1999. The world in 1999: A battle for corporate honesty. *The Economist,* 38: 13–30.
18. Drucker, P. F. 1997. The future that has already happened. *Harvard Business Review,* 75(6): 22.
19. Downes, L. & Nunes, P. 2014. *Big bang disruption.* New York: Penguin.
20. Fahey & Narayanan, op. cit., p. 41.
21. Insights on how to improve predictions can be found in Cross, R., Thomas, R. J., & Light, D. A. 2009. The prediction lover's handbook. *MIT Sloan Management Review,* 50(2): 32–34.
22. Courtney, H., Kirkland, J., & Viguerie, P. 1997. Strategy under uncertainty. *Harvard Business Review,* 75(6): 66–79.
23. Odlyzko, A. 2003. False hopes. *Red Herring,* March: 31.
24. Zweig, J. 2014. Lessons learned from year of shock. *The Wall Street Journal,* December 31: C1–C2; Coy, P. 2009. Worst predictions about 2008. *BusinessWeek,* January 12: 15–16; Pressman, A. 2014. Apple competitors still smarting from iPhone blow. *finance.yahoo.com,* July 17: np; Kowitt, B. Whole Foods takes over America. *Fortune.com,* April 10: 70–77; Basinger, J. 2014. "Gone with the Wind" goes Hollywood. *The Wall Street Journal,* October 4–5: C15; and *www.aarp.org.*
25. Zweig, op. cit.
26. For an interesting perspective on how Accenture practices and has developed its approach to scenario planning, refer to Ferguson, G., Mathur, S., & Shah, B. 2005. Evolving from information to insight. *MIT Sloan Management Review,* 46(2): 51–58.
27. Byrne, J. 2012. Great ideas are hard to come by. *Fortune,* April 7: 69 ff.
28. Dean, T. J., Brown, R. L., & Bamford, C. E. 1998. Differences in large and small firm responses to environmental context: Strategic implications from a comparative analysis of business formations. *Strategic Management Journal,* 19: 709–728.
29. Colvin, G. 2014. Four things that worry business. *Fortune,* October 27: 32.
30. Colvin, G. 1997. How to beat the boomer rush. *Fortune,* August 18: 59–63.
31. Porter, M. E. 2010. Discovering—and lowering—the real costs of health care. *Harvard Business Review,* 89(1/2): 49–50.
32. Farrell, C. 2014. Baby boomers' latest revolution: Unretirement. *Dallas Morning News,* October 19: 4P.
33. Challenger, J. 2000. Women's corporate rise has reduced relocations. *Lexington* (KY) *Herald-Leader,* October 29: D1.
34. Tsao, A. 2005. Retooling home improvement, *Businessweek.com,* February 14; and Grow, B. 2004. Who wears the wallet in the family? *BusinessWeek,* August 16:10.
35. Watkins, M. D. 2003. Government games. *MIT Sloan Management Review,* 44(2): 91–95.
36. A discussion of the political issues surrounding caloric content on meals is in Orey, M. 2008. A food fight over calorie counts. *BusinessWeek,* February 11: 36.
37. For a discussion of the linkage between copyright law and innovation, read Guterman, J. 2009. Does copyright law hinder innovation? *MIT Sloan Management Review,* 50(2): 14–15.
38. Davies, A. 2000. The welcome mat is out for nerds. *BusinessWeek,* May 21: 17; Broache, A. 2007. Annual H-1B visa cap met—already. *news.cnet.com,* April 3: np; and Anonymous. Undated. Cap count for H-1B and H-2B workers for fiscal year 2009. *www.uscis.gov:* np.
39. Weise, K. 2014. How to hack the visa limit. *Bloomberg Businessweek,* May 26–June 1: 39–40.

40. Anonymous. 2014. The 140,000-code question. *The Economist,* May 31: 27.
41. Hout, T. M. & Ghemawat, P. 2010. China vs. the world: Whose technology is it? *Harvard Business Review,* 88(12): 94–103.
42. Business ready for Internet revolution. 1999. *Financial Times,* May 21: 17.
43. A discussion of an alternate energy—marine energy—is the topic of Boyle, M. 2008. Scottish power. *Fortune,* March 17: 28.
44. Baker, S. & Aston, A. 2005. The business of nanotech. *BusinessWeek,* February 14: 64–71.
45. Wilson, H. J. 2013. Wearables in the workplace. *Harvard Business Review,* 91(9): 22–25.
46. For an insightful discussion of the causes of the global financial crisis, read Johnson, S. 2009. The global financial crisis—What really precipitated it? *MIT Sloan Management Review,* 50(2): 16–18.
47. Tyson, L. D. 2011. A better stimulus for the U.S. economy. *Harvard Business Review,* 89(1/2): 53.
48. An interesting and balanced discussion on the merits of multinationals to the U.S. economy is found in Mandel, M. 2008. Multinationals: Are they good for America? *BusinessWeek,* March 10: 41–64.
49. Insights on risk perception across countries are addressed in Purda, L. D. 2008. Risk perception and the financial system. *Journal of International Business Studies,* 39(7): 1178–1196.
50. Thurm, S. 2012. U.S. firms add jobs, but mostly overseas. *wsj.com,* April 27: np.
51. Goll, I. & Rasheed, M. A. 1997. Rational decision-making and firm performance: The moderating role of environment. *Strategic Management Journal,* 18: 583–591.
52. Our discussion of crowdsourcing draws on the first two books that have addressed the concept: Libert, B. & Spector, J. 2008. *We are smarter than me.* Philadelphia: Wharton; and Howe, J. 2008. *Crowdsourcing.* New York: Crown Business. Eric von Hippel addressed similar issues in his 2005 book, *Democraticizing innovation,* Cambridge, MA.: MIT Press.
53. This discussion draws heavily on Porter, M. E. 1980. *Competitive strategy:* chap. 1. New York: Free Press.
54. Ibid.
55. Rivalry in the airline industry is discussed in Foust, D. 2009. Which airlines will disappear in 2009? *BusinessWeek,* January 19: 46–47.
56. Fryer, B. 2001. Leading through rough times: An interview with Novell's Eric Schmidt. *Harvard Business Review,* 78(5): 117–123.
57. For a discussion on the importance of barriers to entry within industries, read Greenwald, B. & Kahn, J. 2005. *Competition demystified: A radically simplified approach to business strategy.* East Rutherford, NJ: Portfolio.
58. A discussion of how the medical industry has erected entry barriers that have resulted in lawsuits is found in Whelan, D. 2008. Bad medicine. *BusinessWeek,* March 10: 86–98.
59. Colvin, G. 2014. Welcome to the era of Lego innovations (some assembly required). *Fortune,* April 14: 52.
60. Wise, R. & Baumgarter, P. 1999. Go downstream: The new profit imperative in manufacturing. *Harvard Business Review,* 77(5): 133–141.
61. Salman, W. A. 2000. The new economy is stronger than you think. *Harvard Business Review,* 77(6): 99–106.
62. Staley, O. 2011. California universities feel the squeeze. *Bloomberg Businessweek,* January 24–January 30: 20–30.
63. Mudambi, R. & Helper, S. 1998. The "close but adversarial" model of supplier relations in the U.S. auto industry. *Strategic Management Journal,* 19: 775–792.
64. Stevens, D. (vice president of Delta Pride Catfish, Inc.). 2014. *personal communication:* October 16; and Fritz, M. 1988. Agribusiness: Catfish story. *Forbes,* December 12: 37.
65. Trends in the solar industry are discussed in Carey, J. 2009. Solar: The sun will come out tomorrow. *BusinessWeek,* January 12: 51.
66. Edelstein, S. 2014. Could U.S. hybrid car sales be peaking already—and if so, why? *greencarreports.com,* June 16: np; and Naughton, K. 2012. Hybrids' unlikely rival: plain old cars. *Bloomberg Businessweek,* February 2: 23–24.
67. An interesting analysis of self-regulation in an industry (chemical) is in Barnett, M. L. & King, A. A. 2008. Good fences make good neighbors: A longitudinal analysis of an industry self-regulatory institution. *Academy of Management Journal,* 51(6): 1053–1078.
68. For an interesting perspective on the intensity of competition in the supermarket industry, refer to Anonymous. 2005. Warfare in the aisles. *The Economist,* April 2: 6–8.
69. Macmillan, D. 2014. Tech's fiercest rivalry: Uber vs. Lyft. *online.wsj.com,* August 11: np.
70. For an interesting perspective on changing features of firm boundaries, refer to Afuah, A. 2003. Redefining firm boundaries in the face of the Internet: Are firms really shrinking? *Academy of Management Review,* 28(1): 34–53.
71. Time to rebuild. 2001. *The Economist,* May 19: 55–56.
72. www.amazon.com.
73. For more on the role of the Internet as an electronic intermediary, refer to Carr, N. G. 2000. Hypermediation: Commerce as clickstream. *Harvard Business Review,* 78(1): 46–48.
74. www.mysimon.com; and www.pricescan.com.
75. www.cnet.com; and www.bizrate.com.
76. For insights into strategies in a low-profit industry, refer to Hopkins, M. S. 2008. The management lessons of a beleaguered industry. *MIT Sloan Management Review,* 50(1): 25–31.
77. Foust, D. 2007. The best performers. *BusinessWeek,* March 26: 58–95; Rosenblum, D., Tomlinson, D., & Scott, L. 2003. Bottom-feeding for blockbuster businesses. *Harvard Business Review,* 81(3): 52–59; Paychex 2006 Annual Report; and WellPoint Health Network 2005 Annual Report.
78. Kumar, N. 1996. The power of trust in manufacturer-retailer relationship. *Harvard Business Review,* 74(6): 92–110.
79. Welch, D. 2006. Renault-Nissan: Say hello to Bo. *BusinessWeek,* July 31: 56–57.
80. Kelleher, J. B. 2014. GM ranked worst automaker by U.S. suppliers—survey. *finance.yahoo.com,* May 12: np; and Welch, D. 2006. Renault-Nissan: Say hello to Bo. *BusinessWeek,* July 31: 56–57.
81. Brandenburger, A. & Nalebuff, B. J. 1995. The right game: Use game theory to shape strategy. *Harvard Business Review,* 73(4): 57–71.
82. For a scholarly discussion of complementary assets and their relationship to competitive advantage, refer to Stieglitz, N. & Heine, K. 2007. Innovations and the role of complementarities in a strategic theory of the firm. *Strategic Management Journal,* 28(1): 1–15.

83. A useful framework for the analysis of industry evolution has been proposed by Professor Anita McGahan of Boston University. Her analysis is based on the identification of the core activities and the core assets of an industry and the threats they face. She suggests that an industry may follow one of four possible evolutionary trajectories—radical change, creative change, intermediating change, or progressive change—based on these two types of threats of obsolescence. Refer to McGahan, A. M. 2004. How industries change. *Harvard Business Review,* 82(10): 87–94.

84. Yoffie, D. B. & Kwak, M. 2006. With friends like these: The art of managing complementors. *Harvard Business Review,* 84(9): 88–98.

85. Porter, M. I. 2008. The five competitive forces that shape strategy. *Harvard Business Review,* 86(1): 79–93.

86. Peteraf, M. & Shanley, M. 1997. Getting to know you: A theory of strategic group identity. *Strategic Management Journal,* 18 (Special Issue): 165–186.

87. An interesting scholarly perspective on strategic groups may be found in Dranove, D., Perteraf, M., & Shanley, M. 1998. Do strategic groups exist? An economic framework for analysis. *Strategic Management Journal,* 19(11): 1029–1044.

88. For an empirical study on strategic groups and predictors of performance, refer to Short, J. C., Ketchen, D. J., Jr., Palmer, T. B., & Hult, T. M. 2007. Firm, strategic group, and industry influences on performance. *Strategic Management Journal,* 28(2): 147–167.

89. This section draws on several sources, including Kerwin, K. R. & Haughton, K. 1997. Can Detroit make cars that baby boomers like? *BusinessWeek,* December 1: 134–148; and Taylor, A., III. 1994. The new golden age of autos. *Fortune,* April 4: 50–66.

90. Csere, C. 2001. Supercar supermarket. *Car and Driver,* January: 118–127.

91. For a discussion of the extent of overcapacity in the worldwide automobile industry, read Roberts, D., Matlack, C., Busyh, J., & Rowley, I. 2009. A hundred factories too many. *BusinessWeek,* January 19: 42–43.

92. McLain, S. 2014. India's middle class embraces minicars. *The Wall Street Journal,* October 9: B2; Anonymous. 2014. Geely GX7 launched after upgrading: Making versatile and comfortable SUV. *www.globaltimes.ch,* April 18: np; Anonymous. 2014. Adequate Guiyang Geely Free Cruiser higher offer 1,000 yuan now. *www.wantinews.com,* February 20: np; Anonymous. 2013. Restyled Chery QQ hit showrooms with a US$6,083 starting price. *www.chinaautoweb.com,* March 4: np; and Doval, P. 2014. Cheapest car tag hit Tata Nano: Creator. *economictimes.indiatimes.com,* August 21: np.

photo credits

Page 36: © Anatoli Styf/Getty Images/RF

Assessing the Internal Environment of the Firm

chapter 3

After reading this chapter, you should have a good understanding of the following learning objectives:

LO3.1 The benefits and limitations of SWOT analysis in conducting an internal analysis of the firm.

LO3.2 The primary and support activities of a firm's value chain.

LO3.3 How value-chain analysis can help managers create value by investigating relationships among activities within the firm and between the firm and its customers and suppliers.

LO3.4 The resource-based view of the firm and the different types of tangible and intangible resources, as well as organizational capabilities.

LO3.5 The four criteria that a firm's resources must possess to maintain a sustainable advantage and how value created can be appropriated by employees and managers.

LO3.6 The usefulness of financial ratio analysis, its inherent limitations, and how to make meaningful comparisons of performance across firms.

LO3.7 The value of the "balanced scorecard" in recognizing how the interests of a variety of stakeholders can be interrelated.

PART 1: STRATEGIC ANALYSIS

Learning from Mistakes

BYD (which stands for Build Your Dreams), founded by Wang Chuanfu in 1995, was originally a low-cost manufacturer of rechargeable lithium ion batteries for cell phones.[1] Wang had considerable expertise in batteries but virtually none in automotive technology. However, that didn't stop him from buying a state-owned automobile maker in 2002. He envisioned a central role for battery technologies in the rise of electric vehicles.

Although the company borrowed ideas from Japanese manufacturing (and reverse-engineered popular Japanese car designs), it shunned Japan's reliance on intensive automation and employed thousands of workers to produce not only cars but also most of the needed parts, from braking systems to CD players. And, in order to boost sales, it rapidly expanded dealerships in China, set aggressive sales targets, and pushed inventory to dealers in pursuit of those targets.

In 2008, Warren Buffett bought 10 percent of the company, dramatically enhancing its brand value and increasing BYD's sales in the United States. In 2009, its F3 model was the best-selling sedan in China, with more than 250,000 cars sold. The company's sales hit a peak of about 500,000 units in 2010. That year it was ranked as the eighth most innovative company in the world by *Businessweek*.

However, soon after, BYD began to falter. Consumer demand for electric vehicles was weak, and China Central Television questioned the company's quality standards. It was not surprising BYD ranked below the industry average on a number of J.D. Power studies, including initial quality and dependability.

Still, BYD did a few things right—from adopting a bold vision to establishing a position as a technology leader. Unfortunately, that vision was not rooted in reality. Widespread consumer adoption of battery-powered passenger vehicles is still far in the future (if it occurs at all). Further, the firm's emphasis on technology made a good start in establishing a strong competitive position, but a vehicle maker must also be known as reliable. *BYD's stumbles resulted from a failure to develop sophisticated capabilities such as new product development, demand forecasting, capacity planning, inventory management, and customer insight.* Going forward, the company may have to accept being a niche player, selling electric passenger cars and buses. And shareholders definitely haven't fared well—by the end of 2014 they had lost about half of the value that they had in 2010!

Discussion Question

1. What were BYD's key strategic mistakes? How could they have been avoided?

In this chapter we will place heavy emphasis on the value-chain concept. That is, we focus on the key value-creating activities (e.g., operations, marketing and sales, and procurement) that a firm must effectively manage and integrate in order to attain competitive advantages in the marketplace. However, firms not only must pay close attention to their own value-creating activities but also must maintain close and effective relationships with key organizations outside the firm boundaries, such as suppliers, customers, and alliance partners.

Although BYD was clearly a technology leader, it faltered because of its weaknesses in many value-creating activities. As noted earlier, these included new product development, inventory management, capacity planning, and customer insight.

LO3.1

The benefits and limitations of SWOT analysis in conducting an internal analysis of the firm.

3.1 STRATEGY SPOTLIGHT

THE LIMITATIONS OF SWOT ANALYSIS

SWOT analysis is a tried-and-true tool of strategic analysis. SWOT (strengths, weaknesses, opportunities, threats) analysis is used regularly in business to initially evaluate the opportunities and threats in the business environment as well as the strengths and weaknesses of a firm's internal environment. Top managers rely on SWOT to stimulate self-reflection and group discussions about how to improve their firm and position it for success.

But SWOT has its limitations. It is just a starting point for discussion. By listing the firm's attributes, managers have the raw material needed to perform more in-depth strategic analysis. However, SWOT cannot show them how to achieve a competitive advantage. They must not make SWOT analysis an end in itself, temporarily raising awareness about important issues but failing to lead to the kind of action steps necessary to enact strategic change.

Let's look at some of the limitations of SWOT analysis.

Strengths May Not Lead to an Advantage

A firm's strengths and capabilities, no matter how unique or impressive, may not enable it to achieve a competitive advantage in the marketplace. It is akin to recruiting a concert pianist to join a gang of thugs—even though such an ability is rare and valuable, it hardly helps the organization attain its goals and objectives! Similarly, the skills of a highly creative product designer would offer little competitive advantage to a firm that produces low-cost commodity products. Indeed, the additional expense of hiring such an individual could erode the firm's cost advantages. If a firm builds its strategy on a capability that cannot, by itself, create or sustain competitive advantage, it is essentially a wasted use of resources.

SWOT's Focus on the External Environment Is Too Narrow

Strategists who rely on traditional definitions of their industry and competitive environment often focus their sights too narrowly on current customers, technologies, and competitors. Hence they fail to notice important changes on the periphery of their environment that may trigger the need to redefine industry boundaries and identify a whole new set of competitive relationships. Consider *Encyclopaedia Britannica,* whose competitive position was severely eroded by a "nontraditional" competitor—CD-based encyclopedias (e.g., Microsoft *Encarta*) that could be used on home computers—and later by online encyclopedias (e.g., Wikipedia).

SWOT Gives a One-Shot View of a Moving Target

A key weakness of SWOT is that it is primarily a static assessment. It focuses too much of a firm's attention on one moment in time. Essentially, this is like studying a single frame of a motion picture. You may be able to identify the principal actors and learn something about the setting, but it doesn't tell you much about the plot. Competition among organizations is played out over time. As circumstances, capabilities, and strategies change, static analysis techniques do not reveal the dynamics of the competitive environment.

SWOT Overemphasizes a Single Dimension of Strategy

Sometimes firms become preoccupied with a single strength or a key feature of the product or service they are offering and ignore other factors needed for competitive success. For example, Toyota, the giant automaker, paid a heavy price for its excessive emphasis on cost control. The resulting problems with quality and the negative publicity led to severe financial losses and an erosion of its reputation in many markets.

SWOT analysis has much to offer, but only as a starting point. By itself, it rarely helps a firm develop competitive advantages that it can sustain over time.

Sources: Shapiro, C. & Varian, H. R. 2000. Versioning: The smart way to sell information. *Harvard Business Review,* 78(1): 99–106; and Picken, J. C. & Dess, G. G. 1997. *Mission critical.* Burr Ridge, IL: Irwin Professional.

Before moving to value-chain analysis, let's briefly revisit the benefits and limitations of SWOT analysis. As discussed in Chapter 2, a SWOT analysis consists of a careful listing of a firm's strengths, weaknesses, opportunities, and threats. While we believe SWOT analysis is very helpful as a starting point, it should not form the primary basis for evaluating a firm's internal strengths and weaknesses or the opportunities and threats in the environment. Strategy Spotlight 3.1 elaborates on the limitations of the traditional SWOT approach.

We will now turn to value-chain analysis. As you will see, it provides greater insights into analyzing a firm's competitive position than SWOT analysis does by itself.

Value-Chain Analysis

> **value-chain analysis**
> a strategic analysis of an organization that uses value-creating activities.

Value-chain analysis views the organization as a sequential process of value-creating activities. The approach is useful for understanding the building blocks of competitive advantage and was described in Michael Porter's seminal book *Competitive Advantage.*[2]

Value is the amount that buyers are willing to pay for what a firm provides them and is measured by total revenue, a reflection of the price a firm's product commands and the quantity it can sell. A firm is profitable when the value it receives exceeds the total costs involved in creating its product or service. Creating value for buyers that exceeds the costs of production (i.e., margin) is a key concept used in analyzing a firm's competitive position.

Porter described two different categories of activities. First, five **primary activities**—inbound logistics, operations, outbound logistics, marketing and sales, and service—contribute to the physical creation of the product or service, its sale and transfer to the buyer, and its service after the sale. Second, **support activities**—procurement, technology development, human resource management, and general administration—either add value by themselves or add value through important relationships with both primary activities and other support activities. Exhibit 3.1 illustrates Porter's value chain.

To get the most out of value-chain analysis, view the concept in its broadest context, without regard to the boundaries of your own organization. That is, place your organization within a more encompassing value chain that includes your firm's suppliers, customers, and alliance partners. Thus, in addition to thoroughly understanding how value is created within the organization, be aware of how value is created for other organizations in the overall supply chain or distribution channel.[3]

Next, we'll describe and provide examples of each of the primary and support activities. Then we'll provide examples of how companies add value by means of relationships among activities within the organization as well as activities outside the organization, such as those activities associated with customers and suppliers.[4]

Primary Activities

Five generic categories of primary activities are involved in competing in any industry, as shown in Exhibit 3.2. Each category is divisible into a number of distinct activities that depend on the particular industry and the firm's strategy.[5]

Inbound Logistics **Inbound logistics** is primarily associated with receiving, storing, and distributing inputs to the product. It includes material handling, warehousing, inventory control, vehicle scheduling, and returns to suppliers.

Just-in-time (JIT) inventory systems, for example, were designed to achieve efficient inbound logistics. In essence, Toyota epitomizes JIT inventory systems, in which parts

> **primary activities**
> sequential activities of the value chain that refer to the physical creation of the product or service, its sale and transfer to the buyer, and its service after sale, including inbound logistics, operations, outbound logistics, marketing and sales, and service.

> **support activities**
> activities of the value chain that either add value by themselves or add value through important relationships with both primary activities and other support activities, including procurement, technology development, human resource management, and general administration.

> **LO3.2**
> The primary and support activities of a firm's value chain.

> **inbound logistics**
> receiving, storing, and distributing inputs of a product.

EXHIBIT 3.1 The Value Chain: Primary and Support Activities

Primary Activities

| Inbound Logistics | Operations | Outbound Logistics | Marketing and Sales | Service |

Support Activities
- General Administration
- Human Resource Management
- Technology Development
- Procurement

Adapted from Competitive Advantage: Creating and Sustaining Superior Performance by Michael E. Porter, 1985, 1998, Free Press.

EXHIBIT 3.2
The Value Chain: Some Factors to Consider in Assessing a Firm's Primary Activities

Inbound Logistics
- Location of distribution facilities to minimize shipping times.
- Warehouse layout and designs to increase efficiency of operations for incoming materials.

Operations
- Efficient plant operations to minimize costs.
- Efficient plant layout and workflow design.
- Incorporation of appropriate process technology.

Outbound Logistics
- Effective shipping processes to provide quick delivery and minimize damages.
- Shipping of goods in large lot sizes to minimize transportation costs.

Marketing and Sales
- Innovative approaches to promotion and advertising.
- Proper identification of customer segments and needs.

Service
- Quick response to customer needs and emergencies.
- Quality of service personnel and ongoing training.

Source: Adapted from Porter, M. E. 1985. *Competitive Advantage: Creating and Sustaining Superior Performance.* New York: Free Press.

deliveries arrive at the assembly plants only hours before they are needed. JIT systems will play a vital role in fulfilling Toyota's commitment to fill a buyer's new-car order in just five days.[6] This standard is in sharp contrast to most competitors that require approximately 30 days' notice to build vehicles. Toyota's standard is three times faster than even Honda Motors, considered to be the industry's most efficient in order follow-through. The five days represent the time from the company's receipt of an order to the time the car leaves the assembly plant. Actual delivery may take longer, depending on where a customer lives.

operations
all activities associated with transforming inputs into the final product form.

Operations Operations include all activities associated with transforming inputs into the final product form, such as machining, packaging, assembly, testing, printing, and facility operations.

Creating environmentally friendly manufacturing is one way to use operations to achieve competitive advantage. Shaw Industries (now part of Berkshire Hathaway), a world-class competitor in the floor-covering industry, is well known for its concern for the environment.[7] It has been successful in reducing the expenses associated with the disposal of dangerous chemicals and other waste products from its manufacturing operations. Its environmental endeavors have multiple payoffs. Shaw has received many awards for its recycling efforts—awards that enhance its reputation.

Efficient operations can also provide a firm with many benefits in virtually any industry—including restaurants. Strategy Spotlight 3.2 discusses Chipotle's rather novel approach to improving its operations.

outbound logistics
collecting, storing, and distributing the product or service to buyers.

Outbound Logistics Outbound logistics is associated with collecting, storing, and distributing the product or service to buyers. These activities include finished goods, warehousing, material handling, delivery vehicle operation, order processing, and scheduling.

3.2 STRATEGY SPOTLIGHT

CHIPOTLE'S EFFICIENT OPERATIONS

Peak hours at restaurants create real challenges that must be addressed. Otherwise, business may be lost and, worse yet, customers may never come back. Lines snaking out the doors have long been a bottleneck to growth at U.S. burrito chain Chipotle. However, the company has a plan—actually a four-step plan, to be exact.

The chain managed to accelerate service by six transactions per hour at peak times during a recent quarter (which is a significant increase over the mere two transactions per hour the previous quarter). "We achieved our fastest throughput ever," claims Steve Ells, co-CEO. However, some of Chipotle's fastest restaurants run more than 350 transactions per hour at lunchtime—more than three times the chainwide average.

How are such remarkable increases in productivity attained? By what the company calls "the four pillars of great throughput." These are:

- **Expediters.** An expediter is the extra person between the one who rolls your burrito and the one who rings up your order. The expediter's job? Getting your drink, asking if your order is "to go," and bagging your food.

- **Linebackers.** These are people who patrol the countertops, serving-ware, and bins of food, so the ones who are actually serving customers never turn their backs on them.

- *Mise en place.* In other restaurants, this means setting out ingredients and utensils ready for use. In Chipotle's case, it means zero tolerance for not having absolutely everything in place ahead of lunch and dinner rush hours.

- **Aces in their places.** This refers to a commitment to having what each branch considers its top servers in the most important positions at peak times. Thus, there are no trainees working at burrito rush hour.

No one can question Chipotle's success: In the past three years, it has experienced 20.5 percent annual sales growth, and its stock has soared 99 percent. And, in 2014, despite raising prices 6.5 percent in the second quarter, same-store sales grew 19.8 percent in the third quarter.

Sources: Ferdman, R. A. 2014. How Chipotle is going to serve burritos faster, and faster, and faster. *www.qz.com*, January 31: np; and Zillman, C. 2014. 2014's top people in business. *Fortune*, December 1: 156.

Campbell Soup uses an electronic network to facilitate its continuous-replenishment program with its most progressive retailers.[8] Each morning, retailers electronically inform Campbell of their product needs and of the level of inventories in their distribution centers. Campbell uses that information to forecast future demand and to determine which products require replenishment (based on the inventory limits previously established with each retailer). Trucks leave Campbell's shipping plant that afternoon and arrive at the retailers' distribution centers the same day. The program cuts the inventories of participating retailers from about a four- to a two-weeks' supply. Campbell Soup achieved this improvement because it slashed delivery time and because it knows the inventories of key retailers and can deploy supplies when they are most needed.

The Campbell Soup example also illustrates the win–win benefits of exemplary value-chain activities. Both the supplier (Campbell) and its buyers (retailers) come out ahead. Since the retailer makes more money on Campbell products delivered through continuous replenishment, it has an incentive to carry a broader line and give the company greater shelf space. After Campbell introduced the program, sales of its products grew twice as fast through participating retailers as through all other retailers. Not surprisingly, supermarket chains love such programs.

Marketing and Sales Marketing and sales activities are associated with purchases of products and services by end users and the inducements used to get them to make purchases.[9] They include advertising, promotion, sales force, quoting, channel selection, channel relations, and pricing.[10,11]

Consider product placement. This is a marketing strategy that many firms are increasingly adopting to reach customers who are not swayed by traditional advertising.

> **marketing and sales**
> activities associated with purchases of products and services by end users and the inducements used to get them to make purchases.

A recent example is the starring role that BMW has in the film *Mission Impossible: Ghost Protocol.*[12]

> In this latest in the series of *Mission Impossible* films, the i8 concept, a next-generation supercar from BMW, helps Tom Cruise and co-star Paul Patton race through Mumbai traffic. The car's appearance highlights the brand's return to Hollywood after a hiatus of more than a decade.
>
> In addition to featuring the upcoming i8, BMW uses the film to promote its current X3 SUV, 6-series convertible, and 1-Series compact. In lieu of an up-front payment, the firm has promised to promote the film in its print and television ads, says Uwe Ellinghaus, head of brand management at BMW. As Ellinghaus claims, "*Mission Impossible* is a whole new dimension for BMW. It's what James Bond used to be."

Strategy Spotlight 3.3 discusses an example that most students are familiar with: how Frito-Lay uses crowdsourcing to create competition for ads. The best ones air during the Super Bowl.

Service The **service** primary activity includes all actions associated with providing service to enhance or maintain the value of the product, such as installation, repair, training, parts supply, and product adjustment.

Let's see how two retailers are providing exemplary customer service. At *Sephora.com*, a customer service representative taking a phone call from a repeat customer has instant access to what shade of lipstick she likes best. This will help the rep cross-sell by suggesting a matching shade of lip gloss. Such personalization is expected to build loyalty and boost sales per customer. Nordstrom, the Seattle-based department store chain, goes even a step further. It offers a cyber-assist: A service rep can take control of a customer's web browser and literally lead her to just the silk scarf that she is looking for. CEO Dan Nordstrom believes that such a capability will close enough additional purchases to pay for the $1 million investment in software.

Support Activities

Support activities in the value chain can be divided into four generic categories, as shown in Exhibit 3.3. Each category of the support activity is divisible into a number of distinct value activities that are specific to a particular industry. For example, technology development's discrete activities may include component design, feature design, field testing, process engineering, and technology selection. Similarly, procurement may include activities such as qualifying new suppliers, purchasing different groups of inputs, and monitoring supplier performance.

Procurement **Procurement** refers to the function of purchasing inputs used in the firm's value chain, not to the purchased inputs themselves.[13] Purchased inputs include raw materials, supplies, and other consumable items as well as assets such as machinery, laboratory equipment, office equipment, and buildings.[14,15]

Microsoft has improved its procurement process (and the quality of its suppliers) by providing formal reviews of its suppliers. One of Microsoft's divisions has extended the review process used for employees to its outside suppliers.[16] The employee services group, which is responsible for everything from travel to 401(k) programs to the on-site library, outsources more than 60 percent of the services it provides. Unfortunately, the employee services group was not providing suppliers with enough feedback. This was feedback that the suppliers wanted to get and that Microsoft wanted to give.

The evaluation system that Microsoft developed helped clarify its expectations to suppliers. An executive noted: "We had one supplier—this was before the new system—that would have scored a 1.2 out of 5. After we started giving this feedback, and the supplier

3.3 STRATEGY SPOTLIGHT — CROWDSOURCING

FRITO-LAY'S SUPER BOWL ADS

While firms have long realized the potential of outsourcing—the practice of sending service and manufacturing jobs overseas and profiting from cheap labor—marketing and sales leaders increasingly pursue a similar concept: crowdsourcing. Although crowdsourcing does not physically send jobs abroad, it uses another pool of cheap labor: everyday people, often amateurs, using their spare time to create content and solve problems.

Take PepsiCo's Frito-Lay division, for example. Frito-Lay has been long known for its Crash the Super Bowl contest, an annual online commercial competition that invites regular consumers to create their own Doritos ads. The contest started in 2006 with a little over 1,000 entries and grew to more than 6,000 entries by 2011. Frito-Lay will air at least one of these fan-made commercials during the Super Bowl. Frito-Lay benefits from this user-generated content on multiple dimensions. The Crash the Super Bowl campaigns are a huge public relations success. In 2007, the International Public Relations Association awarded a Golden World Award to Frito-Lay because the campaign garnered 1.3 billion earned media impressions, created an enthusiastic online community of 1 million users, and helped to generate a 12 percent sales leap for the Doritos brand in January 2007.

One may think that user-generated Super Bowl ads are only a nice marketing gimmick. Think again! The low-budget ads came out on top of the *USA Today* Super Bowl Ad Meter in 2009, 2011, and 2012. The 2007 ad was even named by Time.com as the ninth best commercial of the year. Continuing the crowdsourcing success, Frito-Lay raised the challenge for the 2015 Crash the Super Bowl contest. Doritos once again looked for the best 30-second commercial that would air during Super Bowl XLIX on February 1, 2015. The grand-prize winner not only walked away with $1 million for creating the winning ad but also was invited to work on a "creative project" with Universal Pictures. In addition, the grand-prize winner and all of the finalists got all-expense-paid trips to watch the Super Bowl at the University of Phoenix Stadium in Glendale, Arizona.

The winner and finalists certainly had a good "return on their investments"! In 2014, Ryan Thomas of Scottsdale, Arizona, won $1 million after his commercial, *Time Machine,* was selected. ABC News reported that Anderson, a single dad, spent less than $300 to create the funny commercial that featured his son and their dog.

Sources: Anonymous. 2014. 2015 Doritos Crash the Super Bowl contest: Which ad will be worth $1 million? *inquisitr.com,* November 4: np. Robinson-Jacobs, K. 2012. Crunch time for contest lovers. *Dallas Morning News,* September 21: 1D; Consumer PR—Doritos crashes the Superbowl. 2007. *IPRA:* np; and Keegan, R. W. 2007. Top 10 TV ads. *www.time.com,* December 9: np.

EXHIBIT 3.3 The Value Chain: Some Factors to Consider in Assessing a Firm's Support Activities

General Administration
- Effective planning systems to attain overall goals and objectives.
- Excellent relationships with diverse stakeholder groups.
- Effective information technology to integrate value-creating activities.

Human Resource Management
- Effective recruiting, development, and retention mechanisms for employees.
- Quality relations with trade unions.
- Reward and incentive programs to motivate all employees.

Technology Development
- Effective R&D activities for process and product initiatives.
- Positive collaborative relationships between R&D and other departments.
- Excellent professional qualifications of personnel.

Procurement
- Procurement of raw material inputs to optimize quality and speed and to minimize the associated costs.
- Development of collaborative win–win relationships with suppliers.
- Analysis and selection of alternative sources of inputs to minimize dependence on one supplier.

Source: Adapted from Porter, M.E. 1985. *Competitive Advantage: Creating and Sustaining Superior Performance.* New York: Free Press.

understood our expectations, its performance improved dramatically. Within six months, it scored a 4. If you'd asked me before we began the feedback system, I would have said that was impossible."

Technology Development   Every value activity embodies technology.[17] The array of technologies employed in most firms is very broad, ranging from technologies used to prepare documents and transport goods to those embodied in processes and equipment or the product itself.[18] **Technology development** related to the product and its features supports the entire value chain, while other technology development is associated with particular primary or support activities.

> Techniq, headquartered in Paris, France, with 40,000 employees in 48 countries, is a world leader in project management, engineering, and construction for the energy industry.[19] Its manufacturing plant in Normandy, France, has developed innovative ways to add value for its customers. This division, Subsea Infrastructure, produces subsea flexible pipes for the oil and gas industry. Its technology innovations have added significant value for its customers and has led to operating margins 50 percent higher than those for the company overall.
>
> Its traditional services include installing, inspecting, maintaining, and repairing pipes in locations around the world, from the Arctic to the Arabian Gulf. However, the company now goes much further. In collaboration with oil services giant Schlumberger, Techniq has developed intelligent pipes that can monitor and regulate the temperature throughout an oil pipeline—important value-added activities for its customers, large oil producers. Fluctuating temperatures pose a major problem—they cause changes in pipe diameter, which makes the flow of oil more variable. This compromises drilling efficiency and is a significant source of costs for Techniq's customers. Using intelligent pipes not only keeps temperatures steadier but also reduces the complexity of subsea drilling layouts and shortens pipe installation times.

technology development
activities associated with the development of new knowledge that is applied to the firm's operations.

Human Resource Management   **Human resource management** consists of activities involved in the recruiting, hiring, training, development, and compensation of all types of personnel.[20] It supports both individual primary and support activities (e.g., hiring of engineers and scientists) and the entire value chain (e.g., negotiations with labor unions).[21]

Like all great service companies, JetBlue Airways Corporation is obsessed with hiring superior employees.[22] But the company found it difficult to attract college graduates to commit to careers as flight attendants. JetBlue developed a highly innovative recruitment program for flight attendants—a one-year contract that gives them a chance to travel, meet lots of people, and then decide what else they might like to do. It also introduced the idea of training a friend and employee together so that they could share a job. With such employee-friendly initiatives, JetBlue has been very successful in attracting talent.

Jeffrey Immelt, GE's chairman, addresses the importance of effective human resource management:[23]

> Human resources has to be more than a department. GE recognized early on—50 or 60 years ago—that in a multibusiness company, the common denominators are people and culture. From an employee's first day at GE, she discovers that she's in the people-development business as much as anything else. You'll find that most good companies have the same basic HR processes that we have, but they're discrete. HR at GE is not an agenda item; it is the agenda.

Lise Saari, Ph.D., has held executive positions in human resource management at IBM and Boeing. In addition, she is well known for her prolific academic research and publications. We are pleased that she has shared her perspectives on several issues related to human resource management, or HRM (see Insights from Executives). These include the

human resource management
activities involved in the recruiting, hiring, training, development, and compensation of all types of personnel.

3.1 INSIGHTS FROM EXECUTIVES

LISE M. SAARI, PH.D., FORMER DIRECTOR OF GLOBAL EMPLOYEE RESEARCH, IBM

BIOSKETCH

Lise M. Saari, Ph.D., is the former director of global workforce research at IBM, where her team was responsible for researching employee attitudes and other human resource topics in over 170 countries. Before that, she was the senior manager of people research at the Boeing Company and a research scientist at Battelle Research Institute. In all of these roles, Saari had responsibility for helping design and test human resource management initiatives, such as performance management systems, teaming initiatives, and management development programs. Saari has over 100 publications and presentations and serves on a variety of editorial boards. She is a fellow in the Society for Industrial Organizational Psychology (SIOP), the American Psychological Association, and the Association for Psychological Science. Saari is currently adjunct professor at New York University and Baruch College in their graduate industrial/organizational psychology and international executive programs, teaching in New York City, Singapore, and Taipei. She is also an SIOP representative to the United Nations.

1. *How important is it for human resource management to coordinate its efforts with other areas of the organization?*

   This is extremely important and, frankly, lacking at times. In particular, human resources (HR) needs to ensure its initiatives support people as part of an organization's value-creating activities. HR needs to align to the current strategy of the organization—to ensure the organization's people practices fully support the current direction and goals of the company. This relates to HR being a true partner of the business, with a deep and up-to-date understanding of business realities and objectives, and, in turn, ensuring HR initiatives fully support them at all points of the value chain. A great human resource leader also will know how to be a true partner by being an expert and balanced voice as business strategies are being refined or changed, to ensure they take into account the people side of the business. Thus, to be successful, human resources needs to support and help carry out business strategies, yet at the same time be willing to speak up and offer sound ideas when a proposed strategy may have legitimate issues from a people perspective.

2. *Based on your research and experience in the human resource area, what do you think are the most interesting findings that have important implications for organizational performance?*

   What makes people satisfied in their work, motivates them to perform, and makes them stay or leave are more complex and organizationally unique than we may think they are. Some of the most interesting findings to me are from the so-called linkage research started by Ben Schneider, whereby employee attitudes are statistically related to customer and business measures to see the unique relationships for an organization. We carried out this type of research at IBM with employee attitude data across the globe. The most important employee and workplace topics that contributed value to customers and organizational performance were understanding company objectives and how the employee's own job contributes to it, receiving regular feedback, receiving pay tied to job performance, and having a challenging job with opportunities for development. These are all areas where HR can and should ensure company strategy is clear to all employees; create a performance management system with a clear line of sight to that strategy; provide regular performance feedback; incorporate performance-based pay; and ensure people are challenged in their work with opportunities for learning and job movement. In many cases, managers think pay is the most important, but it is only one of many important areas.

   It is also interesting that some of our long-held beliefs about people at work need continual research to understand the new realities of organizations and the people in them. What has been the case in the past may not hold up for the future of work. As an example, one supposition held for many years—based on solid research—is that employee dissatisfaction is a major cause of turnover/attrition. It was very unlikely to find extremely positive ratings on an employee survey associated with very high turnover. However, this simple truism may no longer be the case. Globalization, economic highs and lows, an elimination of the former employee contract, and a more mobile workforce probably all contribute to a need to rethink this former HR truism. My first encounter with this was looking at country employee survey data relative to turnover rates. The country with the most positive ratings on the employee survey globally also had the highest turnover rate. As it turns out, that country's economy was one of the fastest growing in the world at the time, so jobs were plentiful. As well, job movement was easy. I didn't know how easy until visiting company offices in that country and seeing that competitors were located literally in the same block of the city—it was only a few steps to a new job with a promise of more interesting work, along with likely better pay and a promotion. I now understand that simplistic conclusions about human behavior in organizations may not necessarily hold up in the complexities of the new world of work.

continued

continued

3. ***Based on your experience, what are the greatest challenges in implementing human resource initiatives?***

    HR initiatives that are *well designed, verified as effective and contributing value, fully tested before deployment, cost-effective, easy to use, and not overly time-consuming and that result in positive outcomes for the individual and the organization* should not be a challenge to implement. However, these good design features may not always be present, causing managers and employees to be wary and less than fully supportive of a "new and improved" HR initiative. Even well-designed and thoroughly tested HR initiatives may encounter resistance to implementation because people have learned new HR initiatives are not always good.

    My worst story about poor HR program implementation involves an HR redesign of the online performance appraisal system at an organization. At an HR meeting after full-company deployment, the discussion turned to all the problems and what to do about them; it quickly became clear that many of those engaged in the conversation were ill-equipped to understand the problems because most of them had accessed the "old" system rather than using the new one. When asked why, the reply was, "I knew there would be problems with the new system and I didn't want the headache." Clearly these HR leaders knew it was likely to fail. Had the good design and testing principles described above been followed, many problems could have been avoided. In contrast, in my HR work at Boeing, all HR professionals were trained on the exact same quality themes as the employees in engineering and manufacturing. Thinking about HR initiatives with the same level of rigor and testing as designing and manufacturing a new airplane went a long way toward smooth and effective implementation and, ultimately, the value of HR programs.

    In addition to good design and testing of HR initiatives, having high-level line-executive endorsement can be helpful because it can signify the importance of a new HR initiative and increase manager and employee acceptance and efforts to use it effectively. This is especially the case when the initiative is due to a new company strategy and the HR initiative is in direct support of it. As an example, a company has a new strategy on a leading-edge technology and HR deploys a well-designed and tested training program to bring employees up to speed on that technology. A performance appraisal system is being redesigned, not because so many managers dislike the current one but rather because the company is undergoing an important transformation and the new performance management system aligns and supports it. High-level support helps show the importance of the initiative for more ready acceptance, and a well-designed and well-tested HR program helps ensure success of implementation and its ultimate value.

---

importance of integrating HRM with other value-creating activities in an organization, major challenges in implementing HRM initiatives, and some interesting research findings that have implications for practice.

LO3.3
How value-chain analysis can help managers create value by investigating relationships among activities within the firm and between the firm and its customers and suppliers.

general administration
general management, planning, finance, accounting, legal and government affairs, quality management, and information systems; activities that support the entire value chain and not individual activities.

General Administration **General administration** consists of a number of activities, including general management, planning, finance, accounting, legal and government affairs, quality management, and information systems. Administration (unlike the other support activities) typically supports the entire value chain and not individual activities.[24]

Although general administration is sometimes viewed only as overhead, it can be a powerful source of competitive advantage. In a telephone operating company, for example, negotiating and maintaining ongoing relations with regulatory bodies can be among the most important activities for competitive advantage. Also, in some industries top management plays a vital role in dealing with important buyers.[25]

The strong and effective leadership of top executives can also make a significant contribution to an organization's success. As we discussed in Chapter 1, chief executive officers (CEOs) such as Herb Kelleher, Andrew Grove, and Jack Welch have been credited with playing critical roles in the success of Southwest Airlines, Intel, and General Electric.

Information technology (IT) can also play a key role in enhancing the value that a company can provide its customers and, in turn, increasing its own revenues and profits. Strategy Spotlight 3.4 describes how Schmitz Cargobull, a German truck and trailer manufacturer, uses IT to further its competitive position.

3.4 STRATEGY SPOTLIGHT

SCHMITZ CARGOBULL: ADDING VALUE TO CUSTOMERS VIA IT

Germany's truck and trailer manufacturer, Schmitz Cargobull, mainly serves customers that are operators of truck or trailer fleets. Like its rivals, the company derives a growing share of revenue from support services such as financing, full-service contracts for breakdowns and regular maintenance, and spare-parts supplies.

What sets the company apart is its expertise in telematics (the integrated application of telecommunications data) to monitor the current state of any Schmitz Cargobull–produced trailer. Through telematics, key information is continually available to the driver, the freight agent, and the customer. They can track, for instance, when maintenance is done, how much weight has been loaded, the current cargo temperature, and where the vehicle is on its route. Therefore, Schmitz Cargobull customers can better manage their trailer use and minimize the risk of breakdowns. The decision to introduce telematics, not surprisingly, derived from management's belief that real-time sharing of data would bind the company more closely to customers.

In applying its telematic tools in its products, Schmitz Cargobull is providing clear, tangible benefits. It uses information technology only where it makes sense. On the production line, for example, workers implement statistical quality controls manually, rather than rely on an automated system, because the company found manual control improves engagement and job performance.

That strategy has helped Schmitz Cargobull become an industry leader. In 2013, the company controlled 82 percent of the sales of semitrailer reefers (refrigerated trailers) in Germany, and its market share in Europe was about 50 percent. Further, its results for the fiscal year ending March 2014 are most impressive: sales increased by 7.5 percent and pretax profit soared 66 percent.

Sources: Anonymous. 2014. Schmitz Cargobull AG announces earnings and production results for the year ending March 2014. *www.investing.businessweek.com*, July 31: np; Anonymous. 2014. Premiere at the IAA Show 2014: Increased I-beam stability and payload. *www.cargobull.com*, September: np; and Chick, S. E., Huchzermeier, A., & Netessine, S. 2014. Europe's solution factories. *Harvard Business Review*, 92(4): 11–115.

Interrelationships among Value-Chain Activities within and across Organizations

We have defined each of the value-chain activities separately for clarity of presentation. Managers must not ignore, however, the importance of relationships among value-chain activities.[26] There are two levels: (1) **interrelationships** among activities within the firm and (2) relationships among activities within the firm and with other stakeholders (e.g., customers and suppliers) that are part of the firm's expanded value chain.[27]

With regard to the first level, consider Lise Saari's interview (pages 83–84) on the strategic importance of effective human resource management practices. As she notes: "HR [must be] a true partner of the business, with a deep and up-to-date understanding of business realities and objectives, and, in turn, [must ensure] HR initiatives fully support them at all points of the value chain."

With regard to the second level, Campbell Soup's use of electronic networks enabled it to improve the efficiency of outbound logistics.[28] However, it also helped Campbell manage the ordering of raw materials more effectively, improve its production scheduling, and help its customers better manage their inbound logistics operations.

> **interrelationships** collaborative and strategic exchange relationships between value-chain activities either (a) within firms or (b) between firms. Strategic exchange relationships involve exchange of resources such as information, people, technology, or money that contribute to the success of the firm.

Integrating Customers into the Value Chain

When addressing the value-chain concept, it is important to focus on the interrelationship between the organization and its most important stakeholder—its customers. Some firms find great value by directly incorporating their customers into the value creation process. Firms can do this in one of two ways.

First, they can employ the "prosumer" concept and directly team up with customers to design and build products to satisfy their particular needs. Working directly with customers in this process provides multiple potential benefits for the firm. As the firm develops individualized products and relationship marketing, it can benefit from greater customer satisfaction and loyalty. Additionally, the interactions with customers can generate insights that lead to cost-saving initiatives and more innovative ideas for the producing firm. In discussing this concept, Hartmut Jenner, CEO of Alfred Karcher, a German manufacturing firm, stated:

> In the future, we will be talking more and more about the "prosumer"—a customer/producer who is even more extensively integrated into the value chain. As a consequence, production processes will be customized more precisely and individually.[29]

Second, firms can leverage the power of crowdsourcing. As introduced in Chapter 2, crowdsourcing occurs when firms tap into the knowledge and ideas of a large number of customers and other stakeholders, typically through online forums. The rise of social media has generated tremendous opportunities for firms to engage with customers.[30] In contrast to prosumer interactions, which allow the firm to gain insights on the needs of a particular customer, crowdsourcing offers the opportunity to leverage the wisdom of a larger crowd. Many companies have encouraged customers to participate in value-creating activities, such as brainstorming advertising taglines or product ideas. These activities not only enable firms to innovate at low cost but also engage customers. Clearly, a marketer's dream! At the same time, crowdsourcing has some significant risks.

Understanding the Perils of Crowdsourcing While crowdsourcing offers great promise, in practice such programs are difficult to run. At times, customers can "hijack" them. Instead of offering constructive ideas, customers jump at the chance to raise concerns and even ridicule the company. Such hijacking is one of the biggest challenges companies face. Research has shown about half of such campaigns fail. Consider the following marketing-focused crowdsourcing examples:

- In 2006, General Motors tried a "fun" experiment, one of the first attempts to use user-generated advertising. The company asked the public to create commercials for the Chevy Tahoe—ads the company hoped would go viral. Unfortunately, some of the ads did go viral! These include: "Like this snowy wilderness. Better get your fill of it now. Then say hello to global warming. Chevy Tahoe" and "$70 to fill up the tank, which will last less than 400 miles. Chevy Tahoe."
- McDonald's set up a Twitter campaign to promote positive word of mouth. But this initiative became a platform for people looking to bash the chain. Tweets such as the following certainly didn't help the firm's cause: "I lost 50 lbs in 6 months after I quit working and eating at McDonalds" and "The McRib contains the same chemicals used to make yoga mats, mmmmm."

Research has identified three areas of particular concern:

- **Strong brand reputation.** Companies with strong brands need to protect them. After all, they have the most to lose. They must be aware such efforts provide consumers the opportunity to tarnish the brand. Strong brands are typically built through consistent, effective marketing, and companies need to weigh the potential for misbehaving customers to thwart their careful efforts.
- **High demand uncertainty.** Firms are generally more likely to ask for customer input when market conditions are changing. However, this often backfires when demand is highly uncertain, because customers in such markets often don't know what they want or what they will like. For example, Porsche received a lot of negative feedback when it announced plans to release an SUV, but it went ahead anyway, and the Porsche Cayenne was a great success.
- **Too many initiatives.** Firms typically benefit from working repeatedly with the same customers. Often, the quality, quantity, and variety of inputs decrease as the frequency of engagement increases. A study of the Dell IdeaStorm program (in which customers were encouraged to submit product or service ideas) discovered that the same people submitted ideas repeatedly—including submitting ones

for things the company already provided. And customers whose ideas were implemented tended to return with additional ideas that were quite similar to their initial suggestions.

Applying the Value Chain to Service Organizations

The concepts of inbound logistics, operations, and outbound logistics suggest managing the raw materials that might be manufactured into finished products and delivered to customers. However, these three steps do not apply only to manufacturing. They correspond to any transformation process in which inputs are converted through a work process into outputs that add value. For example, accounting is a sort of transformation process that converts daily records of individual transactions into monthly financial reports. In this example, the transaction records are the inputs, accounting is the operation that adds value, and financial statements are the outputs.

What are the "operations," or transformation processes, of service organizations? At times, the difference between manufacturing and service is in providing a customized solution rather than mass production as is common in manufacturing. For example, a travel agent adds value by creating an itinerary that includes transportation, accommodations, and activities that are customized to your budget and travel dates. A law firm renders services that are specific to a client's needs and circumstances. In both cases, the work process (operation) involves the application of specialized knowledge based on the specifics of a situation (inputs) and the outcome that the client desires (outputs).

The application of the value chain to service organizations suggests that the value-adding process may be configured differently depending on the type of business a firm is engaged in. As the preceding discussion on support activities suggests, activities such as procurement and legal services are critical for adding value. Indeed, the activities that may provide support only to one company may be critical to the primary value-adding activity of another firm.

Exhibit 3.4 provides two models of how the value chain might look in service industries. In the retail industry, there are no manufacturing operations. A firm such as Nordstrom adds value by developing expertise in the procurement of finished goods and by displaying them in its stores in a way that enhances sales. Thus, the value chain makes procurement activities (i.e., partnering with vendors and purchasing goods) a primary rather than a support activity. Operations refer to the task of operating Nordstrom's stores.

EXHIBIT 3.4 Some Examples of Value Chains in Service Industries

Retail: Primary Value-Chain Activities

Partnering with vendors → Purchasing goods → Managing and distributing inventory → Operating stores → Marketing and selling

Engineering Services: Primary Value-Chain Activities

Research and development → Engineering → Designs and solutions → Marketing and sales → Service

For an engineering services firm, research and development provides inputs, the transformation process is the engineering itself, and innovative designs and practical solutions are the outputs. The Beca Group, for example, is a large consulting firm with about 3,000 employees, based in 17 offices throughout the Asia Pacific region. In its technology and innovation management practice, Beca strives to make the best use of the science, technology, and knowledge resources available to create value for a wide range of industries and client sectors. This involves activities associated with research and development, engineering, and creating solutions as well as downstream activities such as marketing, sales, and service. How the primary and support activities of a given firm are configured and deployed will often depend on industry conditions and whether the company is service- and/or manufacturing-oriented.

Resource-Based View of the Firm

> **resource-based view (RBV) of the firm**
> perspective that firms' competitive advantages are due to their endowment of strategic resources that are valuable, rare, costly to imitate, and costly to substitute.

> **LO3.4**
> The resource-based view of the firm and the different types of tangible and intangible resources, as well as organizational capabilities.

The **resource-based view (RBV) of the firm** combines two perspectives: (1) the internal analysis of phenomena within a company and (2) an external analysis of the industry and its competitive environment.[31] It goes beyond the traditional SWOT (strengths, weaknesses, opportunities, threats) analysis by integrating internal and external perspectives. The ability of a firm's resources to confer competitive advantage(s) cannot be determined without taking into consideration the broader competitive context. A firm's resources must be evaluated in terms of how valuable, rare, and hard they are for competitors to duplicate. Otherwise, the firm attains only competitive parity.

As noted earlier (in Strategy Spotlight 3.1), a firm's strengths and capabilities—no matter how unique or impressive—do not necessarily lead to competitive advantages in the marketplace. The criteria for whether advantages are created and whether or not they can be sustained over time will be addressed later in this section. Thus, the RBV is a very useful framework for gaining insights as to why some competitors are more profitable than others. As we will see later in the book, the RBV is also helpful in developing strategies for individual businesses and diversified firms by revealing how core competencies embedded in a firm can help it exploit new product and market opportunities.

In the two sections that follow, we will discuss the three key types of resources that firms possess (summarized in Exhibit 3.5): tangible resources, intangible resources, and organizational capabilities. Then we will address the conditions under which such assets and capabilities can enable a firm to attain a sustainable competitive advantage.[32]

Types of Firm Resources

Firm resources are all assets, capabilities, organizational processes, information, knowledge, and so forth, controlled by a firm that enable it to develop and implement value-creating strategies.

> **tangible resources**
> organizational assets that are relatively easy to identify, including physical assets, financial resources, organizational resources, and technological resources.

Tangible Resources Tangible resources are assets that are relatively easy to identify. They include the physical and financial assets that an organization uses to create value for its customers. Among them are financial resource (e.g., a firm's cash, accounts receivable, and its ability to borrow funds); physical resources (e.g., the company's plant, equipment, and machinery as well as its proximity to customers and suppliers); organizational resources (e.g., the company's strategic planning process and its employee development, evaluation, and reward systems); and technological resources (e.g., trade secrets, patents, and copyrights).

Many firms are finding that high-tech, computerized training has dual benefits: It develops more-effective employees and reduces costs at the same time. Employees at FedEx take computer-based job competency tests every 6 to 12 months.[33] The 90-minute

EXHIBIT 3.5 The Resource-Based View of the Firm: Resources and Capabilities

Tangible Resources	
Financial	• Firm's cash account and cash equivalents. • Firm's capacity to raise equity. • Firm's borrowing capacity.
Physical	• Modern plant and facilities. • Favorable manufacturing locations. • State-of-the-art machinery and equipment.
Technological	• Trade secrets. • Innovative production processes. • Patents, copyrights, trademarks.
Organizational	• Effective strategic planning processes. • Excellent evaluation and control systems.

Intangible Resources	
Human	• Experience and capabilities of employees. • Trust. • Managerial skills. • Firm-specific practices and procedures.
Innovation and creativity	• Technical and scientific skills. • Innovation capacities.
Reputation	• Brand name. • Reputation with customers for quality and reliability. • Reputation with suppliers for fairness, non–zero-sum relationships.

Organizational Capabilities

- Firm competencies or skills the firm employs to transfer inputs to outputs.
- Capacity to combine tangible and intangible resources, using organizational processes to attain desired end.

  EXAMPLES:
  - Outstanding customer service.
  - Excellent product development capabilities.
  - Innovativeness of products and services.
  - Ability to hire, motivate, and retain human capital.

Sources: Adapted from Barney, J. B. 1991. Firm Resources and Sustained Competitive Advantage. *Journal of Management,* 17: 101; Grant, R. M. 1991. *Contemporary Strategy Analysis:* 100–102. Cambridge, England: Blackwell Business; and Hitt, M. A., Ireland, R. D., & Hoskisson, R. E. 2001. *Strategic Management: Competitiveness and Globalization* (4th ed.). Cincinnati: South-Western College Publishing.

computer-based tests identify areas of individual weakness and provide input to a computer database of employee skills—information the firm uses in promotion decisions.

Intangible Resources Much more difficult for competitors (and, for that matter, a firm's own managers) to account for or imitate are **intangible resources,** which are typically embedded in unique routines and practices that have evolved and accumulated over time. These include human resources (e.g., experience and capability of employees, trust, effectiveness of work teams, managerial skills), innovation resources (e.g., technical and scientific expertise, ideas), and reputation resources (e.g., brand name, reputation with suppliers

intangible resources organizational assets that are difficult to identify and account for and are typically embedded in unique routines and practices, including human resources, innovation resources, and reputation resources.

for fairness and with customers for reliability and product quality).[34] A firm's culture may also be a resource that provides competitive advantage.[35]

For example, you might not think that motorcycles, clothes, toys, and restaurants have much in common. Yet Harley-Davidson has entered all of these product and service markets by capitalizing on its strong brand image—a valuable intangible resource.[36] It has used that image to sell accessories, clothing, and toys, and it has licensed the Harley-Davidson Café in New York City to provide further exposure for its brand name and products.

Social networking sites have the potential to play havoc with a firm's reputation. Consider the unfortunate situation Comcast faced when one of its repairmen fell asleep on the job—and it went viral:

> Ben Finkelstein, a law student, had trouble with the cable modem in his home. A Comcast cable repairman arrived to fix the problem. However, when the technician had to call the home office for a key piece of information, he was put on hold for so long that he fell asleep on Finkelstein's couch. Outraged, Finkelstein made a video of the sleeping technician and posted it on YouTube. The clip became a hit—with more than a million viewings. And, for a long time, it undermined Comcast's efforts to improve its reputation for customer service.[37]

organizational capabilities
the competencies and skills that a firm employs to transform inputs into outputs.

Organizational Capabilities **Organizational capabilities** are not specific tangible or intangible assets, but rather the competencies or skills that a firm employs to transform inputs into outputs.[38] In short, they refer to an organization's capacity to deploy tangible and intangible resources over time and generally in combination and to leverage those capabilities to bring about a desired end.[39] Examples of organizational capabilities are outstanding customer service, excellent product development capabilities, superb innovation processes, and flexibility in manufacturing processes.[40]

In the case of Apple, the majority of components used in its products can be characterized as proven technology, such as touch-screen and MP3-player functionality.[41] However, Apple combines and packages these in new and innovative ways while also seeking to integrate the value chain. This is the case with iTunes, for example, where suppliers of downloadable music are a vital component of the success Apple has enjoyed with its iPod series of MP3 players. Thus, Apple draws on proven technologies and its ability to offer innovative combinations of them.

Firm Resources and Sustainable Competitive Advantages

LO3.5

The four criteria that a firm's resources must possess to maintain a sustainable advantage and how value created can be appropriated by employees and managers.

As we have mentioned, resources alone are not a basis for competitive advantages, nor are advantages sustainable over time.[42] In some cases, a resource or capability helps a firm to increase its revenues or to lower costs but the firm derives only a temporary advantage because competitors quickly imitate or substitute for it.[43]

For a resource to provide a firm with the potential for a sustainable competitive advantage, it must have four attributes.[44] First, the resource must be valuable in the sense that it exploits opportunities and/or neutralizes threats in the firm's environment. Second, it must be rare among the firm's current and potential competitors. Third, the resource must be difficult for competitors to imitate. Fourth, the resource must have no strategically equivalent substitutes. These criteria are summarized in Exhibit 3.6. We will now discuss each of these criteria. Then we will examine how Blockbuster's competitive advantage, which seemed secure a decade ago, subsequently eroded, causing the company to file for bankruptcy in 2011.

Is the Resource Valuable? Organizational resources can be a source of competitive advantage only when they are valuable. Resources are valuable when they enable a firm to formulate and implement strategies that improve its efficiency or effectiveness. The SWOT framework suggests that firms improve their performance only when they exploit opportunities or neutralize (or minimize) threats.

EXHIBIT 3.6 Four Criteria for Assessing Sustainability of Resources and Capabilities

Is the resource or capability...	Implications
Valuable?	• Neutralize threats and exploit opportunities
Rare?	• Not many firms possess
Difficult to imitate?	• Physically unique
	• Path dependency (how accumulated over time)
	• Causal ambiguity (difficult to disentangle what it is or how it could be re-created)
	• Social complexity (trust, interpersonal relationships, culture, reputation)
Difficult to substitute?	• No equivalent strategic resources or capabilities

The fact that firm attributes must be valuable in order to be considered resources (as well as potential sources of competitive advantage) reveals an important complementary relationship among environmental models (e.g., SWOT and five-forces analyses) and the resource-based model. Environmental models isolate those firm attributes that exploit opportunities and/or neutralize threats. Thus, they specify what firm attributes may be considered as resources. The resource-based model then suggests what additional characteristics these resources must possess if they are to develop a sustained competitive advantage.

Is the Resource Rare? If competitors or potential competitors also possess the same valuable resource, it is not a source of a competitive advantage because all of these firms have the capability to exploit that resource in the same way. Common strategies based on such a resource would give no one firm an advantage. For a resource to provide competitive advantages, it must be uncommon, that is, rare relative to other competitors.

This argument can apply to bundles of valuable firm resources that are used to formulate and develop strategies. Some strategies require a mix of multiple types of resources—tangible assets, intangible assets, and organizational capabilities. If a particular bundle of firm resources is not rare, then relatively large numbers of firms will be able to conceive of and implement the strategies in question. Thus, such strategies will not be a source of competitive advantage, even if the resource in question is valuable.

Can the Resource Be Imitated Easily? Inimitability (difficulty in imitating) is a key to value creation because it constrains competition.[45] If a resource is inimitable, then any profits generated are more likely to be sustainable.[46] Having a resource that competitors can easily copy generates only temporary value.[47] This has important implications. Since managers often fail to apply this test, they tend to base long-term strategies on resources that are imitable. IBP (Iowa Beef Processors) became the first meatpacking company in the United States to modernize by building a set of assets (automated plants located in cattle-producing states) and capabilities (low-cost "disassembly" of carcasses) that earned returns on assets of 1.3 percent in the 1970s. By the late 1980s, however, ConAgra and Cargill had imitated these resources, and IBP's profitability fell by nearly 70 percent, to 0.4 percent.

Groupon (the company that was the focus of the Learning from Mistakes feature in Chapter 1) is a more recent example of a firm that has suffered because rivals have been able to imitate its strategy rather easily:

> Groupon, which offers online coupons for bargains at local shops and restaurants, created a new market.[48] Although it was initially a boon to consumers, it offers no lasting "first-mover" advantage. Its business model is not patentable and is easy to replicate. Not surprisingly, there are many copycats. For example, there was a tremendous amount of

churn in the industry in 2012. The number of daily deal sites in the United States rose by almost 8 percent (142 sites), according to Daily Deal Media, which tracks the industry. Meanwhile, globally, 560 daily deal sites closed over the same period!

Clearly, an advantage based on inimitability won't last forever. Competitors will eventually discover a way to copy most valuable resources. However, managers can forestall them and sustain profits for a while by developing strategies around resources that have at least one of the following four characteristics.[49]

Physical Uniqueness The first source of inimitability is physical uniqueness, which by definition is inherently difficult to copy. A beautiful resort location, mineral rights, or Pfizer's pharmaceutical patents simply cannot be imitated. Many managers believe that several of their resources may fall into this category, but on close inspection, few do.

Path Dependency A greater number of resources cannot be imitated because of what economists refer to as **path dependency.** This simply means that resources are unique and therefore scarce because of all that has happened along the path followed in their development and/or accumulation. Competitors cannot go out and buy these resources quickly and easily; they must be built up over time in ways that are difficult to accelerate.

The Gerber Products Co. brand name for baby food is an example of a resource that is potentially inimitable. Re-creating Gerber's brand loyalty would be a time-consuming process that competitors could not expedite, even with expensive marketing campaigns. Similarly, the loyalty and trust that Southwest Airlines employees feel toward their firm and its cofounder, Herb Kelleher, are resources that have been built up over a long period of time. Also, a crash R&D program generally cannot replicate a successful technology when research findings cumulate. Clearly, these path-dependent conditions build protection for the original resource. The benefits from experience and learning through trial and error cannot be duplicated overnight.

Causal Ambiguity The third source of inimitability is termed **causal ambiguity.** This means that would-be competitors may be thwarted because it is impossible to disentangle the causes (or possible explanations) of either what the valuable resource is or how it can be re-created. What is the root of 3M's innovation process? You can study it and draw up a list of possible factors. But it is a complex, unfolding (or folding) process that is hard to understand and would be hard to imitate.

Often, causally ambiguous resources are organizational capabilities, involving a complex web of social interactions that may even depend on particular individuals. When Continental and United tried to mimic the successful low-cost strategy of Southwest Airlines, the planes, routes, and fast gate turnarounds were not the most difficult aspects for them to copy. Those were all rather easy to observe and, at least in principle, easy to duplicate. However, they could not replicate Southwest's culture of fun, family, frugality, and focus since no one can clearly specify exactly what that culture is or how it came to be.

Strategy Spotlight 3.5 describes Amazon's continued success as the world's largest online marketplace. Competitors recently tried to imitate Amazon's free-shipping strategy, but with limited success. The reason is that Amazon has developed an array of interrelated elements of strategy which their rivals find too difficult to imitate.

Social Complexity A firm's resources may be imperfectly inimitable because they reflect a high level of **social complexity.** Such phenomena are typically beyond the ability of firms to systematically manage or influence. When competitive advantages are based on social complexity, it is difficult for other firms to imitate them.

A wide variety of firm resources may be considered socially complex. Examples include interpersonal relations among the managers in a firm, its culture, and its reputation with

3.5 STRATEGY SPOTLIGHT

AMAZON PRIME: VERY DIFFICULT FOR RIVALS TO COPY

Amazon Prime, introduced in 2004, is a free-shipping service that guarantees delivery of products within two days for an annual fee of $79. According to *Bloomberg Businessweek*, it may be the most ingenious and effective customer loyalty program in all of e-commerce, if not retail in general. It converts casual shoppers into Amazon addicts who gorge on the gratification of having purchases reliably appear two days after they order. Analysts describe Prime as one of the main factors driving Amazon's stock price up nearly 300 percent from 2008 to 2010. Also, it is one of the main reasons why Amazon's sales grew 30 percent during the recession, while other retailers suffered.

By 2014, Amazon had 25 million Prime members, up from 5 million two years earlier. They are practically addicted to using Amazon—and certainly don't seem to mind the annual membership price boost to $99. Scot Wingo of Channel Advisor, a company that helps online sellers, estimates that people with Prime spend about four times what others do and account for half of all spending at Amazon.

Amazon Prime has proven to be extremely hard for rivals to copy. Why? It enables Amazon to exploit its wide selection, low prices, network of third-party merchants, and finely tuned distribution system. All that while also keying off that faintly irrational human need to maximize the benefits of a club that you have already paid to join. Yet Amazon's success also leads to increased pressure from both public and private entities. For a long time, Amazon was able to avoid collecting local sales taxes because Amazon did not have a local sales presence in many states. This practice distorts competition and strains already tight state coffers. Some states have used a combination of legislation and litigation to convince Amazon to collect sales taxes; Amazon began collecting Texas state sales tax in July 2012.

Moreover, rivals—both online and off—have realized the increasing threat posed by Prime and are rushing to respond. For example, in October 2010, a consortium of more than 20 retailers, including Barnes & Noble, Sports Authority, and Toys 'R' Us, banded together to offer their own copycat $79, two-day shipping program, ShopRunner, which applies to products across their websites. As noted by Fiona Dias, the executive who administers the program, "As Amazon added more merchandising categories to Prime, retailers started feeling the pain. They have finally come to understand that Amazon is an existential threat and that Prime is the fuel of the engine."

Finally, Prime members also gain access to more than 40,000 streaming Instant Video programs and 300,000 free books in the Kindle Owners' Lending Library. And, in April 2014, Amazon paid HBO, a television company, an estimated $200 million to $250 million for a package of shows that Prime members can stream at no extra cost. As annoying as this might be to Netflix, it is not intended primarily as an assault on Netflix. Rather, CEO Jeff Bezos is willing to lose money on shipping and services in exchange for loyalty.

Sources: Anonymous. 2014. Relentless.com. *The Economist*, June 21: 23–26; McCorvey, J. J. 2013. The race has just begun. *Fast Company*, September: 66–76; Stone, B. 2010. What's in the box? Instant gratification. *Bloomberg Businessweek*, November 29–December 5: 39–40; Kaplan, M. 2011. Amazon Prime: 5 million members, 20 percent growth. *www.practicalcommerce.com*, September 16: np; Fowler, G. A. 2010. Retailers team up against Amazon. *www.wsj.com*, October 6: np; and Halkias, M. 2012. Amazon to collect sales tax in Texas. *Dallas Morning News*, April 28: 4A.

---

its suppliers and customers. In many of these cases, it is easy to specify how these socially complex resources add value to a firm. Hence, there is little or no causal ambiguity surrounding the link between them and competitive advantage.

The most recent Edelman Trust Barometer, a comprehensive yearly survey of public trust, found that trust and transparency are more critical than ever.[50] For the first time in the survey's history, impressions of openness, sincerity, and authenticity are more important to corporate reputation in the United States than the quality of products and services. This means trust affects tangible things such as supply chain partnerships and long-term customer loyalty. People want to partner with you because they have heard you are a credible company built through a culture of trust. In a sense, being a great company to work for also makes you a great company to work with.

Are Substitutes Readily Available? The fourth requirement for a firm resource to be a source of sustainable competitive advantage is that there must be no strategically equivalent valuable resources that are themselves not rare or inimitable. Two valuable firm resources (or two bundles of resources) are strategically equivalent when each one can be exploited separately to implement the same strategies.

Substitutability may take at least two forms. First, though it may be impossible for a firm to imitate exactly another firm's resource, it may be able to substitute a similar resource that enables it to develop and implement the same strategy. Clearly, a firm seeking to imitate another firm's high-quality top management team would be unable to copy the team exactly. However, it might be able to develop its own unique management team. Though these two teams would have different ages, functional backgrounds, experience, and so on, they could be strategically equivalent and thus substitutes for one another.

Second, very different firm resources can become strategic substitutes. For example, Internet booksellers such as Amazon.com compete as substitutes for brick-and-mortar booksellers such as Barnes & Noble. The result is that resources such as premier retail locations become less valuable. In a similar vein, several pharmaceutical firms have seen the value of patent protection erode in the face of new drugs that are based on different production processes and act in different ways, but can be used in similar treatment regimes. The coming years will likely see even more radical change in the pharmaceutical industry as the substitution of genetic therapies eliminates certain uses of chemotherapy.[51]

To recap this section, recall that resources and capabilities must be rare and valuable as well as difficult to imitate or substitute in order for a firm to attain competitive advantages that are sustainable over time.[52] Exhibit 3.7 illustrates the relationship among the four criteria of sustainability and shows the competitive implications.

In firms represented by the first row of Exhibit 3.7, managers are in a difficult situation. When their resources and capabilities do not meet any of the four criteria, it would be difficult to develop any type of competitive advantage, in the short or long term. The resources and capabilities they possess enable the firm neither to exploit environmental opportunities nor to neutralize environmental threats. In the second and third rows, firms have resources and capabilities that are valuable as well as rare, respectively. However, in both cases the resources and capabilities are not difficult for competitors to imitate or substitute. Here, the firms could attain some level of competitive parity. They could perform on par with equally endowed rivals or attain a temporary competitive advantage. But their advantages would be easy for competitors to match. It is only in the fourth row, where all four criteria are satisfied, that competitive advantages can be sustained over time. Next, let's look at Blockbuster and see how its competitive advantage, which seemed to be sustainable for a rather long period of time, eventually eroded, leading to the company's bankruptcy in 2011.

Blockbuster Inc.: From Sustainable (?) Advantage to Bankruptcy Blockbuster Video failed to recognize in time the threat posed to its brick-and-mortar business by virtual services such as Netflix.[53] At the time, few thought that consumers would trade the

EXHIBIT 3.7
Criteria for Sustainable Competitive Advantage and Strategic Implications

Is a Resource or Capability ...				
Valuable?	Rare?	Difficult to Imitate?	Without Substitutes?	Implication for Competitiveness
No	No	No	No	Competitive disadvantage
Yes	No	No	No	Competitive parity
Yes	Yes	No	No	Temporary competitive advantage
Yes	Yes	Yes	Yes	Sustainable competitive advantage

Source: Adapted from Barney, J. B. 1991. Firm Resources and Sustained Competitive Advantage. *Journal of Management*, 17: 99–120.

convenience of picking up their videos to waiting for them to arrive in the mail. Interestingly, Blockbuster had the chance to buy Netflix for $50 million in 2000 but turned down the opportunity. Barry McCarthy, Netflix's former chief financial officer, recalls the conversation during a meeting with Blockbuster's top executives: Reed Hastings, Netflix's cofounder, "had the chutzpah to propose to them that we run their brand online and that they run (our) brand in the stores and they just about laughed us out of the office. At least initially, they thought we were a very small niche business."

Users, of course, embraced the automated self-service of Netflix's web-based interface technology that positioned the start-up to transition from mailing DVDs to streaming content over the Internet. As technologies improved broadband speed, reliability, and adoption, Netflix transitioned in just a few years to a cloud-based service.

Blockbuster tried to follow each of Netflix's strategic moves. However, it remained a perennial second in the winner-take-all market for new ways to distribute entertainment content. Blockbuster continued to lag, weighed down by the high labor costs and real estate costs of its once-dominant locations—assets that became liabilities. In 2011, after closing some 900 stores, the company declared bankruptcy.

In the end, Blockbuster's assets were acquired for only $320 million by satellite television maverick Dish Networks, which was mainly interested in Blockbuster's online channel and 3.3 million customers. Had Blockbuster sold out earlier, or found a way to shed the physical assets sooner, that price could have been much higher. In 1999, the year Netflix launched its online subscription service, Blockbuster was valued at nearly $3 billion—nearly 10 times what Dish ultimately paid. Netflix, on the other hand, had a market cap of $21 billion by the end of 2014.

The Generation and Distribution of a Firm's Profits: Extending the Resource-Based View of the Firm

The resource-based view of the firm is useful in determining when firms will create competitive advantages and enjoy high levels of profitability. However, it has not been developed to address how a firm's profits (often referred to as "rents" by economists) will be distributed to a firm's management and employees or other stakeholders such as customers, suppliers, or governments.[54] This is an important issue because firms may be successful in creating competitive advantages that can be sustainable for a period of time. However, much of the profits can be retained (or "appropriated") by a firm's employees and managers or other stakeholders instead of flowing to the firm's owners (i.e., the stockholders).*

Consider Viewpoint DataLabs International, a Salt Lake City–based company that makes sophisticated three-dimensional models and textures for film production houses, video games, and car manufacturers. This example will help to show how employees are often able to obtain (or "appropriate") a high proportion of a firm's profits:

> Walter Noot, head of production, was having trouble keeping his highly skilled Generation X employees happy with their compensation. Each time one of them was lured away for more money, everyone would want a raise. "We were having to give out raises every six months—30 to 40 percent—then six months later they'd expect the same. It was a big struggle to keep people happy."[55]

Here, much of the profits is being generated by the highly skilled professionals working together. They are able to exercise their power by successfully demanding more financial compensation. In part, management has responded favorably because they are united in their demands and their work involves a certain amount of social complexity and causal ambiguity—given the complex, coordinated efforts that their work entails.

---

*Economists define rents as profits (or prices) in excess of what is required to provide a normal return.

Four factors help explain the extent to which employees and managers will be able to obtain a proportionately high level of the profits that they generate:[56]

- ***Employee bargaining power.*** If employees are vital to forming a firm's unique capability, they will earn disproportionately high wages. For example, marketing professionals may have access to valuable information that helps them to understand the intricacies of customer demands and expectations, or engineers may understand unique technical aspects of the products or services. Additionally, in some industries such as consulting, advertising, and tax preparation, clients tend to be very loyal to individual professionals employed by the firm, instead of to the firm itself. This enables them to "take the clients with them" if they leave. This enhances their bargaining power.

- ***Employee replacement cost.*** If employees' skills are idiosyncratic and rare (a source of resource-based advantages), they should have high bargaining power based on the high cost required by the firm to replace them. For example, Raymond Ozzie, the software designer who was critical in the development of Lotus Notes, was able to dictate the terms under which IBM acquired Lotus.

- ***Employee exit costs.*** This factor may tend to reduce an employee's bargaining power. An individual may face high personal costs when leaving the organization. Thus, that individual's threat of leaving may not be credible. In addition, an employee's expertise may be firm-specific and of limited value to other firms.

- ***Manager bargaining power.*** Managers' power is based on how well they create resource-based advantages. They are generally charged with creating value through the process of organizing, coordinating, and leveraging employees as well as other forms of capital such as plant, equipment, and financial capital (addressed further in Chapter 4). Such activities provide managers with sources of information that may not be readily available to others.

Chapter 9 addresses the conditions under which top-level managers (such as CEOs) of large corporations have been, at times, able to obtain levels of total compensation that would appear to be significantly disproportionate to their contributions to wealth generation as well as to top executives in peer organizations. Here, corporate governance becomes a critical control mechanism. Consider shareholders' reaction, in April 2012, to Citigroup's proposed $15 million pay package for then-CEO Vikram Pandit.[57] It was not positive, to say the least. After all, they had suffered a 92 percent decline in the stock's price under Pandit's five-year reign. They rejected the bank's compensation proposal. In October 2012, the board ousted Pandit after the New York–based firm failed to secure Federal Reserve approval to increase its shareholder payouts and Moody's Investors Service cut the bank's credit rating two levels.

Such diversion of profits from the owners of the business to top management is far less likely when the board members are truly independent outsiders (i.e., they do not have close ties to management). In general, given the external market for top talent, the level of compensation that executives receive is based on factors similar to the ones just discussed that determine the level of their bargaining power.[58]

In addition to employees and managers, other stakeholder groups can also appropriate a portion of the rents generated by a firm. If, for example, a critical input is controlled by a monopoly supplier or if a single buyer accounts for most of a firm's sales, this supplier's or buyer's bargaining power can greatly erode the potential profits of a firm. Similarly, excessive taxation by governments can also reduce what is available to a firm's stockholders.

Evaluating Firm Performance: Two Approaches

This section addresses two approaches to use when evaluating a firm's performance. The first is financial ratio analysis, which, generally speaking, identifies how a firm is performing according to its balance sheet, income statement, and market valuation. As we will discuss, when performing a financial ratio analysis, you must take into account the firm's performance from a historical perspective (not just at one point in time) as well as how it compares with both industry norms and key competitors.[59]

The second perspective takes a broader stakeholder view. Firms must satisfy a broad range of stakeholders, including employees, customers, and owners, to ensure their long-term viability. Central to our discussion will be a well-known approach—the balanced scorecard—that has been popularized by Robert Kaplan and David Norton.[60]

Financial Ratio Analysis

The beginning point in analyzing the financial position of a firm is to compute and analyze five different types of financial ratios:

- Short-term solvency or liquidity
- Long-term solvency measures
- Asset management (or turnover)
- Profitability
- Market value

financial ratio analysis
a technique for measuring the performance of a firm according to its balance sheet, income statement, and market valuation.

Exhibit 3.8 summarizes each of these five ratios.

EXHIBIT 3.8 A Summary of Five Types of Financial Ratios

I. Short-term solvency, or liquidity, ratios

$$\text{Current ratio} = \frac{\text{Current assets}}{\text{Current liabilities}}$$

$$\text{Quick ratio} = \frac{\text{Current assets} - \text{Inventory}}{\text{Current liabilities}}$$

$$\text{Cash ratio} = \frac{\text{Cash}}{\text{Current liabilities}}$$

II. Long-term solvency, or financial leverage, ratios

$$\text{Total debt ratio} = \frac{\text{Total assets} - \text{Total equity}}{\text{Total assets}}$$

Debt-equity ratio = Total debt/Total equity

Equity multiplier = Total assets/Total equity

$$\text{Times interest earned ratio} = \frac{\text{EBIT}}{\text{Interest}}$$

$$\text{Cash coverage ratio} = \frac{\text{EBIT} + \text{Depreciation}}{\text{Interest}}$$

III. Asset utilization, or turnover, ratios

$$\text{Inventory turnover} = \frac{\text{Cost of goods sold}}{\text{Inventory}}$$

$$\text{Days' sales in inventory} = \frac{365 \text{ days}}{\text{Inventory turnover}}$$

$$\text{Receivables turnover} = \frac{\text{Sales}}{\text{Accounts receivable}}$$

$$\text{Days' sales in receivables} = \frac{365 \text{ days}}{\text{Receivables turnover}}$$

$$\text{Total asset turnover} = \frac{\text{Sales}}{\text{Total assets}}$$

$$\text{Capital intensity} = \frac{\text{Total assets}}{\text{Sales}}$$

IV. Profitability ratios

$$\text{Profit margin} = \frac{\text{Net income}}{\text{Sales}}$$

$$\text{Return on assets (ROA)} = \frac{\text{Net income}}{\text{Total assets}}$$

$$\text{Return on equity (ROE)} = \frac{\text{Net income}}{\text{Total equity}}$$

$$\text{ROE} = \frac{\text{Net income}}{\text{Sales}} \times \frac{\text{Sales}}{\text{Assets}} \times \frac{\text{Assets}}{\text{Equity}}$$

V. Market value ratios

$$\text{Price-earnings ratio} = \frac{\text{Price per share}}{\text{Earnings per share}}$$

$$\text{Market-to-book ratio} = \frac{\text{Market value per share}}{\text{Book value per share}}$$

Appendix 1 to Chapter 13 (the Case Analysis chapter) provides detailed definitions for and discussions of each of these types of ratios as well as examples of how each is calculated. Refer to pages 441–450.

A meaningful ratio analysis must go beyond the calculation and interpretation of financial ratios.[61] It must include how ratios change over time as well as how they are interrelated. For example, a firm that takes on too much long-term debt to finance operations will see an immediate impact on its indicators of long-term financial leverage. The additional debt will negatively affect the firm's short-term liquidity ratio (i.e., current and quick ratios) since the firm must pay interest and principal on the additional debt each year until it is retired. Additionally, the interest expenses deducted from revenues reduce the firm's profitability.

A firm's financial position should not be analyzed in isolation. Important reference points are needed. We will address some issues that must be taken into account to make financial analysis more meaningful: historical comparisons, comparisons with industry norms, and comparisons with key competitors.

Historical Comparisons When you evaluate a firm's financial performance, it is very useful to compare its financial position over time. This provides a means of evaluating trends. For example, Apple Inc. reported revenues of $171 billion and net income of $37 billion in 2012. Virtually all firms would be very happy with such remarkable financial success. These figures represent a stunning annual growth in revenue and net income of 57 percent and 43 percent, respectively, for the 2011 to 2013 time period. Had Apple's revenues and net income in 2013 been $80 billion and $20 billion, respectively, it would still be a very large and highly profitable enterprise. However, such performance would have significantly damaged Apple's market valuation and reputation as well as the careers of many of its executives.

Exhibit 3.9 illustrates a 10-year period of return on sales (ROS) for a hypothetical company. As indicated by the dotted trend lines, the rate of growth (or decline) differs substantially over time periods.

Comparison with Industry Norms When you are evaluating a firm's financial performance, remember also to compare it with industry norms. A firm's current ratio or profitability may appear impressive at first glance. However, it may pale when compared with industry standards or norms.

LO3.6
The usefulness of financial ratio analysis, its inherent limitations, and how to make meaningful comparisons of performance across firms.

EXHIBIT 3.9 Historical Trends: Return on Sales (ROS) for a Hypothetical Company

Financial Ratio	Semiconductors	Grocery Stores	Skilled-Nursing Facilities
Quick ratio (times)	1.9	0.6	1.3
Current ratio (times)	3.6	1.7	1.7
Total liabilities to net worth (%)	35.1	72.7	82.5
Collection period (days)	48.6	3.3	36.5
Assets to sales (%)	131.7	22.1	58.3
Return on sales (%)	24	1.1	3.1

EXHIBIT 3.10 How Financial Ratios Differ across Industries

Source: Dun & Bradstreet. *Industry Norms and Key Business Ratios, 2010–2011.* One Year Edition, SIC #3600–3699 (Semiconductors); SIC #5400–5499 (Grocery Stores); SIC #8000–8099 (Skilled-Nursing Facilities). New York: Dun & Bradstreet Credit Services.

Comparing your firm with all other firms in your industry assesses relative performance. Banks often use such comparisons when evaluating a firm's creditworthiness. Exhibit 3.10 includes a variety of financial ratios for three industries: semiconductors, grocery stores, and skilled-nursing facilities. Why is there such variation among the financial ratios for these three industries? There are several reasons. With regard to the collection period, grocery stores operate mostly on a cash basis, hence a very short collection period. Semiconductor manufacturers sell their output to other manufacturers (e.g., computer makers) on terms such as 2/15 net 45, which means they give a 2 percent discount on bills paid within 15 days and start charging interest after 45 days. Skilled-nursing facilities also have a longer collection period than grocery stores because they typically rely on payments from insurance companies.

The industry norms for return on sales also highlight differences among these industries. Grocers, with very slim margins, have a lower return on sales than either skilled-nursing facilities or semiconductor manufacturers. But how might we explain the differences between skilled-nursing facilities and semiconductor manufacturers? Health care facilities, in general, are limited in their pricing structures by Medicare/Medicaid regulations and by insurance reimbursement limits, but semiconductor producers have pricing structures determined by the market. If their products have superior performance, semiconductor manufacturers can charge premium prices.

Comparison with Key Competitors Recall from Chapter 2 that firms with similar strategies are members of a strategic group in an industry. Furthermore, competition is more intense among competitors within groups than across groups. Thus, you can gain valuable insights into a firm's financial and competitive position if you make comparisons between a firm and its most direct rivals. Consider a firm trying to diversify into the highly profitable pharmaceutical industry. Even if it was willing to invest several hundred million dollars, it would be virtually impossible to compete effectively against industry giants such as Pfizer and Merck. These two firms have 2013 revenues of $51 billion and $44 billion, respectively, and both had R&D budgets of over $7 billion.[62]

Integrating Financial Analysis and Stakeholder Perspectives: The Balanced Scorecard

LO3.7
The value of the "balanced scorecard" in recognizing how the interests of a variety of stakeholders can be interrelated.

It is useful to see how a firm performs over time in terms of several ratios. However, such traditional approaches can be a double-edged sword.[63] Many important transactions—investments in research and development, employee training and development, and advertising and promotion of key brands—may greatly expand a firm's market potential and create significant long-term shareholder value. But such critical investments are not reflected positively in short-term financial reports. Financial reports typically measure expenses, not the value created. Thus, managers may be penalized for spending money in the short term to improve their firm's long-term competitive viability!

Now consider the other side of the coin. A manager may destroy the firm's future value by dissatisfying customers, depleting the firm's stock of good products coming out of R&D, or damaging the morale of valued employees. Such budget cuts, however, may lead to very good short-term financials. The manager may look good in the short run and even receive credit for improving the firm's performance. In essence, such a manager has mastered "denominator management," whereby decreasing investments makes the return on investment (ROI) ratio larger, even though the actual return remains constant or shrinks.

The Balanced Scorecard: Description and Benefits To provide a meaningful integration of the many issues that come into evaluating a firm's performance, Kaplan and Norton developed a **"balanced scorecard."**[64] This provides top managers with a fast but comprehensive view of the business. In a nutshell, it includes financial measures that reflect the results of actions already taken, but it complements these indicators with measures of customer satisfaction, internal processes, and the organization's innovation and improvement activities—operational measures that drive future financial performance.

The balanced scorecard enables managers to consider their business from four key perspectives: customer, internal, innovation and learning, and financial. These are briefly described in Exhibit 3.11.

Customer Perspective Clearly, how a company is performing from its customers' perspective is a top priority for management. The balanced scorecard requires that managers translate their general mission statements on customer service into specific measures that reflect the factors that really matter to customers. For the balanced scorecard to work, managers must articulate goals for four key categories of customer concerns: time, quality, performance and service, and cost.

Internal Business Perspective Customer-based measures are important. However, they must be translated into indicators of what the firm must do internally to meet customers' expectations. Excellent customer performance results from processes, decisions, and actions that occur throughout organizations in a coordinated fashion, and managers must focus on those critical internal operations that enable them to satisfy customer needs. The internal measures should reflect business processes that have the greatest impact on customer satisfaction. These include factors that affect cycle time, quality, employee skills, and productivity.

Innovation and Learning Perspective Given the rapid rate of markets, technologies, and global competition, the criteria for success are constantly changing. To survive and prosper, managers must make frequent changes to existing products and services as well as introduce entirely new products with expanded capabilities. A firm's ability to do well from an innovation and learning perspective is more dependent on its intangible than tangible assets. Three categories of intangible assets are critically important: human capital (skills, talent, and knowledge), information capital (information systems, networks), and organization capital (culture, leadership).

balanced scorecard
a method of evaluating a firm's performance using performance measures from the customer, internal, innovation and learning, and financial perspectives.

customer perspective
measures of firm performance that indicate how well firms are satisfying customers' expectations.

internal business perspective
measures of firm performance that indicate how well firms' internal processes, decisions, and actions are contributing to customer satisfaction.

innovation and learning perspective
measures of firm performance that indicate how well firms are changing their product and service offerings to adapt to changes in the internal and external environments.

EXHIBIT 3.11
The Balanced Scorecard's Four Perspectives

- How do customers see us? (customer perspective)
- What must we excel at? (internal business perspective)
- Can we continue to improve and create value? (innovation and learning perspective)
- How do we look to shareholders? (financial perspective)

Financial Perspective   Measures of financial performance indicate whether the company's strategy, implementation, and execution are indeed contributing to bottom-line improvement. Typical financial goals include profitability, growth, and shareholder value. Periodic financial statements remind managers that improved quality, response time, productivity, and innovative products benefit the firm only when they result in improved sales, increased market share, reduced operating expenses, or higher asset turnover.[65]

> **financial perspective** measures of firms' financial performance that indicate how well strategy, implementation, and execution are contributing to bottom-line improvement.

Consider how Sears, the retailer, found a strong causal relationship between employee attitudes, customer attitudes, and financial outcomes.[66] Through an ongoing study, Sears developed what it calls its total performance indicators, or TPI—a set of indicators for assessing its performance with customers, employees, and investors. Sears's quantitative model has shown that a 5 percent improvement in employee attitudes leads to a 1.3 percent improvement in customer satisfaction, which in turn drives a 0.5 percent improvement in revenue. Thus, if a single store improved its employee attitude by 5 percent, Sears could predict with confidence that if the revenue growth in the district as a whole were 5 percent, the revenue growth in this particular store would be 5.5 percent. Interestingly, Sears's managers consider such numbers as rigorous as any others that they work with every year. The company's accounting firm audits management as closely as it audits the financial statements.

A key implication is that managers do not need to look at their job as balancing stakeholder demands. They must avoid the following mind-set: "How many units in employee satisfaction do I have to give up to get some additional units of customer satisfaction or profits?" Instead, the balanced scorecard provides a win–win approach—increasing satisfaction among a wide variety of organizational stakeholders, including employees (at all levels), customers, and stockholders.

Limitations and Potential Downsides of the Balanced Scorecard   There is general agreement that there is nothing inherently wrong with the concept of the balanced scorecard.[67] The key limitation is that some executives may view it as a "quick fix" that can be easily installed. If managers do not recognize this from the beginning and fail to commit to it long term, the organization will be disappointed. Poor execution becomes the cause of such performance outcomes. And organizational scorecards must be aligned with individuals' scorecards to turn the balanced scorecards into a powerful tool for sustained performance.

In a study of 50 Canadian medium-size and large organizations, the number of users expressing skepticism about scorecard performance was much greater than the number claiming positive results. A large number of respondents agreed with the statement "Balanced scorecards don't really work." Some representative comments included: "It became just a number-crunching exercise by accountants after the first year," "It is just the latest management fad and is already dropping lower on management's list of priorities as all fads eventually do," and "If scorecards are supposed to be a measurement tool, why is it so hard to measure their results?" There is much work to do before scorecards can become a viable framework to measure sustained strategic performance.

Problems often occur in the balanced scorecard implementation efforts when the commitment to learning is insufficient and employees' personal ambitions are included. Without a set of rules for employees that address continuous process improvement and the personal improvement of individual employees, there will be limited employee buy-in and insufficient cultural change. Thus, many improvements may be temporary and superficial. Often, scorecards that failed to attain alignment and improvements dissipated very quickly. And, in many cases, management's efforts to improve performance were seen as divisive and were viewed by employees as aimed at benefiting senior management compensation. This fostered a "what's in it for me?" attitude.

ISSUE FOR DEBATE

The World Triathlon's Initiatives to Extend Its Brand

World Triathlon Corporation (WTC) is a Florida-based company known for recognizing athletic excellence and performance. It provides events, products, and services under the Ironman and Ironman 70.3* branded names. Since its inception, *Ironman* has been identified with ambitious and courageous individuals who aren't afraid to push their limits. Tapping into athletes' desires to pursue their dream of becoming an Ironman was a successful business strategy for WTC. Given the extreme physical challenge, disciplined training, and camaraderie it offered its clients, WTC was able to grow its revenues and profits over the years.

In 2008, Providence Equity Partners, a private equity firm, acquired WTC for an undisclosed amount. The new owners started expanding the exclusive branding of Ironman to products and events that clearly didn't represent the "spirit" of the brand. For example, those who finished Ironman 70.3 races were allowed to be called "Ironmen," regardless of the shorter length and lesser degree of difficulty. Additionally, products such as cologne, mattresses, and strollers were branded with "Ironman." In October 2010, Ironman Access was launched as a membership program wherein individuals could get preferential registration access to Ironman events for a $1,000 annual fee. The response by the triathlete community was quick and decisive—and overwhelmingly negative. The athletes felt that WTC was losing its values in its pursuit of more profits. The company was trying to expand the brand, but it was alienating its base.

Discussion Questions

1. What actions should WTC take?
2. Is the World Triathlon Corporation acting too aggressively in trying to monetize the brand?
3. What are the long-term implications of the WTC's recent strategic actions?

*Ironman 70.3 is the half triathlon; the number refers to the total distance in miles covered in the race—1.2-mile swim, 56-mile bike ride, and 13.1-mile run.

Sources: Beartini, M. & Gourville, J. T. 2012. Pricing to create share value. *Harvard Business Review*, 90(6): 96–104; and WTC. 2012. Corporate info. www.ironman.com, January 12: np.

Reflecting on Career Implications . . .

- **The Value Chain:** It is important that you develop an understanding of your firm's value chain. What activities are most critical for attaining competitive advantage? Think of ways in which you can add value in your firm's value chain. How might your firm's support activities (e.g., information technology, human resource practices) help you accomplish your assigned tasks more effectively? How will you bring your value-added contribution to the attention of your superiors?

- **The Value Chain:** Consider the most important linkages between the activities you perform in your organization with other activities both within your firm and between your firm and its suppliers, customers, and alliance partners. Understanding and strengthening these linkages can contribute greatly to your career advancement within your current organization.

- **Resource-Based View of the Firm:** Are your skills and talents rare, valuable, and difficult to imitate, and do they have few substitutes? If so, you are in the better position to add value for your firm—and earn rewards and incentives. How can your skills and talents be enhanced to help satisfy these criteria to a greater extent? Get more training? Change positions within the firm? Consider career options at other organizations?

- **Balanced Scorecard:** Can you design a balanced scorecard for your life? What perspectives would you include in it? In what ways would such a balanced scorecard help you attain success in life?

summary

In the traditional approaches to assessing a firm's internal environment, the primary goal of managers would be to determine their firm's relative strengths and weaknesses. Such is the role of SWOT analysis, wherein managers analyze their firm's strengths and weaknesses as well as the opportunities and threats in the external environment. In this chapter, we discussed why this may be a good starting point but hardly the best approach to take in performing a sound analysis. There are many limitations to SWOT analysis, including its static perspective, its potential to overemphasize a single dimension of a firm's strategy, and the likelihood that a firm's strengths do not necessarily help the firm create value or competitive advantages.

We identified two frameworks that serve to complement SWOT analysis in assessing a firm's internal environment: value-chain analysis and the resource-based view of the firm. In conducting a value-chain analysis, first divide the firm into a series of value-creating activities. These include primary activities such as inbound logistics, operations, and service as well as support activities such as procurement and human resource management. Then analyze how each activity adds value as well as how *interrelationships* among value activities in the firm and among the firm and its customers and suppliers add value. Thus, instead of merely determining a firm's strengths and weaknesses per se, you analyze them in the overall context of the firm and its relationships with customers and suppliers—the value system.

The resource-based view of the firm considers the firm as a bundle of resources: tangible resources, intangible resources, and organizational capabilities. Competitive advantages that are sustainable over time generally arise from the creation of bundles of resources and capabilities. For advantages to be sustainable, four criteria must be satisfied: value, rarity, difficulty in imitation, and difficulty in substitution. Such an evaluation requires a sound knowledge of the competitive context in which the firm exists. The owners of a business may not capture all of the value created by the firm. The appropriation of value created by a firm between the owners and employees is determined by four factors: employee bargaining power, replacement cost, employee exit costs, and manager bargaining power.

An internal analysis of the firm would not be complete unless you evaluate its performance and make the appropriate comparisons. Determining a firm's performance requires an analysis of its financial situation as well as a review of how well it is satisfying a broad range of stakeholders, including customers, employees, and stockholders. We discussed the concept of the balanced scorecard, in which four perspectives must be addressed: customer, internal business, innovation and learning, and financial. Central to this concept is the idea that the interests of various stakeholders can be interrelated. We provide examples of how indicators of employee satisfaction lead to higher levels of customer satisfaction, which in turn lead to higher levels of financial performance. Thus, improving a firm's performance does not need to involve making trade-offs among different stakeholders. Assessing the firm's performance is also more useful if it is evaluated in terms of how it changes over time, compares with industry norms, and compares with key competitors.

SUMMARY REVIEW QUESTIONS

1. SWOT analysis is a technique to analyze the internal and external environments of a firm. What are its advantages and disadvantages?
2. Briefly describe the primary and support activities in a firm's value chain.
3. How can managers create value by establishing important relationships among the value-chain activities both within their firm and between the firm and its customers and suppliers?
4. Briefly explain the four criteria for sustainability of competitive advantages.
5. Under what conditions are employees and managers able to appropriate some of the value created by their firm?
6. What are the advantages and disadvantages of conducting a financial ratio analysis of a firm?
7. Summarize the concept of the balanced scorecard. What are its main advantages?

key terms

value-chain analysis 76
primary activities 77
support activities 77
inbound logistics 77
operations 78
outbound logistics 78
marketing and sales 79
service 80
procurement 80
technology development 82
human resource management 82
general administration 84
interrelationships 85
resource-based view of the firm 88
tangible resources 88
intangible resources 89
organizational capabilities 90
path dependency 92
causal ambiguity 92
social complexity 92
financial ratio analysis 97
balanced scorecard 100
customer perspective 100
internal business perspective 100
innovation and learning perspective 100
financial perspective 101

experiential exercise

Caterpillar is a leading firm in the construction and mining equipment industry with extensive global operations. It has approximately 114,000 employees, and its revenues were $55 billion in 2014. In addition to its manufacturing and logistics operations, Caterpillar is well known for its superb service and parts supply, and it provides retail financing for its equipment.

Below, we address several questions that focus on Caterpillar's value-chain activities and the interrelationships among them as well as whether or not the firm is able to attain sustainable competitive advantage(s).

1. Where in Caterpillar's value chain is the firm creating value for its customers?

Value-Chain Activity	Yes/No	How Does Caterpillar Create Value for the Customer?
Primary:		
Inbound logistics		
Operations		
Outbound logistics		
Marketing and sales		
Service		
Support:		
Procurement		
Technology development		
Human resource management		
General administration		

2. What are the important relationships among Caterpillar's value-chain activities? What are the important interdependencies? For each activity, identify the relationships and interdependencies.

	Inbound logistics	Operations	Outbound logistics	Marketing and sales	Service	Procurement	Technology development	Human resource management	General administration
Inbound logistics									
Operations									
Outbound logistics									
Marketing and sales									
Service									
Procurement									
Technology development									
Human resource management									
General administration									

3. What resources, activities, and relationships enable Caterpillar to achieve a sustainable competitive advantage?

Resource/Activity	Is It Valuable?	Is It Rare?	Are There Few Substitutes?	Is It Difficult to Make?
Inbound logistics				
Operations				
Outbound logistics				
Marketing and sales				
Service				
Procurement				
Technology development				
Human resource management				
General administration				

application questions & exercises

1. Using published reports, select two CEOs who have recently made public statements regarding a major change in their firm's strategy. Discuss how the successful implementation of such strategies requires changes in the firm's primary and support activities.
2. Select a firm that competes in an industry in which you are interested. Drawing upon published financial reports, complete a financial ratio analysis. Based on changes over time and a comparison with industry norms, evaluate the firm's strengths and weaknesses in terms of its financial position.
3. How might exemplary human resource practices enhance and strengthen a firm's value-chain activities?
4. Using the Internet, look up your university or college. What are some of its key value-creating activities that provide competitive advantages? Why?

ethics questions

1. What are some of the ethical issues that arise when a firm becomes overly zealous in advertising its products?
2. What are some of the ethical issues that may arise from a firm's procurement activities? Are you aware of any of these issues from your personal experience or businesses you are familiar with?

references

1. Sheehan, M. 2014. How China's electric car dreams became a PR nightmare in America. www.huffingtonpost.com, April 1: np; Jullens, J. 2013. How emerging giants can take on the world. *Harvard Business Review*, 91(12): 121–125; and *finance.yahoo.com*.
2. Our discussion of the value chain will draw on Porter, M. E. 1985. *Competitive advantage:* chap. 2. New York: Free Press.
3. Dyer, J. H. 1996. Specialized supplier networks as a source of competitive advantage: Evidence from the auto industry. *Strategic Management Journal*, 17: 271–291.
4. For an insightful perspective on value-chain analysis, refer to Stabell, C. B. & Fjeldstad, O. D. 1998. Configuring value for competitive advantage: On chains, shops, and networks. *Strategic Management Journal*, 19: 413–437. The authors develop concepts of value chains, value shops, and value networks to extend the value-creation logic across a broad range of industries. Their work builds on the seminal contributions of Porter, 1985, op. cit., and others who have addressed how firms create value through key interrelationships among value-creating activities.
5. Ibid.
6. Maynard, M. 1999. Toyota promises custom order in 5 days. *USA Today*, August 6: B1.
7. Shaw Industries. 1999. Annual report: 14–15.
8. Fisher, M. L. 1997. What is the right supply chain for your product? *Harvard Business Review*, 75(2): 105–116.
9. Jackson, M. 2001. Bringing a dying brand back to life. *Harvard Business Review*, 79(5): 53–61.
10. Anderson, J. C. & Nmarus, J. A. 2003. Selectively pursuing more of your customer's business. *MIT Sloan Management Review*, 44(3): 42–50.
11. Insights on advertising are addressed in Rayport, J. F. 2008. Where is advertising going? Into 'stitials. *Harvard Business Review*, 66(5): 18–20.
12. Reiter, C. 2011. BMW gets its close-up, at Audi's expense. *Bloomberg Businessweek*, December 19–December 25: 24–25.
13. For a scholarly discussion on the procurement of technology components, read Hoetker, G. 2005. How much you know versus how well I know you: Selecting a supplier for a technically innovative component. *Strategic Management Journal*, 26(1): 75–96.

14. For a discussion on criteria to use when screening suppliers for back-office functions, read Feeny, D., Lacity, M., & Willcocks, L. P. 2005. Taking the measure of outsourcing providers. *MIT Sloan Management Review*, 46(3): 41–48.
15. For a study investigating sourcing practices, refer to Safizadeh, M. H., Field, J. M., & Ritzman, L. P. 2008. Sourcing practices and boundaries of the firm in the financial services industry. *Strategic Management Journal*, 29(1): 79–92.
16. Imperato, G. 1998. How to give good feedback. *Fast Company*, September: 144–156.
17. Bensaou, B. M. & Earl, M. 1998. The right mindset for managing information technology. *Harvard Business Review*, 96(5): 118–128.
18. A discussion of R&D in the pharmaceutical industry is in Garnier, J-P. 2008. Rebuilding the R&D engine in big pharma. *Harvard Business Review*, 66(5): 68–76.
19. Chick, S. E., Huchzermeier, A., & Netessine, S. 2014. Europe's solution factories. *Harvard Business Review*, 92(4): 111–115.
20. Ulrich, D. 1998. A new mandate for human resources. *Harvard Business Review*, 96(1): 124–134.
21. A study of human resource management in China is Li, J., Lam, K., Sun, J. J. M., & Liu, S. X. Y. 2008. Strategic resource management, institutionalization, and employment modes: An empirical study in China. *Strategic Management Journal*, 29(3): 337–342.
22. Wood, J. 2003. Sharing jobs and working from home: The new face of the airline industry. *AviationCareer.net:* February 21.
23. Green, S., Hasan, F., Immelt, J. Marks, M., & Meiland, D. 2003. In search of global leaders. *Harvard Business Review*, 81(8): 38–45.
24. For insights on the role of information systems integration in fostering innovation, refer to Cash, J. I. Jr., Earl, M. J., & Morison, R. 2008. Teaming up to crack innovation and enterprise integration. *Harvard Business Review*, 66(11): 90–100.
25. For a cautionary note on the use of IT, refer to McAfee, A. 2003. When too much IT knowledge is a dangerous thing. *MIT Sloan Management Review*, 44(2): 83–90.
26. For an interesting perspective on some of the potential downsides of close customer and supplier relationships, refer to Anderson, E. & Jap, S. D. 2005. The dark side of close relationships. *MIT Sloan Management Review*, 46(3): 75–82.
27. Day, G. S. 2003. Creating a superior customer-relating capability. *MIT Sloan Management Review*, 44(3): 77–82.
28. To gain insights on the role of electronic technologies in enhancing a firm's connections to outside suppliers and customers, refer to Lawrence, T. B., Morse, E. A., & Fowler, S. W. 2005. Managing your portfolio of connections. *MIT Sloan Management Review*, 46(2): 59–66.
29. IBM Global CEO Study, p. 27.
30. Verhoef, P. C., Beckers, S. F. M., & van Doorn, J. 2013. Understand the perils of co-creation. *Harvard Business Review*, 91(9): 28; and Winston, A. S. 2014. *The big pivot.* Boston: Harvard Business Review Press.
31. Collis, D. J. & Montgomery, C. A. 1995. Competing on resources: Strategy in the 1990's. *Harvard Business Review*, 73(4): 119–128; and Barney, J. 1991. Firm resources and sustained competitive advantage. *Journal of Management*, 17(1): 99–120.
32. For critiques of the resource-based view of the firm, refer to Sirmon, D. G., Hitt, M. A., & Ireland, R. D. 2007. Managing firm resources in dynamic environments to create value: Looking inside the black box. *Academy of Management Review*, 32(1): 273–292; and Newbert, S. L. 2007. Empirical research on the resource-based view of the firm: An assessment and suggestions for future research. *Strategic Management Journal*, 28(2): 121–146.
33. Henkoff, R. 1993. Companies that train the best. *Fortune,* March 22: 83; and Dess & Picken, *Beyond productivity,* p. 98.
34. Gaines-Ross, L. 2010. Reputation warfare. *Harvard Business Review,* 88(12): 70–76.
35. Barney, J. B. 1986. Types of competition and the theory of strategy: Towards an integrative framework. *Academy of Management Review*, 11(4): 791–800.
36. Harley-Davidson. 1993. Annual report.
37. Stetler, B. 2008. Griping online? Comcast hears and talks back. *nytimes.com,* July 25: np.
38. For a rigorous, academic treatment of the origin of capabilities, refer to Ethiraj, S. K., Kale, P., Krishnan, M. S., & Singh, J. V. 2005. Where do capabilities come from and how do they matter? A study of the software services industry. *Strategic Management Journal*, 26(1): 25–46.
39. For an academic discussion on methods associated with organizational capabilities, refer to Dutta, S., Narasimhan, O., & Rajiv, S. 2005. Conceptualizing and measuring capabilities: Methodology and empirical application. *Strategic Management Journal*, 26(3): 277–286.
40. Lorenzoni, G. & Lipparini, A. 1999. The leveraging of interfirm relationships as a distinctive organizational capability: A longitudinal study. *Strategic Management Journal*, 20: 317–338.
41. Andersen, M. M. op. cit, p. 209.
42. A study investigating the sustainability of competitive advantage is Newbert, S. L. 2008. Value, rareness, competitive advantages, and performance: A conceptual-level empirical investigation of the resource-based view of the firm. *Strategic Management Journal*, 29(7): 745–768.
43. Arikan, A. M. & McGahan, A. M. 2010. The development of capabilities in new firms. *Strategic Management Journal*, 31(1): 1–18.
44. Barney, J. 1991. Firm resources and sustained competitive advantage. *Journal of Management,* 17(1): 99–120.
45. Barney, 1986, op. cit. Our discussion of inimitability and substitution draws upon this source.
46. A study that investigates the performance implications of imitation is Ethiraj, S. K. & Zhu, D. H. 2008. Performance effects of imitative entry. *Strategic Management Journal*, 29(8): 797–818.
47. Sirmon, D. G., Hitt, M. A., Arregale, J.-L. & Campbell, J. T. 2010. The dynamic interplay of capability strengths and weaknesses: Investigating the bases of temporary competitive advantage. *Strategic Management Journal*, 31(13): 1386–1409.
48. Scherzer, L. 2012. Groupon and deal sites see skepticism replacing promise. *finance.yahoo.com,* November 30: np; The dismal scoop on Groupon. 2011. *The Economist,* October 22: 81; Slater, D. 2012. Are daily deals done? *Fast Company;* and Danna, D. 2012. Groupon & daily deals competition. *beta.fool.com,* June 15: np.
49. Deephouse, D. L. 1999. To be different, or to be the same? It's a question (and theory) of strategic balance. *Strategic Management Journal,* 20: 147–166.

50. Karlgaard, R. 2014. *The soft edge.* San Francisco: Jossey-Bass.
51. Yeoh, P. L. & Roth, K. 1999. An empirical analysis of sustained advantage in the U.S. pharmaceutical industry: Impact of firm resources and capabilities. *Strategic Management Journal,* 20: 637–653.
52. Robins, J. A. & Wiersema, M. F. 2000. Strategies for unstructured competitive environments: Using scarce resources to create new markets. In Bresser, R. F., et al. (Eds.), *Winning strategies in a deconstructing world:* 201–220. New York: Wiley.
53. Graser, M. 2013. Blockbuster chiefs lacked the vision to see how the industry was shifting under the video rental chain's feet. *www.variety.com,* November 12: np; Kellmurray, B. 2013. Learning from Blockbuster's failure to adapt. *www.abovethefoldmag.com,* November 13: np; and Downes, L. & Nunes, P. 2014. *Big bang disruption.* New York: Penguin.
54. Amit, R. & Schoemaker, J. H. 1993. Strategic assets and organizational rent. *Strategic Management Journal,* 14(1): 33–46; Collis, D. J. & Montgomery, C. A. 1995. Competing on resources: Strategy in the 1990's. *Harvard Business Review,* 73(4): 118–128; Coff, R. W. 1999. When competitive advantage doesn't lead to performance: The resource-based view and stakeholder bargaining power. *Organization Science,* 10(2): 119–133; and Blyler, M. & Coff, R. W. 2003. Dynamic capabilities, social capital, and rent appropriation: Ties that split pies. *Strategic Management Journal,* 24: 677–686.
55. Munk, N. 1998. The new organization man. *Fortune,* March 16: 62–74.
56. Coff, op. cit.
57. Anonymous. 2013. "All of them are overpaid": Bank CEOs got average 7.7% raise. *www.moneynews.com,* June 3: np.
58. We have focused our discussion on how internal stakeholders (e.g., employees, managers, and top executives) may appropriate a firm's profits (or rents). For an interesting discussion of how a firm's innovations may be appropriated by external stakeholders (e.g., customers, suppliers) as well as competitors, refer to Grant, R. M. 2002. *Contemporary strategy analysis* (4th ed.): 335–340. Malden, MA: Blackwell.
59. Luehrman, T. A. 1997. What's it worth? A general manager's guide to valuation. *Harvard Business Review,* 45(3): 132–142.
60. See, for example, Kaplan, R. S. & Norton, D. P. 1992. The balanced scorecard: Measures that drive performance. *Harvard Business Review,* 69(1): 71–79.
61. Hitt, M. A., Ireland, R. D., & Stadter, G. 1982. Functional importance of company performance: Moderating effects of grand strategy and industry type. *Strategic Management Journal,* 3: 315–330.
62. *finance.yahoo.com.*
63. Kaplan & Norton, op. cit.
64. Ibid.
65. For a discussion of the relative value of growth versus increasing margins, read Mass, N. J. 2005. The relative value of growth. *Harvard Business Review,* 83(4): 102–112.
66. Rucci, A. J., Kirn, S. P., & Quinn, R. T. 1998. The employee-customer-profit chain at Sears. *Harvard Business Review,* 76(1): 82–97.
67. Our discussion draws upon: Angel, R. & Rampersad, H. 2005. Do scorecards add up? *camagazine.com.* May: np.; and Niven, P. 2002. *Balanced scorecard step by step: Maximizing performance and maintaining results.* New York: John Wiley & Sons.

photo credits

Page 74: © Anatoli Styf/Getty Images/RF

Recognizing a Firm's Intellectual Assets

Moving beyond a Firm's Tangible Resources

chapter 4

After reading this chapter, you should have a good understanding of the following learning objectives:

LO4.1 Why the management of knowledge professionals and knowledge itself are so critical in today's organizations.

LO4.2 The importance of recognizing the interdependence of attracting, developing, and retaining human capital.

LO4.3 The key role of social capital in leveraging human capital within and across the firm.

LO4.4 The importance of social networks in knowledge management and in promoting career success.

LO4.5 The vital role of technology in leveraging knowledge and human capital.

LO4.6 Why "electronic" or "virtual" teams are critical in combining and leveraging knowledge in organizations and how they can be made more effective.

LO4.7 The challenge of protecting intellectual property and the importance of a firm's dynamic capabilities.

PART 1: STRATEGIC ANALYSIS

Learning from Mistakes

In September 2008, Bank of America purchased Merrill Lynch (ML) in the depths of the financial crisis for $50 billion. It seemed like a pretty good deal. However, six months later Bank of America reported $15 billion in losses due to ML's exposure in toxic mortgage-backed securities bonds. This resulted in a class-action lawsuit, with $2.43 billion going to shareholders and $150 million to the Securities and Exchange Commission.[1] Despite these early legal woes, ML has helped bolster Bank of America, contributing roughly half the bank's revenue and the bulk of its profits since 2009, according to bank analysts. From 2009 to 2011, Merrill Lynch made $164.4 billion in revenue and $31.9 billion in total profits. Bank of America over that period, as a total entity, made $326.8 billion in revenue and $5.5 billion in profits. Thus, while the bank was hemorrhaging cash and facing a struggling economy, ML was standing strong and keeping the bank afloat with its army of 16,000 brokers.

Investment bankers, senior executives, and brokers receive Bank of America stock as a significant portion of their compensation in order to align their interests with those of Bank of America. Yet hundreds of high-performing brokers and financial advisers at Merrill Lynch have recently fled the firm. What happened?

Bank of America mismanaged its most valuable asset—its human capital. While it tried to promote the corporate initiative of cross-selling Bank of America's banking products and services to ML's clients, it lost many of its star employees and, of course, their networks of high-net-worth clients in the process.

Leveraging ML's sales force was the focus of Brian Moynihan, chief executive officer. He cited cross-selling as key opportunities for growth, that is, turning brokerage clients into banking clients, and vice versa. However, as Sanford C. Bernstein analyst Brad Hintz pointed out, "The payout on banking products is less to brokers, and they're being asked to share client relationships with Bank of America. That's never a good thing for a broker." Bank of America poorly executed its cross-selling strategy. This left both clients and brokers demanding higher-quality levels of service and questioning why they were associated with Bank of America in the first place. Brokers who were managing over $1 billion in client assets were getting calls from their clients dealing with elementary banking and checking issues. For example, one high-end broker was called about misprinted checks! Additionally, the special white-glove service that ML brokers were accustomed to giving their high-value clients was falling short: Mortgages for ultra-high-net-worth individuals were taking nine months to complete, and the standard practice of charging maintenance fees to cover expenses when accounts fell below their minimum could not be waived at the discretion of the broker.

Bank of America also had some inflexible human resource practices that alienated the brokers. For example, Patrick Rush had been teaching continuing education courses focusing on retirement planning at local colleges. Although Merrill saw value in his teaching and community involvement, Bank of America told him he had to stop. Rush left in 2011 and started his own wealth management firm.

Clearly, Bank of America did not realize that its brokers are highly valuable assets (along with their high-net-worth clients). It paid the price for not fostering the environment for these employees to flourish.

Discussion Questions

1. What actions should Bank of America take to retain its top investment advisers?
2. Can it do this while still leveraging value?
3. Should Bank of America continue to cross-sell?

Managers are always looking for stellar professionals who can take their organizations to the next level. However, attracting talent is a necessary but *not* sufficient condition for success. In today's knowledge economy, it does not matter how big your stock of resources is—whether it be top talent, physical resources, or financial capital. Rather, the question becomes: How good is the organization at attracting top talent and leveraging that talent to produce a stream of products and services valued by the marketplace?

Bank of America's problems with Merrill Lynch, its brokerage division, illustrate issues related to effectively developing and retaining talent. Faced with pressures to cross-sell Bank of America products to their high-net-worth clients, many Merrill brokers have chosen to leave and, of course, taken their clients with them. Restrictive personnel policies, such as barring them from teaching continuing education courses, didn't help either. As a recent article commented, "Merrill's best assets have legs. A heavy corporate hand could send them sprinting."

In this chapter, we also address how human capital can be leveraged in an organization. We point out the important roles of social capital and technology.

The Central Role of Knowledge in Today's Economy

LO4.1
Why the management of knowledge professionals and knowledge itself are so critical in today's organizations.

Central to our discussion is an enormous change that has accelerated over the past few decades and its implications for the strategic management of organizations.[2] For most of the 20th century, managers focused on tangible resources such as land, equipment, and money as well as intangibles such as brands, image, and customer loyalty. Efforts were directed more toward the efficient allocation of labor and capital—the two traditional factors of production.

How times have changed. In the last quarter century, employment in the manufacturing sector declined at a significant rate. Today only 9 percent of the U.S. workforce is employed in this sector, compared to 21 percent in 1980.[3] In contrast, the service sector grew from 73 percent of the workforce in 1980 to 86 percent by 2012.

The knowledge-worker segment, in particular, is growing dramatically. Using a broad definition, it is estimated that knowledge workers currently outnumber other types of workers in the United States by at least four to one—they represent between a quarter and a half of all workers in advanced economies. Recent popular press has gone so far as to suggest that, due to the increased speed and competitiveness of modern business, all modern employees are knowledge workers.

knowledge economy
an economy where wealth is created through the effective management of knowledge workers instead of by the efficient control of physical and financial assets.

In the **knowledge economy,** wealth is increasingly created by effective management of knowledge workers instead of by the efficient control of physical and financial assets. The growing importance of knowledge, coupled with the move by labor markets to reward knowledge work, tells us that investing in a company is, in essence, buying a set of talents, capabilities, skills, and ideas—intellectual capital—not physical and financial resources.[4]

Consider an example. Merck didn't become the "Most Admired" company, for seven consecutive years in *Fortune*'s annual survey, because it can manufacture pills, but because its scientists can discover medicines. P. Roy Vagelos, former CEO of Merck, the $43 billion pharmaceutical giant, during its long run atop the "Most Admired" survey, said, "A low-value product can be made by anyone anywhere. When you have knowledge no one else has access to—that's dynamite. We guard our research even more carefully than our financial assets."[5]

To apply some numbers to our arguments, let's ask, What's a company worth?[6] Start with the "big three" financial statements: income statement, balance sheet, and statement of cash flow. If these statements tell a story that investors find useful, then a company's

EXHIBIT 4.1 Ratio of Market Value to Book Value for Selected Companies

Company	Annual Sales ($ billions)	Market Value ($ billions)	Book Value ($ billions)	Ratio of Market to Book Value
Apple	182.8	641.2	112.5	5.7
Microsoft	86.8	385.4	89.8	4.3
Oracle	38.3	196.4	47.5	4.1
Intel	55.0	175.8	55.0	3.2
Nucor	21.0	15.6	7.6	2.1
General Motors	156.8	56.0	39.5	1.4

Note: The data on market valuations are as of January 5, 2015. All other financial data are based on the most recently available balance sheets and income statements.

Source: *finance.yahoo.com*.

market value* should roughly (but not precisely, because the market looks forward and the books look backward) be the same as the value that accountants ascribe to it—the book value of the firm. However, this is not the case. A study compared the market value with the book value of 3,500 U.S. companies over a period of two decades. In 1978 the two were similar: Book value was 95 percent of market value. However, market values and book values have diverged significantly. By April 2015, the S&P industrials were—on average—trading at 2.89 times book value.[7] Robert A. Howell, an expert on the changing role of finance and accounting, muses, "The big three financial statements . . . are about as useful as an 80-year-old Los Angeles road map."

The gap between a firm's market value and book value is far greater for knowledge-intensive corporations than for firms with strategies based primarily on tangible assets.[8] Exhibit 4.1 shows the ratio of market-to-book value for some well-known companies. In firms where knowledge and the management of knowledge workers are relatively important contributors to developing products and services—and physical resources are less critical—the ratio of market-to-book value tends to be much higher.

As shown in Exhibit 4.1, firms such as Apple, Google, Microsoft, and Oracle have very high market value to book value ratios because of their high investment in knowledge resources and technological expertise. In contrast, firms in more traditional industry sectors such as Nucor and Southwest Airlines have relatively low market-to-book ratios. This reflects their greater investment in physical resources and lower investment in knowledge resources. A firm like Intel has a market-to-book value ratio that falls between the above two groups of firms. This is because its high level of investment in knowledge resources is matched by a correspondingly huge investment in plant and equipment. For example, Intel invested $3 billion to build a fabrication facility in Chandler, Arizona.[9]

Many writers have defined **intellectual capital** as the difference between a firm's market value and book value—that is, a measure of the value of a firm's intangible assets.[10] This broad definition includes assets such as reputation, employee loyalty and commitment, customer relationships, company values, brand names, and the experience and skills of employees.[11] Thus, simplifying, we have:

Intellectual capital = Market value of firm − Book value of firm

intellectual capital the difference between the market value of the firm and the book value of the firm, including assets such as reputation, employee loyalty and commitment, customer relationships, company values, brand names, and the experience and skills of employees.

*The market value of a firm is equal to the value of a share of its common stock times the number of shares outstanding. The book value of a firm is primarily a measure of the value of its tangible assets. It can be calculated by the formula Total assets − Total liabilities.

How do companies create value in the knowledge-intensive economy? The general answer is to attract and leverage human capital effectively through mechanisms that create products and services of value over time.

First, **human capital** is the "*individual* capabilities, knowledge, skills, and experience of the company's employees and managers."[12] This knowledge is relevant to the task at hand, as well as the capacity to add to this reservoir of knowledge, skills, and experience through learning.[13]

Second, **social capital** is "the network of relationships that individuals have throughout the organization." Relationships are critical in sharing and leveraging knowledge and in acquiring resources.[14] Social capital can extend beyond the organizational boundaries to include relationships between the firm and its suppliers, customers, and alliance partners.[15]

Third is the concept of "knowledge," which comes in two different forms. First, there is **explicit knowledge** that is codified, documented, easily reproduced, and widely distributed, such as engineering drawings, software code, and patents.[16] The other type of knowledge is **tacit knowledge.** That is in the minds of employees and is based on their experiences and backgrounds.[17] Tacit knowledge is shared only with the consent and participation of the individual.

New knowledge is constantly created through the continual interaction of explicit and tacit knowledge. Consider two software engineers working together on a computer code. The computer code is the explicit knowledge. By sharing ideas based on each individual's experience—that is, their tacit knowledge—they create new knowledge when they modify the code. Another important issue is the role of "socially complex processes," which include leadership, culture, and trust.[18] These processes play a central role in the creation of knowledge.[19] They represent the "glue" that holds the organization together and helps to create a working environment where individuals are more willing to share their ideas, work in teams, and, in the end, create products and services of value.[20]

Numerous books have been written on the subject of knowledge management and the central role that it has played in creating wealth in organizations and countries throughout the developed world.[21] Here, we focus on some of the key issues that organizations must address to compete through knowledge.

We will now turn our discussion to the central resource itself—human capital—and some guidelines on how it can be attracted/selected, developed, and retained.[22] Tom Stewart, former editor of the *Harvard Business Review,* noted that organizations must also undergo significant efforts to protect their human capital. A firm may "diversify the ownership of vital knowledge by emphasizing teamwork, guard against obsolescence by developing learning programs, and shackle key people with golden handcuffs."[23] In addition, people are less likely to leave an organization if there are effective structures to promote teamwork and information sharing, strong leadership that encourages innovation, and cultures that demand excellence and ethical behavior. Such issues are central to this chapter. Although we touch on these issues throughout this chapter, we provide more detail in later chapters. We discuss organizational controls (culture, rewards, and boundaries) in Chapter 9, organization structure and design in Chapter 10, and a variety of leadership and entrepreneurship topics in Chapters 11 and 12.

Human Capital: The Foundation of Intellectual Capital

Take away my people, but leave my factories and soon grass will grow on the factory floors. . . . Take away my factories, but leave my people and soon we will have a new and better factory.[24]

—Andrew Carnegie, Steel industry legend

The importance of talent to organization success is hardly new. Organizations must recruit talented people—employees at all levels with the proper sets of skills and capabilities coupled with the right values and attitudes. Such skills and attitudes must be continually developed, strengthened, and reinforced, and each employee must be motivated and his or her efforts focused on the organization's goals and objectives.[25]

The rise to prominence of knowledge workers as a vital source of competitive advantage is changing the balance of power in today's organization.[26] Knowledge workers place professional development and personal enrichment (financial and otherwise) above company loyalty. Attracting, recruiting, and hiring the "best and the brightest" is a critical first step in the process of building intellectual capital. As noted by law professor Orly Lobel, *talent wants to be free:*[27]

> Companies like Microsoft, Google, and Facebook are so hungry for talent that they acquire (or, as the tech-buzz is now calling it, acq-hire) entire start-ups only to discard the product and keep the teams, founders, and engineers.

Hiring is only the first of three processes in which all successful organizations must engage to build and leverage their human capital. Firms must also *develop* employees to fulfill their full potential to maximize their joint contributions.[28] Finally, the first two processes are for naught if firms can't provide the working environment and intrinsic and extrinsic rewards to *engage* their best and brightest.[29] Interestingly, a recent Gallup study showed that companies whose workers are the most engaged outperform those with the least engaged by a significant amount: 16 percent higher profitability, 18 percent higher productivity, and 25 to 49 percent lower turnover (depending on the industry).[30] The last benefit can really be significant: Software leader SAP calculated that "for each percentage point that our retention rate goes up or down, the impact on our operating profit is approximately $81 million."

These activities are highly interrelated. We would like to suggest the imagery of a three-legged stool (see Exhibit 4.2).[31] If one leg is weak or broken, the stool collapses.

To illustrate such interdependence, poor hiring impedes the effectiveness of development and retention processes. In a similar vein, ineffective retention efforts place additional burdens on hiring and development. Consider the following anecdote, provided by Jeffrey Pfeffer of the Stanford University Graduate School of Business:

> Not long ago, I went to a large, fancy San Francisco law firm—where they treat their associates like dog doo and where the turnover is very high. I asked the managing partner about the turnover rate. He said, "A few years ago, it was 25 percent, and now we're up to 30 percent." I asked him how the firm had responded to that trend. He said, "We increased our recruiting." So I asked him, "What kind of doctor would you be if your patient was bleeding faster and faster, and your only response was to increase the speed of the transfusion?"[32]

EXHIBIT 4.2 Human Capital: Three Interdependent Activities

Attracting Human Capital ↔ Developing Human Capital
↕ ↕
Retaining Human Capital

4.1 STRATEGY SPOTLIGHT — ENVIRONMENTAL SUSTAINABILITY

CAN GREEN STRATEGIES ATTRACT AND RETAIN TALENT?

Competing successfully for top talent and retaining high-performing employees are critical factors in an organization's success. Employee recruiting and turnover are, of course, very costly. Losing and replacing a top talent can cost companies up to 200 percent of an employee's annual salary, according to *Engaged! Outbehave Your Competition to Create Customers for Life*.

Today, some 40 percent of job seekers read a company's sustainability report, according to a survey commissioned by the Global Reporting Initiative (GRI). Prospective employees can also riffle through Google in seconds and unearth a myriad of sustainability news and accolades, including an Interbrand "Top 50 Global Green Brand" ranking. Further, a poll on green employment by MonsterTRAK.com, a job website geared toward students and entry-level hires, found that 80 percent of young professionals are interested in securing a job that has a positive impact on the environment and 92 percent would be more inclined to work for a company that is environmentally friendly.

Below, we discuss examples of green initiatives by two well-known companies that help attract and retain talent:

- Intel's "Green Intel" intranet portal, environmental sustainability network, and environmental excellence awards are beginning to yield benefits for the company. "Intel's employee engagement has resulted in increased employee loyalty, more company pride, and improved morale," according to Carrie Freeman, a sustainability strategist at the firm. Intel managers expect the next organizational health survey will show increased levels of employee pride and satisfaction with their work, which are considered to be good predictors of employee retention.

- Hewlett-Packard installed a 1.1-megawatt system of 6,256 SunPower solar panels at its San Diego facility. The system is projected to save the company $750,000 during the next 15 years, while providing more than 10 percent of the facility's power. As part of its agreement with SunPower, HP started an employee program offering joint rebates to install solar electricity for employees' homes. The program links the company's initiatives to steps employees can take and provides a unique employee benefit not available at all companies.

Sources: Earley, K. 2014. Sustainabilty gives HR teams an edge in attracting and retaining talent. www.theguardian.com, February 20: np; Anonymous. 2010. The business case for environmental and sustainability employee education. *National Environmental Education Foundation*, November: np; Mattioli, D. 2007. How going green draws talent, cuts costs. *Wall Street Journal*, November 13: B10; and Lederman, G. 2013. *Engaged! Outbehave your competition to create customers for life*. Ashland, OR: Evolve.

Clearly, stepped-up recruiting is a poor substitute for weak retention.[33] Although there are no simple, easy-to-apply answers, we can learn from what leading-edge firms are doing to attract, develop, and retain human capital in today's highly competitive marketplace.[34] Before moving on, Strategy Spotlight 4.1 addresses the importance of a firm's "green" or environmental sustainability strategy in attracting young talent.

Attracting Human Capital

> *In today's world, talent is so critical to the success of what you're doing—their core competencies and how well they fit into your office culture. The combination can be, well, extraordinary. But only if you bring in the right people.*[35]
>
> —Mindy Grossman, CEO of HSN (Home Shopping Network)

The first step in the process of building superior human capital is input control: attracting and selecting the right person.[36] Human resource professionals often approach employee selection from a "lock and key" mentality—that is, fit a key (a job candidate) into a lock (the job). Such an approach involves a thorough analysis of the person and the job. Only then can the right decision be made as to how well the two will fit together. How can you fail, the theory goes, if you get a precise match of knowledge, ability, and skill profiles? Frequently, however, the precise matching approach places its emphasis on task-specific skills (e.g., motor skills, specific information processing capabilities, and communication skills) and puts less emphasis on the broad general knowledge and experience, social skills, values, beliefs, and attitudes of employees.[37]

Many have questioned the precise matching approach. They argue that firms can identify top performers by focusing on key employee mind-sets, attitudes, social skills, and general orientations. If they get these elements right, the task-specific skills can be learned quickly. (This does not imply, however, that task-specific skills are unimportant; rather, it suggests that the requisite skill sets must be viewed as a necessary but not sufficient condition.) This leads us to a popular phrase today that serves as the title of the next section.

"Hire for Attitude, Train for Skill" Organizations are increasingly emphasizing general knowledge and experience, social skills, values, beliefs, and attitudes of employees.[38] Consider Southwest Airlines' hiring practices, which focus on employee values and attitudes. Given its strong team orientation, Southwest uses an "indirect" approach. For example, the interviewing team asks a group of employees to prepare a five-minute presentation about themselves. During the presentations, interviewers observe which candidates enthusiastically support their peers and which candidates focus on polishing their own presentations while the others are presenting.[39] The former are, of course, favored.

Alan Cooper, president of Cooper Software, Inc., in Palo Alto, California, goes further. He cleverly *uses technology* to hone in on the problem-solving ability of his applicants and their attitudes before an interview even takes place. He has devised a "Bozo Filter," an online test that can be applied to any industry. Before you spend time on whether job candidates will work out satisfactorily, find out how their minds work. Cooper advised, "Hiring was a black hole. I don't talk to bozos anymore, because 90 percent of them turn away when they see our test. It's a self-administering bozo filter."[40] How does it work?

> The online test asks questions designed to see how prospective employees approach problem-solving tasks. For example, one key question asks software engineer applicants to design a table-creation software program for Microsoft Word. Candidates provide pencil sketches and a description of the new user interface. Another question used for design communicators asks them to develop a marketing strategy for a new touch-tone phone—directed at consumers in the year 1850. Candidates e-mail their answers back to the company, and the answers are circulated around the firm to solicit feedback. Only candidates with the highest marks get interviews.

Sound Recruiting Approaches and Networking Companies that take hiring seriously must also take recruiting seriously. The number of jobs that successful knowledge-intensive companies must fill is astonishing. Ironically, many companies still have no shortage of applicants. For example, Google, which ranked first on *Fortune*'s 2012 and 2013 "100 Best Companies to Work For," is planning to hire thousands of employees—even though its hiring rate has slowed.[41] The challenge becomes having the right job candidates, not the greatest number of them.

GE Medical Systems, which builds CT scanners and magnetic resonance imaging (MRI) systems, relies extensively on networking. GE has found that current employees are the best source for new ones. Stephen Patscot, VP, human resources, made a few simple changes to double the number of referrals. First, he simplified the process—no complex forms, no bureaucracy, and so on. Second, he increased incentives. Everyone referring a qualified candidate receives a gift certificate from Sears. For referrals who are hired, the "bounty" increases to $2,000. Although this may sound like a lot of money, it is "peanuts" compared to the $15,000 to $20,000 fees that GE typically pays to headhunters for each person hired.[42] Also, when someone refers a former colleague or friend for a job, his or her credibility is on the line. Thus, employees will be careful in recommending people for employment unless they are reasonably confident that these people are good candidates.

Attracting Millennials The Millennial generation has also been termed "Generation Y" or "Echo Boom" and includes people who were born after 1982. Many call them impatient, demanding, or entitled. However, if employers don't provide incentives to attract and retain young workers, somebody else will. Thus, they will be at a competitive disadvantage.[43]

Why? Demographics are on the Millennials' side—within a few years they will outnumber any other generation. The U.S. Bureau of Labor Statistics projects that by 2020 Millennials will make up 40 percent of the workforce. Baby boomers are retiring, and Millennials will be working for the next several decades. Additionally, they have many of the requisite skills to succeed in the future workplace—tech-savviness and the ability to innovate—and they are more racially diverse than any prior generation. Thus, they are better able to relate rapidly to different customs and cultures.

What are some of the "best practices" to attract Millennials and keep them engaged?

- ***Don't fudge the sales pitch.*** High-tech sales presentations and one-on-one attention may be attractive to undergrads. However, the pitch had better match the experience. Consider that today's ultra-connected students can get the lowdown on a company by spending five minutes on a social networking site.
- ***Let them have a life.*** Typically, they are unenthusiastic about their parents' 70- or 80-hour workweeks. Millennials strive for more work-life balance, so liberal vacations become very important. They also want assurances that they can use the vacation time. At KPMG, 80 percent of employees used 40 hours of paid time off in the first six months of a recent year.
- ***No time clocks, please.*** Recent graduates don't mind long hours—if they can work them on their own schedule. Lockheed Martin allows employees to work nine-hour days with every other Friday off. And Chegg, the online textbook service, recently introduced an unlimited vacation policy—turnover rates among the younger workers dropped 50 percent. As noted by its CEO, Dan Rosensweig, "If you provide them with the right environment, they'll work forever."
- ***Give them responsibility.*** A chance to work on fulfilling projects and develop new ones on their own is important. Google urges entry-level employees to spend 20 percent of their time developing new ideas. PepsiCo allows promising young employees to manage small teams in six months.
- ***Feedback and more feedback.*** Career planning advice and frequent performance appraisals are keys to holding on to young hires. Several firms provide new hires with two mentors—a slightly older peer to help them get settled and a senior employee to give long-term guidance.
- ***Giving back matters.*** Today's altruistic young graduates expect to have opportunities for community service. Wells Fargo encourages its employees to teach financial literacy classes in the community. Accenture and Bain allow employees to consult for nonprofits.

A study from the Center for Work-Life Policy sums this issue up rather well: Instead of the traditional plums of prestigious title, powerful position, and concomitant compensation, Millennials value challenging and diverse job opportunities, stimulating colleagues, a well-designed communal workspace, and flexible work options. In fact, 89 percent of Millennials say that flexible work options are an important consideration in choosing an employer.

Developing Human Capital

It is not enough to hire top-level talent and expect that the skills and capabilities of those employees remain current throughout the duration of their employment. Rather, training and development must take place at all levels of the organization.[44] For example, Solectron assembles printed circuit boards and other components for its Silicon Valley clients.[45] Its employees receive an average of 95 hours of company-provided training each year. Chairman Winston Chen observed, "Technology changes so fast that we estimate 20 percent of an engineer's knowledge becomes obsolete each year. Training is an obligation we owe to our employees. If you want high growth and high quality, then training is a big part of the equation."

Leaders who are committed to developing the people who work for them in order to bring out their strengths and enhance their careers will have committed followers. According to James Rogers, CEO of Duke Energy: "One of the biggest things I find in organizations is that people tend to limit their perceptions of themselves and their capabilities, and one of my challenges is to open them up to the possibilities. I have this belief that anybody can do almost anything in the right context."[46]

In addition to training and developing human capital, firms must encourage widespread involvement, monitor and track employee development, and evaluate human capital.[47]

Encouraging Widespread Involvement Developing human capital requires the active involvement of leaders at all levels. It won't be successful if it is viewed only as the responsibility of the human resource department. Each year at General Electric, 200 facilitators, 30 officers, 30 human resource executives, and many young managers actively participate in GE's orientation program at Crotonville, its training center outside New York City. Topics include global competition, winning on the global playing field, and personal examination of the new employee's core values vis-à-vis GE's values. As a senior manager once commented, "There is nothing like teaching Sunday school to force you to confront your own values."

Similarly, A. G. Lafley, Procter & Gamble's former CEO, claimed that he spent 40 percent of his time on personnel.[48] Andy Grove, who was previously Intel's CEO, required all senior people, including himself, to spend at least a week a year teaching high flyers. And Nitin Paranjpe, CEO of Hindustan Unilever, recruits people from campuses and regularly visits high-potential employees in their offices.

Mentoring Mentoring is most often a formal or informal relationship between two people—a senior mentor and a junior protégé.[49] Mentoring can potentially be a valuable influence in professional development in both the public and private sectors. The war for talent is creating challenges within organizations to recruit new talent as well as retain talent.

Mentoring can provide many benefits—to the organization as well as the individual.[50] For the organization, it can help to recruit qualified managers, decrease turnover, fill senior-level positions with qualified professionals, enhance diversity initiatives with senior-level management, and facilitate organizational change efforts. Individuals can also benefit from effective mentoring programs. These benefits include helping newer employees transition into the organization, helping developmental relationships for people who lack access to informal mentoring relationships, and providing support and challenge to people on an organization's "fast track" to positions of higher responsibility.

Mentoring is traditionally viewed as a program to transfer knowledge and experience from more senior managers to up-and-comers. However, many organizations have reinvented it to fit today's highly competitive, knowledge-intensive industries. For example, consider Intel:

> Intel matches people not by job title and years of experience but by specific skills that are in demand. Lory Lanese, Intel's mentor champion at its huge New Mexico plant (with 5,500 employees), states, "This is definitely not a special program for special people." Instead, Intel's program uses an intranet and email to perform the matchmaking, creating relationships that stretch across state lines and national boundaries. Such an approach enables Intel to spread best practices quickly throughout the far-flung organization. Finally, Intel relies on written contracts and tight deadlines to make sure that its mentoring program gets results—and fast.[51]

Intel has also initiated a mentoring program involving its technical assistants (TAs) who work with senior executives. This concept is sometimes referred to as "reverse mentoring" because senior executives benefit from the insights of professionals who have more updated technical skills—but rank lower in the organizational hierarchy. And, not surprisingly, the TAs stand to benefit quite a bit as well. Here are some insights offered by Andy Grove (formerly Intel's CEO):[52]

> In the 1980s I had a marketing manager named Dennis Carter. I probably learned more from him than anyone in my career. He is a genius. He taught me what brands are. I had no idea—I thought a brand was the name on the box. He showed me the connection of brands to strategies. Dennis went on to be Chief Marketing Officer. He was the person responsible for the Pentium name, "Intel Inside;" he came up with all my good ideas.

Monitoring Progress and Tracking Development Whether a firm uses on-site formal training, off-site training (e.g., universities), or on-the-job training, tracking individual progress—and sharing this knowledge with both the employee and key managers—becomes essential. Like many leading-edge firms, GlaxoSmithKline (GSK) places strong emphasis on broader experiences over longer time periods. Dan Phelan, senior vice president and director of human resources, explained, "We ideally follow a two-plus-two-plus-two formula in developing people for top management positions." This reflects the belief that GSK's best people should gain experience in two business units, two functional units (such as finance and marketing), and two countries.

Evaluating Human Capital In today's competitive environment, collaboration and interdependence are vital to organizational success. Individuals must share their knowledge and work constructively to achieve collective, not just individual, goals. However, traditional systems evaluate performance from a single perspective (i.e., "top down") and generally don't address the "softer" dimensions of communications and social skills, values, beliefs, and attitudes.[53]

To address the limitations of the traditional approach, many organizations use **360-degree evaluation and feedback systems.**[54] Here, superiors, direct reports, colleagues, and even internal and external customers rate a person's performance.[55] Managers rate themselves to have a personal benchmark. The 360-degree feedback system complements teamwork, employee involvement, and organizational flattening. As organizations continue to push responsibility downward, traditional top-down appraisal systems become insufficient.[56] For example, a manager who previously managed the performance of 3 supervisors might now be responsible for 10 and is less likely to have the in-depth knowledge needed to appraise and develop them adequately. Exhibit 4.3 provides a portion of GE's 360-degree leadership assessment chart.

At times, a firm's performance assessment methods may get in the way of team success.[57] Microsoft is an example. For many years, the software giant employed a "stack ranking" system as part of its performance evaluation model. With this system, a certain percentage of any team's members would be rated "top performers," "good," "average," "below average," and "poor," regardless of the team's overall performance. Perhaps, in some situations, this type of forced ranking works. However, in Microsoft's case, it had (not too surprisingly!) unintended consequences. Over time, according to inside reports, the stack ranking created a culture in which employees competed with one another rather than against the firm's rivals. And "A" players rarely liked to join groups with other "A" players, because they feared they might be seen as weaker members of the team.

Strategy Spotlight 4.2 provides another cautionary note on evaluation systems: Avoid an overemphasis on internal performance measures that misses the competitive environment a firm faces.

Retaining Human Capital

It has been said that talented employees are like "frogs in a wheelbarrow."[58] They can jump out at any time! By analogy, the organization can either try to force employees to stay in the firm or try to keep them from jumping out by creating incentives.[59] In other

---

360-degree evaluation and feedback systems superiors, direct reports, colleagues, and even external and internal customers rate a person's performance.

4.2 STRATEGY SPOTLIGHT

"I DON'T CARE HOW MANY METRICS YOU GOT RIGHT. YOU FAILED!"

General Motors has long been obsessively inward-looking, according to a writer for *Fortune* magazine. Recently, however, GM has begun to measure success against external rather than internal standards. This represents a major shift in perspective. And it is a good example of the challenge the new CEO, Mary Barra, faces in reversing the firm's competitive position and financial performance.

Bob Lutz, who has been a top executive at all three Detroit carmakers over his 60-year career, provides a colorful example of the flaws inherent in GM's previous approach to performance evaluation. "I had a vehicle line executive come to me with his scorecard. He said, 'I've completed the most successful program in the history of the vehicle line executive system,' and he wanted to talk to me about a bonus. His scorecard had about 50 metrics on it. Each was scored red, yellow, or green, and they were solid green, top to bottom. This was the first time that feat had ever been accomplished."

"I said, 'That's nice. How's the car selling?' He said, 'Oh, it's not selling at all. The public doesn't like it.' I said, 'You failed!'" Lutz believes that the incident illustrates a larger problem—perhaps the most serious of GM's behavioral deficiencies: "Everything was internal criteria. The idiotic assumption was that if you fulfill all the internal criteria, somehow the car will be a success."

Source: Colvin, G. 2014. Mary Barra's (unexpected) opportunity. *Fortune*, September 14: 102–110.

---

words, either today's leaders can provide the challenges, work environment, and incentives to keep productive employees and management from wanting to bail out, or they can use legal means such as employment contracts and noncompete clauses.[60] Firms must prevent the transfer of valuable and sensitive information outside the organization. Failure to do so would be the neglect of a leader's fiduciary responsibility to shareholders. However, greater efforts should be directed at the former (e.g., challenges, good work environment, and incentives), but, as we all know, the latter (e.g., employment contracts and noncompete clauses) have their place.[61]

Vision	• Has developed and communicated a clear, simple, customer-focused vision/direction for the organization.
	• Forward-thinking, stretches horizons, challenges imaginations.
	• Inspires and energizes others to commit to Vision. Captures minds. Leads by example.
	• As appropriate, updates Vision to reflect constant and accelerating change affecting the business.
Customer/Quality Focus	
Integrity	
Accountability/Commitment	
Communication/Influence	
Shared Ownership/Boundaryless	
Team Builder/Empowerment	
Knowledge/Expertise/Intellect	
Initiative/Speed	
Global Mind-Set	

EXHIBIT 4.3 An Excerpt from General Electric's 360-Degree Leadership Assessment Chart

Note: This evaluation system consists of 10 "characteristics"—Vision, Customer/Quality Focus, Integrity, and so on. Each of these characteristics has four "performance criteria." For illustrative purposes, the four performance criteria of "Vision" are included.

Source: Adapted from Slater, R. 1994. *Get Better or Get Beaten:* 152–155. Burr Ridge, IL: Irwin Professional Publishing.

Gary Burnison, CEO of Korn/Ferry International, the world's largest executive search firm, provides an insight on the importance of employee retention:[62]

> How do you extend the life of an employee? This is not an environment where you work for an organization for 20 years. But if you can extend it from three years to six years, that has an enormous impact. Turnover is a huge hidden cost in a profit-and-loss statement that nobody ever focuses on. If there was a line item that showed that, I guarantee you'd have the attention of a CEO.

Identifying with an Organization's Mission and Values People who identify with and are more committed to the core mission and values of the organization are less likely to stray or bolt to the competition. For example, take the perspective of the late Steve Jobs, Apple's widely admired former CEO:[63]

> When I hire somebody really senior, competence is the ante. They have to be really smart. But the real issue for me is: Are they going to fall in love with Apple? Because if they fall in love with Apple, everything else will take care of itself. They'll want to do what's best for Apple, not what's best for them, what's best for Steve, or anyone else.

"Tribal loyalty" is another key factor that links people to the organization.[64] A tribe is not the organization as a whole (unless it is very small). Rather, it is teams, communities of practice, and other groups within an organization or occupation.

Brian Hall, CEO of Values Technology in Santa Cruz, California, documented a shift in people's emotional expectations from work. From the 1950s on, a "task-first" relationship—"Tell me what the job is, and let's get on with it"—dominated employee attitudes. Emotions and personal life were checked at the door. In the past few years, a "relationship-first" set of values has challenged the task orientation. Hall believes that it will become dominant. Employees want to share attitudes and beliefs as well as workspace.

Challenging Work and a Stimulating Environment Arthur Schawlow, winner of the 1981 Nobel Prize in physics, was asked what made the difference between highly creative and less creative scientists. His reply: "The labor of love aspect is very important. The most successful scientists often are not the most talented.[65] But they are the ones impelled by curiosity. They've got to know what the answer is."[66] Such insights highlight the importance of intrinsic motivation: the motivation to work on something because it is exciting, satisfying, or personally challenging.[67]

One way firms keep highly mobile employees motivated and challenged is through opportunities that lower barriers to an employee's mobility within a company. For example, Shell Oil Company has created an "open sourcing" model for talent. Jobs are listed on its intranet, and, with a two-month notice, employees can go to work on anything that interests them.

Financial and Nonfinancial Rewards and Incentives Financial rewards are a vital organizational control mechanism (as we will discuss in Chapter 9). Money—whether in the form of salary, bonus, stock options, and so forth—can mean many different things to people. It might mean security, recognition, or a sense of freedom and independence.

Paying people more is seldom the most important factor in attracting and retaining human capital.[68] Most surveys show that money is not the most important reason why people take or leave jobs and that money, in some surveys, is not even in the top 10. Consistent with these findings, Tandem Computers (part of Hewlett-Packard) typically doesn't tell people being recruited what their salaries would be. People who asked were told that Tandem's salaries were competitive. If they persisted along this line of questioning, they would not be offered a position. Why? Tandem realized a rather simple idea: People who come for money will leave for money.

Another nonfinancial reward is accommodating working families with children. Balancing demands of family and work is a problem at some point for virtually all employees.

Below we discuss how Google attracts and retains talent through financial and nonfinancial incentives. Its unique "Google culture," a huge attraction to potential employees, transforms a traditional workspace into a fun, feel-at-home, and flexible place to work.[69]

> Googlers do not merely work but have a great time doing it. The Mountain View, California, headquarters includes on-site medical and dental facilities, oil change and bike repair, foosball, pool tables, volleyball courts, and free breakfast, lunch, and dinner on a daily basis at 11 gourmet restaurants. Googlers have access to training programs and receive tuition reimbursement while they take a leave of absence to pursue higher education. Google states on its website, "Though Google has grown a lot since it opened in 1998, we still maintain a small company feel."

Enhancing Human Capital: Redefining Jobs and Managing Diversity

Before moving on to our discussion of social capital, it is important to point out that companies are increasingly realizing that the payoff from enhancing their human capital can be substantial. Firms have found that redefining jobs and leveraging the benefits of a diverse workforce can go a long way in improving their performance.

Enhancing Human Capital: Redefining Jobs Recent research by McKinsey Global Institute suggests that by 2020, the worldwide shortage of highly skilled, college-educated workers could reach 38 to 40 million, or about 13 percent of demand.[70] In response, some firms are taking steps to expand their talent pool, for example, by investing in apprenticeships and other training programs. However, some are going further: They are redefining the jobs of their experts and transferring some of their tasks to lower-skilled people inside or outside their companies, as well as outsourcing work that requires less scarce skills and is not as strategically important. Redefining high-value knowledge jobs not only can help organizations address skill shortages but also can lower costs and enhance job satisfaction.

Consider the following examples:

- Orrick, Herrington & Sutcliffe, a San Francisco–based law firm with nine U.S. offices, shifted routine discovery work previously performed by partners and partner-tracked associates to a new service center in West Virginia staffed by lower-paid attorneys.
- In the United Kingdom, a growing number of public schools are relieving head teachers (or principals) of administrative tasks such as budgeting, facilities maintenance, human resources, and community relations so that they can devote more time to developing teachers.
- The Narayana Hrudayalaya Heart Hospital in Bangalore has junior surgeons, nurses, and technicians handle routine tasks such as preparing the patient for surgery and closing the chest after surgery. Senior cardiac surgeons arrive at the operating room only when the patient's chest is open and the heart is ready to be operated on. Such an approach helps the hospital lower the cost to a fraction of the cost of U.S. providers while maintaining U.S.-level mortality and infection rates.

Breaking high-end knowledge work into highly specialized pieces involves several processes. These include identifying the gap between the talent your firm has and what it requires; creating narrower, more-focused job descriptions in areas where talent is scarce; selecting from various options to fill the skills gap; and rewiring processes for talent and knowledge management.

Enhancing Human Capital: Managing Diversity A combination of demographic trends and accelerating globalization of business has made the management of cultural differences a critical issue.[71] Workforces, which reflect demographic changes in the overall population, will be increasingly heterogeneous along dimensions such as gender, race, ethnicity, and nationality.[72] Demographic trends in the United States indicate a growth in Hispanic Americans from 6.9 million in 1960 to over 35 million in 2000, with an expected increase to over 59 million by 2020 and 102 million by 2050. Similarly, the Asian-American population should grow to 20 million in 2020 from 12 million in 2000 and only 1.5 million in 1970. And the African-American population is expected to increase from 12.8 percent of the U.S. population in 2000 to 14.2 percent by 2025.[73]

Such demographic changes have implications not only for the labor pool but also for customer bases, which are also becoming more diverse.[74] This creates important organizational challenges and opportunities.

The effective management of diversity can enhance the social responsibility goals of an organization.[75] However, there are many other benefits as well. Six other areas where sound management of diverse workforces can improve an organization's effectiveness and competitive advantages are (1) cost, (2) resource acquisition, (3) marketing, (4) creativity, (5) problem solving, and (6) organizational flexibility.

- *Cost argument.* As organizations become more diverse, firms effective in managing diversity will have a cost advantage over those that are not.
- *Resource acquisition argument.* Firms with excellent reputations as prospective employers for women and ethnic minorities will have an advantage in the competition for top talent. As labor pools shrink and change in composition, such advantages will become even more important.
- *Marketing argument.* For multinational firms, the insight and cultural sensitivity that members with roots in other countries bring to marketing efforts will be very useful. A similar rationale applies to subpopulations within domestic operations.
- *Creativity argument.* Less emphasis on conformity to norms of the past and a diversity of perspectives will improve the level of creativity.
- *Problem-solving argument.* Heterogeneity in decision-making and problem-solving groups typically produces better decisions because of a wider range of perspectives as well as more thorough analysis. Jim Schiro, former CEO of PricewaterhouseCoopers, explains, "When you make a genuine commitment to diversity, you bring a greater diversity of ideas, approaches, and experiences and abilities that can be applied to client problems. After all, six people with different perspectives have a better shot at solving complex problems than sixty people who all think alike."[76]
- *Organizational flexibility argument.* With effective programs to enhance workplace diversity, systems become less determinant, less standardized, and therefore more fluid. Such fluidity should lead to greater flexibility to react to environmental changes. Reactions should be faster and less costly.

Most managers accept that employers benefit from a diverse workforce. However, this notion can often be very difficult to prove or quantify, particularly when it comes to determining how diversity affects a firm's ability to innovate.[77]

New research provides compelling evidence that diversity enhances innovation and drives market growth. This finding should intensify efforts to ensure that organizations both embody and embrace the power of differences.

Strategy Spotlight 4.3 articulates two kinds of diversity, *inherent* and *acquired,* and the important role they have in driving an organization's innovation.

4.3 STRATEGY SPOTLIGHT

HOW INHERENT AND ACQUIRED DIVERSITY AFFECT INNOVATION

A study explored two kinds of diversity: *inherent* and *acquired*. Its findings were based on a nationally representative survey of 1,800 professionals, 40 case studies, and numerous focus groups and interviews. Inherent diversity involves traits one was born with, such as gender, ethnicity, and sexual orientation. On the other hand, acquired diversity involves traits gained from experience, such as working in another country to understand cultural differences and selling to both male and female consumers to develop "gender smarts." Companies whose leaders exhibited at least three inherent and three acquired traits were viewed as having two-dimensional (2-D) diversity.

The study found that companies with 2-D diversity out-innovated and outperformed the others. Employees in such companies were 45 percent likelier to report their firm's market share grew over the previous year and 70 percent likelier to report the firm captured a new market.

What explains these results? Two-dimensional diversity unlocks innovation by creating a work environment where "outside the box" ideas are heard and minorities form a critical mass. Further, leaders value differences, and all employees can find senior people to go to bat for compelling ideas and can persuade those in charge of budgets to commit resources to develop those ideas.

Inherent diversity, however, is only half of the equation. Acquired diversity provides additional benefits since employees with diverse experiences can provide insights on the needs and preferences of different groups and cultures. They are also more open to the perspectives of the other members on the team. Since acquired diversity increases openness, it also enhances the value of inherent diversity. Minority team members will be more likely to contribute to team discussions, resulting in more creative problem solving. Six behaviors spur innovation across the board: ensuring everyone is heard; making it safe to propose novel ideas; giving team members decision-making authority; sharing credit for success; giving actionable feedback; and implementing feedback from the team.

Sources: Hewlett, S. A., Marshall, M., & Sherbin, L. 2013. How diversity can drive innovation. *Harvard Business Review*, 91(12): 30; and Karlgaard, R. 2014. *The soft edge*. San Francisco: Jossey-Bass.

The Vital Role of Social Capital

Successful firms are well aware that the attraction, development, and retention of talent *is a necessary but not sufficient condition* for creating competitive advantages.[78] In the knowledge economy, it is not the stock of human capital that is important, but the extent to which it is combined and leveraged.[79] In a sense, developing and retaining human capital becomes less important as key players (talented professionals, in particular) take the role of "free agents" and bring with them the requisite skill in many cases. Rather, the development of social capital (that is, the friendships and working relationships among talented individuals) gains importance, because it helps tie knowledge workers to a given firm.[80] Knowledge workers often exhibit greater loyalties to their colleagues and their profession than their employing organization, which may be "an amorphous, distant, and sometimes threatening entity."[81] Thus, a firm must find ways to create "ties" among its knowledge workers.

Let's look at a hypothetical example. Two pharmaceutical firms are fortunate enough to hire Nobel Prize–winning scientists.[82] In one case, the scientist is offered a very attractive salary, outstanding facilities and equipment, and told to "go to it!" In the second case, the scientist is offered approximately the same salary, facilities, and equipment plus one additional ingredient: working in a laboratory with 10 highly skilled and enthusiastic scientists. Part of the job is to collaborate with these peers and jointly develop promising drug compounds. There is little doubt as to which scenario will lead to a higher probability of retaining the scientist. The interaction, sharing, and collaboration will create a situation in which the scientist will develop firm-specific ties and be less likely to "bolt" for a higher salary offer. Such ties are critical because knowledge-based resources tend to be more tacit in nature, as we mentioned early in this chapter. Therefore, they are much more difficult to protect against loss (i.e., the individual quitting the organization) than other types of capital, such as equipment, machinery, and land.

LO4.3
The key role of social capital in leveraging human capital within and across the firm.

Another way to view this situation is in terms of the resource-based view of the firm that we discussed in Chapter 3. That is, competitive advantages tend to be harder for competitors to copy if they are based on "unique bundles" of resources.[83] So, if employees are working effectively in teams and sharing their knowledge and learning from each other, not only will they be more likely to add value to the firm, but they also will be less likely to leave the organization, because of the loyalties and social ties that they develop over time.

How Social Capital Helps Attract and Retain Talent

The importance of social ties among talented professionals creates a significant challenge (and opportunity) for organizations. In *The Wall Street Journal,* Bernard Wysocki described the increase in a type of "Pied Piper effect," in which teams or networks of people are leaving one company for another.[84] The trend is to recruit job candidates at the crux of social relationships in organizations, particularly if they are seen as having the potential to bring with them valuable colleagues.[85] This is a process that is referred to as "hiring via personal networks." Let's look at one instance of this practice.

> Gerald Eickhoff, founder of an electronic commerce company called Third Millennium Communications, tried for 15 years to hire Michael Reene. Why? Mr. Eickhoff says that he has "these Pied Piper skills." Mr. Reene was a star at Andersen Consulting in the 1980s and at IBM in the 1990s. He built his businesses and kept turning down overtures from Mr. Eickhoff.
>
> However, in early 2000, he joined Third Millennium as chief executive officer, with a salary of just $120,000 but with a 20 percent stake in the firm. Since then, he has brought in a raft of former IBM colleagues and Andersen subordinates. One protégé from his time at Andersen, Mary Goode, was brought on board as executive vice president. She promptly tapped her own network and brought along former colleagues.
>
> Wysocki considers the Pied Piper effect one of the underappreciated factors in the war for talent today. This is because one of the myths of the New Economy is rampant individualism, wherein individuals find jobs on the Internet career sites and go to work for complete strangers. Perhaps, instead of Me Inc., the truth is closer to We Inc.[86]

Another example of social relationships causing human capital mobility is the emigration of talent from an organization to form start-up ventures. Microsoft is perhaps the best-known example of this phenomenon.[87] Professionals frequently leave Microsoft en masse to form venture capital and technology start-ups, called "Baby Bills," built around teams of software developers. For example, Ignition Corporation, of Bellevue, Washington, was formed by Brad Silverberg, a former Microsoft senior vice president. Eight former Microsoft executives, among others, founded the company.

Social Networks: Implications for Knowledge Management and Career Success

LO4.4

The importance of social networks in knowledge management and in promoting career success.

Managers face many challenges driven by such factors as rapid changes in globalization and technology. Leading a successful company is more than a one-person job. As Tom Malone put it in *The Future of Work,* "As managers, we need to shift our thinking from command and control to coordinate and cultivate—the best way to gain power is sometimes to give it away."[88] The move away from top-down bureaucratic control to more open, decentralized network models makes it more difficult for managers to understand how work is actually getting done, who is interacting with whom both within and outside the organization, and the consequences of these interactions for the long-term health of the organization.[89]

Malcolm Gladwell, in his best-selling book *The Tipping Point,* used the term *connector* to describe people who have *used* many ties to different social worlds.[90] It's not the number of people that connectors know that makes them significant. Rather, it is their ability to link people, ideas, and resources that wouldn't normally bump into one another. In business, connectors are critical facilitators for collaboration and integration. David Kenny, president of Akamai Technologies, believes that being a connector is one of the most important ways in which he adds value:

> Kenny spends much of his time traveling around the world to meet with employees, partners, and customers. He states, "I spend time with media owners to hear what they think about digital platforms, Facebook, and new pricing models, and with Microsoft leaders to get their views on cloud computing. I'm interested in hearing how our clients feel about macroeconomic issues, the G20, and how debt will affect future generations." These conversations lead to new strategic insights and relationships and help Akamai develop critical external partnerships.

Social networks can also help one bring about important change in an organization—or simply get things done! Consider a change initiative undertaken at the United Kingdom's National Health Care Service—a huge, government-run institution that employs about a million people in hundreds of units and divisions with deeply rooted, bureaucratic, hierarchical systems. This is certainly an organization in which you can't rely solely on your "position power":[91]

> John wanted to set up a nurse-led preoperative assessment service intended to free up time for the doctors who previously led the assessments, reduce cancelled operations (and costs), and improve patient care. Sounds easy enough . . . after all, John was a senior doctor and near the top of the hospital's formal hierarchy. However, he had only recently joined the organization and was not well connected internally.
>
> As he began talking to other doctors and to nurses about the change, he was met with a lot of resistance. He was about to give up when Carol, a well-respected nurse, offered to help. She had even less seniority than John, but many colleagues relied on her advice about navigating hospital politics. She knew many of the people whose support John needed and she eventually converted them to the change.

Social network analysis depicts the pattern of interactions among individuals and helps to diagnose effective and ineffective patterns.[92] It helps identify groups or clusters of individuals that comprise the network, individuals who link the clusters, and other network members. It helps diagnose communication patterns and, consequently, communication effectiveness.[93] Such analysis of communication patterns is helpful because the configuration of group members' social ties within and outside the group affects the extent to which members connect to individuals who:

- Convey needed resources.
- Have the opportunity to exchange information and support.
- Have the motivation to treat each other in positive ways.
- Have the time to develop trusting relationships that might improve the groups' effectiveness.

However, such relationships don't "just happen."[94] Developing social capital requires interdependence among group members. Social capital erodes when people in the network become independent. And increased interactions between members aid in the development and maintenance of mutual obligations in a social network.[95] Social networks such as Facebook may facilitate increased interactions between members in a social network via Internet-based communications.

Let's take a brief look at a simplified network analysis to get a grasp of the key ideas. In Exhibit 4.4, the links depict informal relationships among individuals, such as communication flows, personal support, and advice networks. There may be some individuals with literally no linkages, such as Fred. These individuals are typically labeled "isolates." However, most people do have some linkages with others.

---

social network analysis
analysis of the pattern of social interactions among individuals.

EXHIBIT 4.4 A Simplified Social Network

[Social network diagram showing nodes labeled Fred (isolated), George, Mary, Bill, Frank, and Susan, with Mary serving as a bridge connecting the clusters around Bill, Frank, George, and Susan.]

To simplify, there are two primary types of mechanisms through which social capital will flow: *closure relationships* (depicted by Bill, Frank, George, and Susan) and *bridging relationships* (depicted by Mary). As we can see, in the former relationships one member is central to the communication flows in a group. In contrast, in the latter relationships, one person "bridges" or brings together groups that would have been otherwise unconnected.

Both closure and bridging relationships have important implications for the effective flow of information in organizations and for the management of knowledge. We will now briefly discuss each of these types of relationships. We will also address some of the implications that understanding social networks has for one's career success.

closure
the degree to which all members of a social network have relationships (or ties) with other group members.

Closure With **closure,** many members have relationships (or ties) with other members. As indicated in Exhibit 4.4, Bill's group would have a higher level of closure than Frank's Susan's, or George's groups because more group members are connected to each other. Through closure, group members develop strong relationships with each other, high levels of trust, and greater solidarity. High levels of trust help to ensure that informal norms in the group are easily enforced and there is less "free riding." Social pressure will prevent people from withholding effort or shirking their responsibilities. In addition, people in the network are more willing to extend favors and "go the extra mile" on a colleague's behalf because they are confident that their efforts will be reciprocated by another member in their group. Another benefit of a network with closure is the high level of emotional support. This becomes particularly valuable when setbacks occur that may destroy morale or an unexpected tragedy happens that might cause the group to lose its focus. Social support helps the group to rebound from misfortune and get back on track.

But high levels of closure often come with a price. Groups that become too closed can become insular. They cut themselves off from the rest of the organization and fail to share what they are learning from people outside their group. Research shows that while managers need to encourage closure up to a point, if there is too much closure, they need to encourage people to open up their groups and infuse new ideas through bridging relationships.[96]

Bridging Relationships The closure perspective rests on an assumption that there is a high level of similarity among group members. However, members can be quite heterogeneous with regard to their positions in either the formal or informal structures of the group or the organization. Such heterogeneity exists because of, for example, vertical boundaries (different levels in the hierarchy) and horizontal boundaries (different functional areas).

Bridging relationships, in contrast to closure, stress the importance of ties connecting people. Employees who bridge disconnected people tend to receive timely, diverse information because of their access to a wide range of heterogeneous information flows. Such bridging relationships span a number of different types of boundaries.

The University of Chicago's Ron Burt originally coined the term **"structural holes"** to refer to the social gap between two groups. Structural holes are common in organizations. When they occur in business, managers typically refer to them as "silos" or "stovepipes." Sales and engineering are a classic example of two groups whose members traditionally interact with their peers rather than across groups.

A study that Burt conducted at Raytheon, a $25 billion U.S. electronics company and military contractor, provides further insight into the benefits of bridging.[97]

> Burt studied several hundred managers in Raytheon's supply chain group and asked them to write down ideas to improve the company's supply chain management. Then he asked two Raytheon executives to rate the ideas. The conclusion: *The best suggestions consistently came from managers who discussed ideas outside their regular work group.*
>
> Burt found that Raytheon managers were good at thinking of ideas but bad at developing them. Too often, Burt said, the managers discussed their ideas with colleagues already in their informal discussion network. Instead, he said, they should have had discussions outside their typical contacts, particularly with an informal boss, or someone with enough power to be an ally but not an actual supervisor.

Developing Social Capital: Overcoming Barriers to Collaboration Social capital within a group or organization develops through repeated interactions among its members and the resulting collaboration.[98] However, collaboration does not "just happen." People don't collaborate for various reasons. Effective collaboration requires overcoming four barriers:

- The not-invented-here barrier (people aren't willing to provide help).
- The hoarding barrier (people aren't willing to provide help).
- The search barrier (people are unable to find what they are looking for).
- The transfer barrier (people are unable to work with the people they don't know well).

All four barriers need to be low before effective collaboration can take place. Each one is enough to prevent people from collaborating well. The key is to identify which barriers are present in an organization and then to devise appropriate ways to overcome them.

Different barriers require different solutions. Motivational barriers require leaders to pull levers that make people more willing to collaborate. Ability barriers mean that leaders need to pull levers that enable motivated people to collaborate throughout the organization.

To be effective, leaders can choose a mix of three levers. First, when motivation is the problem, they can use the **unification lever,** wherein they craft compelling common goals, articulate a strong value of cross-company teamwork, and encourage collaboration in order to send strong signals to lift people's sights beyond their narrow interests toward a common goal.

Second, with the **people lever,** the emphasis isn't on getting people to collaborate more. Rather, it's on getting the right people to collaborate on the right projects. This means cultivating what may be called **T-shaped management:** people who simultaneously focus on the performance of their unit (the vertical part of the T) and across boundaries (the horizontal part of the T). People become able to collaborate when needed but are disciplined enough to say no when it's not required.

Third, by using the **network lever,** leaders can build nimble interpersonal networks across the company so that employees are better able to collaborate. Interpersonal networks are more effective than formal hierarchies. However, there is a dark side to networks: When people spend more time networking than getting work done, collaboration can adversely affect results.

---

bridging relationships
relationships in a social network that connect otherwise disconnected people.

structural holes
social gaps between groups in a social network where there are few relationships bridging the groups.

unification lever
method for making people more willing to collaborate by crafting compelling common goals, articulating a strong value of cross-company teamwork, and encouraging collaboration in order to send strong signals to lift people's sights beyond their narrow interests toward a common goal.

people lever
method for making people more willing to collaborate by getting the right people to work on the right projects.

T-shaped management
people's dual focus on the performance of their unit (the vertical part of the T) and across boundaries (the horizontal part of the T).

network lever
method for making people more willing to collaborate by building nimble interpersonal networks across the company.

4.4 STRATEGY SPOTLIGHT

PICASSO VERSUS VAN GOGH: WHO WAS MORE SUCCESSFUL AND WHY?

Vincent van Gogh and Pablo Picasso are two of the most iconoclastic—and famous—artists of modern times. Paintings by both of them have fetched over $100 million. And both of them were responsible for some of the most iconic images in the art world: Van Gogh's *Self-Portrait* (the one sans the earlobe) and *Starry Night* and Picasso's *The Old Guitarist* and *Guernica*. However, there is an important difference between van Gogh and Picasso. Van Gogh died penniless. Picasso's estate was estimated at $750 million when he died in 1973. What was the difference?

Van Gogh's primary connection to the art world was through his brother. Unfortunately, this connection didn't feed directly into the money that could have turned him into a living success. In contrast, Picasso's myriad connections provided him with access to commercial riches. As noted by Gregory Berns in his book *Iconoclast: A Neuroscientist Reveals How to Think Differently*, "Picasso's wide ranging social network, which included artists, writers, and politicians, meant that he was never more than a few people away from anyone of importance in the world."

In effect, van Gogh was a loner, and the charismatic Picasso was an active member of multiple social circles. In social networking terms, van Gogh was a solitary "node" who had few connections. Picasso, on the other hand, was a "hub" who embedded himself in a vast network that stretched across various social lines. Where Picasso smoothly navigated multiple social circles, van Gogh had to struggle just to maintain connections with even those closest to him. Van Gogh inhabited an alien world, whereas Picasso was a social magnet. And because he knew so many people, the world was at Picasso's fingertips. From his perspective, the world was smaller.

Sources: Hayashi, A. M. 2008. Why Picasso out earned van Gogh. *MIT Sloan Management Review*, 50(1): 11–12; and Berns, G. 2008. *A neuroscientist reveals how to think differently*. Boston: Harvard Business Press.

Implications for Career Success Let's go back in time in order to illustrate the value of social networks in one's career success. Consider two of the most celebrated artists of all time: Vincent van Gogh and Pablo Picasso. Strategy Spotlight 4.4 points out why these two artists enjoyed sharply contrasting levels of success during their lifetimes.

Effective social networks provide many advantages for the firm.[99] They can play a key role in an individual's career advancement and success. One's social network potentially can provide three unique advantages: private information, access to diverse skill sets, and power.[100] Managers see these advantages at work every day but might not consider how their networks regulate them.

Private Information We make judgments using both public and private information. Today, public information is available from many sources, including the Internet. However, since it is so accessible, public information offers less competitive advantage than it used to.

In contrast, private information from personal contacts can offer something not found in publicly available sources, such as the release date of a new product or knowledge about what a particular interviewer looks for in candidates. Private information can give managers an edge, though it is more subjective than public information since it cannot be easily verified by independent sources, such as Dunn & Bradstreet. Consequently the value of your private information to others—and the value of others' private information to you—depends on how much trust exists in the network of relationships.

Access to Diverse Skill Sets Linus Pauling, one of only two people to win a Nobel Prize in two different areas and considered one of the towering geniuses of the 20th century, attributed his creative success not to his immense brainpower or luck but to his diverse contacts. He said, "The best way to have a good idea is to have a lot of ideas."

While expertise has become more specialized during the past few decades, organizational, product, and marketing issues have become more interdisciplinary. This means that success is tied to the ability to transcend natural skill limitations through others. Highly diverse network relationships, therefore, can help you develop more complete, creative, and unbiased perspectives on issues. Trading information or skills with people whose experiences differ from your own provides you with unique, exceptionally valuable resources. It is common for people in relationships to share their problems. If you know enough people, you will begin to see how the problems that another person is struggling with can be solved by the solutions being developed by others. If you can bring together problems and solutions, it will greatly benefit your career.

Power Traditionally, a manager's power was embedded in a firm's hierarchy. But when corporate organizations became flatter, more like pancakes than pyramids, that power was repositioned in the network's brokers (people who bridged multiple networks), who could adapt to changes in the organization, develop clients, and synthesize opposing points of view. Such brokers weren't necessarily at the top of the hierarchy or experts in their fields, but they linked specialists in the firm with trustworthy and informative relationships.[101]

Most personal networks are highly clustered; that is, an individual's friends are likely to be friends with one another as well. Most corporate networks are made up of several clusters that have few links between them. Brokers are especially powerful because they connect separate clusters, thus stimulating collaboration among otherwise independent specialists.

In today's knowledge economy, managers must strive to develop a wide range of sources for private information. Unfortunately, we are also a very mobile society. Thus, we often lose touch with people—even those whom we may have been close to for a rather long period of time. However, making contact with such individuals can be very beneficial. Insights from Research 4.1 addresses some very interesting findings on this issue—the benefits of reconnecting with people whom managers had not been in contact with for at least three years (such people are called "dormant ties").

A Cautionary Note: Three Kinds of Network Traps A recent study of over 300 companies explored how management teams can understand and capitalize on the formal and informal social networks of their employees.[102] Six common types of managers who get stuck in three types of network traps were identified. Such findings have important career implications:

- *The wrong structure.* The "formalist" relies too much on his firm's official hierarchy, missing out on the efficiencies and opportunities that come from informal connections. The "overloaded manager" has so much contact with colleagues and external ties that she becomes a bottleneck to progress and burns herself out.
- *The wrong relationships.* The "disconnected expert" sticks with people who keep him focused on safe, existing competencies, rather than those who push him to build new skills. The "biased leader" relies on advisers (same functional background, location, or values) who reinforce her biases, when she should instead seek outsiders to prompt more fully informed decisions.
- *The wrong behavior.* The "superficial networker" engages in surface-level interaction with as many people as possible, mistakenly believing that a bigger network is a better network. The "chameleon" changes his interests, values, and personality to match those of whatever subgroup is his audience, and winds up being disconnected from every group.

The Potential Downside of Social Capital

We'd like to close our discussion of social capital by addressing some of its limitations. First, some firms have been adversely affected by very high levels of social capital because it may breed **"groupthink"**—a tendency not to question shared beliefs.[103] Such thinking may occur in networks with high levels of closure where there is little input from people outside the network. In effect, too many warm and fuzzy feelings among group members

groupthink
a tendency in an organization for individuals not to question shared beliefs.

INSIGHTS FROM RESEARCH

HELLO AGAIN! THE VALUE OF REKINDLING CONNECTIONS

Overview

Reuniting is good for you . . . and for your business. Friends, colleagues, and family members can go different directions geographically, occupationally, and otherwise, leaving those relationships on hold. This research finds dormant ties to be much more valuable than previously thought. The insights gained from reconnecting can add spark to your projects.

What the Research Shows

Researchers from Rutgers University, George Washington University, and Northwestern University published a paper in *Organization Science* in which they compared the value of executives' dormant ties to their existing ties. The research included 129 participants from executive MBA programs and a follow-up with 116 executives. In the follow-up, participants ranked 10 dormant ties (people with whom they had not had any contact for three years or more) from the most to the least preferred. It turns out those ranked low were about as useful as those ranked very high. This means the value of dormant ties is significant. Even those we think are less valuable are still worth pursuing.

Specifically, the researchers found dormant ties were often more "efficient" than current ones. This means time spent consulting with those ties was short and provided efficient access to the person's knowledge. Researchers found reconnecting dormant ties provided greater originality of ideas than consulting current ties. The knowledge accumulated during dormancy, resulting from different experiences, can provide insights if the tie is reconnected.

Finally, in dormant ties where each person was especially motivated to cooperate and had a similar understanding of a problem, trust was higher. There was more of a shared perspective, and this increased the receipt of useful knowledge even more.

Why This Matters

Have you considered reconnecting with people from your past who've changed jobs, moved away, or otherwise gone in another direction? Perhaps you've intended to reach out but have been too overwhelmed by your current obligations to do so.

This research suggests reconnecting to dormant ties is time well spent. Your current connections with customers, friends, and colleagues are valuable but may have diminishing returns. After all, you've probably already exhausted any novel insights for your business—such as marketing ideas of potential customers—from your existing circle. To gather original ideas, a reunion might be in order.

Dormant ties are efficient, so you get more bang for your buck in terms of time spent reconnecting. Because of your previous connection based on common knowledge, business arrangements, or friendship, there's a shared perspective and trust. Often, you can just pick up where you left off because emotional closeness determines a tie's strength more than frequency of communication.

So, what does this mean for management practice? Social networking websites like LinkedIn have reduced the costs of searching for dormant contacts, and such contacts are now much easier to track down. These sites provide a low-cost way to rekindle former relationships while stimulating creativity about current projects.

Top executives stand to gain from revitalizing dormant ties too. Divergent perspectives on how to navigate industry environments can benefit leaders, as can the resurgence of connections between organizations. Corporate heads sometimes even reconnect informal ties, not with individuals but with their replacements, paving the way for future collaboration or strategic alliances.

When you are reconnecting, consultant and *Harvard Business Review* blogger Jodi Glickman suggests acknowledging the lapse in time, explaining the "Why now?" question, and offering a quid pro quo. Her article and the HBR Blog Network include an enlightening example of a dormant tie that paid off, as well as practical advice for reconnecting. One post reads, "I've recently been reaching out to people in my network to build my business and I have been pleasantly surprised at how genuinely happy people are to reconnect. Your insights are spot on."

Key Takeaways

- People lose touch with one another for many reasons. Often, relationships not actively maintained, or "dormant ties," are considered worthless.
- However, reconnecting is a low-cost, high-reward way to gain insights into your business because of experiences and knowledge gained during your loss of contact.
- Dormant ties give you more bang for your buck in the form of ideas and innovations. Even contacts ranked "least preferred" were valuable.
- Former connections are generally delighted to hear from you. Catch up with old friends or associates and you might collaborate on your next big idea.

Apply This Today

Get out of your comfort zone and pursue your old contacts. Reconnecting can add to your current knowledge and give you ideas.

Research Reviewed

Levin, D. Z., Walter, J., & Murnighan, J. K. 2011. Dormant ties: The value of reconnecting. *Organization Science,* 22(4), 923–939.

prevent people from rigorously challenging each other. People are discouraged from engaging in the "creative abrasion" that Dorothy Leonard of Harvard University describes as a key source of innovation.[104] Two firms that were well known for their collegiality, strong sense of employee membership, and humane treatment—Digital Equipment (now part of Hewlett-Packard) and Polaroid—suffered greatly from market misjudgments and strategic errors. The aforementioned aspects of their culture contributed to their problems.

Second, if there are deep-rooted mind-sets, there would be a tendency to develop dysfunctional human resource practices. That is, the organization (or group) would continue to hire, reward, and promote like-minded people who tend to further intensify organizational inertia and erode innovation. Such homogeneity would increase over time and decrease the effectiveness of decision-making processes.

Third, the socialization processes (orientation, training, etc.) can be expensive in terms of both financial resources and managerial commitment. Such investments can represent a significant opportunity cost that should be evaluated in terms of the intended benefits. If such expenses become excessive, profitability would be adversely affected.

Finally, individuals may use the contacts they develop to pursue their own interests and agendas, which may be inconsistent with the organization's goals and objectives. Thus, they may distort or selectively use information to favor their preferred courses of action or withhold information in their own self-interest to enhance their power to the detriment of the common good. Drawing on our discussion of social networks, this is particularly true in an organization that has too many bridging relationships but not enough closure relationships. In high-closure groups, it is easier to watch each other to ensure that illegal or unethical acts don't occur. By contrast, bridging relationships make it easier for a person to play one group or individual off another, with no one being the wiser.[105] We will discuss some behavioral control mechanisms in Chapter 9 (rewards, control, boundaries) that reduce such dysfunctional behaviors and actions.[106]

Using Technology to Leverage Human Capital and Knowledge

LO4.5
The vital role of technology in leveraging knowledge and human capital.

Sharing knowledge and information throughout the organization can be a means of conserving resources, developing products and services, and creating new opportunities. In this section we will discuss how technology can be used to leverage human capital and knowledge within organizations as well as with customers and suppliers beyond their boundaries.

Using Networks to Share Information

As we all know, email is an effective means of communicating a wide variety of information. It is quick, easy, and almost costless. Of course, it can become a problem when employees use it extensively for personal reasons. And we all know how fast jokes or rumors can spread within and across organizations!

Strategy Spotlight 4.5 suggests an innovative approach one firm took to reduce the exorbitant number of emails it had to deal with each day.

Email can also cause embarrassment, or worse, if one is not careful. Consider the plight of a potential CEO—as recalled by Marshall Goldsmith, a well-known executive coach:[107]

> I witnessed a series of e-mails between a potential CEO and a friend inside the company. The first e-mail to the friend provided an elaborate description of "why the current CEO is an idiot." The friend sent a reply. Several rounds of e-mails followed. Then the friend sent an e-mail containing a funny joke. The potential CEO decided that the current CEO would love this joke and forwarded it to him. You can guess what happened next. The CEO scrolled down the e-mail chain and found the "idiot" message. The heir apparent was gone in a week.

4.5 STRATEGY SPOTLIGHT

YES! EMAIL CAN BE REDUCED

Typically, we all have very little control over how many email messages we receive. But we *can* control how many messages we send. That rather obvious insight sparked a huge reduction in one company's email traffic. And, after the executives reduced their output, (surprise!) other employees followed suit.

A seven-person top management team at London-based International Power wanted to increase the firm's efficiency. An analysis suggested a glut of email might be part of the problem. Although executives initially felt the volume was due to others' actions, they were astonished to learn they, themselves, were sending 56 messages a day, on average.

Rather than using email management tools to address the overflow, the firm took a page from lean manufacturing. It decided to treat communications as though they were an industrial process, targeting efficiency killers such as overproduction and defects (confusing, unnecessary, or ineffective messages, which often simply bred other messages). Believing a reduction in executive outflow would prompt a quick reduction in employee outflow, the executives aimed to cut the number of emails sent by the top team members by 20 percent within four months.

Despite a few misgivings, the executives underwent training to reduce their email output by taking more deliberate actions. These included not forwarding messages unless strictly necessary, limiting messages' recipients, and choosing the most efficient form of communication to accomplish the task at hand. A phone call, for example, provides real-time feedback on whether a message is being understood—something that is missing with the low-bandwidth email channel. Also, facial expressions and body language make in-person meetings an even richer method of communication.

The executive team received weekly reports on both their and the top management team's progress. Within three months, the team's total email output dropped by 54 percent. And even though the other 75 London-based employees received no training, their email output dropped by an even greater amount—64 percent. The result was significant: a savings of 10,400 man-hours, which translates to a 7 percent increase in productivity.

Key Lessons

- Teach executives to become more deliberate in their use of email.
- Ask them to set a goal for reducing the number of messages they send and include it in their performance goals.
- Provide weekly feedback.

Source: Brown, C., Killick, A., & Renaud, K. 2013. To reduce email, start at the top. *Harvard Business Review*, 91(9): 26.

Email can, however, be a means for top executives to communicate information efficiently. For example, Martin Sorrell, chairman of WPP Group PLC, the huge $17 billion advertising and public relations firm, is a strong believer in the use of email.[108] He emails all of his employees once a month to discuss how the company is doing, address specific issues, and offer his perspectives on hot issues, such as new business models for the Internet. He believes that it keeps people abreast of what he is working on.

Technology can also enable much more sophisticated forms of communication in addition to knowledge sharing. Cisco, for example, launched Integrated Workforce Experience (IWE) in 2010.[109] It is a social business platform designed to facilitate internal and external collaboration and decentralize decision making. It functions much like a Facebook "wall": A real-time news feed provides updates on employees' status and activities as well as information about relevant communities, business projects, and customer and partner interactions. One manager likens it to Amazon. "It makes recommendations based on what you are doing, the role you are in, and the choices of other people like you. We are taking that to the enterprise level and basically allowing appropriate information to find you," he says.

> **electronic teams**
> a team of individuals that completes tasks primarily through email communication.

> **LO4.6**
> Why "electronic" or "virtual" teams are critical in combining and leveraging knowledge in organizations and how they can be made more effective.

Electronic Teams: Using Technology to Enhance Collaboration

Technology enables professionals to work as part of electronic, or virtual, teams to enhance the speed and effectiveness with which products are developed. For example, Microsoft has concentrated much of its development on **electronic teams** (or e-teams) that are networked together.[110] This helps to accelerate design and testing of new software modules that use the Windows-based framework as their central architecture. Microsoft is able to foster specialized technical expertise while sharing knowledge rapidly throughout the firm. This helps the firm learn how its new technologies can be applied rapidly to new business ventures such as cable television, broadcasting, travel services, and financial services.

What are electronic teams (or e-teams)? There are two key differences between e-teams and more traditional teams:[111]

- E-team members either work in geographically separated workplaces or may work in the same space but at different times. E-teams may have members working in different spaces and time zones, as is the case with many multinational teams.
- Most of the interactions among members of e-teams occur through electronic communication channels such as fax machines and groupware tools such as email, bulletin boards, chat, and videoconferencing.

E-teams have expanded exponentially in recent years.[112] Organizations face increasingly high levels of complex and dynamic change. E-teams are also effective in helping businesses cope with global challenges. Most e-teams perform very complex tasks and most knowledge-based teams are charged with developing new products, improving organizational processes, and satisfying challenging customer problems. For example, Hewlett-Packard's e-teams solve clients' computing problems, and Sun Microsystems' (part of Oracle) e-teams generate new business models.

Advantages   There are multiple advantages of e-teams.[113] In addition to the rather obvious use of technology to facilitate communications, the potential benefits parallel the other two major sections in this chapter—human capital and social capital.

First, e-teams are less restricted by the geographic constraints that are placed on face-to-face teams. Thus, e-teams have the potential to acquire a broader range of "human capital," or the skills and capacities that are necessary to complete complex assignments. So e-team leaders can draw upon a greater pool of talent to address a wider range of problems since they are not constrained by geographic space. Once formed, e-teams can be more flexible in responding to unanticipated work challenges and opportunities because team members can be rotated out of projects when demands and contingencies alter the team's objectives.

Second, e-teams can be very effective in generating "social capital"—the quality of relationships and networks that form. Such capital is a key lubricant in work transactions and operations. Given the broader boundaries associated with e-teams, members and leaders generally have access to a wider range of social contacts than would be typically available in more traditional face-to-face teams. Such contacts are often connected to a broader scope of clients, customers, constituents, and other key stakeholders.

Challenges   However, there are challenges associated with making e-teams effective. Successful action by both traditional teams and e-teams requires that:

- Members *identify* who among them can provide the most appropriate knowledge and resources.
- E-team leaders and key members know how to *combine* individual contributions in the most effective manner for a coordinated and appropriate response.

Group psychologists have termed such activities "identification and combination" activities, and teams that fail to perform them face a "process loss."[114] Process losses prevent teams from reaching high levels of performance because of inefficient interaction dynamics among team members. Such poor dynamics require that some collective energy, time, and effort be devoted to dealing with team inefficiencies, thus diverting the team away from its objectives. For example, if a team member fails to communicate important information at critical phases of a project, other members may waste time and energy. This can lead to conflict and resentment as well as to decreased motivation to work hard to complete tasks.

The potential for process losses tends to be more prevalent in e-teams than in traditional teams because the geographic dispersion of members increases the complexity of establishing effective interaction and exchanges. Generally, teams suffer process loss because of low cohesion, low trust among members, a lack of appropriate norms or standard operating procedures, or a lack of shared understanding among team members about their tasks. With e-teams, members are more geographically or temporally dispersed, and the team becomes more susceptible to the risk factors that can create process loss. Such problems can be exacerbated when team members have less than ideal competencies and social skills. This can erode problem-solving capabilities as well as the effective functioning of the group as a social unit.

A variety of technologies, from email and Internet groups to Skype have facilitated the formation and effective functioning of e-teams as well as a wide range of collaborations within companies. Such technologies greatly enhance the collaborative abilities of employees and managers within a company at a reasonable cost—despite the distances that separate them.

Codifying Knowledge for Competitive Advantage

There are two different kinds of knowledge. Tacit knowledge is embedded in personal experience and shared only with the consent and participation of the individual. Explicit (or codified) knowledge, on the other hand, is knowledge that can be documented, widely distributed, and easily replicated. One of the challenges of knowledge-intensive organizations is to capture and codify the knowledge and experience that, in effect, resides in the heads of its employees. Otherwise, they will have to constantly "reinvent the wheel," which is both expensive and inefficient. Also, the "new wheel" may not necessarily be superior to the "old wheel."[115]

Once a knowledge asset (e.g., a software code or a process) is developed and paid for, it can be reused many times at very low cost, assuming that it doesn't have to be substantially modified each time. Let's take the case of a consulting company, such as Accenture (formerly Andersen Consulting).[116]

> Since the knowledge of its consultants has been codified and stored in electronic repositories, it can be employed in many jobs by a huge number of consultants. Additionally, since the work has a high level of standardization (i.e., there are strong similarities across the numerous client engagements), there is a rather high ratio of consultants to partners. For example, the ratio of consultants to partners is roughly 30, which is quite high. As one might expect, there must be extensive training of the newly hired consultants for such an approach to work. The recruits are trained at Accenture's Center for Professional Education, a 150-acre campus in St. Charles, Illinois. Using the center's knowledge-management respository, the consultants work through many scenarios designed to improve business processes. In effect, the information technologies enable the consultants to be "implementers, not inventors."

Access Health, a call-in medical center, also uses technology to capture and share knowledge. When someone calls the center, a registered nurse uses the company's "clinical decision architecture" to assess the caller's symptoms, rule out possible conditions, and recommend a home remedy, doctor's visit, or trip to the emergency room. The company's knowledge repository contains algorithms of the symptoms of more than 500 illnesses. According to CEO Joseph Tallman, "We are not inventing a new way to cure disease. We are taking available knowledge and inventing processes to put it to better

4.6 STRATEGY SPOTLIGHT — CROWDSOURCING

HOW SAP TAPS KNOWLEDGE WELL BEYOND ITS BOUNDARIES

Traditionally, organizations built and protected their knowledge stocks—proprietary resources that no one else could access. However, the more the business environment changes, the faster the value of what you know at any point in time diminishes. In today's world, success hinges on the ability to access a growing variety of knowledge flows in order to rapidly replenish the firm's knowledge stocks. For example, when an organization tries to improve cycle times in a manufacturing process, it finds far more value in problem solving shaped by the diverse experiences, perspectives, and learning of a tightly knit team (shared through knowledge flows) than in a training manual (knowledge stocks) alone.

Knowledge flows can help companies gain competitive advantage in an age of near-constant disruption. The software company SAP, for example, routinely taps the nearly 3 million participants in its Community Network, which extends well beyond the boundaries of the firm. By providing a virtual platform for customers, developers, system integrators, and service vendors to create and exchange knowledge, SAP has significantly increased the productivity of all the participants in its ecosystem.

According to Mark Yolton, senior vice president of SAP Communications and Social Media, "It's a very robust community with a great deal of activity. We see about 1.2 million unique visitors every month. Hundreds of millions of pages are viewed every year. There are 4,000 discussion forum posts every single day, 365 days a year, and about 115 blogs every day, 365 days a year, from any of the nearly 3 million members."

The site is open to everyone, regardless of whether you are a SAP customer, partner, or newcomer who needs to work with SAP technology. The site offers technical articles, web-based training, code samples, evaluation systems, discussion forums, and excellent blogs for community experts.

Sources: Yolton, M. 2012. SAP: Using social media for building, selling and supporting. *sloanreview.mit.edu*, August 7: np; Hagel, J., III., Brown, J. S., & Davison, L. 2009. The big shift: Measuring the forces of change. *Harvard Business Review*, 87(4): 87; and Anonymous. Undated. SAP developer network. *sap.sys-con.com*: np.

---

use." The software algorithms were very expensive to develop, but the investment has been repaid many times over. The first 300 algorithms that Access Health developed have each been used an average of 8,000 times a year. Further, the company's paying customers—insurance companies and provider groups—save money because many callers would have made expensive trips to the emergency room or the doctor's office had they not been diagnosed over the phone.

The user community can be a major source of knowledge creation for a firm. Strategy Spotlight 4.6 highlights how SAP, in an example of effective crowdsourcing, has been able to leverage the expertise and involvement of its users to develop new knowledge and transmit it to SAP's entire user community.

We close this section with a series of questions managers should consider in determining (1) how effective their organization is in attracting, developing, and retaining human capital and (2) how effective they are in leveraging human capital through social capital and technology. These questions, included in Exhibit 4.5, summarize some of the key issues addressed in this chapter.

Protecting the Intellectual Assets of the Organization: Intellectual Property and Dynamic Capabilities

>**LO4.7**
>The challenge of protecting intellectual property and the importance of a firm's dynamic capabilities.

In today's dynamic and turbulent world, unpredictability and fast change dominate the business environment. Firms can use technology, attract human capital, or tap into research and design networks to get access to pretty much the same information as their competitors. So what would give firms a sustainable competitive advantage?[117] Protecting a firm's intellectual property requires a concerted effort on the part of the company. After all, employees become disgruntled and patents expire. The management of intellectual property (IP) involves, besides patents, contracts with confidentiality and noncompete clauses,

EXHIBIT 4.5 Issues to Consider in Creating Value through Human Capital, Social Capital, and Technology

Human Capital

Recruiting "Top-Notch" Human Capital

- Does the organization assess attitude and "general makeup" instead of focusing primarily on skills and background in selecting employees at all levels?
- How important are creativity and problem-solving ability? Are they properly considered in hiring decisions?
- Do people throughout the organization engage in effective networking activities to obtain a broad pool of worthy potential employees? Is the organization creative in such endeavors?

Enhancing Human Capital through Employee Development

- Does the development and training process inculcate an "organizationwide" perspective?
- Is there widespread involvement, including top executives, in the preparation and delivery of training and development programs?
- Is the development of human capital effectively tracked and monitored?
- Are there effective programs for succession at all levels of the organization, especially at the topmost levels?
- Does the firm effectively evaluate its human capital? Is a 360-degree evaluation used? Why? Why not?
- Are mechanisms in place to ensure that a manager's success does not come at the cost of compromising the organization's core values?

Retaining the Best Employees

- Are there appropriate financial rewards to motivate employees at all levels?
- Do people throughout the organization strongly identify with the organization's mission?
- Are employees provided with a stimulating and challenging work environment that fosters professional growth?
- Are valued amenities provided (e.g., flextime, child care facilities, telecommuting) that are appropriate given the organization's mission, its strategy, and how work is accomplished?
- Is the organization continually devising strategies and mechanisms to retain top performers?

Social Capital

- Are there positive personal and professional relationships among employees?
- Is the organization benefiting (or being penalized) by hiring (or by voluntary turnover) en masse?
- Does an environment of caring and encouragement rather than competition enhance team performance?
- Do the social networks within the organization have the appropriate levels of closure and bridging relationships?
- Does the organization minimize the adverse effects of excessive social capital, such as excessive costs and "groupthink"?

Technology

- Has the organization used technologies such as email and networks to develop products and services?
- Does the organization effectively use technology to transfer best practices across the organization?
- Does the organization use technology to leverage human capital and knowledge both within the boundaries of the organization and among its suppliers and customers?
- Has the organization effectively used technology to codify knowledge for competitive advantage?
- Does the organization try to retain some of the knowledge of employees when they decide to leave the firm?

Source: Adapted from Dess, G. G., & Picken, J. C. 1999. *Beyond Productivity:* 63–64. New York: AMACON.

---

copyrights, and the development of trademarks. Moreover, developing dynamic capabilities is the only avenue providing firms with the ability to reconfigure their knowledge and activities to achieve a sustainable competitive advantage.

Intellectual Property Rights

intellectual property rights
intangible property owned by a firm in the forms of patents, copyrights, trademarks, or trade secrets.

Intellectual property rights are more difficult to define and protect than property rights for physical assets (e.g., plant, equipment, and land). However, if intellectual property rights are not reliably protected by the state, there will be no incentive to develop new products and services. Property rights have been enshrined in constitutions and rules of law in many countries. In the information era, though, adjustments need to be made to accommodate the new realities of knowledge. Knowledge and information are fundamentally different assets from the physical ones that property rights have been designed to protect.

The protection of intellectual rights raises unique issues, compared to physical property rights. IP is characterized by significant development costs and very low marginal costs. Indeed, it may take a substantial investment to develop a software program, an idea, or a digital music tune. Once developed, though, its reproduction and distribution cost may be almost zero, especially if the Internet is used. Effective protection of intellectual property is necessary before any investor will finance such an undertaking. Appropriation of investors' returns is harder to police since possession and deployment are not as readily observable. Unlike physical assets, intellectual property can be stolen by simply broadcasting it. Recall Napster and MP3 as well as the debates about counterfeit software, music CDs, and DVDs coming from developing countries such as China. Part of the problem is that using an idea does not prevent others from simultaneously using it for their own benefit, which is typically impossible with physical assets. Moreover, new ideas are frequently built on old ideas and are not easily traceable.

Given these unique challenges in protecting IP, it comes as no surprise that legal battles over patents become commonplace in IP-heavy industries such as telecommunications. Take the recent patent battles Apple has been fighting against smartphone makers running Android, Google's mobile operating system.[118]

> In 2012, Apple and HTC, a Taiwanese smartphone maker, agreed to dismiss a series of lawsuits filed against each other after Apple accused HTC of copying the iPhone. While this settlement may be a sign that Apple's new CEO, Timothy Cook, is eager to end the distractions caused by IP-related litigation, other patent battles continue, including one between Apple and Samsung, the largest maker of Android phones. This legal battle involves much higher stakes, because Samsung shipped almost eight times as many Android smartphones as HTC in the third quarter of 2012. However, Apple's new leadership seems to be more pragmatic about this issue. In Mr. Cook's words, "It is awkward. I hate litigation. I absolutely hate it," suggesting that he is not as enthusiastic a combatant in the patent wars as was his predecessor, Steve Jobs, who famously promised to "destroy Android, because it's a stolen product."

Countries are attempting to pass new legislation to cope with developments in new pharmaceutical compounds, stem cell research, and biotechnology. However, a firm that is faced with this challenge today cannot wait for the legislation to catch up. New technological developments, software solutions, electronic games, online services, and other products and services contribute to our economic prosperity and the creation of wealth for those entrepreneurs who have the idea first and risk bringing it to the market.

Dynamic Capabilities

Dynamic capabilities entail the capacity to build and protect a competitive advantage.[119] This rests on knowledge, assets, competencies, and complementary assets and technologies as well as the ability to sense and seize new opportunities, generate new knowledge, and reconfigure existing assets and capabilities.[120] According to David Teece, an economist at the University of California at Berkeley, dynamic capabilities are related to the entrepreneurial side of the firm and are built within a firm through its environmental and technological "sensing" apparatus, its choices of organizational form, and its collective ability to strategize. Dynamic capabilities are about the ability of an organization to challenge the conventional wisdom within its industry and market, learn and innovate, adapt to the changing world, and continuously adopt new ways to serve the evolving needs of the market.[121]

> **dynamic capabilities**
> a firm's capacity to build and protect a competitive advantage, which rests on knowledge, assets, competencies, complementary assets, and technologies. Dynamic capabilities include the ability to sense and seize new opportunities, generate new knowledge, and reconfigure existing assets and capabilities.

ISSUE FOR DEBATE

Layoffs or Furloughs: The Action Honeywell Took

Like most companies, Honeywell was faced with severe economic challenges during the deep recession in 2008–2009. However, instead of going the usual route—massive layoffs—the firm decided to use furloughs throughout the company. In a recent *Harvard Business Review* article, David Cote, chairman and CEO of Honeywell, discussed his reasons for taking this seldom-used approach.

When Honeywell began looking at its options, it kept coming back to the idea of furloughs: Workers take unpaid leaves but remain employed. The conventional wisdom was that since furloughs spread the pain across the entire workforce, they hurt everyone's morale, loyalty, and retention, so it is actually better to lay off a smaller number, focusing on the weak performers. Also, furloughs are a challenge logistically. In order to implement them, the firm needed to comply with individual state laws as well as the laws in other countries where the firm did business.

However, Cote felt the benefits of furloughs outweighed the costs. Managers typically overestimate the savings the firm will achieve with layoffs as well as fail to understand that even bad recessions tend to end more quickly than expected. And if a firm has to pay six months of severance, for example, it will have to wait six months before there are any savings. Since recessions may last only 12 to 18 months, it is usually only about a year or so later before the firm must start hiring again. Then, of course, the firm incurs all the usual hiring costs (as well as the earlier costs associated with losing talent and experience). Also, Cote stated he had been through three recessions and seldom heard a management team talk about how choices they make during a downturn will affect performance during the recovery. He kept reiterating that point: "There will be a recovery, and we need to be prepared for it."

Discussion Questions

1. Do you think David Cote made the right decision? Why? Why not?
2. Do you think the decision was well received by the employees? What factors, changes in events, and so on, do you think would affect how employees came to accept (or reject) this decision?

Sources: Cote, D. 2013. Honeywell's CEO on how he avoided layoffs. *Harvard Business Review*, 91 (6): 43-46.

Examples of dynamic capabilities include product development, strategic decision making, alliances, and acquisitions.[122] Some firms have clearly developed internal processes and routines that make them superior in such activities. For example, 3M and Apple are ahead of their competitors in product development. Cisco Systems has made numerous acquisitions over the years. Cisco seems to have developed the capability to identify and evaluate potential acquisition candidates and seamlessly integrate them once the acquisition is completed. Other organizations can try to copy Cisco's practices. However, Cisco's combination of the resources of the acquired companies and their reconfiguration that Cisco has already achieved places it well ahead of its competitors. As markets become increasingly dynamic, traditional sources of long-term competitive advantage become less relevant. In such markets, all that a firm can strive for are a series of temporary advantages. Dynamic capabilities allow a firm to create this series of temporary advantages through new resource configurations.[123]

Reflecting on Career Implications . . .

- **Human Capital:** Identify specific steps taken by your organization to effectively attract, develop, and retain talent. If you cannot identify such steps, you may have fewer career opportunities to develop your human capital at your organization. Do you take advantage of your organization's human resource programs, such as tuition reimbursement, mentoring, and so forth?

- **Human Capital:** As workplaces become more diverse, it is important to reflect on whether your organization values diversity. What kinds of diversity seem to be encouraged (e.g., age-based or ethnicity-based)? In what ways are your colleagues different from and similar to you? If your firm has a homogeneous workforce, there may be limited perspectives on strategic and operational issues and a career at this organization may be less attractive to you.

- **Social Capital:** Does your organization have strong social capital? What is the basis of your conclusion that it has strong or weak social capital? What specific programs are in place to build and develop social capital? What is the impact of social capital on employee turnover in your organization? Alternatively, is social capital so strong that you see effects such as "groupthink"? From your perspective, how might you better leverage social capital toward pursuing other career opportunities?

- **Social Capital:** Are you actively working to build a strong social network at your work organization? To advance your career, strive to build a broad network that gives you access to diverse information.

- **Technology:** Does your organization provide and effectively use technology (e.g., groupware, knowledge management systems) to help you leverage your talents and expand your knowledge base? If your organization does a poor job in this regard, what can you do on your own to expand your knowledge base using technology available outside the organization?

summary

Firms throughout the industrial world are recognizing that the knowledge worker is the key to success in the marketplace. However, they also recognize that human capital, although vital, is still only a necessary, but not a sufficient, condition for creating value. We began the first section of the chapter by addressing the importance of human capital and how it can be attracted, developed, and retained. Then we discussed the role of social capital and technology in leveraging human capital for competitive success. We pointed out that intellectual capital—the difference between a firm's market value and its book value—has increased significantly over the past few decades. This is particularly true for firms in knowledge-intensive industries, especially where there are relatively few tangible assets, such as software development.

The second section of the chapter addressed the attraction, development, and retention of human capital. We viewed these three activities as a "three-legged stool"—that is, it is difficult for firms to be successful if they ignore or are unsuccessful in any one of these activities. Among the issues we discussed in *attracting* human capital were "hiring for attitude, training for skill" and the value of using social networks to attract human capital. In particular, it is important to attract employees who can collaborate with others, given the importance of collective efforts such as teams and task forces. With regard to *developing* human capital, we discussed the need to encourage widespread involvement throughout the organization, monitor progress and track the development of human capital, and evaluate human capital. Among the issues that are widely practiced in evaluating human capital is the 360-degree evaluation system. Employees are evaluated by their superiors, peers, direct reports, and even internal and external customers. We also addressed the value of maintaining a diverse workforce. Finally, some mechanisms for retaining human capital are employees' identification with the organization's mission and values, providing challenging work and a stimulating environment, the importance of financial and nonfinancial rewards and incentives, and providing flexibility and amenities. A key issue here is that a firm should not overemphasize financial rewards. After all, if individuals join an organization for money, they also are likely to leave for money. With money as the primary motivator, there is little chance that employees will develop firm-specific ties to keep them with the organization.

The third section of the chapter discussed the importance of social capital in leveraging human capital. Social capital refers to the network of relationships that individuals have throughout the organization as well as with customers and suppliers. Such ties can be critical in obtaining both information and resources. With regard to recruiting, for example, we saw how some firms are able to hire en masse groups of individuals who are part of social networks. Social relationships can also be very important in the effective functioning of groups. Finally, we discussed some of the potential downsides of social capital. These include the expenses that firms may bear when promoting social and working relationships among individuals as well as the potential for "groupthink," wherein individuals are reluctant to express divergent (or opposing) views on an issue because of social pressures to conform. We also introduced the concept of social networks. The relative advantages of being central in a network versus bridging multiple networks was discussed. We addressed the key role that social networks can play in both improving knowledge management and promoting career success.

The fourth section addressed the role of technology in leveraging human capital. We discussed relatively simple means of using technology, such as email and networks where individuals can collaborate by way of personal computers. We provided suggestions and guidelines on how electronic teams can be effectively managed. We also addressed more sophisticated uses of technology, such as sophisticated management systems. Here, knowledge can be codified and reused at very low cost, as we saw in the examples of firms in the consulting, health care, and high-technology industries.

In the last section we discussed the increasing importance of protecting a firm's intellectual property. Although traditional approaches such as patents, copyrights, and trademarks are important, the development of dynamic capabilities may be the best protection in the long run.

SUMMARY REVIEW QUESTIONS

1. Explain the role of knowledge in today's competitive environment.
2. Why is it important for managers to recognize the interdependence in the attraction, development, and retention of talented professionals?
3. What are some of the potential downsides for firms that engage in a "war for talent"?
4. Discuss the need for managers to use social capital in leveraging their human capital both within and across their firm.
5. Discuss the key role of technology in leveraging knowledge and human capital.

key terms

knowledge economy 110
intellectual capital 111
human capital 112
social capital 112
explicit knowledge 112
tacit knowledge 112
360-degree evaluation and feedback systems 118
social network analysis 125
closure 126
bridging relationships 127
structural holes 127
unification lever 127
people lever 127
T-shaped management 127
network lever 127
groupthink 129
electronic teams 132
intellectual property rights 136
dynamic capabilities 137

experiential exercise

Pfizer, a leading health care firm with $59 billion in revenues, is often rated as one of *Fortune*'s "Most Admired Firms." It is also considered an excellent place to work and has generated high return to shareholders. Clearly, Pfizer values its human capital. Using the Internet and/or library resources, identify some of the actions/strategies Pfizer has taken to attract, develop, and retain human capital. What are their implications? (Fill in the table at bottom of the page.)

application questions & exercises

1. Look up successful firms in a high-technology industry as well as two successful firms in more traditional industries such as automobile manufacturing and retailing. Compare their market values and book values. What are some implications of these differences?
2. Select a firm for which you believe its social capital—both within the firm and among its suppliers and customers—is vital to its competitive advantage. Support your arguments.
3. Choose a company with which you are familiar. What are some of the ways in which it uses technology to leverage its human capital?
4. Using the Internet, look up a company with which you are familiar. What are some of the policies and procedures that it uses to enhance the firm's human and social capital?

ethics questions

1. Recall an example of a firm that recently faced an ethical crisis. How do you feel the crisis and management's handling of it affected the firm's human capital and social capital?
2. Based on your experiences or what you have learned in your previous classes, are you familiar with any companies that used unethical practices to attract talented professionals? What do you feel were the short-term and long-term consequences of such practices?

Activity	Actions/Strategies	Implications
Attracting human capital		
Developing human capital		
Retaining human capital		

references

1. Touryalai, H. 2011. Meddling with Merrill: Merrill Lynch's profits are bolstering BofA. What is Merrill getting in return? *Forbes,* September 26: 45–47; Benoit, D. 2012. BofA-Merrill: Still a bottom-line success. www.wsj.com, September 28: np; Silver-Greenberg, J. & Craig, S. 2012. Bank of America settles suit over Merrill for $2.43 billion. www.nytimes.com, September 28: np.

2. Parts of this chapter draw upon some of the ideas and examples from Dess, G. G. & Picken, J. C. 1999. *Beyond productivity.* New York: AMACOM.

3. Dekas, K. H., et al. 2013. Organizational citizenship behavior, version 2.0: A review and qualitative investigation of OCBs for knowledge workers at Google and beyond. *Academy of Management Perspectives,* 27(3): 219–237.

4. Stewart, T. A. 1997. *Intellectual capital: The new wealth of organizations.* New York: Doubleday/Currency.

5. Leif Edvinsson and Michael S. Malone have a similar, more detailed definition of *intellectual capital:* "the combined knowledge, skill, innovativeness, and ability to meet the task at hand." They consider intellectual capital to equal human capital plus structural capital. *Structural capital* is defined as "the hardware, software, databases, organization structure, patents, trademarks, and everything else of organizational capability that supports those employees' productivity—in a word, everything left at the office when the employees go home." Edvinsson, L. & Malone, M. S. 1997. *Intellectual capital: Realizing your company's true value by finding its hidden brainpower:* 10–14. New York: HarperBusiness.

6. Stewart, T. A. 2001. Accounting gets radical. *Fortune,* April 16: 184–194.

7. Adams, S. & Kichen, S. 2008. Ben Graham then and now. *Forbes,* www.multpl.com/s-p-500-price-to-book, November 10: 56.

8. An interesting discussion of Steve Jobs's impact on Apple's valuation is in Lashinsky, A. 2009. Steve's leave—what does it really mean? *Fortune,* February 2: 96–102.

9. Anonymous. 2007. Intel opens first high volume 45 nm microprocessor manufacturing factory. www.intel.com, October 25: np.

10. Thomas Stewart has suggested this formula in his book *Intellectual capital.* He provides an insightful discussion on pages 224–225, including some of the limitations of this approach to measuring intellectual capital. We recognize, of course, that during the late 1990s and in early 2000, there were some excessive market valuations of high-technology and Internet firms. For an interesting discussion of the extraordinary market valuation of Yahoo!, an Internet company, refer to Perkins, A. B. 2001. The Internet bubble encapsulated: Yahoo! *Red Herring,* April 15: 17–18.

11. Roberts, P. W. & Dowling, G. R. 2002. Corporate reputation and sustained superior financial performance. *Strategic Management Journal,* 23(12): 1077–1095.

12. For a study on the relationships between human capital, learning, and sustainable competitive advantage, read Hatch, N. W. & Dyer, J. H. 2005. Human capital and learning as a source of sustainable competitive advantage. *Strategic Management Journal,* 25: 1155–1178.

13. One of the seminal contributions on knowledge management is Becker, G. S. 1993. *Human capital: A theoretical and empirical analysis with special reference to education* (3rd ed.). Chicago: University of Chicago Press.

14. For an excellent overview of the topic of social capital, read Baron, R. A. 2005. Social capital. In Hitt, M. A. & Ireland, R. D. (Eds.), *The Blackwell encyclopedia of management* (2nd ed.): 224–226. Malden, MA: Blackwell.

15. For an excellent discussion of social capital and its impact on organizational performance, refer to Nahapiet, J. & Ghoshal, S. 1998. Social capital, intellectual capital, and the organizational advantage. *Academy of Management Review,* 23: 242–266.

16. An interesting discussion of how knowledge management (patents) can enhance organizational performance can be found in Bogner, W. C. & Bansal, P. 2007. Knowledge management as the basis of sustained high performance. *Journal of Management Studies,* 44(1): 165–188.

17. Polanyi, M. 1967. *The tacit dimension.* Garden City, NY: Anchor.

18. Barney, J. B. 1991. Firm resources and sustained competitive advantage. *Journal of Management,* 17: 99–120.

19. For an interesting perspective of empirical research on how knowledge can adversely affect performance, read Haas, M. R. & Hansen, M. T. 2005. When using knowledge can hurt performance: The value of organizational capabilities in a management consulting company. *Strategic Management Journal,* 26(1): 1–24.

20. New insights on managing talent are provided in Cappelli, P. 2008. Talent management for the twenty-first century. *Harvard Business Review,* 66(3): 74–81.

21. Some of the notable books on this topic include Edvisson & Malone, op. cit.; Stewart, op. cit.; and Nonaka, I. & Takeuchi, I. 1995. *The knowledge creating company.* New York: Oxford University Press.

22. Segalla, M. & Felton, N. 2010. Find the real power in your organization. *Harvard Business Review,* 88(5): 34–35.

23. Stewart, T. A. 2000. Taking risk to the marketplace. *Fortune,* March 6: 424.

24. Lobel, O. 2014. *Talent wants to be free.* New Haven, CT: Yale University Press.

25. Insights on Generation X's perspective on the workplace are in Erickson, T. J. 2008. Task, not time: Profile of a Gen Y job. *Harvard Business Review,* 86(2): 19.

26. Pfeffer, J. 2010. Building sustainable organizations: The human factor. *Academy of Management Perspectives,* 24(1): 34–45.

27. Lobel, op. cit.

28. Some workplace implications for the aging workforce are addressed in Strack, R., Baier, J., & Fahlander, A. 2008. Managing demographic risk. *Harvard Business Review,* 66(2): 119–128.

29. For a discussion of attracting, developing, and retaining top talent, refer to Goffee, R. & Jones, G. 2007. Leading clever people. *Harvard Business Review,* 85(3): 72–89.

30. Winston, A. S. 2014. *The big pivot.* Boston: Harvard Business Review Press.

31. Dess & Picken, op. cit., p. 34.

32. Webber, A. M. 1998. Danger: Toxic company. *Fast Company,* November: 152–161.

33. Martin, J. & Schmidt, C. 2010. How to keep your top talent. *Harvard Business Review,* 88(5): 54–61.

34. Some interesting insights on why home-grown American talent is going abroad are found in Saffo, P. 2009. A looming American diaspora. *Harvard Business Review,* 87(2): 27.

35. Grossman, M. 2012. The best advice I ever got. *Fortune,* May 12: 119.
36. Davenport, T. H., Harris, J., & Shapiro, J. 2010. Competing on talent analytics. *Harvard Business Review,* 88(10): 62–69.
37. Ployhart, R. E. & Moliterno, T. P. 2011. Emergence of the human capital resource: A multilevel model. *Academy of Management Review,* 36(1): 127–150.
38. For insights on management development and firm performance in several countries, refer to Mabey, C. 2008. Management development and firm performance in Germany, Norway, Spain, and the UK. *Journal of International Business Studies,* 39(8): 1327–1342.
39. Martin, J. 1998. So, you want to work for the best. . . . *Fortune,* January 12: 77.
40. Cardin, R. 1997. Make your own Bozo Filter. *Fast Company,* October–November: 56.
41. Anonymous. 100 best companies to work for. *money.cnn.com*, undated: np.
42. Martin, op. cit.; Henkoff, R. 1993. Companies that train best. *Fortune,* March 22: 53–60.
43. This section draws on: Garg, V. 2012. Here's why companies should give Millennial workers everything they ask for. *buisnessinsider.com*, August 23: np; *worklifepolicy.com*; and Gerdes, L. 2006. The top 50 employers for new college grads. *BusinessWeek,* September 18: 64–81.
44. An interesting perspective on developing new talent rapidly when they join an organization can be found in Rollag, K., Parise, S., & Cross, R. 2005. Getting new hires up to speed quickly. *MIT Sloan Management Review,* 46(2): 35–41.
45. Stewart, T. A. 1998. Gray flannel suit? Moi? *Fortune,* March 18: 80–82.
46. Bryant, A. 2011. *The corner office.* New York: St. Martin's Griffin, 227.
47. An interesting perspective on how Cisco Systems develops its talent can be found in Chatman, J., O'Reilly, C., & Chang, V. 2005. Cisco Systems: Developing a human capital strategy. *California Management Review,* 47(2): 137–166.
48. Anonymous. 2011. Schumpeter: The tussle for talent. *The Economist,* January 8: 68.
49. Training and development policy: Mentoring. *opm.gov:* undated, np.
50. Douglas, C. A. 1997. Formal mentoring programs in organizations. *centerforcreativeleadership.org:* np.
51. Warner, F. 2002. Inside Intel's mentoring movement. *fastcompany.com*, March 31: np.
52. Grove, A. 2011. Be a mentor. *Bloomberg Businessweek,* September 21: 80.
53. For an innovative perspective on the appropriateness of alternate approaches to evaluation and rewards, refer to Seijts, G. H. & Lathan, G. P. 2005. Learning versus performance goals: When should each be used? *Academy of Management Executive,* 19(1): 124–132.
54. The discussion of the 360-degree feedback system draws on the article UPS. 1997. 360-degree feedback: Coming from all sides. *Vision* (a UPS Corporation internal company publication), March: 3; Slater, R. 1994. *Get better or get beaten: Thirty-one leadership secrets from Jack Welch.* Burr Ridge, IL: Irwin; Nexon, M. 1997. General Electric: The secrets of the finest company in the world. *L'Expansion,* July 23: 18–30; and Smith, D. 1996. Bold new directions for human resources. *Merck World* (internal company publication), October: 8.
55. Interesting insights on 360-degree evaluation systems are discussed in Barwise, P. & Meehan, Sean. 2008. So you think you're a good listener. *Harvard Business Review,* 66(4): 22–23.
56. Insights into the use of 360-degree evaluation are in Kaplan, R. E. & Kaiser, R. B. 2009. Stop overdoing your strengths. *Harvard Business Review,* 87(2): 100–103.
57. Mankins, M., Bird, A., & Root, J. 2013. Making star teams out of star players. *Harvard Business Review,* 91(1/2): 74–78.
58. Kets de Vries, M. F. R. 1998. Charisma in action: The transformational abilities of Virgin's Richard Branson and ABB's Percy Barnevik. *Organizational Dynamics,* Winter: 20.
59. For an interesting discussion on how organizational culture has helped Zappos become number one in *Fortune*'s 2009 survey of the best companies to work for, see O'Brien, J. M. 2009. Zappos knows how to kick it. *Fortune,* February 2: 54–58.
60. We have only to consider the most celebrated case of industrial espionage in recent years, wherein José Ignacio Lopez was indicted in a German court for stealing sensitive product planning documents from his former employer, General Motors, and sharing them with his executive colleagues at Volkswagen. The lawsuit was dismissed by the German courts, but Lopez and his colleagues were investigated by the U.S. Justice Department. Also consider the recent litigation involving noncompete employment contracts and confidentiality clauses of *International Paper v. Louisiana-Pacific, Campbell Soup v. H. J. Heinz Co.,* and *PepsiCo v. Quaker Oats's Gatorade.* In addition to retaining valuable human resources and often their valuable network of customers, firms must also protect proprietary information and knowledge. For interesting insights, refer to Carley, W. M. 1998. CEO gets hard lesson in how not to keep his lieutenants. *The Wall Street Journal,* February 11: A1, A10; and Lenzner, R. & Shook, C. 1998. Whose Rolodex is it, anyway? *Forbes,* February 23: 100–103.
61. For an insightful discussion of retention of knowledge workers in today's economy, read Davenport, T. H. 2005. *The care and feeding of the knowledge worker.* Boston, MA: Harvard Business School Press.
62. Weber, L. 2014. Here's what boards want in executives. *The Wall Street Journal,* December 10: B5.
63. Fisher, A. 2008. America's most admired companies. *Fortune,* March 17: 74.
64. Stewart, T. A. 2001. *The wealth of knowledge.* New York: Currency.
65. For insights on fulfilling one's potential, refer to Kaplan, R. S. 2008. Reaching your potential. *Harvard Business Review,* 66(7/8): 45–57.
66. Amabile, T. M. 1997. Motivating creativity in organizations: On doing what you love and loving what you do. *California Management Review,* Fall: 39–58.
67. For an insightful perspective on alternate types of employee–employer relationships, read Erickson, T. J. & Gratton, L. 2007. What it means to work here. *Harvard Business Review,* 85(3): 104–112.
68. Pfeffer, J. 2001. Fighting the war for talent is hazardous to your organization's health. *Organizational Dynamics,* 29(4): 248–259.
69. Best companies to work for 2011. 2011. *finance.yahoo.com*, January 20: np.
70. This section draws on Dewhurst, M., Hancock, B., & Ellsworth, D. 2013. Redesigning knowledge work. *Harvard Business Review,* 91 (1/2): 58–64.

71. Cox, T. L. 1991. The multinational organization. *Academy of Management Executive,* 5(2): 34–47. Without doubt, a great deal has been written on the topic of creating and maintaining an effective diverse workforce. Some excellent, recent books include Harvey, C. P. & Allard, M. J. 2005. *Understanding and managing diversity: Readings, cases, and exercises* (3rd ed.). Upper Saddle River, NJ: Pearson Prentice-Hall; Miller, F. A. & Katz, J. H. 2002. *The inclusion breakthrough: Unleashing the real power of diversity.* San Francisco: Berrett Koehler; and Williams, M. A. 2001. *The 10 lenses: Your guide to living and working in a multicultural world.* Sterling, VA: Capital Books.

72. For an interesting perspective on benefits and downsides of diversity in global consulting firms, refer to Mors, M. L. 2010. Innovation in a global consulting firm: When the problem is too much diversity. *Strategic Management Journal,* 31(8): 841–872.

73. Day, J. C. Undated. National population projections. *cps.ipums.org:* np.

74. Hewlett, S. A. & Rashid, R. 2010. The battle for female talent in emerging markets. *Harvard Business Review,* 88(5): 101–107.

75. This section, including the six potential benefits of a diverse workforce, draws on Cox, T. H. & Blake, S. 1991. Managing cultural diversity: Implications for organizational competitiveness. *Academy of Management Executive,* 5(3): 45–56.

76. www.pwcglobal.com/us/eng/careers/diversity/index.html.

77. Hewlett, S. A., Marshall, M., & Sherbin, L. 2013. How diversity can drive innovation. *Harvard Business Review,* 91(12): 30.

78. This discussion draws on Dess, G. G. & Lumpkin, G. T. 2001. Emerging issues in strategy process research. In Hitt, M. A., Freeman, R. E., & Harrison, J. S. (Eds.), *Handbook of strategic management:* 3–34. Malden, MA: Blackwell.

79. Wong, S.-S. & Boh, W. F. 2010. Leveraging the ties of others to build a reputation for trustworthiness among peers. *Academy of Management Journal,* 53(1): 129–148.

80. Adler, P. S. & Kwon, S. W. 2002. Social capital: Prospects for a new concept. *Academy of Management Review,* 27(1): 17–40.

81. Capelli, P. 2000. A market-driven approach to retaining talent. *Harvard Business Review,* 78(1): 103–113.

82. This hypothetical example draws on Peteraf, M. 1993. The cornerstones of competitive advantage. *Strategic Management Journal,* 14: 179–191.

83. Wernerfelt, B. 1984. A resource-based view of the firm. *Strategic Management Journal,* 5: 171–180.

84. Wysocki, B., Jr. 2000. Yet another hazard of the new economy: The Pied Piper effect. *The Wall Street Journal,* March 20: A1–A16.

85. Ideas on how managers can more effectively use their social network are addressed in McGrath, C. & Zell, D. 2009. Profiles of trust: Who to turn to, and for what. *MIT Sloan Management Review,* 50(2): 75–80.

86. Ibid.

87. Buckman, R. C. 2000. Tech defectors from Microsoft resettle together. *The Wall Street Journal,* October: B1–B6.

88. A study of the relationship between social networks and performance in China is found in Li, J. J., Poppo, L., & Zhou, K. Z. 2008. Do managerial ties in China always produce value? Competition, uncertainty, and domestic vs. foreign firms. *Strategic Management Journal,* 29(4): 383–400.

89. Aime, F., Johnson, S., Ridge, J. W., & Hill, A. D. 2010. The routine may be stable but the advantage is not: Competitive implications of key employee mobility. *Strategic Management Journal,* 31(1): 75–87.

90. Ibarra, H. & Hansen, M. T. 2011. Are you a collaborative leader? *Harvard Business Review,* 89(7/8): 68–74.

91. Battilana, J. & Casciaro, T. 2013. The network secrets of great change agents. *Harvard Business Review,* 91(7/8): 62–68.

92. There has been a tremendous amount of theory building and empirical research in recent years in the area of social network analysis. Unquestionably, two of the major contributors to this domain have been Ronald Burt and J. S. Coleman. For excellent background discussions, refer to Burt, R. S. 1992. *Structural holes: The social structure of competition.* Cambridge, MA: Harvard University Press; Coleman, J. S. 1990. *Foundations of social theory.* Cambridge, MA: Harvard University Press; and Coleman, J. S. 1988. Social capital in the creation of human capital. *American Journal of Sociology,* 94: S95–S120. For a more recent review and integration of current thought on social network theory, consider Burt, R. S. 2005. *Brokerage & closure: An introduction to social capital.* New York: Oxford Press.

93. Our discussion draws on the concepts developed by Burt, 1992, op. cit.; Coleman, 1990, op. cit.; Coleman, 1988, op. cit.; and Oh, H., Chung, M., & Labianca, G. 2004. Group social capital and group effectiveness: The role of informal socializing ties. *Academy of Management Journal,* 47(6): 860–875. We would like to thank Joe Labianca (University of Kentucky) for his helpful feedback and ideas in our discussion of social networks.

94. Arregle, J. L., Hitt, M. A., Sirmon, D. G., & Very, P. 2007. The development of organizational social capital: Attributes of family firms. *Journal of Management Studies,* 44(1): 73–95.

95. A novel perspective on social networks is in Pentland, A. 2009. How social networks network best. *Harvard Business Review,* 87(2): 37.

96. Oh et al., op. cit.

97. Hoppe, op. cit.

98. This section draws on Hansen, M. T. 2009. *Collaboration: How leaders avoid the traps, create unity, and reap big results.* Boston: Harvard Business Press.

99. Perspectives on how to use and develop decision networks are discussed in Cross, R., Thomas, R. J., & Light, D. A. 2009. How "who you know" affects what you decide. *MIT Sloan Management Review,* 50(2): 35–42.

100. Our discussion of the three advantages of social networks draws on Uzzi, B. & Dunlap. S. 2005. How to build your network. *Harvard Business Review,* 83(12): 53–60. For an excellent review on the research exploring the relationship between social capital and managerial performance, read Moran, P. 2005. Structural vs. relational embeddedness: Social capital and managerial performance. *Strategic Management Journal,* 26(12): 1129–1151.

101. A perspective on personal influence is in Christakis, N. A. 2009. The dynamics of personal influence. *Harvard Business Review,* 87(2): 31.

102. Cross, R. & Thomas, R. 2011. A smarter way to network. *Harvard Business Review,* 89(7/8): 149–153.

103. Prusak, L. & Cohen, D. 2001. How to invest in social capital. *Harvard Business Review,* 79(6): 86–93.

104. Leonard, D. & Straus, S. 1997. Putting your company's whole brain to work. *Harvard Business Review,* 75(4): 110–122.

105. For an excellent discussion of public (i.e., the organization) versus private (i.e., the individual manager) benefits of social capital, refer to Leana, C. R. & Van Buren, H. J. 1999. Organizational social capital and employment practices. *Academy of Management Review,* 24(3): 538–555.

106. The authors would like to thank Joe Labianca, University of Kentucky, and John Lin, University of Texas at Dallas, for their very helpful input in our discussion of social network theory and its practical implications.

107. Goldsmith, M. 2009. How not to lose the top job. *Harvard Business Review,* 87(1): 74.

108. Taylor, W. C. 1999. Whatever happened to globalization? *Fast Company,* December: 228–236.

109. Wilson, H. J., Guinan, P. J., Paris, S., & Weinberg, D. 2011. What's your social media strategy? *Harvard Business Review,* 89(7/8): 23–25.

110. Lei, D., Slocum, J., & Pitts, R. A. 1999. Designing organizations for competitive advantage: The power of unlearning and learning. *Organizational Dynamics,* Winter: 24–38.

111. This section draws upon Zaccaro, S. J. & Bader, P. 2002. E-leadership and the challenges of leading e-teams: Minimizing the bad and maximizing the good. *Organizational Dynamics,* 31(4): 377–387.

112. Kirkman, B. L., Rosen, B., Tesluk, P. E., & Gibson, C. B. 2004. The impact of team empowerment on virtual team performance: The moderating role of face-to-face interaction. *Academy of Management Journal,* 47(2): 175–192.

113. The discussion of the advantages and challenges associated with e-teams draws on Zaccaro & Bader, op. cit.

114. For a study exploring the relationship between team empowerment, face-to-face interaction, and performance in virtual teams, read Kirkman, Rosen, Tesluk, & Gibson, op. cit.

115. For an innovative study on how firms share knowledge with competitors and the performance implications, read Spencer, J. W. 2003. Firms' knowledge sharing strategies in the global innovation system: Empirical evidence from the flat panel display industry. *Strategic Management Journal,* 24(3): 217–235.

116. The examples of Andersen Consulting and Access Health draw upon Hansen, M. T., Nohria, N., & Tierney, T. 1999. What's your strategy for managing knowledge? *Harvard Business Review,* 77(2): 106–118.

117. This discussion draws on Conley, J. G. 2005. *Intellectual capital management.* Kellogg School of Management and Schulich School of Business, York University, Toronto, ON; Conley, J. G. & Szobocsan, J. 2001. Snow White shows the way. *Managing Intellectual Property,* June: 15–25; Greenspan, A. 2004. Intellectual property rights. Federal Reserve Board, Remarks by the chairman, February 27; and Teece, D. J. 1998. Capturing value from knowledge assets. *California Management Review,* 40(3): 54–79. The authors would like to thank Professor Theo Peridis, York University, for his contribution to this section.

118. Wingfield, N. 2012. As Apple and HTC end lawsuits, smartphone patent battles continue. *New York Times,* www.nytimes.com, November 11: 57–63; and Tyrangiel, J. 2012. Tim Cook's freshman year: The Apple CEO speaks. *Bloomberg Businessweek,* December 6: 62–76.

119. E. Danneels. 2011. Trying to become a different type of company: Dynamic capability at Smith Corona. *Strategic Management Journal,* 32(1): 1–31.

120. A study of the relationship between dynamic capabilities and related diversification is Doving, E. & Gooderham, P. N. 2008. *Strategic Management Journal,* 29(8): 841–858.

121. A perspective on strategy in turbulent markets is in Sull, D. 2009. How to thrive in turbulent markets. *Harvard Business Review,* 87(2): 78–88.

122. Lee, G. K. 2008. Relevance of organizational capabilities and its dynamics: What to learn from entrants' product portfolios about the determinants of entry timing. *Strategic Management Journal,* 29(12): 1257–1280.

123. Eisenhardt, K. M. & Martin, J. E. 2000. Dynamic capabilities: What are they? *Strategic Management Journal,* 21: 1105–1121.

photo credits

Page 108: © Anatoli Styf/Getty Images/RF

Strategic Formulation

Business-Level Strategy
Creating and Sustaining Competitive Advantages

chapter 5

After reading this chapter, you should have a good understanding of the following learning objectives:

LO5.1 The central role of competitive advantage in the study of strategic management and the three generic strategies: overall cost leadership, differentiation, and focus.

LO5.2 How the successful attainment of generic strategies can improve a firm's relative power vis-à-vis the five forces that determine an industry's average profitability.

LO5.3 The pitfalls managers must avoid in striving to attain generic strategies.

LO5.4 How firms can effectively combine the generic strategies of overall cost leadership and differentiation.

LO5.5 What factors determine the sustainability of a firm's competitive advantage.

LO5.6 The importance of considering the industry life cycle to determine a firm's business-level strategy and its relative emphasis on functional area strategies and value-creating activities.

LO5.7 The need for turnaround strategies that enable a firm to reposition its competitive position in an industry.

PART 2: STRATEGIC FORMULATION

Learning from Mistakes

Crumbs Bake Shop rode the gourmet cupcake boom to great heights. The company was founded in 2003 in the Upper West Side of New York City by Jason Bauer, who designed and baked giant, high-quality cupcakes with decadent flavors, such as cookie dough, caramel macchiato, and red velvet. The cupcakes came with a hefty calorie count of 600 calories and a premium price of $3.50 to $4.50 each. Crumbs grew quickly from a single bakery in 2003 to nearly 80 bakeries in 10 states by 2013 and hoped to grow to 200 stores by 2014. The firm was honored by *Inc.* magazine as a "breakout company" in 2010. It went public in 2011 and saw its stock price rise to $13 per share. However, as fast as the company rose, it fell even more quickly. The firm lost $18.2 million on $47 million in sales in 2013 and saw its cash reserves dwindle from $6.3 million to $893,000. The chain closed nine stores in late 2013 and six more in early 2014 as managers tried to save the company. However, it all came crashing down in July 2014 when Crumbs was delisted by the NASDAQ Stock Exchange after its stock dropped to 30 cents a share. The firm then filed for bankruptcy and closed all of its remaining 48 stores.[1] What went wrong?

> Crumbs experienced two of the pitfalls differentiators can fall into. First, the rapid growth of the company strained its ability to sustain the high quality of its products. As it moved from an entrepreneurial firm in which the entire baking process was overseen by the founder to a publicly traded company in which the baking was done by low-wage workers, customers started to question whether their cupcakes were worth $4.50 each. As one customer, Ari Stern, commented, "It's impossible to control quality when you're worrying about your shareholders instead of your product." Second, customer tastes can be fickle. As a result, a highly desirable differentiated product can fall out of favor before firms can react. Crumbs differentiated itself from other bakeries by offering large, 4-inch cupcakes with rich flavors. While demand for these types of cupcakes took off after they were featured in *Sex in the City,* demand quickly slackened as people became more concerned about the calorie count in them and the gluten-free craze took hold.

Crumbs may not be done yet. The firm emerged from bankruptcy in August 2014 with a new ownership team led by self-styled turnaround guru Marcus Lemonis. The new owners planned to reopen about two dozen Crumbs locations in major cities, such as New York, Los Angeles, Chicago, and Boston.

Discussion Questions

1. What lessons can we take from Crumbs Bake Shop's experience?
2. What actions can Crumbs take to increase its chances of survival in a market that no longer puts as high a premium on high-end cupcakes?

In order to create and sustain a competitive advantage, companies such as Crumbs need to stay focused on their customers' evolving wants and needs and not sacrifice their strategic position as they grow. By becoming too growth-oriented and not focusing on customer needs, Crumbs and many other firms have seen their performance drop and even their existence challenged.

business-level strategy
a strategy designed for a firm or a division of a firm that competes within a single business.

Types of Competitive Advantage and Sustainability

L05.1

The central role of competitive advantage in the study of strategic management and the three generic strategies: overall cost leadership, differentiation, and focus.

generic strategies
basic types of business-level strategies based on breadth of target market (industrywide versus narrow market segment) and type of competitive advantage (low cost versus uniqueness).

Michael Porter presented three **generic strategies** that a firm can use to overcome the five forces and achieve competitive advantage.[2] Each of Porter's generic strategies has the potential to allow a firm to outperform rivals in their industry. The first, *overall cost leadership,* is based on creating a low-cost position. Here, a firm must manage the relationships throughout the value chain and lower costs throughout the entire chain. Second, *differentiation* requires a firm to create products and/or services that are unique and valued. Here, the primary emphasis is on "nonprice" attributes for which customers will gladly pay a premium.[3] Third, a *focus* strategy directs attention (or "focus") toward narrow product lines, buyer segments, or targeted geographic markets, and they must attain advantages through either differentiation or cost leadership.[4] Whereas the overall cost leadership and differentiation strategies strive to attain advantages industrywide, focusers have a narrow target market in mind. Exhibit 5.1 illustrates these three strategies on two dimensions: competitive advantage and markets served.

Both casual observation and research support the notion that firms that identify with one or more of the forms of competitive advantage outperform those that do not.[5] There has been a rich history of strategic management research addressing this topic. One study analyzed 1,789 strategic business units and found that businesses combining multiple forms of competitive advantage (differentiation and overall cost leadership) outperformed businesses that used only a single form. The lowest performers were those that did not identify with any type of advantage. They were classified as "stuck in the middle." Results of this study are presented in Exhibit 5.2.[6]

For an example of the dangers of being stuck in the middle, consider the traditional supermarket.[7] The major supermarket chains, such as Kroger, Ralphs, and Albertsons, used to be the main source of groceries for consumers. However, they find themselves in a situation today where affluent customers are going upmarket to get their organic and gourmet foods at retailers like Whole Foods Market and budget-conscious consumers are drifting to discount chains such as Walmart, Aldi, and Dollar General.

overall cost leadership
a firm's generic strategy based on appeal to the industrywide market using a competitive advantage based on low cost.

Overall Cost Leadership

The first generic strategy is **overall cost leadership.** Overall cost leadership requires a tight set of interrelated tactics that include:

- Aggressive construction of efficient-scale facilities.
- Vigorous pursuit of cost reductions from experience.

EXHIBIT 5.1 Three Generic Strategies

	Competitive Advantage	
Markets Served	Low Cost Position	Superior Perceived Value by Customer
Broad Target Market	Overall Cost Leadership	Broad Differentiation
Narrow Target Markets	Cost Focus	Differentiation Focus

Source: Adapted from *Competitive Strategy: Techniques for Analyzing Industries and Competitors* by Michael E. Porter, 1980, 1998, Free Press.

EXHIBIT 5.2 Competitive Advantage and Business Performance

	Competitive Advantage					
	Differentiation and Cost	Differentiation	Cost	Differentiation and Focus	Cost and Focus	Stuck in the Middle
Performance						
Return on investment (%)	35.5	32.9	30.2	17.0	23.7	17.8
Sales growth (%)	15.1	13.5	13.5	16.4	17.5	12.2
Gain in market share (%)	5.3	5.3	5.5	6.1	6.3	4.4
Sample size	123	160	100	141	86	105

- Tight cost and overhead control.
- Avoidance of marginal customer accounts.
- Cost minimization in all activities in the firm's value chain, such as R&D, service, sales force, and advertising.

Exhibit 5.3 draws on the value-chain concept (see Chapter 3) to provide examples of how a firm can attain an overall cost leadership strategy in its primary and support activities.

One factor often central to an overall cost leadership strategy is the **experience curve,** which refers to how business "learns" to lower costs as it gains experience with production processes. With experience, unit costs of production decline as output increases in most industries. The experience curve, developed by the Boston Consulting Group in 1968, is a way of looking at efficiency gains that come with experience. For a range of products, as cumulative experience doubles, costs and labor hours needed to produce a unit of product decline by 10 to 30 percent. There are a number of reasons why we find this effect. Among the most common factors are workers getting better at what they do, product designs being simplified as the product matures, and production processes being automated and streamlined. However, experience curve gains will be the foundation for a cost advantage only if the firm knows the source of the cost reduction and can keep these gains proprietary.

To generate above-average performance, a firm following an overall cost leadership position must attain **competitive parity** on the basis of differentiation relative to competitors.[8] In other words, a firm achieving parity is similar to its competitors, or "on par," with respect to differentiated products.[9] Competitive parity on the basis of differentiation permits a cost leader to translate cost advantages directly into higher profits than competitors. Thus, the cost leader earns above-average returns.[10]

The failure to attain parity on the basis of differentiation can be illustrated with an example from the automobile industry—the ill-fated Yugo. Below is an excerpt from a speech by J. W. Marriott, Jr., chairman of the Marriott Corporation:[11]

> Money is a big thing. But it's not the only thing. In the 1980s, a new automobile reached North America from behind the Iron Curtain. It was called the Yugo, and its main attraction was price. About $3,000 each. But the only way they caught on was as the butt of jokes. Remember the guy who told his mechanic, "I want a gas cap for my Yugo." "OK," the mechanic replied, "that sounds like a fair trade."

Yugo was offering a lousy value proposition. The cars literally fell apart before your eyes. And the lesson was simple. Price is just one component of value. No matter how good the price, the most cost-sensitive consumer won't buy a bad product.

> **experience curve**
> the decline in unit costs of production as cumulative output increases.

> **competitive parity**
> a firm's achievement of similarity, or being "on par," with competitors with respect to low cost, differentiation, or other strategic product characteristic.

EXHIBIT 5.3
Value-Chain Activities: Examples of Overall Cost Leadership

Support Activities

Firm Infrastructure
- Few management layers to reduce overhead costs.
- Standardized accounting practices to minimize personnel required.

Human Resource Management
- Minimize costs associated with employee turnover through effective policies.
- Effective orientation and training programs to maximize employee productivity.

Technology Development
- Effective use of automated technology to reduce scrappage rates.
- Expertise in process engineering to reduce manufacturing costs.

Procurement
- Effective policy guidelines to ensure low-cost raw materials (with acceptable quality levels).
- Shared purchasing operations with other business units.

Primary Activities

Inbound Logistics
- Effective layout of receiving dock operations.

Operations
- Effective use of quality control inspectors to minimize rework.

Outbound Logistics
- Effective utilization of delivery fleets.

Marketing and Sales
- Purchase of media in large blocks.
- Sales-force utilization is maximized by territory management.

Service
- Thorough service repair guidelines to minimize repeat maintenance calls.
- Use of single type of vehicle to minimize repair costs.

Source: Adapted from Porter, M. E. 1985. *Competitive Advantage: Creating and Sustaining Superior Performance.* New York: Free Press.

Gordon Bethune, the former CEO of Continental Airlines, summed up the need to provide good products or services when employing a low-cost strategy this way: "You can make a pizza so cheap, nobody will buy it."[12]

Next, we discuss some examples of how firms enhance a cost leadership position.

Aldi, a discount supermarket retailer, has grown from its German base to the rest of Europe, Australia, and the United States by replicating a simple business format. Aldi limits the number of products (SKUs in the grocery business) in each category to ensure product turn, to ease stocking shelves, and to increase its power over suppliers. It also sells mostly private-label products to minimize cost. It has small, efficient, and simply designed stores. It offers limited services and expects customers to bring their own bags and bag their own groceries. As a result, Aldi can offer its products at prices 40 percent lower than competing supermarkets.[13]

Tesco, Britain's largest grocery retailer, has changed how it views waste in order to become more efficient. To cut its costs, Tesco has begun shipping off food waste to

5.1 STRATEGY SPOTLIGHT

RENAULT FINDS LOW COST WORKS WELL IN THE NEW EUROPE

The European economic crisis has changed how Renault, a French carmaker, designs and produces cars for European customers. Historically, European car buyers have been sophisticated, demanding well-designed, feature-laden cars from manufacturers. When the economic crisis hit Europe in 2007, automakers saw a dramatic shift in demand. Overall demand dropped, and the customers who did come in to buy became much more cost-conscious.

In these difficult conditions, Renault has been able to carve out a profitable market for itself, selling low-cost, no-frills cars. Renault responded to this shift by creating an entry-level car group that was charged with designing and producing cars for these more cost-conscious consumers. For example, the group took an ultra-cheap car, the Logan, that was originally aimed for emerging markets and redesigned it to meet the new needs of the European market. The boxy sedan, which sells for around $10,000, is now one of Renault's best sellers. Its entry-level cars accounted for 30 percent of the cars sold by Renault in 2011 and generated operating profit margins over twice the profit margins of the higher-priced cars Renault sold.

What is the recipe for success Renault has found to generate high profits on low-priced cars? It uses simple designs that incorporate components from older car designs at Renault and employs a no-discount retail policy. At the center of its design procedure is a "design-to-cost" philosophy. In this process, designers and engineers no longer strive for the cutting edge. Instead, they focus on choosing parts and materials for simplicity, ease of manufacturing, and availability. This often involves using components that were engineered for prior vehicle designs. When needing a new component, Renault begins by assessing how much customers would be willing to pay for certain features, such as air conditioning or power door locks, and then asks suppliers whether they can propose a way to offer this feature at a cost that matches what customers are willing to pay.

As it faces imitation of this strategy by Volkswagen and Toyota, Renault is not sitting idle. As Carlos Ghosn, Renault's CEO, stated, "Our low-cost offering isn't low-cost enough. So we're working on a new platform that will be ultra low-cost."

Sources: Pearson, D. 2012. Renault takes low-cost lead. *wsj.com*, April 16: np; and Ciferri, L. 2013. How Renault's low-cost Dacia has become a "cash cow." *Automotive News Europe*, January 3: np.

---

bioenergy plants to convert the waste onto electricity. This allows Tesco to both avoid landfill taxes of $98 per ton and also save on the cost of its electricity by providing the fuel for the power plant. Tesco is saving $3 million a year alone in landfill taxes by simply sending its used cooking oil and chicken fat to be used to generate bioenergy rather than putting it in a landfill. Overall, Tesco estimates that energy-saving efforts are shaving over $300 million a year from its energy bills.[14]

Zulily, an online retailer, has built its business model around lower-cost operations in order to carve out a unique position relative to Amazon and other online retailers. Zulily keeps very little inventory and typically orders products from vendors only when customers purchase the product. It also has developed a bare-bones distribution system. Together, these actions result in deliveries that take an average of 11.5 days to get to customers and can sometimes stretch out to several weeks. Due to its reduced operational costs, Zulily is able to offer attractive prices to customers who are willing to wait.[15]

A business that strives for a low-cost advantage must attain an absolute cost advantage relative to its rivals.[16] This is typically accomplished by offering a no-frills product or service to a broad target market using standardization to derive the greatest benefits from economies of scale and experience. However, such a strategy may fail if a firm is unable to attain parity on important dimensions of differentiation such as quick responses to customer requests for services or design changes. Strategy Spotlight 5.1 discusses how Renault is leveraging a low-cost strategy to draw in auto buyers in Europe.

Overall Cost Leadership: Improving Competitive Position vis-à-vis the Five Forces An overall low-cost position enables a firm to achieve above-average returns despite strong competition. It protects a firm against rivalry from competitors, because lower costs allow a firm to earn returns even if its competitors eroded their profits through intense rivalry. A low-cost position also protects firms against powerful buyers. Buyers can exert power to drive down prices only to the level of the next most efficient producer. Also, a low-cost position provides more flexibility to cope with demands from powerful suppliers for input cost

LO5.2

How the successful attainment of generic strategies can improve a firm's relative power vis-à-vis the five forces that determine an industry's average profitability.

increases. The factors that lead to a low-cost position also provide a substantial entry barriers position with respect to substitute products introduced by new and existing competitors.[17]

A few examples will illustrate these points. Zulily's close attention to costs helps to protect the company from buyer power and intense rivalry from competitors. Thus, Zulily is able to drive down costs and reduce the bargaining power of its customers. By increasing productivity and lowering unit costs, Renault both lessens the degree of rivalry it faces and increases entry barriers for new entrants. Aldi's extreme focus on minimizing costs across its operations makes it less vulnerable to substitutes, such as discount retailers like Walmart and dollar stores.

Potential Pitfalls of Overall Cost Leadership Strategies Potential pitfalls of an overall cost leadership strategy include:

> **LO5.3**
> The pitfalls managers must avoid in striving to attain generic strategies.

- *Too much focus on one or a few value-chain activities.* Would you consider a person to be astute if he canceled his newspaper subscription and quit eating out to save money but then "maxed out" several credit cards, requiring him to pay hundreds of dollars a month in interest charges? Of course not. Similarly, firms need to pay attention to all activities in the value chain.[18] Too often managers make big cuts in operating expenses but don't question year-to-year spending on capital projects. Or managers may decide to cut selling and marketing expenses but ignore manufacturing expenses. Managers should explore *all* value-chain activities, including relationships among them, as candidates for cost reductions.

- *Increase in the cost of the inputs on which the advantage is based.* Firms can be vulnerable to price increases in the factors of production. For example, consider manufacturing firms based in China that rely on low labor costs. Due to demographic factors, the supply of workers 16 to 24 years old has peaked and will drop by a third in the next 12 years, thanks to stringent family-planning policies that have sharply reduced China's population growth.[19] This is leading to upward pressure on labor costs in Chinese factories, undercutting the cost advantage of firms producing there.

- *A strategy that can be imitated too easily.* One of the common pitfalls of a cost leadership strategy is that a firm's strategy may consist of value-creating activities that are easy to imitate.[20] Such has been the case with online brokers in recent years.[21] As of early 2015, there were over 200 online brokers listed on allstocks.com, hardly symbolic of an industry where imitation is extremely difficult. And according to Henry McVey, financial services analyst at Morgan Stanley, "We think you need five to ten" online brokers.

- *A lack of parity on differentiation.* As noted earlier, firms striving to attain cost leadership advantages must obtain a level of parity on differentiation.[22] Firms providing online degree programs may offer low prices. However, they may not be successful unless they can offer instruction that is perceived as comparable to traditional providers. For them, parity can be achieved on differentiation dimensions such as reputation and quality and through signaling mechanisms such as accreditation agencies.

- *Reduced flexibility.* Building up a low-cost advantage often requires significant investments in plant and equipment, distribution systems, and large, economically scaled operations. As a result, firms often find that these investments limit their flexibility, leading to great difficulty responding to changes in the environment. For example, Coors Brewing developed a highly efficient, large-scale brewery in Golden, Colorado. Coors was one of the most efficient brewers in the world, but its plant was designed to mass-produce one or two types of beer. When the craft brewing craze started to grow, the plant was not well equipped to produce smaller batches of craft beer, and Coors found it difficult to meet this opportunity. Ultimately, Coors had to buy its way into this movement by acquiring small craft breweries.[23]

- **Obsolescence of the basis of cost advantage.** Ultimately, the foundation of a firm's cost advantage may become obsolete. In such circumstances, other firms develop new ways of cutting costs, leaving the old cost leaders at a significant disadvantage. The older cost leaders are often locked into their way of competing and are unable to respond to the newer, lower-cost means of competing. This is what happened to the U.S. auto industry in the 1970s. Ford, GM, and Chrysler had built up efficient mass-manufacturing auto plants. However, when Toyota and other Japanese manufacturers moved into the North American car market using lean manufacturing, a new and more efficient means of production, the U.S. firms found themselves at a significant cost disadvantage. It took the U.S. firms over 30 years to redesign and retool their plants and restructure the responsibilities of line workers to get to a position where they were on cost parity with the Japanese firms.

Differentiation

As the name implies, a **differentiation strategy** consists of creating differences in the firm's product or service offering by creating something that is perceived *industrywide* as unique and valued by customers.[24] Differentiation can take many forms:

- Prestige or brand image (Hotel Monaco, BMW automobiles).[25]
- Quality (Apple, Ruth's Chris steak houses, Michelin tires).
- Technology (Martin guitars, Marantz stereo components, North Face camping equipment).
- Innovation (Medtronic medical equipment, Apple's iPhones and iPads).
- Features (Cannondale mountain bikes, Honda Goldwing motorcycles).
- Customer service (Nordstrom department stores, USAA financial services).
- Dealer network (Lexus automobiles, Caterpillar earthmoving equipment).

> **differentiation strategy**
> a firm's generic strategy based on creating differences in the firm's product or service offering by creating something that is perceived *industrywide* as unique and valued by customers.

Exhibit 5.4 draws on the concept of the value chain as an example of how firms may differentiate themselves in primary and support activities.

Firms may differentiate themselves along several different dimensions at once.[26] For example, the Cheesecake Factory, an upscale casual restaurant, differentiates itself by offering high-quality food, the widest and deepest menu in its class of restaurants, and premium locations.[27]

Firms achieve and sustain differentiation advantages and attain above-average performance when their price premiums exceed the extra costs incurred in being unique.[28] For example, the Cheesecake Factory must increase consumer prices to offset the higher cost of premium real estate and producing such a wide menu. Thus, a differentiator will always seek out ways of distinguishing itself from similar competitors to justify price premiums greater than the costs incurred by differentiating.[29] Clearly, a differentiator cannot ignore costs. After all, its premium prices would be eroded by a markedly inferior cost position. Therefore, it must attain a level of cost *parity* relative to competitors. Differentiators can do this by reducing costs in all areas that do not affect differentiation. Porsche, for example, invests heavily in engine design—an area in which its customers demand excellence—but it is less concerned and spends fewer resources in the design of the instrument panel or the arrangement of switches on the radio.[30] Although a differentiation firm needs to be mindful of costs, it must also regularly and consistently reinforce the foundations of its differentiation advantage. In doing so, the firm builds a stronger reputation for differentiation, and this reputation can be an enduring source of advantage in its market.[31] As seen

EXHIBIT 5.4 Value-Chain Activities: Examples of Differentiation

Support Activities

Firm Infrastructure
- Superior MIS—to integrate value-creating activities to improve quality.
- Facilities that promote firm image.
- Widely respected CEO who enhances firm reputation.

Human Resource Management
- Programs to attract talented engineers and scientists.
- Provision of training and incentives to ensure a strong customer service orientation.

Technology Development
- Superior material handling and sorting technology.
- Excellent applications engineering support.

Procurement
- Purchase of high-quality components to enhance product image.
- Use of most-prestigious outlets.

Primary Activities

Inbound Logistics
- Superior material handling operations to minimize damage.
- Quick transfer of inputs to manufacturing process.

Operations
- Flexibility and speed in responding to changes in manufacturing specifications.
- Low defect rates to improve quality.

Outbound Logistics
- Accurate and responsive order processing.
- Effective product replenishment to reduce customer inventory.

Marketing and Sales
- Creative and innovative advertising programs.
- Fostering of personal relationship with key customers.

Service
- Rapid response to customer service requests.
- Complete inventory of replacement parts and supplies.

Source: Adapted from Porter, M. E. 1985. *Competitive Advantage: Creating and Sustaining Superior Performance.* New York: Free Press.

in Spotlight 5.2, Quiznos is a firm that provided mixed messages to its customers as to how focused the firm was on retaining a differentiated advantage, and this led to declining performance that ultimately resulted in bankruptcy.

Many companies successfully follow a differentiation strategy. For example, Zappos may sell shoes, but it sees the core element of its differentiation advantage as service. Zappos CEO Tony Hsieh puts it this way:[32]

> We hope that 10 years from now people won't even realize that we started out selling shoes online, and that when you say "Zappos," they'll think, "Oh, that's the place with the

5.2 STRATEGY SPOTLIGHT

QUIZNOS LOSES ITS EDGE

Quiznos was once one of the fastest-growing quick-service restaurants in the world. Founded in 1981, the chain had grown to nearly 5,000 restaurants worldwide by 2008. The secret to the chain's success was its subs. It built its reputation for differentiated subs by using a unique toasting technique and offering meatier subs than its competitors. But three factors led to a quick decline in the firm's differentiation and its financial performance. First, when the Great Recession hit in 2008, Quiznos entered into a price competition with Subway. This was damaging to the firm on two levels. It eroded the chain's differentiation image. Additionally, since it had a higher cost structure than Subway, the price war left it financially wounded. Second, Quiznos did not reinforce its differentiation advantage with an adequate marketing campaign, leading to a decline in customer perceptions about the chain. Third, the chain had a very tense relationship with its franchisees. Franchisee groups sued Quiznos, claiming the chain overcharged them for supplies and provided insufficient marketing. Due to their concerns and also the financial distress they faced, franchisees did not heavily invest in their stores, thus reinforcing the perception that Quiznos was no longer a premium, differentiated sub chain. In 2012, Quiznos reversed course and tried to reassert its product differentiation by introducing a new menu that included artisan breads, all-natural chicken, natural cheeses, and raw vegetables. But the damage was done, and Quiznos found it hard to rebuild its reputation with customers.

While Quiznos struggled, competing chains pushed forward with their own differentiation elements. For example, Jimmy John's emphasized its speedy service, and Potbelly Sandwich Shops positioned itself as the chain with better condiments, side elements such as milkshakes, and a restaurant environment that feels more like a coffee shop, even at times including a musician in the corner. Thus, as Quiznos slid in customers' eyes, other firms were willing to step in and take its place. Quiznos now has less than half the stores it once had and filed for bankruptcy in March 2014.

Quiznos serves as a cautionary tale of what happens when a differentiation-oriented firm fails to reinforce its differentiation over time and across all elements of its value chain. By entering into a price war with Subway, Quiznos eroded its own image with customers and the value of its brand. By not building strong, cooperative relationships with its franchisees, Quiznos limited the franchisees' willingness to invest in the restaurants and in the service they provided customers. As Elizabeth Friend, a senior food service analyst at Euromonitor International, states, "It's hard to remain successful and implement new menu items if you can't keep the franchisees happy. It speaks to there being something broken in the basic business model."

Sources: Zillman, C. 2014. Quiznos and Potbelly: A tale of two sandwich chains. *CNNMoney.com*, March 18: np; and Jargon, J. & Glazer, E. 2014. Crisis quickens at Quiznos. *wsj.com*, December 6: np.

---

absolute best customer service." And that doesn't even have to be limited to being an online experience. We've had customers email us and ask us if we would please start an airline, or run the IRS.

This emphasis on service has led to great success. Growing from an idea to a billion-dollar company in only a dozen years, Zappos is seeing the benefits of providing exemplary service. In Insights from Research, we see that firms are better able to provide excellent customer service when corporate leaders model a service orientation and customer service representatives are given the latitude to react genuinely and creatively with customers.

INSIGHTS FROM RESEARCH

SERVICE REPRESENTATIVES MUST GET REAL WITH CUSTOMERS

Overview
Customer service organizations expect their representatives to act in positive ways toward customers, even if they have to manufacture the positive interactions. Yet standardizing these expectations can create internal psychological conflicts in employees, so companies benefit from experimenting with alternatives.

What the Research Shows
Psychologists have long understood that people have a strong need for genuine self-expression and authentic functioning. In a 2013 study, researchers at the University of Haifa and the Academic College of Tel-Aviv-Yaffo acknowledge that customer service representatives must do a great deal of "acting" to complete positive service encounters with customers.

continued

continued

They used a grounded theory approach in their article, published in the *Academy of Management Journal*. This entailed interviewing 44 employees from 27 organizations providing cellular and Internet services, along with a few employees from travel agencies.

The research reveals that employees were drawn to being sincere with customers if they associated with them personally or if the employees had a strong identification with the company's message or product. In these genuine interactions, the employees spontaneously expressed their natural emotions with authentic behaviors such as being completely honest with customers or performing above and beyond what the company expected. Most of the genuine interactions were positive. However, if the employees' behavior was in conflict with the organization's rules and expectations, the employees felt strong internal conflicts, including a sense of disloyalty to the company.

Why This Matters

To ensure standard and pleasant customer service experiences, executives of many organizations tightly control employee interactions with rules, scripts, and monitoring. For example, in 2009, researchers from the University of Central Oklahoma found that if a complaint letter was sent to American Airlines, an automatic "apology" letter was sent to the customer. Each letter was exactly the same, leaving no opportunity for an authentic reaction to the customer's dissatisfaction, further devaluing the customer's experience. These types of scripted responses tend to drive employees into distancing their real emotions from their encounters with customers and becoming "numb" to their authentic feelings. These coping mechanisms are harmful to the psychological well-being of the employees and often result in behaviors counterproductive to the company's aim.

Business leaders in customer service organizations would be better served by focusing less on controlling the service interaction and more on creating a positive disposition toward customers. Then, in unpredictable situations, employees will behave in genuinely positive ways. Here is a near-perfect real-life example: Jia Jiang is afraid of rejection and decided to beat his fear by going to different shops, restaurants, and so forth, and making outrageous requests that readily deserve a "No, we can't do that" response, all the while secretly videoing all interactions for his YouTube channel. Jiang experienced an above-and-beyond customer-care moment when he walked into a Krispy Kreme Doughnuts store and requested that a doughnut shaped like an Olympic symbol, featuring accurate frosting colors, be made especially for him—within 15 minutes. Krispy Kreme employee Jackie met Jia Jiang's challenge, apologized for the doughnut not looking as perfect as she wished, and didn't charge him since it didn't meet her own expectations for the company's product. This video went viral, and Krispy Kreme publicists seized the opportunity to make a Twitter shout-out to Jackie, thanking her for her fantastic customer care.

How can you utilize social media to encourage such excellent customer care?

Former Wachovia Corp. CEO Ken Thompson said, "If [a great service culture] is not important to the CEO, it won't be important to others in the company." As a leader, you have the ability to set the example for your employees' interactions with customers. Try rewarding your employees for every positive comment they make about a customer. Additionally, Greg Gianforte, founder and CEO of RightNow Technologies Inc., says product and customer knowledge allow employees to have a personal experience with the customers, focusing on their core needs more quickly.

Key Takeaways

- Requiring employees to obey rules about behaving positively toward customers may cause them to become "numb" to their real feelings or to experience negative inner conflicts.
- Rewarding employees for being positive with customers may cause their behavior to be externally motivated rather than genuine.
- Employees act in genuine ways toward customers when they have a strong personal association with the customer or a strong personal identification with the task.
- When employees act in genuine ways toward customers, they may experience a sense of disloyalty to the company if their actions are in conflict with organizational expectations.
- When employees act in genuine ways toward customers, they may experience social rejection if their actions are in conflict with customers' expectations.
- A positive disposition toward customers must be modeled and rewarded by leaders.

Apply This Today

Superb service begins with leaders. Create a positive response to customers, reward employees who emulate it, and ensure that employees have the knowledge to exceed customers' expectations. To learn more, visit businessminded.com.

Research Reviewed

Walker, H. J., Bauer, T.N., Cole, M.S., Bernerth, J. B., Field, H. S., & Short, J. C. 2013. Is this how I will be treated? Reducing uncertainty through recruitment interactions. *Academy of Management Journal,* 56(5): 1325–1347. We thank Matthew Gilley, Ph.D., of *businessminded.com* for contributing this Research Brief.

5.3 STRATEGY SPOTLIGHT

ENVIRONMENTAL SUSTAINABILITY / CROWDSOURCING

CROWDSOURCING FOR DIFFERENTIATION IDEAS: UNILEVER'S EFFORTS TO PROPEL FORWARD ITS SUSTAINABILITY INITIATIVES

Unilever, a global manufacturer of consumer products such as Dove soap, Ben and Jerry's ice cream, Lipton ice tea, Axe deodorants, and many other widely used products, is aiming to lead the market in its ability to run a sustainable business enterprise. As part of this effort, the company published its Sustainable Living Plan in November 2010. Included in this plan were Unilever's ambitious goals to reduce its environmental footprint by 50 percent and source all of its agricultural inputs from sustainable growers by 2020.

Knowing that these goals will be challenging to achieve, Unilever turned to the power of the crowd to develop initiatives to meet these targets. In April 2012, it hosted a 24-hour global crowdsourcing event, called the Sustainable Living Lab, to generate creative ideas on how to improve Unilever's sustainability. Speaking of the challenges facing Unilever as it strives to lead the market in sustainability, Miguel Pestana, VP of Global External Affairs at Unilever, stated, "We can't solve these issues on our own. We need to engage with civil society, companies, government, and other key stakeholders." Unilever designed the lab as an invitation-only event where it would get input from sustainability leaders and experts. The response it received from invited participants was very positive, with over 2,200 individuals, including over 100 Unilever managers, coming together to co-create ideas and solutions to advance Unilever's agenda of increasing the sustainability of its business and product line. Unilever hosted discussion groups on four broad topics that encompassed activities across the company's entire value chain. The topics discussed were sustainable sourcing, sustainable production and distribution, consumer behavior change, and recycling and waste.

The boards generated a large volume of discussion and also triggered a follow-up survey completed by over 400 participants. Unilever then used the discussions as a basis for extending current partnerships and developing new ones with participating firms and organizations to help it achieve its sustainability goals.

Unilever's efforts for sustainability appear to be paying off. According to a GlobalScan survey, Unilever is the corporate leader in sustainability, being ranked the top firm by 33 sustainability experts, nearly four times as frequently as the second-highest-mentioned firm.

Sources: Holme, C. 2012. How Unilever crowdsourced creativity to meet its sustainability goals. *Greenbiz.com*, June 7, np; Peluso, M. 2012. Unilever to crowdsource sustainability. *MarketingWeek*, April 10, np; and Coulter, C. & Guenther, C. 2014. The expert view: Top corporate sustainability leaders of 2014. *Theguardian.com*, May 14: np.

Strategy Spotlight 5.3 discusses how Unilever, a global consumer products firm, uses crowdsourcing to differentiate itself through increased sustainability.

Differentiation: Improving Competitive Position vis-à-vis the Five Forces Differentiation provides protection against rivalry since brand loyalty lowers customer sensitivity to price and raises customer switching costs.[33] By increasing a firm's margins, differentiation also avoids the need for a low-cost position. Higher entry barriers result because of customer loyalty and the firm's ability to provide uniqueness in its products or services.[34] Differentiation also provides higher margins that enable a firm to deal with supplier power. And it reduces buyer power, because buyers lack comparable alternatives and are therefore less price-sensitive.[35] Supplier power is also decreased because there is a certain amount of prestige associated with being the supplier to a producer of highly differentiated products and services. Last, differentiation enhances customer loyalty, thus reducing the threat from substitutes.[36]

Our examples illustrate these points. Porsche has enjoyed enhanced power over buyers because its strong reputation makes buyers more willing to pay a premium price. This lessens rivalry, since buyers become less price-sensitive. The prestige associated with its brand name also lowers supplier power since margins are high. Suppliers would probably desire to be associated with prestige brands, thus lessening their incentives to drive up prices. Finally, the loyalty and "peace of mind" associated with a service provider such as Zappos makes such firms less vulnerable to rivalry or substitute products and services.

Potential Pitfalls of Differentiation Strategies Potential pitfalls of a differentiation strategy include:

- *Uniqueness that is not valuable.* A differentiation strategy must provide unique bundles of products and/or services that customers value highly. It's not enough just to be "different." An example is Gibson's Dobro bass guitar. Gibson came up with a unique idea: Design and build an acoustic bass guitar with sufficient sound volume so that amplification wasn't necessary. The problem with other acoustic bass guitars was that they did not project enough volume because of the low-frequency bass notes. By adding a resonator plate on the body of the traditional acoustic bass, Gibson increased the sound volume. Gibson believed this product would serve a particular niche market—bluegrass and folk artists who played in small group "jams" with other acoustic musicians. Unfortunately, Gibson soon discovered that its targeted market was content with the existing options: an upright bass amplified with a microphone or an acoustic electric guitar. Thus, Gibson developed a unique product, but it was not perceived as valuable by its potential customers.[37]
- *Too much differentiation.* Firms may strive for quality or service that is higher than customers desire.[38] Thus, they become vulnerable to competitors that provide an appropriate level of quality at a lower price. For example, consider the expensive Mercedes-Benz S-Class, which ranged in price between $93,650 and $138,000 for the 2011 models.[39] *Consumer Reports* described it as "sumptuous," "quiet and luxurious," and a "delight to drive." The magazine also considered it to be the least reliable sedan available in the United States. According to David Champion, who runs the testing program, the problems are electronic. "The engineers have gone a little wild," he says. "They've put every bell and whistle that they think of, and sometimes they don't have the attention to detail to make these systems work." Some features include a computer-driven suspension that reduces body roll as the vehicle whips around a corner; cruise control that automatically slows the car down if it gets too close to another car; and seats that are adjustable 14 ways and are ventilated by a system that uses eight fans.
- *Too high a price premium.* This pitfall is quite similar to too much differentiation. Customers may desire the product, but they are repelled by the price premium. For example, Duracell recently charged too much for batteries.[40] The firm tried to sell consumers on its superior-quality products, but the mass market wasn't convinced. Why? The price differential was simply too high. At one CVS drugstore, a four-pack of Energizer AA batteries was on sale at $2.99 compared with a Duracell four-pack at $4.59. Duracell's market share dropped 2 percent in a recent two-year period, and its profits declined over 30 percent. Clearly, the price/performance proposition Duracell offered customers was not accepted.
- *Differentiation that is easily imitated.* As we noted in Chapter 3, resources that are easily imitated cannot lead to sustainable advantages. Similarly, firms may strive for, and even attain, a differentiation strategy that is successful for a time. However, the advantages are eroded through imitation. Consider Cereality's innovative differentiation strategy of stores that offer a wide variety of cereals and toppings for around $4.[41] As one would expect, once the idea proved successful, competitors entered the market because much of the initial risk had already been taken. These new competitors included stores with the following names: the Cereal Cabinet, The Cereal Bowl, and Bowls: A Cereal Joint. Says David Roth, one of Cereality's founders: "With any good business idea, you're faced with people who see you've cracked the code and who try to cash in on it."
- *Dilution of brand identification through product-line extensions.* Firms may erode their quality brand image by adding products or services with lower prices

and less quality. Although this can increase short-term revenues, it may be detrimental in the long run. Consider Gucci.[42] In the 1980s Gucci wanted to capitalize on its prestigious brand name by launching an aggressive strategy of revenue growth. It added a set of lower-priced canvas goods to its product line. It also pushed goods heavily into department stores and duty-free channels and allowed its name to appear on a host of licensed items such as watches, eyeglasses, and perfumes. In the short term, this strategy worked. Sales soared. However, the strategy carried a high price. Gucci's indiscriminate approach to expanding its products and channels tarnished its sterling brand. Sales of its high-end goods (with higher profit margins) fell, causing profits to decline.

Overall Cost Leadership

- Too much focus on one or a few value-chain activities.
- Increase in the cost of the inputs on which the advantage is based.
- A strategy that can be imitated too easily.
- A lack of parity on differentiation.
- Reduced flexibility.
- Obsolescence of the basis of cost advantage.

Differentiation

- Uniqueness that is not valuable.
- Too much differentiation.
- A price premium that is too high.
- Differentiation that is easily imitated.
- Dilution of brand identification through product-line extensions.
- Perceptions of differentiation that vary between buyers and sellers.

EXHIBIT 5.5
Potential Pitfalls of Overall Cost Leadership and Differentiation Strategies

- *Perceptions of differentiation that vary between buyers and sellers.* The issue here is that "beauty is in the eye of the beholder." Companies must realize that although they may perceive their products and services as differentiated, their customers may view them as commodities. Indeed, in today's marketplace, many products and services have been reduced to commodities.[43] Thus, a firm could overprice its offerings and lose margins altogether if it has to lower prices to reflect market realities.

Exhibit 5.5 summarizes the pitfalls of overall cost leadership and differentiation strategies. In addressing the pitfalls associated with these two generic strategies, there is one common, underlying theme: Managers must be aware of the dangers associated with concentrating so much on one strategy that they fail to attain parity on the other.

Focus

A **focus strategy** is based on the choice of a narrow competitive scope within an industry. A firm following this strategy selects a segment or group of segments and tailors its strategy to serve them. The essence of focus is the exploitation of a particular market niche. As you might expect, narrow focus itself (like merely "being different" as a differentiator) is simply not sufficient for above-average performance.

The focus strategy, as indicated in Exhibit 5.1, has two variants. In a cost focus, a firm strives to create a cost advantage in its target segment. In a differentiation focus, a firm seeks to differentiate in its target market. Both variants of the focus strategy rely on providing better service than broad-based competitors that are trying to serve the focuser's target segment. Cost focus exploits differences in cost behavior in some segments, while differentiation focus exploits the special needs of buyers in other segments.

Let's look at examples of two firms that have successfully implemented focus strategies. LinkedIn has staked out a position as the business social media site of choice. Rather than compete with Facebook head on, LinkedIn created a strategy that focuses on individuals who wish to share their business experience and make connections with individuals with whom they share or could potentially share business ties. In doing so, it has created an extremely strong business model. LinkedIn monetizes its user information in three ways: subscription fees from some users, advertising fees, and recruiter fees. The first two are fairly standard for social media sites, but the advertising fees are higher for LinkedIn since

focus strategy
a firm's generic strategy based on appeal to a narrow market segment within an industry.

5.4 STRATEGY SPOTLIGHT

LUXURY IN THE E-COMMERCE WORLD

Traditionally, luxury retailers have relied on high levels of personal touch in their stores as well as a sense of exclusivity in order to differentiate themselves from the mass retail markets. As a result, many luxury retailers have looked on the Internet retail market skeptically, thinking it didn't fit their products and the needs of their customers. Rather than offering an indulgent and exclusive retail experience, the Internet promotes accessibility and efficiency. Yoox, an Italian firm, appears to have solved the mystery of how to turn e-commerce into a luxury experience. Yoox designs and manages online stores for nearly 40 luxury brands, including Armani, Diesel, Emilio Pucci, and Brunello Cucinelli. In 2013, the firm booked over 3 million orders for over 1 million customers in 100 countries, generating $563 million in sales and $15.6 million in net income.

How has Yoox translated the luxury retail experience to the online world? Its expertise at creating the right experience cuts across the value chain. First, Yoox views itself as a craftsperson, designing each website specifically to the brand. Second, it focuses on the details. This includes training its 60 photographers to create images for each product that match the specific guidelines of each brand. For one clothing retailer, this included using flamenco dancers in its designer images, rather than fashion models. The attention to detail flows through to the packaging. Packers at Yoox's five fulfillment centers are trained on the specific angle of the ribbons for a box containing an Alexander Wang dress versus one containing a Bottega Veneta bag. Third, Yoox has developed innovative algorithms to predict which products will sell at which times and in which geographic regions, allowing effective stocking to meet the needs of customers and providing guidance to retailers on optimal pricing. Finally, Yoox has insisted on exclusive contracts with luxury brands to ensure that it can control the brands' images in the online retail space. These luxury brands have grown reliant on Yoox. About one-third of Yoox's revenue derives from the creation and management of the luxury brands' websites, while the remainder comes from its order-fulfillment services.

Sources: Fairchild, C. 2014. A luxe look for e-commerce. *Fortune*, June 16: 83–84; and Clark, N. 2014. Success draws competition for luxury e-retailer Yoox. *nytimes.com*, December 6: np.

---

the ads can be more effectively targeted as a result of LinkedIn's focus. The third income source is fairly unique for LinkedIn. Headhunters and human resource departments pay significant user fees, up to $8,200 a year, to have access to LinkedIn's recruiting search engine, which can sift through LinkedIn profiles to identify individuals with desired skills and experiences. The power of this business model can be seen in the difference in user value for LinkedIn when compared to Facebook. For every hour that a user spends on the site, LinkedIn generates $1.30 in income. For Facebook, it is a paltry 6.2 cents.[44]

Marlin Steel Wire Products, a Baltimore-based manufacturing company, has also seen great benefit from developing a niche-differentiator strategy. Marlin, a manufacturer of commodity wire products, faced stiff and ever-increasing competition from rivals based in China and other emerging markets. These rivals had labor-based cost advantages that Marlin found hard to counter. Marlin responded by changing the game it played. Drew Greenblatt, Marlin's president, decided to go upmarket, automating his production and specializing in high-end products. For example, Marlin produces antimicrobial baskets for restaurant kitchens and exports its products globally. Marlin provides products to customers in 36 countries and, in 2012, was listed as the 162nd fastest-growing private manufacturing company in the United States.[45]

Strategy Spotlight 5.4 illustrates how Yoox has carved out a profitable niche in the online retailing world as a luxury goods provider.

Focus: Improving Competitive Position vis-à-vis the Five Forces Focus requires that a firm have either a low-cost position with its strategic target, high differentiation, or both. As we discussed with regard to cost and differentiation strategies, these positions provide defenses against each competitive force. Focus is also used to select niches that are least vulnerable to substitutes or where competitors are weakest.

Let's look at our examples to illustrate some of these points. First, by providing a platform for a targeted customer group, businesspeople, to share key work information, LinkedIn insulated itself from rivalrous pressure from existing social networks, such as

Facebook. It also felt little threat from new generalist social networks, such as Google +. Similarly, the new focus of Marlin Steel lessened the power of buyers since the company provides specialized products. Also, it is insulated from competitors, which manufacture the commodity products Marlin used to produce.

Potential Pitfalls of Focus Strategies   Potential pitfalls of focus strategies include:

- *Cost advantages may erode within the narrow segment.* The advantages of a cost focus strategy may be fleeting if the cost advantages are eroded over time. For example, early pioneers in online education, such as the University of Phoenix, have faced increasing challenges as traditional universities have entered with their own online programs that allow them to match the cost benefits associated with online delivery systems. Similarly, other firms have seen their profit margins drop as competitors enter their product segment.
- *Even product and service offerings that are highly focused are subject to competition from new entrants and from imitation.* Some firms adopting a focus strategy may enjoy temporary advantages because they select a small niche with few rivals. However, their advantages may be short-lived. A notable example is the multitude of dot-com firms that specialize in very narrow segments such as pet supplies, ethnic foods, and vintage automobile accessories. The entry barriers tend to be low, there is little buyer loyalty, and competition becomes intense. And since the marketing strategies and technologies employed by most rivals are largely nonproprietary, imitation is easy. Over time, revenues fall, profits margins are squeezed, and only the strongest players survive the shakeout.
- *Focusers can become too focused to satisfy buyer needs.* Some firms attempting to attain advantages through a focus strategy may have too narrow a product or service. Consider many retail firms. Hardware chains such as Ace and True Value are losing market share to rivals such as Lowe's and Home Depot that offer a full line of home and garden equipment and accessories. And given the enormous purchasing power of the national chains, it would be difficult for such specialty retailers to attain parity on costs.

Combination Strategies: Integrating Overall Low Cost and Differentiation

Perhaps the primary benefit to firms that integrate low-cost and differentiation strategies is the difficulty for rivals to duplicate or imitate.[46] This strategy enables a firm to provide two types of value to customers: differentiated attributes (e.g., high quality, brand identification, reputation) and lower prices (because of the firm's lower costs in value-creating activities). The goal is thus to provide unique value to customers in an efficient manner.[47] Some firms are able to attain both types of advantages simultaneously.[48] For example, superior quality can lead to lower costs because of less need for rework in manufacturing, fewer warranty claims, a reduced need for customer service personnel to resolve customer complaints, and so forth. Thus, the benefits of combining advantages can be additive, instead of merely involving trade-offs. Next, we consider four approaches to combining overall low cost and differentiation.

L05.4
How firms can effectively combine the generic strategies of overall cost leadership and differentiation.

combination strategies
firms' integrations of various strategies to provide multiple types of value to customers.

Adopting Automated and Flexible Manufacturing Systems   Given the advances in manufacturing technologies such as CAD/CAM (computer aided design and computer aided manufacturing) as well as information technologies, many firms have been able to manufacture unique products in relatively small quantities at lower costs—a concept known as **mass customization**.[49]

mass customization
a firm's ability to manufacture unique products in small quantities at low cost.

Let's consider Andersen Windows of Bayport, Minnesota—a $2.3 billion manufacturer of windows for the building industry.[50] Until about 20 years ago, Andersen was a mass producer, in small batches, of a variety of standard windows. However, to meet changing customer needs, Andersen kept adding to its product line. The result was catalogs of ever-increasing size and a bewildering set of choices for both homeowners and contractors. Over a six-year period, the number of products tripled, price quotes took several hours, and the error rate increased. This not only damaged the company's reputation but also added to its manufacturing expenses.

To bring about a major change, Andersen developed an interactive computer version of its paper catalogs that it sold to distributors and retailers. Salespersons can now customize each window to meet the customer's needs, check the design for structural soundness, and provide a price quote. The system is virtually error-free, customers get exactly what they want, and the time to develop the design and furnish a quotation has been cut by 75 percent. Each showroom computer is connected to the factory, and customers are assigned a code number that permits them to track the order. The manufacturing system has been developed to use some common finished parts, but it also allows considerable variation in the final products. Despite its huge investment, Andersen has been able to lower costs, enhance quality and variety, and improve its response time to customers.

Using Data Analytics Corporations are increasingly collecting and analyzing data on their customers, including data on customer characteristics, purchasing patterns, employee productivity, and physical asset utilization. These efforts, commonly referred to as "Big Data," have the potential to allow firms to better customize their product and service offerings to customers while more efficiently and fully using the resources of the company. For example, Pepsi used data analytics to develop an algorithm that lowers the rate of inventory out-of-stocks and has shared the algorithm with partners and retailers. Similarly, Kaiser Permanente collects petabytes of data on the health treatment of its 8 million health care members. This has allowed Kaiser to develop insights on the cost, efficacy, and safety of the treatments provided by doctors and procedures in hospitals—leading to more effective and cost-conscious treatment patterns.[51]

| profit pool
| the total profits in an industry at all points along the industry's value chain.

Exploiting the Profit Pool Concept for Competitive Advantage A **profit pool** is defined as the total profits in an industry at all points along the industry's value chain.[52] Although the concept is relatively straightforward, the structure of the profit pool can be complex.[53] The potential pool of profits will be deeper in some segments of the value chain than in others, and the depths will vary within an individual segment. Segment profitability may vary widely by customer group, product category, geographic market, or distribution channel. Additionally, the pattern of profit concentration in an industry is very often different from the pattern of revenue generation. Strategy Spotlight 5.5 outlines how airlines have expanded the profit pools of their market by adding fees for a variety of services.

Coordinating the "Extended" Value Chain by Way of Information Technology
Many firms have achieved success by integrating activities throughout the "extended value chain" by using information technology to link their own value chain with the value chains of their customers and suppliers. As noted in Chapter 3, this approach enables a firm to add value not only through its own value-creating activities but also for its customers and suppliers.

Such a strategy often necessitates redefining the industry's value chain. A number of years ago, Walmart took a close look at its industry's value chain and decided to reframe the competitive challenge. Although its competitors were primarily focused on retailing—merchandising and promotion—Walmart determined that it was not so much in the retailing industry as in the transportation logistics and communications industries.

5.5 STRATEGY SPOTLIGHT

EXPANDING THE PROFIT POOL IN THE SKY

Commercial airlines find themselves in a very competitive market, facing a number of competitors, having high fixed costs, and experiencing demand that is largely driven by economic conditions. As a result, profits in the airline industry are typically fairly low and often negative. The challenges in this industry are evident in the 23 separate bankruptcies that have occurred in the U.S. airline industry since 2000. However, as anyone who has flown in recent years can attest, airlines have found new sources of profit to augment their income beyond what customers are willing to pay when purchasing a ticket. The fees airlines have added on for ancillary services accounted for $27.1 billion in additional revenue for global airlines in 2012, up from a paltry $2.5 billion in 2008.

The range of revenue sources has expanded in recent years. The most obvious source of service revenue is baggage fees. However, airlines also generate revenue by charging booking fees and by selling premium economy seating, the right to assigned seats, exit-row seating, guarantees that family members can all sit together, earlier boarding of flights, premium meals, pillow and blanket sets, Internet access on board, and the right to hold a reservation before making a purchase commitment. Outside the flight experience itself, airlines are generating revenue by charging fees for credit cards, frequent-flyer programs, and access to airport lounges. The importance of these fees is staggering for some airlines. While Emirates Air relies on these service fees for less than 1 percent of its revenue, 22 percent of Ryanair's revenue and 38 percent of Spirit Airlines' revenue is accounted for by these fees.

By separating the value of the actual flight from the services associated with flying, airlines have greatly expanded the profit pool associated with flying. They have found that flyers may be very price-conscious when purchasing tickets but are willing to shell out more for a range of services. While this does increase their revenue, it may also provide benefits for at least some customers. As Jay Sorensen, CEO of IdeaWorks, notes, "It offers the potential for an airline to better tailor service to the needs of individual customers. They can click and buy the amenities they want rather than the airline deciding what is bundled in the base fare."

Sources: Akasie, J. 2013. With a fee for everything, airlines jet toward a new business model. *minyanville.com*, October 1: np; and Perera, J. 2014. Looking at airline fees in 2008 compared to 2014. *chron.com*, November 25: np.

Here, linkages in the extended value chain became central. That became Walmart's chosen battleground. By redefining the rules of competition that played to its strengths, Walmart has attained competitive advantages and dominates its industry.

Integrated Overall Low-Cost and Differentiation Strategies: Improving Competitive Position vis-à-vis the Five Forces Firms that successfully integrate both differentiation and cost advantages create an enviable position. For example, Walmart's integration of information systems, logistics, and transportation helps it to drive down costs and provide outstanding product selection. This dominant competitive position serves to erect high entry barriers to potential competitors that have neither the financial nor physical resources to compete head-to-head. Walmart's size—with over $475 billion in sales in 2014—provides the chain with enormous bargaining power over suppliers. Its low pricing and wide selection reduce the power of buyers (its customers), because there are relatively few competitors that can provide a comparable cost/value proposition. This reduces the possibility of intense head-to-head rivalry, such as protracted price wars. Finally, Walmart's overall value proposition makes potential substitute products (e.g., Internet competitors) a less viable threat.

Pitfalls of Integrated Overall Cost Leadership and Differentiation Strategies The pitfalls of integrated overall cost leadership and differentiation include:

- *Failing to attain both strategies and possibly ending up with neither, leaving the firm "stuck in the middle."* A key issue in strategic management is the creation of competitive advantages that enable a firm to enjoy above-average returns. Some firms may become stuck in the middle if they try to attain both cost and differentiation advantages. As mentioned earlier in this chapter, mainline supermarket chains find themselves stuck in the middle as their cost structure is higher than discount retailers offering groceries and their products and services are not seen by consumers as being as valuable as those of high-end grocery chains, such as Whole Foods.

- *Underestimating the challenges and expenses associated with coordinating value-creating activities in the extended value chain.* Integrating activities across a firm's value chain with the value chain of suppliers and customers involves a significant investment in financial and human resources. Firms must consider the expenses linked to technology investment, managerial time and commitment, and the involvement and investment required by the firm's customers and suppliers. The firm must be confident that it can generate a sufficient scale of operations and revenues to justify all associated expenses.
- *Miscalculating sources of revenue and profit pools in the firm's industry.* Firms may fail to accurately assess sources of revenue and profits in their value chain. This can occur for several reasons. For example, a manager may be biased due to his or her functional area background, work experiences, and educational background. If the manager's background is in engineering, he or she might perceive that proportionately greater revenue and margins were being created in manufacturing, product, and process design than a person whose background is in a "downstream" value-chain activity such as marketing and sales. Or politics could make managers "fudge" the numbers to favor their area of operations. This would make them responsible for a greater proportion of the firm's profits, thus improving their bargaining position.

A related problem is directing an overwhelming amount of managerial time, attention, and resources to value-creating activities that produce the greatest margins—to the detriment of other important, albeit less profitable, activities. For example, a car manufacturer may focus too much on downstream activities, such as warranty fulfillment and financing operations, to the detriment of differentiation and cost of the cars themselves.

Can Competitive Strategies Be Sustained? Integrating and Applying Strategic Management Concepts

LO5.5
What factors determine the sustainability of a firm's competitive advantage.

Thus far this chapter has addressed how firms can attain competitive advantages in the marketplace. We discussed the three generic strategies—overall cost leadership, differentiation, and focus—as well as combination strategies. Next we discussed the importance of linking value-chain activities (both those within the firm and those linkages between the firm's suppliers and customers) to attain such advantages. We also showed how successful competitive strategies enable firms to strengthen their position vis-à-vis the five forces of industry competition as well as how to avoid the pitfalls associated with the strategies.

Competitive advantages are, however, often short-lived. As we discussed in the beginning of Chapter 1, the composition of the firms that constitute the Fortune 500 list has experienced significant turnover in its membership over the years—reflecting the temporary nature of competitive advantages. Consider Dell's fall from grace. Here was a firm whose advantages in the marketplace seemed unassailable in the early 2000s. In fact, it was *Fortune*'s "Most Admired Firm" in 2005. However, cracks began to appear in 2007, and its competitive position has recently been severely eroded both by its traditional competitors and by an onslaught of firms selling tablets and other mobile devices. In short, Dell focused so much on operational efficiency and perfecting its "direct model" that it failed to deliver innovations that an increasingly sophisticated market demanded.[54]

Clearly, "nothing is forever" when it comes to competitive advantages. Rapid changes in technology, globalization, and actions by rivals from within—as well as outside—the industry can quickly erode a firm's advantages. It is becoming increasingly important to recognize that the duration of competitive advantages is declining, especially in technology-intensive industries.[55] Even in industries that are normally viewed as "low tech," the increasing use of technology has suddenly made competitive advantages less sustainable.[56] Amazon's success in book retailing at the cost of Barnes & Noble, the former industry leader, as well as BlackBerry's difficulties in responding to Apple's innovations in the smartphone market, serves to illustrate how difficult it has become for industry leaders to sustain competitive advantages that they once thought would last forever.

In this section, we will discuss some factors that help determine whether a strategy is sustainable over a long period of time. We will draw on some strategic management concepts from the first five chapters. To illustrate our points, we will look at a company, Atlas Door, which created an innovative strategy in its industry and enjoyed superior performance for several years. Our discussion of Atlas Door draws on a *Harvard Business Review* article by George Stalk, Jr.[57] It was published some time ago (1988), which provides us the benefit of hindsight to make our points about the sustainability of competitive advantage. After all, the strategic management concepts we have been addressing in the text are quite timeless in their relevance to practice. A brief summary follows.

Atlas Door: A Case Example

Atlas Door, a U.S.-based company, has enjoyed remarkable success. It has grown at an average annual rate of 15 percent in an industry with an overall annual growth rate of less than 5 percent. Recently, its pretax earnings were 20 percent of sales—about five times the industry average. Atlas is debt-free, and by its 10th year, the company achieved the number-one competitive position in its industry.

Atlas produces industrial doors—a product with almost infinite variety, involving limitless choices of width and height and material. Given the importance of product variety, inventory is almost useless in meeting customer orders. Instead, most doors can be manufactured only after the order has been placed.

How Did Atlas Door Create Its Competitive Advantages in the Marketplace? *First,* Atlas built just-in-time factories. Although simple in concept, they require extra tooling and machinery to reduce changeover times. Further, the manufacturing process must be organized by product and scheduled to start and complete with all of the parts available at the same time.

Second, Atlas reduced the time to receive and process an order. Traditionally, when customers, distributors, or salespeople called a door manufacturer with a request for price and delivery, they would have to wait more than one week for a response. In contrast, Atlas first streamlined and then automated its entire order-entry, engineering, pricing, and scheduling process. Atlas can price and schedule 95 percent of its incoming orders while the callers are still on the telephone. It can quickly engineer new special orders because it has preserved on computer the design and production data of all previous special orders—which drastically reduces the amount of reengineering necessary.

Third, Atlas tightly controlled logistics so that it always shipped only fully complete orders to construction sites. Orders require many components, and gathering all of them at the factory and making sure that they are with the correct order can be a time-consuming task. Of course, it is even more time-consuming to get the correct parts to the job site after the order has been shipped! Atlas developed a system to track the parts in production and the purchased parts for each order. This helped to ensure the arrival of all necessary parts at the shipping dock in time—a just-in-time logistics operation.

The Result? When Atlas began operations, distributors had little interest in its product. The established distributors already carried the door line of a much larger competitor and saw little to no reason to switch suppliers except, perhaps, for a major price concession. But as a start-up, Atlas was too small to compete on price alone. Instead, it positioned itself as the door supplier of last resort—the company people came to if the established supplier could not deliver or missed a key date.

Of course, with an average industry order-fulfillment time of almost four months, some calls inevitably came to Atlas. And when it did get the call, Atlas commanded a higher price because of its faster delivery. Atlas not only got a higher price, but its effective integration of value-creating activities saved time and lowered costs. Thus, it enjoyed the best of both worlds.

In 10 short years, the company replaced the leading door suppliers in 80 percent of the distributors in the United States. With its strategic advantage, the company could be selective—becoming the supplier for only the strongest distributors.

Are Atlas Door's Competitive Advantages Sustainable?

We will now take both the "pro" and "con" positions as to whether or not Atlas Door's competitive advantages will be sustainable for a very long time. It is important, of course, to assume that Atlas Door's strategy is unique in the industry, and the central issue becomes whether or not rivals will be able to easily imitate its strategy or create a viable substitute strategy.

"Pro" Position: The Strategy Is Highly Sustainable Drawing on Chapter 2, it is quite evident that Atlas Door has attained a very favorable position vis-à-vis the five forces of industry competition. For example, it is able to exert power over its customers (distributors) because of its ability to deliver a quality product in a short period of time. Also, its dominance in the industry creates high entry barriers for new entrants. It is also quite evident that Atlas Door has been able to successfully integrate many value-chain activities within the firm—a fact that is integral to its just-in-time strategy. As noted in Chapter 3, such integration of activities provides a strong basis for sustainability, because rivals would have difficulty in imitating this strategy due to causal ambiguity and path dependency (i.e., it is difficult to build up in a short period of time the resources that Atlas Door has accumulated and developed as well as disentangle the causes of what the valuable resources are or how they can be re-created). Further, as noted in Chapter 4, Atlas Door benefits from the social capital that it has developed with a wide range of key stakeholders (Chapter 1). These would include customers, employees, and managers (a reasonable assumption, given how smoothly the internal operations flow and the company's long-term relationships with distributors). It would be very difficult for a rival to replace Atlas Door as the supplier of last resort—given the reputation that it has earned over time for "coming through in the clutch" on time-sensitive orders. Finally, we can conclude that Atlas Door has created competitive advantages in both overall low cost and differentiation (Chapter 5). Its strong linkages among value-chain activities—a requirement for its just-in-time operations—not only lower costs but enable the company to respond quickly to customer orders. As noted in Exhibit 5.4, many of the value-chain activities associated with a differentiation strategy reflect the element of speed or quick response.

"Con" Position: The Strategy Can Be Easily Imitated or Substituted An argument could be made that much of Atlas Door's strategy relies on technologies that are rather well known and nonproprietary. Over time, a well-financed rival could imitate its strategy (via trial and error), achieve a tight integration among its value-creating activities, and implement a just-in-time manufacturing process. Because human capital is highly mobile (Chapter 4), a rival could hire away Atlas Door's talent, and these individuals could aid the rival in transferring Atlas Door's best practices. A new rival could also enter the industry with a large resource base, which might enable it to price its doors well under Atlas Door to build market share (but this would likely involve pricing below cost and would be a risky and nonsustainable strategy). Finally, a rival could potentially "leapfrog" the technologies and processes that Atlas Door has employed and achieve competitive superiority. With the benefit of hindsight, it could use the Internet to further speed up the linkages among its value-creating activities and the order-entry processes with its customers and suppliers. (But even this could prove to be a temporary advantage, since rivals could relatively easily do the same thing.)

What Is the Verdict? Both positions have merit. Over time, it would be rather easy to see how a new rival could achieve parity with Atlas Door—or even create a superior competitive position with new technologies or innovative processes. However, two factors make it extremely difficult for a rival to challenge Atlas Door in the short term: (1) The success that Atlas Door has enjoyed with its just-in-time scheduling and production systems—which involve the successful integration of many value-creating activities—helps the firm not only lower costs but also respond quickly to customer needs, and (2) the strong, positive reputational effects that it has earned with its customers increases their loyalty and would take significant time for rivals to match.

Finally, it is important to also understand that it is Atlas Door's ability to appropriate most of the profits generated by its competitive advantages that make it a highly successful company. As we discussed in Chapter 3, profits generated by resources can be appropriated by a number of stakeholders such as suppliers, customers, employees, or rivals. The structure of the industrial door industry makes such value appropriation difficult: The suppliers provide generic parts, no one buyer is big enough to dictate prices, the tacit nature of the knowledge makes imitation difficult, and individual employees may be easily replaceable. Still, even with the advantages that Atlas Door enjoys, it needs to avoid becoming complacent or will suffer the same fate as the dominant firm it replaced.

Industry Life-Cycle Stages: Strategic Implications

>**L05.6**
>
>The importance of considering the industry life cycle to determine a firm's business-level strategy and its relative emphasis on functional area strategies and value-creating activities.
>
>**industry life cycle**
>the stages of introduction, growth, maturity, and decline that typically occur over the life of an industry.

The **industry life cycle** refers to the stages of introduction, growth, maturity, and decline that occur over the life of an industry. In considering the industry life cycle, it is useful to think in terms of broad product lines such as personal computers, photocopiers, or long-distance telephone service. Yet the industry life-cycle concept can be explored from several levels, from the life cycle of an entire industry to the life cycle of a single variation or model of a specific product or service.

Why are industry life cycles important?[58] The emphasis on various generic strategies, functional areas, value-creating activities, and overall objectives varies over the course of an industry life cycle. Managers must become even more aware of their firm's strengths and weaknesses in many areas to attain competitive advantages. For example, firms depend on their research and development (R&D) activities in the introductory stage. R&D is the source of new products and features that everyone hopes will appeal to customers. Firms develop products and services to stimulate consumer demand. Later, during the maturity phase, the functions of the product have been defined, more competitors have entered the market, and competition is intense. Managers then place greater emphasis on production efficiencies and process (as opposed to the product) engineering in order to lower manufacturing costs. This helps to protect the firm's market position and to extend the product life cycle because the firm's lower costs can be passed on to consumers in the form of lower prices, and price-sensitive customers will find the product more appealing.

Exhibit 5.6 illustrates the four stages of the industry life cycle and how factors such as generic strategies, market growth rate, intensity of competition, and overall objectives change over time. Managers must strive to emphasize the key functional areas during each of the four stages and to attain a level of parity in all functional areas and value-creating activities. For example, although controlling production costs may be a primary concern

EXHIBIT 5.6 Stages of the Industry Life Cycle

Stage / Factor	Introduction	Growth	Maturity	Decline
Generic strategies	Differentiation	Differentiation	Differentiation Overall cost leadership	Overall cost leadership Focus
Market growth rate	Low	Very large	Low to moderate	Negative
Number of segments	Very few	Some	Many	Few
Intensity of competition	Low	Increasing	Very intense	Changing
Emphasis on product design	Very high	High	Low to moderate	Low
Emphasis on process design	Low	Low to moderate	High	Low
Major functional area(s) of concern	Research and development	Sales and marketing	Production	General management and finance
Overall objective	Increase market awareness	Create consumer demand	Defend market share and extend product life cycles	Consolidate, maintain, harvest, or exit

during the maturity stage, managers should not totally ignore other functions such as marketing and R&D. If they do, they can become so focused on lowering costs that they miss market trends or fail to incorporate important product or process designs. Thus, the firm may attain low-cost products that have limited market appeal.

It is important to point out a caveat. While the life-cycle idea is analogous to a living organism (i.e., birth, growth, maturity, and death), the comparison has limitations.[59] Products and services go through many cycles of innovation and renewal. Typically, only fad products have a single life cycle. Maturity stages of an industry can be "transformed" or followed by a stage of rapid growth if consumer tastes change, technological innovations take place, or new developments occur. The cereal industry is a good example. When medical research indicated that oat consumption reduced a person's cholesterol, sales of Quaker Oats increased dramatically.[60]

Strategies in the Introduction Stage

In the **introduction stage,** products are unfamiliar to consumers.[61] Market segments are not well defined, and product features are not clearly specified. The early development of an industry typically involves low sales growth, rapid technological change, operating losses, and the need for strong sources of cash to finance operations. Since there are few players and not much growth, competition tends to be limited.

Success requires an emphasis on research and development and marketing activities to enhance awareness. The challenge becomes one of (1) developing the product and finding a way to get users to try it and (2) generating enough exposure so the product emerges as the "standard" by which all other rivals' products are evaluated.

There's an advantage to being the "first mover" in a market.[62] It led to Coca-Cola's success in becoming the first soft-drink company to build a recognizable global brand and enabled Caterpillar to get a lock on overseas sales channels and service capabilities.

However, there can also be a benefit to being a "late mover." Target carefully considered its decision to delay its Internet strategy. Compared to its competitors Walmart and Kmart, Target was definitely an industry laggard. But things certainly turned out well:[63]

> By waiting, Target gained a late-mover advantage. The store was able to use competitors' mistakes as its own learning curve. This saved money, and customers didn't seem to mind the wait: When Target finally opened its website, it quickly captured market share from both Kmart and Walmart Internet shoppers. Forrester Research Internet analyst Stephen Zrike commented, "There's no question, in our mind, that Target has a far better understanding of how consumers buy online."

Examples of products currently in the introductory stages of the industry life cycle include electric vehicles and space tourism.

> **introduction stage**
> the first stage of the industry life cycle, characterized by (1) new products that are not known to customers, (2) poorly defined market segments, (3) unspecified product features, (4) low sales growth, (5) rapid technological change, (6) operating losses, and (7) a need for financial support.

Strategies in the Growth Stage

The **growth stage** is characterized by strong increases in sales. Such potential attracts other rivals. In the growth stage, the primary key to success is to build consumer preferences for specific brands. This requires strong brand recognition, differentiated products, and the financial resources to support a variety of value-chain activities such as marketing and sales, and research and development. Whereas marketing and sales initiatives were mainly directed at spurring *aggregate* demand—that is, demand for all such products in the introduction stage—efforts in the growth stage are directed toward stimulating *selective* demand, in which a firm's product offerings are chosen instead of a rival's.

Revenues increase at an accelerating rate because (1) new consumers are trying the product and (2) a growing proportion of satisfied consumers are making repeat purchases.[64] In general, as a product moves through its life cycle, the proportion of repeat buyers to new purchasers increases. Conversely, new products and services often fail if there are relatively few repeat purchases. For example, Alberto-Culver introduced Mr. Culver's Sparklers, which were solid air fresheners that looked like stained glass. Although the product quickly went from the introductory to the growth stage, sales collapsed. Why? Unfortunately, there were few repeat purchasers because buyers treated them as inexpensive window decorations, left them there, and felt little need to purchase new ones. Examples of products currently in the growth stage include cloud computing data storage services and ultra-high-definition television (UHD TV).

> **growth stage**
> the second stage of the product life cycle, characterized by (1) strong increases in sales; (2) growing competition; (3) developing brand recognition; and (4) a need for financing complementary value-chain activities such as marketing, sales, customer service, and research and development.

Strategies in the Maturity Stage

In the **maturity stage** aggregate industry demand softens. As markets become saturated, there are few new adopters. It's no longer possible to "grow around" the competition, so direct competition becomes predominant.[65] With few attractive prospects, marginal competitors exit the market. At the same time, rivalry among existing rivals intensifies because

> **maturity stage**
> the third stage of the product life cycle, characterized by (1) slowing demand growth, (2) saturated markets, (3) direct competition, (4) price competition, and (5) strategic emphasis on efficient operations.

of fierce price competition at the same time that expenses associated with attracting new buyers are rising. Advantages based on efficient manufacturing operations and process engineering become more important for keeping costs low as customers become more price-sensitive. It also becomes more difficult for firms to differentiate their offerings, because users have a greater understanding of products and services.

An article in *Fortune* magazine that addressed the intensity of rivalry in mature markets was aptly titled "A Game of Inches." It stated, "Battling for market share in a slowing industry can be a mighty dirty business. Just ask laundry soap archrivals Unilever and Procter & Gamble."[66] These two firms have been locked in a battle for market share since 1965. Why is the competition so intense? There is not much territory to gain and industry sales were flat. An analyst noted, "People aren't getting any dirtier." Thus, the only way to win is to take market share from the competition. To increase its share, Procter & Gamble (P&G) spends $100 million a year promoting its Tide brand on television, billboards, buses, magazines, and the Internet. But Unilever isn't standing still. Armed with an $80 million budget, it launched a soap tablet product named Wisk Dual Action Tablets. For example, it delivered samples of this product to 24 million U.S. homes in Sunday newspapers, followed by a series of TV ads. P&G launched a counteroffensive with Tide Rapid Action Tablets ads showed in side-by-side comparisons of the two products dropped into beakers of water. In the promotion, P&G claimed that its product is superior because it dissolves faster than Unilever's product.

Although this is only one example, many product classes and industries, including consumer products such as beer, automobiles, and athletic shoes, are in maturity.

Firms do not need to be "held hostage" to the life-cycle curve. By positioning or repositioning their products in unexpected ways, firms can change how customers mentally categorize them. Thus, firms are able to rescue products floundering in the maturity phase of their life cycles and return them to the growth phase.

Two positioning strategies that managers can use to affect consumers' mental shifts are **reverse positioning,** which strips away "sacred" product attributes while adding new ones, and **breakaway positioning,** which associates the product with a radically different category.[67] We discuss each of these positioning strategies below and then provide an example of each in Strategy Spotlight 5.6.

reverse positioning a break in the industry tendency to continuously augment products, characteristic of the product life cycle, by offering products with fewer product attributes and lower prices.

breakaway positioning a break in the industry tendency to incrementally improve products along specific dimensions, characteristic of the product life cycle, by offering products that are still in the industry but are perceived by customers as being different.

Reverse Positioning This strategy assumes that although customers may desire more than the baseline product, they don't necessarily want an endless list of features. With reverse positioning, companies make the creative decision to step off the augmentation treadmill and shed product attributes that the rest of the industry considers sacred. Then, once a product is returned to its baseline state, the stripped-down product adds one or more carefully selected attributes that would usually be found only in a highly augmented product. Such an unconventional combination of attributes allows the product to assume a new competitive position within the category and move backward from maturity into a growth position on the life-cycle curve.

Breakaway Positioning As noted above, with reverse positioning, a product establishes a unique position in its category but retains a clear category membership. However, with breakaway positioning, a product escapes its category by deliberately associating with a different one. Thus, managers leverage the new category's conventions to change both how products are consumed and with whom they compete. Instead of merely seeing the breakaway product as simply an alternative to others in its category, consumers perceive it as altogether different.

When a breakaway product is successful in leaving its category and joining a new one, it is able to redefine its competition. Similar to reverse positioning, this strategy permits the product to shift backward on the life-cycle curve, moving from the rather dismal maturity phase to a thriving growth opportunity.

5.6 STRATEGY SPOTLIGHT

REVERSE AND BREAKAWAY POSITIONING: HOW TO AVOID BEING HELD HOSTAGE TO THE LIFE-CYCLE CURVE

When firms adopt a reverse or breakaway positioning strategy, there is typically no pretense about what they are trying to accomplish. In essence, they subvert convention through unconventional promotions, prices, and attributes. That becomes a large part of their appeal—a cleverly positioned product offering. Next, we discuss Commerce Bank's reverse positioning and Swatch's breakaway positioning.

Commerce Bank

While most banks offer dozens of checking and savings accounts and compete by trying to offer the highest interest rates, Commerce Bank, a regional bank on the East Coast, took a totally different approach. It paid among the lowest rates in its market. Further, it offered a limited product line—just four checking accounts, for example. One would think that such a stingy approach would have scared off customers. However, Commerce Bank was very successful. Between 1999 and 2007, it expanded from 120 to 435 branches. Growing from a single branch in 1973, it was purchased by TD Bank in 2007 for $8.5 billion.

Why was it so successful? It stripped away all of what customers expected—lots of choices and peak interest rates and it *reverse positioned* itself as "the most convenient bank in America." It was open seven days a week, including evenings until 8 p.m. You could get a debit card while you waited. And when it rained, an escort with an umbrella walked you to your car. Further, the bank offered free coffee and newspapers for customers. Not too surprisingly, despite the inferior rates and few choices, customers regularly flocked to the bank, making it an attractive target for a larger bank to buy.

Swatch

Interestingly, the name "Swatch" is often misconstrued as a contraction of the words *Swiss watch*. However, Nicolas Hayek, chairman, affirms that the original contraction was *second watch*—the new watch was introduced as a new concept of watches as casual, fun, and relatively disposable accessories. And therein lies Swatch's *breakaway positioning*.

When Swatch was launched in 1983, Swiss watches were marketed as a form of jewelry. They were serious, expensive, enduring, and discreetly promoted. Once a customer purchased one, it lasted a lifetime. Swatch changed all of that by defining its watches as playful fashion accessories which were showily promoted. They inspired impulse buying—customers would often purchase half a dozen in different designs. Their price—$40 when the brand was introduced—expanded Swatch's reach beyond its default category (watches as high-end jewelry) and moved it into the fashion accessory category, where it has different customers and competitors. Swatch became the official timekeeper of the Summer Olympics in 1996, has continued to support the Olympics since, and has already signed on as a top sponsor of the 2016 Olympic Games in Rio.

Today, The Swatch Group is the largest watch company in the world. It has acquired many brands over the years, including Omega, Longines, Harry Winston, Calvin Klein, and Hamilton. Revenues have grown to $8.5 billion in 2013, and net income has increased to $1.9 billion. These figures represent increases of 65 percent and 153 percent, respectively, since 2009.

Sources: Moon, Y. 2005. Break free from the product life cycle. *Harvard Business Review*, 83(5): 87–94; www.hoovers.com; and http://rio2016.com/en/sponsors/omega.

Strategies in the Decline Stage

Although all decisions in the phases of an industry life cycle are important, they become particularly difficult in the **decline stage.** Firms must face up to the fundamental strategic choices of either exiting or staying and attempting to consolidate their position in the industry.[68]

The decline stage occurs when industry sales and profits begin to fall. Typically, changes in the business environment are at the root of an industry or product group entering this stage.[69] Changes in consumer tastes or a technological innovation can push a product into decline. Compact discs forced cassette tapes into decline in the prerecorded music industry in the 1980s, and now digital devices have pushed CDs into decline.

Products in the decline stage often consume a large share of management time and financial resources relative to their potential worth. Sales and profits decline. Also, competitors may start drastically cutting their prices to raise cash and remain solvent. The situation is further aggravated by the liquidation of assets, including inventory, of some of the competitors that have failed. This further intensifies price competition.

In the decline stage, a firm's strategic options become dependent on the actions of rivals. If many competitors leave the market, sales and profit opportunities increase. On the other hand, prospects are limited if all competitors remain.[70] If some competitors merge,

> **decline stage**
> the fourth stage of the product life cycle, characterized by (1) falling sales and profits, (2) increasing price competition, and (3) industry consolidation.

their increased market power may erode the opportunities for the remaining players. Managers must carefully monitor the actions and intentions of competitors before deciding on a course of action.

Four basic strategies are available in the decline phase: *maintaining, harvesting, exiting,* and *consolidating.*[71]

- ***Maintaining*** refers to keeping a product going without significantly reducing marketing support, technological development, or other investments, in the hope that competitors will eventually exit the market. Many offices, for example, still use typewriters for filling out forms and other purposes that cannot be completed on a PC. In some rural areas, rotary (or dial) telephones persist because of the older technology used in central switching offices. Thus, there may still be the potential for revenues and profits.

- **Harvesting** involves obtaining as much profit as possible and requires that costs be reduced quickly. Managers should consider the firm's value-creating activities and cut associated budgets. Value-chain activities to consider are primary (e.g., operations, sales and marketing) and support (e.g., procurement, technology development). The objective is to wring out as much profit as possible.

- ***Exiting the market*** involves dropping the product from a firm's portfolio. Since a residual core of consumers exist, eliminating it should be carefully considered. If the firm's exit involves product markets that affect important relationships with other product markets in the corporation's overall portfolio, an exit could have repercussions for the whole corporation. For example, it may involve the loss of valuable brand names or human capital with a broad variety of expertise in many value-creating activities such as marketing, technology, and operations.

- **Consolidation** involves one firm acquiring at a reasonable price the best of the surviving firms in an industry. This enables firms to enhance market power and acquire valuable assets. One example of a consolidation strategy took place in the defense industry in the early 1990s. As the cliché suggests, "peace broke out" at the end of the Cold War and overall U.S. defense spending levels plummeted.[72] Many companies that make up the defense industry saw more than 50 percent of their market disappear. Only one-quarter of the 120,000 companies that once supplied the Department of Defense still serve in that capacity; the others have shut down their defense business or dissolved altogether. But one key player, Lockheed Martin, became a dominant rival by pursuing an aggressive strategy of consolidation. During the 1990s, it purchased 17 independent entities, including General Dynamics' tactical aircraft and space systems divisions, GE Aerospace, Goodyear Aerospace, and Honeywell Electro-Optics. These combinations enabled Lockheed Martin to emerge as the top provider to three governmental customers: the Department of Defense, the Department of Energy, and NASA.

Examples of products currently in the decline stage of the industry life cycle include the video-rental business (being replaced by video on demand), hard disk drives (being replaced by solid-state memory and cloud storage), and desktop computers (being replaced by notebook and tablet computers).

The introduction of new technologies and associated products does not always mean that old technologies quickly fade away. Research shows that in a number of cases, old technologies actually enjoy a very profitable "last gasp."[73] Examples include personal computers (versus tablet computers and other mobile devices), coronary artery bypass graft surgery (versus angioplasty), and vinyl records (versus CDs and digital downloads of music). In each case, the advent of new technology prompted predictions of the demise of the older technology, but each of these has proved to be a resilient survivor. What accounts for their continued profitability and survival?

> **harvesting strategy**
> a strategy of wringing as much profit as possible out of a business in the short to medium term by reducing costs.

> **consolidation strategy**
> a firm's acquiring or merging with other firms in an industry in order to enhance market power and gain valuable assets.

Retreating to more defensible ground is one strategy that firms specializing in technologies threatened with rapid obsolescence have followed. For example, while angioplasty may be appropriate for relatively healthier patients with blocked arteries, sicker, higher-risk patients seem to benefit more from coronary artery bypass graft surgery. This enabled the surgeons to concentrate on the more difficult cases and improve the technology itself. The advent of television unseated the radio as the major source of entertainment from American homes. However, the radio has survived and even thrived in venues where people are also engaged in other activities, such as driving.

Using the new to improve the old is a second approach. Microsoft has integrated elements of mobile technology into the Windows operating system to address the challenge of Google's Android and Apple's iOS.

Improving the price-performance trade-off is a third approach. IBM continues to make money selling mainframes long after their obituary was written. It retooled the technology using low-cost microprocessors and cut their prices drastically. Further, it invested and updated the software, enabling it to offer clients such as banks better performance and lower costs.

Turnaround Strategies

A **turnaround strategy** involves reversing performance decline and reinvigorating growth toward profitability.[74] A need for turnaround may occur at any stage in the life cycle but is more likely to occur during maturity or decline.

> **turnaround strategy**
> a strategy that reverses a firm's decline in performance and returns it to growth and profitability.

Most turnarounds require a firm to carefully analyze the external and internal environments.[75] The external analysis leads to identification of market segments or customer groups that may still find the product attractive.[76] Internal analysis results in actions aimed at reduced costs and higher efficiency. A firm needs to undertake a mix of both internally and externally oriented actions to effect a turnaround.[77] In effect, the cliché "You can't shrink yourself to greatness" applies.

A study of 260 mature businesses in need of a turnaround identified three strategies used by successful companies.[78]

- *Asset and cost surgery.* Very often, mature firms tend to have assets that do not produce any returns. These include real estate, buildings, and so on. Outright sales or sale and leaseback free up considerable cash and improve returns. Investment in new plants and equipment can be deferred. Firms in turnaround situations try to aggressively cut administrative expenses and inventories and speed up collection of receivables. Costs also can be reduced by outsourcing production of various inputs for which market prices may be cheaper than in-house production costs.

- *Selective product and market pruning.* Most mature or declining firms have many product lines that are losing money or are only marginally profitable. One strategy is to discontinue such product lines and focus all resources on a few core profitable areas. For example, in 2014, Procter & Gamble announced that it would sell off or close down up to 100 of its brands, allowing the firm to improve its efficiency and its innovativeness as it focused on its core brands. The remaining 70 to 80 "core" brands accounted for 90 percent of the firm's sales.

- *Piecemeal productivity improvements.* There are many ways in which a firm can eliminate costs and improve productivity. Although individually these are small gains, they cumulate over a period of time to substantial gains. Improving business processes by reengineering them, benchmarking specific activities against industry leaders, encouraging employee input to identify excess costs, increasing capacity utilization, and improving employee productivity lead to a significant overall gain.

> **LO5.7**
> The need for turnaround strategies that enable a firm to reposition its competitive position in an industry.

Strategy Spotlight 5.7 provides an illustration of a turnaround effort by focusing on the dramatic strategic realignment that Mindy Grossman undertook at HSN (formerly the Home Shopping Network).

5.7 STRATEGY SPOTLIGHT

HOW MINDY GROSSMAN LED HSN'S REMARKABLE TURNAROUND

Mindy Grossman took over the helm of HSN, formerly known as the Home Shopping Network, in 2008, at a very trying time. The Home Shopping Network was falling behind the times as retailing technology changed rapidly in the digital age and was saddled with the reputation of being the home for C-list celebrities hawking relatively low-grade jewelry, fashion, and health and beauty products to couch potatoes. The firm had experienced significant leadership turmoil, with seven CEOs in the prior 10 years. It was also facing some of the worst economic conditions since the 1930s. Not surprisingly, the firm experienced a multibillion-dollar loss in 2008.

However, things have changed dramatically since those dark days. HSN generated $178 million in profit on $3.4 billion in 2013. The firm's stock price, which traded as low as $1.42 in 2008, was trading at over $70 a share in late 2014.

At the center of HSN's turnaround is Mindy Grossman, the firm's CEO. She came to HSN after working for a number of clothing manufacturers, including Ralph Lauren, Tommy Hilfiger, and, most recently, Nike. Her recipe for the turnaround reflects a mix of hard business acumen combined with an ability to engage stakeholders in the firm to move the turnaround forward. With her changes, she's moved HSN from being a dowdy cable TV channel to a retailer that meets the needs of busy women by providing them a place to shop wherever they are—at home through their TVs or while traveling for work or at their kids' soccer games through their phones or tablets.

What are Grossman's lessons for managing a turnaround? First, she found value in engaging with employees. Her first day at HSN, she chose to go through the same new-employee orientation that all employees go through. She felt this humanized her in the minds of other employees. On her second day, she held a town-hall meeting so that she could directly introduce herself and set the tone that she was accessible and that all employees were valued and could have a future at HSN. She also set up a policy to regularly have breakfasts and lunches with employees and says, "I learn more from those than from reading any report."

Second, she got the lineup of employees right. She categorizes workers into three categories. "Evangelists" are the employees who are truly enthusiastic about the company and try to rally others. The "Interested" are those who are invested in the firm's success but have something of a wait-and-see attitude. The "Blockers" are toxic and work to limit the firm's ability to change. She saw the need to rid the company of toxicity and pushed out the Blockers quickly. This allowed her to develop a management team, which largely stayed intact for several years, that reflected the strong skills and commitment she desired.

She tailored the company's offerings to meet the changing needs of her customer base. In the deep days of the recession in 2008–2009, this meant shifting from offering high-priced jewelry and fashions to providing products and services that helped HSN's customers save time and money. Later, this meant dramatically growing the company's mobile platforms. Today, over half the new customers come to HSN through their mobile phones. One of the new services attracting them is HSN's online arcade, where customers can play games that allow them to win HSN merchandise, which generated over 100 million plays in its first year.

Key to it all is staying focused on what HSN's strategy is and who its customers are. In the words of Grossman, "We're not trying to be Amazon, all things to all people. We have a highly specialized customer and want to give her the best experience somewhere she can trust."

Sources: Goudreau, J. 2012. How Mindy Grossman is transforming HSN. *forbes.com*, August 29: np; Banjo, S. 2013. HSN enjoys a mobile-shopping rebirth in the digital age. *wsj.com*, July 5: np; and Snyder, B. 2014. How Mindy Grossman turned around HSN. *gsb.stanford.edu/insights*, June 5: np.

ISSUE FOR DEBATE

Uncertain Course for Jet Blue

JetBlue appears to be stuck in the middle. The airline has grown rapidly since its founding in 1999 to become the fifth-largest airline in the United States. It has long positioned itself as the "egalitarian" airline, where customers all get the same level of service at largely the same price-point. It structured itself as a low-cost airline but one that provided a higher level of service that included more legroom than competitors, individual TV screens, and Wi-Fi access in its all-coach cabins. In essence, it was the "cheap chic" airline that generated great customer appreciation and commitment.

But JetBlue now faces some challenges. Internally, its costs are rising. After being pressured by its pilots, JetBlue collectively raised pilot pay by $145 million from 2014 through 2017.

But its pilots decided to unionize anyway—which suggests future cost increases. Externally, JetBlue faces increasing pressures on both ends of the strategy spectrum. At the low-cost end, hard-discount airlines, most notably Spirit Airlines, are effectively undercutting JetBlue's prices and stealing the price-conscious consumer. At the differentiation end, the mainline airlines, such as Delta and American, have expanded the services and amenities they provide, especially for higher-fare business travelers. And JetBlue has difficulty matching the global network of routes these airlines can provide business travelers. As a result, JetBlue's sales growth and profitability have lagged its main competitors.

JetBlue has responded by moving to become more like the mainline airlines. The firm ordered new jets that have first-class cabins for use on their flights between the east and west coasts. JetBlue restructured its pricing system to offer different levels of service, with the lowest level requiring that passengers pay to check luggage and providing lower frequent-flyer credit than other fares. JetBlue is also adding seats to its planes by reducing legroom. Airline executives argue JetBlue isn't abandoning its core customers, but others argue the changes will erode the airline's reputation and customer loyalty.

Discussion Questions
1. Is it wise for JetBlue to change its strategy to become more like Delta, American, and United?
2. What are the risks and benefits of this change?
3. What does JetBlue need to do to retain its distinctiveness in customers' eyes?

Sources: Carey, S. 2013. Discount carrier JetBlue goes upmarket. *wsj.com*, August 5: np; Carey, S. 2014. JetBlue CEO in hot seat as airline lags rivals. *wsj.com*, May 13: np; and *finance.yahoo.com*.

Reflecting on Career Implications . . .

- **Types of Competitive Advantage:** Are you aware of your organization's business-level strategy? What do you do to help your firm either increase differentiation or lower costs? Can you demonstrate to your superiors how you have contributed to the firm's chosen business-level strategy?

- **Types of Competitive Advantage:** What is your own competitive advantage? What opportunities does your current job provide to enhance your competitive advantage? Are you making the best use of your competitive advantage? If not, what organizations might provide you with better opportunities for doing so? Does your résumé clearly reflect your competitive advantage? Or are you "stuck in the middle"?

- **Understanding *Your* Differentiation:** When looking for a new job or for advancement in your current firm, be conscious of being able to identify what differentiates you from other applicants. Consider the items in Exhibit 5.4 as you work to identify what distinguishes you from others.

- **Industry Life Cycle:** Before you go for a job interview, identify the life-cycle stage of the industry within which your firm is located. You are more likely to have greater opportunities for career advancement in an industry in the growth stage than one in the decline stage.

- **Industry Life Cycle:** If you sense that your career is maturing (or in the decline phase!), what actions can you take to restore career growth and momentum (e.g., training, mentoring, professional networking)? Should you actively consider professional opportunities in other industries?

summary

How and why firms outperform each other goes to the heart of strategic management. In this chapter, we identified three generic strategies and discussed how firms are able not only to attain advantages over competitors but also to sustain such advantages over time. Why do some advantages become long-lasting while others are quickly imitated by competitors?

The three generic strategies—overall cost leadership, differentiation, and focus—form the core of this chapter. We began by providing a brief description of each generic strategy (or competitive advantage) and furnished examples of firms that have successfully implemented these strategies. Successful generic strategies invariably enhance a firm's position vis-à-vis the five forces of that industry—a point that we stressed and illustrated with examples. However, as we pointed out, there are pitfalls to each of the generic strategies. Thus, the sustainability of a firm's advantage is always challenged because of imitation or substitution by new or existing rivals. Such competitor moves erode a firm's advantage over time.

We also discussed the viability of combining (or integrating) overall cost leadership and generic differentiation strategies. If successful, such integration can enable a firm to enjoy superior performance and improve its competitive position. However, this is challenging, and managers must be aware of the potential downside risks associated with such an initiative.

We addressed the challenges inherent in determining the sustainability of competitive advantages. Drawing on an example from a manufacturing industry, we discussed both the "pro" and "con" positions as to why competitive advantages are sustainable over a long period of time.

The concept of the industry life cycle is a critical contingency that managers must take into account in striving to create and sustain competitive advantages. We identified the four stages of the industry life cycle—introduction, growth, maturity, and decline—and suggested how these stages can play a role in decisions that managers must make at the business level. These include overall strategies as well as the relative emphasis on functional areas and value-creating activities.

When a firm's performance severely erodes, turnaround strategies are needed to reverse its situation and enhance its competitive position. We have discussed three approaches—asset cost surgery, selective product and market pruning, and piecemeal productivity improvements.

SUMMARY REVIEW QUESTIONS

1. Explain why the concept of competitive advantage is central to the study of strategic management.
2. Briefly describe the three generic strategies—overall cost leadership, differentiation, and focus.
3. Explain the relationship between the three generic strategies and the five forces that determine the average profitability within an industry.
4. What are some of the ways in which a firm can attain a successful turnaround strategy?
5. Describe some of the pitfalls associated with each of the three generic strategies.
6. Can firms combine the generic strategies of overall cost leadership and differentiation? Why or why not?
7. Explain why the industry life-cycle concept is an important factor in determining a firm's business-level strategy.

key terms

business-level strategy 147
generic strategies 148
overall cost leadership 148
experience curve 149
competitive parity 149
differentiation strategy 153
focus strategy 159
combination strategies 161
mass customization 161
profit pool 162
industry life cycle 167
introduction stage 169
growth stage 169
maturity stage 169
reverse positioning 170
breakaway positioning 170
decline stage 171
harvesting strategy 172
consolidation strategy 172
turnaround strategy 173

experiential exercise

What are some examples of primary and support activities that enable Nucor, a $21 billion steel manufacturer, to achieve a low-cost strategy? (Fill in the table below.)

Value-Chain Activity	Yes/No	How Does Nucor Create Value for the Customer?
Primary:		
Inbound logistics		
Operations		
Outbound logistics		
Marketing and sales		
Service		
Support:		
Procurement		
Technology development		
Human resource management		
General administration		

application questions & exercises

1. Go to the Internet and look up www.walmart.com. How has this firm been able to combine overall cost leadership and differentiation strategies?
2. Choose a firm with which you are familiar in your local business community. Is the firm successful in following one (or more) generic strategies? Why or why not? What do you think are some of the challenges it faces in implementing these strategies in an effective manner?
3. Think of a firm that has attained a differentiation focus or cost focus strategy. Are its advantages sustainable? Why? Why not? (*Hint:* Consider its position vis-à-vis Porter's five forces.)
4. Think of a firm that successfully achieved a combination overall cost leadership and differentiation strategy. What can be learned from this example? Are the advantages sustainable? Why? Why not? (*Hint:* Consider its competitive position vis-à-vis Porter's five forces.)

ethics questions

1. Can you think of a company that suffered ethical consequences as a result of an overemphasis on a cost leadership strategy? What do you think were the financial and nonfinancial implications?
2. In the introductory stage of the product life cycle, what are some of the unethical practices that managers could engage in to enhance their firm's market position? What could be some of the long-term implications of such actions?

references

1. Randazzo, S. 2014. Sticky time for Crumbs Bake Shop. *wsj.com,* July 8: np; O'Donnell, J. 2014. Here's why the cupcake crumbled at Crumbs. *nydailynews.com,* np; and Randazzo, S. 2014. Crumbs Bake Shop to reopen stores after court approval. *wsj.com,* np.
2. For a perspective by Porter on competitive strategy, refer to Porter, M. E. 1996. What is strategy? *Harvard Business Review,* 74(6): 61–78.
3. For insights into how a start-up is using solar technology, see Gimbel, B. 2009. Plastic power. *Fortune,* February 2: 34.
4. Useful insights on strategy in an economic downturn are in Rhodes, D. & Stelter, D. 2009. Seize advantage in a downturn. *Harvard Business Review,* 87(2): 50–58.
5. Some useful ideas on maintaining competitive advantages can be found in Ma, H. & Karri, R. 2005. Leaders beware: Some sure ways to lose your competitive advantage. *Organizational Dynamics,* 343(1): 63–76.
6. Miller, A. & Dess, G. G. 1993. Assessing Porter's model in terms of its generalizability, accuracy, and simplicity. *Journal of Management Studies,* 30(4): 553–585.
7. Gasparro, A. & Martin, T. 2012. What's wrong with America's supermarkets? *wsj.com,* July 12: np.
8. For insights on how discounting can erode a firm's performance, read Stibel, J. M. & Delgrosso, P. 2008. Discounts can be dangerous. *Harvard Business Review,* 66(12): 31.
9. For a scholarly discussion and analysis of the concept of competitive parity, refer to Powell, T. C. 2003. Varieties of competitive parity. *Strategic Management Journal,* 24(1): 61–86.
10. Rao, A. R., Bergen, M. E., & Davis, S. 2000. How to fight a price war. *Harvard Business Review,* 78(2): 107–120.
11. Marriot, J. W., Jr. Our competitive strength: Human capital. A speech given to the Detroit Economic Club on October 2, 2000.
12. Burrus, D. 2011. *Flash foresight: How to see the invisible and do the impossible.* New York: HarperCollins.
13. Corstjens, M. & Lal, R. 2012. Retail doesn't cross borders. *Harvard Business Review,* April: 104–110.
14. Downing, L. 2012. Finally, a use for sandwich crusts. *Bloomberg Businessweek,* June 18: 18–19.
15. Ng, S. 2014. Zulily customers play the waiting game. *wsj.com,* May 4: np.
16. Interesting insights on Walmart's effective cost leadership strategy are found in Palmeri, C. 2008. Wal-Mart is up for this downturn. *BusinessWeek,* November 6: 34.
17. An interesting perspective on the dangers of price discounting is Mohammed, R. 2011. Ditch the discounts. *Harvard Business Review,* 89(1/2): 23–25.
18. Dholakia, U. M. 2011. Why employees can wreck promotional offers. *Harvard Business Review,* 89(1/2): 28.
19. Jacobs, A. 2010. Workers in China voting with their feet. *International Herald Tribune,* July 13: 1, 14.
20. For a perspective on the sustainability of competitive advantages, refer to Barney, J. 1995. Looking inside for competitive advantage. *Academy of Management Executive,* 9(4): 49–61.
21. Thornton, E. 2001. Why e-brokers are broker and broker. *BusinessWeek,* January 22: 94.
22. Mohammed, R. 2011. Ditch the discounts. *Harvard Business Review,* 89(1/2): 23–25.
23. Wilson, D. 2012. Big Beer dresses up in craft brewers' clothing. *Fortune.com,* November 15: np.
24. For an "ultimate" in differentiated services, consider time-shares in exotic automobiles such as Lamborghinis and Bentleys. Refer to Stead, D. 2008. My Lamborghini—today, anyway. *BusinessWeek,* January 18:17.
25. For an interesting perspective on the value of corporate brands and how they may be leveraged, refer to Aaker, D. A. 2004, *California Management Review,* 46(3): 6–18.
26. A unique perspective on differentiation strategies is Austin, R. D. 2008. High margins and the quest for aesthetic coherence. *Harvard Business Review,* 86(1): 18–19.
27. Eng, D. 2011. Cheesecake Factory's winning formula. *Fortune,* May 2: 19–20.
28. For a discussion on quality in terms of a company's software and information systems, refer to

28. Prahalad, C. K. & Krishnan, M. S. 1999. The new meaning of quality in the information age. *Harvard Business Review,* 77(5): 109–118.
29. The role of design in achieving differentiation is addressed in Brown, T. 2008. Design thinking. *Harvard Business Review,* 86(6): 84–92.
30. Taylor, A., III. 2001. Can you believe Porsche is putting its badge on this car? *Fortune,* February 19: 168–172.
31. Roberts, P. & Dowling, G. 2008. Corporate reputation and sustained superior financial performance. *Strategic Management Journal,* 23: 1077–1093.
32. Mann, J. 2010. The best service in the world. *Networking Times,* January: np.
33. Bonnabeau, E., Bodick, N., & Armstrong, R. W. 2008. A more rational approach to new-product development. *Harvard Business Review,* 66(3): 96–102.
34. Insights on Google's innovation are in Iyer, B. & Davenport, T. H. 2008. Reverse engineering Google's innovation machine. *Harvard Business Review,* 66(4): 58–68.
35. A discussion of how a firm used technology to create product differentiation is in Mehta, S. N. 2009. Under Armour reboots. *Fortune,* February 2: 29–33 (5).
36. Bertini, M. & Wathieu, L. 2010. How to stop customers from fixating on price. *Harvard Business Review,* 88(5): 84–91.
37. The authors would like to thank Scott Droege, a faculty member at Western Kentucky University, for providing this example.
38. Dixon, M., Freeman, K., & Toman, N. 2010. Stop trying to delight your customers. *Harvard Business Review,* 88(7/8).
39. Flint, J. 2004. Stop the nerds. *Forbes,* July 5: 80; and Fahey, E. 2004. Over-engineering 101. *Forbes,* December 13: 62.
40. Symonds, W. C. 2000. Can Gillette regain its voltage? *BusinessWeek,* October 16: 102–104.
41. Caplan, J. 2006. In a real crunch. *Inside Business,* July: A37–A38.
42. Gadiesh, O. & Gilbert, J. L. 1998. Profit pools: A fresh look at strategy. *Harvard Business Review,* 76(3): 139–158.
43. Colvin, G. 2000. Beware: You could soon be selling soybeans. *Fortune,* November 13: 80.
44. Anders, G. 2012. How LinkedIn has turned your resume into a cash machine. *Forbes.com,* July 16: np.
45. Burrus, D. 2011. *Flash foresight: How to see the invisible and do the impossible.* New York: HarperCollins.
46. Hall, W. K. 1980. Survival strategies in a hostile environment, *Harvard Business Review,* 58: 75–87; on the paint and allied products industry, see Dess, G. G. & Davis, P. S. 1984. Porter's (1980) generic strategies as determinants of strategic group membership and organizational performance. *Academy of Management Journal,* 27: 467–488; for the Korean electronics industry, see Kim, L. & Lim, Y. 1988. Environment, generic strategies, and performance in a rapidly developing country: A taxonomic approach. *Academy of Management Journal,* 31: 802–827; Wright, P., Hotard, D., Kroll, M., Chan, P., & Tanner, J. 1990. Performance and multiple strategies in a firm: Evidence from the apparel industry. In Dean, B. V. & Cassidy, J. C. (Eds.), *Strategic management: Methods and studies:* 93–110. Amsterdam: Elsevier-North Holland; and Wright, P., Kroll, M., Tu, H., & Helms, M. 1991. Generic strategies and business performance: An empirical study of the screw machine products industry. *British Journal of Management,* 2: 1–9.
47. Gilmore, J. H. & Pine, B. J., II. 1997. The four faces of customization. *Harvard Business Review,* 75(1): 91–101.
48. Heracleous, L. & Wirtz, J. 2010. Singapore Airlines' balancing act. *Harvard Business Review,* 88(7/8): 145–149.
49. Gilmore & Pine, op. cit. For interesting insights on mass customization, refer to Cattani, K., Dahan, E., & Schmidt, G. 2005. Offshoring versus "spackling." *MIT Sloan Management Review,* 46(3): 6–7.
50. Goodstein, L. D. & Butz, H. E. 1998. Customer value: The linchpin of organizational change. *Organizational Dynamics,* Summer: 21–34.
51. Kiron, D. 2013. From value to vision: Reimagining the possible with data analytics. *MIT Sloan Management Review Research Report,* Spring: 1–19.
52. Gadiesh & Gilbert, op. cit., pp. 139–158.
53. Insights on the profit pool concept are addressed in Reinartz, W. & Ulaga, W. 2008. How to sell services more profitably. *Harvard Business Review,* 66(5): 90–96.
54. A rigorous and thorough discussion of the threats faced by industries due to the commoditization of products and services and what strategic actions firms should consider is found in D'Aveni, R. A. 2010. *Beating the commodity trap.* Boston: Harvard Business Press.
55. For an insightful, recent discussion on the difficulties and challenges associated with creating advantages that are sustainable for any reasonable period of time and suggested strategies, refer to D'Aveni, R. A., Dagnino, G. B., & Smith, K. G. 2010. The age of temporary advantage. *Strategic Management Journal,* 31(13): 1371–1385. This is the lead article in a special issue of this journal that provides many ideas that are useful to both academics and practicing managers. For an additional examination of declining advantage in technologically intensive industries, see Vaaler, P. M. & McNamara, G. 2010. Are technology-intensive industries more dynamically competitive? No and yes. *Organization Science,* 21: 271–289.
56. Rita McGrath provides some interesting ideas on possible strategies for firms facing highly uncertain competitive environments: McGrath, R. G. 2011. When your business model is in trouble. *Harvard Business Review,* 89(1/2): 96–98.
57. The Atlas Door example draws on Stalk, G., Jr. 1988. Time—the next source of competitive advantage. *Harvard Business Review,* 66(4): 41–51.
58. For an interesting perspective on the influence of the product life cycle and rate of technological change on competitive strategy, refer to Lei, D. & Slocum, J. W., Jr. 2005. Strategic and organizational requirements for competitive advantage. *Academy of Management Executive,* 19(1): 31–45.
59. Dickson, P. R. 1994. *Marketing management:* 293. Fort Worth, TX: Dryden Press; Day, G. S. 1981. The product life cycle: Analysis and application. *Journal of Marketing Research,* 45: 60–67.
60. Bearden, W. O., Ingram, T. N., & LaForge, R. W. 1995. *Marketing principles and practices.* Burr Ridge, IL: Irwin.
61. MacMillan, I. C. 1985. Preemptive strategies. In Guth, W. D. (Ed.), *Handbook of business strategy:* 9-1–9-22. Boston: Warren,

Gorham & Lamont; Pearce, J. A. & Robinson, R. B. 2000. *Strategic management* (7th ed.). New York: McGraw-Hill; and Dickson, op. cit., pp. 295–296.

62. Bartlett, C. A. & Ghoshal, S. 2000. Going global: Lessons for late movers. *Harvard Business Review,* 78(2): 132–142.

63. Neuborne, E. 2000. E-tailers hit the relaunch key. *BusinessWeek,* October 17: 62.

64. Berkowitz, E. N., Kerin, R. A., & Hartley, S. W. 2000. *Marketing* (6th ed.). New York: McGraw-Hill.

65. MacMillan, op. cit.

66. Brooker, K. 2001. A game of inches. *Fortune,* February 5: 98–100.

67. Our discussion of reverse and breakaway positioning draws on Moon, Y. 2005. Break free from the product life cycle. *Harvard Business Review,* 83(5): 87–94. This article also discusses stealth positioning as a means of overcoming consumer resistance and advancing a product from the introduction to the growth phase.

68. MacMillan, op. cit.

69. Berkowitz et al., op. cit.

70. Bearden et al., op. cit.

71. The discussion of these four strategies draws on MacMillan, op. cit.; Berkowitz et al., op. cit.; and Bearden et al., op. cit.

72. Augustine, N. R. 1997. Reshaping an industry: Lockheed Martin's survival story. *Harvard Business Review,* 75(3): 83–94.

73. Snow, D. C. 2008. Beware of old technologies' last gasps. *Harvard Business Review,* January: 17–18; Lohr, S. 2008. Why old technologies are still kicking. *New York Times,* March 23: np; and McGrath, R. G. 2008. Innovation and the last gasps of dying technologies. *ritamcgrath. com,* March 18: np.

74. Coyne, K. P., Coyne, S. T., & Coyne, E. J., Sr. 2010. When you've got to cut costs—now. *Harvard Business Review,* 88(5): 74–83.

75. A study that draws on the resource-based view of the firm to investigate successful turnaround strategies is Morrow, J. S., Sirmon, D. G., Hitt, M. A., & Holcomb, T. R. 2007. Creating value in the face of declining performance: Firm strategies and organizational recovery. *Strategic Management Journal,* 28(3): 271–284.

76. For a study investigating the relationship between organizational restructuring and acquisition performance, refer to Barkema, H. G. & Schijven, M. Toward unlocking the full potential of acquisitions: The role of organizational restructuring. *Academy of Management Journal,* 51(4): 696–722.

77. For some useful ideas on effective turnarounds and handling downsizings, refer to Marks, M. S. & De Meuse, K. P. 2005. Resizing the organization: Maximizing the gain while minimizing the pain of layoffs, divestitures and closings. *Organizational Dynamics,* 34(1): 19–36.

78. Hambrick, D. C. & Schecter, S. M. 1983. Turnaround strategies for mature industrial product business units. *Academy of Management Journal,* 26(2): 231–248.

Corporate-Level Strategy
Creating Value through Diversification

chapter 6

After reading this chapter, you should have a good understanding of the following learning objectives:

LO6.1 The reasons for the failure of many diversification efforts.

LO6.2 How managers can create value through diversification initiatives.

LO6.3 How corporations can use related diversification to achieve synergistic benefits through economies of scope and market power.

LO6.4 How corporations can use unrelated diversification to attain synergistic benefits through corporate restructuring, parenting, and portfolio analysis.

LO6.5 The various means of engaging in diversification—mergers and acquisitions, joint ventures/strategic alliances, and internal development.

LO6.6 Managerial behaviors that can erode the creation of value.

PART 2: STRATEGIC FORMULATION

Learning from Mistakes

The Flip video camera burst onto the scene in 2007 and took off, selling over 2 million of the simple, small, and easy-to-use cameras in two years. Sensing opportunity in the digital video market, Cisco Systems snapped up Pure Digital Technologies, the parent company of Flip, in 2009 for $590 million.[1] Just two years later, Cisco announced that it was pulling the plug on the Flip video camera and shutting down the Flip division. Why did Cisco, an experienced acquirer, fail with the Flip acquisition?

Cisco, a computer networking giant, has been extremely successful over the last several years, producing over $47 billion in sales and $7.9 billion in net income in 2014. As part of its business model, Cisco regularly undertakes acquisitions to extend its technology base and product portfolio. In the last decade, Cisco acquired over 80 firms as it extended its product portfolio.

Even with this experience with acquisitions, Cisco was unable to avoid failure with Flip for two reasons. First, Cisco's core business operations are in business networking equipment and software. Flip's business was selling video cameras to individual customers. This is a very different business, where Cisco's knowledge and other competencies were of little value. While Cisco has had some success extending into the consumer market, such as with its acquisition of Linksys, this success has come in the home networking business, a market to which Cisco can transfer some of its business networking competencies.

Second, in large, widely diversified firms, decision making can become slow and remote to market conditions. Cisco competes in a wide range of markets and had nearly 60 decision-making groups in its structure, with several layers separating John Chambers, the CEO of Cisco, from the individual markets. In such a large and diversified firm, the decision making in a small division with only $400 million in annual sales, 1 percent of the overall sales of Cisco, was not the top priority of corporate managers. Stephen Baker, an analyst with NPD Group, saw this and commented that "Cisco was never really committed to the product." As a result, Flip was slower and less responsive to market pressures than it was when it was an entrepreneurial firm.

These two factors left Flip unable to respond to the rapid changes occurring in the home market. Flip experienced a meteoric rise from 2007 to 2009, but this simply triggered an onslaught of competing cameras. Flip also faced an increasing threat from video-camera-enabled smartphones and tablets. There was also a shift in how customers used video devices during this period. Users increasingly wanted the ability to share videos in real time and also upload videos easily to YouTube, Flickr, and other social media sites. Cisco failed to see this shift and didn't add wireless transmission technology into the cameras. John Chambers, Cisco's CEO, admitted this failure. "With Flip, we missed the transition. . . . it was about software that goes into the cloud—the way you're going to really deliver information in the future. We should have been developing our software for the cloud as opposed to the device. And we missed the window of opportunity."

In the end, Cisco didn't have the necessary vision to succeed in this market or the ability to respond quickly enough to the dynamic changes in customer desires.

Discussion Questions

1. Would Flip have had a better chance at success as a stand-alone firm than it did as part of Cisco? Why or why not?
2. Cisco didn't have the right market focus or competencies to win with Flip. What firms could have succeeded by acquiring Flip?

LO6.1

The reasons for the failure of many diversification efforts.

corporate-level strategy
a strategy that focuses on gaining long-term revenue, profits, and market value through managing operations in multiple businesses.

Cisco's experience with Flip is more the rule than the exception. Research shows that a majority of acquisitions of public corporations result in value destruction rather than value creation. Many large multinational firms have also failed to effectively integrate their acquisitions, paid too high a premium for the target's common stock, or were unable to understand how the acquired firm's assets would fit with their own lines of business.[2] And, at times, top executives may not have acted in the best interests of shareholders. That is, the motive for the acquisition may have been to enhance the executives' power and prestige rather than to improve shareholder returns. At times, the only other people who may have benefited were the shareholders of the *acquired* firms—or the investment bankers who advise the acquiring firm, because they collect huge fees up front regardless of what happens afterward![3]

There have been several studies that were conducted over a variety of time periods that show how disappointingly acquisitions have typically turned out. For example:

- A study evaluated the stock market reaction of 600 acquisitions over the period between 1975 and 1991. The results indicated that the acquiring firms suffered an average 4 percent drop in market value (after adjusting for market movements) in the three months following the acquisitions announcement.[4]
- In a study by Salomon Smith Barney of U.S. companies acquired since 1997 in deals for $15 billion or more, the stocks of the acquiring firms have, on average, underperformed the S&P stock index by 14 percentage points and underperformed their peer group by 4 percentage points after the deals were announced.[5]
- A study investigated 270 mergers that took place between 2000 and 2003 in multiple countries and regions. It found that after a merger, sales growth decreased by 6 percent, earnings growth dropped 9.4 percent, and market valuations declined 2.5 percent (figures are adjusted for industry trends and refer to three years pre- or postmerger).[6]
- A study that investigated 86 completed takeover bids that took place between 1993 and 2008 noted a negative return of 2 percent per month in long-term performance for the three-year postacquisition period.[7]

Exhibit 6.1 lists some well-known examples of failed acquisitions and mergers.

EXHIBIT 6.1 Some Well-Known M&A Blunders

Examples of Some Very Expensive Blunders

- Sprint and Nextel merged in 2005. On January 31, 2008, the firm announced a merger-related charge of $31 billion. Its stock had lost 76 percent of its value by late 2012 when it was announced that Sprint Nextel would be purchased by SoftBank, a Japanese telecommunications and Internet firm. SoftBank's stock price dropped 20 percent in the week after announcing it would acquire Sprint.
- AOL paid $114 billion to acquire Time Warner in 2001. Over the next two years, AOL Time Warner lost $150 billion in market valuation.
- Conseco paid $5.8 billion to buy Green Tree, a mobile home mortgage lender, in 1998 though the company's net worth was not even $1 billion. In the next two years, Conseco lost 90 percent of its market value!
- Daimler Benz paid $36 billion to acquire Chrysler in 1998. After years of losses, it sold 80.1 percent of the unit to Cerberus Capital Management for $7.4 billion in 2007. Cerberus didn't do any better, losing its ownership stake when Chrysler went into a government-managed bankruptcy in 2009.
- In 2012, Hewlett-Packard wrote off $9 billion of the $11 billion it paid for Autonomy, a software company that it purchased one year earlier. After the purchase, HP realized that Autonomy's accounting statements were not accurate, resulting in a nearly 80 percent drop in the value of Autonomy once those accounting irregularities were corrected.
- Similarly, in 2012, Microsoft admitted to a major acquisition mistake when it wrote off essentially the entire $6.2 billion it paid for a digital advertising firm, aQuantive, that it purchased in 2007.

Sources: Ante, S. E. 2008. Sprint's wake-up call. *businessweek.com*, February 21: np; Gupta, P. 2008. Daimler may sell remaining Chrysler stake. *www.reuters.com*, September 24: np; Tully, S. 2006. The (second) worst deal ever. *Fortune*, October 16: 102–119; and Wakabayashi, D., Troianovski, A., & Ante, S. 2012. Bravado behind Softbank's Sprint deal. October 16, *wsj.com*: np.

Many acquisitions ultimately result in divestiture—an admission that things didn't work out as planned. In fact, some years ago, a writer for *Fortune* magazine lamented, "Studies show that 33 percent to 50 percent of acquisitions are later divested, giving corporate marriages a divorce rate roughly comparable to that of men and women."[8]

Admittedly, we have been rather pessimistic so far.[9] Clearly, many diversification efforts have worked out very well—whether through mergers and acquisitions, strategic alliances and joint ventures, or internal development. We will discuss many success stories throughout this chapter. Next, we will discuss the primary rationales for diversification.

Making Diversification Work: An Overview

LO6.2
How managers can create value through diversification initiatives.

Clearly, not all **diversification** moves, including those involving mergers and acquisitions, erode performance. For example, acquisitions in the oil industry, such as British Petroleum's purchases of Amoco and Arco, are performing well, as is the Exxon-Mobil merger. MetLife was able to dramatically expand its global footprint by acquiring Alico, a global player in the insurance business, from AIG in 2010 when AIG was in financial distress. Since AIG was desperate to sell assets, MetLife was able to acquire this business at an attractive price. With this acquisition, MetLife expanded its global reach from 17 to 64 countries and increased its non-U.S. revenue from 15 to 40 percent.[10] Many leading high-tech firms such as Google, Apple, and Intel have dramatically enhanced their revenues, profits, and market values through a wide variety of diversification initiatives, including acquisitions, strategic alliances, and joint ventures, as well as internal development.

diversification
the process of firms expanding their operations by entering new businesses.

So the question becomes: Why do some diversification efforts pay off and others produce poor results? This chapter addresses two related issues: (1) What businesses should a corporation compete in? and (2) How should these businesses be managed to jointly create more value than if they were freestanding units?

Diversification initiatives—whether through mergers and acquisitions, strategic alliances and joint ventures, or internal development—must be justified by the creation of value for shareholders.[11] But this is not always the case.[12] Acquiring firms typically pay high premiums when they acquire a target firm. For example, in 2006 Freeport-McMoRan paid a 30 percent premium to acquire Phelps Dodge in order to create the largest metals and mining concern in the U.S. In contrast, you and I, as private investors, can diversify our portfolio of stocks very cheaply. With an intensely competitive online brokerage industry, we can acquire hundreds (or thousands) of shares for a transaction fee of as little as $10 or less—a far cry from the 30 to 40 percent (or higher) premiums that corporations typically must pay to acquire companies.

Given the seemingly high inherent downside risks and uncertainties, one might ask: Why should companies even bother with diversification initiatives? The answer, in a word, is *synergy*, derived from the Greek word *synergos*, which means "working together." This can have two different, but not mutually exclusive, meanings.

First, a firm may diversify into *related* businesses. Here, the primary potential benefits to be derived come from *horizontal relationships*, that is, businesses sharing intangible resources (e.g., core competencies such as marketing) and tangible resources (e.g., production facilities, distribution channels).[13] Firms can also enhance their market power via pooled negotiating power and vertical integration. For example, Procter & Gamble enjoys many synergies from having businesses that share distribution resources.

Second, a corporation may diversify into *unrelated* businesses.[14] Here, the primary potential benefits are derived largely from *hierarchical relationships*, that is, value creation derived from the corporate office. Examples of the latter would include leveraging some of the support activities in the value chain that we discussed in Chapter 3, such as information systems or human resource practices.

EXHIBIT 6.2
Creating Value through Related and Unrelated Diversification

Related Diversification: Economies of Scope

Leveraging core competencies
- 3M leverages its competencies in adhesives technologies to many industries, including automotive, construction, and telecommunications.

Sharing activities
- Polaris, a manufacturer of snowmobiles, motorcycles, watercraft, and off-road vehicles, shares manufacturing operations across its businesses. It also has a corporate R&D facility and staff departments that support all of Polaris's operating divisions.

Related Diversification: Market Power

Pooled negotiating power
- ConAgra, a diversified food producer, increases its power over suppliers by centrally purchasing huge quantities of packaging materials for all of its food divisions.

Vertical integration
- Shaw Industries, a giant carpet manufacturer, increases its control over raw materials by producing much of its own polypropylene fiber, a key input to its manufacturing process.

Unrelated Diversification: Parenting, Restructuring, and Financial Synergies

Corporate restructuring and parenting
- The corporate office of Cooper Industries adds value to its acquired businesses by performing such activities as auditing their manufacturing operations, improving their accounting activities, and centralizing union negotiations.

Portfolio management
- Novartis, formerly Ciba-Geigy, uses portfolio management to improve many key activities, including resource allocation and reward and evaluation systems.

Please note that such benefits derived from horizontal (related diversification) and hierarchical (unrelated diversification) relationships are not mutually exclusive. Many firms that diversify into related areas benefit from information technology expertise in the corporate office. Similarly, unrelated diversifiers often benefit from the "best practices" of sister businesses even though their products, markets, and technologies may differ dramatically.

Exhibit 6.2 provides an overview of how we will address the various means by which firms create value through both related and unrelated diversification and also includes a summary of some examples that we will address in this chapter.[15]

Related Diversification: Economies of Scope and Revenue Enhancement

related diversification
a firm entering a different business in which it can benefit from leveraging core competencies, sharing activities, or building market power.

economies of scope
cost savings from leveraging core competencies or sharing related activities among businesses in a corporation.

LO6.3
How corporations can use related diversification to achieve synergistic benefits through economies of scope and market power.

Related diversification enables a firm to benefit from horizontal relationships across different businesses in the diversified corporation by leveraging core competencies and sharing activities (e.g., production and distribution facilities). This enables a corporation to benefit from economies of scope. **Economies of scope** refers to cost savings from leveraging core competencies or sharing related activities among businesses in the corporation. A firm can also enjoy greater revenues if two businesses attain higher levels of sales growth combined than either company could attain independently.

Leveraging Core Competencies

The concept of core competencies can be illustrated by the imagery of the diversified corporation as a tree.[16] The trunk and major limbs represent core products; the smaller branches are business units; and the leaves, flowers, and fruit are end products. The core competencies are represented by the root system, which provides nourishment, sustenance, and stability. Managers often misread the strength of competitors by looking only at their end products, just as we can fail to appreciate the strength of a tree by looking only at its leaves. Core competencies may also be viewed as the "glue" that binds existing businesses together or as the engine that fuels new business growth.

Core competencies reflect the collective learning in organizations—how to coordinate diverse production skills, integrate multiple streams of technologies, and market diverse products and services.[17] Casio, a giant electronic products producer, synthesizes its abilities in miniaturization, microprocessor design, material science, and ultrathin precision castings to produce digital watches. These are the same skills it applies to design and produce its miniature card calculators, digital cameras, pocket electronic dictionaries, and other small electronics.

> **core competencies**
> a firm's strategic resources that reflect the collective learning in the organization.

For a core competence to create value and provide a viable basis for synergy among the businesses in a corporation, it must meet three criteria:[18]

- *The core competence must enhance competitive advantage(s) by creating superior customer value.* Every value-chain activity has the potential to provide a viable basis for building on a core competence.[19] At Gillette, for example, scientists have developed a series of successful new razors, including the Sensor, Fusion, Mach 3, and ProGlide, building on a thorough understanding of several phenomena that underlie shaving. These include the physiology of facial hair and skin, the metallurgy of blade strength and sharpness, the dynamics of a cartridge moving across skin, and the physics of a razor blade severing hair. Such innovations are possible only with an understanding of such phenomena and the ability to combine such technologies into innovative products. Customers are willing to pay more for such technologically differentiated products.

- *Different businesses in the corporation must be similar in at least one important way related to the core competence.* It is not essential that the products or services themselves be similar. Rather, at least one element in the value chain must require similar skills in creating competitive advantage if the corporation is to capitalize on its core competence. At first glance you might think that computers and health care have little in common. However, Strategy Spotlight 6.1 discusses how IBM is combining its competencies in computing technology with crowdsourced knowledge to provide health care services.

- *The core competencies must be difficult for competitors to imitate or find substitutes for.* As we discussed in Chapter 5, competitive advantages will not be sustainable if the competition can easily imitate or substitute them. Similarly, if the skills associated with a firm's core competencies are easily imitated or replicated, they are not a sound basis for sustainable advantages.

Consider Amazon's retailing operations. Amazon developed strong competencies in Internet retailing, website infrastructure, warehousing, and order fulfillment to dominate the online book industry. It used these competencies along with its brand name to expand into a range of online retail businesses. Competitors in these other market areas have had great difficulty imitating Amazon's competencies, and many have simply stopped trying. Instead, they have partnered with Amazon and contracted with Amazon to provide these services for them.[20]

Steve Jobs provided insight on the importance of a firm's core competence. The Apple CEO was considered one of the world's most respected business leaders:[21]

> One of our biggest insights (years ago) was that we didn't want to get into any business where we didn't own or control the primary technology, because you'll get your head handed to you. We realized that for almost all future consumer electronics, the primary technology was going to be software. And we were pretty good at software. We could

6.1 STRATEGY SPOTLIGHT — CROWDSOURCING

IBM: THE NEW HEALTH CARE EXPERT

Watson, the supercomputer IBM used to win a competition against the best players on the quiz show *Jeopardy!* is now working toward becoming Dr. Watson. Over the decades, IBM has developed strong competencies in raw computing power. With Watson, a computer named after IBM founder Thomas J. Watson, IBM engineers and scientists set out to extend IBM's competencies by building a computing system that can process natural language. Their goal was to build a system that could rival a human's ability to answer questions posed in natural language with speed, accuracy, and confidence. They took four years to develop the system and demonstrated its capabilities in beating two of the greatest champions of *Jeopardy!* in 2011.

Now IBM is aiming to leverage its competencies in the health care arena. In 2013, IBM introduced three applications, one which recommends cancer treatment options and two for reviewing and authorizing treatments and related insurance claims. IBM developed the cancer treatment application with Memorial Sloan-Kettering, one of the world's premier cancer treatment clinics. IBM chose to work on cancer treatment since the volume of research on cancer doubles every five years. As a result, oncologists, the doctors treating cancer, can easily fall behind the cutting edge of research. As Dr. Mark Kris, chief of Memorial Sloan Kettering's Thoracic Oncology Service, stated, "There has been an explosion in medical research, and doctors can't possibly keep up." That is not a problem for Watson. IBM sees this massive volume of research as an opportunity to crowdsource knowledge to develop new, integrated insights. IBM regularly feeds massive amounts of data from medical studies into Watson. In a one-year period, Watson absorbed and analyzed more than 600,000 pieces of medical data and 2 million pages of text from 42 medical journals and clinical trials of cancer treatments. IBM then adds the individual patient's health history and current symptoms to the system. With its natural-language capabilities, Watson can easily process and codify all of the information fed into it. Doctors access the system, using an iPad, enter the patient's symptoms, and within three seconds receive a personalized diagnosis and a prioritized list of recommended tests and treatment options.

While oncology is the first medical specialty for Watson, IBM is looking to take the same approach to providing guidance for the treatment of diabetes, kidney disease, heart disease, and many other areas of medicine. It has enlisted leading health care partners, such as the Cleveland Clinic and Cedars-Sinai Hospital, in its efforts to expand into other treatment areas.

Sources: Frier, S. 2012. IBM wants to put a Watson in your pocket. *Bloomberg Businessweek*, September 17: 41–42; Groenfeldt, T. 2012. IBM's Watson, Cedars-Sinai and WellPoint take on cancer. *forbes.com*, February 1: np; Henschen, D. 2013. IBM's Watson could be healthcare game changer. *informationweek.com*, February 3: np; and *ibm.com*.

---

do the operating system software. We could write applications like iTunes on the Mac or even PC. And we could write the back-end software that runs on a cloud like iTunes. So we could write all these different kinds of software and tweed it all together and make it work seamlessly. And you ask yourself: What other companies can do that? It's a pretty short list.

Sharing Activities

As we saw above, leveraging core competencies involves transferring accumulated skills and expertise across business units in a corporation. Corporations also can achieve synergy by **sharing activities** across their business units. These include value-creating activities such as common manufacturing facilities, distribution channels, and sales forces. As we will see, sharing activities can potentially provide two primary payoffs: cost savings and revenue enhancements.

sharing activities
having activities of two or more businesses' value chains done by one of the businesses.

Deriving Cost Savings Typically, this is the most common type of synergy and the easiest to estimate. Peter Shaw, head of mergers and acquisitions at the British chemical and pharmaceutical company ICI, refers to cost savings as "hard synergies" and contends that the level of certainty of their achievement is quite high. Cost savings come from many sources, including from the elimination of jobs, facilities, and related expenses that are no longer needed when functions are consolidated and from economies of scale in purchasing. Cost savings are generally highest when one company acquires another from the same industry in the same country. Shaw Industries, a division of Berkshire Hathaway, is the nation's largest carpet producer. Over the years, it has dominated the competition through a strategy of acquisition that has enabled Shaw, among other things, to consolidate its manufacturing operations in a few, highly efficient plants and to lower costs through higher capacity utilization.

Sharing activities inevitably involve costs that the benefits must outweigh such as the greater coordination required to manage a shared activity. Even more important is the need to compromise on the design or performance of an activity so that it can be shared. For example, a salesperson handling the products of two business units must operate in a way that is usually not what either unit would choose if it were independent. If the compromise erodes the unit's effectiveness, then sharing may reduce rather than enhance competitive advantage.

Enhancing Revenue and Differentiation

Often an acquiring firm and its target may achieve a higher level of sales growth together than either company could on its own. For example, Starbucks has acquired a number of small firms, including La Boulange, a small bakery chain; Teavana, a tea producer; and Evolution Fresh, a juice company. Starbucks can add value to all of these firms by expanding their market exposure as Starbucks offers these products for sale in its national retail chain.[22]

Firms also can enhance the effectiveness of their differentiation strategies by means of sharing activities among business units. A shared order-processing system, for example, may permit new features and services that a buyer will value. As another example, financial service providers strive to provide differentiated bundles of services to customers. By having a single point of contact where customers can manage their checking accounts, investment accounts, insurance policies, bill-payment services, mortgages, and many other services, they create value for their customers.

As a cautionary note, managers must keep in mind that sharing activities among businesses in a corporation can have a negative effect on a given business's differentiation. For example, when Ford owned Jaguar, customers had lower perceived value of Jaguar automobiles when they learned that the entry-level Jaguar shared its basic design with and was manufactured in the same production plant as the Ford Mondeo, a European midsize car. Perhaps it is not too surprising that Jaguar was divested by Ford in 2008.

Related Diversification: Market Power

We now discuss how companies achieve related diversification through **market power.** We also address the two principal means by which firms achieve synergy through market power: *pooled negotiating power* and *vertical integration.* Managers do, however, have limits on their ability to use market power for diversification, because government regulations can sometimes restrict the ability of a business to gain very large shares of a particular market. For example, in 2011 AT&T attempted to acquire T-Mobile, a wireless service provider, but the acquisition was blocked by federal regulators who feared the combined firm would have too much market power in the telecommunications industry.

market power
firms' abilities to profit through restricting or controlling supply to a market or coordinating with other firms to reduce investment.

Pooled Negotiating Power

Similar businesses working together or the affiliation of a business with a strong parent can strengthen an organization's bargaining position relative to suppliers and customers and enhance its position vis-à-vis competitors. Compare, for example, the position of an independent food manufacturer with that of the same business within Nestlé. Being part of Nestlé provides the business with significant clout—greater bargaining power with suppliers and customers—since it is part of a firm that makes large purchases from suppliers and provides a wide variety of products. Access to the parent's deep pockets

pooled negotiating power
the improvement in bargaining position relative to suppliers and customers.

increases the business's strength, and the Nestlé unit enjoys greater protection from substitutes and new entrants. Not only would rivals perceive the unit as a more formidable opponent, but the unit's association with Nestlé would also provide greater visibility and improved image.

When acquiring related businesses, a firm's potential for pooled negotiating power vis-à-vis its customers and suppliers can be very enticing. However, managers must carefully evaluate how the combined businesses may affect relationships with actual and potential customers, suppliers, and competitors. For example, when PepsiCo diversified into the fast-food industry with its acquisitions of Kentucky Fried Chicken, Taco Bell, and Pizza Hut (now part of Yum! Brands), it clearly benefited from its position over these units that served as a captive market for its soft-drink products. However, many competitors, such as McDonald's, refused to consider PepsiCo as a supplier of its own soft-drink needs because of competition with Pepsi's divisions in the fast-food industry. Simply put, McDonald's did not want to subsidize the enemy! Thus, although acquiring related businesses can enhance a corporation's bargaining power, it must be aware of the potential for retaliation.

Vertical Integration

> **vertical integration**
> an expansion or extension of the firm by integrating preceding or successive production processes.

Vertical integration occurs when a firm becomes its own supplier or distributor. That is, it represents an expansion or extension of the firm by integrating preceding or successive production processes.[23] The firm incorporates more processes toward the original source of raw materials (backward integration) or toward the ultimate consumer (forward integration). For example, a car manufacturer might supply its own parts or make its own engines to secure sources of supply or control its own system of dealerships to ensure retail outlets for its products. Similarly, an oil refinery might secure land leases and develop its own drilling capacity to ensure a constant supply of crude oil. Or it could expand into retail operations by owning or licensing gasoline stations to guarantee customers for its petroleum products.

Vertical integration can be a viable strategy for many firms. Strategy Spotlight 6.2 discusses Nutriva, a Canadian dairy firm, that has backward integrated in order to ensure that the inputs it uses in its dairy business support and reinforce the firm's differentiated market position.

Benefits and Risks of Vertical Integration Vertical integration is a means for an organization to reduce its dependence on suppliers or its channels of distribution to end users. However, the benefits associated with vertical integration—backward or forward—must be carefully weighed against the risks.[24] The primary benefits and risks of vertical integration are listed in Exhibit 6.3.

Winnebago, the leader in the market for drivable recreational vehicles, with a 20.6 percent market share, illustrates some of vertical integration's benefits.[25] The word *Winnebago* means "big RV" to most Americans. And the firm has a sterling reputation for great quality. The firm's huge northern Iowa factories do everything from extruding aluminum for body parts to molding plastics for water and holding tanks to dashboards. Such vertical integration at the factory may appear to be outdated and expensive, but it guarantees excellent quality. The Recreational Vehicle Dealer Association started giving a quality award in 1996, and Winnebago has won it every year.

In making vertical integration decisions, five issues should be considered:[26]

1. ***Is the company satisfied with the quality of the value that its present suppliers and distributors are providing?*** If the performance of organizations in the vertical chain—both suppliers and distributors—is satisfactory, it may not, in general, be appropriate for a company to perform these activities itself. Nike and

6.2 STRATEGY SPOTLIGHT — ENVIRONMENTAL SUSTAINABILITY

VERTICAL INTEGRATION AT NUTRIVA

After graduating with a master's degree in animal science from Michigan State University, Bill Vanderkooi returned to British Columbia to help run his family's dairy business. He saw the need to break out of the low-margin, commodity nature of the dairy business. His desire was to build a brand that emphasized health consciousness and environmental sustainability. He developed a line of organic dairy products enriched with DHA, an omega-3 fatty acid that is thought to provide several health benefits. To ensure that his dairy products met his desire for healthy differentiation, he backward integrated into a number of businesses that provide high-quality feed designed to result in higher nutrient qualities in the firm's dairy products. First, he started a business that developed seeds that produce nutrient-rich grains to feed his cows without the use of pesticides. He also built a feed business in which samples of grain are analyzed and graded on their nutrient values. He founded an organic-milk trucking company so that he can be sure the milk he receives from supplier farms is not contaminated by being transported in trucks that also carry nonorganic milk. Finally, he built a demonstration dairy farm at which Nutriva can educate consumers on the health attributes of its dairy products and the environmental consciousness of the company's dairy operations. In Vanderkooi's words, all of these efforts allow the firm to have "traceable quality control." His desire is to have transparency so that customers can have confidence in the health attributes of the products they purchase and in the environmental sustainability efforts of the supplier farms and dairy operations.

These efforts appear to be paying off. The firm's sales doubled from 2009 to 2013. Vanderkooi's desire to provide healthy food products and increase consumer demand has led the firm to expand its offerings to other food products, such as vitamin-rich eggs from free-range chickens, and consulting services for other food producers.

Sources: Vanderkooi, B. 2012. Bill Vanderkooi, president of Bakerview Ecodairy and CEO of Nutriva Group. *dairyindustries.com*, August 12: np; Ebner, D. 2012. Farmer rips page from corporate strategy handbook. *theglobeandmail.com*, August 23: np; and *nutrivagroup.com*.

EXHIBIT 6.3 Benefits and Risks of Vertical Integration

Benefits

- A secure source of raw materials or distribution channels.
- Protection of and control over valuable assets.
- Proprietary access to new technologies developed by the unit.
- Simplified procurement and administrative procedures.

Risks

- Costs and expenses associated with increased overhead and capital expenditures.
- Loss of flexibility resulting from large investments.
- Problems associated with unbalanced capacities along the value chain. (For example, the in-house supplier has to be larger than your needs in order to benefit from economies of scale in that market.)
- Additional administrative costs associated with managing a more complex set of activities.

Reebok have outsourced the manufacture of their shoes for years, because they have found the independent suppliers capable of providing low-cost, acceptable-quality shoes.

2. *Are there activities in the industry value chain presently being outsourced or performed independently by others that are a viable source of future profits?*
   Even if a firm is outsourcing value-chain activities to companies that are doing a credible job, it may be missing out on substantial profit opportunities. Consider Best Buy. When it realized that the profit potential of providing installation and service was substantial, Best Buy forward integrated into this area by acquiring Geek Squad.

3. *Is there a high level of stability in the demand for the organization's products?*
   High demand or sales volatility is not conducive to vertical integration. With the high level of fixed costs in plant and equipment as well as operating costs that accompany endeavors toward vertical integration, widely fluctuating sales demand

can either strain resources (in times of high demand) or result in unused capacity (in times of low demand). The cycles of "boom and bust" in the automobile industry are a key reason why the manufacturers have increased the amount of outsourced inputs.

4. ***Does the company have the necessary competencies to execute the vertical integration strategies?*** As many companies would attest, successfully executing strategies of vertical integration can be very difficult. For example, Boise Cascade, a lumber firm, once forward integrated into the home-building industry but found that it didn't have the design and marketing competencies needed to compete in this market.

5. ***Will the vertical integration initiative have potential negative impacts on the firm's stakeholders?*** Managers must carefully consider the impact that vertical integration may have on existing and future customers, suppliers, and competitors. After Lockheed Martin, a dominant defense contractor, acquired Loral Corporation, an electronics supplier, for $9.1 billion, it had an unpleasant and unanticipated surprise. Loral, as a subsidiary of Lockheed, was viewed as a rival by many of its previous customers. Thus, while Lockheed Martin may have seen benefits by being able to coordinate operations with Loral as a captive supplier, it also saw a decline in business for Loral with other defense contractors.

Analyzing Vertical Integration: The Transaction Cost Perspective Another approach that has proved very useful in understanding vertical integration is the **transaction cost perspective**.[27] According to this perspective, every market transaction involves some *transaction costs*. First, a decision to purchase an input from an outside source leads to *search* costs (i.e., the cost to find where it is available, the level of quality, etc.). Second, there are costs associated with *negotiating*. Third, a *contract* needs to be written spelling out future possible contingencies. Fourth, parties in a contract have to *monitor* each other. Finally, if a party does not comply with the terms of the contract, there are *enforcement* costs. Transaction costs are thus the sum of search costs, negotiation costs, contracting costs, monitoring costs, and enforcement costs. These transaction costs can be avoided by internalizing the activity, in other words, by producing the input in-house.

A related problem with purchasing a specialized input from outside is the issue of *transaction-specific investments*. For example, when an automobile company needs an input specifically designed for a particular car model, the supplier may be unwilling to make the investments in plant and machinery necessary to produce that component for two reasons. First, the investment may take many years to recover but there is no guarantee the automobile company will continue to buy from the supplier after the contract expires, typically in one year. Second, once the investment is made, the supplier has no bargaining power. That is, the buyer knows that the supplier has no option but to supply at ever-lower prices because the investments were so specific that they cannot be used to produce alternative products. In such circumstances, again, vertical integration may be the only option.

Vertical integration, however, gives rise to a different set of costs. These costs are referred to as *administrative costs*. Coordinating different stages of the value chain now internalized within the firm causes administrative costs to go up. Decisions about vertical integration are, therefore, based on a comparison of transaction costs and administrative costs. If transaction costs are lower than administrative costs, it is best to resort to market transactions and avoid vertical integration. For example, McDonald's may be the world's biggest buyer of beef, but it does not raise cattle. The market for beef has low transaction costs and requires no transaction-specific investments. On the other hand, if transaction costs are higher than administrative costs, vertical integration becomes an attractive strategy. Most automobile manufacturers produce their own engines because the market for engines involves high transaction costs and transaction-specific investments.

---

transaction cost perspective
a perspective that the choice of a transaction's governance structure, such as vertical integration or market transaction, is influenced by transaction costs, including search, negotiating, contracting, monitoring, and enforcement costs, associated with each choice.

Unrelated Diversification: Financial Synergies and Parenting

With **unrelated diversification,** unlike related diversification, few benefits are derived from *horizontal relationships*—that is, the leveraging of core competencies or the sharing of activities across business units within a corporation. Instead, potential benefits can be gained from *vertical (or hierarchical) relationships*—the creation of synergies from the interaction of the corporate office with the individual business units. There are two main sources of such synergies. First, the corporate office can contribute to "parenting" and restructuring of (often acquired) businesses. Second, the corporate office can add value by viewing the entire corporation as a family or "portfolio" of businesses and allocating resources to optimize corporate goals of profitability, cash flow, and growth. Additionally, the corporate office enhances value by establishing appropriate human resource practices and financial controls for each of its business units.

Corporate Parenting and Restructuring

We have discussed how firms can add value through related diversification by exploring sources of synergy *across* business units. Now, we discuss how value can be created *within* business units as a result of the expertise and support provided by the corporate office.

Parenting The positive contributions of the corporate office are called the **"parenting advantage."**[28] Many firms have successfully diversified their holdings without strong evidence of the more traditional sources of synergy (i.e., horizontally across business units). Diversified public corporations such as Berkshire Hathaway and Virgin Group and leveraged buyout firms such as KKR and Clayton, Dubilier & Rice are a few examples.[29] These parent companies create value through management expertise. How? They improve plans and budgets and provide especially competent central functions such as legal, financial, human resource management, procurement, and the like. They also help subsidiaries make wise choices in their own acquisitions, divestitures, and new internal development decisions. Such contributions often help business units to substantially increase their revenues and profits. For example, KKR, a private equity firm, has a team of parenting experts, called KKR Capstone, that works with newly acquired firms for 12 to 24 months to enhance the acquired firm's value. The team works to improve a range of operating activities, such as new product development processes, sales force activities, quality improvement, and supply chain management.

Restructuring Restructuring is another means by which the corporate office can add value to a business.[30] The central idea can be captured in the real estate phrase "Buy low and sell high." Here, the corporate office tries to find either poorly performing firms with unrealized potential or firms in industries on the threshold of significant, positive change. The parent intervenes, often selling off parts of the business; changing the management; reducing payroll and unnecessary sources of expenses; changing strategies; and infusing the company with new technologies, processes, reward systems, and so forth. When the restructuring is complete, the firm can either "sell high" and capture the added value or keep the business and enjoy financial and competitive benefits.[31]

Loews Corporation, a conglomerate with $15 billion in revenues, competes in such industries as oil and gas, tobacco, watches, insurance, and hotels. It provides an exemplary example of how firms can successfully "buy low and sell high" as part of their corporate strategy.[32]

> Energy accounts for 33 percent of Loews' $30 billion in total assets. In the 1980s it bought six oil tankers for only $5 million each during a sharp slide in oil prices. The downside was limited. After all, these huge hulks could easily have been sold as scrap steel. However,

LO6.4
How corporations can use unrelated diversification to attain synergistic benefits through corporate restructuring, parenting, and portfolio analysis.

unrelated diversification
a firm entering a different business that has little horizontal interaction with other businesses of a firm.

parenting advantage
the positive contributions of the corporate office to a new business as a result of expertise and support provided and not as a result of substantial changes in assets, capital structure, or management.

restructuring
the intervention of the corporate office in a new business that substantially changes the assets, capital structure, and/or management, including selling off parts of the business, changing the management, reducing payroll and unnecessary sources of expenses, changing strategies, and infusing the new business with new technologies, processes, and reward systems.

that didn't have to happen. Eight years after Loews purchased the tankers, it sold them for $50 million each.

Loews was also extremely successful with its next energy play—drilling equipment. Although wildcatting for oil is very risky, selling services to wildcatters is not, especially if the assets are bought during a down cycle. Loews did just that. It purchased 10 offshore drilling rigs for $50 million in 1989 and formed Diamond Offshore Drilling. In 1995 Loews received $338 million after taking a 30 percent piece of this operation public!

For the restructuring strategy to work, the corporate management must have the insight to detect undervalued companies (otherwise, the cost of acquisition would be too high) or businesses competing in industries with a high potential for transformation.[33] Additionally, of course, it must have the requisite skills and resources to turn the businesses around, even if they may be in new and unfamiliar industries.

Restructuring can involve changes in assets, capital structure, or management.

- *Asset restructuring* involves the sale of unproductive assets, or even whole lines of businesses, that are peripheral. In some cases, it may even involve acquisitions that strengthen the core business.
- *Capital restructuring* involves changing the debt-equity mix, or the mix between different classes of debt or equity. Although the substitution of equity with debt is more common in buyout situations, occasionally the parent may provide additional equity capital.
- *Management restructuring* typically involves changes in the composition of the top management team, organizational structure, and reporting relationships. Tight financial control, rewards based strictly on meeting short- to medium-term performance goals, and reduction in the number of middle-level managers are common steps in management restructuring. In some cases, parental intervention may even result in changes in strategy as well as infusion of new technologies and processes.

Portfolio Management

During the 1970s and early 1980s, several leading consulting firms developed the concept of **portfolio management** to achieve a better understanding of the competitive position of an overall portfolio (or family) of businesses, to suggest strategic alternatives for each of the businesses, and to identify priorities for the allocation of resources. Several studies have reported widespread use of these techniques among American firms.[34]

While portfolio management tools have been widely used in corporations, research on their use has offered mixed support. However, recent research has suggested that strategically channeling resources to units with the most promising prospects can lead to corporate advantage. Research suggests that many firms do not adjust their capital allocations in response to changes in the performance of units or the attractiveness of the markets in which units of the corporation compete. Instead, allocations are fairly consistent from year to year. However, firms that assess the attractiveness of markets in which the firm competes and the capabilities of each division and then choose allocations of corporate resources based on these assessments exhibit higher levels of corporate survival, overall corporate performance, stock market performance, and the performance of individual business units within the corporation. These effects have also been shown to be stronger when firms compete in more competitive markets and in times of economic distress.[35] These findings have shown that the ability to effectively allocate financial capital is a key competence of high-performance diversified firms.

Description and Potential Benefits The key purpose of portfolio models is to assist a firm in achieving a balanced portfolio of businesses.[36] This consists of businesses whose

> **portfolio management**
> a method of (a) assessing the competitive position of a portfolio of businesses within a corporation, (b) suggesting strategic alternatives for each business, and (c) identifying priorities for the allocation of resources across the businesses.

profitability, growth, and cash flow characteristics complement each other and adds up to a satisfactory overall corporate performance. Imbalance, for example, could be caused either by excessive cash generation with too few growth opportunities or by insufficient cash generation to fund the growth requirements in the portfolio.

The Boston Consulting Group's (BCG's) growth/share matrix is among the best known of these approaches.[37] In the BCG approach, each of the firm's strategic business units (SBUs) is plotted on a two-dimensional grid in which the axes are relative market share and industry growth rate. The grid is broken into four quadrants. Exhibit 6.4 depicts the BCG matrix. Following are a few clarifications:

1. Each circle represents one of the corporation's business units. The size of the circle represents the relative size of the business unit in terms of revenues.
2. Relative market share, measured by the ratio of the business unit's size to that of its largest competitor, is plotted along the horizontal axis.
3. Market share is central to the BCG matrix. This is because high relative market share leads to unit cost reduction due to experience and learning curve effects and, consequently, superior competitive position.

Each of the four quadrants of the grid has different implications for the SBUs that fall into the category:

- **Stars** are SBUs competing in high-growth industries with relatively high market shares. These firms have long-term growth potential and should continue to receive substantial investment funding.
- **Question marks** are SBUs competing in high-growth industries but having relatively weak market shares. Resources should be invested in them to enhance their competitive positions.
- **Cash cows** are SBUs with high market shares in low-growth industries. These units have limited long-run potential but represent a source of current cash flows to fund investments in "stars" and "question marks."
- **Dogs** are SBUs with weak market shares in low-growth industries. Because they have weak positions and limited potential, most analysts recommend that they be divested.

EXHIBIT 6.4 The Boston Consulting Group (BCG) Portfolio Matrix

In using portfolio strategy approaches, a corporation tries to create shareholder value in a number of ways.[38] First, portfolio analysis provides a snapshot of the businesses in a corporation's portfolio. Therefore, the corporation is in a better position to allocate resources among the business units according to prescribed criteria (e.g., use cash flows from the cash cows to fund promising stars). Second, the expertise and analytical resources in the corporate office provide guidance in determining what firms may be attractive (or unattractive) acquisitions. Third, the corporate office is able to provide financial resources to the business units on favorable terms that reflect the corporation's overall ability to raise funds. Fourth, the corporate office can provide high-quality review and coaching for the individual businesses. Fifth, portfolio analysis provides a basis for developing strategic goals and reward/evaluation systems for business managers. For example, managers of cash cows would have lower targets for revenue growth than managers of stars, but the former would have higher threshold levels of profit targets on proposed projects than the managers of star businesses. Compensation systems would also reflect such realities. Managers of cash cows understandably would be rewarded more on the basis of cash that their businesses generate than would managers of star businesses. Similarly, managers of star businesses would be held to higher standards for revenue growth than managers of cash cow businesses.

Limitations Despite the potential benefits of portfolio models, there are also some notable downsides. First, they compare SBUs on only two dimensions, making the implicit but erroneous assumption that (1) those are the only factors that really matter and (2) every unit can be accurately compared on that basis. Second, the approach views each SBU as a stand-alone entity, ignoring common core business practices and value-creating activities that may hold promise for synergies across business units. Third, unless care is exercised, the process becomes largely mechanical, substituting an oversimplified graphical model for the important contributions of the CEO's (and other corporate managers') experience and judgment. Fourth, the reliance on "strict rules" regarding resource allocation across SBUs can be detrimental to a firm's long-term viability. Finally, while colorful and easy to comprehend, the imagery of the BCG matrix can lead to some troublesome and overly simplistic prescriptions. For example, division managers are likely to want to jump ship as soon as their division is labeled a "dog."

To see what can go wrong, consider Cabot Corporation.

> Cabot Corporation supplies carbon black for the rubber, electronics, and plastics industries. Following the BCG matrix, Cabot moved away from its cash cow, carbon black, and diversified into stars such as ceramics and semiconductors in a seemingly overaggressive effort to create more revenue growth for the corporation. Predictably, Cabot's return on assets declined as the firm shifted away from its core competence to unrelated areas. The portfolio model failed by pointing the company in the wrong direction in an effort to spur growth—away from its core business. Recognizing its mistake, Cabot Corporation returned to its mainstay carbon black manufacturing and divested unrelated businesses. Today the company is a leader in its field with $3.6 billion in revenues in 2014.[39]

Caveat: Is Risk Reduction a Viable Goal of Diversification?

One of the purposes of diversification is to reduce the risk that is inherent in a firm's variability in revenues and profits over time. That is, if a firm enters new products or markets that are affected differently by seasonal or economic cycles, its performance over time will be more stable. For example, a firm manufacturing lawn mowers may diversify into snowblowers to even out its annual sales. Or a firm manufacturing a luxury line of household furniture may introduce a lower-priced line since affluent and lower-income customers are affected differently by economic cycles.

At first glance the above reasoning may make sense, but there are some problems with it. First, a firm's stockholders can diversify their portfolios at a much lower cost than a corporation, and they don't have to worry about integrating the acquisition into their portfolio. Second, economic cycles as well as their impact on a given industry (or firm) are difficult to predict with any degree of accuracy.

Notwithstanding the above, some firms have benefited from diversification by lowering the variability (or risk) in their performance over time. Consider GE, a firm that manufactures a wide range of products, including aircraft engines, power-generation equipment, locomotive trains, large appliances, healthcare equipment, lighting, water treatment equipment, oil well drilling equipment, and many other products. Offering such a wide range of products has allowed GE to generate stable earnings and a low-risk profile. Due to its earning stability, GE is able to borrow money at favorable rates which it then uses to invest in its own operations and to extend its portfolio even further by acquiring other manufacturers.

Risk reduction in and of itself is rarely viable as a means to create shareholder value. It must be undertaken with a view of a firm's overall diversification strategy.

The Means to Achieve Diversification

LO6.5

The various means of engaging in diversification—mergers and acquisitions, joint ventures/strategic alliances, and internal development.

We have addressed the types of diversification (e.g., related and unrelated) that a firm may undertake to achieve synergies and create value for its shareholders. Now, we address the means by which a firm can go about achieving these desired benefits.

There are three basic means. First, through acquisitions or mergers, corporations can directly acquire a firm's assets and competencies. Although the terms *mergers* and *acquisitions* are used quite interchangeably, there are some key differences. With **acquisitions**, one firm buys another through a stock purchase, cash, or the issuance of debt.[40] **Mergers**, on the other hand, entail a combination or consolidation of two firms to form a new legal entity. Mergers are relatively rare and entail a transaction among two firms on a relatively equal basis. Despite such differences, we consider both mergers and acquisitions to be quite similar in terms of their implications for a firm's corporate-level strategy.[41]

acquisitions
the incorporation of one firm into another through purchase.

mergers
the combining of two or more firms into one new legal entity.

Second, corporations may agree to pool the resources of other companies with their resource base, commonly known as a joint venture or strategic alliance. Although these two forms of partnerships are similar in many ways, there is an important difference. Joint ventures involve the formation of a third-party legal entity where by the two (or more) firms each contribute equity, whereas strategic alliances do not.

Third, corporations may diversify into new products, markets, and technologies through internal development. Called corporate entrepreneurship, it involves the leveraging and combining of a firm's own resources and competencies to create synergies and enhance shareholder value. We address this subject in greater length in Chapter 12.

Mergers and Acquisitions

The most visible and often costly means to diversify is through acquisitions. Over the past several years, several large acquisitions were announced. These include:[42]

- InBev's acquisition of Anheuser-Busch for $52 billion.
- Pfizer's acquisition of Wyeth for $68 billion.
- AT&T's acquisition of DirecTV for $67 billion.
- Boston Scientific's $27 billion acquisition of medical device maker Guidant.
- Facebook's acquisition of WhatsApp for $19.4 billion.
- Duke Energy's acquisition of Progress Energy for $25.5 billion.
- Softbank's acquisition of Sprint for $20 billion.

Exhibit 6.5 illustrates the volatility in worldwide M&A activity over the last several years. Several factors influence M&A activity. Julia Coronado, the chief economist at the investment bank BNP Paribas, highlights two of the key determinants, stating, "When mergers and acquisitions pick up, that's a good sign that businesses are feeling confident

EXHIBIT 6.5 Global Value of Mergers and Acquisitions ($ trillions)

Source: Thomson Financial, Institute of Mergers, Acquisitions, and Alliances (IMAA) analysis.

enough about the future that they're willing to become aggressive, look for deals, look for ways to grow and expand their operations. And it's also an indication that markets are willing to finance these transactions. So it's optimism from the markets and from the businesses themselves."[43] Thus, the general economic conditions and level of optimism about the future influence managers' willingness to take on the risk of acquisitions. Additionally, the availability of financing can influence acquisition activity. During boom periods, financing is typically widely available. In contrast, during recessionary periods, potential acquirers typically find it difficult to borrow money to finance acquisitions.

Governmental policies such as regulatory actions and tax policies can also make the M&A environment more or less favorable. For example, increased antitrust enforcement will decrease the ability of firms to acquire their competitors or possibly firms in closely related markets. In contrast, increased regulatory pressures for good corporate governance may leave boards of directors more open to acquisition offers.

Finally, currency fluctuations can influence the rate of cross-border acquisitions, with firms in countries with stronger currencies being in a stronger position to acquire. For example, the U.S. dollar has increased in value from just over 75 to nearly 120 Japanese Yen from 2012 to the mid-2015, making it relatively cheaper for U.S. firms to acquire Japanese firms.

Motives and Benefits Growth through mergers and acquisitions has played a critical role in the success of many corporations in a wide variety of high-technology and knowledge-intensive industries. Here, market and technology changes can occur very quickly and unpredictably.[44] Speed—speed to market, speed to positioning, and speed to becoming a viable company—is critical in such industries. For example, in 2010, Apple acquired Siri Inc. so that it could quickly fully integrate Siri's natural-language voice recognition software into iOS, Apple's operating system.

Mergers and acquisitions also can be a means of *obtaining valuable resources that can help an organization expand its product offerings and services.* As noted earlier in the chapter, Cisco Systems, a computer networking firm, has undertaken over 80 acquisitions in the last decade. Cisco uses these acquisitions to quickly add new technology to its product offerings to meet changing customer needs. Then it uses its excellent sales force to market the new technology to its corporate customers. Cisco also provides strong incentives to the staff of acquired companies to stay on. To realize the greatest value from its acquisitions, Cisco also has learned to integrate acquired companies efficiently and effectively.[45]

Acquiring firms often use acquisitions to acquire critical human capital. These acquisitions have been referred to as acq-hires. In an acq-hire, the acquiring firm believes it needs the specific technical knowledge or the social network contacts of individuals in the target firm. This is especially important in settings where the technology or consumer preferences are highly dynamic. For example, in 2014, Apple purchased Beats Electronics for $3 billion. While Apple valued the product portfolio of Beats, its primary aim was to pull the founders of Beats, Jimmy Iovine and Dr. Dre (aka Andrew Young), into the Apple family. With Apple's iTunes business having hit a wall in growth, experiencing a 1 percent decline in 2013, Apple wanted to acquire new management talent to turn this business around. In addition to their experience at Beats, Iovine and Dr. Dre both have over 20 years of experience in the music industry, with Iovine founding and heading InterScope Records and Dr. Dre being a hip-hop pioneer and music producer. With this acquisition, Apple believes it brought in a wealth of knowledge about the music business, the ability to identify music trends, up-and-coming talent, and industry contacts needed to rejuvenate Apple's music business.[46]

Mergers and acquisitions also can *provide the opportunity for firms to attain the three bases of synergy—leveraging core competencies, sharing activities, and building market power.* Consider some of eBay's acquisitions. eBay has purchased a range of businesses in related product markets, such as GSI Commerce, a company that designs and runs online shopping sites for brick-and-mortar retailers, and StubHub, an online ticket broker. Additionally, it has purchased Korean online auction company Gmarket to expand its geographic scope. Finally, it has purchased firms providing related services, such as Shutl, a rapid-order-fulfillment service provider.

These acquisitions offer the opportunity to leverage eBay's competencies.[47] For example, with the acquisition of GSI, eBay saw opportunities to leverage its core competencies in online systems as well as its reputation to strengthen GSI while also expanding eBay's ability to work with medium to large merchants and brands. eBay can also benefit from these acquisitions by sharing activities. In acquiring firms in related product markets and in new geographic markets, eBay has built a set of businesses that can share in the development of e-commerce and mobile commerce systems. Finally, by expanding into new geographic markets and offering a wider range of services, eBay can build market power as one of the few online retailer systems that provide a full set of services on a global platform.

Merger and acquisition activity also can *lead to consolidation within an industry and can force other players to merge.*[48] The airline industry has seen a great deal of consolidation in the last several years. With a number of large-scale acquisitions, including Delta's acquisition of Northwest Airlines in 2008, United's acquisition of Continental in 2010, and American's purchase of US Airways in 2013, the U.S. airlines industry has been left with only four major players. In combining, these airlines are both seeking greater efficiencies by combining their networks and hoping that consolidation will dampen the rivalry in the industry.[49]

Corporations can also *enter new market segments by way of acquisitions.* As mentioned above, eBay, a firm that specialized in providing services to individuals and small businesses, moved into providing online retail systems for large merchants with its acquisition of GSI Commerce. Similarly, one of the reasons Fiat acquired Chrysler was to gain access to the U.S. auto market. Exhibit 6.6 summarizes the benefits of mergers and acquisitions.

EXHIBIT 6.6
Benefits of Mergers and Acquisitions

- Obtain valuable resources, such as critical human capital, that can help an organization expand its product offerings.
- Provide the opportunity for firms to attain three bases of synergy: leveraging core competencies, sharing activities, and building market power.
- Lead to consolidation within an industry and force other players to merge.
- Enter new market segments.

Potential Limitations As noted in the previous section, mergers and acquisitions provide a firm with many potential benefits. However, at the same time, there are many potential drawbacks or limitations to such corporate activity.[50]

First, *the takeover premium that is paid for an acquisition typically is very high.* Two times out of three, the stock price of the acquiring company falls once the deal is made public. Since the acquiring firm often pays a 30 percent or higher premium for the target company, the acquirer must create synergies and scale economies that result in sales and market gains exceeding the premium price. Firms paying higher premiums set the performance hurdle even higher. For example, Household International paid an 82 percent premium to buy Beneficial, and Conseco paid an 83 percent premium to acquire Green Tree Financial. Historically, paying a high premium over the stock price has been a poor strategy.

Second, *competing firms often can imitate any advantages realized or copy synergies that result from the M&A.*[51] Thus, a firm can often see its advantages quickly erode. Unless the advantages are sustainable and difficult to copy, investors will not be willing to pay a high premium for the stock. Similarly, the time value of money must be factored into the stock price. M&A costs are paid up front. Conversely, firms pay for R&D, ongoing marketing, and capacity expansion over time. This stretches out the payments needed to gain new competencies. The M&A argument is that a large initial investment is worthwhile because it creates long-term advantages. However, stock analysts want to see immediate results from such a large cash outlay. If the acquired firm does not produce results quickly, investors often divest the stock, driving the price down.

Third, *managers' credibility and ego can sometimes get in the way of sound business decisions.* If the M&A does not perform as planned, managers who pushed for the deal find their reputation tarnished. This can lead them to protect their credibility by funneling more money, or escalating their commitment, into an inevitably doomed operation. Further, when a merger fails and a firm tries to unload the acquisition, the firm often must sell at a huge discount. These problems further compound the costs and erode the stock price.

Fourth, *there can be many cultural issues that may doom the intended benefits from M&A endeavors.* Consider the insights of Joanne Lawrence, who played an important role in the merger between SmithKline and the Beecham Group.[52]

> The key to a strategic merger is to create a new culture. This was a mammoth challenge during the SmithKline Beecham merger. We were working at so many different cultural levels, it was dizzying. We had two national cultures to blend—American and British—that compounded the challenge of selling the merger in two different markets with two different shareholder bases. There were also two different business cultures: One was very strong, scientific, and academic; the other was much more commercially oriented. And then we had to consider within both companies the individual businesses, each of which has its own little culture.

Exhibit 6.7 summarizes the limitations of mergers and acquisitions.

Strategy Spotlight 6.3 discusses the characteristics of acquisitions that lead investors to see greater value in the combinations. In Insights from Executives, Archie Jones, a senior executive at IBM, offers further insight on the factors that impact the likelihood of the success of an acquisition.

EXHIBIT 6.7
Limitations of Mergers and Acquisitions

- Takeover premiums paid for acquisitions are typically very high.
- Competing firms often can imitate any advantages or copy synergies that result from the merger or acquisition.
- Managers' egos sometimes get in the way of sound business decisions.
- Cultural issues may doom the intended benefits from M&A endeavors.

6.3 STRATEGY SPOTLIGHT

THE WISDOM OF CROWDS: WHEN DO INVESTORS SEE VALUE IN ACQUISITIONS?

By some estimates, 70 to 90 percent of acquisitions destroy shareholder value. But investors do see value in some acquisitions. The question is, When does the wisdom of the investment crowd indicate there is value with acquisitions? Recent research suggests it rests in both the characteristics of the deal and the motivation of the acquiring firm.

The Characteristics of the Deal

Research has identified several deal characteristics that lead to positive investor reactions. Not surprisingly, investors see greater value in acquisitions when the acquiring and the acquired (target) firm are in the same or closely related industries. This is consistent with there being greater potential for synergies when the firms are in similar markets. Second, investors see greater value potential when acquiring managers are seen as responding quickly to new opportunities, such as those provided by the emergence of new technologies or market deregulation. Third, investors have a more positive reaction when the acquiring firm used cash to buy the target, as opposed to giving the target shareholders stock in the combined firm. Acquiring firms often use stock to finance acquisitions when they think their own stock is overvalued. Thus, the use of cash signals that the acquiring firm's managers have confidence in the value of the deal. Fourth, the less the acquiring firm relies on outside advisers, such as investment banks, the more investors see value in the deal. As with the use of cash, managers who rely primarily on their own knowledge and abilities to manage deals are seen as more confident. Finally, when the target firm tries to avoid the acquisition, investors see less value potential. Defense actions by targets are seen as signals that the target firm will not be open to easy integration with the acquiring firm. Thus, it may be difficult to leverage synergies.

The Motivation of the Acquirer

How much value investors see in the deal is also affected by the motivation of the acquirer. Interestingly, if the acquiring firm is highly profitable, investors see less value in the acquisition. The concern here is that strong performance likely leads managers to become overconfident and more likely to undertake "empire building" acquisitions as opposed to acquisitions that generate shareholder value. Second, if the acquiring firm is highly leveraged, having a high debt-equity ratio, investors see more value in the acquisition. Since the acquiring firm is at a higher risk of bankruptcy, managers of highly leveraged firms are likely to undertake acquisitions only if they are low risk and likely to generate synergistic benefits.

In total, the stock investors look to logical clues about the potential value of the deal and the motives of the acquiring firm managers to assess the value they see. Thus, there appears to be simple but logical wisdom in the crowd.

Sources: McNamara, G., Haleblian, J., & Dykes, B. 2008. Performance implications of participating in an acquisition wave: Early mover advantages, bandwagon effects, and the moderating influence of industry characteristics and acquirer tactics. *Academy of Management Journal*, 51: 113–130; and Schijven, M. & Hitt, M. 2012. The vicarious wisdom of crowds: Toward a behavioral perspective on investor reactions to acquisition announcements. *Strategic Management Journal*, 33: 1247–1268.

6.1 INSIGHTS FROM EXECUTIVES

ARCHIE L. JONES, VICE PRESIDENT OF BUSINESS DEVELOPMENT AT KENEXA, A SUBSIDIARY OF IBM

BIOSKETCH

Archie L. Jones is the vice president of business development at Kenexa, a subsidiary of IBM that provides workforce management and recruitment service solutions to a wide range of corporations. Kenexa has grown from a start-up firm in 1987 to a company with over 2,600 employees providing services to clients in over 20 countries. Jones began his career in private equity in 1993 after graduating from Morehouse College. After completing his MBA at Harvard Business School, Jones invested in Kenexa and served on its board of directors. He brought his expertise in strategic planning and M&A management inside Kenexa in 2005 and has helped guide Kenexa to expand into new product and geographic markets through organic growth, strategic alliances, and acquisitions.

1. *The value of acquisitions is often easy to see in capital-intensive industries, where acquisitions allow for the development of market power and economies of scale and scope. The value can be more difficult to see in service industries, such as in talent management consulting. How has Kenexa used acquisitions to build and extend its competencies, and how has this helped you better serve your customers?*

   As our strategy calls for us to have a comprehensive suite of solutions, we use acquisitions to broaden and strengthen our suite of offerings. Most of our customers are looking to buy from fewer suppliers to simplify their supply chain. By offering our clients the broadest suite of solutions in our market, we are able to better serve our clients and differentiate from the competition.

   We also use M&A to expand Kenexa's global footprint. We have purchased seven companies outside the

   continued

continued

U.S., including in Canada, Europe, and Asia Pacific, and formed a joint venture in China. By acquiring local market knowledge and delivery capabilities in key international markets, we are able to serve the world's largest employers in their home market and abroad, creating another level of differentiation.

The most valuable asset in most of our acquisitions is the human capital that is acquired. A growing talent pool is our greatest source of growth, innovation, and thought leadership. The core of the Kenexa Leadership Institute, a recognized center for human capital research, was acquired as part of an M&A transaction.

2. *Differences in the cultures of acquiring and target firms can make integrating firms challenging. What have you found to be the most critical steps to take to ensure that these cultural differences don't derail acquisitions and destroy their value-creating potential?*

Understanding the human capital of the firm we are considering acquiring is key to our success. Therefore, assessing talent and its fit is integral in our due diligence. If you plan to retain and engage key employees, you have to meet them early in the acquisition process. At Kenexa, we routinely use leadership assessments of the key managers of the target company to better understand their strengths and motivations. In our experience, CEOs have a low survival rate postclosing. Quite simply, most CEO/founders find it difficult to have a boss again. Thus, we don't make acquisitions that are heavily dependent on the target CEO/founder. We have found it critical to get to know the senior team beyond the C-suite. Also, we openly share our company's values and culture up front and are prepared for some of the target company employees to self-select out. We have found that the sooner we figure out who will stay and assimilate well, the better the acquisition will go.

3. *What do you see as the most important drivers of acquisition success, and what are the steps you take to make sure you maximize the opportunities for success with an acquisition?*

The acquisition has to be tightly aligned with the firm's overall strategy. Your board or investment committee should be "presold" on the type of businesses you are targeting because it is explicitly called for in your strategy. The M&A team must work closely with the business unit leaders to understand their strategic needs and how M&A can play a role. This also allows you to identify and engage targets directly and proactively.

You have to get the price right. Establish minimum guidelines regarding how quickly an acquisition has to contribute to the growth in the firm's sales and earnings as well as the length of the payback period. Don't pay the seller for your synergies. Develop a downside case, a realistic/likely case, and an upside case. You should still be able to hit your minimum guidelines in the downside case.

Conduct a full due diligence to avoid later surprises. Start with a well-developed and comprehensive investment logic. Clearly outline the rationale for and expected benefits of the purchase and then test that rationale in due diligence. This is where you have to be brutally honest with yourself. Did the majority of the reasons for the acquisition survive diligence? If not, adjust the price or exit the process.

Undertake early integration planning. Integration starts during due diligence. Business unit managers and key functional leaders should develop the financial and strategic postclose plan and understand that these postclose numbers will be a part of their future targets and compensation plans.

Divestment: The Other Side of the "M&A Coin" When firms acquire other businesses, it typically generates quite a bit of "press" in business publications such as *The Wall Street Journal, Bloomberg Businessweek,* and *Fortune.* It makes for exciting news, and one thing is for sure—large acquiring firms automatically improve their standing in the Fortune 500 rankings (since it is based solely on total revenues). However, managers must also carefully consider the strategic implications of exiting businesses.

divestment
the exit of a business from a firm's portfolio.

Divestments, the exit of a business from a firm's portfolio, are quite common. One study found that large, prestigious U.S. companies divested more acquisitions than they kept.[53]

Divesting a business can accomplish many different objectives.* It can be used to help a firm reverse an earlier acquisition that didn't work out as planned. Often, this is simply to

---

*Firms can divest their businesses in a number of ways. Sell-offs, spin-offs, equity carve-outs, asset sales/dissolution, and split-ups are some such modes of divestment. In a sell-off, the divesting firm privately negotiates with a third party to divest a unit/subsidiary for cash/stock. In a spin-off, a parent company distributes shares of the unit/subsidiary being divested pro rata to its existing shareholders and a new company is formed. Equity carve-outs are similar to spin-offs except that shares in the unit/subsidiary being divested are offered to new shareholders. Dissolution involves sale of redundant assets, not necessarily as an entire unit/subsidiary as in sell-offs but a few bits at a time. A split-up, on the other hand, is an instance of divestiture where by the parent company is split into two or more new companies and the parent ceases to exist. Shares in the parent company are exchanged for shares in new companies, and the exact distribution varies case by case.

6.4 STRATEGY SPOTLIGHT

SLIMMING DOWN BRISTOL-MYERS SQUIBB

From 2011 to 2014, Bristol-Myers Squibb saw its sales decline from $21 billion to $16 billion. For most firms, a 22 percent decline in sales would be seen as a disaster and a call for action. For Bristol-Myers Squibb, a global pharmaceutical firm, this was the successful implementation of its corporate strategy.

Rather than striving to be a pharmaceutical firm that provides solutions for a wide range of medical conditions and diseases, Bristol-Myers Squibb divested a number of its businesses, including selling its diabetes division, which provided over 10 percent of the corporation's sales, to a rival firm, AstraZeneca, as it focused on a few treatment areas where it could truly excel. The slimming of Bristol allowed it to reduce its costs by $2.5 billion, lower its workforce size by one-third, and close over half of its manufacturing operations. The sale of some of the firm's assets also generated resources that it used to invest in its remaining areas of business focus. For example, while the firm shrunk in size, its investment in R&D increased from 2011 to 2014. Also, while closing numerous plants, Bristol-Myers Squibb simultaneously committed to invest $900 million in a new biologics plant in Ireland to provide a more global manufacturing footprint in this growing medical treatment segment.

Bristol-Myers Squibb decided to focus on pharmaceutical segments that met three conditions. First, it invested in segments where it would face a limited number of competitors. Second, it focused on areas where it could find partners to share the development costs. Third, the firm emphasized product segments where it had expertise. The firm has settled on immune system treatments for chronic diseases (such as Crohn's disease and arthritis), virology (including treatments for HIV and hepatitis), and oncology (cancer treatments). Bristol-Myers Squibb's former chairman, Jim Cornelius, referred to the remaining businesses as the firm's "string of pearls." Recently, the firm has leveraged its expertise in immunology and oncology to develop potentially revolutionary immune system–based treatments for cancer.

One industry analyst, Jami Rubin, commented that the transformation at Bristol has been "really quite startling. It's a completely different company today than it was back in 2007. They've gone from a big, diversified drug company to a highly focused biopharma firm." The stock market appears to like the change. The firm's stock price doubled from early 2012 to the end of 2014.

Sources: Fry, E. 2014. Big pharma's small wonder. *Fortune*, June 16: 178-186; Calia, M. 2014. Bristol-Myers Squibb to build biologics plant in Ireland. *wsj.com*, November 14: np; and *finance.yahoo.com*.

---

help "cut their losses." Other objectives include (1) enabling managers to focus their efforts more directly on the firm's core businesses,[54] (2) providing the firm with more resources to spend on more attractive alternatives, and (3) raising cash to help fund existing businesses. Strategy Spotlight 6.4 discusses how Bristol-Myers Squibb has experienced these benefits of divestment.

Divesting can enhance a firm's competitive position only to the extent that it reduces its tangible (e.g., maintenance, investments, etc.) or intangible (e.g., opportunity costs, managerial attention) costs without sacrificing a current competitive advantage or the seeds of future advantages.[55] To be effective, divesting requires a thorough understanding of a business unit's current ability and future potential to contribute to a firm's value creation. However, since such decisions involve a great deal of uncertainty, it is very difficult to make such evaluations. In addition, because of managerial self-interests and organizational inertia, firms often delay divestments of underperforming businesses.

The Boston Consulting Group has identified seven principles for successful divestiture.[56]

1. ***Remove the emotion from the decision.*** Managers need to consider objectively the prospects for each unit in the firm and how this unit fits with the firm's overall strategy. Issues related to personal relationships with the managers of the unit, the length of time the unit has been part of the company, and other emotional elements should not be considered in the decision.[57]
2. ***Know the value of the business you are selling.*** Divesting firms can generate greater interest in and higher bids for units they are divesting if they can clearly articulate the strategic value of the unit.
3. ***Time the deal right.*** This involves both internal timing, where by the firm regularly evaluates all its units so that it can divest units when they are no longer highly valued in the firm but will still be of value to the outside market, and external timing, being ready to sell when the market conditions are right.

4. ***Maintain a sizable pool of potential buyers.*** Divesting firms should not focus on a single potential buyer. Instead, they should discuss possible deals with several hand-picked potential bidders.
5. ***Tell a story about the deal.*** For each potential bidder it talks with, the divesting firm should develop a narrative about how the unit it is interested in selling will create value for that buyer.
6. ***Run divestitures systematically through a project office.*** Firms should look at developing the ability to divest units as a distinct form of corporate competencies. While many firms have acquisition units, they often don't have divesting units even though there is significant potential value in divestitures.
7. ***Communicate clearly and frequently.*** Corporate managers need to clearly communicate to internal stakeholders, such as employees, and external stakeholders, such as customers and stockholders, what their goals are with divestment activity, how it will create value, and how the firm is moving forward strategically with these decisions.

Strategic Alliances and Joint Ventures

> **strategic alliance**
> a cooperative relationship between two or more firms.

> **joint ventures**
> new entities formed within a strategic alliance in which two or more firms, the parents, contribute equity to form the new legal entity.

A **strategic alliance** is a cooperative relationship between two (or more) firms.[58] Alliances may be either informal or formal—that is, involving a written contract. **Joint ventures** represent a special case of alliances, wherein two (or more) firms contribute equity to form a new legal entity.

Strategic alliances and joint ventures are assuming an increasingly prominent role in the strategy of leading firms, both large and small.[59] Such cooperative relationships have many potential advantages.[60] Among these are entering new markets, reducing manufacturing (or other) costs in the value chain, and developing and diffusing new technologies.[61]

Entering New Markets Often a company that has a successful product or service wants to introduce it into a new market. However, it may not have the financial resources or the requisite marketing expertise because it does not understand customer needs, know how to promote the product, or have access to the proper distribution channels.[62]

Zara, a Spanish clothing company, operates stores in over 70 countries. Still, when entering markets very distant from its home markets, Zara often uses local alliance partners to help it negotiate the different cultural and regulatory environments. For example, when Zara expanded into India in 2010, it did it in cooperation with Tata, an Indian conglomerate.[63]

Strategy Spotlight 6.5 discusses how a strategic alliance between Lionsgate and Alibaba provides Lionsgate with a strong partner to expand its business in China.

Reducing Manufacturing (or Other) Costs in the Value Chain Strategic alliances (or joint ventures) often enable firms to pool capital, value-creating activities, or facilities in order to reduce costs. For example, SABMiller and Molson Coors, the number-two and number-three brewers in the United States, created a joint venture to combine their U.S. brewing operations in 2007. In combining brewery and distribution operations, they would benefit from economies of scale and better utilization of their facilities. The two firms projected $500 million in annual cost savings as a result of the integration of their operations.[64]

Developing and Diffusing New Technologies Strategic alliances also may be used to build jointly on the technological expertise of two or more companies. This may enable them to develop products technologically beyond the capability of the companies acting independently.[65] IBM's alliances with Memorial Sloan Kettering, the Cleveland Clinic, and Cedars-Sinai, which were discussed in Strategic Spotlight 6.1, provide IBM with expert medical knowledge necessary for the computing giant to be able to leverage its technological skills in order to develop new medical insights.

6.5 STRATEGY SPOTLIGHT

LIONSGATE'S ALLIANCE WITH ALIBABA OFFERS ACCESS TO THE CHINESE MARKET

Lionsgate has been one of the most successful Hollywood studios over the last several years, with movie and TV hits such as the *Twilight* films, *The Hunger Games,* and *Mad Men.* Still, it faced challenges expanding its footprint on a global scale. To gain better access in the world's largest market, Lionsgate has allied with Alibaba, the Chinese Internet giant. Through this alliance, Alibaba gains exclusive rights in the Chinese market to stream Lionsgate's shows and movies through Alibaba's set-top boxes. Viewers will get to see not only Lionsgate's television shows and movies but also behind-the-scenes footage, as well as related merchandise and invitations to private screenings. This alliance allows Lionsgate to overcome a number of challenges in entering the Chinese market. By using Internet streaming of movies, it overcomes China's quota system for theatrical release. It also lessens the likelihood of having a movie blocked by Chinese censors, as occurred with both *Django Unchained* and *Noah*. Finally, having a strong local partner also lessens concerns about intellectual property rights protection in China.

The alliance also brings benefits to Alibaba. The Internet retailing firm is expanding into media content in order to increase demand for and traffic on its set-top boxes. In addition to the alliance with Lionsgate, Alibaba has acquired a controlling stake in ChinaVision Media Group, has developed an online gaming business, and has ties with Wasu, an online video business. The Lionsgate alliance fits into its efforts to expand beyond retailing into a range of digital content.

Sources: McNary, D. 2014. Lionsgate, Alibaba teaming on streaming service for China. *variety.com*, July 14: np; Miller, D., Faughnder, R., & Chang, A. 2014. Alibaba could give Hollywood studios new pipeline into China. *latimes.com*, October 24: np; and Chen, L. & Palazzo, A. 2014. Alibaba joins Lionsgate for video service in China. *bloomberg.com*, July 15: np.

Potential Downsides Despite their promise, many alliances and joint ventures fail to meet expectations for a variety of reasons.[66] First, without the proper partner, a firm should never consider undertaking an alliance, even for the best of reasons.[67] Each partner should bring the desired complementary strengths to the partnership. Ideally, the strengths contributed by the partners are unique; thus synergies created can be more easily sustained and defended over the longer term. The goal must be to develop synergies between the contributions of the partners, resulting in a win–win situation. Moreover, the partners must be compatible and willing to trust each other.[68] Unfortunately, often little attention is given to nurturing the close working relationships and interpersonal connections that bring together the partnering organizations.[69]

Internal Development

Firms can also diversify by means of corporate entrepreneurship and new venture development. **In today's economy, internal development is such an important means by which companies expand their businesses that we have devoted a whole chapter to it (see Chapter 12).** Sony and the Minnesota Mining & Manufacturing Co. (3M), for example, are known for their dedication to innovation, R&D, and cutting-edge technologies. For example, 3M has developed its entire corporate culture to support its ongoing policy of generating at least 25 percent of total sales from products created within the most recent four-year period. While 3M exceeded this goal for decades, a push for improved efficiency that began in the early 2000s resulted in a drop to generating only 21 percent of sales from newer products in 2005. By refocusing on innovation, 3M raised that value back up to 30 percent in 2011.

Biocon, the largest Indian biotechnology firm, shows the power of internal development. Kiran Mazumdar-Shaw, the firm's founder, took the knowledge she learned while studying malting and brewing in college to start a small firm that produced enzymes for the beer industry in her Bangalore garage in 1978. The firm first expanded into providing enzymes for other food and textile industries. From there, Biocon expanded on to producing generic drugs and is now the largest producer of insulin in Asia.[70]

Compared to mergers and acquisitions, firms that engage in internal development capture the value created by their own innovative activities without having to "share the wealth" with alliance partners or face the difficulties associated with combining activities across the value chains of several firms or merging corporate cultures.[71] Also, firms can

> **internal development** entering a new business through investment in new facilities, often called corporate enterpreneurship and new venture development.

often develop new products or services at a relatively lower cost and thus rely on their own resources rather than turning to external funding.⁷²

There are also potential disadvantages. It may be time-consuming; thus, firms may forfeit the benefits of speed that growth through mergers or acquisitions can provide. This may be especially important among high-tech or knowledge-based organizations in fast-paced environments where being an early mover is critical. Thus, firms that choose to diversify through internal development must develop capabilities that allow them to move quickly from initial opportunity recognition to market introduction.

How Managerial Motives Can Erode Value Creation

LO6.6
Managerial behaviors that can erode the creation of value.

Thus far in the chapter, we have implicitly assumed that CEOs and top executives are "rational beings"; that is, they act in the best interests of shareholders to maximize long-term shareholder value. In the real world, however, they may often act in their own self-interest. We now address some **managerial motives** that can serve to erode, rather than enhance, value creation. These include "growth for growth's sake," excessive egotism, and the creation of a wide variety of antitakeover tactics.

managerial motives
managers acting in their own self-interest rather than to maximize long-term shareholder value.

Growth for Growth's Sake

growth for growth's sake
managers' actions to grow the size of their firms not to increase long-term profitability but to serve managerial self-interest.

There are huge incentives for executives to increase the size of their firm. And these are not consistent with increasing shareholder wealth. Top managers, including the CEO, of larger firms typically enjoy more prestige, higher rankings for their firms on the Fortune 500 list (based on revenues, *not* profits), greater incomes, more job security, and so on. There is also the excitement and associated recognition of making a major acquisition. As noted by Harvard's Michael Porter, "There's a tremendous allure to mergers and acquisitions. It's the big play, the dramatic gesture. With one stroke of the pen you can add billions to size, get a front-page story, and create excitement in markets."⁷³

In recent years many high-tech firms have suffered from the negative impact of their uncontrolled growth. Consider, for example, Priceline.com's ill-fated venture into an online service to offer groceries and gasoline.⁷⁴ A myriad of problems—perhaps most importantly, a lack of participation by manufacturers—caused the firm to lose more than $5 million a *week* prior to abandoning these ventures. Such initiatives are often little more than desperate moves by top managers to satisfy investor demands for accelerating revenues. Unfortunately, the increased revenues often fail to materialize into a corresponding hike in earnings.

At times, executives' overemphasis on growth can result in a plethora of ethical lapses, which can have disastrous outcomes for their companies. A good example (of bad practice) is Joseph Berardino's leadership at Andersen Worldwide. Berardino had a chance early on to take a hard line on ethics and quality in the wake of earlier scandals at clients such as Waste Management and Sunbeam. Instead, according to former executives, he put too much emphasis on revenue growth. Consequently, the firm's reputation quickly eroded when it audited and signed off on the highly flawed financial statements of such infamous firms as Enron, Global Crossing, and WorldCom. Berardino ultimately resigned in disgrace in March 2002, and his firm was dissolved later that year.⁷⁵

Egotism

egotism
managers' actions to shape their firms' strategies to serve their selfish interests rather than to maximize long-term shareholder value.

A healthy ego helps make a leader confident, clearheaded, and able to cope with change. CEOs, by their very nature, are intensely competitive people in the office as well as on the tennis court or golf course. But sometimes when pride is at stake, individuals will go to great lengths to win.

Egos can get in the way of a "synergistic" corporate marriage. Few executives (or lower-level managers) are exempt from the potential downside of excessive egos. Consider, for example, the reflections of General Electric's former CEO Jack Welch, considered by many to be the world's most admired executive. He admitted to a regrettable decision: "My hubris got in the way in the Kidder Peabody deal. [He was referring to GE's buyout of the soon-to-be-troubled Wall Street firm.] I got wise advice from Walter Wriston and other directors who said, 'Jack, don't do this.' But I was bully enough and on a run to do it. And I got whacked right in the head."[76] In addition to poor financial results, Kidder Peabody was wracked by a widely publicized trading scandal that tarnished the reputations of both GE and Kidder Peabody. Welch ended up selling Kidder.

The business press has included many stories of how egotism and greed have infiltrated organizations.[77] Some incidents are considered rather astonishing, such as Tyco's former (and now convicted) CEO Dennis Kozlowski's purchase of a $6,000 shower curtain and vodka-spewing, full-size replica of Michelangelo's *David*.[78] Other well-known examples of power grabs and extraordinary consumption of compensation and perks include executives at Enron, the Rigas family who were convicted of defrauding Adelphia of roughly $1 billion, former CEO Bernie Ebbers's $408 million loan from WorldCom, and so on.

A more recent example of excess and greed was exhibited by John Thain.[79] On January 22, 2009, he was ousted as head of Merrill Lynch by Bank of America's CEO, Ken Lewis:

> Thain embarrassingly doled out $4 billion in discretionary year-end bonuses to favored employees just before Bank of America's rescue purchase of failing Merrill. The bonuses amounted to about 10 percent of Merrill's 2008 losses.
>
> Obviously, John Thain believed that he was entitled. When he took over ailing Merrill in early 2008, he began planning major cuts, but he also ordered that his office be redecorated. He spent $1.22 million of company funds to make it "livable," which, in part, included $87,000 for a rug, $87,000 for a pair of guest chairs, $68,000 for a 19th-century credenza, and (what really got the attention of the press) $35,000 for a "commode with legs."
>
> He later agreed to repay the decorating costs. However, one might still ask: What kind of person treats other people's money like this? And who needs a commode that costs as much as a new Lexus? Finally, a comment by Bob O'Brien, stock editor at Barrons.com, clearly applies: "The sense of entitlement that's been engendered in this group of people has clearly not been beaten out of them by the brutal performance of the financial sector over the course of the last year."

Antitakeover Tactics

Unfriendly or hostile takeovers can occur when a company's stock becomes undervalued. A competing organization can buy the outstanding stock of a takeover candidate in sufficient quantity to become a large shareholder. Then it makes a tender offer to gain full control of the company. If the shareholders accept the offer, the hostile firm buys the target company and either fires the target firm's management team or strips the team members of their power. Thus, **antitakeover tactics** are common, including greenmail, golden parachutes, and poison pills.[80]

The first, **greenmail,** is an effort by the target firm to prevent an impending takeover. When a hostile firm buys a large block of outstanding target company stock and the target firm's management feels that a tender offer is impending, it offers to buy the stock back from the hostile company at a higher price than the unfriendly company paid for it. Although this often prevents a hostile takeover, the same price is not offered to preexisting shareholders. However, it protects the jobs of the target firm's management.

Second, a **golden parachute** is a prearranged contract with managers specifying that, in the event of a hostile takeover, the target firm's managers will be paid a significant severance package. Although top managers lose their jobs, the golden parachute provisions protect their income.

Third, **poison pills** are used by a company to give shareholders certain rights in the event of a takeover by another firm. They are also known as shareholder rights plans.

Clearly, antitakeover tactics can often raise some interesting ethical—and legal—issues. Strategy Spotlight 6.6 addresses how antitakeover measures can benefit multiple stakeholders—not just management.

antitakeover tactics
managers' actions to avoid losing wealth or power as a result of a hostile takeover.

greenmail
a payment by a firm to a hostile party for the firm's stock at a premium, made when the firm's management feels that the hostile party is about to make a tender offer.

golden parachute
a prearranged contract with managers specifying that, in the event of a hostile takeover, the target firm's managers will be paid a significant severance package.

poison pill
used by a company to give shareholders certain rights in the event of takeover by another firm.

6.6 STRATEGY SPOTLIGHT

HOW ANTITAKEOVER MEASURES MAY BENEFIT MULTIPLE STAKEHOLDERS, NOT JUST MANAGEMENT

Antitakeover defenses represent a gray area, because management can often legitimately argue that such actions are not there solely to benefit themselves. Rather, they can benefit other stakeholders, such as employees, customers, and the community.

In the late 1980s, takeovers were very popular. The Dayton Hudson Corporation (now Target) even appealed to the Minnesota legislature to pass an antitakeover bill to help Dayton Hudson in its struggle with Hafts—the former owners of Dart, a drugstore chain on the east coast. History had shown that the Dayton Hudson management in place at the time was much better able to manage Dayton Hudson in the long run. In addition to Minnesota, many states now have laws that allow firms to take the interests of all stakeholders into account when considering a takeover bid.

In the summer of 2003, Oracle launched a hostile bid for PeopleSoft. Many analysts charged that the tactics of Oracle CEO Larry Ellison had been unfair, and many of PeopleSoft's customers took its side, indicating that Oracle ownership would not be of benefit to them. PeopleSoft was concerned that Oracle was merely seeking to buy PeopleSoft for its lucrative base of application software and was not interested in supporting the company's products. Oracle, on the other hand, sued PeopleSoft in an attempt to have the latter's so-called poison pill takeover defense removed.

In December 2004, Oracle struck a deal to buy PeopleSoft—ending a bitter 18-month hostile takeover battle. Oracle's $10.3 billion acquisition valued the firm at $26.50 a share—an increase of 66 percent over its initial offer of $16 a share. Noted analyst John DiFucci: "This is a financial acquisition primarily. Oracle is buying PeopleSoft for its maintenance stream." And, worth noting, PeopleSoft executives, including CEO and company founder David Duffield, did not join Oracle during the conference call announcing the acquisition. Oracle dropped its suit against PeopleSoft in which the former charged that PeopleSoft's "poison pill" takeover defense should be dismissed.

On moral grounds, some antitakeover defenses are not undertaken to entrench and protect management, but often they are. When such defenses are used simply to keep management in power, they are wrong. However, when they are used to defend the long-term financial health of the company and to protect broader stakeholder interests, they will be morally permissible.

Sources: Bowie, N. E. & Werhane, P. H. 2005. *Management ethics*. Malden, MA: Blackwell; and La Monica, P. R. 2004. Finally, Oracle to buy PeopleSoft. *CNNMoney.com*, December 13: np.

ISSUE FOR DEBATE

Starbucks Moves Far Outside the Coffeehouse

When you say Starbucks, most people instantly think of coffee, specifically coffee prepared by a barista just the way you want it—once you get the Starbucks lingo down. Starbucks is available in over 20,000 coffeehouses in more than 60 countries. Starbucks has experienced amazing growth over the last 30 years as it moved from a small chain of coffeehouses in Seattle to the global powerhouse that it is now. However, the firm faces more limited prospects for growth in its coffee business from this point forward. The coffee market is fairly mature, and Starbucks sees a limited number of new markets in which to expand.

In recent years, Starbucks has diversified into a number of new products and distribution channels to stoke up its growth potential. This has included diversifying into new products to sell through its cafes. Starbucks purchased La Boulange Bakery and now produces baked goods to sell in its cafes. Similarly, it purchased Teavana and is adding tea bars to its cafes. It also purchased Evolution Fresh juice company and now supplies the juices it sells in Starbucks coffeehouses. It is also test marketing additional new products in its cafes—beer and wine in Starbucks Evening concept stores and carbonated beverages in several markets. Starbucks is also making a major push in the grocery aisle. The firm has developed a "signature aisle" which features wood shelving that reflects the appearance of a Starbucks Café. The aisle's desirable end cap (the high-traffic shelf area at the end of an aisle) attracts shoppers' attention to products such as Starbucks' bagged coffee, its single-serve K-cups, and its Via brand instant coffee. But selling coffee in grocery stores is just the first step. Starbucks aims to also distribute its La Boulange bakery products, Teavana teas, and Evolution Fresh juices in grocery stores. It has even been looking further afield as it developed Evolution Harvest snack bars for the grocery aisle and also crafted an alliance with Danone to produce and sell Evolution Fresh yogurt products in grocery stores. The grocery aisle business now accounts for about 7 percent of Starbucks' business, but CEO Howard Schultz envisions the grocery aisle business producing half of the company's sales.

While the growth potential is enticing, there are some potential pitfalls associated with Starbucks' push into new arenas. The perceived differentiation of its coffee products could erode as they become a grocery aisle staple. Also, the growth of grocery sales could cannibalize the sales at cafes as people simply brew their K-cup coffee at home rather than swinging through the Starbucks drive-through on the way to work. In moving into noncoffee products, the question becomes whether or not Starbucks has the competencies to manage other businesses well. While Starbucks has mastered the management of the coffee supply chain and developed a distinctive product, it is not clear that the company has the competencies to produce bakery products, juice, tea, beer, and wine better than outside suppliers. Finally, managing all of these new businesses may distract Starbucks from its core coffee cafe business. The challenge for Starbucks is to know what its core competencies are and to focus on markets that allow it to best exploit those competencies.

Discussion Questions

1. What are Starbucks' core competencies? Do the new businesses allow Starbucks to leverage those competencies?
2. Do Starbucks' diversification efforts appear to be primarily about increasing growth or increasing shareholder value by sharing activities, building market power, and/or leveraging core competencies?
3. Where do you think Starbucks should draw boundaries on what businesses to compete in? Should it keep the new products in the corporate family? Should it continue to move into the grocery retailing space?

Sources: Levine-Weinberg, A. 2014. Starbucks has decades of growth ahead. *money.cnn.com*, November 19: np; Kowitt, B. 2013. Starbucks' grocery gambit. *Fortune*, December 23: np; Strom, S. 2013. Starbucks aims to move beyond beans. *nytimes.com*, October 8: np; and s*tarbucks.com*.

Reflecting on Career Implications . . .

- **Corporate-Level Strategy:** Is your current employer a single business firm or a diversified firm? If it is diversified, does it pursue related or unrelated diversification? Does its diversification provide you with career opportunities, especially lateral moves? What organizational policies are in place to either encourage or discourage you from moving from one business unit to another?
- **Core Competencies:** What do you see as your core competencies? How can you leverage them within your business unit as well as across other business units?
- **Sharing Infrastructures:** Identify what infrastructure activities and resources (e.g., information systems, legal) are available in the corporate office that are shared by various business units in the firm. How often do you take advantage of these shared resources? Identify ways in which you can enhance your performance by taking advantage of these shared infrastructure resources.
- **Diversification:** From your career perspective, what actions can you take to diversify your employment risk (e.g., doing coursework at a local university, obtaining professional certification such as a CPA, networking through professional affiliation, etc.)? In periods of retrenchment, such actions will provide you with a greater number of career options.

summary

A key challenge for today's managers is to create "synergy" when engaging in diversification activities. As we discussed in this chapter, corporate managers do not, in general, have a very good track record in creating value in such endeavors when it comes to mergers and acquisitions. Among the factors that serve to erode shareholder values are paying an excessive premium for the target firm, failing to integrate the activities of the newly acquired businesses into the corporate family, and undertaking diversification initiatives that are too easily imitated by the competition.

We addressed two major types of corporate-level strategy: related and unrelated diversification. With *related diversification* the corporation strives to enter into areas in which key resources and capabilities of the corporation can be shared or leveraged. Synergies come from horizontal relationships between business units. Cost savings and enhanced revenues can be derived from two major sources. First, economies of scope can be achieved from the leveraging of core competencies and the sharing of activities. Second, market power can be attained from greater, or pooled, negotiating power and from vertical integration.

When firms undergo *unrelated diversification,* they enter product markets that are dissimilar to their present businesses. Thus, there is generally little opportunity to either leverage core competencies or share activities across business units. Here, synergies are created from vertical relationships between the corporate office and the individual business units. With unrelated diversification, the primary ways to create value are corporate restructuring and parenting, as well as the use of portfolio analysis techniques.

Corporations have three primary means of diversifying their product markets—mergers and acquisitions, joint ventures/strategic alliances, and internal development. There are key trade-offs associated with each of these. For example, mergers and acquisitions are typically the quickest means to enter new markets and provide the corporation with a high level of control over the acquired business. However, with the expensive premiums that often need to be paid to the shareholders of the target firm and the challenges associated with integrating acquisitions, they can also be quite expensive. Not surprisingly, many poorly performing acquisitions are subsequently divested. At times, however, divestitures can help firms refocus their efforts and generate resources. Strategic alliances and joint ventures between two or more firms, on the other hand, may be a means of reducing risk since they involve the sharing and combining of resources. But such joint initiatives also provide a firm with less control (than it would have with an acquisition) since governance is shared between two independent entities. Also, there is a limit to the potential upside for each partner because returns must be shared as well. Finally, with internal development, a firm is able to capture all of the value from its initiatives (as opposed to sharing it with a merger or alliance partner). However, diversification by means of internal development can be very time-consuming—a disadvantage that becomes even more important in fast-paced competitive environments.

Finally, some managerial behaviors may serve to erode shareholder returns. Among these are "growth for growth's sake," egotism, and antitakeover tactics. As we discussed, some of these issues—particularly antitakeover tactics—raise ethical considerations because the managers of the firm are not acting in the best interests of the shareholders.

SUMMARY REVIEW QUESTIONS

1. Discuss how managers can create value for their firm through diversification efforts.
2. What are some of the reasons that many diversification efforts fail to achieve desired outcomes?
3. How can companies benefit from related diversification? Unrelated diversification? What are some of the key concepts that can explain such success?
4. What are some of the important ways in which a firm can restructure a business?
5. Discuss some of the various means that firms can use to diversify. What are the pros and cons associated with each of these?
6. Discuss some of the actions that managers may engage in to erode shareholder value.

key terms

corporate-level strategy 182
diversification 183
related diversification 184
economies of scope 184
core competencies 185
sharing activities 186
market power 187
pooled negotiating power 187
vertical integration 188
transaction cost perspective 190
unrelated diversification 191
parenting advantage 191
restructuring 191
portfolio management 192
acquisitions 195
mergers 195
divestment 200
strategic alliance 202
joint ventures 202
internal development 203
managerial motives 204
growth for growth's sake 204
egotism 204
antitakeover tactics 205
greenmail 205
golden parachute 205
poison pill 205

application questions & exercises

1. What were some of the largest mergers and acquisitions over the last two years? What was the rationale for these actions? Do you think they will be successful? Explain.
2. Discuss some examples from business practice in which an executive's actions appear to be in his or her self-interest rather than the corporation's well-being.
3. Discuss some of the challenges that managers must overcome in making strategic alliances successful. What are some strategic alliances with which you are familiar? Were they successful or not? Explain.
4. Use the Internet and select a company that has recently undertaken diversification into new product markets. What do you feel were some of the reasons for this diversification (e.g., leveraging core competencies, sharing infrastructures)?

experiential exercise

Time Warner (formerly AOL Time Warner) is a firm that follows a strategy of related diversification. Evaluate its success (or lack thereof) with regard to how well it has (1) built on core competencies, (2) shared infrastructures, and (3) increased market power. (Fill answers in table below.)

ethics questions

1. In recent years there has been a rash of corporate downsizing and layoffs. Do you feel that such actions raise ethical considerations? Why or why not?
2. What are some of the ethical issues that arise when managers act in a manner that is counter to their firm's best interests? What are the long-term implications for both the firms and the managers themselves?

Rationale for Related Diversification	Successful/Unsuccessful?	Why?
1. Build on core competencies		
2. Share infrastructures		
3. Increase market power		

references

1. Grobart, S. & Rusli, E. 2011. For Flip video camera, four years from hot start-up to obsolete. *NYTimes.com,* April 4: np; Chen, B. 2011. Why Cisco's Flip flopped in the camera business. *Wired.com,* April 11: np; Rose, C. 2012. Charlie Rose talks to Cisco's John Chambers. *Bloomberg Businessweek,* April 24: 41; and www.cisco.com.
2. Insights on measuring M&A performance are addressed in Zollo, M. & Meier, D. 2008. What is M&A performance? *BusinessWeek,* 22(3): 55–77.
3. Insights on how and why firms may overpay for acquisitions are addressed in Malhotra, D., Ku, G., & Murnighan, J. K. 2008. When winning is everything. *Harvard Business Review,* 66(5): 78–86.
4. Dr. G. William Schwert, University of Rochester study cited in Pare, T. P. 1994. The new merger boom. *Fortune,* November 28: 96.
5. Lipin, S. & Deogun, N. 2000. Big mergers of the 1990's prove disappointing to shareholders. *The Wall Street Journal,* October 30: C1.
6. Rothenbuecher, J. & Schrottke, J. 2008. To get value from a merger, grow sales. *Harvard Business Review,* 86(5): 24–25; and Rothenbuecher, J. 2008. Personal communication, October 1.
7. Kyriazis, D. 2010. The long-term post acquisition performance of Greek acquiring firms. *International Research Journal of Finance and Economics,* 43: 69–79.
8. Pare, T. P. 1994. The new merger boom. *Fortune,* November 28: 96.
9. A discussion of the effects of director experience and acquisition performance is in McDonald, M. L. & Westphal, J. D. 2008. What do they know? The effects of outside director acquisition experience on firm acquisition performance. *Strategic Management Journal,* 29(11): 1155–1177.
10. Finance and economics: Snoopy sniffs an opportunity; MetLife buys Alico. 2010. *Economist.com,* March 13: np.
11. For a study that investigates several predictors of corporate diversification, read Wiersema, M. F. & Bowen, H. P. 2008. Corporate diversification: The impact of foreign competition, industry globalization, and product diversification. *Strategic Management Journal,* 29(2): 114–132.
12. Kumar, M. V. S. 2011. Are joint ventures positive sum games? The relative effects of cooperative and non-cooperative behavior. *Strategic Management Journal,* 32(1): 32–54.
13. Makri, M., Hitt, M. A., & Lane, P. J. 2010. Complementary technologies, knowledge relatedness, and invention outcomes in high technology mergers and acquisitions. *Strategic Management Journal,* 31(6): 602–628.
14. A discussion of Tyco's unrelated diversification strategy is in Hindo, B. 2008. Solving Tyco's identity crisis. *BusinessWeek,* February 18: 62.
15. Our framework draws upon a variety of sources, including Goold, M. & Campbell, A. 1998. Desperately seeking synergy. *Harvard Business Review,* 76(5): 131–143; Porter, M. E. 1987. From advantage to corporate strategy. *Harvard Business Review,* 65(3): 43–59; and Hitt, M. A., Ireland, R. D., & Hoskisson, R. E. 2001. *Strategic management: Competitiveness and globalization* (4th ed.). Cincinnati, OH: South-Western.
16. This imagery of the corporation as a tree and related discussion draws on Prahalad, C. K. & Hamel, G. 1990. The core competence of the corporation. *Harvard Business Review,* 68(3): 79–91. Parts of this section also draw on Picken, J. C. & Dess, G. G. 1997. *Mission critical:* chap. 5. Burr Ridge, IL: Irwin Professional.
17. Graebner, M. E., Eisenhardt, K. M., & Roundy, P. T. 2010. Success and failure in technology acquisitions: Lessons for buyers and sellers. *Academy of Management Perspectives,* 24(3): 73–92.
18. This section draws on Prahalad & Hamel, op. cit.; and Porter, op. cit.
19. A study that investigates the relationship between a firm's technology resources, diversification, and performance can be found in Miller, D. J. 2004. Firms' technological resources and the performance effects of diversification. A longitudinal study. *Strategic Management Journal,* 25: 1097–1119.
20. Chesbrough, H. 2011. Bringing open innovation to services. *MIT Sloan Management Review,* 52(2): 85–90.
21. Fisher, A. 2008. America's most admired companies. *Fortune,* March 17: 74.
22. Levine-Weinberg, A. 2014. Starbucks has decades of growth ahead. *money.cnn.com,* November 19: np.

23. This section draws on Hrebiniak, L. G. & Joyce, W. F. 1984. *Implementing strategy.* New York: Macmillan; and Oster, S. M. 1994. *Modern competitive analysis.* New York: Oxford University Press.

24. The discussion of the benefits and costs of vertical integration draws on Hax, A. C. & Majluf, N. S. 1991. *The strategy concept and process: A pragmatic approach:* 139. Englewood Cliffs, NJ: Prentice Hall.

25. Fahey, J. 2005. Gray winds. *Forbes,* January 10: 143.

26. This discussion draws on Oster, op. cit.; and Harrigan, K. 1986. Matching vertical integration strategies to competitive conditions. *Strategic Management Journal,* 7(6): 535–556.

27. For a scholarly explanation on how transaction costs determine the boundaries of a firm, see Oliver E. Williamson's pioneering books *Markets and hierarchies: Analysis and antitrust implications* (New York: Free Press, 1975) and *The economic institutions of capitalism* (New York: Free Press, 1985).

28. Campbell, A., Goold, M., & Alexander, M. 1995. Corporate strategy: The quest for parenting advantage. *Harvard Business Review,* 73(2): 120–132; and Picken & Dess, op. cit.

29. Anslinger, P. A. & Copeland, T. E. 1996. Growth through acquisition: A fresh look. *Harvard Business Review,* 74(1): 126–135.

30. This section draws on Porter, op. cit.; and Hambrick, D. C. 1985. Turnaround strategy. In Guth, W. D. (Ed.), *Handbook of business strategy:* 10-1–10-32. Boston: Warren, Gorham & Lamont.

31. There is an important delineation between companies that are operated for a long-term profit and those that are bought and sold for short-term gains. The latter are sometimes referred to as "holding companies" and are generally more concerned about financial issues than strategic issues.

32. Lenzner, R. 2007. High on Loews. *Forbes,* February 26: 98–102.

33. Casico, W. F. 2002. Strategies for responsible restructuring. *Academy of Management Executive,* 16(3): 80–91; and Singh, H. 1993. Challenges in researching corporate restructuring. *Journal of Management Studies,* 30(1): 147–172.

34. Hax & Majluf, op. cit. By 1979, 45 percent of Fortune 500 companies employed some form of portfolio analysis, according to Haspelagh, P. 1982. Portfolio planning: Uses and limits. *Harvard Business Review,* 60: 58–73. A later study conducted in 1993 found that over 40 percent of the respondents used portfolio analysis techniques, but the level of usage was expected to increase to more than 60 percent in the near future: Rigby, D. K. 1994. Managing the management tools. *Planning Review,* September–October: 20–24.

35. Fruk, M., Hall, S., & Mittal, D. 2013. Never let a good crisis go to waste. *mckinsey.com,* October: np; and Arrfelt, M., Wiseman, R., McNamara, G., & Hult, T., 2015. Examining a key corporate role: The influence of capital allocation competency on business unit performance. *Strategic Management Journal,* in press.

36. Goold, M. & Luchs, K. 1993. Why diversify? Four decades of management thinking. *Academy of Management Executive,* 7(3): 7–25.

37. Other approaches include the industry attractiveness–business strength matrix developed jointly by General Electric and McKinsey and Company, the life-cycle matrix developed by Arthur D. Little, and the profitability matrix proposed by Marakon. For an extensive review, refer to Hax & Majluf, op. cit.: 182–194.

38. Porter, op. cit.: 49–52.

39. Picken & Dess, op. cit.; Cabot Corporation. 2001. 10-Q filing, Securities and Exchange Commission, May 14.

40. Insights on the performance of serial acquirers is found in Laamanen, T. & Keil, T. 2008. Performance of serial acquirers: Toward an acquisition program perspective. *Strategic Management Journal,* 29(6): 663–672.

41. Some insights from Lazard's CEO on mergers and acquisitions are addressed in Stewart, T. A. & Morse, G. 2008. Giving great advice. *Harvard Business Review,* 66(1): 106–113.

42. Coy, P., Thornton, E., Arndt, M., & Grow, B. 2005. Shake, rattle, and merge. *BusinessWeek,* January 10: 32–35; and Anonymous. 2005. Love is in the air. *The Economist,* February 5: 9.

43. Hill, A. 2011. Mergers indicate market optimism. *www.marketplace.org,* March 21: np.

44. For an interesting study of the relationship between mergers and a firm's product-market strategies, refer to Krishnan, R. A., Joshi, S., & Krishnan, H. 2004. The influence of mergers on firms' product-mix strategies. *Strategic Management Journal,* 25: 587–611.

45. Like many high-tech firms during the economic slump that began in mid-2000, Cisco Systems experienced declining performance. On April 16, 2001, it announced that its revenues for the quarter closing April 30 would drop 5 percent from a year earlier—and a stunning 30 percent from the previous three months—to about $4.7 billion. Furthermore, Cisco announced that it would lay off 8,500 employees and take an enormous $2.5 billion charge to write down inventory. By late October 2002, its stock was trading at around $10, down significantly from its 52-week high of $70. Elstrom, op. cit.: 39.

46. Sisario, B. 2014. Jimmy Iovine, a master of Beats, lends Apple a skilled ear. *nytimes.com,* May 28: np; and Dickey, M. 2014. Meet the executives Apple is paying $3 billion to get. *businessinsider.com,* May 28: np.

47. Ignatius, A. 2011. How eBay developed a culture of experimentation. *Harvard Business Review,* 89(3): 92–97.

48. For a discussion of the trend toward consolidation of the steel industry and how Lakshmi Mittal is becoming a dominant player, read Reed, S. & Arndt, M. 2004. The raja of steel. *BusinessWeek,* December 20: 50–52.

49. Colvin, G. 2011. Airline king. *Fortune,* May 2: 50–57.

50. This discussion draws upon Rappaport, A. & Sirower, M. L. 1999. Stock or cash? The trade-offs for buyers and sellers in mergers and acquisitions. *Harvard Business Review,* 77(6): 147–158; and Lipin, S. & Deogun, N. 2000. Big mergers of 90s prove disappointing to shareholders. *The Wall Street Journal,* October 30: C1.

51. The downside of mergers in the airline industry is found in Gimbel, B. 2008. Why airline mergers don't fly. *BusinessWeek,* March 17: 26.

52. Mouio, A. (Ed.). 1998. Unit of one. *Fast Company,* September: 82.

53. Porter, M. E. 1987. From competitive advantage to corporate strategy. *Harvard Business Review,* 65(3): 43.

54. The divestiture of a business that is undertaken in order to enable managers to better focus on its core business has been termed "downscoping." Refer to Hitt, M. A., Harrison, J. S., & Ireland, R. D. 2001. *Mergers and acquisitions: A guide to creating value for stakeholders.* New York: Oxford University Press.

55. Sirmon, D. G., Hitt, M. A., & Ireland, R. D. 2007. Managing firm resources in dynamic environments to create value: Looking inside the black box. *Academy of Management Review*, 32(1): 273–292.
56. Kengelbach, J., Klemmer, D., & Roos, A. 2012. Plant and prune: How M&A can grow portfolio value. *BCG Report*, September: 1–38.
57. Berry, J., Brigham, B., Bynum, A., Leu, C., & McLaughlin, R. 2012. Creating value through divestitures—Deans Foods: Theory in practice. *Unpublished manuscript*.
58. A study that investigates alliance performance is Lunnan, R. & Haugland, S. A. 2008. Predicting and measuring alliance performance: A multidimensional analysis. *Strategic Management Journal*, 29(5): 545–556.
59. For scholarly perspectives on the role of learning in creating value in strategic alliances, refer to Anard, B. N. & Khanna, T. 2000. Do firms learn to create value? *Strategic Management Journal*, 12(3): 295–317; and Vermeulen, F. & Barkema, H. P. 2001. Learning through acquisitions. *Academy of Management Journal*, 44(3): 457–476.
60. For a detailed discussion of transaction cost economics in strategic alliances, read Reuer, J. J. & Arno, A. 2007. Strategic alliance contracts: Dimensions and determinants of contractual complexity. *Strategic Management Journal*, 28(3): 313–330.
61. This section draws on Hutt, M. D., Stafford, E. R., Walker, B. A., & Reingen, P. H. 2000. Case study: Defining the strategic alliance. *Sloan Management Review*, 41(2): 51–62; and Walters, B. A., Peters, S., & Dess, G. G. 1994. Strategic alliances and joint ventures: Making them work. *Business Horizons*, 4: 5–10.
62. A study that investigates strategic alliances and networks is Tiwana, A. 2008. Do bridging ties complement strong ties? An empirical examination of alliance ambidexterity. *Strategic Management Journal*, 29(3): 251–272.
63. Fashion chain Zara opens its first Indian store. 2010. *bbc.co.uk/news/*, May 31: np.
64. Martin, A. 2007. Merger for SABMiller and Molson Coors. *nytimes.com*, October 10: np.
65. Phelps, C. 2010. A longitudinal study of the influence of alliance network structure and composition on firm exploratory innovation. *Academy of Management Journal*, 53(4): 890–913.
66. For an institutional theory perspective on strategic alliances, read Dacin, M. T., Oliver, C., & Roy, J. P. 2007. The legitimacy of strategic alliances: An institutional perspective. *Strategic Management Journal*, 28(2): 169–187.
67. A study investigating factors that determine partner selection in strategic alliances is found in Shah, R. H. & Swaminathan, V. 2008. *Strategic Management Journal*, 29(5): 471–494.
68. Arino, A. & Ring, P. S. 2010. The role of fairness in alliance formation. *Strategic Management Journal*, 31(6): 1054–1087.
69. Greve, H. R., Baum, J. A. C., Mitsuhashi, H. & Rowley, T. J. 2010. Built to last but falling apart: Cohesion, friction, and withdrawal from interfirm alliances. *Academy of Management Journal*, 53(4): 302–322.
70. Narayan, A. 2011. From brewing, an Indian biotech is born. *Bloomberg Businessweek*, February 28: 19–20.
71. For an insightful perspective on how to manage conflict between innovation and ongoing operations in an organization, read Govindarajan, V. & Trimble, C. 2010. *The other side of innovation: Solving the execution challenge*. Boston: Harvard Business School Press.
72. Dunlap-Hinkler, D., Kotabe, M., & Mudambi, R. 2010. A story of breakthrough versus incremental innovation: Corporate entrepreneurship in the global pharmaceutical industry. *Strategic Entrepreneurship Journal*, 4(2): 106–127.
73. Porter, op. cit.: 43–59.
74. Angwin, J. S. & Wingfield, N. 2000. How Jay Walker built WebHouse on a theory that he couldn't prove. *The Wall Street Journal*, October 16: A1, A8.
75. The fallen. 2003. *BusinessWeek*, January 13: 80–82.
76. The Jack Welch example draws upon Sellers, P. 2001. Get over yourself. *Fortune*, April 30: 76–88.
77. Li, J. & Tang, Y. 2010. CEO hubris and firm risk taking in China: The moderating role of managerial discretion. *Academy of Management Journal*, 53(1): 45–68.
78. Polek, D. 2002. The rise and fall of Dennis Kozlowski. *BusinessWeek*, December 23: 64–77.
79. John Thain and his golden commode. 2009. Editorial. *Dallasnews.com*, January 26: np; Task, A. 2009. Wall Street's $18.4B bonus: The sense of entitlement has not been beaten out. *finance.yahoo.com*, January 29: np; and Exit Thain. 2009. *Newsfinancialcareers.com*, January 22: np.
80. This section draws on Weston, J. F., Besley, S., & Brigham, E. F. 1996. *Essentials of managerial finance* (11th ed.): 18–20. Fort Worth, TX: Dryden Press, Harcourt Brace.

International Strategy
Creating Value in Global Markets

chapter 7

After reading this chapter, you should have a good understanding of the following learning objectives:

LO7.1 The importance of international expansion as a viable diversification strategy.

LO7.2 The sources of national advantage; that is, why an industry in a given country is more (or less) successful than the same industry in another country.

LO7.3 The motivations (or benefits) and the risks associated with international expansion, including the emerging trend for greater offshoring and outsourcing activity.

LO7.4 The two opposing forces—cost reduction and adaptation to local markets—that firms face when entering international markets.

LO7.5 The advantages and disadvantages associated with each of the four basic strategies: international, global, multidomestic, and transnational.

LO7.6 The difference between regional companies and truly global companies.

LO7.7 The six basic types of entry strategies and the relative benefits and risks associated with each of them.

PART 2: STRATEGIC FORMULATION

Learning from Mistakes

SAIC, a major Chinese automaker, wanted to grow outside its home market. As a step to achieve this aim, it acquired a controlling interest in SsangYong, a struggling Korean automaker, in 2004.[1] However, this investment didn't turn out as SAIC had hoped. After five tumultuous years and $618 million in investment, SAIC decided to stop any further investments in SsangYong and saw its ownership stake erode when SsangYong went into bankruptcy in 2009. Why did SAIC's takeover of SsangYong turn out so badly?

SAIC, formerly known as Shanghai Automotive Industry Corporation, grew from a small firm in the 1970s to the largest Chinese-based automaker by 2010. It has leveraged relationships with major global automakers, including Volkswagen and GM, to develop its resources to design and build world-class cars. Building off its success at home, SAIC wanted to grow its global footprint.

As a first step in this effort, SAIC undertook its first acquisition of a non-Chinese firm. In 2004, SAIC paid $500 million to acquire 49 percent of SsangYong, the number-four auto manufacturer in South Korea. SsangYong had a 10 percent share of the Korean car market and was especially strong in the small SUV market. In addition to its Korean sales base, it was building its export business.

Analysts saw the acquisition as one with strong promise. SAIC would gain access to its first foreign markets and also access to SsangYong's advanced technologies. Of great potential value was SsangYong's hybrid engine technology. SsangYong, which was burdened by heavy debt, would be recapitalized by SAIC. Additionally, SAIC, which had very efficient plant operations, could help improve SsangYong's production efficiency.

Even with all of the potential, problems quickly arose. Cultural differences between Chinese and Korean managers hampered their ability to agree on how to restructure SsangYong. SAIC had even greater difficulties negotiating with SsangYong's unions. South Korea has a heritage of strong unions and difficult management–labor relations, something that was entirely new to SAIC.

These differences were exacerbated by a steep drop in demand for SsangYong's vehicles. When gasoline prices spiked in 2006, SUV sales dropped dramatically. Further, when the global recession hit in late 2007, global auto sales tanked. SsangYong's sales were cut in half by the end of 2008.

SAIC proposed a dramatic overhaul at SsangYong, with major changes in shop-floor practices to improve efficiency and a 36 percent reduction in SsangYong's workforce. SsangYong's unions rebelled and charged that SAIC was illegally transferring technology designs and technology to China. Without any further cash infusion from SAIC, SsangYong filed for bankruptcy in January 2009. The unions went on strike and barricaded themselves in SsangYong's plants for 77 days. SAIC wrote off its investments in SsangYong and blamed the experience for its 26 percent drop in profits in the first half of 2009.

Discussion Questions

1. What lessons should SAIC learn from its acquisition of SsangYong?
2. When buying a firm in another country, what issues should the acquiring firm think about to limit the risks it will face with the acquisition?
3. How can a firm bridge cultural differences between its home market and a country it is moving into?

In this chapter we discuss how firms create value and achieve competitive advantage in the global marketplace. Multinational firms are constantly faced with the dilemma of choosing between local adaptation—in product offerings, locations, advertising, and pricing—and global integration. We discuss how firms can avoid pitfalls such as those experienced by SAIC, a major Chinese automaker. In addition, we address factors that can influence a nation's success in a particular industry. In our view, this is an important context in determining how well firms might eventually do when they compete beyond their nation's boundaries.

The Global Economy: A Brief Overview

LO7.1
The importance of international expansion as a viable diversification strategy.

Managers face many opportunities and risks when they diversify abroad.[2] The trade among nations has increased dramatically in recent years, and it is estimated that by 2015 the trade *across* nations will exceed the trade within nations. In a variety of industries such as semiconductors, automobiles, commercial aircraft, telecommunications, computers, and consumer electronics, it is almost impossible to survive unless firms scan the world for competitors, customers, human resources, suppliers, and technology.[3]

GE's wind energy business benefits by tapping into talent around the world. The firm has built research centers in China, Germany, India, and the U.S. "We did it," says CEO Jeffrey Immelt, "to access the best brains everywhere in the world." All four centers have played a key role in GE's development of huge 92-ton turbines:[4]

- Chinese researchers in Shanghai designed the microprocessors that control the pitch of the blade.
- Mechanical engineers from India (Bangalore) devised mathematical models to maximize the efficiency of materials in the turbine.
- Power-systems experts in the U.S. (Niskayuna, New York), which has researchers from 55 countries, do the design work.
- Technicians in Munich, Germany, have created a "smart" turbine that can calculate wind speeds and signal sensors in other turbines to produce maximum electricity.

globalization
a term that has two meanings: (1) the increase in international exchange, including trade in goods and services as well as exchange of money, ideas, and information; (2) the growing similarity of laws, rules, norms, values, and ideas across countries.

The rise of **globalization**—meaning the rise of market capitalism around the world—has undeniably created tremendous business opportunities for multinational corporations. For example, while smartphone sales declined in Western Europe in the third quarter of 2014, they grew at a 50 percent rate in Eastern Europe, the Middle East, and Africa.[5]

This rapid rise in global capitalism has had dramatic effects on the growth in different economic zones. As shown in Exhibit 7.1, the growth experienced by developed economies in the first decade of the 2000s was anemic, while the growth in developing economies was robust.[6] This has resulted in a dramatic shift in the structure of the global economy. Over half the world's output now comes from emerging markets. This is leading to a convergence of living standards across the globe and is changing the face of business. One example of this is the shift in the global automobile market. China supplanted the United States as the largest market for automobiles in 2009.

One of the challenges with globalization is determining how to meet the needs of customers at very different income levels. In many developing economies, distributions of income remain much wider than they do in the developed world, leaving many impoverished even as the economies grow. The challenge for multinational firms is to tailor their products and services to meet the needs of the "bottom of the pyramid." Global corporations are increasingly changing their product offerings to meet the needs of the nearly 5 billion poor people in the world who inhabit developing countries. Collectively, this represents a very large market with $14 trillion in purchasing power.

Next, we will address in more detail the question of why some nations and their industries are more competitive.[7] This establishes an important context or setting for the

EXHIBIT 7.1 Rate of Growth in GDP per Person, 2001–2011, by Region

[Bar chart showing GDP per person growth rates by region: United States ~1.8, European Union ~1.8, Japan ~0.6, Latin America ~4.6, Central and Eastern Europe ~4.3, Sub-Saharan Africa ~5.8, Middle East ~5.0, Russia ~4.8, India ~8.1, China ~10.7]

Source: A game of catch-up. 2011. *The Economist,* September 24: 3–6.

remainder of the chapter. After we discuss why some *nations and their industries* outperform others, we will be better able to address the various strategies that *firms* can take to create competitive advantage when they expand internationally.

Factors Affecting a Nation's Competitiveness

Michael Porter of Harvard University conducted a four-year study in which he and a team of 30 researchers looked at the patterns of competitive success in 10 leading trading nations. He concluded that there are four broad attributes of nations that individually, and as a system, constitute what is termed the **diamond of national advantage.** In effect, these attributes jointly determine the playing field that each nation establishes and operates for its industries. These factors are:

- *Factor endowments.* The nation's position in factors of production, such as skilled labor or infrastructure, necessary to compete in a given industry.
- *Demand conditions.* The nature of home-market demand for the industry's product or service.
- *Related and supporting industries.* The presence or absence in the nation of supplier industries and other related industries that are internationally competitive.
- *Firm strategy, structure, and rivalry.* The conditions in the nation governing how companies are created, organized, and managed, as well as the nature of domestic rivalry.

Factor Endowments[8,9]

Classical economics suggests that factors of production such as land, labor, and capital are the building blocks that create usable consumer goods and services.[10] However, companies in advanced nations seeking competitive advantage over firms in other nations *create* many of the factors of production. For example, a country or industry dependent on scientific innovation must have a skilled human resource pool to draw upon. This resource pool is not inherited; it is created through investment in industry-specific knowledge and talent. The supporting infrastructure of a country—that is, its transportation and communication systems as well as its banking system—is also critical.

diamond of national advantage
a framework for explaining why countries foster successful multinational corporations; consists of four factors—factor endowments; demand conditions; related and supporting industries; and firm strategy, structure, and rivalry.

factor endowments (national advantage)
a nation's position in factors of production.

LO7.2
The sources of national advantage; that is, why an industry in a given country is more (or less) successful than the same industry in another country.

Factors of production must be developed that are industry- and firm-specific. In addition, the pool of resources is less important than the speed and efficiency with which these resources are deployed. Thus, firm-specific knowledge and skills created within a country that are rare, valuable, difficult to imitate, and rapidly and efficiently deployed are the factors of production that ultimately lead to a nation's competitive advantage.

For example, the island nation of Japan has little landmass, making the warehouse space needed to store inventory prohibitively expensive. But by pioneering just-in-time inventory management, Japanese companies managed to create a resource from which they gained advantage over companies in other nations that spent large sums to warehouse inventory.

Demand Conditions

demand conditions (national advantage) the nature of home-market demand for the industry's product or service.

Demand conditions refer to the demands that consumers place on an industry for goods and services. Consumers who demand highly specific, sophisticated products and services force firms to create innovative, advanced products and services to meet the demand. This consumer pressure presents challenges to a country's industries. But in response to these challenges, improvements to existing goods and services often result, creating conditions necessary for competitive advantage over firms in other countries.

Countries with demanding consumers drive firms in that country to meet high standards, upgrade existing products and services, and create innovative products and services. The conditions of consumer demand influence how firms view a market. This, in turn, helps a nation's industries to better anticipate future global demand conditions and proactively respond to product and service requirements.

Denmark, for instance, is known for its environmental awareness. Demand from consumers for environmentally safe products has spurred Danish manufacturers to become leaders in water pollution control equipment—products it successfully exported.

Related and Supporting Industries

related and supporting industries (national advantage) the presence, absence, and quality in the nation of supplier industries and other related industries that supply services, support, or technology to firms in the industry value chain.

Related and supporting industries enable firms to manage inputs more effectively. For example, countries with a strong supplier base benefit by adding efficiency to downstream activities. A competitive supplier base helps a firm obtain inputs using cost-effective, timely methods, thus reducing manufacturing costs. Also, close working relationships with suppliers provide the potential to develop competitive advantages through joint research and development and the ongoing exchange of knowledge.

Related industries offer similar opportunities through joint efforts among firms. In addition, related industries create the probability that new companies will enter the market, increasing competition and forcing existing firms to become more competitive through efforts such as cost control, product innovation, and novel approaches to distribution. Combined, these give the home country's industries a source of competitive advantage.

In the Italian footwear industry the supporting industries enhance national competitive advantage. In Italy, shoe manufacturers are geographically located near their suppliers. The manufacturers have ongoing interactions with leather suppliers and learn about new textures, colors, and manufacturing techniques while a shoe is still in the prototype stage. The manufacturers are able to project future demand and gear their factories for new products long before companies in other nations become aware of the new styles.

Firm Strategy, Structure, and Rivalry

firm strategy, structure, and rivalry (national advantage) the conditions in the nation governing how companies are created, organized, and managed, as well as the nature of domestic rivalry.

Rivalry is particularly intense in nations with conditions of strong consumer demand, strong supplier bases, and high new-entrant potential from related industries. This competitive rivalry in turn increases the efficiency with which firms develop, market, and distribute products and services within the home country. Domestic rivalry thus provides a strong impetus for firms to innovate and find new sources of competitive advantage.

This intense rivalry forces firms to look outside their national boundaries for new markets, setting up the conditions necessary for global competitiveness. Among all the points on Porter's diamond of national advantage, domestic rivalry is perhaps the strongest indicator of global competitive success. Firms that have experienced intense domestic competition are more likely to have designed strategies and structures that allow them to successfully compete in world markets.

In the European grocery retail industry, intense rivalry has led firms such as Aldi and Tesco to tighten their supply chains and improve store efficiency. Thus, it is no surprise that these firms are also strong global players.

The Indian software industry offers a clear example of how the attributes in Porter's "diamond" interact to lead to the conditions for a strong industry to grow. Exhibit 7.2 illustrates India's "software diamond," and Strategy Spotlight 7.1 further discusses the mutually reinforcing elements at work in this market.

7.1 STRATEGY SPOTLIGHT

INDIA AND THE DIAMOND OF NATIONAL ADVANTAGE

The Indian software industry has become one of the leading global markets for software. The industry has grown to over $60 billion, and Indian IT firms provide software and services to over half the Fortune 500 firms. What are the factors driving this success? Porter's diamond of national advantage helps clarify this question. See Exhibit 7.2.

First, *factor endowments* are conducive to the rise of India's software industry. Through investment in human resource development with a focus on industry-specific knowledge, India's universities and software firms have literally created this essential factor of production. For example, India produces the second-largest annual output of scientists and engineers in the world, behind only the United States. In a knowledge-intensive industry such as software, development of human resources is fundamental to both domestic and global success.

EXHIBIT 7.2 India's Software Diamond

- **Domestic rivalry**: No regulatory barriers to entry or start-up; 800 firms, mostly small, in fierce rivalry; growing number of MNC software-development centers in India.
- Dashed lines represent weaker interactions.
- **Factor endowments**: Large pool of skilled labor; low salaries; English-language capability.
- **Domestic demand conditions**
- **U.S. demand conditions**: Large, growing market; sophisticated customers; cutting-edge applications.
- **Related and supporting industries**: Large network of public and private educational institutions; weak but rapidly improving communications infrastructure; duty-free access to imported computers and software, following economic liberalization.

Source: From Kampur D. and Ramamurti R., "India's Emerging Competition Advantage in Services," *Academy of Management Executive: The Thinking Manager's Source.* Copyright © 2001 by Academy of Management.

continued

continued

Second, *demand conditions* require that software firms stay on the cutting edge of technological innovation. India has already moved toward globalization of its software industry; consumer demand conditions in developed nations such as Germany, Denmark, parts of Southeast Asia, and the United States created the consumer demand necessary to propel India's software makers toward sophisticated software solutions.*

Third, India has the *supplier base as well as the related industries* needed to drive competitive rivalry and enhance competitiveness. In particular, information technology (IT) hardware prices declined rapidly in the 1990s. Furthermore, rapid technological change in IT hardware meant that latecomers like India were not locked into older-generation technologies. Thus, both the IT hardware and software industries could "leapfrog" older technologies. In addition, relationships among knowledge workers in these IT hardware and software industries offer the social structure for ongoing knowledge exchange, promoting further enhancement of existing products. Further infrastructure improvements are occurring rapidly.

Fourth, with over 800 firms in the software services industry in India, *intense rivalry forces firms to develop competitive strategies and structures.* Although firms like TCS, Infosys, and Wipro have become large, they still face strong competition from dozens of small and midsize companies aspiring to catch them. This intense rivalry is one of the primary factors driving Indian software firms to develop overseas distribution channels, as predicted by Porter's diamond of national advantage.

It is interesting to note that the cost advantage of Indian firms has eroded. For example, TCS's engineers' compensation soared 13 percent in 2010. Further, IBM and Accenture are aggressively building up their Indian operations, hiring tens of thousands of sought-after Indians by paying them more, thereby lowering their costs while raising those of TCS. Finally, many low-labor-cost countries, such as China, the Philippines, and Vietnam, are emerging as threats to the Indian competitors.

*Although India's success cannot be explained in terms of its home-market demand (according to Porter's model), the nature of the industry enables software to be transferred among different locations simultaneously by way of communications links. Thus, competitiveness of markets outside India can be enhanced without a physical presence in those markets.

Sources: Sachitanand, R. 2010. The new face of IT. *Business Today*, 19: 62; Anonymous. 2010. Training to lead. *www.Dqindia.com*, October 5: np; Nagaraju, B. 2011. India's software exports seen up 16–18 pct. in Fy12. *www.reuters.com*, February 2: np; Ghemawat, P. & Hout, T. 2008. Tomorrow's global giants. *Harvard Business Review*, 86(11): 80–88; Mathur, S. K. 2007. Indian IT industry: A performance analysis and a model for possible adoption. *ideas.repec.org*, January 1: np; Kripalani, M. 2002. Calling Bangalore: Multinationals are making it a hub for high-tech research *BusinessWeek*, November 25: 52–54; Kapur, D. & Ramamurti, R. 2001. India's emerging competitive advantage in services. 2001. *Academy of Management Executive*, 15(2): 20–33; World Bank. 2001 *World Development Report:* 6. New York: Oxford University Press; and Reuters. 2001. Oracle in India push, taps software talent. *Washington Post Online*, July 3.

Concluding Comment on Factors Affecting a Nation's Competitiveness

Porter drew his conclusions based on case histories of firms in more than 100 industries. Despite the differences in strategies employed by successful global competitors, a common theme emerged: Firms that succeeded in global markets had first succeeded in intensely competitive home markets. We can conclude that competitive advantage for global firms typically grows out of relentless, continuing improvement, and innovation.[11]

International Expansion: A Company's Motivations and Risks

LO7.3 The motivations (or benefits) and the risks associated with international expansion, including the emerging trend for greater offshoring and outsourcing activity.

Motivations for International Expansion

Increase Market Size There are many motivations for a company to pursue international expansion. The most obvious one is to *increase the size of potential markets* for a firm's products and services.[12] The world's population approached 7.5 billion in early 2015, with the U.S. representing less than 5 percent.

Many **multinational firms** are intensifying their efforts to market their products and services to countries such as India and China as the ranks of their middle class have increased over the past decade. The potential is great. An OECD study predicts that consumption by middle-class consumers in Asian markets will grow from $4.9 trillion in 2009 to over $30 trillion by 2020. At that point, Asia will make up 60 percent of global middle-class consumption, up from 20 percent in 2009.[13]

Expanding a firm's global presence also automatically increases its scale of operations, providing it with a larger revenue and asset base.[14] As we noted in Chapter 5 in discussing overall cost leadership strategies, such an increase in revenues and asset base

multinational firms firms that manage operations in more than one country.

potentially enables a firm to *attain economies of scale*. This provides multiple benefits. One advantage is the spreading of fixed costs such as R&D over a larger volume of production. Examples include the sale of Boeing's commercial aircraft and Microsoft's operating systems in many foreign countries.

Filmmaking is another industry in which international sales can help amortize huge developmental costs.[15] For example, 77 percent of the $1.1 billion box-office take for *Transformers: Age of Extinction* came from overseas moviegoers. Similarly, the market for kids' movies is largely outside the U.S., with 70 percent of *Frozen*'s $1.3 billion in box-office take coming from overseas.

Take Advantage of Arbitrage *Taking advantage of* **arbitrage opportunities** is a second advantage of international expansion. In its simplest form, arbitrage involves buying something where it is cheap and selling it where it commands a higher price. A big part of Walmart's success can be attributed to the company's expertise in arbitrage. The possibilities for arbitrage are not necessarily confined to simple trading opportunities. It can be applied to virtually any factor of production and every stage of the value chain. For example, a firm may locate its call centers in India, its manufacturing plants in China, and its R&D in Europe, where the specific types of talented personnel may be available at the lowest possible cost. In today's integrated global financial markets, a firm can borrow anywhere in the world where capital is cheap and use it to fund a project in a country where capital is expensive. Such arbitrage opportunities are even more attractive to global corporations because their larger size enables them to buy in huge volume, thus increasing their bargaining power with suppliers.

> **arbitrage opportunities**
> an opportunity to profit by buying and selling the same good in different markets.

Enhancing a Product's Growth Potential *Enhancing the growth rate of a product* that is in its maturity stage in a firm's home country but that has greater demand potential elsewhere is another benefit of international expansion. As we noted in Chapter 5, products (and industries) generally go through a four-stage life cycle of introduction, growth, maturity, and decline. In recent decades, U.S. soft-drink producers such as Coca-Cola and PepsiCo have aggressively pursued international markets to attain levels of growth that simply would not be available in the United States. The differences in market growth potential have even led some firms to restructure their operations. For example, Procter & Gamble relocated its global skin, cosmetics, and personal care unit headquarters from Cincinnati to Singapore to be closer to the fast-growing Asian market.[16]

Optimize the Location of Value-Chain Activities *Optimizing the physical location for every activity in the firm's value chain* is another benefit. Recall from our discussions in Chapters 3 and 5 that the value chain represents the various activities in which all firms must engage to produce products and services. It includes primary activities, such as inbound logistics, operations, and marketing, as well as support activities, such as procurement, R&D, and human resource management. All firms have to make critical decisions as to where each activity will take place.[17] Optimizing the location for every activity in the value chain can yield one or more of three strategic advantages: performance enhancement, cost reduction, and risk reduction. We will now discuss each of these.

Performance Enhancement Microsoft's decision to establish a corporate research laboratory in Cambridge, England, is an example of a location decision that was guided mainly by the goal of building and sustaining world-class excellence in selected value-creating activities.[18] This strategic decision provided Microsoft with access to outstanding technical and professional talent. Location decisions can affect the quality with which any activity is performed in terms of the availability of needed talent, speed of learning, and the quality of external and internal coordination.

Cost Reduction Two location decisions founded largely on cost-reduction considerations are (1) Nike's decision to source the manufacture of athletic shoes from Asian countries such as China, Vietnam, and Indonesia and (2) the decision of Volkswagen to locate a new auto production plant in Chattanooga, Tennessee, to leverage the relatively low labor costs in the area as well as low shipping costs due to Chattanooga's close proximity to both rail and river transportation. Such location decisions can affect the cost structure in terms of local manpower and other resources, transportation and logistics, and government incentives and the local tax structure.

Performance enhancement and cost-reduction benefits parallel the business-level strategies (discussed in Chapter 5) of differentiation and overall cost leadership. They can at times be attained simultaneously. Consider our example in the previous section on the Indian software industry. When Oracle set up a development operation in that country, the company benefited both from lower labor costs and operational expenses and from performance enhancements realized through the hiring of superbly talented professionals.

Risk Reduction Given the erratic swings in the exchange ratios between the U.S. dollar and the Japanese yen (in relation to each other and to other major currencies), an important basis for cost competition between Ford and Toyota has been their relative ingenuity at managing currency risks. One way for such rivals to manage currency risks has been to spread the high-cost elements of their manufacturing operations across a few select and carefully chosen locations around the world. Location decisions such as these can affect the overall risk profile of the firm with respect to currency, economic, and political risks.[19]

Learning Opportunities By expanding into new markets, corporations expose themselves to differing market demands, R&D capabilities, functional skills, organizational processes, and managerial practices. This provides opportunities for managers to transfer the knowledge that results from these exposures back to their home office and to other divisions in the firm. Thus, expansion into new markets provides a range of learning opportunities. For example, when L'Oréal, a French personal care product manufacturer, acquired two U.S. firms that developed and sold hair care products to African-American customers, L'Oréal gained knowledge on what is referred to in the industry as "ethnic hair care." It then took this knowledge and built a new ethnic hair care division in Europe and later began making inroads in African markets. More generally, research suggests that overseas expansion leads to valuable learning at home. One study found that, rather than distracting the firm in its efforts in its home market, overseas acquisitions led to substantial performance improvements, an average of a 12 percent increase, in home markets.[20]

reverse innovation
new products developed by developed-country multinational firms for emerging markets that have adequate functionality at a low cost.

Explore Reverse Innovation Finally, *exploring possibilities for* **reverse innovation** has become a major motivation for international expansion. Many leading companies are discovering that developing products specifically for emerging markets can pay off in a big way. In the past, multinational companies typically developed products for their rich home markets and then tried to sell them in developing countries with minor adaptations. However, as growth slows in rich nations and demand grows rapidly in developing countries such as India and China, this approach becomes increasingly inadequate. Instead, companies like GE have committed significant resources to developing products that meet the needs of developing nations, products that deliver adequate functionality at a fraction of the cost. Interestingly, these products have subsequently found considerable success in value segments in wealthy countries as well. Hence, this process is referred to as reverse innovation, a new motivation for international expansion.

7.2 STRATEGY SPOTLIGHT

REVERSE INNOVATION: HOW DEVELOPING COUNTRIES ARE BECOMING HOTBEDS OF INNOVATION

A number of firms have seen the need to develop technologies and products that are appropriate to developing markets, only to find that these innovations are valuable in their home markets as well. Here are a few examples of firms that have leveraged or are striving to leverage "reverse innovation."

- GE Healthcare developed a portable, inexpensive ultrasound device, called the Vscan, in China. This device cost one-tenth what a full-scale ultrasound device would cost in the United States. The product is a hit in China as well as in other developing markets. GE also sees tremendous potential for the product in developed markets. The main unit of the device is small enough and cheap enough to put one in the pocket of every physician, paramedic, and emergency room nurse. GE's vision is to have the Vscan become as indispensable as the stethoscope as a diagnostic tool.

- Moline, Illinois–based Deere & Co. opened a center in Pune, India, almost a decade ago with the intention to penetrate the Indian market. Deere, a firm known for its heavy-duty farm equipment and big construction gear, used the Pune facility to design four no-frills models. Though lacking first-world features like GPS and air conditioning, they were sturdy enough to handle the rigors of commercial farming. The tractors cost as little as $7,000, compared to over $300,000 for a fully loaded 8360R tractor in the United States. Subsequently, Deere targeted a segment of the home market that it had previously largely ignored—hobbyists as well as bargain hunters. These buyers do not care for advanced features but covet the same qualities as Indian farmers: affordability and maneuverability. Today, half of the no-frills models that Deere produces in India are exported to other countries.

- The potential even exists in service industries. Walmart developed "small mart stores" to meet the needs of customers in Argentina, Brazil, and Mexico but is now transferring this idea back to the United States to compete in areas, such as urban markets, where a full-size Walmart is not workable.

- PepsiCo is now seeing potential with this model. It built a global innovation center in India in 2010 and hopes to develop products and packaging that will meet the needs of the Indian market and other markets as well.

Sources: Frugal ideas are spreading from East to West. 2012. *The Economist,* March 24: 68; and Singh, S. & Nagarajan, G. 2011. Small is beautiful for John Deere. *Bloomberg Businessweek,* September 26: 33–34.

As $3,000 cars, $300 computers, and $30 mobile phones bring what were previously considered as luxuries within the reach of the middle class of emerging markets, it is important to understand the motivations and implications of reverse innovation. *First,* it is impossible to sell first-world versions of products with minor adaptations in countries where the average annual income per person is between $1,000 and $4,000, as is the case in most developing countries. To sell in these markets, entirely new products must be designed and developed by local technical talent and manufactured with local components. *Second,* although these countries are relatively poor, they are growing rapidly. *Third,* if the innovation does not come from first-world multinationals, there are any number of local firms that are ready to grab the market with low-cost products. *Fourth,* as the consumers and governments of many first-world countries are rediscovering the virtues of frugality and are trying to cut down expenses, these products and services originally developed for the first world may gain significant market shares in developing countries as well.

Strategy Spotlight 7.2 describes some examples of reverse innovation.

Potential Risks of International Expansion

When a company expands its international operations, it does so to increase its profits or revenues. As with any other investment, however, there are also potential risks.[21] To help companies assess the risk of entering foreign markets, rating systems have been developed to evaluate political and economic, as well as financial and credit, risks.[22] *Euromoney* magazine publishes a semiannual "Country Risk Rating" that evaluates political, economic, and other risks that entrants potentially face.[23] Exhibit 7.3 presents a sample of country risk ratings, published by AM Best. Note that the overall ratings range from 1 to 5, with higher risk receiving the higher score.

EXHIBIT 7.3 A Sample of Country Risk Ratings, August 2014

Country Score	Overall Country Rating	Economic Risk	Political Risk	Financial System Risk
Norway	1	1	1	1
Canada	1	1	1	1
United States	1	1	1	1
Singapore	1	2	1	1
Hong Kong	2	2	1	1
South Korea	2	1	2	2
South Africa	3	3	3	2
China	3	2	3	3
Bahrain	3	3	4	3
Kazakhstan	4	3	4	4
Colombia	4	3	4	4
Russia	4	3	4	4
Argentina	5	4	4	5
Libya	5	5	5	5

Source: A.M. Best Company - Used by permission.

Next we will discuss the four main types of risk: political risk, economic risk, currency risk, and management risk.

Political and Economic Risk Generally speaking, the business climate in the United States is very favorable. However, some countries around the globe may be hazardous to the health of corporate initiatives because of **political risk**.[24] Forces such as social unrest, military turmoil, demonstrations, and even violent conflict and terrorism can pose serious threats.[25] Consider, for example, the ongoing tension and violence in the Middle East associated with the revolutions and civil wars in Egypt, Libya, Syria, and other countries. Such conditions increase the likelihood of destruction of property and disruption of operations as well as nonpayment for goods and services. Thus, countries that are viewed as high risk are less attractive for most types of business.[26]

political risk
potential threat to a firm's operations in a country due to ineffectiveness of the domestic political system.

Another source of political risk in many countries is the absence of the **rule of law.** The absence of rules or the lack of uniform enforcement of existing rules leads to what might often seem to be arbitrary and inconsistent decisions by government officials. This can make it difficult for foreign firms to conduct business.

rule of law
a characteristic of legal systems where by behavior is governed by rules that are uniformly enforced.

For example, consider Renault's experience in Russia. Renault paid $1 billion to acquire a 25 percent ownership stake in the Russian automaker AvtoVAZ in 2008. Just one year later, Russian Prime Minister Vladimir Putin threatened to dilute Renault's ownership stake unless it contributed more money to prop up AvtoVAZ, which was then experiencing a significant slide in sales. Renault realized its ownership claim may not have held up in the corrupt Russian court system. Therefore, it was forced to negotiate and eventually agreed to transfer over $300 million in technology and expertise to the Russian firm to ensure its ownership stake would stay at 25 percent.[27]

Interestingly, while corporations have historically been concerned about rule-of-law issues in developing markets, such issues have also become a significant concern in developed markets, most critically in the United States. In a 2012 World Economic Forum Global Competitive Report that examined the quality of governmental institutions and the rule of law, the United

States fared poorly. Starkly, the United States was ranked among the top 20 countries on only 1 of the 22 measures of institutional quality the survey included. In line with these findings, the International Finance Corporation (IFC) found that governmental hurdles businesses face have become a greater challenge in the U.S. in recent years. The IFC compiles data annually on the burdens of doing business that are put in place by governments and found that the U.S. is one of only a few countries surveyed in which doing business has become more burdensome. In nearly 90 percent of countries, governmental burdens have eased since 2006, but the U.S. has bucked that trend and become a more difficult location in which to operate. As institutions deteriorate, the U.S. loses its luster as a place to base operations. This sentiment was reflected in a survey of business executives who are alumni of the Harvard Business School. When asked whether they had recently favored basing new operations in the U.S. or in a foreign location, an overwhelming majority, 84 percent, responded that they had chosen the foreign location. Thus, advanced economies, such as the U.S., risk losing out to other countries if they fail to reinforce and strengthen their legal and political institutions.[28]

The laws, and the enforcement of laws, associated with the protection of intellectual property rights can be a major potential **economic risk** in entering new countries.[29] Microsoft, for example, has lost billions of dollars in potential revenue through piracy of its software products in many countries, including China. Other areas of the globe, such as the former Soviet Union and some eastern European nations, have piracy problems as well.[30] Firms rich in intellectual property have encountered financial losses as imitations of their products have grown due to a lack of law enforcement of intellectual property rights.[31]

Counterfeiting, a direct form of theft of intellectual property rights, is a significant and growing problem. The International Chamber of Commerce estimated that the value of counterfeit goods will exceed $1.7 trillion in 2015. "The whole business has just exploded," said Jeffrey Hardy, head of the anticounterfeiting program at ICC. "And it goes way beyond music and Gucci bags." Counterfeiting has moved well beyond handbags and shoes to include chemicals, pharmaceuticals, and aircraft parts. According to a University of Florida study, 25 percent of the pesticide market in some parts of Europe is estimated to be counterfeit. This is especially troubling since these chemicals are often toxic.[32] In Strategy Spotlight 7.3, we discuss the challenge of fighting counterfeiting in the pharmaceutical business and how Pfizer is attempting to fight this threat to its business.

Currency Risks Currency fluctuations can pose substantial risks. A company with operations in several countries must constantly monitor the exchange rate between its own currency and that of the host country to minimize **currency risks.** Even a small change in the exchange rate can result in a significant difference in the cost of production or net profit when doing business overseas. When the U.S. dollar appreciates against other currencies, for example, U.S. goods can be more expensive to consumers in foreign countries. At the same time, however, appreciation of the U.S. dollar can have negative implications for American companies that have branch operations overseas. The reason for this is that profits from abroad must be exchanged for dollars at a more expensive rate of exchange, reducing the amount of profit when measured in dollars. For example, consider an American firm doing business in Italy. If this firm had a 20 percent profit in euros at its Italian center of operations, this profit would be totally wiped out when converted into U.S. dollars if the euro had depreciated 20 percent against the U.S. dollar. (U.S. multinationals typically engage in sophisticated "hedging strategies" to minimize currency risk. The discussion of this is beyond the scope of this section.)

Below, we discuss how Israel's strong currency—the shekel—forced a firm to reevaluate its strategy.

> For years O.R.T. Technologies resisted moving any operations outside Israel. However, when faced with a sharp rise in the value of the shekel, the maker of specialized software for managing gas stations froze all local hiring and decided to transfer some

> **economic risk**
> potential threat to a firm's operations in a country due to economic policies and conditions, including property rights laws and enforcement of those laws.

> **counterfeiting**
> selling of trademarked goods without the consent of the trademark holder.

> **currency risk**
> potential threat to a firm's operations in a country due to fluctuations in the local currency's exchange rate.

7.3 STRATEGY SPOTLIGHT — ETHICS

COUNTERFEIT DRUGS: A DANGEROUS AND GROWING PROBLEM

Brian Donnelly has an interesting background. He's both a cop and a pharmacist. He worked as a special agent for the FBI for 21 years, but he also has a PhD in pharmacology. Now he's on the front lines of an important fight: keeping counterfeit drugs from the market. He works as an investigator for Pfizer, one of the world's largest pharmaceutical companies, putting both his pharmacology and law enforcement skills at work to blunt the growing flow of counterfeit drugs. He is one of a small army of former law enforcement officers employed by the pharmaceutical companies working for the same aim.

This is an important fight for two reasons. First, it is of economic consequence for the pharmaceutical companies. Counterfeit drugs are big business. In the United States alone, counterfeit drugs generated around $75 billion in revenue in 2010. They are enticing to customers. For example, while Pfizer's erectile dysfunction pill, Viagra, sells for $15 per tablet, fake versions sold online can be gotten for as little as $1 a pill. The sales of counterfeit drugs cut into the sales and profits of Pfizer and the other pharmaceutical firms. Second and more importantly, these fake drugs are potentially dangerous. The danger comes from both what they contain and what they don't contain. Fake pills have been found to contain chalk, brick dust, paint, and even pesticides. Thus, they may be toxic, and ingesting them may cause significant health problems. On the other side, they may not contain the correct dose or even any of the active ingredients they are supposed to have. This may lead to severe health consequences. For example, fake Zithromax, an antibiotic, may contain none of the necessary chemical components, leaving the patient unable to fight the infection. According to one estimate, counterfeit drugs contribute to the death of upward of 100,000 people a year globally.

The pharmaceutical firms are fighting back with Donnelly and his colleagues. They use a common law enforcement technique. The fake drugs are sold by local dealers in the United States, who typically sell through websites, such as hardtofindrx.com and even Craigslist. These local dealers, called drop dealers, are the easiest to catch. From there, the investigators try to gain information on the major dealers from whom the drop dealers order. If they can get to these folks, they try to take it back to the kingpins manufacturing the drugs. This typically takes them through multiple law enforcement agencies in multiple countries, often back to manufacturing plants in China and India. To find the source, the pharmaceutical companies also use advanced technology. They determine the chemical composition of fake drugs they seize to search for common chemical signatures that point to the possible sourcing plant.

Pfizer is also fighting the fight from another angle. It is now tagging every bottle of Viagra and many other pharmaceuticals with radio-frequency identification (RFID) tags. Pharmacies can read these tags and input the data into Pfizer's system to confirm that these bottles are legitimate Pfizer drugs. This won't stop shady websites from delivering counterfeit drugs, but it will help keep the counterfeits out of legitimate pharmacies.

Sources: O'Connor, M. 2006. Pfizer using RFID to fight fake Viagra. *RFIDjournal.com*, January 6: np; and Gillette, F. 2013. Inside Pfizer's fight against counterfeit drugs. *Bloomberg Businessweek*, January 17: np.

---

developmental work to Eastern Europe. Laments CEO Alex Milner, "I never thought I'd see the day when we would have to move R&D outside of Israel, but the strong shekel has forced us to do so."[33]

Management Risks Management risks may be considered the challenges and risks that managers face when they must respond to the inevitable differences that they encounter in foreign markets. These take a variety of forms: culture, customs, language, income levels, customer preferences, distribution systems, and so on.[34] As we will note later in the chapter, even in the case of apparently standard products, some degree of local adaptation will become necessary.[35]

Differences in cultures across countries can also pose unique challenges for managers.[36] Cultural symbols can evoke deep feelings.[37] For example, in a series of advertisements aimed at Italian vacationers, Coca-Cola executives turned the Eiffel Tower, Empire State Building, and Tower of Pisa into the familiar Coke bottle. So far, so good. However, when the white marble columns of the Parthenon that crowns the Acropolis in Athens were turned into Coke bottles, the Greeks became outraged. Why? Greeks refer to the Acropolis as the "holy rock," and a government official said the Parthenon is an "international symbol of excellence" and that "whoever insults the Parthenon insults international culture." Coca-Cola apologized. Below are some cultural tips for conducting business in HongKong:

- Handshakes when greeting and before leaving are customary.
- After the initial handshake, business cards are presented with both hands on the card. Carefully read the card before putting it away.

---

management risk
potential threat to a firm's operations in a country due to the problems that managers have making decisions in the context of foreign markets.

- In Hong Kong, Chinese people should be addressed by their professional title (or Mr., Mrs., Miss) followed by their surname.
- Appointments should be made as far in advance as possible.
- Punctuality is very important and demonstrates respect.
- Negotiations in Hong Kong are normally very slow, with much attention to detail. The same negotiating team should be kept throughout the proceedings.
- Tea will be served during the negotiations. Always accept and wait for the host to begin drinking before you partake.
- Be aware that "yes" may just be an indication that the person heard you rather than indicating agreement. A Hong Kong Chinese businessperson will have a difficult time saying "no" directly.

Below, we discuss a rather humorous example of how a local custom can affect operations at a manufacturing plant in Singapore.

> Larry Henderson, plant manager, and John Lichthental, manager of human resources, were faced with a rather unique problem. They were assigned by Celanese Chemical Corp. to build a plant in Singapore, and the plant was completed in July. However, according to local custom, a plant should be christened only on "lucky" days. Unfortunately, the next lucky day was not until September 3.
>
> The managers had to convince executives at Celanese's Dallas headquarters to delay the plant opening. As one might expect, it wasn't easy. But after many heated telephone conversations and flaming emails, the president agreed to open the new plant on a lucky day—September 3.[38]

In the nearby Insights from Executives box, Terrie Campbell, a senior executive at Ricoh Americas, offers further thoughts on the opportunities and risks for multinational firms.

Global Dispersion of Value Chains: Outsourcing and Offshoring

A major recent trend has been the dispersion of the value chains of multinational corporations across different countries; that is, the various activities that constitute the value chain of a firm are now spread across several countries and continents. Such dispersion of value occurs mainly through increasing offshoring and outsourcing.

A report issued by the World Trade Organization described the production of a particular U.S. car as follows: "30 percent of the car's value goes to Korea for assembly, 17.5 percent to Japan for components and advanced technology, 7.5 percent to Germany for design, 4 percent to Taiwan and Singapore for minor parts, 2.5 percent to U.K. for advertising and marketing services, and 1.5 percent to Ireland and Barbados for data processing. This means that only 37 percent of the production value is generated in the U.S."[39] In today's economy, we are increasingly witnessing two interrelated trends: outsourcing and offshoring.

Outsourcing occurs when a firm decides to utilize other firms to perform value-creating activities that were previously performed in-house.[40] It may be a new activity that the firm is perfectly capable of doing but chooses to have someone else perform for cost or quality reasons. Outsourcing can be to either a domestic or foreign firm.

Offshoring takes place when a firm decides to shift an activity that it was performing in a domestic location to a foreign location.[41] For example, both Microsoft and Intel now have R&D facilities in India, employing a large number of Indian scientists and engineers. Often, offshoring and outsourcing go together; that is, a firm may outsource an activity to a foreign supplier, thereby causing the work to be offshored as well.[42]

The recent explosion in the volume of outsourcing and offshoring is due to a variety of factors. Up until the 1960s, for most companies, the entire value chain was in one location. Further, the production took place close to where the customers were in order to keep transportation costs under control. In the case of service industries, it was generally believed that offshoring was not possible because the producer and consumer had to be

> **outsourcing**
> using other firms to perform value-creating activities that were previously performed in-house.
>
> **offshoring**
> shifting a value-creating activity from a domestic location to a foreign location.

7.1 INSIGHTS FROM EXECUTIVES

TERRIE CAMPBELL, VICE PRESIDENT OF STRATEGIC MARKETING AT RICOH AMERICAS CORPORATION

BIOSKETCH

Terrie Campbell serves as vice president of strategic marketing for Ricoh Americas Corporation. In this role, she is responsible for the strategy, direction, and execution of Ricoh's Managed Document Services approach, as well as key vertical marketing strategies and programs, for both direct and dealer channels. Campbell is also the global lead for the development of tools and processes to ensure consistent execution of Ricoh Managed Document Services around the world. Prior to this appointment, Campbell served as vice president of Managed Document Services for Ricoh USA.

1. *Ricoh has significant international operations. What do you see as some of the primary opportunities and threats in global expansion?*

   Opportunities are primarily found in the area of being able to leverage our global footprint and support customers that want a level of consistency from region to region. We also find that by having such a significant number of locations and customers, we are very well positioned to understand the best practices, benchmarks, and trends that help us continue to innovate and find new ways to solve our customer problems. With such a large network of resources, there are very few issues or challenges in our space that we have not addressed somewhere in our organization before.

   The challenges include regional culture differences and time-zone management when trying to collaborate via conference calls or video. There are also limitations on what our systems are allowed to pass from region to region due to legislation and regional regulations. There is also the dynamic that as an organization, a significant portion of our growth came through acquisitions, which may create headwind from assimilation issues. For our model to work, we have also embraced a distributor model in some of our noncore markets. This brings us a high degree of flexibility to meet our customer needs, but it also adds a new level of oversight to ensure consistency in the delivery of services and support. The biggest challenge is around the ability of systems to speak to one another when translation and currency conversions are needed. The reality is that it requires a lot of heavy lifting to get a global view of business when you take these issues into consideration.

2. *What are some of the challenges associated with adapting your marketing strategies to local tastes and cultures?*

   Different words have different meanings from region to region. It is critical to define the vision first for the organization and then allow the resources that best understand the regional connotation to edit for final copy. The risk, when this happens, is that the message may lose some of the nuance that brings "punch" to the story. Getting everyone to understand the intent of the message must be the first order of business. You will often find that an entirely different approach is needed in a region, but given flexibility, it will achieve even stronger alignment and customer engagement.

   Another challenge that is fairly typical is that the "not invented here" mentality may set in when one region proposes an idea across the globe. There is no question that the passion for an idea is typically going to lie with the originator; as a result, it may be difficult for that person to understand or accept resistance from another region when that region does not feel the same passion for the idea or concept. It may turn into a long, emotional battle of wills if the other region believes it has a superior idea, concept, or current way of operating. This is often a surprise to a person new to global marketing or communications. The key to success is to ensure that the key stakeholders have a voice in the process early and can see their "fingerprints" on the finished idea. The time invested in the up-front collaboration and engagement is well worth your effort to ensure adoption and success.

3. *How does Ricoh facilitate the transmission of knowledge and learning from one market to another?*

   Facilitation of learning across markets begins with a strong best-practice collection and development process. Additionally, tools to enable the organization to share wins and learning that may be part of an innovation process ensure that new ideas and successes are formalized and shared. Once an idea is defined as a repeatable solution or process, then leveraging field deployment teams and training tools will instill knowledge, manage testing, and report certifications. These tools will include online, self-paced courses, classroom courses, and facilitator-led, manager-led, or virtual-classroom options. There is also the need to proliferate casual or "tribal" knowledge, which can be facilitated through social platforms or knowledge libraries that provide access to the appropriate employees.

4. *What are some of the human resource management challenges and opportunities with regard to Ricoh's different international operations?*

   As a global company, it would be ideal to have all employees in common job descriptions, with common pay grades, incentives, and so on. The idea is great, but the fact is that with local competition for talent and local pay practices, regional variation is required in these areas. Additionally, the job title in one region may not make sense at all in another. We do seek to have relevant technical certifications and cross-leverage training to ensure consistency where possible in knowledge, but how the roles are managed from a human resource perspective requires local direction. We also find that unemployment is different across the operations so turnover dynamics are not the same, and that has an impact on the cost of doing business in an area. We are fortunate to have strong alignment of the human resource leadership across the regions so best practices are shared to take advantage of them where possible.

---

present at the same place at the same time. After all, a haircut could not be performed if the barber and the client were separated!

For manufacturing industries, the rapid decline in transportation and coordination costs has enabled firms to disperse their value chains over different locations. For example, Nike's R&D takes place in the U.S., raw materials are procured from a multitude of countries, actual manufacturing takes place in China, Indonesia, or Vietnam, advertising is produced in the U.S., and sales and service take place in practically all the countries. Each value-creating activity is performed in the location where the cost is the lowest or the quality is the best. Without finding optimal locations for each activity, Nike could not have attained its position as the world's largest shoe company.

The experience of the manufacturing sector was also repeated in the service sector by the mid-1990s. A trend that began with the outsourcing of low-level programming and data entry work to countries such as India and Ireland suddenly grew manyfold, encompassing a variety of white-collar and professional activities ranging from call centers to R&D.

Bangalore, India, in recent years, has emerged as a location where more and more U.S. tax returns are prepared. In India, U.S.-trained and licensed radiologists interpret chest X-rays and CT scans from U.S. hospitals for half the cost. The advantages from offshoring go beyond mere cost savings today. In many specialized occupations in science and engineering, there is a shortage of qualified professionals in developed countries, whereas countries like India, China, and Singapore have what seems like an inexhaustible supply.[43]

While offshoring offers the potential to cut costs in corporations across a wide range of industries, many firms are finding the benefits of offshoring to be more elusive and the costs greater than they anticipated.[44] A study by AMR Research found that 56 percent of companies moving production offshore experienced an increase in total costs, contrary to their expectations of cost savings. In a more focused study, 70 percent of managers said sourcing in China is more costly than they initially estimated.

The cause of this contrary outcome is actually not all that surprising. Common savings from offshoring, such as lower wages, benefits, energy costs, regulatory costs, and taxes, are all easily visible and immediate. In contrast, there are a host of hidden costs that arise over time and often overwhelm the cost savings of offshoring. These hidden costs include:

- ***Total wage costs.*** Labor cost per hour may be significantly lower in developing markets, but this may not translate into lower overall costs. If workers in these markets are less productive or less skilled, firms end up with a higher number of hours needed to produce the same quantity of product. This necessitates hiring more workers and having employees work longer hours.
- ***Indirect costs.*** In addition to higher labor costs, there are also a number of indirect costs that pop up. If there are problems with the skill level of workers, the firm will find the need for more training and supervision of workers, more raw material and greater scrap due to the lower skill level, and greater rework to fix quality problems. The firm may also experience greater need for security staff in its facilities.
- ***Increased inventory.*** Due to the longer delivery times, firms often need to tie up more capital in work in progress and inventory.

7.4 STRATEGY SPOTLIGHT

RESHORING OPERATIONS: OTIS STRUGGLES TO LIFT ITS U.S. MANUFACTURING OFF THE GROUND

United Technologies Corporation has found that reshoring manufacturing to the United States is a very challenging experience. In late 2012, the firm announced with great fanfare that it would relocate an Otis elevator plant from Mexico to South Carolina. The relocation was seen both as a boon to the community, since it would generate nearly 400 good-paying jobs, and as another signal of the renaissance of American manufacturing. For Otis, the move promised to save the firm money, streamline operations, and speed up order fulfillment by bringing manufacturing closer to customers and locating manufacturing right next to the engineering staff. The firm anticipated seeing a 17 percent reduction in freight and logistics costs and a 20 percent efficiency gain by co-locating all staff involved in elevator design and manufacturing.

However, it has proved to be a challenging transition. Due to production delays as Otis ramped up U.S. production, a large backlog in orders arose. Some customers canceled their orders after waiting months for delivery. Otis was forced to keep its Nogales, Mexico, plant open six months longer than it had anticipated due to delays in ramping up the manufacturing unit in South Carolina. All totaled, the problems led to a $60 million hit to Otis's bottom line in 2013 and continued to weigh on earnings through the first half of 2014.

The key challenge Otis faced was constructing the skilled labor pool it needed. Although the firm transferred some workers from operations in Arizona and Indiana, it had difficulty finding skilled manufacturing workers in South Carolina. Florence, South Carolina, the town Otis moved to, had a long history of being a manufacturing town but saw its manufacturing base decline rapidly in the 1980s and 1990s. It is a geographically attractive location, with available manufacturing sites and easy access to rail and port locations. As a result, Otis was able to move into an empty facility that used to house a Maytag plant. However, Otis found that the current manufacturing systems required higher technology-based skills than those in the past and that the skill set of the region's workers was not up to the demands of the job.

In the words of Robert McDonough, COO of the business unit that includes Otis, "I think we failed on both the planning and the execution side." To address these issues, Otis brought in new leadership for its North American operations. At the plant level, Otis brought in additional workers and invested in greater training than it had anticipated. Otis is still committed to the Florence plant and has brought the backlog down, but its experience does highlight some of the challenges firms face as they bring manufacturing operations back to the U.S.

Sources: Mann, T. 2014. Otis finds reshoring manufacturing is not easy. *wsj.com*, May 2: np; and Anonymous. 2014. Supply chain news: When it comes to reshoring, detailed planning and expectation setting is key, Otis elevators learns the hard way. *scdigest.com*, May 5: np.

- ***Reduced market responsiveness.*** The long supply lines from low-cost countries may leave firms less responsive to shifts in customer demands. This may damage their brand image and also increase product obsolescence costs, as they may have to scrap or sell at a steep discount products that fail to meet quickly changing technology standards or customer tastes.
- ***Coordination costs.*** Coordinating product development and manufacturing can be difficult with operations undertaking different tasks in different countries. This may hamper innovation. It may also trigger unexpected costs, such as paying overtime in some markets so that staff across multiple time zones can meet to coordinate their activities.
- ***Intellectual property rights.*** Firms operating in countries with weak IP protection can wind up losing their trade secrets or taking costly measures to protect these secrets.
- ***Wage inflation.*** In moving overseas, firms often assume some level of wage stability, but wages in developing markets can be volatile and spike dramatically. For example, minimum wages set by provinces in China increased at an average of 18 percent per year in the 2010–2014 period.[45] As Roger Meiners, chairman of the Department of Economics at the University of Texas at Arlington, stated, "The U.S. is more competitive on a wage basis because average wages have come down, especially for entry-level workers, and wages in China have been increasing."

Firms need to take into account all of these costs in determining whether or not to move their operations offshore. Strategy Spotlight 7.4 discusses the experience Otis, the elevator manufacturer, had when it decided to "reshore" its manufacturing.

Achieving Competitive Advantage in Global Markets

>LO7.4
>The two opposing forces—cost reduction and adaptation to local markets—that firms face when entering international markets.

We now discuss the two opposing forces that firms face when they expand into global markets: cost reduction and adaptation to local markets. Then we address the four basic types of international strategies that they may pursue: international, global, multidomestic, and transnational. The selection of one of these four types of strategies is largely dependent on a firm's relative pressure to address each of the two forces.

Two Opposing Pressures: Reducing Costs and Adapting to Local Markets

Many years ago, the famed marketing strategist Theodore Levitt advocated strategies that favored global products and brands. He suggested that firms should standardize all of their products and services for all of their worldwide markets. Such an approach would help a firm lower its overall costs by spreading its investments over as large a market as possible. Levitt's approach rested on three key assumptions:

1. Customer needs and interests are becoming increasingly homogeneous worldwide.
2. People around the world are willing to sacrifice preferences in product features, functions, design, and the like for lower prices at high quality.
3. Substantial economies of scale in production and marketing can be achieved through supplying global markets.[46]

However, there is ample evidence to refute these assumptions.[47] Regarding the first assumption—the increasing worldwide homogeneity of customer needs and interests—consider the number of product markets, ranging from watches and handbags to soft drinks and fast foods. Companies have identified global customer segments and developed global products and brands targeted to those segments. Also, many other companies adapt lines to idiosyncratic country preferences and develop local brands targeted to local market segments. For example, Nestlé's line of pizzas marketed in the United Kingdom includes cheese with ham and pineapple topping on a French bread crust. Similarly, Coca-Cola in Japan markets Georgia (a tonic drink) as well as Classic Coke and Hi-C.

Consider the second assumption—the sacrifice of product attributes for lower prices. While there is invariably a price-sensitive segment in many product markets, there is no indication that this is increasing. In contrast, in many product and service markets—ranging from watches, personal computers, and household appliances to banking and insurance—there is a growing interest in multiple product features, product quality, and service.

Finally, the third assumption is that significant economies of scale in production and marketing could be achieved for global products and services. Although standardization may lower manufacturing costs, such a perspective does not consider three critical and interrelated points. First, as we discussed in Chapter 5, technological developments in flexible factory automation enable economies of scale to be attained at lower levels of output and do not require production of a single standardized product. Second, the cost of production is only one component, and often not the critical one, in determining the total cost of a product. Third, a firm's strategy should not be product-driven. It should also consider other activities in the firm's value chain, such as marketing, sales, and distribution.

Based on the above, we would have a hard time arguing that it is wise to develop the same product or service for all markets throughout the world. While there are some exceptions, such as Boeing airplanes and some of Coca-Cola's soft-drink products, managers

EXHIBIT 7.4 Opposing Pressures and Four Strategies

	Pressures for Local Adaptation	
Pressures to Lower Costs High	Global strategy	Transnational strategy
Low	International strategy	Multidomestic strategy
	Low	High

must also strive to tailor their products to the culture of the country in which they are attempting to do business. Few would argue that "one size fits all" generally applies.

The opposing pressures that managers face place conflicting demands on firms as they strive to be competitive.[48] On the one hand, competitive pressures require that firms do what they can to *lower unit costs* so that consumers will not perceive their product and service offerings as too expensive. This may lead them to consider locating manufacturing facilities where labor costs are low and developing products that are highly standardized across multiple countries.

In addition to responding to pressures to lower costs, managers must strive to be *responsive to local pressures* in order to tailor their products to the demand of the local market in which they do business. This requires differentiating their offerings and strategies from country to country to reflect consumer tastes and preferences and making changes to reflect differences in distribution channels, human resource practices, and governmental regulations. However, since the strategies and tactics to differentiate products and services to local markets can involve additional expenses, a firm's costs will tend to rise.

The two opposing pressures result in four different basic strategies that companies can use to compete in the global marketplace: international, global, multidomestic, and transnational. The strategy that a firm selects depends on the degree of pressure that it is facing for cost reductions and the importance of adapting to local markets. Exhibit 7.4 shows the conditions under which each of these strategies would be most appropriate.

It is important to note that we consider these four strategies to be "basic" or "pure"; that is, in practice, all firms will tend to have some elements of each strategy.

LO7.5

The advantages and disadvantages associated with each of the four basic strategies: international, global, multidomestic, and transnational.

International Strategy

There are a small number of industries in which pressures for both local adaptation and lowering costs are rather low. An extreme example of such an industry is the "orphan" drug industry. These are medicines for diseases that are severe but affect only a small number of people. Diseases such as Gaucher disease and Fabry disease fit into this category. Companies such as Genzyme and Oxford GlycoSciences are active in this segment of the drug industry. There is virtually no need to adapt their products to the local markets. And the pressures to reduce costs are low; even though only a few thousand patients are affected, the revenues and margins are significant, because patients are charged up to $100,000 per year.

An **international strategy** is based on diffusion and adaptation of the parent company's knowledge and expertise to foreign markets. Country units are allowed to make some minor adaptations to products and ideas coming from the head office, but they have far less independence and autonomy compared to multidomestic companies. The primary goal of the strategy is worldwide exploitation of the parent firm's knowledge and capabilities. All sources of core competencies are centralized.

The majority of large U.S. multinationals pursued the international strategy in the decades following World War II. These companies centralized R&D and product development but established manufacturing facilities as well as marketing organizations abroad. Companies such as McDonald's and Kellogg are examples of firms following such a strategy. Although these companies do make some local adaptations, they are of a very limited nature. With increasing pressures to reduce costs due to global competition, especially from low-cost countries, opportunities to successfully employ an international strategy are becoming more limited. This strategy is most suitable in situations where a firm has distinctive competencies that local companies in foreign markets lack.

> **international strategy**
> a strategy based on firms' diffusion and adaptation of the parent companies' knowledge and expertise to foreign markets; used in industries where the pressures for both local adaptation and lowering costs are low.

Risks and Challenges Below are some of the risks and challenges associated with an international strategy.

- Different activities in the value chain typically have different optimal locations. That is, R&D may be optimally located in a country with an abundant supply of scientists and engineers, whereas assembly may be better conducted in a low-cost location. Nike, for example, designs its shoes in the United States, but all the manufacturing is done in countries like China or Thailand. The international strategy, with its tendency to concentrate most of its activities in one location, fails to take advantage of the benefits of an optimally distributed value chain.
- The lack of local responsiveness may result in the alienation of local customers. Worse still, the firm's inability to be receptive to new ideas and innovation from its foreign subsidiaries may lead to missed opportunities.

Exhibit 7.5 summarizes the strengths and limitations of international strategies in the global marketplace.

Global Strategy

As indicated in Exhibit 7.4, a firm whose emphasis is on lowering costs tends to follow a **global strategy.** Competitive strategy is centralized and controlled to a large extent by the corporate office. Since the primary emphasis is on controlling costs, the corporate office strives to achieve a strong level of coordination and integration across the various businesses.[49] Firms following a global strategy strive to offer standardized products and services as well as to locate manufacturing, R&D, and marketing activities in only a few locations.[50]

A global strategy emphasizes economies of scale due to the standardization of products and services and the centralization of operations in a few locations. As such, one advantage may be that innovations that come about through efforts of either a business unit or the

> **global strategy**
> a strategy based on firms' centralization and control by the corporate office, with the primary emphasis on controlling costs; used in industries where the pressure for local adaptation is low and the pressure for lowering costs is high.

EXHIBIT 7.5 Strengths and Limitations of International Strategies in the Global Marketplace

Strengths	Limitations
• Leverage and diffusion of a parent firm's knowledge and core competencies. • Lower costs because of less need to tailor products and services.	• Limited ability to adapt to local markets. • Inability to take advantage of new ideas and innovations occurring in local markets.

corporate office can be transferred more easily to other locations. Although costs may be lower, the firm following a global strategy may, in general, have to forgo opportunities for revenue growth since it does not invest extensive resources in adapting product offerings from one market to another.

A global strategy is most appropriate when there are strong pressures for reducing costs and comparatively weak pressures for adaptation to local markets. Economies of scale become an important consideration.[51] Advantages to increased volume may come from larger production plants or runs as well as from more efficient logistics and distribution networks. Worldwide volume is also especially important in supporting high levels of investment in research and development. As we would expect, many industries requiring high levels of R&D, such as pharmaceuticals, semiconductors, and jet aircraft, follow global strategies.

Another advantage of a global strategy is that it can enable a firm to create a standard level of quality throughout the world. Let's look at what Tom Siebel, former chairman of Siebel Systems (now part of Oracle), the $2 billion developer of e-business application software, said about global standardization:

> Our customers—global companies like IBM, Zurich Financial Services, and Citicorp—expect the same high level of service and quality, and the same licensing policies, no matter where we do business with them around the world. Our human resources and legal departments help us create policies that respect local cultures and requirements worldwide, while at the same time maintaining the highest standards. We have one brand, one image, one set of corporate colors, and one set of messages, across every place on the planet. An organization needs central quality control to avoid surprises.[52]

Risks and Challenges There are, of course, some risks associated with a global strategy:[53]

- A firm can enjoy scale economies only by concentrating scale-sensitive resources and activities in one or few locations. Such concentration, however, becomes a "double-edged sword." For example, if a firm has only one manufacturing facility, it must export its output (e.g., components, subsystems, or finished products) to other markets, some of which may be a great distance from the operation. Thus, decisions about locating facilities must weigh the potential benefits from concentrating operations in a single location against the higher transportation and tariff costs that result from such concentration.
- The geographic concentration of any activity may also tend to isolate that activity from the targeted markets. Such isolation may be risky since it may hamper the facility's ability to quickly respond to changes in market conditions and needs.
- Concentrating an activity in a single location also makes the rest of the firm dependent on that location. Such dependency implies that, unless the location has world-class competencies, the firm's competitive position can be eroded if problems arise. A European Ford executive, reflecting on the firm's concentration of activities during a global integration program in the mid-1990s, lamented, "Now if you misjudge the market, you are wrong in 15 countries rather than only one."

Exhibit 7.6 summarizes the strengths and limitations of global strategies.

EXHIBIT 7.6 Strengths and Limitations of Global Strategies

Strengths	Limitations
• Strong integration occurs across various businesses.	• Limited ability exists to adapt to local markets.
• Standardization leads to higher economies of scale, which lower costs.	• Concentration of activities may increase dependence on a single facility.
• Creation of uniform standards of quality throughout the world is facilitated.	• Single locations may lead to higher tariffs and transportation costs.

Multidomestic Strategy

According to Exhibit 7.4, a firm whose emphasis is on differentiating its product and service offerings to adapt to local markets follows a **multidomestic strategy**.[54] Decisions evolving from a multidomestic strategy tend to be decentralized to permit the firm to tailor its products and respond rapidly to changes in demand. This enables a firm to expand its market and to charge different prices in different markets. For firms following this strategy, differences in language, culture, income levels, customer preferences, and distribution systems are only a few of the many factors that must be considered. Even in the case of relatively standardized products, at least some level of local adaptation is often necessary.

> **multidomestic strategy**
> a strategy based on firms' differentiating their products and services to adapt to local markets; used in industries where the pressure for local adaptation is high and the pressure for lowering costs is low.

Consider, for example, the Oreo cookie.[55] Kraft has tailored the iconic cookie to better meet the tastes and preferences in different markets. For example, Kraft has created green tea Oreos in China, chocolate and peanut butter Oreos for Indonesia, and banana and dulce de leche Oreos for Argentina. Kraft has also lowered the sweetness of the cookie for China and reduced the bitterness of the cookie for India. The shape is also on the table for change. Kraft has even created wafer-stick-style Oreos.

Kraft has tailored other products to meet local market needs. For example, with its Tang drink product, it developed local flavors, such as a lime and cinnamon flavor for Mexico and mango Tang for the Philippines. It also looked to the nutritional needs in different countries. True to the heritage of the brand, Kraft has kept the theme that Tang is a good source of vitamin C. But in Brazil, where children often have iron deficiencies, it added iron as well as other vitamins and minerals. The local-focus strategy has worked well, with Tang's sales almost doubling in five years.

To meet the needs of local markets, companies need to go beyond just product designs. One of the simple ways firms have worked to meet market needs is by finding appropriate names for their products. For example, in China, the names of products imbue them with strong meanings and can be significant drivers of their success. As a result, firms have been careful with how they translate their brands. For example, Reebok became *Rui bu,* which means "quick steps." Lay's snack foods became *Le shi,* which means "happy things." And Coca-Cola's Chinese name, *Ke Kou Ke Le,* translates to "tasty fun."

Strategy Spotlight 7.5 discusses how Honda experienced challenges in moving fully to multidomestic operations and how it responded.

Risks and Challenges As you might expect, there are some risks associated with a multidomestic strategy. Among these are the following:

- Typically, local adaptation of products and services will increase a company's cost structure. In many industries, competition is so intense that most firms can ill afford any competitive disadvantages on the dimension of cost. A key challenge of managers is to determine the trade-off between local adaptation and its cost structure. For example, cost considerations led Procter & Gamble to standardize its diaper design across all European markets. This was done despite research data indicating that Italian mothers, unlike those in other countries, preferred diapers that covered the baby's navel. Later, however, P&G recognized that this feature was critical to these mothers, so the company decided to incorporate this feature for the Italian market despite its adverse cost implications.
- At times, local adaptations, even when well intentioned, may backfire. When the American restaurant chain TGI Fridays entered the South Korean market, it purposely incorporated many local dishes, such as kimchi (hot, spicy cabbage), in its menu. This responsiveness, however, was not well received. Company analysis of the weak market acceptance indicated that Korean customers anticipated a visit

7.5 STRATEGY SPOTLIGHT

HONDA ACTS TO IMPROVE ITS MARKET RESPONSIVENESS

Two attributes have set Honda apart in the automobile industry. First, it has always had outstanding engineering skills. Second, it has built an organization oriented to design and build cars that meet the needs of the markets in which it operates. Honda expanded its R&D and engineering staff globally and was the first automaker to create new models in the markets it served. For several decades, this had provided a basis for continued success in the market. But Honda's position took a downturn with the Great Recession of 2008. Honda saw its U.S. market share peak in 2009 at 11.1 percent and then fall to 9 percent by 2011. In the words of Ian Fletcher, senior analyst with IHS automotive, "Honda's management has lost its way somewhat. Over the past decade, they've lost track of what the fundamental basis of their business is and what appeal they hold on the market."

What led to this crisis? With its engineering-centered organizational culture, Honda had developed local engineering staffs but had never developed fully integrated operations in the North American market. Some R&D and engineering issues were initially handled solely with R&D staffs in the local market and then reviewed and approved in corporate headquarters in Japan before the decisions were communicated to the manufacturing and marketing staffs. This worked well until Honda faced market turbulence associated with the Great Recession and was unable to effectively coordinate engineering, manufacturing, and marketing to launch new models that met the evolving customer demands in a timely way.

Honda's answer was to change the organization's structure to better coordinate the functions in each region and to bring in new talent to raise the profile of the marketing staff in the company. First, the company created a seven-member North American regional operating board that includes key members from all of the major functional areas. The board was tasked with overseeing and coordinating the design process for new models to speed decision making and shorten time to market. At lower levels in the organization, instead of having engineering drive the initial stages of new product development, sales, manufacturing, engineering, and purchasing, associates now work as an integrated team and make decisions on their own. Second, Honda went outside and hired a new chief marketing officer for North American operations, tapping Mike Accavitti, a marketing executive from Chrysler. Honda signaled the importance of having a marketing perspective driving the design process by promoting him to senior vice president of automobile operations in North America.

The goal of all of these changes is to develop a more integrated operation in North America to allow Honda to be more responsive to local market needs and to be swifter in meeting ever-evolving market needs.

Sources: Reed, J. & Simon, B. 2012. Honda faces challenges in the U.S. market. *ft.com*, January 5: np; and Taylor, A. 2013. Honda gets its mojo back. *Fortune*, August 12: 68–72.

---

to TGI Fridays as a visit to America. Thus, finding Korean dishes was inconsistent with their expectations.

- The optimal degree of local adaptation evolves over time. In many industry segments, a variety of factors, such as the influence of global media, greater international travel, and declining income disparities across countries, may lead to increasing global standardization. On the other hand, in other industry segments, especially where the product or service can be delivered over the Internet (such as music), the need for even greater customization and local adaptation may increase over time. Firms must recalibrate the need for local adaptation on an ongoing basis; excessive adaptation extracts a price as surely as underadaptation.

Exhibit 7.7 summarizes the strengths and limitations of multidomestic strategies.

EXHIBIT 7.7 Strengths and Limitations of Multidomestic Strategies

Strengths	Limitations
• Ability to adapt products and services to local market conditions.	• Decreased ability to realize cost savings through scale economies.
• Ability to detect potential opportunities for attractive niches in a given market, enhancing revenue.	• Greater difficulty in transferring knowledge across countries.
	• Possibility of leading to "overadaptation" as conditions change.

Transnational Strategy

A **transnational strategy** strives to optimize the trade-offs associated with efficiency, local adaptation, and learning.[56] It seeks efficiency not for its own sake but as a means to achieve global competitiveness.[57] It recognizes the importance of local responsiveness as a tool for flexibility in international operations.[58] Innovations are regarded as an outcome of a larger process of organizational learning that includes the contributions of everyone in the firm.[59] Also, a core tenet of the transnational model is that a firm's assets and capabilities are dispersed according to the most beneficial location for each activity. Thus, managers avoid the tendency to either concentrate activities in a central location (a global strategy) or disperse them across many locations to enhance adaptation (a multidomestic strategy). Peter Brabeck, chairman of Nestlé, the giant food company, provides such a perspective:

> We believe strongly that there isn't a so-called global consumer, at least not when it comes to food and beverages. People have local tastes based on their unique cultures and traditions—a good candy bar in Brazil is not the same as a good candy bar in China. Therefore, decision making needs to be pushed down as low as possible in the organization, out close to the markets. Otherwise, how can you make good brand decisions? That said, decentralization has its limits. If you are too decentralized, you can become too complicated—you get too much complexity in your production system. The closer we come to the consumer, in branding, pricing, communication, and product adaptation, the more we decentralize. The more we are dealing with production, logistics, and supply-chain management, the more centralized decision making becomes. After all, we want to leverage Nestlé's size, not be hampered by it.[60]

The Nestlé example illustrates a common approach in determining whether or not to centralize or decentralize a value-chain activity. Typically, primary activities that are "downstream" (e.g., marketing and sales, and service), or closer to the customer, tend to require more decentralization in order to adapt to local market conditions. On the other hand, primary activities that are "upstream" (e.g., logistics and operations), or further away from the customer, tend to be centralized. This is because there is less need for adapting these activities to local markets and the firm can benefit from economies of scale. Additionally, many support activities, such as information systems and procurement, tend to be centralized in order to increase the potential for economies of scale.

A central philosophy of the transnational organization is enhanced adaptation to all competitive situations as well as flexibility by capitalizing on communication and knowledge flows throughout the organization.[61] A principal characteristic is the integration of unique contributions of all units into worldwide operations. Thus, a joint innovation by headquarters and by one of the overseas units can lead potentially to the development of relatively standardized and yet flexible products and services that are suitable for multiple markets. Strategy Spotlight 7.6 discusses how Panasonic benefited from moving from a global to a transnational strategy.

Risks and Challenges As with the other strategies, there are some unique risks and challenges associated with a transnational strategy:

- **The choice of a seemingly optimal location cannot guarantee that the quality and cost of factor inputs (i.e., labor, materials) will be optimal.** Managers must ensure that the relative advantage of a location is actually realized, not squandered because of weaknesses in productivity and the quality of internal operations. Ford Motor Co., for example, has benefited from having some of its manufacturing operations in Mexico. While some have argued that the benefits of lower wage rates will be partly offset by lower productivity, this does not always have to be the case. Since unemployment in Mexico is higher than in the United States, Ford

> **transnational strategy**
> a strategy based on firms' optimizing the trade-offs associated with efficiency, local adaptation, and learning; used in industries where the pressures for both local adaptation and lowering costs are high.

7.6 STRATEGY SPOTLIGHT

PANASONIC'S CHINA EXPERIENCE SHOWS THE BENEFITS OF BEING A TRANSNATIONAL

Panasonic moved into China in the late 1980s, seeing it as a low-cost region in which to manufacture its products. Traditionally, Panasonic had used a global strategy in its operations. It designed standardized products in Japan, manufactured them in low-cost markets, and sold its products primarily in developed markets. China simply served as a manufacturing location.

This worked well until the Chinese economy started to grow and mature. As the Chinese middle class began to emerge, local competitors, such as Haier, quickly jumped in with products designed for the Chinese market and outcompeted Panasonic in the growing market. This led Panasonic to radically change its way of competing in the global market.

Panasonic embraced the need to balance global integration with local adaptation. It set up a Lifestyle Research Center in China. In this center, marketing and product development staff compiled and interpreted data on customer wants and needs. Their charge was to uncover hidden needs in the Chinese market and design products to meet those needs. At the same time, country managers emphasized the need for the center staff to design products that benefited from global integration. For example, staff members were told to regularly work with engineers in Japan to ensure that product designs used standard global parts in the Panasonic system and also leveraged technologies being developed in Japan. Over time, this built trust with the Japanese engineers, who began to discuss how to draw on their knowledge to help design products that could be sold in other markets. Thus, knowledge flowed in both directions: from Japan to China and from China to Japan and, by extension, the rest of the world. The system has worked so well in China that Panasonic has expanded its policies and built lifestyle research centers in Europe and India.

There are five key elements of Panasonic's transnational initiatives. Each allows Panasonic to manage the tension for global integration and local adaptation.

- **Establish a dedicated unit.** One organization should be devoted to embracing the tension. The aim of Panasonic's China Lifestyle Research Center was to both understand Chinese consumers and draw on Panasonic Japan's R&D capabilities.
- **Create an on-the-ground mission.** The unit's mission should state explicitly how local adaptation and cross-border integration support company strategy. The lifestyle center's mission was "data interpretation," not just data collection, to ensure that insights led to viable product proposals that leveraged Panasonic's technology assets.
- **Develop core local staff.** The unit should develop local staff who can engage in both localization and integration activities. At the lifestyle center, each staff member spent a year getting training and extensive coaching in fieldwork and proposal writing for products that leverage Panasonic's technology to meet local needs.
- **Extend the reach.** The unit must constantly push to expand its influence. The lifestyle center's leader ratcheted up communication and interaction between the center and engineers at Panasonic's headquarters to broaden the organization's scope and influence.
- **Strengthen local authority.** Sufficient authority should be given to overseas subsidiaries to enhance their autonomy while ensuring sound global integration. Seeing the early successes of the lifestyle center, Panasonic gave increasing authority to its Chinese operations for deeper local adaptation while also maintaining integrated working relationships between Japan and China.

Sources: Wakayama, T., Shintaku, J., & Amano, T. 2012. What Panasonic learned in China. *Harvard Business Review*, December: 109–113; and Osawa, J. 2012. Panasonic pins hopes on home appliances. *wsj.com*, March 25: np.

---

can be more selective in its hiring practices for its Mexican operations. And, given the lower turnover among its Mexican employees, Ford can justify a high level of investment in training and development. Thus, the net result can be not only lower wage rates but also higher productivity than in the United States.

- **Although knowledge transfer can be a key source of competitive advantage, it does not take place "automatically."** For knowledge transfer to take place from one subsidiary to another, it is important for the source of the knowledge, the target units, and the corporate headquarters to recognize the potential value of such unique know-how. Given that there can be significant geographic, linguistic, and cultural distances that typically separate subsidiaries, the potential for knowledge transfer can become very difficult to realize. Firms must create mechanisms to systematically and routinely uncover the opportunities for knowledge transfer.

Exhibit 7.8 summarizes the relative advantages and disadvantages of transnational strategies.

EXHIBIT 7.8 Strengths and Limitations of Transnational Strategies

Strengths	Limitations
• Ability to attain economies of scale. • Ability to adapt to local markets. • Ability to locate activities in optimal locations. • Ability to increase knowledge flows and learning.	• Unique challenges in determining optimal locations of activities to ensure cost and quality. • Unique managerial challenges in fostering knowledge transfer.

Global or Regional? A Second Look at Globalization

Thus far, we have suggested four possible strategies from which a firm must choose once it has decided to compete in the global marketplace. In recent years, many writers have asserted that the process of globalization has caused national borders to become increasingly irrelevant.[62] However, some scholars have questioned this perspective, and they have argued that it is unwise for companies to rush into full-scale globalization.[63]

Before answering questions about the extent of firms' globalization, let's try to clarify what "globalization" means. Traditionally, a firm's globalization is measured in terms of its foreign sales as a percentage of total sales. However, this measure can be misleading. For example, consider a U.S. firm that has expanded its activities into Canada. Clearly, this initiative is qualitatively different from achieving the same sales volume in a distant country such as China. Similarly, if a Malaysian firm expands into Singapore or a German firm starts selling its products in Austria, this would represent an expansion into a geographically adjacent country. Such nearby countries would often share many common characteristics in terms of language, culture, infrastructure, and customer preferences. In other words, this is more a case of regionalization than globalization.

Extensive analysis of the distribution data of sales across different countries and regions led Alan Rugman and Alain Verbeke to conclude that there is a stronger case to be made in favor of **regionalization** than globalization. According to their study, a company would have to have at least 20 percent of its sales in each of the three major economic regions—North America, Europe, and Asia—to be considered a global firm. However, they found that only 9 of the world's 500 largest firms met this standard! Even when they relaxed the criterion to 20 percent of sales each in at least two of the three regions, the number only increased to 25. *Thus, most companies are regional or, at best, biregional—not global—even today.*

In a world of instant communication, rapid transportation, and governments that are increasingly willing to open up their markets to trade and investment, why are so few firms "global"? The most obvious answer is that distance still matters. After all, it is easier to do business in a neighboring country than in a faraway country, all else being equal. Distance, in the final analysis, may be viewed as a concept with many dimensions, not just a measure of geographic distance. For example, both Canada and Mexico are the same distance from the U.S. However, U.S. companies find it easier to expand operations into Canada than into Mexico. Why? Canada and the U.S. share many commonalities in terms of language, culture, economic development, legal and political systems, and infrastructure development. Thus, if we view distance as having many dimensions, the U.S. and Canada are very close, whereas there is greater distance between the U.S. and Mexico. Similarly, when we look at what we might call the "true" distance between the U.S. and China, the effects of geographic distance are multiplied by distance in terms of culture, language, religion, and legal and political systems between the two countries. On the other hand, although U.S. and Australia are geographically distant, the "true" distance is somewhat less when one considers distance along the other dimensions.

>**LO7.6**
>The difference between regional companies and truly global companies.

>**regionalization**
>increasing international exchange of goods, services, money, people, ideas, and information; and the increasing similarity of culture, laws, rules, and norms within a region such as Europe, North America, or Asia.

trading blocs
groups of countries agreeing to increase trade between them by lowering trade barriers.

Another reason for regional expansion is the rise of **trading blocs** and free trade zones. A number of regional agreements have been created that facilitate the growth of business within these regions by easing trade restrictions and taxes and tariffs. These have included the European Union (EU), North American Free Trade Agreement (NAFTA), Association of Southeast Asian Nations (ASEAN), and MERCOSUR (a South American trading block).

Regional economic integration has progressed at a faster pace than global economic integration, and the trade and investment patterns of the largest companies reflect this reality. After all, regions represent the outcomes of centuries of political and cultural history that results in not only commonalities but also mutual affinity. For example, stretching from Algeria and Morocco in the West to Oman and Yemen in the East, more than 30 countries share the Arabic language and the Muslim religion, making these countries a natural regional bloc. Similarly, the countries of South and Central America share the Spanish language (except Brazil), the Catholic religion, and a history of Spanish colonialism. No wonder firms find it easier and less risky to expand within their region than to other regions.

Entry Modes of International Expansion

LO7.7
The six basic types of entry strategies and the relative benefits and risks associated with each of them.

A firm has many options available to it when it decides to expand into international markets. Given the challenges associated with such entry, many firms first start on a small scale and then increase their level of investment and risk as they gain greater experience with the overseas market in question.[64]

Exhibit 7.9 illustrates a wide variety of modes of foreign entry, including exporting, licensing, franchising, joint ventures, strategic alliances, and wholly owned subsidiaries.[65] As the exhibit indicates, the various types of entry form a continuum ranging from exporting (low investment and risk, low control) to a wholly owned subsidiary (high investment and risk, high control).[66]

There can be frustrations and setbacks as a firm evolves its international entry strategy from exporting to more expensive types, including wholly owned subsidiaries. For example, according to the CEO of a large U.S. specialty chemical company:

> In the end, we always do a better job with our own subsidiaries; sales improve, and we have greater control over the business. But we still need local distributors for entry, and we are still searching for strategies to get us through the transitions without battles over control and performance.[67]

EXHIBIT 7.9 Entry Modes for International Expansion

Exporting

Exporting consists of producing goods in one country to sell in another.[68] This entry strategy enables a firm to invest the least amount of resources in terms of its product, its organization, and its overall corporate strategy. Many host countries dislike this entry strategy because it provides less local employment than other modes of entry.[69]

Multinationals often stumble onto a stepwise strategy for penetrating markets, beginning with the exporting of products. This often results in a series of unplanned actions to increase sales revenues. As the pattern recurs with entries into subsequent markets, this approach, named a "beachhead strategy," often becomes official policy.[70]

Benefits Such an approach definitely has its advantages. After all, firms start from scratch in sales and distribution when they enter new markets. Because many foreign markets are nationally regulated and dominated by networks of local intermediaries, firms need to partner with local distributors to benefit from their valuable expertise and knowledge of their own markets. Multinationals, after all, recognize that they cannot master local business practices, meet regulatory requirements, hire and manage local personnel, or gain access to potential customers without some form of local partnership.

Multinationals also want to minimize their own risk. They do this by hiring local distributors and investing very little in the undertaking. In essence, the firm gives up control of strategic marketing decisions to the local partners—much more control than they would be willing to give up in their home market.

Risks and Limitations Exporting is a relatively inexpensive way to enter foreign markets. However, it can still have significant downsides. Most centrally, the ability to tailor the firm's products to meet local market needs is typically very limited. In a study of 250 instances in which multinational firms used local distributors to implement their exporting entry strategy, the results were dismal. In the vast majority of the cases, the distributors were bought (to increase control) by the multinational firm or were fired. In contrast, successful distributors shared two common characteristics:

- They carried product lines that complemented, rather than competed with, the multinational's products.
- They behaved as if they were business partners with the multinationals. They shared market information with the corporations, they initiated projects with distributors in neighboring countries, and they suggested initiatives in their own or nearby markets. Additionally, these distributors took on risk themselves by investing in areas such as training, information systems, and advertising and promotion in order to increase the business of their multinational partners.

The key point is the importance of developing collaborative, win–win relationships.

To ensure more control over operations without incurring significant risks, many firms have used licensing and franchising as a mode of entry. Let's now discuss these and their relative advantages and disadvantages.

Licensing and Franchising

Licensing and franchising are both forms of contractual arrangements. **Licensing** enables a company to receive a royalty or fee in exchange for the right to use its trademark, patent, trade secret, or other valuable item of intellectual property.[71]

Franchising contracts generally include a broader range of factors in an operation and have a longer time period during which the agreement is in effect. Franchising remains a primary form of American business. According to a survey, more than 400 U.S. franchisers have international exposure.[72] This is greater than the combined totals of the next four largest franchiser home countries—France, the United Kingdom, Mexico, and Austria.

---

exporting
producing goods in one country to sell to residents of another country.

licensing
a contractual arrangement in which a company receives a royalty or fee in exchange for the right to use its trademark, patent, trade secret, or other valuable intellectual property.

franchising
a contractual arrangement in which a company receives a royalty or fee in exchange for the right to use its intellectual property; franchising usually involves a longer time period than licensing and includes other factors, such as monitoring of operations, training, and advertising.

Benefits In international markets, an advantage of licensing is that the firm granting a license incurs little risk, since it does not have to invest any significant resources into the country itself. In turn, the licensee (the firm receiving the license) gains access to the trademark, patent, and so on, and is able to potentially create competitive advantages. In many cases, the country also benefits from the product being manufactured locally. For example, Yoplait yogurt is licensed by General Mills from Sodima, a French cooperative, for sale in the United States. The logos of college and professional athletic teams in the United States are another source of trademarks that generate significant royalty income domestically and internationally.

Franchising has the advantage of limiting the risk exposure that a firm has in overseas markets. At the same time, the firm is able to expand the revenue base of the company.

Risks and Limitations The licensor gives up control of its product and forgoes potential revenues and profits. Furthermore, the licensee may eventually become so familiar with the patent and trade secrets that it may become a competitor; that is, the licensee may make some modifications to the product and manufacture and sell it independently of the licensor without having to pay a royalty fee. This potential situation is aggravated in countries that have relatively weak laws to protect intellectual property. Additionally, if the licensee selected by the multinational firm turns out to be a poor choice, the brand name and reputation of the product may be tarnished.[73]

With franchising, the multinational firm receives only a portion of the revenues, in the form of franchise fees. Had the firm set up the operation itself (e.g., a restaurant through direct investment), it would have had the entire revenue to itself.

Companies often desire a closer collaboration with other firms in order to increase revenue, reduce costs, and enhance their learning—often through the diffusion of technology. To achieve such objectives, they enter into strategic alliances or joint ventures, two entry modes we will discuss next.

Strategic Alliances and Joint Ventures

Joint ventures and strategic alliances have recently become increasingly popular.[74] These two forms of partnership differ in that joint ventures entail the creation of a third-party legal entity, whereas strategic alliances do not. In addition, strategic alliances generally focus on initiatives that are smaller in scope than joint ventures.[75]

Benefits As we discussed in Chapter 6, these strategies have been effective in helping firms increase revenues and reduce costs as well as enhance learning and diffuse technologies.[76] These partnerships enable firms to share the risks as well as the potential revenues and profits. Also, by gaining exposure to new sources of knowledge and technologies, such partnerships can help firms develop core competencies that can lead to competitive advantages in the marketplace.[77] Finally, entering into partnerships with host-country firms can provide very useful information on local market tastes, competitive conditions, legal matters, and cultural nuances.[78]

Risks and Limitations Managers must be aware of the risks associated with strategic alliances and joint ventures and how they can be minimized.[79] First, there needs to be a clearly defined strategy that is strongly supported by the organizations that are party to the partnership. Otherwise, the firms may work at cross-purposes and not achieve any of their goals. Second, and closely allied to the first issue, there must be a clear understanding of capabilities and resources that will be central to the partnership. Without such clarification, there will be fewer opportunities for learning and developing competencies that could lead to competitive advantages. Third, trust is a vital element. Phasing in the relationship between alliance partners permits them to get to know each other better and develop trust. Without trust, one party may take advantage of the other by, for example, withholding its fair share of resources and gaining access to privileged information through unethical (or illegal) means.

Fourth, cultural issues that can potentially lead to conflict and dysfunctional behaviors need to be addressed. An organization's culture is the set of values, beliefs, and attitudes that influence the behavior and goals of its employees.[80] Thus, recognizing cultural differences, as well as striving to develop elements of a "common culture" for the partnership, is vital. Without a unifying culture, it will become difficult to combine and leverage resources that are increasingly important in knowledge-intensive organizations (discussed in Chapter 4).[81]

Finally, the success of a firm's alliance should not be left to chance.[82] To improve their odds of success, many companies have carefully documented alliance-management knowledge by creating guidelines and manuals to help them manage specific aspects of the entire alliance life cycle (e.g., partner selection and alliance negotiation and contracting). For example, Hewlett-Packard developed 60 different tools and templates, which it placed in a 300-page manual for guiding decision making. The manual included such tools as a template for making the business case for an alliance, a partner evaluation form, a negotiation template outlining the roles and responsibilities of different departments, a list of the ways to measure alliance performance, and an alliance termination checklist.

When a firm desires the highest level of control, it develops wholly owned subsidiaries. Although wholly owned subsidiaries can generate the greatest returns, they also have the highest levels of investment and risk. We will now discuss them.

Wholly Owned Subsidiaries

A **wholly owned subsidiary** is a business in which a multinational company owns 100 percent of the stock. Two ways a firm can establish a wholly owned subsidiary are to (1) acquire an existing company in the home country or (2) develop a totally new operation (often referred to as a "greenfield venture").

> **wholly owned subsidiary**
> a business in which a multinational company owns 100 percent of the stock.

Benefits Establishing a wholly owned subsidiary is the most expensive and risky of the various entry modes. However, it can also yield the highest returns. In addition, it provides the multinational company with the greatest degree of control of all activities, including manufacturing, marketing, distribution, and technology development.[83]

Wholly owned subsidiaries are most appropriate where a firm already has the appropriate knowledge and capabilities that it can leverage rather easily through multiple locations. Examples range from restaurants to semiconductor manufacturers. To lower costs, for example, Intel Corporation builds semiconductor plants throughout the world—all of which use virtually the same blueprint. Knowledge can be further leveraged by hiring managers and professionals from the firm's home country, often through hiring talent from competitors.

Risks and Limitations As noted, wholly owned subsidiaries are typically the most expensive and risky entry mode. With franchising, joint ventures, or strategic alliances, the risk is shared with the firm's partners. With wholly owned subsidiaries, the entire risk is assumed by the parent company. The risks associated with doing business in a new country (e.g., political, cultural, and legal) can be lessened by hiring local talent.

For example, Wendy's avoided committing two blunders in Germany by hiring locals to its advertising staff.[84] In one case, the firm wanted to promote its "old-fashioned" qualities. However, a literal translation would have resulted in the company promoting itself as "outdated." In another situation, Wendy's wanted to emphasize that its hamburgers could be prepared 256 ways. The problem? The German word that Wendy's wanted to use for "ways" usually meant "highways" or "roads." Although such errors may sometimes be entertaining to the public, it is certainly preferable to catch these mistakes before they confuse the consumer or embarrass the company.

We have addressed entry strategies as a progression from exporting to the creation of wholly owned subsidiaries. However, we must point out that many firms do not follow such an evolutionary approach.

ISSUE FOR DEBATE

The Ethicality of Tax Inversions

In June 2014, Medtronic, a Minneapolis-based medical device manufacturer, announced that it would join the tax-inversion acquisition parade. A tax-inversion acquisition occurs when a corporation acquires a target firm based in a lower-tax country and, as part of the transaction, moves its legal headquarters to the target firm's nation. After making this move, the combined corporation's taxes are based on the lower rate of its new home country. This move is perfectly legal according to U.S. law as long as the target firm's shareholders own at least 20 percent of the combined firm. About 50 U.S. corporations have undertaken tax inversions over the last 10 years, but the rate of occurrence appears to be increasing.

Medtronic's plan is to acquire Covidien, an Irish-based medical equipment manufacturer, for $43 billion and move its legal home to Ireland. Not much else will change. Medtronic will keep its corporate headquarters in Minneapolis. But Medtronic benefits from the move in two primary ways. First, while the tax rate on profits of U.S. corporations is 35 percent, the tax rate on Ireland-based corporate profits is only 12.5 percent. Additionally, the U.S. is one of only six developed economies that tax the global profits of corporations. If a multinational corporation makes profits in a foreign country, the firm pays taxes on those profits to the foreign government at the rate the foreign country charges. For corporations based in most countries, that is the end of their tax obligations. However, if a U.S.-based firm wants to bring those profits back to its home country either to invest in new facilities or to distribute dividends to its stockholders, it has to pay income tax on the profits earned in foreign markets. The rate the firm pays is the difference in the tax rate in the foreign country and the U.S. rate. For example, if Medtronic earned income in Ireland and then repatriated the profits to the U.S., it would face a 22.5 percent additional tax rate, the difference between the U.S. and Irish corporate tax rates. Since Medtronic has accumulated $13 billion in earned profits abroad, it could face $3.5 billion to $4 billion in taxes if it brought those profits home. Thus, corporations, such as Medtronic, undertake tax inversions to save on taxes and, by extension, benefit their shareholders by being able to invest more in the firm to help it grow and/or return higher levels of dividends to shareholders.

Critics, however, point out that these firms are choosing not to pay taxes at the U.S. rates even though they have benefited and will continue to benefit from being American corporations. While inverters change their legal residence, they typically keep their corporate headquarters in the U.S. and stay listed on a U.S. stock exchange. As a result, they benefit from America's deep financial markets, military might, intellectual property rights and other legal protections, intellectual and physical infrastructure, substantial human capital base, and national research programs. For example, Medtronic won $484 million in contracts with the U.S. government in recent years and plans to complete these contracts even though it will no longer be an American company; it hires students from top-notch American universities; and it files patents for all of its new technologies in the United States. Critics see the decision to move to a lower-tax country as unethical and unpatriotic. Jack Lew, the U.S. Treasury secretary, echoed this perspective when he stated, "We should prevent companies from effectively renouncing their citizenship to get out of paying taxes. What we need is a new sense of economic patriotism, where we all rise and fall together."

Discussion Questions

1. Is Medtronic justified in moving its legal home to Ireland?
2. How should firms balance the desire to limit taxes to maximize cash generation with the need to be a good corporate citizen?
3. How should the U.S. government respond to the increasing frequency of tax inversions?

Sources: Sloan, A. 2014. Positively un-American. *fortune.com*, July 7: np; McKinnon, J. 2014. Obama administration urges immediate action on "inversion." *wsj.com*, July 15: np; Sahadi, J. 2014. When U.S. companies dodge taxes, is it unpatriotic? *finance.yahoo.com*, July 23: np; Anonymous. 2014. Medtronic's tax inversion lesson. *wsj.com*, August 13: np; and Gleckman, H. 2014. The tax-shopping backstory of the Medtronic-Covidien inversion. *forbes.com*, June 17: np.

Reflecting on Career Implications . . .

- **International Strategy:** Be aware of your organization's international strategy. What percentage of the total firm activity is international? What skills are needed to enhance your company's international efforts? How can you get more involved in your organization's international strategy? For your career, what conditions in your home country might cause you to seek a career abroad?

- **Outsourcing and Offshoring:** More and more organizations have resorted to outsourcing and offshoring in recent years. To what extent has your firm engaged in either? What activities in your organization can/should be outsourced or offshored? Be aware that you are competing in the global marketplace for employment and professional advancement. What is the likelihood that your own job may be outsourced or offshored? In what ways can you enhance your talents, skills, and competencies to reduce the odds that your job may be offshored or outsourced?

- **International Career Opportunities:** Taking on overseas assignments in other countries can often provide a career boost. There are a number of ways in which you can improve your odds of being selected for an overseas assignment. Studying abroad for a semester or doing an overseas internship are two obvious strategies. Learning a foreign language can also greatly help. Anticipate how such opportunities will advance your short- and long-term career aspirations.

- **Management Risks:** Explore ways in which you can develop cultural sensitivity. Interacting with people from other cultures, foreign travel, reading about foreign countries, watching foreign movies, and similar activities can increase your cultural sensitivity. Identify ways in which your perceptions and behaviors have changed as a result of increased cultural sensitivity.

summary

We live in a highly interconnected global community where many of the best opportunities for growth and profitability lie beyond the boundaries of a company's home country. Along with the opportunities, of course, there are many risks associated with diversification into global markets.

The first section of the chapter addressed the factors that determine a nation's competitiveness in a particular industry. The framework was developed by Professor Michael Porter of Harvard University and was based on a four-year study that explored the competitive success of 10 leading trading nations. The four factors, collectively termed the "diamond of national advantage," were factor endowments, demand conditions, related and supporting industries, and firm strategy, structure, and rivalry.

The discussion of Porter's "diamond" helped, in essence, to set the broader context for exploring competitive advantage at the firm level. In the second section, we discussed the primary motivations and the potential risks associated with international expansion. The primary motivations included increasing the size of the potential market for the firm's products and services, achieving economies of scale, extending the life cycle of the firm's products, and optimizing the location for every activity in the value chain. On the other hand, the key risks included political and economic risks, currency risks, and management risks. Management risks are the challenges associated with responding to the inevitable differences that exist across countries such as customs, culture, language, customer preferences, and distribution systems. We also addressed some of the managerial challenges and opportunities associated with offshoring and outsourcing.

Next, we addressed how firms can go about attaining competitive advantage in global markets. We began by discussing the two opposing forces—cost reduction and adaptation to local markets—that managers must contend with when entering global markets. The relative importance of these two factors plays a major part in determining which of the four basic types of strategies to select: international, global, multidomestic, or transnational. The chapter covered the benefits and risks associated with each type of strategy.

The final section discussed the four types of entry strategies that managers may undertake when entering international markets. The key trade-off in each of these strategies is the level of investment or risk versus the level of control. In order of their progressively greater investment/risk and control, the strategies range from exporting to licensing and franchising, to strategic alliances and joint ventures, to wholly owned subsidiaries. The relative benefits and risks associated with each of these strategies were addressed.

SUMMARY REVIEW QUESTIONS

1. What are some of the advantages and disadvantages associated with a firm's expansion into international markets?
2. What are the four factors described in Porter's diamond of national advantage? How do the four factors explain why some industries in a given country are more successful than others?
3. Explain the two opposing forces—cost reduction and adaptation to local markets—that firms must deal with when they go global.
4. There are four basic strategies—international, global, multidomestic, and transnational. What are the advantages and disadvantages associated with each?
5. What is the basis of Alan Rugman's argument that most multinationals are still more regional than global? What factors inhibit firms from becoming truly global?
6. Describe the basic entry strategies that firms have available when they enter international markets. What are the relative advantages and disadvantages of each?

key terms

globalization 214
diamond of national advantage 215
factor endowments (national advantage) 215
demand conditions (national advantage) 216
related and supporting industries (national advantage) 216
firm strategy, structure, and rivalry (national advantage) 216
multinational firms 218
arbitrage opportunities 219
reverse innovation 220
political risk 222
rule of law 222
economic risk 223
counterfeiting 223
currency risk 223
management risk 224
outsourcing 225
offshoring 225
international strategy 231
global strategy 231
multidomestic strategy 233
transnational strategy 235
regionalization 237
trading blocs 238
exporting 239
licensing 239
franchising 239
wholly owned subsidiary 241

experiential exercise

The United States is considered a world leader in the motion picture industry. Using Porter's diamond framework for national competitiveness, explain the success of this industry. (Fill in the chart on page 245.)

application questions & exercises

1. Data on the "competitiveness of nations" can be found at www.imd.org/research/publications/wcy/index.cfm. This website provides a ranking on 329 criteria for 59 countries. How might Porter's diamond of national advantage help to explain the rankings for some of these countries for certain industries that interest you?
2. The Internet has lowered the entry barriers for smaller firms that wish to diversify into international markets. Why is this so? Provide an example.
3. Many firms fail when they enter into strategic alliances with firms that link up with companies based in other countries. What are some reasons for this failure? Provide an example.
4. Many large U.S.-based management consulting companies such as McKinsey and Company and the BCG Group have been very successful in the international marketplace. How can Porter's diamond explain their success?

ethics questions

1. Over the past few decades, many American firms have relocated most or all of their operations from the United States to countries such as Mexico and China that pay lower wages. What are some of the ethical issues that such actions may raise?
2. Business practices and customs vary throughout the world. What are some of the ethical issues concerning payments that must be made in a foreign country to obtain business opportunities?

Diagram

- **Domestic rivalry**
  1.
  2.
  3.
- **Factor conditions**
  1.
  2.
  3.
- **Demand conditions**
  1.
  2.
  3.
- **Related and supporting industries**
  1.
  2.
  3.

references

1. Williamson, P. & Raman, A. 2011. How China reset its global acquisition agenda. *Harvard Business Review,* April: 109–114; and SAIC under pressure to help save SsangYong. 2009. *nytimes.com,* January 12: np.
2. For a discussion on globalization by one of international business's most respected authors, read Ohmae, K. 2005. *The next global stage: Challenges and opportunities in our borderless world.* Philadelphia: Wharton School.
3. Our discussion of globalization draws upon Engardio, P. & Belton, C. 2000. Global capitalism: Can it be made to work better? *BusinessWeek,* November 6: 72–98.
4. Sellers, P. 2005. Blowing in the wind. *Fortune,* July 25: 63.
5. Rivera, J. 2014. Gartner says sales of smartphones grew 20 percent in third quarter of 2014. *gartner.com,* December 15: np.
6. A game of catch-up. 2011. *The Economist,* September 24: 3–6.
7. Some insights into how winners are evolving in emerging markets are addressed in Ghemawat, P. & Hout, T. 2008. Tomorrow's global giants: Not the usual suspects. *Harvard Business Review,* 66(11): 80–88.
8. For another interesting discussion on a country perspective, refer to Makino, S. 1999. MITI Minister Kaora Yosano on reviving Japan's competitive advantages. *Academy of Management Executive,* 13(4): 8–28.
9. The following discussion draws heavily upon Porter, M. E. 1990. The competitive advantage of nations. *Harvard Business Review,* March–April: 73–93.
10. Landes, D. S. 1998. *The wealth and poverty of nations.* New York: W. W. Norton.
11. A study that investigates the relationship between international diversification and firm performance is Lu, J. W. & Beamish, P. W. 2004. International diversification and firm performance: The s-curve hypothesis. *Academy of Management Journal,* 47(4): 598–609.
12. Part of our discussion of the motivations and risks of international expansion draws upon Gregg, F. M. 1999. International strategy. In Helms, M. M. (Ed.), *Encyclopedia of management:* 434–438. Detroit: Gale Group.
13. Anthony, S. 2012. Singapore sessions. *Harvard Business Review,* 90(4): np.
14. Eyring, M. J., Johnson, M. W., & Nair, H. 2011. New business models in emerging markets. *Harvard Business Review,* 89 (1/2): 88–98.
15. Cieply, M. & Barnes, B. 2010. After rants, skepticism over Gibson bankability grows in non-U.S. markets. *International Herald Tribune,* July 23: 1.
16. Glazer, E. 2012. P&G unit bids goodbye to Cincinnati, hello to Asia. *wsj.com,* May 10: np.
17. This discussion draws upon Gupta, A. K. & Govindarajan, V. 2001. Converting global presence into global competitive advantage. *Academy of Management Executive,* 15(2): 45–56.
18. Stross, R. E. 1997. Mr. Gates builds his brain trust. *Fortune,* December 8: 84–98.
19. For a good summary of the benefits and risks of international expansion, refer to Bartlett, C. A. & Ghoshal, S. 1987. Managing across borders:

New strategic responses. *Sloan Management Review,* 28(5): 45–53; and Brown, R. H. 1994. *Competing to win in a global economy.* Washington, DC: U.S. Department of Commerce.

20. Capron, L. & Bertrand, O. 2014. Going abroad in search of higher productivity at home. *Harvard Business Review,* 92(6): 26.

21. For an interesting insight into rivalry in global markets, refer to MacMillan, I. C., van Putten, A. B., & McGrath, R. G. 2003. Global gamesmanship. *Harvard Business Review,* 81(5): 62–73.

22. It is important for firms to spread their foreign operations and outsourcing relationships with a broad, well-balanced mix of regions and countries to reduce risk and increase potential reward. For example, refer to Vestring, T., Rouse, T., & Reinert, U. 2005. Hedge your offshoring bets. *MIT Sloan Management Review,* 46(3): 27–29.

23. An interesting discussion of risks faced by Lukoil, Russia's largest oil firm, is in Gimbel, B. 2009. Russia's king of crude. *Fortune,* February 2: 88–92.

24. For a discussion of some of the challenges associated with government corruption regarding entry strategies in foreign markets, read Rodriguez, P., Uhlenbruck, K., & Eden, L. 2005. Government corruption and entry strategies of multinationals. *Academy of Management Review,* 30(2): 383–396.

25. For a discussion of the political risks in China for United States companies, refer to Garten, J. E. 1998. Opening the doors for business in China. *Harvard Business Review,* 76(3): 167–175.

26. Insights on how forensic economics can be used to investigate crimes and wrongdoing are in Fisman, R. 2009. The rise of forensic economics. *Harvard Business Review,* 87(2): 26.

27. Iosebashvili, I. 2012. Renault-Nissan buy into Russia's aged auto giant. *wsj.com,* May 3: np.

28. Ferguson, N. 2013. Is the business of America still business? *Harvard Business Review,* 91(6): 40.

29. For an interesting perspective on the relationship between diversification and the development of a nation's institutional environment, read Chakrabarti, A., Singh, K., & Mahmood, I. 2007. Diversification and performance: Evidence from East Asian firms. *Strategic Management Journal,* 28(2): 101–120.

30. A study looking into corruption and foreign direct investment is Brouthers, L. E., Gao, Y., & McNicol, J. P. 2008. *Strategic Management Journal,* 29(6): 673–680.

31. Gikkas, N. S. 1996. International licensing of intellectual property: The promise and the peril. *Journal of Technology Law & Policy,* 1(1): 1–26.

32. Hargreaves, S. 2012. Counterfeit goods becoming more dangerous. *cnnmoney.com,* September 27: np.

33. Sandler, N. 2008. Israel: Attack of the super-shekel. *BusinessWeek,* Februrary 25: 38.

34. For an excellent theoretical discussion of how cultural factors can affect knowledge transfer across national boundaries, refer to Bhagat, R. S., Kedia, B. L., Harveston, P. D., & Triandis, H. C. 2002. Cultural variations in the cross-border transfer of organizational knowledge: An integrative framework. *Academy of Management Review,* 27(2): 204–221.

35. An interesting discussion on how local companies compete effectively with large multinationals is in Bhatacharya, A. K. & Michael, D. C. 2008. *Harvard Business Review,* 66(3): 84–95.

36. To gain insights on the role of national and regional cultures on knowledge management models and frameworks, read Pauleen, D. J. & Murphy, P. 2005. In praise of cultural bias. *MIT Sloan Management Review,* 46(2): 21–22.

37. Berkowitz, E. N. 2000. *Marketing* (6th ed.). New York: McGraw-Hill.

38. Harvey, M. & Buckley, M. R. 2002. Assessing the "conventional wisdoms" of management for the 21st century organization. *Organization Dynamics,* 30(4): 368–378.

39. World Trade Organization. *Annual Report 1998.* Geneva: World Trade Organization.

40. Lei, D. 2005. Outsourcing. In Hitt, M. A. & Ireland, R. D. (Eds.), *The Blackwell encyclopedia of management,* Entrepreneurship: 196–199. Malden, MA: Blackwell.

41. Future trends in offshoring are addressed in Manning, S., Massini, S., & Lewin, A. Y. 2008. A dynamic perspective on next-generation offshoring: The global sourcing of science and engineering talent. *Academy of Management Perspectives,* 22(3): 35–54.

42. An interesting perspective on the controversial issue regarding the offshoring of airplane maintenance is in Smith, G. & Bachman, J. 2008. Flying in for a tune-up overseas. *BusinessWeek,* April 21: 26–27.

43. The discussion draws from Colvin, J. 2004. Think your job can't be sent to India? Just watch. *Fortune,* December 13: 80; Schwartz, N. D. 2004. Down and out in white collar America. *Fortune,* June 23: 321–325; and Hagel, J. 2004. Outsourcing is not just about cost cutting. *The Wall Street Journal,* March 18: A3.

44. Porter, M. & Rivkin, J. 2012 Choosing the United States. *Harvard Business Review,* 90(3): 80–93; Bussey, J. 2012. U.S. manufacturing, defying naysayers. *wsj.com,* April 19: np; and Jean, S. & Alcott, K. 2013. Manufacturing jobs have slid steadily as work has moved offshore. *Dallas Morning News,* January 14: 1D.

45. Wong, C. 2014. As China's economy slows, so too does growth in workers' wages. *blogs.wsj.com,* December 17: np.

46. Levitt, T. 1983. The globalization of markets. *Harvard Business Review,* 61(3): 92–102.

47. Our discussion of these assumptions draws upon Douglas, S. P. & Wind, Y. 1987. The myth of globalization. *Columbia Journal of World Business,* Winter: 19–29.

48. Ghoshal, S. 1987. Global strategy: An organizing framework. *Strategic Management Journal,* 8: 425–440.

49. For insights on global branding, refer to Aaker, D. A. & Joachimsthaler, E. 1999. The lure of global branding. *Harvard Business Review,* 77(6): 137–146.

50. Dawar, N. & Frost, T. 1999. Competing with Giants: Survival Strategies for Local Companies in Emerging Markets. *Harvard Business Review,* 77(3): 119–129.

51. Hout, T., Porter, M. E., & Rudden, E. 1982. How global companies win out. *Harvard Business Review,* 60(5): 98–107.

52. Fryer, B. 2001. Tom Siebel of Siebel Systems: High tech the old-fashioned way. *Harvard Business Review,* 79(3): 118–130.

53. The risks that are discussed for the global, multidomestic, and transnational strategies draw upon Gupta & Govindarajan, op. cit.

54. A discussion on how McDonald's adapts its products to overseas markets is in Gumbel, P. 2008. Big

Mac's local flavor. *Fortune,* May 5: 115–121.

55. Einhorn, B. & Winter, C. 2012. Want some milk with your green tea Oreos? *Bloomberg Businessweek,* May 7: 25–26; Khosla, S. & Sawhney, M. 2012. Blank checks: Unleashing the potential of people and business. *Strategy-Business.com,* Autumn: np; and In China, brands more than symbolic. 2012. *Dallas Morning News,* November 27: 3D.

56. Prahalad, C. K. & Doz, Y. L. 1987. *The multinational mission: Balancing local demands and global vision.* New York: Free Press.

57. For an insightful discussion on knowledge flows in multinational corporations, refer to Yang, Q., Mudambi, R., & Meyer, K. E. 2008. Conventional and reverse knowledge flows in multinational corporations. *Journal of Management,* 34(5): 882–902.

58. Kidd, J. B. & Teramoto, Y. 1995. The learning organization: The case of Japanese RHQs in Europe. *Management International Review,* 35 (Special Issue): 39–56.

59. Gupta, A. K. & Govindarajan, V. 2000. Knowledge flows within multinational corporations. *Strategic Management Journal,* 21(4): 473–496.

60. Wetlaufer, S. 2001. The business case against revolution: An interview with Nestlé's Peter Brabeck. *Harvard Business Review,* 79(2): 112–121.

61. Nobel, R. & Birkinshaw, J. 1998. Innovation in multinational corporations: Control and communication patterns in international R&D operations. *Strategic Management Journal,* 19(5): 461–478.

62. Chan, C. M., Makino, S., & Isobe, T. 2010. Does subnational region matter? Foreign affiliate performance in the United States and China. *Strategic Management Journal,* 31(11): 1226–1243.

63. This section draws upon Ghemawat, P. 2005. Regional strategies for global leadership. *Harvard Business Review,* 84(12): 98–108; Ghemawat, P. 2006. Apocalypse now? *Harvard Business Review,* 84(12): 32; Ghemawat, P. 2001. Distance still matters: The hard reality of global expansion. *Harvard Business Review,* 79(8): 137–147; Peng, M. W. 2006. *Global strategy:* 387. Mason, OH: Thomson South-Western; and Rugman, A. M. & Verbeke, A. 2004. A perspective on regional and global strategies of multinational enterprises. *Journal of International Business Studies,* 35: 3–18.

64. For a rigorous analysis of performance implications of entry strategies, refer to Zahra, S. A., Ireland, R. D., & Hitt, M. A. 2000. International expansion by new venture firms: International diversity, modes of entry, technological learning, and performance. *Academy of Management Journal,* 43(6): 925–950.

65. Li, J. T. 1995. Foreign entry and survival: The effects of strategic choices on performance in international markets. *Strategic Management Journal,* 16: 333–351.

66. For a discussion of how home-country environments can affect diversification strategies, refer to Wan, W. P. & Hoskisson, R. E. 2003. Home country environments, corporate diversification strategies, and firm performance. *Academy of Management Journal,* 46(1): 27–45.

67. Arnold, D. 2000. Seven rules of international distribution. *Harvard Business Review,* 78(6): 131–137.

68. Sharma, A. 1998. Mode of entry and ex-post performance. *Strategic Management Journal,* 19(9): 879–900.

69. This section draws upon Arnold, op. cit., pp. 131–137; and Berkowitz, op. cit.

70. Salomon, R. & Jin, B. 2010. Do leading or lagging firms learn more from exporting? *Strategic Management Journal,* 31(6): 1088–1113.

71. Kline, D. 2003. Strategic licensing. *MIT Sloan Management Review,* 44(3): 89–93.

72. Martin, J. 1999. Franchising in the Middle East. *Management Review,* June: 38–42.

73. Arnold, op. cit.; and Berkowitz, op. cit.

74. An in-depth case study of alliance dynamics is found in Faems, D., Janssens, M., Madhok, A., & Van Looy, B. 2008. Toward an integrative perspective on alliance governance: Connecting contract design, trust dynamics, and contract application. *Academy of Management Journal,* 51(6): 1053–1078.

75. Knowledge transfer in international joint ventures is addressed in Inkpen, A. 2008. Knowledge transfer and international joint ventures. *Strategic Management Journal,* 29(4): 447–453.

76. Wen, S. H. & Chuang, C.-M. 2010. To teach or to compete? A strategic dilemma of knowledge owners in international alliances. *Asia Pacific Journal of Management,* 27(4): 697–726.

77. Manufacturer–supplier relationships can be very effective in global industries such as automobile manufacturing. Refer to Kotabe, M., Martin, X., & Domoto, H. 2003. Gaining from vertical partnerships: Knowledge transfer, relationship duration, and supplier performance improvement in the U.S. and Japanese automotive industries. *Strategic Management Journal,* 24(4): 293–316.

78. For a good discussion, refer to Merchant, H. & Schendel, D. 2000. How do international joint ventures create shareholder value? *Strategic Management Journal,* 21(7): 723–738.

79. This discussion draws upon Walters, B. A., Peters, S., & Dess, G. G. 1994. Strategic alliances and joint ventures: Making them work. *Business Horizons,* 37(4): 5–11.

80. Some insights on partnering in the global area are discussed in MacCormack, A. & Forbath, T. 2008. *Harvard Business Review,* 66(1): 24, 26.

81. For a rigorous discussion of the importance of information access in international joint ventures, refer to Reuer, J. J. & Koza, M. P. 2000. Asymmetric information and joint venture performance: Theory and evidence for domestic and international joint ventures. *Strategic Management Journal,* 21(1): 81–88.

82. Dyer, J. H., Kale, P., & Singh, H. 2001. How to make strategic alliances work. *MIT Sloan Management Review,* 42(4): 37–43.

83. For a discussion of some of the challenges in managing subsidiaries, refer to O'Donnell, S. W. 2000. Managing foreign subsidiaries: Agents of headquarters, or an independent network? *Strategic Management Journal,* 21(5): 525–548.

84. Ricks, D. 2006. *Blunders in international business* (4th ed.). Malden, MA: Blackwell.

Entrepreneurial Strategy and Competitive Dynamics

chapter 8

After reading this chapter, you should have a good understanding of the following learning objectives:

LO8.1 The role of opportunities, resources, and entrepreneurs in successfully pursuing new ventures.

LO8.2 Three types of entry strategies—pioneering, imitative, and adaptive—commonly used to launch a new venture.

LO8.3 How the generic strategies of overall cost leadership, differentiation, and focus are used by new ventures and small businesses.

LO8.4 How competitive actions, such as the entry of new competitors into a marketplace, may launch a cycle of actions and reactions among close competitors.

LO8.5 The components of competitive dynamics analysis—new competitive action, threat analysis, motivation and capability to respond, types of competitive actions, and likelihood of competitive reaction.

PART 2: STRATEGIC FORMULATION

Learning from Mistakes

Digg was an early social network pioneer. In 2004, its founder, Kevin Rose, had an innovative idea. Rather than allow major news services to decide what the big news stories of the day were, Rose figured that people could make that choice. He founded Digg, a news-sharing site, to give them that choice.[1] Users would post news articles they found interesting. Other users would then vote the story up or down and also post comments about the article. Articles that were voted up moved up in prominence on the site. Those voted down sank and eventually disappeared. The business took off and served as a front-page article in *BusinessWeek* in 2006. Notable venture capitalists like Marc Andreessen, Ron Conway, and Greylock Partners invested $45 million in Digg. It was rumored that Google was interested in buying Digg in 2008 for a reported $200 million.

But the deal never happened, and Digg quickly fell from favor. It struggled due to two major issues—new competition and poor operational decisions. As we'll discuss later in this chapter, innovative business ideas are typically quickly imitated. Digg faced two forms of imitation. First, Reddit and other sites came online to challenge Digg by implementing similar business models. Second, other social network sites, such as Facebook and Twitter, ate away at Digg's business by letting users share news articles they found interesting with their friends and followers. This seemed much more personalized to many, since they would be more interested in what their friends recommended than how the general population voted on Digg.

Digg also suffered by not building the resource set needed to serve its users effectively. The company struggled to handle the volume of traffic on its site, leaving users frustrated when the site kept going down. When Digg finally went to a wholesale upgrade of its systems in 2010, there were a number of technical glitches that drove users away. Digg also didn't make the site as easy to use as it should have or as easy as its competitors' sites. As Rose himself noted, "It took eight steps to post a link on Digg."[2]

What was the cost of Digg's missteps? Even though Digg was still drawing over 7 million visitors a month in early 2012, it was no longer a valued brand or corporation. The firm, which was at one time thought to be worth $200 million, was sold to Betaworks in July 2012 for the whopping sum of $500,000.

Discussion Questions

1. What lessons can we learn from Digg?
2. Can you think of other Internet firms that have failed and recovered? If so, what lessons can Betaworks draw from these experiences to help Digg recover?

By offering a service allowing users to share and vote on news stories, Digg seemed to have identified an attractive opportunity. But the start-up's failure shows what can go wrong when—even though a good opportunity and a skilled entrepreneurial team are brought together—a business opportunity disappears as quickly as it appeared.

The Digg case illustrates how important it is for new entrepreneurial entrants—whether they are start-ups or incumbents—to think and act strategically. Even with a strong initial resource base, entrepreneurs are unlikely to succeed if their business ideas are easily imitated or the execution of the strategy falls short.

In this chapter we address entrepreneurial strategies. The previous three chapters have focused primarily on the business-level, corporate-level, and international strategies of incumbent firms. Here we ask: What about the strategies of those entering into a market or industry for the first time? Whether it's a fast-growing start-up such as Digg or an existing company seeking growth opportunities, new entrants need effective strategies.

Companies wishing to launch new ventures must also be aware that, consistent with the five-forces model in Chapter 2, new entrants are a threat to existing firms in an industry. Entry into a new market arena is intensely competitive from the perspective of incumbents in that arena. Therefore, new entrants can nearly always expect a competitive response from other companies in the industry they are entering. Knowledge of the competitive dynamics that are at work in the business environment is an aspect of entrepreneurial new entry that will be addressed later in this chapter.

Before moving on, it is important to highlight the role that entrepreneurial start-ups and small businesses play in entrepreneurial value creation. Small businesses, those defined as having 500 employees or fewer, create about 65 percent of all new jobs in the United States and also generate 13 times as many new patents per employee as larger firms.[3]

Recognizing Entrepreneurial Opportunities

entrepreneurship
the creation of new value by an existing organization or new venture that involves the assumption of risk.

Defined broadly, **entrepreneurship** refers to new value creation. Even though entrepreneurial activity is usually associated with start-up companies, new value can be created in many different contexts, including:

- Start-up ventures
- Major corporations
- Family-owned businesses
- Nonprofit organizations
- Established institutions

LO8.1

The role of opportunities, resources, and entrepreneurs in successfully pursuing new ventures.

For an entrepreneurial venture to create new value, three factors must be present—an entrepreneurial opportunity, the resources to pursue the opportunity, and an entrepreneur or entrepreneurial team willing and able to undertake the opportunity.[4] The entrepreneurial strategy that an organization uses will depend on these three factors. Thus, beyond merely identifying a venture concept, the opportunity recognition process also involves organizing the key people and resources that are needed to go forward. Exhibit 8.1 depicts the three factors that are needed to successfully proceed—opportunity, resources, and entrepreneur(s). In the sections that follow, we address each of these factors.

Entrepreneurial Opportunities

The starting point for any new venture is the presence of an entrepreneurial opportunity. Where do opportunities come from? For new business start-ups, opportunities come from many sources—current or past work experiences, hobbies that grow into businesses or lead to inventions, suggestions by friends or family, or a chance event that makes an entrepreneur aware of an unmet need. Terry Tietzen, founder and CEO of Edatanetworks, puts it this way, "You get ideas through watching the world and through relationships. You get ideas from looking down the road."[5] For established firms, new business opportunities come from the needs of existing customers, suggestions by suppliers, or technological developments that lead to new advances.[6] For all firms, there is a major, overarching factor behind all viable opportunities that emerge in the business landscape: change. Change creates opportunities. Entrepreneurial firms make the most of changes brought about by new technology, sociocultural trends, and shifts in consumer demand.

How do changes in the external environment lead to new business creation? They spark creative new ideas and innovation. Businesspeople often have ideas for entrepreneurial ventures. However, not all such ideas are good ideas—that is, viable business opportunities. To determine which ideas are strong enough to become new ventures, entrepreneurs

EXHIBIT 8.1 Opportunity Analysis Framework

```
         Opportunity
          /      \
         /        \
    Resources —— Entrepreneur(s)
```

Sources: Based on Timmons, J. A. & Spinelli, S. 2004. *New Venture Creation* (6th ed.). New York: McGraw-Hill/Irwin; and Bygrave, W. D. 1997. The Entrepreneurial Process. In W. D. Bygrave (Ed.), *The Portable MBA in Entrepreneurship* (2nd ed.). New York: Wiley.

must go through a process of identifying, selecting, and developing potential opportunities. This is the process of **opportunity recognition**.[7]

Opportunity recognition refers to more than just the "Eureka!" feeling that people sometimes experience at the moment they identify a new idea. Although such insights are often very important, the opportunity recognition process involves two phases of activity—discovery and evaluation—that lead to viable new venture opportunities.[8]

The discovery phase refers to the process of becoming aware of a new business concept.[9] Many entrepreneurs report that their idea for a new venture occurred to them in an instant, as a sort of "Aha!" experience—that is, they had some insight or epiphany, often based on their prior knowledge, that gave them an idea for a new business. The discovery of new opportunities is often spontaneous and unexpected. For example, Howard Schultz, CEO of Starbucks, was in Milan, Italy, when he suddenly realized that the coffee-and-conversation cafe model that was common in Europe would work in the U.S. as well. According to Schultz, he didn't need to do research to find out if Americans would pay $3 for a cup of coffee—he just *knew*. Starbucks was just a small business at the time but Schultz began literally shaking with excitement about growing it into a bigger business.[10] Strategy Spotlight 8.1 tells how two brothers took the realization that many people wanted to wear their optimism and turned it into a growing business empire.

Opportunity discovery also may occur as the result of a deliberate search for new venture opportunities or creative solutions to business problems. Viable opportunities often emerge only after a concerted effort. The search process is very similar to a creative process, which may be unstructured and "chaotic" at first but eventually leads to a practical solution or business innovation. To stimulate the discovery of new opportunities, companies often encourage creativity, out-of-the-box thinking, and brainstorming. While a deliberate search can aim to identify truly novel and creative entrepreneurial opportunities, it can also be more focused to look for "obvious" opportunities that others have failed to see. Experienced entrepreneurs discussing ways to look for new entrepreneurial opportunities identify several ways to undertake a structured search for entrepreneurial ideas:[11]

- ***Look at what's bugging you.*** What are the frustrations you have with current products or processes? Search for ideas on how to address these annoyances to identify entrepreneurial opportunities. For example, David Cohen found an idea for an entrepreneurial venture in his frustration with finding news regarding music groups he followed. Normal web search engines and news compilers didn't provide

> **opportunity recognition**
> the process of discovering and evaluating changes in the business environment, such as a new technology, sociocultural trends, or shifts in consumer demand, that can be exploited.

8.1 STRATEGY SPOTLIGHT

SEEING OPPORTUNITY IN THE BRIGHT SIDE

People were craving something positive that focused on the good, instead of what is wrong with the world.

—John Jacobs

That simple inspiration was the insight that has driven the success of Life is Good T-shirts. Beginning in 1989, John Jacobs and his brother, Bert, had been selling T-shirts out of their van, scraping out a living. They used their own artwork on the shirts and found an audience for their funky designs, especially on college campuses. But after five and a half years in the business, they had a whopping $78 in the bank.

Their business turned with a simple conversation. As John explained, "Then in 1994, we talked about how people seemed worn down by the media's constant focus on the negative side of information." They had a keg party at which they asked friends to comment on drawings they were considering for new shirts. The design that received the most buzz was a simple stick figure that smiled. They paired this design with a simple slogan, "Life is Good," to offer a positive message. They printed up 48 shirts with the new design and sold out within an hour at a street fair. Their inspiration seemed correct. People craved a sense of positivity.

They started working with retailers to sell the shirts. The retailers liked the design but also started asking questions, such as, "Does the smiley guy eat ice cream? Does he roller-skate?" Bert and John responded by starting to draw designs that reflected what made life good. In Bert's words, "Our concept was that optimism is powerful." What they found out was that optimism is a powerful sales slogan. Their sales topped $250,000 within two years.

It's been over 20 years since they had the simple but profound insight that people buy into a positive message. Life is Good now generates nearly $150 million in sales and distributes its clothing through more than 4,500 retail stores in over 30 countries. The firm also has strategic alliances with Hallmark and Smucker's that extend its message to additional products, and John and Bert see further opportunities in publishing and filmmaking with their message that life is good. The brothers have also set up a foundation that hosts festivals to benefit kids overcoming poverty, illness, and violence. Their goal is clear. As Bert stated, "We can be a billion dollar company driving positive social change, teaching, and reinforcing the values we think are most important in the world." The message isn't that life is great or life is perfect but that even in hard times, life is good.

Sources: Buchanan, L. 2006. Life lessons. *inc.com*, October 1: np; Eng, D. 2014. Life is good in the T-shirt business. *Fortune*, May 19: 39–42; and *hoovers.com*.

---

what he wanted. In response, he developed earFeeder, a program that checks computers for music that is stored on the hard drive and feeds listeners news, tour, and ticket information on the bands they like.

- **Talk to the people who know.** These people can include your suppliers, customers, and frontline employees. Interactions can include visits with them, group discussions, and even role playing, such as having senior executives take shifts in frontline jobs or use the firm's online ordering system. These discussions and role-playing exercises can lead to insights on how these stakeholders' needs aren't being met and can also open avenues to hearing from these people regarding what they would like to see in new products and processes. For example, Sam Palmisano, former CEO of IBM, realized there was tremendous potential in providing outsourced services, such as IT and accounting systems, when he had a conversation with the CEO of Procter & Gamble. In this conversation, A. G. Lafley, the CEO of P&G, discussed the possibility of improving firm efficiency by focusing his firm on its core operations and outsourcing a range of services to specialized service firms.
- **Look to other markets.** One of the most powerful ways of finding new ideas is by borrowing ideas from other markets. This could involve looking at other industries or other geographic markets to identify new ideas. For example, in developing the idea for CarMax, the used-car superstore chain, Richard Sharp drew on his experience leading a major consumer electronics retailer to lay out the logic for his "big box" used-car lots, which allowed him to streamline operations and improve the efficiency of the used-car market. In essence, he decided to build the Best Buy or the Home Depot of the used-car market.
- **Get inspired by history.** Sometimes, the best ideas are not actually new ideas. Opportunities in industries can often be discovered by looking to the past to find good ideas that have slipped out of practice but might now be valued by the

market again. For example, Sam Calagione, founder of Ancient Ales, developed an innovative line of craft beers by using ancient brewing techniques and ingredients that differ from modern brews.

Opportunity evaluation, which occurs after an opportunity has been identified, involves analyzing an opportunity to determine whether it is viable and strong enough to be developed into a full-fledged new venture. Ideas developed by new product groups or in brainstorming sessions are tested by various methods, including talking to potential target customers and discussing operational requirements with production or logistics managers. A technique known as feasibility analysis is used to evaluate these and other critical success factors. This type of analysis often leads to the decision that a new venture project should be discontinued. If the venture concept continues to seem viable, a more formal business plan may be developed.[12]

Among the most important factors to evaluate is the market potential for the product or service. Established firms tend to operate in established markets. They have to adjust to market trends and to shifts in consumer demand, of course, but they usually have a customer base for which they are already filling a marketplace need. New ventures, in contrast, must first determine whether a market exists for the product or service they are contemplating. Thus, a critical element of opportunity recognition is assessing to what extent the opportunity is viable *in the marketplace.*

For an opportunity to be viable, it needs to have four qualities:[13]

- *Attractive.* The opportunity must be attractive in the marketplace; that is, there must be market demand for the new product or service.
- *Achievable.* The opportunity must be practical and physically possible.
- *Durable.* The opportunity must be attractive long enough for the development and deployment to be successful; that is, the window of opportunity must be open long enough for it to be worthwhile.
- *Value creating.* The opportunity must be potentially profitable; that is, the benefits must surpass the cost of development by a significant margin.

If a new business concept meets these criteria, two other factors must be considered before the opportunity is launched as a business: the resources available to undertake it and the characteristics of the entrepreneur(s) pursuing it. In the next section, we address the issue of entrepreneurial resources; following that, we address the importance of entrepreneurial leaders and teams. But first, consider the opportunities that have been created by the recent surge in interest in environmental sustainability. Strategy Spotlight 8.2 discusses how an entrepreneurial firm is building a strong market position with eco-friendly cleaning products.

Entrepreneurial Resources

As Exhibit 8.1 indicates, resources are an essential component of a successful entrepreneurial launch. For start-ups, the most important resource is usually money because a new firm typically has to expend substantial sums just to start the business. However, financial resources are not the only kind of resource a new venture needs. Human capital and social capital are also important. Many firms also rely on government resources to help them thrive.[14]

Financial Resources Hand-in-hand with the importance of markets (and marketing) to new venture creation, entrepreneurial firms must also have financing. In fact, the level of available financing is often a strong determinant of how the business is launched and its eventual success. Cash finances are, of course, highly important. But access to capital, such as a line of credit or favorable payment terms with a supplier, can also help a new venture succeed.

The types of financial resources that may be needed depend on two factors: the stage of venture development and the scale of the venture.[15] Entrepreneurial firms that are starting from scratch—start-ups—are at the earliest stage of development. Most start-ups also begin on a relatively small scale. The funding available to young and small firms tends to be quite limited. In fact, the majority of new firms are low-budget start-ups launched with

8.2 STRATEGY SPOTLIGHT — ENVIRONMENTAL SUSTAINABILITY

SOAKING IN THE MARKET WITH GREEN CLEANERS

Adam Lowry wanted to put his Stanford University chemical engineering degree to work to help create a more sustainable world. He searched for a consumer product market that was large and established but had not yet responded to the desire of many for a healthier and more sustainable planet. He had an inspiration when he opened a bottle of Snapple Element to drink and wondered, "Why can't Pine-Sol smell like this?" This was the thought that led Lowry and his childhood friend and roommate, Eric Ryan, to start their eco-friendly cleaner products firm, Method Products. They took their personal savings and contributions from family and friends to cobble together $90,000 to launch the firm in 2000. Lowry's logic for the business was clear: "Before us, you got either a toxic product that got the job done or a green product that didn't."

Lowry and Ryan developed their first four products—kitchen, shower, glass, and bathroom cleaners—and tested the products themselves, as well as enlisting friends to try them out. Ryan jokes that this was the time when their apartment "was the cleanest it'd ever been." It took six months before they convinced a single store to carry their products. Mollie Stone's Market in Burlingame, California, first put their products on its shelves in February 2001. By the end of 2002, Method products were in 700 stores and the founders were growing their product line. In addition to their first four products, they added dish soap, laundry detergent, automotive cleaners, air fresheners, and room sprays. Across all of the products, Method aims to use natural ingredients, ensures that no animal testing was used in developing its products, uses a third-party laboratory to test all of its product components for health and environmental safety, and bottles its products in recycled plastic containers. The firm has also worked to reduce its carbon footprint as much as possible.

Method now generates over $100 million in sales per year. The strength of its idea and market position is evident in the reaction of its major competitors. Most of its primary competitors, including S.C. Johnson and Clorox, have launched their own green cleaning-products lines. In spite of the increased competition, Method Products continues to grow at a healthy 10 percent rate.

Sources: Eng, D. 2013. Mopping up with green cleaners. *Fortune*, October 28: 47–50; *methodhome.com*; and *privco.com*.

---

angel investors
private individuals who provide equity investments for seed capital during the early stages of a new venture.

venture capitalists
companies organized to place their investors' funds in lucrative business opportunities.

personal savings and the contributions of family and friends.[16] Among firms included in the *Entrepreneur* list of the 100 fastest-growing new businesses, 61 percent reported that their start-up funds came from personal savings.[17]

Although bank financing, public financing, and venture capital are important sources of small business finance, these types of financial support are typically available only after a company has started to conduct business and generate sales. Even **angel investors**—private individuals who provide equity investments for seed capital during the early stages of a new venture—favor companies that already have a winning business model and dominance in a market niche.[18] According to Cal Simmons, coauthor of *Every Business Needs an Angel*, "I would much rather talk to an entrepreneur who has already put his money and his effort into proving the concept."[19]

Thus, while the press commonly talks about the role of **venture capitalists** and angel investors in start-up firms, the majority of external funding for young and small firms comes from informal sources such as family and friends. Based on a Kauffman Foundation survey

EXHIBIT 8.2 Sources of Capital for Start-Up Firms

	Capital Invested in Their First Year	Percentage of Capital Invested in Their First Year	Capital Invested in Their Fifth Year	Percentage of Capital Invested in Their Fifth Year
Insider equity	$33,034	41.1	$13,914	17.9
Investor equity	$ 4,108	5.1	$ 3,108	4.0
Personal debt of owners	$23,353	29.1	$21,754	28.0
Business debt	$19,867	24.7	$39,009	50.1
Total average capital invested	$80,362		$77,785	

Source: From Robb, A., Reedy, E. J., Ballou, J., DesRoches, D., Potter, F., & Zhao, A. 2010. An Overview of the Kauffman Firm Survey. Reproduced with permission from the Ewing Marion Kauffman Foundation.

of entrepreneurial firms, Exhibit 8.2 identifies the source of funding used by start-up businesses and by ongoing firms that are five years old. The survey shows that most start-up funding, about 70 percent, comes from either equity investments by the entrepreneur and the entrepreneur's family and friends or personal loans taken out by the entrepreneur.

Once a venture has established itself as a going concern, other sources of financing become readily available. Banks, for example, are more likely to provide later-stage financing to companies with a track record of sales or other cash-generating activity. According to the Kauffman Foundation study, after five years of operation, the largest source of funding is from loans taken out by the business.

At both stages, 5 percent or less of the funding comes from outside investors, such as angel investors or venture capitalists. In fact, few firms ever receive venture capital investments—only 7 of 2,606 firms in the Kauffman study received money from outside investors. But when they do, these firms receive a substantial level of investment—over $1 million on average in the survey—because they tend to be the firms that are the most innovative and have the greatest growth potential. These start-ups typically involve large capital investments or extensive development costs—such as manufacturing or engineering firms trying to commercialize an innovative product—and have high cash requirements soon after they are founded. Since these investments are typically well beyond the capability of the entrepreneur or even a local bank to fund, entrepreneurs running these firms turn to the venture capital market. Other firms turn to venture capitalists when they are on the brink of rapid growth.

Venture capital is a form of private equity financing through which entrepreneurs raise money by selling shares in the new venture. In contrast to angel investors, who invest their own money, venture capital companies are organized to place the funds of private investors into lucrative business opportunities. Venture capitalists nearly always have high performance expectations from the companies they invest in, but they also provide important managerial advice and links to key contacts in an industry.[20]

In recent years, a new source of funding, **crowdfunding,** has emerged as a means for start-ups to amass significant pools of capital.[21] In these peer-to-peer investment systems, individuals striving to grow their business post their business ideas on a crowdfunding website. Potential investors who go to the site evaluate the proposals listed and decide which, if any, to fund. Typically, no individual makes a very sizable funding allotment. Most investors contribute up to a few hundred dollars to any investment, but the power of the crowd is at work. If a few thousand investors sign up for a venture, it can potentially raise over a million dollars.

The crowdfunding market has taken off since the term was first coined in 2006. The total value of crowdfunding investments passed $5 billion in 2013, and according to a World Bank study, it could reach $90 billion by 2025.[22] Some crowdfunding websites allow investors to own actual equity in the firms they fund. Others, such as Kickstarter, don't offer investors equity. Instead, they get a reward from the entrepreneurial firm. For example, Mystery Brewing Company gave its investors logoed bottle openers, tulip-shaped beer glasses, T-shirts, posters, and home-brew recipes.

While crowdfunding offers a new avenue for corporations to raise funding, there are some potential downsides. First, the crowdfunding sites take a slice of the funds raised—typically 4 to 9 percent. Second, while crowdfunding offers a marketplace in which to raise funds, it also puts additional pressure on entrepreneurs. The social network–savvy investors who fund these ventures are quick to comment on their social media websites if the firm misses deadlines or falls short of its revenue projections. Finally, entrepreneurs can struggle with how much information to share about their business ideas. They want to share enough information without releasing critical information that competitors trolling these sites can benefit from. They also may be concerned about posting their financials, since these statements give their suppliers and customers access to sensitive information about margins and earnings.

There are also some concerns that the loose rules in the regulation of crowdfunding could lead to significant fraud by firms soliciting investment. According to Stephen

> **crowdfunding**
> funding a venture by pooling small investments from a large number of investors; often raised on the Internet.

8.3 STRATEGY SPOTLIGHT — CROWDSOURCING

EVALUATING CROWDFUNDING OPPORTUNITIES

Because the requirements for firms raising funds through crowdfunding are lax, investors need to do their homework. Here are some simple recommendations to keep from getting burned.

- *Financial statements.* Be sure to closely review the corporate tax returns that firms are required to post. Better yet, have your accountant review them to see if anything looks fishy.
- *Licenses and registrations.* You should check to see if the company has current licenses and registrations needed to operate in its chosen industry. This can often be done through online checks with the secretary of state's office or the state's corporation department. Sometimes, it will take a phone call or two. This provides a simple check to see if the company is legitimate.
- *Litigation.* Check to see if the company has been sued. You can search online at the free site justia.com and the law-oriented information sites Westlaw and Lexis. Be sure to check under current and former names of the firm and its principals (top managers).
- *Better Business Bureau.* Check the firm's BBB report. Does the firm appear to exist? What is the grade the BBB gives it? Is the firm a BBB member? All of this information gives insight into the firm's current operations and its customer relations.
- *Employment and educational history.* This is a bit tricky because of privacy issues, but you can typically contact colleges listed on the filing forms and inquire if the principals of the firm attended and graduated from the schools they list. You can also search employment histories on the websites of the companies the principals used to work at as well as social network sites, such as LinkedIn and Facebook.
- *Required disclosures.* Read all of the documentation carefully. This includes the shareholder rights statement. This statement will provide information on how much of a stake in the firm you get and how this will be diluted by future offerings. Also, read statements on the company's competition and risks it faces.

Sources: Wasik, J. 2012. The brilliance (and madness) of crowdfunding. *Forbes*, June 25: 144–146; and Burke, A. 2012. Crowdfunding set to explode with passage of Entrepreneur Access to Capital Act. *Forbes.com*, February 29: np.

Goodman, an attorney with Pryor Cashman LLP, "The SEC has been extremely skeptical of this [crowdfunding] process." Others have faith in the wisdom of the crowd to catch fraud. They point to the experience with Little Monster Productions, a video game developer. Little Monster was set to raise funds on Kickstarter, but the fund call was closed by Kickstarter when potential investors noticed and commented that Little Monster had stolen some of the images it was using in its game from another game site. Even with potential investors identifying glaring problems with some crowdfunding projects, the likelihood of success with crowdfunded projects is somewhat low. One study found that 75 percent of crowdfunded projects failed to meet their anticipated launch dates.[23] Strategy Spotlight 8.3 provides a checklist for investors considering participating in a crowdfunding effort. Regardless of their source, financial resources are essential for entrepreneurial ventures.[24]

Human Capital Bankers, venture capitalists, and angel investors agree that the most important asset an entrepreneurial firm can have is strong and skilled management.[25] According to Stephen Gaal, founding member of Walnut Venture Associates, venture investors do not invest in businesses; instead, "We invest in people . . . very smart people with very high integrity." Managers need to have a strong base of experience and extensive domain knowledge, as well as an ability to make rapid decisions and change direction as shifting circumstances may require. In the case of start-ups, more is better. New ventures that are started by teams of three, four, or five entrepreneurs are more likely to succeed in the long run than are ventures launched by "lone wolf" entrepreneurs.[26]

Social Capital New ventures founded by entrepreneurs who have extensive social contacts are more likely to succeed than are ventures started without the support of a social network.[27] Even though a venture may be new, if the founders have contacts who will vouch for them, they gain exposure and build legitimacy faster.[28] This support can come from several sources: prior jobs, industry organizations, and local business groups such as the chamber of commerce. These contacts can all contribute to a growing network that provides support for the entrepreneurial firm. Janina Pawlowski, cofounder of the online lending company E-Loan, attributes part of her success to the strong advisers she persuaded to serve on her board of directors, including Tim Koogle, former CEO of Yahoo![29]

Strategic alliances represent a type of social capital that can be especially important to young and small firms.[30] Strategic alliances can provide a key avenue for growth by entrepreneurial firms.[31] By partnering with other companies, young or small firms can expand or give the appearance of entering numerous markets or handling a range of operations. According to the National Federation of Independent Business (NFIB), nearly two-thirds of small businesses currently hold or have held some type of alliance. Here are a few types of alliances that have been used to extend or strengthen entrepreneurial firms:

- *Technology alliances.* Tech-savvy entrepreneurial firms often benefit from forming alliances with older incumbents. The alliance allows the larger firm to enhance its technological capabilities and expands the revenue and reach of the smaller firm.
- *Manufacturing alliances.* The use of outsourcing and other manufacturing alliances by small firms has grown dramatically in recent years. Internet-enabled capabilities such as collaborating online about delivery and design specifications have greatly simplified doing business, even with foreign manufacturers.
- *Retail alliances.* Licensing agreements allow one company to sell the products and services of another in different markets, including overseas. Specialty products—the types sometimes made by entrepreneurial firms—often seem more exotic when sold in another country.

Although such alliances often sound good, there are also potential pitfalls. Lack of oversight and control is one danger of partnering with foreign firms. Problems with product quality, timely delivery, and receiving payments can also sour an alliance relationship if it is not carefully managed. With technology alliances, there is a risk that big firms may take advantage of the technological know-how of their entrepreneurial partners. However, even with these potential problems, strategic alliances provide a good means for entrepreneurial firms to develop and grow.

Government Resources In the U.S., the federal government provides support for entrepreneurial firms in two key arenas—financing and government contracting. The Small Business Administration (SBA) has several loan guarantee programs designed to support the growth and development of entrepreneurial firms. The government itself does not typically lend money but underwrites loans made by banks to small businesses, thus reducing the risk associated with lending to firms with unproven records. The SBA also offers training, counseling, and support services through its local offices and Small Business Development Centers.[32] State and local governments also have hundreds of programs to provide funding, contracts, and other support for new ventures and small businesses. These programs are often designed to grow the economy of a region.

Another key area of support is government contracting. Programs sponsored by the SBA and other government agencies ensure that small businesses have the opportunity to bid on contracts to provide goods and services to the government. Although working with the government sometimes has its drawbacks in terms of issues of regulation and time-consuming decision making, programs to support small businesses and entrepreneurial activity constitute an important resource for entrepreneurial firms.

Entrepreneurial Leadership

Whether a venture is launched by an individual entrepreneur or an entrepreneurial team, effective leadership is needed. Launching a new venture requires a special kind of

entrepreneurial leadership
leadership appropriate for new ventures that requires courage, belief in one's convictions, and the energy to work hard even in difficult circumstances and that embodies vision, dedication and drive, and commitment to excellence.

leadership. Research indicates that entrepreneurs tend to have characteristics that distinguish them from corporate managers. Differences include:

- **Higher core self-evaluation.** Successful entrepreneurs evidence higher levels of self-confidence and a higher assessment of the degree to which an individual controls his or her own destiny.[33]
- **Higher conscientiousness.** Entrepreneurs tend to have a higher degree of organization, persistence, hard work, and pursuit of goal accomplishment.
- **Higher openness to experience.** Entrepreneurs also tend to score higher on openness to experience, a personality trait associated with intellectual curiosity and a desire to explore novel ideas.
- **Higher emotional stability.** Entrepreneurs exhibit a higher ability to handle ambiguity and maintain even emotions during stressful periods, and they are less likely to be overcome by anxieties.
- **Lower agreeableness.** Finally, entrepreneurs tend to score lower on agreeableness. This suggests they typically look out primarily for their own self-interest and also are willing to influence or manipulate others for their own advantage.[34]

These personality traits are embodied in the behavioral attributes necessary for successful entrepreneurial leadership—vision, dedication and drive, and commitment to excellence:

- **Vision.** This may be an entrepreneur's most important asset. Entrepreneurs envision realities that do not yet exist. But without a vision, most entrepreneurs would never even get their venture off the ground. With vision, entrepreneurs are able to exercise a kind of transformational leadership that creates something new and, in some way, changes the world. Just having a vision, however, is not enough. To develop support, get financial backing, and attract employees, entrepreneurial leaders must share their vision with others.
- **Dedication and drive.** Dedication and drive are reflected in hard work. Drive involves internal motivation; dedication calls for an intellectual commitment that keeps an entrepreneur going even in the face of bad news or poor luck. They both require patience, stamina, and a willingness to work long hours. However, a business built on the heroic efforts of one person may suffer in the long run. That's why the dedicated entrepreneur's enthusiasm is also important—like a magnet, it attracts others to the business to help with the work.[35]
- **Commitment to excellence.** Excellence requires entrepreneurs to commit to knowing the customer, providing quality goods and services, paying attention to details, and continuously learning. Entrepreneurs who achieve excellence are sensitive to how these factors work together. However, entrepreneurs may flounder if they think they are the only ones who can create excellent results. The most successful, by contrast, often report that they owe their success to hiring people smarter than themselves.

In his book *Good to Great,* Jim Collins makes another important point about entrepreneurial leadership: Ventures built on the charisma of a single person may have trouble growing "from good to great" once that person leaves.[36] Thus, the leadership that is needed to build a great organization is usually exercised by a team of dedicated people working together rather than a single leader. Another aspect of this team approach is attracting team members who fit with the company's culture, goals, and work ethic. Thus, for a venture's leadership to be a valuable resource and not a liability, it must be cohesive in its vision, drive and dedication, and commitment to excellence.

David Drews is a senior executive at the entrepreneurial marketing firm Project: WorldWide. In the Insights from Executives box, he provides additional thoughts on both identifying entrepreneurial opportunities and leading entrepreneurial firms.

8.1 INSIGHTS FROM EXECUTIVES

DAVID DREWS, EXECUTIVE VICE PRESIDENT AND CFO OF PROJECT: WORLDWIDE

BIOSKETCH

David Drews has been executive vice president and CFO of Project: WorldWide for over 20 years. Project: WorldWide is an independent, global network of complementary, wholly owned marketing agencies that has grown from $30 million in annual revenue in the mid-1980s to nearly $1 billion in revenue today. Drews began his career in public accounting after graduating from Michigan State University in 1982. He received his MBA from the University of Michigan in 1987. He joined the company in 1986, has served on the executive committee since 1993, and has been a board member since 2005. He has helped guide Project: WorldWide's expansion into new product and geographic markets through organic growth, strategic alliances, and acquisitions, as well as completing an employee-led, S corporation ESOP buyout of the company in 2005.

1. *You've been involved with multiple situations in which your firm has identified attractive opportunities for growth. What has been the source of insight that you and your colleagues have drawn on to identify these profitable opportunities?*

   Attractive growth always begins with our clients' needs. Listening carefully to their needs—and anticipating their needs—is the key driver for strategic initiatives. Knowing the competitive landscape and leaning forward, adopting new offerings before they're widely available in the market, creates opportunity for profitable growth. Hiring staff with diverse backgrounds has allowed new thinking to broaden our offering. Hiring talent—world-class talent—leads to winning business from much larger competitors. The key across all opportunities for growth centers on finding the right talent that can bring tremendous value to our clients.

2. *Adequate financial capital is a key resource for growing firms. Firms can access this resource from a variety of sources, including the personal investment of entrepreneurs, bank loans, angel investors, venture capital, crowdfunding, and many other sources. What sources of financing have your firms used? What have you found to be the advantages and disadvantages of each source?*

   Wealth is created with equity. Equity provides the opportunity for tremendous returns for angel investors, private equity, venture capital, and the like. It also provides the most upside for entrepreneurs. Inasmuch as salary, short-term incentives, and long-term incentives are important, real wealth comes from owning the business. Before sharing equity with others, entrepreneurs should very carefully evaluate the alternatives. If the business can be financed another way, through debt and the entrepreneur's own capital, for instance, that should be a much more attractive alternative—unless other capital sources multiply earnings growth. Project: WorldWide has used past earnings and debt to finance growth. This creates the most upside for our employee-owners. In the end, the owner of equity will be rewarded for the risk taken by achieving a multiple of EBITDA when the business is sold. Be slow to give up equity. It is the crown jewel of finance for entrepreneurs.

3. *By some estimates, up to 90 percent of new ventures fail. What do you see as the most common drivers of venture failure? What steps as an entrepreneur did you take to enhance your chances of success?*

   As the saying goes, "Failure to plan means you are planning to fail." That said, only so much analysis can be done before launching a new venture. Analyzing the market demand is critical. Coming up short on revenue is the number-one reason for failure. Having enough—but not too much—top-end talent is critical. Revenue must be able to support the staff load. As a result, staff need to be able to wear multiple "hats." The "burn rate" needs to be determined to see how long the business can sustain itself before the next injection of capital—or when revenue is adequate to achieve break-even. Knowing your business model and key success factors is critical. Entrepreneurs who lead, inspire, and recruit outstanding people greatly enhance the chance of success.

4. *How have ventures you've been involved in drawn on ties in social networks to create competitive advantages? This could include informal ties, such as personal ties of the firm's founders with potential customers, investors, or government officials, or more formal social capital, such as strategic alliances with suppliers, customers, or technology partners.*

   Social networks can provide excellent background information on people your business is looking to do business with. However, nothing replaces a personal relationship. Strong personal relationships lead to opportunities which lead to sustainable revenue. In a service-based business, these relationships are key. Becoming a trusted adviser means solving real business problems for clients, addressing their current needs, and anticipating their future needs. Social networks aid in cataloging contacts, but they don't create the foundation for long-term success with clients. This must be done personally, with great work earning trust over an extended period of time. The same can be said for suppliers and technology partners. Finding partners, through social networks or diligent research, that fulfill the outsourced portion of your product offering is key to sustained success. A common thread of successful entrepreneurs is the ability to develop truly trusted relationships across the entire spectrum of clients, suppliers, employees, and other business contracts.

Once an opportunity has been recognized, and an entrepreneurial team and resources have been assembled, a new venture must craft a strategy. Prior chapters have addressed the strategies of incumbent firms. In the next section, we highlight the types of strategies and strategic considerations faced by new entrants.

Entrepreneurial Strategy

> **entrepreneurial strategy**
> a strategy that enables a skilled and dedicated entrepreneur, with a viable opportunity and access to sufficient resources, to successfully launch a new venture.

Successfully creating new ventures requires several ingredients. As indicated in Exhibit 8.1, three factors are necessary—a viable opportunity, sufficient resources, and a skilled and dedicated entrepreneur or entrepreneurial team. Once these elements are in place, the new venture needs a strategy. In this section, we consider several different strategic factors that are unique to new ventures and also how the generic strategies introduced in Chapter 5 can be applied to entrepreneurial firms. We also indicate how combination strategies might benefit entrepreneurial firms and address the potential pitfalls associated with launching new venture strategies.

To be successful, new ventures must evaluate industry conditions, the competitive environment, and market opportunities in order to position themselves strategically. However, a traditional strategic analysis may have to be altered somewhat to fit the entrepreneurial situation. For example, five-forces analysis (as discussed in Chapter 2) is typically used by established firms. It can also be applied to the analysis of new ventures to assess the impact of industry and competitive forces. But you may ask: How does a new entrant evaluate the threat of other new entrants?

First, the new entrant needs to examine barriers to entry. If the barriers are too high, the potential entrant may decide not to enter or to gather more resources before attempting to do so. Compared to an older firm with an established reputation and available resources, the barriers to entry may be insurmountable for an entrepreneurial start-up. Therefore, understanding the force of these barriers is critical in making a decision to launch.

A second factor that may be especially important to a young venture is the threat of retaliation by incumbents. In many cases, entrepreneurial ventures *are* the new entrants that pose a threat to incumbent firms. Therefore, in applying the five-forces model to new ventures, the threat of retaliation by established firms needs to be considered.

Part of any decision about what opportunity to pursue is a consideration of how a new entrant will actually enter a new market. The concept of entry strategies provides a useful means of addressing the types of choices that new ventures have.

Entry Strategies

> **LO8.2**
> Three types of entry strategies—pioneering, imitative, and adaptive—commonly used to launch a new venture.

One of the most challenging aspects of launching a new venture is finding a way to begin doing business that quickly generates cash flow, builds credibility, attracts good employees, and overcomes the liability of newness. The idea of an entry strategy or "entry wedge" describes several approaches that firms may take to get a foothold in a market.[37] Several factors will affect this decision:

- Is the product/service high-tech or low-tech?
- What resources are available for the initial launch?
- What are the industry and competitive conditions?
- What is the overall market potential?
- Does the venture founder prefer to control the business or to grow it?

In some respects, any type of entry into a market for the first time may be considered entrepreneurial. But the entry strategy will vary depending on how risky and innovative the new business concept is.[38] New-entry strategies typically fall into one of three categories—pioneering new entry, imitative new entry, or adaptive new entry.[39]

Pioneering New Entry New entrants with a radical new product or highly innovative service may change the way business is conducted in an industry. This kind of

8.4 STRATEGY SPOTLIGHT

ROCKET INTERNET FINDS THAT IMITATION IS THE MOST PROFITABLE FORM OF FLATTERY

Since its founding in 2007, Rocket Internet has funded over 100 start-ups in 50 countries that now generate over $4 billion in revenue. What is the secret to Rocket's success? It is blatant imitation. Employees of the firm scour the Internet looking for successful businesses and then create copies of these existing e-commerce sites, typically in underserved European and emerging markets. For example, one of the firm's most successful ventures is Lamoda, a retailing fashion site in Russia that is modeled after Zappos. Similarly, it created Food Panda, a GrubHub-clone food-delivery service in Asia, and Linio, a site that has been called the "Amazon of Latin America." More recently, it launched Helpling, a system to book and rate home cleaning services in Germany that copies the formula of San Francisco–based Homejoy.

While the stereotype of a successful entrepreneur is one who creates bold and novel products and services, Rocket Internet demonstrates that taking a proven idea to new and underserved markets is a very viable form of entrepreneurship. In the words of Jennifer Binder-LePape, a partner in the consulting firm Bain & Company, "The reality is that not everyone can be Elon Musk. Rocket's play is just another form of innovation." Rocket Internet pushes for speed and efficiency in launching its businesses. Rocket's U.K. managing director, Ian Marsh, asserts that the firm can launch a new business in 60 days. Rocket reduces costs and risk by imitating established business models that it tweaks slightly for each market and by hiring seasoned, professional managers to run each site. The success of the business was evident when it listed its stock on the Frankfurt Stock Exchange in October 2014, at a firm market value of $8 billion.

Sources: Cava, M. 2014. Berlin's copycats. *Lansing State Journal,* June 1: 8B; and Williams-Grut, O. 2014. Rocket Internet: Attack of the online clone. *independent.co.uk,* December 18: np.

---

breakthrough—creating new ways to solve old problems or meeting customers' needs in a unique new way—is referred to as a **pioneering new entry.** If the product or service is unique enough, a pioneering new entrant may actually have little direct competition. The first personal computer was a pioneering product; there had never been anything quite like it, and it revolutionized computing. The first Internet browser provided a type of pioneering service. These breakthroughs created whole new industries and changed the competitive landscape. And breakthrough innovations continue to inspire pioneering entrepreneurial efforts.

> **pioneering new entry**
> a firm's entry into an industry with a radical new product or highly innovative service that changes the way business is conducted.

The pitfalls associated with a pioneering new entry are numerous. For one thing, there is a strong risk that the product or service will not be accepted by consumers. The history of entrepreneurship is littered with new ideas that never got off the launching pad. Take, for example, Smell-O-Vision, an invention designed to pump odors into movie theaters from the projection room at preestablished moments in a film. It was tried only once (for the film *Scent of a Mystery*) before it was declared a major flop. Innovative? Definitely. But hardly a good idea at the time.[40]

A pioneering new entry is disruptive to the status quo of an industry. It is likely based on a technological breakthrough. If it is successful, other competitors will rush in to copy it. This can create issues of sustainability for an entrepreneurial firm, especially if a larger company with greater resources introduces a similar product. For a new entrant to sustain its pioneering advantage, it may be necessary to protect its intellectual property, advertise heavily to build brand recognition, form alliances with businesses that will adopt its products or services, and offer exceptional customer service.

Imitative New Entry Whereas pioneers are often inventors or tinkerers with new technology, imitators usually have a strong marketing orientation. They look for opportunities to capitalize on proven market successes. An **imitative new entry** strategy is used by entrepreneurs who see products or business concepts that have been successful in one market niche or physical locale and introduce the same basic product or service in another segment of the market. Strategy Spotlight 8.4 discusses how Rocket Internet has built an imitative business empire.

> **imitative new entry**
> a firm's entry into an industry with products or services that capitalize on proven market successes and that usually have a strong marketing orientation.

Sometimes the key to success with an imitative strategy is to fill a market space where the need had previously been filled inadequately. Entrepreneurs are also prompted to be imitators when they realize that they have the resources or skills to do a job better than an existing competitor. This can actually be a serious problem for entrepreneurial start-ups if the imitator is an established company. Consider the example of Square.[41] Founded in 2010, Square provides a means for small businesses to process credit and debit card sales without signing up for a traditional credit card arrangement that typically includes monthly fees and minimum charges. Square provides a small credit card reader that plugs into a smartphone to users who sign up for its service. Users swipe the card and input the charge amount. Square does the rest for a 2.75 percent transaction fee. As of 2014, Square was processing $30 billion in transactions annually. But success triggers imitation. A host of both upstart and established firms have moved into this new segment. While Square has quickly established itself in the market, it now faces strong competition from major competitors, including Apple, Google, and PayPal. With the strong competition it faces and the thin margins in its business, Square is bleeding cash. This has led to persistent rumors that it will look for a larger firm to buy it out.[42]

Adaptive New Entry Most new entrants use a strategy somewhere between "pure" imitation and "pure" pioneering. That is, they offer a product or service that is somewhat new and sufficiently different to create new value for customers and capture market share. Such firms are adaptive in the sense that they are aware of marketplace conditions and conceive entry strategies to capitalize on current trends.

According to business creativity coach Tom Monahan, "Every new idea is merely a spin of an old idea. [Knowing that] takes the pressure off from thinking [you] have to be totally creative. You don't. Sometimes it's one slight twist to an old idea that makes all the difference."[43] An **adaptive new entry** approach does not involve "reinventing the wheel," nor is it merely imitative either. It involves taking an existing idea and adapting it to a particular situation. Exhibit 8.3 presents examples of four young companies that successfully modified or adapted existing products to create new value.

There are several pitfalls that might limit the success of an adaptive new entrant. First, the value proposition must be perceived as unique. Unless potential customers believe a

> **adaptive new entry** a firm's entry into an industry by offering a product or service that is somewhat new and sufficiently different to create value for customers by capitalizing on current market trends.

EXHIBIT 8.3 Examples of Adaptive New Entrants

Company Name	Product	Adaptation	Result
Under Armour, Inc. Founded in 1995	Undershirts and other athletic gear	Used moisture-wicking fabric to create better gear for sweaty sports.	Under Armour generated nearly $3 billion in 2014 and is now the number-two athletic-clothing firm in the U.S. after Nike.
Mint.com Founded in 2005	Comprehensive online money management	Created software that tells users what they are spending by aggregating financial information from online bank and credit card accounts.	Mint has over 10 million users and is helping them manage over $1 billion in assets.
Plum Organics Founded in 2005	Organic baby food and snack foods for children	Made convenient line of baby food using organic ingredients.	Plum now has over 20 products and is ranked number 19 on Forbes's "Most Promising Companies" list.
Spanx Founded in 2000	Footless pantyhose and other undergarments for women	Combined nylon and Lycra to create a new type of undergarment that is comfortable and eliminates panty lines.	Spanx now produces over 200 products generating over $250 million in sales annually.

Sources: Bryan, M. 2007. Spanx Me, Baby! *www.observer.com*, December 10, np.; Carey, J. 2006. Perspiration Inspiration. *BusinessWeek,* June 5: 64; Palanjian, A. 2008. A Planner Plumbs for a Niche. *www.wsj.com,* September 30, np.; Worrell, D. 2008. Making Mint. *Entrepreneur,* September: 55; *www.mint.com; www.spanx.com; www.underarmour.com;* Buss, D. 2010. The Mothers of Invention. *Wall Street Journal,* February 8: R7; Crook, J. 2012. Mint.com Tops 10 Million Registered Users, 70% Use Mobile. *techcrunch.com,* August 29: np; *plumorganics.com; forbes.com/companies/plum-organics/;* and Germano, S. 2015. Under Armour Overtakes Adidas in U.S. Sportswear Market. *wsj.com,* January 8: np.

new product or service does a superior job of meeting their needs, they will have little motivation to try it. Second, there is nothing to prevent a close competitor from mimicking the new firm's adaptation as a way to hold on to its customers. Third, once an adaptive entrant achieves initial success, the challenge is to keep the idea fresh. If the attractive features of the new business are copied, the entrepreneurial firm must find ways to adapt and improve the product or service offering.

Considering these choices, an entrepreneur or entrepreneurial team might ask, Which new entry strategy is best? The choice depends on many competitive, financial, and marketplace considerations. Nevertheless, research indicates that the greatest opportunities may stem from being willing to enter new markets rather than seeking growth only in existing markets. One study found that companies that ventured into arenas that were new to the world or new to the company earned total profits of 61 percent. In contrast, companies that made only incremental improvements, such as extending an existing product line, grew total profits by only 39 percent.[44]

However, whether to be pioneering, imitative, or adaptive when entering markets is only one question the entrepreneur faces. A new entrant must also decide what type of strategic positioning will work best as the business goes forward. The strategic choices can be informed by the guidelines suggested for the generic strategies. We turn to that subject next.

Generic Strategies

Typically, a new entrant begins with a single business model that is equivalent in scope to a business-level strategy (Chapter 5). In this section we address how overall low cost, differentiation, and focus strategies can be used to achieve competitive advantages.

Overall Cost Leadership One of the ways entrepreneurial firms achieve success is by doing more with less. By holding down costs or making more efficient use of resources than larger competitors, new ventures are often able to offer lower prices and still be profitable. Thus, under the right circumstances, a low-cost leader strategy is a viable alternative for some new ventures. The way most companies achieve low-cost leadership, however, is typically different for young or small firms.

Recall from Chapter 5 that three of the features of a low-cost approach include operating at a large-enough scale to spread costs over many units of production (economies of scale), making substantial capital investments in order to increase scale economies, and using knowledge gained from experience to make cost-saving improvements. These elements of a cost-leadership strategy may be unavailable to new ventures. Because new ventures are typically small, they usually don't have high economies of scale relative to competitors. Because they are usually cash strapped, they can't make large capital investments to increase their scale advantages. And because many are young, they often don't have a wealth of accumulated experience to draw on to achieve cost reductions.

Given these constraints, how can new ventures successfully deploy cost-leader strategies? Compared to large firms, new ventures often have simple organizational structures that make decision making both easier and faster. The smaller size also helps young firms change more quickly when upgrades in technology or feedback from the marketplace indicate that improvements are needed. They are also able to make decisions at the time they are founded that help them deal with the issue of controlling costs. For example, they may source materials from a supplier that provides them more cheaply or set up manufacturing facilities in another country where labor costs are especially low. Thus, new firms have several avenues for achieving low-cost leadership.

Strategy Spotlight 8.5 highlights the success of Tuft and Needle, a growing mattress manufacturer with an overall cost leadership strategy. Whatever methods young firms use to achieve a low-cost advantage, this has always been a way that entrepreneurial firms take business away from incumbents—by offering a comparable product or service at a lower price.

>LO8.3
>How the generic strategies of overall cost leadership, differentiation, and focus are used by new ventures and small businesses.

8.5 STRATEGY SPOTLIGHT

TUFT AND NEEDLE CONSTRUCTS A LOW-COST MATTRESS

J. T. Marino had to buy a new mattress. He researched the options online and was overwhelmed by the competing claims and marketing lingo. He visited mattress stores and found even more confusion. He saw dozens of competing mattresses and couldn't figure out why two models that appeared identical could have prices that varied by several hundred dollars. "Honestly, it was a lot like the Taco Bell menu," Marino quips. "It's all these same ingredients mixed around with different formats, like a different mix of fabric, springs and thicknesses." In the end, he laid down $3,200 to buy a memory-foam mattress that he realized he didn't find comfortable once he started using it. Marino concluded, "It was a terrible experience."

This experience led Marino and a college buddy, Daehee Park, on the path to launching a low-cost mattress manufacturer. They researched the industry, discussed mattress manufacturing with component suppliers, and dissected mattresses they bought. What they realized was that the expensive mattress Marino purchased cost only about $300 to manufacture, including materials and labor. Considering all of the markups across the supply chain, they realized big-brand mattresses are priced up to 1,000 percent of their actual cost.

Their response was to build a cheaper mattress. Their company, Tuft and Needle, sells mattresses through its own website and on Amazon for a fraction of the cost of a brand-name mattress at a furniture store. Tuft and Needle reduces cost by removing the retailer and salespeople's commissions, having a limited marketing campaign, offering a narrow range of models built with standardized components, and cutting back on some of the plush extras on store mattresses that do little to add to the comfort or durability of the mattress. The company also sucks all of the air out of the foam in a mattress and vacuum seal it so that it can be shipped cheaply in small boxes. Its mattresses are priced from $200 to $600, less than one-third of the price of a typical foam mattress at retailers.

So far, the company is having great success. Launched in 2012, Tuft and Needle surpassed $1 million in sales in 2013 and was expected to gross $5 million in sales in 2014. Customers also seem to appreciate both the service Tuft and Needle provides and the quality of its products. Its mattresses are the top-rated mattresses on Amazon. What is left to be seen is when and how the major players in the industry will respond to Tuft and Needle.

Sources: Helft, M. 2014. Meet the Warby Parker of mattresses. *cnnmoney.com*, January 22: np; and Daley, J. 2014. How Tuft & Needle disrupted a tired mattress marketplace. *entrepreneur.com*, October 20: np.

Differentiation Both pioneering and adaptive entry strategies involve some degree of differentiation. That is, the new entry is based on being able to offer a differentiated value proposition. In the case of pioneers, the new venture is attempting to do something strikingly different, either by using a new technology or by deploying resources in a way that radically alters the way business is conducted. Often, entrepreneurs do both.

Amazon founder Jeff Bezos set out to use Internet technology to revolutionize the way books are sold. He garnered the ire of other booksellers and the attention of the public by making bold claims about being the "earth's largest bookseller." As a bookseller, Bezos was not doing anything that had not been done before. But two key differentiating features—doing it on the Internet and offering extraordinary customer service—made Amazon a differentiated success.

There are several factors that make it more difficult for new ventures to be successful as differentiators. For one thing, the strategy is generally thought to be expensive to enact. Differentiation is often associated with strong brand identity, and establishing a brand is usually considered to be expensive because of the cost of advertising and promotion, paid endorsements, exceptional customer service, and so on. Differentiation successes are sometimes built on superior innovation or use of technology. These are also factors that might make it challenging for young firms to excel relative to established competitors.

Nevertheless, all of these areas—innovation, technology, customer service, distinctive branding—are also arenas where new ventures have sometimes made a name for themselves even though they must operate with limited resources and experience. To be successful, according to Garry Ridge, CEO of the WD-40 Company, "You need to have a great product, make the end user aware of it, and make it easy to buy."[45] It sounds simple, but it is a difficult challenge for new ventures with differentiation strategies.

Focus Focus strategies are often associated with small businesses because there is a natural fit between the narrow scope of the strategy and the small size of the firm. A focus strategy may include elements of differentiation and overall cost leadership, as well as combinations of these approaches. But to be successful within a market niche, the key strategic requirement is to stay focused. Let's consider why that is so.

Despite all the attention given to fast-growing new industries, most start-ups enter industries that are mature.[46] In mature industries, growth in demand tends to be slow and there are often many competitors. Therefore, if a start-up wants to get a piece of the action, it often has to take business away from an existing competitor. If a start-up enters a market with a broad or aggressive strategy, it is likely to evoke retaliation from a more powerful competitor. Young firms can often succeed best by finding a market niche where they can get a foothold and make small advances that erode the position of existing competitors.[47] From this position, they can build a name for themselves and grow.

Consider, for example, the "Miniature Editions" line of books launched by Running Press, a small Philadelphia publisher. The books are palm-size minibooks positioned at bookstore cash registers as point-of-sale impulse items costing about $4.95. Beginning with just 10 titles in 1993, Running Press grew rapidly and within 10 years had sold over 20 million copies. Even though these books represent just a tiny fraction of total sales in the $23 billion publishing industry, they have been a mainstay for Running Press.[48] As the Running Press example indicates, many new ventures are successful even though their share of the market is quite small.

Combination Strategies

One of the best ways for young and small businesses to achieve success is by pursuing combination strategies. By combining the best features of low-cost, differentiation, and focus strategies, new ventures can often achieve something truly distinctive.

Entrepreneurial firms are often in a strong position to offer a combination strategy because they have the flexibility to approach situations uniquely. For example, holding down expenses can be difficult for big firms because each layer of bureaucracy adds to the cost of doing business across the boundaries of a large organization.[49]

A similar argument could be made about entrepreneurial firms that differentiate. Large firms often find it difficult to offer highly specialized products or superior customer services. Entrepreneurial firms, by contrast, can often create high-value products and services through their unique differentiating efforts.

For nearly all new entrants, one of the major dangers is that a large firm with more resources will copy what they are doing. Well-established incumbents that observe the success of a new entrant's product or service will copy it and use their market power to overwhelm the smaller firm. The threat may be lessened for firms that use combination strategies. Because of the flexibility of entrepreneurial firms, they can often enact combination strategies in ways that the large firms cannot copy. This makes the new entrant's strategies much more sustainable.

Perhaps more threatening than large competitors are close competitors, because they have similar structural features that help them adjust quickly and be flexible in decision making. Here again, a carefully crafted and executed combination strategy may be the best way for an entrepreneurial firm to thrive in a competitive environment. Nevertheless, competition among rivals is a key determinant of new venture success. To address this, we turn next to the topic of competitive dynamics.

Competitive Dynamics

New entry into markets, whether by start-ups or by incumbent firms, nearly always threatens existing competitors. This is true in part because, except in very new markets, nearly every market need is already being met, either directly or indirectly, by existing firms. As a result, the competitive actions of a new entrant are very likely to provoke a competitive response from companies that feel threatened. This, in turn, is likely to evoke a reaction to

LO8.4

How competitive actions, such as the entry of new competitors into a marketplace, may launch a cycle of actions and reactions among close competitors.

the response. As a result, a competitive dynamic—action and response—begins among the firms competing for the same customers in a given marketplace.

Competitive dynamics—intense rivalry among similar competitors—has the potential to alter a company's strategy. New entrants may be forced to change their strategies or develop new ones to survive competitive challenges by incumbent rivals. New entry is among the most common reasons why a cycle of competitive actions and reactions gets started. It might also occur because of threatening actions among existing competitors, such as aggressive cost cutting. Thus, studying competitive dynamics helps explain why strategies evolve and reveals how, why, and when to respond to the actions of close competitors. Exhibit 8.4 identifies the factors that competitors need to consider when determining how to respond to a competitive act.

> **competitive dynamics**
> intense rivalry, involving actions and responses, among similar competitors vying for the same customers in a marketplace.

New Competitive Action

Entry into a market by a new competitor is a good starting point to begin describing the cycle of actions and responses characteristic of a competitive dynamic process.[50] However, new entry is only one type of competitive action. Price cutting, imitating successful products, and expanding production capacity are other examples of competitive acts that might provoke competitors to react.

> **LO8.5**
> The components of competitive dynamic analysis—new competitive action, threat analysis, motivation and capability to respond, types of competitive actions, and likelihood of competitive reaction.

Why do companies launch new competitive actions? There are several reasons:

- Improve market position
- Capitalize on growing demand
- Expand production capacity
- Provide an innovative new solution
- Obtain first-mover advantages

Underlying all of these reasons is a desire to strengthen financial outcomes, capture some of the extraordinary profits that industry leaders enjoy, and grow the business. Some companies are also motivated to launch competitive challenges because they want to build their reputation for innovativeness or efficiency. For example, Toyota's success with the Prius signaled to its competitors the potential value of high-fuel-economy cars, and these firms have responded with their own hybrids, electric cars, high-efficiency diesel engines, and even more fuel-efficient traditional gasoline engines. This is indicative of the competitive dynamic cycle. As former Intel chairman Andy Grove stated, "Business success contains the seeds of its own destruction. The more successful you are, the more people want a chunk of your business and then another chunk and then another until there is nothing left."[51]

> **new competitive action**
> acts that might provoke competitors to react, such as new market entry, price cutting, imitating successful products, and expanding production capacity.

EXHIBIT 8.4 Model of Competitive Dynamics

New competitive action → Threat analysis → Motivation and capability to respond → Types of competitive action → Likelihood of competitive reaction → (back to New competitive action)

Sources: Adapted from Chen, M. J. 1996. Competitor Analysis and Interfirm Rivalry: Toward a Theoretical Integration. *Academy of Management Review,* 21(1): 100–134; Ketchen, D. J., Snow, C. C., & Hoover, V. L. 2004. Research on Competitive Dynamics: Recent Accomplishments and Future Challenges. *Journal of Management,* 30(6): 779–804; and Smith, K. G., Ferrier, W. J., & Grimm, C. M. 2001. King of the Hill: Dethroning the Industry Leader. *Academy of Management Executive,* 15(2): 59–70.

When a company enters into a market for the first time, it is an attack on existing competitors. As indicated earlier in the chapter, any of the entry strategies can be used to take competitive action. But competitive attacks come from many sources besides new entrants. Some of the most intense competition is among incumbent rivals intent on gaining strategic advantages. "Winners in business play rough and don't apologize for it," according to Boston Consulting Group authors George Stalk, Jr., and Rob Lachenauer in their book *Hardball: Are You Playing to Play or Playing to Win?*[52] Exhibit 8.5 outlines their five strategies.

The likelihood that a competitor will launch an attack depends on many factors.[53] In the remaining sections, we discuss factors such as competitor analysis, market conditions, types of strategic actions, and the resource endowments and capabilities companies need to take competitive action.

EXHIBIT 8.5 Five "Hardball" Strategies

Strategy	Description	Examples
Devastate rivals' profit sanctuaries	Not all business segments generate the same level of profits for a company. Through focused attacks on a rival's most profitable segments, a company can generate maximum leverage with relatively smaller-scale attacks. Recognize, however, that companies closely guard the information needed to determine just what their profit sanctuaries are.	In 2005, Walmart began offering low-priced extended warranties on home electronics after learning that its rivals such as Best Buy derived most of their profits from extended warranties.
Plagiarize with pride	Just because a close competitor comes up with an idea first does not mean it cannot be successfully imitated. Second movers, in fact, can see how customers respond, make improvements, and launch a better version without all the market development costs. Successful imitation is harder than it may appear and requires the imitating firm to keep its ego in check.	In designing its smartphones, Samsung copied the look, feel, and technological attributes of Apple's IPhone. Samsung lost a patent infringement lawsuit to Apple, but by copying Apple, Samsung was able to improve its market position.
Deceive the competition	A good gambit sends the competition off in the wrong direction. This may cause the rivals to miss strategic shifts, spend money pursuing dead ends, or slow their responses. Any of these outcomes support the deceiving firms' competitive advantage. Companies must be sure not to cross ethical lines during these actions.	Max Muir knew that Australian farmers liked to buy from family-firm suppliers but also wanted efficient suppliers. To meet both needs, he quietly bought a number of small firms to build economies of scale but didn't consolidate brands or his sales force so that, to his customers and rivals, they still looked like independent family firms.
Unleash massive and overwhelming force	While many hardball strategies are subtle and indirect, this one is not. This is a full-frontal attack where by a firm commits significant resources to a major campaign to weaken rivals' positions in certain markets. Firms must be sure they have the mass and stamina required to win before they declare war against a rival.	Unilever has taken a dominant position, with 65 percent market share, in the Vietnamese laundry detergent market by employing a massive investment and marketing campaign. In doing so, it decimated the market position of the local, incumbent competitors.
Raise competitors' costs	If a company has superior insight into the complex cost and profit structure of the industry, it can compete in a way that steers its rivals into relatively higher cost/lower profit arenas. This strategy uses deception to make the rivals think they are winning, when in fact they are not. Again, companies using this strategy must be confident that they understand the industry better than their rivals.	Ecolab, a company that sells cleaning supplies to businesses, encouraged a leading competitor, Diversity, to adopt a strategy to go after the low-volume, high-margin customers. What Ecolab knew that Diversity didn't is that the high servicing costs involved with this segment make the segment unprofitable—a situation Ecolab ensured by bidding high enough to lose the contracts to Diversity but low enough to ensure the business lost money for Diversity.

Sources: Berner, R. 2005. Watch Out, Best Buy and Circuit City. *BusinessWeek,* November 10; Stalk, G., Jr. 2006. Curveball Strategies to Fool the Competition. *Harvard Business Review,* 84(9): 114–121; and Stalk, G., Jr., & Lachenauer, R. 2004. *Hardball: Are You Playing to Play or Playing to Win?* Cambridge, MA: Harvard Business School Press. Reprinted by permission of Harvard Business School Press from G. Stalk, Jr., and R. Lachenauer. Copyright 2004 by the Harvard Business School Publishing Corporation; all rights reserved; Lam, Y. 2013. FDI Companies Dominate Vietnam's Detergent Market. *www.saigon-gpdaily.com.vn,* January 22: np; Vascellaro, J. 2012. Apple Wins Big in Patent Case. *www.wsj.com,* August 25: np; and Pech, R. & Stamboulidis, G. 2010. How Strategies of Deception Facilitate Business Growth. *Journal of Business Strategy,* 31(6): 37–45.

Threat Analysis

threat analysis
a firm's awareness of its closest competitors and the kinds of competitive actions they might be planning.

Prior to actually observing a competitive action, companies may need to become aware of potential competitive threats. That is, companies need to have a keen sense of who their closest competitors are and the kinds of competitive actions they might be planning.[54] This may require some environmental scanning and monitoring of the sort described in Chapter 2. Awareness of the threats posed by industry rivals allows a firm to understand what type of competitive response, if any, may be necessary.

Being aware of competitors and cognizant of whatever threats they might pose is the first step in assessing the level of competitive threat. Once a new competitive action becomes apparent, companies must determine how threatening it is to their business. Competitive dynamics are likely to be most intense among companies that are competing for the same customers or that have highly similar sets of resources.[55] Two factors are used to assess whether or not companies are close competitors:

market commonality
the extent to which competitors are vying for the same customers in the same markets.

- **Market commonality.** Whether or not competitors are vying for the same customers and how many markets they share in common. For example, aircraft manufacturers Boeing and Airbus have a high degree of market commonality because they make very similar products and have many buyers in common.

resource similarity
the extent to which rivals draw from the same types of strategic resources.

- **Resource similarity.** The degree to which rivals draw on the same types of resources to compete. For example, the home pages of Google and Yahoo! may look very different, but behind the scenes, they both rely on the talent pool of high-caliber software engineers to create the cutting-edge innovations that help them compete.

When any two firms have both a high degree of market commonality and highly similar resource bases, a stronger competitive threat is present. Such a threat, however, may not lead to competitive action. On the one hand, a market rival may be hesitant to attack a company that it shares a high degree of market commonality with because it could lead to an intense battle. On the other hand, once attacked, rivals with high market commonality will be much more motivated to launch a competitive response. This is especially true in cases where the shared market is an important part of a company's overall business.

How strong a response an attacked rival can mount will be determined by its strategic resource endowments. In general, the same set of conditions holds true with regard to resource similarity. Companies that have highly similar resource bases will be hesitant to launch an initial attack but pose a serious threat if required to mount a competitive response.[56] Greater strategic resources increase a firm's capability to respond.

Motivation and Capability to Respond

Once attacked, competitors are faced with deciding how to respond. Before deciding, however, they need to evaluate not only how they will respond but also their reasons for responding and their capability to respond. Companies need to be clear about what problems a competitive response is expected to address and what types of problems it might create.[57] There are several factors to consider.

First, how serious is the impact of the competitive attack to which they are responding? For example, a large company with a strong reputation that is challenged by a small or unknown company may elect to simply keep an eye on the new competitor rather than quickly react or overreact. Part of the story of online retailer Amazon's early success is attributed to Barnes & Noble's overreaction to Amazon's claim that it was "earth's biggest bookstore." Because Barnes & Noble was already using the phrase "world's largest bookstore," it sued Amazon, but lost. The confrontation made it to the front pages of *The Wall Street Journal*, and Amazon was on its way to becoming a household name.[58]

Companies planning to respond to a competitive challenge must also understand their motivation for responding. What is the intent of the competitive response? Is it merely to blunt the attack of the competitor, or is it an opportunity to enhance its competitive position? Sometimes the most a company can hope for is to minimize the damage caused by a competitive action.

A company that seeks to improve its competitive advantage may be motivated to launch an attack rather than merely respond to one. For example, a few years ago, the *Wall Street Journal (WSJ)* attacked the *New York Times* by adding a local news section to the New York edition of the *WSJ*. Its aim was to become a more direct competitor of the *Times*. The publishers of the *WSJ* undertook this attack when they realized the *Times* was in a weakened financial condition and would be unable to respond to the attack.[59] A company must also assess its capability to respond. What strategic resources can be deployed to fend off a competitive attack? Does the company have an array of internal strengths it can draw on, or is it operating from a position of weakness?

Consider the role of firm age and size in calculating a company's ability to respond. Most entrepreneurial new ventures start out small. The smaller size makes them more nimble compared to large firms so they can respond quickly to competitive attacks. Because they are not well-known, start-ups also have the advantage of the element of surprise in how and when they attack. Innovative uses of technology, for example, allow small firms to deploy resources in unique ways.

Because they are young, however, start-ups may not have the financial resources needed to follow through with a competitive response.[60] In contrast, older and larger firms may have more resources and a repertoire of competitive techniques they can use in a counterattack. Large firms, however, tend to be slower to respond. Older firms tend to be predictable in their responses because they often lose touch with the competitive environment and rely on strategies and actions that have worked in the past.

Other resources may also play a role in whether a company is equipped to retaliate. For example, one avenue of counterattack may be launching product enhancements or new product/service innovations. For that approach to be successful, it requires a company to have both the intellectual capital to put forward viable innovations and the teamwork skills to prepare a new product or service and get it to market. Resources such as cross-functional teams and the social capital that makes teamwork production effective and efficient represent the type of human capital resources that enhance a company's capability to respond.

Types of Competitive Actions

Once an organization determines whether it is willing and able to launch a competitive action, it must determine what type of action is appropriate. The actions taken will be determined by both its resource capabilities and its motivation for responding. There are also marketplace considerations. What types of actions are likely to be most effective given a company's internal strengths and weaknesses as well as market conditions?

Two broadly defined types of competitive action include strategic actions and tactical actions. **Strategic actions** represent major commitments of distinctive and specific resources. Examples include launching a breakthrough innovation, building a new production facility, or merging with another company. Such actions require significant planning and resources and, once initiated, are difficult to reverse.

Tactical actions include refinements or extensions of strategies. Examples of tactical actions include cutting prices, improving gaps in service, or strengthening marketing efforts. Such actions typically draw on general resources and can be implemented quickly. Exhibit 8.6 identifies several types of strategic and tactical competitive actions that illustrate the range of actions that can occur in a rivalrous relationship.

Some competitive actions take the form of frontal assaults, that is, actions aimed directly at taking business from another company or capitalizing on industry weaknesses. This can be especially effective when firms use a low-cost strategy. The airline industry provides a good example of this head-on approach. When Southwest Airlines began its no-frills, no-meals strategy in the late-1960s, it represented a direct assault on the major carriers of the

> **strategic actions**
> major commitments of distinctive and specific resources to strategic initiatives.

> **tactical actions**
> refinements or extensions of strategies usually involving minor resource commitments.

EXHIBIT 8.6 Strategic and Tactical Competitive Actions

	Actions	Examples
Strategic Actions	• Entering new markets	• Make geographical expansions • Expand into neglected markets • Target rivals' markets • Target new demographics
	• New product introductions	• Imitate rivals' products • Address gaps in quality • Leverage new technologies • Leverage brand name with related products • Protect innovation with patents
	• Changing production capacity	• Create overcapacity • Tie up raw materials sources • Tie up preferred suppliers and distributors • Stimulate demand by limiting capacity
	• Mergers/Alliances	• Acquire/partner with competitors to reduce competition • Tie up key suppliers through alliances • Obtain new technology/intellectual property • Facilitate new market entry
Tactical Actions	• Price cutting (or increases)	• Maintain low-price dominance • Offer discounts and rebates • Offer incentives (e.g., frequent flyer miles) • Enhance offering to move upscale
	• Product/service enhancements	• Address gaps in service • Expand warranties • Make incremetal product improvements
	• Increased marketing efforts	• Use guerilla marketing • Conduct selective attacks • Change product packaging • Use new marketing channels
	• New distribution channels	• Access suppliers directly • Access customers directly • Develop multiple points of contact with customers • Expand Internet presence

Sources: Chen, M. J. & Hambrick, D. 1995. Speed, Stealth, and Selective Attack: How Small Firms Differ from Large Firms in Competitive Behavior. *Academy of Management Journal,* 38: 453–482; Davies, M. 1992. Sales Promotions as a Competitive Strategy. *Management Decision,* 30(7): 5–10; Ferrier, W., Smith, K., & Grimm, C. 1999. The Role of Competitive Action in Market Share Erosion and Industry Dethronement: A Study of Industry Leaders and Challengers. *Academy of Management Journal,* 42(4): 372–388; and Garda, R. A. 1991. Use Tactical Pricing to Uncover Hidden Profits. *Journal of Business Strategy,* 12(5): 17–23.

day. In Europe, Ryanair has similarly directly challenged the traditional carriers with an overall cost leadership strategy.

Guerilla offensives and selective attacks provide an alternative for firms with fewer resources.[61] These draw attention to products or services by creating buzz or generating enough shock value to get some free publicity. TOMS Shoes has found a way to generate interest in its products without a large advertising budget to match Nike. Its policy of donating one pair of shoes to those in need for every pair of shoes purchased by customers has generated a lot of buzz on the Internet.[62] Over 3 million people have given a "like" rating on TOMS's Facebook page. The policy has a real impact as well, with over 35 million shoes donated as of January 2015.[63]

Some companies limit their competitive response to defensive actions. Such actions rarely improve a company's competitive advantage, but a credible defensive action can lower the risk of being attacked and deter new entry.

Several of the factors discussed earlier in the chapter, such as types of entry strategies and the use of cost leadership versus differentiation strategies, can guide the decision about what types of competitive actions to take. Before launching a given strategy, however, assessing the likely response of competitors is a vital step.[64]

Likelihood of Competitive Reaction

The final step before initiating a competitive response is to evaluate what a competitor's reaction is likely to be. The logic of competitive dynamics suggests that once competitive actions are initiated, it is likely they will be met with competitive responses.[65] The last step before mounting an attack is to evaluate how competitors are likely to respond. Evaluating potential competitive reactions helps companies plan for future counterattacks. It may also lead to a decision to hold off—that is, not to take any competitive action at all because of the possibility that a misguided or poorly planned response will generate a devastating competitive reaction.

How a competitor is likely to respond will depend on three factors: market dependence, competitor's resources, and the reputation of the firm that initiates the action (actor's reputation). The implications of each of these are described briefly in the following sections.

Market Dependence If a company has a high concentration of its business in a particular industry, it has more at stake because it must depend on that industry's market for its sales. Single-industry businesses or those where one industry dominates are more likely to mount a competitive response. Young and small firms with a high degree of **market dependence** may be limited in how they respond due to resource constraints.

> **market dependence**
> degree of concentration of a firm's business in a particular industry.

Competitor's Resources Previously, we examined the internal resource endowments that a company must evaluate when assessing its capability to respond. Here, it is the competitor's resources that need to be considered. For example, a small firm may be unable to mount a serious attack due to lack of resources. As a result, it is more likely to react to tactical actions such as incentive pricing or enhanced service offerings because they are less costly to attack than large-scale strategic actions. In contrast, a firm with financial "deep pockets" may be able to mount and sustain a costly counterattack.

Actor's Reputation Whether a company should respond to a competitive challenge will also depend on who launched the attack against it. Compared to relatively smaller firms with less market power, competitors are more likely to respond to competitive moves by market leaders. Another consideration is how successful prior attacks have been. For example, price cutting by the big automakers usually has the desired result—increased sales to price-sensitive buyers—at least in the short run. Given that history, when GM offers discounts or incentives, rivals Ford and Chrysler cannot afford to ignore the challenge and quickly follow suit.

Choosing Not to React: Forbearance and Co-opetition

The above discussion suggests that there may be many circumstances in which the best reaction is no reaction at all. This is known as **forbearance**—refraining from reacting at

> **forbearance**
> a firm's choice of not reacting to a rival's new competitive action.

8.6 STRATEGY SPOTLIGHT — ETHICS

CLEANING UP IN THE SOAP BUSINESS

Consumer product companies Colgate-Palmolive, Unilever, Procter & Gamble (P&G), and Henkel compete with each other globally in the soap business. But as regulators found after a long investigation, this wasn't true in France. The firms in this market had colluded to fix prices for nearly a decade. In the words of a Henkel executive, the detergent makers wanted "to limit the intensity of competition between them and clean up the market." The Autorité de la Concurrance, the French antitrust watchdog, hit these four firms with fines totaling $484 million after completing its investigation.

The firms started sharing pricing information in the 1980s, but by the 1990s their cooperation got bolder, morphing into behavior that sounds like something out of a spy novel. In 1996, four brand directors secretly met in a restaurant in a suburb of Paris and agreed to coordinate the pricing of their soap products. They agreed to prearranged prices at which they would sell to retailers and agreed to notify each other of any planned special offers. They gave each firm a secret alias: Pierre for Procter & Gamble, Laurence for Unilever, Hugues for Henkel, and Christian for Colgate-Palmolive. From that point forward, they allegedly scheduled clandestine meetings four times a year. The meetings, which they called "store checks" in their schedules to limit any questioning they may have received, often lasted an entire afternoon. They would set complex pricing schemes. For example, P&G sold its Ariel brand as an upscale product and coordinated with Unilever to keep Ariel at a 3 percent markup over Unilever's Skip brand. At these meetings, they would also hash out any complaints about whether and how any of the participants had been bending the rules.

The collusion lasted for almost 10 years until it broke down in 2004. Unilever was the first to defect, offering a 10 percent "D-Day" price cut without negotiating it with the three other firms. Other competitors quickly responded with actions that violated the pricing norms they had set.

Sources: Colchester, M. & Passariello, C. 2011. Dirty secrets in soap prices. *wsj.com*, December 9: np; and Smith, H. & White, A. 2011. P&G, Colgate fined by France in $484 million detergent cartel. *Bloomberg.com*, December 11: np.

---

all as well as holding back from initiating an attack. The decision of whether a firm should respond or show forbearance is not always clear.

Related to forbearance is the concept of **co-opetition.** This is a term that was coined by network software company Novell's founder and former CEO Raymond Noorda to suggest that companies often benefit most from a combination of competing and cooperating.[66] Close competitors that differentiate themselves in the eyes of consumers may work together behind the scenes to achieve industrywide efficiencies.[67] For example, breweries in Sweden cooperate in recycling used bottles but still compete for customers on the basis of taste and variety. Similarly, several competing Hollywood studios came together and agreed to cooperate on buying movie film. They negotiated promises to buy certain quantities of film to keep Kodak from closing down its film manufacturing business.[68] As long as the benefits of cooperating are enjoyed by all participants in a co-opetition system, the practice can aid companies in avoiding intense and damaging competition.[69]

Despite the potential benefits of co-opetition, companies need to guard against cooperating to such a great extent that their actions are perceived as collusion, a practice that has legal ramifications in the United States. In Strategy Spotlight 8.6, we see an example of crossing the line into illegal cooperation.

Once a company has evaluated a competitor's likelihood of responding to a competitive challenge, it can decide what type of action is most appropriate. Competitive actions can take many forms: the entry of a start-up into a market for the first time, an attack by a lower-ranked incumbent on an industry leader, or the launch of a breakthrough innovation that disrupts the industry structure. Such actions forever change the competitive dynamics of a marketplace. Thus, the cycle of actions and reactions that occur in business every day is a vital aspect of entrepreneurial strategy that leads to continual new value creation and the ongoing advancement of economic well-being.

> **co-opetition**
> a firm's strategy of both cooperating and competing with rival firms.

ISSUE FOR DEBATE

Where Have the Entrepreneurs Gone?

The United States has long been seen as the home of a vibrant entrepreneurial economy, but the statistics call this into question. From 1977 to 2011, the number of new start-up firms in the U.S. declined by 28 percent. More dramatically, relative to the size of the working population, the number of new start-ups has fallen by half. Even Silicon Valley has seen the rate of new business start-ups decline by 50 percent over the last three decades. Entrepreneurial actions have fallen most sharply among younger adults. People age 20 to 34 created only 22.7 percent of all new companies in 2013, down from 34.8 percent in 1996. This is an ironic change given that enrollment in college entrepreneurship programs has been growing.

This declining rate of entrepreneurship is setting off warning bells for many. It leads to less innovation in the economy and slower job opportunity growth. Over the long run, it would lead to lower living standards and stagnant economic growth.

Concerns on this issue have led to a discussion of the underlying causes of this change. The causes of this decline may be emotional or institutional. On the emotional level, it may be that the aftereffects of the Great Recession have tilted society toward risk aversion. Additionally, many would-be entrepreneurs are saddled with significant student loan debt, leaving them less willing to take on the risk of entrepreneurship. Consistent with this view, Audrey Baxter, a woman who won a business proposal award as a student at UCLA, opted to take a corporate job when she graduated rather than pushing her small business forward. "Having a secure job with a really good salary was something to be considered carefully," Baxter said.

It may also be that institutional factors are reducing people's willingness or ability to start a business. Weakened antitrust enforcement may be playing a role. Firms have been able to grow and combine in a range of markets, leading to extremely large competitors that dominate markets, increasing the entry barriers for entrepreneurs. Also, lax antitrust enforcement has made it easier for large incumbent firms to respond very aggressively to newcomers, increasing the risk for entrepreneurs. Government red tape is another institutional barrier to entrepreneurs. For example, Celeste Kelly opened a business offering horse massage but had to shut down the business when the Arizona State Veterinary Medical Examining Board ordered her to "cease and desist" because it ruled she was practicing veterinary medicine without a license—even though no veterinarians in the area offered horse massage as a treatment. This may seem like an obscure example, but many businesses, including barbers, bartenders, cosmetologists, and even tour guides, are required to obtain licenses. Less than 5 percent of workers required licenses in the 1950s. That number is now 35 percent. According to economists Morris Kleiner and Alan Krueger, licenses increase the wage costs for a business by 18 percent.

Discussion Questions

1. How concerned are you about the drop in the rate of entrepreneurship?
2. What do you think are the primary causes of the decline?
3. What actions should be taken to increase the rate of new business start-ups? How effective will these actions be?
4. What factors influence your desire to work in an entrepreneurial firm versus an established firm?

Sources: Hamilton, W. 2014. A drop-off in start-ups: Where are all the entrepreneurs? latimes.com, September 7: np; Anonymous. 2014. Red tape blues: The best and worst states for small business. *The Economist*, July 5: 23–24; and Anonymous. 2014. Unshackle the entrepreneurs; America's license raj. *The Economist*, July 5: 14.

Reflecting on Career Implications . . .

- **Opportunity Recognition:** What ideas for new business activities are actively discussed in your work environment? Could you apply the four characteristics of an opportunity to determine whether they are viable opportunities? If no one in your organization is excited about or even considering new opportunities, you may want to ask yourself if you want to continue with your current firm.
- **Entrepreneurial New Entry:** Are there opportunities to launch new products or services that might add value to the organization? What are the best ways for you to bring these opportunities to the attention of key managers? Or might this provide an opportunity for you to launch your own entrepreneurial venture?
- **Entrepreneurial Resources:** Evaluate your resources in terms of financial resources, human capital, and social capital. Are these enough to launch your own venture? If you are deficient in one area, are there ways to compensate for it? Even if you are not interested in starting a new venture, can you use your entrepreneurial resources to advance your career within your firm?
- **Competitive Dynamics:** There is always internal competition within organizations: among business units and sometimes even individuals within the same unit. What types of strategic and tactical actions are employed in these internal rivalries? What steps have you taken to strengthen your own position given the "competitive dynamics" within your organization?

summary

New ventures and entrepreneurial firms that capitalize on marketplace opportunities make an important contribution to the U.S. economy. They are leaders in terms of implementing new technologies and introducing innovative products and services. Yet entrepreneurial firms face unique challenges if they are going to survive and grow.

To successfully launch new ventures or implement new technologies, three factors must be present: an entrepreneurial opportunity, the resources to pursue the opportunity, and an entrepreneur or entrepreneurial team willing and able to undertake the venture. Firms must develop a strong ability to recognize viable opportunities. Opportunity recognition is a process of determining which venture ideas are, in fact, promising business opportunities.

In addition to strong opportunities, entrepreneurial firms need resources and entrepreneurial leadership to thrive. The resources that start-ups need include financial resources as well as human and social capital. Many firms also benefit from government programs that support new venture development and growth. New ventures thrive best when they are led by founders or owners who have vision, drive and dedication, and a commitment to excellence.

Once the necessary opportunities, resources, and entrepreneur skills are in place, new ventures still face numerous strategic challenges. Decisions about the strategic positioning of new entrants can benefit from conducting strategic analyses and evaluating the requirements of niche markets. Entry strategies used by new ventures take several forms, including pioneering new entry, imitative new entry, and adaptive new entry. Entrepreneurial firms can benefit from using overall low cost, differentiation, and focus strategies although each of these approaches has pitfalls that are unique to young and small firms. Entrepreneurial firms are also in a strong position to benefit from combination strategies.

The entry of a new company into a competitive arena is like a competitive attack on incumbents in that arena. Such actions often provoke a competitive response, which may, in turn, trigger a reaction to the response. As a result, a competitive dynamic—action and response—begins among close competitors. In deciding whether to attack or counterattack, companies must analyze the seriousness of the competitive threat, their ability to mount a competitive response, and the type of action—strategic or tactical—that the situation requires. At times, competitors find it is better not to respond at all or to find avenues to cooperate with, rather than challenge, close competitors.

SUMMARY REVIEW QUESTIONS

1. Explain how the combination of opportunities, resources, and entrepreneurs helps determine the character and strategic direction of an entrepreneurial firm.
2. What is the difference between discovery and evaluation in the process of opportunity recognition? Give an example of each.
3. Describe the three characteristics of entrepreneurial leadership: vision, dedication and drive, and commitment to excellence.
4. Briefly describe the three types of entrepreneurial entry strategies: pioneering, imitative, and adaptive.
5. Explain why entrepreneurial firms are often in a strong position to use combination strategies.
6. What does the term *competitive dynamics* mean?
7. Explain the difference between strategic actions and tactical actions and provide examples of each.

key terms

entrepreneurship 250
opportunity recognition 251
angel investors 254
venture capitalists 254
crowdfunding 255
entrepreneurial leadership 257
entrepreneurial strategy 260
pioneering new entry 261
imitative new entry 261
adaptive new entry 262
competitive dynamics 266
new competitive
   action 266
threat analysis 268
market commonality 268
resource similarity 268
strategic actions 269
tactical actions 269
market dependence 271
forbearance 271
co-opetition 272

application questions & exercises

1. E-Loan and Lending Tree are two entrepreneurial firms that offer lending services over the Internet. Evaluate the features of these two companies. (Fill in the table below.)
   a. Evaluate their characteristics and assess the extent to which they are comparable in terms of market commonality and resource similarity.
   b. Based on your analysis, what strategic and/or tactical actions might these companies take to improve their competitive position? Could E-Loan and Lending Tree improve their performance more through co-opetition than competition? Explain your rationale.
2. Using the Internet, research the Small Business Administration's website (*www.sba.gov*). What different types of financing are available to small firms? Besides financing, what other programs are available to support the growth and development of small businesses?
3. Think of an entrepreneurial firm that has been successfully launched in the last 10 years. What kind of entry strategy did it use—pioneering, imitative, or adaptive? Since the firm's initial entry, how has it used or combined overall low-cost, differentiation, and/or focus strategies?
4. Select an entrepreneurial firm you are familiar with in your local community. Research the company and discuss how it has positioned itself relative to its close competitors. Does it have a unique strategic advantage? Disadvantage? Explain.

ethics questions

1. Imitation strategies are based on the idea of copying another firm's idea and using it for your own purposes. Is this unethical or simply a smart business practice? Discuss the ethical implications of this practice (if any).
2. Intense competition such as price wars are an accepted practice in the United States, but cooperation between companies has legal ramifications because of antitrust laws. Should price wars that drive small businesses or new entrants out of business be illegal? What ethical considerations are raised (if any)?

Company	Market Commonality	Resource Similarity
E-Loan		
Lending Tree		

Company	Strategic Actions	Tactical Actions
E-Loan		
Lending Tree		

references

1. Pepitone, J. 2012. Digg sold to Betaworks for pocket change. *cnnmoney.com,* July 12: np.
2. Ante, S. & Walker, J. 2012. Digg admits missteps. *wsj.com,* July 16: np.
3. http://web.sba.gov.
4. Timmons, J. A. & Spinelli, S. 2004. *New venture creation* (6th ed.). New York: McGraw-Hill/Irwin; and Bygrave, W. D. 1997. The entrepreneurial process. In W. D. Bygrave (Ed.), *The portable MBA in entrepreneurship* (2nd ed.). New York: Wiley.
5. Bryant, A. 2012. Want to innovate? Feed a cookie to the monster. *nytimes.com,* March 24: np.
6. Fromartz, S. 1998. How to get your first great idea. *Inc. Magazine,* April 1: 91–94; and Vesper, K. H. 1990. *New venture strategies* (2nd ed.). Englewood Cliffs, NJ: Prentice Hall.
7. For an interesting perspective on the nature of the opportunity recognition process, see Baron, R. A. 2006. Opportunity recognition as pattern recognition: How entrepreneurs "connect the dots" to identify new business opportunities. *Academy of*

Management Perspectives, February: 104–119.

8. Gaglio, C. M. 1997. Opportunity identification: Review, critique and suggested research directions. In Katz, J. A. (Ed.), *Advances in entrepreneurship, firm emergence and growth,* vol. 3. Greenwich, CT: JAI Press: 139–202; Lumpkin, G. T., Hills, G. E., & Shrader, R. C. 2004. Opportunity recognition. In Welsch, H. L. (Ed.), *Entrepreneurship: The road ahead:* 73–90. London: Routledge; and Long, W. & McMullan, W. E. 1984. Mapping the new venture opportunity identification process. *Frontiers of entrepreneurship research, 1984:* 567–590. Wellesley, MA: Babson College.

9. For an interesting discussion of different aspects of opportunity discovery, see Shepherd, D. A. & De Tienne, D. R. 2005. Prior knowledge, potential financial reward, and opportunity identification. *Entrepreneurship Theory & Practice,* 29(1): 91–112; and Gaglio, C. M. 2004. The role of mental simulations and counterfactual thinking in the opportunity identification process. *Entrepreneurship Theory & Practice,* 28(6): 533–552.

10. Stewart, T. A. 2002. How to think with your gut. *Business 2.0,* November: 99–104.

11. Anonymous. 2013. How entrepreneurs come up with great ideas. *wsj.com,* April 29: np.

12. For more on the opportunity recognition process, see Smith, B. R., Matthews, C. H., & Schenkel, M. T. 2009. Differences in entrepreneurial opportunities: The role of tacitness and codification in opportunity identification. *Journal of Small Business Management,* 47(1): 38–57.

13. Timmons, J. A. 1997. Opportunity recognition. In Bygrave, W. D. (Ed.), *The portable MBA in entrepreneurship* (2nd ed.): 26–54. New York: Wiley.

14. Social networking is also proving to be an increasingly important type of entrepreneurial resource. For an interesting discussion, see Aldrich, H. E. & Kim, P. H. 2007. Small worlds, infinite possibilities? How social networks affect entrepreneurial team formation and search. *Strategic Entrepreneurship Journal,* 1(1): 147–166.

15. Bhide, A. V. 2000. *The origin and evolution of new businesses.* New York: Oxford University Press.

16. Small business 2001: Where are we now? 2001. *Inc.,* May 29: 18–19; and Zacharakis, A. L., Bygrave, W. D., & Shepherd, D. A. 2000. *Global entrepreneurship monitor—National entrepreneurship assessment: United States of America 2000 Executive Report.* Kansas City, MO: Kauffman Center for Entrepreneurial Leadership.

17. Cooper, S. 2003. Cash cows. *Entrepreneur,* June: 36.

18. Seglin, J. L. 1998. What angels want. *Inc.,* 20(7): 43–44.

19. Torres, N. L. 2002. Playing an angel. *Entrepreneur,* May: 130–138.

20. For an interesting discussion of how venture capital practices vary across different sectors of the economy, see Gaba, V. & Meyer, A. D. 2008. Crossing the organizational species barrier: How venture capital practices infiltrated the information technology sector. *Academy of Management Journal,* 51(5): 391–412.

21. Our discussion of crowdfunding draws on Wasik, J. 2012. The brilliance (and madness) of crowdfunding. *Forbes,* June 25: 144–146; Anonymous. 2012. Why crowdfunding may not be path to riches. *Finance.yahoo.com,* October 23: np; and Espinoza, J. 2012. Doing equity crowd funding right. *The Wall Street Journal,* May 21: R3.

22. Noyes, K. 2014. Why investors are pouring millions into crowdfunding. *fortune.com,* April 17. np.

23. Shchetko, N. 2014. There's no refunding in crowdfunding. *The Wall Street Journal,* November 26: B1, B4.

24. For more on how different forms of organizing entrepreneurial firms as well as different stages of new firm growth and development affect financing, see Cassar, G. 2004. The financing of business start-ups. *Journal of Business Venturing,* 19(2): 261–283.

25. Kroll, M., Walters, B., & Wright, P. 2010. The impact of insider control and environment on post-IPO performance. *Academy of Management Journal,* 53: 693–725.

26. Eisenhardt, K. M. & Schoonhoven, C. B. 1990. Organizational growth: Linking founding team, strategy, environment, and growth among U.S. semiconductor ventures, 1978–1988. *Administrative Science Quarterly,* 35: 504–529.

27. Dubini, P. & Aldrich, H. 1991. Personal and extended networks are central to the entrepreneurship process. *Journal of Business Venturing,* 6(5): 305–333.

28. For more on the role of social contacts in helping young firms build legitimacy, see Chrisman, J. J. & McMullan, W. E. 2004. Outside assistance as a knowledge resource for new venture survival. *Journal of Small Business Management,* 42(3): 229–244.

29. Vogel, C. 2000. Janina Pawlowski. *Working Woman,* June: 70.

30. For a recent perspective on entrepreneurship and strategic alliances, see Rothaermel, F. T. & Deeds, D. L. 2006. Alliance types, alliance experience and alliance management capability in high-technology ventures. *Journal of Business Venturing,* 21(4): 429–460; and Lu, J. W. & Beamish, P. W. 2006. Partnering strategies and performance of SMEs' international joint ventures. *Journal of Business Venturing,* 21(4): 461–486.

31. Monahan, J. 2005. All systems grow. *Entrepreneur,* March: 78–82; Weaver, K. M. & Dickson, P. 2004. Strategic alliances. In Dennis, W. J., Jr. (Ed.), *NFIB national small business poll.* Washington, DC: National Federation of Independent Business; and Copeland, M. V. & Tilin, A. 2005. Get someone to build it. *Business 2.0,* 6(5): 88.

32. For more information, go to the Small Business Administration website at *www.sba.gov.*

33. Simsek, Z., Heavey, C., & Veiga, J. 2009. The impact of CEO core self-evaluation on entrepreneurial orientation. *Strategic Management Journal,* 31: 110–119.

34. Zhao, H. & Seibert, S. 2006. The big five personality dimensions and entrepreneurial status: A meta-analytic review. *Journal of Applied Psychology,* 91: 259–271.

35. For an interesting study of the role of passion in entrepreneurial success, see Chen, X-P., Yao, X., & Kotha, S. 2009. Entrepreneur passion and preparedness in business plan presentations: A persuasion analysis of venture capitalists' funding decisions. *Academy of Management Journal,* 52(1): 101–120.

36. Collins, J. 2001. *Good to great.* New York: HarperCollins.

37. The idea of entry wedges was discussed by Vesper, K. 1990. *New venture strategies* (2nd ed.). Englewood Cliffs, NJ: Prentice Hall; and Drucker, P. F. 1985. *Innovation and entrepreneurship.* New York: HarperBusiness.

38. See Dowell, G. & Swaminathan, A. 2006. Entry timing, exploration, and firm survival in the early U.S. bicycle industry. *Strategic Management Journal,* 27:

1159–1182, for a recent study of the timing of entrepreneurial new entry.

39. Dunlap-Hinkler, D., Kotabe, M., & Mudambi, R. 2010. A story of breakthrough vs. incremental innovation: Corporate entrepreneurship in the global pharmaceutical industry. *Strategic Entrepreneurship Journal,* 4: 106–127.

40. Maiello, M. 2002. They almost changed the world. *Forbes,* December 22: 217–220.

41. Pogue, D. 2012. Pay by app: No cash or card needed. *International Herald Tribune,* July 19: 18.

42. Helft, M. 2014. Square's status? It's complicated. *fortune.com,* May 14: np.

43. Williams, G. 2002. Looks like rain. *Entrepreneur,* September: 104–111.

44. Pedroza, G. M. 2002. Tech tutors. *Entrepreneur,* September: 120.

45. Romanelli, E. 1989. Environments and strategies of organization start-up: Effects on early survival. *Administrative Science Quarterly,* 34(3): 369–387.

46. Wallace, B. 2000. Brothers. *Philadelphia Magazine,* April: 66–75.

47. Buchanan, L. 2003. The innovation factor: A field guide to innovation. *www.forbes.com,* April 21.

48. Kim, W. C. & Mauborgne, R. 2005. *Blue ocean strategy.* Boston: Harvard Business School Press.

49. For more on how unique organizational combinations can contribute to competitive advantages of entrepreneurial firms, see Steffens, P., Davidsson, P., & Fitzsimmons, J. Performance configurations over time: Implications for growth- and profit-oriented strategies. *Entrepreneurship Theory & Practice,* 33(1): 125–148.

50. Smith, K. G., Ferrier, W. J., & Grimm, C. M. 2001. King of the hill: Dethroning the industry leader. *Academy of Management Executive,* 15(2): 59–70.

51. Grove, A. 1999. *Only the paranoid survive: How to exploit the crisis points that challenge every company.* New York: Random House.

52. Stalk, G., Jr., & Lachenauer, R. 2004. *Hardball: Are you playing to play or playing to win?* Cambridge, MA: Harvard Business School Press.

53. Chen, M. J., Lin, H. C, & Michel, J. G. 2010. Navigating in a hypercompetitive environment: The roles of action aggressiveness and TMT integration. *Strategic Management Journal,* 31: 1410–1430.

54. Peteraf, M. A. & Bergen, M. A. 2003. Scanning competitive landscapes: A market-based and resource-based framework. *Strategic Management Journal,* 24: 1027–1045.

55. Chen, M. J. 1996. Competitor analysis and interfirm rivalry: Toward a theoretical integration. *Academy of Management Review,* 21(1): 100–134.

56. Chen, 1996, op.cit.

57. Chen, M. J., Su, K. H, & Tsai, W. 2007. Competitive tension: The awareness-motivation-capability perspective. *Academy of Management Journal,* 50(1): 101–118.

58. St. John, W. 1999. Barnes & Noble's epiphany. *www.wired.com,* June.

59. Anonymous. 2010. Is the *Times* ready for a newspaper war? *Bloomberg Businessweek,* April 26: 30–31.

60. Souder, D. & Shaver, J. M. 2010. Constraints and incentives for making long horizon corporate investments. *Strategic Management Journal,* 31: 1316–1336.

61. Chen, M. J. & Hambrick, D. 1995. Speed, stealth, and selective attack: How small firms differ from large firms in competitive behavior. *Academy of Management Journal,* 38: 453–482.

62. Fenner, L. 2009. TOMS Shoes donates one pair of shoes for every pair purchased. *America.gov,* October 19: np.

63. *www.facebook.com/tomsshoes.*

64. For a discussion of how the strategic actions of Apple Computer contribute to changes in the competitive dynamics in both the cellular phone and music industries, see Burgelman, R. A. & Grove, A. S. 2008. Cross-boundary disruptors: Powerful interindustry entrepreneurial change agents. *Strategic Entrepreneurship Journal,* 1(1): 315–327.

65. Smith, K. G., Ferrier, W. J., & Ndofor, H. 2001. Competitive dynamics research: Critique and future directions. In Hitt, M. A., Freeman, R. E., & Harrison, J. S. (Eds.), *The Blackwell handbook of strategic management:* 315–361. Oxford, UK: Blackwell.

66. Gee, P. 2000. Co-opetition: The new market milieu. *Journal of Healthcare Management,* 45: 359–363.

67. Ketchen, D. J., Snow, C. C., & Hoover, V. L. 2004. Research on competitive dynamics: Recent accomplishments and future challenges. *Journal of Management,* 30(6): 779–804.

68. Fritz, B. 2014. Movie film, at death's door, gets a reprieve. *wsj.com,* July 29: np.

69. Khanna, T., Gulati, R., & Nohria, N. 2000. The economic modeling of strategy process: Clean models and dirty hands. *Strategic Management Journal,* 21: 781–790.

Strategic Implementation

Strategic Control and Corporate Governance

chapter 9

After reading this chapter, you should have a good understanding of the following learning objectives:

LO9.1 The value of effective strategic control systems in strategy implementation.

LO9.2 The key difference between "traditional" and "contemporary" control systems.

LO9.3 The imperative for contemporary control systems in today's complex and rapidly changing competitive and general environments.

LO9.4 The benefits of having the proper balance among the three levers of behavioral control: culture, rewards and incentives, and boundaries.

LO9.5 The three key participants in corporate governance: shareholders, management (led by the CEO), and the board of directors.

LO9.6 The role of corporate governance mechanisms in ensuring that the interests of managers are aligned with those of shareholders from both the United States and international perspectives.

PART 3: STRATEGIC IMPLEMENTATION

Learning from Mistakes

Just a few years ago, Tesco was a high-flying global retailer. Throughout the 1990s and early 2000s, Tesco grew to dominate the U.K. retailing market, attaining a 33 percent market share, and successfully expanded into new geographic markets. However, over the last several years, Tesco has faced increasing pressures at home and large struggles outside the U.K. This included a failed entry into the U.S. market and increasing pressure at home from hard-discounting competitors, most notably Lidl and Aldi. In recent years, Tesco has seen its stock price drop by nearly 40 percent, major investors including Warren Buffett bail out, and pressures from investors that forced the ousting of the firm's CEO.

In September 2014, the situation for Tesco got much worse.[1] After an employee alerted the firm's general counsel of accounting irregularities, a full-blown accounting scandal erupted. Senior managers in the U.K. food business had been booking income early and delaying the booking of costs to shore up the financial performance of the firm. The firm was forced to restate its earnings for the first half of 2014, initially to the tune of $408 million, which was later increased to $431 million as the scope of the problem increased. The scandal led to the suspension or dismissal of eight senior executives at Tesco, the suspension of retirement packages for the firm's prior CEO and CFO, and the eventual resignation of the chairman of the board of Tesco. It also triggered an investigation by the U.K.'s accounting watchdog, the Financial Reporting Council, into Tesco's accounting practices for the years 2012, 2013, and 2014.

The scandal has triggered commentators to reassert some long-standing concerns about Tesco's governance and also led them to point out some new concerns. Industry analysts have long been critical of Tesco's board of directors, especially noting that the board lacks retail experience. This likely played a role in the scandal, since the board would have had limited ability to notice the arcane, retail-related accounting practices at the center of the accounting deception. Interestingly, four months before the scandal arose, Tesco's auditor, PricewaterhouseCoopers, warned of the "risk of manipulation" in the accounting of promotional events, the areas that were manipulated, but the board appeared to take no action in its following meeting. The accounting irregularities also arose at a time of limited oversight within the firm. Laurie McIlwee, the firm's chief financial officer, stepped down in April 2014, but her replacement didn't take up the CFO position until December 2014. During that time, Tesco's finances were managed by the CEO's office. Thus, the firm did not have a senior executive whose primary task was to ensure the validity of the firm's financial reporting. Finally, the most senior leadership of the firm was distracted by other tasks. The firm's prior CEO was dismissed in July, and the new CEO took the reins in August 2014. Thus, Dave Lewis, the new CEO, was focusing on learning the business and the firm's operations just as the scandal broke.

The scandal has been quite damaging to the firm, with Tesco's already battered stock price plunging an additional 28 percent during the period the scandal unfolded.

Discussion Questions

1. What changes should Tesco make to avoid future similar scandals?
2. To what degree do you think the scandal at Tesco was related to how the firm had been performing?

strategic control
the process of monitoring and correcting a firm's strategy and performance.

We first explore two central aspects of **strategic control:**[2] (1) *informational control,* which is the ability to respond effectively to environmental change, and (2) *behavioral control,* which is the appropriate balance and alignment among a firm's culture, rewards, and boundaries. In the final section of this chapter, we focus on strategic control from a much broader perspective—what is referred to as *corporate governance.*[3] Here, we direct our attention to the need for a firm's shareholders (the owners) and their elected representatives (the board of directors) to ensure that the firm's executives (the management team) strive to fulfill their fiduciary duty of maximizing long-term shareholder value. As we just saw in the Tesco example, poor governance and control can lead to damaging scandals in firms.

LO9.1
The value of effective strategic control systems in strategy implementation.

Ensuring Informational Control: Responding Effectively to Environmental Change

We discuss two broad types of control systems: "traditional" and "contemporary." As both general and competitive environments become more unpredictable and complex, the need for contemporary systems increases.

A Traditional Approach to Strategic Control

traditional approach to strategic control
a sequential method of organizational control in which (1) strategies are formulated and top management sets goals, (2) strategies are implemented, and (3) performance is measured against the predetermined goal set.

The **traditional approach to strategic control** is sequential: (1) strategies are formulated and top management sets goals, (2) strategies are implemented, and (3) performance is measured against the predetermined goal set, as illustrated in Exhibit 9.1.

Control is based on a feedback loop from performance measurement to strategy formulation. This process typically involves lengthy time lags, often tied to a firm's annual planning cycle. Such traditional control systems, termed "single-loop" learning by Harvard's Chris Argyris, simply compare actual performance to a predetermined goal.[4] They are most appropriate when the environment is stable and relatively simple, goals and objectives can be measured with a high level of certainty, and there is little need for complex measures of performance. Sales quotas, operating budgets, production schedules, and similar quantitative control mechanisms are typical. The appropriateness of the business strategy or standards of performance is seldom questioned.[5]

LO9.2
The key difference between "traditional" and "contemporary" control systems.

James Brian Quinn of Dartmouth College has argued that grand designs with precise and carefully integrated plans seldom work.[6] Rather, most strategic change proceeds incrementally—one step at a time. Leaders should introduce some sense of direction, some logic in incremental steps.[7] Similarly, McGill University's Henry Mintzberg has written about leaders "crafting" a strategy.[8] Drawing on the parallel between the potter at her wheel and the strategist, Mintzberg pointed out that the potter begins work with some general idea of the artifact she wishes to create, but the details of design—even possibilities for a different design—emerge as the work progresses. For businesses facing complex and turbulent business environments, the craftsperson's method helps us deal with the uncertainty about how a design will work out in practice and allows for a creative element.

LO9.3
The imperative for contemporary control systems in today's complex and rapidly changing competitive and general environments.

Mintzberg's argument, like Quinn's, questions the value of rigid planning and goal-setting processes. Fixed strategic goals also become dysfunctional for firms competing in highly unpredictable competitive environments. Strategies need to change frequently and opportunistically. An inflexible commitment to predetermined goals and milestones can prevent the very adaptability that is required of a good strategy.

EXHIBIT 9.1 Traditional Approach to Strategic Control

Formulate strategies → Implement strategies → Strategic control

A Contemporary Approach to Strategic Control

Adapting to and anticipating both internal and external environmental change is an integral part of strategic control. The relationships between strategy formulation, implementation, and control are highly interactive, as suggested by Exhibit 9.2. The exhibit also illustrates two different types of strategic control: informational control and behavioral control. **Informational control** is primarily concerned with whether or not the organization is "doing the right things." **Behavioral control,** on the other hand, asks if the organization is "doing things right" in the implementation of its strategy. Both the informational and behavioral components of strategic control are necessary, but not sufficient, conditions for success. What good is a well-conceived strategy that cannot be implemented? Or what use is an energetic and committed workforce if it is focused on the wrong strategic target?

John Weston is the former CEO of ADP Corporation, the largest payroll and tax-filing processor in the world. He captures the essence of contemporary control systems:

> At ADP, 39 plus 1 adds up to more than 40 plus 0. The 40-plus-0 employee is the harried worker who at 40 hours a week just tries to keep up with what's in the "in" basket.... Because he works with his head down, he takes zero hours to think about what he's doing, why he's doing it, and how he's doing it.... On the other hand, the 39-plus-1 employee takes at least 1 of those 40 hours to think about what he's doing and why he's doing it. That's why the other 39 hours are far more productive.[9]

Informational control deals with the internal environment as well as the external strategic context. It addresses the assumptions and premises that provide the foundation for an organization's strategy. Do the organization's goals and strategies still "fit" within the context of the current strategic environment? Depending on the type of business, such assumptions may relate to changes in technology, customer tastes, government regulation, and industry competition.

This involves two key issues. First, managers must scan and monitor the external environment, as we discussed in Chapter 2. Also, conditions can change in the internal environment of the firm, as we discussed in Chapter 3, requiring changes in the strategic direction of the firm. These may include, for example, the resignation of key executives or delays in the completion of major production facilities.

In the contemporary approach, information control is part of an ongoing process of organizational learning that continuously updates and challenges the assumptions that underlie the organization's strategy. In such double-loop learning, the organization's assumptions, premises, goals, and strategies are continuously monitored, tested, and reviewed. The benefits of continuous monitoring are evident—time lags are dramatically shortened, changes in the competitive environment are detected earlier, and the organization's ability to respond with speed and flexibility is enhanced.

Contemporary control systems must have four characteristics to be effective:[10]

1. The focus is on constantly changing information that has potential strategic importance.
2. The information is important enough to demand frequent and regular attention from all levels of the organization.

informational control
a method of organizational control in which a firm gathers and analyzes information from the internal and external environment in order to obtain the best fit between the organization's goals and strategies and the strategic environment.

behavioral control
a method of organizational control in which a firm influences the actions of employees through culture, rewards, and boundaries.

EXHIBIT 9.2 Contemporary Approach to Strategic Control

Formulate strategies ↔ Implement strategies

Informational control ↘ ↙ Behavioral control

Strategic control

> ### 9.1 STRATEGY SPOTLIGHT
>
> #### HOW DO MANAGERS AND EMPLOYEES VIEW THEIR FIRM'S CONTROL SYSTEM?
>
> Top executives of organizations often assert that they are pushing for more contemporary control systems. The centralized, periodic setting of objectives and rules with top-down implementation processes is ineffective for organizations facing heterogeneous and dynamic environments. For example, Walmart has, in recent years, realized its top-down, rule-based leadership system was too rigid for a firm emphasizing globalization and technological change. Like many other firms, Walmart is moving to a more decentralized, values-based leadership system where lower-level managers make key decisions, keeping the values of the firm in mind as they do so.
>
> Managers of firms see the need to make this transition, but do lower-level managers and workers see a change in the control systems at their organizations? To get at this question, the Boston Research Group conducted a study of 36,000 managers and employees to get their views on their firm's control systems. Their findings are enlightening. Only 3 percent of employees saw their firm's culture as "self-governing," in which decision making is driven by a "set of core principles and values." In contrast, 43 percent of employees saw their firm as operating using a top-down, command-and-control decision process, what the authors of the study labeled as the "blind-obedience" model; and 53 percent of employees saw their firm following an "informed-acquiescence" model, in which the overall style is top-down but with skilled management that used a mix of rewards and rules to get the desired behavior. In total, 97 percent of employees saw their firm's culture and decision style as being top-down.
>
> Interestingly, managers had a different view. The survey found that 24 percent of managers believed their organizations used the values-driven, decentralized "self-governing" model. Thus, managers were eight times more likely than employees to see the firm employing a contemporary, values-driven control system. Similarly, while 41 percent of managers said that their firm rewarded performance based on values and not just financial outcomes, only 14 percent of employees saw this.
>
> The cynicism employees expressed regarding the control systems in their firms had important consequences for the firm. Almost half of the employees who had described their firms as blind-obedience firms had witnessed unethical behavior in the firm within the last year. Only one in four employees in firms with the other two control types said they had witnessed unethical behavior. Additionally, only one-fourth of the employees in blind-obedience firms would blow the whistle on unethical behavior, but this rate went up to nine in ten if the firm relied on self-governance. Finally, the impressions of employees influence the ability of the firm to be responsive and innovative. Among those surveyed, 90 percent of employees in self-governing and 67 percent of employees in informed-acquiescence firms agreed with the statement that "good ideas are readily adopted by my company." Less than 20 percent of employees in blind-obedience firms agreed with the same statement.
>
> These findings indicate that managers need to be aware of how the actions they take to improve the control systems in their firms are being received by employees. If the employees see the pronouncements of management regarding moving toward a decentralized, culture-centered control system as simply propaganda, the firm is unlikely to experience the positive changes it desires.
>
> Sources: Anonymous. 2011. The view from the top and bottom. *The Economist*, September 24: 76; and Levit, A. 2012. Your employees aren't wearing your rose colored glasses. *openforum.com*, November 12: np.

3. The data and information generated are best interpreted and discussed in face-to-face meetings.
4. The control system is a key catalyst for an ongoing debate about underlying data, assumptions, and action plans.

An executive's decision to use the control system interactively—in other words, to invest the time and attention to review and evaluate new information—sends a clear signal to the organization about what is important. The dialogue and debate that emerge from such an interactive process can often lead to new strategies and innovations. Strategy Spotlight 9.1 discusses how managers and employees each see the control systems at work in their companies and identifies some of the consequences of those impressions.

Attaining Behavioral Control: Balancing Culture, Rewards, and Boundaries

LO9.4 The benefits of having the proper balance among the three levers of behavioral control: culture, rewards and incentives, and boundaries.

Behavioral control is focused on implementation—doing things right. Effectively implementing strategy requires manipulating three key control "levers": culture, rewards, and boundaries (see Exhibit 9.3). There are two compelling reasons for an increased emphasis on culture and rewards in a system of behavioral controls.[11]

EXHIBIT 9.3 Essential Elements of Behavioral Control

[Diagram: Three circles connected by double-headed arrows forming a triangle — Boundaries (top), Culture (bottom left), Rewards (bottom right)]

First, the competitive environment is increasingly complex and unpredictable, demanding both flexibility and quick response to its challenges. As firms simultaneously downsize and face the need for increased coordination across organizational boundaries, a control system based primarily on rigid strategies, rules, and regulations is dysfunctional. The use of rewards and culture to align individual and organizational goals becomes increasingly important.

Second, the implicit long-term contract between the organization and its key employees has been eroded.[12] Today's younger managers have been conditioned to see themselves as "free agents" and view a career as a series of opportunistic challenges. As managers are advised to "specialize, market yourself, and have work, if not a job," the importance of culture and rewards in building organizational loyalty claims greater importance.

Each of the three levers—culture, rewards, and boundaries—must work in a balanced and consistent manner. Let's consider the role of each.

Building a Strong and Effective Culture

Organizational culture is a system of shared values (what is important) and beliefs (how things work) that shape a company's people, organizational structures, and control systems to produce behavioral norms (the way we do things around here).[13] How important is culture? Very. Over the years, numerous best sellers, such as *Theory Z, Corporate Cultures, In Search of Excellence,* and *Good to Great,*[14] have emphasized the powerful influence of culture on what goes on within organizations and how they perform.

Collins and Porras argued in *Built to Last* that the key factor in sustained exceptional performance is a cultlike culture.[15] You can't touch it or write it down, but it's there in every organization; its influence is pervasive; it can work for you or against you.[16] Effective leaders understand its importance and strive to shape and use it as one of their important levers of strategic control.[17]

The Role of Culture Culture wears many different hats, each woven from the fabric of those values that sustain the organization's primary source of competitive advantage. Some examples are:

- FedEx and Amazon focus on customer service.
- Lexus (a division of Toyota) and Apple emphasize product quality.
- Google and 3M place a high value on innovation.
- Nucor (steel) and Walmart are concerned, above all, with operational efficiency.

Culture sets implicit boundaries—unwritten standards of acceptable behavior—in dress, ethical matters, and the way an organization conducts its business.[18] By creating a

> **organizational culture**
> a system of shared values and beliefs that shape a company's people, organizational structures, and control systems to produce behavioral norms.

framework of shared values, culture encourages individual identification with the organization and its objectives. Culture acts as a means of reducing monitoring costs.[19]

Strong culture can lead to greater employee engagement and provide a common purpose and identity. Firms have typically relied on economic incentives for workers, using a combination of rewards (carrots) and rules and threats (sticks) to get employees to act in desired ways. But these systems rely on the assumption that individuals are fundamentally self-interested and selfish. However, research suggests that this assumption is overstated.[20] When given a chance to act selfishly or cooperatively with others, over half of employees choose to cooperate, while only 30 percent consistently choose to act selfishly. Thus, cultural systems that build engagement, communication, and a sense of common purpose and identity would allow firms to leverage these collaborative workers.

Sustaining an Effective Culture Powerful organizational cultures just don't happen overnight, and they don't remain in place without a strong commitment—in terms of both words and deeds—by leaders throughout the organization.[21] A viable and productive organizational culture can be strengthened and sustained. However, it cannot be "built" or "assembled"; instead, it must be cultivated, encouraged, and "fertilized."[22]

Storytelling is one way effective cultures are maintained. 3M is a company that uses powerful stories to reinforce the culture of the firm. One of those is the story of Francis G. Okie.[23] In 1922 Okie came up with the idea of selling sandpaper to men as a replacement for razor blades. The idea obviously didn't pan out, but Okie was allowed to remain at 3M. Interestingly, the technology developed by Okie led 3M to develop its first blockbuster product: a waterproof sandpaper that became a staple of the automobile industry. Such stories foster the importance of risk taking, experimentation, freedom to fail, and innovation—all vital elements of 3M's culture. Strategy Spotlight 9.2 discusses the power of pictures and stories in building a customer-centric culture.

Rallies or "pep talks" by top executives also serve to reinforce a firm's culture. The late Sam Walton was known for his pep rallies at local Walmart stores. Four times a year, the founders of Home Depot—Bernard Marcus and Arthur Blank—used to don orange aprons and stage Breakfast with Bernie and Arthur, a 6:30 a.m. pep rally, broadcast live over the firm's closed-circuit TV network to most of its 45,000 employees.[24]

Southwest Airlines' "Culture Committee" is a unique vehicle designed to perpetuate the company's highly successful culture. The following excerpt from an internal company publication describes its objectives:

> The goal of the Committee is simple—to ensure that our unique Corporate Culture stays alive. . . . Culture Committee members represent all regions and departments across our system and they are selected based upon their exemplary display of the "Positively Outrageous Service" that won us the first-ever Triple Crown; their continual exhibition of the "Southwest Spirit" to our Customers and to their fellow workers; and their high energy level, boundless enthusiasm, unique creativity, and constant demonstration of teamwork and love for their fellow workers.[25]

Motivating with Rewards and Incentives

Reward and incentive systems represent a powerful means of influencing an organization's culture, focusing efforts on high-priority tasks, and motivating individual and collective task performance.[26] Just as culture deals with influencing beliefs, behaviors, and attitudes of people within an organization, the **reward system**—by specifying who gets rewarded and why—is an effective motivator and control mechanism.[27] The managers at Not Your Average Joe's, a Massachusetts-based restaurant chain, changed their staffing procedures both to let their servers better understand their performance and to better motivate them.[28] The chain uses sophisticated software to track server performance—in both per customer sales and customer satisfaction as seen in tips. Highly rated servers are given more tables

| reward system |
| policies that specify who gets rewarded and why. |

9.2 STRATEGY SPOTLIGHT

USING PICTURES AND STORIES TO BUILD A CUSTOMER-ORIENTED CULTURE

Most firms tout that customers are their most important stakeholders. In firms that have value statements, these statements typically list the firms' responsibilities to their customers first. But it is hard to build and maintain a customer-centric culture. Using visual imagery and stories can help firms put customers at the center of their culture.

The old saying is that "a picture is worth a thousand words." This is certainly true when building a culture. A simple snapshot of a customer or end user can be a powerful motivating tool for workers to care about that customer. For example, radiologists rarely see patients. They look at X-rays from the files of patients, but these patients are typically faceless and anonymous to them. However, when pictures of the patients were added to their files, one study found that radiologists increased the length of their reports on the patients' X-rays by 29 percent and improved the accuracy of their diagnoses by 46 percent. Other firms have found the same effect. Microfinance provider Kiva includes pictures of the entrepreneurs whom it is trying to fund, believing that potential donors feel more of a connection with an entrepreneur when they have seen a picture of him or her.

Stories can also help build a customer-centric culture. Inside the firm, the stories that employees share with each other become imprinted on the organizational mind. Thus, as employees share their positive stories of experiences with customers, they not only provide encouragement for other employees to better meet the needs of customers but also reinforce the storytelling employee's desire to work hard to serve customers. For example, at Ritz-Carlton hotels, employees meet each day for 15 minutes to share stories about how they went the extra yard to meet customers' needs. These stories can even be more significant for new employees, helping them learn about the values of the firm. With outside stories, firms can draw on the accounts of customers to reinvigorate their employees. These can be based on personal statements from customers or even from news stories. To test these effects, one researcher gave lifeguards a few short news stories about swimmers who were saved by lifeguards on other beaches. The lifeguards who heard these stories reported that they found their job more meaningful, volunteered to work more hours, and were rated by their supervisors as being more vigilant in their work one month later.

Managers can help ensure that the stories told support the firm's customer-centric culture by taking the following steps:

- Tell positive stories about employees' interactions with customers.
- Share positive customer feedback with employees.
- Tie employee recognition to positive employee actions.
- Weave stories into the employee handbook and new employee orientation.
- Make sure that mentors in the firm know about the importance of using stories in their mentoring efforts.

The "short story" here is that firms can help build and reinforce a customer-centric culture if they just keep the customer in the center of the stories they tell and make the customer personally relevant to workers.

Sources: Grant, A. 2011. How customers rally your troops. *Harvard Business Review*, 89(6): 96–103; and Heathfield, S. 2014. How stories strengthen your work culture—or not. *humanresources.about.com*, December 29: np.

---

and preferred schedules. In shifting more work and better schedules to the best workers, the chain hopes to improve profitability and motivate all workers.

The Potential Downside While they can be powerful motivators, reward and incentive policies can also result in undesirable outcomes in organizations. At the individual level, incentives can go wrong for multiple reasons. First, if individual workers don't see how their actions relate to how they are compensated, incentives can be demotivating. For example, if the rewards are related to the firm's stock price, workers may feel that their efforts have little if any impact and won't perceive any benefit from working harder. On the other hand, if the incentives are too closely tied to their individual work, they may lead to dysfunctional outcomes. For example, if a sales representative is rewarded for sales volume, she will be incentivized to sell at all costs. This may lead her to accept unprofitable sales or push sales through distribution channels the firm would rather avoid. Thus, the collective sum of individual behaviors of an organization's employees does not always result in what is best for the organization; individual rationality is no guarantee of organizational rationality.

Reward and incentive systems can also cause problems across organizational units. As corporations grow and evolve, they often develop different business units with multiple reward systems. These systems may differ based on industry contexts, business situations, stage of product life cycles, and so on. Subcultures within organizations may reflect differences among functional areas, products, services, and divisions. To the extent that reward systems reinforce such behavioral norms, attitudes, and belief systems, cohesiveness is reduced; important information is hoarded rather than shared, individuals begin working at cross-purposes, and they lose sight of overall goals.

Such conflicts are commonplace in many organizations. For example, sales and marketing personnel promise unrealistically quick delivery times to bring in business, much to the dismay of operations and logistics; overengineering by R&D creates headaches for manufacturing; and so on. Conflicts also arise across divisions when divisional profits become a key compensation criterion. As ill will and anger escalate, personal relationships and performance may suffer.

Creating Effective Reward and Incentive Programs To be effective, incentive and reward systems need to reinforce basic core values, enhance cohesion and commitment to goals and objectives, and meet with the organization's overall mission and purpose.[29]

At General Mills, to ensure a manager's interest in the overall performance of his or her unit, half of a manager's annual bonus is linked to business unit results and half to individual performance.[30] For example, if a manager simply matches a rival manufacturer's performance, his or her salary is roughly 5 percent lower. However, if a manager's product ranks in the industry's top 10 percent in earnings growth and return on capital, the manager's total pay can rise to nearly 30 percent beyond the industry norm.

Effective reward and incentive systems share a number of common characteristics[31] (see Exhibit 9.4). The perception that a plan is "fair and equitable" is critically important. The firm must have the flexibility to respond to changing requirements as its direction and objectives change. In recent years many companies have begun to place more emphasis on growth. To ensure that managers focus on growth, a number of firms have changed their compensation systems to move from a bottom-line focus to one that emphasizes growth, new products, acquisitions, and international expansion.

However, incentive and reward systems don't have to be all about money. Employees respond not only to monetary compensation but also to softer forms of incentives and rewards. In fact, a number of studies have found that for employees who are satisfied with their base salary, nonfinancial motivators are more effective than cash incentives in building long-term employee motivation.[32] Three key reward systems appear to provide the greatest incentives. First, employees respond to managerial praise. This can include formal recognition policies and events. For example, at Mars Central Europe, the company holds an event twice a year at which they celebrate innovative ideas generated by employees. Recognition at the Mars "Make a Difference" event is designed to motivate the winners and also other employees who want to receive the same recognition. Employees also respond well to informal recognition rewards, such as personal praise, written praise, and public praise. This is especially effective when it includes small perks, such as a gift certificate for dinner, some scheduling flexibility, or even an extra day off. Positive words and actions are especially powerful since almost two-thirds of employees in one study said management was much more likely to criticize them for poor performance than praise them for good work. Second, employees feel rewarded when they receive attention from

EXHIBIT 9.4
Characteristics of Effective Reward and Incentive Systems

- Objectives are clear, well understood, and broadly accepted.
- Rewards are clearly linked to performance and desired behaviors.
- Performance measures are clear and highly visible.
- Feedback is prompt, clear, and unambiguous.
- The compensation "system" is perceived as fair and equitable.
- The structure is flexible; it can adapt to changing circumstances.

INSIGHTS FROM RESEARCH

INSPIRE PASSION—MOTIVATE TOP PERFORMANCE

Overview

Often, managers approach and strive to motivate employees with extrinsic rewards. These produce some results; however, employees tend to perform best when their intrinsic needs are met. Think of ways to highlight the purpose of your employees' work. Allow employees to work on projects that ignite their passions.

What the Research Shows

Employees who are passionate about their jobs are more engaged in their jobs. And employees who are more engaged in their jobs perform them better, according to investigators from the University of Richmond, Nanyang Technological University, and Keppel Offshore and Marine Ltd. in Singapore. Their 2011 research, published in the *Journal of Management Studies,* utilized the performance appraisals of 509 headquarters employees of a large insurance company. The employees were given a survey to identify their attitudes toward their jobs. Using structural equations modeling, the researchers found a relationship between the employees' passion for their jobs and their performance of their jobs. However, the effect was significant only when mediated by the employees' absorption in their jobs.

Employees who had job passion identified with their jobs intrinsically and believed their work was meaningful. Therefore, they were able to feel passionate about their jobs while balancing that passion with other aspects of their lives that were also important to them. This resulted in an intensity of focus on and deep immersion in their tasks while they were working. When they were deeply engrossed in work, the employees were not distracted by other activities or roles in their lives. In turn, this job absorption resulted in superior performance on the job.

Why This Matters

While many managers attempt to tap into their employees' passions to motivate them to perform their jobs, external incentives are not the best way to engender internal identification with work. Even positive feedback can become an external incentive if employees work toward receiving that recognition rather than working simply because they identify with and enjoy their jobs. A better way to nurture employees' identification with their work is to provide them with a sense of ownership of their work and, more importantly, to help them see how meaningful their jobs are. For example, to help their employees see the impact of their work on others, Cancer Treatment Centers of America in the Tulsa, Oklahoma, area recruits spouses of employees to form and run a nonprofit organization to raise money for cancer patients' nonmedical expenses.

Kevin Cleary, CEO of Clif Bar and Co., says success is contingent upon an "engaged, inspired and outrageously committed team." He breaks this down into these steps:

1. Engage your employees with the company's mission and vision. If you don't have a mission and vision statement, get employees' contributions to create one you believe in.
2. Once people understand the mission and vision, trust your employees to work. Do not micromanage or assume they need a held hand.
3. Have a business model in which people come first, second, and third.

Cleary says exceptional talent is valuable only when employees believe in the organization's mission.

Key Takeaways

- Employees who are passionate about their jobs will be more engaged and absorbed in them and will perform better.
- When employees like their jobs and view them as important, they will be more passionate about their work.
- Employees whose jobs are significant to their personal identities—relative to the other roles they play in their lives—will be more passionate about their jobs.
- When employees are passionate about their jobs, they become deeply engrossed in their job tasks and aren't easily distracted by other activities.
- Although job passion must be voluntary and driven by employees' internal identities, managers can encourage it by helping employees see the significance of their work.

Apply This Today

Managers can fuel employees' intrinsic motivation by helping them see the meaning in their tasks, the company, and its mission. If employees can find personal meaning and passion in their jobs, the company will be rewarded with significant improvements in performance. To learn more about motivating your employees, visit *businessminded.com.*

Research Reviewed

Ho, V. T., Wong, S. S., & Lee, C. H. 2011. A tale of passion: Linking job passion and cognitive engagement to employee work performance. *Journal of Management Studies,* 48(1): 26–47.

leaders and, as a result, feel valued and involved. One survey found that the number-one factor employees valued was "managerial support and involvement"—having their managers ask for their opinions, involve them in decisions, and give them authority to complete tasks. Third, managers can reward employees by giving them opportunities to lead projects or task forces. In sum, incentives and rewards can go well beyond simple pay to include formal recognition, praise, and the self-esteem that comes from feeling valued.

The Insights from Research box provides further evidence that employees are motivated more when they feel a sense of purpose in their work and feel valued by their employers than when they are only monetarily rewarded for their work.

Setting Boundaries and Constraints

In an ideal world, a strong culture and effective rewards should be sufficient to ensure that all individuals and subunits work toward the common goals and objectives of the whole organization.[33] However, this is not usually the case. Counterproductive behavior can arise because of motivated self-interest, lack of a clear understanding of goals and objectives, or outright malfeasance. **Boundaries and constraints** can serve many useful purposes for organizations, including:

> **boundaries and constraints**
> rules that specify behaviors that are acceptable and unacceptable.

- Focusing individual efforts on strategic priorities.
- Providing short-term objectives and action plans to channel efforts.
- Improving efficiency and effectiveness.
- Minimizing improper and unethical conduct.

Focusing Efforts on Strategic Priorities Boundaries and constraints play a valuable role in focusing a company's strategic priorities. For example, in 2015, GE sold off its financial services businesses in order to refocus on its manufacturing businesses. Similarly, Pfizer sold its infant formula business as it refocused its attention on core pharmaceutical products.[34] This concentration of effort and resources provides the firm with greater strategic focus and the potential for stronger competitive advantages in the remaining areas.

Steve Jobs would use whiteboards to set priorities and focus attention at Apple. For example, he would take his "top 100" people on a retreat each year. One year, he asked the group what 10 things Apple should do next. The group identified ideas. Ideas went up on the board and then got erased or revised; new ones were added, revised, and erased. The group argued about it for a while and finally identified their list of top 10 initiatives. Jobs proceeded to slash the bottom seven, stating, "We can only do three."[35]

Boundaries also have a place in the nonprofit sector. For example, a British relief organization uses a system to monitor strategic boundaries by maintaining a list of companies whose contributions it will neither solicit nor accept. Such boundaries are essential for maintaining legitimacy with existing and potential benefactors.

Providing Short-Term Objectives and Action Plans In Chapter 1 we discussed the importance of a firm having a vision, mission, and strategic objectives that are internally consistent and that provide strategic direction. In addition, short-term objectives and action plans provide similar benefits. That is, they represent boundaries that help to allocate resources in an optimal manner and to channel the efforts of employees at all levels throughout the organization.[36] To be effective, short-term objectives must have several attributes. They should:

- Be specific and measurable.
- Include a specific time horizon for their attainment.
- Be achievable, yet challenging enough to motivate managers who must strive to accomplish them.

Research has found that performance is enhanced when individuals are encouraged to attain specific, difficult, yet achievable, goals (as opposed to vague "do your best" goals).[37]

9.3 STRATEGY SPOTLIGHT — ENVIRONMENTAL SUSTAINABILITY

BREAKING DOWN SUSTAINABILITY INTO MEASURABLE GOALS

Marks and Spencer (M&S) laid out an ambitious goal in early 2010 to become "the world's most sustainable retailer" by 2015. To meet this goal, M&S needed to substantially change how it undertook nearly all of its business operations. To make this process more tractable and to provide opportunities to identify a range of actions managers could take, M&S developed an overarching plan for its sustainability efforts, dubbed Plan A. They called it Plan A because, as M&S managers put it, when it comes to building environmental sustainability, there is no Plan B. Everyone in the firm needed to be committed to the one vision. In this plan, M&S identified three broad themes:

- Aim for all M&S products to have at least one Plan A quality.
- Help our customers make a difference to the social and environmental causes that matter to them.
- Help our customers live a more sustainable life.

Thus, M&S aimed not only to improve its own operations but also to change the lives of its customers and the operations of its suppliers and other partners. Marc Bolland, M&S's CEO, fleshed out the general Plan A goal with 180 environmental commitments. These commitments all had time targets associated with them, some short term and some longer term. For example, one commitment was to make the company carbon-neutral, a goal it achieved in 2014. To meet its goal, M&S estimated it needed to achieve a 25 percent reduction in energy use in its stores by 2012 and extended it to 35 percent by 2015. This provided clear targets for store managers to work toward. Similarly, M&S set a goal to improve its water use efficiency in stores by 25 percent by the year 2015. Additionally, M&S set out to design new stores that used 35 percent less water than current stores. These targets provided clear metrics for store managers as well as architects and designers working on new stores.

In working with its suppliers, M&S similarly rolled out a series of time-based commitments. For example, it conducted a review with all suppliers on the Plan A initiatives in the first year of the plan. M&S required all suppliers of fresh meat, dairy, produce, and flowers to engage in a sustainable agriculture program by 2012. All clothing suppliers were required to install energy-efficient lighting and improved insulation by 2015 to attain a 10 percent reduction in energy usage. These types of efforts spanned across the firm and its supply chain. As of 2014, 85 of M&S's top 100 suppliers had introduced energy-efficient best practices.

With its Plan A, M&S broke down a huge initiative into clear targets that were actionable by managers across the firm and in its partner firms. Interestingly, while this initiative was hatched as a means to achieve environmental sustainability gains, it has also turned out to be an economic win for M&S. In the first year of the plan, the firm experienced an $80 million profit on the actions it undertook. The surplus has resulted from gains in energy efficiency, lower packaging costs, lower waste bills, and profit from a sustainable energy business it set up that relies on burning biowaste to generate electricity.

Sources: Felsted, A. 2011. Marks and Spencer's green blueprint. *ft.com*, March 17: np; Anonymous. 2012. Marks & Spencer's ambitious sustainability goals. *sustainablebusiness.com*, March 3: np; and *planareport.marksandspencer.com*.

Short-term objectives must provide proper direction and also provide enough flexibility for the firm to keep pace with and anticipate changes in the external environment, new government regulations, a competitor introducing a substitute product, or changes in consumer taste. Unexpected events within a firm may require a firm to make important adjustments in both strategic and short-term objectives. The emergence of new industries can have a drastic effect on the demand for products and services in more traditional industries.

Action plans are critical to the implementation of chosen strategies. Unless action plans are specific, there may be little assurance that managers have thought through all of the resource requirements for implementing their strategies. In addition, unless plans are specific, managers may not understand what needs to be implemented or have a clear time frame for completion. This is essential for the scheduling of key activities that must be implemented. Finally, individual managers must be held accountable for the implementation. This helps to provide the necessary motivation and "sense of ownership" to implement action plans on a timely basis. Strategy Spotlight 9.3 illustrates how Marks and Spencer puts its sustainability mission into action by creating clear, measurable goals.

Improving Operational Efficiency and Effectiveness Rule-based controls are most appropriate in organizations with the following characteristics:

- Environments are stable and predictable.
- Employees are largely unskilled and interchangeable.

- Consistency in product and service is critical.
- The risk of malfeasance is extremely high (e.g., in banking or casino operations).[38]

McDonald's Corp. has extensive rules and regulations that regulate the operation of its franchises.[39] Its policy manual from a number of years ago stated, "Cooks must turn, never flip, hamburgers. If they haven't been purchased, Big Macs must be discarded in 10 minutes after being cooked and French fries in 7 minutes. Cashiers must make eye contact with and smile at every customer."

Guidelines can also be effective in setting spending limits and the range of discretion for employees and managers, such as the $2,500 limit that hotelier Ritz-Carlton uses to empower employees to placate dissatisfied customers.

Minimizing Improper and Unethical Conduct Guidelines can be useful in specifying proper relationships with a company's customers and suppliers.[40] Many companies have explicit rules regarding commercial practices, including the prohibition of any form of payment, bribe, or kickback. For example, Singapore Airlines has a 17-page policy outlining its anticorruption and antibribery policies.[41]

Regulations backed up with strong sanctions can also help an organization avoid conducting business in an unethical manner. Since the passing of the Sarbanes-Oxley Act (which provides for stiffer penalties for financial reporting misdeeds) in 2002, many chief financial officers (CFOs) have taken steps to ensure ethical behavior in the preparation of financial statements. For example, Home Depot's CFO, Carol B. Tomé, strengthened the firm's code of ethics and developed stricter guidelines. Now all 25 of her subordinates must sign personal statements that all of their financial statements are correct—just as she and her CEO have to do.[42]

Behavioral Control in Organizations: Situational Factors

Here, the focus is on ensuring that the behavior of individuals at all levels of an organization is directed toward achieving organizational goals and objectives. The three fundamental types of control are culture, rewards and incentives, and boundaries and constraints. An organization may pursue one or a combination of them on the basis of a variety of internal and external factors.

Not all organizations place the same emphasis on each type of control.[43] In high-technology firms engaged in basic research, members may work under high levels of autonomy. An individual's performance is generally quite difficult to measure accurately because of the long lead times involved in R&D activities. Thus, internalized norms and values become very important.

When the measurement of an individual's output or performance is quite straightforward, control depends primarily on granting or withholding rewards. Frequently, a sales manager's compensation is in the form of a commission and bonus tied directly to his or her sales volume, which is relatively easy to determine. Here, behavior is influenced more strongly by the attractiveness of the compensation than by the norms and values implicit in the organization's culture. The measurability of output precludes the need for an elaborate system of rules to control behavior.[44]

Control in bureaucratic organizations is dependent on members following a highly formalized set of rules and regulations. Most activities are routine, and the desired behavior can be specified in a detailed manner because there is generally little need for innovative or creative activity. Managing an assembly plant requires strict adherence to many rules as well as exacting sequences of assembly operations. In the public sector, the Department of Motor Vehicles in most states must follow clearly prescribed procedures when issuing or renewing driver licenses. Strategy Spotlight 9.4 highlights how Digital Reasoning is using data analytics to strengthen control in major financial firms.

Exhibit 9.5 provides alternative approaches to behavioral control and some of the situational factors associated with them.

9.4 STRATEGY SPOTLIGHT

USING DATA ANALYTICS TO ENHANCE ORGANIZATIONAL CONTROL

Tim Estes's goal was to develop cognitive computing as a useful business tool. Cognitive computing strives to integrate raw computing power with natural-language processing and pattern recognition to build powerful computer systems that mimic human problem solving and learning. He first found a ready home for his vision in national security. The U.S. Army's Ground Intelligence Center contracted with Digital Reasoning to develop systems to identify potential terrorists on the basis of analyses of large volumes of different sources of data, including emails, travel information, and other data.

More recently, Digital Reasoning has taken its expertise to the financial services industry and, in doing so, is providing a new type of control system to catch potential rogue traders and market manipulators within the firms. Digital Reasoning provides systems Estes refers to as "proactive compliance" to a number of major financial services providers, including Credit Suisse and Goldman Sachs. Digital Reasoning has developed software that looks for information in and patterns across billions of emails, instant messages, media reports, and memos that suggest an employee's intention to engage in illegal or prohibited behavior before the employee crosses the line. Rather than looking for evidence of actions already taken, Digital Reasoning's software looks into ongoing patterns of correspondence to search for evolving personal relationships within the company, putting up red flags when it sees unexpected patterns, such as people in different units of the firm suddenly communicating with unusual frequency or a heightened level of discussion on topics that may be tied to unethical or illegal behavior. Any unusual patterns are then investigated by analysts in each of the financial services' firms. The goal for the firms is to both control employee behavior to stay on the right side of the law and also to send signals to customers and regulators that they are taking steps to stay on the right side of legal and ethical boundaries.

Sources: McGee, J. 2014. When crisis strikes, Digital Reasoning takes action. *tennessean.com*, October 9: np; McGee, J. 2014. Digital reasoning gains $24M from Goldman, Credit Suisse. *tennessean.com*, October 9: np; and Dillow, C. 2014. Nothing to hide, everything to fear. *Fortune*, September 1: 45–48.

Evolving from Boundaries to Rewards and Culture

In most environments, organizations should strive to provide a system of rewards and incentives, coupled with a culture strong enough that boundaries become internalized. This reduces the need for external controls such as rules and regulations.

First, hire the right people—individuals who already identify with the organization's dominant values and have attributes consistent with them. Kroger, a supermarket chain, uses a preemployment test to assess the degree to which potential employees will be friendly and communicate well with customers.[45] Microsoft's David Pritchard is well aware of the consequences of failing to hire properly:

> If I hire a bunch of bozos, it will hurt us, because it takes time to get rid of them. They start infiltrating the organization and then they themselves start hiring people of lower quality. At Microsoft, we are always looking for people who are better than we are.

Second, training plays a key role. For example, in elite military units such as the Green Berets and Navy SEALs, the training regimen so thoroughly internalizes the culture that

EXHIBIT 9.5 Organizational Control: Alternative Approaches

Approach	Some Situational Factors
Culture: A system of unwritten rules that forms an internalized influence over behavior.	• Often found in professional organizations. • Associated with high autonomy. • Norms are the basis for behavior.
Rules: Written and explicit guidelines that provide external constraints on behavior.	• Associated with standardized output. • Most appropriate when tasks are generally repetitive and routine. • Little need for innovation or creative activity.
Rewards: The use of performance-based incentive systems to motivate.	• Measurement of output and performance is rather straightforward. • Most appropriate in organizations pursuing unrelated diversification strategies. • Rewards may be used to reinforce other means of control.

individuals, in effect, lose their identity. The group becomes the overriding concern and focal point of their energies. At firms such as FedEx, training not only builds skills but also plays a significant role in building a strong culture on the foundation of each organization's dominant values.

Third, managerial role models are vital. Andy Grove, former CEO and cofounder of Intel, didn't need (or want) a large number of bureaucratic rules to determine who is responsible for what, who is supposed to talk to whom, and who gets to fly first class (no one does). He encouraged openness by not having many of the trappings of success—he worked in a cubicle like all the other professionals. Can you imagine any new manager asking whether or not he can fly first class? Grove's personal example eliminated such a need.

Fourth, reward systems must be clearly aligned with the organizational goals and objectives. For example, as part of its efforts to drive sustainability efforts down through its suppliers, Marks and Spencer pushes the suppliers to develop employee reward systems that support a living wage and team collaboration.

The Role of Corporate Governance

LO9.5

The three key participants in corporate governance: shareholders, management (led by the CEO), and the board of directors.

We now address the issue of strategic control in a broader perspective, typically referred to as "corporate governance." Here we focus on the need for both shareholders (the owners of the corporation) and their elected representatives, the board of directors, to actively ensure that management fulfills its overriding purpose of increasing long-term shareholder value.[46]

Robert Monks and Nell Minow, two leading scholars in **corporate governance,** define it as "the relationship among various participants in determining the direction and performance of corporations. The primary participants are (1) the shareholders, (2) the management (led by the CEO), and (3) the board of directors."* Our discussion will center on how corporations can succeed (or fail) in aligning managerial motives with the interests of the shareholders and their elected representatives, the board of directors.[47] As you will recall from Chapter 1, we discussed the important role of boards of directors and provided some examples of effective and ineffective boards.[48]

corporate governance
the relationship among various participants in determining the direction and performance of corporations. The primary participants are (1) the shareholders, (2) the management, and (3) the board of directors.

Good corporate governance plays an important role in the investment decisions of major institutions, and a premium is often reflected in the price of securities of companies that practice it. The corporate governance premium is larger for firms in countries with sound corporate governance practices compared to countries with weaker corporate governance standards.[49]

Sound governance practices often lead to superior financial performance. However, this is not always the case. For example, practices such as independent directors (directors who are not part of the firm's management) and stock options are generally assumed to result in better performance. But in many cases, independent directors may not have the necessary expertise or involvement, and the granting of stock options to the CEO may lead to decisions and actions calculated to prop up share price only in the short term.

At the same time, few topics in the business press are generating as much interest (and disdain!) as corporate governance.

Some recent notable examples of flawed corporate governance include:[50]

- In 2014, three senior executives at Walmart resigned from the firm in the wake of accusations of bribery of government officials in Mexico. In response, Walmart changed both the leadership in this region and its compliance structure.[51]

---

*Management cannot ignore the demands of other important firm stakeholders such as creditors, suppliers, customers, employees, and government regulators. At times of financial duress, powerful creditors can exert strong and legitimate pressures on managerial decisions. In general, however, the attention to stakeholders other than the owners of the corporation must be addressed in a manner that is still consistent with maximizing long-term shareholder returns. For a seminal discussion on stakeholder management, refer to Freeman, R. E. 1984. *Strategic Management: A Stakeholder Approach*. Boston: Pitman.

- In 2012 Japanese camera and medical equipment maker Olympus Corporation and three of its former executives pleaded guilty to charges that they falsified accounting records over a five-year period to inflate the financial performance of the firm. The total value of the accounting irregularities came to $1.7 billion.[52]
- In October 2010, Angelo Mozilo, the cofounder of Countrywide Financial, agreed to pay $67.5 million to the Securities and Exchange Commission (SEC) to settle fraud charges. He was charged with deceiving the home loan company's investors while reaping a personal windfall. He was accused of hiding risks about Countrywide's loan portfolio as the real estate market soured. Former Countrywide president David Sambol and former chief financial officer Eric Sieracki were also charged with fraud, as they failed to disclose the true state of Countrywide's deteriorating mortgage portfolio. The SEC accused Mozilo of insider trading, alleging that he sold millions of dollars worth of Countrywide stock after he knew the company was doomed.

Because of the many lapses in corporate governance, we can see the benefits associated with effective practices.[53] However, corporate managers may behave in their own self-interest, often to the detriment of shareholders. Next we address the implications of the separation of ownership and management in the modern corporation, and some mechanisms that can be used to ensure consistency (or alignment) between the interests of shareholders and those of the managers to minimize potential conflicts.

The Modern Corporation: The Separation of Owners (Shareholders) and Management

Some of the proposed definitions for a *corporation* include:

- "The business corporation is an instrument through which capital is assembled for the activities of producing and distributing goods and services and making investments. Accordingly, a basic premise of corporation law is that a business corporation should have as its objective the conduct of such activities with a view to enhancing the corporation's profit and the gains of the corporation's owners, that is, the shareholders." (Melvin Aron Eisenberg, *The Structure of Corporation Law*)
- "A body of persons granted a charter legally recognizing them as a separate entity having its own rights, privileges, and liabilities distinct from those of its members." (*American Heritage Dictionary*)
- "An ingenious device for obtaining individual profit without individual responsibility." (Ambrose Bierce, *The Devil's Dictionary*)[54]

All of these definitions have some validity and each one reflects a key feature of the corporate form of business organization—its ability to draw resources from a variety of groups and establish and maintain its own persona that is separate from all of them. As Henry Ford once said, "A great business is really too big to be human."

Simply put, a **corporation** is a mechanism created to allow different parties to contribute capital, expertise, and labor for the maximum benefit of each party.[55] The shareholders (investors) are able to participate in the profits of the enterprise without taking direct responsibility for the operations. The management can run the company without the responsibility of personally providing the funds. The shareholders have limited liability as well as rather limited involvement in the company's affairs. However, they reserve the right to elect directors who have the fiduciary obligation to protect their interests.

Over 80 years ago, Columbia University professors Adolf Berle and Gardiner C. Means addressed the divergence of the interests of the owners of the corporation from the professional managers who are hired to run it. They warned that widely dispersed ownership "released management from the overriding requirement that it serve stockholders." The separation of

corporation
a mechanism created to allow different parties to contribute capital, expertise, and labor for the maximum benefit of each party.

ownership from management has given rise to a set of ideas called "agency theory." Central to agency theory is the relationship between two primary players—the *principals,* who are the owners of the firm (stockholders), and the *agents,* who are the people paid by principals to perform a job on their behalf (management). The stockholders elect and are represented by a board of directors that has a fiduciary responsibility to ensure that management acts in the best interests of stockholders to ensure long-term financial returns for the firm.

Agency theory is concerned with resolving two problems that can occur in agency relationships.[56] *The first is the agency problem that arises (1) when the goals of the principals and agents conflict and (2) when it is difficult or expensive for the principal to verify what the agent is actually doing.*[57] The board of directors would be unable to confirm that the managers were actually acting in the shareholders' interests because managers are "insiders" with regard to the businesses they operate and thus are better informed than the principals. Thus, managers may act "opportunistically" in pursuing their own interests—to the detriment of the corporation.[58] Managers may spend corporate funds on expensive perquisites (e.g., company jets and expensive art), devote time and resources to pet projects (initiatives in which they have a personal interest but that have limited market potential), engage in power struggles (where they may fight over resources for their own betterment and to the detriment of the firm), and negate (or sabotage) attractive merger offers because they may result in increased employment risk.[59]

The second issue is the problem of risk sharing. This arises when the principal and the agent have different attitudes and preferences toward risk. The executives in a firm may favor additional diversification initiatives because, by their very nature, they increase the size of the firm and thus the level of executive compensation.[60] At the same time, such diversification initiatives may erode shareholder value because they fail to achieve some synergies that we discussed in Chapter 6 (e.g., building on core competencies, sharing activities, or enhancing market power). Agents (executives) may have a stronger preference toward diversification than shareholders because it reduces their personal level of risk from potential loss of employment. Executives who have large holdings of stock in their firms were more likely to have diversification strategies that were more consistent with shareholder interests—increasing long-term returns.[61]

At times, top-level managers engage in actions that reflect their self-interest rather than the interests of shareholders. We provide two examples below:

- Steve Wynn, the CEO of Wynn Resorts, had a great year in 2011, even though his stockholders barely broke even. He received a starting salary of $3.9 million. On top of that, he received two bonuses, one worth $2 million and another for $9 million. In addition to cash compensation, he received over $900,000 worth of personal flying time on the corporate jet and over $500,000 worth of use of the company's villa.[62]
- John Sperling retired as chairman emeritus of Apollo Group in early 2013. He founded Apollo, the for-profit education company best known for its University of Phoenix unit, in 1973. Even though he already owned stock in Apollo worth in excess of $200 million, the board of directors, which includes his son as a member, granted him a "special retirement bonus" of $5 million, gave him two cars, and awarded him a lifetime annuity of $71,000 a month. He received all of these benefits even though Apollo's stock at the time of his retirement was worth one-fourth of its value in early 2009.[63]

Governance Mechanisms: Aligning the Interests of Owners and Managers

As noted above, a key characteristic of the modern corporation is the separation of ownership from control. To minimize the potential for managers to act in their own self-interest,

agency theory
a theory of the relationship between principals and their agents, with emphasis on two problems: (1) the conflicting goals of principals and agents, along with the difficulty of principals to monitor the agents, and (2) the different attitudes and preferences toward risk of principals and agents.

LO9.6

The role of corporate governance mechanisms in ensuring that the interests of managers are aligned with those of shareholders from both the United States and international perspectives.

or "opportunistically," the owners can implement some governance mechanisms.[64] First, there are two primary means of monitoring the behavior of managers. These include (1) a committed and involved *board of directors* that acts in the best interests of the shareholders to create long-term value and (2) *shareholder activism,* wherein the owners view themselves as share*owners* instead of share*holders* and become actively engaged in the governance of the corporation. Finally, there are managerial incentives, sometimes called "contract-based outcomes," which consist of *reward and compensation agreements.* Here the goal is to carefully craft managerial incentive packages to align the interests of management with those of the stockholders.[65]

We close this section with a brief discussion of one of the most controversial issues in corporate governance—duality. Here, the question becomes: Should the CEO also be chairman of the board of directors? In many Fortune 500 firms, the same individual serves in both roles. However, in recent years, we have seen a trend toward separating these two positions. The key issue is what implications CEO duality has for firm governance and performance.

A Committed and Involved Board of Directors The **board of directors** acts as a fulcrum between the owners and controllers of a corporation. The directors are the intermediaries who provide a balance between a small group of key managers in the firm based at the corporate headquarters and a sometimes vast group of shareholders.[66] In the United States, the law imposes on the board a strict and absolute fiduciary duty to ensure that a company is run consistent with the long-term interests of the owners—the shareholders. The reality, as we have seen, is somewhat more ambiguous.[67]

The Business Roundtable, representing the largest U.S. corporations, describes the duties of the board as follows:

1. Making decisions regarding the selection, compensation and evaluation of a well-qualified and ethical CEO. The board also appoints or approves other members of the senior management team.
2. Directors monitor management on behalf of the corporation's shareholders. Exercise vigorous and diligent oversight of the corporation's affairs. This includes the following activities.
   a. Plan for senior management development and succession.
   b. Review, understand and monitor the implementation of the corporation's strategic plans.
   c. Review and understand the corporation's risk assessment and oversee the corporation's risk management processes.
   d. Review, understand and oversee annual operating plans and budgets.
   e. Ensure the integrity and clarity of the corporation's financial statements and financial reporting.
   f. Advise management on significant issues facing the corporation.
   g. Review and approve significant corporate actions.
   h. Nominate directors and committee members and oversee effective corporate governance.
   i. Oversee legal and ethical compliance.
3. Represent the interests of all shareholders.[68]

> **board of directors**
> a group that has a fiduciary duty to ensure that the company is run consistently with the long-term interests of the owners, or shareholders, of a corporation and that acts as an intermediary between the shareholders and management.

While the roles of the board are fairly clear, following these guidelines does not guarantee that the board will be effective. To be effective, the board needs to allocate its scarce time to the most critical issues to which its members can add value. A survey of several hundred corporate board members revealed dramatic differences in how the most and least effective boards allocated their time. Boards that were seen as being ineffective, meaning they had limited impact on the direction and success of the firm, spent almost all of their time on the basic requirements of ensuring compliance, reviewing financial reports,

9.5 STRATEGY SPOTLIGHT

MOVING THE BOARD FROM AUDITOR TO ADVISER

Boards of directors are given the formal role of representing shareholders of a corporation and overseeing corporate managers to make sure managers act to enhance shareholder value. However, for decades, boards were often little more than cozy clubs, populated by the friends of the CEO who would meet every few months to rubber-stamp the CEO's plans for the firm. Financial scandals and corporate failures in the late 1990s and early 2000s changed this. New regulations came about, pushing for stronger oversight by the board, more independent directors, and greater penalties for boards that failed to fulfill their duties. This has resulted in stronger boards that more diligently oversee and discipline firm management. But it doesn't mean that the firm is leveraging all of the talent on the board, unless the firm finds a way to effectively draw on the experiences and expertise of its board.

Ram Charan, Dennis Carey, and Michael Useem argue in their book *Boards That Lead* that boards need to change, and are dramatically changing, their role, moving away from being auditors that check on the performance of managers and, instead, becoming strategic partners with firm management. The key change is that rather than reviewing and ratifying managers' decisions, the board can serve as a panel of strategic advisers to the firm, aiding in the formulation of the firm's strategy and not simply reviewing the firm's strategy. To do so, board members work to build strong relationships with the firm's CEO, actively mentor the CEO by providing advice from the wealth of their experience, and serve as talent scouts to help identify new executives for the firm. For example, the board of Ford Motor Company was instrumental in the firm's turnaround by convincing the firm's CEO, Bill Ford, of the need for new leadership, recruiting Alan Mulally from Boeing to be Ford's new CEO, and working with and advising Ford management as it worked to reorient the firm. More generally, research on a broad range of companies has found that boards that have the skills and knowledge to advise CEOs on potential key strategic initiatives are able to add more value to the firm.

The potential benefits of a leading board are clear, but so are the risks of this change. Can boards that work with and advise the CEO also serve as effective overseers of firm management, or will they end up in the cozy relationships seen in the past? Will the CEO be comfortable sharing power with the board, or will there be a power struggle as the board weighs in with advice? Finding the right balance will require not only negotiations between the board and the CEO to define the roles effectively but also the efforts of institutional investors and regulators to ensure the board doesn't get too friendly with the CEO.

Sources: McDonald, M., Westphal, J., & Graebner, M. 2008. What do they know? The effects of outside director acquisition experience on firm acquisition performance. *Strategic Management Journal*, 29: 1155–1177; Haynes, K. & Hillman, A. 2010. The effect of board capital and CEO power on strategic change. *Strategic Management Journal*, 31: 1145–1163; and Anonymous. 2013. From cuckolds to captains. *The Economist*, December 7: 72.

---

assessing corporate diversification, and evaluating current performance metrics. Effective boards examined these issues but also expanded the range of issues they discussed to include more forward-looking strategic issues. Effective boards discussed potential performance synergies and the value of strategic alternatives open to the firm, assessed the firm's value drivers, and evaluated potential resource reallocation options. In the end, effective and ineffective boards spent about the same time on their basic board roles, but effective boards spent additional time together to discuss more forward-looking, strategic issues. As a result, board members of effective boards spent twice as many days, about 40 per year, in their role as a board member compared to only about 19 days per year for members of ineffective boards.[69]

Strategy Spotlight 9.5 extends our discussion of the growing role of the effective boards as strategic advisers to firm management.

Although boards in the past were often dismissed as CEOs' rubber stamps, increasingly they are playing a more active role by forcing out CEOs who cannot deliver on performance.[70] Not only are they dismissing CEOs, but boards are more willing to make strong public statements about CEOs they dismissed. In the past, firms would often announce that a CEO was leaving the position to spend more time with family or pursue new opportunities. More frequently, boards are unambiguously labeling the action a dismissal to signal that they are active and engaged boards. For example, when Symantec's board removed the firm's CEO in March 2014, the board announced it was bringing in an interim CEO following "the termination of Steve Bennett." Sanofi, a French pharmaceutical firm, went even further when it fired CEO Christopher Viehbacher. In a conference call with stock analysts, the firm's board chairman discussed how a "lack of trust" between the board and Viehbacher led to his dismissal. Sometimes even the CEO clarifies the situation. When Andrew Mason was ousted as head of Groupon, he released a humorous statement saying, "After four and a half intense and wonderful years as CEO of Groupon, I've decided to spend more time with my family. Just kidding—I was fired today."[71]

Another key component of top-ranked boards is director independence.[72] Governance experts believe that a majority of directors should be free of all ties to either the CEO or the company.[73] This means that a minimum of "insiders" (past or present members of the management team) should serve on the board and that directors and their firms should be barred from doing consulting, legal, or other work for the company.[74] Interlocking directorships—in which CEOs and other top managers serve on each other's boards—are not desirable. But perhaps the best guarantee that directors act in the best interests of shareholders is the simplest: Most good companies now insist that directors own significant stock in the company they oversee.[75]

Taking it one step further, research and simple observations of boards indicate that simple prescriptions, such as having a majority of outside directors, are insufficient to lead to effective board operations. Firms need to cultivate engaged and committed boards. There are several actions that can have a positive influence on board dynamics as the board works to both oversee and advise management.[76]

1. ***Build in the right expertise on the board.*** Outside directors can bring in experience that the management team is missing. For example, corporations that are considering expanding into a new region of the globe may want to add a board member who brings expertise on and connections in that region. Similarly, research suggests that firms that are focusing on improving their operational efficiency benefit from having an external board member whose full-time position is as a chief operating officer, a position that typically focuses on operational activities.

2. ***Keep your board size manageable.*** Small, focused boards, generally with 5 to 11 members, are preferable to larger ones. As boards grow in size, the ability for them to function as a team declines. The members of the board feel less connected with each other, and decision making can become unwieldy.

3. ***Choose directors who can participate fully.*** The time demands on directors have increased as their responsibilities have grown to include overseeing management, verifying the firm's financial statements, setting executive compensation, and advising on the strategic direction of the firm. As a result, the average number of hours per year spent on board duties has increased to over 350 hours for directors of large firms. Directors have to dedicate significant time to their roles—not just for scheduled meetings but also to review materials between meetings and to respond to time-sensitive challenges. Thus, firms should strive to include directors who are not currently overburdened by their core occupation or involvement on other boards.

4. ***Balance the need to focus on the past, the present, and the future.*** Boards have a three-tiered role. They need to focus on the recent performance of the firm, how the firm is meeting current milestones and operational targets, and what the strategic direction of the firm will be moving forward. Under current regulations, boards are required to spend a great amount of time on the past as they vet the firm's financials. However, effective boards balance this time and ensure that they give adequate consideration to the present and the future.

5. ***Consider management talent development.*** As part of their future-oriented focus, effective boards develop succession plans for the CEO but also focus on talent development at other upper echelons of the organization. In a range of industries,

human capital is an increasingly important driver of firm success, and boards should be involved in evaluating and developing the top management core.

6. ***Get a broad view.*** In order to better understand the firm and make contact with key managers, the meetings of the board should rotate to different operating units and sites of the firm.

7. ***Maintain norms of transparency and trust.*** Highly functioning boards maintain open, team-oriented dialogue wherein information flows freely and questions are asked openly. Directors respect each other and trust that they are all working in the best interests of the corporation.

Because of financial crises and corporate scandals, regulators and investors have pushed for significant changes in the structure and actions of boards. Exhibit 9.6 highlights some of the changes seen among firms in the S&P 500.

Shareholder Activism As a practical matter, there are so many owners of the largest American corporations that it makes little sense to refer to them as "owners" in the sense of

EXHIBIT 9.6

The Changing Face of the Board of Firms in the S&P 500

Issue	Then and Now		Explanation
	1987	2011	
Percentage of boards that have an average age of 64 or older	3	37	Fewer sitting CEOs are willing to serve on the boards of other firms. As a result, companies are raising the retirement age for directors and pulling in retired executives to their boards.
Average pay for directors	$36,667	$95,262	Board work has taken greater time and commitment. Additionally, the personal liability directors face has increased. As a result, compensation has increased to attract and retain board members.
Percentage of board members who are female	9	16.2	While the number of boards with women and minorities has increased, these groups are still underrepresented. Still, companies have emphasized including female directors in key roles. For example, over half the audit and compensation committees of S&P 500 firms have at least one female member.
Percentage of boards with 12 or fewer members	22	83	As the strategic role and the legal requirements of the board have increased, firms have opted for smaller boards since these smaller boards better operate as true decision-making groups.
Percentage of the directors who are independent	68	84	The Sarbanes-Oxley Act and pressure from investors have led to an increase in the number of independent directors. In fact, over half the S&P 500 firms now have no insiders other than the CEO on the board.

Sources: Anonymous. 2011. Corporate boards: Now and then. *Harvard Business Review,* 89(11): 38–39; and Dalton, D. & Dalton, C. 2010. Women and corporate boards of directors: The promise of increased, and substantive, participation in the post Sarbanes-Oxley era. *Business Horizons,* 53: 257–268.

individuals becoming informed and involved in corporate affairs.[77] However, even an individual shareholder has several rights, including (1) the right to sell the stock, (2) the right to vote the proxy (which includes the election of board members), (3) the right to bring suit for damages if the corporation's directors or managers fail to meet their obligations, (4) the right to certain information from the company, and (5) certain residual rights following the company's liquidation (or its filing for reorganization under bankruptcy laws), once creditors and other claimants are paid off.[78]

Collectively, shareholders have the power to direct the course of corporations.[79] This may involve acts such as being party to shareholder action suits and demanding that key issues be brought up for proxy votes at annual board meetings.[80] The power of shareholders has intensified in recent years because of the increasing influence of large institutional investors such as mutual funds (e.g., T. Rowe Price and Fidelity Investments) and retirement systems such as TIAA-CREF (for university faculty members and school administrative staff).[81] Institutional investors hold over 50 percent of all listed corporate stock in the United States.[82]

Shareholder activism refers to actions by large shareholders, both institutions and individuals, to protect their interests when they feel that managerial actions diverge from shareholder value maximization.

Many institutional investors are aggressive in protecting and enhancing their investments. They are shifting from traders to owners. They are assuming the role of permanent shareholders and rigorously analyzing issues of corporate governance. In the process they are reinventing systems of corporate monitoring and accountability.[83]

Consider the proactive behavior of CalPERS, the California Public Employees' Retirement System, which manages nearly $300 billion in assets and is the third-largest pension fund in the world.[84] Every year CalPERS reviews the performance of the 1,000 firms in which it retains a sizable investment.[85] It reviews each firm's short- and long-term performance, governance characteristics, and financial status, as well as market expectations for the firm. CalPERS then meets with selected companies to better understand their governance and business strategy. If needed, CalPERS requests changes in the firm's governance structure and works to ensure shareholders' rights. If CalPERS does not believe that the firm is responsive to its concerns, it considers filing proxy actions at the firm's next shareholders meeting and possibly even court actions. CalPERS's research suggests that these actions lead to superior performance. The portfolio of firms it has included in its review program produced a cumulative return that was 11.59 percent higher than a respective set of benchmark firms over a three-year period. Thus, CalPERS has seen a real benefit of acting as an interested owner, rather than as a passive investor.

Strategy Spotlight 9.6 discusses how institutional investors have moved beyond only filing proxy actions designed to create shareholder value. In addition to pushing for changes in executive pay and increasing stock buyback initiatives, institutional investors are now pushing social initiatives.

Managerial Rewards and Incentives As we discussed earlier in the chapter, incentive systems must be designed to help a company achieve its goals.[86] From the perspective of governance, one of the most critical roles of the board of directors is to create incentives that align the interests of the CEO and top executives with the interests of owners of the corporation—long-term shareholder returns.[87] Shareholders rely on CEOs to adopt policies and strategies that maximize the value of their shares.[88] A combination of three basic policies may create the right monetary incentives for CEOs to maximize the value of their companies:[89]

1. Boards can require that the CEOs become substantial owners of company stock.
2. Salaries, bonuses, and stock options can be structured so as to provide rewards for superior performance and penalties for poor performance.
3. Dismissal for poor performance should be a realistic threat.

> **shareholder activism**
> actions by large shareholders to protect their interests when they feel that managerial actions of a corporation diverge from shareholder value maximization.

9.6 STRATEGY SPOTLIGHT — ENVIRONMENTAL SUSTAINABILITY

INSTITUTIONAL INVESTORS PUSH SOCIAL CONCERNS

Traditionally, activist investors have been very bottom-line-focused. They've pushed firms to unlock more value for shareholders. This led firms to take actions such as appointing a nonexecutive chairman of the board, altering compensation for top managers, divesting business units, increasing dividends, adding activist representatives to the board of directors, changing CEOs, and undertaking stock buyback programs. However, activist investors are now pushing a broader range of issues with managers, most notably pushing social initiatives. In the first quarter of 2014, 56 percent of shareholder proposals related to environmental and social issues. These proposals have resulted in shareholders voting on issues related to greenhouse gas emissions, political spending, and labor rights.

These initiatives rarely find strong support from shareholders, with environmental and social resolutions garnering only 21 percent support from shareholders when they get to an actual vote. About 30 percent of these proposals never get to a vote. Instead, corporate leaders and the activist investors negotiate an agreement on the issue. Corporations are often open to finding a negotiated solution to avoid unnecessary negative press coverage of the firm. For example, after being pressured by the $160 billion New York State Common Retirement Fund, Safeway, a major grocery retailer, agreed to buy only palm oil produced in ways that don't harm rainforests. Similarly, after being pressured by Greenpeace and associated activist investors, Lego agreed to not renew a contract with Royal Dutch Shell that had allowed Lego to sell kits with the Shell logo on trucks and gas pumps. The activists were concerned that Shell was not developing Arctic drilling areas in an environmentally responsible way and pressured Lego to disassociate itself from Shell. The effects of such activist investors can be seen more broadly as well. For example, 53 percent of firms in the S&P 500 now publish sustainability reports, and 80 percent publish data on their political giving—both of which are common concerns of social-oriented activist investors.

These pressures also put managers in a difficult position as they potentially face competing pressures. One class of activist investors may be pushing the firm to take aggressive, profitability-oriented actions, while other activist investors may be pushing competing initiatives for the firm to take social or environmental actions.

Sources: Studzinski, J. 2014. Shareholder activists up their game. *Fortune,* April 28: 20; Chasan, E. 2014. More companies bow to investors with a social cause. *wsj.com,* March 31: np; and Hansegard, J. 2014. Lego to stop making Shell play sets after Greenpeace campaign. *wsj.com,* October 9: np.

In recent years the granting of stock options has enabled top executives of publicly held corporations to earn enormous levels of compensation. In 2013, the average CEO in the Standard & Poor's 500 stock index took home 330 times the pay of the average worker—up from 40 times the average in 1980.[90] The counterargument, that the ratio is down from the 514 multiple in 2000, doesn't get much traction.[91]

Many boards have awarded huge option grants despite poor executive performance, and others have made performance goals easier to reach. However, stock options can be a valuable governance mechanism to align the CEO's interests with those of the shareholders. The extraordinarily high level of compensation can, at times, be grounded in sound governance principles.[92] Research by Steven Kaplan at the University of Chicago found that firms with CEOs in the top quintile of pay generated stock returns 60 percent higher than their direct competitors, while firms with CEOs in the bottom quintile of pay saw their stock underperform their rivals by almost 20 percent.[93] For example, Robert Kotik, CEO of video game firm Activision Blizzard, made $64.9 million in 2013, but the firm's stock price rose by over 60 percent that year, producing a strong return for stockholders as well.

That doesn't mean that executive compensation systems can't or shouldn't be improved. Exhibit 9.7 outlines a number of ways to build effective compensation packages for executives.[94]

CEO Duality: Is It Good or Bad?

CEO duality is one of the most controversial issues in corporate governance. It refers to the dual-leadership structure wherein the CEO acts simultaneously as the chair of the board of directors.[95] Scholars, consultants, and executives who are interested in determining the best way to manage a corporation are divided on the issue of the roles and responsibilities of a CEO. Two schools of thought represent the alternative positions.

EXHIBIT 9.7 Six Policies for Effective Top-Management Compensation

Boards need to be diligent in building executive compensation packages that will incentivize executives to build long-term shareholder value and to address the concerns that regulators and the public have about excessive compensation. The key is to have open, fair, and consistent pay plans. Here are six policies to achieve that.

1. **Increase transparency.** Principles and pay policies should be consistent over time and fully disclosed in company documents. For example, Novartis has emphasized making its compensation policies fully transparent and not altering the targets used for incentive compensation in midstream.
2. **Build long-term performance with long-term pay.** The timing of compensation can be structured to force executives to think about the long-term success of the organization. For example, ExxonMobil times two-thirds of its senior executives' incentive compensation so that they don't receive it until they retire or for 10 years, whichever is longer. Similarly, in 2009, Goldman Sachs replaced its annual bonuses for its top managers with restricted stock grants that executives could sell in three to five years.
3. **Reward executives for performance, not simply for changes in the company's stock price.** To keep them from focusing only on stock price, Target includes a component in its executives' compensation plan for same-store sales performance over time.
4. **Have executives put some "skin in the game."** Firms should create some downside risk for managers. Relying more on restricted stock, rather than stock options, can achieve this. But some experts suggest that top executives should purchase sizable blocks of the firm's stock with their own money.
5. **Avoid overreliance on simple metrics.** Rather than rewarding for short-term financial performance metrics, firms should include future-oriented qualitative measures to incentivize managers to build for the future. Companies could include criteria such as customer retention rates, innovation and new product launch milestones, and leadership development criteria. For example, IBM added bonuses for executives who evidenced actions fostering global cooperation.
6. **Increase equity between workers and executives.** Top executives, with their greater responsibilities, should and will continue to make more than frontline employees, but firms can signal equity by dropping special perks, plans, and benefits for top managers. Additionally, companies can give employees the opportunity to share in the success of the firm by establishing employee stock ownership plans.

Sources: George, B. 2010. Executive pay: Rebuilding trust in an era of rage. *Bloomberg Businessweek,* September 13: 56; and Barton, D. 2011. Capitalism for the long term. *Harvard Business Review,* 89(3): 85.

Unity of Command Advocates of the unity-of-command perspective believe that when one person holds both roles, he or she is able to act more efficiently and effectively. CEO duality provides firms with a clear focus on both objectives and operations as well as eliminates confusion and conflict between the CEO and the chairman. Thus, it enables smoother, more effective strategic decision making. Holding dual roles as CEO/chairman creates unity across a company's managers and board of directors and ultimately allows the CEO to serve the shareholders even better. Having leadership focused in a single individual also enhances a firm's responsiveness and ability to secure critical resources. This perspective maintains that separating the two jobs—that of a CEO and that of the chairperson of the board of directors—may produce all types of undesirable consequences. CEOs may find it harder to make quick decisions. Ego-driven chief executives and chairmen may squabble over who is ultimately in charge. The shortage of first-class business talent may mean that bosses find themselves second-guessed by people who know little about the business.[96] Companies like Coca-Cola, JPMorgan, and Time Warner have refused to divide the CEO's and chairman's jobs and support this duality structure.

Agency Theory Supporters of agency theory argue that the positions of CEO and chairman should be separate. The case for separation is based on the simple principle of the separation of power. How can a board discharge its basic duty—monitoring the boss—if the boss is chairing its meetings and setting its agenda? How can a board act as a safeguard against corruption or incompetence when the possible source of that corruption and incompetence is sitting at the head of the table? CEO duality can create a conflict of interest that could negatively affect the interests of the shareholders.

Duality also complicates the issue of CEO succession. In some cases, a CEO/chairman may choose to retire as CEO but keep his or her role as the chairman. Although this splits up the roles, which appeases an agency perspective, it nonetheless puts the new CEO in a difficult position. The chairman is bound to question some of the new changes put in place, and the board as a whole might take sides with the chairman they trust and with whom they have a history. This conflict of interest would make it difficult for the new CEO to institute any changes, as the power and influence would still remain with the former CEO.[97]

Duality also serves to reinforce popular doubts about the legitimacy of the system as a whole and evokes images of bosses writing their own performance reviews and setting their own salaries. A number of the largest corporations, including Ford Motor Company, General Motors, Citigroup, Oracle, Apple, and Microsoft, have divided the roles between the CEO and chairman and eliminated duality. Finally, more than 90 percent of S&P 500 companies with CEOs who also serve as chairman of the board have appointed "lead" or "presiding" directors to act as a counterweight to a combined chairman and chief executive.

Research suggests that the effects of going from having a joint CEO/chairman to separating the two positions is contingent on how the firm is doing. When the positions are broken apart, there is a clear shift in the firm's performance. If the firm has been performing well, its performance declines after the separation. If the firm has been doing poorly, it experiences improvement after separating the two roles. This research suggests that there is no one correct answer on duality, but that firms should consider its current position and performance trends when deciding whether to keep the CEO and chairman positions in the hands of one person.[98]

External Governance Control Mechanisms

Thus far, we've discussed internal governance mechanisms. Internal controls, however, are not always enough to ensure good governance. The separation of ownership and control that we discussed earlier requires multiple control mechanisms, some internal and some external, to ensure that managerial actions lead to shareholder value maximization. Further, society-at-large wants some assurance that this goal is met without harming other stakeholder groups. Now we discuss several **external governance control mechanisms** that have developed in most modern economies. These include the market for corporate control, auditors, banks and analysts, governmental regulatory bodies, media, and public activists.

external governance control mechanisms
methods that ensure that managerial actions lead to shareholder value maximization and do not harm other stakeholder groups that are outside the control of the corporate governance system.

The Market for Corporate Control Let us assume for a moment that internal control mechanisms in a company are failing. This means that the board is ineffective in monitoring managers and is not exercising the oversight required of it and that shareholders are passive and are not taking any actions to monitor or discipline managers. Under these circumstances managers may behave opportunistically.[99] Opportunistic behavior can take many forms. First, managers can *shirk* their responsibilities. Shirking means that managers fail to exert themselves fully, as is required of them. Second, they can engage in *on-the-job consumption*. Examples of on-the-job consumption include private jets, club memberships, expensive artwork in the offices, and so on. Each of these represents consumption by managers that does not in any way increase shareholder value. Instead, they actually diminish shareholder value. Third, managers may engage in *excessive product-market diversification*.[100] As we discussed in Chapter 6, such diversification serves to reduce only the employment risk of the managers rather than the financial risk of the shareholders, who can more cheaply diversify their risk by owning a portfolio of investments. Is there any external mechanism to stop managers from shirking, consumption on the job, and excessive diversification?

market for corporate control
an external control mechanism in which shareholders dissatisfied with a firm's management sell their shares.

The **market for corporate control** is one external mechanism that provides at least some partial solution to the problems described. If internal control mechanisms fail and the management is behaving opportunistically, the likely response of most shareholders will be to sell their stock rather than engage in activism.[101] As more stockholders vote with their feet, the value of the stock begins to decline. As the decline continues, at some point the market value of the firm becomes less than the book value. A corporate raider can take over the company for a price less than the book value of the assets of the company. The first thing that the raider may do on assuming control over the company is fire the underperforming management. The risk of being acquired by a hostile raider is often referred to as the **takeover constraint.** The takeover constraint deters management from engaging in opportunistic behavior.[102]

> **takeover constraint**
> the risk to management of the firm being acquired by a hostile raider.

Although in theory the takeover constraint is supposed to limit managerial opportunism, in recent years its effectiveness has become diluted as a result of a number of defense tactics adopted by incumbent management (see Chapter 6). Foremost among them are poison pills, greenmail, and golden parachutes. Poison pills are provisions adopted by the company to reduce its worth to the acquirer. An example would be payment of a huge one-time dividend, typically financed by debt. Greenmail involves buying back the stock from the acquirer, usually at an attractive premium. Golden parachutes are employment contracts that cause the company to pay lucrative severance packages to top managers fired as a result of a takeover, often running to several million dollars.

Auditors Even when there are stringent disclosure requirements, there is no guarantee that the information disclosed will be accurate. Managers may deliberately disclose false information or withhold negative financial information as well as use accounting methods that distort results based on highly subjective interpretations. Therefore, all accounting statements are required to be audited and certified to be accurate by external auditors. These auditing firms are independent organizations staffed by certified professionals who verify the firm's books of accounts. Audits can unearth financial irregularities and ensure that financial reporting by the firm conforms to standard accounting practices.

However, these audits often fail to catch accounting irregularities. In the past, auditing failures played an important part in the failures of firms such as Enron and WorldCom. A recent study by the Public Company Accounting Oversight Board (PCAOB) found that audits conducted by the Big 4 accounting firms were often deficient. For example, 20 percent of the Ernst & Young audits examined by the PCAOB failed. And this was the best of the Big 4! The PCAOB found fault with 45 percent of the Deloitte audits it examined. Why do these reputable firms fail to find all of the issues in audits they conduct? First, auditors are appointed by the firm being audited. The desire to continue that business relationship sometimes makes them overlook financial irregularities. Second, most auditing firms also do consulting work and often have lucrative consulting contracts with the firms that they audit. Understandably, some of them tend not to ask too many difficult questions, because they fear jeopardizing the consulting business, which is often more profitable than the auditing work.

Banks and Analysts Commercial and investment banks have lent money to corporations and therefore have to ensure that the borrowing firm's finances are in order and that the loan covenants are being followed. Stock analysts conduct ongoing in-depth studies of the firms that they follow and make recommendations to their clients to buy, hold, or sell. Their rewards and reputation depend on the quality of these recommendations. Their access to information, their knowledge of the industry and the firm, and the insights they gain from interactions with the management of the company enable them to alert the investing community of both positive and negative developments relating to a company.

It is generally observed that analyst recommendations are often more optimistic than warranted by facts. "Sell" recommendations tend to be exceptions rather than the norm. Many analysts failed to grasp the gravity of the problems surrounding failed companies such as Lehman Brothers and Countrywide till the very end. Part of the explanation may lie in the fact that most analysts work for firms that also have investment banking relationships with the companies they follow. Negative recommendations by analysts can displease the management, who may decide to take their investment banking business to a rival firm. Otherwise independent and competent analysts may be pressured to overlook negative information or tone down their criticism.

Governmental Regulatory Bodies The extent of government regulation is often a function of the type of industry. Banks, utilities, and pharmaceuticals are subject to more regulatory oversight because of their importance to society. Public corporations are subject to more regulatory requirements than private corporations.[103]

All public corporations are required to disclose a substantial amount of financial information by bodies such as the Securities and Exchange Commission. These include quarterly and annual filings of financial performance, stock trading by insiders, and details of executive compensation packages. There are two primary reasons behind such requirements. First, markets can operate efficiently only when the investing public has faith in the market system. In the absence of disclosure requirements, the average investor suffers from a lack of reliable information and therefore may completely stay away from the capital market. This will negatively impact an economy's ability to grow. Second, disclosure of information such as insider trading protects the small investor to some extent from the negative consequences of information asymmetry. The insiders and large investors typically have more information than the small investor and can therefore use that information to buy or sell before the information becomes public knowledge.

The failure of a variety of external control mechanisms led the U.S. Congress to pass the Sarbanes-Oxley Act in 2002. This act calls for many stringent measures that would ensure better governance of U.S. corporations. Some of these measures include:[104]

- *Auditors* are barred from certain types of nonaudit work. They are not allowed to destroy records for five years. Lead partners auditing a client should be changed at least every five years.
- *CEOs* and *CFOs* must fully reveal off-balance-sheet finances and vouch for the accuracy of the information revealed.
- *Executives* must promptly reveal the sale of shares in firms they manage and are not allowed to sell when other employees cannot.
- *Corporate lawyers* must report to senior managers any violations of securities law lower down.

Media and Public Activists The press is not usually recognized as an external control mechanism in the literature on corporate governance. There is no denying that in all developed capitalist economies, the financial press and media play an important indirect role in monitoring the management of public corporations. In the United States, business magazines such as *Bloomberg Businessweek* and *Fortune,* financial newspapers such as *The Wall Street Journal* and *Investor's Business Daily,* as well as television networks like Fox Business Network and CNBC are constantly reporting on companies. Public perceptions about a company's financial prospects and the quality of its management are greatly influenced by the media. Food Lion's reputation was sullied when ABC's *Prime Time Live* in 1992 charged the company with employee exploitation, false package dating, and unsanitary meat-handling practices. Bethany McLean of *Fortune* magazine is often credited as the first to have raised questions about Enron's long-term financial viability.[105]

Similarly, consumer groups and activist individuals often take a crusading role in exposing corporate malfeasance.[106] Well-known examples include Ralph Nader and Erin Brockovich, who played important roles in bringing to light the safety issues related to GM's Corvair and environmental pollution issues concerning Pacific Gas and Electric Company, respectively. Ralph Nader has created over 30 watchdog groups, including:[107]

- *Aviation Consumer Action Project.* Works to propose new rules to prevent flight delays, impose penalties for deceiving passengers about problems, and push for higher compensation for lost luggage.

- **Center for Auto Safety.** Helps consumers find plaintiff lawyers and agitate for vehicle recalls, increased highway safety standards, and lemon laws.
- **Center for Study of Responsive Law.** This is Nader's headquarters. Home of a consumer project on technology, this group sponsored seminars on Microsoft remedies and pushed for tougher Internet privacy rules. It also took on the drug industry over costs.
- **Pension Rights Center.** This center helped employees of IBM, General Electric, and other companies to organize themselves against cash-balance pension plans.

Corporate Governance: An International Perspective

The topic of corporate governance has long been dominated by agency theory and based on the explicit assumption of the separation of ownership and control.[108] The central conflicts are principal–agent conflicts between shareholders and management. However, such an underlying assumption seldom applies outside the United States and the United Kingdom. This is particularly true in emerging economies and continental Europe. Here, there is often concentrated ownership, along with extensive family ownership and control, business group structures, and weak legal protection for minority shareholders. Serious conflicts tend to exist between two classes of principals: controlling shareholders and minority shareholders. Such conflicts can be called **principal–principal (PP) conflicts,** as opposed to *principal–agent* conflicts (see Exhibits 9.8 and 9.9).

Strong family control is one of the leading indicators of concentrated ownership. In East Asia (excluding China), approximately 57 percent of the corporations have board chairmen and CEOs from the controlling families. In continental Europe, this number is 68 percent. A very common practice is the appointment of family members as board chairmen, CEOs, and other top executives. This happens because the families are controlling (not necessarily majority) shareholders. In 2003, 30-year-old James Murdoch was appointed CEO of British Sky Broadcasting (BSkyB), Europe's largest satellite broadcaster. There was very vocal resistance by minority shareholders. Why was he appointed in the first place? James's father just happened to be Rupert Murdoch, who controlled 35 percent of BSkyB and chaired the board. Clearly, this is a case of a PP conflict.

> **principal–principal conflicts**
> conflicts between two classes of principals—controlling shareholders and minority shareholders—within the context of a corporate governance system.

EXHIBIT 9.8 Traditional Principal–Agent Conflicts versus Principal–Principal Conflicts: How They Differ along Dimensions

	Principal–Agent Conflicts	**Principal–Principal Conflicts**
Goal incongruence	Between shareholders and professional managers who own a relatively small portion of the firm's equity.	Between controlling shareholders and minority shareholders.
Ownership pattern	Dispersed—5%–20% is considered "concentrated ownership."	Concentrated—often greater than 50% of equity is controlled by controlling shareholders.
Manifestations	Strategies that benefit entrenched managers at the expense of shareholders in general (e.g., shirking, pet projects, excessive compensation, and empire building).	Strategies that benefit controlling shareholders at the expense of minority shareholders (e.g., minority shareholder expropriation, nepotism, and cronyism).
Institutional protection of minority shareholders	Formal constraints (e.g., judicial reviews and courts) set an upper boundary on potential expropriation by majority shareholders. Informal norms generally adhere to shareholder wealth maximization.	Formal institutional protection is often lacking, corrupted, or unenforced. Informal norms are typically in favor of the interests of controlling shareholders ahead of those of minority investors.

Source: Adapted from Young, M., Peng, M. W., Ahlstrom, D., & Bruton, G. 2002. Governing the Corporation in Emerging Economies: A Principal–Principal Perspective. *Academy of Management Best Papers Proceedings,* Denver.

EXHIBIT 9.9 Principal–Agent Conflicts and Principal–Principal Conflicts: A Diagram

Source: Young, M. N., Peng, M. W., Ahlstrom, D., Bruton, G. D., & Jiang, 2008. Principal–Principal Conflicts in Corporate Governance. *Journal of Management Studies*, 45(1): 196–220; and Peng, M. V. 2006. *Global Strategy*. Cincinnati: Thomson South-Western. We are very appreciative of the helpful comments of Mike Young of Hong Kong Baptist University and Mike Peng of the University of Texas at Dallas.

In general, three conditions must be met for PP conflicts to occur:

- A dominant owner or group of owners who have interests that are distinct from minority shareholders.
- Motivation for the controlling shareholders to exercise their dominant positions to their advantage.
- Few formal (such as legislation or regulatory bodies) or informal constraints that would discourage or prevent the controlling shareholders from exploiting their advantageous positions.

expropriation of minority shareholders
activities that enrich the controlling shareholders at the expense of the minority shareholders.

The result is often that family managers, who represent (or actually are) the controlling shareholders, engage in **expropriation of minority shareholders,** which is defined as activities that enrich the controlling shareholders at the expense of minority shareholders. What is their motive? After all, controlling shareholders have incentives to maintain firm value. But controlling shareholders may take actions that decrease aggregate firm performance if their personal gains from expropriation exceed their personal losses from their firm's lowered performance.

Another ubiquitous feature of corporate life outside the United States and United Kingdom is *business groups* such as the keiretsus of Japan and the chaebols of South Korea. This is particularly dominant in emerging economies. A **business group** is "a set of firms that, though legally independent, are bound together by a constellation of formal and informal ties and are accustomed to taking coordinated action."[109] Business groups are especially common in emerging economies, and they differ from other organizational forms in that they are communities of firms without clear boundaries.

business groups
a set of firms that, though legally independent, are bound together by a constellation of formal and informal ties and are accustomed to taking coordinated action.

Business groups have many advantages that can enhance the value of a firm. They often facilitate technology transfer or intergroup capital allocation that otherwise might be impossible because of inadequate institutional infrastructure such as excellent financial services firms. On the other hand, informal ties—such as cross-holdings, board interlocks, and coordinated actions—can often result in intragroup activities and transactions, often at very favorable terms to member firms. Expropriation can be legally done through *related transactions,* which can occur when controlling owners sell firm assets to another firm they own at below-market prices or spin off the most profitable part of a public firm and merge it with another of their private firms.

ISSUE FOR DEBATE

CEO Pay: Appropriate Incentives or Always Dealing the CEO a Winning Hand

Alpha Natural Resources had its worst ever financial performance in 2011. The firm shut six mines, laid off over 1,500 workers, and saw its stock price drop by 66 percent. Still, the board of directors granted the firm's CEO a $528,000 bonus on top of his over $6 million pay package, noting his "tremendous efforts" to improve worker safety. Stories like these leave commentators questioning if the game is stacked to ensure that CEOs receive high pay regardless of their firm's performance.

Most large firms structure the pay packages of their top executives so that the CEO and other senior executives' pay is tied to firm performance. A large part of their pay is stock-based. The value of the stock options they receive goes up and down with the price of the firm's stock. Their annual bonuses are conditional on meeting preset performance targets. However, boards often change the rules if the firm performs poorly. If the stock price drops, leaving the options held by the CEO "underwater" and worthless, they often reprice the options the CEO holds to a lower price, making them potentially much more valuable to the CEO if the stock price bounces back. As noted above, boards also often find reasons to grant bonuses to CEOs even if the firm underperforms.

At first blush, this suggests the boards of directors are ineffective and serve to meet the desires of the CEO. But there is a logical reason why boards reprice options and grant bonuses when firms perform poorly. Boards may reprice options or change the goals that justify bonuses as a means to protect CEOs from being harmed by events out of their control. For example, if a spike in fuel prices hurts the performance of an airline or a major hurricane results in a loss for an insurance firm, the boards of these firms may argue that underperformance isn't the fault of the CEO and shouldn't result in less pay.

However, critics of this practice argue that it's wrong to protect CEOs from bad luck but not withhold benefits if the firm benefits from good luck. Boards rarely, if ever, raise the standards on CEO pay when the firm benefits from an unanticipated event. A study by researchers at Claremont Graduate University and Washington University found that executives lost less pay when their firms experienced bad luck than they gained when the firm experienced good luck. Additionally, critics point out that most workers, such as the 1,500 who were laid off by Alpha, don't receive the same protection from adverse events that the CEO does.

Discussion Questions

1. Is it appropriate for firms to insulate their CEOs' pay from bad luck?
2. How can firms restructure pay to ensure that the CEOs also don't benefit from good luck?

Sources: Mider, Z. & Green, J. 2012. Heads or tails, some CEOs win the pay game. *Bloomberg Businessweek,* October 8: 23; and Devers, C., McNamara, G., Wiseman, R., & Arrfelt, M. 2008. Moving closer to the action: Examining compensation design effects on firm risk. *Organization Science,* 19: 548–566.

Reflecting on Career Implications . . .

- **Behavioral Control:** What types of behavioral control does your organization employ? Do you find these behavioral controls helping or hindering you from doing a good job? Some individuals are comfortable with and even desire rules and procedures for everything. Others find that they inhibit creativity and stifle initiative. Evaluate your own level of comfort with the level of behavioral control and then assess the match between your own optimum level of control and the level and type of control used by your organization. If the gap is significant, you might want to consider other career opportunities.

- **Setting Boundaries and Constraints:** Your career success depends to a great extent on you monitoring and regulating your own behavior. Setting boundaries and constraints on yourself can help you focus on strategic priorities, generate short-term objectives and action plans, improve efficiency and effectiveness, and minimize improper conduct. Identify the boundaries and constraints you have placed on yourself and evaluate how each of those contributes to your personal growth and career development. If you do not have boundaries and constraints, consider developing them.

- **Rewards and Incentives:** Is your organization's reward structure fair and equitable? On what criteria do you base your conclusions? How does the firm define outstanding performance and reward it? Are these financial or nonfinancial rewards? The absence of rewards that are seen as fair and equitable can result in the long-term erosion of morale, which may have long-term adverse career implications for you.

- **Culture:** Given your career goals, what type of organizational culture would provide the best work environment? How does your organization's culture deviate from this concept? Does your organization have a strong and effective culture? In the long run, how likely are you to internalize the culture of your organization? If you believe that there is a strong misfit between your values and the organization's culture, you may want to reconsider your relationship with the organization.

summary

For firms to be successful, they must practice effective strategic control and corporate governance. Without such controls, the firm will not be able to achieve competitive advantages and outperform rivals in the marketplace.

We began the chapter with the key role of informational control. We contrasted two types of control systems: what we termed "traditional" and "contemporary" information control systems. Whereas traditional control systems may have their place in placid, simple competitive environments, there are fewer of those in today's economy. Instead, we advocated the contemporary approach wherein the internal and external environment are constantly monitored so that when surprises emerge, the firm can modify its strategies, goals, and objectives.

Behavioral controls are also a vital part of effective control systems. We argued that firms must develop the proper balance between culture, rewards and incentives, and boundaries and constraints. Where there are strong and positive cultures and rewards, employees tend to internalize the organization's strategies and objectives. This permits a firm to spend fewer resources on monitoring behavior, and assures the firm that the efforts and initiatives of employees are more consistent with the overall objectives of the organization.

In the final section of this chapter, we addressed corporate governance, which can be defined as the relationship between various participants in determining the direction and performance of the corporation. The primary participants include shareholders, management (led by the chief executive officer), and the board of directors. We reviewed studies that indicated a consistent relationship between effective corporate governance and financial performance. There are also several internal and external control mechanisms that can serve to align managerial interests and shareholder interests. The internal mechanisms include a committed and involved board of directors, shareholder activism, and effective managerial incentives and rewards. The external mechanisms include the market for corporate control, banks and analysts, regulators, the media, and public activists. We also addressed corporate governance from both a United States and an international perspective.

SUMMARY REVIEW QUESTIONS

1. Why are effective strategic control systems so important in today's economy?
2. What are the main advantages of contemporary control systems over traditional control systems? What are the main differences between these two systems?
3. Why is it important to have a balance between the three elements of behavioral control—culture, rewards and incentives, and boundaries?
4. Discuss the relationship between types of organizations and their primary means of behavioral control.
5. Boundaries become less important as a firm develops a strong culture and reward system. Explain.
6. Why is it important to avoid a "one best way" mentality concerning control systems? What are the consequences of applying the same type of control system to all types of environments?
7. What is the role of effective corporate governance in improving a firm's performance? What are some of the key governance mechanisms that are used to ensure that managerial and shareholder interests are aligned?
8. Define principal–principal (PP) conflicts. What are the implications for corporate governance?

key terms

strategic control 280
traditional approach to strategic control 280
informational control 281
behavioral control 281
organizational culture 283
reward system 284
boundaries and constraints 288
corporate governance 292
corporation 293
agency theory 294
board of directors 295
shareholder activism 299
external governance control mechanisms 302
market for corporate control 302
takeover constraint 303
principal–principal conflicts 305
expropriation of minority shareholders 306
business groups 306

experiential exercise

McDonald's Corporation, the world's largest fast-food restaurant chain, with 2014 revenues of $27 billion, but the firm has stumbled recently. Sales in 2014 dropped by 2%, and its shareholder value declined by 4% from May 2014 to May 2015. Using the Internet, evaluate the quality of the corporation in terms of management, the board of directors, and shareholder activism. (Fill in the chart below.) Are the issues you list favorable or unfavorable for sound corporate governance?

application questions & exercises

1. The problems of many firms may be attributed to a traditional control system that failed to continuously monitor the environment and make necessary changes in their strategy and objectives. What companies are you familiar with that responded appropriately (or inappropriately) to environmental change?
2. How can a strong, positive culture enhance a firm's competitive advantage? How can a weak, negative culture erode competitive advantages? Explain and provide examples.
3. Use the Internet to research a firm that has an excellent culture and/or reward and incentive system. What are this firm's main financial and nonfinancial benefits?
4. Using the Internet, go to the website of a large, publicly held corporation in which you are interested. What evidence do you see of effective (or ineffective) corporate governance?

ethics questions

1. Strong cultures can have powerful effects on employee behavior. How does this create inadvertent control mechanisms? That is, are strong cultures an ethical way to control behavior?
2. Rules and regulations can help reduce unethical behavior in organizations. To be effective, however, what other systems, mechanisms, and processes are necessary?

Management
1.
2.
3.

Board of directors
1.
2.
3.

Shareholder activism
1.
2.
3.

references

1. Anonymous. 2014. Not so funny. *economist.com,* September 27: np; Evans, P. & Fleisher, L. 2014. Tesco investigates accounting error. *wsj.com,* September 23: np; Rosenblum, P. 2014. Tesco's accounting irregularities are mind blowing. *forbes.com,* September 22: np; and Davey, J. 2014. UK watchdog to investigate Tesco accounts and auditor PwC. *reuters.com,* December 22: np.
2. This chapter draws upon Picken, J. C. & Dess, G. G. 1997. *Mission critical.* Burr Ridge, IL: Irwin Professional.
3. For a unique perspective on governance, refer to Carmeli, A. & Markman, G. D. 2011. Capture, governance, and resilience: Strategy implications from the history of Rome. *Strategic Management Journal,* 32(3): 332–341.

4. Argyris, C. 1977. Double-loop learning in organizations. *Harvard Business Review,* 55: 115–125.

5. Simons, R. 1995. Control in an age of empowerment. *Harvard Business Review,* 73: 80–88. This chapter draws on this source in the discussion of informational control.

6. Goold, M. & Quinn, J. B. 1990. The paradox of strategic controls. *Strategic Management Journal,* 11: 43–57.

7. Quinn, J. B. 1980. *Strategies for change.* Homewood, IL: Irwin.

8. Mintzberg, H. 1987. Crafting strategy. *Harvard Business Review,* 65: 66–75.

9. Weston, J. S. 1992. Soft stuff matters. *Financial Executive,* July–August: 52–53.

10. This discussion of control systems draws upon Simons, op. cit.

11. Ryan, M. K., Haslam, S. A., & Renneboog, L. D. R. 2011. Who gets the carrot and who gets the stick? Evidence of gender discrimination in executive remuneration. *Strategic Management Journal,* 32(3): 301–321.

12. For an interesting perspective on this issue and how a downturn in the economy can reduce the tendency toward "free agency" by managers and professionals, refer to Morris, B. 2001. White collar blues. *Fortune,* July 23: 98–110.

13. For a colorful example of behavioral control in an organization, see Beller, P. C. 2009. Activision's unlikely hero. *Forbes,* February 2: 52–58.

14. Ouchi, W. 1981. *Theory Z.* Reading, MA: Addison-Wesley; Deal, T. E. & Kennedy, A. A. 1982. *Corporate cultures.* Reading, MA: Addison-Wesley; Peters, T. J. & Waterman, R. H. 1982. *In search of excellence.* New York: Random House; and Collins, J. 2001. *Good to great.* New York: HarperCollins.

15. Collins, J. C. & Porras, J. I. 1994. *Built to last: Successful habits of visionary companies.* New York: Harper Business.

16. Lee, J. & Miller, D. 1999. People matter: Commitment to employees, strategy, and performance in Korean firms. *Strategic Management Journal,* 6: 579–594.

17. For an insightful discussion of IKEA's unique culture, see Kling, K. & Goteman, I. 2003. IKEA CEO Anders Dahlvig on international growth and IKEA's unique corporate culture and brand identity. *Academy of Management Executive,* 17(1): 31–37.

18. For a discussion of how professionals inculcate values, refer to Uhl-Bien, M. & Graen, G. B. 1998. Individual self-management: Analysis of professionals' self-managing activities in functional and cross-functional work teams. *Academy of Management Journal,* 41(3): 340–350.

19. A perspective on how antisocial behavior can erode a firm's culture can be found in Robinson, S. L. & O'Leary-Kelly, A. M. 1998. Monkey see, monkey do: The influence of work groups on the antisocial behavior of employees. *Academy of Management Journal,* 41(6): 658–672.

20. Benkler, Y. 2011. The unselfish gene. *Harvard Business Review,* 89(7): 76–85.

21. An interesting perspective on organizational culture is in Mehta, S. N. 2009. Under Armour reboots. *Fortune,* February 2: 29–33.

22. For insights on social pressure as a means for control, refer to Goldstein, N. J. 2009. Harnessing social pressure. *Harvard Business Review,* 87(2): 25.

23. Mitchell, R. 1989. Masters of innovation. *BusinessWeek,* April 10: 58–63.

24. Sellers, P. 1993. Companies that serve you best. *Fortune,* May 31: 88.

25. Southwest Airlines Culture Committee. 1993. *Luv Lines* (company publication), March–April: 17–18; for an interesting perspective on the "downside" of strong "cultlike" organizational cultures, refer to Arnott, D. A. 2000. *Corporate cults.* New York: AMACOM.

26. Kerr, J. & Slocum, J. W., Jr. 1987. Managing corporate culture through reward systems. *Academy of Management Executive,* 1(2): 99–107.

27. For a unique perspective on leader challenges in managing wealthy professionals, refer to Wetlaufer, S. 2000. Who wants to manage a millionaire? *Harvard Business Review,* 78(4): 53–60.

28. Netessine, S. & Yakubovich, V. 2012. The Darwinian workplace. *Harvard Business Review,* 90(5): 25–28.

29. For a discussion of the benefits of stock options as executive compensation, refer to Hall, B. J. 2000. What you need to know about stock options. *Harvard Business Review,* 78(2): 121–129.

30. Tully, S. 1993. Your paycheck gets exciting. *Fortune,* November 13: 89.

31. Carter, N. M. & Silva, C. 2010. Why men still get more promotions than women. *Harvard Business Review,* 88(9): 80–86.

32. Sirota, D., Mischkind, L. & Meltzer, I. 2008. Stop demotivating your employees! *Harvard Management Update,* July: 3–5; Nelson, B. 2003. Five questions about employee recognition and reward. *Harvard Management Update;* Birkinshaw, J., Bouquet, C., & Barsaoux, J. 2011. The 5 myths of innovation. *MIT Sloan Management Review.* Winter, 43–50; and Dewhurst, M. Guthridge, M., & Mohr, E. 2009. Motivating people: Getting beyond money. *mckinsey.com.* November: np.

33. This section draws on Picken & Dess, op. cit., chap. 5.

34. Anonymous. 2012. Nestle set to buy Pfizer unit. *Dallas Morning News,* April 19: 10D.

35. Isaacson, W. 2012. The real leadership lessons of Steve Jobs. *Harvard Business Review,* 90(4): 93–101.

36. This section draws upon Dess, G. G. & Miller, A. 1993. *Strategic management.* New York: McGraw-Hill.

37. For a good review of the goal-setting literature, refer to Locke, E. A. & Latham, G. P. 1990. *A theory of goal setting and task performance.* Englewood Cliffs, NJ: Prentice Hall.

38. For an interesting perspective on the use of rules and regulations that is counter to this industry's (software) norms, refer to Fryer, B. 2001. Tom Siebel of Siebel Systems: High tech the old fashioned way. *Harvard Business Review,* 79(3): 118–130.

39. Thompson, A. A., Jr., & Strickland, A. J., III. 1998. *Strategic management: Concepts and cases* (10th ed.): 313. New York: McGraw-Hill.

40. Weaver, G. R., Trevino, L. K., & Cochran, P. L. 1999. Corporate ethics programs as control systems: Influences of executive commitment and environmental factors. *Academy of Management Journal,* 42(1): 41–57.

41. www.singaporeair.com/pdf/media-centre/anti-corruption-policy-procedures.pdf.

42. Weber, J. 2003. CFOs on the hot seat. *BusinessWeek,* March 17: 66–70.

43. William Ouchi has written extensively about the use of clan control (which is viewed as an alternative to bureaucratic or market control). Here, a powerful culture results in people aligning their individual interests with those of the firm. Refer to Ouchi, op. cit.

This section also draws on Hall, R. H. 2002. *Organizations: Structures, processes, and outcomes* (8th ed.). Upper Saddle River, NJ: Prentice Hall.

44. Poundstone, W. 2003. *How would you move Mount Fuji?* New York: Little, Brown: 59.

45. Abby, E. 2012. Woman sues over personality test job rejection. *abcnews.go.com,* October 1: np.

46. Interesting insights on corporate governance are in Kroll, M., Walters, B. A., & Wright, P. 2008. Board vigilance, director experience, and corporate outcomes. *Strategic Management Journal,* 29(4): 363–382.

47. For a brief review of some central issues in corporate governance research, see Hambrick, D. C., Werder, A. V., & Zajac, E. J. 2008. New directions in corporate governance research. *Organization Science,* 19(3): 381–385.

48. Monks, R. & Minow, N. 2001. *Corporate governance* (2nd ed.). Malden, MA: Blackwell.

49. Pound, J. 1995. The promise of the governed corporation. *Harvard Business Review,* 73(2): 89–98.

50. Maurer, H. & Linblad, C. 2009. Scandal at Satyam. *BusinessWeek,* January 19: 8; Scheck, J. & Stecklow, S. 2008. Brocade ex-CEO gets 21 months in prison. *The Wall Street Journal,* January 17: A3; Levine, D. & Graybow, M. 2010. Mozilo to pay millions in Countrywide settlement. *finance. yahoo.com,* October 15: np; Ellis, B. 2010. Countrywide's Mozilo to pay $67.5 million settlement. *cnnmoney .com,* October 15: np; Frank, R., Efrati, A., Lucchetti, A., & Bray, C. 2009. Madoff jailed after admitting epic scam. *The Wall Street Journal,* March 13: A1; and Henriques, D. B. 2009. Madoff is sentenced to 150 years for Ponzi scheme. *www. nytimes.com,* June 29: np.

51. Harris, E. 2014. After bribery scandal, high-level departures at Walmart. *nytimes.com,* June 4: np.

52. Anonymous. 2012. Olympus and ex-executives plead guilty in accounting fraud. *nytimes.com,* September 25: np.

53. Corporate governance and social networks are discussed in McDonald, M. L., Khanna, P., & Westphal, J. D. 2008. *Academy of Management Journal,* 51(3): 453–475.

54. This discussion draws upon Monks & Minow, op. cit.

55. For an interesting perspective on the politicization of the corporation, read Palazzo, G. & Scherer, A. G. 2008. Corporate social responsibility, democracy, and the politicization of the corporation. *Academy of Management Review,* 33(3): 773–774.

56. Eisenhardt, K. M. 1989. Agency theory: An assessment and review. *Academy of Management Review,* 14(1): 57–74. Some of the seminal contributions to agency theory include Jensen, M. & Meckling, W. 1976. Theory of the firm: Managerial behavior, agency costs, and ownership structure. *Journal of Financial Economics,* 3: 305–360; Fama, E. & Jensen, M. 1983. Separation of ownership and control. *Journal of Law and Economics,* 26: 301, 325; and Fama, E. 1980. Agency problems and the theory of the firm. *Journal of Political Economy,* 88: 288–307.

57. Nyberg, A. J., Fulmer, I. S., Gerhart, B., & Carpenter, M. 2010. Agency theory revisited: CEO return and shareholder interest alignment. *Academy of Management Journal,* 53(5): 1029–1049.

58. Managers may also engage in "shirking"—that is, reducing or withholding their efforts. See, for example, Kidwell, R. E., Jr. & Bennett, N. 1993. Employee propensity to withhold effort: A conceptual model to intersect three avenues of research. *Academy of Management Review,* 18(3): 429–456.

59. For an interesting perspective on agency and clarification of many related concepts and terms, visit www.encycogov.com.

60. The relationship between corporate ownership structure and export intensity in Chinese firms is discussed in Filatotchev, I., Stephan, J., & Jindra, B. 2008. Ownership structure, strategic controls and export intensity of foreign-invested firms in transition economies. *Journal of International Business,* 39(7): 1133–1148.

61. Argawal, A. & Mandelker, G. 1987. Managerial incentives and corporate investment and financing decisions. *Journal of Finance,* 42: 823–837.

62. Gross, D. 2012. Outrageous CEO compensation: Wynn, Adelson, Dell and Abercrombie shockers. *finance. yahoo.com,* June 7: np.

63. Anonymous. 2013. Too early for the worst footnote of 2013? *footnoted. com,* January 18: np.

64. For an insightful, recent discussion of the academic research on corporate governance, and in particular the role of boards of directors, refer to Chatterjee, S. & Harrison, J. S. 2001. Corporate governance. In Hitt, M. A., Freeman, R. E., & Harrison, J. S. (Eds.), *Handbook of strategic management:* 543–563. Malden, MA: Blackwell.

65. For an interesting theoretical discussion on corporate governance in Russia, see McCarthy, D. J. & Puffer, S. M. 2008. Interpreting the ethicality of corporate governance decisions in Russia: Utilizing integrative social contracts theory to evaluate the relevance of agency theory norms. *Academy of Management Review,* 33(1): 11–31.

66. Haynes, K. T. & Hillman, A. 2010. The effect of board capital and CEO power on strategic change. *Strategic Management Journal,* 31(110): 1145–1163.

67. This opening discussion draws on Monks & Minow, op. cit. pp. 164, 169; see also Pound, op. cit.

68. Business Roundtable. 2012. Principles of corporate governance.

69. Bhagat, C. & Kehoe, C. 2014. High performing boards: What's on their agenda? *mckinsey.com,* April: np.

70. The role of outside directors is discussed in Lester, R. H., Hillman, A., Zardkoohi, A., & Cannella, A. A., Jr. 2008. Former government officials as outside directors: The role of human and social capital. *Academy of Management Journal,* 51(5): 999–1013.

71. Feintzeig, R. 2014. You're fired! And we really mean it. *The Wall Street Journal,* November 5: B1, B6.

72. For an analysis of the effects of outside directors' compensation on acquisition decisions, refer to Deutsch, T., Keil, T., & Laamanen, T. 2007. Decision making in acquisitions: The effect of outside directors' compensation on acquisition patterns. *Journal of Management,* 33(1): 30–56.

73. Director interlocks are addressed in Kang, E. 2008. Director interlocks and spillover effects of reputational penalties from financial reporting fraud. *Academy of Management Journal,* 51(3): 537–556.

74. There are benefits, of course, to having some insiders on the board of directors. Inside directors would be more aware of the firm's strategies. Additionally, outsiders may rely too often on financial performance indicators because of information asymmetries. For an interesting discussion, see Baysinger, B. D. & Hoskisson, R. E. 1990. The composition of boards of directors and strategic control: Effects on

corporate strategy. *Academy of Management Review,* 15: 72–87.

75. Hambrick, D. C. & Jackson, E. M. 2000. Outside directors with a stake: The linchpin in improving governance. *California Management Review,* 42(4): 108–127.

76. Corsi, C., Dale, G., Daum, J., Mumm, J., & Schoppen, W. 2010. 5 things board directors should be thinking about. *spencerstuart.com,* December: np; Evans, B. 2007. Six steps to building an effective board. *inc.com:* np; Beatty, D. 2009. New challenges for corporate governance. *Rotman Magazine,* Fall: 58–63; and Krause, R., Semadeni, M., & Cannella, A. 2013. External COO/presidents as expert directors: A new look at the service role of boards. *Strategic Management Journal,* 34(13): 1628–1641.

77. A discussion on the shareholder approval process in executive compensation is presented in Brandes, P., Goranova, M., & Hall, S. 2008. Navigating shareholder influence: Compensation plans and the shareholder approval process. *Academy of Management Perspectives,* 22(1): 41–57.

78. Monks and Minow, op. cit., p. 93.

79. A discussion of the factors that lead to shareholder activism is found in Ryan, L. V. & Schneider, M. 2002. The antecedents of institutional investor activism. *Academy of Management Review,* 27(4): 554–573.

80. For an insightful discussion of investor activism, refer to David, P., Bloom, M., & Hillman, A. 2007. Investor activism, managerial responsiveness, and corporate social performance. *Strategic Management Journal,* 28(1): 91–100.

81. There is strong research support for the idea that the presence of large-block shareholders is associated with value-maximizing decisions. For example, refer to Johnson, R. A., Hoskisson, R. E., & Hitt, M. A. 1993. Board of director involvement in restructuring: The effects of board versus managerial controls and characteristics. *Strategic Management Journal,* 14: 33–50.

82. Anonymous. 2011. Institutional ownership nears all-time highs. Good or bad for alpha-seekers? *allaboutalpha.com,* February 2: np.

83. For an interesting perspective on the impact of institutional ownership on a firm's innovation strategies, see Hoskisson, R. E., Hitt, M. A., Johnson, R. A., & Grossman, W. 2002. *Academy of Management Journal,* 45(4): 697–716.

84. *calpers.ca.gov.*

85. *www.calpers-governance.org.*

86. For a study of the relationship between ownership and diversification, refer to Goranova, M., Alessandri, T. M., Brandes, P., & Dharwadkar, R. 2007. Managerial ownership and corporate diversification: A longitudinal view. *Strategic Management Journal,* 28(3): 211–226.

87. Jensen, M. C. & Murphy, K. J. 1990. CEO incentives—It's not how much you pay, but how. *Harvard Business Review,* 68(3): 138–149.

88. For a perspective on the relative advantages and disadvantages of "duality"—that is, one individual serving as both chief executive office and chairman of the board, see Lorsch, J. W. & Zelleke, A. 2005. Should the CEO be the chairman? *MIT Sloan Management Review,* 46(2): 71–74.

89. A discussion of knowledge sharing is addressed in Fey, C. F. & Furu, P. 2008. Top management incentive compensation and knowledge sharing in multinational corporations. *Strategic Management Journal,* 29(12): 1301–1324.

90. Dill, K. 2014. Report: CEOs earn 331 times as much as average workers, 774 times as much as minimum wage earners. *forbes.com,* April 15: np.

91. Sasseen, J. 2007. A better look at the boss's pay. *BusinessWeek,* February 26: 44–45; and Weinberg, N., Maiello, M., & Randall, D. 2008. Paying for failure. *Forbes,* May 19: 114, 116.

92. Research has found that executive compensation is more closely aligned with firm performance in companies with compensation committees and boards dominated by outside directors. See, for example, Conyon, M. J. & Peck, S. I. 1998. Board control, remuneration committees, and top management compensation. *Academy of Management Journal,* 41: 146–157.

93. Anonymous. 2012. American chief executives are not overpaid. *The Economist,* September 8: 67.

94. George, B. 2010. Executive pay: Rebuilding trust in an era of rage. *Bloomberg Businessweek,* September 13: 56.

95. Chahine, S. & Tohme, N. S. 2009. Is CEO duality always negative? An exploration of CEO duality and ownership structure in the Arab IPO context. *Corporate Governance: An International Review,* 17(2): 123–141; and McGrath, J. 2009. How CEOs work. *HowStuffWorks.com.* January 28: np.

96. Anonymous. 2009. Someone to watch over them. *The Economist,* October 17: 78; Anonymous. 2004. Splitting up the roles of CEO and chairman: Reform or red herring? *Knowledge@Wharton,* June 2: np; and Kim, J. 2010. Shareholders reject split of CEO and chairman jobs at JPMorgan. *FierceFinance.com,* May 18: np.

97. Tuggle, C. S., Sirmon, D. G., Reutzel, C. R., & Bierman, L. 2010. Commanding board of director attention: Investigating how organizational performance and CEO duality affect board members' attention to monitoring. *Strategic Management Journal,* 31: 946–968; Weinberg, N. 2010. No more lapdogs. *Forbes,* May 10: 34–36; and Anonymous. 2010. Corporate constitutions. *The Economist,* October 30: 74.

98. Semadeni, M. & Krause, R. 2012. Splitting the CEO and chairman roles: It's complicated . . . *businessweek.com,* November 1: np.

99. Such opportunistic behavior is common in all principal–agent relationships. For a description of agency problems, especially in the context of the relationship between shareholders and managers, see Jensen, M. C. & Meckling, W. H. 1976. Theory of the firm: Managerial behavior, agency costs, and ownership structure. *Journal of Financial Economics,* 3: 305–360.

100. Hoskisson, R. E. & Turk, T. A. 1990. Corporate restructuring: Governance and control limits of the internal market. *Academy of Management Review,* 15: 459–477.

101. For an insightful perspective on the market for corporate control and how it is influenced by knowledge intensity, see Coff, R. 2003. Bidding wars over R&D-intensive firms: Knowledge, opportunism, and the market for corporate control. *Academy of Management Journal,* 46(1): 74–85.

102. Walsh, J. P. & Kosnik, R. D. 1993. Corporate raiders and their disciplinary role in the market for corporate control. *Academy of Management Journal,* 36: 671–700.

103. The role of regulatory bodies in the banking industry is addressed in Bhide, A. 2009. Why bankers got so reckless. *BusinessWeek,* February 9: 30–31.

104. Wishy-washy: The SEC pulls its punches on corporate-governance rules. 2003. *The Economist,* February 1: 60.

105. McLean, B. 2001. Is Enron overpriced? *Fortune,* March 5: 122–125.
106. Swartz, J. 2010. Timberland's CEO on standing up to 65,000 angry activists. *Harvard Business Review,* 88(9): 39–43.
107. Bernstein, A. 2000. Too much corporate power. *BusinessWeek,* September 11: 35–37.
108. This section draws upon Young, M. N., Peng, M. W., Ahlstrom, D., Bruton, G. D., & Jiang, Y. 2005. Principal–principal conflicts in corporate governance (unpublished manuscript); and, Peng, M. W. 2006. *Global Strategy.* Cincinnati: Thomson South-Western. We appreciate the helpful comments of Mike Young of Hong Kong Baptist University and Mike Peng of the University of Texas at Dallas.
109. Khanna, T. & Rivkin, J. 2001. Estimating the performance effects of business groups in emerging markets. *Strategic Management Journal,* 22: 45–74.

Creating Effective Organizational Designs

chapter 10

After reading this chapter, you should have a good understanding of the following learning objectives:

LO10.1 The growth patterns of major corporations and the relationship between a firm's strategy and its structure.

LO10.2 Each of the traditional types of organizational structure: simple, functional, divisional, and matrix.

LO10.3 The implications of a firm's international operations for organizational structure.

LO10.4 The different types of boundaryless organizations—barrier-free, modular, and virtual—and their relative advantages and disadvantages.

LO10.5 The need for creating ambidextrous organizational designs that enable firms to explore new opportunities and effectively integrate existing operations.

PART 3: STRATEGIC IMPLEMENTATION

Learning from Mistakes

The Boeing 787 Dreamliner is a game changer in the aircraft market.[1] It is the first commercial airliner that doesn't have an aluminum skin. Instead, Boeing designed it to have a composite exterior, which provides a weight savings that allows the plane to use 20 percent less fuel than the 767, the plane it is designed to replace. The increased fuel efficiency and other design advancements made the 787 very popular with airlines. Boeing received orders for over 900 Dreamliners before the first 787 ever took flight.

It was also a game changer for Boeing. In 2003, when Boeing announced the development of the new plane, it also decided to design and manufacture the 787 in a way that was different from what it had ever done before. In the past, Boeing had internally designed and engineered the major components of its planes. Boeing would then provide detailed engineering designs and specifications to its key suppliers. The suppliers would then build the components to Boeing's specifications. To limit the up-front investment it would need to make with the 787, Boeing moved to a modular structure and outsourced much of the engineering of the components to suppliers. Boeing provided them with basic specifications and left it to the suppliers to undertake the detailed design, engineering, and manufacturing of components and subsystems. Boeing's operations in Seattle were then responsible for assembling the pieces into a completed aircraft.

Working with about 50 suppliers on four continents, Boeing found the coordination and integration of the work of suppliers to be very challenging. Some of the contracted suppliers didn't have the engineering expertise needed to do the work and outsourced the engineering to subcontractors. This made it especially difficult to monitor the engineering work for the plane. Jim Albaugh, Boeing's commercial aviation chief, identified a core issue with this change in responsibility and stated, "We gave work to people that had never really done this kind of technology before, and we didn't provide the oversight that was necessary." With the geographic stretch of the supplier set, Boeing also had difficulty monitoring the progress of the supplying firms. Boeing even ended up buying some of the suppliers once it became apparent they couldn't deliver the designs and products on schedule. For example, Boeing spent about $1 billion to acquire the Vought Aircraft Industries unit responsible for the plane's fuselage. When the suppliers finally delivered the parts, Boeing sometimes found they had difficulty assembling or combining the components. With its first 787, it found that the nose section and the fuselage didn't initially fit together, leaving a sizable gap between the two sections. To address these issues, Boeing was forced to co-locate many of its major suppliers together for six months to smooth out design and integration issues.

In the end, the decision to outsource cost Boeing dearly. The plane was three years behind schedule when the first 787 was delivered to a customer. The entire process took billions of dollars more than originally projected and also more than what it would have cost Boeing to design in-house. In early 2013, all 49 of the 787s that had been delivered to customers were grounded because of concerns about onboard fires in the lithium ion batteries used to power the plane—parts that were not designed by Boeing. The efforts Boeing had to make to fix the supply problems were still being felt in 2014, when it was still losing an estimated $45 million on each 787 it delivered. As Boeing CEO Jim McNerney concluded, "In retrospect, our 787 game plan may have been overly ambitious, incorporating too many firsts all at once—in the application of new technologies, in revolutionary design and build processes, and in increased global sourcing of engineering and manufacturing content."

Discussion Questions

1. A number of firms benefit from outsourcing design and manufacturing. What is different with Boeing that makes it so much harder to be successful?
2. What lessons does its experience with the 787 offer Boeing for its next plane development effort?

One of the central concepts in this chapter is the importance of boundaryless organizations. Successful organizations create permeable boundaries among the internal activities as well as between the organization and its external customers, suppliers, and alliance partners. We introduced this idea in Chapter 3 in our discussion of the value-chain concept, which consisted of several primary (e.g., inbound logistics, marketing and sales) and support activities (e.g., procurement, human resource management). There are a number of possible benefits to outsourcing activities as part of becoming an effective boundaryless organization. However, outsourcing can also create challenges. As in the case of Boeing, the firm lost a large amount of control by using independent suppliers to design and manufacture key subsystems of the 787.

Today's managers are faced with two ongoing and vital activities in structuring and designing their organizations.[2] First, they must decide on the most appropriate type of organizational structure. Second, they need to assess what mechanisms, processes, and techniques are most helpful in enhancing the permeability of both internal and external boundaries.

Traditional Forms of Organizational Structure

> **organizational structure**
> the formalized patterns of interactions that link a firm's tasks, technologies, and people.

Organizational structure refers to the formalized patterns of interactions that link a firm's tasks, technologies, and people.[3] Structures help to ensure that resources are used effectively in accomplishing an organization's mission. Structure provides a means of balancing two conflicting forces: a need for the division of tasks into meaningful groupings and the need to integrate such groupings in order to ensure efficiency and effectiveness.[4] Structure identifies the executive, managerial, and administrative organization of a firm and indicates responsibilities and hierarchical relationships. It also influences the flow of information as well as the context and nature of human interactions.[5]

Most organizations begin very small and either die or remain small. Those that survive and prosper embark on strategies designed to increase the overall scope of operations and enable them to enter new product-market domains. Such growth places additional pressure on executives to control and coordinate the firm's increasing size and diversity. The most appropriate type of structure depends on the nature and magnitude of growth.

> **LO10.1**
> The growth patterns of major corporations and the relationship between a firm's strategy and its structure.

Patterns of Growth of Large Corporations: Strategy-Structure Relationships

A firm's strategy and structure change as it increases in size, diversifies into new product markets, and expands its geographic scope.[6] Exhibit 10.1 illustrates common growth patterns of firms.

A new firm with a *simple structure* typically increases its sales revenue and volume of outputs over time. It may also engage in some vertical integration to secure sources of supply (backward integration) as well as channels of distribution (forward integration). The simple-structure firm then implements a *functional structure* to concentrate efforts on both increasing

EXHIBIT 10.1 Dominant Growth Patterns of Large Corporations

```
                              ┌──────────┐
                              │  Simple  │
                              │Structure │
                              └─────┬────┘
    → Strategies leading             │ Growth in revenues
      to new structure               │ and employees
    ⇒ Dominant growth                ▼
      path for U.S. firms       ┌──────────┐
                                │Functional│
         Diversification into   │Structure │  Vertical integration
         unrelated areas       ┌┴──────────┴┐
                              ▼              ▼
                  ┌─────────┐    Diversification    ┌──────────┐
                  │ Holding │    into related        │Functional│
                  │ Company │    products and        │Structure │
                  │Structure│    markets             └────┬─────┘
                  └────┬────┘         │                   │
                       │              ▼                   │
      International    │         ┌──────────┐   Related   │ International
      expansion        │ Increase│ Divisional│ diversif.   │ expansion
                       │ related-│ Structure │             │
                       │ ness    └─────┬─────┘             ▼
                       ▼                │            ┌──────────┐
                  ┌─────────┐           │            │Worldwide │
                  │Worldwide│           │ Internat'l │Functional│
                  │ Holding │           │ expansion  │Structure │
                  │ Company │           ▼            └────┬─────┘
                  │Structure│      ┌──────────┐    Related│
                  └────┬────┘      │Internat'l│  diversif.│
                       │           │Structures│←──────────┘
                       └──────────►└──────────┘
                    Increase relatedness of
                    products and markets
```

Source: Adapted from J.R. Galbraith and R.K. Kazanjian, *Strategy Implementation: Structure, Systems and Process* 2nd ed., 1986, St. Paul, MN: West Publishing Company.

efficiency and enhancing its operations and products. This structure enables the firm to group its operations into functions, departments, or geographic areas. As its initial markets mature, a firm looks beyond its present products and markets for possible expansion.

A strategy of related diversification requires a need to reorganize around product lines or geographic markets. This leads to a *divisional structure.* As the business expands in terms of sales revenues, and domestic growth opportunities become somewhat limited, a firm may seek opportunities in international markets. A firm has a wide variety of structures to choose from. These include *international division, geographic area, worldwide product division, worldwide functional,* and *worldwide matrix.* Deciding upon the most appropriate structure when a firm has international operations depends on three primary factors: the extent of international expansion, type of strategy (global, multidomestic, or transnational), and degree of product diversity.[7]

Some firms may find it advantageous to diversify into several product lines rather than focus their efforts on strengthening distributor and supplier relationships through vertical integration. They would organize themselves according to product lines by implementing a divisional structure. Also, some firms may choose to move into unrelated product areas, typically by acquiring existing businesses. Frequently, their rationale is that acquiring assets and competencies is more economical or expedient than developing them internally.

Such an unrelated, or conglomerate, strategy requires relatively little integration across businesses and sharing of resources. Thus, a *holding company structure* becomes appropriate. There are many other growth patterns, but these are the most common.*

Now we will discuss some of the most common types of organizational structures—simple, functional, divisional (including two variants: *strategic business unit* and *holding company*), and matrix—and their advantages and disadvantages. We will close the section with a discussion of the structural implications when a firm expands its operations into international markets.[8]

Simple Structure

LO10.2

Each of the traditional types of organizational structure: simple, functional, divisional, and matrix.

simple organizational structure
an organizational form in which the owner-manager makes most of the decisions and controls activities, and the staff serves as an extension of the top executive.

The **simple organizational structure** is the oldest, and most common, organizational form. Most organizations are very small and have a single or very narrow product line in which the owner-manager (or top executive) makes most of the decisions. The owner-manager controls all activities, and the staff serves as an extension of the top executive.

Advantages The simple structure is highly informal, and the coordination of tasks is accomplished by direct supervision. Characteristics of this structure include highly centralized decision making, little specialization of tasks, few rules and regulations, and an informal evaluation and reward system. Although the owner-manager is intimately involved in almost all phases of the business, a manager is often employed to oversee day-to-day operations.

Disadvantages A simple structure may foster creativity and individualism since there are generally few rules and regulations. However, such "informality" may lead to problems. Employees may not clearly understand their responsibilities, which can lead to conflict and confusion. Employees may take advantage of the lack of regulations and act in their own self-interest, which can erode motivation and satisfaction and lead to the possible misuse of organizational resources. Small organizations have flat structures that limit opportunities for upward mobility. Without the potential for future advancement, recruiting and retaining talent may become very difficult.

Functional Structure

functional organizational structure
an organizational form in which the major functions of the firm, such as production, marketing, R&D, and accounting, are grouped internally.

When an organization is small (15 or fewer employees), it is not necessary to have a variety of formal arrangements and groupings of activities. However, as firms grow, excessive demands may be placed on the owner-manager in order to obtain and process all of the information necessary to run the business. Chances are the owner will not be skilled in all specialties (e.g., accounting, engineering, production, marketing). Thus, he or she will need to hire specialists in the various functional areas. Such growth in the overall scope and complexity of the business necessitates a **functional organizational structure** wherein the major functions of the firm are grouped internally. The coordination and integration of the functional areas becomes one of the most important responsibilities of the chief executive of the firm (see Exhibit 10.2).

Functional structures are generally found in organizations in which there is a single or closely related product or service, high production volume, and some vertical integration. Initially, firms tend to expand the overall scope of their operations by penetrating existing markets, introducing similar products in additional markets, or increasing the level of vertical integration. Such expansion activities clearly increase the scope and complexity of the

---

*The lowering of transaction costs and globalization have led to some changes in the common historical patterns that we have discussed. Some firms are, in effect, bypassing the vertical integration stage. Instead, they focus on core competencies and outsource other value-creation activities. Also, even relatively young firms are going global early in their history because of lower communication and transportation costs. For an interesting perspective on global start-ups, see McDougall, P. P. & Oviatt, B. M. 1996. New Venture Internationalization, Strategic Change and Performance: A Follow-Up Study. *Journal of Business Venturing,* 11: 23–40; and McDougall, P. P. & Oviatt, B. M. (Eds.). 2000. The Special Research Forum on International Entrepreneurship. *Academy of Management Journal,* October: 902–1003.

EXHIBIT 10.2 Functional Organizational Structure

```
                    Chief Executive
                   Officer or President
    ┌──────────┬──────────┬──────────┬──────────┬──────────┐
 Manager    Manager    Manager    Manager    Manager    Manager
Production Engineering Marketing    R&D     Personnel  Accounting

       Lower-level managers, specialists, and operating personnel
```

operations. The functional structure provides for a high level of centralization that helps to ensure integration and control over the related product-market activities or multiple primary activities (from inbound logistics to operations to marketing, sales, and service) in the value chain (addressed in Chapters 3 and 4).

Advantages By bringing together specialists into functional departments, a firm is able to enhance its coordination and control within each of the functional areas. Decision making in the firm will be centralized at the top of the organization. This enhances the organizational-level (as opposed to functional area) perspective across the various functions in the organization. In addition, the functional structure provides for a more efficient use of managerial and technical talent since functional area expertise is pooled in a single department (e.g., marketing) instead of being spread across a variety of product-market areas. Finally, career paths and professional development in specialized areas are facilitated.

Disadvantages The differences in values and orientations among functional areas may impede communication and coordination. Edgar Schein of MIT has argued that shared assumptions, often based on similar backgrounds and experiences of members, form around functional units in an organization. This leads to what are often called "stove pipes" or "silos," in which departments view themselves as isolated, self-contained units with little need for interaction and coordination with other departments. This erodes communication because functional groups may have not only different goals but also differing meanings of words and concepts. According to Schein:

> The word "marketing" will mean product development to the engineer, studying customers through market research to the product manager, merchandising to the salesperson, and constant change in design to the manufacturing manager. When they try to work together, they will often attribute disagreements to personalities and fail to notice the deeper, shared assumptions that color how each function thinks.[9]

Such narrow functional orientations also may lead to short-term thinking based largely upon what is best for the functional area, not the entire organization. In a manufacturing firm, sales may want to offer a wide range of customized products to appeal to the firm's customers; R&D may overdesign products and components to achieve technical elegance; and manufacturing may favor no-frills products that can be produced at low cost by means of long production runs. Functional structures may overburden the top executives in the firm because conflicts have a tendency to be "pushed up" to the top of the organization since there are no managers who are responsible for the specific product lines. Functional structures make it difficult to establish uniform performance standards across the entire organization. It may be relatively easy to evaluate production managers on the basis of production volume and cost control, but establishing performance measures for engineering, R&D, and accounting becomes more problematic.

Divisional Structure

divisional organizational structure
an organizational form in which products, projects, or product markets are grouped internally.

The **divisional organizational structure** (sometimes called the multidivisional structure or M-Form) is organized around products, projects, or markets. Each of the divisions, in turn, includes its own functional specialists who are typically organized into departments.[10] A divisional structure encompasses a set of relatively autonomous units governed by a central corporate office. The operating divisions are relatively independent and consist of products and services that are different from those of the other divisions.[11] Operational decision making in a large business places excessive demands on the firm's top management. In order to attend to broader, longer-term organizational issues, top-level managers must delegate decision making to lower-level managers. Divisional executives play a key role: They help to determine the product-market and financial objectives for the division as well as their division's contribution to overall corporate performance.[12] The rewards are based largely on measures of financial performance such as net income and revenue. Exhibit 10.3 illustrates a divisional structure.

General Motors was among the earliest firms to adopt the divisional organizational structure.[13] In the 1920s the company formed five major product divisions (Cadillac, Buick, Oldsmobile, Pontiac, and Chevrolet) as well as several industrial divisions. Since then, many firms have discovered that as they diversified into new product-market activities, functional structures—with their emphasis on single functional departments—were unable to manage the increased complexity of the entire business.

Advantages By creating separate divisions to manage individual product markets, there is a separation of strategic and operating control. Divisional managers can focus their efforts on improving operations in the product markets for which they are responsible, and corporate officers can devote their time to overall strategic issues for the entire corporation. The focus on a division's products and markets—by the divisional executives—provides the corporation with an enhanced ability to respond quickly to important changes. Since there are functional departments within each division of the corporation, the problems associated with sharing resources across functional departments are minimized. Because there are multiple levels of general managers (executives responsible for integrating and coordinating all functional areas), the development of general management talent is enhanced.

EXHIBIT 10.3 Divisional Organizational Structure

```
                    Chief Executive
                   Officer or President
                           |
                           |———— Corporate Staff
                           |
      ┌────────────────────┼────────────────────┐
      |                    |                    |
  Division A           Division B           Division C
General Manager      General Manager      General Manager
      |                    |                    |
┌──┬──┬──┬──┬──┐           |                    |
M  M  M  M  M  M       Organized            Organized
Prod Eng Mkt R&D Pers Acct   similarly to         similarly to
                         Division A           Division A

Lower-level managers, specialists, and operating personnel
```

STRATEGY SPOTLIGHT 10.1

BREAKING DOWN DIVISIONAL BOUNDARIES: LEARNING FROM YOUR TWIN

On the edge of Lake Michigan in Burns Harbor, Indiana, sits a 50-year-old steel mill that produces steel for the automotive, appliance, and other industries with midwestern production plants. The steel mill struggled through the 1980s and 1990s and went bankrupt in 2002. It was bought out of bankruptcy and has been owned by ArcelorMittal, the world's largest steel producer, since 2005. However, the plant faced another crisis in 2007 when it was threatened with closure unless it became more productive and efficient.

Today, this plant requires 1.32 man-hours per ton of steel produced, which is 34 percent more efficient than the average in U.S. steel mills. Further, in 2011, the plant was 19 percent more efficient than it was in 2007 and produced twice the quantity of steel it produced in 2009. Its future as a productive steel plant is now secure.

How did ArcelorMittal achieve these gains and rejuvenate an old steel mill? It did it by breaking down the barriers between organization units to facilitate knowledge transfer and learning. One of the disadvantages of a divisional structure is that the divisions often perceive themselves as being in competition with each other and are therefore unwilling to share information to help other divisions improve. ArcelorMittal has overcome this by "twinning" different steel mills, one efficient and one struggling, and challenging the efficient plant to help out its twin. The Burns Harbor mill was paired with a mill in Ghent, Belgium. Over 100 engineers and managers from Burns Harbor traveled to Belgium to tour the Ghent plant and learn from their colleagues there how to improve operations. They copied routines from that plant, implemented an advanced computer control system used in the Belgian mill, and employed automated machines similar to the ones used in Belgium. ArcelorMittal also provided $150 million in capital investments to upgrade the operations to bring the facilities up to par with the Ghent plant. These changes resulted in dramatic improvements in the efficiency of the Burns Harbor mill. The Belgians take pride in the improvements in Burns Harbor and now find themselves striving to improve their own operations to stay ahead of the Americans. The Ghent plant now produces 950 tons of steel per employee each year, only 50 tons per employee more than Burns Harbor, but the Ghent managers boast they will soon increase productivity to 1,100 tons per employee. Thus, Ghent cooperates and is willing to help Burns Harbor, but the managers and employees at Ghent have a competitive streak as well.

The experience of ArcelorMittal demonstrates how firms can act to overcome the typical disadvantages of their divisional structure.

Source: Miller, J. 2012. Indiana steel mill revived with lessons from abroad. *wsj.com*, May 21: np; *www.nishp.org/bh-history.htm;* and Markovich, S. 2012. Morning brief: Foreign investment revives Indiana steel mill. *blogs.cfr.org*, May 21: np.

Disadvantages It can be very expensive; there can be increased costs due to the duplication of personnel, operations, and investment since each division must staff multiple functional departments. There also can be dysfunctional competition among divisions since each division tends to become concerned solely about its own operations. Divisional managers are often evaluated on common measures such as return on assets and sales growth. If goals are conflicting, there can be a sense of a "zero-sum" game that would discourage sharing ideas and resources among the divisions for the common good of the corporation. Ghoshal and Bartlett, two leading strategy scholars, note:

> As their label clearly warns, divisions divide. The divisional model fragmented companies' resources; it created vertical communication channels that insulated business units and prevented them from sharing their strengths with one another. Consequently, the whole of the corporation was often less than the sum of its parts.[14]

With many divisions providing different products and services, there is the chance that differences in image and quality may occur across divisions. One division may offer no-frills products of lower quality that may erode the brand reputation of another division that has top-quality, highly differentiated offerings. Since each division is evaluated in terms of financial measures such as return on investment and revenue growth, there is often an urge to focus on short-term performance. If corporate management uses quarterly profits as the key performance indicator, divisional management may tend to put significant emphasis on "making the numbers" and minimizing activities, such as advertising, maintenance, and capital investments, which would detract from short-term performance measures. Strategy Spotlight 10.1 discusses how ArcelorMittal works to overcome some of the disadvantages of the divisional structure by "twinning" its plants.

10.2 STRATEGY SPOTLIGHT

CARGILL TAILORS ITS SBU STRUCTURE TO BREAK DOWN BOUNDARIES

Cargill is a $130 billion family-owned agribusiness behemoth with over 70 business units. It sells to a range of customer groups, including food, beverage, industrial, pharmaceutical, and personal care product makers, as well as farmers and food service providers. It strives for both efficiency and responsiveness to market opportunities. Greg Page, the firm's chairman and former CEO, strives to find the balance between corporate financial discipline and synergistic opportunities across the business units. He's created a novel SBU structure to help find that balance.

At the top is the company's senior corporate governing body, the Cargill Leadership Team (CLT). This group has only six people. The CLT's role is to set the broad strategy of the firm, set growth goals and directions, and allocate human and financial capital. The next layer is the Corporate Center, which includes CLT members and about 25 others who head up the firm's SBUs. The non-CLT Corporate Center members are "tagged," using Cargill's terminology, to a CLT member to ensure that administrative matters and lines of responsibility are aligned and clear. Members of the Corporate Center, along with some division heads and next-level functional leaders, populate 12 committees, including the Food Risk Committee, Technology Committee, Strategy and Capital Committee, and the Cargill Brand Reputation Committee. These committees work to leverage economies of scope, to transfer competencies between units, and to maintain consistency across the SBUs.

Page asserts that "by keeping the CLT too small to conduct the day-to-day affairs of the company, it forces that accountability and ownership down the line. With it comes a lot of engagement and shared, or collective, leadership."

Sources: Neilson, G. L. & Wulf, J. 2012. How many direct reports? *Harvard Business Review*, 90(4): 113–118; Anonymous. 2014. Cargill announces additions to board, leadership team. *world-grain.com*, December 9: np; and *yahoo.finance.com*.

We'll discuss two variations of the divisional form: the strategic business unit (SBU) and holding company structures.

Strategic Business Unit (SBU) Structure Highly diversified corporations such as ConAgra, a $13 billion food producer, may consist of dozens of different divisions.[15] If ConAgra were to use a purely divisional structure, it would be nearly impossible for the corporate office to plan and coordinate activities, because the span of control would be too large. To attain synergies, ConAgra has put its diverse businesses into three primary SBUs: food service (restaurants), retail (grocery stores), and agricultural products.

> **strategic business unit (SBU) structure**
> an organizational form in which products, projects, or product-market divisions are grouped into homogeneous units.

With an **SBU structure,** divisions with similar products, markets, and/or technologies are grouped into homogeneous units to achieve some synergies. These include those discussed in Chapter 6 for related diversification, such as leveraging core competencies, sharing infrastructures, and market power. Generally the more related businesses are within a corporation, the fewer SBUs will be required. Each of the SBUs in the corporation operates as a profit center. Strategy Spotlight 10.2 discusses how Cargill has built an SBU structure that fosters consistency across units but also learning and collaboration across unit boundaries.

Advantages The SBU structure makes the task of planning and control by the corporate office more manageable. Also, with greater decentralization of authority, individual businesses can react more quickly to important changes in the environment than if all divisions had to report directly to the corporate office.

Disadvantages Since the divisions are grouped into SBUs, it may become difficult to achieve synergies across SBUs. If divisions in different SBUs have potential sources of synergy, it may become difficult for them to be realized. The additional level of management increases the number of personnel and overhead expenses, while the additional hierarchical level removes the corporate office further from the individual divisions. The corporate office may become unaware of key developments that could have a major impact on the corporation.

Holding Company Structure The **holding company structure** (sometimes referred to as a *conglomerate*) is also a variation of the divisional structure. Whereas the SBU structure is often used when similarities exist between the individual businesses (or divisions), the holding company structure is appropriate when the businesses in a corporation's portfolio do not have much in common. Thus, the potential for synergies is limited.

Holding company structures are most appropriate for firms with a strategy of unrelated diversification. Companies such as Berkshire Hathaway and Loews use a holding company structure to implement their unrelated diversification strategies. Since there are few similarities across the businesses, the corporate offices in these companies provide a great deal of autonomy to operating divisions and rely on financial controls and incentive programs to obtain high levels of performance from the individual businesses. Corporate staffs at these firms tend to be small because of their limited involvement in the overall operation of their various businesses.[16]

Advantages The holding company structure has the cost savings associated with fewer personnel and the lower overhead resulting from a small corporate office and fewer hierarchical levels. The autonomy of the holding company structure increases the motivational level of divisional executives and enables them to respond quickly to market opportunities and threats.

Disadvantages There is an inherent lack of control and dependence that corporate-level executives have on divisional executives. Major problems could arise if key divisional executives leave the firm, because the corporate office has very little "bench strength"—additional managerial talent ready to quickly fill key positions. If problems arise in a division, it may become very difficult to turn around individual businesses because of limited staff support in the corporate office.

Matrix Structure

One approach that tries to overcome the inadequacies inherent in the other structures is the **matrix organizational structure.** It is a combination of the functional and divisional structures. Most commonly, functional departments are combined with product groups on a project basis. For example, a product group may want to develop a new addition to its line; for this project, it obtains personnel from functional departments such as marketing, production, and engineering. These personnel work under the manager of the product group for the duration of the project, which can vary from a few weeks to an open-ended period of time. The individuals who work in a matrix organization become responsible to two managers: the project manager and the manager of their functional area. Exhibit 10.4 illustrates a matrix structure.

Some large multinational corporations rely on a matrix structure to combine product groups and geographic units. Product managers have global responsibility for the development, manufacturing, and distribution of their own line, while managers of geographic regions have responsibility for the profitability of the businesses in their regions. Vodafone, the wireless service provider, utilizes this type of structure.

Other organizations, such as Cisco, use a matrix structure to try to maintain flexibility. In these firms, individual workers have a permanent functional home but also are assigned to and work within temporary project teams.[17]

Advantages The matrix structure facilitates the use of specialized personnel, equipment, and facilities. Instead of duplicating functions, as would be the case in a divisional structure based on products, the resources are shared. Individuals with high expertise can divide their time among multiple projects. Such resource sharing and collaboration enable a firm to use resources more efficiently and to respond more quickly and effectively to changes in

---

holding company structure
an organizational form that is a variation of the divisional organizational structure in which the divisions have a high degree of autonomy both from other divisions and from corporate headquarters.

matrix organizational structure
an organizational form in which there are multiple lines of authority and some individuals report to at least two managers.

EXHIBIT 10.4 Matrix Organizational Structure

the competitive environment. The flexibility inherent in a matrix structure provides professionals with a broader range of responsibility. Such experience enables them to develop their skills and competencies.

Disadvantages The dual-reporting structures can result in uncertainty and lead to intense power struggles and conflict over the allocation of personnel and other resources. Working relationships become more complicated. This may result in excessive reliance on group processes and teamwork, along with a diffusion of responsibility, which in turn may erode timely decision making.

Let's look at Procter & Gamble (P&G) to see some of the disadvantages associated with a matrix structure:

> After 50 years with a divisional structure, P&G went to a matrix structure in 1987. In this structure, it had product categories, such as soaps and detergents, on one dimension and functional managers on the other dimension. Within each product category, country managers reported to regional managers who then reported to product managers. The structure became complex to manage, with 13 layers of management and significant power struggles as the functional managers developed their own strategic agendas that often were at odds with the product managers' agendas. After seeing its growth rate decline from 8.5 percent in the 1980s to 2.6 percent in the late 1990s, P&G scrapped the matrix structure to go to a global product structure with three major product categories to offer unity in direction and more responsive decision making.[18]

Exhibit 10.5 briefly summarizes the advantages and disadvantages of the functional, divisional, and matrix organizational structures.

International Operations: Implications for Organizational Structure

LO10.3

The implications of a firm's international operations for organizational structure.

Today's managers must maintain an international outlook on their firm's businesses and competitive strategies. In the global marketplace, managers must ensure consistency between their strategies (at the business, corporate, and international levels) and the structure of their organization. As firms expand into foreign markets, they generally follow a pattern of change

EXHIBIT 10.5 Functional, Divisional, and Matrix Organizational Structures: Advantages and Disadvantages

Functional Structure	
Advantages	**Disadvantages**
• Pooling of specialists enhances coordination and control.	• Differences in functional area orientation impede communication and coordination.
• Centralized decision making enhances an organizational perspective across functions.	• Tendency for specialists to develop short-term perspective and narrow functional orientation.
• Efficient use of managerial and technical talent.	• Functional area conflicts may overburden top-level decision makers.
• Facilitates career paths and professional development in specialized areas.	• Difficult to establish uniform performance standards.

Divisional Structure	
Advantages	**Disadvantages**
• Increases strategic and operational control, permitting corporate-level executives to address strategic issues.	• Increased costs incurred through duplication of personnel, operations, and investment.
• Quick response to environmental changes.	• Dysfunctional competition among divisions may detract from overall corporate performance.
• Increases focus on products and markets.	• Difficult to maintain uniform corporate image.
• Minimizes problems associated with sharing resources across functional areas.	• Overemphasis on short-term performance.
• Facilitates development of general managers.	

Matrix Structure	
Advantages	**Disadvantages**
• Increases market responsiveness through collaboration and synergies among professional colleagues.	• Dual-reporting relationships can result in uncertainty regarding accountability.
• Allows more efficient utilization of resources.	• Intense power struggles may lead to increased levels of conflict.
• Improves flexibility, coordination, and communication.	• Working relationships may be more complicated and human resources duplicated.
• Increases professional development through a broader range of responsibility.	• Excessive reliance on group processes and teamwork may impede timely decision making.

in structure that parallels the changes in their strategies.[19] Three major contingencies that influence the chosen structure are (1) the type of strategy that is driving a firm's foreign operations, (2) product diversity, and (3) the extent to which a firm is dependent on foreign sales.[20]

As international operations become an important part of a firm's overall operations, managers must make changes that are consistent with their firm's structure. The primary types of structures used to manage a firm's international operations are:[21]

- International division
- Geographic-area division
- Worldwide functional
- Worldwide product division
- Worldwide matrix

Multidomestic strategies are driven by political and cultural imperatives requiring managers within each country to respond to local conditions. The structures consistent with

international division structure
an organizational form in which international operations are in a separate, autonomous division. Most domestic operations are kept in other parts of the organization.

geographic-area division structure
a type of divisional organizational structure in which operations in geographic regions are grouped internally.

worldwide matrix structure
a type of matrix organizational structure that has one line of authority for geographic-area divisions and another line of authority for worldwide product divisions.

worldwide functional structure
a functional structure in which all departments have worldwide reponsibilities.

worldwide product division structure
a product division structure in which all divisions have worldwide responsibilities.

global start-up
a business organization that, from inception, seeks to derive significant advantage from the use of resources and the sale of outputs in multiple countries.

such a strategic orientation are the **international division** and **geographic-area division structures.** Here, local managers are provided with a high level of autonomy to manage their operations within the constraints and demands of their geographic market. As a firm's foreign sales increase as a percentage of its total sales, it will likely change from an international division to a geographic-area division structure. And, as a firm's product and/or market diversity becomes large, it is likely to benefit from a **worldwide matrix structure.**

Global strategies are driven by economic pressures that require managers to view operations in different geographic areas to be managed for overall efficiency. The structures consistent with the efficiency perspective are the **worldwide functional** and **worldwide product division structures.** Here, division managers view the marketplace as homogeneous and devote relatively little attention to local market, political, and economic factors. The choice between these two types of structures is guided largely by the extent of product diversity. Firms with relatively low levels of product diversity may opt for a worldwide product division structure. However, if significant product-market diversity results from highly unrelated international acquisitions, a worldwide holding company structure should be implemented. Such firms have very little commonality among products, markets, or technologies and have little need for integration.

Global Start-Ups: A Recent Phenomenon

International expansion occurs rather late for most corporations, typically after possibilities of domestic growth are exhausted. Increasingly, we are seeing two interrelated phenomena. First, many firms now expand internationally relatively early in their history. Second, some firms are "born global"—that is, from the very beginning, many start-ups are global in their activities. For example, Logitech International, a leading producer of personal computer accessories, was global from day one. Founded in 1982 by a Swiss national and two Italians, the company was headquartered in both California and Switzerland. R&D and manufacturing were also conducted in both locations and, subsequently, in Taiwan and Ireland.[22]

The success of companies such as Logitech challenges the conventional wisdom that a company must first build up assets, internal processes, and experience before venturing into faraway lands. It also raises a number of questions: What exactly is a global start-up? Under what conditions should a company start out as a global start-up? What does it take to succeed as a global start-up?

A **global start-up** has been defined as a business organization that, from inception, seeks to derive significant competitive advantage from the use of resources and the sale of outputs in multiple countries. Right from the beginning, it uses inputs from around the world and sells its products and services to customers around the world. Geographic boundaries of nation-states are irrelevant for a global start-up.

There is no reason for every start-up to be global. Being global necessarily involves higher communication, coordination, and transportation costs. Therefore, it is important to identify the circumstances under which going global from the beginning is advantageous.[23] First, if the required human resources are globally dispersed, going global may be the best way to access those resources. For example, Italians are masters in fine leather and Europeans in ergonomics. Second, in many cases foreign financing may be easier to obtain and more suitable. Traditionally, U.S. venture capitalists have shown greater willingness to bear risk, but they have shorter time horizons in their expectations for return. If a U.S. start-up is looking for patient capital, it may be better off looking overseas. Third, the target customers in many specialized industries are located in other parts of the world. Fourth, in many industries a gradual move from domestic markets to foreign markets is no longer possible because, if a product is successful, foreign competitors may immediately imitate it. Therefore, preemptive entry into foreign markets may be the only option. Finally, because of high up-front development costs, a global market is often necessary to recover the costs. This is particularly true for start-ups from smaller nations that do not have access to large domestic markets.

10.3 STRATEGY SPOTLIGHT

GLOBAL START-UP, BRCK, WORKS TO BRING RELIABLE INTERNET CONNECTIVITY TO THE WORLD

BRCK is a notable technology pioneer. It's bringing a novel and potentially very valuable product to market, and it is doing so as a truly global start-up. BRCK's first product is a surge-resistant, battery-powered router to provide Internet service, which the firm is simply calling the BRCK. In many parts of the world, power systems are unreliable and offer only intermittent service. Additionally, they are prone to generate power surges that can fry many electronic products, including Internet routers. For example, in 2013, a single power-surge event in Nairobi, Kenya, blew out more than 3,000 routers. BRCK has developed a product to address these issues. Its router has a built-in battery that charges up whenever the power grid is operating and that runs off the battery for up to eight hours when the power grid goes down. It can also handle power surges up to 400 volts. The BRCK is also flexible as to how it connects to the Internet. It can connect directly to an ethernet line, can link up with a Wi-Fi network in its area, and can connect via a wireless phone connection. BRCK is aiming to sell its product to small and medium-size businesses, schools, and medical facilities. Its routers allow up to 20 users to simultaneously connect to the Internet. The technologies it uses are not cutting-edge, but the end product itself is innovative and meets a market need.

What really sets BRCK apart is that it is a global start-up that turns the table on typical global structures. Most tech-oriented global firms design their products in a technology center in the developed world and manufacture the products in a developing country. BRCK has flipped this model. BRCK designs its products in a developing country and manufactures in a developed country. Its corporate headquarters are in Nairobi, Kenya, at a technology center that houses a small group of entrepreneurs. The firm employs a dozen engineers to design its products in its corporate headquarters, and while its offices look a bit like those in Silicon Valley, the building has backup power for times when the Kenyan power grid inevitably goes down. The firm sources most of the components for its routers from Asia and manufactures its products in Austin, Texas. Even its sales are also going global right from the start. As of mid-2014, the firm had sold 700 BRCKs to customers in 45 countries.

Sources: Cary, J. 2014. Made in Kenya, assembled in America: This Internet-anywhere company innovates from silicon savannah. *fastcoexist.com*, September 4: np; and Vogt, H. 2014. Made in Africa: A gadget startup. *wsj.com*, July 10: np.

Successful management of a global start-up presents many challenges. Communication and coordination across time zones and cultures are always problematic. Since most global start-ups have far less resources than well-established corporations, one key for success is to internalize few activities and outsource the rest. Managers of such firms must have considerable prior international experience so that they can successfully handle the inevitable communication problems and cultural conflicts. Another key for success is to keep the communication and coordination costs low. The only way to achieve this is by creating less costly administrative mechanisms. The boundaryless organizational designs that we discuss in the next section are particularly suitable for global start-ups because of their flexibility and low cost.

Strategy Spotlight 10.3 discusses a Kenyan technology start-up with a global vision and scope of operations.

How an Organization's Structure Can Influence Strategy Formulation

Discussions of the relationship between strategy and structure usually strongly imply that structure follows strategy. The strategy that a firm chooses (e.g., related diversification) dictates such structural elements as the division of tasks, the need for integration of activities, and authority relationships within the organization. However, an existing structure can influence strategy formulation. Once a firm's structure is in place, it is very difficult and expensive to change.[24] Executives may not be able to modify their duties and responsibilities greatly or may not welcome the disruption associated with a transfer to a new location. There are costs associated with hiring, training, and replacing executive, managerial, and operating personnel. Strategy cannot be formulated without considering structural elements.

An organization's structure can also have an important influence on how it competes in the marketplace. It can also strongly influence a firm's strategy, day-to-day operations, and performance.[25]

10.4 STRATEGY SPOTLIGHT

BOUNDARY TYPES

There are primarily four types of boundaries that place limits on organizations. In today's dynamic business environment, different types of boundaries are needed to foster high degrees of interaction with outside influences and varying levels of permeability.

1. **Vertical boundaries between levels in the organization's hierarchy.** SmithKline Beecham asks employees at different hierarchical levels to brainstorm ideas for managing clinical trial data. The ideas are incorporated into action plans that significantly cut the new product approval time of its pharmaceuticals. This would not have been possible if the barriers between levels of individuals in the organization had been too high.

2. **Horizontal boundaries between functional areas.** Fidelity Investments makes the functional barriers more porous and flexible among divisions, such as marketing, operations, and customer service, in order to offer customers a more integrated experience when conducting business with the company. Customers can take their questions to one person, reducing the chance that customers will "get the run-around" from employees who feel customer service is not their responsibility. At Fidelity, customer service is everyone's business, regardless of functional area.

3. **External boundaries between the firm and its customers, suppliers, and regulators.** GE Lighting, by working closely with retailers, functions throughout the value chain as a single operation. This allows GE to track point-of-sale purchases, giving it better control over inventory management.

4. **Geographic boundaries between locations, cultures, and markets.** The global nature of today's business environment spurred PricewaterhouseCoopers to use a global groupware system. This allows the company to instantly connect to its 26 worldwide offices.

Source: Ashkenas, R. 1997. The organization's new clothes. In Hesselbein, F., Goldsmith, M., and Beckhard, R. (Eds.), *The organization of the future:* 104–106. San Francisco: Jossey-Bass.

Boundaryless Organizational Designs

LO10.4

The different types of boundaryless organizations—barrier-free, modular, and virtual—and their relative advantages and disadvantages.

boundaryless organizational designs
organizations in which the boundaries, including vertical, horizontal, external, and geographic boundaries, are permeable.

The term *boundaryless* may bring to mind a chaotic organizational reality in which "anything goes." This is not the case. As Jack Welch, GE's former CEO, has suggested, boundaryless does not imply that all internal and external boundaries vanish completely, but that they become more open and permeable.[26] Strategy Spotlight 10.4 discusses four types of boundaries.

We are not suggesting that **boundaryless organizational designs** replace the traditional forms of organizational structure, but they should complement them. Strategy Spotlight 10.5 discusses how Dr. Tracy Gaudet is working to integrate different units in the Veterans Administration to more effectively provide holistic medical services to veterans.

We will discuss three approaches to making boundaries more permeable that help to facilitate the widespread sharing of knowledge and information across both the internal and external boundaries of the organization. The *barrier-free* type involves making all organizational boundaries—internal and external—more permeable. Teams are a central building block for implementing the boundaryless organization. The *modular* and *virtual* types of organizations focus on the need to create seamless relationships with external organizations such as customers or suppliers. While the modular type emphasizes the outsourcing of noncore activities, the virtual (or network) organization focuses on alliances among independent entities formed to exploit specific market opportunities.

The Barrier-Free Organization

The "boundary" mind-set is ingrained deeply into bureaucracies. It is evidenced by such clichés as "That's not my job" and "I'm here from corporate to help" or by endless battles over transfer pricing. In the traditional company, boundaries are clearly delineated in the design of an organization's structure. Their basic advantage is that the roles of managers and employees are simple, clear, well defined, and long-lived. A major shortcoming was pointed out to the authors during an interview with a high-tech executive: "Structure tends to be divisive; it leads to territorial fights."

10.5 STRATEGY SPOTLIGHT

BREAKING BARRIERS TO BETTER SERVE VETERANS

The Veterans Administration (VA) is the largest health care service provider in the United States, with over 280,000 employees and a budget of more than $150 billion. But it has struggled mightily to meet the growing needs of veterans. This includes the traditional medical care needs of the aging veterans of World War II, the Korean War, and the Vietnam War, and it also includes the complex needs of veterans from Iraq and Afghanistan, who may have both physical and psychological challenges.

Medical care has historically been oriented around reacting to the diseases or injuries of patients. When health problems arise, doctors and other health care providers offer focused treatment to address the current challenge. To provide expertise in each medical area, most medical systems, including the VA, have traditionally been structured functionally along medical specialty lines, such as cardiology, dermatology, and orthopedics. Thus, medical systems in the United States have typically offered effective disease treatment but not effective holistic care for patients. This limitation is especially acute for the VA since veterans often need a more holistic treatment because their physical scars and maladies may be tied into the psychological scars they carry from their time at war.

Dr. Tracy Gaudet has taken on this challenge in her role as the director of the Office of Patient-Centered Care and Cultural Transformation at the VA. Dr. Gaudet is a proponent of integrative medicine, a field that works to treat the whole person and not just a diseased or broken body part. To provide better service, she is pushing for transformation at the VA that will break down traditional medical discipline boundaries in the organization to provide integrative health services to veterans. This includes traditional medical fields but also related supporting services and nontraditional medical disciplines. To pilot test how to do this, the VA has created nine centers of innovation. These centers work to integrate a range of physical and psychological medical services along with health maintenance and lifestyle services. Some centers have nutritionists on staff, along with vegetable gardens; while others offer yoga instruction, massage therapy, acupuncture, and mindfulness instruction. Thus, they strive to meet not only the traditional medical needs but also the lifestyle and emotional needs of veterans to better battle PTSD, substance-abuse problems, sleep disorders, and pain management. The leaders of these centers of innovation will then serve as consultants to facilitate cultural and organizational change in other VA facilities.

The challenge is huge, but the issue is personal for Dr. Gaudet. She recalls her father as a loving man, but also a man who carried pain from his experiences fighting in World War II that led to a long battle with alcoholism. Thus she sees it as a personal challenge, one about which she says, "We need to and can do better" to meet the needs of veterans.

Sources: Kowitt, B. 2013. Can caring cure? *Fortune*, October 28: 22–26; and Whited, R. 2011. VA office developing innovative patient-centered model of care for veterans. *examiner.com*, January 21: np.

Such structures are being replaced by fluid, ambiguous, and deliberately ill-defined tasks and roles. Just because work roles are no longer clearly defined, however, does not mean that differences in skills, authority, and talent disappear. A **barrier-free organization** enables a firm to bridge real differences in culture, function, and goals to find common ground that facilitates information sharing and other forms of cooperative behavior. Eliminating the multiple boundaries that stifle productivity and innovation can enhance the potential of the entire organization.

barrier-free organization
an organizational design in which firms bridge real differences in culture, function, and goals to find common ground that facilitates information sharing and other forms of cooperative behavior.

Creating Permeable Internal Boundaries For barrier-free organizations to work effectively, the level of trust and shared interests among all parts of the organization must be raised.[27] The organization needs to develop among its employees the skill level needed to work in a more democratic organization. Barrier-free organizations also require a shift in the organization's philosophy from executive to organizational development and from investments in high-potential individuals to investments in leveraging the talents of all individuals.

Teams can be an important aspect of barrier-free structures.[28] Jeffrey Pfeffer, author of several insightful books, including *The Human Equation*, suggests that teams have three primary advantages.[29] First, teams substitute peer-based control for hierarchical control of work activities. Employees control themselves, reducing the time and energy management needs to devote to control. Second, teams frequently develop more creative solutions to problems because they encourage the sharing of the tacit knowledge held by individuals.[30] Brainstorming, or group problem solving, involves the pooling of ideas and expertise to enhance the chances that at least one group member will think of a way to solve the problems at hand. Third, by substituting peer control for hierarchical control, teams permit the removal of layers of hierarchy and absorption of administrative tasks previously performed by specialists. This avoids the costs of having people whose sole job is to watch the people who watch other people do the work. Novartis, the Swiss pharmaceutical giant, is leveraging the power of teams by consolidating its R&D activities in four locations. Novartis believes that grouping together and teaming up researchers from different disciplines into self-managed work teams will foster creativity and cooperation.[31]

Some have argued for the need to move more radically to discard formal hierarchical structures and work toward a more democratic team organizational structure.[32] One version of such systems is called a "holacracy." In a holacracy, there is no formal organizational structure in the traditional sense. Instead, employees self-identify into roles, undertaking the types of tasks that they are highly skilled at and interested in. Most employees will have multiple roles. Employees then group together into self-organized teams—or, in the terminology of holacracy, circles—in which they work together to complete tasks, such as circles for service delivery or product development. Since individual employees have multiple roles, they typically belong to multiple circles. This overlapping membership facilitates communication and coordination between circles. The circles within a firm change over time to meet the evolving situation of the firm. Each circle elects a lead, called a "lead link." This lead link guides meetings and sets the general agenda for the circle, although the members of the circle decide democratically on how the circle will complete tasks. The lead link also serves as a member of a higher-level circle. Overseeing it all is the general company circle, a collection of lead links who serve as the leadership team for the firm.

Most firms that have moved to a holacracy way of organizing are small technology firms. These firms see little need for hierarchical authority, and they are attracted to the promises of improved agility and creativity, as well as higher employee morale, with this flexible, autonomous type of structure. However, in 2014, Zappos decided to transition its entire 1,500 employees to a holacracy structure. The new structure initially consisted of 250 circles, and it may grow to 400 circles as the new system gets fully implemented. Tony Hsieh, who was Zappos' CEO and is now lead link of the Experiential SWAT Team, says he wants "Zappos to function more like a city and less like a top-down bureaucratic organization." In making this change, Zappos is serving as a natural experiment to see if a larger firm can operate as a holacracy.

Developing Effective Relationships with External Constituencies In barrier-free organizations, managers must also create flexible, porous organizational boundaries and establish communication flows and mutually beneficial relationships with internal (e.g., employees) and external (e.g., customers) constituencies.[33] IBM has worked to develop a long-standing cooperative relationship with the Mayo Clinic. The clinic is a customer but more importantly a research partner. IBM has placed staff at the Mayo Clinic, and the two organizations have worked together on technology for the early identification of aneurysms, the mining of data in electronic health records to develop customized treatment plans for patients, and other medical issues.[34]

Barrier-free organizations create successful relationships between both internal and external constituencies, but there is one additional constituency—competitors—with whom some organizations have benefited as they developed cooperative relationships. For example, Coca-Cola and PepsiCo, often argued to be the most intense rivals in business, work together to develop new, environmentally conscious refrigerants for use in their vending machines.[35]

By joining and actively participating in the Business Roundtable—an organization consisting of CEOs of leading U.S. corporations—Walmart has been able to learn about cutting-edge sustainable initiatives of other major firms. This free flow of information has enabled Walmart to undertake a number of steps that increased the energy efficiency of its operations. These are described in Strategy Spotlight 10.6.

10.6 STRATEGY SPOTLIGHT — ENVIRONMENTAL SUSTAINABILITY

THE BUSINESS ROUNDTABLE: A FORUM FOR SHARING BEST ENVIRONMENTAL SUSTAINABILITY PRACTICES

The Business Roundtable is a group of chief executive officers of major U.S. corporations that was created to promote probusiness public policy. It was formed in 1972 through the merger of three existing organizations: The March Group, the Construction Users Anti-Inflation Roundtable, and the Labor Law Study Committee. The group has been called President Obama's "closest ally in the business community."

The Business Roundtable became the first broad-based business group to agree on the need to address climate change through collective action, and it remains committed to limiting greenhouse gas emissions and setting the United States on a more sustainable path. The organization considers that threats to water quality and quantity, rising greenhouse gas emissions, and the risk of climate change—along with increasing energy prices and growing demand—are of great concern.

Its recent report "Create, Grow, Sustain" provides best practices and metrics from Business Roundtable member companies that represent nearly all sectors of the economy with $6 trillion in annual revenues. CEOs from Walmart, FedEx, PepsiCo, Whirlpool, and Verizon are among the 126 executives from leading U.S. companies that shared some of their best sustainability initiatives in this report. These companies are committed to reducing emissions, increasing energy efficiency, and developing more sustainable business practices.

Let's look, for example, at some of Walmart's initiatives. The firm's CEO, Mike Duke, says it is working with suppliers, partners, and consumers to drive its sustainability program. It has helped establish the Sustainability Consortium to drive metrics for measuring the environmental effects of consumer products across their life cycle. The retailer also helped lead the creation of a Sustainable Product Index to provide product information to consumers about the environmental impact of the products they purchase.

As part of its sustainability efforts, Walmart either had initiated or was in the process of developing over 180 renewable energy projects. Combined, these efforts resulted in more than 1 billion kilowatt-hours of renewable energy production each year, enough power to provide the electrical needs of 78,000 homes.

Walmart's renewable energy efforts have focused on three general initiatives:

- It has invested in developing distributed electrical generation systems on its property. As part of this effort, Walmart has installed rooftop solar panels on 127 locations in seven countries. It also has 26 fuel cell installations, 11 micro-wind projects, and 7 solar thermal projects.

- Expanding its contracts with suppliers for renewable energy has also been a focus of Walmart. Thus, Walmart bypasses the local utility to go directly to renewable energy suppliers to sign long-term contracts for renewable energy. With long-term contracts, Walmart has found that providers will give it more favorable terms. Walmart also believes that the long-term contracts give suppliers the incentive to invest in their generation systems, increasing the availability of renewable power for other users.

- In regions where going directly to renewable energy suppliers is difficult or impossible, Walmart has engaged the local utilities to increase their investment in renewable energy.

Sources: Anonymous. 2010. Leading CEOs share best sustainability practices. *www.environmentalleader.com*, April 26: np; Hopkins, M. No date. Sustainable growth. *www.businessroundtable*, np; Anonymous. 2012. Create, grow, sustain. *www.businessroundtable.org*, April 18: 120; and Business Roundtable. *www.en.wikipedia.org*.

Risks, Challenges, and Potential Downsides Many firms find that creating and managing a barrier-free organization can be frustrating.[36] Puritan-Bennett Corporation, a manufacturer of respiratory equipment, found that its product development time more than doubled after it adopted team management. Roger J. Dolida, director of R&D, attributed this failure to a lack of top management commitment, high turnover among team members, and infrequent meetings. Often, managers trained in rigid hierarchies find it difficult to make the transition to the more democratic, participative style that teamwork requires.

The pros and cons of barrier-free structures are summarized in Exhibit 10.6.

The Modular Organization

As Charles Handy, author of *The Age of Unreason,* has noted:

> While it may be convenient to have everyone around all the time, having all of your workforce's time at your command is an extravagant way of marshaling the necessary resources. It is cheaper to keep them outside the organization . . . and to buy their services when you need them.[37]

EXHIBIT 10.6 Pros and Cons of Barrier-Free Structures

Pros	Cons
• Leverages the talents of all employees. • Enhances cooperation, coordination, and information sharing among functions, divisions, SBUs, and external constituencies. • Enables a quicker response to market changes through a single-goal focus. • Can lead to coordinated win–win initiatives with key suppliers, customers, and alliance partners.	• Difficult to overcome political and authority boundaries inside and outside the organization. • Lacks strong leadership and common vision, which can lead to coordination problems. • Time-consuming and difficult-to-manage democratic processes. • Lacks high levels of trust, which can impede performance.

modular organization
an organization in which nonvital functions are outsourced, using the knowledge and expertise of outside suppliers while retaining strategic control.

The **modular organization** outsources nonvital functions, tapping into the knowledge and expertise of "best in class" suppliers, but retains strategic control. Outsiders may be used to manufacture parts, handle logistics, or perform accounting activities.[38] The value chain can be used to identify the key primary and support activities performed by a firm to create value: Which activities do we keep in-house and which activities do we outsource to suppliers?[39] The organization becomes a central hub surrounded by networks of outside suppliers and specialists, and parts can be added or taken away. Both manufacturing and service units may be modular.[40]

Apparel is an industry in which the modular type has been widely adopted. Nike and Reebok, for example, concentrate on their strengths: designing and marketing high-tech, fashionable footwear. Nike has few production facilities and Reebok owns no plants. These two companies contract virtually all their footwear production to suppliers in China, Vietnam, and other countries with low-cost labor. Avoiding large investments in fixed assets helps them derive large profits on minor sales increases. Nike and Reebok can keep pace with changing tastes in the marketplace because their suppliers have become expert at rapidly retooling to produce new products.[41]

In a modular company, outsourcing the noncore functions offers three advantages:

1. A firm can decrease overall costs, stimulate new product development by hiring suppliers with talent superior to that of in-house personnel, avoid idle capacity, reduce inventories, and avoid being locked into a particular technology.
2. A company can focus scarce resources on the areas where it holds a competitive advantage. These benefits can translate into more funding for R&D to hire the best engineers and for sales and service to provide continuous training for staff.
3. An organization can tap into the knowledge and expertise of its specialized supply chain partners, adding critical skills and accelerating organizational learning.[42]

The modular type enables a company to leverage relatively small amounts of capital and a small management team to achieve seemingly unattainable strategic objectives.[43] Certain preconditions are necessary before the modular approach can be successful. First, the company must work closely with suppliers to ensure that the interests of each party are being fulfilled. Companies need to find loyal, reliable vendors who can be trusted with trade secrets. They also need assurances that suppliers will dedicate their financial, physical, and human resources to satisfy strategic objectives such as lowering costs or being first to market.

Second, the modular company must be sure that it selects the proper competencies to keep in-house. For Nike and Reebok, the core competencies are design and marketing, not shoe manufacturing; for Honda, the core competence is engine technology. An organization must avoid outsourcing components that may compromise its long-term competitive advantages.

Strategic Risks of Outsourcing The main strategic concerns are (1) loss of critical skills or developing the wrong skills, (2) loss of cross-functional skills, and (3) loss of control over a supplier.[44]

Too much outsourcing can result in a firm "giving away" too much skill and control.[45] Outsourcing relieves companies of the requirement to maintain skill levels needed to manufacture essential components.[46] At one time, semiconductor chips seemed like a simple technology to outsource, but they have now become a critical component of a wide variety of products. Companies that have outsourced the manufacture of these chips run the risk of losing the ability to manufacture them as the technology escalates. They become more dependent upon their suppliers.

Cross-functional skills refer to the skills acquired through the interaction of individuals in various departments within a company.[47] Such interaction assists a department in solving problems as employees interface with others across functional units. However, if a firm outsources key functional responsibilities, such as manufacturing, communication across departments can become more difficult. A firm and its employees must now integrate their activities with a new, outside supplier.

The outsourced products may give suppliers too much power over the manufacturer. Suppliers that are key to a manufacturer's success can, in essence, hold the manufacturer "hostage." Nike manages this potential problem by sending full-time "product expatriates" to work at the plants of its suppliers. Also, Nike often brings top members of supplier management and technical teams to its headquarters. This way, Nike keeps close tabs on the pulse of new developments, builds rapport and trust with suppliers, and develops long-term relationships with suppliers to prevent hostage situations.

Exhibit 10.7 summarizes the pros and cons of modular structures.[48]

The Virtual Organization

In contrast to the "self-reliant" thinking that guided traditional organizational designs, the strategic challenge today has become doing more with less and looking outside the firm for opportunities and solutions to problems. The virtual organization provides a new means of leveraging resources and exploiting opportunities.[49]

The **virtual organization** can be viewed as a continually evolving network of independent companies—suppliers, customers, even competitors—linked together to share skills, costs, and access to one another's markets.[50] The members of a virtual organization, by pooling and sharing the knowledge and expertise of each of the component organizations, simultaneously "know" more and can "do" more than any one member of the group could do alone. By working closely together, each gains in the long run from individual and organizational learning.[51] The term *virtual,* meaning "being in effect but not actually so,"

> **virtual organization**
> a continually evolving network of independent companies that are linked together to share skills, costs, and access to one another's markets.

EXHIBIT 10.7 Pros and Cons of Modular Structures

Pros	Cons
• Directs a firm's managerial and technical talent to the most critical activities.	• Inhibits common vision through reliance on outsiders.
• Maintains full strategic control over most critical activities—core competencies.	• Diminishes future competitive advantages if critical technologies or other competencies are outsourced.
• Achieves "best in class" performance at each link in the value chain.	• Increases the difficulty of bringing back into the firm activities that now add value due to market shifts.
• Leverages core competencies by outsourcing with smaller capital commitment.	• Leads to an erosion of cross-functional skills.
• Encourages information sharing and accelerates organizational learning.	• Decreases operational control and potential loss of control over a supplier.

is commonly used in the computer industry. A computer's ability to appear to have more storage capacity than it really possesses is called virtual memory. Similarly, by assembling resources from a variety of entities, a virtual organization may seem to have more capabilities than it really possesses.[52]

Virtual organizations need not be permanent, and participating firms may be involved in multiple alliances. Virtual organizations may involve different firms performing complementary value activities or different firms involved jointly in the same value activities, such as production, R&D, and distribution. The percentage of activities that are jointly performed with partners may vary significantly from alliance to alliance.[53]

How does the virtual type of structure differ from the modular type? Unlike the modular type, in which the focal firm maintains full strategic control, the virtual organization is characterized by participating firms that give up part of their control and accept interdependent destinies. Participating firms pursue a collective strategy that enables them to cope with uncertainty through cooperative efforts. The benefit is that, just as virtual memory increases storage capacity, the virtual organizations enhance the capacity or competitive advantage of participating firms.

Each company that links up with others to create a virtual organization contributes only what it considers its core competencies. It will mix and match what it does best with the best of other firms by identifying its critical capabilities and the necessary links to other capabilities.[54]

In addition to linking a set of organizations in a virtual organization, firms can create internal virtual organizations, in which individuals who are not located together and may not even be in the same traditional organizational unit are joined together in virtual teams. These teams may be permanent but often are flexible, with changing membership as business needs evolve. The Insights from Research box offers evidence on how to effectively manage these virtual teams.

Challenges and Risks The virtual organization demands that managers build relationships both within the firm and with other companies, negotiate win–win deals for all parties, find the right partners with compatible goals and values, and provide the right balance of freedom and control. Information systems must be designed and integrated to facilitate communication with current and potential partners.

Managers must be clear about the strategic objectives while forming alliances. Some objectives are time-bound, and those alliances need to be dissolved once the objective is fulfilled. Some alliances may have relatively long-term objectives and will need to be clearly monitored and nurtured to produce mutual commitment and avoid bitter fights for control. The highly dynamic personal computer industry is characterized by multiple temporary alliances among hardware, operating system, and software producers.[55] But alliances in the more stable automobile industry have long-term objectives and tend to be relatively stable.

The virtual organization is a logical culmination of joint venture strategies of the past. Shared risks, costs, and rewards are the facts of life in a virtual organization.[56] When virtual organizations are formed, they involve tremendous challenges for strategic planning. As with the modular corporation, it is essential to identify core competencies. However, for virtual structures to be successful, a strategic plan is also needed to determine the effectiveness of combining core competencies.

The strategic plan must address the diminished operational control and overwhelming need for trust and common vision among the partners. This new structure may be appropriate for firms whose strategies require merging technologies (e.g., computing and communication) or for firms exploiting shrinking product life cycles that require simultaneous entry into multiple geographic markets. It may be effective for firms that desire to be quick to the market with a new product or service. The recent profusion of alliances

INSIGHTS FROM RESEARCH

HOW TO LEAD VIRTUAL TEAMS

Overview

Because team members in different locations work together virtually, traditional leadership styles are less effective. What works instead? Emphasize fair rewards, and make sure information sharing and communication are managed well. Empower your team members to serve as substitute leaders for each other, and ensure that everyone has access to functional technology.

What the Research Shows

Researchers from Michigan State University investigated the effectiveness of virtual teams in a 2012 article published in the *Journal of Applied Psychology*. Using structural equation modeling, they studied 101 research and development teams made up of 565 team members from global manufacturing industries. Team members worked across geographic distances, time zones, and cultures using electronic communication. Some teams were more virtual than others in terms of geographic dispersion, electronic versus face-to-face communication, and number of nationalities per team. The study's authors wanted to determine what happens as teams become more virtual. In other words, do changes in leadership behaviors, structures, and communication help teams produce a sufficient quality of work within budget and on schedule?

First, the researchers found that teams performed better under shared leadership, regardless of whether or not they were virtual. This means team members sought feedback to improve their performance, supported one another, and understood their teammates' problems and needs.

Additionally, the researchers determined that hierarchical leaders lost effectiveness as teams became more virtual. Without face-to-face meetings, formal leaders in headquarters lacked opportunities for personal influence or mentoring. On the other hand, structural supports became more important for team performance. For example, the following structural supports facilitated better employee performance:

- A "fair" performance appraisal system.
- Clear information about task completion.
- Details about rewards.

Why This Matters

Virtual teams, virtual meetings, and virtual offices are a reality in many companies today. Reducing travel and overhead expenses seems like a great idea, but what do virtual offices mean for managers? This study shows that leaders must evolve their management techniques to keep up with the technological and organizational changes created by virtual environments.

If you manage a virtual team, you should ease up on traditional leadership methods. For instance, resist the temptation to exert authority via a Lone Ranger approach. A single leader isn't in a position to exert face-to-face influence and may lack the information to effectively monitor behaviors. Instead, you should focus on providing effective structural supports. Make sure your appraisal system is fair and transparent, team members have as much information as they need, and the link between specific efforts and rewards is clear. Team members should hold one another accountable for results and for making sure all employees have the resources they need.

Consultant Jessica Lipnack, chief executive officer of NetAge Inc., says virtual team members should feel they're contributing to meaningful goals. She once worked with a team of rocket scientists who never met face-to-face yet came up with a new rocket design in a fraction of the typical time—at one-tenth of the normal budget. The team reduced the parts used from hundreds to a few and brought the project in ahead of schedule.

Lipnack says the following have become essential supports for virtual teams: good communication, an online "team room," regular meetings, consulting teleconferences, and a clear plan for what to accomplish. Technology remains critical, especially video, but videoconferences can lose effectiveness if the number of participants rises above 15.

Key Takeaways

- Members of virtual teams work together from different locations using electronic communication. Organizations across the globe are using virtual teams more often.
- These arrangements pose a challenge to formal, hierarchical leadership. Teams with far-flung members find substitute leaders help them perform better.
- As hierarchical leaders become less effective, the management of rewards becomes more important. Communication and information sharing become critical.
- Shared leadership among team members helps performance, regardless of how virtual the group is.
- As your teams rely more on electronic communication to bridge distance and cultures, technological acumen grows more valuable. Remain flexible about exercising traditional management behaviors, but be sure your employees have the leadership they need.

Apply This Today

Leaders need to keep up with the times. When it comes to virtual teams, leaders should empower others to manage through rewards and provide information where most needed. Take action based on these research findings, and you could be the most skilled leader at the virtual table.

Research Reviewed

Hoch, J. E. & Kozlowski, S. W. 2012. Leading virtual teams: Hierarchical leadership, structural supports, and shared team leadership. *Journal of Applied Psychology,* doi: 10.1037/a0030264.

EXHIBIT 10.8 Pros and Cons of Virtual Structures

Pros	Cons
• Enables the sharing of costs and skills.	• Harder to determine where one company ends and another begins, due to close interdependencies among players.
• Enhances access to global markets.	
• Increases market responsiveness.	• Leads to potential loss of operational control among partners.
• Creates a "best of everything" organization since each partner brings core competencies to the alliance.	• Results in loss of strategic control over emerging technology.
	• Requires new and difficult-to-acquire managerial skills.
• Encourages both individual and organizational knowledge sharing and accelerates organizational learning.	

Source: Miles, R. E., & Snow, C. C. 1986. Organizations: New Concepts for New Forms. *California Management Review,* Spring: 62–73; Miles & Snow. 1999. Causes of Failure in Network Organizations. *California Management Review,* Summer: 53–72; and Bahrami, H. 1991. The Emerging Flexible Organization: Perspectives from Silicon Valley. *California Management Review,* Summer: 33–52.

among airlines was primarily motivated by the need to provide seamless travel demanded by the full-fare-paying business traveler. Exhibit 10.8 summarizes the pros and cons of virtual structures.

Boundaryless Organizations: Making Them Work

Designing an organization that simultaneously supports the requirements of an organization's strategy, is consistent with the demands of the environment, and can be effectively implemented by the people around the manager is a tall order for any manager.[57] The most effective solution is usually a combination of organizational types. That is, a firm may outsource many parts of its value chain to reduce costs and increase quality, engage simultaneously in multiple alliances to take advantage of technological developments or penetrate new markets, and break down barriers within the organization to enhance flexibility.

When an organization faces external pressures, resource scarcity, and declining performance, it tends to become more internally focused, rather than directing its efforts toward managing and enhancing relationships with existing and potential external stakeholders. This may be the most opportune time for managers to carefully analyze their value-chain activities and evaluate the potential for adopting elements of modular, virtual, and barrier-free organizational types.

In this section, we will address two issues managers need to be aware of as they work to design an effective boundaryless organization. First, managers need to develop mechanisms to ensure effective coordination and integration. Second, managers need to be aware of the benefits and costs of developing strong and long-term relationships with both internal and external stakeholders.

Facilitating Coordination and Integration Achieving the coordination and integration necessary to maximize the potential of an organization's human capital involves much more than just creating a new structure. Techniques and processes to ensure the coordination and integration of an organization's key value-chain activities are critical. Teams are key building blocks of the new organizational forms, and teamwork requires new and flexible approaches to coordination and integration.

Managers trained in rigid hierarchies may find it difficult to make the transition to the more democratic, participative style that teamwork requires. As Douglas K. Smith, co-author of *The Wisdom of Teams,* pointed out, "A completely diverse group must agree on a goal, put the notion of individual accountability aside and figure out how to work with each other. Most of all, they must learn that if the team fails, it's everyone's fault."[58] Within the framework of an appropriate organizational design, managers must select a mix and balance of tools and techniques to facilitate the effective coordination and integration of key activities. Some of the factors that must be considered include:

- Common culture and shared values.
- Horizontal organizational structures.
- Horizontal systems and processes.
- Communications and information technologies.
- Human resource practices.

Common Culture and Shared Values Shared goals, mutual objectives, and a high degree of trust are essential to the success of boundaryless organizations. In the fluid and flexible environments of the new organizational architectures, common cultures, shared values, and carefully aligned incentives are often less expensive to implement and are often a more effective means of strategic control than rules, boundaries, and formal procedures. Tony Hsieh, the founder of Zappos, echoes this need for a shared culture and values when he describes his role this way: "I think of myself less as a leader and more of being an architect of an environment that enables employees to come up with their own ideas."[59]

Horizontal Organizational Structures These structures, which group similar or related business units under common management control, facilitate sharing resources and infrastructures to exploit synergies among operating units and help to create a sense of common purpose. Consistency in training and the development of similar structures across business units facilitates job rotation and cross-training and enhances understanding of common problems and opportunities. Cross-functional teams and interdivisional committees and task groups represent important opportunities to improve understanding and foster cooperation among operating units.

> **horizontal organizational structures** organizational forms that group similar or related business units under common management control and facilitate sharing resources and infrastructures to exploit synergies among operating units and help to create a sense of common purpose.

Horizontal Systems and Processes Organizational systems, policies, and procedures are the traditional mechanisms for achieving integration among functional units. Existing policies and procedures often do little more than institutionalize the barriers that exist from years of managing within the framework of the traditional model. Beginning with an understanding of basic business processes in the context of "a collection of activities that takes one or more kinds of input and creates an output that is of value to the customer," Michael Hammer and James Champy's 1993 best-selling *Reengineering the Corporation* outlined a methodology for redesigning internal systems and procedures that has been embraced by many organizations.[60] Successful reengineering lowers costs, reduces inventories and cycle times, improves quality, speeds response times, and enhances organizational flexibility. Others advocate similar benefits through the reduction of cycle times, total quality management, and the like.

Communications and Information Technology (IT) The effective use of IT can play an important role in bridging gaps and breaking down barriers between organizations. Email and videoconferencing can improve lateral communications across long distances and multiple time zones and circumvent many of the barriers of the traditional model. Information technology can be a powerful ally in the redesign and streamlining of internal business processes and in improving coordination and integration between suppliers and customers. Internet technologies have eliminated the paperwork in many buyer–supplier relationships, enabling cooperating organizations to reduce inventories, shorten delivery cycles, and reduce operating costs. Information technology must be viewed more as a prime component of an organization's overall strategy than simply in terms of administrative support.

Human Resource Practices Change always involves and affects the human dimension of organizations. The attraction, development, and retention of human capital are vital to value creation. As boundaryless structures are implemented, processes are reengineered, and organizations become increasingly dependent on sophisticated ITs, the skills of workers and managers alike must be upgraded to realize the full benefits.

The Benefits and Costs of Developing Lasting Internal and External Relationships
Successful boundaryless organizations rely heavily on the relational aspects of organizations. Rather than relying on strict hierarchical and bureaucratic systems, these firms are flexible and coordinate action by leveraging shared social norms and strong social relationships between both internal and external stakeholders.[61] At the same time, it is important to acknowledge that relying on relationships can have both positive and negative effects. To successfully move to a more boundaryless organization, managers need to acknowledge and attend to both the costs and benefits of relying on relationships and social norms to guide behavior.

There are three primary benefits that organizations accrue when relying on relationships:

- *Agency costs within the firm can be dramatically cut through the use of relational systems.* Managers and employees in relationship-oriented firms are guided by social norms and relationships they have with other managers and employees. As a result, the firm can reduce the degree to which it relies on monitoring, rules and regulations, and financial incentives to ensure that workers put in a strong effort and work in the firm's interests. A relational view leads managers and employees to act in a supportive manner and makes them more willing to step out of their formal roles when needed to accomplish tasks for others and for the organization. They are also less likely to shirk their responsibilities.
- *There is also likely to be a reduction in the transaction costs between a firm and its suppliers and customers.* If firms have built strong relationships with partnering firms, they are more likely to work cooperatively with these firms and build trust that their partners will work in the best interests of the alliance. This will reduce the need for the firms to write detailed contracts and set up strict bureaucratic rules to outline the responsibilities and define the behavior of each firm. Additionally, partnering firms with strong relationships are more likely to invest in assets that specifically support the partnership. Finally, they will have much less fear that their partner will try to take advantage of them or seize the bulk of the benefits from the partnership.
- *Since they feel a sense of shared ownership and goals, individuals within the firm as well as partnering firms will be more likely to search for win–win rather than win–lose solutions.* When taking a relational view, individuals are less likely to look out solely for their personal best interests. They will also be considerate of the benefits and costs to other individuals in the firm and to the overall firm. The same is true at the organizational level. Firms with strong relationships with their partners are going to look for solutions that not only benefit themselves but also provide equitable benefits and limited downside for the partnering firms. Such a situation was evident with a number of German firms during the economic crisis of 2008–2010. The German government, corporations, and unions worked together to find the fairest way to respond to the crisis. The firms agreed not to lay off workers. The unions agreed to reduce workweeks. The government kicked in a subsidy to make up for some of the lost wages. In other words, they negotiated a shared sacrifice to address the challenge. This positioned the German firms to bounce back quickly once the crisis passed.

While there are a number of benefits with using a relational view, there can also be some substantial costs:

- *As the relationships between individuals and firms strengthen, they are also more likely to fall prey to suboptimal lock-in effects.* The problem here is that as decisions become driven by concerns about relationships, economic factors become less important. As a result, firms become less likely to make decisions that could benefit the firm since those decisions may harm employees or partnering firms. For example, firms may see the economic logic in exiting a market, but the ties they feel with employees that work in that division and partnering firms in that market may reduce their willingness to make the hard decision to exit the market. This can be debilitating to firms in rapidly changing markets where successful firms add, reorganize, and sometimes exit operations and relationships regularly.

- *Since there are no formal guidelines, conflicts between individuals and units within firms, as well as between partnering firms, are typically resolved through ad hoc negotiations and processes.* In these circumstances, there are no legal means or bureaucratic rules to guide decision making. Thus, when firms face a difficult decision where there are differences of opinion about the best course of action, the ultimate choices made are often driven by the inherent power of the individuals or firms involved. This power use may be unintentional and subconscious, but it can result in outcomes that are deemed unfair by one or more of the parties.
- *The social capital of individuals and firms can drive their opportunities.* Thus, rather than identifying the best person to put in a leadership role or the optimal supplier to contract with, these choices are more strongly driven by the level of social connection the person or supplier has. This also increases the entry barriers for potential new suppliers or employees with whom a firm can contract since new firms likely don't have the social connections needed to be chosen as a worthy partner with whom to contract. This also may limit the likelihood that new innovative ideas will enter into the conversations at the firm.

As mentioned earlier in the chapter, the solution may be to effectively integrate elements of formal structure and reward systems with stronger relationships. This may influence specific relationships so that a manager will want employees to build relationships while still maintaining some managerial oversight and reward systems that motivate the desired behavior. This may also result in different emphases with different relationships. For example, there may be some units, such as accounting, where a stronger role for traditional structures and forms of evaluation may be optimal. However, in new product development units, a greater emphasis on relational systems may be more appropriate.

Creating Ambidextrous Organizational Designs

In Chapter 1, we introduced the concept of "ambidexterity," which incorporates two contradictory challenges faced by today's managers.[62] First, managers must explore new opportunities and adjust to volatile markets in order to avoid complacency. They must ensure that they maintain **adaptability** and remain proactive in expanding and/or modifying their product-market scope to anticipate and satisfy market conditions. Such competencies are especially challenging when change is rapid and unpredictable.

Second, managers must also effectively exploit the value of their existing assets and competencies. They need to have **alignment,** which is a clear sense of how value is being created in the short term and how activities are integrated and properly coordinated. Firms that achieve both adaptability and alignment are considered *ambidextrous organizations*—aligned and efficient in how they manage today's business but flexible enough to changes in the environment so that they will prosper tomorrow.

Handling such opposing demands is difficult because there will always be some degree of conflict. Firms often suffer when they place too strong a priority on either adaptability

LO10.5
The need for creating ambidextrous organizational designs that enable firms to explore new opportunities and effectively integrate existing operations.

adaptability
managers' exploration of new opportunities and adjustment to volatile markets in order to avoid complacency.

alignment
managers' clear sense of how value is being created in the short term and how activities are integrated and properly coordinated.

or alignment. If it places too much focus on adaptability, the firm will suffer low profitability in the short term. If managers direct their efforts primarily at alignment, they will likely miss out on promising business opportunities.

Ambidextrous Organizations: Key Design Attributes

A study by Charles O'Reilly and Michael Tushman[63] provides some insights into how some firms were able to create successful **ambidextrous organizational designs.** They investigated companies that attempted to simultaneously pursue modest, incremental innovations as well as more dramatic, breakthrough innovations. The team investigated 35 attempts to launch breakthrough innovations undertaken by 15 business units in nine different industries. They studied the organizational designs and the processes, systems, and cultures associated with the breakthrough projects as well as their impact on the operations and performance of the traditional businesses.

> **ambidextrous organizational designs**
> organizational designs that attempt to simultaneously pursue modest, incremental innovations as well as more dramatic, breakthrough innovations.

Companies structured their breakthrough projects in one of four primary ways:

- Seven were carried out within existing *functional organizational structures*. The projects were completely integrated into the regular organizational and management structure.
- Nine were organized as *cross-functional teams*. The groups operated within the established organization but outside the existing management structure.
- Four were organized as *unsupported teams*. Here, they became independent units set up outside the established organization and management hierarchy.
- Fifteen were conducted within *ambidextrous organizations*. Here, the breakthrough efforts were organized within structurally independent units, each having its own processes, structures, and cultures. However, they were integrated into the existing senior management structure.

The performance results of the 35 initiatives were tracked along two dimensions:

- Their success in creating desired innovations was measured by either the actual commercial results of the new product or the application of practical market or technical learning.
- The performance of the existing business was evaluated.

The study found that the organizational structure and management practices employed had a direct and significant impact on the performance of both the breakthrough initiative and the traditional business. The ambidextrous organizational designs were more effective than the other three designs on both dimensions: launching breakthrough products or services (i.e., adaptation) and improving the performance of the existing business (i.e., alignment).

Why Was the Ambidextrous Organization the Most Effective Structure?

The study found that there were many factors. A clear and compelling vision, consistently communicated by the company's senior management team, was critical in building the ambidextrous designs. The structure enabled cross-fertilization while avoiding cross-contamination. The tight coordination and integration at the managerial levels enabled the newer units to share important resources from the traditional units, such as cash, talent, and expertise. Such sharing was encouraged and facilitated by effective reward systems that emphasized overall company goals. The organizational separation ensured that the new units' distinctive processes, structures, and cultures were not overwhelmed by the forces of "business as usual." The established units were shielded from the distractions of launching new businesses, and they continued to focus all of their attention and energy on refining their operations, enhancing their products, and serving their customers.

ISSUE FOR DEBATE

McDonald's New Structure

Growing from a single restaurant in 1955 to over 14,000 restaurants in the United States in 2014, McDonald's has experienced nearly continuous growth and success. With over $35 billion in sales in the U.S., McDonald's generates nearly three times the revenue of its closest competitor, Subway. But that doesn't mean that McDonald's is immune to struggles. In 2014, it faced a real challenge to remain relevant as an attractive option for customers and saw its U.S. sales drop by 4.1 percent compared to sales in 2013. This negative turn in the firm's performance is likely related to the surprise retirement of McDonald's CEO, Don Thompson, in February 2015.

To consumers, McDonald's menu appears stale and unhealthy. As a result, customers are flocking to competing restaurants, such as Chipotle and Panera, that are seen as offering healthier food and having fresher ingredients and more interesting menu items. As McDonald's U.S.A. president, Mike Andres, stated, "What has worked for McDonald's for the past decade is not sufficient to propel the business forward in the future."

McDonald's believes that one of the causes of its struggles is the structure of the firm. McDonald's has long aimed for consistency across its units. To maintain this consistency, McDonald's has used a central testing kitchen to develop new products that could be rolled out across the firm. The firm has also relied on a regional structure, with Eastern, Central, and Western divisions. When a new initiative or product was rolled out, the firm would introduce it in each region, moving from north to south. Thus, customers in Minnesota and Louisiana would have the same menu, but new products would first be introduced in Minnesota and later in Louisiana. But this structure is hampering the firm since it is unable to be very responsive to regional taste differences and is very slow in responding to changing customer tastes and preferences. As a result, within McDonald's, "there are too many layers, redundancies in planning and communication, competing priorities, barriers to efficient decision making, and too much talking to ourselves instead of to and about our customers," according to Andres. Thus, the firm has been burdened by organizational boundaries that slow communication and the ability to talk to and respond to customers and other stakeholders.

To shake things up, McDonald's announced it would eliminate layers of management and create a new organizational structure in October 2014. The aim of the changes is to allow the firm to be more responsive to local tastes and to changes in customer demands. At the top level, the chain is moving to four regional divisions: Northeast, South, Central, and West. In McDonald's assessment, this new structure more effectively clusters together customers with similar tastes and preferences. At a lower level, McDonald's is giving leaders in 22 regional groups greater autonomy in making local menu and marketing decisions. In Andres's words, "We need to be more sophisticated in how we use local intelligence to address specific consumer needs . . . and to put decision making closer to our customers." As part of this effort, McDonald's is looking to the regions to learn about emerging customer preferences, and it created a learning lab on the west coast to better understand what consumers in that region want.

The open question is whether or not these structural changes will allow McDonald's to refresh its image and pull in more customers.

Discussion Questions
1. Is this structural change likely to be beneficial to McDonald's as it aims to stop sliding sales?
2. What are the potential costs and benefits of increasing regional autonomy?

continued

continued

3. New initiatives or menu changes in one region may be valuable in another region. What actions can McDonald's take to break through regional boundaries to facilitate learning?
4. What other actions does McDonald's need to take to turn around its sales?

Sources: Lorenzetti, L. 2014. McDonald's struggling to stay relevant with millennials. *fortune.com*, August 25: np; Anonymous. 2014. McDonald's profit, sales decline amid ongoing struggles around the world. *foxbusiness.com*, October 21: np; Jargon, J. 2014. McDonald's plans to change U.S. structure. *wsj.com*, October 30: np; and Jargon, J. & Prior, A. 2014. McDonald's expects further challenges. *wsj.com*, July 22: np.

Reflecting on Career Implications . . .

- **Boundaryless Organizational Designs:** Does your firm have structural mechanisms (e.g., culture, human resource practices) that facilitate sharing information across boundaries? Regardless of the level of boundarylessness of your organization, a key issue for your career is the extent to which you are able to cut across boundaries within your organization. Such boundaryless behavior on your part will enable you to enhance and leverage your human capital. Evaluate how boundaryless you are within your organizational context. What actions can you take to become even more boundaryless?

- **Horizontal Systems and Processes:** One of the approaches suggested in the chapter to improve boundarylessness within organizations is *reengineering*. Analyze the work you are currently doing and think of ways in which it can be reengineered to improve quality, accelerate response time, and lower cost. Consider presenting the results of your analysis to your immediate superiors. Do you think they will be receptive to your suggestions?

- **Ambidextrous Organizations:** Firms that achieve *adaptability* and *alignment* are considered ambidextrous. As an individual, you can also strive to be ambidextrous. Evaluate your own ambidexterity by assessing your adaptability (your ability to change in response to changes around you) and alignment (how good you are at exploiting your existing competencies). What steps can you take to improve your ambidexterity?

summary

Successful organizations must ensure that they have the proper type of organizational structure. Furthermore, they must ensure that their firms incorporate the necessary integration and processes so that the internal and external boundaries of their firms are flexible and permeable. Such a need is increasingly important as the environments of firms become more complex, changing rapidly and unpredictably.

In the first section of the chapter, we discussed the growth patterns of large corporations. Although most organizations remain small or die, some firms continue to grow in terms of revenues, vertical integration, and diversity of products and services. In addition, their geographic scope may increase to include international operations. We traced the dominant pattern of growth, which evolves from a simple structure to a functional structure as a firm grows in terms of size and increases its level of vertical integration. After a firm expands into related products and services, its structure changes from a functional to a divisional form of organization. Finally, when the firm enters international markets, its structure again changes to accommodate the change in strategy.

We also addressed the different types of organizational structure—simple, functional, divisional (including two variations: strategic business unit and holding company), and matrix—as well as their relative advantages and disadvantages. We closed the section with a discussion of the implications for structure that arise when a firm enters international markets. The three primary factors to take into account when determining the appropriate structure are type of international strategy, product diversity, and the extent to which a firm is dependent on foreign sales.

The second section of the chapter introduced the concept of the boundaryless organization. We did not suggest that the concept of the boundaryless organization replaces the traditional forms of organizational structure. Rather, it should complement them. This is necessary to cope with the increasing complexity and change in the competitive environment. We addressed three types of boundaryless organizations. The barrier-free type focuses on the need for the internal and external boundaries of a firm to be more flexible and permeable. The modular type emphasizes the strategic outsourcing of noncore activities. The virtual type centers on the strategic benefits of alliances and the forming of network organizations. We discussed both the advantages and disadvantages of each type of boundaryless organization, and we suggested some techniques and processes that are necessary to successfully implement each type. These are common culture and values, horizontal organizational structures, horizontal systems and processes, communications and information technologies, and human resource practices.

The final section addressed the need for managers to develop ambidextrous organizations. In today's rapidly changing global environment, managers must be responsive and proactive in order to take advantage of new opportunities. At the same time, they must effectively integrate and coordinate existing operations. Such requirements call for organizational designs that establish project teams that are structurally independent units, with each having its own processes, structures, and cultures. But, at the same time, each unit needs to be effectively integrated into the existing management hierarchy.

SUMMARY REVIEW QUESTIONS

1. Why is it important for managers to carefully consider the type of organizational structure that they use to implement their strategies?
2. Briefly trace the dominant growth pattern of major corporations from simple structure to functional structure to divisional structure. Discuss the relationship between a firm's strategy and its structure.
3. What are the relative advantages and disadvantages of the types of organizational structure—simple, functional, divisional, matrix—discussed in the chapter?
4. When a firm expands its operations into foreign markets, what are the three most important factors to take into account in deciding what type of structure is most appropriate? What are the types of international structures discussed in the text, and what are the relationships between strategy and structure?
5. Briefly describe the three different types of boundaryless organizations: barrier-free, modular, and virtual.
6. What are some of the key attributes of effective groups? Ineffective groups?
7. What are the advantages and disadvantages of the three types of boundaryless organizations: barrier-free, modular, and virtual?
8. When are ambidextrous organizational designs necessary? What are some of their key attributes?

key terms

organizational structure 316
simple organizational structure 318
functional organizational structure 318
divisional organizational structure 320
strategic business unit (SBU) structure 322
holding company structure 323
matrix organizational structure 323
international division structure 326
geographic-area division structure 326
worldwide matrix structure 326
worldwide functional structure 326
worldwide product division structure 326
global start-up 326
boundaryless organizational designs 328
barrier-free organization 329
modular organization 332
virtual organization 333
horizontal organizational structures 337
adaptability 339
alignment 339
ambidextrous organizational designs 340

experiential exercise

Many firms have recently moved toward a modular structure. For example, they have increasingly outsourced many of their information technology (IT) activities. Identify three such organizations. Using secondary sources, evaluate (1) the firm's rationale for IT outsourcing and (2) the implications for performance.

Firm	Rationale	Implication(s) for Performance
1.		
2.		
3.		

application questions & exercises

1. Select an organization that competes in an industry in which you are particularly interested. Go on the Internet and determine what type of organizational structure this organization has. In your view, is it consistent with the strategy that it has chosen to implement? Why? Why not?
2. Choose an article from *Bloomberg Businessweek, Fortune, Forbes, Fast Company,* or any other well-known publication that deals with a corporation that has undergone a significant change in its strategic direction. What are the implications for the structure of this organization?
3. Go on the Internet and look up some of the public statements or speeches of an executive in a major corporation about a significant initiative such as entering into a joint venture or launching a new product line. What do you feel are the implications for making the internal and external barriers of the firm more flexible and permeable? Does the executive discuss processes, procedures, integrating mechanisms, or cultural issues that should serve this purpose? Or are other issues discussed that enable a firm to become more boundaryless?
4. Look up a recent article in the publications listed in question 2 that addresses a firm's involvement in outsourcing (modular organization) or in strategic alliance or network organizations (virtual organization). Was the firm successful or unsuccessful in this endeavor? Why? Why not?

ethics questions

1. If a firm has a divisional structure and places extreme pressures on its divisional executives to meet short-term profitability goals (e.g., quarterly income), could this raise some ethical considerations? Why? Why not?
2. If a firm enters into a strategic alliance but does not exercise appropriate behavioral control of its employees (in terms of culture, rewards and incentives, and boundaries—as discussed in Chapter 9) who are involved in the alliance, what ethical issues could arise? What could be the potential long-term and short-term downside for the firm?

references

1. Wilson, K. & Doz, Y. 2012. 10 rules for managing global innovation. *Harvard Business Review,* 90(10): 84–92; Wallace, J. 2007. Update on problems joining 787 fuselage sections. *Seattlepi.com,* June 7: np; Peterson, K. 2011. Special report: A wing and a prayer: Outsourcing at Boeing. *Reuters.com,* January 20: np; Hiltzik, M. 2011. 787 Dreamliner teaches Boeing costly lesson on outsourcing. *Latimes.com,* February 15: np; Gates, D. 2013. Boeing 787's problems blamed on outsourcing, lack of oversight. *Seattletimes.com,* February 2: np; and Ostrower, J. 2014. Boeing's Key Mission: Cut Dreamliner cost. *wsj.com.* January 7: np.
2. For a unique perspective on organization design, see Rao, R. 2010. What 17th century pirates can teach us about job design. *Harvard Business Review,* 88(10): 44.
3. This introductory discussion draws upon Hall, R. H. 2002. *Organizations: Structures, processes, and outcomes* (8th ed.). Upper Saddle River, NJ: Prentice Hall; and Duncan, R. E. 1979. What is the right organization structure? Decision-tree analysis provides the right answer. *Organizational Dynamics,* 7(3): 59–80. For an insightful discussion of strategy-structure relationships in the organization theory and strategic management literatures, refer to Keats, B. & O'Neill, H. M. 2001. Organization structure: Looking through a strategy lens. In Hitt, M. A., Freeman, R. E., & Harrison, J. S. 2001. *The Blackwell handbook of strategic management:* 520–542. Malden, MA: Blackwell.
4. Gratton, L. 2011. The end of the middle manager. *Harvard Business Review,* 89(1/2): 36.
5. An interesting discussion on the role of organizational design in strategy execution is in Neilson, G. L., Martin, K. L., & Powers, E. 2009. The secrets to successful strategy execution. *Harvard Business Review,* 87(2): 60–70.
6. This discussion draws upon Chandler, A. D. 1962. *Strategy and structure.* Cambridge, MA: MIT Press; Galbraith J. R. & Kazanjian, R. K. 1986. *Strategy implementation: The role of structure and process.* St. Paul, MN: West; and Scott, B. R. 1971. Stages of corporate development. Intercollegiate Case Clearing House, 9-371-294, BP 998. Harvard Business School.
7. Our discussion of the different types of organizational structures draws on a variety of sources, including Galbraith & Kazanjian, op. cit.; Hrebiniak, L. G. & Joyce, W. F. 1984. *Implementing strategy.* New York: Macmillan; Distelzweig, H. 2000. Organizational structure. In Helms, M. M. (Ed.), *Encyclopedia of management:* 692–699. Farmington Hills, MI: Gale; and Dess, G. G. & Miller, A. 1993. *Strategic management.* New York: McGraw-Hill.
8. A discussion of an innovative organizational design is in Garvin, D. A. & Levesque, L. C. 2009. The multiunit enterprise. *Harvard Business Review,* 87(2): 106–117.
9. Schein, E. H. 1996. Three cultures of management: The key to organizational learning. *Sloan Management Review,* 38(1): 9–20.
10. Insights on governance implications for multidivisional forms are in Verbeke, A. & Kenworthy, T. P. 2008. Multidivisional vs. metanational governance. *Journal of International Business,* 39(6): 940–956.
11. Martin, J. A. & Eisenhardt, K. 2010. Rewiring: Cross-business-unit collaborations in multibusiness organizations. *Academy of Management Journal,* 53(2): 265–301.
12. For a discussion of performance implications, refer to Hoskisson, R. E. 1987. Multidivisional structure and performance: The contingency of diversification strategy. *Academy*

of *Management Journal,* 29: 625–644.

13. For a thorough and seminal discussion of the evolution toward the divisional form of organizational structure in the United States, refer to Chandler, op. cit. A rigorous empirical study of the strategy and structure relationship is found in Rumelt, R. P. 1974. *Strategy, structure, and economic performance.* Cambridge, MA: Harvard Business School Press.

14. Ghoshal S. & Bartlett, C. A. 1995. Changing the role of management: Beyond structure to processes. *Harvard Business Review,* 73(1): 88.

15. Koppel, B. 2000. Synergy in ketchup? *Forbes,* February 7: 68–69; and Hitt, M. A., Ireland, R. D., & Hoskisson, R. E. 2001. *Strategic management: Competitiveness and globalization* (4th ed.). Cincinnati, OH: South-Western.

16. Pitts, R. A. 1977. Strategies and structures for diversification. *Academy of Management Journal,* 20(2): 197–208.

17. Silvestri, L. 2012. The evolution of organizational structure. *footnote1.com,* June 6: np.

18. Andersen, M. M., Froholdt, M., & Poulfelt, F. 2010. *Return on strategy: How to achieve it.* New York: Routledge.

19. Haas, M. R. 2010. The double-edged swords of autonomy and external knowledge: Analyzing team effectiveness in a multinational organization. *Academy of Management Journal,* 53(5): 989–1008.

20. Daniels, J. D., Pitts, R. A., & Tretter, M. J. 1984. Strategy and structure of U.S. multinationals: An exploratory study. *Academy of Management Journal,* 27(2): 292–307.

21. Habib, M. M. & Victor, B. 1991. Strategy, structure, and performance of U.S. manufacturing and service MNCs: A comparative analysis. *Strategic Management Journal,* 12(8): 589–606.

22. Our discussion of global start-ups draws from Oviatt, B. M. & McDougall, P. P. 2005. The internationalization of entrepreneurship. *Journal of International Business Studies,* 36(1): 2–8; Oviatt, B. M. & McDougall, P. P. 1994. Toward a theory of international new ventures. *Journal of International Business Studies,* 25(1): 45–64; and Oviatt, B. M. & McDougall, P. P. 1995. Global start-ups: Entrepreneurs on a worldwide stage. *Academy of Management Executive,* 9(2): 30–43.

23. Some useful guidelines for global start-ups are provided in Kuemmerle, W. 2005. The entrepreneur's path for global expansion. *MIT Sloan Management Review,* 46(2): 42–50.

24. See, for example, Miller, D. & Friesen, P. H. 1980. Momentum and revolution in organizational structure. *Administrative Science Quarterly,* 13: 65–91.

25. Many authors have argued that a firm's structure can influence its strategy and performance. These include Amburgey, T. L. & Dacin, T. 1995. As the left foot follows the right? The dynamics of strategic and structural change. *Academy of Management Journal,* 37: 1427–1452; Dawn, K. & Amburgey, T. L. 1991. Organizational inertia and momentum: A dynamic model of strategic change. *Academy of Management Journal,* 34: 591–612; Fredrickson, J. W. 1986. The strategic decision process and organization structure. *Academy of Management Review,* 11: 280–297; Hall, D. J. & Saias, M. A. 1980. Strategy follows structure! *Strategic Management Journal,* 1: 149–164; and Burgelman, R. A. 1983. A model of the interaction of strategic behavior, corporate context, and the concept of strategy. *Academy of Management Review,* 8: 61–70.

26. An interesting discussion on how the Internet has affected the boundaries of firms can be found in Afuah, A. 2003. Redefining firm boundaries in the face of the Internet: Are firms really shrinking? *Academy of Management Review,* 28(1): 34–53.

27. Govindarajan, V. G. & Trimble, C. 2010. Stop the innovation wars. *Harvard Business Review,* 88(7/8): 76–83.

28. For a discussion of the role of coaching on developing high-performance teams, refer to Kets de Vries, M. F. R. 2005. Leadership group coaching in action: The zen of creating high performance teams. *Academy of Management Executive,* 19(1): 77–89.

29. Pfeffer, J. 1998. *The human equation: Building profits by putting people first.* Cambridge, MA: Harvard Business School Press.

30. For a discussion on how functional area diversity affects performance, see Bunderson, J. S. & Sutcliffe, K. M. 2002. Comparing alternative conceptualizations of functional diversity in management teams: Process and performance effects. *Academy of Management Journal,* 45(5): 875–893.

31. Falconi, M. 2014. Novartis chairman stresses need for R&D investment. *wsj.com,* March 24: np.

32. Groth, A. 2015. Holacracy at Zappos: It's either the future of management or a social experiment gone awry. *qz.com,* January 14: np; Anonymous. 2014. The holes in holacracy. *economist.com,* July 5: np; and Van De Kamp, P. 2014. Holacracy—A radical approach to organizational design. *medium.com,* August 2: np.

33. Public-private partnerships are addressed in Engardio, P. 2009. State capitalism. *BusinessWeek,* February 9: 38–43.

34. Aller, R., Weiner, H., & Weilart, M. 2005. IBM and Mayo collaborating to customize patient treatment plans. *cap.org,* January: np; and McGee, M. 2010. IBM, Mayo partner on aneurysm diagnostics. *informationweek.com,* January 25: np.

35. Winston, A. 2014: *The big pivot.* Boston: Harvard Business Review Press.

36. Dess, G. G., Rasheed, A. M. A., McLaughlin, K. J., & Priem, R. 1995. The new corporate architecture. *Academy of Management Executive,* 9(3): 7–20.

37. Handy, C. 1989. The age of unreason. Boston: Harvard Business School Press; Ramstead, E. 1997. APC maker's low-tech formula: Start with the box. *The Wall Street Journal,* December 29: B1; Mussberg, W. 1997. Thin screen PCs are looking good but still fall flat. *The Wall Street Journal,* January 2: 9; Brown, E. 1997. Monorail: Low cost PCs. *Fortune,* July 7: 106–108; and Young, M. 1996. Ex-Compaq executives start new company. *Computer Reseller News,* November 11: 181.

38. An original discussion on how open sourcing could help the Big 3 automobile companies is in Jarvis, J. 2009. How the Google model could help Detroit. *BusinessWeek,* February 9: 32–36.

39. For a discussion of some of the downsides of outsourcing, refer to Rossetti, C. & Choi, T. Y. 2005. On the dark side of strategic sourcing: Experiences from the aerospace industry. *Academy of Management Executive,* 19(1): 46–60.

40. Tully, S. 1993. The modular corporation. *Fortune,* February 8: 196.

41. Offshoring in manufacturing firms is addressed in Coucke, K. & Sleuwaegen, L. 2008. Offshoring as a survival strategy: Evidence from manufacturing firms in Belgium. *Journal of International Business Studies,* 39(8): 1261–1277.
42. Quinn, J. B. 1992. *Intelligent enterprise: A knowledge and service based paradigm for industry.* New York: Free Press.
43. For an insightful perspective on outsourcing and its role in developing capabilities, read Gottfredson, M., Puryear, R., & Phillips, C. 2005. Strategic sourcing: From periphery to the core. *Harvard Business Review,* 83(4): 132–139.
44. This discussion draws upon Quinn, J. B. & Hilmer, F. C. 1994. Strategic outsourcing. *Sloan Management Review,* 35(4): 43–55.
45. Reitzig, M. & Wagner, S. 2010. The hidden costs of outsourcing: Evidence from patent data. *Strategic Management Journal,* 31(11): 1183–1201.
46. Insights on outsourcing and private branding can be found in Cehn, S-F. S. 2009. A transaction cost rationale for private branding and its implications for the choice of domestic vs. offshore outsourcing. *Journal of International Business Strategy,* 40(1): 156–175.
47. For an insightful perspective on the use of outsourcing for decision analysis, read Davenport, T. H. & Iyer, B. 2009. Should you outsource your brain? *Harvard Business Review,* 87(2): 38.
48. See also Stuckey, J. & White, D. 1993. When and when not to vertically integrate. *Sloan Management Review,* Spring: 71–81; Harrar, G. 1993. Outsource tales. *Forbes ASAP,* June 7: 37–39, 42; and Davis, E. W. 1992. Global outsourcing: Have U.S. managers thrown the baby out with the bath water? *Business Horizons,* July–August: 58–64.
49. For a discussion of knowledge creation through alliances, refer to Inkpen, A. C. 1996. Creating knowledge through collaboration. *California Management Review,* 39(1): 123–140; and Mowery, D. C., Oxley, J. E., & Silverman, B. S. 1996. Strategic alliances and interfirm knowledge transfer. *Strategic Management Journal,* 17 (Special Issue, Winter): 77–92.
50. Doz, Y. & Hamel, G. 1998. *Alliance advantage: The art of creating value through partnering.* Boston: Harvard Business School Press.
51. DeSanctis, G., Glass, J. T., & Ensing, I. M. 2002. Organizational designs for R&D. *Academy of Management Executive,* 16(3): 55–66.
52. Barringer, B. R. & Harrison, J. S. 2000. Walking a tightrope: Creating value through interorganizational alliances. *Journal of Management,* 26: 367–403.
53. One contemporary example of virtual organizations is R&D consortia. For an insightful discussion, refer to Sakaibara, M. 2002. Formation of R&D consortia: Industry and company effects. *Strategic Management Journal,* 23(11): 1033–1050.
54. Bartness, A. & Cerny, K. 1993. Building competitive advantage through a global network of capabilities. *California Management Review,* Winter: 78–103. For an insightful historical discussion of the usefulness of alliances in the computer industry, see Moore, J. F. 1993. Predators and prey: A new ecology of competition. *Harvard Business Review,* 71(3): 75–86.
55. See Lorange, P. & Roos, J. 1991. Why some strategic alliances succeed and others fail. *Journal of Business Strategy,* January–February: 25–30; and Slowinski, G. 1992. The human touch in strategic alliances. *Mergers and Acquisitions,* July–August: 44–47. A compelling argument for strategic alliances is provided by Ohmae, K. 1989. The global logic of strategic alliances. *Harvard Business Review,* 67(2): 143–154.
56. Some of the downsides of alliances are discussed in Das, T. K. & Teng, B. S. 2000. Instabilities of strategic alliances: An internal tensions perspective. *Organization Science,* 11: 77–106.
57. This section draws upon Dess, G. G. & Picken, J. C. 1997. *Mission critical.* Burr Ridge, IL: Irwin Professional.
58. Katzenbach, J. R. & Smith, D. K. 1994. *The wisdom of teams: Creating the high performance organization.* New York: HarperBusiness.
59. Bryant, A. 2011. *The corner office:* 230. New York: St. Martin's Griffin.
60. Hammer, M. & Champy, J. 1993. *Reengineering the corporation: A manifesto for business revolution.* New York: HarperCollins.
61. Gupta, A. 2011. The relational perspective and east meets west. *Academy of Management Perspectives,* 25(3): 19–27.
62. This section draws on Birkinshaw, J. & Gibson, C. 2004. Building ambidexterity into an organization. *MIT Sloan Management Review,* 45(4): 47–55; and Gibson, C. B. & Birkinshaw, J. 2004. The antecedents, consequences, and mediating role of organizational ambidexterity. *Academy of Management Journal,* 47(2): 209–226. Robert Duncan is generally credited with being the first to coin the term "ambidextrous organizations" in his article entitled: Designing dual structures for innovation. In Kilmann, R. H., Pondy, L. R., & Slevin, D. (Eds.). 1976. *The management of organizations,* vol. 1: 167–188. For a seminal academic discussion of the concept of exploration and exploitation, which parallels adaptation and alignment, refer to March, J. G. 1991. Exploration and exploitation in organizational learning. *Organization Science,* 2: 71–86.
63. This section is based on O'Reilly, C. A. & Tushman, M. L. 2004. The ambidextrous organization. *Harvard Business Review,* 82(4): 74–81.

Strategic Leadership
Creating a Learning Organization and an Ethical Organization

chapter 11

After reading this chapter, you should have a good understanding of the following learning objectives:

LO11.1 The three key interdependent activities in which all successful leaders must be continually engaged.

LO11.2 Two elements of effective leadership: overcoming barriers to change and using power effectively.

LO11.3 The crucial role of emotional intelligence (EI) in successful leadership, as well as its potential drawbacks.

LO11.4 The importance of creating a learning organization.

LO11.5 The leader's role in establishing an ethical organization.

LO11.6 The difference between integrity-based and compliance-based approaches to organizational ethics.

LO11.7 Several key elements that organizations must have to become ethical organizations.

PART 3: STRATEGIC IMPLEMENTATION

Learning from Mistakes

It took four generations to build Stroh's Brewing into a major player in the beer industry and just one generation to tear it down. Stroh's was founded in Detroit by Bernard Stroh, who had emigrated from Germany in 1850. Bernard took the $150 he had and a cherished family beer recipe and began selling beer door to door. By 1890, his sons, Julius and Bernard, had grown the family business and were shipping beer around the Great Lakes region. The family business survived prohibition by making ice cream and maple syrup. After World War II ended, the business grew along with the industrial Midwest, seeing its sales surge from 500,000 barrels of beer in 1950 to 2.7 million barrels in 1956. The firm succeeded by following a simple business recipe: catering to the needs of working-class tastes by brewing a simple, drinkable, and affordable beer and treating its employees well. Following this business blueprint, the company found success and growth, resulting in a business that was worth an estimated $700 million in the mid-1980s. A little over a decade later, the firm was out of business.[1]

Its rapid descent from a successful and growing firm to failure is tied to a series of disastrous decisions made by Peter Stroh, representing the fifth generation of the family to lead the firm, who took on the role of CEO in 1980. Rather than stick to the tried-and-true business plan of catering to the needs of the Midwest working class, Peter stepped out to build a larger, national beer empire. He purchased F&M Schaefer, a New York–based brewer, in 1981. He followed this up in 1982 by purchasing Joseph Schlitz Brewing, a firm that was much bigger than Stroh's. To undertake this acquisition, Stroh's borrowed $500 million, five times the value of Stroh's itself. Peter's acquisitions hampered the firm in two key ways. First, working to combine the firms distracted Stroh's from seeing the evolving needs of customers. Most notably, it completely missed the most significant shift in customer tastes in a generation—the emergence of light beer. Also, the heavy debt load taken on to finance the acquisitions left the firm with little money to launch the national advertising campaigns needed to support a company that was now the third-largest brewer in the United States. In the words of Greg Stroh, a cousin of Peter and an employee of the firm, "We made the decision to go national without having the budget. It was like going to a gunfight with a knife. We didn't have a chance."

Stroh's tried various tactics to improve its situation. It tried undercutting the price of its major rivals, Anheuser-Busch and Miller, by offering 15 cans of beer for the price of 12. It laid off hundreds of employees to save on cost. It then changed course, raising prices and nixing the 15-pack containers. Customers rebelled, pushing sales down 40 percent in a single year. The firm was left with 6 million barrels of excess brewing capacity. Finally, the firm took on one last, disastrous acquisition. Stroh's purchased another struggling brewer, G. Heileman, for $300 million, saddling itself with even more debt. While the firm struggled in its core beer business, Peter tried to diversify Stroh's into biotechnology and real estate investing. The almost inevitable end came in 1999 when Stroh's assets were purchased by Pabst Brewing for $350 million—$250 million of which went to the debtholders of the firm.

Discussion Questions

1. Why were the acquisitions so debilitating for Stroh's?
2. What would have been the likely outcome for Stroh's if it hadn't purchased other brands?

Under Peter Stroh's leadership, Stroh's Brewing went from being a successful and growing family business to a failed firm. He took the firm away from its traditional strategy and also missed seeing key shifts in the beer industry. This led him to change the firm's strategy in ways that undercut the value of its brand and its culture, ultimately leading to Stroh's demise and the loss of the family's legacy. In contrast to Peter's ineffective leadership, effective leaders set a clear direction for the firm, create and reinforce valuable strategies, and strengthen firm values and culture.

This chapter provides insights into the role of strategic leadership in managing, adapting, and coping in the face of increased environmental complexity and uncertainty. First, we define leadership and its three interdependent activities—setting a direction, designing the organization, and nurturing a culture dedicated to excellence and ethical behavior. Then, we identify two elements of leadership that contribute to success—overcoming barriers to change and using power effectively. The third section focuses on emotional intelligence, a trait that is increasingly acknowledged to be critical to successful leadership. Next, we emphasize the importance of leaders developing competency companions and creating a learning organization. Here, we focus on empowerment wherein employees and managers throughout an organization develop a sense of self-determination, competence, meaning, and impact that is centrally important to learning. Finally, we address the leader's role in building an ethical organization and the elements of an ethical culture that contribute to firm effectiveness.

Leadership: Three Interdependent Activities

In today's chaotic world, few would argue against the need for leadership, but how do we go about encouraging it? Is it enough to merely keep an organization afloat, or is it essential to make steady progress toward some well-defined objective? We believe custodial management is not leadership. Leadership is proactive, goal-oriented, and focused on the creation and implementation of a creative vision. **Leadership** is the process of transforming organizations from what they are to what the leader would have them become. This definition implies a lot: *dissatisfaction* with the status quo, a *vision* of what should be, and a *process* for bringing about change. An insurance company executive shared the following insight: "I lead by the Noah Principle: It's all right to know when it's going to rain, but, by God, you had better build the ark."

Doing the right thing is becoming increasingly important. Many industries are declining; the global village is becoming increasingly complex, interconnected, and unpredictable; and product and market life cycles are becoming increasingly compressed. When asked to describe the life cycle of his company's products, the CEO of a supplier of computer components replied, "Seven months from cradle to grave—and that includes three months to design the product and get it into production!" Richard D'Aveni, author of *Hypercompetition*, argued that in a world where all dimensions of competition appear to be compressed in time and heightened in complexity, *sustainable* competitive advantages are no longer possible.

Despite the importance of doing the "right thing," leaders must also be concerned about "doing things right." Charan and Colvin strongly believe that execution, that is, the implementation of strategy, is also essential to success:

> Mastering execution turns out to be the odds-on best way for a CEO to keep his job. So what's the right way to think about that sexier obsession, strategy? It's vitally important—obviously. The problem is that our age's fascination feeds the mistaken belief that developing exactly the right strategy will enable a company to rocket past competitors. In reality, that's less than half the battle.[2]

Thus, leaders are change agents whose success is measured by how effectively they formulate *and* implement a strategic vision and mission.[3]

---

leadership
the process of transforming organizations from what they are to what the leader would have them become.

LO11.1
The three key interdependent activities in which all successful leaders must be continually engaged.

EXHIBIT 11.1 Three Interdependent Leadership Activities

- Setting a direction
- Designing the organization
- Nurturing a culture dedicated to excellence and ethical behavior

Many authors contend that successful leaders must recognize three interdependent activities that must be continually reassessed for organizations to succeed. As shown in Exhibit 11.1, these are (1) setting a direction, (2) designing the organization, and (3) nurturing a culture dedicated to excellence and ethical behavior.[4]

The interdependent nature of these three activities is self-evident. Consider an organization with a great mission and a superb organizational structure but a culture that implicitly encourages shirking and unethical behavior. Or one with a sound direction and strong culture but counterproductive teams and a "zero-sum" reward system that leads to the dysfunctional situation in which one party's gain is viewed as another party's loss and collaboration and sharing are severely hampered. Clearly, such combinations would be ineffective.

Often, failure of today's organizations can be attributed to a lack of equal consideration of these three activities. The imagery of a three-legged stool is instructive: The stool will collapse if one leg is missing or broken. Let's briefly look at each of these activities as well as the value of an ambicultural approach to leadership.

Setting a Direction

A holistic understanding of an organization's stakeholders requires an ability to scan the environment to develop a knowledge of all of the company's stakeholders and other salient environmental trends and events. Managers must integrate this knowledge into a vision of what the organization could become.[5] This necessitates the capacity to solve increasingly complex problems, become proactive in approach, and develop viable strategic options. A strategic vision provides many benefits: a clear future direction; a framework for the organization's mission and goals; and enhanced employee communication, participation, and commitment.

Strategy Spotlight 11.1 discusses how Alan Mulally exhibited the three key leadership activities as he brought Ford Motor Company back from the brink.

> **setting a direction**
> a strategic leadership activity of strategy analysis and strategy formulation.

Designing the Organization

At times, almost all leaders have difficulty implementing their vision and strategies.[6] Such problems may stem from a variety of sources:

- Lack of understanding of responsibility and accountability among managers.
- Reward systems that do not motivate individuals (or collectives such as groups and divisions) toward desired organizational goals.
- Inadequate or inappropriate budgeting and control systems.
- Insufficient mechanisms to integrate activities across the organization.

Successful leaders are actively involved in building structures, teams, systems, and organizational processes that facilitate the implementation of their vision and strategies. Without

> **designing the organization**
> a strategic leadership activity of building structures, teams, systems, and organizational processes that facilitate the implementation of the leader's vision and strategies.

11.1 STRATEGY SPOTLIGHT

ALAN MULALLY'S LEADERSHIP OF FORD

When Alan Mulally took over Ford Motor Company in 2006, there were a lot of questions about whether he was the right man for the job. He was taking over an automotive firm that had a proud heritage but was struggling mightily, losing money and market share. Yet he had no experience in the automobile industry. He had been successful as the head of Boeing's aircraft division but hadn't impressed Boeing's board of directors enough to be seen as CEO material and had been passed over in the search for Boeing's CEO the year before.

But as he retired from Ford in June 2014, the imprint of his leadership was easy to see. Ford had made more money under his leadership than it had in the history of the firm—$42 billion in profits over the prior five years. The value of the firm had risen from $15 billion to $63 billion under his tenure. More importantly for the long run, he had built a much more driven, focused, and collaborative Ford Motor Company.

The three interdependent activities of a successful leader were easily seen with Mulally. First, he set a clear direction for Ford. Starting with a simple motto, "One Ford," he set the firm on a trajectory to create a unified global firm built around the Blue Oval—Ford's logo. Mulally's One Ford platform included four main points: (1) He emphasized bringing all Ford employees together as a global team. (2) He wanted to globally leverage Ford's unique automotive knowledge and assets. (3) He emphasized building cars and trucks that people wanted and valued, focusing on new technology, safety, and fuel economy as key differentiators. (4) He arranged the financing necessary for the plan to succeed. To make it work, he met with employees and other stakeholders to explain and sell the new direction.

Second, he designed an organization to move Ford forward. Part of this included shedding parts of the organization that didn't fit the new Ford. He shut down the Mercury division and sold off the Volvo, Land Rover, Aston Martin, and Jaguar brands. The new, streamlined structure kept the Ford brand at the center. In the past, different geographic divisions developed completely distinct products for each market. He changed that by developing global-platform teams that designed products that could sell on a global basis. These changes allowed Ford to become much more efficient in developing and maintaining its product portfolio, which now includes 20 different car models, down from 97 when he first took over as CEO.

Third, he nurtured the culture of Ford. Prior to his arrival, Ford had a reputation as a cutthroat place to work. Managers would look for and openly discuss the weaknesses and failures of their peers, practicing self-preservation over collaboration. Mulally set out to change that. He instituted weekly meetings at which managers would openly discuss the status of programs they were managing, using a series of green-, yellow-, and red-light ratings of different aspects of the projects. Early on, when one senior manager, Mark Fields, noted areas of concern—red lights—on a project in his unit, Mulally applauded him and turned to the rest of the team for suggestions to address the problems. This quickly became the norm in the firm—open discussion with collaborative problem solving, making executive meetings a safe environment where data could be shared without blame, improving collaboration, and setting the stage for innovation success.

Through his leadership, Ford moved from being a firm that, in Mulally's own words, had "been going out of business for 40 years" to being a highly profitable and growing firm. Jeff Carlson, a Ford dealership owner, put it this way: "He came with one plan and stayed with one plan, and that continuity of leadership allowed him to manage the company out of dire straits."

Sources: Boudette, N., Rogers, C., & Lublin, J. 2014. Mulally's legacy: Setting Ford on a stronger course. *wsj.com*, April 21: np; and Caldicott, S. 2014. Why Ford's Alan Mulally is an innovation CEO for the record books. *forbes.com*, June 25: np.

---

appropriately structuring organizational activities, a firm would generally be unable to attain an overall low-cost advantage by closely monitoring its costs through detailed and formalized cost and financial control procedures. With regard to corporate-level strategy, a related diversification strategy would necessitate reward systems that emphasize behavioral measures because interdependence among business units tends to be very important. In contrast, reward systems associated with an unrelated diversification strategy should rely more on financial indicators of performance because business units are relatively autonomous.

These examples illustrate the important role of leadership in creating systems and structures to achieve desired ends. As Jim Collins says about the importance of designing the organization, "Along with figuring out what the company stands for and pushing it to understand what it's really good at, building mechanisms is the CEO's role—the leader as architect."[7]

Nurturing a Culture Committed to Excellence and Ethical Behavior

excellent and ethical organizational culture
an organizational culture focused on core competencies and high ethical standards.

Organizational culture can be an effective means of organizational control.[8] Leaders play a key role in changing, developing, and sustaining an organization's culture. Brian Chesky, cofounder and CEO of Airbnb, clearly understands the role of the leader in building and maintaining an organization's culture. In October 2013, as Airbnb was growing rapidly,

> ### 11.2 STRATEGY SPOTLIGHT · ETHICS
>
> **INSTILLING ETHICS AND A FIRM'S VALUES: WALKING THE TALK**
>
> Firms often draft elaborate value statements and codes of conduct, yet many firms do not live up to their own standards—or, in other words, fail to "walk the talk." Take the positive example of N. R. Narayana Murthy, chairman and one of the founders of Infosys (a giant Indian technology company). In February 1984, shortly after the firm was founded, Infosys decided to import a super minicomputer so that it could start developing software for overseas clients. When the machine landed at Bangalore Airport, the local customs official refused to clear it unless the company "took care of him"—the Indian euphemism for demanding a bribe. A delay at customs could have threatened the project. Yet, instead of caving in to the unethical customs official's demands, Murthy kept true to his values and took the more expensive formal route of paying a customs duty of 135 percent with dim chances of successfully appealing the duty and receiving a refund.
>
> Reflecting on these events, Murthy reasons, "We didn't have enough money to pay the duty and had to borrow it. However, because we had decided to do business ethically, we didn't have a choice. We would not pay bribes. We effectively paid twice for the machine and had only a slim chance of recovering our money. But a clear conscience is the softest pillow on which you can lay your head down at night. . . . It took a few years for corrupt officials to stop approaching us for favors."
>
> Source: Raman, A. P. 2011. "Why don't we try to be India's most respected company?" *Harvard Business Review*, 89(11): 82.

Chesky sent out an email to his leadership team imploring the team members to be very conscious to maintain the culture of the firm.[9] He stated, "The culture is what creates the foundation for all future innovation. If you break the culture, you break the machine that creates your products." He then went on to comment that they needed to uphold the firm's values in all they do: who they hire, how they work on a project, how they treat other employees in the hallway, and what they write in emails. Chesky then laid out the power of firm culture in the following words:

> The stronger the culture, the less corporate process a company needs. When the culture is strong, you can trust everyone to do the right thing. People can be independent and autonomous. They can be entrepreneurial. And if we have a company that is entrepreneurial in spirit, we will be able to take our next "(wo)man on the moon" leap. . . . In organizations (or even in a society) where the culture is weak, you need an abundance of heavy, precise rules, and processes.

In sharp contrast, leaders can also have a very detrimental effect on a firm's culture and ethics. Imagine the negative impact that Todd Berman's illegal activities have had on a firm that he cofounded—New York's private equity firm Chartwell Investments.[10] He stole more than $3.6 million from the firm and its investors. Berman pleaded guilty to fraud charges brought by the Justice Department. For 18 months he misled Chartwell's investors concerning the financial condition of one of the firm's portfolio companies by falsely claiming it needed to borrow funds to meet operating expenses. Instead, Berman transferred the money to his personal bank account, along with fees paid by portfolio companies.

Clearly, a leader's behavior and values can make a strong impact on an organization—for good or for bad. Strategy Spotlight 11.2 provides a positive example. It discusses how the chairman of Infosys created an ethical culture by "walking the talk."

Managers and top executives must accept personal responsibility for developing and strengthening ethical behavior throughout the organization. They must consistently demonstrate that such behavior is central to the vision and mission of the organization. Several elements must be present and reinforced for a firm to become highly ethical, including role models, corporate credos and codes of conduct, reward and evaluation systems, and policies and procedures. Given the importance of these elements, we address them in detail in the last section of this chapter.

Michael Williams, a former senior executive at Biggby Coffee, offers further insight on the attributes of effective leaders in Insights from Executives.

11.1 INSIGHTS FROM EXECUTIVES

MICHAEL WILLIAMS, FORMER CHIEF FINANCIAL OFFICER FOR BIGGBY COFFEE

BIOSKETCH

Michael Williams is the director of Entrepreneurship Activities and the director of the Business and Entrepreneurship Clinic at the University of Wisconsin–Madison School of Business. Prior to working in higher education, Williams was the chief financial officer for Biggby Coffee, a coffee shop franchising company. Prior to Biggby, Williams owned Kismetic Enterprises East, LLC, a consulting business that provided interim-CFO duties, prepared business and financial plans, and strategically prepared small to midsize companies to raise capital. Prior to Kismetic, Williams held various C-level positions with Voyager.net, an entrepreneurial Internet company that experienced explosive growth and went public in 1999.

1. *One of the key roles of a leader is to set the direction for an organization. In your experience, what do effective leaders do to formulate and communicate a vision or direction for the firm?*

   In my experience, the best leaders surround themselves with exceptional people who are not afraid to disagree and give good, constructive feedback. Formulating and executing the vision is always an iterative and fluid process with the top management team and also with the employee base. The vision of a company can change, and the best leaders are not afraid of modifying it, but not whimsically so.

   The best leaders are always fantastic communicators who are trusted by their employees. This is an earned trust because the leaders hold themselves accountable to the goals, mission, and vision of the company. The most effective leaders are not afraid to admit they made mistakes and change course, if needed. This shows the employees that the leaders are honest and have the best interests of the firm and its employees at heart.

   I also had experience with some bad leaders. It was quickly apparent to me these ineffectual leaders were out for themselves and didn't care about the employees or the long-term fate of the company. The most glaring difference between these types of leaders and the best leaders was that the bad leaders held everyone accountable except themselves. These leaders never garnered the trust of the employees, and every facet of the company suffered because of it.

2. *Leaders must also design an organization to achieve the direction they've laid out for the business. What have you found to be the key elements in designing an effective organization?*

   The highest priority of a company trying to design an effective organization is to create *core values* that are simple, clear, and direct. Core values are those values that guide the way employees interact with each other, and the rest of the world, and they also guide the way the company interacts with the most important "person" of all: *the customer.*

   Two other key elements in designing an effective organization are transparency and accountability. I have found that when employees believe they are working in a "fair" environment, they will buy in to the company's vision and mission and work extremely hard to make sure the company succeeds. Their loyalty to the company will be unwavering.

3. *Most successful organizations have a culture that is committed to excellence and ethical behaviors. How can leaders help build, support, and reinforce such a culture in their organizations?*

   This is actually very simple. The leaders must do as they say. They must walk the talk. If they hold themselves to a different standard, then the firm culture will quickly erode. If the company has a strict policy that it will not pay for liquor at a business dinner, then the CEO needs to reach into his or her own pocket to pay for that bottle of wine. It doesn't matter that the CEO is entertaining the biggest client the company has ever entertained. A good CEO walks the talk every single day.

4. *Competitive environments are not static. As a result, even when firms are doing well, they need to change to respond to market dynamics and other changes in their environment. What are the types of actions leaders can take to improve their firm's openness to change?*

   It could be argued that the competitive environment in most industries has never been as fierce as it is now. In an environment where a bad experience could reach millions at the touch of a "Tweet" that goes viral, the ability to change and move has never been more important. But change can be difficult and scary for many people. If something happens in a firm, the first thing most people will think is "How will this affect me?"

   A leader can create an environment that is ready for change by being completely honest and open. Most of the anxiety surrounding change comes from the unknown, which stems from lack of information. The more information that a leader can share with his or her employees, the better. I have found that it is best to have "buy-in" from employees on changes that need to occur. Buy-in comes from the employees feeling like they are engaged and their concerns are heard and taken into consideration. Even if their suggestions are not used, they should still feel like they are part of the process and they will be more accepting of the needed change. Creating an employee feedback loop for difficult situations can build trust and also minimize the unproductive anxiety that gut-wrenching change can create.

5. *Emotional intelligence is a key managerial attribute. Think of a strong leader you have had an opportunity to work with and observe. Discuss which of these traits you saw in that leader and how these traits helped him or her effectively lead his or her organization.*

   I have had the pleasure to work with many strong leaders over the years. One of the strongest is Michael McFall, cofounder and president of Biggby Coffee. When we first met in fall 1999, Biggby had just opened its first franchised coffee shop. Now, it is nearing 200 open stores with 50 more under contract to be opened in the next 12 to 18 months. Michael's strengths come from self-awareness, empathy, and a strong motivation to do what is right. He runs the company with honesty, transparency, simplicity, and swift action.

   He and his cofounder, Robert Fish, have split responsibilities based on what each one does extremely well (self-awareness), and this has had a huge positive effect on the company's productivity, employee satisfaction and retention, customer loyalty, and, ultimately, on profitability. Michael is a wizard at understanding the economics and financials of a growing company. He designed reports and metrics that the company uses on a daily basis to understand where it may have issues. If it does have issues, Michael requests honest feedback from the employees and takes that into consideration while creating a swift action plan. Michael and Robert have created a culture of "Fun but Serious," and this enabled Biggby to be honored as one of the fastest-growing franchises in the United States in 2012.

Getting Things Done: Overcoming Barriers and Using Power

LO11.2

Two elements of effective leadership: overcoming barriers to change and using power effectively.

The demands on leaders in today's business environment require them to perform a variety of functions. The success of their organizations often depends on how they as individuals meet challenges and deliver on promises. What practices and skills are needed to get the job done effectively? In this section, we focus on two capabilities that are marks of successful leadership—overcoming barriers to change and using power effectively. Then, in the next section, we will examine an important human trait that helps leaders be more effective—emotional intelligence.

Overcoming Barriers to Change

What are the **barriers to change** that leaders often encounter, and how can leaders best bring about organizational change?[11] After all, people generally have some level of choice about how strongly they support or resist a leader's change initiatives. Why is there often so much resistance? Organizations at all levels are prone to inertia and are slow to learn, adapt, and change because:

1. Many people have **vested interests in the status quo.** People tend to be risk-averse and resistant to change. There is a broad stream of research on "escalation," wherein certain individuals continue to throw "good money at bad decisions" despite negative performance feedback.[12]
2. There are **systemic barriers.** The design of the organization's structure, information processing, reporting relationships, and so forth impedes the proper flow and evaluation of information. A bureaucratic structure with multiple layers, onerous requirements for documentation, and rigid rules and procedures will often "inoculate" the organization against change. Lou Gerstner, the former

barriers to change
characteristics of individuals and organizations that prevent a leader from transforming an organization.

vested interest in the status quo
a barrier to change that stems from people's risk aversion.

systemic barriers
barriers to change that stem from an organizational design that impedes the proper flow and evaluation of information.

CEO of IBM, described the challenge of systemic barriers in successful firms the following way:

> Rather than changing, they find it easier to just keep doing the same things that brought them success. They codify why they're successful. They write guidebooks. They create teaching manuals.[13]

behavioral barriers
barriers to change associated with the tendency for managers to look at issues from a biased or limited perspective based on their prior education and experience.

3. **Behavioral barriers** cause managers to look at issues from a biased or limited perspective due to their education, training, work experiences, and so forth. Consider an incident shared by David Lieberman, marketing director at GVO, an innovation consulting firm:

> A company's creative type had come up with a great idea for a new product. Nearly everybody loved it. However, it was shot down by a high-ranking manufacturing representative who exploded: "A new color? Do you have any idea of the spare-parts problem that it will create?" This was not a dimwit exasperated at having to build a few storage racks at the warehouse. He'd been hearing for years about cost cutting, lean inventories, and "focus." Lieberman's comment: "Good concepts, but not always good for innovation."

political barriers
barriers to change related to conflicts arising from power relationships.

4. **Political barriers** refer to conflicts arising from power relationships. This can be the outcome of a myriad of symptoms such as vested interests, refusal to share information, conflicts over resources, conflicts between departments and divisions, and petty interpersonal differences.

personal time constraints
a barrier to change that stems from people's not having sufficient time for strategic thinking and reflection.

5. **Personal time constraints** bring to mind the old saying about "not having enough time to drain the swamp when you are up to your neck in alligators." Gresham's law of planning states that operational decisions will drive out the time necessary for strategic thinking and reflection. This tendency is accentuated in organizations experiencing severe price competition or retrenchment wherein managers and employees are spread rather thin.

Strategy Spotlight 11.3 discusses the challenges Mary Barra faces as she works to change the culture and values of General Motors.

Leaders must draw on a range of personal skills as well as organizational mechanisms to move their organizations forward in the face of such barriers. Two factors mentioned earlier—building a learning organization and building an ethical organization—provide the kind of climate within which a leader can advance the organization's aims and make progress toward its goals.

One of the most important tools a leader has for overcoming barriers to change is his or her personal and organizational power. On the one hand, good leaders must be on guard not to abuse power. On the other hand, successful leadership requires the measured exercise of power. We turn to that topic next.

Using Power Effectively

Successful leadership requires the effective use of power in overcoming barriers to change.[14] As humorously noted by Mark Twain, "I'm all for progress. It's change I object to." **Power** refers to a leader's ability to get things done in a way he or she wants them to be done. It is the ability to influence other people's behavior, to persuade them to do things that they otherwise would not do, and to overcome resistance and opposition. Effective exercise of power is essential for successful leadership.[15]

power
a leader's ability to get things done in a way he or she wants them to be done.

A leader derives his or her power from several sources or bases. The simplest way to understand the bases of power is by classifying them as organizational and personal, as shown in Exhibit 11.2.

organizational bases of power
a formal management position that is the basis of a leader's power.

Organizational bases of power refer to the power that a person wields because of her formal management position.[16] These include legitimate, reward, coercive, and information

11.3 STRATEGY SPOTLIGHT

MARY BARRA AND THE NEED FOR CHANGE AT GENERAL MOTORS

Mary Barra took over as CEO of General Motors in January 2014 and soon found herself facing an unanticipated crisis that reinforced the widely held view that GM is a company in need of major change. The question is whether or not Barra is up to the task.

GM has struggled for a number of decades, seeing its share of the U.S. market decline from 40 percent in 1985 to 18 percent in 2013. More recently, GM was rocked by the financial crisis of 2008 and only survived due to a government bailout. Just after Barra was appointed CEO, a new crisis arose—a problem with faulty ignition switches in GM cars. While the problem came to light in 2014, engineers at GM knew as early as 2001 that an ignition switch used across a wide range of GM cars could fail and cause crashes, but the firm didn't recall the cars to fix their switches. According to the attorney managing claims for GM, crashes caused by the faulty switches have cost at least 50 lives. Critics say the death toll is much higher.

The problems at GM run deep. Analysts have long criticized the firm for having plodding decision making, with rival departments refusing to share information and being more focused on shifting blame for failures than on working together to solve problems. Further, an internal report on GM's decision making noted that GM was hampered by a "proliferation of committees" whose conclusions were "reported to yet further committees." Analysts also accuse the company of being more cost-conscious than customer-focused.

The near death of GM in 2008 could have provided the setting for major changes to the firm, but leadership turmoil has limited the degree of change. Over the five years prior to Barra's appointment, GM had five different CEOs. None appeared to have the drive or power necessary to undertake major changes in GM's culture and operations. The prior CEO and chairman, Dan Akerson, who had no experience in the auto industry before becoming GM's leader, managed to repay the government for bailing out GM but left abruptly without undertaking a major reorganization effort at the company. He was replaced as CEO by Barra and as chairman of the board by Tim Solso.

Is Barra the right person to bring about the necessary change? Some argue she is too much of a GM insider. She is a second-generation GM lifetime employee. Her father was a die maker who worked at the company for 39 years. Barra has worked at GM for 33 years. She began her career while still a student, worked her way up the ladder in the engineering function at GM, and served as a plant manager, VP of Global Manufacturing, and VP of Global Human Resources before becoming CEO. Yet she may not have the positional power necessary, since she doesn't also carry the role of chairman of the board. Others argue she is the perfect candidate to take on the task. She can act quickly and decisively since she knows the organization inside and out. Her career has taken her through various units of the firm, and she has relationships with people throughout the firm who trust her judgment. Also, at only 52 years of age, she is likely to be at the helm for a while, making it difficult for managers to resist her change efforts and try to wait her out.

So far, Barra is taking some actions that are bold for the GM culture. She fired 15 employees associated with the ignition-failure debacle. She also moved out seven high-level GM managers in her first few months as CEO. While these may seem like minor actions for such a large firm, they are quite bold for the conservative GM culture. She's also championing the use of external measures to assess the success of GM's products and financials. Up to now, GM has almost exclusively used internal measures, such as whether projects are meeting scheduling milestones and whether new-model sales are meeting internal benchmarks. Barra wants the firm to compare itself to its competitors and be much more aggressive and competitive. "I accept no excuses for why we can't be the best," Barra says.

Commentators suggest a major restructuring and turnaround at GM is a monumental task and could take 5 to 10 years. What is unclear at this point is whether or not Barra can be the leader to finally change GM.

Sources: Levin, D. 2014. New GM: Same as it ever was? *Fortune*, April 10: 64–67; Colvin, G. 2014. Mary Barra's (unexpected) opportunity. *Fortune*, October 6: 102–108; and Anonymous. 2009. A giant falls. *economist.com*, June 9: np.

---

power. *Legitimate power* is derived from organizationally conferred decision-making authority and is exercised by virtue of a manager's position in the organization. *Reward power* depends on the ability of the leader or manager to confer rewards for positive behaviors or outcomes. *Coercive power* is the power a manager exercises over employees using fear of punishment for errors of omission or commission. *Information power* arises from a manager's access, control, and distribution of information that is not freely available to everyone in an organization.

A leader might also be able to influence subordinates because of his or her personality characteristics and behavior. These would be considered the **personal bases of power**, including referent power and expert power. The source of *referent power* is a subordinate's

> **personal bases of power**
> a leader's personality characteristics and behavior that are the basis of the leader's power.

EXHIBIT 11.2 A Leader's Bases of Power

- **Bases of Power**
  - **Organizational**
    - Legitimate power
    - Reward power
    - Coercive power
    - Information power
  - **Personal**
    - Referent power
    - Expert power

identification with the leader. A leader's personal attributes or charisma might influence subordinates and make them devoted to that leader. The source of *expert power* is the leader's expertise and knowledge. The leader is the expert on whom subordinates depend for information that they need to do their jobs successfully.

Successful leaders use the different bases of power, and often a combination of them, as appropriate to meet the demands of a situation, such as the nature of the task, the personality characteristics of the subordinates, and the urgency of the issue.[17] Persuasion and developing consensus are often essential, but so is pressing for action. At some point stragglers must be prodded into line.[18] Peter Georgescu, former CEO of Young & Rubicam (an advertising and media subsidiary of the U.K.-based WPP Group), summarized a leader's dilemma brilliantly (and humorously), "I have knee pads and a .45. I get down and beg a lot, but I shoot people too."[19]

Strategy Spotlight 11.4 addresses some of the subtleties of power. Here, the CEO of Siemens successfully brought about organizational change by the effective use of peer pressure.

Emotional Intelligence: A Key Leadership Trait

LO11.3

The crucial role of emotional intelligence (EI) in successful leadership, as well as its potential drawbacks.

In the previous sections, we discussed skills and activities of strategic leadership. The focus was on "what leaders do and how they do it." Now the issue becomes "who leaders *are*," that is, what leadership traits are the most important. Clearly, these two issues are related, because successful leaders possess the valuable traits that enable them to perform effectively in order to create value for their organization.[20]

There has been a vast amount of literature on the successful traits of leaders.[21] These traits include integrity, maturity, energy, judgment, motivation, intelligence, expertise, and so on. For simplicity, these traits may be grouped into three broad sets of capabilities:

emotional intelligence (EI)
an individual's capacity for recognizing his or her own emotions and those of others, including the five components of self-awareness, self-regulation, motivation, empathy, and social skills.

- Purely technical skills (like accounting or operations research).
- Cognitive abilities (like analytical reasoning or quantitative analysis).
- Emotional intelligence (like self-management and managing relationships).

Emotional intelligence (EI) has been defined as the capacity for recognizing one's own emotions and those of others.[22]

11.4 STRATEGY SPOTLIGHT

THE USE OF "SOFT" POWER AT SIEMENS

Until 1999, not only was paying bribes in international markets legally allowed in Germany, but German corporations could also deduct bribes from taxable income. However, once those laws changed, German industrial powerhouse Siemens found it hard to break its bribing habit in its sprawling global operations. Eventually a major scandal forced many top executives out of the firm, including CEO Klaus Kleinfeld. As the successor to Kleinfeld, Peter Löscher became the first outside CEO in the more than 160-year history of Siemens in 2007. As an outsider Löscher found it challenging to establish himself as a strong leader inside the bureaucratic Siemens organization. However, he eventually found a way to successfully transition into his new position.

Naturally, in the early stage of his tenure, he lacked internal connections and the bases of power associated with inside knowledge of people and processes. Yet Siemens faced tremendous challenges, such as a lack of customer orientation, and required a strong leader with the ability to change the status quo. Absent a more formal power base, he turned to more informal means to accomplish his mandate of organizational change and increasing customer orientation.

Once a year, all 700 of Siemens top managers come together for a leadership conference in Berlin. Given the historical lack of customer focus, Löscher used peer pressure as an informal (or soft) form of power in order to challenge and eventually change the lack of customer orientation. As he recalls from his first leadership conference as CEO, "I collected the Outlook calendars for the previous year from all my division CEOs and board members. Then I mapped how much time they had spent with customers and I ranked them. There was a big debate in my inner circle over whether I should use names. Some felt we would embarrass people, but I decided to put the names on the screen anyway."

The results of this exercise were quite remarkable: Löscher spent around 50 percent of his time with customers, more than any other top executive. Clearly, the people who were running the business divisions should rank higher on customer interaction than the CEO. This confirmed the lack of customer orientation in the organization. This ranking has been repeated at every Siemens leadership conference since Löscher took office. Over time, customer orientation has improved because nobody wants to fall short on this metric and endure potential ridicule. Löscher's leadership style and use of soft power during his early time in office seemed to have paid off, as the Siemens board extended his contract as CEO of the German industry icon a year early.

Source: Löscher, P. 2012. The CEO of Siemens on using a scandal to drive change. *Harvard Business Review*, 90(11): 42; and Anonymous. 2011. Löscher soll vorstandschef bleiben. www.manager-magazin.de, July 25: np.

Research suggests that effective leaders at all levels of organizations have high levels of EI.[23] After controlling for cognitive abilities and manager personality attributes, EI leads to stronger job performance across a wide range of professions, with stronger effects for professions that require a great deal of human interaction. Interestingly, there is only partial support for the catchy phrase "IQ gets you hired, but EQ (emotional quotient) gets you promoted." Evidence indicates that high levels of EI increase the likelihood of being promoted up to the middle-manager level. However, managers at high levels of the corporate hierarchy tend to evidence lower levels of EI, with the CEOs having, on average, lower levels of EI than managers at any other level. This is troubling given that firms led by CEOs high in EI outperform firms led by CEOs lower in EI. High-EI CEOs excel in managing relationships, influencing people, and forging alliances both inside and outside the firm. These CEOs can also benefit the firm since their ability to connect with and relate to outside stakeholders helps build the firm's reputation. Thus, firms would benefit from considering more than cognitive ability and easily measured performance metrics when choosing corporate leaders. Including EI as an element to consider would help firms choose superior corporate leaders.

Exhibit 11.3 identifies the five components of EI: self-awareness, self-regulation, motivation, empathy, and social skill.

Self-Awareness

Self-awareness is the first component of EI and brings to mind that Delphic oracle who gave the advice "Know thyself" thousands of years ago. Self-awareness involves a person having a deep understanding of his or her emotions, strengths, weaknesses, and drives.

EXHIBIT 11.3 The Five Components of Emotional Intelligence at Work

- **Self-awareness**: The ability to know your own emotions, drives, values, and goals as well as recognize their impact on others
- **Self-regulation**: The ability to control or redirect disruptive emotions and impulses and adapt to changing circumstances
- **Motivation**: Being driven to achieve for the sake of achievement, not simply for money or status
- **Empathy**: The ability to see and consider other people's feelings especially when making decisions
- **Social Skill**: The ability to build and manage relationships to move people in the desired direction

People with strong self-awareness are neither overly critical nor unrealistically optimistic. Instead, they are honest with themselves and others.

People generally admire and respect candor. Leaders are constantly required to make judgment calls that require a candid assessment of capabilities—their own and those of others. People who assess themselves honestly (i.e., self-aware people) are well suited to do the same for the organizations they run.[24]

Self-Regulation

Biological impulses drive our emotions. Although we cannot do away with them, we can strive to manage them. Self-regulation, which is akin to an ongoing inner conversation, frees us from being prisoners of our feelings.[25] People engaged in such conversation feel bad moods and emotional impulses just as everyone else does. However, they find ways to control them and even channel them in useful ways.

Self-regulated people are able to create an environment of trust and fairness where political behavior and infighting are sharply reduced and productivity tends to be high. People who have mastered their emotions are better able to bring about and implement change in an organization. When a new initiative is announced, they are less likely to panic; they are able to suspend judgment, seek out information, and listen to executives explain the new program.

Motivation

Successful executives are driven to achieve beyond expectations—their own and everyone else's. Although many people are driven by external factors, such as money and prestige, those with leadership potential are driven by a deeply embedded desire to achieve for the sake of achievement.

Motivated people show a passion for the work itself, such as seeking out creative challenges, a love of learning, and taking pride in a job well done. They also have a high level of energy to do things better as well as a restlessness with the status quo. They are eager to explore new approaches to their work.

Empathy

Empathy is probably the most easily recognized component of EI. Empathy means thoughtfully considering an employee's feelings, along with other factors, in the process of making intelligent decisions. Empathy is particularly important in today's business environment for at least three reasons: the increasing use of teams, the rapid pace of globalization, and the growing need to retain talent.[26]

When leading a team, a manager is often charged with arriving at a consensus—often in the face of a high level of emotions. Empathy enables a manager to sense and understand the viewpoints of everyone around the table.

Globalization typically involves cross-cultural dialogue that can easily lead to miscues. Empathetic people are attuned to the subtleties of body language; they can hear the message beneath the words being spoken. They have a deep understanding of the existence and importance of cultural and ethnic differences.

Empathy also plays a key role in retaining talent. Human capital is particularly important to a firm in the knowledge economy when it comes to creating advantages that are sustainable. Leaders need empathy to develop and keep top talent, because when high performers leave, they take their tacit knowledge with them.

Social Skill

While the first three components of EI are all self-management skills, the last two—empathy and social skill—concern a person's ability to manage relationships with others. Social skill may be viewed as friendliness with a purpose: moving people in the direction you desire, whether that's agreement on a new marketing strategy or enthusiasm about a new product.

Socially skilled people tend to have a wide circle of acquaintances as well as a knack for finding common ground and building rapport. They recognize that nothing gets done alone, and they have a network in place when the time for action comes.

Social skill can be viewed as the culmination of the other dimensions of EI. People will be effective at managing relationships when they can understand and control their own emotions and empathize with others' feelings. Motivation also contributes to social skill. People who are driven to achieve tend to be optimistic, even when confronted with setbacks. And when people are upbeat, their "glow" is cast upon conversations and other social encounters. They are popular, and for good reason.

A key to developing social skill is to become a good listener—a skill that many executives find to be quite challenging. Teresa Taylor, chief operating officer at Qwest Communications, says:[27]

> Over the years, something I really try to focus on is truly listening. When I say that, I mean sometimes people act like they're listening but they're really formulating their own thoughts in their heads. I'm trying to put myself into someone else's shoes, trying to figure out what's motivating them, and why they are in the spot they are in.

Emotional Intelligence: Some Potential Drawbacks and Cautionary Notes

Many great leaders have great reserves of empathy, interpersonal astuteness, awareness of their own feelings, and an awareness of their impact on others.[28] More importantly, they know how to apply these capabilities judiciously as best benefits the situation. Having some minimum level of EI will help a person be effective as a leader as long as it is channeled appropriately. However, if a person has a high level of these capabilities it may become "too much of a good thing" if he or she is allowed to drive inappropriate behaviors. Some additional potential drawbacks of EI can be gleaned by considering the flip side of its benefits.

Effective Leaders Have Empathy for Others   However, they also must be able to make the "tough decisions." Leaders must be able to appeal to logic and reason and acknowledge others' feelings so that people feel the decisions are correct. However, it is easy to overidentify with others or confuse empathy with sympathy. This can make it more difficult to make the tough decisions.

Effective Leaders Are Astute Judges of People   A danger is that leaders may become judgmental and overly critical about the shortcomings they perceive in others. They are likely to dismiss other people's insights, making them feel undervalued.

Effective Leaders Are Passionate about What They Do, and They Show It   This doesn't mean that they are always cheerleaders. Rather, they may express their passion as persistence in pursuing an objective or a relentless focus on a valued principle. However, there is a fine line between being excited about something and letting your passion close your mind to other possibilities or cause you to ignore realities that others may see.

Effective Leaders Create Personal Connections with Their People   Most effective leaders take time to engage employees individually and in groups, listening to their ideas, suggestions, and concerns and responding in ways that make people feel that their ideas are respected and appreciated. However, if the leader makes too many unannounced visits, it may create a culture of fear and micromanagement. Clearly, striking a correct balance is essential.

From a moral standpoint, emotional leadership is neither good nor bad. On the one hand, emotional leaders can be altruistic, focused on the general welfare of the company and its employees, and highly principled. On the other hand, they can be manipulative, selfish, and dishonest. For example, if a person is using leadership solely to gain power, that is not leadership at all.[29] Rather, that person is using his or her EI to grasp what people want and pander to those desires in order to gain authority and influence. After all, easy answers sell.

Creating a Learning Organization

LO11.4

The importance of creating a learning organization.

To enhance the long-term viability of organizations, leaders also need to build a learning organization. Such an organization is capable of adapting to change, fostering creativity, and succeeding in highly competitive markets.

Successful, innovative organizations recognize the importance of having everyone involved in the process of actively learning and adapting. As noted by today's leading expert on learning organizations, MIT's Peter Senge, the days when Henry Ford, Alfred Sloan, and Tom Watson *"learned for the organization"* are gone:

> In an increasingly dynamic, interdependent, and unpredictable world, it is simply no longer possible for anyone to "figure it all out at the top." The old model, "the top thinks and the local acts," must now give way to integrating thinking and acting at all levels. While the challenge is great, so is the potential payoff. "The person who figures out how to harness the collective genius of the people in his or her organization," according to former Citibank CEO Walter Wriston, "is going to blow the competition away."[30]

Learning and change typically involve the ongoing questioning of an organization's status quo or method of procedure. This means that all individuals throughout the organization must be reflective.[31] Many organizations get so caught up in carrying out their day-to-day work that they rarely, if ever, stop to think objectively about themselves and their businesses. They often fail to ask the probing questions that might lead them to call into question their basic assumptions, to refresh their strategies, or to reengineer their work

> **EXHIBIT 11.4** Key Elements of a Learning Organization
>
> These are the six key elements of a learning organization. Each of these items should be viewed as *necessary, but not sufficient*. That is, successful learning organizations need all six elements.
>
> 1. Inspiring and motivating people with a mission or purpose.
> 2. Developing leaders.
> 3. Empowering employees at all levels.
> 4. Accumulating and sharing internal knowledge.
> 5. Gathering and integrating external information.
> 6. Challenging the status quo and enabling creativity.

processes. According to Michael Hammer and Steven Stanton, the pioneer consultants who touched off the reengineering movement:

> Reflection entails awareness of self, of competitors, of customers. It means thinking without preconception. It means questioning cherished assumptions and replacing them with new approaches. It is the only way in which a winning company can maintain its leadership position, by which a company with great assets can ensure that they continue to be well deployed.[32]

To adapt to change, foster creativity, and remain competitive, leaders must build learning organizations. Exhibit 11.4 lists the six key elements of a learning organization.

Inspiring and Motivating People with a Mission or Purpose

Successful **learning organizations** create a proactive, creative approach to the unknown, actively solicit the involvement of employees at all levels, and enable all employees to use their intelligence and apply their imagination. Higher-level skills are required of everyone, not just those at the top.[33] A learning environment involves organizationwide commitment to change, an action orientation, and applicable tools and methods.[34] It must be viewed by everyone as a guiding philosophy and not simply as another change program.

A critical requirement of all learning organizations is that everyone feels and supports a compelling purpose. In the words of William O'Brien, CEO of Hanover Insurance, "Before there can be meaningful participation, people must share certain values and pictures about where we are trying to go. We discovered that people have a real need to feel that they're part of an enabling mission."[35] Such a perspective is consistent with an intensive study by Kouzes and Posner, authors of *The Leadership Challenge*.[36] They analyzed data from nearly 1 million respondents who were leaders at various levels in many organizations throughout the world. A major finding was that what leaders struggle with most is communicating an image of the future that draws others in—that is, it speaks to what others see and feel. To illustrate:

> Buddy Blanton, a principal program manager at Rockwell Collins, learned this lesson firsthand. He asked his team for feedback on his leadership, and the vast majority of it was positive. However, he got some strong advice from his team about how he could be more effective in inspiring a shared vision. "You would benefit by helping us, as a team, to understand how you go to your vision. We want to walk with you while you create the goals and vision, so we all get to the end of the vision together."[37]

Inspiring and motivating people with a mission or purpose is a necessary but not sufficient condition for developing an organization that can learn and adapt to a rapidly changing, complex, and interconnected environment.

Developing Leaders

Leadership development programs aid in the building of a learning organization in two different ways. First, programs help the participants learn new skills that help them be more capable in their current roles and more able to take on additional responsibility.

learning organizations
organizations that create a proactive, creative approach to the unknown; characterized by (1) inspiring and motivating people with a mission and purpose, (2) developing leaders, (3) empowering employees at all levels, (4) accumulating and sharing internal knowledge, (5) gathering and integrating external information, and (6) challenging the status quo and enabling creativity.

In short, this helps enhance individual learning and, thus, increases the human capital of the firm. Second, these development programs can also train employees to be more effective at learning over time by giving them the skills to incorporate new information and better learn from their experiences.

Not all leadership development programs are equally effective. Research suggests that successful development programs share four common traits.[38] First, the programs are designed to fit the firm's overall strategy. For example, if a firm emphasizes organic growth, its leadership development program should emphasize building the skills to see opportunities in the firm's industry and related markets and developing internal talent. This will channel the learning capabilities of its leaders. Second, effective leadership development programs combine real-world experiences with classroom learning to build the desired skills. In line with this concept, one major engineering and construction firm emphasized developing skills in interacting with customers to build additional business. Participants were tasked to identify new business opportunities in their home units. One participant committed his team to develop a new order with a customer that spanned more than one of the group's business lines. Third, leader development programs need to have hard conversations to identify and overcome organizational biases that keep the firm from learning and being more flexible. One European industrial firm included frameworks for driving capital allocation decisions lower in the organization, but the entrenched culture of the firm left managers reluctant to relinquish control. Once the trainers took this issue head-on, enlisting open-minded managers to take the leap first and report back to the team and also emphasizing the learning opportunity for lower-level managers, participants more widely implemented the decentralization program. Fourth, top managers and trainers need to assess the impact of the training by following up with participants several months after the training to assess how effectively they have implemented the training, overcome the barriers to marking it work, and learned from the process.

Empowering Employees at All Levels

"The great leader is a great servant," asserted Ken Melrose, former CEO and chairman of Toro Company and author of *Making the Grass Greener on Your Side*.[39] A manager's role becomes one of creating an environment where employees can achieve their potential as they help move the organization toward its goals. Instead of viewing themselves as resource controllers and power brokers, leaders must envision themselves as flexible resources willing to assume numerous roles as coaches, information providers, teachers, decision makers, facilitators, supporters, or listeners, depending on the needs of their employees.[40]

The central key to empowerment is effective leadership. Empowerment can't occur in a leadership vacuum. According to Melrose, "You best lead by serving the needs of your people. You don't do their jobs for them; you enable them to learn and progress on the job."

Leading-edge organizations recognize the need for trust, cultural control, and expertise at all levels instead of the extensive and cumbersome rules and regulations inherent in hierarchical control.[41] Some commentators have argued that too often organizations fall prey to the "heroes-and-drones syndrome," wherein the value of those in powerful positions is exalted and the value of those who fail to achieve top rank is diminished. Such an attitude is implicit in phrases such as "Lead, follow, or get out of the way" or, even less appealing, "Unless you're the lead horse, the view never changes." Few will ever reach the top hierarchical positions in organizations, but in the information economy, the strongest organizations are those that effectively use the talents of all the players on the team.

Empowering individuals by soliciting their input helps an organization to enjoy better employee morale. It also helps create a culture in which middle- and lower-level employees feel that their ideas and initiatives will be valued and enhance firm performance, as explained in Strategy Spotlight 11.5.

STRATEGY SPOTLIGHT 11.5 — CROWDSOURCING

USING THE WISDOM OF YOUR EMPLOYEES TO MAKE BETTER DECISIONS

CEOs are often surrounded by an aura of unfailing business acumen. Yet few CEOs live up to these high expectations over the long run, suggesting that even the most able CEOs have limited abilities. Ironically, shattering the image of the almighty CEO by realizing and identifying cognitive limitations may help us to improve organizational decision making. Consider WBG Construction, a small home builder west of Boston. When important decisions need to be made, Greg Burrill, the president, asks all employees with relevant knowledge or a stake in the outcome for their thoughts. This collaborative approach recently led to a decision that not only sold a house but also inspired a new floor plan that appealed to a whole new segment of buyers.

As another example, EMC, the data storage giant, enables participation by a social media platform called EMC One. When the recession hit and cost cutting became imperative, EMC used this social media platform to do something most companies would leave to top management: decide where to cut costs. Several thousand employees participated and identified cost savings that were largely unknown to top management. The resulting cuts were less painful because employees had a say in the cost reduction. Empowering employees in this manner utilizes the day-to-day insights of lower-level employees and benefits both the firm and the workforce.

In some other cases, bad decisions not only cost money but also can lead to heartbreaking accidents. NASA can look back at some 50 years of pioneering success, but also tragic accidents caused by bad judgment. In February 2009, the flight of space shuttle *Discovery* was overshadowed by uncertainties about whether an issue with the fuel system should delay the launch. Prior space shuttle launch decisions were made by a small group of individuals supported by a culture of complacency born of many prior successes and communication breakdowns. But NASA finally implemented a much-needed change of culture that now values input from all group members. As Mike Ryschkewitsch, NASA's chief engineer, observed, "One of the things that NASA strongly emphasizes now is that any individual who works here, if they see something that doesn't look right, they have a responsibility to raise it, and they can raise it." By utilizing the insights of individuals in their organizations, leaders hope to improve organizational decision making and secure the long-term success of their businesses.

Sources: Davenport, T. H. 2012. The wisdom of your in-house crowd. *Harvard Business Review*, 90(10): 40; and Davenport, T. H., & Manville, B. 2012. *Judgment calls: Twelve stories of big decisions and the teams that got them right:* 25–38. Boston: Harvard Business Review Press.

Accumulating and Sharing Internal Knowledge

Effective organizations must also *redistribute information, knowledge* (skills to act on the information), and *rewards*.[42] A company might give frontline employees the power to act as "customer advocates," doing whatever is necessary to satisfy customers. The company needs to disseminate information by sharing customer expectations and feedback as well as financial information. The employees must know about the goals of the business as well as how key value-creating activities in the organization are related to each other. Finally, organizations should allocate rewards on how effectively employees use information, knowledge, and power to improve customer service quality and the company's overall performance.[43]

Let's take a look at Whole Foods Market, Inc., the largest natural-foods grocer in the United States.[44] An important benefit of the sharing of internal information at Whole Foods becomes the active process of *internal benchmarking.* Competition is intense at Whole Foods. Teams compete against their own goals for sales, growth, and productivity; they compete against different teams in their stores; and they compete against similar teams at different stores and regions. There is an elaborate system of peer reviews through which teams benchmark each other. The "Store Tour" is the most intense. On a periodic schedule, each Whole Foods store is toured by a group of as many as 40 visitors from another region. Lateral learning—discovering what your colleagues are doing right and carrying those practices into your organization—has become a driving force at Whole Foods.

In addition to enhancing the sharing of company information both up and down as well as across the organization, leaders also have to develop means to tap into some of the more informal sources of internal information. In a survey of presidents, CEOs, board members, and top executives in a variety of nonprofit organizations, respondents were asked what differentiated the successful candidates for promotion. The consensus: The executive was seen as a person who listens. According to Peter Meyer, the author of the study, "The value of listening is clear: You cannot succeed in running a company if you do not hear what your people, customers, and suppliers are telling you. . . . Listening and understanding well are key to making good decisions."[45]

Gathering and Integrating External Information

Recognizing opportunities, as well as threats, in the external environment is vital to a firm's success. As organizations *and* environments become more complex and evolve rapidly, it is far more critical for employees and managers to become more aware of environmental trends and events—both general and industry-specific—and more knowledgeable about their firm's competitors and customers. Next, we will discuss some ideas on how to do it.

First, company employees at all levels can use a variety of sources to acquire external information. Much can be gleaned by reading trade and professional journals, books, and popular business magazines. Other venues for gathering external information include membership in professional or trade organizations, attendance at meetings and conventions, and networking among colleagues inside and outside your industry. Online social networks, such as LinkedIn, can also provide access to contacts to learn about changes in the external environment. To gain up-to-date information on particular rivals, firms can monitor the direct communications from rival firms and their executives, such as press releases and quarterly-earnings calls. These communications can provide insight on the rival's actions and intended actions. It may also be valuable to follow rival-firm employees' online postings, on Twitter and other platforms, to gain insights on rivals' investments and actions.

Second, **benchmarking** *can be a useful means of employing external information.* Here managers seek out the best examples of a particular practice as part of an ongoing effort to improve the corresponding practice in their own organization.[46] There are two primary types of benchmarking. **Competitive benchmarking** restricts the search for best practices to competitors, while **functional benchmarking** endeavors to determine best practices regardless of industry. Industry-specific standards (e.g., response times required to repair power outages in the electric utility industry) are typically best handled through competitive benchmarking, whereas more generic processes (e.g., answering 1-800 calls) lend themselves to functional benchmarking because the function is essentially the same in any industry.

Ford Motor Company works with its suppliers on benchmarking its competitors' products during product redesigns. At the launch of the redesign, Ford and its suppliers identify a few key components they want to focus on improving. They then do a "tear down" of Ford's components as well as matching components from three or four rivals. The idea is to get early input from suppliers so that Ford can design components that are best in class—lighter, cheaper, and more reliable.[47]

Third, focus directly on customers for information. For example, William McKnight, head of 3M's Chicago sales office, required that salesmen of abrasives products talk directly to the workers in the shop to find out what they needed, instead of calling on only front-office executives.[48] This was very innovative at the time—1909! But it illustrates the need to get to the end user of a product or service. (McKnight went on to become 3M's president from 1929 to 1949 and chairman from 1949 to 1969.)

Challenging the Status Quo and Enabling Creativity

Earlier in this chapter we discussed some of the barriers that leaders face when trying to bring about change in an organization: vested interests in the status quo, systemic barriers, behavioral barriers, political barriers, and personal time constraints. For a firm to become a learning organization, it must overcome such barriers in order to foster creativity and

---

benchmarking
managers seeking out best examples of a particular practice as part of an ongoing effort to improve the corresponding practice in their own organization.

competitive benchmarking
benchmarking in which the examples are drawn from competitors in the industry.

functional benchmarking
benchmarking in which the examples are drawn from any organization, even those outside the industry.

enable it to permeate the firm. This becomes quite a challenge if the firm is entrenched in a status quo mentality.

Perhaps the best way to challenge the status quo is for the leader to forcefully create a sense of urgency. For example, when Tom Kasten was vice president of Levi Strauss, he had a direct approach to initiating change:

> You create a compelling picture of the risks of *not* changing. We let our people hear directly from customers. We videotaped interviews with customers and played excerpts. One big customer said, "We trust many of your competitors implicitly. We sample their deliveries. We open *all* Levi's deliveries." Another said, "Your lead times are the worst. If you weren't Levi's, you'd be gone." It was powerful. I wish we had done more of it.[49]

Such initiative, if sincere and credible, establishes a shared mission and the need for major transformations. It can channel energies to bring about both change and creative endeavors.

Establishing a "culture of dissent" can be another effective means of questioning the status quo and serving as a spur toward creativity. Here norms are established whereby dissenters can openly question a superior's perspective without fear of retaliation or retribution.

Closely related to the culture of dissent is the fostering of a culture that encourages risk taking. "If you're not making mistakes, you're not taking risks, and that means you're not going anywhere," claimed John Holt, coauthor of *Celebrate Your Mistakes*.[50] "The key is to make errors faster than the competition, so you have more chances to learn and win."

Companies that cultivate cultures of experimentation and curiosity make sure that *failure* is not, in essence, an obscene word. They encourage mistakes as a key part of their competitive advantage. It has been said that innovation has a great paradox: Success—that is, true breakthroughs—usually come through failure. Below are some approaches to encourage risk taking and learning from mistakes in an organization:[51]

- ***Formalize forums for failure.*** To keep failures and the important lessons that they offer from getting swept under the rug, carve out time for reflection. GE formalized the sharing of lessons from failure by bringing together managers whose "Imagination Breakthrough" efforts were put on the shelf.
- ***Move the goalposts.*** Innovation requires flexibility in meeting goals, since early predictions are often little more than educated guesses. Intuit's Scott Cook even goes so far as to suggest that teams developing new products ignore forecasts in the early days. "For every one of our failures, we had spreadsheets that looked awesome," he claims.
- ***Bring in outsiders.*** Outsiders can help neutralize the emotions and biases that prop up a flop. Customers can be the most valuable. After its DNA chip failed, Corning brought pharmaceutical companies in early to test its new drug-discovery technology, Epic.
- ***Prove yourself wrong, not right.*** Development teams tend to look for supporting, rather than countervailing, evidence. "You have to reframe what you're seeking in the early days," says Innosight's Scott Anthony. "You're not really seeking proof that you have the right answer. It's more about testing to prove yourself wrong."

Finally, failure can play an important and positive role in one's professional development. John Donahue, eBay's CEO, draws on the sport of baseball in recalling the insight (and inspiration!) one of his former bosses shared with him:[52]

> The best hitters in Major League Baseball, world class, they can strike out six times out of ten and still be the greatest hitters of all time. That's my philosophy—the key is to get up in that batter's box and take a swing. And all you have to do is hit one single, a couple of doubles, and an occasional home run out of every ten at-bats, and you're going to be the best hitter or the best business leader around. You can't play in the major leagues without having a lot of failures.

Creating an Ethical Organization

LO11.5

The leader's role in establishing an ethical organization.

ethics
a system of right and wrong that assists individuals in deciding when an act is moral or immoral and/or socially desirable or not.

Ethics may be defined as a system of right and wrong.[53] Ethics assists individuals in deciding when an act is moral or immoral, socially desirable or not. The sources for an individual's ethics include religious beliefs, national and ethnic heritage, family practices, community standards, educational experiences, and friends and neighbors. Business ethics is the application of ethical standards to commercial enterprise.

Individual Ethics versus Organizational Ethics

Many leaders think of ethics as a question of personal scruples, a confidential matter between employees and their consciences. Such leaders are quick to describe any wrongdoing as an isolated incident, the work of a rogue employee. They assume the company should not bear any responsibility for individual misdeeds. In their view, ethics has nothing to do with leadership.

organizational ethics
the values, attitudes, and behavioral patterns that define an organization's operating culture and that determine what an organization holds as acceptable behavior.

Ethics has everything to do with leadership. Seldom does the character flaw of a lone actor completely explain corporate misconduct. Instead, unethical business practices typically involve the tacit, if not explicit, cooperation of others and reflect the values, attitudes, and behavior patterns that define an organization's operating culture. Ethics is as much an organizational as a personal issue. Leaders who fail to provide proper leadership to institute proper systems and controls that facilitate ethical conduct share responsibility with those who conceive, execute, and knowingly benefit from corporate misdeeds.[54]

ethical orientation
the practices that firms use to promote an ethical business culture, including ethical role models, corporate credos and codes of conduct, ethically based reward and evaluation systems, and consistently enforced ethical policies and procedures.

The **ethical orientation** of a leader is a key factor in promoting ethical behavior. Ethical leaders must take personal, ethical responsibility for their actions and decision making. Leaders who exhibit high ethical standards become role models for others and raise an organization's overall level of ethical behavior. Ethical behavior must start with the leader before the employees can be expected to perform accordingly.

There has been a growing interest in corporate ethical performance. Some reasons for this trend may be the increasing lack of confidence regarding corporate activities, the growing emphasis on quality-of-life issues, and a spate of recent corporate scandals. Without a strong ethical culture, the chance of ethical crises occurring is enhanced. Ethical crises can be very expensive—both in terms of financial costs and in the erosion of human capital and overall firm reputation. Merely adhering to the minimum regulatory standards may not be enough to remain competitive in a world that is becoming more socially conscious. Strategy Spotlight 11.6 highlights potential ethical problems at utility companies that are trying to capitalize on consumers' desire to participate in efforts to curb global warming.

The past two decades have been characterized by numerous examples of unethical and illegal behavior by many top-level corporate executives. These include executives of firms such as Enron, Tyco, WorldCom, Adelphia, and HealthSouth, who were all forced to resign and are facing (or have been convicted of) criminal charges. Perhaps the most glaring example is Bernie Madoff, whose Ponzi scheme, which unraveled in 2008, defrauded investors of $50 billion in assets they had set aside for retirement and charitable donations.

The ethical organization is characterized by a conception of ethical values and integrity as a driving force of the enterprise.[55] Ethical values shape the search for opportunities, the design of organizational systems, and the decision-making process used by individuals and groups. They provide a common frame of reference that serves as a unifying force across different functions, lines of business, and employee groups. Organizational ethics helps to define what a company is and what it stands for.

There are many potential benefits of an ethical organization, but they are often indirect. Research has found somewhat inconsistent results concerning the overall relationship between ethical performance and measures of financial performance.[56] However, positive relationships have generally been found between ethical performance and strong

11.6 STRATEGY SPOTLIGHT
ENVIRONMENTAL SUSTAINABILITY · **ETHICS**

GREEN ENERGY: REAL OR JUST A MARKETING PLOY?

Many consumers want to "go green" and are looking for opportunities to do so. Utility companies that provide heat and electricity are one of the most obvious places to turn, because they often use fossil fuels that could be saved through energy conservation or replaced by using alternative energy sources. In fact, some consumers are willing to pay a premium to contribute to environmental sustainability efforts if paying a little more will help curb global warming. Knowing this, many power companies in the United States have developed alternative energy programs and appealed to customers to help pay for them.

Unfortunately, many of the power companies that are offering eco-friendly options are falling short on delivering on them. Some utilities have simply gotten off to a slow start or found it difficult to profitably offer alternative power. Others, however, are suspected of committing a new type of fraud—"greenwashing." This refers to companies that make unsubstantiated claims about how environmentally friendly their products or services really are. In the case of many power companies, their claims of "green power" are empty promises. Instead of actually generating additional renewable energy, most of the premiums are going for marketing costs.

"They are preying on people's goodwill," says Stephen Smith, executive director of the Southern Alliance for Clean Energy, an advocacy group in Knoxville, Tennessee.

Consider what two power companies offered and how the money was actually spent:

- Duke Power of Indiana created a program called "GoGreen Power." Customers were told that they could pay a green-energy premium and a specific amount of electricity would be obtained from renewable sources. What actually happened? Less than 18 percent of voluntary customer contributions in a recent year went to renewable energy development.

- Alliant Energy of Iowa established a program dubbed "Second Nature." Customers were told that they would "support the growth of earth-friendly 'green power' created by wind and biomass." What actually happened? More than 56 percent of expenditures went to marketing and administrative costs, not green-energy development.

Sources: Elgin, B. & Holden, D. 2008. Green power: Buyers beware. *BusinessWeek*, September 29: 68–70; www.cleanenergy.org; duke-energy.com; and alliantenergy.com.

---

organizational culture, increased employee efforts, lower turnover, higher organizational commitment, and enhanced social responsibility.

The advantages of a strong ethical orientation can have a positive effect on employee commitment and motivation to excel. This is particularly important in today's knowledge-intensive organizations, where human capital is critical in creating value and competitive advantages. Positive, constructive relationships among individuals (i.e., social capital) are vital in leveraging human capital and other resources in an organization. Drawing on the concept of stakeholder management, an ethically sound organization can also strengthen its bonds among its suppliers, customers, and governmental agencies.

Integrity-Based versus Compliance-Based Approaches to Organizational Ethics

>**LO11.6**
>The difference between integrity-based and compliance-based approaches to organizational ethics.

Before discussing the key elements of an ethical organization, one must understand the links between organizational integrity and the personal integrity of an organization's members.[57] There cannot be high-integrity organizations without high-integrity individuals. However, individual integrity is rarely self-sustaining. Even good people can lose their bearings when faced with pressures, temptations, and heightened performance expectations in the absence of organizational support systems and ethical boundaries. Organizational integrity rests on a concept of purpose, responsibility, and ideals for an organization as a whole. An important responsibility of leadership is to create this ethical framework and develop the organizational capabilities to make it operational.[58]

Lynn Paine, an ethics scholar at Harvard, identifies two approaches: the compliance-based approach and the integrity-based approach. (See Exhibit 11.5 for a comparison of

EXHIBIT 11.5 Approaches to Ethics Management

Characteristics	Approach	Actions
Ethos	Compliance-based	Conformity with externally imposed standards
	Integrity-based	Self-governance according to chosen standards
Objective	Compliance-based	Prevent criminal misconduct
	Integrity-based	Enable responsible conduct
Leadership	Compliance-based	Driven by legal office
	Integrity-based	Driven by management, with input from functional staff
Methods	Compliance-based	Reduced discretion, training, controls, audits, and penalties
	Integrity-based	Education, leadership, accountability, decision processes, auditing, and penalties
Behavioral Assumptions	Compliance-based	Individualistic, self-interested actors
	Integrity-based	Social actors, guided by a combination of self-interest, ideals, values, and social expectations

compliance-based ethics programs programs for building ethical organizations that have the goal of preventing, detecting, and punishing legal violations.

integrity-based ethics programs programs for building ethical organizations that combine a concern for law with an emphasis on managerial responsibility for ethical behavior, including (1) enabling ethical conduct; (2) examining the organization's and members' core guiding values, thoughts, and actions; and (3) defining the responsibilities and aspirations that constitute an organization's ethical compass.

compliance-based and integrity-based strategies.) Faced with the prospect of litigation, several organizations reactively implement **compliance-based ethics programs.** Such programs are typically designed by a corporate counsel with the goal of preventing, detecting, and punishing legal violations. But being ethical is much more than being legal, and an integrity-based approach addresses the issue of ethics in a more comprehensive manner.

An **integrity-based ethics program** combines a concern for law with an emphasis on managerial responsibility for ethical behavior. It is broader, deeper, and more demanding than a legal compliance initiative. It is broader in that it seeks to enable responsible conduct. It is deeper in that it cuts to the ethos and operating systems of an organization and its members—their core guiding values, thoughts, and actions. It is more demanding because it requires an active effort to define the responsibilities that constitute an organization's ethical compass. Most importantly, organizational ethics is seen as the responsibility of management.

A corporate counsel may play a role in designing and implementing integrity strategies, but it is managers at all levels and across all functions who are involved in the process. Once integrated into the day-to-day operations, such strategies can prevent damaging ethical lapses, while tapping into powerful human impulses for moral thought and action. Ethics becomes the governing ethos of an organization and not burdensome constraints. Here is an example of an organization that goes beyond mere compliance to laws in building an ethical organization:

> In teaching ethics to its employees, Texas Instruments, the $12 billion chip and electronics manufacturer, asks them to run an issue through the following steps: Is it legal? Is it consistent with the company's stated values? Will the employee feel bad doing it? What will the public think if the action is reported in the press? Does the employee think it is wrong? If the employees are not sure of the ethicality of the issue, they are encouraged to ask someone until they are clear about it. In the process, employees can approach high-level personnel and even the company's lawyers. At TI, the question of ethics goes much beyond merely being legal. It is no surprise that this company is a benchmark for corporate ethics and has been a recipient of three ethics awards: the David C. Lincoln Award for Ethics and Excellence in Business, American Business Ethics Award, and Bentley College Center for Business Ethics Award.[59]

Compliance-based approaches are externally motivated—that is, based on the fear of punishment for doing something unlawful. On the other hand, integrity-based approaches are driven by a personal and organizational commitment to ethical behavior.

A firm must have several key elements to become a highly ethical organization:

- Role models.
- Corporate credos and codes of conduct.
- Reward and evaluation systems.
- Policies and procedures.

These elements are highly interrelated. Reward structures and policies will be useless if leaders are not sound role models. That is, leaders who implicitly say, "Do as I say, not as I do," will quickly have their credibility eroded and such actions will sabotage other elements that are essential to building an ethical organization.

>LO11.7
>
>Several key elements that organizations must have to become ethical organizations.

Role Models

For good or for bad, leaders are role models in their organizations. Perhaps few executives can share an experience that better illustrates this than Linda Hudson, former president of General Dynamics.[60] Right after she was promoted to become the firm's first female president, she went to Nordstrom and bought some new suits to wear to work. A lady at the store showed her how to tie a scarf in a very unique way. The day after she wore it to work, guess what: No fewer than a dozen women in the organization were wearing scarves tied exactly the same way! She reflects:

> And that's when I realized that life was never going to be the way it had been before, that people were watching everything I did. And it wasn't just going to be about how I dressed. It was about my behavior, the example I set, the tone I set, the way I carried myself, and how confident I was—all those kinds of things. . . . As the leader, people are looking at you in a way you could not have imagined in other roles.

Clearly, leaders must "walk the talk"; they must be consistent in their words and deeds. The values as well as the character of leaders become transparent to an organization's employees through their behaviors. When leaders do not believe in the ethical standards that they are trying to inspire, they will not be effective as good role models. Being an effective leader often includes taking responsibility for ethical lapses within the organization—even though the executives themselves are not directly involved. Consider the perspective of Dennis Bakke, former CEO of AES, a $16 billion global electricity company based in Arlington, Virginia:

> There was a major breach (in 1992) of the AES values. Nine members of the water treatment team in Oklahoma lied to the EPA about water quality at the plant. There was no environmental damage, but they lied about the test results. A new, young chemist at the plant discovered it, told a team leader, and we then were notified. Now, you could argue that the people who lied were responsible and were accountable, but the senior management team also took responsibility by taking pay cuts. My reduction was about 30 percent.[61]

Such action enhances the loyalty and commitment of employees throughout the organization. Many would believe that it would have been much easier (and personally less expensive!) for Bakke and his management team to merely take strong punitive action against the nine individuals who were acting contrary to the behavior expected in AES's ethical culture. However, by sharing responsibility for the misdeeds, the top executives—through their highly visible action—made it clear that responsibility and penalties for ethical lapses go well beyond the "guilty" parties. Such courageous behavior by leaders helps to strengthen an organization's ethical environment.

corporate credo
a statement of the beliefs typically held by managers in a corporation.

Corporate Credos and Codes of Conduct

Corporate credos and codes of conduct are mechanisms that provide statements of norms and beliefs as well as guidelines for decision making. They provide employees with a clear understanding of the organization's policies and ethical position. Such guidelines also provide the basis for employees to refuse to commit unethical acts and help to make them aware of issues before they are faced with the situation. For such codes to be truly effective, organization members must be aware of them and what behavioral guidelines they contain.[62]

Large corporations are not the only ones to develop and use codes of conduct. Consider the example of Wetherill Associates (WAI), a small, privately held supplier of electrical parts to the automotive market:

> Rather than a conventional code of conduct, WAI has a Quality Assurance Manual—a combination of philosophy text, conduct guide, technical manual, and company profile—that describes the company's commitment to honesty, ethical action, and integrity. WAI doesn't have a corporate ethics officer, because the company's corporate ethics officer is Marie Bothe, WAI's CEO. She sees her main function as keeping the 350-employee company on the path of ethical behavior and looking for opportunities to help the community. She delegates the "technical" aspects of the business—marketing, finance, personnel, and operations—to other members of the organization.[63]

Reward and Evaluation Systems

It is entirely possible for a highly ethical leader to preside over an organization that commits several unethical acts. How? A flaw in the organization's reward structure may inadvertently cause individuals to act in an inappropriate manner if rewards are seen as being distributed on the basis of outcomes rather than the means by which goals and objectives are achieved.[64]

Generally speaking, unethical (or illegal) behaviors are also more likely to take place when competition is intense. Some researchers have called this the "dark side of competition." Consider a couple of examples:[65]

- Competition among educational institutions for the best students is becoming stiffer. A senior admissions officer at Claremont McKenna College resigned after admitting to inflating SAT scores of the incoming classes for six years. The motive, of course, was to boost the school's rankings in the *U.S. News & World Report*'s annual listing of top colleges and universities in the United States. Carmen Nobel, who reported the incident in *Working Knowledge* (a Harvard Business School publication), suggested that the scandal "questions the value of competitive rankings."
- A study of 11,000 New York vehicle emission test facilities found that companies with a greater number of local competitors passed cars with considerably high emission rates and lost customers when they failed to pass the tests. The authors of the study concluded, "In contexts when pricing is restricted, firms use illicit quality as a business strategy."

Many companies have developed reward and evaluation systems that evaluate whether a manager is acting in an ethical manner. For example, Raytheon, a $24 billion defense contractor, incorporated the following items in its "Leadership Assessment Instrument":[66]

- Maintains unequivocal commitment to honesty, truth, and ethics in every facet of behavior.
- Conforms with the letter and intent of company policies while working to affect any necessary policy changes.

- Actions are consistent with words; follows through on commitments; readily admits mistakes.
- Is trusted and inspires others to be trusted.

As noted by Dan Burnham, Raytheon's former CEO: "What do we look for in a leadership candidate with respect to integrity? What we're really looking for are people who have developed an inner gyroscope of ethical principles. We look for people for whom ethical thinking is part of what they do—no different from 'strategic thinking' or 'tactical thinking.'"

Policies and Procedures

Many situations that a firm faces have regular, identifiable patterns. Leaders tend to handle such routine by establishing a policy or procedure to be followed that can be applied uniformly to each occurrence. Such guidelines can be useful in specifying the proper relationships with a firm's customers and suppliers. For example, Levi Strauss has developed stringent global sourcing guidelines, and Chemical Bank (part of JPMorgan Chase Bank) has a policy of forbidding any review that would determine if suppliers are Chemical customers when the bank awards contracts.

Carefully developed policies and procedures guide behavior so that all employees will be encouraged to behave in an ethical manner. However, they must be reinforced with effective communication, enforcement, and monitoring, as well as sound corporate governance practices. In addition, the Sarbanes-Oxley Act of 2002 provides considerable legal protection to employees of publicly traded companies who report unethical or illegal practices. Provisions in the act:[67]

- Make it unlawful to "discharge, demote, suspend, threaten, harass, or in any manner discriminate against 'a whistleblower.'"
- Establish criminal penalties of up to 10 years in jail for executives who retaliate against whistleblowers.
- Require board audit committees to establish procedures for hearing whistleblower complaints.
- Allow the secretary of labor to order a company to rehire a terminated whistleblower with no court hearings whatsoever.
- Give a whistleblower the right to a jury trial, bypassing months or years of cumbersome administrative hearings.

ISSUE FOR DEBATE

JPMorgan Responds to a Request

In June 2012, Jamie Dimon, the CEO of JPMorgan Chase, met with a Chinese insurance regulatory official, Xiang Junbo, at the bank's headquarters in New York. JPMorgan was seeking to win lucrative work from a Chinese insurance company. Xiang would have a say in whether or not JPMorgan would win the business. Also at that meeting was a woman brought by Xiang who served as the interpreter between Dimon and Xiang.

continued

continued

As the meeting drew to a close, Xiang changed the subject of the meeting and focused on his young interpreter, noting that she was the daughter of a close friend and promoting her as a potential employee at JPMorgan. JPMorgan employees in Hong Kong knew that Xiang hoped to see the woman hired by JPMorgan and had brought her to New York to introduce her to Dimon. Following the meeting, a banker in the Hong Kong office sent an email that outlined how Xiang asked Dimon "for a favor to retain her." In discussing the need to maintain good rapport with Xiang, the banker also emphasized "the importance of this relationship" and the need to "find a solution for her quickly." Dimon passed information on the applicant to others in the bank but took no direct action on whether or not to hire her. After conducting a series of interviews and gaining approval from the bank's compliance department, the bank created a special internship for the woman. She later was hired into a full-time position. But she is not alone. In filings with federal regulators, JPMorgan has reported that it has hired several dozen individuals with close ties to Chinese regulators, government officials, and corporate executives.

In the months after the meeting between Dimon and Xiang, JPMorgan worked on deals with at least four insurance companies overseen by Xiang to take the insurers public via an IPO. More recently, five top insurance companies in China became clients of JPMorgan.

Federal regulators have opened investigations of the hiring practices of JPMorgan as well as several other leading Wall Street firms, including Citigroup, Credit Suisse, Deutsche Bank, Goldman Sachs, Morgan Stanley, and UBS. Banks are not prohibited from hiring individuals with ties to Chinese government officials. They would be in violation of the Foreign Corrupt Practices Act only if they can be shown to have explicitly traded job offers for approval of business deals. In the words of the statute, the banks would have had to act with "corrupt intent" to influence a Chinese official.

Officials at JPMorgan defend their hiring of the interpreter. They argue that she was well qualified, having a graduate degree from NYU, and note that she has received very positive evaluations from her supervisors.

JPMorgan has had ongoing discussions over the years about how to respond to requests for preferential treatment of job candidates with close ties to powerful Chinese officials. In July 2006, JPMorgan executives held a meeting in Hong Kong at which they discussed how to stay in compliance with antibribery laws while pursuing recruits with ties to officials. In response to questions from managers in its Chinese offices, the bank developed new guidelines that were included as part of a broader set of anticorruption measures approved by the board in late 2011. In a January 2014 interview on CNBC, Dimon weighed in on the challenge with such hires, stating it has been a "norm of business for years" for banks to hire "sons and daughters of companies, and to give them proper jobs and don't violate, you know, [the] American Foreign Corrupt Practices Act."

Discussion Questions

1. Was JPMorgan ethical in hiring the friend of the Chinese government official?
2. What should the hiring policies of banks be to meet the needs of being ethical while also building their business in China? Should banks strive to follow their legal requirements, or should their standards be higher?
3. How responsible are senior managers of banks for ensuring that hiring done in regional operations is ethical and in line with legal requirements?

Sources: Barboza, D. & Gough, N. 2014. Chinese official made job plea to JPMorgan Chase chief. *nytimes.com*, February 10: np; and Glazer, E., Fitzpatrick, D., & Eaglesham, J. 2014. J.P. Morgan knew of China hiring concerns before probe. *wsj.com*, October 23: np.

Reflecting on Career Implications . . .

- **Strategic Leadership:** The chapter identifies three interdependent activities that are central to strategic leadership; namely, setting direction, designing the organization, and nurturing a culture dedicated to excellence and ethical behavior. Both during your life as a student and in organizations at which you have worked, you have often assumed leadership positions. To what extent have you consciously and successfully engaged in each of these activities? Observe the leaders in your organization and assess to what extent you can learn from them the qualities of strategic leadership that you can use to advance your own career.

- **Power:** Identify the sources of power used by your superior at work. How do this person's primary source of power and the way he or she uses it affect your own creativity, morale, and willingness to stay with the organization? In addition, identify approaches you will use to enhance your power as you move up your career ladder. Explain why you chose these approaches.

- **Emotional Intelligence:** The chapter identifies the five components of emotional intelligence (self-awareness, self-regulation, motivation, empathy, and social skills). How do you rate yourself on each of these components? What steps can you take to improve your emotional intelligence and achieve greater career success?

- **Creating an Ethical Organization:** Identify an ethical dilemma that you personally faced in the course of your work. How did you respond to it? Was your response compliance-based, integrity-based, or even unethical? If your behavior was compliance-based, speculate on how it would have been different if it were integrity-based. What have you learned from your experience that would make you a more ethical leader in the future?

summary

Strategic leadership is vital in ensuring that strategies are formulated and implemented in an effective manner. Leaders must play a central role in performing three critical and interdependent activities: setting the direction, designing the organization, and nurturing a culture committed to excellence and ethical behavior. If leaders ignore or are ineffective at performing any one of the three, the organization will not be very successful. We identified two elements of leadership that contribute to success—overcoming barriers to change and using power effectively.

For leaders to effectively fulfill their activities, emotional intelligence (EI) is very important. Five elements that contribute to EI are self-awareness, self-regulation, motivation, empathy, and social skill. The first three elements pertain to self-management skills, whereas the last two are associated with a person's ability to manage relationships with others. We addressed some of the potential drawbacks from the ineffective use of EI. These include the dysfunctional use of power as well as a tendency to become overly empathetic, which may result in unreasonably lowered performance expectations.

Leaders need to play a central role in creating a learning organization. Gone are the days when the top-level managers "think" and everyone else in the organization "does." With rapidly changing, unpredictable, and complex competitive environments, leaders must engage everyone in the ideas and energies of people throughout the organization. Great ideas can come from anywhere in the organization—from the executive suite to the factory floor. The five elements that we discussed as central to a learning organization are inspiring and motivating people with a mission or purpose, empowering people at all levels throughout the organization, accumulating and sharing internal knowledge, gathering external information, and challenging the status quo to stimulate creativity.

In the final section of the chapter, we addressed a leader's central role in instilling ethical behavior in the organization. We discussed the enormous costs that firms face when ethical crises arise—costs in terms of financial and reputational loss as well as the erosion of human capital and relationships with suppliers, customers, society at large, and governmental agencies. And, as we would expect, the benefits of having a strong ethical organization are also numerous. We contrasted compliance-based and integrity-based approaches to organizational ethics. Compliance-based approaches are largely externally motivated; that is, they are motivated by the fear of punishment for doing something that is unlawful. Integrity-based approaches, on the other hand, are driven by a personal and organizational commitment to ethical behavior. We also addressed the four key elements of an ethical organization: role models, corporate credos and codes of conduct, reward and evaluation systems, and policies and procedures.

SUMMARY REVIEW QUESTIONS

1. Three key activities—setting a direction, designing the organization, and nurturing a culture and ethics—are all part of what effective leaders do on a regular basis. Explain how these three activities are interrelated.
2. Define emotional intelligence (EI). What are the key elements of EI? Why is EI so important to successful strategic leadership? Address potential "downsides."

3. The knowledge a firm possesses can be a source of competitive advantage. Describe ways that a firm can continuously learn to maintain its competitive position.
4. How can the five central elements of "learning organizations" be incorporated into global companies?
5. What are the benefits to firms and their shareholders of conducting business in an ethical manner?
6. Firms that fail to behave in an ethical manner can incur high costs. What are these costs, and what is their source?
7. What are the most important differences between an "integrity organization" and a "compliance organization" in a firm's approach to organizational ethics?
8. What are some of the important mechanisms for promoting ethics in a firm?

experiential exercise

Select two well-known business leaders—one you admire and one you do not. Evaluate each of them on the five characteristics of emotional intelligence in the table at the bottom of the page.

application questions & exercises

1. Identify two CEOs whose leadership you admire. What is it about their skills, attributes, and effective use of power that causes you to admire them?
2. Founders have an important role in developing their organization's culture and values. At times, their influence persists for many years. Identify and describe two organizations in which the cultures and values established by the founder(s) continue to flourish. You may find research on the Internet helpful in answering this question.
3. Some leaders place a great emphasis on developing superior human capital. In what ways does this help a firm to develop and sustain competitive advantages?
4. In this chapter we discussed the five elements of a "learning organization." Select a firm with which you are familiar and discuss whether or not it epitomizes some (or all) of these elements.

ethics questions

1. Sometimes organizations must go outside the firm to hire talent, thus bypassing employees already working for the firm. Are there conditions under which this might raise ethical considerations?
2. Ethical crises can occur in virtually any organization. Describe some of the systems, procedures, and processes that can help to prevent such crises.

key terms

leadership 350
setting a direction 351
designing the organization 351
excellent and ethical organizational culture 352
barriers to change 355
vested interest in the status quo 355
systemic barriers 355
behavioral barriers 356
political barriers 356
personal time constraints 356
power 356
organizational bases of power 356
personal bases of power 357
emotional intelligence (EI) 358
learning organizations 363
benchmarking 366
competitive benchmarking 366
functional benchmarking 366
ethics 368
organizational ethics 368
ethical orientation 368
compliance-based ethics programs 370
integrity-based ethics programs 370
corporate credo 372

Emotional Intelligence Characteristics	Admired Leader	Leader Not Admired
Self-awareness		
Self-regulation		
Motivation		
Empathy		
Social skills		

references

1. Dolan, K. 2014. How to blow $9 billion. *Forbes,* July 21: 74–77; Woo, E. 2002. Peter Stroh, 74, head of brewery, philanthropist. *latimes.com,* September 21: np; and Anonymous. 2014. How to lose $700 million: The rise and fall of Stroh's. *finance.yahoo.com,* July 15: np.
2. Charan, R. & Colvin, G. 1999. Why CEOs fail. *Fortune,* June 21: 68–78.
3. Yukl, G. 2008. How leaders influence organizational effectiveness. *Leadership Quarterly,* 19(6): 708–722.
4. These three activities and our discussion draw from Kotter, J. P. 1990. What leaders really do. *Harvard Business Review,* 68(3): 103–111; Pearson, A. E. 1990. Six basics for general managers. *Harvard Business Review,* 67(4): 94–101; and Covey, S. R. 1996. Three roles of the leader in the new paradigm. In Hesselbein, M., Goldsmith, M., & Beckhard, R. (Eds.), *The leader of the future:* 149–160. San Francisco: Jossey-Bass. Some of the discussion of each of the three leadership activity concepts draws on Dess, G. G. & Miller, A. 1993. *Strategic management:* 320–325. New York: McGraw-Hill.
5. García-Morales, V. J., Lloréns-Montes, F. J., & Verdú-Jover, A. J. 2008. The effects of transformational leadership on organizational performance through knowledge and innovation. *British Journal of Management,* 19(4): 299–319.
6. Martin, R. 2010. The execution trap. *Harvard Business Review,* 88(7/8): 64–71.
7. Collins, J. 1997. What comes next? *Inc.,* October: 34–45.
8. Hsieh, T. 2010. Zappos's CEO on going to extremes for customers. *Harvard Business Review,* 88(7/8): 41–44.
9. Chesky, B. 2014. Don't f*ck up the culture. *linkedin.com,* April 24: np.
10. Anonymous. 2006. Looking out for number one. *BusinessWeek,* October 30: 66.
11. Schaffer, R. H. 2010. Mistakes leaders keep making. *Harvard Business Review,* 88(9): 86–91.
12. For insightful perspectives on escalation, refer to Brockner, J. 1992. The escalation of commitment to a failing course of action. *Academy of Management Review,* 17(1): 39–61; and Staw, B. M. 1976. Knee-deep in the big muddy: A study of commitment to a chosen course of action. *Organizational Behavior and Human Decision Processes,* 16: 27–44. The discussion of systemic, behavioral, and political barriers draws on Lorange, P. & Murphy, D. 1984. Considerations in implementing strategic control. *Journal of Business Strategy,* 5: 27–35. In a similar vein, Noel M. Tichy has addressed three types of resistance to change in the context of General Electric: technical resistance, political resistance, and cultural resistance. See Tichy, N. M. 1993. Revolutionalize your company. *Fortune,* December 13: 114–118. Examples draw from O'Reilly, B. 1997. The secrets of America's most admired corporations: New ideas and new products. *Fortune,* March 3: 60–64.
13. Davis, I. 2014. Lou Gerstner on corporate reinvention and values. *mckinsey.com,* September: np.
14. This section draws on Champoux, J. E. 2000. *Organizational behavior: Essential tenets for a new millennium.* London: South-Western; and The mature use of power in organizations. 2003. *RHR International-Executive Insights,* May 29, *12.19.168.197/execinsights/8-3.htm.*
15. An insightful perspective on the role of power and politics in organizations is provided in Ciampa, K. 2005. Almost ready: How leaders move up. *Harvard Business Review,* 83(1): 46–53.
16. Pfeffer, J. 2010. Power play. *Harvard Business Review,* 88(7/8): 84–92.
17. Westphal, J. D., & Graebner, M. E. 2010. A matter of appearances: How corporate leaders manage the impressions of financial analysts about the conduct of their boards. *Academy of Management Journal,* 53(4): 15–44.
18. A discussion of the importance of persuasion in bringing about change can be found in Garvin, D. A. & Roberto, M. A. 2005. Change through persuasion. *Harvard Business Review,* 83(4): 104–113.
19. Lorsch, J. W. & Tierney, T. J. 2002. *Aligning the stars: How to succeed when professionals drive results.* Boston: Harvard Business School Press.
20. Some consider EI to be a "trait," that is, an attribute that is stable over time. However, many authors, including Daniel Goleman, have argued that it can be developed through motivation, extended practice, and feedback. For example, in D. Goleman, 1998, What makes a leader? *Harvard Business Review,* 76(5): 97, Goleman addresses this issue in a sidebar: "Can emotional intelligence be learned?"
21. For a review of this literature, see Daft, R. 1999. *Leadership: Theory and practice.* Fort Worth, TX: Dryden Press.
22. EI has its roots in the concept of "social intelligence" that was first identified by E. L. Thorndike in 1920 (Intelligence and its uses. *Harper's Magazine,* 140: 227–235). Psychologists have been uncovering other intelligences for some time now and have grouped them into such clusters as abstract intelligence (the ability to understand and manipulate verbal and mathematical symbols), concrete intelligence (the ability to understand and manipulate objects), and social intelligence (the ability to understand and relate to people). See Ruisel, I. 1992. Social intelligence: Conception and methodological problems. *Studia Psychologica,* 34(4–5): 281–296. Refer to *trochim.human.cornell.edu/gallery.*
23. Joseph, D. & Newman, D. 2010. Emotional intelligence: An integrative meta-analysis and cascading model. *Journal of Applied Psychology,* 95(1): 54–78; Brusman, M. 2013. Leadership effectiveness through emotional intelligence. *workingresourcesblog.com,* September 18: np; and Bradberry, T. 2015. Why your boss lacks emotional intelligence. *forbes.com,* January 6: np.
24. Tate, B. 2008. A longitudinal study of the relationships among self-monitoring, authentic leadership, and perceptions of leadership. *Journal of Leadership & Organizational Studies,* 15(1): 16–29.
25. Moss, S. A., Dowling, N., & Callanan, J. 2009. Towards an integrated model of leadership and self-regulation. *Leadership Quarterly,* 20(2): 162–176.
26. An insightful perspective on leadership, which involves

discovering, developing, and celebrating what is unique about each individual, is found in Buckingham, M. 2005. What great managers do. *Harvard Business Review,* 83(3): 70–79.

27. Bryant, A. 2011. *The corner office:* 197. New York: St. Martin's Griffin.

28. This section draws upon Klemp. G. 2005. *Emotional intelligence and leadership: What really matters.* Cambria Consulting, Inc., *www.cambriaconsulting.com.*

29. Heifetz, R. 2004. Question authority. *Harvard Business Review,* 82(1): 37.

30. Senge, P. M. 1990. The leader's new work: Building learning organizations. *Sloan Management Review,* 32(1): 7–23.

31. Bernoff, J. & Schandler, T. 2010. Empowered. *Harvard Business Review,* 88(7/8): 94–101.

32. Hammer, M. & Stanton, S. A. 1997. The power of reflection. *Fortune,* November 24: 291–296.

33. Hannah, S. T. & Lester, P. B. 2009. A multilevel approach to building and leading learning organizations. *Leadership Quarterly,* 20(1): 34–48.

34. For some guidance on how to effectively bring about change in organizations, refer to Wall, S. J. 2005. The protean organization: Learning to love change. *Organizational Dynamics,* 34(1): 37–46.

35. Covey, S. R. 1989. *The seven habits of highly effective people: Powerful lessons in personal change.* New York: Simon & Schuster.

36. Kouzes, J. M. & Posner, B. Z. 2009. To lead, create a shared vision. *Harvard Business Review,* 87(1): 20–21.

37. Ibid.

38. Gurdjian, P. & Halbeisen, T. 2014. Why leadership-development programs fail. *mckinsey.com,* January: np.

39. Melrose, K. 1995. *Making the grass greener on your side: A CEO's journey to leading by servicing.* San Francisco: Barrett-Koehler.

40. Tekleab, A. G., Sims, H. P., Jr., Yun, S., Tesluk, P. E., & Cox, J. 2008. Are we on the same page? Effects of self-awareness of empowering and transformational leadership. *Journal of Leadership & Organizational Studies,* 14(3): 185–201.

41. Helgesen, S. 1996. Leading from the grass roots. In Hesselbein et al., The *leader of the future:* 19–24. San Francisco: Jossey-Bass.

42. Bowen, D. E. & Lawler, E. E., III. 1995. Empowering service employees. *Sloan Management Review,* 37: 73–84.

43. Easterby-Smith, M. & Prieto, I. M. 2008. Dynamic capabilities and knowledge management: An integrative role for learning? *British Journal of Management,* 19(3): 235–249.

44. Schafer, S. 1997. Battling a labor shortage? It's all in your imagination. *Inc.,* August: 24.

45. Meyer, P. 1998. So you want the president's job . . . *Business Horizons,* January–February: 2–8.

46. The introductory discussion of benchmarking draws on Miller, A. 1998. *Strategic management:* 142–143. New York: McGraw-Hill.

47. Sedgwick, D. 2014. Ford and suppliers jointly benchmark competitors' vehicles. *automotivenews.com,* October 19: np.

48. Main, J. 1992. How to steal the best ideas around. *Fortune,* October 19: 102–106.

49. Sheff, D. 1996. Levi's changes everything. *Fast Company,* June–July: 65–74.

50. Holt, J. W. 1996. *Celebrate your mistakes.* New York: McGraw-Hill.

51. McGregor, J. 2006. How failure breeds success. *Bloomberg Businessweek,* July 10: 42–52.

52. Bryant, A. 2011. *The corner office:* 34. New York: St. Martin's Griffin.

53. This opening discussion draws upon Conley, J. H. 2000. Ethics in business. In Helms, M. M. (Ed.), *Encyclopedia of management* (4th ed.): 281–285. Farmington Hills, MI: Gale Group; Paine, L. S. 1994. Managing for organizational integrity. *Harvard Business Review,* 72(2): 106–117; and Carlson, D. S. & Perrewe, P. L. 1995. Institutionalization of organizational ethics through transformational leadership. *Journal of Business Ethics,* 14: 829–838.

54. Pinto, J., Leana, C. R., & Pil, F. K. 2008. Corrupt organizations or organizations of corrupt individuals? Two types of organization-level corruption. *Academy of Management Review,* 33(3): 685–709.

55. Soule, E. 2002. Managerial moral strategies—In search of a few good principles. *Academy of Management Review,* 27(1): 114–124.

56. Carlson & Perrewe, op. cit.

57. This discussion is based upon Paine, Managing for organizational integrity; Paine, L. S. 1997. *Cases in leadership, ethics, and organizational integrity: A Strategic approach.* Burr Ridge, IL: Irwin; and Fontrodona, J. 2002. Business ethics across the Atlantic. Business Ethics Direct, *www.ethicsa.org/BED_art_fontrodone.html.*

58. For more on operationalizing capabilities to sustain an ethical framework, see Largay, J. A., III, & Zhang, R. 2008. Do CEOs worry about being fired when making investment decisions? *Academy of Management Perspectives,* 22(1): 60–61.

59. See *www.ti.com/corp/docs/company/citizen/ethics/benchmark.shtml;* and *www.ti.com/corp/docs/company/citizen/ethics/quicktest.shtml.*

60. Bryant, A. 2011. *The corner office:* 91. New York: St. Martin's Griffin.

61. Wetlaufer, S. 1999. Organizing for empowerment: An interview with AES's Roger Sant and Dennis Bakke. *Harvard Business Review,* 77(1): 110–126.

62. For an insightful, academic perspective on the impact of ethics codes on executive decision making, refer to Stevens, J. M., Steensma, H. K., Harrison, D. A., & Cochran, P. S. 2005. Symbolic or substantive document? The influence of ethics code on financial executives' decisions. *Strategic Management Journal,* 26(2): 181–195.

63. Paine, Managing for organizational integrity.

64. For a study on the effects of goal setting on unethical behavior, read Schweitzer, M. E., Ordonez, L., & Douma, B. 2004. Goal setting as a motivator of unethical behavior. *Academy of Management Journal,* 47(3): 422–432.

65. Williams, R. 2012. How competition can encourage unethical business practices. *business.financialpost.com,* July 31: np.

66. Fulmer, R. M. 2004. The challenge of ethical leadership. *Organizational Dynamics,* 33(3): 307–317.

67. *www.sarbanes-oxley.com.*

Managing Innovation and Fostering Corporate Entrepreneurship

chapter 12

After reading this chapter, you should have a good understanding of the following learning objectives:

LO12.1 The importance of implementing strategies and practices that foster innovation.

LO12.2 The challenges and pitfalls of managing corporate innovation processes.

LO12.3 How corporations use new venture teams, business incubators, and product champions to create an internal environment and culture that promote entrepreneurial development.

LO12.4 How corporate entrepreneurship achieves both financial goals and strategic goals.

LO12.5 The benefits and potential drawbacks of real options analysis in making resource deployment decisions in corporate entrepreneurship contexts.

LO12.6 How an entrepreneurial orientation can enhance a firm's efforts to develop promising corporate venture initiatives.

PART 3: STRATEGIC IMPLEMENTATION

Learning from Mistakes

If you ask a group of students to name a successful company, Google is likely to be one of the first firms mentioned. It dominates online search and advertising, has developed a successful browser, and developed the operating system that powers 85 percent of the smartphones sold in the second quarter of 2014.[1] Its success is evident in its stock price, which rose from about $150 in early 2009 to over $525 a share in early 2015. But that doesn't mean that Google has been successful at all it has tried. One of Google's most notable failures occurred when it tried to venture outside the online and wireless markets. In 2006, Google decided to expand its advertising business to radio advertising. After spending several hundred million dollars on its entrepreneurial effort in the radio advertising market, Google pulled the plug on this business in 2009.

Google saw great potential in applying its business model to the radio advertising industry. In the traditional radio advertising model, companies that wished to advertise their products and services contracted with an advertising agency to develop a set of radio spots (commercials). They then bought blocks of advertising time from radio stations. Advertisers paid based on the number of listeners on each station. Google believed that it could develop a stronger model. Its design was to purchase large blocks of advertising time from stations. It would then sell the time in a competitive auction to companies that wished to advertise. Google believed it could sell ad time to advertisers at a higher rate if it could identify what ads on what stations had the greatest impact for advertisers. Thus, rather than charging based on audience size, Google would follow the model it used on the web and charge based on ad effectiveness. To develop the competency to measure ad effectiveness, Google purchased dMarc, a company that developed technology to manage and measure radio ads, for $102 million.

Google's overall vision was even broader. The company also planned to enter print and TV advertising. It could then provide a "dashboard" to marketing executives at firms that would provide information on the effectiveness of advertising on the web, on TV, in print, and on radio. Google would then sell them a range of advertising space among all four to maximize a firm's ad expenditures.

However, Google found that its attempt to innovate the radio market bumped up against two core challenges. First, the radio advertising model was based much more on relationships than online advertising was. Radio stations, advertising firms, and advertising agencies had long-standing relationships that limited Google's ability to break into the market. In fact, few radio stations were willing to sell advertising time to Google. Also, advertising agencies saw Google as a threat to their business model and were unwilling to buy time from Google. Second, Google found that its ability to measure the effectiveness of radio ads was limited. Unlike the case with online markets, where it could measure whether people clicked on ads, the company found it difficult to measure whether listeners responded to ads. Google tried ads that mentioned specific websites that listeners could go to, but it found few people accessed these sites. In the end, Google was able to sell radio time at only a fraction of what radio stations could get from working their traditional advertising deals. This led stations to abandon Google's radio business.

Google found that it had the initiative to innovate the radio market but didn't have the knowledge, experience, or social connections needed to win in this market.

Discussion Questions

1. Why didn't the lessons Google learned in the online advertising market apply to the radio market?
2. Radio is increasingly moving to satellite and streaming systems. Is this a new opportunity for Google, or should it steer clear of radio altogether?

LO12.1

The importance of implementing strategies and practices that foster innovation.

Managing change is one of the most important functions performed by strategic leaders. There are two major avenues through which companies can expand or improve their business—innovation and corporate entrepreneurship. These two activities go hand-in-hand because they both have similar aims. The first is strategic renewal. Innovations help an organization stay fresh and reinvent itself as conditions in the business environment change. This is why managing innovation is such an important strategic implementation issue. The second is the pursuit of venture opportunities. Innovative breakthroughs, as well as new product concepts, evolving technologies, and shifting demand, create opportunities for corporate venturing. In this chapter we will explore these topics—how change and innovation can stimulate strategic renewal and foster corporate entrepreneurship.

Managing Innovation

innovation
the use of new knowledge to transform organizational processes or create commercially viable products and services.

One of the most important sources of growth opportunities is innovation. **Innovation** involves using new knowledge to transform organizational processes or create commercially viable products and services. The sources of new knowledge may include the latest technology, the results of experiments, creative insights, or competitive information. However it comes about, innovation occurs when new combinations of ideas and information bring about positive change.

The emphasis on newness is a key point. For example, for a patent application to have any chance of success, one of the most important attributes it must possess is novelty. You can't patent an idea that has been copied. This is a central idea. In fact, the root of the word *innovation* is the Latin *novus*, which means "new." Innovation involves introducing or changing to something new.[2]

Among the most important sources of new ideas is new technology. Technology creates new possibilities. Technology provides the raw material that firms use to make innovative products and services. But technology is not the only source of innovations. There can be innovations in human resources, firm infrastructure, marketing, service, or many other value-adding areas that have little to do with anything "high-tech." Strategy Spotlight 12.1 highlights a simple but effective innovation by Dutch Boy paints. As the Dutch Boy example suggests, innovation can take many forms.

Types of Innovation

Although innovations are not always high-tech, changes in technology can be an important source of change and growth. When an innovation is based on a sweeping new technology, it often has a more far-reaching impact. Sometimes even a small innovation can add value and create competitive advantages. Innovation can and should occur throughout an organization—in every department and all aspects of the value chain.

product innovation
efforts to create product designs and applications of technology to develop new products for end users.

process innovation
efforts to improve the efficiency of organizational processes, especially manufacturing systems and operations.

One distinction that is often used when discussing innovation is between process innovation and product innovation.[3] **Product innovation** refers to efforts to create product designs and applications of technology to develop new products for end users. Recall from Chapter 5 how generic strategies were typically different depending on the stage of the industry life cycle. Product innovations tend to be more common during the earlier stages of an industry's life cycle. Product innovations are also commonly associated with a differentiation strategy. Firms that differentiate by providing customers with new products or services that offer unique features or quality enhancements often engage in product innovation.

Process innovation, by contrast, is typically associated with improving the efficiency of an organizational process, especially manufacturing systems and operations. By drawing on new technologies and an organization's accumulated experience (Chapter 5), firms

12.1 STRATEGY SPOTLIGHT

DUTCH BOY'S SIMPLE PAINT CAN INNOVATION

Sometimes a simple change can make a vast improvement in a product. Any painter knows that getting the paint can open and pouring out paint without drips are two of the challenges of painting. Dutch Boy addressed this issue by developing a twist and pour paint container. The all-plastic container has a large, easy-to-use twist-off top and a handle on the side. The result was a consumer-friendly product that made painting easier and less messy. The handle also reduces the need for a paint stirring stick since you can mix the paint by shaking the container. Even though Dutch Boy's innovation was simple and nontechnological and had nothing to do with the core product, the launch of the new packaging led to articles in 30 national consumer magazines and 60 major newspapers as well as a story on *Good Morning America.* The Twist and Pour can was also named "Product of the Year" by *USA Today, Bloomberg Businessweek,* and *Better Homes & Gardens.* It was also named a winner of the 2011 Good Housekeeping VIP Awards, which commemorate the most innovative products from the past decade.

Sources: 11 innovative products from the past decade. 2011 *The Good Housekeeping Research Institute;* and www.fallscommunications.com.

---

can often improve materials utilization, shorten cycle time, and increase quality. Process innovations are more likely to occur in the later stages of an industry's life cycle as companies seek ways to remain viable in markets where demand has flattened out and competition is more intense. As a result, process innovations are often associated with overall cost leader strategies, because the aim of many process improvements is to lower the costs of operations.

Another way to view the impact of an innovation is in terms of its degree of innovativeness, which falls somewhere on a continuum that extends from incremental to radical.[4]

- **Radical innovations** produce fundamental changes by evoking major departures from existing practices. These breakthrough innovations usually occur because of technological change. They tend to be highly disruptive and can transform a company or even revolutionize a whole industry. They may lead to products or processes that can be patented, giving a firm a strong competitive advantage. Examples include electricity, the telephone, the transistor, desktop computers, fiber optics, artificial intelligence, and genetically engineered drugs.

> **radical innovation**
> an innovation that fundamentally changes existing practices.

- **Incremental innovations** enhance existing practices or make small improvements in products and processes. They may represent evolutionary applications within existing paradigms of earlier, more radical innovations. Because they often sustain a company by extending or expanding its product line or manufacturing skills, incremental innovations can be a source of competitive advantage by providing new capabilities that minimize expenses or speed productivity. Examples include frozen food, sports drinks, steel-belted radial tires, electronic bookkeeping, shatterproof glass, and digital thermometers.

> **incremental innovation**
> an innovation that enhances existing practices or makes small improvements in products and processes.

Some innovations are highly radical; others are only slightly incremental. But most innovations fall somewhere between these two extremes (see Exhibit 12.1).

Harvard Business School Professor Clayton M. Christensen identified another useful approach to characterize types of innovations.[5] Christensen draws a distinction between sustaining and disruptive innovations. *Sustaining innovations* are those that extend sales in an existing market, usually by enabling new products or services to be sold at higher margins. Such innovations may include either incremental or radical innovations. For example, the Internet was a breakthrough technology that transformed retail selling. But rather than disrupting the activities of catalog companies such as Lands' End and L.L. Bean, the Internet energized their existing business by extending their reach and making their operations more efficient.

EXHIBIT 12.1 Continuum of Radical and Incremental Innovations

- Fiber-optic cable
- Internet browser
- Online auction exchanges
- Bubble wrap

Radical Innovation ←————————————————————————→ **Incremental Innovation**

- Laparoscopic "keyhole" surgery
- Speech recognition software
- Polyester
- Enterprise resource planning (ERP)
- Frozen yogurt

By contrast, *disruptive innovations* are those that overturn markets by providing an altogether new approach to meeting customer needs. The features of a disruptive innovation make it somewhat counterintuitive. Disruptive innovations:

- Are technologically simpler and less sophisticated than currently available products or services.
- Appeal to less demanding customers who are seeking more convenient, less expensive solutions.
- Take time to take effect and only become disruptive once they have taken root in a new market or low-end part of an existing market.

Christensen cites Walmart and Southwest Airlines as two disruptive examples. Walmart started with a single store, Southwest with a few flights. But because they both represented major departures from existing practices and tapped into unmet needs, they steadily grew into ventures that appealed to a new category of customers and eventually overturned the status quo. "Instead of sustaining the trajectory of improvement that has been established in a market," says Christensen, a disruptive innovation "disrupts it and redefines it by bringing to the market something that is simpler."[6]

Spotlight 12.2 discusses how a new technology, graphene, may disrupt the electronics and computer industries.

Innovation is both a force in the external environment (technology, competition) and a factor affecting a firm's internal choices (generic strategy, value-adding activities).[7] Nevertheless, innovation can be quite difficult for some firms to manage, especially those that have become comfortable with the status quo.

Challenges of Innovation

LO12.2

The challenges and pitfalls of managing corporate innovation processes.

Innovation is essential to sustaining competitive advantages. Recall from Chapter 3 that one of the four elements of the balanced scorecard is the innovation and learning perspective. The extent and success of a company's innovation efforts are indicators of its overall performance. As management guru Peter Drucker warned, "An established company which, in an age demanding innovation, is not capable of innovation is doomed to decline and extinction."[8] In today's competitive environment, most firms have only one choice: "Innovate or die."

As with change, however, firms are often resistant to innovation. Only those companies that actively pursue innovation, even though it is often difficult and uncertain, will get a payoff from their innovation efforts. But managing innovation is challenging.[9] As former

12.2 STRATEGY SPOTLIGHT

WILL GRAPHENE RADICALLY CHANGE THE ELECTRONICS INDUSTRY?

The consumer electronics industry is often thought of as one of the most dynamic industries around, with new product innovations being launched on a regular basis. With this in mind, it is interesting to realize that the base technology standards of the components used to make consumer electronic products have been unchanged for a number of years. For example, the semiconductor chips used in consumer electronics are made from silicon wafers, the same as was the case 30 years ago. The chips have gotten more complex, packed with more and narrower channels in the silicon chip, but the basic technology is the same. Similarly, the screens of devices are primarily LCD panels, which have been widely used in electronic products for over 15 years.

However, a new technology, graphene, may radically change the consumer electronics industry. Graphene, which is produced in a sheet form and is a very thin layer of graphite atoms in a honeycomb lattice, is a product with amazing qualities. In the words of Jeanie Lau, professor of physics at the University of California at Riverside, "Graphene is a wonderful material. It conducts heat 10 times better than copper and electricity, 100 times better than silicon, is transparent like plastic, extremely lightweight, extremely strong, yet flexible and elastic." Additionally, researchers have discovered that they can magnetize graphene. This raises the possibility of building computer systems that use spintronics—that's shorthand for "spin transport electronics." Spintronics involves processing a signal using magnetic spin rather than electric charge. It is still a number of years away, but eventual consumer and business applications for spintronics technology could be faster processors and memory with vastly higher capacities. With such amazing properties, it is not surprising that major players, such as Samsung, have invested heavily in graphene, secured patents related to its use, developed prototypes that use graphene, and plan to produce a number of graphene-based products in the coming years. Its most promising initial use may be as a transparent electrode in monitors, displays, and touch screens. It also has the potential to be used in semiconductor chips in the future, possibly replacing silicon as the primary component of the chip.

As with any radical innovation, it is not yet clear if graphene will live up to its promise. Firms have not yet figured out how to manufacture it on a large scale or at a reasonable cost. It costs around $100 to produce a 1-inch-diameter wafer. There are also questions about whether researchers can figure out how to effectively turn transistors on a graphene chip on and off, an essential element if graphene will ever be used in semiconductor chips. Michael Patterson, CEO of Graphene Frontiers, commented that researchers are "really pushing the edges of technology" with graphene, and it may take 10 years before we know if it will replace current technologies.

Sources: Noyes, K. 2014. The business potential of (amazing, wonderful, futuristic) graphene. *cnnmoney.com*, May 12: np; and Whitwam, R., 2015. Researchers make graphene magnetic, clearing the way for faster everything. *extremetech.com*, January 29: np.

Pfizer former chairman and CEO William Steere puts it: "In some ways, managing innovation is analogous to breaking in a spirited horse. You are never sure of success until you achieve your goal. In the meantime, everyone takes a few lumps."[10]

What is it that makes innovation so difficult? The uncertainty about outcomes is one factor. Companies are often reluctant to invest time and resources in activities with an unknown future. Another factor is that the innovation process involves so many choices. These choices present five dilemmas that companies must wrestle with when pursuing innovation:[11]

- *Seeds versus weeds.* Most companies have an abundance of innovative ideas. They must decide which of these is most likely to bear fruit—the "seeds"—and which should be cast aside—the "weeds." This is complicated by the fact that some innovation projects require a considerable level of investment before a firm can fully evaluate whether they are worth pursuing. Firms need a mechanism with which they can choose among various innovation projects.
- *Experience versus initiative.* Companies must decide who will lead an innovation project. Senior managers may have experience and credibility but tend to be more risk-averse. Midlevel employees, who may be the innovators themselves, may have more enthusiasm because they can see firsthand how an innovation would address specific problems. Firms need to support and reward organizational members who bring new ideas to light.
- *Internal versus external staffing.* Innovation projects need competent staffs to succeed. People drawn from inside the company may have greater social capital

12.3 STRATEGY SPOTLIGHT

PROCTER & GAMBLE STRIVES TO REMAIN INNOVATIVE

From the development of Ivory Soap in 1879; to Crisco Oil, the first all-vegetable shortening, in 1911; to Crest, the first fluoridated toothpaste in 1955; to the stackable Pringles chips in 1968; to the Swiffer mop in 1998, Procter & Gamble (P&G) has long been known as a successful innovative firm. It led the market with these products and used these innovative products to build up its position as a differentiated consumer products firm. By all measures, P&G is a very successful company and was honored as the Fifth Most Admired Company by *Fortune* magazine in 2012. Still, P&G has found it challenging to remain innovative. The last major innovative blockbuster product P&G launched was Crest Whitestrips, and this product was introduced in 2001. Instead, in recent years, its new products have been extensions of current products, such as adding whitening flecks to Crest toothpaste, or derivatives of current products, such as taking the antihistamine in Nyquil and using it as a sleeping aid, labeled ZzzQuil. With ZzzQuil, P&G is not an innovator in this market, since there were a number of earlier entrants in the sleep market, such as Johnson & Johnson with its Tylenol PM product. One portfolio manager at a mutual fund derided the ZzzQuil product, saying, "It's a sign of what passes for innovation at P&G. It's not enough. It's incremental, derivative."

The factors leading to P&G's struggles to remain innovative should not be surprising. They largely grow out of the success the firm has had. First, with its wide range of products, P&G has a wide range of potential new product extensions and derivatives from which to choose. Though these are unlikely to be blockbusters, they look much safer than truly new innovative ideas. Second, while lower-level managers at P&G may be excited about new, innovative ideas, the division heads of P&G units, who are responsible for developing new products, are likely to shy away from big-bet product launches. These unit heads are also responsible for and rewarded on current division performance, a metric that will be negatively affected by the large costs associated with developing and marketing truly innovative new products. Third, due to its large size, P&G moved R&D responsibilities down to the divisions. While this enhances the divisions' abilities to quickly launch incrementally new products, it doesn't facilitate the collaboration across units often needed to develop boldly new products.

P&G is trying to address these issues by centralizing 20 to 30 percent of its research efforts within a new corporate-level business creation and innovation unit. Having a corporate effort at innovation separates the budget for product development from divisional profit numbers, enhancing the firm's willingness to invest in long-term product development efforts. Also, the corporate unit will be able to foster collaboration between units to develop blockbuster products.

Sources: Coleman-Lochner, L. & Hymowitz, C. 2012. At P&G, the innovation well runs dry. *Bloomberg Businessweek*, September 10: 24–26; and Bussey, J. 2012. The innovator's enigma. *wsj.com*, October 4: np.

---

and know the organization's culture and routines. But this knowledge may actually inhibit them from thinking outside the box. Staffing innovation projects with external personnel requires that project managers justify the hiring and spend time recruiting, training, and relationship building. Firms need to streamline and support the process of staffing innovation efforts.

- **Building capabilities versus collaborating.** Innovation projects often require new sets of skills. Firms can seek help from other departments and/or partner with other companies that bring resources and experience as well as share costs of development. However, such arrangements can create dependencies and inhibit internal skills development. Further, struggles over who contributed the most or how the benefits of the project are to be allocated may arise. Firms need a mechanism for forging links with outside parties to the innovation process.

- **Incremental versus preemptive launch.** Companies must manage the timing and scale of new innovation projects. An incremental launch is less risky because it requires fewer resources and serves as a market test. But a launch that is too tentative can undermine the project's credibility. It also opens the door for a competitive response. A large-scale launch requires more resources, but it can effectively preempt a competitive response. Firms need to make funding and management arrangements that allow for projects to hit the ground running, and they need to be responsive to market feedback.

These dilemmas highlight why the innovation process can be daunting even for highly successful firms. Strategy Spotlight 12.3 discusses how Procter & Gamble has been struggling with these challenges to improve its innovativeness. Next, we consider five steps that firms can take to improve the innovation process within the firm.[12]

Cultivating Innovation Skills

Some firms, such as Apple, Google, and Amazon, regularly produce innovative products and services, while other firms struggle to generate new, marketable products. What separates these innovative firms from the rest of the pack? Jeff Dyer, Hal Gregersen, and Clayton Christensen argue it is the innovative DNA of the leaders of these firms.[13] The leaders of these firms have exhibited "discovery skills" that allow them to see the potential in innovations and to move the organization forward in leveraging the value of those innovations.[14] These leaders spend 50 percent more time on these discovery activities than the leaders of less innovative firms. To improve their innovative processes, firms need to cultivate the innovation skills of their managers.

The key attribute that firms need to develop in their managers in order to improve their innovative potential is creative intelligence. Creative intelligence is driven by a core skill of associating—the ability to see patterns in data and integrate different questions, information, and insights—and four patterns of action: questioning, observing, experimenting, and networking. As managers practice the four patterns of action, they will begin to develop the skill of association. Dyer and his colleagues offer the following illustration to demonstrate that individuals using these skills are going to develop more creative, higher-potential innovations:

> Imagine that you have an identical twin, endowed with the same brains and natural talents that you have. You're both given one week to come up with a creative new business-venture idea. During that week, you come up with ideas alone in your room. In contrast, your twin (1) talks with 10 people—including an engineer, a musician, a stay-at-home dad, and a designer—about the venture, (2) visits three innovative start-ups to observe what they do, (3) samples five "new to the market" products, (4) shows a prototype he's built to five people, and (5) asks the questions "What if I tried this?" and "Why do you do that?" at least 10 times each day during these networking, observing, and experimenting activities. Who do you bet will come up with the more innovative (and doable) ideas?

The point is that by questioning, observing, experimenting, and networking as part of the innovative process, managers will not only make better innovation decisions now but, more importantly, start to build the innovative DNA needed to be more successful innovators in the future. As they get into the practice of these habits, decision makers will see opportunities and be more creative as they associate information from different parts of their life, different people they come in contact with, and different parts of their organizations. The ability to innovate is not hard-wired into our brains at birth. Research suggests that only one-third of our ability to think creatively is genetic. The other two-thirds is developed over time. Neuroscience research indicates that the brain is "plastic," meaning it changes over time due to experiences. As managers build up the ability to ask creative questions, develop a wealth of experiences from diverse settings, and link together insights from different arenas of their lives, their brains will follow suit and will build the ability to easily see situations creatively and draw upon a wide range of experiences and knowledge to identify creative solutions. The five traits of the effective innovator are described and examples of each trait are presented in Exhibit 12.2.

Defining the Scope of Innovation

Firms must have a means to focus their innovation efforts. By defining the "strategic envelope"—the scope of a firm's innovation efforts—firms ensure that their innovation efforts are not wasted on projects that are outside the firm's domain of interest. Strategic enveloping defines the range of acceptable projects. A **strategic envelope** creates a firm-specific view of innovation that defines how a firm can create new knowledge and learn from an

> **strategic envelope**
> a firm-specific view of innovation that defines how a firm can create new knowledge and learn from an innovation initiative even if the project fails.

EXHIBIT 12.2 The Innovator's DNA

Trait	Description	Example
Associating	Innovators have the ability to connect seemingly unrelated questions, problems, and ideas from different fields. This allows them to creatively see opportunities that others miss.	Pierre Omidyar saw the opportunity that led to eBay when he linked three items: (1) a personal fascination with creating more efficient markets, (2) his fiancee's desire to locate hard-to-find collectible Pez dispensers, and (3) the ineffectiveness of local classified ads in locating such items.
Questioning	Innovators constantly ask questions that challenge common wisdom. Rather than accept the status quo, they ask "Why not?" or "What if?" This gets others around them to challenge the assumptions that limit the possible range of actions the firm can take.	After witnessing the emergence of eBay and Amazon, Marc Benioff questioned why computer software was still sold in boxes rather than leased with a subscription and downloaded through the Internet. This was the genesis of Salesforce.com, a firm with over $4.1 billion in sales in 2014.
Observing	Discovery-driven executives produce innovative business ideas by observing regular behavior of individuals, especially customers and potential customers. Such observations often identify challenges customers face and previously unidentified opportunities.	From watching his wife struggle to keep track of the family's finances, Intuit founder Scott Cook identified the need for easy-to-use financial software that provided a single place for managing bills, bank accounts, and investments.
Experimenting	Thomas Edison once said, "I haven't failed. I've simply found 10,000 ways that do not work." Innovators regularly experiment with new possibilities, accepting that many of their ideas will fail. Experimentation can include new jobs, living in different countries, and new ideas for their businesses.	Founders Larry Page and Sergey Brin provide time and resources for Google employees to experiment. Some, such as the Android cell phone platform, have been big winners. Others, such as the Orkut and Buzz social networking systems, have failed. But Google will continue to experiment with new products and services.
Networking	Innovators develop broad personal networks. They use this diverse set of individuals to find and test radical ideas. This can be done by developing a diverse set of friends. It can also be done by attending idea conferences where individuals from a broad set of backgrounds come together to share their perspectives and ideas, such as the Technology, Entertainment, and Design (TED) Conference or the Aspen Ideas Festival.	Michael Lazaridis got the idea for a wireless email device that led him to found Research in Motion, now called BlackBerry, from a conference he attended. At the conference, a speaker was discussing a wireless system Coca-Cola was using that allowed vending machines to send a signal when they needed refilling. Lazaridis saw the opportunity to use the same concept with email communications, and the idea for the BlackBerry was hatched.

Source: Adapted from J.H. Dyer, H.G. Gregerson and C.M. Christensen, "The Innovator's DNA," Harvard Business Review, December 2009, pp. 61–67.

innovation initiative even if the project fails. It also gives direction to a firm's innovation efforts, which helps separate seeds from weeds and builds internal capabilities.

One way to determine which projects to work on is to focus on a common technology. Then innovation efforts across the firm can aim at developing skills and expertise in a given technical area. Another potential focus is on a market theme. Consider how DuPont responded to a growing concern for environmentally sensitive products:

> In the early 1990s, DuPont sought to use its knowledge of plastics to identify products to meet a growing market demand for biodegradable products. It conducted numerous experiments with a biodegradable polyester resin it named Biomax. By trying different applications and formulations demanded by potential customers, the company was finally able to create a product that could be produced economically and had market appeal. DuPont has continued to extend the Biomax brand and now produces a large line of environmentally sensitive plastics.[15]

Companies must be clear about not only the kinds of innovation they are looking for but also the expected results. Each company needs to develop a set of questions to ask itself about its innovation efforts:

- How much will the innovation initiative cost?
- How likely is it to actually become commercially viable?
- How much value will it add; that is, what will it be worth if it works?
- What will be learned if it does not pan out?

However a firm envisions its innovation goals, it needs to develop a systematic approach to evaluating its results and learning from its innovation initiatives. Viewing innovation from this perspective helps firms manage the process.[16]

Managing the Pace of Innovation

Along with clarifying the scope of an innovation by defining a strategic envelope, firms also need to regulate the pace of innovation. How long will it take for an innovation initiative to realistically come to fruition? The project timeline of an incremental innovation may be 6 months to 2 years, whereas a more radical innovation is typically long term—10 years or more.[17] Radical innovations often begin with a long period of exploration in which experimentation makes strict timelines unrealistic. In contrast, firms that are innovating incrementally in order to exploit a window of opportunity may use a milestone approach that is more stringently driven by goals and deadlines. This kind of sensitivity to realistic time frames helps companies separate dilemmas temporally so they are easier to manage.

Time pacing can also be a source of competitive advantage because it helps a company manage transitions and develop an internal rhythm.[18] Time pacing does not mean the company ignores the demands of market timing; instead, companies have a sense of their own internal clock in a way that allows them to thwart competitors by controlling the innovation process. With time pacing, the firm works to develop an internal rhythm that matches the buying practices of customers. For example, for years, Intel worked to develop new microprocessor chips every 18 months. The company would have three chips in process at any point in time—one it was producing and selling, one it was currently developing, and one that was just on the drawing board. This pacing also matched the market, because most corporate customers bought new computers about every three years. Thus, customers were then two generations behind in their computing technology, leading them to feel the need to upgrade at the three-year point. In the post-PC era, Apple has developed a similar but faster internal cycle, allowing it to launch a new generation of the iPhone on an annual basis.

This doesn't mean the aim is always to be faster when innovating. Some projects can't be rushed. Companies that hurry their research efforts or go to market before they are ready can damage their ability to innovate—and their reputation. Thus, managing the pace of innovation can be an important factor in long-term success.

Staffing to Capture Value from Innovation

People are central to the processes of identifying, developing, and commercializing innovations effectively. They need broad sets of skills as well as experience—experience working with teams and experience working on successful innovation projects. To capture value from innovation activities, companies must provide strategic decision makers with staff members who make it possible.

This insight led strategy experts Rita Gunther McGrath and Thomas Keil to research the types of human resource management practices that effective firms use to capture value from their innovation efforts.[19] Four practices are especially important:

- Create innovation teams with experienced players who know what it is like to deal with uncertainty and can help new staff members learn venture management skills.

- Require that employees seeking to advance their career with the organization serve in the new venture group as part of their career climb.
- Once people have experience with the new venture group, transfer them to mainstream management positions where they can use their skills and knowledge to revitalize the company's core business.
- Separate the performance of individuals from the performance of the innovation. Otherwise, strong players may feel stigmatized if the innovation effort they worked on fails.

There are other staffing practices that may sound as if they would benefit a firm's innovation activities but may, in fact, be counterproductive:

- Creating a staff that consists only of strong players whose primary experience is related to the company's core business. This provides too few people to deal with the uncertainty of innovation projects and may cause good ideas to be dismissed because they do not appear to fit with the core business.
- Creating a staff that consists only of volunteers who want to work on projects they find interesting. Such players are often overzealous about new technologies or overly attached to product concepts, which can lead to poor decisions about which projects to pursue or drop.
- Creating a climate where innovation team members are considered second-class citizens. In companies where achievements are rewarded, the brightest and most ambitious players may avoid innovation projects with uncertain outcomes.

Unless an organization can align its key players into effective new venture teams, it is unlikely to create any differentiating advantages from its innovation efforts.[20] An enlightened approach to staffing a company's innovation efforts provides one of the best ways to ensure that the challenges of innovation will be effectively met. The nearby Insights from Research box discusses actions a firm can take to enhance the creativity of its employees in order to increase the innovative potential of the firm.

Collaborating with Innovation Partners

It is rare for any one organization to have all the information it needs to carry an innovation from concept to commercialization. Even a company that is highly competent with its current operations usually needs new capabilities to achieve new results. Innovation partners provide the skills and insights that are needed to make innovation projects succeed.[21]

Innovation partners may come from many sources, including research universities and the federal government. Each year the federal government issues requests for proposals (RFPs) asking private companies for assistance in improving services or finding solutions to public problems. Universities are another type of innovation partner. Chip-maker Intel, for example, has benefited from underwriting substantial amounts of university research. Rather than hand universities a blank check, Intel bargains for rights to patents that emerge from Intel-sponsored research. The university retains ownership of the patent, but Intel gets royalty-free use of it.[22]

Strategic partnering requires firms to identify their strengths and weaknesses and make choices about which capabilities to leverage, which need further development, and which are outside the firm's current or projected scope of operations.

To choose partners, firms need to ask what competencies they are looking for and what the innovation partner will contribute.[23] These might include knowledge of markets, technology expertise, or contacts with key players in an industry. Innovation partnerships also typically need to specify how the rewards of the innovation will be shared and who will own the intellectual property that is developed.[24]

Innovation efforts that involve multiple partners and the speed and ease with which partners can network and collaborate are changing the way innovation is conducted.[25] Strategy

INSIGHTS FROM RESEARCH

STIMULATING YOUR EMPLOYEES' CREATIVITY: WHAT LEADERS CAN DO

Overview

Business leaders consider creativity a prized characteristic in job candidates. The research suggests that qualities of certain individuals predispose them to produce creative work. How leaders interact with these employees can either promote or hinder employee creativity.

What the Research Shows

Are you wondering how to help your employees boost their creativity? Research conducted by scholars at Monash University and Aston University, as well as ISCTE Business School, provides insights into whom organizations should hire and how to best manage employees to promote creativity. The researchers carried out a questionnaire study of 213 employees and 49 leaders in manufacturing companies in China. This study, published in a 2012 article in the *Journal of Organizational Behavior,* found that employees are generally motivated at work by the achievement of one of two types of goals: Employees driven to achieve positive outcomes such as career advancement and growth were referred to as having a *promotion focus,* and employees whose goals push them to achieve personal security or to fulfill a duty or obligation were referred to as having a *prevention focus.*

Overall, employees with a promotion focus were more creative than employees with a prevention focus. Leaders can improve promotion-focused employees' creativity even further when they allow employees to participate in company decision-making processes and engage employees in intellectually stimulating leadership practices. For instance, they can encourage employees to come up with new ways to complete work tasks.

By hiring the right employees and engaging them through effective management practices, leaders can encourage their employees to flex their creative muscles.

Why This Matters

The results of this research suggest that if you want employees to be innovative, first make sure that you hire people with a promotion focus—those motivated by the achievement of career advancement, growth, and positive outcomes. With that in mind, HR procedures could feature personnel selection processes such as personality diagnostic tests and interview questions to help you, as the hiring manager, understand the promotion or prevention focus of prospective employees. Second, as a leader, you play a key role in helping your employees to produce creative outcomes. By empowering your employees to actively engage in the decision-making processes of the organization and by intellectually stimulating employees with challenges, you can bolster employee creativity.

The e-commerce technology development company iGo-Digital uses employee empowerment and intellectually stimulating leadership practices to inspire employee creativity. The company regularly hosts "Innovation Days." Employees go off-site and participate in idea-generation sessions. During Innovation Days, employees are encouraged to take on new roles in the company to understand how different functional areas work. All iGoDigital employees are treated equally and encouraged to come up with ideas and ways of getting work done, thus promoting a sense of empowerment. Finally, the organization tries to integrate some fun personal growth time into the Innovation Days to allow employees to gain a sense of personal growth and enjoyment. iGoDigital's techniques work, as is evidenced by new product launches including a technology product that helps companies manage email signatures across their businesses.

Key Takeaways

- The factors motivating employees' work efforts, in combination with how leaders interact with workers, can affect employees' creativity on the job.
- Employees are motivated by different outcomes such as achieving career advancement, growth, and personal security and fulfilling obligations. These motivators relate to how creative employees are.
- The researchers say that employees motivated by achieving career advancement and growth have a promotion focus and are more creative than employees motivated by personal security and obligations.
- Leaders can further enhance the creativity of promotion-focused employees by allowing them to participate in decision making and to engage in intellectually stimulating leadership behaviors.

Apply This Today

By hiring employees motivated by the achievement of career advancement and growth and by engaging employees via effective management practices, leaders can support the development of their workers' creativity. To learn more about how iGoDigital and other companies inspire employee creativity, visit BusinessMinded.com.

Research Reviewed

Zhou, Q., Hirst, G., & Shipton, H. (2012). Context matters: Combined influence of participation and intellectual stimulation on the promotion focus–employee creativity relationship. *Journal of Organizational Behavior,* 33(7): 894–909.

12.4 STRATEGY SPOTLIGHT — CROWDSOURCING

NASA WORKS WITH INNOCENTIVE TO ADDRESS CHALLENGES OF SPACE MISSIONS

NASA, the American space agency, regularly faces technological hurdles with space missions it is considering undertaking. Even with a staff of 18,000, its knowledge base is limited and unable to identify all of the innovative ways the agency could overcome the technological hurdles it faces.

One solution NASA has identified is to work with InnoCentive, an open innovation company that specializes in crowdsourcing innovative ideas. InnoCentive draws upon the knowledge and insight of over a quarter of a million "solvers" who have signed up on its site to provide innovative solutions for subscribing firms.

Between 2009 and 2014, NASA ran 13 innovation "challenges" with InnoCentive and awarded prizes up to $20,000 to the "solvers" who came up with the best ideas. Challenges have involved issues ranging from doing laundry in microgravity, to noninvasive ways of measuring intracranial pressure, to systems for better predicting solar events.

In a recent competition, NASA asked InnoCentive to help it identify ways to reduce radiation exposure during extended deep-space exploration missions. Addressing this issue is critical to NASA as it moves forward with plans for manned space missions to Mars and beyond. The challenge resulted in nearly 600 potential solutions, with NASA promising to grant awards of up to $12,000 to at least three of the submitters.

Working with InnoCentive offers NASA a low-cost avenue to crowdsource innovative ideas to address technological challenges the agency faces.

Sources: Anonymous. 2014. NASA joins InnoCentive, seeks ideas from public to reduce radiation exposure. *microfinancemonitor.com*, November 20: np; Hane, P. 2011. Innocentive links problems and problem-solvers. *newsbreaks.infotoday.com*, April 25: np; and *innocentive.com*.

Spotlight 12.4 outlines how NASA is working with an innovation partner, InnoCentive, to crowdsource ideas for overcoming space exploration challenges.

The Value of Unsuccessful Innovation

Companies are often reluctant to pursue innovations due to the high uncertainty associated with innovative efforts. They are torn about whether to invest in emerging technologies, wondering which, if any, will win in the market and offer the best payoff for the firm. Conventional wisdom suggests that firms pay dearly if they bet on the wrong technology or new product direction. However, research by NYU professor J. P. Eggers suggests that betting on a losing technology and then switching to the winner can position a company to come out ahead of competitors that were on the right track all along.[26]

His research shows that firms that initially invest in an unsuccessful innovative effort often end up dominating the market in the long run. The key is that the firm remains open to change and to learning from both its mistakes and the experience of the innovators that initially chose to pursue the winning technology. Eggers offers the following insights for companies competing in a dynamic market where it is uncertain which technology will emerge triumphant:

1. ***Avoid overcommitting.*** This can be difficult as the firm sees the need to build specific expertise and stake out a decisive position to be seen as a leader in the market. However, managers can become entrenched as confirmation bias leads them to focus only on data that suggest they've made the right choice. Eggers suggests firms consider joint ventures and other alliances to avoid overinvestments they may come to regret.
2. ***Don't let shame or despair knock you out of the game.*** Shame has been shown to be a particularly destructive reaction to failure. Remember that it is very likely no one could have had complete confidence regarding which technology would win. And try to avoid seeing things as worse than they are. Some companies that bet on the wrong technology decide, unnecessarily, to get out of the market entirely, missing out on any future market opportunities.
3. ***Pivot quickly.*** Once they realized they made a mistake, firms that were ultimately successful changed course and moved quickly. Studies have shown that the ideal

moment to enter a high-tech industry is just as the dominant design emerges. So missing the target initially doesn't have to mean that a firm is doomed to failure if the firm moves swiftly as the dominant technology becomes clear.

4. ***Transfer knowledge.*** Successful firms use the information they gathered in a losing bet to exploit other market opportunities. For example, when flat-panel computer displays were first emerging, it was unclear if plasma or LCD technology would win. IBM initially invested heavily in plasma displays, a bet that turned out to be wrong when LCD technology won out. But IBM took away valuable knowledge from its plasma investments. For example, the heavy glass required by plasma technology forced IBM to become skilled at glass design, which helped it push glass technology in new directions in products such as the original ThinkPad laptop.

5. ***Be aware that it can be dangerous to be right at the outset.*** Managers in firms that initially select the winning technology have a tendency to interpret their ability to choose the most promising technology as an unconditional endorsement of everything they had been doing. As a result, they fail to recognize the need to rethink some details of their product and the underlying technology. Their complacency can give firms that initially chose the wrong technology the space to catch up and then pull ahead, since the later-moving firms are more open to see the need for improvements and are hungry and aggressive in their actions. The key to who wins typically isn't who is there first. Instead, the winning firm is the one that continuously incrementally innovates on the initial bold innovation to offer the best product at the best price.

Corporate Entrepreneurship

Corporate entrepreneurship (CE) has two primary aims: the pursuit of new venture opportunities and strategic renewal.[27] The innovation process keeps firms alert by exposing them to new technologies, making them aware of marketplace trends, and helping them evaluate new possibilities. Corporate entrepreneurship uses the fruits of the innovation process to help firms build new sources of competitive advantage and renew their value propositions. Just as the innovation process helps firms to make positive improvements, CE helps firms identify opportunities and launch new ventures.

Corporate new venture creation was labeled "intrapreneuring" by Gifford Pinchot because it refers to building entrepreneurial businesses within existing corporations.[28] However, to engage in corporate entrepreneurship that yields above-average returns and contributes to sustainable advantages, it must be done effectively. In this section we will examine the sources of entrepreneurial activity within established firms and the methods large corporations use to stimulate entrepreneurial behavior.

In a typical corporation, what determines how entrepreneurial projects will be pursued? The answer depends on many factors, including:

- Corporate culture.
- Leadership.
- Structural features that guide and constrain action.
- Organizational systems that foster learning and manage rewards.

All of the factors that influence the strategy implementation process will also shape how corporations engage in internal venturing.

Other factors will also affect how entrepreneurial ventures will be pursued:

- The use of teams in strategic decision making.
- Whether the company is product- or service-oriented.
- Whether its innovation efforts are aimed at product or process improvements.
- The extent to which it is high-tech or low-tech.

> **corporate entrepreneurship (CE)**
> the creation of new value for a corporation through investments that create either new sources of competitive advantage or renewal of the value proposition.

Because these factors are different in every organization, some companies may be more involved than others in identifying and developing new venture opportunities.[29] These factors will also influence the nature of the CE process.

Successful CE typically requires firms to reach beyond their current operations and markets in the pursuit of new opportunities. It is often the breakthrough opportunities that provide the greatest returns. Such strategies are not without risks, however. In the sections that follow, we will address some of the strategic choice and implementation issues that influence the success or failure of CE activities.

Two distinct approaches to corporate venturing are found among firms that pursue entrepreneurial aims. The first is *focused* corporate venturing, in which CE activities are isolated from a firm's existing operations and worked on by independent work units. The second approach is *dispersed,* in which all parts of the organization and every organization member are engaged in intrapreneurial activities.

Focused Approaches to Corporate Entrepreneurship

Firms using a **focused approach** typically separate the corporate venturing activity from the other ongoing operations of the firm. CE is usually the domain of autonomous work groups that pursue entrepreneurial aims independent of the rest of the firm. The advantage of this approach is that it frees entrepreneurial team members to think and act without the constraints imposed by existing organizational norms and routines. This independence is often necessary for the kind of open-minded creativity that leads to strategic breakthroughs. The disadvantage is that, because of their isolation from the corporate mainstream, the work groups that concentrate on internal ventures may fail to obtain the resources or support needed to carry an entrepreneurial project through to completion. Two forms—new venture groups (NVGs) and business incubators—are among the most common types of focused approaches.

New Venture Groups Corporations often form **new venture groups (NVGs)** whose goal is to identify, evaluate, and cultivate venture opportunities. These groups typically function as semiautonomous units with little formal structure. The NVG may simply be a committee that reports to the president on potential new ventures. Or it may be organized as a corporate division with its own staff and budget. The aims of the NVG may be open-ended in terms of what ventures it may consider. Alternatively, some corporations use an NVG to promote concentrated effort on a specific problem. In both cases, NVGs usually have a substantial amount of freedom to take risks and a supply of resources to do it with.[30]

New venture groups usually have a larger mandate than a typical R&D department. Their involvement extends beyond innovation and experimentation to coordinating with other corporate divisions, identifying potential venture partners, gathering resources, and actually launching the venture. Strategy Spotlight 12.5 shows how Taco Bell has used an NVG to improve its CE efforts.

Business Incubators The term *incubator* was originally used to describe a device in which eggs are hatched. **Business incubators** are designed to "hatch" new businesses. They are a type of corporate NVG with a somewhat more specialized purpose—to support and nurture fledgling entrepreneurial ventures until they can thrive on their own as stand-alone businesses. Corporations use incubators as a way to grow businesses identified by the NVG. Although they often receive support from many parts of the corporation, they still operate independently until they are strong enough to go it alone. Depending on the type of business, they either are integrated into an existing corporate division or continue to operate as a subsidiary of the parent firm.

12.5 STRATEGY SPOTLIGHT

TACO BELL COOKS UP SOME NEW IDEAS

When people think of highly innovative industries, it is unlikely that fast food is going to be one of the first industries that comes to mind. However, that doesn't mean that firms in this market see no need to innovate. One of the most innovative fast-food chains is Taco Bell. Many firms in the fast-food market, such as In-N-Out Burger, are content to deliver a consistent lineup of popular items, but Taco Bell regularly launches new products to keep customers coming back and to try to find the next big-hit product. One example of this occurred, in 2012, when Taco Bell sold over 100 million Doritos Locos Tacos in the first 10 weeks after the product was launched.

The responsibility for coming up with new food ideas falls on Taco Bell's 40-person innovation center team. Their charge, in the words of Greg Creed, CEO of Yum! Brands, the parent corporation of Taco Bell, is to craft the "industry's next big thing." The team tries out new recipes nearly every day and, as a result, is very well fed. Elizabeth Matthews, Taco Bell's chief food and beverage innovation officer, states, "Sometimes, before 10 a.m., I'm sure I've had 3,000 calories." To avoid packing on the Taco Bell 12 (pounds), the innovation center houses a fully equipped gym and offers 20 exercise classes a week for center employees.

To generate new ideas, the center's employees follow social media, consider new ingredients, and track what the firm's rivals are doing. They take field trips to grocery stores to see what new products and flavors are hitting the market. In developing new products, the team must always keep in mind Taco Bell's drive for taste, value, and speed.

A great example of how this works is the process that led to the Waffle Taco. Heather Mottershaw, director of product development, was scrolling through Facebook status updates one morning when a photo a friend posted caught her eye. The photo was of a meal her friend had ordered in a restaurant. The main course looked like a folded-over waffle sandwich stuffed with eggs and avocado. Her reaction was "huh, that's an interesting idea." She ran out to the store and bought a package of waffles and brought them into the office at 7 a.m. on Monday morning. She thawed a waffle out, folded it into a U shape, and flash-fried it in a chalupa basket. She then filled it with eggs, sausage, and cheese. By 9 a.m., executives at Taco Bell were evaluating the idea. The verdict, in Mottershaw's words, was "This is a cool idea, this is a big idea." Even with a "big idea," the development process can be long and arduous. The team first tested the Waffle Taco in the lab and then in test restaurants. The team went through 80 iterations of the new product before it was finalized. But the excitement for it remained, and the Waffle Taco, along with the A.M. Crunchwrap, became the centerpiece menu item in Taco Bell's nationwide breakfast launch in March 2014.

Sources: Rosenfeld, E., 2012. Taco Bell's Doritos Locos Tacos are an insanely huge hit. *time.com*, June 5: np; and Wong, V. 2014. Taco Bell's secret recipe for new products. *bloomberg.com*, May 29: np.

Incubators typically provide some or all of the following five functions:[31]

- *Funding.* This includes capital investments as well as in-kind investments and loans.
- *Physical space.* Incubators in which several start-ups share space often provide fertile ground for new ideas and collaboration.
- *Business services.* Along with office space, young ventures need basic services and infrastructure, which may include anything from phone systems and computer networks to public relations and personnel management.
- *Mentoring.* Senior executives and skilled technical personnel often provide coaching and experience-based advice.
- *Networking.* Contact with other parts of the firm and external resources such as suppliers, industry experts, and potential customers facilitates problem solving and knowledge sharing.

Because Microsoft has struggled to reinvigorate its entrepreneurial capabilities, the company has created a business incubator to enhance corporate entrepreneurship efforts.

To encourage entrepreneurship, corporations sometimes need to do more than create independent work groups or venture incubators to generate new enterprises. In some firms, the entrepreneurial spirit is spread throughout the organization.

Dispersed Approaches to Corporate Entrepreneurship

The second type of CE is dispersed. For some companies, a dedication to the principles and practices of entrepreneurship is spread throughout the organization. One advantage of

dispersed approaches to corporate entrepreneurship
corporate entrepreunership in which a dedication to the principles and policies of entrepreneurship is spread throughout the organization.

this **dispersed approach** is that organizational members don't have to be reminded to think entrepreneurially or be willing to change. The ability to change is considered to be a core capability. This leads to a second advantage: Because of the firm's entrepreneurial reputation, stakeholders such as vendors, customers, or alliance partners can bring new ideas or venture opportunities to anyone in the organization and expect them to be well received. Such opportunities make it possible for the firm to stay ahead of the competition. However, there are disadvantages as well. Firms that are overzealous about CE sometimes feel they must change for the sake of change, causing them to lose vital competencies or spend heavily on R&D and innovation to the detriment of the bottom line. Three related aspects of dispersed entrepreneurship include entrepreneurial cultures that have an overarching commitment to CE activities, resource allotments to support entrepreneurial actions, and the use of product champions in promoting entrepreneurial behaviors.

Entrepreneurial Culture In some large corporations, the corporate culture embodies the spirit of entrepreneurship. A culture of entrepreneurship is one in which the search for venture opportunities permeates every part of the organization. The key to creating value successfully is viewing every value-chain activity as a source of competitive advantage. The effect of CE on a firm's strategic success is strongest when it animates all parts of an organization. It is found in companies where the strategic leaders and the culture together generate a strong impetus to innovate, take risks, and seek out new venture opportunities.[32]

entrepreneurial culture
corporate culture in which change and renewal are a constant focus of attention.

In companies with an **entrepreneurial culture,** everyone in the organization is attuned to opportunities to help create new businesses. Many such firms use a top-down approach to stimulate entrepreneurial activity. The top leaders of the organization support programs and incentives that foster a climate of entrepreneurship. Many of the best ideas for new corporate ventures, however, come from the bottom up. Catherine Winder, president of Rainmaker Entertainment, discussed how she welcomes any employee to generate and pitch innovative ideas this way:[33]

> We have an open-door policy for anyone in the company to pitch ideas . . . to describe their ideas in 15 to 30 seconds. If we like the core idea, we'll work with them. If you can be concise and come up with your idea in a really clear way, it means you're on to something.

An entrepreneurial culture is one in which change and renewal are on everybody's mind. Amazon, 3M, Intel, and Cisco are among the corporations best known for their corporate venturing activities. Many fast-growing young corporations also attribute much of their success to an entrepreneurial culture. But other successful firms struggle in their efforts to remain entrepreneurial. For example, Microsoft has had great difficulty increasing its innovativeness. One of the challenges has been that the conservatism of the firm's culture has led to a focus on short-term profitability over innovation.[34]

Resource Allotments Corporate entrepreneurship requires the willingness of the firm to invest in the generation and execution of innovative ideas. On the generation side, employees are much more likely to develop these ideas if they have the time to do so. For decades, 3M allowed its engineers free time, up to 15 percent of their work schedule, to work on developing new products.[35] Intuit follows a similar model, offering employees the opportunity to spend 10 percent of their time on ideas that improve Intuit's processes or on products that address user problems. According to Brad Smith, Intuit's CEO, this time is critical for the future success of Intuit since "innovation is not going to come from me. It's going to come from challenging people to think about new and different ways of solving big, important problems."[36] In addition to time, firms can foster CE by providing monetary investment to fund entrepreneurial ideas. Johnson & Johnson (J&J) uses its Internal Ventures Group to support entrepreneurial ideas developed inside the firm. Entrepreneurs within J&J submit proposals to the group. The review board decides which proposals to fund and then solicits further investments from J&J's operating divisions. Nike's Sustainable Business and Innovation Lab and Google's Ventures Group have a similar charter to review and fund promising corporate entrepreneurship activities. The availability of these time and financing sources can enhance the likelihood of successful entrepreneurial activities within the firm.

Product Champions Corporate entrepreneurship does not always involve making large investments in start-ups or establishing incubators to spawn new divisions. Often, innovative ideas emerge in the normal course of business and are brought forth and become part of the way of doing business. Entrepreneurial champions are often needed to take charge of internally generated ventures. **Product champions** (or project champions) are those individuals working within a corporation who bring entrepreneurial ideas forward, identify what kind of market exists for the product or service, find resources to support the venture, and promote the venture concept to upper management.[37]

> product champion
> an individual working within a corporation who brings entrepreneurial ideas forward, identifies what kind of market exists for the product or service, finds resources to support the venture, and promotes the venture concept to upper management.

When lower-level employees identify a product idea or novel solution, they will take it to their supervisor or someone in authority. A new idea that is generated in a technology lab may be introduced to others by its inventor. If the idea has merit, it gains support and builds momentum across the organization.[38] Even though the corporation may not be looking for new ideas or have a program for cultivating internal ventures, the independent behaviors of a few organizational members can have important strategic consequences.

No matter how an entrepreneurial idea comes to light, however, a new venture concept must pass through two critical stages or it may never get off the ground:

1. *Project definition.* An opportunity has to be justified in terms of its attractiveness in the marketplace and how well it fits with the corporation's other strategic objectives.
2. *Project impetus.* For a project to gain impetus, its strategic and economic impact must be supported by senior managers who have experience with similar projects. It then becomes an embryonic business with its own organization and budget.

For a project to advance through these stages of definition and impetus, a product champion is often needed to generate support and encouragement. Champions are especially important during the time after a new project has been defined but before it gains momentum. They form a link between the definition and impetus stages of internal development, which they do by procuring resources and stimulating interest for the product among potential customers.[39] Often, they must work quietly and alone. Consider the example of Ken Kutaragi, the Sony engineer who championed the PlayStation.

> Even though Sony had made the processor that powered the first Nintendo video games, no one at Sony in the mid-1980s saw any future in such products. "It was a kind of snobbery," Kutaragi recalled. "For Sony people, the Nintendo product would have been very embarrassing to make because it was only a toy." But Kutaragi was convinced he could make a better product. He began working secretly on a video game. Kutaragi said, "I realized that if it was visible, it would be killed." He quietly began enlisting the support of senior executives, such as the head of R&D. He made a case that Sony could use his project to develop capabilities in digital technologies that would be important in the future. It was not until 1994, after years of "underground" development and quiet building of support, that Sony introduced the PlayStation. By the year 2000, Sony had sold 55 million of them, and Kutaragi became CEO of Sony Computer Entertainment. By 2005, Kutaragi was Sony's chief operating officer, and was supervising efforts to launch PS3, the next generation version of the market-leading PlayStation video game console.[40]

Product champions play an important entrepreneurial role in a corporate setting by encouraging others to take a chance on promising new ideas.[41]

Measuring the Success of Corporate Entrepreneurship Activities

At this point in the discussion, it is reasonable to ask whether CE is successful. Corporate venturing, like the innovation process, usually requires a tremendous effort. Is it worth it? We consider factors that corporations need to take into consideration when evaluating the success of CE programs. We also examine techniques that companies can use to limit the expense of venturing or to cut their losses when CE initiatives appear doomed.

LO12.4
How corporate entrepreneurship achieves both financial goals and strategic goals.

Comparing Strategic and Financial CE Goals   Not all corporate venturing efforts are financially rewarding. In terms of financial performance, slightly more than 50 percent of corporate venturing efforts reach profitability (measured by ROI) within six years of their launch.[42] If this were the only criterion for success, it would seem to be a rather poor return. On the one hand, these results should be expected, because CE is riskier than other investments such as expanding ongoing operations. On the other hand, corporations expect a higher return from corporate venturing projects than from normal operations. Thus, in terms of the risk–return trade-off, it seems that CE often falls short of expectations.[43]

There are several other important criteria, however, for judging the success of a corporate venture initiative. Most CE programs have strategic goals.[44] The strategic reasons for undertaking a corporate venture include strengthening competitive position, entering into new markets, expanding capabilities by learning and acquiring new knowledge, and building the corporation's base of resources and experience. Three questions should be used to assess the effectiveness of a corporation's venturing initiatives:[45]

1. *Are the products or services offered by the venture accepted in the marketplace?* Is the venture considered to be a market success? If so, the financial returns are likely to be satisfactory. The venture may also open doors into other markets and suggest avenues for other venture projects.
2. *Are the contributions of the venture to the corporation's internal competencies and experience valuable?* Does the venture add to the worth of the firm internally? If so, strategic goals such as leveraging existing assets, building new knowledge, and enhancing firm capabilities are likely to be met.[46]
3. *Is the venture able to sustain its basis of competitive advantage?* Does the value proposition offered by the venture insulate it from competitive attack? If so, it is likely to place the corporation in a stronger position relative to competitors and provide a base from which to build other advantages.

These criteria include both strategic and financial goals of CE. Another way to evaluate a corporate venture is in terms of the four criteria from the balanced scorecard (Chapter 3). In a successful venture, not only are financial and market acceptance (customer) goals met but so are the internal business and innovation and learning goals. Thus, when assessing the success of corporate venturing, it is important to look beyond simple financial returns and consider a well-rounded set of criteria.[47]

Exit Champions   Although a culture of championing venture projects is advantageous for stimulating an ongoing stream of entrepreneurial initiatives, many—in fact, most—of the ideas will not work out. At some point in the process, a majority of initiatives will be abandoned. Sometimes, however, companies wait too long to terminate a new venture and do so only after large sums of resources are used up or, worse, result in a marketplace failure. Motorola's costly global satellite telecom project known as Iridium provides a useful illustration. Even though problems with the project existed during the lengthy development process, Motorola refused to pull the plug. Only after investing $5 billion and years of effort was the project abandoned.[48]

One way to avoid these costly and discouraging defeats is to support a key role in the CE process: **exit champions.** In contrast to product champions and other entrepreneurial enthusiasts within the corporation, exit champions are willing to question the viability of

exit champion
an individual working within a corporation who is willing to question the viability of a venture project by demanding hard evidence of venture success and challenging the belief system that carries a venture forward.

a venture project.[49] By demanding hard evidence and challenging the belief system that is carrying an idea forward, exit champions hold the line on ventures that appear shaky.

Both product champions and exit champions must be willing to energetically stand up for what they believe. Both put their reputations on the line. But they also differ in important ways.[50] Product champions deal in uncertainty and ambiguity. Exit champions reduce ambiguity by gathering hard data and developing a strong case for why a project should be killed. Product champions are often thought to be willing to violate procedures and operate outside normal channels. Exit champions often have to reinstate procedures and reassert the decision-making criteria that are supposed to guide venture decisions. Whereas product champions often emerge as heroes, exit champions run the risk of losing status by opposing popular projects.

The role of exit champion may seem unappealing. But it is one that could save a corporation both financially and in terms of its reputation in the marketplace. It is especially important because one measure of the success of a firm's CE efforts is the extent to which it knows when to cut its losses and move on.

Real Options Analysis: A Useful Tool

>**LO12.5**
>The benefits and potential drawbacks of real options analysis in making resource deployment decisions in corporate entrepreneurship contexts.

One way firms can minimize failure and avoid losses from pursuing faulty ideas is to apply the logic of real options. **Real options analysis (ROA)** is an investment analysis tool from the field of finance. It has been slowly, but increasingly, adopted by consultants and executives to support strategic decision making in firms. What does ROA consist of and how can it be appropriately applied to the investments required to initiate strategic decisions? To understand *real* options it is first necessary to have a basic understanding of what *options* are.

Options exist when the owner of the option has the right but not the obligation to engage in certain types of transactions. The most common are stock options. A stock option grants the holder the right to buy (call option) or sell (put option) shares of the stock at a fixed price (strike price) at some time in the future.[51] The investment to be made immediately is small, whereas the investment to be made in the future is generally larger. An option to buy a rapidly rising stock currently priced at $50 might cost as little as $.50.[52] Owners of such a stock option have limited their losses to $.50 per share, while the upside potential is unlimited. This aspect of options is attractive, because options offer the prospect of high gains with relatively small up-front investments that represent limited losses.

>**real options analysis (ROA)** an investment analysis tool that looks at an investment or activity as a series of sequential steps, and for each step the investor has the option of (a) investing additional funds to grow or accelerate, (b) delaying, (c) shrinking the scale of, or (d) abandoning the activity.

The phrase "real options" applies to situations where options theory and valuation techniques are applied to real assets or physical things as opposed to financial assets. Applied to entrepreneurship, real options suggest a path that companies can use to manage the uncertainty associated with launching new ventures. Some of the most common applications of real options are with property and insurance. A real estate option grants the holder the right to buy or sell a piece of property at an established price some time in the future. The actual market price of the property may rise above the established (or strike) price—or the market value may sink below the strike price. If the price of the property goes up, the owner of the option is likely to buy it. If the market value of the property drops below the strike price, the option holder is unlikely to execute the purchase. In the latter circumstance, the option holder has limited his or her loss to the cost of the option but during the life of the option retains the right to participate in whatever the upside potential might be.

Applications of Real Options Analysis to Strategic Decisions

The concept of options can also be applied to strategic decisions where management has flexibility. Situations arise where management must decide whether to invest additional funds to grow or accelerate the activity, perhaps delay in order to learn more, shrink the scale of the activity, or even abandon it. Decisions to invest in new ventures or other business activities such as R&D, motion pictures, exploration and production of oil wells, and the opening and closing of copper mines often have this flexibility.[53] Important issues to note are:

- ROA is appropriate to use when investments can be staged; a smaller investment up front can be followed by subsequent investments. Real options can be applied to an investment decision that gives the company the right, but not the obligation, to make follow-on investments.
- Strategic decision makers have "tollgates," or key points at which they can decide whether to continue, delay, or abandon the project. Executives have flexibility. There are opportunities to make other go or no-go decisions associated with each phase.
- It is expected that there will be increased knowledge about outcomes at the time of the next investment and that additional knowledge will help inform the decision makers about whether to make additional investments (i.e., whether the option is in the money or out of the money).

Many strategic decisions have the characteristic of containing a series of options. The phenomenon is called "embedded options," a series of investments in which at each stage of the investment there is a go/no-go decision. Consider the real options logic that Johnson Controls, a maker of car seats, instrument panels, and interior control systems, uses to advance or eliminate entrepreneurial ideas.[54] Johnson options each new innovative idea by making a small investment in it. To receive additional funding, the idea must continue to prove itself at each stage of development. Here's how Jim Geschke, former vice president and general manager of electronics integration at Johnson, described the process:

> Think of Johnson as an innovation machine. The front end has a robust series of gates that each idea must pass through. Early on, we'll have many ideas and spend a little money on each of them. As they get more fleshed out, the ideas go through a gate where a go or no-go decision is made. A lot of ideas get filtered out, so there are far fewer items, and the spending on each goes up. . . . Several months later each idea will face another gate. If it passes, that means it's a serious idea that we are going to develop. Then the spending goes way up, and the number of ideas goes way down. By the time you reach the final gate, you need to have a credible business case in order to be accepted. At a certain point in the development process, we take our idea to customers and ask them what they think. Sometimes they say, "That's a terrible idea. Forget it." Other times they say, "That's fabulous. I want a million of them."

This process of evaluating ideas by separating winning ideas from losing ones in a way that keeps investments low has helped Johnson Controls grow its revenues to over $43 billion a year. Using real options logic to advance the development process is a key way that firms reduce uncertainty and minimize innovation-related failures.[55] Real options logic can also be used with other types of strategic decisions. Strategy Spotlight 12.6 discusses how Intel uses real options logic in making capacity expansion decisions.

Potential Pitfalls of Real Options Analysis

Despite the many benefits that can be gained from using ROA, managers must be aware of its potential limitations or pitfalls. Below we will address three major issues.[56]

back-solver dilemma
problem with investment decisions in which managers scheme to have a project meet investment approval criteria, even though the investment may not enhance firm value.

Agency Theory and the Back-Solver Dilemma Let's assume that companies adopting a real options perspective invest heavily in training and that their people understand how to effectively estimate variance—the amount of dispersion or range that is estimated for potential outcomes. Such training can help them use ROA. However, it does not solve another inherent problem: Managers may have an incentive and the know-how to "game the system." Most electronic spreadsheets permit users to simply back-solve any formula; that is, you can type in the answer you want and ask what values are needed in a formula to get that answer. If managers know that a certain option value must be met in order for the proposal to get approved, they can back-solve the model to find a variance estimate needed to arrive at the answer that upper management desires.

12.6 STRATEGY SPOTLIGHT

SAVING MILLIONS WITH REAL OPTIONS AT INTEL

The semiconductor business is complex and dynamic. This makes it a difficult one to manage. On the one hand, both the technology in the chips and the consumer demand for chips are highly volatile. This makes it difficult to plan for the future as far as the need for chip designs and production plants is concerned. On the other hand, it is incredibly expensive to build new chip plants, about $5 billion each, and chip manufacturing equipment needs to be ordered well ahead of when it is needed. The lead time for ordering new equipment can be up to three years. This creates a great challenge. Firms have to decide how much and what type of equipment to purchase long before they have a good handle on what the demand for semiconductor chips will be. Guessing wrong leaves the firm with too much or too little capacity.

Intel has figured out a way to limit the risk it faces by using option contracts. Intel pays an up-front fee for the right to purchase key pieces of equipment at a specific future date. At that point, Intel either purchases the equipment or releases the supplier from the contract. In these cases, the supplier is then free to sell the equipment to someone else. This all seems fairly simple. A number of commodities, such as wheat and sugar, have robust option markets. The challenge isn't in setting up the contracts. It is in pricing those contracts. Unlike wheat and sugar, where a large number of suppliers and buyers results in an efficient market that sets the prices of standard commodity products, there are few buyers and suppliers of chip manufacturing equipment. Further, the equipment is not a standard commodity. As a result, prices for equipment options are the outcome of difficult negotiations.

Karl Kempf, a mathematician with Intel, has figured out how to make this process smoother. Along with a group of mathematicians at Stanford, Kempf has developed a computing logic for calculating the price of options. He and his colleagues create a forecasting model for potential demand. They calculate the likelihood of a range of potential demand levels. They also set up a computer simulation of a production plant. They then use the possible demand levels to predict how many pieces of production equipment they will need in the plant to meet the demand. They run this over and over again, thousands of times, to generate predictions about the likelihood they will need to purchase a specific piece of equipment. They use this information to identify what equipment they definitely need to order. Where there is significant uncertainty about the need for equipment, they use the simulation results to identify the specific equipment for which they need option contracts and the value of those options to Intel. This helps with the pricing.

Intel estimates that in the five years from 2008 to 2012, the use of options in equipment purchases saved the firm in excess of $125 million and provided the firm with at least $2 billion in revenue upside for expansions it could have quickly made using optioned equipment.

Sources: Kempf, K., Erhun, F., Hertzler, E., Rosenberg, T., & Peng, C. 2013. Optimizing capital investment decisions at Intel Corporation. *Interfaces*, 43(1): 62–78; and King, I. 2012. A chipmaker's model mathematician. *Bloomberg Businessweek*, June 4: 35.

Agency problems are typically inherent in investment decisions. They may occur when the managers of a firm are separated from its owners—when managers act as "agents" rather than "principals" (owners). A manager may have something to gain by not acting in the owner's best interests, or the interests of managers and owners are not co-aligned. Agency theory suggests that as managerial and owner interests diverge, managers will follow the path of their own self-interests. Sometimes this is to secure better compensation: Managers who propose projects may believe that if their projects are approved, they stand a much better chance of getting promoted. So while managers have an incentive to propose projects that *should* be successful, they also have an incentive to propose projects that *might* be successful. And because of the subjectivity involved in formally modeling a real option, managers may have an incentive to choose variance values that increase the likelihood of approval.

Managerial Conceit: Overconfidence and the Illusion of Control Often, poor decisions are the result of such traps as biases, blind spots, and other human frailties. Much of this literature falls under the concept of **managerial conceit**.[57]

First, managerial conceit occurs when decision makers who have made successful choices in the past come to believe that they possess superior expertise for managing uncertainty. They believe that their abilities can reduce the risks inherent in decision making to a much greater extent than they actually can. Such managers are more likely to shift

> **managerial conceit**
> biases, blind spots, and other human frailties that lead to poor managerial decisions.

away from analysis to trusting their own judgment. In the case of real options, they can simply declare that any given decision is a real option and proceed as before. If asked to formally model their decision, they are more likely to employ variance estimates that support their viewpoint.

Second, employing the real options perspective can encourage decision makers toward a bias for action. Such a bias may lead to carelessness. Managerial conceit is as much a problem (if not more so) for small decisions as for big ones. Why? The cost to write the first stage of an option is much smaller than the cost of full commitment, and managers pay less attention to small decisions than to large ones. Because real options are designed to minimize potential losses while preserving potential gains, any problems that arise are likely to be smaller at first, causing less concern for the manager. Managerial conceit could suggest that managers will assume that those problems are the easiest to solve and control—a concern referred to as the illusion of control. Managers may fail to respond appropriately because they overlook the problem or believe that since it is small, they can easily resolve it. Thus, managers may approach each real option decision with less care and diligence than if they had made a full commitment to a larger investment.

Managerial Conceit: Irrational Escalation of Commitment A strength of a real options perspective is also one of its Achilles heels. Both real options and decisions involving **escalation of commitment** require specific environments with sequential decisions.[58] As the escalation-of-commitment literature indicates, simply separating a decision into multiple parts does not guarantee that decisions made will turn out well. This condition is potentially present whenever the exercise decision retains some uncertainty, which most still do. The decision to abandon also has strong psychological factors associated with it that affect the ability of managers to make correct exercise decisions.[59]

An option to exit requires reversing an initial decision made by someone in the organization. Organizations typically encourage managers to "own their decisions" in order to motivate them. As managers invest themselves in their decision, it proves harder for them to lose face by reversing course. For managers making the decision, it feels as if they made the wrong decision in the first place, even if it was initially a good decision. The more specific the manager's human capital becomes, the harder it is to transfer it to other organizations. Hence, there is a greater likelihood that managers will stick around and try to make an existing decision work. They are more likely to continue an existing project even if it should perhaps be ended.[60]

Despite the potential pitfalls of a real options approach, many of the strategic decisions that product champions and top managers must make are enhanced when decision makers have an entrepreneurial mind-set.

Entrepreneurial Orientation

Firms that want to engage in successful CE need to have an entrepreneurial orientation (EO).[61] **Entrepreneurial orientation** refers to the strategy-making practices that businesses use in identifying and launching corporate ventures. It represents a frame of mind and a perspective toward entrepreneurship that is reflected in a firm's ongoing processes and corporate culture.[62]

An EO has five dimensions that permeate the decision-making styles and practices of the firm's members: autonomy, innovativeness, proactiveness, competitive aggressiveness, and risk taking. These factors work together to enhance a firm's entrepreneurial performance. But even those firms that are strong in only a few aspects of EO can be very successful.[63] Exhibit 12.3 summarizes the dimensions of entrepreneurial orientation. Below, we discuss the five dimensions of EO and how they have been used to enhance internal venture development.

---

escalation of commitment
the tendency for managers to irrationally stick with an investment, even one that is broken down into a sequential series of decisions, when investment criteria are not being met.

LO12.6
How an entrepreneurial orientation can enhance a firm's efforts to develop promising corporate venture initiatives.

entrepreneurial orientation
the practices that businesses use in identifying and launching corporate ventures.

EXHIBIT 12.3 Dimensions of Entrepreneurial Orientation

Dimension	Definition
Autonomy	Independent action by an individual or team aimed at bringing forth a business concept or vision and carrying it through to completion.
Innovativeness	A willingness to introduce novelty through experimentation and creative processes aimed at developing new products and services as well as new processes.
Proactiveness	A forward-looking perspective characteristic of a marketplace leader that has the foresight to seize opportunities in anticipation of future demand.
Competitive aggressiveness	An intense effort to outperform industry rivals characterized by a combative posture or an aggressive response aimed at improving position or overcoming a threat in a competitive marketplace.
Risk taking	Making decisions and taking action without certain knowledge of probable outcomes; some undertakings may also involve making substantial resource commitments in the process of venturing forward.

Sources: Dess, G. G. & Lumpkin, G. T. 2005. The Role of Entrepreneurial Orientation in Stimulating Effective Corporate Entrepreneurship. *Academy of Management Executive,* 19(1): 147–156; Covin, J. G. & Slevin, D. P. 1991. A Conceptual Model of Entrepreneurship as Firm Behavior. *Entrepreneurship Theory & Practice,* Fall: 7–25; Lumpkin, G. T. and Dess, G. G. 1996. Clarifying the Entrepreneurial Orientation Construct and Linking It to Performance. *Academy of Management Review,* 21: 135–172; and Miller, D. 1983. The Correlates of Entrepreneurship in Three Types of Firms. *Management Science,* 29: 770–791.

Autonomy

Autonomy refers to a willingness to act independently in order to carry forward an entrepreneurial vision or opportunity. It applies to both individuals and teams that operate outside an organization's existing norms and strategies. In the context of corporate entrepreneurship, autonomous work units are often used to leverage existing strengths in new arenas, identify opportunities that are beyond the organization's current capabilities, and encourage development of new ventures or improved business practices.[64]

The need for autonomy may apply to either dispersed or focused entrepreneurial efforts. Because of the emphasis on venture projects that are being developed outside the normal flow of business, a focused approach suggests a working environment that is relatively autonomous. But autonomy may also be important in an organization where entrepreneurship is part of the corporate culture. Everything from the methods of group interaction to the firm's reward system must make organizational members feel as if they can think freely about venture opportunities, take time to investigate them, and act without fear of condemnation. This implies a respect for the autonomy of each individual and an openness to the independent thinking that goes into championing a corporate venture idea. Thus, autonomy represents a type of empowerment (see Chapter 11) that is directed at identifying and leveraging entrepreneurial opportunities. Exhibit 12.4 identifies two techniques that organizations often use to promote autonomy.

Creating autonomous work units and encouraging independent action may have pitfalls that can jeopardize their effectiveness. Autonomous teams often lack coordination. Excessive decentralization has a strong potential to create inefficiencies, such as duplicating effort and wasting resources on projects with questionable feasibility. For example, Chris Galvin, former CEO of Motorola, scrapped the skunkworks approach the company had been using to develop new wireless phones. Fifteen teams had created 128 different phones, which led to spiraling costs and overly complex operations.[65]

For autonomous work units and independent projects to be effective, such efforts have to be measured and monitored. This requires a delicate balance: Companies must have the patience and budget to tolerate the explorations of autonomous groups and the strength to cut back efforts that are not bearing fruit. Efforts must be undertaken with a clear sense of purpose—namely, to generate new sources of competitive advantage.

autonomy
independent action by an individual or a team aimed at bringing forth a business concept or vision and carrying it through to completion.

EXHIBIT 12.4 Autonomy Techniques

Autonomy		
Technique	**Description/Purpose**	**Example**
Use skunkworks to foster entrepreneurial thinking.	Skunkworks are independent work units, often physically separate from corporate headquarters. They allow employees to get out from under the pressures of their daily routines to engage in creative problem solving.	Overstock.com created a skunkworks to address the problem of returned merchandise. The solution was a business within a business: Overstock auctions. The unit has grown by selling products returned to Overstock and offers fees 30 percent lower than eBay's auction service.
Design organizational structures that support independent action.	Established companies with traditional structures often need to break out of such old forms to compete more effectively.	Deloitte Consulting, a division of Deloitte Touche Tohmatsu, found it difficult to compete against young agile firms. So it broke the firm into small autonomous units called "chip-aways" that operate with the flexibility of a start-up. In its first year, revenues were $40 million—10 percent higher than its projections.

Sources: Conlin, M. 2006. Square Feet. Oh How Square! *BusinessWeek,* www.businessweek.com, July 3; Cross, K. 2001. Bang the Drum Quickly. *Business 2.0,* May: 28–30; Sweeney, J. 2004. A Firm for All Reasons. *Consulting Magazine,* www.consultingmag.com; and Wagner, M. 2005. Out of the Skunkworks. *Internet Retailer,* January, www.internetretailer.com.

Innovativeness

innovativeness
a willingness to introduce novelty through experimentation and creative processes aimed at developing new products and services as well as new processes.

Innovativeness refers to a firm's efforts to find new opportunities and novel solutions. In the beginning of this chapter we discussed innovation; here the focus is on innovativeness—a firm's attitude toward innovation and willingness to innovate. It involves creativity and experimentation that result in new products, new services, or improved technological processes.[66] Innovativeness is one of the major components of an entrepreneurial strategy. As indicated at the beginning of the chapter, however, the job of managing innovativeness can be very challenging.

Innovativeness requires that firms depart from existing technologies and practices and venture beyond the current state of the art. Inventions and new ideas need to be nurtured even when their benefits are unclear. However, in today's climate of rapid change, effectively producing, assimilating, and exploiting innovations can be an important avenue for achieving competitive advantages. Interest in global warming and other ecological concerns has led many corporations to focus their innovativeness efforts on solving environmental problems.

As our earlier discussion of CE indicated, many corporations owe their success to an active program of innovation-based corporate venturing.[67] Exhibit 12.5 highlights two of the methods companies can use to enhance their competitive position through innovativeness.

Innovativeness can be a source of great progress and strong corporate growth, but there are also major pitfalls for firms that invest in innovation. Expenditures on R&D aimed at identifying new products or processes can be a waste of resources if the effort does not yield results. Another danger is related to the competitive climate. Even if a company innovates a new capability or successfully applies a technological breakthrough, another company may develop a similar innovation or find a use for it that is more profitable. Finally R&D and other innovation efforts are among the first to be cut back during an economic downturn.

Even though innovativeness is an important means of internal corporate venturing, it also involves major risks, because investments in innovations may not pay off. For strategic managers of entrepreneurial firms, successfully developing and adopting innovations can generate competitive advantages and provide a major source of growth for the firm.

Proactiveness

proactiveness
a forward-looking perspective characteristic of a marketplace leader that has the foresight to seize opportunities in anticipation of future demand.

Proactiveness refers to a firm's efforts to seize new opportunities. Proactive organizations monitor trends, identify the future needs of existing customers, and anticipate changes in demand or emerging problems that can lead to new venture opportunities. Proactiveness involves not only

EXHIBIT 12.5 Innovativeness Techniques

	Innovativeness	
Technique	**Description/Purpose**	**Example**
Foster creativity and experimentation.	Companies that support idea exploration and allow employees to express themselves creatively enhance innovation outcomes.	To tap into its reserves of innovative talent, Royal Dutch Shell created "GameChanger" to help employees develop promising ideas. The process provides funding up to $600,000 for would-be entrepreneurs to pursue innovative projects and conduct experiments.
Invest in new technology, R&D, and continuous improvement.	The latest technologies often provide sources of new competitive advantages. To extract value from a new technology, companies must invest in it.	Dell Computer Corporation's OptiPlex manufacturing system revolutionized the traditional assembly line. Hundreds of custom-built computers can be made in an eight-hour shift using state-of-the-art automation techniques that increased productivity per person by 160 percent.

Sources: Breen, B. 2004. Living in Dell Time. *Fast Company,* November: 88–92: Hammonds, K. H. 2002. Size Is Not a Strategy. *Fast Company,* August: 78–83; Perman, S. 2001. Automate or Die. *eCompanyNow.com,* July; Dell, M. 1999. *Direct from Dell.* New York: HarperBusiness; and Watson, R. 2006. Expand Your Innovation Horizons. *Fast Company, www.fastcompany.com,* May.

recognizing changes but also being willing to act on those insights ahead of the competition.[68] Strategic managers who practice proactiveness have their eye on the future in a search for new possibilities for growth and development. Such a forward-looking perspective is important for companies that seek to be industry leaders. Many proactive firms seek out ways not only to be future-oriented but also to change the very nature of competition in their industry.

Proactiveness puts competitors in the position of having to respond to successful initiatives. The benefit gained by firms that are the first to enter new markets, establish brand identity, implement administrative techniques, or adopt new operating technologies in an industry is called first-mover advantage.[69]

First movers usually have several advantages. First, industry pioneers, especially in new industries, often capture unusually high profits because there are no competitors to drive prices down. Second, first movers that establish brand recognition are usually able to retain their image and hold on to the market share gains they earned by being first. Sometimes these benefits also accrue to other early movers in an industry, but, generally speaking, first movers have an advantage that can be sustained until firms enter the maturity phase of an industry's life cycle.[70]

First movers are not always successful. The customers of companies that introduce novel products or embrace breakthrough technologies may be reluctant to commit to a new way of doing things. In his book *Crossing the Chasm,* Geoffrey A. Moore noted that most firms seek evolution, not revolution, in their operations. This makes it difficult for a first mover to sell promising new technologies.[71]

Even with these caveats, however, companies that are first movers can enhance their competitive position. Exhibit 12.6 illustrates two methods firms can use to act proactively.

Being an industry leader does not always lead to competitive advantages. Some firms that have launched pioneering new products or staked their reputation on new brands have failed to get the hoped-for payoff. Coca-Cola and PepsiCo invested $75 million to launch sodas that would capitalize on the low-carb diet trend. But with half the carbohydrates taken out, neither *C2,* Coke's entry, nor *Pepsi Edge* tasted very good. The two new brands combined never achieved more than 1 percent market share. PepsiCo halted production in 2005 and Coca-Cola followed suit in 2007.[72] Such missteps are indicative of the dangers of trying to proactively anticipate demand. Another danger for opportunity-seeking companies is that they will take their proactiveness efforts too far. For example, Porsche has tried to extend its brand images outside the automotive arena. While some efforts have worked, such as Porsche-designed T-shirts and sunglasses, other efforts have failed, such as the Porsche-branded golf clubs.

EXHIBIT 12.6 Proactiveness Techniques

	Proactiveness	
Technique	**Description/Purpose**	**Example**
Introduce new products or technological capabilities ahead of the competition.	Being a first mover provides companies with an ability to shape the playing field and shift competitive advantages in their favor.	Amazon was able to define the online bookselling market by entering the market early and defining the user experience. It further leveraged its position as an early mover when moving into other retailing ventures and later into cloud computing.
Continuously seek out new product or service offerings.	Firms that provide new resources or sources of supply can benefit from a proactive stance.	Costco seized a chance to leverage its success as a warehouse club that sells premium brands when it introduced Costco Home Stores. The home stores are usually located near its warehouse stores, and its rapid inventory turnover gives it a cost advantage of 15 to 25 percent over close competitors such as Bassett Furniture and the Bombay Company.

Sources: Bryce, D. J. & Dyer, J. H. 2007. Strategies to Crack Well-Guarded Markets. *Harvard Business Review,* May: 84–92; Collins, J. C. & Porras, J. I. 1997. *Built to Last.* New York: HarperBusiness; Robinson, D. 2005. Sony Pushes Reliability in Vaio Laptops. *IT Week, www.itweek.co.uk,* October 12; and *www.sony.com.*

Careful monitoring and scanning of the environment, as well as extensive feasibility research, are needed for a proactive strategy to lead to competitive advantages. Firms that do it well usually have substantial growth and internal development to show for it. Many of them have been able to sustain the advantages of proactiveness for years.

Competitive Aggressiveness

Competitive aggressiveness refers to a firm's efforts to outperform its industry rivals. Companies with an aggressive orientation are willing to "do battle" with competitors. They might slash prices and sacrifice profitability to gain market share or spend aggressively to obtain manufacturing capacity. As an avenue of firm development and growth, competitive aggressiveness may involve being very assertive in leveraging the results of other entrepreneurial activities such as innovativeness or proactiveness.

Competitive aggressiveness is directed toward competitors. The SWOT analysis discussed in Chapters 2 and 3 provides a useful way to distinguish between these different approaches to CE. Proactiveness, as we saw in the previous section, is a response to opportunities—the O in SWOT. Competitive aggressiveness, by contrast, is a response to threats—the T in SWOT. A competitively aggressive posture is important for firms that seek to enter new markets in the face of intense rivalry.

Strategic managers can use competitive aggressiveness to combat industry trends that threaten their survival or market position. Sometimes firms need to be forceful in defending the competitive position that has made them an industry leader. Firms often need to be aggressive to ensure their advantage by capitalizing on new technologies or serving new market needs. Exhibit 12.7 suggests two of the ways competitively aggressive firms enhance their entrepreneurial position.

Another practice companies use to overcome the competition is to make preannouncements of new products or technologies. This type of signaling is aimed not only at potential customers but also at competitors to see how they will react or to discourage them from launching similar initiatives. Sometimes the preannouncements are made just to scare off competitors, an action that has potential ethical implications.

Competitive aggressiveness may not always lead to competitive advantages. Some companies (or their CEOs) have severely damaged their reputations by being overly aggressive. Although Microsoft continues to be a dominant player, its highly aggressive profile makes it the subject of scorn by some businesses and individuals. Efforts to find viable

---

competitive aggressiveness
an intense effort to outperform industry rivals; characterized by a combative posture or an aggressive response aimed at improving position or overcoming a threat in a competitive marketplace.

EXHIBIT 12.7 Competitive Aggressiveness Techniques

Competitive Aggressiveness		
Technique	**Description/Purpose**	**Example**
Enter markets with drastically lower prices.	Narrow operating margins make companies vulnerable to extended price competition.	Using open-source software, California-based Zimbra, Inc. has become a leader in messaging and collaboration software. Its product costs about one-third less than its direct competitor Microsoft Exchange. Zimbra generated $4.3 billion in sales in 2012.
Find successful business models and copy them.	As long as a practice is not protected by intellectual property laws, it's probably OK to imitate it. Finding solutions to existing problems is generally quicker and cheaper than inventing them.	Best Practices LLC is a North Carolina consulting group that seeks out best practices and then repackages and resells them. With annual revenues in excess of $8 million, Best Practices has become a leader in continuous improvement and benchmarking strategies.

Sources: Guth, R. A. 2006. Trolling the Web for Free Labor, Software Upstarts Are New Force. *The Wall Street Journal*, November 12: 1; Mochari, I. 2001. Steal This Strategy. *Inc.*, July: 62–67; www.best-in-class.com; and www.zimbra.com.

replacements for the Microsoft products have helped fuel interest in alternative options provided by Google, Apple, and the open-source software movement.[73]

Competitive aggressiveness is a strategy that is best used in moderation. Companies that aggressively establish their competitive position and vigorously exploit opportunities to achieve profitability may, over the long run, be better able to sustain their competitive advantages if their goal is to defeat, rather than decimate, their competitors.

Risk Taking

Risk taking refers to a firm's willingness to seize a venture opportunity even though it does not know whether the venture will be successful—to act boldly without knowing the consequences. To be successful through corporate entrepreneurship, firms usually have to take on riskier alternatives, even if it means forgoing the methods or products that have worked in the past. To obtain high financial returns, firms take such risks as assuming high levels of debt, committing large amounts of firm resources, introducing new products into new markets, and investing in unexplored technologies.

All of the approaches to internal development that we have discussed are potentially risky. Whether they are being aggressive, proactive, or innovative, firms on the path of CE must act without knowing how their actions will turn out. Before launching their strategies, corporate entrepreneurs must know their firm's appetite for risk.[74]

Three types of risk that organizations and their executives face are business risk, financial risk, and personal risk:

- **Business risk taking** involves venturing into the unknown without knowing the probability of success. This is the risk associated with entering untested markets or committing to unproven technologies.
- **Financial risk taking** requires that a company borrow heavily or commit a large portion of its resources in order to grow. In this context, risk is used to refer to the risk–return trade-off that is familiar in financial analysis.
- **Personal risk taking** refers to the risks that an executive assumes in taking a stand in favor of a strategic course of action. Executives who take such risks stand to influence the course of their whole company, and their decisions also can have significant implications for their careers.

Even though risk taking involves taking chances, it is not gambling. The best-run companies investigate the consequences of various opportunities and create scenarios of likely outcomes. A key to managing entrepreneurial risks is to evaluate new venture opportunities

> **risk taking**
> making decisions and taking action without certain knowledge of probable outcomes. Some undertakings may also involve making substantial resource commitments in the process of venturing forward.

EXHIBIT 12.8 Risk-Taking Techniques

	Risk Taking	
Technique	**Description/Purpose**	**Example**
Research and assess risk factors to minimize uncertainty.	Companies that "do their homework"—that is, carefully evaluate the implications of bold actions—reduce the likelihood of failure.	Graybar Electric Co. took a risk when it invested $144 million to revamp its distribution system. It consolidated 231 small centers into 16 supply warehouses and installed the latest communications network. Graybar is now considered a leader in facility redesign, and its sales have increased steadily since the consolidation, topping $5 billion in sales in a recent year.
Use techniques that have worked in other domains.	Risky methods that other companies have tried may provide an avenue for advancing company goals.	Autobytel.com, one of the first companies to sell cars online, decided on an approach that worked well for others—advertising during the Super Bowl. It was the first dot-com ever to do so, and its $1.2 million 30-second ad paid off well by generating weeks of free publicity and favorable business press.

Sources: Anonymous. 2006. Graybar Offers Data Center Redesign Seminars. *Cabling Installation and Maintenance,* www.cim.pennnet.com, September 1; Keenan, F. & Mullaney, T. J. 2001. Clicking at Graybar. *BusinessWeek,* June 18: 132–134; Weintraub, A. 2001. Make or break for Autobytel. *BusinessWeek e.biz,* July 9: EB30–EB32; www.autobytel.com; and www.graybar.com.

thoroughly enough to reduce the uncertainty surrounding them. Exhibit 12.8 indicates two methods companies can use to strengthen their competitive position through risk taking.

Risk taking, by its nature, involves potential dangers and pitfalls. Only carefully managed risk is likely to lead to competitive advantages. Actions that are taken without sufficient forethought, research, and planning may prove to be very costly. Therefore, strategic managers must always remain mindful of potential risks. In his book *Innovation and Entrepreneurship,* Peter Drucker argued that successful entrepreneurs are typically not risk takers. Instead, they take steps to minimize risks by carefully understanding them. That is how they avoid focusing on risk and remain focused on opportunity.[75] Risk taking is a good place to close this chapter on corporate entrepreneurship. Companies that choose to grow through internal corporate venturing must remember that entrepreneurship always involves embracing what is new and uncertain.

ISSUE FOR DEBATE

The Internet of Things

From activity bracelets that upload metrics of your physical activity to the web, to meat thermometers monitored with a smartphone, to door locks that can be locked and unlocked from a tablet computer anywhere in the world, devices and appliances are increasingly being connected to the Internet. The "Internet of things" is a rapidly growing market space. Cisco estimates that the number of devices connected to the Internet will explode from 10 billion in 2014 to 50 billion by 2020.

Some of the devices are already generating significant interest and sales. For example, over 3 million fitness-tracking devices were sold in the April 2013 to March 2014 period. Additionally, Google saw so much promise with Nest Labs, a company that manufactures Internet-enabled thermostats and smoke detectors, it purchased the firm for $3.2 billion in 2014. Both of these types of devices appear to have significant potential since they benefit from being tied to sociological forces in advanced economies. Fitness-tracking devices tie very directly into desires to lose weight and improve fitness. Similarly, Nest Labs' products are designed to aid in improving the energy efficiency of homes and respond to the desires of many individuals to reduce their carbon footprint. However, the degree of customer demand for such products is still uncertain. In a survey done by Forrester Research in mid-2013, 28 percent of respondents said they were interested in controlling appliances from a smartphone, while 53 percent said they weren't.

Such mixed sentiment isn't stopping other firms from taking the "Internet of things" trend to new classes of products. For example, Procter & Gamble (P&G) introduced a prototype of the world's first web-enabled toothbrush in early 2014. It reports the user's brushing habits to a smartphone. The associated app uses the data to provide mouth-care tips. The toothbrush, which came to market in June 2015, carries a suggested retail price tag of $219. P&G executives believe the toothbrush will be a big hit. "I truly believe that 10 years from now, it's going to be hard to think you didn't have something like it," said Michael Cohen-Dumani, P&G's associate marketing director. Others are skeptical of the market for Internet-enabled products. "We are just at the beginning of seeing a bunch of really ridiculous products that tie pretty much anything to a smartphone," said Stacey Higgenbotham, a writer for the tech website Gigaom.

One overarching concern associated with all Internet-enabled products is privacy. With the devices transmitting information to the web, users' personal data are potentially open for all to see. The default settings on some devices make the data available to the public. For example, some fitness trackers send the data unencrypted, which makes it possible for others to access the fitness data of the users. Additionally, there are fears that devices could be hacked, leaving users vulnerable to thieves. By tracking when users remotely act to control home appliances, thieves could learn information on whether the users are at home.

Thus, while it is a potentially exciting market, there are significant uncertainties about the opportunities and challenges with Internet-enabled products.

Discussion Questions

1. Is the "Internet of things" a market with tremendous growth potential or just a bunch of hype?
2. What types of products are likely to be successful in this market? What characteristics enhance the potential for Internet-enabled products?
3. How much of a concern is the privacy issue with these products?

Sources: Clark, D. 2014. "Internet of Things" in reach. *wsj.com*, January 5: np; Shechner, S. 2014. Web-enabled toothbrushes join the Internet of things. *wsj.com*, March 2: np; and Anonymous. 2015. P&G's smart toothbrush keeps tabs on tooth care. *cnbc.com*, February 20.

Reflecting on Career Implications . . .

- **Innovation:** Identify the types of innovations being pursued by your company. Do they tend to be incremental or radical? Product-related or process-related? Are there ways in which you can add value to such innovations, no matter how minor your contributions are?

- **Cultivating Innovation Skills:** Exhibit 12.2 describes the five traits of an effective innovator (associating, questioning, observing, experimenting, and networking). Assess yourself on each of these traits. Practice the skills in your work and professional life to build your skills as an innovator. If you are interviewing for a job with an organization that is considered high on innovation, it might be in your interest to highlight these traits.

- **Real Options Analysis:** Success in your career often depends on creating and exercising career "options." However, creation of options involves costs as well, such as learning new skills, obtaining additional certifications, and so on. Consider what options you can create for yourself. Evaluate the cost of these options.

- **Entrepreneurial Orientation:** Consider the five dimensions of entrepreneurial orientation. Evaluate yourself on each of these dimensions (autonomy, innovativeness, proactiveness, competitive aggressiveness, and risk taking). If you are high on entrepreneurial orientation, you may have a future as an entrepreneur. Consider the ways in which you can use the experience and learning from your current job to become a successful entrepreneur in later years.

summary

To remain competitive in today's economy, established firms must find new avenues for development and growth. This chapter has addressed how innovation and corporate entrepreneurship can be a means of internal venture creation and strategic renewal, and how an entrepreneurial orientation can help corporations enhance their competitive position.

Innovation is one of the primary means by which corporations grow and strengthen their strategic position. Innovations can take several forms, ranging from radical breakthrough innovations to incremental improvement innovations. Innovations are often used to update products and services or to improve organizational processes. Managing the innovation process is often challenging, because it involves a great deal of uncertainty and there are many choices to be made about the extent and type of innovations to pursue. By cultivating innovation skills, defining the scope of innovation, managing the pace of innovation, staffing to capture value from innovation, and collaborating with innovation partners, firms can more effectively manage the innovation process.

We also discussed the role of corporate entrepreneurship in venture development and strategic renewal. Corporations usually take either a focused or dispersed approach to corporate venturing. Firms with a focused approach usually separate the corporate venturing activity from the ongoing operations of the firm in order to foster independent thinking and encourage entrepreneurial team members to think and act without the constraints imposed by the corporation. In corporations where venturing activities are dispersed, a culture of entrepreneurship permeates all parts of the company in order to induce strategic behaviors by all organizational members. In measuring the success of corporate venturing activities, both financial and strategic objectives should be considered. Real options analysis is often used to make better-quality decisions in uncertain entrepreneurial situations. However, a real options approach has potential drawbacks.

Most entrepreneurial firms need to have an entrepreneurial orientation: the methods, practices, and decision-making styles that strategic managers use to act entrepreneurially. Five dimensions of entrepreneurial orientation are found in firms that pursue corporate venture strategies. Autonomy, innovativeness, proactiveness, competitive aggressiveness, and risk taking each make a unique contribution to the pursuit of new opportunities. When deployed effectively, the methods and practices of an entrepreneurial orientation can be used to engage successfully in corporate entrepreneurship and new venture creation. However, strategic managers must remain mindful of the pitfalls associated with each of these approaches.

SUMMARY REVIEW QUESTIONS

1. What is meant by the concept of a continuum of radical and incremental innovations?
2. What are the dilemmas that organizations face when deciding what innovation projects to pursue? What steps can organizations take to effectively manage the innovation process?
3. What is the difference between focused and dispersed approaches to corporate entrepreneurship?
4. How are business incubators used to foster internal corporate venturing?
5. What is the role of the product champion in bringing a new product or service into existence in a corporation? How can companies use product champions to enhance their venture development efforts?
6. Explain the difference between proactiveness and competitive aggressiveness in terms of achieving and sustaining competitive advantage.
7. Describe how the entrepreneurial orientation (EO) dimensions of innovativeness, proactiveness, and risk taking can be combined to create competitive advantages for entrepreneurial firms.

key terms

innovation 382
product innovation 382
process innovation 382
radical innovation 383
incremental innovation 383
strategic envelope 387
corporate entrepreneurship (CE) 393
focused approaches to corporate entrepreneurship 394
new venture group (NVG) 394
business incubator 394
dispersed approaches to corporate entrepreneurship 396
entrepreneurial culture 396
product champion 397
exit champion 398
real options analysis (ROA) 399
back-solver dilemma 400
managerial conceit 401
escalation of commitment 402
entrepreneurial orientation 402
autonomy 403
innovativeness 404
proactiveness 404
competitive aggressiveness 406
risk taking 407

experiential exercise

Select two different major corporations from two different industries (you might use Fortune 500 companies to make your selection). Compare and contrast these organizations in terms of their entrepreneurial orientation. (Fill in the table below.)

Based on your comparison:

1. How is the corporation's entrepreneurial orientation reflected in its strategy?
2. Which corporation would you say has the stronger entrepreneurial orientation?
3. Is the corporation with the stronger entrepreneurial orientation also stronger in terms of financial performance?

Entrepreneurial Orientation	Company A	Company B
Autonomy		
Innovativeness		
Proactiveness		
Competitive aggressiveness		
Risk taking		

application questions & exercises

1. Select a firm known for its corporate entrepreneurship activities. Research the company and discuss how it has positioned itself relative to its close competitors. Does it have a unique strategic advantage? Disadvantage? Explain.
2. Explain the difference between product innovations and process innovations. Provide examples of firms that have recently introduced each type of innovation. What are the types of innovations related to the strategies of each firm?
3. Using the Internet, select a company that is listed on the NASDAQ or New York Stock Exchange. Research the extent to which the company has an entrepreneurial culture. Does the company use product champions? Does it have a corporate venture capital fund? Do you believe its entrepreneurial efforts are sufficient to generate sustainable advantages?
4. How can an established firm use an entrepreneurial orientation to enhance its overall strategic position? Provide examples.

ethics questions

1. Innovation activities are often aimed at making a discovery or commercializing a technology ahead of the competition. What are some of the unethical practices that companies could engage in during the innovation process? What are the potential long-term consequences of such actions?
2. Discuss the ethical implications of using entrepreneurial policies and practices to pursue corporate social responsibility goals. Are these efforts authentic and genuine or just an attempt to attract more customers?

references

1. Eddy, N. 2014. Android captures 85 percent of smartphone market worldwide. *eweek.com,* August 8: np; Vascellaro, J. 2009. Radio tunes out Google in rare miss for web titan. *wsj.com,* May 12: np; and McGrath, R. 2011. Failing by design. *Harvard Business Review,* 89(4): 76–83.
2. For an interesting discussion, see Johannessen, J. A., Olsen, B., & Lumpkin, G. T. 2001. Innovation as newness: What is new, how new, and new to whom? *European Journal of Innovation Management,* 4(1): 20–31.
3. The discussion of product and process innovation is based on Roberts, E. B. (Ed.). 2002. *Innovation: Driving product, process, and market change.* San Francisco: Jossey-Bass; Hayes, R. & Wheelwright, S. 1985. Competing through manufacturing. *Harvard Business Review,* 63(1): 99–109; and Hayes, R. & Wheelwright, S. 1979. Dynamics of product–process life cycles. *Harvard Business Review,* 57(2): 127–136.
4. The discussion of radical and incremental innovations draws from Leifer, R., McDermott, C. M., Colarelli, G., O'Connor, G. C., Peters, L. S., Rice, M. P., & Veryzer, R. W. 2000. *Radical innovation: How mature companies can outsmart upstarts.* Boston: Harvard Business School Press; Damanpour, F. 1996. Organizational complexity and innovation: Developing and testing multiple contingency models. *Management Science,* 42(5): 693–716; and Hage, J. 1980. *Theories of organizations.* New York: Wiley.
5. Christensen, C. M. & Raynor, M. E. 2003. *The innovator's solution.*

Boston: Harvard Business School Press.

6. Dressner, H. 2004. The Gartner Fellows interview: Clayton M. Christensen. *www.gartner.com*, April 26.

7. For another perspective on how different types of innovation affect organizational choices, see Wolter, C. & Veloso, F. M. 2008. The effects of innovation on vertical structure: Perspectives on transactions costs and competences. *Academy of Management Review,* 33(3): 586–605.

8. Drucker, P. F. 1985. *Innovation and entrepreneurship.* New York: Harper & Row.

9. Birkinshaw, J., Hamel, G., & Mol, M. J. 2008. Management innovation. *Academy of Management Review,* 33(4): 825–845.

10. Steere, W. C., Jr. & Niblack, J. 1997. Pfizer, Inc. In Kanter, R. M., Kao, J., & Wiersema, F. (Eds.), *Innovation: Breakthrough thinking at 3M, DuPont, GE, Pfizer, and Rubbermaid:* 123–145. New York: HarperCollins.

11. Morrissey, C. A. 2000. Managing innovation through corporate venturing. *Graziadio Business Report,* Spring, *gbr.pepperdine.edu;* and Sharma, A. 1999. Central dilemmas of managing innovation in large firms. *California Management Review,* 41(3): 147–164.

12. Sharma, op. cit.

13. Dyer, J. H., Gregersen, H. B., & Christensen, C. M. 2009. The innovator's DNA. *Harvard Business Review,* December: 61–67.

14. Eggers, J. P. & Kaplan, S. 2009. Cognition and renewal: Comparing CEO and organizational effects on incumbent adaptation to technical change. *Organization Science,* 20: 461–477.

15. Biodegradable Products Institute. 2003. "Compostable Logo" of the Biodegradable Products Institute gains momentum with approval of DuPont Biomax resin, *www.bpiworld.org,* June 12; Leifer et al., op. cit.

16. For more on defining the scope of innovation, see Valikangas, L. & Gibbert, M. 2005. Boundary-setting strategies for escaping innovation traps. *MIT Sloan Management Review,* 46(3): 58–65.

17. Leifer et al., op. cit.

18. Bhide, A. V. 2000. *The origin and evolution of new businesses.* New York: Oxford University Press; Brown, S. L. & Eisenhardt, K. M. 1998. *Competing on the edge: Strategy as structured chaos.* Cambridge, MA: Harvard Business School Press.

19. McGrath, R. G. & Keil, T. 2007. The value captor's process: Getting the most out of your new business ventures. *Harvard Business Review,* May: 128–136.

20. For an interesting discussion of how sharing technology knowledge with different divisions in an organization can contribute to innovation processes, see Miller, D. J., Fern, M. J., & Cardinal, L. B. 2007. The use of knowledge for technological innovation within diversified firms. *Academy of Management Journal,* 50(2): 308–326.

21. Ketchen, D. J., Jr., Ireland, R. D., & Snow, C. C. 2007 Strategic entrepreneurship, collaborative innovation, and wealth creation. *Strategic Entrepreneurship Journal,* 1(3–4): 371–385.

22. Chesbrough, H. 2003. *Open innovation: The new imperative for creating and profiting from technology.* Boston: Harvard Business School Press.

23. For a study of what makes alliance partnerships successful, see Sampson, R. C. 2007. R&D alliances and firm performance: The impact of technological diversity and alliance organization on innovation. *Academy of Management Journal,* 50(2): 364–386.

24. For an interesting perspective on the role of collaboration among multinational corporations, see Hansen, M. T. & Nohria, N. 2004. How to build collaborative advantage. *MIT Sloan Management Review,* 46(1): 22–30.

25. Wells, R. M. J. 2008. The product innovation process: Are managing information flows and cross-functional collaboration key? *Academy of Management Perspectives,* 22(1): 58–60; Dougherty, D. & Dunne, D. D. 2011. Organizing ecologies of complex innovation. *Organization Science,* 22(5): 1214–1223; and Kim, H. E. & Pennings, J. M. 2009. Innovation and strategic renewal in mature markets: A study of the tennis racket industry. *Organization Science,* 20: 368–383.

26. Eggers, J. P. 2014. Get ahead by betting wrong. *Harvard Business Review,* 92(7/8): 26; and Lepore, J. 2014. The disruption machine. *newyorker.com,* June 23: np.

27. Guth, W. D. & Ginsberg, A. 1990. Guest editor's introduction: Corporate entrepreneurship. *Strategic Management Journal,* 11: 5–15.

28. Pinchot, G. 1985. *Intrapreneuring.* New York: Harper & Row.

29. For an interesting perspective on the role of context on the discovery and creation of opportunities, see Zahra, S. A. 2008. The virtuous cycle of discovery and creation of entrepreneurial opportunities. *Strategic Entrepreneurship Journal,* 2(3): 243–257.

30. Birkinshaw, J. 1997. Entrepreneurship in multinational corporations: The characteristics of subsidiary initiatives. *Strategic Management Journal,* 18(3): 207–229; and Kanter, R. M. 1985. *The change masters.* New York: Simon & Schuster.

31. Hansen, M. T., Chesbrough, H. W., Nohria, N., & Sull, D. 2000. Networked incubators: Hothouses of the new economy. *Harvard Business Review,* 78(5): 74–84.

32. For more on the importance of leadership in fostering a climate of entrepreneurship, see Ling, Y., Simsek, Z., Lubatkin, M. H., & Veiga, J. F. 2008. Transformational leadership's role in promoting corporate entrepreneurship: Examining the CEO-TMT interface. *Academy of Management Journal,* 51(3): 557–576.

33. Bryant, A. 2011. Got an idea? Sell it to me in 30 seconds. *nytimes.com,* January 1: np.

34. Ovide, S. 2013. Next CEO's biggest job: Fixing Microsoft's culture. *wsj.com,* August 25: np.

35. Gunther, M. 2010. 3M's innovation revival. *cnnmoney.com,* September 24: np; Byrne, J. 2012. The 12 greatest entrepreneurs of our time. *Fortune,* April 9: 76; and Anonymous. 2007. Johnson & Johnson turns to internal venturing. *silico.wordpress.com,* July 16: np.

36. Colvin, G. 2014. Brad Smith: Getting rid of friction. *Fortune,* July 21: 24.

37. For an interesting discussion, see Davenport, T. H., Prusak, L., & Wilson, H. J. 2003. Who's bringing you hot ideas and how are you responding? *Harvard Business Review,* 80(1): 58–64.

38. Howell, J. M. 2005. The right stuff. Identifying and developing effective champions of innovation. *Academy of Management Executive,* 19(2): 108–119. See also Greene, P., Brush, C., & Hart, M. 1999. The corporate venture champion: A resource-based approach to role and process.

Entrepreneurship Theory & Practice, 23(3): 103–122; and Markham, S. K. & Aiman-Smith, L. 2001. Product champions: Truths, myths and management. *Research Technology Management,* May–June: 44–50.

39. Burgelman, R. A. 1983. A process model of internal corporate venturing in the diversified major firm. *Administrative Science Quarterly,* 28: 223–244.

40. Hamel, G. 2000. *Leading the revolution.* Boston: Harvard Business School Press.

41. Greene, Brush, & Hart, op. cit.; and Shane, S. 1994. Are champions different from non-champions? *Journal of Business Venturing,* 9(5): 397–421.

42. Block, Z. & MacMillan, I. C. 1993. *Corporate venturing—Creating new businesses with the firm.* Cambridge, MA: Harvard Business School Press.

43. For an interesting discussion of these trade-offs, see Stringer, R. 2000. How to manage radical innovation. *California Management Review,* 42(4): 70–88; and Gompers, P. A. & Lerner, J. 1999. *The venture capital cycle.* Cambridge, MA: MIT Press.

44. Cardinal, L. B., Turner, S. F., Fern, M. J., & Burton, R. M. 2011. Organizing for product development across technological environments: Performance trade-offs and priorities. *Organization Science,* 22: 1000–1025.

45. Albrinck, J., Hornery, J., Kletter, D., & Neilson, G. 2001. Adventures in corporate venturing. *Strategy + Business,* 22: 119–129; and McGrath, R. G. & MacMillan, I. C. 2000. *The entrepreneurial mind-set.* Cambridge, MA: Harvard Business School Press.

46. Kiel, T., McGrath, R. G., & Tukiainen, T. 2009. Gems from the ashes: Capability creation and transforming in internal corporate venturing. *Organization Science,* 20: 601–620.

47. For an interesting discussion of how different outcome goals affect organizational learning and employee motivation, see Seijts, G. H. & Latham, G. P. 2005. Learning versus performance goals: When should each be used? *Academy of Management Executive,* 19(1): 124–131.

48. Crockett, R. O. 2001. Motorola. *BusinessWeek,* July 15: 72–78.

49. The ideas in this section are drawn from Royer, I. 2003. Why bad projects are so hard to kill. *Harvard Business Review,* 80(1): 48–56.

50. For an interesting perspective on the different roles that individuals play in the entrepreneurial process, see Baron, R. A. 2008. The role of affect in the entrepreneurial process. *Academy of Management Review,* 33(2): 328–340.

51. Hoskin, R. E. 1994. *Financial accounting.* New York: Wiley.

52. We know stock options as derivative assets—that is, "an asset whose value depends on or is derived from the value of another, the underlying asset": Amram, M. & Kulatilaka, N. 1999. *Real options: Managing strategic investment in an uncertain world: 34.* Boston: Harvard Business School Press.

53. For an interesting discussion on why it is difficult to "kill options," refer to Royer, I. 2003. Why bad projects are so hard to kill. *Harvard Business Review,* 81(2): 48–57.

54. Slywotzky, A. & Wise, R. 2003. Double-digit growth in no-growth times. *Fast Company,* April: 66–72; www.hoovers.com; and www.johnsoncontrols.com.

55. For more on the role of real options in entrepreneurial decision making, see Folta, T. B. & O'Brien, J. P. 2004. Entry in the presence of dueling options. *Strategic Management Journal,* 25: 121–138.

56. This section draws on Janney, J. J. & Dess, G. G. 2004. Can real options analysis improve decision-making? Promises and pitfalls. *Academy of Management Executive,* 18(4): 60–75. For additional insights on pitfalls of real options, consider McGrath, R. G. 1997. A real options logic for initiating technology positioning investment. *Academy of Management Review,* 22(4): 974–994; Coff, R. W. & Laverty, K. J. 2001. Real options on knowledge assets: Panacea or Pandora's box? *Business Horizons,* 73: 79; McGrath, R. G. 1999. Falling forward: Real options reasoning and entrepreneurial failure. *Academy of Management Review,* 24(1): 13–30; and Zardkoohi, A. 2004. Do real options lead to escalation of commitment? *Academy of Management Review,* 29(1): 111–119.

57. For an understanding of the differences between how managers say they approach decisions and how they actually do, March and Shapira's discussion is perhaps the best. March, J. G. & Shapira, Z. 1987. Managerial perspectives on risk and risk-taking. *Management Science,* 33(11): 1404–1418.

58. A discussion of some factors that may lead to escalation in decision making is included in Choo, C. W. 2005. Information failures and organizational disasters. *MIT Sloan Management Review,* 46(3): 8–10.

59. For an interesting discussion of the use of real options analysis in the application of wireless communications, which helped to lower the potential for escalation, refer to McGrath, R. G., Ferrier, W. J., & Mendelow, A. L. 2004. Real options as engines of choice and heterogeneity. *Academy of Management Review,* 29(1): 86–101.

60. One very useful solution for reducing the effects of managerial conceit is to incorporate an exit champion into the decision process. Exit champions provide arguments for killing off the firm's commitment to a decision. For a very insightful discussion on exit champions, refer to Royer, I. 2003. Why bad projects are so hard to kill. *Harvard Business Review,* 81(2): 49–56.

61. For more on how entrepreneurial orientation influences organizational performance, see Wang, L. 2008. Entrepreneurial orientation, learning orientation, and firm performance. *Entrepreneurship Theory & Practice,* 32(4): 635–657; and Runyan, R., Droge, C., & Swinney, J. 2008. Entrepreneurial orientation versus small business orientation: What are their relationships to firm performance? *Journal of Small Business Management,* 46(4): 567–588.

62. Covin, J. G. & Slevin, D. P. 1991. A conceptual model of entrepreneurship as firm behavior. *Entrepreneurship Theory and Practice,* 16(1): 7–24; Lumpkin, G. T. & Dess, G. G. 1996. Clarifying the entrepreneurial orientation construct and linking it to performance. *Academy of Management Review,* 21(1): 135–172; and McGrath, R. G. & MacMillan, I. C. 2000. *The entrepreneurial mind-set.* Cambridge, MA: Harvard Business School Press.

63. Lumpkin, G. T. & Dess, G. G. 2001. Linking two dimensions of entrepreneurial orientation to firm performance: The moderating role of environment and life cycle. *Journal of Business Venturing,* 16: 429–451.

64. For an interesting discussion, see Day, J. D., Mang, P. Y., Richter, A., & Roberts, J. 2001. The innovative organization: Why new ventures need more than a room of their own. *McKinsey Quarterly,* 2: 21–31.

65. Crockett, R. O. 2001. Chris Galvin shakes things up—again. *BusinessWeek,* May 28: 38–39.

66. For insights into the role of information technology in innovativeness, see Dibrell, C., Davis, P. S., & Craig, J. 2008. Fueling innovation through information technology in SMEs. *Journal of Small Business Management,* 46(2): 203–218.
67. For an interesting discussion of the impact of innovativeness on organizational outcomes, see Cho, H. J. & Pucik, V. 2005. Relationship between innovativeness, quality, growth, profitability, and market value. *Strategic Management Journal,* 26(6): 555–575.
68. Danneels, E. & Sethi, R. 2011. New product exploration under environmental turbulence. *Organization Science,* 22(4): 1026–1039.
69. Lieberman, M. B. & Montgomery, D. B. 1988. First mover advantages. *Strategic Management Journal,* 9 (Special Issue): 41–58.
70. The discussion of first-mover advantages is based on several articles, including Lambkin, M. 1988. Order of entry and performance in new markets. *Strategic Management Journal,* 9: 127–140; Lieberman & Montgomery, op. cit., pp. 41–58; and Miller, A. & Camp, B. 1985. Exploring determinants of success in corporate ventures. *Journal of Business Venturing,* 1(2): 87–105.
71. Moore, G. A. 1999. *Crossing the chasm* (2nd ed.). New York: HarperBusiness.
72. Mallas, S. 2005. PepsiCo loses its Edge. *Motley Fool,* June 1, www.fool.com.
73. Lyons, D. 2006. The cheap revolution. *Forbes,* September 18: 102–111.
74. Miller, K. D. 2007. Risk and rationality in entrepreneurial processes. *Strategic Entrepreneurship Journal,* 1(1–2): 57–74.
75. Drucker, op. cit., pp. 109–110.

Case Analysis

Analyzing Strategic Management Cases

chapter 13

After reading this chapter, you should have a good understanding of the following learning objectives:

LO13.1 How strategic case analysis is used to simulate real-world experiences.

LO13.2 How analyzing strategic management cases can help develop the ability to differentiate, speculate, and integrate when evaluating complex business problems.

LO13.3 The steps involved in conducting a strategic management case analysis.

LO13.4 How to get the most out of case analysis.

LO13.5 How integrative thinking and conflict-inducing discussion techniques can lead to better decisions.

LO13.6 How to use the strategic insights and material from each of the 12 previous chapters in the text to analyze issues posed by strategic management cases.

PART 4: CASE ANALYSIS

Why Analyze Strategic Management Cases?

If you don't ask the right questions, then you're never going to get the right solution. I spent too much of my career feeling like I'd done a really good job answering the wrong question. And that was because I was letting other people give me the question. One of the things that I've tried to do more and more—and I obviously have the opportunity to do as a leader—is to take ownership of the question. And so I'm much more interested these days in having debates about what the questions should be than I necessarily am about the solutions.[1]

—Tim Brown, CEO of IDEO (a leading design consulting firm)

LO13.1
How strategic case analysis is used to simulate real-world experiences.

It is often said that the key to finding good answers is to ask good questions. Strategic managers and business leaders are required to evaluate options, make choices, and find solutions to the challenges they face every day. To do so, they must learn to ask the right questions. The study of strategic management poses the same challenge. The process of analyzing, decision making, and implementing strategic actions raises many good questions:

- Why do some firms succeed and others fail?
- Why are some companies higher performers than others?
- What information is needed in the strategic planning process?
- How do competing values and beliefs affect strategic decision making?
- What skills and capabilities are needed to implement a strategy effectively?

How does a student of strategic management answer these questions? By strategic case analysis. **Case analysis** simulates the real-world experience that strategic managers and company leaders face as they try to determine how best to run their companies. It places students in the middle of an actual situation and challenges them to figure out what to do.[2]

case analysis
a method of learning complex strategic management concepts—such as environmental analysis, the process of decision making, and implementing strategic actions—through placing students in the middle of an actual situation and challenging them to figure out what to do.

Asking the right questions is just the beginning of case analysis. In the previous chapters we have discussed issues and challenges that managers face and provided analytical frameworks for understanding the situation. But once the analysis is complete, decisions have to be made. Case analysis forces you to choose among different options and set forth a plan of action based on your choices. But even then the job is not done. Strategic case analysis also requires that you address how you will implement the plan and the implications of choosing one course of action over another.

A strategic management case is a detailed description of a challenging situation faced by an organization.[3] It usually includes a chronology of events and extensive support materials, such as financial statements, product lists, and transcripts of interviews with employees. Although names or locations are sometimes changed to provide anonymity, cases usually report the facts of a situation as authentically as possible.

One of the main reasons to analyze strategic management cases is to develop an ability to evaluate business situations critically. In case analysis, memorizing key terms and conceptual frameworks is not enough. To analyze a case, it is important that you go beyond textbook prescriptions and quick answers. It requires you to look deeply into the information that is provided and root out the essential issues and causes of a company's problems.

The types of skills that are required to prepare an effective strategic case analysis can benefit you in actual business situations. Case analysis adds to the overall learning experience by helping you acquire or improve skills that may not be taught in a typical lecture course.

LO13.2

How analyzing strategic management cases can help develop the ability to differentiate, speculate, and integrate when evaluating complex business problems.

Three capabilities that can be learned by conducting case analysis are especially useful to strategic managers—the ability to differentiate, speculate, and integrate.[4] Here's how case analysis can enhance those skills:

1. ***Differentiate.*** Effective strategic management requires that many different elements of a situation be evaluated at once. This is also true in case analysis. When analyzing cases, it is important to isolate critical facts, evaluate whether assumptions are useful or faulty, and distinguish between good and bad information. Differentiating between the factors that are influencing the situation presented by a case is necessary for making a good analysis. Strategic management also involves understanding that problems are often complex and multilayered. This applies to case analysis as well. Ask whether the case deals with operational, business-level, or corporate issues. Do the problems stem from weaknesses in the internal value chain or threats in the external environment? Dig deep. Being too quick to accept the easiest or least controversial answer will usually fail to get to the heart of the problem.

2. ***Speculate.*** Strategic managers need to be able to use their imagination to envision an explanation or solution that might not readily be apparent. The same is true with case analysis. Being able to imagine different scenarios or contemplate the outcome of a decision can aid the analysis. Managers also have to deal with uncertainty since most decisions are made without complete knowledge of the circumstances. This is also true in case analysis. Case materials often seem to be missing data or the information provided is contradictory. The ability to speculate about details that are unknown or the consequences of an action can be helpful.

3. ***Integrate.*** Strategy involves looking at the big picture and having an organizationwide perspective. Strategic case analysis is no different. Even though the chapters in this textbook divide the material into various topics that may apply to different parts of an organization, all of this information must be integrated into one set of recommendations that will affect the whole company. A strategic manager needs to comprehend how all the factors that influence the organization will interact. This also applies to case analysis. Changes made in one part of the organization affect other parts. Thus, a holistic perspective that integrates the impact of various decisions and environmental influences on all parts of the organization is needed.

In business, these three activities sometimes "compete" with each other for your attention. For example, some decision makers may have a natural ability to differentiate among elements of a problem but are not able to integrate them very well. Others have enough innate creativity to imagine solutions or fill in the blanks when information is missing. But they may have a difficult time when faced with hard numbers or cold facts. Even so, each of these skills is important. The mark of a good strategic manager is the ability to simultaneously make distinctions and envision the whole, and to imagine a future scenario while staying focused on the present. Thus, another reason to conduct case analysis is to help you develop and exercise your ability to differentiate, speculate, and integrate. David C. Novak, the chairman and CEO of Yum! Brands, provides a useful insight on this matter:[5]

> I think what we need in our leaders, the people who ultimately run our companies and run our functions, is whole-brained people—people who can be analytical but also have the creativity, the right-brain side of the equation. There's more and more of a premium on that today than ever before.

Case analysis takes the student through the whole cycle of activity that a manager would face. Beyond the textbook descriptions of concepts and examples, case analysis asks you to "walk a mile in the shoes" of the strategic decision maker and learn to evaluate situations

> ### 13.1 STRATEGY SPOTLIGHT
>
> #### ANALYSIS, DECISION MAKING, AND CHANGE AT SAPIENT HEALTH NETWORK
>
> Sapient Health Network (SHN) had gotten off to a good start. CEO Jim Kean and his two cofounders had raised $5 million in investor capital to launch their vision: an Internet-based health care information subscription service. The idea was to create an Internet community for people suffering from chronic diseases. It would provide members with expert information, resources, a message board, and chat rooms so that people suffering from the same ailments could provide each other with information and support. "Who would be more voracious consumers of information than people who are faced with life-changing, life-threatening illnesses?" thought Bill Kelly, one of SHN's cofounders. Initial market research and beta tests had supported that view.
>
> During the beta tests, however, the service had been offered for free. The troubles began when SHN tried to convert its trial subscribers into paying ones. Fewer than 5 percent signed on, far less than the 15 percent the company had projected. Sapient hired a vice president of marketing who launched an aggressive promotion, but after three months of campaigning SHN still had only 500 members. SHN was now burning through $400,000 per month, with little revenue to show for it.
>
> At that point, according to SHN board member Susan Clymer, "there was a lot of scrambling around trying to figure out how we could wring value out of what we'd already accomplished." One thing SHN had created was an expert software system which had two components: an "intelligent profile engine" (IPE) and an "intelligent query engine" (IQE). SHN used this system to collect detailed information from its subscribers.
>
> SHN was sure that the expert system was its biggest selling point. But how could the company use it? Then the founders remembered that the original business plan had suggested there might be a market for aggregate data about patient populations gathered from the website. Could they turn the business around by selling patient data? To analyze the possibility, Kean tried out the idea on the market research arm of a huge east coast health care conglomerate. The officials were intrigued. SHN realized that its expert system could become a market research tool.
>
> Once the analysis was completed, the founders made the decision: They would still create Internet communities for chronically ill patients, but the service would be free. And they would transform SHN from a company that processed subscriptions to one that sold market research.
>
> Finally, they enacted the changes. Some of the changes were painful, including laying off 18 employees. However, SHN needed more health care industry expertise. It even hired an interim CEO, Craig Davenport, a 25-year veteran of the industry, to steer the company in its new direction. Finally, SHN had to communicate a new message to its members. It began by reimbursing the $10,000 of subscription fees they had paid.
>
> All of this paid off dramatically in a matter of just two years. Revenues jumped to $1.9 million, and early in the third year SHN was purchased by WebMD. Less than a year after that, WebMD merged with Healtheon. The combined company still operates a thriving office out of SHN's original location in Portland, Oregon.
>
> Sources: Ferguson, S. 2007. Health care gets a better IT prescription. *Baseline*, www.baselinemag.com, May 24. Brenneman, K. 2000. Healtheon/WebMD's local office is thriving. *Business Journal of Portland*, June 2; and Raths, D. 1998. Reversal of fortune. *Inc. Technology*, 2: 52–62.

critically. Executives and owners must make decisions every day with limited information and a swirl of business activity going on around them. Consider the example of Sapient Health Network, an Internet start-up that had to undergo some analysis and problem solving just to survive. Strategy Spotlight 13.1 describes how this company transformed itself after a serious self-examination during a time of crisis.

As you can see from the experience of Sapient Health Network, businesses are often faced with immediate challenges that threaten their lives. The Sapient case illustrates how the strategic management process helped it survive. First, the company realistically assessed the environment, evaluated the marketplace, and analyzed its resources. Then it made tough decisions, which included shifting its market focus, hiring and firing, and redeploying its assets. Finally, it took action. The result was not only firm survival but also a quick turnaround leading to rapid success.

How to Conduct a Case Analysis

The process of analyzing strategic management cases involves several steps. In this section we will review the mechanics of preparing a case analysis. Before beginning, there are two things to keep in mind that will clarify your understanding of the process and make the results of the process more meaningful.

LO13.3

The steps involved in conducting a strategic management case analysis.

First, unless you prepare for a case discussion, there is little you can gain from the discussion and even less that you can offer. Effective strategic managers don't enter into problem-solving situations without doing some homework—investigating the situation, analyzing and researching possible solutions, and sometimes gathering the advice of others. Good problem solving often requires that decision makers be immersed in the facts, options, and implications surrounding the problem. In case analysis, this means reading and thoroughly comprehending the case materials before trying to make an analysis.

The second point is related to the first. To get the most out of a case analysis, you must place yourself "inside" the case—that is, think like an actual participant in the case situation. However, there are several positions you can take. These are discussed in the following paragraphs:

- *Strategic decision maker.* This is the position of the senior executive responsible for resolving the situation described in the case. It may be the CEO, the business owner, or a strategic manager in a key executive position.
- *Board of directors.* Since the board of directors represents the owners of a corporation, it has a responsibility to step in when a management crisis threatens the company. As a board member, you may be in a unique position to solve problems.
- *Outside consultant.* Either the board or top management may decide to bring in outsiders. Consultants often have an advantage because they can look at a situation objectively. But they also may be at a disadvantage since they have no power to enforce changes.

Before beginning the analysis, it may be helpful to envision yourself assuming one of these roles. Then, as you study and analyze the case materials, you can make a diagnosis and recommend solutions in a way that is consistent with your position. Try different perspectives. You may find that your view of the situation changes depending on the role you play. As an outside consultant, for example, it may be easy for you to conclude that certain individuals should be replaced in order to solve a problem presented in the case. However, if you take the role of the CEO who knows the individuals and the challenges they have been facing, you may be reluctant to fire them and will seek another solution instead.

The idea of assuming a particular role is similar to the real world in various ways. In your career, you may work in an organization where outside accountants, bankers, lawyers, or other professionals are advising you about how to resolve business situations or improve your practices. Their perspective will be different from yours, but it is useful to understand things from their point of view. Conversely, you may work as a member of the audit team of an accounting firm or the loan committee of a bank. In those situations, it would be helpful if you understood the situation from the perspective of the business leader who must weigh your views against all the other advice that he or she receives. Case analysis can help develop an ability to appreciate such multiple perspectives.

One of the most challenging roles to play in business is as a business founder or owner. For small businesses or entrepreneurial start-ups, the founder may wear all hats at once—key decision maker, primary stockholder, and CEO. Hiring an outside consultant may not be an option. However, the issues faced by young firms and established firms are often not that different, especially when it comes to formulating a plan of action. Business plans that entrepreneurial firms use to raise money or propose a business expansion typically revolve around a few key issues that must be addressed no matter what the size or age of the business. Strategy Spotlight 13.2 reviews business planning issues that are most important to consider when evaluating any case, especially from the perspective of the business founder or owner.

13.2 STRATEGY SPOTLIGHT

USING A BUSINESS PLAN FRAMEWORK TO ANALYZE STRATEGIC CASES

Established businesses often have to change what they are doing in order to improve their competitive position or sometimes simply to survive. To make the changes effectively, businesses usually need a plan. Business plans are no longer just for entrepreneurs. The kind of market analysis, decision making, and action planning that is considered standard practice among new ventures can also benefit going concerns that want to make changes, seize an opportunity, or head in a new direction.

The best business plans, however, are not those that are loaded with decades of month-by-month financial projections or that depend on rigid adherence to a schedule of events that is impossible to predict. The good ones are focused on four factors that are critical to new venture success. These same factors are important in case analysis as well because they get to the heart of many of the problems found in strategic cases.

1. **The people.** "When I receive a business plan, I always read the résumé section first," says Harvard Professor William Sahlman. The people questions that are critically important to investors include: What are their skills? How much experience do they have? What is their reputation? Have they worked together as a team? These same questions also may be used in case analysis to evaluate the role of individuals in the strategic case.

2. **The opportunity.** Business opportunities come in many forms. They are not limited to new ventures. The chance to enter new markets, introduce new products, or merge with a competitor provides many of the challenges that are found in strategic management cases. What are the consequences of such actions? Will the proposed changes affect the firm's business concept? What factors might stand in the way of success? The same issues are also present in most strategic cases.

3. **The context.** Things happen in contexts that cannot be controlled by a firm's managers. This is particularly true of the general environment, where social trends, economic changes, or events such as the September 11, 2001, terrorist attacks can change business overnight. When evaluating strategic cases, ask: Is the company aware of the impact of context on the business? What will it do if the context changes? Can it influence the context in a way that favors the company?

4. **Risk and reward.** With a new venture, the entrepreneurs and investors take the risks and get the rewards. In strategic cases, the risks and rewards often extend to many other stakeholders, such as employees, customers, and suppliers. When analyzing a case, ask: Are the managers making choices that will pay off in the future? Are the rewards evenly distributed? Will some stakeholders be put at risk if the situation in the case changes? What if the situation remains the same? Could that be even riskier?

Whether a business is growing or shrinking, large or small, industrial or service-oriented, the issues of people, opportunities, context, and risks and rewards will have a large impact on its performance. Therefore, you should always consider these four factors when evaluating strategic management cases.

Sources: Wasserman, E. 2003. A simple plan. *MBA Jungle*, February: 50–55; DeKluyver, C. A. 2000. *Strategic thinking: An executive perspective*. Upper Saddle River, NJ: Prentice Hall; and Sahlman, W. A. 1997. How to write a great business plan. *Harvard Business Review*, 75(4): 98–108.

Next we will review five steps to follow when conducting a strategic management case analysis: becoming familiar with the material, identifying the problems, analyzing the strategic issues using the tools and insights of strategic management, proposing alternative solutions, and making recommendations.[6]

Become Familiar with the Material

Written cases often include a lot of material. They may be complex and include detailed financials or long passages. Even so, to understand a case and its implications, you must become familiar with its content. Sometimes key information is not immediately apparent. It may be contained in the footnotes to an exhibit or in an interview with a lower-level employee. In other cases the important points may be difficult to grasp because the subject matter is so unfamiliar. When you approach a strategic case, try the following technique to enhance comprehension:

- Read quickly through the case one time to get an overall sense of the material.
- Use the initial read-through to assess possible links to strategic concepts.
- Read through the case again, in depth. Make written notes as you read.

- Evaluate how strategic concepts might inform key decisions or suggest alternative solutions.
- After formulating an initial recommendation, thumb through the case again quickly to help assess the consequences of the actions you propose.

Identify Problems

When conducting case analysis, one of your most important tasks is to identify the problem. Earlier we noted that one of the main reasons to conduct case analysis is to find solutions. But you cannot find a solution unless you know the problem. Another saying you may have heard is "A good diagnosis is half the cure." In other words, once you have determined what the problem is, you are well on your way to identifying a reasonable solution.

Some cases have more than one problem. But the problems are usually related. For a hypothetical example, consider the following: Company A was losing customers to a new competitor. Upon analysis, it was determined that the competitor had a 50 percent faster delivery time even though its product was of lower quality. The managers of company A could not understand why customers would settle for an inferior product. It turns out that no one was marketing to company A's customers that its product was superior. A second problem was that falling sales resulted in cuts in company A's sales force. Thus, there were two related problems: inferior delivery technology and insufficient sales effort.

When trying to determine the problem, avoid getting hung up on symptoms. Zero in on the problem. For example, in the company A example above, the symptom was losing customers. But the problems were an underfunded, understaffed sales force combined with an outdated delivery technology. Try to see beyond the immediate symptoms to the more fundamental problems.

Another tip when preparing a case analysis is to articulate the problem.[7] Writing down a problem statement gives you a reference point to turn to as you proceed through the case analysis. This is important because the process of formulating strategies or evaluating implementation methods may lead you away from the initial problem. Make sure your recommendation actually addresses the problems you have identified.

One more thing about identifying problems: Sometimes problems are not apparent until *after* you do the analysis. In some cases the problem will be presented plainly, perhaps in the opening paragraph or on the last page of the case. But in other cases the problem does not emerge until after the issues in the case have been analyzed. We turn next to the subject of strategic case analysis.

Conduct Strategic Analyses

This textbook has presented numerous analytical tools (e.g., five-forces analysis and value-chain analysis), contingency frameworks (e.g., when to use related rather than unrelated diversification strategies), and other techniques that can be used to evaluate strategic situations. The previous 12 chapters have addressed practices that are common in strategic management, but only so much can be learned by studying the practices and concepts. The best way to understand these methods is to apply them by conducting analyses of specific cases.

The first step is to determine which strategic issues are involved. Is there a problem in the company's competitive environment? Or is it an internal problem? If it is internal, does it have to do with organizational structure? Strategic controls? Uses of technology? Or perhaps the company has overworked its employees or underutilized its intellectual capital. Has the company mishandled a merger? Chosen the wrong diversification strategy? Botched a new product introduction? Each of these issues is linked to one or more of the concepts discussed earlier in the text. Determine what strategic issues are associated with the problems you have identified. Remember also that most real-life case situations involve issues that are highly interrelated. Even in cases where there is only one major problem, the strategic processes required to solve it may involve several parts of the organization.

Once you have identified the issues that apply to the case, conduct the analysis. For example, you may need to conduct a five-forces analysis or dissect the company's competitive strategy. Perhaps you need to evaluate whether its resources are rare, valuable, difficult to imitate, or difficult to substitute. Financial analysis may be needed to assess the company's economic prospects. Perhaps the international entry mode needs to be reevaluated because of changing conditions in the host country. Employee empowerment techniques may need to be improved to enhance organizational learning. Whatever the case, all the strategic concepts introduced in the text include insights for assessing their effectiveness. Determining how well a company is doing these things is central to the case analysis process.

Financial ratio analysis is one of the primary tools used to conduct case analysis. Appendix 1 to Chapter 13 includes a discussion and examples of the financial ratios that are often used to evaluate a company's performance and financial well-being. Exhibit 13.1 provides a summary of the financial ratios presented in Appendix 1 to this chapter.

In this part of the overall strategic analysis process, it is also important to test your own assumptions about the case.[8] First, what assumptions are you making about the case materials? It may be that you have interpreted the case content differently than your team

> **financial ratio analysis**
> a method of evaluating a company's performance and financial well-being through ratios of accounting values, including short-term solvency, long-term solvency, asset utilization, profitability, and market value ratios.

EXHIBIT 13.1 Summary of Financial Ratio Analysis Techniques

Ratio	What It Measures
Short-term solvency, or liquidity, ratios:	
Current ratio	Ability to use assets to pay off liabilities.
Quick ratio	Ability to use liquid assets to pay off liabilities quickly.
Cash ratio	Ability to pay off liabilities with cash on hand.
Long-term solvency, or financial leverage, ratios:	
Total debt ratio	How much of a company's total assets are financed by debt.
Debt-equity ratio	Compares how much a company is financed by debt with how much it is financed by equity.
Equity multiplier	How much debt is being used to finance assets.
Times interest earned ratio	How well a company has its interest obligations covered.
Cash coverage ratio	A company's ability to generate cash from operations.
Asset utilization, or turnover, ratios:	
Inventory turnover	How many times each year a company sells its entire inventory.
Days' sales in inventory	How many days on average inventory is on hand before it is sold.
Receivables turnover	How frequently each year a company collects on its credit sales.
Days' sales in receivables	How many days on average it takes to collect on credit sales (average collection period).
Total asset turnover	How much of sales is generated for every dollar in assets.
Capital intensity	The dollar investment in assets needed to generate $1 in sales.
Profitability ratios:	
Profit margin	How much profit is generated by every dollar of sales.
Return on assets (ROA)	How effectively assets are being used to generate a return.
Return on equity (ROE)	How effectively amounts invested in the business by its owners are being used to generate a return.
Market value ratios:	
Price-earnings ratio	How much investors are willing to pay per dollar of current earnings.
Market-to-book ratio	Compares market value of the company's investments to the cost of those investments.

members or classmates. Being clear about these assumptions will be important in determining how to analyze the case. Second, what assumptions have you made about the best way to resolve the problems? Ask yourself why you have chosen one type of analysis over another. This process of assumption checking can also help determine if you have gotten to the heart of the problem or are still just dealing with symptoms.

As mentioned earlier, sometimes the critical diagnosis in a case can be made only after the analysis is conducted. However, by the end of this stage in the process, you should know the problems and have completed a thorough analysis of them. You can now move to the next step: finding solutions.

Propose Alternative Solutions

It is important to remember that in strategic management case analysis, there is rarely one right answer or one best way. Even when members of a class or a team agree on what the problem is, they may not agree upon how to solve the problem. Therefore, it is helpful to consider several different solutions.

After conducting strategic analysis and identifying the problem, develop a list of options. What are the possible solutions? What are the alternatives? First, generate a list of all the options you can think of without prejudging any one of them. Remember that not all cases call for dramatic decisions or sweeping changes. Some companies just need to make small adjustments. In fact, "Do nothing" may be a reasonable alternative in some cases. Although that is rare, it might be useful to consider what will happen if the company does nothing. This point illustrates the purpose of developing alternatives: to evaluate what will happen if a company chooses one solution over another.

Thus, during this step of a case analysis, you will evaluate choices and the implications of those choices. One aspect of any business that is likely to be highlighted in this part of the analysis is strategy implementation. Ask how the choices made will be implemented. It may be that what seems like an obvious choice for solving a problem creates an even bigger problem when implemented. But remember also that no strategy or strategic "fix" is going to work if it cannot be implemented. Once a list of alternatives is generated, ask:

- Can the company afford it? How will it affect the bottom line?
- Is the solution likely to evoke a competitive response?
- Will employees throughout the company accept the changes? What impact will the solution have on morale?
- How will the decision affect other stakeholders? Will customers, suppliers, and others buy into it?
- How does this solution fit with the company's vision, mission, and objectives?
- Will the culture or values of the company be changed by the solution? Is it a positive change?

The point of this step in the case analysis process is to find a solution that both solves the problem and is realistic. A consideration of the implications of various alternative solutions will generally lead you to a final recommendation that is more thoughtful and complete.

Make Recommendations

The basic aim of case analysis is to find solutions. Your analysis is not complete until you have recommended a course of action. In this step the task is to make a set of recommendations that your analysis supports. Describe exactly what needs to be done. Explain why this course of action will solve the problem. The recommendation should also include suggestions for how best to implement the proposed solution because the recommended actions and their implications for the performance and future of the firm are interrelated.

Recall that the solution you propose must solve the problem you identified. This point cannot be overemphasized; too often students make recommendations that treat only symptoms or fail to tackle the central problems in the case. Make a logical argument that shows how the problem led to the analysis and the analysis led to the recommendations you are proposing. Remember, an analysis is not an end in itself; it is useful only if it leads to a solution.

The actions you propose should describe the very next steps that the company needs to take. Don't say, for example, "If the company does more market research, then I would recommend the following course of action. . . ." Instead, make conducting the research part of your recommendation. Taking the example a step further, if you also want to suggest subsequent actions that may be different *depending* on the outcome of the market research, that's OK. But don't make your initial recommendation conditional on actions the company may or may not take.

In summary, case analysis can be a very rewarding process but, as you might imagine, it can also be frustrating and challenging. If you will follow the steps described above, you will address the different elements of a thorough analysis. This approach can give your analysis a solid footing. Then, even if there are differences of opinion about how to interpret the facts, analyze the situation, or solve the problems, you can feel confident that you have not missed any important steps in finding the best course of action.

Students are often asked to prepare oral presentations of the information in a case and their analysis of the best remedies. This is frequently assigned as a group project. Or you may be called upon in class to present your ideas about the circumstances or solutions for a case the class is discussing. Exhibit 13.2 provides some tips for preparing an oral case presentation.

EXHIBIT 13.2 Preparing an Oral Case Presentation

Rule	Description
Organize your thoughts.	Begin by becoming familiar with the material. If you are working with a team, compare notes about the key points of the case and share insights that other team members may have gleaned from tables and exhibits. Then make an outline. This is one of the best ways to organize the flow and content of the presentation.

Emphasize strategic analysis.	The purpose of case analysis is to diagnose problems and find solutions. In the process, you may need to unravel the case material as presented and reconfigure it in a fashion that can be more effectively analyzed. Present the material in a way that lends itself to analysis—don't simply restate what is in the case. This involves three major categories with the following emphasis:
	
	    Background/Problem Statement 10–20%
	    Strategic Analysis/Options 60–75%
	    Recommendations/Action Plan 10–20%
	
	As you can see, the emphasis of your presentation should be on analysis. This will probably require you to reorganize the material so that the tools of strategic analysis can be applied.

Be logical and consistent.	A presentation that is rambling and hard to follow may confuse the listener and fail to evoke a good discussion. Present your arguments and explanations in a logical sequence. Support your claims with facts. Include financial analysis where appropriate. Be sure that the solutions you recommend address the problems you have identified.
Defend your position.	Usually an oral presentation is followed by a class discussion. Anticipate what others might disagree with, and be prepared to defend your views. This means being aware of the choices you made and the implications of your recommendations. Be clear about your assumptions. Be able to expand on your analysis.
Share presentation responsibilities.	Strategic management case analyses are often conducted by teams. Each member of the team should have a clear role in the oral presentation, preferably a speaking role. It's also important to coordinate the different parts of the presentation into a logical, smooth-flowing whole. How well team members work together is usually very apparent during an oral presentation.

How to Get the Most from Case Analysis

LO13.4

How to get the most out of case analysis.

One of the reasons case analysis is so enriching as a learning tool is that it draws on many resources and skills besides just what is in the textbook. This is especially true in the study of strategy. Why? Because strategic management itself is a highly integrative task that draws on many areas of specialization at several levels, from the individual to the whole of society. Therefore, to get the most out of case analysis, expand your horizons beyond the concepts in this text and seek insights from your own reservoir of knowledge. Here are some tips for how to do that:[9]

- ***Keep an open mind.*** Like any good discussion, a case analysis discussion often evokes strong opinions and high emotions. But it's the variety of perspectives that makes case analysis so valuable: Many viewpoints usually lead to a more complete analysis. Therefore, avoid letting an emotional response to another person's style or opinion keep you from hearing what he or she has to say. Once you evaluate what is said, you may disagree with it or dismiss it as faulty. But unless you keep an open mind in the first place, you may miss the importance of the other person's contribution. Also, people often place a higher value on the opinions of those they consider to be good listeners.

- ***Take a stand for what you believe.*** Although it is vital to keep an open mind, it is also important to state your views proactively. Don't try to figure out what your friends or the instructor wants to hear. Analyze the case from the perspective of your own background and belief system. For example, perhaps you feel that a decision is unethical or that the managers in a case have misinterpreted the facts. Don't be afraid to assert that in the discussion. For one thing, when a person takes a strong stand, it often encourages others to evaluate the issues more closely. This can lead to a more thorough investigation and a more meaningful class discussion.

- ***Draw on your personal experience.*** You may have experiences from work or as a customer that shed light on some of the issues in a case. Even though one of the purposes of case analysis is to apply the analytical tools from this text, you may be able to add to the discussion by drawing on your outside experiences and background. Of course, you need to guard against carrying that to extremes. In other words, don't think that your perspective is the only viewpoint that matters! Simply recognize that firsthand experience usually represents a welcome contribution to the overall quality of case discussions.

- ***Participate and persuade.*** Have you heard the phrase "Vote early . . . and often"? Among loyal members of certain political parties, it has become rather a joke. Why? Because a democratic system is built on the concept of one person, one vote. Even though some voters may want to vote often enough to get their candidate elected, doing so is against the law. Not so in a case discussion. People who are persuasive and speak their mind can often influence the views of others. But to do so, you have to be prepared and convincing. Being persuasive is more than being loud or long-winded. It involves understanding all sides of an argument and being able to overcome objections to your own point of view. These efforts can make a case discussion more lively. And they parallel what happens in the real world; in business, people frequently share their opinions and attempt to persuade others to see things their way.

- ***Be concise and to the point.*** In the previous point, we encouraged you to speak up and "sell" your ideas to others in a case discussion. But you must be clear about what you are selling. Make your arguments in a way that is explicit and direct. Zero in on the most important points. Be brief. Don't try to make a lot of points at once by jumping around between topics. Avoid trying to explain the whole case situation at once. Remember, other students usually resent classmates who go on and on, take up a lot of "airtime," or repeat themselves unnecessarily. The best way to avoid this is to stay focused and be specific.

- ***Think out of the box.*** It's OK to be a little provocative; sometimes that is the consequence of taking a stand on issues. But it may be equally important to be imaginative and creative when making a recommendation or determining how to implement a solution. Albert Einstein once stated, "Imagination is more important than knowledge." The reason is that managing strategically requires more than memorizing concepts. Strategic management insights must be applied to each case differently—just knowing the principles is not enough. Imagination and out-of-the-box thinking help to apply strategic knowledge in novel and unique ways.

- ***Learn from the insights of others.*** Before you make up your mind about a case, hear what other students have to say. Get a second opinion, and a third, and so forth. Of course, in a situation where you have to put your analysis in writing, you may not be able to learn from others ahead of time. But in a case discussion, observe how various students attack the issues and engage in problem solving. Such observation skills also may be a key to finding answers within the case. For example, people tend to believe authority figures, so they would place a higher value on what a company president says. In some cases, however, the statements of middle managers may represent a point of view that is even more helpful for finding a solution to the problems presented by the case.

- ***Apply insights from other case analyses.*** Throughout the text, we have used examples of actual businesses to illustrate strategy concepts. The aim has been to show you how firms think about and deal with business problems. During the course, you may be asked to conduct several case analyses as part of the learning experience. Once you have performed a few case analyses, you will see how the concepts from the text apply in real-life business situations. Incorporate the insights learned from the text examples and your own previous case discussions into each new case that you analyze.

- ***Critically analyze your own performance.*** Performance appraisals are a standard part of many workplace situations. They are used to determine promotions, raises, and work assignments. In some organizations, everyone from the top executive down is subject to such reviews. Even in situations where the owner or CEO is not evaluated by others, top executives often find it useful to ask themselves regularly, Am I being effective? The same can be applied to your performance in a case analysis situation. Ask yourself, Were my comments insightful? Did I make a good contribution? How might I improve next time? Use the same criteria on yourself that you use to evaluate others. What grade would you give yourself? This technique not only will make you more fair in your assessment of others but also will indicate how your own performance can improve.

- ***Conduct outside research.*** Many times, you can enhance your understanding of a case situation by investigating sources outside the case materials. For example, you may want to study an industry more closely or research a company's close competitors. Recent moves such as mergers and acquisitions or product introductions may be reported in the business press. The company itself may provide useful information on its website or in its annual reports. Such information can usually spur additional discussion and enrich the case analysis. (*Caution:* It is best to check with your instructor in advance to be sure this kind of additional research is encouraged. Bringing in outside research may conflict with the instructor's learning objectives.)

EXHIBIT 13.3 Preparing a Written Case Analysis

Rule	Description
Be thorough.	Many of the ideas presented in Exhibit 13.2 about oral presentations also apply to written case analysis. However, a written analysis typically has to be more complete. This means writing out the problem statement and articulating assumptions. It is also important to provide support for your arguments and reference case materials or other facts more specifically.
Coordinate team efforts.	Written cases are often prepared by small groups. Within a group, just as in a class discussion, you may disagree about the diagnosis or the recommended plan of action. This can be healthy if it leads to a richer understanding of the case material. But before committing your ideas to writing, make sure you have coordinated your responses. Don't prepare a written analysis that appears contradictory or looks like a patchwork of disconnected thoughts.
Avoid restating the obvious.	There is no reason to restate material that everyone is familiar with already, namely, the case content. It is too easy for students to use up space in a written analysis with a recapitulation of the details of the case—this accomplishes very little. Stay focused on the key points. Restate only the information that is most central to your analysis.
Present information graphically.	Tables, graphs, and other exhibits are usually one of the best ways to present factual material that supports your arguments. For example, financial calculations such as break-even analysis, sensitivity analysis, or return on investment are best presented graphically. Even qualitative information such as product lists or rosters of employees can be summarized effectively and viewed quickly by using a table or graph.
Exercise quality control.	When presenting a case analysis in writing, it is especially important to use good grammar, avoid misspelling words, and eliminate typos and other visual distractions. Mistakes that can be glossed over in an oral presentation or class discussion are often highlighted when they appear in writing. Make your written presentation appear as professional as possible. Don't let the appearance of your written case keep the reader from recognizing the importance and quality of your analysis.

Several of the points suggested above for how to get the most out of case analysis apply only to an open discussion of a case, like that in a classroom setting. Exhibit 13.3 provides some additional guidelines for preparing a written case analysis.

Useful Decision-Making Techniques in Case Analysis

LO13.5
How integrative thinking and conflict-inducing discussion techniques can lead to better decisions.

The demands on today's business leaders require them to perform a wide variety of functions. The success of their organizations often depends on how they as individuals—and as part of groups—meet the challenges and deliver on promises. In this section we address three different techniques that can help managers make better decisions and, in turn, enable their organizations to achieve higher performance.

First, we discuss integrative thinking, a technique that helps managers make better decisions through the resolution of competing demands on resources, multiple contingencies, and diverse opportunities. Second, we address the concept of "asking heretical questions." These are questions that challenge conventional wisdom and may even seem odd or unusual—but they can often lead to valuable innovations. Third, we introduce two approaches to decision making that involve the effective use of conflict in the decision-making process. These are devil's advocacy and dialectical inquiry.

Integrative Thinking

integrative thinking
a process of reconciling opposing thoughts by generating new alternatives and creative solutions rather than rejecting one thought in favor of another.

How does a leader make good strategic decisions in the face of multiple contingencies and diverse opportunities? A study by Roger L. Martin reveals that executives who have a capability known as **integrative thinking** are among the most effective leaders. In his book *The Opposable Mind,* Martin contends that people who can consider two conflicting ideas simultaneously, without dismissing one of the ideas or becoming discouraged about

EXHIBIT 13.4 Integrative Thinking: The Process of Thinking and Deciding

```
          SALIENCE
      Consider more-salient
            factors.

RESOLUTION              CAUSALITY
Strive for a creative   Consider both
resolution of conflicts. multidirectional
                        and nonlinear
                        causality.

          ARCHITECTURE
         When working on
         parts, visualize
            the whole.
```

Source: Adaption from Harvard Business School Press from R. L. Martin. *The Opposable Mind*, 2007.

reconciling them, often make the best problem solvers because of their ability to creatively synthesize the opposing thoughts. In explaining the source of his title, Martin quotes F. Scott Fitzgerald, who observed, "The test of a first-rate intelligence is the ability to hold two opposing ideas in mind at the same time and still retain the ability to function. One should, for example, be able to see that things are hopeless yet be determined to make them otherwise."[10]

In contrast to conventional thinking, which tends to focus on making choices between competing ideas from a limited set of alternatives, integrative thinking is the process by which people reconcile opposing thoughts to identify creative solutions that provide them with more options and new alternatives. Exhibit 13.4 outlines the four stages of the integrative thinking and deciding process. Martin uses the admittedly simple example of deciding where to go on vacation to illustrate the stages:

- *Salience.* Take stock of what features of the decision you consider relevant and important. For example: Where will you go? What will you see? Where will you stay? What will it cost? Is it safe? Other features may be less important, but try to think of everything that may matter.
- *Causality.* Make a mental map of the causal relationships between the features, that is, how the various features are related to one another. For example, is it worth it to invite friends to share expenses? Will an exotic destination be less safe?
- *Architecture.* Use the mental map to arrange a sequence of decisions that will lead to a specific outcome. For example, will you make the hotel and flight arrangements first, or focus on which sightseeing tours are available? No particular

decision path is right or wrong, but considering multiple options simultaneously may lead to a better decision.
- **Resolution.** Make your selection. For example, choose which destination, which flight, and so forth. Your final resolution is linked to how you evaluated the first three stages; if you are dissatisfied with your choices, the dotted arrows in the diagram (Exhibit 13.4) suggest you can go back through the process and revisit your assumptions.

Applied to business, an integrative thinking approach enables decision makers to consider situations not as forced trade-offs—either decrease costs or invest more; either satisfy shareholders or please the community—but as a method for synthesizing opposing ideas into a creative solution. The key is to think in terms of "both-and" rather than "either-or." "Integrative thinking," says Martin, "shows us that there's a way to integrate the advantages of one solution without canceling out the advantages of an alternative solution."

Although Martin found that integrative thinking comes naturally to some people, he also believes it can be taught. But it may be difficult to learn, in part because it requires people to *un*learn old patterns and become aware of how they think. For executives willing to take a deep look at their habits of thought, integrative thinking can be developed into a valuable skill. Strategy Spotlight 13.3 tells how Red Hat Inc. cofounder Bob Young made his company a market leader by using integrative thinking to resolve a major problem in the domain of open-source software.

Asking Heretical Questions

In his recent book *The Big Pivot,* Andrew Winston introduced the concept of heretical innovation to help address the challenges associated with environmental sustainability in today's world.[11] He describes the need to pursue a deeper level of innovation that challenges long-held beliefs about how things work. Central to addressing these challenges is the need to pose "heretical questions"—those that challenge conventional wisdom. Typically, they may make us uncomfortable or may seem odd (or even impossible)—but they often become the means of coming up with major innovations. Although the context of Winston's discussion was environmental sustainability, we believe that his ideas have useful implications for major challenges faced by today's managers in a wide range of firms and industries.

Heretical questions can address issues that are both small and large—from redesigning a single process or product to rethinking the whole business model. One must not discount the value of the approach in considering small matters. After all, the vast majority of people in a company don't have the mandate to rethink strategy. However, anyone in an organization can ask disruptive questions that profoundly change one aspect of a business. What makes this heretical is how deeply it challenges the conventional wisdom.

Consider the fascinating story of UPS's "no left turns," a classic tale in the sustainability world that has become rather well known. The catchy phrase became a rallying cry for mapping out new delivery routes that avoided crossing traffic and idling at stoplights. UPS is saving time, money, and energy—about 85 million miles and 8 million gallons of fuel annually.

Also, take the example of dyeing clothing—a tremendously water-intensive process. Somebody at Adidas asked a heretical question: Could we dye clothes with no water? The answer was yes. However, the company needed to partner with a small Thailand-based company, Yeh Group. The DreDye process Adidas is now piloting uses heat and pressure to force pigment into the fibers. The process uses no water and also cuts energy and chemical use by 50 percent!

Finally, in 2010, Kimberly-Clark, the $21 billion firm that is behind such brands as Kleenex and Scott, questioned the simple assumption that toilet paper rolls must have cardboard tubes to hold their shape. It created the Scott Naturals Tube-Free line, which

13.3 STRATEGY SPOTLIGHT

INTEGRATIVE THINKING AT RED HAT, INC.

How can a software developer make money giving away free software? That was the dilemma Red Hat founder Bob Young was facing during the early days of the open-source software movement. A Finnish developer named Linus Torvalds, using freely available UNIX software, had developed an operating system dubbed "Linux" that was being widely circulated in the freeware community. The software was intended specifically as an alternative to the pricey proprietary systems sold by Microsoft and Oracle. To use proprietary software, corporations had to pay hefty installation fees and were required to call Microsoft or Oracle engineers to fix it when anything went wrong. In Young's view it was a flawed and unsustainable business model.

But the free model was flawed as well. Although several companies had sprung up to help companies use Linux, there were few opportunities to profit from using it. As Young said, "You couldn't make any money selling [the Linux] operating system because all this stuff was free, and if you started to charge money for it, someone else would come in and price it lower. It was a commodity in the truest sense of the word." To complicate matters, hundreds of developers were part of the software community that was constantly modifying and debugging Linux—at a rate equivalent to three updates per day. As a result, systems administrators at corporations that tried to adopt the software spent so much time keeping track of updates that they didn't enjoy the savings they expected from using free software.

Young saw the appeal of both approaches but also realized a new model was needed. While contemplating the dilemma, he realized a salient feature that others had overlooked—because most major corporations have to live with software decisions for at least 10 years, they will nearly always choose to do business with the industry leader. Young realized he had to position Red Hat as the top provider of Linux software. To do that, he proposed a radical solution: provide the authoritative version of Linux and deliver it in a new way—as a download rather than on CD. He hired programmers to create a downloadable version—still free—and promised, in essence, to maintain its quality (for a fee, of course) by dealing with all the open-source programmers who were continually suggesting changes. In the process, he created a product companies could trust and then profited by establishing ongoing service relationships with customers. Red Hat's version of Linux became the de facto standard. By 2000, Linux was installed in 25 percent of server operating systems worldwide and Red Hat had captured over 50 percent of the global market for Linux systems.

By recognizing that a synthesis of two flawed business models could provide the best of both worlds, Young exhibited the traits of integrative thinking. He pinpointed the causal relationships between the salient features of the marketplace and Red Hat's path to prosperity. He then crafted an approach that integrated aspects of the two existing approaches into a new alternative. By resolving to provide a free downloadable version, Young also took responsibility for creating his own path to success. The payoff was substantial: When Red Hat went public in 1999, Young became a billionaire on the first day of trading. And by 2015 Red Hat had over $1.5 billion in annual revenues and a market capitalization of nearly $13 billion.

Sources: Martin, R. L. 2007. *The opposable mind.* Boston: Harvard Business School Press; and *finance.yahoo.com*.

---

offers this household staple in the familiar cylindrical shape. But it comes with no cardboard core—just a hole the same size. It's been very successful—a key part of the now $100 million Scott Naturals brand. While this product may not save the world, if it became the industry standard, we could eliminate 17 billion tubes that are used in the United States every year and save fuel by shipping lighter rolls. This is a good example of heretical thinking. After all, the product doesn't incrementally use less cardboard—it uses none.

The concept of accepting failure and aiming for deep, heretical innovation is difficult for most organizations to embrace. Ed Catmull, the president and cofounder of animation pioneer Pixar, claims that when you are doing something new, you are by definition doing something you don't know very well, and that means mistakes. However, if you don't encourage mistakes, he says, you won't encourage anything new: "We're very conscientious about making it so that mistakes really aren't thought of as bad . . . they're just learning."

Conflict-Inducing Techniques

Next we address some techniques often used to improve case analyses that involve the constructive use of conflict. In the classroom—as well as in the business world—you will frequently be analyzing cases or solving problems in groups. While the word *conflict* often has a negative connotation (e.g., rude behavior, personal affronts), it can be very helpful in arriving at better solutions to cases. It can provide an effective means for new insights as well as for rigorously questioning and analyzing assumptions and strategic alternatives. In fact, if you don't have constructive conflict, you may get only consensus. When this happens, decisions tend to be based on compromise rather than collaboration.

In your organizational behavior classes, you probably learned the concept of "groupthink."[12] *Groupthink,* a term coined by Irving Janis after he conducted numerous studies on executive decision making, is a condition in which group members strive to reach agreement or consensus without realistically considering other viable alternatives. In effect, group norms bolster morale at the expense of critical thinking, and decision making is impaired.[13]

Many of us have probably been "victims" of groupthink at one time or another in our life. We may be confronted with situations when social pressure, politics, or "not wanting to stand out" may prevent us from voicing our concerns about a chosen course of action. Nevertheless, decision making in groups is a common practice in the management of many businesses. Most companies, especially large ones, rely on input from various top managers to provide valuable information and experience from their specialty area as well as their unique perspectives. Organizations need to develop cultures and reward systems that encourage people to express their perspectives and create open dialogues. Constructive conflict can be very helpful in that it emphasizes the need for managers to consider other people's perspectives and not simply become a strong advocate for positions that they may prefer.

Chapter 11 emphasized the importance of empowering individuals at all levels to participate in decision-making processes. After all, many of us have experienced situations where there is not a perfect correlation between one's rank and the viability of one's ideas! In terms of this course, case analysis involves a type of decision making that is often conducted in groups. Strategy Spotlight 13.4 provides guidelines for making team-based approaches to case analysis more effective.

Clearly, understanding how to work in groups and the potential problems associated with group decision processes can benefit the case analysis process. Therefore, let's first look at some of the symptoms of groupthink and suggest ways of preventing it. Then we will suggest some conflict-inducing decision-making techniques—devil's advocacy and dialectical inquiry—that can help to prevent groupthink and lead to better decisions.

Symptoms of Groupthink and How to Prevent It   Irving Janis identified several symptoms of groupthink, including:

- *An illusion of invulnerability.* This reassures people about possible dangers and leads to overoptimism and failure to heed warnings of danger.
- *A belief in the inherent morality of the group.* Because individuals think that what they are doing is right, they tend to ignore ethical or moral consequences of their decisions.
- *Stereotyped views of members of opposing groups.* Members of other groups are viewed as weak or not intelligent.
- *The application of pressure to members who express doubts about the group's shared illusions or question the validity of arguments proposed.*
- *The practice of self-censorship.* Members keep silent about their opposing views and downplay to themselves the value of their perspectives.
- *An illusion of unanimity.* People assume that judgments expressed by members are shared by all.
- *The appointment of mindguards.* People sometimes appoint themselves as mindguards to protect the group from adverse information that might break the climate of consensus (or agreement).

Clearly, groupthink is an undesirable and negative phenomenon that can lead to poor decisions. Irving Janis considers it to be a key contributor to such faulty decisions as the failure to prepare for the attack on Pearl Harbor, the escalation of the Vietnam conflict, and

13.4 STRATEGY SPOTLIGHT

MAKING CASE ANALYSIS TEAMS MORE EFFECTIVE

Working in teams can be very challenging. Not all team members have the same skills, interests, or motivations. Some team members just want to get the work done. Others see teams as an opportunity to socialize. Occasionally, there are team members who think they should be in charge and make all the decisions; other teams have freeloaders—team members who don't want to do anything except get credit for the team's work.

One consequence of these various styles is that team meetings can become time wasters. Disagreements about how to proceed, how to share the work, or what to do at the next meeting tend to slow down teams and impede progress toward the goal. While the dynamics of case analysis teams are likely to always be challenging depending on the personalities involved, one thing nearly all members realize is that, ultimately, the team's work must be completed. Most team members also aim to do the highest-quality work possible. The following guidelines provide some useful insights about how to get the work of a team done more effectively.

Spend More Time Together

One of the factors that prevents teams from doing a good job with case analysis is their failure to put in the necessary time. Unless teams really tackle the issues surrounding case analysis—both the issues in the case itself and organizing how the work is to be conducted—the end result will probably be lacking because decisions that are made too quickly are unlikely to get to the heart of the problem(s) in the case. "Meetings should be a precious resource, but they're treated like a necessary evil," says Kenneth Sole, a consultant who specializes in organizational behavior. As a result, teams that care more about finishing the analysis than getting the analysis right often make poor decisions.

Therefore, expect to have a few meetings that run long, especially at the beginning of the project, when the work is being organized and the issues in the case are being sorted out, and again at the end, when the team must coordinate the components of the case analysis that will be presented. Without spending this kind of time together, it is doubtful that the analysis will be comprehensive and the presentation is likely to be choppy and incomplete.

Make a Focused and Disciplined Agenda

To complete tasks and avoid wasting time, meetings need to have a clear purpose. To accomplish this at Roche, the Swiss drug and diagnostic product maker, CEO Franz Humer implemented a "decision agenda." The agenda focuses only on Roche's highest-value issues, and discussions are limited to these major topics. In terms of case analysis, the major topics include sorting out the issues of the case, linking elements of the case to the strategic issues presented in class or the text, and assigning roles to various team members. Such objectives help keep team members on track.

Agendas also can be used to address issues such as the timeline for accomplishing work. Otherwise, the purpose of meetings may only be to manage the "crisis" of getting the case analysis finished on time. One solution is to assign a team member to manage the agenda. That person could make sure the team stays focused on the tasks at hand and remains mindful of time constraints. Another role could be to link the team's efforts to the steps presented in Exhibit 13.2 and Exhibit 13.3 on how to prepare a case analysis.

Pay More Attention to Strategy

Teams often waste time by focusing on unimportant aspects of a case. These may include details that are interesting but irrelevant or operational issues rather than strategic issues. It is true that useful clues to the issues in the case are sometimes embedded in the conversations of key managers or the trends evident in a financial statement. But once such insights are discovered, teams need to focus on the underlying strategic problems in the case. To solve such problems, major corporations such as Cadbury Schweppes and Boeing hold meetings just to generate strategic alternatives for solving their problems. This gives managers time to consider the implications of various courses of action. Separate meetings are held to evaluate alternatives, make strategic decisions, and approve an action plan.

Once the strategic solutions or "course corrections" are identified—as is common in most cases assigned—the operational implications and details of implementation will flow from the strategic decisions that companies make. Therefore, focusing primarily on strategic issues will provide teams with insights for making recommendations that are based on a deeper understanding of the issues in the case.

Produce Real Decisions

Too often, meetings are about discussing rather than deciding. Teams often spend a lot of time talking without reaching any conclusions. As Raymond Sanchez, CEO of Florida-based Security Mortgage Group, says, meetings are often used to "rehash the hash that's already been hashed." To be efficient and productive, team meetings need to be about more than just information sharing and group input. For example, an initial meeting may result in the team realizing that it needs to study the case in greater depth and examine links to strategic issues more carefully. Once more analysis is conducted, the team needs to reach a consensus so that the decisions that are made will last once the meeting is over. Lasting decisions are more actionable because they free team members to take the next steps.

One technique for making progress in this way is recapping each meeting with a five-minute synthesis report. According to Pamela Schindler, director of the Center for Applied Management at Wittenberg University, it's important to think through the implications of the meeting before ending it. "The real joy of synthesis," says Schindler, "is realizing how many meetings you won't need."

continued

continued

Not only are these guidelines useful for helping teams finish their work, but they can also help resolve some of the difficulties that teams often face. By involving every team member, using a meeting agenda, and focusing on the strategic issues that are critical to nearly every case, the discussion is limited and the criteria for making decisions become clearer. This allows the task to dominate rather than any one personality. And if the team finishes its work faster, this frees up time to focus on other projects or put the finishing touches on a case analysis presentation.

Sources: Mankins, M. C. 2004. Stop wasting valuable time. *Harvard Business Review*, September: 58–65; and Sauer, P. J. 2004. Escape from meeting hell. *Inc.*, May, www.inc.com.

the failure to prepare for the consequences of the Iraqi invasion. Many of the same sorts of flawed decision making occur in business organizations. Janis has provided several suggestions for preventing groupthink that can be used as valuable guides in decision making and problem solving:

- Leaders must encourage group members to address their concerns and objectives.
- When higher-level managers assign a problem for a group to solve, they should adopt an impartial stance and not mention their preferences.
- Before a group reaches its final decision, the leader should encourage members to discuss their deliberations with trusted associates and then report the perspectives back to the group.
- The group should invite outside experts and encourage them to challenge the group's viewpoints and positions.
- The group should divide into subgroups, meet at various times under different chairpersons, and then get together to resolve differences.
- After reaching a preliminary agreement, the group should hold a "second chance" meeting that provides members a forum to express any remaining concerns and rethink the issue prior to making a final decision.

Using Conflict to Improve Decision Making In addition to the above suggestions, the effective use of conflict can be a means of improving decision making. Although conflict can have negative outcomes, such as ill will, anger, tension, and lowered motivation, both leaders and group members must strive to ensure that it is managed properly and used in a constructive manner.

Two conflict-inducing decision-making approaches that have become quite popular are *devil's advocacy* and *dialectical inquiry*. Both approaches incorporate conflict into the decision-making process through formalized debate. A group charged with making a decision or solving a problem is divided into two subgroups, and each will be involved in the analysis and solution.

With **devil's advocacy,** one of the groups (or individuals) acts as a critic to the plan. The devil's advocate tries to come up with problems with the proposed alternative and suggest reasons why it should not be adopted. The role of the devil's advocate is to create dissonance. This ensures that the group will take a hard look at its original proposal or alternative. By having a group (or individual) assigned the role of devil's advocate, it becomes clear that such an adversarial stance is legitimized. It brings out criticisms that might otherwise not be made.

Some authors have suggested that the use of a devil's advocate can help boards of directors to ensure that decisions are addressed comprehensively and to avoid groupthink.[14] And Charles Elson, a director of Sunbeam Corporation, has argued:

> Devil's advocates are terrific in any situation because they help you to figure a decision's numerous implications. . . . The better you think out the implications prior to making the decision, the better the decision ultimately turns out to be. That's why a devil's advocate is always a great person, irritating sometimes, but a great person.

devil's advocacy
a method of introducing conflict into a decision-making process by having specific individuals or groups act as a critic to an analysis or planned solution.

As one might expect, there can be some potential problems with using the devil's advocate approach. If one's views are constantly criticized, one may become demoralized. Thus, that person may come up with "safe solutions" in order to minimize embarrassment or personal risk and become less subject to criticism. Additionally, even if the devil's advocate is successful with finding problems with the proposed course of action, there may be no new ideas or counterproposals to take its place. Thus, the approach sometimes may simply focus on what is wrong without suggesting other ideas.

Dialectical inquiry attempts to accomplish the goals of the devil's advocate in a more constructive manner. It is a technique whereby a problem is approached from two alternative points of view. The idea is that out of a critique of the opposing perspectives—a thesis and an antithesis—a creative synthesis will occur. Dialectical inquiry involves the following steps:

1. Identify a proposal and the information that was used to derive it.
2. State the underlying assumptions of the proposal.
3. Identify a counterplan (antithesis) that is believed to be feasible, politically viable, and generally credible. However, it rests on assumptions that are opposite to the original proposal.
4. Engage in a debate in which individuals favoring each plan provide their arguments and support.
5. Identify a synthesis which, hopefully, includes the best components of each alternative.

> **dialectical inquiry**
> a method of introducing conflict into a decision-making process by devising different proposals that are feasible, politically viable, and credible but rely on different assumptions and then debating the merits of each.

There are some potential downsides associated with dialectical inquiry. It can be quite time-consuming and involve a good deal of training. Further, it may result in a series of compromises between the initial proposal and the counterplan. In cases where the original proposal was the best approach, this would be unfortunate.

Despite some possible limitations associated with these conflict-inducing decision-making techniques, they have many benefits. Both techniques force debate about underlying assumptions, data, and recommendations between subgroups. Such debate tends to prevent the uncritical acceptance of a plan that may seem to be satisfactory after a cursory analysis. The approach serves to tap the knowledge and perspectives of group members and continues until group members agree on both assumptions and recommended actions. Given that both approaches serve to use, rather than minimize or suppress, conflict, higher-quality decisions should result. Exhibit 13.5 briefly summarizes these techniques.

EXHIBIT 13.5 Two Conflict-Inducing Decision-Making Processes

Alternative #1 → Alternative #1 Critiqued by Devil's Advocate → Revised Alternative

Alternative #1 (Thesis) / Alternative #2 (Antithesis) → Structural Debate → Alternative #3 (Synthesis)

LO13.6

How to use the strategic insights and material from each of the 12 previous chapters in the text to analyze issues posed by strategic management cases.

Following the Analysis-Decision-Action Cycle in Case Analysis

In Chapter 1 we defined strategic management as the analysis, decisions, and actions that organizations undertake to create and sustain competitive advantages. It is no accident that we chose that sequence of words because it corresponds to the sequence of events that typically occurs in the strategic management process. In case analysis, as in the real world, this cycle of events can provide a useful framework. First, an analysis of the case in terms of the business environment and current events is needed. To make such an analysis, the case background must be considered. Next, based on that analysis, decisions must be made. This may involve formulating a strategy, choosing between difficult options, moving forward aggressively, or retreating from a bad situation. There are many possible decisions, depending on the case situation. Finally, action is required. Once decisions are made and plans are set, the action begins. The recommended action steps and the consequences of implementing these actions are the final stage.

Each of the previous 12 chapters of this book includes techniques and information that may be useful in a case analysis. However, not all of the issues presented will be important in every case. As noted earlier, one of the challenges of case analysis is to identify the most critical points and sort through material that may be ambiguous or unimportant.

In this section we draw on the material presented in each of the 12 chapters to show how it informs the case analysis process. The ideas are linked sequentially and in terms of an overarching strategic perspective. One of your jobs when conducting case analysis is to see how the parts of a case fit together and how the insights from the study of strategy can help you understand the case situation.

1. *Analyzing organizational goals and objectives.* A company's vision, mission, and objectives keep organization members focused on a common purpose. They also influence how an organization deploys its resources, relates to its stakeholders, and matches its short-term objectives with its long-term goals. The goals may even impact how a company formulates and implements strategies. When exploring issues of goals and objectives, you might ask:

    - Has the company developed short-term objectives that are inconsistent with its long-term mission? If so, how can management realign its vision, mission, and objectives?
    - Has the company considered all of its stakeholders equally in making critical decisions? If not, should the views of all stakeholders be treated the same or are some stakeholders more important than others?
    - Is the company being faced with an issue that conflicts with one of its long-standing policies? If so, how should it compare its existing policies to the potential new situation?

2. *Analyzing the external environment.* The business environment has two components. The general environment consists of demographic, sociocultural, political/legal, technological, economic, and global conditions. The competitive environment includes rivals, suppliers, customers, and other factors that may directly affect a company's success. Strategic managers must monitor the environment to identify opportunities and threats that may have an impact on performance. When investigating a firm's external environment, you might ask:

    - Does the company follow trends and events in the general environment? If not, how can these influences be made part of the company's strategic analysis process?

- Is the company effectively scanning and monitoring the competitive environment? If so, how is it using the competitive intelligence it is gathering to enhance its competitive advantage?
- Has the company correctly analyzed the impact of the competitive forces in its industry on profitability? If so, how can it improve its competitive position relative to these forces?

3. *Analyzing the internal environment.* A firm's internal environment consists of its resources and other value-adding capabilities. Value-chain analysis and a resource-based approach to analysis can be used to identify a company's strengths and weaknesses and determine how they are contributing to its competitive advantages. Evaluating firm performance can also help make meaningful comparisons with competitors. When researching a company's internal analysis, you might ask:
   - Does the company know how the various components of its value chain are adding value to the firm? If not, what internal analysis is needed to determine its strengths and weakness?
   - Has the company accurately analyzed the source and vitality of its resources? If so, is it deploying its resources in a way that contributes to competitive advantages?
   - Is the company's financial performance as good as or better than that of its close competitors? If so, has it balanced its financial success with the performance criteria of other stakeholders such as customers and employees?

4. *Assessing a firm's intellectual assets.* Human capital is a major resource in today's knowledge economy. As a result, attracting, developing, and retaining talented workers is a key strategic challenge. Other assets such as patents and trademarks are also critical. How companies leverage their intellectual assets through social networks and strategic alliances, and how technology is used to manage knowledge, may be a major influence on a firm's competitive advantage. When analyzing a firm's intellectual assets, you might ask:
   - Does the company have underutilized human capital? If so, what steps are needed to develop and leverage its intellectual assets?
   - Is the company missing opportunities to forge strategic alliances? If so, how can it use its social capital to network more effectively?
   - Has the company developed knowledge-management systems that capture what it learns? If not, what technologies can it employ to retain new knowledge?

5. *Formulating business-level strategies.* Firms use the competitive strategies of differentiation, focus, and overall cost leadership as a basis for overcoming the five competitive forces and developing sustainable competitive advantages. Combinations of these strategies may work best in some competitive environments. Additionally, an industry's life cycle is an important contingency that may affect a company's choice of business-level strategies. When assessing business-level strategies, you might ask:
   - Has the company chosen the correct competitive strategy given its industry environment and competitive situation? If not, how should it use its strengths and resources to improve its performance?
   - Does the company use combination strategies effectively? If so, what capabilities can it cultivate to further enhance profitability?
   - Is the company using a strategy that is appropriate for the industry life cycle in which it is competing? If not, how can it realign itself to match its efforts to the current stage of industry growth?

6. ***Formulating corporate-level strategies.*** Large firms often own and manage portfolios of businesses. Corporate strategies address methods for achieving synergies among these businesses. Related and unrelated diversification techniques are alternative approaches to deciding which business should be added to or removed from a portfolio. Companies can diversify by means of mergers, acquisitions, joint ventures, strategic alliances, and internal development. When analyzing corporate-level strategies, you might ask:

    - Is the company competing in the right businesses given the opportunities and threats that are present in the environment? If not, how can it realign its diversification strategy to achieve competitive advantages?
    - Is the corporation managing its portfolio of businesses in a way that creates synergies among the businesses? If so, what additional business should it consider adding to its portfolio?
    - Are the motives of the top corporate executives who are pushing diversification strategies appropriate? If not, what action can be taken to curb their activities or align them with the best interests of all stakeholders?

7. ***Formulating international-level strategies.*** Foreign markets provide both opportunities and potential dangers for companies that want to expand globally. To decide which entry strategy is most appropriate, companies have to evaluate the trade-offs between two factors that firms face when entering foreign markets: cost reduction and local adaptation. To achieve competitive advantages, firms will typically choose one of three strategies: global, multidomestic, or transnational. When evaluating international-level strategies, you might ask:

    - Is the company's entry into an international marketplace threatened by the actions of local competitors? If so, how can cultural differences be minimized to give the firm a better chance of succeeding?
    - Has the company made the appropriate choices between cost reduction and local adaptation to foreign markets? If not, how can it adjust its strategy to achieve competitive advantages?
    - Can the company improve its effectiveness by embracing one international strategy over another? If so, how should it choose between a global, multidomestic, or transnational strategy?

8. ***Formulating entrepreneurial strategies.*** New ventures add jobs and create new wealth. To do so, they must identify opportunities that will be viable in the marketplace as well as gather resources and assemble an entrepreneurial team to enact the opportunity. New entrants often evoke a strong competitive response from incumbent firms in a given marketplace. When examining the role of strategic thinking on the success of entrepreneurial ventures and the role of competitive dynamics, you might ask:

    - Is the company engaged in an ongoing process of opportunity recognition? If not, how can it enhance its ability to recognize opportunities?
    - Do the entrepreneurs who are launching new ventures have vision, dedication and drive, and a commitment to excellence? If so, how have these affected the performance and dedication of other employees involved in the venture?
    - Have strategic principles been used in the process of developing strategies to pursue the entrepreneurial opportunity? If not, how can the venture apply tools such as five-forces analysis and value-chain analysis to improve its competitive position and performance?

9. *Achieving effective strategic control.* Strategic controls enable a firm to implement strategies effectively. Informational controls involve comparing performance to stated goals and scanning, monitoring, and being responsive to the environment. Behavioral controls emerge from a company's culture, reward systems, and organizational boundaries. When assessing the impact of strategic controls on implementation, you might ask:

    - Is the company employing the appropriate informational control systems? If not, how can it implement a more interactive approach to enhance learning and minimize response times?
    - Does the company have a strong and effective culture? If not, what steps can it take to align its values and rewards system with its goals and objectives?
    - Has the company implemented control systems that match its strategies? If so, what additional steps can be taken to improve performance?

10. *Creating effective organizational designs.* Organizational designs that align with competitive strategies can enhance performance. As companies grow and change, their structures must also evolve to meet new demands. In today's economy, firm boundaries must be flexible and permeable to facilitate smoother interactions with external parties such as customers, suppliers, and alliance partners. New forms of organizing are becoming more common. When evaluating the role of organizational structure on strategy implementation, you might ask:

    - Has the company implemented organizational structures that are suited to the type of business it is in? If not, how can it alter the design in ways that enhance its competitiveness?
    - Is the company employing boundaryless organizational designs where appropriate? If so, how are senior managers maintaining control of lower-level employees?
    - Does the company use outsourcing to achieve the best possible results? If not, what criteria should it use to decide which functions can be outsourced?

11. *Creating a learning organization and an ethical organization.* Strong leadership is essential for achieving competitive advantages. Two leadership roles are especially important. The first is creating a learning organization by harnessing talent and encouraging the development of new knowledge. Second, leaders play a vital role in motivating employees to excellence and inspiring ethical behavior. When exploring the impact of effective strategic leadership, you might ask:

    - Do company leaders promote excellence as part of the overall culture? If so, how has this influenced the performance of the firm and the individuals in it?
    - Is the company committed to being a learning organization? If not, what can it do to capitalize on the individual and collective talents of organizational members?
    - Have company leaders exhibited an ethical attitude in their own behavior? If not, how has their behavior influenced the actions of other employees?

12. *Fostering corporate entrepreneurship.* Many firms continually seek new growth opportunities and avenues for strategic renewal. In some corporations, autonomous work units such as business incubators and new venture groups are used to focus corporate venturing activities. In other corporate settings, product champions and

other firm members provide companies with the impetus to expand into new areas. When investigating the impact of entrepreneurship on strategic effectiveness, you might ask:

- Has the company resolved the dilemmas associated with managing innovation? If so, is it effectively defining and pacing its innovation efforts?
- Has the company developed autonomous work units that have the freedom to bring forth new product ideas? If so, has it used product champions to implement new venture initiatives?
- Does the company have an entrepreneurial orientation? If not, what can it do to encourage entrepreneurial attitudes in the strategic behavior of its organizational members?

summary

Strategic management case analysis provides an effective method of learning how companies analyze problems, make decisions, and resolve challenges. Strategic cases include detailed accounts of actual business situations. The purpose of analyzing such cases is to gain exposure to a wide variety of organizational and managerial situations. By putting yourself in the place of a strategic decision maker, you can gain an appreciation of the difficulty and complexity of many strategic situations. In the process you can learn how to ask good strategic questions and enhance your analytical skills. Presenting case analyses can also help develop oral and written communication skills.

In this chapter we have discussed the importance of strategic case analysis and described the five steps involved in conducting a case analysis: becoming familiar with the material, identifying problems, analyzing strategic issues, proposing alternative solutions, and making recommendations. We have also discussed how to get the most from case analysis. Finally, we have described how the case analysis process follows the analysis-decision-action cycle of strategic management and outlined issues and questions that are associated with each of the previous 12 chapters of the text.

key terms

case analysis 416
financial ratio analysis 423
integrative thinking 428
devil's advocacy 434
dialectical inquiry 435

references

1. Bryant, A. 2011. *The corner office:* 15. New York: St. Martin's.
2. The material in this chapter is based on several sources, including Barnes, L. A., Nelson, A. J., & Christensen, C. R. 1994. *Teaching and the case method: Text, cases and readings.* Boston: Harvard Business School Press; Guth, W. D. 1985. Central concepts of business unit and corporate strategy. In Guth, W. D. (Ed.), *Handbook of business strategy:* 1–9. Boston: Warren, Gorham & Lamont; Lundberg, C. C., & Enz, C. 1993. A framework for student case preparation. *Case Research Journal,* 13 (Summer): 129–140; and Ronstadt, R. 1980. *The art of case analysis: A guide to the diagnosis of business situations.* Dover, MA: Lord.
3. Edge, A. G. & Coleman, D. R. 1986. *The guide to case analysis and reporting* (3rd ed.). Honolulu, HI: System Logistics.
4. Morris, E. 1987. Vision and strategy: A focus for the future. *Journal of Business Strategy,* 8: 51–58.
5. Bryant, A. 2011. *The corner office:* 15. New York: St. Martin's.
6. This section is based on Lundberg & Enz, op. cit., and Ronstadt, op. cit.
7. The importance of problem definition was emphasized in Mintzberg, H., Raisinghani, D., & Theoret, A. 1976. The structure of "unstructured" decision processes. *Administrative Science Quarterly,* 21(2): 246–275.
8. Drucker, P. F. 1994. The theory of the business. *Harvard Business Review,* 72(5): 95–104.
9. This section draws on Edge & Coleman, op. cit.
10. Evans, R. 2007. The either/or dilemma. *www.ft.com,* December 19: np; and Martin, R. L. 2007. *The opposable mind.* Boston: Harvard Business School Press.
11. This section draws on Winston, A. S. 2014. *The big pivot.* Boston: Harvard Business Review Press.
12. Irving Janis is credited with coining the term *groupthink,* and he applied it primarily to fiascos in government (such as the Bay of Pigs incident in 1961). Refer to Janis, I. L. 1982. *Victims of groupthink* (2nd ed.). Boston: Houghton Mifflin.
13. Much of our discussion is based upon Finkelstein, S. & Mooney, A. C. 2003. Not the usual suspects: How to use board process to make boards better. *Academy of Management Executive,* 17(2): 101–113; Schweiger, D. M., Sandberg, W. R., & Rechner, P. L. 1989. Experiential effects of dialectical inquiry, devil's advocacy, and consensus approaches to strategic decision making. *Academy of Management Journal,* 32(4): 745–772; and Aldag, R. J. & Stearns, T. M. 1987. *Management.* Cincinnati: South-Western.
14. Finkelstein and Mooney, op. cit.

APPENDIX 1 TO CHAPTER 13

Financial Ratio Analysis*

Standard Financial Statements

One obvious thing we might want to do with a company's financial statements is to compare them to those of other, similar companies. We would immediately have a problem, however. It's almost impossible to directly compare the financial statements of two companies because of differences in size.

For example, Oracle and IBM are obviously serious rivals in the computer software market, but IBM is much larger (in terms of assets), so it is difficult to compare them directly. For that matter, it's difficult to even compare financial statements from different points in time for the same company if the company's size has changed. The size problem is compounded if we try to compare IBM and, say, SAP (of Germany). If SAP's financial statements are denominated in euros, then we have a size *and* a currency difference.

To start making comparisons, one obvious thing we might try to do is to somehow standardize the financial statements. One very common and useful way of doing this is to work with percentages instead of total dollars. The resulting financial statements are called *common-size statements*. We consider these next.

Common-Size Balance Sheets

For easy reference, Prufrock Corporation's 2014 and 2015 balance sheets are provided in Exhibit 13A.1. Using these, we construct common-size balance sheets by expressing each item as a percentage of total assets. Prufrock's 2014 and 2015 common-size balance sheets are shown in Exhibit 13A.2.

Notice that some of the totals don't check exactly because of rounding errors. Also notice that the total change has to be zero since the beginning and ending numbers must add up to 100 percent.

In this form, financial statements are relatively easy to read and compare. For example, just looking at the two balance sheets for Prufrock, we see that current assets were 19.7 percent of total assets in 2015, up from 19.1 percent in 2014. Current liabilities declined from 16 percent to 15.1 percent of total liabilities and equity over that same time. Similarly, total equity rose from 68.1 percent of total liabilities and equity to 72.2 percent.

Overall, Prufrock's liquidity, as measured by current assets compared to current liabilities, increased over the year. Simultaneously, Prufrock's indebtedness diminished as a percentage of total assets. We might be tempted to conclude that the balance sheet has grown "stronger."

Common-Size Income Statements

A useful way of standardizing the income statement, shown in Exhibit 13A.3, is to express each item as a percentage of total sales, as illustrated for Prufrock in Exhibit 13A.4.

This income statement tells us what happens to each dollar in sales. For Prufrock, interest expense eats up $.061 out of every sales dollar and taxes take another $.081. When all is said and done, $.157 of each dollar flows through to the bottom line (net income), and that amount is split into $.105 retained in the business and $.052 paid out in dividends.

These percentages are very useful in comparisons. For example, a relevant figure is the cost percentage. For Prufrock, $.582 of each $1 in sales goes to pay for goods sold. It would be interesting to compute the same percentage for Prufrock's main competitors to see how Prufrock stacks up in terms of cost control.

---

*This entire appendix is adapted from Rows, S. A., Westerfield, R. W., & Jordan, B. D. 1999. *Essentials of Corporate Finance* (2nd ed.), chap. 3. New York: McGraw-Hill.

EXHIBIT 13A.1
Prufrock Corporation

	2014	2015
Assets		
Current assets		
Cash	$ 84	$ 98
Accounts receivable	165	188
Inventory	393	422
Total	$ 642	$ 708
Fixed assets		
Net plant and equipment	$ 2,731	$ 2,880
Total assets	$ 3,373	$ 3,588
Liabilities and Owners' Equity		
Current liabilities		
Accounts payable	$ 312	$ 344
Notes payable	231	196
Total	$ 543	$ 540
Long-term debt	$ 531	$ 457
Owners' equity		
Common stock and paid-in surplus	$ 500	$ 550
Retained earnings	1,799	2,041
Total	$ 2,299	$ 2,591
Total liabilities and owners' equity	$ 3,373	$ 3,588

Balance sheets as of December 31, 2014 and 2015 ($ millions).

Ratio Analysis

Another way of avoiding the problems involved in comparing companies of different sizes is to calculate and compare *financial ratios*. Such ratios are ways of comparing and investigating the relationships between different pieces of financial information. We cover some of the more common ratios next, but there are many others that we don't touch on.

One problem with ratios is that different people and different sources frequently don't compute them in exactly the same way, and this leads to much confusion. The specific definitions we use here may or may not be the same as others you have seen or will see elsewhere. If you ever use ratios as a tool for analysis, you should be careful to document how you calculate each one, and, if you are comparing your numbers to those of another source, be sure you know how its numbers are computed.

For each of the ratios we discuss, several questions come to mind:

1. How is it computed?
2. What is it intended to measure, and why might we be interested?
3. What is the unit of measurement?
4. What might a high or low value be telling us? How might such values be misleading?
5. How could this measure be improved?

EXHIBIT 13A.2
Prufrock Corporation

	2014	2015	Change
Assets			
Current assets			
Cash	2.5%	2.7%	+ .2%
Accounts receivable	4.9	5.2	+ .3
Inventory	11.7	11.8	+ .1
Total	19.1	19.7	+ .6
Fixed assets			
Net plant and equipment	80.9	80.3	− .6
Total assets	100.0%	100.0%	.0%
Liabilities and Owners' Equity			
Current liabilities			
Accounts payable	9.2%	9.6%	+ .4%
Notes payable	6.8	5.5	−1.3
Total	16.0	15.1	− .9
Long-term debt	15.7	12.7	−3.0
Owners' equity			
Common stock and paid-in surplus	14.8	15.3	+ .5
Retained earnings	53.3	56.9	+3.6
Total	68.1	72.2	+4.1
Total liabilities and owners' equities	100.0%	100.0%	.0%

Common-size balance sheets as of December 31, 2014 and 2015 (%).

Note: Numbers may not add up to 100.0% due to rounding.

EXHIBIT 13A.3
Prufrock Corporation

Sales		$2,311
Cost of goods sold		1,344
Depreciation		276
Earnings before interest and taxes		$ 691
Interest paid		141
Taxable income		$ 550
Taxes (34%)		187
Net income		$ 363
Dividends	$121	
Addition to retained earnings	242	

2015 income statement ($ millions).

EXHIBIT 13A.4
Prufrock Corporation

Sales	100.0%
Cost of goods sold	58.2
Depreciation	11.9
Earnings before interest and taxes	29.9
Interest paid	6.1
Taxable income	23.8
Taxes (34%)	8.1
Net income	15.7%
Dividends	5.2%
Addition to retained earnings	10.5

2015 Common-size income statement (%).

Financial ratios are traditionally grouped into the following categories:

1. Short-term solvency, or liquidity, ratios.
2. Long-term solvency, or financial leverage, ratios.
3. Asset management, or turnover, ratios.
4. Profitability ratios.
5. Market value ratios.

We will consider each of these in turn. In calculating these numbers for Prufrock, we will use the ending balance sheet (2015) figures unless we explicitly say otherwise. The numbers for the various ratios come from the income statement and the balance sheet.

Short-Term Solvency, or Liquidity, Measures

As the name suggests, short-term solvency ratios as a group are intended to provide information about a firm's liquidity, and these ratios are sometimes called *liquidity measures*. The primary concern is the firm's ability to pay its bills over the short run without undue stress. Consequently, these ratios focus on current assets and current liabilities.

For obvious reasons, liquidity ratios are particularly interesting to short-term creditors. Since financial managers are constantly working with banks and other short-term lenders, an understanding of these ratios is essential.

One advantage of looking at current assets and liabilities is that their book values and market values are likely to be similar. Often (though not always), these assets and liabilities just don't live long enough for the two to get seriously out of step. On the other hand, like any type of near cash, current assets and liabilities can and do change fairly rapidly, so today's amounts may not be a reliable guide to the future.

Current Ratio One of the best-known and most widely used ratios is the *current ratio*. As you might guess, the current ratio is defined as:

$$\text{Current ratio} = \frac{\text{Current assets}}{\text{Current liabilities}}$$

For Prufrock, the 2015 current ratio is:

$$\text{Current ratio} = \frac{\$708}{\$540} = 1.31 \text{ times}$$

Because current assets and liabilities are, in principle, converted to cash over the following 12 months, the current ratio is a measure of short-term liquidity. The unit of measurement is either dollars or times. So we could say Prufrock has $1.31 in current assets for every $1 in current liabilities, or we could say Prufrock has its current liabilities covered 1.31 times over.

To a creditor, particularly a short-term creditor such as a supplier, the higher the current ratio, the better. To the firm, a high current ratio indicates liquidity, but it also may indicate an inefficient use of cash and other short-term assets. Absent some extraordinary circumstances, we would expect to see a current ratio of at least 1, because a current ratio of less than 1 would mean that net working capital (current assets less current liabilities) is negative. This would be unusual in a healthy firm, at least for most types of businesses.

The current ratio, like any ratio, is affected by various types of transactions. For example, suppose the firm borrows over the long term to raise money. The short-run effect would be an increase in cash from the issue proceeds and an increase in long-term debt. Current liabilities would not be affected, so the current ratio would rise.

Finally, note that an apparently low current ratio may not be a bad sign for a company with a large reserve of untapped borrowing power.

Quick (or Acid-Test) Ratio Inventory is often the least liquid current asset. It's also the one for which the book values are least reliable as measures of market value, since the quality of the inventory isn't considered. Some of the inventory may later turn out to be damaged, obsolete, or lost.

More to the point, relatively large inventories are often a sign of short-term trouble. The firm may have overestimated sales and overbought or overproduced as a result. In this case, the firm may have a substantial portion of its liquidity tied up in slow-moving inventory.

To further evaluate liquidity, the *quick*, or *acid-test, ratio* is computed just like the current ratio, except inventory is omitted:

$$\text{Quick ratio} = \frac{\text{Current assets} - \text{Inventory}}{\text{Current liabilities}}$$

Notice that using cash to buy inventory does not affect the current ratio, but it reduces the quick ratio. Again, the idea is that inventory is relatively illiquid compared to cash.

For Prufrock, this ratio in 2015 was:

$$\text{Quick ratio} = \frac{\$708 - 422}{\$540} = .53 \text{ times}$$

The quick ratio here tells a somewhat different story than the current ratio, because inventory accounts for more than half of Prufrock's current assets. To exaggerate the point, if this inventory consisted of, say, unsold nuclear power plants, then this would be a cause for concern.

Cash Ratio A very short-term creditor might be interested in the *cash ratio:*

$$\text{Cash ratio} = \frac{\text{Cash}}{\text{Current liabilities}}$$

You can verify that this works out to be .18 times for Prufrock.

Long-Term Solvency Measures

Long-term solvency ratios are intended to address the firm's long-run ability to meet its obligations, or, more generally, its financial leverage. These ratios are sometimes called *financial leverage ratios* or just *leverage ratios*. We consider three commonly used measures and some variations.

Total Debt Ratio The *total debt ratio* takes into account all debts of all maturities to all creditors. It can be defined in several ways, the easiest of which is:

$$\text{Total debt ratio} = \frac{\text{Total assets} - \text{Total equity}}{\text{Total assets}}$$

$$= \frac{\$3{,}588 - 2{,}591}{\$3{,}588} = .28 \text{ times}$$

In this case, an analyst might say that Prufrock uses 28 percent debt.[1] Whether this is high or low or whether it even makes any difference depends on whether or not capital structure matters.

Prufrock has $.28 in debt for every $1 in assets. Therefore, there is $.72 in equity ($1 − .28) for every $.28 in debt. With this in mind, we can define two useful variations on the total debt ratio, the *debt-equity ratio* and the *equity multiplier:*

$$\text{Debt-equity ratio} = \text{Total debt/Total equity}$$
$$= \$.28/\$.72 = .39 \text{ times}$$
$$\text{Equity multiplier} = \text{Total assets/Total equity}$$
$$= \$1/\$.72 = 1.39 \text{ times}$$

The fact that the equity multiplier is 1 plus the debt-equity ratio is not a coincidence:

$$\text{Equity multiplier} = \text{Total assets/Total equity} = \$1/\$.72 = 1.39$$
$$= (\text{Total equity} + \text{Total debt})/\text{Total equity}$$
$$= 1 + \text{Debt-equity ratio} = 1.39 \text{ times}$$

The thing to notice here is that given any one of these three ratios, you can immediately calculate the other two, so they all say exactly the same thing.

Times Interest Earned Another common measure of long-term solvency is the *times interest earned* (TIE) *ratio*. Once again, there are several possible (and common) definitions, but we'll stick with the most traditional:

$$\text{Times interest earned ratio} = \frac{\text{EBIT}}{\text{Interest paid}}$$

$$= \frac{\$691}{\$141} = 4.9 \text{ times}$$

As the name suggests, this ratio measures how well a company has its interest obligations covered, and it is often called the *interest coverage ratio*. For Prufrock, the interest bill is covered 4.9 times over.

Cash Coverage A problem with the TIE ratio is that it is based on earnings before interest and taxes (EBIT), which is not really a measure of cash available to pay interest. The reason is that depreciation, a noncash expense, has been deducted. Since interest is most definitely a cash outflow (to creditors), one way to define the *cash coverage ratio* is:

$$\text{Cash coverage ratio} = \frac{\text{EBIT} + \text{Depreciation}}{\text{Interest paid}}$$

$$= \frac{\$691 + 276}{\$141} = \frac{\$967}{\$141} = 6.9 \text{ times}$$

---

[1] Total equity here includes preferred stock, if there is any. An equivalent numerator in this ratio would be (Current liabilities + Long-term debt).

The numerator here, EBIT plus depreciation, is often abbreviated EBDIT (earnings before depreciation, interest, and taxes). It is a basic measure of the firm's ability to generate cash from operations, and it is frequently used as a measure of cash flow available to meet financial obligations.

Asset Management, or Turnover, Measures

We next turn our attention to the efficiency with which Prufrock uses its assets. The measures in this section are sometimes called *asset utilization ratios*. The specific ratios we discuss can all be interpreted as measures of turnover. What they are intended to describe is how efficiently, or intensively, a firm uses its assets to generate sales. We first look at two important current assets: inventory and receivables.

Inventory Turnover and Days' Sales in Inventory   During the year, Prufrock had a cost of goods sold of $1,344. Inventory at the end of the year was $422. With these numbers, *inventory turnover* can be calculated as:

$$\text{Inventory turnover} = \frac{\text{Cost of goods sold}}{\text{Inventory}}$$

$$= \frac{\$1,344}{\$422} = 3.2 \text{ times}$$

In a sense, we sold off, or turned over, the entire inventory 3.2 times. As long as we are not running out of stock and thereby forgoing sales, the higher this ratio is, the more efficiently we are managing inventory.

If we know that we turned our inventory over 3.2 times during the year, then we can immediately figure out how long it took us to turn it over on average. The result is the average *days' sales in inventory:*

$$\text{Days' sales in inventory} = \frac{365 \text{ days}}{\text{Inventory turnover}}$$

$$= \frac{365}{3.2} = 114 \text{ days}$$

This tells us that, on average, inventory sits 114 days before it is sold. Alternatively, assuming we used the most recent inventory and cost figures, it will take about 114 days to work off our current inventory.

For example, we frequently hear things like "Majestic Motors has a 60 days' supply of cars." This means that, at current daily sales, it would take 60 days to deplete the available inventory. We could also say that Majestic has 60 days of sales in inventory.

Receivables Turnover and Days' Sales in Receivables   Our inventory measures give some indication of how fast we can sell products. We now look at how fast we collect on those sales. The *receivables turnover* is defined in the same way as inventory turnover:

$$\text{Receivables turnover} = \frac{\text{Sales}}{\text{Accounts receivable}}$$

$$= \frac{\$2,311}{\$188} = 12.3 \text{ times}$$

Loosely speaking, we collected our outstanding credit accounts and reloaned the money 12.3 times during the year.[2]

---

[2]Here we have implicitly assumed that all sales are credit sales. If they were not, then we would simply use total credit sales in these calculations, not total sales.

This ratio makes more sense if we convert it to days, so the *days' sales in receivables* is:

$$\text{Days' sales in receivables} = \frac{365 \text{ days}}{\text{Receivables turnover}}$$

$$= \frac{365}{12.3} = 30 \text{ days}$$

Therefore, on average, we collect on our credit sales in 30 days. For obvious reasons, this ratio is very frequently called the *average collection period* (ACP).

Also note that if we are using the most recent figures, we can also say that we have 30 days' worth of sales currently uncollected.

Total Asset Turnover Moving away from specific accounts like inventory or receivables, we can consider an important "big picture" ratio, the *total asset turnover ratio*. As the name suggests, total asset turnover is:

$$\text{Total asset turnover} = \frac{\text{Sales}}{\text{Total assets}}$$

$$= \frac{\$2,311}{\$3,588} = .64 \text{ times}$$

In other words, for every dollar in assets, we generated $.64 in sales.

A closely related ratio, the *capital intensity ratio,* is simply the reciprocal of (i.e., 1 divided by) total asset turnover. It can be interpreted as the dollar investment in assets needed to generate $1 in sales. High values correspond to capital-intensive industries (e.g., public utilities). For Prufrock, total asset turnover is .64, so, if we flip this over, we get that capital intensity is $1/.64 = $1.56. That is, it takes Prufrock $1.56 in assets to create $1 in sales.

Profitability Measures

The three measures we discuss in this section are probably the best known and most widely used of all financial ratios. In one form or another, they are intended to measure how efficiently the firm uses its assets and how efficiently the firm manages its operations. The focus in this group is on the bottom line, net income.

Profit Margin Companies pay a great deal of attention to their *profit margin:*

$$\text{Profit margin} = \frac{\text{Net income}}{\text{Sales}}$$

$$= \frac{\$363}{\$2,311} = 15.7\%$$

This tells us that Prufrock, in an accounting sense, generates a little less than 16 cents in profit for every dollar in sales.

All other things being equal, a relatively high profit margin is obviously desirable. This situation corresponds to low expense ratios relative to sales. However, we hasten to add that other things are often not equal.

For example, lowering our sales price will usually increase unit volume, but will normally cause profit margins to shrink. Total profit (or, more importantly, operating cash flow) may go up or down; so the fact that margins are smaller isn't necessarily bad. After all, isn't it possible that, as the saying goes, "Our prices are so low that we lose money on everything we sell, but we make it up in volume!"[3]

---

[3] No, it's not; margins can be small, but they do need to be positive!

Return on Assets *Return on assets* (ROA) is a measure of profit per dollar of assets. It can be defined several ways, but the most common is:

$$\text{Return on assets} = \frac{\text{Net income}}{\text{Total assets}}$$

$$= \frac{\$363}{\$3{,}588} = 10.12\%$$

Return on Equity *Return on equity* (ROE) is a measure of how the stockholders fared during the year. Since benefiting shareholders is our goal, ROE is, in an accounting sense, the true bottom-line measure of performance. ROE is usually measured as:

$$\text{Return on equity} = \frac{\text{Net income}}{\text{Total equity}}$$

$$= \frac{\$363}{\$2{,}591} = 14\%$$

For every dollar in equity, therefore, Prufrock generated 14 cents in profit, but, again, this is only correct in accounting terms.

Because ROA and ROE are such commonly cited numbers, we stress that it is important to remember they are accounting rates of return. For this reason, these measures should properly be called *return on book assets* and *return on book equity*. In addition, ROE is sometimes called *return on net worth*. Whatever it's called, it would be inappropriate to compare the results to, for example, an interest rate observed in the financial markets.

The fact that ROE exceeds ROA reflects Prufrock's use of financial leverage. We will examine the relationship between these two measures in more detail below.

Market Value Measures

Our final group of measures is based, in part, on information not necessarily contained in financial statements—the market price per share of the stock. Obviously, these measures can be calculated directly only for publicly traded companies.

We assume that Prufrock has 33 million shares outstanding and the stock sold for $88 per share at the end of the year. If we recall that Prufrock's net income was $363 million, then we can calculate that its earnings per share were:

$$\text{EPS} = \frac{\text{Net income}}{\text{Shares outstanding}} = \frac{\$363}{33} = \$11$$

Price-Earnings Ratio The first of our market value measures, the *price-earnings,* or PE, *ratio* (or multiple), is defined as:

$$\text{PE ratio} = \frac{\text{Price per share}}{\text{Earnings per share}}$$

$$= \frac{\$88}{\$11} = 8 \text{ times}$$

In the vernacular, we would say that Prufrock shares sell for eight times earnings, or we might say that Prufrock shares have, or "carry," a PE multiple of 8.

Since the PE ratio measures how much investors are willing to pay per dollar of current earnings, higher PEs are often taken to mean that the firm has significant prospects for future growth. Of course, if a firm had no or almost no earnings, its PE would probably be quite large; so, as always, be careful when interpreting this ratio.

Market-to-Book Ratio A second commonly quoted measure is the *market-to-book ratio:*

$$\text{Market-to-book ratio} = \frac{\text{Market value per share}}{\text{Book value per share}}$$

$$= \frac{\$88}{(\$2{,}591/33)} = \frac{\$88}{\$78.5} = 1.12 \text{ times}$$

Notice that book value per share is total equity (not just common stock) divided by the number of shares outstanding.

Since book value per share is an accounting number, it reflects historical costs. In a loose sense, the market-to-book ratio therefore compares the market value of the firm's investments to their cost. A value less than 1 could mean that the firm has not been successful overall in creating value for its stockholders.

Conclusion

This completes our definition of some common ratios. Exhibit 13A.5 summarizes the ratios we've discussed.

EXHIBIT 13A.5 A Summary of Five Types of Financial Ratios

I. Short-term solvency, or liquidity, ratios

$$\text{Current ratio} = \frac{\text{Current assets}}{\text{Current liabilities}}$$

$$\text{Quick ratio} = \frac{\text{Current assets} - \text{Inventory}}{\text{Current liabilities}}$$

$$\text{Cash ratio} = \frac{\text{Cash}}{\text{Current liabilities}}$$

II. Long-term solvency, or financial leverage, ratios

$$\text{Total debt ratio} = \frac{\text{Total assets} - \text{Total equity}}{\text{Total assets}}$$

$$\text{Debt-equity ratio} = \text{Total debt/Total equity}$$

$$\text{Equity multiplier} = \text{Total assets/Total equity}$$

$$\text{Times interest earned ratio} = \frac{\text{EBIT}}{\text{Interest paid}}$$

$$\text{Cash coverage ratio} = \frac{\text{EBIT} + \text{Depreciation}}{\text{Interest paid}}$$

III. Asset utilization, or turnover, ratios

$$\text{Inventory turnover} = \frac{\text{Cost of goods sold}}{\text{Inventory}}$$

$$\text{Days' sales in inventory} = \frac{365 \text{ days}}{\text{Inventory turnover}}$$

$$\text{Receivables turnover} = \frac{\text{Sales}}{\text{Accounts receivable}}$$

$$\text{Days' sales in receivables} = \frac{365 \text{ days}}{\text{Receivables turnover}}$$

$$\text{Total asset turnover} = \frac{\text{Sales}}{\text{Total assets}}$$

$$\text{Capital intensity} = \frac{\text{Total assets}}{\text{Sales}}$$

IV. Profitability ratios

$$\text{Profit margin} = \frac{\text{Net income}}{\text{Sales}}$$

$$\text{Return on assets (ROA)} = \frac{\text{Net income}}{\text{Total assets}}$$

$$\text{Return on equity (ROE)} = \frac{\text{Net income}}{\text{Total equity}}$$

$$\text{ROE} = \frac{\text{Net income}}{\text{Sales}} \times \frac{\text{Sales}}{\text{Assets}} \times \frac{\text{Assets}}{\text{Equity}}$$

V. Market value ratios

$$\text{Price-earnings ratio} = \frac{\text{Price per share}}{\text{Earnings per share}}$$

$$\text{Market-to-book ratio} = \frac{\text{Market value per share}}{\text{Book value per share}}$$

APPENDIX 2 TO CHAPTER 13

Sources of Company and Industry Information*

In order for business executives to make the best decisions when developing corporate strategy, it is critical for them to be knowledgeable about their competitors and about the industries in which they compete. The process used by corporations to learn as much as possible about competitors is often called "competitive intelligence." This appendix provides an overview of important and widely available sources of information that may be useful in conducting basic competitive intelligence. Much information of this nature is available in libraries in article databases and business reference books and on websites. This appendix will recommend a variety of them. Ask a librarian for assistance, because library collections and resources vary.

The information sources are organized into 10 categories:

Competitive Intelligence
Public or Private—Subsidiary or Division—U.S. or Foreign?
Finding Public-Company Information
Guides and Tutorials
SEC Filings/EDGAR—Company Disclosure Reports
Company Rankings
Business Websites
Strategic and Competitive Analysis—Information Sources
Sources for Industry Research and Analysis
Search Engines

Competitive Intelligence

Students and other researchers who want to learn more about the value and process of competitive intelligence should see four recent books on this subject. Ask a librarian about electronic (ebook) versions of the following titles.

Rainer Michaeli. *Competitive Intelligence: Competitive Advantage through Analysis of Competition, Markets and Technologies.* London: Springer-Verlag, 2012.
Erik Jannesson, Fredrik Nilsson, and Birger Rapp (Eds.). *Strategy, Control and Competitive Advantage.* Heidelberg: Springer, 2014.
Hans Hedin, Irmeli Hirvensalo, and Markko Vaarnas. *Handbook of Market Intelligence: Understand, Compete and Grow in Global Markets.* Chichester, West Sussex, U.K.: John Wiley & Sons, 2011.
Benjamin Gilad. *Early Warning: Using Competitive Intelligence to Anticipate Market Shifts, Control Risk, and Create Powerful Strategies.* New York: American Management Association, 2004.

Public or Private—Subsidiary or Division—U.S. or Foreign?

Companies traded on stock exchanges in the United States are required to file a variety of reports that disclose information about the company. This begins the process that produces a wealth of data on public companies and, at the same time, distinguishes them from private companies, which often lack available data. Similarly, financial data of subsidiaries and divisions are typically filed in a consolidated financial statement by the parent company, rather than treated independently, thus limiting the kind of data available on them. On the other hand, foreign companies that trade on U.S. stock exchanges are required to file 20F reports, similar

---

*This information was compiled by Ruthie Brock and Carol Byrne, business librarians at The University of Texas at Arlington. We greatly appreciate their valuable contribution.

to the 10-K for U.S. companies, the most comprehensive of the required reports. The following directories provide brief facts about companies, including whether they are public or private, subsidiary or division, U.S. or foreign.

Corporate Affiliations. New Providence, NJ: LexisNexis, 2014.
> This eight-volume directory features brief profiles of major U.S. and foreign corporations, both public and private, as well as their subsidiaries, divisions, and affiliates. The directory also indicates hierarchies of corporate relationships. An online version of the directory allows retrieval of a list of companies that meet specific criteria. Results can be downloaded to a spreadsheet. The online version requires a subscription, available in some libraries.

ReferenceUSA. Omaha, NE: Infogroup.Inc.
> *ReferenceUSA* is an online directory of more than 14 million businesses located in the United States. This resource is unique in that it includes both public and private companies regardless of how small or large, as well as educational, medical, and nonprofit organizations. Results can be summarized visually in chart format. Job opportunities are provided in search results when available. Specialized modules include consumer lifestyles, historical records, and health care. Check with a librarian regarding availability of specialized modules at your location.

Finding Public-Company Information

Most companies have their annual report to shareholders and other financial reports available on their corporate website. Note that some companies use a variation of their company name in their web address, such as Procter & Gamble: www.pg.com. A few "aggregators" have also conveniently provided an accumulation of links to many reports of U.S. and international corporations or include a PDF document as part of their database, although these generally do not attempt to be comprehensive.

The Public Register Online. Woodstock Valley, CT: Bay Tact Corp.
> *Public Register Online* includes over 5,000 public-company shareholder annual reports and 10-K filings for online viewing. Links are provided to reports on individual companies' websites, official filings from the Securities and Exchange Commission website, stock information from the NYSE Euronext exchange, or some combination of these sources. A link is also provided on this website for ordering personal copies of hard-copy annual reports.
> www.annualreportservice.com/

Mergent Online. New York: Mergent, Inc.
> *Mergent Online* is a database that provides company reports and financial statements for both U.S. and foreign public companies. Mergent's database has up to 25 years of quarterly and annual financial data that can be downloaded into a spreadsheet for analysis across time or across companies. Students should check with a librarian to determine the availability of this database at their college or university library.
> http://mergentonline.com

Guides & Tutorials for Researching Companies and Industries

Guide to Financial Statements and *How to Read Annual Reports.* Armonk, NY: IBM.
> These two educational guides, located on IBM's website, provide basic information on how to read and make sense of financial statements and other information in 10-K and shareholder annual reports for companies in general, not IBM specifically.
> www.ibm.com/investor/help/guide/introduction.wss
> www.ibm.com/investor/help/reports/introduction.wss

EDGAR Full-Text Search Frequently Asked Questions (FAQ). Washington, DC: U.S. Securities and Exchange Commission.
> The capability to search full-text SEC filings (popularly known as EDGAR filings) was vastly improved when the SEC launched its new search form in late 2006. Features are explained at the FAQ page.
> www.sec.gov/edgar/searchedgar/edgarfulltextfaq.htm

Ten Steps to Industry Intelligence Research. Industry Tutorial. George A. Smathers Libraries, University of Florida, Gainesville, FL.

This tutorial provides a step-by-step approach for finding information about industries, with embedded links to recommended sources.

http://businesslibrary.uflib.ufl.edu/industryresearch

Conducting Business Research.

This tutorial provides a step-by-step process for business research.

www.lib.utexas.edu/services/instruction/learningmodules/businessresearch/intro.html

Guide to Financial Statements. Armonk, NY: IBM.

International Business Machines (IBM) created an educational guide for beginners to learn how to understand and interpret a typical financial statement.

How to Read Annual Reports. Armonk, NY: IBM.

International Business Machines (IBM) created an educational guide to help novices make sense of information that is typically included in annual 10-K and shareholder reports.

Ten Steps to Company Intelligence. Company Research Tutorial. William and Joan Schreyer Business Library, Penn State University, University Park, PA.

This tutorial provides a step-by-step approach to finding company intelligence information.

http://businesslibrary.uflib.ufl.edu/companyresearch

SEC Filings/EDGAR—Company Disclosure Reports

SEC Filings are the various reports that publicly traded companies must file with the Securities and Exchange Commission to disclose information about their corporation. These are often referred to as "EDGAR" filings, an acronym for the Electronic Data Gathering, Analysis and Retrieval System. Some websites and commercial databases improve access to these reports by offering additional retrieval features not available on the official (*www.sec.gov*) website.

EDGAR Database Full-Text Search. U.S. Securities and Exchange Commission (SEC), Washington, DC.

10-K reports and other required corporate documents are quickly made available in the SEC's EDGAR database. The 10-K is the most comprehensive disclosure document for company information. Some companies also include the annual report to shareholders as part of the 10-K filing, although it is not required. The SEC made changes to its search engine in 2013, improving visual layout, navigation, and search results. The SEC's legacy search engine is still available.

www.sec.gov/edgar/searchedgar/companysearch.html

OneSource. Concord, MA: Avention.

OneSource provides a recent year or so of SEC filings, but it includes a longer history of the shareholder annual reports.

LexisNexis Academic. SEC Filings & Reports. Bethesda, MD: LexisNexis.

SEC filings are available in *LexisNexis Academic* by selecting "Search by Content Type." A company-name search or an advanced search can be conducted at that point.

Mergent Online—Government Filings Search.

This database also provides an alternative search interface for SEC filings. *Mergent's Government Filings* search allows searching by company name, ticker, CIK (Central Index Key) number, or industry SIC number. The search can be limited by date and by type of SEC file. Ask a librarian whether your library subscribes to *Mergent Online* for this feature.

www.mergentonline.com/filingsearch.php?type=edgar&criteriatype=findall&submitvalues

Company Rankings

Fortune 500. New York: Time Inc.

The *Fortune 500* list and other company rankings are published in the printed edition of *Fortune* magazine and are also available online.

http://money.cnn.com/magazines/fortune/fortune500/2014/full_list/index.html

Forbes Global 2000. Forbes, Inc.
> The companies listed on the Forbes Global 2000 are the biggest and most powerful in the world.
> www.forbes.com/global2000/

Business Websites

Big Charts. San Francisco: MarketWatch, Inc.
> *BigCharts* is a comprehensive and easy-to-use investment research website, providing access to professional-level research tools such as interactive charts, current and historical quotes, industry analysis, and intraday stock screeners, as well as market news and commentary. MarketWatch operates this website, a service of Dow Jones & Company. Supported by site sponsors, it is free to self-directed investors.
> http://bigcharts.marketwatch.com/

GlobalEdge. East Lansing, MI: Michigan State University.
> *GlobalEdge* is a web portal providing a significant amount of information about international business, countries around the globe, the U.S. states, industries, and news.
> http://globaledge.msu.edu/

Yahoo Finance. Sunnyvale, CA: Yahoo! Inc.
> This website links to information on U.S. markets, world markets, data sources, finance references, investment editorials, financial news, and other helpful websites.
> http://finance.yahoo.com

Strategic and Competitive Analysis—Information Sources

Analyzing a company can take the form of examining its internal and external environments. In the process, it is useful to identify the company's strengths, weaknesses, opportunities, and threats (SWOT). Sources for this kind of analysis are varied, but perhaps the best would be articles from *The Wall Street Journal,* business magazines, and industry trade publications. Publications such as these can be found in the following databases available at many public and academic libraries. When using a database that is structured to allow it, try searching the company name combined with one or more keywords, such as "IBM and competition" or "Microsoft and lawsuits" or "AMR and fuel costs" to retrieve articles relating to the external environment.

ABI/INFORM Complete. Ann Arbor, MI: ProQuest LLC.
> *ABI/INFORM Complete* provides abstracts and full-text articles covering disciplines such as management, law, taxation, economics, health care, and information technology from more than 6,800 scholarly, business, and trade publications. Other types of resources include company and industry reports, case studies, market research reports, and a variety of downloadable economic data.

Business Insights: Essentials. Farmington Hills, MI: Gale CENGAGE Learning.
> *Business Insights* provides company and industry intelligence for a selection of public and private companies. Company profiles include parent-subsidiary relationships, industry rankings, products and brands, industry statistics, and financial ratios. Selections of SWOT analysis reports are also available. The Company and Industry comparison tool allows a researcher to compare up to six companies' revenues, employees, and sales data over time. Results are available as an image, chart, or spreadsheet.

Business Source Complete. Ipswich, MA: EBSCO Publishing.
> *Business Source Complete* is a full-text database with over 3,800 scholarly business journals covering management, economics, finance, accounting, international business, and more. The database also includes detailed company profiles for the world's 10,000 largest companies, as well as selected country economic reports provided by the Economist Intelligence Unit (EIU). The database includes case studies, investment and market research reports, SWOT analyses, and more. *Business Source Complete* contains over 2,400 peer-reviewed business journals.

Hoover's Academic. Short Hills, NJ: Dun & Bradstreet.

Hoover's provides company and industry information for over 85 million public and private U.S. and international companies. The company profiles include the company's history, key financials, and executive information, as well as access to the latest news stories and SEC filings. Over 600 industries are covered in *Hoover's*. Custom reports can be created and downloaded.

OneSource. Concord, MA: Avention, Inc.

OneSource provides a wealth of information about U.S. and international public and private companies. The profiles include key executives, a financial report, and the corporate family structure. Also available are recent analyst reports, company SWOT analyses, industry reports, news and SEC filings information. Custom reports can be created and downloaded.

Thomson ONE Research.

Thomson ONE Research offers full-text analytical reports on more than 65,000 companies worldwide. The research reports are excellent sources for strategic and financial profiles of a company and its competitors and of industry trends. Developed by a global roster of brokerage, investment banking, and research firms, these full-text investment reports include a wealth of current and historical information useful for evaluating a company or industry over time.

International Directory of Company Histories. Detroit, MI: St. James Press, 1988–present. 163 volumes to date.

This directory covers more than 11,000 multinational companies, and the series is still adding volumes. Each company history is approximately three to five pages in length and provides a summary of the company's mission, goals, and ideals, followed by company milestones, principal subsidiaries, and competitors. Strategic decisions made during the company's period of existence are usually noted. This series covers public and private companies and nonprofit entities. Entry information includes a company's legal name, headquarters information, URL, incorporation date, ticker symbol, stock exchange listing, sales figures, and the primary North American Industry Classification System (NAICS) code. Further reading selections complete the entry information. Volumes 59 to the most recent are available electronically in the Gale Virtual Reference Library database from Gale CENGAGE Learning.

LexisNexis Academic. Bethesda, MD: LexisNexis.

LexisNexis Academic provides access to legal, company, and industry information, news sources, and public records. Industry information is available through the Company Info tab or the "Search by content type" selection. The Company Dossier tool allows a researcher to compare up to five companies' financial statements at one time with download capabilities.

The Wall Street Journal. New York: Dow Jones & Co.

This respected business newspaper is available in searchable full text from 1984 to the present in the *Factiva* database. The "News Pages" link provides access to current articles and issues of *The Wall Street Journal*. Dow Jones, publisher of the print version of the *Wall Street Journal,* also has an online subscription available at *wsj.com*. Some libraries provide access to *The Wall Street Journal* through the ProQuest Newspapers database.

Sources for Industry Research and Analysis

Factiva. New York: Dow Jones & Co.

The *Factiva* database has several options for researching an industry. One would be to search the database for articles in the business magazines and industry trade publications. A second option in *Factiva* would be to search in the Companies/Markets category for company/industry comparison reports.

Mergent Online. New York: Mergent Inc.

Mergent Online is a searchable database of over 60,000 global public companies. The database offers worldwide industry reports, U.S. and global competitors, and executive biographical information. *Mergent*'s Basic Search option permits searching by primary industry codes (either SIC or NAICS). Once the search is executed, companies in that industry should be listed. A comparison or standard peer-group analysis can be created to analyze companies in the same industry on various criteria. The Advanced Search allows the user to search a wider range of financial and textual information. Results, including ratios for a company and its competitors, can be downloaded to a spreadsheet.

North American Industry Classification System (NAICS)

The North American Industry Classification System has officially replaced the Standard Industrial Classification (SIC) as the numerical structure used to define and analyze industries, although some publications and databases offer both classification systems. The NAICS codes are used in Canada, the United States, and Mexico. In the United States, the NAICS codes are used to conduct an Economic Census every five years providing a snapshot of the U.S. economy at a given moment in time.

NAICS: *www.census.gov/eos/www/naics/*

Economic Census: *www.census.gov/econ/census/*

NetAdvantage. New York: S & P Capital IQ.

The database includes company, financial, and investment information as well as the well-known publication called *Industry Surveys.* Each industry report includes information on the current environment, industry trends, key industry ratios and statistics, and comparative company financial analysis. Available in HTML, PDF, or Excel formats.

Business Insights: Essentials. Farmington Hills, MI: Gale CENGAGE Learning.

Business Insights provides company and industry intelligence for a selection of public and private companies. Company profiles include parent-subsidiary relationships, industry rankings, products and brands, industry statistics, and financial ratios. Selections of SWOT analysis reports are also available. The Company and Industry comparison tool allows a researcher to compare up to six companies' revenues, employees, and sales data over time. Results are available as an image, chart, or spreadsheet.

Plunkett Research Online. Houston, TX: Plunkett Research, Ltd.

Plunkett's provides industry-specific market research, trends analysis, and business intelligence for 34 industries.

Search Engines

Google. Mountain View, CA: Google, Inc.

Recognized for its advanced technology, quality of results, and simplicity, the search engine Google is highly recommended by librarians and other expert web surfers.
www.google.com

Dogpile. Bellevue, WA: InfoSpace, Inc.

Dogpile is a metasearch engine that searches and compiles the most relevant results from more than 12 individual search engines.
http://www.dogpile.com/

Cases

PART 5: CASES

CASE 1	Robin Hood	C2
CASE 2	Edward Marshall Boehm, Inc.	C3
CASE 3	American International Group and the Bonus Fiasco	C4
CASE 4	Southwest: Is Luv Soaring?	C7
CASE 5	Jetblue Airlines: Getting Over the "Blues"?	C14
CASE 6	Backers Beware: Kickstarter Is Not a Store	C21
CASE 7	Weight Watchers International, Inc.	C27
CASE 8	Dippin' Dots: Is the Future Frozen?	C38
CASE 9	Jamba Juice: Feeling the Squeeze or Juicing Up?	C48
CASE 10	Ann Taylor: Survival in Specialty Retail	C57
CASE 11	GreenWood Resources: A Global Sustainable Venture in the Making	C68
CASE 12	Tata Starbucks: How to Brew a Sustainable Blend for India	C82
CASE 13	Avon: A New Era?	C89
CASE 14	The Boston Beer Company: Poised for Growth	C99
CASE 15	Zynga: Room for a Final Round or is the Game Over?	C111
CASE 16	Apple Inc.: Still Taking a Bite Out of the Competition?	C117
CASE 17	Campbell: How to Keep the Soup Simmering	C130
CASE 18	United Way Worldwide	C143
CASE 19	The Global Casino Industry	C152
CASE 20	Ebay	C156
CASE 21	Yahoo!	C168
CASE 22	World Wrestling Entertainment	C173
CASE 23	QVC	C179
CASE 24	Nintendo's Wii U	C184
CASE 25	McDonald's	C194
CASE 26	Procter & Gamble	C200
CASE 27	Microfinance	C206
CASE 28	Samsung Electronics	C209
CASE 29	Heineken	C215
CASE 30	FreshDirect: Is It Really Fresh?	C220
CASE 31	Johnson & Johnson	C233
CASE 32	General Motors	C239
CASE 33	Is One Ford Really Working?	C245
CASE 34	Emirates Airline	C262
CASE 35	Cirque Du Soleil	C270
CASE 36	Pixar	C274

CASES

CASE 1
ROBIN HOOD*

It was in the spring of the second year of his insurrection against the High Sheriff of Nottingham that Robin Hood took a walk in Sherwood Forest. As he walked he pondered the progress of the campaign, the disposition of his forces, the Sheriff's recent moves, and the options that confronted him.

The revolt against the Sheriff had begun as a personal crusade, erupting out of Robin's conflict with the Sheriff and his administration. Alone, however, Robin Hood could do little. He therefore sought allies, men with grievances and a deep sense of justice. Later he welcomed all who came, asking few questions, and only demanding a willingness to serve. Strength, he believed, lay in numbers.

He spent the first year forging the group into a disciplined band, united in enmity against the Sheriff, and willing to live outside the law. The band's organization was simple. Robin ruled supreme, making all important decisions. He delegated specific tasks to his lieutenants. Will Scarlett was in charge of intelligence and scouting. His main job was to shadow the Sheriff and his men, always alert to their next move. He also collected information on the travel plans of rich merchants and tax collectors. Little John kept discipline among the men, and saw to it that their archery was at the high peak that their profession demanded. Scarlock took care of the finances, converting loot into cash, paying shares of the take, and finding suitable hiding places for the surplus. Finally, Much the Miller's son had the difficult task of provisioning the ever-increasing band of Merrymen.

The increasing size of the band was a source of satisfaction for Robin, but also a source of concern. The fame of his Merrymen was spreading, and new recruits poured in from every corner of England. As the band grew larger, their small bivouac became a major encampment. Between raids the men milled about, talking and playing games. Vigilance was in decline, and discipline was becoming harder to enforce. "Why," Robin reflected, "I don't know half the men I run into these days."

The growing band was also beginning to exceed the food capacity of the forest. Game was becoming scarce, and supplies had to be obtained from outlying villages. The cost of buying food was beginning to drain the band's financial reserves at the very moment when revenues were in decline. Travelers, especially those with the most to lose, were now giving the forest a wide berth. This was costly and inconvenient to them, but it was preferable to having all their goods confiscated.

Robin believed that the time had come for the Merrymen to change their policy of outright confiscation of goods to one of a fixed transit tax. His lieutenants strongly resisted this idea. They were proud of the Merrymen's famous motto: "Rob the rich and give to the poor." "The farmers and the townspeople," they argued, "are our most important allies. How can we tax them, and still hope for their help in our fight against the Sheriff?"

Robin wondered how long the Merrymen could keep to the ways and methods of their early days. The Sheriff was growing stronger and better organized. He now had the money and the men, and was beginning to harass the band, probing for its weaknesses.

The tide of events was beginning to turn against the Merrymen. Robin felt that the campaign must be decisively concluded before the Sheriff had a chance to deliver a mortal blow. "But how," he wondered, "could this be done?"

Robin had often entertained the possibility of killing the Sheriff, but the chances for this seemed increasingly remote. Besides, while killing the Sheriff might satisfy his personal thirst for revenge, it would not improve the situation. Robin had hoped that the perpetual state of unrest, and the Sheriff's failure to collect taxes, would lead to his removal from office. Instead, the Sheriff used his political connections to obtain reinforcement. He had powerful friends at court, and was well regarded by the regent, Prince John.

Prince John was vicious and volatile. He was consumed by his unpopularity among the people, who wanted the imprisoned King Richard back. He also lived in constant fear of the barons, who had first given him the regency, but were now beginning to dispute his claim to the throne. Several of these barons had set out to collect the ransom that would release King Richard the Lionheart from his jail in Austria. Robin was invited to join the conspiracy in return for future amnesty. It was a dangerous proposition. Provincial banditry was one thing, court intrigue another. Prince John's spies were everywhere. If the plan failed, the pursuit would be relentless and retribution swift.

The sound of the supper horn startled Robin from his thoughts. There was the smell of roasting venison in the air. Nothing was resolved or settled. Robin headed for camp promising himself that he would give these problems his utmost attention after tomorrow's raid.

---

* Prepared by Joseph Lampel, City University, London. Copyright Joseph Lampel © 1985, revised 1991. Reprinted with permission.

CASES

CASE 2
EDWARD MARSHALL BOEHM, INC.*

Edward Marshall Boehm—a farmer, veterinarian, and nature lover living near New York City—was convinced by his wife and friends to translate some of his clay animal sculptures into pieces for possible sale to the gift and art markets. Boehm recognized that porcelain was the best medium for portraying his creations because of its translucent beauty, permanence, and fidelity of color as well as form. But the finest of the porcelains, hard paste porcelain, was largely a secret art about which little technical literature existed. Boehm studied this art relentlessly, absorbing whatever knowledge artbooks, museums, and the few U.S. ceramic factories offered. Then, after months of experimentation in a dingy Trenton, New Jersey, basement, Boehm and some chemist friends developed a porcelain clay equal to the finest in the world.

Next Boehm had to master the complex art of porcelain manufacture. Each piece of porcelain sculpture is a technical as well as artistic challenge. A 52-step process is required to convert a plasticine sculpture into a completed porcelain piece. For example, one major creation took 509 mold sections to make 151 parts, and consumed 8 tons of plaster in the molds. Sculptural detail included 60,000 individually carved feather barbs. Each creation had to be kiln-fired to 2400° where heat could change a graceful detail into a twisted mass. Then it had to be painted, often in successive layers, and perhaps fired repeatedly to anneal delicate colors. No American had excelled in hard paste porcelains. And when Boehm's creations first appeared, no one understood the quality of the porcelain or even believed it was hard paste porcelain.

But Boehm began to create in porcelain what he knew and loved best—nature, particularly the more delicate forms of animals, birds, and flowers. In his art Boehm tried "to capture that special moment and setting which conveys the character, charm, and loveliness of a bird or animal in its natural habitat." After selling his early creations for several years during her lunch hours, his talented wife, Helen, left an outstanding ophthalmic marketing career to "peddle" Boehm's porcelains full time. Soon Mrs. Boehm's extraordinary merchandising skills, promotional touch, and sense for the art market began to pay off. People liked Boehm's horses and dogs, but bought his birds. And Boehm agreeably complied, striving for ever greater perfection on ever more exotic and natural bird creations.

By 1968 some Boehm porcelains (especially birds) had become recognized as collector's items. An extremely complex piece like "Fondo Marino" might sell for $28,500 at retail, and might command much more upon resale. Edward Marshall Boehm, then 55—though flattered by his products' commercial success—considered his art primarily an expression of his love for nature. He felt the ornithological importance of portraying vanishing species like U.S. prairie chickens with fidelity and traveled to remote areas to bring back live samples of rare tropical birds for study and later rendering into porcelain. A single company, Minton China, was the exclusive distributor of Boehm products to some 175 retail outlets in the United States. Boehm's line included (1) its "Fledgling" series of smaller, somewhat simpler pieces, usually selling for less than $100, (2) its profitable middle series of complex sculptures like the "Snowy Owl" selling from $800 to $5,000, and (3) its special artistic pieces (like "Fondo Marino" or "Ivory Billed Woodpeckers") which might sell initially for over $20,000.

Individual Boehm porcelains were increasingly being recognized as outstanding artistic creations and sought by some sophisticated collectors. Production of such designs might be sold out for years in advance, but it was difficult to anticipate which pieces might achieve this distinction. Many of the company's past policies no longer seemed appropriate. And the Boehms wanted to further position the company for the long run. When asked what they wanted from the company, they would respond, "to make the world aware of Mr. Boehm's artistic talent, to help world wildlife causes by creating appreciation and protection for threatened species, and to build a continuing business that could make them comfortably wealthy, perhaps millionaires." No one goal had great precedence over the others.

---

* Republished with permission from H. Mintzberg and J. B. Quinn, *The Strategy Process*, Prentice Hall, New York, 1996.

CASE 3

AMERICAN INTERNATIONAL GROUP AND THE BONUS FIASCO*

After two decades of rapid growth and expansion in an environment of very little regulatory oversight and unbounded optimism about the power of the markets to create limitless wealth, the U.S. financial system came crashing down in the second half of 2008. What started as a sudden decline in housing prices after years of speculative growth very soon snowballed into a full-fledged financial crisis. Major banking companies such as Citicorp and Bank of America found their equity base wiped out by loan losses. Investment banking firms such as Merrill Lynch and Bear Stearns, which operate largely outside the regulatory framework of the Federal Reserve, were in even bigger trouble because they were highly leveraged. Fearing a complete financial meltdown, Henry Paulson, secretary of the Treasury in the Bush administration, announced a bailout package of $750 billion on September 16, 2008, to restore confidence in the banks and to jump-start the credit markets.

What exactly does the government do in a bailout? A bailout can take many forms. For example, the government can buy stock in a troubled institution, thus shoring up its equity base.

The very fact that the government has an equity stake may be taken as an implicit government guarantee by creditors, suppliers, and clients because concerns about solvency and ability to stay in business are assuaged. Alternatively, the government can extend a loan to the institution, to be paid back when the company becomes profitable again. Another approach is for the government to buy preferred stock in the company. In this case the government is entitled to a fair return on the investment. Finally, the government can buy distressed assets of the institution, thereby helping it to clean up its balance sheet. Irrespective of the form of the bailout, all bailouts represent a temporary or, in some cases, long-term commitment of public money to private companies.

As the economic crisis gathered momentum and the credit markets came to a standstill in the fall of 2008, it became clear that banks were not the only institutions in trouble. American International Group (AIG), one of the largest and most respected insurance companies in the world, found itself in even bigger financial distress in September 2008 when the rating agencies suddenly lowered its credit rating. Not only did this cause the cost of borrowing to go up for AIG, but it also triggered the requirement that the company post collateral with its counterparties. Unable to do so, AIG approached the government for a bailout. In the next few months, the government pumped an astounding $85 billion into AIG alone to prevent it from going bankrupt. Insurance companies are generally supposed to be risk-averse and prudent. How did AIG get into such a big mess?

The primary culprit for the problems of AIG was a somewhat exotic financial product called credit default swaps (CDSs). In simple terms, these swaps represented an insurance cover to holders of mortgage-backed securities: If the value of the securities went down, AIG would make good the losses suffered by the owners. In good times, when real estate prices were climbing steadily each year, the CDSs were pure profits for AIG. Emboldened by what it perceived as negligible risk and motivated by the prospect of ever-increasing profits, AIG sold hundreds of billions of dollars' worth of these instruments. Although insurance is a business regulated by the states, these products were outside the range of regulation.

Right from the beginning, there was considerable controversy about whether the government should try to bail out any failing firm in a market economy. Even those who were not ideologically opposed to the bailout were skeptical whether the government efforts would be enough to save the company. There were also concerns about how the company would spend the bailout money.

Immediately after the first bailout was announced, AIG attracted considerable negative press when it was reported that AIG executives attended a lavish retreat in California that featured spa treatments, banquets, and golf outings. Total tab: $444,000. Immediately thereafter, AP reported that AIG executives spent $86,000 on a luxurious English hunting trip.[1] This was only days after the Fed had extended a $37.8 billion loan on top of the $85 billion mentioned earlier. The company's response: "We regret that this event was not canceled."[2]

In March 2009, it was disclosed that AIG had paid $218 million in bonus payments to employees of the financial services division, the very division that was responsible for issuing the credit default swaps that got the firm into trouble. Overall, 418 managers were the beneficiaries of these "retention" bonuses, although 53 of them were no longer with the company! The highest bonus was $6.4 million. Six managers received more than $4 million each, and 51 people received between $1 million and $2 million.

---

* This case was prepared by Professor Abdul A. Rasheed of the University of Texas at Arlington, Graduate Student Brian Pinkham, and Professor Gregory G. Dess of the University of Texas at Dallas. This case was based solely on library research and was developed for class discussion rather than to illustrate either effective or ineffective handling of an administrative situation. Copyright © 2009 Abdul A. Rasheed and Gregory G. Dess.

The announcement of these bonuses sparked instant outrage among the public. President Barack Obama accused the company of "recklessness and greed." Noting that AIG had "received substantial sums" of federal aid, the president announced that he was asking Treasury Secretary Timothy Geithner "to use that leverage and pursue every legal avenue to block these bonuses and make the American taxpayers whole."[3] Andrew Cuomo, New York State's attorney general, threatened to subpoena the executives and engage in a "name and shame" campaign by making the list of bonus recipients public.[4] The House even passed a bill that effectively imposed a punitive 90 percent tax on the bonuses.[5]

At the same time, there were others who felt that the payments represented contractual obligations and therefore populist sentiments should not be allowed to violate the sanctity of contracts. Many of the employees felt that they had every right to receive the payments they were promised and worked for. Their feelings were best expressed in the following resignation letter sent by Jake DeSantis, an executive vice president of the American International Group's financial products unit, to Edward M. Liddy, the chief executive of AIG.

> Dear Mr. Liddy:
>
> It is with deep regret that I submit my notice of resignation from A.I.G. Financial Products. I hope you take the time to read this entire letter. Before describing the details of my decision, I want to offer some context:
>
> I am proud of everything I have done for the commodity and equity divisions of A.I.G.-F.P. I was in no way involved in—or responsible for—the credit default swap transactions that have hamstrung A.I.G. Nor were more than a handful of the 400 current employees of A.I.G.-F.P. Most of those responsible have left the company and have conspicuously escaped the public outrage.
>
> After 12 months of hard work dismantling the company—during which A.I.G. reassured us many times we would be rewarded in March 2009—we in the financial products unit have been betrayed by A.I.G. and are being unfairly persecuted by elected officials. In response to this, I will now leave the company and donate my entire post-tax retention payment to those suffering from the global economic downturn. My intent is to keep none of the money myself.
>
> I take this action after 11 years of dedicated, honorable service to A.I.G. I can no longer effectively perform my duties in this dysfunctional environment, nor am I being paid to do so. Like you, I was asked to work for an annual salary of $1, and I agreed out of a sense of duty to the company and to the public officials who have come to its aid. Having now been let down by both, I can no longer justify spending 10, 12, 14 hours a day away from my family for the benefit of those who have let me down.
>
> You and I have never met or spoken to each other, so I'd like to tell you about myself. I was raised by schoolteachers working multiple jobs in a world of closing steel mills. My hard work earned me acceptance to M.I.T., and the institute's generous financial aid enabled me to attend. I had fulfilled my American dream.
>
> I started at this company in 1998 as an equity trader, became the head of equity and commodity trading and, a couple of years before A.I.G.'s meltdown last September, was named the head of business development for commodities. Over this period the equity and commodity units were consistently profitable—in most years generating net profits of well over $100 million. Most recently, during the dismantling of A.I.G.-F.P., I was an integral player in the pending sale of its well-regarded commodity index business to UBS. As you know, business unit sales like this are crucial to A.I.G.'s effort to repay the American taxpayer.
>
> The profitability of the businesses with which I was associated clearly supported my compensation. I never received any pay resulting from the credit default swaps that are now losing so much money. I did, however, like many others here, lose a significant portion of my life savings in the form of deferred compensation invested in the capital of A.I.G.-F.P. because of those losses. In this way I have personally suffered from this controversial activity—directly as well as indirectly with the rest of the taxpayers.
>
> I have the utmost respect for the civic duty that you are now performing at A.I.G. You are as blameless for these credit default swap losses as I am. You answered your country's call and you are taking a tremendous beating for it.
>
> But you also are aware that most of the employees of your financial products unit had nothing to do with the large losses. And I am disappointed and frustrated over your lack of support for us. I and many others in the unit feel betrayed that you failed to stand up for us in the face of untrue and unfair accusations from certain members of Congress last Wednesday and from the press over our retention payments, and that you didn't defend us against the baseless and reckless comments made by the attorneys general of New York and Connecticut.
>
> My guess is that in October, when you learned of these retention contracts, you realized that the employees of the financial products unit needed some incentive to stay and that the contracts, being both ethical and useful, should be left to stand. That's probably why A.I.G. management assured us on three occasions during that month that the company would "live up to its commitment" to honor the contract guarantees.
>
> That may be why you decided to accelerate by three months more than a quarter of the amounts due under the contracts. That action signified to us your support, and was hardly something that one would do if he truly found the contracts "distasteful."
>
> That may also be why you authorized the balance of the payments on March 13.
>
> At no time during the past six months that you have been leading A.I.G. did you ask us to revise,

renegotiate or break these contracts—until several hours before your appearance last week before Congress.

I think your initial decision to honor the contracts was both ethical and financially astute, but it seems to have been politically unwise. It's now apparent that you either misunderstood the agreements that you had made—tacit or otherwise—with the Federal Reserve, the Treasury, various members of Congress and Attorney General Andrew Cuomo of New York, or were not strong enough to withstand the shifting political winds.

You've now asked the current employees of A.I.G.-F.P. to repay these earnings. As you can imagine, there has been a tremendous amount of serious thought and heated discussion about how we should respond to this breach of trust.

As most of us have done nothing wrong, guilt is not a motivation to surrender our earnings. We have worked 12 long months under these contracts and now deserve to be paid as promised. None of us should be cheated of our payments any more than a plumber should be cheated after he has fixed the pipes but a careless electrician causes a fire that burns down the house.

Many of the employees have, in the past six months, turned down job offers from more stable employers, based on A.I.G.'s assurances that the contracts would be honored. They are now angry about having been misled by A.I.G.'s promises and are not inclined to return the money as a favor to you.

The only real motivation that anyone at A.I.G.-F.P. now has is fear. Mr. Cuomo has threatened to "name and shame," and his counterpart in Connecticut, Richard Blumenthal, has made similar threats—even though attorneys general are supposed to stand for due process, to conduct trials in courts and not the press.

So what am I to do? There's no easy answer. I know that because of hard work I have benefited more than most during the economic boom and have saved enough that my family is unlikely to suffer devastating losses during the current bust. Some might argue that members of my profession have been overpaid, and I wouldn't disagree.

That is why I have decided to donate 100 percent of the effective after-tax proceeds of my retention payment directly to organizations that are helping people who are suffering from the global downturn. This is not a tax-deduction gimmick; I simply believe that I at least deserve to dictate how my earnings are spent, and do not want to see them disappear back into the obscurity of A.I.G.'s or the federal government's budget. Our earnings have caused such a distraction for so many from the more pressing issues our country faces, and I would like to see my share of it benefit those truly in need.

On March 16 I received a payment from A.I.G. amounting to $742,006.40, after taxes. In light of the uncertainty over the ultimate taxation and legal status of this payment, the actual amount I donate may be less—in fact, it may end up being far less if the recent House bill raising the tax on the retention payments to 90 percent stands. Once all the money is donated, you will immediately receive a list of all recipients.

This choice is right for me. I wish others at A.I.G.-F.P. luck finding peace with their difficult decision, and only hope their judgment is not clouded by fear.

Mr. Liddy, I wish you success in your commitment to return the money extended by the American government, and luck with the continued unwinding of the company's diverse businesses—especially those remaining credit default swaps. I'll continue over the short term to help make sure no balls are dropped, but after what's happened this past week I can't remain much longer—there is too much bad blood. I'm not sure how you will greet my resignation, but at least Attorney General Blumenthal should be relieved that I'll leave under my own power and will not need to be "shoved out the door."

Sincerely,

Jake DeSantis

Liddy was clearly in an unwinnable situation. On the one hand, the politicians and the press were pillorying him for authorizing lavish bonuses while the company was essentially on welfare payments from the taxpayer. On the other hand, his own employees were upset at him that he was pandering to the politicians by describing these contractual payments as "distasteful."

ENDNOTES

1. AIG executives spent thousands during hunting trip. Associated Press, October 17, 2008, http://ap.google.com/article/ALeqM5g3InVeHoYnmXZnM2ACXSgjG0nIQD93R68VO0.
2. A. Taylor. AIG execs' retreat after bailout angers lawmakers. Associated Press, October 11, 2008, http://thecoffeedesk.com/news/index.php/archives/76kers.
3. T. Raum. Obama: AIG can't justify "outrage" of exec bonuses with taxpayer money keeping company afloat. Associated Press, March 16, 2009, http://finance.yahoo.com/news/Frank-assails-bonuses-paid-to-apf-14646988.html.
4. Cuomo issues subpoena to AIG on credit derivatives data. March 27, 2009, www.rttnews.com/Content/BreakingNews.aspx?Node=B1&Id=895234%20&Category=Breaking%20News.
5. J. D. McKinnon and A. Jones. Laws may not hinder effort to tax AIG bonuses. Wall Street Journal, March 18, 2009, http://online.wsj.com/article/SB123742691757579925.html.

CASES

CASE 4

SOUTHWEST: IS LUV SOARING?*

Southwest Airlines announced record earnings of $1.1 billion in 2014. This was the first time that the Dallas-based carrier crossed the billion-dollar mark, although the company had been profitable throughout its history, for 44 consecutive years. Its previous best year was 2013, when its net income reached $754 million. "Our strategic plan has come together successfully, and we have realized significant contributions from the AirTran integration, fleet modernization efforts and the continued growth of our Rapid Rewards program," said Gary Kelly, chairman and CEO of Southwest Airlines. Reviewing Southwest's performance and accomplishments in 2014, he also said, "We have been very pleased with the overall performance of our markets under development, most notably, Dallas Love Field, New York LaGuardia, and [Washington] Reagan National."[1] Going forward, Southwest should save $1.7 billion in fuel costs in 2015 compared to 2014 as the carrier would enjoy the sharp decline in energy prices, said CFO Tammy Romo. Southwest had readjusted its hedging program after realizing the depth of the energy price drop and was "essentially unhedged for 2015," said Kelly, although it retained hedging positions for 2016 and 2017.[2]

At pretty much the same time that Southwest was relishing its continued success, some chinks in the armor seemed to be widening. On January 15, 2015, the U.S. Department of Transportation announced it was imposing a $1.6 million fine on Southwest Airlines for keeping passengers on airplanes too long at Chicago Midway in January 2014. This fine was the largest imposed since DOT implemented a regulation in 2010 requiring that airlines give their passengers an opportunity to get off airplanes that are delayed on tarmacs for three hours or more. Southwest had 16 airplanes that were delayed beyond the maximum wait time. The DOT order stated:

> In addition to severe weather on January 2, Southwest experienced a malfunctioning of its crew scheduling system and an unexpected shortage of staff, particularly the carrier's ramp-crew.... Southwest's ramp crew is responsible for baggage handling, de-icing, snow removal, and marshaling aircraft to and from the gates. The absence of some of Southwest's ramp crew inhibited the carrier's ability to clear aircraft from Southwest's gates in a timely manner to accommodate arriving flights.... At the time the sixteen flights at issue arrived at MDW [Chicago Midway], between 10:15 p.m. and 11:01 p.m., an employee shift change had taken place and the small ramp crew that remained made it impossible for Southwest to clear and prepare gates for the arriving flights in a timely manner.

The order further said: "The Enforcement Office is not disputing, nor is this order based upon, Southwest's assertion that it could not safely deplane passengers at that time."

Is Southwest growing too big and ignoring essential investments that made the airline so successful for so long? Will the success saga continue under Kelly when the core elements of the company's strategy—low-cost, organic, and domestic point-to-point short-haul growth and customer-centric culture—are all simultaneously changing?

An Exemplary Market Disruption: The Kelleher Era

The inconvenience and expense of ground travel by bus or automobile between the cities of Houston, Dallas, and San Antonio—the Golden Triangle that was experiencing rapid economic and population growth during the late 1960s—offered an opportunity for an intrastate airline. The idea was suggested by Rollin King, a San Antonio entrepreneur who owned a small commuter air service, when his banker, John Parker, complained about the issue. King then talked to Herb Kelleher—a New Jersey–born, New York University Law School graduate who had moved to San Antonio in 1967 to practice law. They soon pooled the seed money to start Southwest Airlines. The infant Southwest Airlines (SWA) fought long-drawn-out legal battles, primarily engineered by the major airlines, for over four years before it got its first flight off the ground in 1971. Later on, the company had to work around a regulation intended to penalize SWA's decision to operate out of Dallas Love Field instead of moving to the new Dallas–Fort Worth (DFW) airport. With Kelleher's brilliant legal expertise and extensive lobbying of the House of Representatives, the issue was settled and SWA was allowed to operate out of Love Field in 1979. The struggle for existence in the initial years worked to the advantage of the company, as the struggle created the esprit de corps for which the airline became so well known. The employees were caught up in fighting for

---

* This case study was prepared by Professor Naga Lakshmi Damaraju of the Indian School of Business, Professor Alan B. Eisner at Pace University, and Professor Gregory G. Dess at the University of Texas at Dallas. The purpose of the case is to stimulate class discussion rather than to illustrate effective or ineffective handling of a business situation. The authors thank Mr. Arun Bhambhu, Indian School of Business, for his research assistance, and Professor Michael Oliff at the University of Texas at Dallas for his valuable comments on an earlier version of this case. Several parts of the case are from an earlier version. Copyright © 2015 Damaraju, Eisner, and Dess.

the "SWA cause" that created "the warrior mentality, the very fight to survive," according to Colleen Barrett, who became the president and chief operating officer of SWA in 2001 (she now is the president emeritus).[3]

Southwest (or the "LUV" airline) was unique in many ways from its inception. It pioneered point-to-point short-haul flights, bypassing the expensive hub-and-spoke operations. It chose less popular, less congested airports to achieve quicker turnarounds. Further, it's "no-frills" operations included no meals, no baggage transfers, no assigned seating, and only peanuts as snacks. All these policies contributed to lowering the turnaround times at gates to ensure timely departures and increase aircraft utilization. Southwest also operated a single aircraft type, the Boeing 737, and thereby kept training costs low and personnel utilization high. This saved plenty of money and work. Southwest hired employees for "attitude" rather than "skills" and created a unique cost-conscious culture that was driven by positive peer pressure focused on hard work along with fun. Under Kelleher's "walk the talk" leadership, the company grew by leaps and bounds from the time he took the CEO position in 1982. From being an underdog (with a fleet of 3 Boeing 737s in 1971 and with only 27 planes and $270 million in revenues, flying to only 14 cities, in 1982),[4] it became the largest and most consistently profitable discount carrier in the United States. In May 1988 Southwest became the first airline to win the coveted Triple Crown for a month: Best On-Time Record, Best Baggage Handling, and Fewest Customer Complaints. Southwest crossed its $1 billion revenue mark in 1990, thereby becoming a major airline. It continued winning the monthly Triple Crown more than 30 times, and it won five annual Triple Crowns for 1992, 1993, 1994, 1995, and 1996. (See Exhibit 1 for Southwest's mission statement.)

From Kelleher to Kelly

Southwest Airlines had a change in leadership in August 2001 when Herb Kelleher relinquished power to two of his close aides. Unlike most corporate positions, his was a very hard position to fill because Kelleher had won the hearts of all his employees during his tenure. Colleen C. Barrett, vice president for customers, became the president and chief operating officer; and James F. Parker, general counsel, became the chief executive officer.

The growth of the company and the consequent increase in the number of employees also posed challenges to keeping the culture intact. The distance between the rank and file and top management was growing. In addition, the warm employee relations at Southwest seemed to chill over time. In July 2004 James Parker abruptly resigned as CEO of Southwest amid strained labor negotiations with the flight attendants. Kelleher stepped into the negotiations, and the flight attendants walked away smiling, with a 31 percent pay raise.[5]

Gary Kelly: The Beginning of the Change

At this point, Gary C. Kelly, former chief financial officer of Southwest, took the helm. In many ways, Kelly fully subscribed to Southwest's low-cost culture and was the backbone of operational and financial discipline that propelled Southwest's consistent success. After becoming the CEO, Kelly made some very bold moves, some of which marked a significant departure from the original Southwest strategy.

Among the most important changes was the audacious acquisition of six gates at Chicago's Midway Airport from bankrupt carrier ATA. Southwest signed its first-ever code-share agreement with ATA, primarily in response to AirTran eyeing a move into Chicago. Code sharing is a commercial agreement between two airlines that allows an airline to put its two-letter identification code on another airline's flight numbers in computerized reservation systems. This was a significant departure from Southwest's going-alone and going-organic policy, which had been a key trait of the company for several decades. Meanwhile, Southwest entered the Philadelphia market, a stronghold of USAir, in May 2004. The Philadelphia market was one of the most overpriced and underserved. Southwest aimed to capture the market with its tried-and-tested low-cost, no-frills formula, albeit with leather seats on some of its newer planes. USAir responded, "We will be a vigorous competitor to Southwest in Philadelphia on every route they fly."[6]

In addition to establishing the ATA code share for Chicago's Midway,[7] Kelly added Phoenix to the code share in April 2005.[8] Then Kelly directed Southwest's entry into Pittsburgh in May 2005, and service to Florida began in October 2005.[9] Denver, Colorado, and Washington Dulles International Airport were added to the list in 2006.

EXHIBIT 1 Mission Statement of Southwest Airlines

The mission of Southwest Airlines is dedication to the highest quality of Customer Service delivered with a sense of warmth, friendliness, individual pride, and Company Spirit.

To Our Employees

We are committed to provide our Employees a stable work environment with equal opportunity for learning and personal growth. Creativity and innovation are encouraged for improving the effectiveness of Southwest Airlines. Above all, Employees will be provided the same concern, respect, and caring attitude within the organization that they are expected to share externally with every Southwest Customer.

Source: Southwest Airlines. www.southwest.com/html/about-southwest/index.html.

Kelly also pushed for the repeal of the Wright amendment.[10] Southwest entered into an agreement with the City of Dallas, the City of Fort Worth, American Airlines Inc. (which had its hub at Dallas–Fort Worth airport), and the DFW International Airport Board, following which these five parties sought enactment of legislation that would amend the original Wright amendment. In October 2006, Congress responded with a reform act that substantially reduced earlier restrictions. This worked to Southwest's advantage, enabling the company to fly to many more destinations from Love Field than it could earlier, provided the flights stopped first in a state within the Wright perimeter: New Mexico, Oklahoma, Missouri, Arkansas, Louisiana, Mississippi, Kansas, and Alabama, along with Texas.[11] Since the Wright restrictions were loosened, Southwest has gained control of about 90 percent of the Love Field market and its passenger traffic at Love Field has risen by about 18 percent. This, of course, has led to significant price competition between American and Southwest.[12]

Southwest's move toward adding international destinations started in December 2008 when the company agreed to provide an online link to WestJet's booking portal to helps its customers book flights to Canada. Later, Southwest formally filed an application with the Department of Transportation for the right to fly its own planes to Canada.[13]

By January 2015, Southwest had expanded its fleet to 683 Boeing jets (including 47 Boeing 717s from AirTran); it offered 3,400 flights a day, with service to 93 cities in 40 states and to destinations in five nearby countries (see Exhibits 2 and 3).[14] Subject to government approvals, service to San Jose (Costa Rica), Puerto Vallarta (Mexico), and Belize City (Belize) were expected to begin in March 2015, June 2015, and October 2015, respectively.[15]

By this time, Southwest had been experiencing cost increases per average seat-mile (ASM)—a key metric used to measure performance in the industry—primarily due to increases in fuel costs and wages. The cost per ASM went up from 7.07 cents in 1995 to 12.6 cents in 2013, with fuel costs, wages, and benefits being the major contributors.

EXHIBIT 2 Financial and Operating Data for Southwest Airlines, 2010–2014 (year-end December 31)*

	2014	2013	2012	2011	2010
Financial Data (in millions, except per share amounts):					
Operating revenues	$18,605	$17,699	$17,088	$15,658	$12,104
Operating expenses	$16,380	$16,421	$16,465	$14,965	$11,116
Operating income	$ 2,225	$ 1,278	$ 623	$ 693	$ 988
Other expenses (income) net	$ 409	$ 69	$ (62)	$ 370	$ 243
Income before taxes	$ 1,816	$ 1,209	$ 685	$ 323	$ 745
Provision for income taxes	$ 680	$ 455	$ 264	$ 145	$ 286
Net income	$ 1,136	$ 754	$ 421	$ 178	$ 459
Net income per share, basic	$ 1.65	$ 1.06	$ 0.56	$ 0.23	$ 0.62
Net income per share, diluted	$ 1.64	$ 1.05	$ 0.56	$ 0.23	$ 0.61
Cash dividends per common share		$0.1300	$0.0345	$0.0180	$0.0180
Total assets at period-end	$20,064	$19,345	$18,596	$18,068	$15,463
Long-term obligations at period-end	$ 2,434	$ 2,191	$ 2,883	$ 3,107	$ 2,875
Stockholders' equity at period-end	$ 6,775	$ 7,336	$ 6,992	$ 6,877	$ 6,237
Operating Data:					
Revenue passengers carried	11,04,96,912	10,80,75,976	10,93,46,509	10,39,73,759	8,81,91,322
Enplaned passengers	13,57,67,188	13,31,55,030	13,39,78,100	12,75,51,012	10,62,27,521
Revenue passenger-miles (RPMs) (000s)	10,80,35,133	10,43,48,216	10,28,74,979	9,75,82,530	7,80,46,967
Available seat miles (ASMs) (000s)	13,10,03,957	13,03,44,072	12,81,37,110	12,05,78,736	9,84,37,092

*Refer to the appendix at the end of this case for a glossary of the terms used in this table.

continued

EXHIBIT 2 *Continued*

	2014	2013	2012	2011	2010
Load factor	82.5%	80.1%	80.3%	80.9%	79.3%
Average length of passenger haul (miles)	978	966	941	939	885
Average aircraft stage length (miles)	721	703	693	679	648
Trips flown	12,55,502	13,12,785	13,61,558	13,17,977	11,14,451
Average passenger fare	$159.80	$154.72	$147.17	$141.90	$130.27
Passenger revenue yield per RPM (cents)	16.34	16.02	15.64	15.12	14.72
Operating revenue per ASM (cents)	14.2	13.58	13.34	12.99	12.3
Passenger revenue per ASM (cents)	13.48	12.83	12.56	12.24	11.67
Operating expenses per ASM (cents)	12.5	12.6	12.85	12.41	11.29
Operating expenses per ASM, excluding fuel (cents)	8.46	8.18	8.07	7.73	7.61
Operating expenses per ASM, excluding fuel and profit sharing (cents)	8.19	8.01	7.98	7.65	7.45
Fuel costs per gallon, including fuel tax	$ 2.93	$ 3.16	$ 3.30	$ 3.19	$ 2.51
Fuel costs per gallon, including fuel tax, economic	$ 2.92	$ 3.12	$ 3.28	$ 3.19	$ 2.39
Fuel consumed, in gallons (millions)	1,801	1,818	1,847	1,764	1,437
Active full-time equivalent Employees	46,278	44,831	45,861	45,392	34,901
Aircraft in service at period-end	665	680	694	698	548

Source: Southwest Airlines. SEC filings, Form 10-K, *www.sec.gov.*

Southwest's cost per average seat-mile, however, remained below that of the big carriers. The company was already working hard on controlling costs. With more of its customers making reservations online and the labor cost advantage narrowing between major airlines after restructuring, further cost squeezing appeared to be a difficult proposition. Though Kelly did not concede it openly, he understood that further cost reductions were hard to come by without modest fare increases and possible employee layoffs—something that was totally against Southwest's culture.[16]

Intensifying competition in the low-fare segment was another factor that Kelly had to acknowledge. Southwest's investments to automate and significantly streamline the ticketing and boarding process (with computer-generated bag tags, automated boarding passes, and self-service boarding-pass kiosks), and its investments to increase the functionality of its website, along with its moves to enhance aircraft interiors with leather seats, can hardly be described as *not* being motivated by competition.[17]

To further control expenses, Southwest reconfigured its cabins, reducing legroom to squeeze in six extra seats on every plane in its fleet. In December 2011, Southwest signed a deal with Boeing for 208 Boeing 737 Max jets for $19 billion.[18] The Boeing 737 Max jet will seat up to 200 passengers (11 more than the current 737 model), and the passengers may lose another 2 inches of legroom. The 737 Max will provide 20 percent better fuel efficiency per seat compared to the second most fuel-efficient jet.[19]

In 2007, a new fare structure was introduced that included Business Select, which gave customers the option of priority in boarding.[20] With a new $40 fee that allowed customers to be among the first 15 passengers to board the plane, this new fare structure was definitely targeted at wooing some of the business travelers who wanted a little more than no frills. However, with this move, Southwest managed to irritate some of its most loyal customers.[21] While Southwest continued its bags-fly-free policy, which had contributed to increasing its market share, Kelly declared "Never say never" when probed about his company's plans to start charging baggage check-in fees in 2013.[22] Southwest introduced an in-flight entertainment portal with free live and on-demand television, offering 20 live channels and 75 television episodes from popular series. It also introduced Internet access for $8 a day per device on Wi-Fi-enabled aircraft.[23]

In another significant departure from standard policy, Southwest abandoned its organic growth strategy and

EXHIBIT 3 Cities Served by Southwest Airlines

Source: Printed with permission from Southwest Airlines, www.southwest.com/travel_center/routemap_dyn.html?int5GSUBNAV-AIR-ROUTEMAP.

acquired AirTran Holdings Inc., the parent company of AirTran Airways (AirTran), for a combination of $1.4 billion cash and Southwest Airlines common stock.[24] The acquisition, which was announced in September 2010, was only the third in Southwest's history. It gave the discounter its first service in Atlanta, a Delta Air Lines fortress for decades, and more flights from New York and Washington, DC.[25] Little more than a year after the transaction officially closed, Southwest was dehubbing AirTran's Atlanta hub and conceding markets to Delta. AirTran's Atlanta hub had been Southwest's motivation in acquiring AirTran in the first place. While the AirTran acquisition gave access to Atlanta, Southwest converted the Atlanta hub to a point-to-point model. Southwest also finalized a deal to lease 88 Boeing 717 AirTran planes to Delta because Southwest did not want to use any plane other than the Boeing 737.[26] Another key reason behind the AirTran acquisition was to help Southwest push further into international markets. On July 1, 2014, Southwest started international flights to Aruba, Jamaica, and the Bahamas by integrating AirTran's overseas routes. "To make that shift in strategy has taken a huge effort, but as a leading domestic carrier, it was time 'that we think about stepping out,'" said Kelly.[27] Following what could possibly be the slowest merger in history, Southwest successfully completed the merger on December 28, 2014, when the last AirTran flight flew, retracing its original Atlanta-to-Tampa route of October 1993 (AirTran was called ValueJet at that time).[28] "The company expects total acquisition and integration costs to be approximately $550 million (before profit-sharing and taxes) upon completing the transition of AirTran 717-200s out of the fleet in 2015," said company officials.

Southwest would have been under even greater pressure for profitability, particularly in view of the majority of oil hedges that expired in 2013, but for the rise in U.S. shale oil production from 1 percent of domestic gas production to over 20 percent by 2010.[29] By 2014, domestic fields in the U.S. produced 1.1 million barrels of shale oil per day compared to the 8.6-million-barrel production of crude oil by Saudi Arabia.[30] This resulted in lower demand for crude oil internationally. In the past, Saudi Arabia had decreased its oil production to control oil prices, although such a move resulted in loss of market share. However, in 2014, Saudi Arabia declared that it would not cut oil production. The expectation was that this approach would weed out high-cost oil producers. The result was a 40 percent oil price drop in the second half of 2014.[31] Southwest readjusted its hedges in view of this situation. Going forward, as CFO Tammy Romo said, Southwest should save about $1.7 billion in fuel costs in 2015.

Yet another positive development for Southwest was the complete elimination of the Wright amendment, the law that had limited nonstop flights out of the Dallas airport, as of October 13, 2014. Since then, Southwest expanded its schedule from 118 daily departures to 153, including 4 that began in early January 2015. Southwest controlled 16 of the 20 gates at Love Field. Its traffic increased 36.1 percent, from 688,290 passengers in December 2013 to 936,886 in December 2014. Nevertheless, its market share at Love Field declined from 96.8 percent of the traffic in December 2013 to 89.9 percent in December 2014, which leaves further room for growth. Kelly stated:

> We're at the point where we need more than 16 gates. We do have a use agreement with United that allows us access to a 17th gate to support this level of flight activity. Hopefully, we can add some more flights, but I'm not willing to commit to that yet. . . . The operation, we're happy with. We're real busy. Load factors are where they need to be, and [we'd] love to be able to have more capacity at the airport obviously within the 20 gates. So we're working on that.[32]

Herb Kelleher continued to be in the limelight when he accepted the Lifetime Aviation Entrepreneur Award at the 12th-annual Living Legends of Aviation Awards at the Beverly Hilton in Los Angeles 2015. The awards are considered among the most prestigious and important recognition events in aviation.[33]

Southwest's stocks continued to surge ahead, standing at $46.99 on January 29, 2015. Should Southwest ride on the shale oil revolution and focus on low cost, creating the "Southwest effect" as it did in the oil price hedging days, or should it continue on the new path of reaping the consumer surplus? How should Kelly move forward?

ENDNOTES

1. Maxon, Terry. Southwest Airlines tops $1 billion in annual profits for the first time. http://aviationblog.dallasnews.com/2015/01/southwest-airlines-tops-1-billion-in-annual-profits-for-first-time.html/.
2. Maxon, Terry. Dallas Love Field traffic jumps 46.5% in December, 11.1% for year. http://aviationblog.dallasnews.com/tag/southwest-airlines/.
3. Freiberg, K., & Freiberg, J. 1996. Nuts! Southwest Airlines' crazy recipe for personal and business success. Austin, TX: Bard Press, 20–27. archives.californiaaviation.org/airport/msg15249.html.
4. Ibid.
5. Gimbel, B. 2005. Southwest's new flight plan. Fortune, May 16: 93–97.
6. Serwer, A. 2004. Southwest Airlines: The hottest thing in the sky. Fortune, March 8: 86–88.
7. Zellner. 2005. Dressed to kill . . . competitors. BusinessWeek, February 21: 60.
8. Southwest Airlines. 2005. Press releases, March 7 and June 28.
9. Southwest Airlines. 2005. Press releases, May 4, June 27, and July 14.
10. The federal law that limited airlines operating at Dallas Love Field to serving destinations in Texas and seven nearby states, primarily with an intention to protect the then-new Dallas–Fort Worth International Airport. Southwest was not initially a part of the agreement, and therefore its original quest for existence led to its "underdog" mentality.
11. Southwest Airlines. 2006. SEC filing.
12. Mutzabaugh, B. 2007. Southwest soars at Dallas Love following relaxed Wright rules. USAToday, March 23, blogs.usatoday.com/sky/wright_amendment/index.html.
13. Southwest. 2008. Press release, December 16, www.blogsouthwest.com/news/southwest-airlines-offer-online-link-westjet-southwestcom/.
14. Southwest Airlines. Fact sheet. http://swamedia.com/channels/Corporate-Fact-Sheet/pages/corporate-fact-sheet.
15. http://southwest.investorroom.com/?clk=GFOOTER-ABOUT-INVESTOR.
16. Southwest Airlines. Company press releases.
17. Southwest Airlines. SEC Form 10-K filings.
18. Gates, Dominic. Southwest's order gives huge boost to Boeing's 737 Max program. http://seattletimes.com/html/businesstechnology/2017003166_boeing14.html.
19. Boeing. www.boeing.com/boeing/commercial/737family/737max.page.
20. Gimbel, op. cit.
21. Murray, Lance. 2013. Southwest: Some customers ask where has LUV gone? Dallas Business Journal, February 11, www.bizjournals.com/dallas/blog/morning_call/2013/02/southwest-some-customers-ask-where.html.
22. Murray, Lance. 2013. Southwest Airlines CEO: "Never say Never" to charging bag fees. Dallas Business Journal, January 25, www.bizjournals.com/denver/morning_call/2013/01/southwest-airlines-ceo-never-say.html.
23. Southwest Airlines. www.southwest.com/html/air/products/wifi-access.html.
24. Schlangenstein, M., & Hughes, J. 2010. Southwest CEO risks keep-it-simple strategy to reignite growth. Bloomberg, September 28, www.bloomberg.com/news/2010-09-27/southwest-airlines-agrees-to-buy-airtran-for-1-4-billion-in-cash-shares.html.
25. Rappeport, A., & Lemer, J. 2010. Southwest acquires AirTran for $3.4 bn. Financial Times, September 27, www.ft.com/cms/s/0/14ff99a0-ca2e-11df-87b8-00144feab49a.html#axzz1ODSbX63E.
26. http://travel.usatoday.com/flights/post/2012/07/southwest-leases-planes-to-delta/800171/1.
27. Jones, Charisse. Southwest announces first international flights. www.usatoday.com/story/travel/flights/2014/01/27/southwest-launches-international-services/4938011/.
28. Maxon, Southwest Airlines tops $1 billion.
29. Stevens, Paul. The "shale gas revolution": Developments and changes. www.chathamhouse.org/sites/files/chathamhouse/public/Research/Energy,%20Environment%20and%20Development/bp0812_stevens.pdf.
30. U.S. production: www.eia.gov/todayinenergy/detail.cfm?id=19411; Saudi Arabia production: https://ycharts.com/indicators/saudi_arabia_crude_oil_production.
31. Stefanova, Katina. Do falling oil prices foreshadow a slump in the stock market in 2015? www.forbes.com/sites/katinastefanova/2014/12/31/do-falling-oil-prices-foreshadow-a-slump-in-the-stock-market-in-2015/.
32. Maxon, Terry. Dallas Love Field carries over a million passengers in December. www.dallasnews.com/business/airline-industry/20150125-dallas-love-field-carries-over-a-million-passengers-in-december.ece.
33. Rutherford, Linda. Herb collects more hardware: Lifetime aviation entrepreneur award. www.blogsouthwest.com/herb-collects-more-hardware-lifetime-aviation-entrepreneur-award/.

APPENDIX A
GLOSSARY OF KEY TERMS USED

aircraft utilization   The average number of block hours operated per day per aircraft for the total fleet of aircraft.

available seat-miles   The number of seats available for passengers multiplied by the number of miles the seats are flown.

average fare   The average one-way fare paid per flight segment by a revenue passenger.

average stage length   The average number of miles flown per flight.

break-even load factor   The passenger load factor that will result in operating revenues being equal to operating expenses, assuming constant revenue per passenger-mile and expenses.

load factor   The percentage of aircraft seating capacity actually used (revenue passenger-miles divided by available seat-miles).

operating expense per available seat-mile   Operating expenses divided by available seat-miles.

operating revenue per available seat-mile   Operating revenues divided by available seat-miles.

revenue passenger-miles   The number of miles flown by revenue passengers.

revenue passengers   The total number of paying passengers flown on all flight segments.

yield per passenger-mile   The average amount one passenger pays to fly 1 mile.

CASES

CASE 5

JETBLUE AIRLINES: GETTING OVER THE "BLUES"?*

In September 2014, JetBlue announced that its chief executive, Dave Barger, would step down from the position on February 15, 2015. JetBlue's current president, Robin Hayes, would replace him and join the board on February 16, 2015.[1] Barger, an employee since the inception of JetBlue in 1998, had replaced the founding CEO, David Neeleman, in 2007 when Neeleman was ousted by the board after an ice storm severely disrupted the airline's operations.

Equity analysts tended to view Dave Barger "as being overly concerned" with customer service and comfort.[2] During Barger's tenure, JetBlue earned accolades for customer service. However, its low-fare business model was being threatened as its costs started going up. In April 2014, its pilots, long nonunion, voted to join the Air Line Pilots Association.[3] The airline was racked again in winter by weather-driven cancellations. JetBlue's stock under Barger's leadership lagged behind that of both big legacy carriers, Delta Air Lines and fellow discounter Southwest Airlines. Even with a rise in recent months, the shares were up just 9 percent since Barger became CEO.[4] In the same period, Southwest's shares gained more than 140 percent and the overall Bloomberg U.S. Airline index gained 49 percent.[5]

In promoting President Robin Hayes to be the airline's next CEO, JetBlue's board signaled its readiness to focus on investor-friendly changes (see Exhibit 1). With this news, the share price immediately soared by 5 percent, but JetBlue loyalists who loved the company for its customers-first policies were getting uncomfortable.[6] Would JetBlue soar in clearer skies, or would it sink into the blues again?

---

* This case study was prepared by Professor Naga Lakshmi Damaraju of the Indian School of Business, Professor Alan B. Eisner at Pace University, and Professor Gregory G. Dess at the University of Texas at Dallas. The purpose of the case is to stimulate class discussion rather than to illustrate effective or ineffective handling of a business situation. The authors thank Ms. Parul Agarwal, Indian School of Business, for her research assistance and Professor Michael Oliff at the University of Texas at Dallas for his valuable comments on an earlier version of this case. Several parts of the case are from an earlier version. Copyright © 2015 Damaraju, Eisner, and Dess.

EXHIBIT 1 JetBlue's Stock Performance versus S&P 500

Open 16.45
Close 15.77
Low 15.69
High 16.52
Vol 9.2M
% Chg 80.02%

JBLU 15.77 — 80.02%
^GSPC 2,002.16 — 12.32%

Source: finance.yahoo.com.

The U.S. Airline Industry[7]

The U.S. airline industry consisted of three primary segments: major airlines, regional airlines, and low-fare airlines. Major U.S. airlines, as defined by the Department of Transportation, were those with annual revenues of over $1 billion. Most major airlines had adopted the hub-and-spoke route system. In this system, the operations were concentrated in a limited number of hub cities, while other destinations were served by providing one-stop or connecting service through the hub. Scheduled flights served most large cities within the United States and abroad and also served numerous smaller cities.

Regional airlines typically operated smaller aircraft on lower-volume routes than did major airlines. Unlike the low-fare airlines, the regional airlines did not have an independent route system. They typically entered into relationships with major airlines and carried their passengers on the "spoke"—that is, between a hub or larger city and a smaller city.

Deregulation of the U.S. airline industry in 1978 ushered in competition in the previously protected industry. Several low-cost, low-fare operators entered the competitive landscape that Southwest had pioneered in 1971. The low-fare airlines operated from point to point and had their own route systems. The target segment of low-fare airlines was fare-conscious leisure and business travelers who might otherwise have used alternative forms of transportation or not traveled at all. Low-fare airlines stimulated demand in this segment and were successful in weaning business travelers from the major airlines. Southwest remained an outstanding example that has long been a major line, having crossed the $1 billion mark in 1990.[8]

The main bases of competition in the airline industry were fare pricing, customer service, routes, flight schedules, types of aircraft, safety record and reputation, code-sharing relationships, in-flight entertainment systems, and frequent-flier programs. The economic downturn in the late 1990s and the terrorist attacks on the World Trade Center and the Pentagon on September 11, 2001, severely affected the airline industry and changed the competitive relationships among carriers. The demand for air travel dropped significantly, leading to a reduction in traffic and revenue. Security concerns, security costs, and liquidity concerns increased. Lower fares and the increased capacity of the low-cost airlines created a very unprofitable environment for traditional networks. Since 2011 most of the traditional network airlines filed for bankruptcy or underwent financial restructuring, mergers, or consolidations.[9] With these restructurings, many of them were able to significantly reduce labor costs, restructure debt, and generally gain a more competitive cost structure. This enabled the major airlines to provide innovative offerings similar to those of low-cost airlines while still maintaining their alliances, frequent-flier programs, and expansive route networks. The gap between low-cost airlines and traditional network airlines was diminishing drastically.

JetBlue: The Humble Beginnings and the Great Rise[10]

Born in São Paulo, Brazil, and brought up in Salt Lake City, David Neeleman, along with June Morris, launched Utah-based Morris Air, a charter operation, in 1984. Morris Air was closely modeled after Southwest Airlines, the legendary discount airline. Neeleman considered Herb Kelleher, Southwest's founder, his idol.

While following the Southwest model, Neeleman brought his own innovations into the business. He pioneered the use of at-home reservation agents, routing calls to agents' homes to save money on office rent and infrastructure expense. He also developed the first electronic ticketing system in the airline industry. Impressed by Morris's low costs and high revenue, Southwest bought the company for $129 million in 1992. Neeleman became the executive vice president of Southwest. However, he could not adjust to Southwest's pace of doing things. By 1994 he was at odds with the top executives, and he left after signing a five-year noncompete agreement.

After the noncompete agreement with Southwest Airlines ended in 1999, Neeleman launched his own airline. He raised about $130 million of capital in two weeks.[11] With such strong support from venture capitalists, JetBlue began as the highest-funded start-up airline in U.S. aviation history. JetBlue commenced operations in August 2000, with John F. Kennedy International Airport (JFK) as its primary base of operations. In 2001 JetBlue extended its operations to the West Coast with its base at Long Beach Municipal Airport, which served the Los Angeles area. In 2002 the company went public and was listed on NASDAQ as JBLU. JetBlue's stock offering was one of the hottest IPOs of the year.[12]

JetBlue had been established with the goal of being a leading low-fare passenger airline that offered customers a differentiated product and high-quality customer service on point-to-point routes. JetBlue had a geographically diversified flight schedule that included both short-haul and long-haul routes. The mission of the company, according to Neeleman, was "to bring humanity back to air travel." To stimulate demand, the airline focused on underserved markets and large metropolitan areas that had high average fares.

JetBlue was committed to keeping its costs low. To achieve this objective, the company originally operated a single-type aircraft fleet comprising Airbus A320 planes as opposed to the more popular but costly Boeing 737. The A320s had 162 seats, compared to 132 seats in the Boeing 737. According to JetBlue, the A320 was cheaper to maintain and also more fuel-efficient. Since all of JetBlue's planes were new, the maintenance costs were also lower. In addition, the single type of aircraft kept training costs low and increased personnel utilization. JetBlue was the first to introduce the "paperless cockpit," in which pilots, equipped with laptops, had ready access to flight manuals that were constantly updated at headquarters. As a result, pilots could quickly calculate the weight, balance, and takeoff performance of the aircraft instead of having to download and print the manuals to make the calculations. The paperless cockpit ensured faster takeoffs by reducing paperwork and thus helped the airline achieve quicker turnarounds and higher aircraft utilization.[13] No meals were served on the planes, and pilots even had to be ready, if need be, to do the cleanup work on the plane to minimize the time the aircraft was on the ground. Turnaround time was also reduced by the airline's choice of less congested airports.[14] Innovation was everywhere. For example, there were no paper tickets to lose and no mileage statements to mail to frequent fliers.

With friendly, customer service–oriented employees; new aircraft; roomy leather seats with 36 channels of free LiveTV, 100 channels of free XM satellite radio, and movie channel offerings from FOXInflight; and more legroom (one row of seats was removed to create additional space), JetBlue promised its customers a distinctive flying experience, the "JetBlue experience." With virtually no incidences of passengers being denied boarding; high completion factors (99.6 percent as compared to 98.3 percent at other major airlines); the lowest incidence of delayed, mishandled, or lost bags; and the third-lowest number of customer complaints, the company was indeed setting standards for low-cost operations in the industry. JetBlue was voted the best domestic airline in the *Condé Nast Traveler*'s Readers' Choice Awards for five consecutive years. It was also rated the World's Best Domestic Airline by readers of *Travel + Leisure Magazine* in 2006. In addition, it earned the Passenger Service Award from *Air Transport World*.[15]

Nevertheless, high fuel prices, the competitive pricing environment, and other cost increases made it increasingly difficult to fund JetBlue's growth profitability. The airline suffered its first-ever losses after its IPO in 2005. It posted net losses of $1 million and $20 million for 2006 and 2005, respectively.[16]

The 2007 Valentine's Day Disaster[17]

Valentine's Day 2007 was a nightmare in JetBlue's hitherto glorious history for more than one reason. Not only did the event destroy JetBlue's reputation for customer friendliness and cost Neeleman his job, but it also exposed the critical weaknesses in the systems that had kept the airline's operations going.

Although there was trouble in the Midwest for several days before the Valentine's Day storm reached the East Coast and several other airlines canceled dozens of their flights in preparation for the storm, JetBlue opted to wait it out. Several of its outbound planes were on the runway at John F. Kennedy airport in New York at about 8 a.m. This positioning was done to ensure that the planes would be ready to take off as soon as the bad weather let up. However, with further weather deterioration, by about 3 p.m., with no hope of getting the planes off the ground, the airline began calling in buses to bring the passengers back to the terminal.

By then, however, the damage had been done. Airport terminals, especially the JFK hub, were filled with passengers still expecting to get on flights, and, compounding the problem, the waiting passengers were now being joined by hundreds of infuriated passengers returning from the JetBlue planes. In addition, communications broke down and the airline could not contact other passengers, so they continued to arrive at the airport and this had a cascading effect.

A number of shortcomings in the company's information systems were responsible for this debacle, according to Charles Mees, the CIO who had joined the company a few months before the event. The reservation system, for example, was not expanded enough to meet the extreme customer call volume, and last-minute quick fixes did not work. Also in a mess was the baggage-handling mechanism, which was not computerized and therefore led to mounds of bags piling up. Neeleman said:

> We had so many people in the company who wanted to help who weren't trained to help. We had an emergency control center full of people who didn't know what to do. I had flight attendants sitting in hotel rooms for three days who couldn't get a hold of us. I had pilots e-mailing me saying, "I'm available, what do I do?"

Southwest, by contrast, handled the Valentine's Day weather disaster with ease by simply canceling most services during the disrupted period. It looked as though JetBlue had completely missed out on this obvious solution.

The airline's reputation hit rock bottom. To limit the damage, JetBlue announced huge compensations to customers—refunds and future flights, which were to cost the airline about $30 million. Neeleman quickly followed up with a new Customer Bill of Rights. The Customer Bill of Rights basically outlined self-imposed penalties for JetBlue and major rewards for its passengers if the airline experienced operational problems and could not adjust to weather-related cancellations within a "reasonable" amount of time. All these announcements and even a public apology could not, of course, restore things to normalcy. Neeleman was pushed out as CEO on May 10, 2007. Dave Barger, the president, assumed the position of chief executive officer.

Subsequently, a few additional incidents further tarnished JetBlue. Its flight from Pittsburgh to New York's JFK Airport made an unscheduled landing after a control panel indicator warned against landing in icy conditions at JFK. The passengers on the flight were put on hold for about four hours in Philadelphia. Adding to its problems, JetBlue had to ground 25 of its Embraer jets to fix persistent software problems.[18]

Resurrecting JetBlue?

Under the new CEO, Dave Barger, JetBlue added several new services and embarked on capacity expansion to give the airline a new boost. In July 2007, it became the first U.S. carrier to let passengers send free email and text messages from wireless handheld devices, a technology developed through its LiveTV LLC subsidiary.[19] Later, in September 2007, it expanded to smaller cities that did not have sufficient demand for the larger planes flown by Southwest, Virgin America, and Skybus Airlines. It also introduced Embraer jets along the way.[20]

In 2007, JetBlue had its first full-year profit in three years as an increase in traffic and operational improvements helped the discount airline compensate for skyrocketing fuel costs. Profits tanked again in 2008, and JetBlue reported a net loss of $85 million.[21] Nevertheless, the company returned to profitability in 2009 (see Exhibit 2). In April 2010, JetBlue successfully completed the International Air Transport Association's (IATA's) Operational Safety Audit (IOSA) and achieved IOSA registration, meeting the same highest industry benchmarks as other world-class airlines.[22]

The "Interline" Model

Unlike many other carriers around the world, JetBlue chose to stay independent. The carrier relied on signing a series of interline agreements instead of joining an airline alliance. While the interline agreements do not fit into a strict hub-and-spoke model, they nearly amount to the same thing, allowing JetBlue passengers in New York, Boston, and San Juan to connect to destinations around the world. On February 6, 2007, JetBlue announced its plans to enter into an alliance with Aer Lingus, an Irish flag carrier. The alliance was expected to facilitate easy transfers for both airlines' customers, but, unlike traditional code-share alliances, it did not allow either airline to sell seats on the other airline, meaning customers had to make individual reservations with both carriers (the agreement was converted into a full code-share agreement in 2011).[23]

In February 2007, JetBlue announced its first code-share agreement, with Cape Air. Under this agreement, JetBlue passengers from Boston's Logan Airport were carried to Cape Air's destinations throughout Cape Cod and the surrounding islands, and customers were able to purchase seats on both airlines under one reservation.[24] While Lufthansa's January 2008 acquisition of a minority equity stake (42.6 million shares of common stock) in JetBlue did not

EXHIBIT 2 Financial Statements of JetBlue (in millions, except per share amounts)

Statements of Operations Data:	2014 (unaudited)	2013	2012	2011	2010	2009
Operating revenues	$5,817	$5,441	$4,982	$4,504	$3,779	$3,292
Aircraft fuel and related taxes	1,912	1,899	1,806	1,664	1,115	945
Salaries, wages and benefits	1,294	1,135	1,044	947	891	776
Landing fees and other rents	321	305	277	245	228	213
Depreciation and amortization	320	290	258	233	220	228
Aircraft rent	124	128	130	135	126	126
Sales and marketing	231	223	204	199	179	151
Maintenance materials and repairs	418	432	338	227	172	149
Other operating expenses	682	601	549	532	515	419
Total operating expenses	5,302	5,013	4,606	4,182	3,446	3,007
Operating income	515	428	376	322	333	285
Other income (expense)	108	−149	−167	−177	−172	−181
Income before income taxes	623	279	209	145	161	104
Income tax expense	222	111	81	59	64	43
Net income	$ 401	$ 168	$ 128	$ 86	$ 97	$ 61
Earnings per common share:						
Basic	$1.36	0.59	$0.45	$0.31	$0.36	$0.24
Diluted	$1.19	0.52	$0.4	$0.28	$0.31	$0.21

Source: JetBlue SEC filings; 2014 data from company website (investor relations).

automatically lead to any code-share agreements, Lufthansa expected to have "operational cooperation" with JetBlue.[25]

JetBlue continued on the path of signing more interline agreements. In March 2011, it announced an interline agreement with Virgin Atlantic. Virgin Atlantic and Virgin America have some shared ownership, with Virgin Group owning 25 percent of Virgin America. Virgin America is a major competitor of JetBlue.[26] In March 2013, JetBlue entered its 22nd code-share agreement, with Qatar Airways, which followed its partnerships with the UAE-based Emirates airline, Korean Air, Air China, and the Indian carrier Jet Airways, allowing JetBlue to expand its reach far beyond the Americas, into India, China, the Middle East, and other parts of Asia.[27] Etihad Airways and El Al Israel joined this list in January 2014 and November 2014, respectively.[28]

More Goodies for Customers

Over the years, JetBlue constantly maintained its customer-first attitude. In 2011, it introduced the "Go Places" application on Facebook, which rewarded customers with TrueBlue points and special discounts so they could earn free trips faster. The "Even More" suite of products and services—including early boarding, early access, expedited security experience, and extra legroom offers—was also introduced in the same year. In 2012, JetBlue added more benefits for its frequent fliers through its "TrueBlue Mosaic" loyalty program. The services included a free second checked bag, a dedicated 24-hour customer service line, and bonus points, among many other offers.[29]

In June 2012, JetBlue became the first Federal Aviation Administration–certified carrier in the U.S. to utilize the new satellite-based Special Required Navigation Performance Authorization Required (RNP AR) approaches at its home base at New York's JFK airport. These unique procedures resulted in stabilized approach paths, shorter flight times, and reduced noise levels and greenhouse gas emissions, and they increased fuel savings by as much as 18 gallons per flight.[30]

Nevertheless, in October 2013, amid costs cutting into earnings, JetBlue announced a fleet modernization program that included deferral of 24 Embraer aircraft from 2014–2018 to 2020–2022 so that capital expenditures could be reduced over the near term. It also converted 18 orders with Airbus from A320 to A321 aircraft. It said its future focus would be on adding aircraft with more fuel-efficient engines. JetBlue also shrunk legroom, adding 15 more seats to its Airbus A320 planes.[31] However, in December 2014, JetBlue was ranked among the companies with the lowest operating margins. With an operating margin of only 10.7 percent, JetBlue was behind only Delta Air Lines, which had an operating margin of 7.5 percent (see Exhibit 2 for the financial performance of JetBlue). Southwest Airlines (12.8 percent) was ahead of the bottom five and behind United Continental Holdings (11.3 percent) and Allegiant Travel (10.9 percent).[32] This was despite the general decreases in fuel prices during the year.

Reinventing JetBlue?

On January 29, 2015, with the new CEO yet to take charge, Hayes announced that JetBlue was testing a new pricing model and would unveil three new fare families in the second quarter of 2015. Under the new fare structure, passengers were able to choose which features they did or didn't want included in the ticket price. At the low end of the pricing spectrum, tickets did not include a checked bag. Passengers who paid higher fares were entitled to checked bags (one bag at the middle level, two at the high end) and also got bonus loyalty points. At the high end of the pricing, "Even More" seats offered extra legroom (38 inches of pitch), expedited security clearance, and priority dibs at overhead bin space. With this fare structure, seats were subject to variable pricing not only by flight but also by their specific position in the aircraft. Hayes said that the airline is committed to delivering "the best travel experience for our customers. . . . JetBlue's core mission to Inspire Humanity and its differentiated model of serving underserved customers remain unchanged."[33]

In 2014, the J.D. Power and Associates Airline Satisfaction Study ranked JetBlue as the most customer-friendly airline for the ninth consecutive year.[34] Will JetBlue be able to hold on to its core mission and still be able to make its stakeholders happy? Does JetBlue have a strong and clear strategic position and coherent business model to support it? Or, with too many complexities being introduced into its simple model of success, will JetBlue sink into the blues once again?

ENDNOTES

1. Schlangenstein, M., & Sasso, M. 2014. Investor-friendly skies; JetBlue with new CEO poised to add revenue with bag fee. *Worcester Telegram & Gazette,* September 22, www.thefreelibrary.com/Investor-friendly+skies%3B+JetBlue+with+new+CEO+poised+to+add+revenue...-a0383201056.
2. Tuttle, B. 2014. A new era has begun for JetBlue, and travelers will hate it. *Time,* November 19, www.time.com/money/3595360/jetblue-fees-legroom-hates/.
3. Nicas, J. 2014. Jetblue's pilots vote to unionize. *Wall Street Journal,* April 22, www.wsj.com/articles/SB10001424052702304049904579517911131169286.
4. Carey, S. 2014. JetBlue CEO Barger to retire in February. *Wall Street Journal,* September 18, www.wsj.com/articles/jetblue-ceo-barger-to-retire-in-february-1411072958.
5. Schlangenstein & Sasso, op. cit.
6. Tuttle, op. cit.
7. This section draws heavily on the SEC filings of JetBlue for the years 2008 and 2009. Other sources include Zellner, W. 2003. Look who's buzzing the discounters. *BusinessWeek,* November 24; Zellner, W. 2004. Folks are finally packing their bags. *BusinessWeek,* January 12; and a joint study by A. T. Kearney and the Society of British Aerospace Companies, www.atkearney.com/shared_res/pdf/Emerging_Airline_Industry_S.pdf.
8. Serwer, A., & Bonamici, K. 2004. Southwest Airlines: The hottest thing in the sky through change at the top, through 9/11, in a lousy industry, it keeps winning most admired kudos. How? *Fortune,* March 8: 88–106, money.cnn.com/magazines/fortune/fortune_archive/2004/03/08/363700/index.htm.
9. Peterson, K., and Daily, M. 2011. American Airlines files for bankruptcy. *Reuters,* November 29, www.reuters.com/article/2011/11/29/us-americanairlines-idUSTRE7AS0T220111129.

10. This section draws heavily on Gajilan, A. T. 2004. The amazing JetBlue. *Fortune Small Business, www.fortune/smallbusiness/articles/0.15114,444298-2,00.html.*
11. Gale/Cengage Learning. Undated. JetBlue Airways Corporation. In *International directory of company histories, galenet.galegroup.com.*
12. *CNNMoney.* 2002. JetBlue IPO soars. April 12, *money.cnn.com/2002/04/12/markets/ipo/jetblue.*
13. *BusinessWeek.* 2003. WEBSMART50. November 24: 92.
14. Bay, W., & Neeleman, D. 2002. JetBlue reaches new heights in airline industry (interview with David Neeleman by Willow Bay of CNN Business Unusual). Aired June 23, *www.cnn.com/TRANSCRIPTS/0206/23/bun.00.html.*
15. JetBlue. SEC filings, 2006.
16. JetBlue. SEC filings, 2007 and 2008.
17. This section draws heavily on the following sources: Bartholomew, D., & Duvall, M. 2007. What really happened at JetBlue? *www.baselinemag.com,* April 5; and Bailey, J. 2007. Long delays hurt image of JetBlue. *New York Times,* February 17: 1.
18. Schlangenstein, M. 2007. JetBlue to repair 25 of its jets. *Deseret Morning News,* March.
19. Associated Press. 2007. N.Y. discount carrier JetBlue to detail wireless email plans. *Toronto Star,* July 6.
20. Ray, S. 2007. Repaired planes boost JetBlue expansion plan. *Bloomberg News,* September 1.
21. JetBlue. SEC filings, 2008–2010.
22. From the company's press releases, 2010. JetBlue completes top international safety audit. April 19, *www.jetblue.com.*
23. *USAToday.* 2007. JetBlue, Aer Lingus to forge world's first international discount alliance. *USAToday.com,* February 6; and Mulligan, J. 2013. Aer Lingus and JetBlue sign full codeshare agreement. *Independent,* February 22, *www.independent.ie/business/irish/aer-lingus-and-jetblue-sign-full-codeshare-agreement-29087072.html.*
24. Compart, A. 2007. JetBlue's pact with Cape Air is airline's first codeshare deal. February 19, *www.travelweekly.com/Travel-News/Airline-News/JetBlue-s-pact-with-Cape-Air-is-airline-s-first-codeshare-deal/.*
25. Associated Press. 2007. Lufthansa pays $300 million for JetBlue stake.
26. Associated Press. 2011. JetBlue partners with Virgin Atlantic; and Blank, D. 2011. JetBlue and Virgin Atlantic (finally) announce interline agreement. *Online Travel Review,* March 22, *www.onlinetravelreview.com/2011/03/22/jetblue-and-virgin-atlantic-finally-announce-interline-agreement/.*
27. Unnikrishnan, M. 2012. JetBlue signs codeshare agreement with Air China. *Aviation Week,* June 12, *www.aviationweek.com/Article.aspx?id=/article-xml/awx_06_12_2012_p0-467058.xml.*
28. Associated Press. 2014. JetBlue, Etihad Airlines announce partnership. *New Zealand Herald,* January 22; and JetBlue Airways and El Al Israel Airlines sign codeshare agreement, November 21, 2014, *www.heritagefl.com/story/2014/11/21/features/jetblue-airways-and-el-al-israel-airlines-sign-codeshare-agreement/3600.html.*
29. JetBlue. Press releases.
30. Drum, B. 2012. JetBlue Airways becomes first FAA-certified carrier to fly Special (non-public) RNP AR approaches with Airbus A320s at New York's JFK Airport. June 20, *http://worldairlinenews.com/2012/06/20/jetblue-airways-becomes-first-faa-certified-carrier-to-fly-special-non-public-rnp-ar-approaches-with-airbus-a320s-at-new-yorks-jfk-airport/.*
31. Tuttle, op. cit.
32. Quinn, J. 2014. Lowest operating margin in the airlines industry detected in shares of Delta Air Lines (DAL, JBLU, ALGT, UAL, LUV). *Comtex News Network,* December 22.
33. Schaal, D. 2014. The new JetBlue will have more bag fees and less legroom. November 19, *http://skift.com/2015/01/29/jetblue-to-unveil-bag-fees-and-new-types-of-fares-in-the-second-quarter/.*
34. J.D. Power. Press release, May 2014. *http://india.jdpower.com/press-releases/2014-north-america-airline-satisfaction-study.*

APPENDIX A

GLOSSARY OF KEY TERMS USED*

aircraft utilization   The average number of block hours operated per day per aircraft for the total fleet of aircraft.

available seat-miles   The number of seats available for passengers multiplied by the number of miles the seats are flown.

average fare   The average one-way fare paid per flight segment by a revenue passenger.

average stage length   The average number of miles flown per flight.

break-even load factor   The passenger load factor that will result in operating revenues being equal to operating expenses, assuming constant revenue per passenger-mile and expenses.

*From JetBlue SEC filings, 2008.

load factor   The percentage of aircraft seating capacity that is actually utilized (revenue passenger-miles divided by available seat-miles).

operating expense per available seat-mile   Operating expenses divided by available seat-miles.

operating revenue per available seat-mile   Operating revenues divided by available seat-miles.

passenger revenue per available seat-mile   Passenger revenue divided by available seat-miles.

revenue passenger-miles   The number of miles flown by revenue passengers.

revenue passengers   The total number of paying passengers flown on all flight segments.

yield per passenger-mile   The average amount one passenger pays to fly 1 mile.

CASES

CASE 6
BACKERS BEWARE: KICKSTARTER IS NOT A STORE*

By 2015, the concept of "crowdfunding" had matured. According to Wharton School researcher Ethan Mollick, crowdfunding allowed "founders of for-profit, artistic, and cultural ventures to fund their efforts by drawing on relatively small contributions from a relatively large number of individuals using the Internet, without standard financial intermediaries." It was considered "a novel method for funding a variety of new ventures," but it was not without its problems. Although billions of dollars had been raised for projects ranging from something as small as an artist's video diary to large endeavors such as the development of a new product for accessing email or an award-winning film documentary, very little was known about the kinds of mechanisms that made funding efforts successful or whether "existing projects ultimately deliver the products they promise." One example of this "new phenomena in entrepreneurship"[1] was the story of Kickstarter. As of January 2015, Kickstarter was the largest U.S. crowdfunding site, with over 201,000 launched projects, over 7 million backers, and over $1.49 billion in pledged dollars—87 projects had raised over $1 million each. Kickstarter also had a success rate of just nearly 40 percent, meaning 60 percent of the time the backers got nothing in return for their donations.[2] What was this crowdfunding thing all about, and was Kickstarter truly a boon for entrepreneurs, or a bust for backers?

"Kickstarter = Dumb people giving money to anonymous people in hope of some goodies in an unspecified amount of time."[3] So read a comment posted in response to a story about one nine-year-old girl's Kickstarter campaign. Mackenzie Wilson wanted to raise $829 so that she could go to computer camp and create her own video game. (She said her older brothers were making fun of her, and she wanted to prove that girls could do "tech stuff" too.) The trouble was that Kickstarter rules said someone had to be at least 18 years old in order to list a project, so Mackenzie's mom, Susan Wilson, created the information listing. And Susan Wilson was a Harvard graduate and a known entrepreneur and had allegedly promoted her daughter's Kickstarter campaign by tweeting celebrities like Lady Gaga and Ellen DeGeneres to elicit support.

Whatever promotion Wilson did worked. The project launched on March 20, 2013, and within 24 hours it not only had reached its $829 goal but was on its way to getting 1,247 backers and $22,562 in pledges.[4] It also received headlines because of the extreme public response—accusations of a scam and death threats against Wilson and her family. The majority of negative responses seemed to come from those who believed that Susan Wilson had misrepresented the nature of the project, that she had acted in bad faith—intending to profit from her daughter's story—and thereby had violated Kickstarter's project guidelines.

Kickstarter clearly stated that its crowdfunding service could not be used for "charity or cause funding" such as an awareness campaign or scholarship; nor could a project be used to "fund my life"—things like going on vacation, buying a new camera, or paying for tuition. And a project had to have a clear goal, "like making an album, a book, or a work of art. . . . A project is not open-ended. Starting a business, for example, does not qualify as a project." In addition, for Kickstarter to maintain its reputation as one of the top crowdfunding services, it had to make sure it kept control of how the projects were promoted: "Sharing your project with friends, fans, and followers is one thing, but invading inboxes and social networks is another."[5]

Kickstarter responded to comments on the Wilson project by affirming its support, saying, "Kickstarter is a funding platform for creative projects. The goal of this project is to create a video game, which backers are offered for a $10 pledge. On Kickstarter backers ultimately decide the validity and worthiness of a project by whether they decide to fund it."[6] However, backers and Kickstarter fans were concerned, with one user commenting, "It's all of our jobs to be on the lookout for shady Kickstarters and personally I don't want to see it devolve into a make a wish foundation for already privileged kids to learn how to sidestep rules of a website to profit."[7] And therein lay Kickstarter's dilemma—how to provide a service that allowed funding for obvious commercial ventures while also providing safeguards for backers.

Kickstarter had remained a service business, collecting 5 percent of funded projects as a fee for this service, and had kept itself hands-off otherwise. However, in addition to getting comments such as the ones in response to the Wilsons' project, Kickstarter had come under fire for providing no guarantees that funded projects would actually produce promised items or deliver on the project's goals. In September 2012, Kickstarter's three founders had even had to create a specific blog post titled "Kickstarter Is Not

---

* This case was prepared by graduate student Eric Engelson of Pace University, Professor Alan B. Eisner of Pace University, Professor Dan Baugher of Pace University, and Associate Professor Pauline Assenza, Western Connecticut State University. This case was solely based on library research and was developed for class discussion rather than to illustrate either effective or ineffective handling of an administrative situation. Copyright © 2015 Alan B. Eisner.

a Store"—reminding backers that the ventures were *projects* and, as such, would be subject to delays, sometimes long ones, while in development.[8] Kickstarter made it clear that it was the project *creators'* responsibility to complete projects and that it would pull projects from its web pages if project promises were obviously unrealistic or violated copyright or patent law, but otherwise it gave no other protection to backers. And even if a project couldn't fully deliver, Kickstarter collected its fee. By keeping its business model as a fee-for-service commercial venture, was it in danger of losing its reputation and therefore its future business stream?

More competitors were entering the crowdfunding, crowdinvesting, or peer-to-peer lending space, partly because of the Jumpstart Our Business Startups (JOBS) Act passed by Congress in April 2012. The JOBS Act was designed to encourage small business and start-up funding by easing federal regulations, allowing individuals to become investors; and crowdfunding by the likes of Kickstarter was a "major catalyst in shifting the way small businesses" operated and found start-up capital.[9] Crowdsourcing had already changed the way businesses interacted with consumers; crowdfunding needed to figure out "how to build a community of supporters before, during, and after" a business launched.[10] But Kickstarter's founders seemed to believe "a big part of the value backers enjoy throughout the Kickstarter experience" was to get "a closer look at the creative process as the project comes to life."[11] Kickstarter seemed to want to be a place where people could "participate in something"—something they "held dear"—and ultimately become a "cultural institution" that would outlive its founders.[12] Was that the vision of a commercial venture, or was it a wish to eventually become a not-for-profit legitimate cause-funding organization? What did Kickstarter want to be when it ultimately grew up?

The Kickstarter Business Model

By 2015 Kickstarter had become a popular "middleman"—acting as a go-between, connecting the entrepreneur and the capital needed to turn an idea into a reality. The Kickstarter platform had launched on April 28, 2009, created by Perry Chen, Yancey Strickler, and Charles Adler, and was one of the first to introduce the new concept of crowdfunding: raising capital from the general public in small denominations. In a social media–filled world, an opportunity had been recognized—you could count on your peers to help you fund your big idea. Many creators, who were young, inexperienced, low on capital, or any combination of the above, turned to websites such as Kickstarter for financial support for their projects. The site acted as a channel, enabling them to call on their friends, family, and other intrigued peers to help them raise money.

When establishing a listing on Kickstarter, the creator could place his or her project offering in one of 13 different categories: art, comics, dance, design, fashion, film & video, food, games, music, photography, publishing, technology, and theater. The project "owner" filled out some basic information, and the listing was on its way. However, certain standards had to be met before the listing could go live. If the project met those requirements, it was approved by the Kickstarter team and listed.

The guidelines were surprisingly basic and straightforward. First, and foremost, the listing had to be for a project. It could not be for a charity or involve cause funding, nor could it be a "fund my life" project. The guidelines also disallowed prohibited content. Other than that, the project simply had to fit into one of the 13 designated categories.

More recently, however, a few more cautious measures were added to ensure that only real and recognizable listings were created (see the section on rules and regulations later in this case). The project creator now had to set a deadline for the fund-raising, as well as a monetary goal, stating how much money he or she hoped to raise for the project. If that goal was met, the funds were then transferred to the project creator/owner. If the goal was not met, however, all donating parties were given refunds and the project was not funded. Additionally, the project owner could create rewards as incentives for different levels of donations, to be received by the donor if the project met its goal and was therefore funded. The more a donor pledged, the better the reward, which was usually related in some way to the project at hand, such as being the first backer to receive the finished product.

If the project succeeded in reaching its goal, payment was collected through Amazon. The project creator had to have an active Amazon Payments account when setting up his or her project. If a project was successfully funded, the money was transferred from the backers' credit cards to the creator's Amazon Payments account. If the project was not successfully funded, Amazon released the funds back to the backers' credit cards and no charges were issued; Kickstarter never actually possessed the funds at all. Once a project was successfully funded, Kickstarter took 5 percent of the total funds raised, while Amazon took around 3 to 5 percent for its services. After both parties deducted their commissions, the project creator/owner could still expect a payout of about 90 percent of the total money that was raised.[13]

Kickstarter History

The company was launched in April 2009 by its three cofounders: Perry Chen, Yancey Strickler, and Charles Adler. Originally based in Brooklyn, New York, Kickstarter initially raised $10 million from Union Square Ventures and angel investors, including Jack Dorsey of Twitter, Zach Klein of Vimeo, Scott Heiferman of Meetup, and Caterina Fake of Flickr.[14] It all started with the hope of a musical success—a $20,000 late-night concert that Perry Chen was trying to organize at the 2002 New Orleans Jazz Fest. Chen had hopes of bringing a pair of DJs into town to perform. He had found a perfect venue for the concert and even gotten in touch with the DJs' management, yet the show never happened. The problem was the lack of capital, and, even if he had found willing backers, Chen had wondered what he would do if the show was unable to attract sufficient interest to pay back any investment.

This dilemma brought Chen to the realization that the world needed a better way to fund the arts. He thought to himself, "What if people could go to a site and pledge to buy tickets for a show? And if enough money was pledged they would be charged and the show would happen. If not, it wouldn't."[15] Although Chen loved this initial idea, he put it on the back burner at the time, being more focused on making music and not on starting an Internet company. Three years later, in 2005, Chen moved back to New York and began to reconsider the potential for his business idea, but he was unsure how to go about building it. That fall, Chen met Yancey Strickler, the editor-in-chief of *eMusic*, through a mutual friend and approached him with the idea of Kickstarter. Strickler was intrigued, and the two began brainstorming. Then, about a year later, Chen was introduced to Charles Adler. Adler was also intrigued and began working with Chen and Strickler.[16] After months of work, the team had created specifications for an Internet site, yet one major problem remained: None of them knew HTML coding, so the project was put on hold. Adler moved to San Francisco to do some freelance work, and Strickler remained at his day job.

Finally, in the summer of 2008, Chen was introduced to Andy Baio, who joined the team remotely as an adviser, since he was living in Portland, Oregon, at the time. Soon after, Baio and Adler contacted some developers, including Lance Ivy in Walla Walla, Washington, and the site started to take shape. Although the team was scattered throughout the country, they were well connected through Skype and email and finally began building the web portal. By April 28, 2009, Kickstarter had been created and was launched to the public. The idea for creating a new channel for artistic entrepreneurs of all kinds to explore their creativity was finally realized.[17]

Crowdfunding Competition

Although by 2015 Kickstarter had become a well-known name in crowdfunding, many other companies had had the same idea. Not all of them had attracted as much media attention, but this meant that they had also avoided some of the negative press. Also, being market followers rather than leaders gave Kickstarter a prime opportunity to maintain a clean track record.

One of the better-known Kickstarter competitors was Indiegogo, founded in January 2008 in San Francisco. Indiegogo was initially funded with $1.5 million from investors such as Zynga cofounder Steve Schoettler. As of June 2012, the company had attracted over 100,000 projects from 196 countries. Aiming to "make an even bigger impact," in 2012 Indiegogo raised an additional $15 million in a "Series A" private equity stock offering.[18] CEO Slava Rubin said that the money was needed mostly to hire, build out, and increase resources to take on other crowdsourcing competitors such as Kickstarter. However, while Kickstarter focused on individuals' creative projects, Indiegogo was much more business-oriented. Projects on Indiegogo were not regulated as they were on Kickstarter. Indiegogo used an algorithm that decided which projects to promote on the basis of activity and engagement metrics like "funding velocity."[19]

Additionally, Indiegogo projects followed the "keep it all" model—all funds collected were handed over to the project creator, regardless of any goal achievement. If the project fund-raising goal was never met, or the project's objectives were never achieved, it was up to the project creator to refund collected funds to the contributors. Indiegogo was also available for use internationally, while Kickstarter required backers to have either a U.S. or U.K. bank account.[20]

Other online crowdfunding companies, which raised funds for either charitable or creative projects, included ArtistShare for musicians[21] and Fundly for charitable projects and political campaigns—Meg Whitman used Fundly to raise $20 million for her 2010 campaign for governor of California.[22] Illustrating the degree of competition, ArtistShare and Kickstarter had been in a patent dispute since 2011 over ownership of the "methods and apparatuses for financing and marketing a creative work," with ArtistShare claiming Kickstarter infringement.[23] Meanwhile, similar companies that created some buzz in the area of business investment were Crowdfunder and Grow VC. While only in start-up mode, Crowdfunder had made enough noise to grab some attention. This platform enabled funders to participate in three different ways: They could simply donate to a project, lend to a project and receive a return, or purchase equity. However, the third option, purchasing equity through crowdfunding, was still not allowed in the U.S. as of 2013.[24]

Grow VC, similar to Kickstarter, made funds accessible to the company or entrepreneur only when the goal had been reached. One important difference between the two was that Grow VC enabled companies to collect monthly installments from investors, allowing a growing business to collect a continuous influx of funds rather than just a one-time investment. The cap for funding was set at $1 million.[25] Other recognizable competitors were EarlyShares and Bolstr in the United States, CrowdCube in the United Kingdom, and Symbid, based in the Netherlands. These were only a few of the more publicized newcomers to the industry—there were at least 50 legitimate crowdfunding platforms operating worldwide.[26]

Kickstarter Successes

By January 2015, Kickstarter had launched 200,988 projects, raising $1.49 billion, of which $1.28 billion was successfully collected by project owners, $186 million was unsuccessful, and $20 million was currently in "live" donation status on the site.[27] On February 8, 2012, the first project to ever get a million dollars funded from the site was a project in the design category, an iPod dock created by ElevationLab. Its goal was set at $75,000, and backers reached this goal almost instantly, raising a total of $1,464,706. However, as impressive as this feat was, its top-funding status was short-lived. Six hours later, in the game category, Double Fine beat that goal, receiving $3,336,371 to fund its new adventure game, far exceeding the initial request for $400,000.[28]

Other notable projects with over $1 million in funding included the TikTok and LunaTik multitouch watch kits and the Pebble Watch in the design category; the OUYA TV console and Project Eternity in the games category; the FORM1 3-D printer and the Oculus Rift virtual reality headset in the technology category; and a new Amanda Palmer record, art book, and tour in the music category. Gustin premium men's wear and Ministry of Supply men's dress shirts, in the fashion category, were notably successful offerings, with over $400,000 in pledges.[29] In the movie category, in 2013, *Inocente* became the first Kickstarter crowdfunded film to win an Oscar—for Best Documentary (Short Subject)[30]—and Kickstarter backers donated over $2 million in 12 hours to fund a movie based on the popular *Veronica Mars* franchise.[31] Kickstarter was becoming a source of major support for independent films: According to the company, as of 2013 it had facilitated over $100 million in donations to various "indie" films and had funded 10 percent of all the films shown at the 2013 Sundance Film Festival.[32]

These projects had made contributions to Kickstarter's business model. Even with an office on the Lower East Side of Manhattan, large amounts of capital raised, and about 50 employees, Kickstarter had to have been profitable. Based on the April 2013 statistics, at an average 3 percent cut, Kickstarter should have grossed over $6 million in its five years of operation.

Kickstarter Failures

However, as in all sectors of capital investment, some Kickstarter projects did not work out as planned. In the world of start-ups, many venture capitalists or angel investors made investments in projects that were inherently risky. Some were lucky and achieved their intended goals or did even better. Others fell short. There were many possible reasons for the failures, including lack of industry knowledge, unrealistic projections of cost, lack of managerial experience, manufacturing capabilities, or simply a lack of competence for the task at hand. These possibilities existed for Kickstarter projects as well, but in the Kickstarter model, investors/backers/donators didn't "own" anything—project creators kept ownership of their work. As Kickstarter pointed out, "Backers are supporting projects to help them come to life, not to profit financially."[33]

This disclaimer didn't stop backers or the media from highlighting Kickstarter's risks. Eyez was one of the better-known project failures on Kickstarter. More than 2,000 backers collectively contributed more than $300,000 to the entrepreneurs developing the high-tech glasses, meant for recording live video. Eyez's product creators promised delivery of the glasses ahead of the fall 2011 goal, yet by 2013 Eyez glasses still weren't being produced and none of the individual backers had received a pair. Meanwhile, the entrepreneurs had stopped providing online updates on the project and wouldn't answer questions from backers.[34] Other failed projects included TechSync Power Systems, whose project creators took $27,000 in pledges before Kickstarter canceled the offering under odd circumstances. Others, such as the group behind MYTHIC, a nonexistent game from an imaginary team, continued to try to scam the crowdfunding scene.[35]

Ongoing Issues—Backers' Concerns; Rules and Regulations

Despite the success Kickstarter had achieved, the company was under fire for many things, particularly regarding false projects, the collection of funds with no end product, and the failure of backers to receive the stated rewards set by project creators. Kickstarter followed the "all or nothing" approach to funding—pledged dollars were collected only if the fund-raising goal was met. In the beginning, Kickstarter had tried to explain that the company had no control over the donated funds once these funds were in the hands of the developer—there was no guarantee of product or project "delivery." Additionally, if the fund-raising goal was met but the project never made it to fruition, Kickstarter had no ability to issue refunds. These explanations didn't keep backers from complaining of "delays, deception, and broken promises."[36]

In 2012 the Kickstarter founders felt it was necessary to reiterate "Kickstarter Is Not a Store" and point out, yet again, that "in addition to rewards, a big part of the value backers enjoy throughout the Kickstarter experience is getting a closer look at the creative process as the project comes to life."[37] Kickstarter then implemented a new set of rules, designed to prevent creators from promising a product they couldn't deliver. The goal, Kickstarter said, was to help prevent entrepreneurs from overpromising and disappointing backers by not delivering. By forcing creators to be transparent about their progress, Kickstarter hoped to discourage unrealistic projects and encourage the participation of more creative individuals who had the skills to ship products as promised.

These new rules required Kickstarter's project creators to list all potential problems involved in seeing their projects through to completion; to submit proper supporting materials—no simulations or "renderings," just technical drawings or photos of the actual current prototype; and to create a "reasonable" reward system in which backers received a reward based on their level of participation, which in most cases included a working version of the project in question. Kickstarter prohibited the use of multiple quantities at any reward level: Kickstarter was not a store, but an opportunity to invest in good ideas. The company also included the use of investors' funds in the project creator agreement. The regulations stated that if funds were collected, the creator was required to use those funds toward the creation of the project. If the funds were used for any other purpose, legal repercussions would follow.[38] In 2013 Kickstarter did a "major overhaul" on the set of tools project creators used to communicate with backers, including a "rewards sent" checklist, a tool to survey backers regarding rewards, and a project "dashboard" so that creators could track where their pledges were coming from.[39]

Even if Kickstarter was able to sustain its success with the implementation of tougher approval policies on its end, the future of the size and success of projects was also to be determined by the government and its ability to police the crowdfunding world through its own set of regulations. Recent federal legislation showed the government's intentions to do just that.

The JOBS Act

Signed into law in April 2012 by President Obama, the Jumpstart Our Business Startups (JOBS) Act supported entrepreneurship and the growth of small businesses in the United States and emphasized the new phenomenon of crowdfunding. The act eased federal regulations in regard to crowdfunding by allowing individuals to become investors in new business efforts. However, it also set out specific provisions to regulate just how much funding was acceptable, in order to ensure the financial safety and security of the investors. The new act stated that, as of January 2013, an equity-based company could raise no more than $1 million a year. Additionally, a company could sell to investors only through a middleman—a broker or website—that was registered with the Securities and Exchange Commission (SEC). The middleman could sell only shares that had originated from the company.

The JOBS Act did not yet apply to Kickstarter, because there were no equity sales under its current business model—on its platform, the project creator maintained 100 percent ownership of the product or service.[40] Although it was too early to tell, as long as Kickstarter didn't change its approach to doing business, in the future this could lead to a competitive advantage for Kickstarter over companies that were equity-based. With no cap to investments and minimal federal regulations, people could be more inclined to contribute to a Kickstarter project than invest in an equity-based competitor.

The Future for Kickstarter

Perry Chen, the cofounder and person responsible for the idea behind Kickstarter, was interviewed in May 2012 and spoke about Kickstarter's future. Chen talked about funding business start-ups and stated that Kickstarter was not interested in that model: "We're going to keep funding creative projects in the way we currently do it. We're not gearing up for the equity wave if it comes. The real disruption is doing it without equity."[41] Regarding one of the more basic details of Kickstarter's business model, Chen commented on expanding beyond 13 categories. Particularly, he spoke about focusing on more public-service projects: "We're also looking at . . . expanding a little bit into urban design and things like bike lanes and bike racks and community gardens. A lot of cities have approached us, talking to us about projects in that space."[42]

As *Time* magazine said when it voted Kickstarter one of the 50 best inventions of 2010: "Think of Kickstarter as crowdsourced philanthropy."[43] Chen had said, back when Kickstarter was founded, that the concept was "not an investment, lending or a charity. . . . It's something else in the middle: a sustainable marketplace where people exchange goods for services or some other benefit and receive some value."[44] Cofounder Yancey Strickler pointed out that "everyday people" had pledged over half a billion dollars to Kickstarter projects in the five years since its founding and said that this "shows the power and passion of the human spirit." As Strickler explained it, "We want to become part of things bigger than ourselves."[45]

What *would* Kickstarter become? While it seemed to have a clear mission and was certainly profitable, as Wharton School researcher Mollick warned, "Crowdfunding represents a potentially disruptive change in the way that new ventures are funded."[46] Going forward, the Kickstarter founders needed to consider whether they had the right business model for the future.

ENDNOTES

1. Mallick, E. R. 2013. The dynamics of crowdfunding: Determinants of success and failure. University of Pennsylvania–Wharton School. March 25. Available at SSRN: *http://ssrn.com/abstract=2088298* or *http://dx.doi.org/10.2139/ssrn.2088298;* from the abstract.
2. Statistics gathered on March 31, 2013, 6:50 p.m. EDT, from *www.kickstarter.com/help/stats.*
3. Reader comment by Devlin1776, attached to news story: Bindley, K. 2013. 9-year-old's $20,000 Kickstarter campaign draws scam accusations. *Huffington Post,* March 26, *www.huffingtonpost.com/2013/03/26/9-year-old-kickstarter-campaign_n_2949294.html#slide=1240691.*
4. See the full Kickstarter project listing, plus current status, and both backer and general comments at *www.kickstarter.com/projects/susanwilson/9-year-old-building-an-rpg-to-prove-her-brothers-w.*
5. See Kickstarter funding guidelines at *www.kickstarter.com/help/guidelines.* See also comments on the Wilson project as a scam: Multi-millionaire scams Kickstarter for over $22,000—"Sending daughter to game dev camp," *http://imgur.com/zwyRWCa.*
6. Bindley. 2013. 9-year-old's $20,000 Kickstarter campaign.
7. Ibid.
8. See Chen, P., Strickler, Y., & Adler, C. 2012. Kickstarter is not a store. September 20, *www.kickstarter.com/blog/kickstarter-is-not-a-store.*
9. Farrell, J. 2012. The JOBS Act: What startups and small businesses need to know. *Forbes,* September 9, *www.forbes.com/sites/work-in-progress/2012/09/21/the-jobs-act-what-startups-and-small-businesses-need-to-know-infographic/.*
10. Ibid.
11. An, J. 2013. Dude, where's my Kickstarter stuff? Dealing with delays, deception and broken promises. *Digital Trends,* March 20, *www.digitaltrends.com/social-media/dude-wheres-my-kickstarter-stuff/#ixzz2OmMqQ4dq.*

12. From Strickler, Y. 2013. Talk given at Expand Engadget Conference, March 16, *www.youtube.com/watch?v=thlaPwpobMk.* Also see the conversation liveblog at *www.engadget.com/2013/03/16/kickstarter-yancey-strickler-expand-liveblog/;* and the interview with Myriam Joire, Engadget editor, linked at the *Huffington Post* story at *www.huffingtonpost.com/2013/03/26/9-year-old-kickstarter-campaign_n_2949294.html#slide=1240691.*
13. Nick D. 2012. The history of Kickstarter: "Crowdfunding" at its best. *1Up.com,* May 14, *www.1up.com/do/blogEntry?publicUserId=6111503&bId=9097349.*
14. Kafka, P. 2011. Kickstarter fesses up: The crowdsourcing funding start-up has funding, too. *All Things D,* March 17, *allthingsd.com/20110317/kickstarter-fesses-up-the-crowd-sourced-funding-startup-had-funding-too/.*
15. See Kickstarter Pressroom at *www.kickstarter.com/press.*
16. Vinh, K. 2012. An interview with Charles Adler of Kickstarter. *Subtraction,* June 28, *www.subtraction.com/2012/06/28/an-interview-with-charles-adler-of-kickstarter.*
17. *Details.* 2010. 2010 mavericks: Yancey Strickler, Perry Chen, John Auerback & Chris Wong. October, *www.details.com/culture-trends/critical-eye/201010/strickler-chen-kickstarter-auerbach-wong-gilt-man.*
18. Taylor, C. 2012. Indiegogo raises $15 million series A to make crowdfunding go mainstream. *TechCrunch.com,* June 6, *techcrunch.com/2012/06/06/indiegogo-funding-15-million-crowdfunding/.*
19. Jeffries, A. 2012. Kickstarter competitor Indiegogo raises $15M., staffing up in New York. *BetaBeat,* June 6, *betabeat.com/2012/06/kickstarter-competitor-indiegogo-raises-15-m-staffing-up-in-new-york/.*
20. Taylor, C. 2011. Indiegogo wants to give Kickstarter a run for its money. *Gigaom.com,* August 5, *gigaom.com/2011/08/05/indiegogo/.*
21. See the *Wikipedia* entry at *en.wikipedia.org/wiki/ArtistShare.*
22. See the *Wikipedia* entry at *en.wikipedia.org/wiki/Fundly.*
23. Jeffries, A. 2012. Kickstarter wins small victory in patent lawsuit with 2000-era crowdfunding site. *BetaBeat,* May 14, *betabeat.com/2012/05/kickstarter-artistshare-fan-funded-patent-lawsuit/.*
24. See Crowdfunder: How it works, *www.crowdfunder.com/how-it-works#a-1.*
25. See Loikkanen, V. 2011. What is Grow VC? *GrowVC.com,* September 8, *www.growvc.com/help/2011/09/08/what-is-grow-vc/.*
26. See the list of crowdfunding services as of April 1, 2013, on *Wikipedia* at *en.wikipedia.org/wiki/Comparison_of_crowd_funding_services;* see also Fiegerman, S. 2012. 8 Kickstarter alternatives you should know about. *Mashable.com,* December 6, *mashable.com/2012/12/06/kickstarter-alternatives/.*
27. See current Kickstarter stats at *www.kickstarter.com/help/stats.*
28. See Strickler, Y. 2012. The history of #1. *Kickstarter Blog,* April 18, *www.kickstarter.com/blog/the-history-of-1-0.*
29. See The most funded projects in Kickstarter history (since 2009!), *www.kickstarter.com/discover/most-funded.*
30. Watercutter, A. 2013. The first Kickstarter film to win an Oscar takes home crowdsourced gold. *Wired,* February 15, *www.wired.com/underwire/2013/02/kickstarter-first-oscar/.*
31. McMillan, G. 2013. *Veronica Mars.* Kickstarter breaks records, raises over $2M in 12 hours. *Wired,* March 14, *www.wired.com/underwire/2013/03/veronica-mars-kickstarter-record/.*
32. Watercutter. 2013. The first Kickstarter film.
33. See What is Kickstarter? at *www.kickstarter.com/hello.*
34. Krantz, M. 2012. Crowd-funding dark side: Sometimes investments go down drain. *USA Today,* August 14, *usatoday30.usatoday.com/money/markets/story/2012-08-14/crowd-funding-raising-money/57058678/1.*
35. Koetsier, J. 2012. Kickstarter dodges responsibility for failed projects. *Venture Beat,* September 4, *venturebeat.com/2012/09/04/kickstarter-co-founder-failed-projects/.*
36. An. 2013. Dude, where's my Kickstarter stuff?
37. Ibid.
38. Boris, C. 2012. Kickstarter's new rules for entrepreneurs. *Entrepreneur,* September 28, *www.entrepreneur.com/blog/224524.*
39. See Better tools for project creators, *www.kickstarter.com/blog/better-tools-for-project-creators.*
40. Farrell. 2012. The JOBS Act.
41. Malik, O. 2012. Kickstarted: My conversation with Kickstarter co-founder Perry Chen. *Gigaom.com,* May 22, *gigaom.com/2012/05/22/kickstarter-founder-perry-chen-intervie/#3.*
42. Ibid.
43. Snyder, S. J. 2010. Kickstarter one of 50 best inventions of 2010. *Time,* November 11, *www.time.com/time/specials/packages/article/0,28804,2029497_2030652_2029823,00.html#ixzz2P9t9PunP.*
44. Worthan, J. 2009. A few dollars at a time, patrons support artists on the web. *New York Times,* August 24, *www.nytimes.com/2009/08/25/technology/start-ups/25kick.html?_r=1&em.*
45. Strickler. 2013. Talk given at Expand Engadget Conference.
46. Mallick. 2013. The dynamics of crowdfunding.

CASES

CASE 7
WEIGHT WATCHERS INTERNATIONAL, INC.*

In February 2015, Weight Watchers advertised during the Super Bowl for the very first time. The 30-second "All You Can Eat" spot was meant to highlight the challenges everyday people face when popular culture reinforces an unhealthy relationship with food. The ad was part of a larger "Help with the Hard Part" campaign launched at the end of 2014 that was meant to help people deal with an environment that sometimes sabotages the decision to lose weight. Customized help was now available via Weight Watchers Online *Plus* and a Personal Coaching feature that offered live help from a coach who had successfully shed pounds. To boost membership, Weight Watchers was also offering a "Lose 10 lbs on us" incentive: Anyone joining the program by Valentine's Day, February 14, 2015, who lost at least 10 pounds within two months would receive a refund of two months' membership fees.[1] Would this new campaign work to boost the company's weight-loss business?

The media and programmatic push, plus a newly redesigned magazine offered in late 2014, was all part of a rebranding effort that failed to impress investors. The price of Weight Watchers shares (ticker symbol: WTW) dropped in the early days of January 2015, just when most might expect New Year's resolutions to kick in and bolster the weight-loss stock. This price decline echoed the financial reality: seven straight quarters of declining sales.[2] Although Weight Watchers had been working to update its image and offerings, and was still able to boast a high gross profit margin, the reality was that revenue and cash generation, and therefore firm growth, was significantly lower than the industry average. Weight Watchers was in trouble.[3]

Weight Watchers had recently celebrated 50 years of success in helping people lose weight, and this celebration had come after some significant financial gain as well. In 2011 Weight Watchers had hit a new revenue record of $1.8 billion.[4] In 2012 the company saw a slight reduction in revenue but still beat all pre-2011 numbers; however, by 2013 things started to slide. Weight Watchers, while still the undeniable industry standard, had lost some of its luster.

Originally started in 1963 by Jean Nidetch as a women's support group in her home, Weight Watchers International, Inc. grew into a multibillion-dollar weight-loss goliath in four decades' time. In November 2010 Weight Watchers introduced the new PointsPlus system. It replaced the old calorie-counting system by considering where the calories came from. Even though calories still counted, PointsPlus encouraged people to eat a wide variety of healthy foods—split between three meals plus snacks within an individualized calorie level. With a counting system based on dietary guidelines, dieters were encouraged to maximize their PointsPlus allowance by choosing more "Power Foods"—the healthiest, most filling foods, such as whole grains, lean meats, low-fat dairy, and unlimited quantities of fresh fruit and nonstarchy vegetables.

Although doctors and nutritionists gave the Points program (both the original and the subsequent PointsPlus version) a thumbs up,[5] Weight Watchers' then-CEO David Kirchhoff felt it wasn't enough. Citing evidence from behavioral scientists, in 2012 Kirchhoff said he "realized that Weight Watchers needed to take into account social, environmental and behavioral factors that led members to fail."[6] Weight Watchers had always believed in behavior change, encouraging people to be mindful of what they ate, but just counting calories, as the PointsPlus system did, was not enough.

In 2013, Weight Watchers created the 360-degree program—the "Points Plus program with a 21st-century makeover." By monitoring the amount of carbohydrates, fats, fiber, and proteins in the food choices people make on a daily basis, and using current scientific research on why people eat what they eat, Weight Watchers could help guide members toward making healthier eating decisions in all sorts of situations.[7] The 360-degree program added two new components to tracking caloric intake: "spaces," which included tips for how to handle eating situations in the different environments members might encounter, and "routines," which encouraged members to create new habits for themselves—for instance, changing just three small behaviors a day, such as walking an extra five minutes, eating lunch at the same time, and drinking an additional glass of water. These 360-degree components—tracking, spaces, and routines—were even available as apps on the Weight Watchers website as well as on Apple and Android mobile devices. By adding the mobile apps and other online social networking support to the direct face-to-face support of the weekly meetings, Kirchhoff believed that Weight Watchers finally had a program that tied everything together and that people would be willing to pay for it.[8]

However, in August 2013, Kirchhoff resigned in order to "pursue other opportunities." This left the company floundering to reinvent itself in the Internet age, a time when community social support for weight loss could be

---

* This case was developed by Professor Alan B. Eisner, Pace University; Professor Helaine J. Korn, Baruch College–City University of New York; Associate Professor Pauline Assenza, Western Connecticut State University; and graduate student Jennifer M. DiChiara, Pace University. Material has been drawn from published sources to be used for class discussion. Copyright © 2015 Alan B. Eisner.

provided virtually rather than at a physical weekly meeting. Also, the next generation of diet programs and online apps, like MyFitnessPal and the FitBit activity monitor, were providing this support basically for free, since the companies offering them didn't need to charge meeting fees or employ trained support staff.[9] In January 2014, new CEO Jim Chambers admitted, "The consumer has changed and we haven't kept pace. . . . We need to turn this company inside out."[10]

The market for weight-loss products was growing and obesity levels were on the rise in more and more parts of the world, and this made weight management an attractive industry for firms, especially deeply entrenched firms such as Weight Watchers. However, faced with increased competition from traditional rivals Nutrisystem and Medifast and other weight-loss programs such as Jenny Craig and the *Biggest Loser* franchise, Weight Watchers had to increase customer value and seek new target segments to preempt the competition and stay on top of its industry. In the highly competitive weight-management industry, Weight Watchers International was in a position where it had to remain cognizant of the major trends that had the potential to adversely affect industry and firm profitability and revenues. Those trends, as they related to Weight Watchers and the weight-loss industry as a whole, included the temporary emergence of fad diets; decreased effectiveness of marketing and advertising programs; the need for developing new and innovative products and services, many of which had to be delivered via online or mobile apps; the development of more favorably perceived or more effective weight-management methods (e.g., pharmaceuticals and surgical options such as the Lap-Band); and the threat of impairment of the Weight Watchers brand.[11] The challenge for Weight Watchers was repositioning itself and creating a forward-focused diet plan for the 21st century while staying true to the mission initially established by Jean Nidetch, its founder. The brand needed to remain relevant and, at the same time, pursue additional medium- to long-term initiatives, such as reaching out to new market segments.[12]

History and Expansion

Jean Nidetch began Weight Watchers in an unlikely, and unintended, way. The origins of the company started when Jean invited six women into her home to help both herself and her neighbors and friends lose weight by communally discussing their weight-loss issues. Nidetch's belief, which became the core of the Weight Watchers philosophy, was that anyone could be given a "diet" but the group and social setting of "talk therapy" was the true component not only to losing weight but also *to keeping it off*. She believed in fostering success through group support, and she created a simple reward system that included pins and tie bars to reward increments of weight loss. The idea was simple, yet very effective![13]

The basic concept of the Weight Watchers plan consisted of two components: the Weight Watchers program and the group support. The program was essentially a food plan and an activity plan. The food plan was intended to provide people with the educational tools they needed for weight loss as well as to provide control mechanisms so that individuals could find their way to healthier food choices. The company radically simplified the food selection process involved in dieting by assigning each food a corresponding point value, which eliminated the need to tally calories.[14]

Nidetch accomplished what she set out to do and much more. Weight Watchers, originally targeting primarily women, ages 25 to 55, experienced a rapid expansion. Of the behemoth that Weight Watchers came to be, Nidetch said, "My little group became an industry. I really didn't mean it to—it was really just a club for me and my fat friends." She continued by commenting on something a lecturer once said: "It's a place where you walk in fat and hope nobody notices you, and four or five months later you walk out thin and hope that everyone sees you." Nidetch believed that the love, information, companionship, and commiseration of fellow overweight individuals were the key components in an effective formula many people needed to succeed at weight loss.[15]

What Weight Watchers evolved into was a globally branded company providing weight-management services worldwide. By 2015, approximately 1 million members attended almost 40,000 Weight Watchers meetings around the world each week. Expansion and the onset of the dot-com era had inevitably led to the creation of *WeightWatchers.com*, an Internet-based version of the Weight Watchers plan. Weight Watchers was selling a wide range of branded products and services, including meetings conducted by Weight Watchers International and its franchisees (and the products sold at the meetings), subscriptions to *WeightWatchers.com*, licensed products sold by retailers, magazine subscriptions, and other publications.[16] In addition, the company had put its name and point values on a variety of food products sold in supermarkets, such as Progresso soups,[17] and it had created a separate Weight Watchers menu for certain restaurants.[18]

Reflecting the growing move to the use of online apps and activity monitors for weight control, by the end of 2014 Weight Watchers announced that its members could sync with third-party open APIs such as Fitbit and Jawbone for a more complete and integrated weight-loss experience. Also in 2014, as part of a new technology strategy, Weight Watchers acquired Silicon Valley–based weight-loss start-up Wello, an app that enabled people to attend fitness classes or one-on-one fitness training through any Internet or webcam-enabled device. This acquisition was part of Weight Watchers' strategy to compete in "an increasingly digital weight loss market." As explained by CTO Dan Crowe:

> [Weight Watchers will] become a 21st-century technology organization, engineered for the digital era, whose innovative technology fundamentally

improves the way people manage their weight, health and wellness. We will be agile service-oriented, data-driven, cloud-enabled and efficient. We will be a model for digital technology in the markets in which we compete and we will be a magnet for talented innovators both inside and outside the company.[19]

Echoing the long-term strength of the brand, in 2015 Weight Watchers was ranked the "Best Weight-Loss Diet" for the fifth consecutive year, "Best Commercial Diet Plan," and "Easiest Diet to Follow" (for the fourth year in a row) by *U.S. News & World Report*.[20]

Industry and Competitive Environment

Weight Watchers International had experienced stock price volatility in the past, as had the majority of its competitors, because of rival weight-management options—such as the over-the-counter weight-loss drug *Alli*, launched by GlaxoSmithKline in June 2006, and the development of Allergan's Lap-Band device. However, there had yet to be a widely supported "magic pill" or surgical option to weight management. In the absence of a safe and effective pharmaceutical or surgical alternative for weight loss, Weight Watchers and its competitors had faced a weight-management industry characterized by not only competition but threats and opportunity as well.

Obesity was on the rise in the developed countries, especially in North America, and by 2011 weight loss, including the overall health and fitness industry, constituted a $60 billion–a-year industry in the United States alone.[21] But by 2013 the industry revenue had declined at an annual rate of 3.7 percent, and by the end of 2013 Weight Watchers itself had seen a 15 percent drop in meeting attendance while online paid subscribers were down by 2.6 percent. According to research by NPD Group, the number of Americans dieting had dropped by 12 percent since the peak in 1991. This study opined that Americans might have become more accepting of overweight people's appearance and that possibly people were "starting to realize that diets alone don't work."[22] However, this didn't mean there were no profits to be made. In part due to an improving economy and a growing awareness of men as a target group, the weight-loss industry alone was projected to grow from $2.4 billion in 2013 to over $2.7 billion by 2018.[23] In addition, the obesity problem was not confined to the United States, and this made geographic expansion a possibility for weight-loss firms. Worldwide, the World Health Organization predicted 2.3 billion people would be overweight by 2015 and more than 700 million would be obese.[24] Overall, the statistics proved there were still opportunities, and therefore competition, in the weight-loss industry.

Weight Watchers was attempting to reinvent itself while still paying close attention to the moves of its weight-loss rivals. Competition for Weight Watchers International included both price competition and competition from self-help, pharmaceutical, surgical, dietary supplement, and meal-replacement products, as well as other weight-management brands, diets, programs, and products.[25] The main competitors for Weight Watchers had traditionally included Jenny Craig, Slim-Fast, Nutrisystem (NASDAQ: NTRI), and Medifast, as well as programs from fitness gurus such as *The Biggest Loser* star Jillian Michaels.[26]

Over the years, among the commercial plans, Weight Watchers had consistently earned the highest overall rating, according to various surveys, because of its nutritionally based diet, weekly meetings, and weigh-ins for behavioral support. In 2015, according to *U.S. News & World Report*, Jenny Craig's prepackaged-food diet plan came in second with its rapid weight loss and easy-to-follow features, followed by the Biggest Loser Diet. Other traditional competitors, Nutrisystem and Medifast, came in much further down the list. Going into 2015, competitors included those listed in Exhibit 1.

One important factor in all these diets was the extent to which they were do-it-yourself efforts. Many of the successful diets, including the DASH and Mayo Clinic diets, required consistent self-control without any external support system. Obviously, Weight Watchers was different there, as were Jenny Craig and Nutrisystem.

Another differentiating factor was cost. The cost of plans in which people bought their own food depended, of course, on each person's food choices. The cost of the commercial plans also varied widely. Weight Watchers' cost depended on whether the member chose to attend weekly in-person meetings or use only the online tools. A monthly pass to unlimited in-person meetings could cost up to $42.95, which also included access to eTools. Or members could pay per meeting; meetings were $12 to $15 per week, with a one-time $20 registration fee. For online-only access, a three-month plan was $65. None of the costs included food. With Jenny Craig, the initial registration fee could exceed $400, and a week's worth of Jenny's Cuisine might cost at least $100. Nutrisystem, which had basically fallen off the survey charts due to complaints about costs and the poor taste of the food, had a 28-day Select Plan, which included 10 days of frozen meals and 18 days of pantry food, and generally cost between $300 and $340. Packaged diets such as Slim-Fast didn't have a personal support system, but food supplements could be customized to achieve a "satisfied feeling" that reduced regular food intake. A 24-pack of shakes cost about $35, and 24 snack bars cost about $17. One major advantage Weight Watchers had was the extent of research done on its results. Two studies published in 2012 found that Weight Watchers was just as good as clinical weight-loss programs under a physician's control and that some Weight Watchers participants lost more than twice as much weight as individuals following clinical advice.[27] A physician from the Mayo Clinic said, "It's only natural that the weekly weigh-ins and 'group spirit' of programs such as Weight Watchers would prove more effective than occasional guidance from a doctor or nurse, since research has shown that dieters are more likely to stick with weight-loss programs that stress accountability."[28]

EXHIBIT 1 Competitors for Weight Watchers

Diet Plan	Diet Type	Good For	Ratings*	Price	Comments
Weight Watchers	Commercial diet	Weight loss, heart health	First for weight loss; tied for third as best diet overall	Membership costs less than $40/mo.; buy-it-yourself food is extra	Rated easiest to follow
HMR Diet	Commercial diet	Weight loss	Second best at weight loss	Shakes and entrees starter kit: $295; 2-week reorder: $180; plus fruits and vegs	Phased approach gives quick weight loss; shakes can get boring
Jenny Craig	Commercial diet	Weight loss	Second-best commercial diet plan	Membership and food can run as high as $400/mo.	Customized meal plan plus weekly one-on-one counseling
Biggest Loser Diet	Commercial diet	Weight loss, diabetes	Third-best commercial diet plan	Need to buy the book, $22, plus buy-it-yourself food	6-week program of self-directed food and exercise
Slim-Fast Diet	Commercial diet	Weight loss	Good-Fair rating	$35 for 24 shakes	Easy to follow
Nutrisystem	Commercial diet	Weight loss, *not* heart healthy	Fair rating	Meals cost up to $340/mo.	Taste isn't as good as Jenny Craig meals
Medifast	Commercial diet	Weight loss	Poor rating; hard to stay on it	Meals cost up to $315/mo.	Need to supplement with your own food
The Mediterranean Diet	Developed by Harvard School of Public Health	Overall healthy eating	Third-best diet overall (tie)	Buy-it-yourself food; fresh produce, olive oil, and nuts are expensive	Plant based, do it yourself, easy to follow
The Ornish Diet	Developed by Dr. Ornish for overall nutrition	Heart health, diabetes	Third for heart health and diabetes control	Buy-it-yourself food	Plant based, from book by Dean Ornish
The TLC Diet	Developed by National Institutes of Health	Heart health	One of the best do-it-yourself diets overall	Buy-it-yourself food	Stands for "Therapeutic Lifestyle Changes"
The DASH Diet	Government-developed suggested eating plan	Heart health, diabetes	First for heart health and diabetes control; best do-it-yourself diet	Buy-it-yourself food	Stands for "Dietary Approaches to Stop Hypertension"
Mayo Clinic Diet	Nutritionist-developed, do-it-yourself plan	Diabetes	Third for diabetes control	Buy-it-yourself food	Best for health, not necessarily weight control

*Ratings are from *U.S. News & World Report,* Best diets methodology: How we rated 35 eating plans, January 6, 2015, http://health.usnews.com/health-news/health-wellness/articles/2015/01/06/us-news-best-diets-how-we-rated-35-eating-plans?int=9c2508; and *Consumer Reports,* Weight Loss Programs Reviews, January 2015, www.consumersearch.com/weight-loss-programs.

Business Model

Revenues for Weight Watchers International, Inc., as shown in Exhibit 2, were principally gained from meeting fees (members paid to attend weekly meetings), product sales (bars, cookbooks, and the like, sold as complements to weight-management plans), online revenues (from Internet subscription products), and revenues gained from licensing (the placement of the Weight Watchers logo on certain foods and other products) and franchising (franchisees typically paid a royalty fee of 10 percent of their meeting fee).[29]

The costs of running meetings were low, with part-time class instructors paid on a commission basis, and many meeting locations were rented hourly in inexpensive local facilities such as churches. This lean organizational structure allowed wide profit margins.[30] Meeting fees were paid up front or at the time of the meeting by attendees, resulting in net negative working capital for Weight Watchers—an indication of cash-flow efficiency.[31]

What was perhaps most important about Weight Watchers' business model was its flexibility. The number of meetings could be adjusted according to demand

	2014	2013	2012	2011	2010	2009
Meeting fees	$ 744.6	$ 851.6	$ 934.9	$ 990.3	$ 819.6	$ 817.5
Product sales	169.1	212.0	253.2	281.8	260.5	251.4
Online revenues	437.4	522.2	504.3	399.5	238.8	196.0
Licensing, franchise royalties, and others	128.9	138.3	147.0	160.9	145.2	147.7
Total	$1,479.9	$1,724.1	$1,839.4	$1,832.5	$1,464.1	$1,412.6

EXHIBIT 2 Weight Watchers' Revenue Sources ($ millions)

Go to library tab in Connect to access Case Financials.

Source: Weight Watchers 10-K filings.

and seasonal fluctuations. The business model's reliance on a variable cost structure had enabled the company to maintain high margins even as the number of meetings over the same time period was expanded. When attendance growth outpaced meeting growth, the gross margins of Weight Watchers typically improved. Since fiscal year 2005, Weight Watchers International had maintained an annual gross margin in the operating segment of 50 percent or more.[32] Weight Watchers' business model yielded high profit margins as a result of the company's low variable expenses and low capital expenditure requirements. By allowing its meetings to be held anywhere, Weight Watchers kept its capital costs low—unlike Jenny Craig, which maintained its own centers with food inventories. This model also allowed Weight Watchers to gain entry into the workplace at wellness-minded companies via its Weight Watchers at Work Program.[33] Exhibits 3 to 5 show financial statements of the firm.

Innovation

Domestically and abroad, Weight Watchers was fortunate enough to build on a foundation of five decades of weight-management expertise that had allowed the company to become one of the most recognized and trusted brand names among weight-conscious consumers worldwide.[34] The innovation initiatives at Weight Watchers were focused on three main objectives: (1) rejuvenating the brand through more effective marketing, (2) providing more customer value by introducing new products, and (3) broadening the customer mix by targeting new customer segments.

The Brand

With regard to its brand, Weight Watchers was fortunate that consumers considered its brand credible and effective. The company needed to more adequately differentiate its lifestyle-based approach from the strictly dieting orientation utilized by many of its competitors. In a focus group for Weight Watchers, a woman who had considered joining expressed concern that her weight would be called out in public and that she would have to tell her whole weight-loss struggle as if she were at an Alcoholics Anonymous meeting. Thus, one of the primary challenges for Weight Watchers was to correct such types of misperceptions as to what Weight Watchers actually was.[35] Weight Watchers had the challenge of dispelling concerns that the meeting experience was something akin to a *Biggest Loser* weigh-in and competition.

The second thing that Weight Watchers was trying to do was to reenergize the brand with more effective and differentiated marketing. Weight Watchers believed that its advertising needed to accomplish three basic tasks. First, it had to be noticed when it was seen. Second, on noticing it, people had to associate the advertising with the Weight Watchers brand. Third, it had to accomplish both the first and the second aims while communicating something new about Weight Watchers that would cause consumers to reconsider Weight Watchers as their *solution*—a plan at which they could be successful.[36] Weight Watchers had to actively emphasize the innovative things that it was doing in order to overcome consumers' preconceived notions. The company needed to show its consumers that its approach was different from the other diets out there to unleash the power that Weight Watchers believed had become a little dormant in its brand. Weight Watchers also had to consider the potential of marketing to relay relevant information that would appeal to a wider net of demographic groups.

The Program

To increase customer value, Weight Watchers had introduced programs that provided members with more flexibility and satisfaction. One innovation was a Monthly Pass payment option. When a member became a Monthly Pass subscriber, he or she participated in an eight-month recurring billing commitment in exchange for complete access to the full range of product offerings. So the underlying benefit was customization—members could utilize the different options as they saw fit in meeting their weight-loss needs. And it seemed to work. People on the Monthly Pass were losing 30 percent more weight since the pass's implementation. Further, there was a higher attendance intensity for Monthly Pass holders than for those who paid per meeting.[37] If a member canceled his Monthly Pass because

EXHIBIT 3 Income Statements ($ thousands)

Go to library tab in Connect to access Case Financials.

	2014	2013	2012	2011	2010
Total revenue	1,479,916	1,724,123	1,839,432	1,832,494	1,452,037
Cost of revenue	677,365	723,011	745,614	773,989	661,407
Gross profit	802,551	1,001,112	1,093,818	1,058,505	790,630
Operating expenses:					
Marketing, Selling, general, and administrative	529,294	540,355	583,013	512,177	400,285
Operating income or loss	273,257	460,757	510,805	546,328	390,345
Income, continuing operations:					
Other income/expenses net	(3,206)	(599)	(1,979)	(3,386)	(963)
Earnings before interest and taxes	216,621	460,158	508,826	542,942	389,382
Interest expense	122,964	103,108	90,537	59,850	76,204
Early debt extinguishment	—	21,685	1,328	—	—
Income before tax	157,607	335,365	416,961	483,092	313,178
Income tax expense	59,014	130,640	159,535	178,748	120,656
Minority interest	—	—	—	523	1,713
Net income	98,647	204,725	257,426	304,867	194,235

EXHIBIT 4 Balance Sheets ($ thousands)

Go to library tab in Connect to access Case Financials.

	2014	2013	2012	2011	2010
Assets					
Current assets:					
Cash and cash equivalents	$ 301,212	$ 174,557	$ 70,215	$ 47,469	$ 40,534
Net receivables	31,960	36,248	37,363	71,787	63,522
Inventory	32,382	40,939	46,846	53,437	40,571
Deferred income taxes	23,744	24,457	21,757	—	—
Other current assets	38,430	39,524	41,786	41,833	45,815
Total current assets	427,728	315,725	217,967	214,526	190,442
Property plant and equipment	74,650	87,052	71,768	41,072	30,930
Franchise rights acquired	799,795	836,835	783,695	—	—
Goodwill	106,820	79,294	62,726	50,012	51,425
Intangible assets	68,115	45,297	52,480	801,487	795,826
Other assets	5,337	2,682	3,400	5,811	9,973
Deferred long-term asset charges	32,742	42,046	26,571	8,720	13,391
Total assets	$1,515,187	$1,408,931	$1,218,607	$1,121,628	$1,091,987

EXHIBIT 4 Continued

	2014	2013	2012	2011	2010
Liabilities					
Current liabilities:					
Accounts payable	$ 54,474	$ 45,496	$ 49,349	$ 217,232	$ 187,388
Short/current long-term debt	24,000	30,000	114,695	149,546	237,277
Salaries & wages payable	64,785	65,810	56,490	—	—
Accrued marketing & advertising	20,540	15,509	27,437	—	—
Accrued interest	22,965	22,776	13,552	—	—
Other current liabilities	124,076	89,899	100,171	127,429	114,470
Deferred revenue	66,190	76,330	86,161	—	—
Total current liabilities	**377,030**	**345,820**	**447,855**	**494,207**	**539,135**
Long-term debt	2,334,000	2,358,000	2,291,669	926,868	1,167,561
Other liabilities	16,883	15,669	15,111	9,596	13,208
Deferred income taxes	171,529	164,064	129,431	100,723	62,807
Monthly interest	—	—	—	—	4,042
Total liabilities	**2,899,442**	**2,883,553**	**2,884,066**	**1,531,394**	**1,786,753**
Stockholders' equity:					
Retained earnings	1,883,349	1,773,267	1,603,513	1,378,616	1,103,817
Treasury stock	(3,253,597)	(3,256,406)	(3,281,831)	(1,793,983)	(1,794,066)
Other comprehensive income	(19,560)	8,517	12,859	5,601	(4,517)
Total Deficit	**(1,389,808)**	**(1,474,622)**	**(1,665,459)**	**(409,766)**	**(694,766)**
Total Liabilities & Deficit	**$1,515,187**	**$1,408,931**	**$1,218,607**	**$1,121,628**	**$1,091,987**

EXHIBIT 5 Cash Flow Statements ($ thousands)

Go to library tab in Connect to access Case Financials.

	2014	2013	2012	2011	2010
Net income	**$98,593**	**$204,725**	**$257,426**	**$304,867**	**$194,235**
Depreciation	49,234	44,904	36,640	30,995	33,671
Amortization deferred financing costs	9,305	7,672	7,070	4,825	—
Impairment of assets	26,709	5,426	—	—	—
Share-based compensation expense	10,533	4,255	8,845	9,067	—
Deferred tax provision	22,182	35,380	26,765	25,291	—
Allowance doubtful accounts	99	596	(1,067)	1,441	—
Reserve inventory obsolescence	11,822	9,580	10,491	13,203	—
Foreign currency rate	(7,592)	659	(722)	(80)	—
Loss disposal of assets	171	1,417	590	500	—

Continued

EXHIBIT 5 *Continued*

	2014	2013	2012	2011	2010
Loss investment	—	—	2,697	3,585	—
Early extinguishment of debt	—	21,685	1,328	—	—
Adjustments to net income	(184)	—	—	105	41,493
Changes in accounts receivables	3,777	345	5,870	(563)	(6,764)
Changes in inventories	(3,218)	(2,226)	(1,341)	(24,456)	(15,490)
Prepaid expenses	(722)	1,037	(639)	2,531	—
Accounts payable	9,870	(3,607)	(11,794)	17,495	—
U.K. self-employment liability	—	(7,272)	(37,441)	2,931	—
Accrued liabilities	10,361	4,988	28,042	2,348	22,225
Deferred revenue	(7,915)	(10,521)	1,539	10,555	—
Income taxes	(1,442)	4,473	2,408	2,922	—
Changes in other operating activities	—	—	—	—	14,027
Total cash flow from operating activities	**231,619**	**323,516**	**336,707**	**407,039**	**281,484**
Investing activities, cash flows provided by/used in:					
Capital expenditures	(9,097)	(40,657)	(48,807)	(21,750)	(9,137)
Capitalized software	(42,589)	(21,277)	(29,926)	(23,086)	—
Cash paid for acquisitions	(16,678)	(83,825)	(30,400)	—	—
Other cash flows from investing activities	(628)	411	(323)	(374)	(19,509)
Total cash flows from investing activities	**(68,992)**	**(145,348)**	**(109,456)**	**(45,210)**	**(28,646)**
Proceeds new term loans	—	2,400,000	1,449,397	—	—
Net borrowings/payments on revolver	—	70,000	30,000	(174,000)	—
Long-term debt paid	(30,000)	(2,488,364)	(124,833)	(139,285)	—
Dividends paid	(80)	(29,571)	(51,961)	(51,624)	(53,409)
Sale/purchase of stock	—	—	(1,504,189)	(34,924)	2,513
Deferred financing costs	—	(44,817)	(26,248)	—	—
Proceeds from stock options exercised	658	16,187	12,688	42,040	—
Tax benefit restricted stock units/options	1	2,132	4,026	5,831	—
Net borrowings	—	—	—	—	(205,916)
Total cash flows from financing activities	**(29,421)**	**(74,433)**	**(211,120)**	**(351,962)**	**(256,812)**
Effect of exchange rate changes	(6,551)	607	885	(13)	(1,629)
Change in cash & cash equivalents	**126,655**	**104,342**	**17,016**	**9,854**	**(5,603)**
Cash & cash equivalents, beginning of fiscal year	**174,557**	**70,215**	**53,199**	**43,345**	**—**
Cash & cash equivalents, end of fiscal year	**$301,212**	**$174,557**	**$70,215**	**$53,199**	**—**

Source: Weight Watchers 10-K filings.

he had reached his goal weight, and then later regained weight, he knew that he could always return to Weight Watchers because the plan had worked in the past.

PointsPlus, introduced at the end of 2010, was a revision of the traditional Points program. The revised program was designed to educate and encourage people to make choices that favored foods the body worked harder to convert into energy, resulting in fewer net calories absorbed. Users were encouraged to focus on foods that created a sense of fullness and satisfaction and were more healthful; they were nudged toward natural foods, rather than foods with excess added sugars and fats, but were allowed flexibility for indulgences, special occasions, and eating out. While calorie counting had been the foundation of many weight-loss programs, including the Weight Watchers original Points system, the new PointsPlus program went beyond just calories to help people make healthful and satisfying choices. It took into account the energy contained in each of the components that made up calories—protein, carbohydrates, fat, and fiber—and it also factored how hard the body worked to process them (conversion cost) as well as their respective eating satisfaction (satiety).[38]

The next program innovation, introduced in December 2012, was the 360-degree plan. This plan built on the PointsPlus program, with members still encouraged to track their food intake with numbers based on the content of protein, fiber, carbohydrates, and fat. In addition, however, the program helped participants make better food-related decisions and did more to incorporate physical activity. For instance, an optional physical activity monitor, called Active Link, could track physical movements. This monitor, costing $40 plus a $5 monthly charge, measured all activity and converted it into PointsPlus values. Also, members were encouraged to use more of the Weight Watchers smartphone apps and website tools during the meetings while participating in hands-on demonstrations such as learning to estimate portion sizes. Other new tips included teaching people to better manage food environments at home, at work, on their travels, or at restaurants. According to Karen Miller-Kovach, chief scientific officer for the company, the emphasis on controlling food in the spaces where people live and work was based on research on "hedonic hunger—the desire to seek out high-sugar, high-fat foods that bring pleasure . . . you have to control your environment to avoid that drive."[39]

The newest program, Weight Watchers Personal Coaching, included on-demand 24/7 Expert Chat with Weight Watchers–certified coaches to "Help with the Hard Part" of managing weight loss. Supporting this program was a new ad campaign that dropped the celebrity spokesperson, formerly Jessica Simpson or Jennifer Hudson, in favor of showing regular people dealing with difficult food choices. The point was "not to pass judgment on anyone eating in an unhealthy way, but rather to demonstrate that Weight Watchers understands that eating can be emotionally charged . . . that at the end of the day, we get it and we're here to help." One former *Biggest Loser* contestant felt that Weight Watchers' new approach could "cause a stir in the category" and agreed that celebrity before-and-after pictures aren't realistic, while using real people shows "what it's really like for the millions with weight issues."[40]

The Customer

Innovation at Weight Watchers also involved broadening the customer mix and targeting new customer segments. Weight Watchers was expanding beyond its target consumer market of women, ages 25 to 55.[41] In an attempt to appeal to other demographic groups, such as men and the Hispanic community in the United States, Weight Watchers retooled its offerings and approach to appear more relevant to weight-loss consumers who sought different methods of weight management.

In terms of the Hispanic community, the company worked to better serve the growing Hispanic population. For example, it improved its Spanish-language meeting materials and increased the number of Spanish meetings offered.[42] Men, another attractive market segment, appeared to be more the self-help type and were not as much in favor of a group-support experience.[43] Weight Watchers meetings had been attended mostly by women, with men making up only 5 percent of members. Morgan Stanley analyst Catherine Lewis said, "Weight Watchers has a pipeline of unpenetrated and underpenetrated markets" and, thus, was testing home weight-loss services for men.[44]

To attract this segment, Weight Watchers Online, the step-by-step online guide to following the Weight Watchers plan, was intentionally customized for men and their unique set of weight-loss challenges.[45] The Weight Watchers Online for Men customization was born of the realization that Weight Watchers needed to be more culturally relevant to more groups of people who wanted different things.[46] For instance, a research study showed that about 70 percent of men were overweight and about 30 percent of men were obese. Yet, according to the study, only 28 percent of men were actively engaged in weight loss. Weight Watchers sought to provide the weight-loss answer for men by applying its 40 years of experience to its customized Internet offerings for men.

While the fundamental concepts of weight loss—eat less and exercise more—were the same for both genders, the approach to weight loss for each gender was different. As Chief Scientific Officer Miller-Kovach noted, "Men and women are biologically and emotionally different, and multiple variables factor into how each loses weight." However, the same underlying motivators for weight loss were shared between the genders: "appearance and health."[47] Thus, while the preferred means might be different, the desired end was the same. Weight Watchers Online for Men allowed men to follow the Weight Watchers plan and get food and fitness ideas, as well as other content and resources, tailored specifically to them. These products afforded Weight Watchers a new opportunity to appeal to a large market segment that might not have otherwise considered giving the program a try.[48] The percentage of men as a percentage of the Weight Watchers total market had been on the rise. Weight Watchers was pleased with the results of the male-focused products and continued working to identify the proper levers for building that part of the business.[49] One of those levers was spokesman–sports legend Charles Barkley, whose humorous approach was intended to appeal to the everyday man.

Questions Remain

Following the onslaught and subsequent demise of fad diets such as the low-carbohydrate-focused Atkins Challenge and South Beach Diet, Weight Watchers had attempted to reinvent itself in several ways. It began to look beyond its core market of women, to include men, and expanded its business model to include not only in-person meetings but also online weight-management tools. Weight Watchers also was transitioning into a business-to-business model by partnering with major health care plans and large self-insured corporations, which offered subsidized Weight Watchers memberships to eligible members and employees. Weight Watchers was actively promoting its larger health message. Colin Watts, senior vice president of health solutions and global innovation, pointed out:

> The *American Journal of Preventive Medicine* indicates that obesity has become an equal, if not greater, contributor to the burden of disease than smoking, and with alarming predictions for 2030, it's more important than ever to provide practical solutions that are not only proven effective, but that are also accessible and scalable.[50]

Weight Watchers intended to be that provider.

The question remains, then: Will Weight Watchers be effective in staying true to the core of Jean Nidetch's goals while still expanding to different target groups, different dieting platforms, and different means of offering them? Only time will tell, but one thing is certain: The weight-loss industry is not going away, and members of Weight Watchers' senior management continue to have many tough decisions to make.

ENDNOTES

1. Weight Watchers. 2015. Weight Watchers advertises during the super bowl for the first time ever; launches "Lose 10 lbs on us" offer. *PRNewswire,* February 2, http://finance.yahoo.com/news/weight-watchers-advertises-during-super-130000381.html.
2. Rupp, L., Coleman-Lochner, L., & Hwang, I. 2015. Weight Watchers tumbles as rebranding fails to wow investors. *BloombergBusiness,* January 2, www.bloomberg.com/news/articles/2015-01-02/weight-watchers-tumbles-as-rebranding-fails-to-impress-investors?cmpid=yhoo.
3. Ingram, S. 2015. There's a reason why Weight Watchers (WTW) stock is falling today. *The Street,* January 2, www.thestreet.com/story/12998430/1/weight-watchers-wtw-stock-is-falling-today-after-magazine-redesign.html?puc=yahoo&cm_ven=YAHOO.
4. Weight Watchers International, Inc. (Weight Watchers). 2012. Form 10-K, 2011 annual report, April 9, www.weightwatchersinternational.com/phoenix.zhtml?c=130178&p=irol-reportsAnnual.
5. Zelman, K. M. Undated. Weight Watchers diet. *WebMD Expert Review.* www.webmd.com/diet/features/weight-watchers-diet.
6. Kosner, A. W. 2012. Weight Watchers 360: Mobile apps can break hard habits with easy-to-follow steps. *Forbes,* December 17, www.forbes.com/sites/anthonykosner/2012/12/17/weight-watchers-360-mobile-apps-can-break-hard-habits-with-easy-to-follow-steps/.
7. Lane, C. 2013. Weight Watchers: 50 years of losing. *TimesUnion,* January 11, www.timesunion.com/living/article/Weight-Watchers-50-years-of-losing-4187277.php#page-1.
8. Ibid.
9. DePillis, L. 2013. Internet killed the dieting star: Why Weight Watchers is floundering. *Washington Post,* August 4, www.washingtonpost.com/blogs/wonkblog/wp/2013/08/04/internet-killed-the-dieting-star-why-weight-watchers-is-floundering/.
10. Berr, J. 2014. The flabby business of shrinking waistlines. *The Fiscal Times,* February 3, www.thefiscaltimes.com/Articles/2014/02/03/Weight-Watchers-and-Flabby-Business-Shrinking-Waistlines.
11. Weight Watchers. 2011. Form 10-K, 2010 annual report.
12. Ibid.
13. Nidetch, J. T., & Rattner, J. 1979. *The story of Weight Watchers.* New York: Penguin.
14. Weight Watchers. 2010. Weight Watchers introduces revolutionary new program to help Americans improve their eating habits and successfully lose weight. November 29, www.weightwatchersinternational.com/phoenix.zhtml?c=30178&p=irol-newsArticle&ID=1500758.
15. Weight Watchers. 2011. Form 10-K, 2010 annual report.
16. Ibid.
17. Let the countdown to soup begin! 2007. *Business Wire,* August 14.
18. Perrenot, G., & Durnan, K. 2005. Lunch ladies: Applebee's Weight Watchers menu. *Dallas Morning News,* April 11.
19. Dolan, B. 2014. Weight Watchers confirms Wello acquisition, plans API-enabled fitness platform. *MobileHealthNews,* May 6, http://mobihealthnews.com/32838/weight-watchers-confirms-wello-acquisition-plans-api-enabled-fitness-platform/.
20. Weight Watchers. 2015. 2015 marks the fifth consecutive year Weight Watchers is ranked "Best Weight-Loss Diet" by *U.S. News & World Report.* PRNewswire, January 6, www.weightwatchersinternational.com/phoenix.zhtml?c=130178&p=irol-newsArticle&ID=2003574.
21. Williams, G. 2011. Made in the USA: The weight-loss industry makes huge gains. *AOL Small Business,* February 16, smallbusiness.aol.com/2011/02/16/made-in-the-usa-the-weight-loss-industry-makes-huge-gains/.
22. Hill, C. 2014. 10 things the weight-loss industry won't tell you. *MarketWatch,* January 14, www.marketwatch.com/story/10-things-the-weight-loss-industry-wont-tell-you-2014-01-10?page=7.
23. Ibid.
24. Weight Watchers. 2010. Tackling the growing obesity epidemic: New research shows Weight Watchers works globally. July 13, www.weightwatchersinternational.com/phoenix.zhtml?c=130178&p=irol-newsArticle&ID=1446897.
25. Weight Watchers. 2011. Form 10-K, 2010 annual report.
26. Lee, J. 2010. Diet plan review: Best ways to lose 20 pounds. *MoneyWatch,* January 4, moneywatch.bnet.com/saving-money/article/diet-plan-review-best-ways-to-lose-weight/377880/.
27. Salahi, L. 2012. Study: Weight Watchers as successful as clinical weight-loss programs. *ABC News,* October 9, abcnews.go.com/Health/w_DietAndFitness/study-weight-watchers-successful-clinical-weight-loss-programs/story?id=17424647#.UOeEE6zNl8E.
28. MacMillan, A. 2012. Dieters in Weight Watchers study drop up to 15 pounds in a year. *Health.com,* January 4, www.cnn.com/2011/09/07/health/weight-watchers-lancet/index.html.
29. Weight Watchers. Form 10-K, annual reports.
30. Florian, E. 2002. When it comes to fat, they're huge. *Fortune,* October 14: 54.
31. Choe. 2004. Weight Watchers' attractive figures.

32. Weight Watchers. Form 10-K, annual reports.
33. Serafin. 2006. The fat of the land.
34. Weight Watchers. Form 10-K, annual reports.
35. Weight Watchers. 2007. Event brief of Q2 2007 Weight Watchers International, Inc. earnings conference call—final.
36. Weight Watchers. 2007. Event brief of Q1 2007 Weight Watchers International, Inc. earnings conference call.
37. Ibid.
38. Weight Watchers. 2010. Weight Watchers introduces revolutionary new program to help Americans improve their eating habits and successfully lose weight. November 29, *www.weightwatchersinternational.com/phoenix.zhtml?c=130178&p=irol-newsArticle&ID=1500758*.
39. Hellmich, N. 2012. New Weight Watchers 360 plan unveiled. *USA Today*, December 2, *www.usatoday.com/story/news/nation/2012/12/02/weight-watchers-new-program/1732297/*.
40. Newman, A. A. 2014. Weight Watchers serving up understanding to those who eat their feelings. *New York Times*, November 24, *www.nytimes.com/2014/11/25/business/media/weight-watchers-serving-up-understanding-to-those-who-eat-their-feelings.html?_r=0*.
41. Sunoo, B. P. 1997. Changing behavior at Weight Watchers. *Workforce*, July: 27–29.
42. Weight Watchers. 2006. Event brief of Q4 2006 Weight Watchers International, Inc. earnings conference call.
43. Ibid.
44. Marcial, G. G. 2002. Hefty gains for Weight Watchers? *BusinessWeek*, October 21: 168.
45. Weight Watchers. 2007. Weight loss: Announcing the launch of Weight Watchers Online for Men and Weight Watchers eTools for Men. *Women's Health Law Weekly*, April 22: 251.
46. Weight Watchers. Form 10-K, annual reports.
47. Weight Watchers. 2007. Weight loss: Announcing the launch of Weight Watchers Online for Men.
48. Weight Watchers. 2007. Event brief of Q1 2007 Weight Watchers International, Inc. earnings conference call—final. *Fair Disclosure Wire*, May 3.
49. Weight Watchers. 2007. Event brief of Q2 2007 Weight Watchers International, Inc. earnings conference call—final. *Fair Disclosure Wire*, August 1.
50. Weight Watchers. 2012. Weight Watchers and WellCare join forces to support better health for Georgians. *PRNewswire*, December 6, *www.weightwatchersinternational.com/phoenix.zhtml?c=130178&p=irol-newsArticle&ID=1765083&highlight=*.

CASES

CASE 8

DIPPIN' DOTS: IS THE FUTURE FROZEN?*

The year 2015 presented challenges and opportunities for Dippin' Dots, the "Ice Cream of the Future." Despite the introduction of innovative new products, record-setting promotional events, and enticing franchise expansion opportunities, the future of the company remained uncertain. When the company was bailed out of bankruptcy in 2012, there seemed to be a lot of potential to grow Dippin' Dots. The vision and creativity of the company founder and CEO, Curt Jones, appeared to be supplemented perfectly by the business acumen and experience of its president, Scott Fischer.[1] However, the number of Dippin' Dots U.S. franchises was not growing steadily, and the number of international franchises remained stagnant.

A year earlier, Dippin' Dots had decided to celebrate the 30th anniversary of National Ice Cream Month[†] by attempting to set a new world record in the world of ice cream. On July 4, 2014, Dippin' Dots, the maker of the iconic flash-frozen ice cream and frozen treats, achieved a Guinness World Records title for the number of ice cream cups prepared by a team of five in three minutes. Curt Jones, Dippin' Dots founder and CEO, was part of the record-setting team. "Our record attempt was a fun and unique way to commemorate the 30th anniversary of National Ice Cream Month," said Jones.

In 2014, the company also launched the Monster Munch, Kettle Corn Dippin' Dots, and Dinner Dots ice cream lines. The Monster Munch line included eight monster-themed flavors with what the company called "crazy names and crazy ingredients," while the Dinner Dots line included dot-size portions of five savory meals.

In addition, the company promoted the low cost of entry and flexibility of its franchising options. In an interview with *CNN Money* in 2013, Steve Rothenstein, Dippin' Dots' director of franchising, said the company had a lot of opportunities to suit a variety of business models. With a franchise start-up fee of only $15,000, the company offered an economic option for budding entrepreneurs. Dippin' Dots also was flexible with alternate delivery models in addition to its more traditional brick-and-mortar locations. These included kiosks at malls and carts at community events (e.g., fairs and festivals).

What remained to be seen was whether these fixes would have a lasting impact on reversing the softness in company revenues and give the financials a much needed boost. Were these enhancements to the product portfolio, promotions, and business expansion efforts clever ways of growing the business? Or were they merely a last-ditch effort before it was rendered obsolete?

Company Overview

Dippin' Dots had produced and distributed its flash-frozen tiny beads of ice cream, yogurt, sherbet, and flavored-ice products since microbiologist Curt Jones invented the cryogenic process in 1988. Made at the company's production facility in Paducah, Kentucky, Dippin' Dots' unique frozen products were distributed in all 50 states and 11 countries, and the company employed nearly 200 people.

In May 2012, Dippin' Dots LLC, a newly formed company based in Oklahoma and funded by private capital, acquired the Paducah, Kentucky–based Dippin' Dots Inc. A motion to approve the proposed sale was filed in April 2012 in the U.S. Bankruptcy Court in Louisville, Kentucky. In November 2011, Dippin' Dots Inc. had filed for Chapter 11 bankruptcy protection in federal court in Kentucky, due to a combination of reasons, including owing millions to lenders from costly patent litigation, as well as having increased operating costs and plummeting sales. In the bankruptcy filing, the company listed about $20.2 million in assets and more than $12 million in liabilities.[2] The acquisition was approved shortly after, in May of the same year.

Dippin' Dots employed approximately 165 workers at its facility in Paducah, Kentucky, and Scott Fischer, president of Dippin' Dots LLC, had no particular plan to move the facility or let go of any existing employees. Dippin' Dots LLC was unaffiliated with the existing Dippin' Dots Inc. entity. Fischer said:

> We are looking forward to working with the Dippin' Dots management team and employees to maximize the opportunity of the business and realize the company's growth potential in a global market. We are committed to ensuring that Dippin' Dots reclaims its status, not as a novelty of the past, but as the ice cream of the future. This transaction has become a very equitable solution to the parties involved, and we expect a very smooth transition.[3]

---

* This case was prepared by Professor Alan B. Eisner of Pace University and graduate student Brian R. Callahan of Pace University as a basis for class discussion rather than to illustrate either effective or ineffective handling of an administrative situation. Copyright © 2015 Alan B. Eisner.

† July was designated National Ice Cream Month by the U.S. government in 1984.

Fischer took the opportunity to acquire Dippin' Dots Inc. in order to rescue the frozen novelty and keep it afloat. Fischer added:

> We are looking forward to rolling up our sleeves and personally meeting with all of the employees, franchisees, and business associates of the company and moving forward in a very stable and productive manner. We see substantial value in the Dippin' Dots brand, one of the most well-known brand names in the retail market.[4]

Showing their enthusiasm for growth, in January 2013 Fischer and the new executive team decided to invest over $3.1 million in the company's home facility in Kentucky, expanding operations and creating 30 new full-time jobs. Prior to the expansion, Dippin' Dots employed 170 workers, 60 of whom lived in the Paducah area. Fischer stated, "This investment underscores our long-term commitment to market the wonderful Dippin' Dots brand, introduce new products to complement existing ones, and maintain the historic ties to Kentucky."[5] Other improvements were to include purchasing energy-efficient equipment, upgrading processes, and renovating the facility. Dippin' Dots products, all of which were manufactured in Paducah, were distributed in 50 states and 11 countries. Available in many tastes and types—such as Original Dots, Dots 'n Cream, Coffee, and Dot Treats—Dippin' Dots' innovative take on frozen food had changed the public's way of looking at ice cream.

Yet despite its unique twist on the classic frozen novelty, prior to the acquisition Dippin' Dots had been encountering abysmal revenues and having trouble maintaining attention in the market. Feeling the pressure, the company looked to innovative new products, promotions, and business-expansion efforts as the hope for a turnaround.

In 2014, it launched the Monster Munch ice cream line. The line featured "crazy flavors, crazy names and some crazy ingredients." Earlier, Dippin' Dots had expanded its product line from ice creams to uniquely brewed coffees. Founder Curt Jones took a colder-than-cold instant-freezing process, similar to the one that made Dippin' Dots ice creams so delectable, and redirected that technology to fresh-brewed coffee. Just as he had dubbed Dippin' Dots the "Ice Cream of the Future" two decades earlier, he said the new "coffee dots" would adopt the slogan "Coffee of the Future." Real espresso was made from fresh, high-quality arabica beans and then flash-frozen into dots immediately, capturing the flavor and aroma. Named "Forty Below Joe edible coffee," the coffee dots could be eaten with a spoon, heated with water and milk to make a hot "fresh-brewed" coffee without brewing, or blended with Frappé beads to make a Dippin' Dots Frappé. Jones's once-kid-targeted dots now had a very adult twist.

However, Jones was also thinking about more kid-friendly treats. For years he had been thinking of coming out with low-calorie, low-fat Dippin' Dots that could meet the nutrition requirements and regulations set by public schools and thus be sold at the schools. The result was "Chillz," a lower-calorie alternative to ice cream. Dippin' Dots Chillz was a low-fat frozen-beaded dessert made with Truvia, an all-natural sweetener. This healthier alternative to ice cream was also an excellent source of vitamin C and was available in three flavors: Sour Blue Razz, Wango Rainbo, and Chocolate.[6] In the words of Dippin' Dots' vice president of sales, Michael Barrette:

> We're starting to distribute Chillz through the vending channel. We already have two contracts underway and expect to get more. Vending companies know and love the Dippin' Dots brand. With Chillz and other products, it's a great opportunity for them. Schools need that revenue. They've thrown out a lot of products in recent times that have no nutritional value. So we feel bullish about Chillz.[7]

An Innovative Product

The company's chief operation was the sale of BB-size pellets of flash-frozen ice cream in some two-dozen flavors to franchisees and national accounts throughout the world. As a Six Flags customer commented, "I gotta say, man, they're pretty darn good. . . . Starts off like a rock candy but ends up like ice cream."[8]

Dippin' Dots was the marriage between old-fashioned handmade ice cream and space-age technology. Dippin' Dots were tiny round beads of ice cream that were made at super-cold temperatures, served at subzero temperatures in a soufflé cup, and eaten with a spoon. The super-cold freezing of Dippin' Dots ice cream, done by liquid nitrogen, cryogenically locked in both flavor and freshness in a way that no other manufactured ice cream could offer. The process virtually eliminated the presence of trapped ice and air, giving the ice cream a fresh flavor and a hard texture. Not only had Jones discovered a new way of making ice cream, but many felt his product proved to be much more flavorful and richer than regular ice cream. According to Jones, "I created a way . . . [to] get a quicker freeze so the ice cream wouldn't get large ice crystals. . . . About six months later, I decided to quit my job and go into business."

Jones was a microbiologist by trade, with an area of expertise in cryogenics. His first job was researching and engineering as a microbiologist for ALLtech Inc., a bioengineering company based in Lexington, Kentucky. During his days at ALLtech, Jones worked with different types of bacteria to find new ways of preserving them so that they could be transported throughout the world. He applied a method of freezing using super-cold temperatures with substances such as liquid CO_2 and liquid nitrogen—the same method he later used to create Dippin' Dots.

One process Jones developed was "microencapsulating" the bacteria by freezing their medium with liquid nitrogen. Other scientists thought he was crazy, because nothing like that had ever been done before. Jones, however, was convinced his idea would work. He spent months trying to perfect the process and continued to make progress. While

Jones was working over 80 hours a week in ALLtech's labs to perfect the microencapsulating process, he made the most influential decision of his life. He took a weekend off and attended a family barbeque at his parents' house. It just so happened that his mother was making ice cream the day of the barbeque. Jones began to reminisce about homemade ice cream prepared the slow, old-fashioned way. Then Jones wondered if it was possible to flash-freeze ice cream. Instead of using a bacteria medium, was it possible to microencapsulate ice cream?

The answer was yes. After virtually reinventing a frozen dessert that had been around since the second century BC,[9] Jones patented his idea to flash-freeze liquid cream, and he opened the first Dippin' Dots store.[10] Once franchising was offered in 2000, the "Ice Cream of the Future" could be found at thousands of shopping malls, amusement parks, water parks, fairs, and festivals worldwide. Dippin' Dots ice cream was transported coast to coast and around the world by truck, train, plane, and ship. In addition to being transported in specially designed cryogenic transport containers, the product was transported in refrigerated boxes known as pallet reefers. Both types of containers ensured fast and efficient delivery to franchisees around the world. The product was served in 4-, 5-, and 8-ounce cups and in 5-ounce vending prepacks.

Product Specifics

Dippin' Dots were flash-frozen beads of ice cream typically served in a cup or vending package. The ice cream averaged 90 calories per serving, depending on the flavor, and had 9 grams of fat. The ice cream was produced by a patented process that introduced flavored liquid cream into a vat of 2,325-degree liquid nitrogen, where it was flash-frozen to produce the bead or dot shape. Once frozen, the dots were collected and either mixed with other flavors or packaged separately for delivery to retail locations. The product had to be stored at subzero temperatures to maintain the consistency of the dots. Subzero storage temperatures were achieved by utilizing special equipment and freezers supplemented with dry ice. Although storage was a challenge for international shipping, the beads could maintain their shape for up to 15 days in their special containers. To maintain product integrity and consistency, the ice cream had to be served at 10 to 20 degrees below zero. A retail location had to have special storage and serving freezers. Because the product had to be stored and served at such low temperatures, it was unavailable in regular frozen-food cases and could not be stored in a typical household freezer. Therefore, it could be consumed only at or near a retail location, unless stored with dry ice to maintain the necessary storage temperature.

Industry Overview

The frozen dairy industry has traditionally been occupied by family-owned businesses such as Dippin' Dots, full-line dairies, and a couple of large international companies that focused on only a single sales region. The year 2015 was a relatively flat year for the production and sale of ice cream, as volume in traditional varieties remained flat and new types of ice cream emerged. Despite higher ingredient costs, manufacturers were continually churning out new products, though at a slower rate than in the previous year. These ranged from super-premium selections to good-for-you varieties to cobranded packages and novelties. Most novelty ice creams could be found together in supermarket freezer cases, in small freezers in convenience stores, and in carts, kiosks, or trucks at popular summertime events. Ice cream makers had been touched by consolidation trends affecting the overall food and beverage industry that extended beyond their products, as even the big names were folded into global conglomerates.

The ice cream segment in the United States had become a battleground for two huge international consumer-product companies seeking to corner the ice cream market. Those two industry giants were Nestlé SA of Switzerland, the world's largest food company, with more than $101 billion in annual sales, and Unilever PLC of London and Rotterdam, with over $71 billion in annual revenues.[11] Both had been buying into U.S. firms for quite a while, but Nestlé, which already owned the Häagen-Dazs product line, upped the ante with its June 2003 merger with Dreyer's Grand/Edy's Ice Cream Inc. of Oakland, California. But even as the two giants dominated the U.S. ice cream industry, about 500 small businesses continued to produce and distribute frozen treats. As one commentator said, "Like microbrewers and small-scale chocolate makers, entrepreneurs are drawn to ice cream as a labor of love."[12] Some of the better-known brands were regional ones, such as Blue Bell, based in Brenham, Texas (see Exhibit 1).

Approximately $10 billion was spent on ice cream in recent years,[13] and ice cream and related frozen desserts were consumed by more than 90 percent of households in the United States.[14] Consumers spent $8.9 billion on products for at-home consumption, while $13.9 billion went toward away-from-home purchases. Harry Balzar, of the market research firm NPD Group, said about ice cream in general, "It's not a small category, but one that has remained flat for more than a decade, and is not likely to grow."[15] The challenge for producers was to woo customers away from competitors and sustain a loyal fan base by continuing to innovate. The trend toward more healthy treats had spurred the major players, Nestlé and Unilever, to develop reduced-fat product lines that still had the taste and texture of full-fat ice cream. Edy's/Dreyer's, Breyers, and Häagen-Dazs had all continued to experiment, and the "slow churned," "double-churn," and "light" products were seeing increased sales since their introduction in 2004.[16]

In October 2002 it was announced that Good Humor–Breyers Ice Cream of Green Bay, Wisconsin, and Ben & Jerry's of Vermont had formed a unified retail sales division named Unilever Ice Cream. The new organization brought together both companies and represented the five Unilever North American ice cream brands, which

EXHIBIT 1 Top 10 Ice Cream Brands, 2014

Brand	Sales in million U.S. dollars
Private label	1,103.41
Blue Bell	628.19
Ben & Jerry's	488.92
Häagen-Dazs	424.99
Breyers	374.15
Dreyer's Edy's Slow Churned	282.05
Dreyer's Edy's Grand	262.97
Wells Blue Bunny	217.73
Turkey Hill	211.74
Talenti	132.49

included Ben & Jerry's, Breyers, Good Humor, Popsicle, and Klondike. Good Humor–Breyers had created several new cobranded novelties specifically for convenience-store and vending locations. The company had also set out to expand the availability of single-serve novelties by placing freezers of its products in Blockbuster video stores and Breyers-branded kiosks in 30 Chicago-area Loews theaters. In addition to prepackaged products, freshly scooped ice cream was served at the kiosks. The new sales team would focus solely on the out-of-home ice cream business and, therefore, exclude grocery channels.

Another novelty product delivery system in the independent scoop shop was the "slab" concept. Employees at franchises such as Marble Slab Creamery and Cold Stone Creamery worked ingredients on a cold granite or marble slab to blend premium ice cream with the customer's choice of tasty additives, such as crumbled cookies, fruits, and nuts, before serving it in a cup or cone. The novelty was the entertainment of watching the preparation. Both chains ranked in *Entrepreneur* magazine's list of the top 500 franchise opportunities, but commentators were skeptical of their sustainability once the novelty wore off, especially since the average price was $5 for a medium serving.[17] As of 2015, both Cold Stone Creamery and Marble Slab Creamery were able to maintain spots in *Entrepreneur's* list of the top 500 franchises, ranked in the 54th and 261st positions, respectively.[18]

Industry Segmentation

Frozen desserts come in many forms. Each of the following foods has its own definition, and many are standardized by federal regulations.[19]

- **Ice cream** consists of a mixture of dairy ingredients, such as cream, milk, and nonfat milk, and ingredients for sweetening and flavoring, such as fruits, nuts, and chocolate chips. Functional ingredients, such as stabilizers and emulsifiers, are often included in the product to promote proper texture and enhance the eating experience. By federal law, ice cream must contain at least 10 percent butterfat before the addition of bulky ingredients, and it must weigh a minimum of 4.5 pounds to the gallon.
- **Novelties** are separately packaged single servings of a frozen dessert, such as ice cream sandwiches, fudge sticks, and juice bars, which may or may not contain dairy ingredients.
- **Frozen custard** or **french ice cream** must also contain a minimum of 10 percent butterfat as well as at least 1.4 percent egg yolk solids.
- **Sherbets** have a butterfat content of between 1 and 2 percent and have a slightly higher sweetener content than ice cream. Sherbet weighs a minimum of 6 pounds to the gallon and is flavored with either fruit or other characterizing ingredients.
- **Gelato** is characterized by an intense flavor and is served in a semifrozen state. Gelato contains sweeteners, milk, cream, egg yolks, and flavoring.
- **Sorbet** and **water ices** are similar to sherbets, but they contain no dairy ingredients.
- A **quiescently frozen confection** is a frozen novelty such as a water-ice novelty on a stick.

- **Frozen yogurt** consists of a mixture of dairy ingredients, such as milk and nonfat milk, that have been cultured, as well as ingredients for sweetening and flavoring.

Dippin' Dots' Growth[20]

The growth of Dippin' Dots Inc. was recognized in the United States and the world by industry watchdogs such as *Inc.* magazine, which ranked Dippin' Dots as one of the 500 fastest-growing companies two years in a row, 1996 and 1997. Dippin' Dots Franchising Inc. ranked number 4 on *Entrepreneur* magazine's 2004 list of the top 50 new franchise companies, and it achieved the 101st spot on *Entrepreneur*'s Franchise 500 for 2004. In 2005 Dippin' Dots ranked number 2 as a top new franchise opportunity and climbed to number 93 on the Franchise 500 list. By the end of 2009, Dippin' Dots had slid to the 175th position on *Entrepreneur*'s Franchise 500 list.[21] And by 2015 Dippin' Dots had fallen off the list. Exhibit 2 shows the growth of franchises for Dippin' Dots, and Exhibit 3 explains key corporate milestones.

Despite the company's initial success, the achievements of Curt Jones and Dippin' Dots had not come without obstacles. Once Jones had perfected his idea, he needed to start a company for the new process of flash-freezing ice cream. Like many new entrepreneurs, Jones enlisted the help of his family to support his endeavor. It was essential to start selling his product, but he had no protection for his idea from competitors.

The first obstacle confronting Jones was the need to locate funding to accomplish his goals. He needed money for the patent to protect his intellectual property, and he needed seed money to start manufacturing the ice cream once the patent was granted. At the same time that Jones was perfecting the flash-freezing process for his ice cream, he was also working on a Small Business Administration (SBA) loan to convert the family farm into one that would manufacture ethanol. However, instead of using the farm to produce the alternative fuel, Jones's parents took out a first, and then a second, mortgage to help fund Jones's endeavor. Thus, Jones initiated the entire venture by self-funding his company with personal and family assets.

Unfortunately, the money from Jones's parents was enough to pay for only the patent and some crude manufacturing facilities (a liquid nitrogen tank in his parents' garage). He next had to open a store, and doing so required even more money—money that Jones and his family did not have. They were unable to get the SBA loan because, while the product was novel and looked promising, there was no proof that it would sell. So Jones and his newly appointed CFO (his sister) went to an alternative lender who lent them cash at an exorbitant interest rate that was tacked on to the principal weekly if unpaid.

Now in possession of the seed money they needed, Jones and his family opened their first store. Its summertime opening created a buzz in the community. The store was mobbed every night, and Dippin' Dots was legitimized by public demand. With the influx of cash, Jones was able to move his manufacturing operation from his family's garage into a vacant warehouse. There he set up shop and personally made flash-frozen ice cream for 12 hours every day to supply the store.

After the store had been operating for a few months, the Joneses were able to secure small business loans from local banks to cover the expenses of a modest manufacturing plant and office. At the same time, Jones's sister made calls to fairs and other events to learn whether Dippin' Dots products could be sold at them. Luckily for the Joneses, the amusement park at Opryland in Nashville, Tennessee, was willing to have Dippin' Dots as a vendor. Unfortunately, the first Dippin' Dots stand was placed in front of a roller coaster, and people generally did not want ice cream before they went on a ride. After a few unsuccessful weeks, Jones moved the stand and business picked up considerably. Eventually, the Joneses were able to move to an inline location, which was similar to a store, where Dippin' Dots had its own personnel and sitting area to serve customers.

Through word of mouth, interest in Curt Jones and Dippin' Dots spread. Soon other entrepreneurs contacted Jones about opening up stores to sell Dippin' Dots. A dealership network was developed to sell ice cream to authorized vendors and provide support with equipment and marketing. During that time, Jones employed friends in corporate jobs. Dippin' Dots grew into a multimillion-dollar company with authorized dealers operating in all 50 states and internationally.

A franchise location was any mall, fair, national account, or large family entertainment center. According to the franchising information in 2015, the initial franchise fee was $15,000, with an estimated initial investment ranging from $119,704 to $366,950. The result was a cash

EXHIBIT 2 Dippin' Dots Franchise Growth

Year	U.S. Franchises	Canadian Franchises	Foreign Franchises	Company Owned
2014	116	1	13	1
2013	112	1	13	1
2012	114	1	13	1

Source: *www.entrepreneur.com* and author estimates.

EXHIBIT 3 Dippin' Dots Milestones

Year	Milestone
1988	Dippin' Dots is established as a company in Grand Chain, Illinois.
1989	First amusement park account debuts at Opryland USA in Nashville.
1990	Production facility moves to Paducah, Kentucky.
1991	Dealer network is established for fair, festival, and commercial retail locations.
1994	First international licensee is set up (Japan).
1995	New 32,000-square-foot production facility opens in Paducah.
1997	Production facility expands by 20,000 square feet; company earns spot on *Inc.* 500 list of fastest-growing private companies in the United States.
2000	Dippin' Dots Franchising Inc. is established, and first franchise is offered; litigation against competitors is initiated to protect patent.
2001	Dippin' Dots enlists 30 new franchisees. *Franchise Times* magazine lists Dippin' Dots third in the United States in number of ice cream franchise locations, behind Baskin-Robbins and Dairy Queen.
2002	Dippin' Dots Franchising Inc. achieves 112th spot on *Entrepreneur* magazine's Franchise 500 list, ranks 69th on its list of the fastest-growing franchise companies, and is named the number 1 new franchise company. Dippin' Dots becomes a regular menu offering at McDonald's restaurants in the San Francisco Bay Area.
2003	Dippin' Dots Franchising Inc. achieves 144th spot on *Entrepreneur* magazine's Franchise 500 list and number 4 on *Entrepreneur*'s list of the top 50 new franchise companies. Dippin' Dots opens the Ansong manufacturing plant, 80 miles south of Seoul, South Korea.
2004	Dippin' Dots Franchising Inc. ranks number 4 on *Entrepreneur*'s Top 50 New Franchise Companies list and achieves 101st spot on *Entrepreneur* magazine's Franchise 500 list. Curt Jones and Dippin' Dots are featured on a segment of the *Oprah Winfrey Show,* appearing in 110 countries. Dippin' Dots is featured among the top 10 ice cream palaces on the Travel Channel. Curt Jones is quoted in Donald Trump's best-selling *The Way to the Top* (p. 131).
2005	International Dairy Foods Association names Dippin' Dots Best in Show for Dot Delicacies. Dippin' Dots also wins three awards for package design. Dippin' Dots Franchising Inc. ranks number 1 on *Franchise Times* magazine's Fast 55 list of the fastest-growing young franchises in the nation. Ice cream cake and ice cream sandwiches (Dotwiches) are introduced to launch the Dot Delicacies program.
2006	Company leadership is restructured. Curt Jones becomes chairman of the board. Tom Leonard becomes president of Dippin' Dots Inc. Dots 'n Cream, conventional ice cream enhanced by beads of Dippin' Dots, is introduced for market testing in Kroger stores in the Midwest. The 200th franchisee begins operations.
2007	Dippin' Dots is available in Colombia, and *www.dippindots.com* V.5 is launched.
2008	Dippin' Dots Franchising Inc. ranks 112th on *Entrepreneur*'s Franchise 500 list.
2009	Curt Jones returns to running the day-to-day operations of the firm. Dippin' Dots slides to 175th on *Entrepreneur*'s Franchise 500 list.
2010	Dippin' Dots has 3 million Facebook fans.
2011	On November 4, 2011, Dippin' Dots files for chapter 11 bankruptcy.
2012	On May 18, 2012, the purchase of Dippin' Dots by Scott Fischer, president of Dippin' Dots LLC, is approved by U.S. Bankruptcy Court; Scott Fischer joins the team as president.
2013	Dippin' Dots begins distribution to pharmacies and convenience stores to increase access.
2014	Dippin' Dots enters *Guinness World Records* book for producing the largest number of ice cream cups with a team of five in 3 minutes.

Source: Dippin' Dots Inc. Undated. History. *www.dippindots.com/more-info/history.html.*

inflow for Dippin' Dots franchising. In addition, franchisees were required to pay a variable royalty fee.

The Ice Cream of the Future

Dippin' Dots was counting on youthful exuberance to expand growth. "Our core demographic was pretty much 8- to 18-year-olds," said Terry Reeves, former corporate communications director. "On top of that, we're starting to see a generation of parents who grew up on Dippin' Dots and are starting to introduce the products to their kids." Although Dippin' Dots seemed to appeal more to youngsters, the product still had to have staying power as customers grew older. As one individual commented, "How can this stuff keep continuing to call itself the 'ice cream of the future'? Well the future is now, folks, and they have been pushing this sorry excuse for ice cream off on me at amusement parks and zoos since I was a little kid."[22]

In 2002 McDonald's reportedly spent $1.2 million on advertising to roll out Dippin' Dots in about 250 restaurants in the San Francisco area. Jones called the deal "open-ended" if it worked favorably for both firms. However, by 2007 Dippin' Dots was available only at a few McDonald's franchises in southern California. Storage and transportation issues were problematic, and the price of the product, 5 ounces for $5, was too steep for all but the die-hard Dippin' Dots fans.

In other marketing efforts, Dippin' Dots ads were running in issues of *Seventeen* and *Nickelodeon* magazines. Additionally, Dippin' Dots hired a Hollywood firm to place its ice cream in the background of television and movie scenes, including the 2003 *Cheaper by the Dozen*. In 2002 the Food Network's *Summer Foods: Unwrapped* showcased Dippin' Dots as one of the most unique and coolest ice cream treats. 'N Sync member Joey Fatone ordered a Dippin' Dots freezer for his home after seeing a Dots vending machine at a theater the band rented in Orlando. Caterers also sought Dippin' Dots for their star clients. A birthday party at the home of NBA star Shaquille O'Neal featured Dippin' Dots ice cream. Dippin' Dots also continued to pursue the celebrity word-of-mouth route by serving its products at events such as the MTV awards and celebrity charity functions.

Dippin' Dots' sales came from approximately 131 franchisees, 90 percent of which had multiple locations.[23]

Dippin' Dots had met increased competition in the out-of-home ice cream market. The major threats to Dippin' Dots were other franchise operations, such as Ben & Jerry's, Häagen-Dazs, Baskin-Robbins, Carvel, Dairy Queen, and newcomers such as Cold Stone Creamery, Maggie Moo's, and Marble Slab Creamery (see Exhibit 4).

Although one dealer commented that Dippin' Dots used incoming franchise fees from royalties on sales for its own corporate means rather than for improvements in franchise support, most dealers did convert to the new franchise system. Dippin' Dots Franchising Inc. grandfathered existing dealers' locations by issuing a franchise and waiving the franchise fee for the first contract period of five years. Many dealers had to renew their contracts in 2004; while many were initially apprehensive of converting to a franchised system, less than 2 percent left the system, and the firm showed franchise growth.

Meltdown?

In an attempt to counteract the copycat threats from Frosty Bites and Mini Melts, Dippin' Dots brought a patent infringement lawsuit against them in 2005. However, during the jury trial, Dippin' Dots' testimony in support of the original patent revealed that Jones had made sales of the beaded ice cream product to over 800 customers more than a year before submitting the patent application. Even though Jones argued that these sales were for the purpose of market testing and that the production method had subsequently been further refined, and therefore deserving of a patented process, the court rendered the patent nonenforceable because these sales were not disclosed to the Patent Office. An appeal by Dippin' Dots was denied in 2007, and the patent was declared invalid.[24]

Mini Melts, released from the lawsuit, continued to expand its manufacturing facilities throughout the world; it had plants in South Korea, the Philippines, the United Arab Emirates, Hong Kong, and China as well as the United Kingdom and the United States. Instead of having franchises, Mini Melts sold dealerships for vending machines and kiosks carrying its products. Mini Melts CEO Tom Mosey was nominated by Ernst and Young as Entrepreneur of the Year and was listed in the *Inc. 500* for two separate ventures over the years.

By 2009 Dippin' Dots had billed itself as the "Ice Cream of the Future" for over 20 years. However, Dippin' Dots was close to a meltdown. Founder Curt Jones said that Dippin' Dots "just got hit by a perfect storm" of soaring operating costs and plummeting sales. Jones then resumed daily control over the troubled Dippin' Dots after a three-year break from operations. He let go of President Tom Leonard, who had run Samsonite before joining Dippin' Dots in August 2006, and Operations Vice President Dominic Fontana, who had spent about 17 years with Häagen-Dazs. Jones described the separations as amicable and regrettable.

In spite of these challenges, Jones, always the inventor, was investing in R&D to create a conventional ice cream product that had super-frozen dots embedded in it. He was developing a new product that could withstand conventional freezers while preserving the super-frozen dots in the ice cream. Called Dots 'n Cream and available in berry crème, caramel cappuccino, mint chocolate, orange crème de la crème, vanilla bean, vanilla over the rainbow, wild about chocolate, and banana split, this product was introduced for market testing in Kroger stores in the Midwest in 2006. Thus, Dippin' Dots was finally on the verge of having a take-home ice cream option. As of April 2011, the Dots 'n Cream product was still available only in a few locations and could be bought online.

EXHIBIT 4 Ice Cream Franchises, 2014

Franchise	Start-Up Costs	Number of Franchises
Baskin-Robbins	$103K–389K	7,412
Ice cream, frozen yogurt, frozen beverages		
Ben & Jerry's	$156K–486K	594
Ice cream, frozen yogurt, sorbet, smoothies		
Bruster's Real Ice Cream	$188K–1M	181
Ice cream, frozen yogurt, ices, sherbets		
Camille's Ice Cream Bars	$152K–553K	2
Ice cream, shakes, frozen yogurt		
Carvel	$249K–381K	445
Ice cream, ice cream cakes		
Cold Stone Creamery	$277K–464K	1,423
Ice cream, sorbet		
Culver Franchising System Inc.	$2M–4M	519
Frozen custard, specialty burgers		
Dairy Queen	$362K–2M	6,388
Ice cream, burgers, chicken		
Dippin' Dots Franchising LLC	$120K–367K	131
Specialty ice cream, frozen yogurt, ices, sorbet		
Freddy's Frozen Custard LLC	$522K–1M	119
Frozen custard, steakburgers, hot dogs		
Fro.Zen.Yo	$355K–588K	9
Frozen yogurt		
The Haagen-Dazs Shoppe Co. Inc.	$145K–457K	216
Ice cream, frozen yogurt		
Happy Joe's	$189K–993K	53
Pizza, pasta, sandwiches, salads, frozen yogurt		
Kona Ice	$109K–125K	574
Shaved-ice truck		
Marble Slab Creamery	$230K–372K	349
Ice cream, frozen yogurt, baked goods		
Menchie's	$231K–393K	457
Self-serve frozen yogurt		
Milani Gelateria	$176K–243K	1
Gelato		

Continued

EXHIBIT 4 *Continued*

Franchise	Start-Up Costs	Number of Franchises
Paciugo Gelato Caffè	$200K–435K	36
Gelato, beverages		
Popbar	$233K–429K	9
Gelato, sorbetto and frozen yogurt on a stick		
Red Mango - Yogurt Cafe & Juice Bar	$195K–492K	322
Frozen yogurt, smoothies, juices, wraps		
Repicci's Italian Ice	$58K–150K	44
Italian ice and gelato		
Rita's Italian Ice	$140K–414K	555
Italian ice, frozen custard, gelato		
Ritter's Frozen Custard	$234K–775K	25
Frozen custard		
Sloan's Ice Cream	$588K–897K	5
Ice cream, candy, toys, novelty items		
Stricklands Frozen Custard	$189K–315K	5
Frozen custard, ice cream, yogurt, sorbet		
Sub Zero Ice Cream	$160K–381K	39
Ice cream, yogurt, custard, smoothies		
Tasti D-Lite	$234K–423K	60
Frozen desserts		
Yogurtland Franchising Inc.	$337K–789K	296
Self-serve frozen yogurt		

Source: *Entrepreneur*. Ice cream franchises. December 17, 2014, www.entrepreneur.com/franchises/categories/ffqicecr.html.

The other new product introduced by Dippin' Dots was Dot Delicacies. The new product to be introduced in this category was Dot Treats. As of April 2011, there were seven different Dot Treats: Solar Freeze, sundaes, floats, shakes, Clusterz, Quakes, and LOL (lots of layers). These products were available at most of the retail locations where Dippin' Dots ice cream was sold.

By 2010, Dippin' Dots had started an online venture by selling some of its products through its website. Customers could order ice creams, yogurts, and sherbets online, and the items would be delivered to their doors. The company had also branched out and released a series of coffee-based products. The "coffee dots" were new concepts in coffee—frappé and espresso that could be eaten by spoon or could be made into hot coffee drinks by just adding water and milk. Another untapped market Jones and his team tried to enter was the market of healthy ice cream. The low-fat frozen beaded dessert named "Chillz," made with an all-natural sweetener, was introduced by Dippin' Dots as a healthier alternative to ice cream. This product was developed with public schools in mind and was being distributed in schools through vending channels.

Despite the development of new products, the company's experience and resource base were clearly in the ice cream manufacturing and scoop-shop retailing businesses. Dealing with supermarket chains and vending distribution firms was an ongoing challenge for this relatively small firm. However, with a penchant for innovation (from Curt Jones) and an infusion of business acumen and capital (from Scott Fischer), Dippin' Dots was optimistic about the future, focusing on what it was good at and looking to recapture attention in the frozen novelty industry.

ENDNOTES

1. Saving the ice cream of the future. *Profile Magazine,* http://profilemagazine.com/2013/dippin-dots/.
2. *www.nydailynews.com/life-style/eats/dippin-dots-maker-declares-bankruptcy-ice-cream-future-files-chapter-11-reorganization-article-1.973683.*
3. *www.dippindots.com/news/2012/04/Purchase-Agreement.html.*
4. Ibid.
5. *www.dippindots.com/news/2013/01/Expand-Manufacturing.html.*
6. Dippin' Dots Inc. 2010. Dippin' Dots Chillz frozen treat. *VendingMarketWatch.com,* January 7, *www.vendingmarketwatch.com/product/10110602/dippin-dots-chillz-frozen-treat.*
7. Perna, G., & Fairbanks, B. 2010. From the future to the present. *Food and Drink Digital,* March 24, *www.foodanddrinkdigital.com/reports/dippin'-dots-future-present.*
8. Associated Press. 2006. Business blazing for supercold Dippin' Dots. July 23, *www.msnbc.msn.com/id/14001806.*
9. Ice cream's origins are known to reach back as far as the second century BC, although no specific date of origin is known and no inventor has been indisputably credited with its discovery. We know that Alexander the Great enjoyed snow and ice flavored with honey and nectar. Biblical references also show that King Solomon was fond of iced drinks during harvesting. During the Roman Empire, Nero (AD 54–86) frequently sent runners into the mountains for snow, which was then flavored with fruits and juices. Information from International Dairy Foods Association, Ice Cream Media Kit.
10. The idea of using liquid nitrogen to make ice cream had been around in scientific circles for some time. To learn how to make ice cream this way at home, see *www.polsci.wvu.edu/henry/icecream/icecream.html.* See also Kurti, N., & This-Benckhard, H. 1994. Chemistry and physics in the kitchen. *Scientific American,* April: 66–71; and *www.subzeroicecream.com/press/coldfacts2006.pdf.*
11. *www.reuters.com.*
12. Anderson, G. 2005. America's favorite ice cream. *CNN/Money.com,* July 29, *money.cnn.com/2005/07/25/pf/goodlife/summer_ice_cream.*
13. Gagliardi, N. 2014. What's cool and hot about today's ice cream market. *Forbes,* October 30.
14. Author estimates; and Dairy Facts, International Ice Cream Association, *www.idfa.org.*
15. Murphy, K. 2006. Slabs are joining scoops in ice cream retailing. *New York Times,* October 26, *www.nytimes.com/2006/10/26/business/26sbiz.html.*
16. Moskin, J. 2006. Creamy, healthier ice cream? What's the catch? *New York Times,* July 26, *www.nytimes.com/2006/07/26/dining/26cream.html.* Note: *Slow churned* and *double churned* refer to a process called low-temperature extrusion, which significantly reduces the size of the fat globules and ice crystals in ice cream.
17. Murphy. 2006. Slabs are joining scoops in ice cream retailing.
18. *Entrepreneur.* 2011. 2011 Franchise 500 rankings. *www.entrepreneur.com/franchises/rankings/franchise500-115608/2011,-2.html.*
19. All definitions are taken from International Dairy Foods Organization (IDFA). Undated. What's in the ice cream aisle? *www.idfa.org/news—views/media-kits/ice-cream/whats-in-the-ice-cream-aisle/.*
20. Dippin' Dots 10th anniversary promotional video.
21. *Entrepreneur.* 2015. 2015 Franchise 500 rankings. *www.entrepreneur.com/franchises/rankings/franchise500-115608/2009,-4.html.*
22. Michelle, S. 2006. Review. *Yelp Reviews–Chicago,* November 17, *www.yelp.com/biz/qnA4ml7Lu-9W4SDJOF1YPA.*
23. *www.entrepreneur.com.*
24. Jones, L. 2010. Dippin' Dots spends millions on patent invalidity. *Noro IP,* November 15, *www.noroip.com/news-blog/dippin-dots-spends-millions-on-patent-invalidity/.*

CASES

CASE 9

JAMBA JUICE: FEELING THE SQUEEZE OR JUICING UP?*

James D. White, chairman, president, and CEO of Jamba, saw Jamba's momentum building behind the success of the juice and whole-food blending platform: "Our juice sales are up more than three times over last year and we expect sales will continue to grow as trial and awareness increase. Our new line of ready-to-drink juices, now available in California, provides consumers with fresh-squeezed juices in the store and cold-pressed juices for later." In addition, the company planned to enhance shareholder value by using the liquidity generated from juice sales to fund a stock repurchase plan. These efforts were expected to result in accelerated accomplishments and a transition in Jamba's product mix to juice.[1]

Nearly two years earlier, Jamba Juice CEO James D. White had rung the opening bell at NASDAQ in New York City. Headlines announced "Jamba Juice Rings in the New Year with the Unveiling of Brand-New Jamba Kids Meals." This new menu, targeting Jamba's newest and youngest customers, involved smaller 9.5-ounce sizes of fruit smoothies—Strawberries Gone Bananas, Blueberry Strawberry Blast-off, Popp'in Peach Mango, and Berry Beet It—plus two new food items: a Pizza Swirl with Turkey and a Cheesy Stuffed Pretzel. The idea for this kids' menu came from listening to customers, who had struggled to share the larger smoothie drinks with their young children. It also meshed with Jamba's overall strategy: to create "good-for-you food that tastes good" and to continue to add more full-meal options to the menu for both kids and adults.[2]

The Jamba Juice Company had gradually expanded its product line over the years to offer Jamba products that pleased a broader palate. In addition, Jamba had been pursuing an aggressive expansion program, evolving from a made-to-order smoothie company into a healthy, active-lifestyle company. However, was it biting off more than it could chew? After all, the continued menu expansion had put Jamba Juice in direct play against the likes of McDonald's and Starbucks, and Jamba was just emerging from six straight years of net financial losses. Although CEO James White had worked to build Jamba's position as a popular health-and-wellness brand, 2012 was the chain's first year of profitability in six years as a public company and going into 2015 White still had his work cut out for him.

Just after his arrival as the new Jamba Juice CEO nearly six years ago, White instituted a new set of strategic priorities. Believing it was necessary to revitalize the company, White outlined the following goals:[3]

- Transform the chain through refranchising existing stores.
- Initiate international growth.
- Build a retail presence with branded consumer packaged goods and licensing.
- Bring more food offerings to the menu across all dayparts—breakfast, lunch, afternoon, dinner.
- Implement a disciplined expense-reduction plan and improve comparable sales.

Within a few years, Jamba Juice pronounced this turnaround complete and began to focus on achieving a second phase of growth. CEO White called this next set of initiatives an accelerated-growth BLEND Plan 2.0. This plan included the following:

- Become a top-of-mind brand by simplifying and sharpening Jamba's healthy food and beverage marketing message to better clarify value and make the brand more relevant.
- Embody health by engaging company workers in programs that would allow them to embody healthful living and improve their knowledge of nutrition, and extend this lifestyle message broadly across the enterprise.
- Accelerate global retail growth through new and existing formats. Focus franchise growth on more nontraditional venues, such as airports, transportation hubs, grocery stores, big-box outlets, school cafeterias, and college campuses. Build a global consumer packaged-goods platform in Jamba-relevant categories.
- Continue to reduce operational costs by using technology to drive store-level productivity and improve efficiency in the supply, sourcing, and distribution process.[4]

According to White, these strategic priorities supported the company's mission to "accelerate growth and development of Jamba as a premier healthy, active lifestyle brand."[5] Could Jamba Juice succeed with its strategic growth plans, especially now that McDonald's, Starbucks, and even Burger King were selling smoothies?

---

* This case was developed by Professor Alan B. Eisner, Pace University; Professor Jerome C. Kuperman, Minnesota State University–Moorhead; Professor James Gould, Pace University; Associate Professor Pauline Assenza, Western Connecticut State University; and doctoral student Dev Das, Pace University. Material has been drawn from published sources to be used for class discussion. Copyright © 2015 Alan B. Eisner.

Company Background

Juice Club was founded by Kirk Perron and opened its first store in San Luis Obispo, California, in April 1990.[6] While many small health-food stores had juice bars offering fresh carrot juice, wheat germ, and protein powder, dedicated juice and smoothie bars were sparse in 1990 and didn't gain widespread popularity until the mid- to late 1990s.

Juice Club began with a franchise strategy and opened its second and third stores in northern and southern California in 1993. In 1994 management decided that an expansion strategy focusing on company stores would provide a greater degree of quality and operating control. In 1995 the company changed its name to Jamba Juice Company to provide a point of differentiation as competitors began offering similar healthy juices and smoothies in the marketplace.

In March 1999 Jamba Juice Company merged with Zuka Juice Inc., a smoothie retail chain with 98 smoothie retail units in the western United States. On March 13, 2006, Jamba Juice Company agreed to be acquired by Services Acquisition Corp. International (headed by Steven Berrard, former CEO of Blockbuster Inc.) for $265 million.[7] The company went public in November 2006 as NASDAQ-traded JMBA. Jamba Juice stores were owned and franchised by Jamba Juice Company, which was a wholly owned subsidiary of Jamba Inc.

In August 2008 Jamba Juice faced significant leadership changes. Steven Berrard agreed to assume the responsibilities of interim CEO.[8] In December 2008, James White was named CEO and president, while Berrard remained chairman of the board of directors. Prior to joining Jamba Juice, White had been senior vice president of consumer brands at Safeway, a publicly traded Fortune 100 food and drug retailer. During what CEO White called the turnaround years, from 2009 to 2011, he worked to eliminate short-term debt, innovate and expand the menu, and change the business model by refranchising stores, growing internationally, and commercializing product lines.

Going into 2015, Jamba Juice had 862 locations, consisting of 272 company-owned and -operated stores and 535 franchise stores, with 55 licensed sites overseas.[9] On the fiscal front, Jamba Inc. was able to:

- Deliver a marginally positive company-owned comparable-store sales increase of 0.5 percent.
- Produce adjusted operating profit margins of 1 percent, and decrease general and administrative expenses by 7.4 percent.[10]

Overall, Jamba had over $229 million in revenue, a huge increase compared to the just over $22 million in revenue during fiscal year 2006 (see Exhibits 1 and 2).[11]

Top-of-Mind Brand Marketing

According to data presented by Jamba Inc. in early 2015, Jamba Juice was the smoothie brand leader and number-one retailer for fresh-squeezed made-to-order juices. Jamba also boasted over 1.8 million Facebook fans and over 100 million annual visits to its stores.

Menu Items

One of the ways Jamba intended to grow "top-of-mind" was by creating innovative and "craveable" menu items it could offer throughout the day—for breakfast, lunch, afternoon, and dinner. Jamba Juice stores offered customers a range of fresh-squeezed fruit juices, blended beverages, baked goods and meals, nutritional supplements, and healthy snacks. Jamba smoothie and juice options were made with real fruit and 100 percent fruit juices. Jamba smoothies were rich in vitamins, minerals, proteins, and fiber; were blended to order; and provided four to six servings of fruits and vegetables. In addition to the natural nutrients in Jamba smoothies, Jamba offered supplements in the form of boosts and shots. Boosts included 10 combinations of vitamins, minerals, proteins, and extracts designed to give the mind and body a nutritious boost. Shots included three combinations of wheatgrass, green tea, orange juice, and soymilk designed to give customers a natural concentrate of vitamins, minerals, and antioxidants.

As a complement to its smoothie and boost offerings, Jamba also offered baked goods and other meal items. Each of these items was made with natural ingredients and was high in protein or fiber. One popular item added was steel-cut hot oatmeal with fruit, a low-calorie organic product that captured a "best of" rating by nutritionists when compared against offerings from McDonald's, Starbucks, Au Bon Pain, and Cosi.[12] Jamba also offered a variety of grab-and-go wraps, sandwiches, and California flatbread food offerings.

Jamba also added an organic brew-by-the-cup coffee service and a line of Whirl'ns frozen yogurt and sorbet bar treats, with probiotic fruit and yogurt blends. In 2012 Jamba added to the hot-beverage category by acquiring premium tea blender Talbott Teas. This acquisition was championed by ABC TV's *Shark Tank* venture capitalists Kevin O'Leary, Daymond John, and Barbara Corcoran, who convinced Jamba CEO James White that the acquisition would be a good fit for Jamba's strategy to "accelerate growth through the acquisition of specialty lifestyle brands that support the company's expansion into new and relevant product categories."[13]

Next, Jamba introduced its first line of fruit and vegetable smoothies with three offerings: the Berry UpBEET, combining strawberries and blueberries with the juices from carrots, beets, broccoli, and lettuce; the Apple 'n Greens blend of apple and strawberry juice mixed with the juice from dark leafy green vegetables, carrots, and lettuce and with spirulina (a microscopic blue-green algae used as a dietary supplement), peaches, mangos, and bananas; and the Orange Carrot Karma—a simple blend of carrot juice, orange juice, mangos, and bananas. The same year saw the introduction of Fit 'N Fruitful smoothie offerings

EXHIBIT 1
Income Statements
($ thousands)

Period Ending	2014	2013	2012
Total Revenue	218,048	229,249	228,789
Cost of Revenue	174,704	178,378	176,298
Gross Profit	43,344	50,871	52,491
Operating Expenses			
Research Development	—	—	—
Selling General and Administrative	36,560	37,529	40,816
Non Recurring	1,608	1,315	2,256
Others	10,084	10,974	11,062
Total Operating Expenses	—	—	—
Operating Income or Loss	(3,300)	2,368	613
Income from Continuing Operations			
Total Other Income/Expenses Net	74	9	61
Earnings Before Interest and Taxes	(3,226)	2,377	674
Interest Expense	195	242	217
Income Before Tax	(3,421)	2,135	457
Income Tax Expense	168	55	155
Minority Interest	(43)	—	—
Net Income from Continuing Ops	(3,632)	2080	302
Non-recurring Events			
Discontinued Operations	—	—	—
Extraordinary Items	—	—	—
Effect of Accounting Changes	—	—	—
Other Items	—	—	—
Net Income	(3,632)	2,080	302
Preferred Stock and Other Adjustments	—	(588)	(2,181)
Net Income Applicable to Common Shares	(3,632)	1,492	(1,879)

Source: Jamba 10-K reports.

EXHIBIT 2
Balance Sheets
($ thousands)

Period Ending	2014	2013	2012
Assets			
Current Assets			
Cash and Cash Equivalents	17,750	32,386	31,691
Short Term Investments	—	—	—
Net Receivables	16,977	14,110	11,327
Inventory	2,300	2,670	3,143
Other Current Assets	20,304	17,236	5,416

Continued

EXHIBIT 2
Continued

Period Ending	2014	2013	2012
Total Current Assets	57,331	66,402	51,577
Long Term Investments	—	—	—
Property Plant and Equipment	29,575	27,961	38,442
Goodwill	982	1,038	1,336
Intangible Assets	2,360	1,317	1,412
Accumulated Amortization	—	—	—
Other Assets	2,241	1,198	846
Deferred Long Term Asset Charges	—	—	—
Total Assets	92,489	97,916	93,613
Liabilities			
Current Liabilities			
Accounts Payable	49,746	48,791	50,493
Short/Current Long Term Debt	—	—	—
Other Current Liabilities	16,454	13,082	11,141
Total Current Liabilities	66,200	61,873	61,634
Long Term Debt	—	—	—
Other Liabilities	—	—	—
Deferred Long Term Liability Charges	9,544	9,201	10,467
Minority Interest	131	—	—
Negative Goodwill	—	—	—
Total Liabilities	75,875	71,074	72,101
Stockholders' Equity			
Misc Stocks Options Warrants	—	—	—
Redeemable Preferred Stock	—	—	7916
Preferred Stock	—	—	—
Common Stock	17	17	78
Retained Earnings	(368,041)	(364,409)	(366,489)
Treasury Stock	(11,991)	—	—
Capital Surplus	396,629	391,234	380,007
Other Stockholder Equity	—	—	—
Total Stockholder Equity	16,614	26,842	13,596
Net Tangible Assets	13,272	24,487	10,848

Source: Jamba 10-K reports.

with 14 added vitamins and minerals, protein and fiber from Balance Boost, two or more servings of fruit, and the added benefit of a "Weight Burner Boost" made with conjugated linoleic acid, or CLA, to help manage weight "tastefully."

Later, Jamba Juice launched a "Make It Light" option for its 10 classic smoothies, which cut calories, sugar, and carbohydrates by one-third. The Make It Light version replaced the nonfat frozen yogurt or sherbet used in classic smoothies with a lower-calorie dairy base sweetened with Splenda. A 16-ounce classic Banana Berry smoothie, for example, had 290 calories and 60 grams of sugar. The Make It Light version, however, had 170 calories and 32 grams of sugar.

Simultaneously, Jamba announced plans to "re-concept" existing stores in selected markets with a fresh-squeezed-juice emphasis. This was planned to address competition from both Juice It Up! and Starbucks, which were expanding their premium juice-bar businesses. But the big announcement was Jamba's introduction of its kids meals. This new menu was targeted toward children ages 4 to 8, with a complete meal—a smoothie plus a food item—containing fewer than 500 calories. The items included whole grains, 2.5 servings of fruit or vegetables, and no added sugar.

In more recent years, the company continued to innovate with whole-food blends, capitalizing on changes in consumer eating habits and the need for healthier on-the-go options.[14]

Innovative Tactics

Regarding its marketing efforts, historically, Jamba had not engaged in any mass-media promotional programs, relying instead on word of mouth and in-store promotions to increase customer awareness. However, Jamba was featured in stories appearing in the *Wall Street Journal*, the *New York Times*, *USA Today*, and a host of local newspapers and magazines, as well as in profiled spots on TV news shows such as *Good Morning America*. Jamba also ran an "Ambassadors of WOW" contest nationwide, encouraging fans to nominate themselves or worthy friends or family members to be the new faces of Jamba Juice, creating "wow" through support and involvement within their communities. These ambassadors would have the opportunity to appear in Jamba Juice advertisements and promotional campaigns.[15]

Jamba also capitalized on the openings of new sites as opportunities to reach out to the media and secure live local television coverage, radio broadcasts, and articles in local print media. Openings were frequently associated with a charitable event, thus serving to reinforce Jamba Juice Company's strong commitment to its communities. In addition, Jamba aligned itself with "active-living" spokespeople, such as tennis star Venus Williams, who partnered with Jamba to open two stores in the Maryland–Washington, D.C., area.[16]

One of the key objectives of Jamba's growth strategy was to market itself in a way that would increase sales year-round and significantly decrease weather and seasonal vulnerabilities. Seasonal issues were serious, since the traditional driver of Jamba's revenue and profit was the sale of smoothies during hot weather. In southern states (e.g., California), where the weather remained warm year-round, Jamba experienced fairly steady sales. However, in the northern states (e.g., New York), where there was a cold and fairly long winter season, Jamba experienced severe seasonal variability. To counter the seasonal slump, Jamba pushed to increase the presence of nontraditional stores inside existing venues.

Transition from Company-Owned to Franchise and Nontraditional Formats

Originally, Jamba Juice Company had followed a strategy of expanding its store locations in existing markets and opening stores only in select new markets. Jamba soon began acquiring the assets of Jamba Juice franchised stores in an attempt to gain more control over growth direction. It acquired several franchise stores and expected to continue making additional franchise acquisitions as part of its ongoing growth strategy. However, the company-owned franchises were not as productive and accounted for a disproportionately low portion of company revenues.[17] As the majority of Jamba stores became company-owned, financial analysts predicted that Jamba's widely recognized brand poised the company to "expand in an underpenetrated and growing health food market."[18] However, the same analysts recognized that Jamba was experiencing declines in store traffic and store-level margins due to the subprime crisis and that Jamba therefore needed to slow its expansion until the economy had a chance to recover. Jamba subsequently announced its plans to close underperforming company-owned stores and terminate signed leases for unbuilt locations.[19]

CEO Paul E. Clayton stepped down after eight years in the role and was ultimately replaced by James White. White subsequently reversed the trajectory of the growth strategy, focusing on the acceleration of franchise and nontraditional store growth. The more heavily franchised business model tended to require less capital investment and reduced the volatility of cash flow performance over time. However, revenue then came more from royalties and franchise fees than from retail sales. Within five years of White taking charge, there were twice as many independent franchises as company-owned stores (see Exhibit 3).

International growth was also a horizon priority. Starting with the first South Korean location in January 2011, Jamba Juice grew to 48 stores internationally by 2014, with 27 outlets in South Korea, 12 in Canada, and 9 in the Philippines. International stores were located in prominent locations like the Mall of Asia, the largest integrated shopping, dining, and leisure destination in the Philippines.[20] Jamba and its partners were poised to open more than 200 stores

EXHIBIT 3 Store Types and Locations

	2014		2013	
	Domestic	International	Domestic	International
Company Stores:				
Beginning of period	268	—	301	—
Company Stores opened	—	—	2	—
Company Stores closed	(13)	—	(4)	—
Company Stores sold to franchisees	(18)	—	(31)	—
Total Company Stores	263	—	268	—
Franchise and International Stores:				
Beginning of period	535	48	473	35
Stores opened	43	24	52	15
Stores closed	(27)	(10)	(21)	(2)
Stores purchased from Company	18	—	31	—
Total Franchise Stores	543	62	535	48

Source: Jamba 10-K reports.

in South Korea and 40 more in the Philippines within the next 10 years. In addition, Jamba's Canadian partner was projected to develop 80 Jamba Juice stores by 2022.

Jamba Inc. was also aggressively pursuing licensing agreements for commercialized product lines in the areas of Jamba-branded make-at-home frozen-smoothie kits, frozen-yogurt novelty bars, all-natural energy drinks, coconut water fruit-juice beverages, Brazilian super fruit shots, trail mixes, and fruit cups. The objective was to reinforce the Jamba better-for-you message with convenient and portable products available at multiple consumer locations. By the end of 2013, there were nearly 50 license agreements in place.

Nontraditional Locations

Jamba had generally characterized its stores as either traditional or nontraditional. Traditional locations included suburban strip malls and various retail locations in urban centers. Traditional stores averaged approximately 1,400 square feet in size and were designed to be fun, friendly, energetic, and colorful to represent the active, healthy lifestyle that Jamba Juice promoted.

Nontraditional stores were considered those located in areas that allowed Jamba to generate awareness and try out new products to fuel the core business. Jamba's nontraditional opportunities included store-within-a-store locations, airports, shopping malls, and colleges and universities:

Store-within-a-store: Jamba Juice Company was developing franchise-partner relationships with major grocers and retailers to develop store-within-a-store concepts. The franchise partnerships provided it with the opportunity to reach new customers and enhance the brand without making significant capital investments.

Airports: Jamba operated several airport locations and had the opportunity to develop stores in numerous additional airports. Jamba Juice Company's highly portable product appealed to travelers on the go and provided them with an energizing boost.

Shopping malls: Jamba had opportunistically established stores in shopping malls that presented attractive expansion opportunities. In addition, as with the airport locations, the indoor setting helped to alleviate weather and seasonal vulnerabilities that challenged traditional locations.

Colleges and universities: The Jamba brand was believed to be extremely appealing to the average college student's active, on-the-go lifestyle, and Jamba expected to continue to develop on-campus locations.

Other Potential Nontraditional Store Locations

Additional high-traffic, nontraditional locations existed for Jamba to explore. Many large health clubs included a juice and smoothie bar within their buildings. There was an opportunity for Jamba to partner with a major gym chain or individual private gyms with high membership rates. Another possibility was to partner with a large school district. Schools across the country were under increasing scrutiny to offer healthy alternatives to the traditional fat-, carbohydrate-, and preservative-rich foods served in cafeterias, especially as a growing number of states were prohibiting the sale of junk food on K–12 campuses.

Jamba also introduced self-service JambaGO automated drink stations in nontraditional locations, including schools. The move into schools was seen as a real growth opportunity—with Jamba products in front of a captive audience on a daily basis, "generations will grow up knowing the brand."[21] Taking roughly the space of a soda-fountain beverage dispenser, the JambaGO format, which CEO White called a wellness center, included the chain's branded packaged products, as well as the option of several preblended smoothies. The JambaGO concept was a way to reinforce Jamba as a healthy, active-lifestyle brand that was also convenient and portable. This licensed concept represented no capital investment for Jamba and used the razor/razor blade net profit model. White was hoping Jamba would become "the go-to resource for healthy solutions for school foodservice directors."[22]

Building a Global Consumer Packaged-Goods Platform

Jamba Juice Company's strong association with premium, flavorful beverages translated well into ready-to-drink beverages available in a variety of retail locations. For instance, Jamba Juice developed an agreement with Nestlé under which Nestlé would manufacture three flavors of Jamba's juice and smoothie ready-to-drink products. Jamba All-Natural Energy Drinks were rolled out in multiple retail locations in the Northeast and in 600 Jamba Juice retail stores.[23] Kraft had had a similar deal with Starbucks to distribute its Frappuccino drinks, but the deal eventually ended. The 90-calorie Jamba energy drinks contained no artificial preservatives, flavors, or colors and were made with 70 percent real fruit juice and 80 milligrams of caffeine derived from natural sources. However, Jamba Juice soon followed Starbucks' lead and split from Nestlé. Jamba acquired the product formulation and intellectual property under a licensing agreement with Nestlé, explaining that Jamba wanted more control over the growth of its consumer packaged goods.[24]

In aggressive moves, Jamba expanded licensing agreements to include a line of fruit-infused coconut water to be distributed through the Pepsi Beverage Company, Brazilian super fruit shots, and all-natural fruit cups to be produced in partnership with Zola and Sundia Corporation. Other Jamba-branded consumer products included yogurt and sorbet frozen novelty items manufactured under license by Oregon Ice Cream LLC of Eugene, Oregon, and Jamba-branded apparel, including cotton T-shirts, beanies, and a canvas tote bag, developed in partnership with licensee Headline Entertainment.

Engage Company Workers—Embody a Healthy, Active Lifestyle

To meet the goal of being a top-of-mind brand, Jamba Juice believed it had to build a customer-first, operationally focused service culture. Attracting and developing team members who provided superior service was important to reinforcing Jamba's brand image. Jamba sought to hire customer service–oriented people and provided team members with extensive training, financial incentives, and opportunities for advancement when they fulfilled service expectations.

Jamba participated in the Obama administration's Summer Jobs Initiative, holding National Hiring Days in more than 70 stores to attract nearly 6,000 team members for the busy May to September summer season. Over 10 percent of those hires were subsequently retained for ongoing employment with Jamba. In addition, Jamba established partnerships with the San Francisco–based Job Corps Culinary Arts Center and the Bay Area chapter of the United Way to develop internship programs in culinary skills. Job Corps interns were able to work side by side with Jamba's product innovation team developing new menu concepts. This helped build product knowledge and encourage employee long-term loyalty to the brand.[25]

Jamba also created a new Healthy Living Council of nutritionists and dietary experts to help the brand evolve with more healthful offerings, as well as to educate both employees and consumers and to work with schools on healthy-living and antiobesity efforts. The timing of this effort coincided with New York mayor Bloomberg's ban on sugary drinks larger than 16 ounces. Jamba's All Fruit smoothies were all under 250 calories at 16 ounces and offered multiple servings of fruit. According to Jamba's Healthy Living Council member, dietician Elizabeth Ward:

> When you use whole fruit and 100-percent pure fruit juice, you're getting vitamins and minerals and fiber that you're not getting from a smoothie base or blend that a lot of places [like McDonald's] start with. . . . We want you to get away from drinks that are offering nothing for the calories. When you're consuming 200 calories, you want to get vitamins and minerals and protein, [as you do with Jamba Juice drinks].[26]

This information helped Jamba employees educate consumers about the Jamba difference.

Expense Reduction Plan

As a major part of CEO White's strategic initiative, and partly due to the weakness of consumer spending at the time, Jamba planned to increase operating margins by reducing store-level costs. This would be done over several years by reducing costs of goods sold, simplifying operations to reduce labor costs, better managing wages and benefits, implementing a labor-planning system, increasing occupancy savings, and improving management of controllable costs, store costs, and marketing expenditures. In addition, Jamba took several measures to reduce general and administrative costs. The company was also looking for ways to better use technology to improve store-level productivity; for instance, it was testing a program with Google Wallet that allowed guests to pay and redeem coupons with their smartphones.[27]

Competition

Jamba was the smoothie industry leader and initially had several competitors with similar health and fitness focuses, such as Juice It Up!, Planet Smoothie, and Smoothie King, but over time that changed. Starbucks and Panera Bread entered the smoothie market, and McDonald's brought its marketing machine into the frozen-drink category, launching its line of smoothies with a value pitch. When McDonald's introduced a 12-ounce smoothie for $2.29, Jamba Juice's berry smoothies started at $3.55 for 16 ounces. When asked about the McDonald's push into its competitive space, Jamba Juice CEO White said, "We view the entry of McDonald's into the smoothie category as an overall validation of the potential of smoothies. Their advertising will expand interest in the category."

Burger King also entered the smoothie market, and Starbucks, with its smoothies already in place, acquired both Evolution Fresh, the premium juice-bar operator, and Teavana Teas. This positioned Starbucks as a head-to-head competitor of Jamba Juice.

On the international market, Canadian-based Tim Hortons had been offering smoothies in its U.S. market for several years and was beginning to sell berry smoothies in Canada. Analysts there believed the smoothie market was "hot," with a lot of potential for growth.[28] Jamba Juice, therefore, expanded into Canada and planned additional franchise development.

Can Jamba grow without losing its "Healthy Alternatives" brand identity?

Jamba Juice Company's desire to grow by expanding its selection of nonjuice menu items seemed to follow the Starbucks model. Although originally just a coffeehouse, by 2012 most Starbucks stores offered a variety of muffins, fruit plates, sandwiches, quiches, and desserts. And with the 2012 acquisition of juice-bar operator Evolution Fresh and premium loose-tea purveyor Teavana, Starbucks was pushing boundaries even further. This menu expansion helped Starbucks attract customers who were looking for a light meal or dessert to go with their coffee, and it also attracted non-coffee drinkers who just came in for the food, tea, and juice beverages. Offering iced coffees, teas, and juices helped Starbucks overcome some of its seasonal variability, giving customers a cool-drink offering during hot-weather months. Offering ready-to-go-drinks in grocery and convenience stores also enabled Starbucks to get its products to a wider customer base.

Likewise, Jamba had set out to strengthen its customer reach by offering ready-to-drink products, hot food and drink items to attract customers during the cold-weather months, and a range of breakfast and lunch food items to complement its juice-based offerings and satisfy customer desires all day and year-round. Could Jamba follow Starbucks' path of broadening its menu base but still maintaining its brand identity?

One of the issues with growth is how to manage the pace of innovation—by choosing a direction that capitalizes on the organization's core competencies and then validating new ideas by testing them in the marketplace—and then make sure the financial and human assets are available to invest in sustaining needed operational components. Consultant Robert Sher advises CEOs of midmarket companies who are trying to plan for growth. He pointed to Jamba CEO James White as one who seemed to get it, explaining that White's team uses "a well-disciplined 'stage-gate' process to de-risk each idea, from conception through testing." As an example, Sher pointed to Jamba's launch of its steel-cut oatmeal, a product that took two years of field testing but ended up a winner.[29]

With White at the helm, the Jamba turnaround seemed to be on track. However, even with no debt and increased margins going into 2015, there was still speculation about whether Jamba could sustain itself as a brand well recognized enough to compete with the likes of Starbucks and McDonald's. With Burger King also entering the smoothie category, the drive-through chains might be able to slash prices on their smoothies and use them as loss leaders. And Starbucks, with its move into the juice-bar business, might be able to attract the family dollar as well as the company's traditional adult customer.[30]

However, going into 2015, Jamba CEO White believed his company might actually benefit from these increased entries into the juice market, as they reminded the market that Jamba had been offering healthy alternatives for over two decades; he stated, "The bigger players that have entered the fresh juice and smoothie market have done nothing but elevate the importance of healthier on-the-go solutions."[31] At the time, the investment community seemed to agree. It was likely Jamba's competitors weren't losing sight of Jamba either. There was still speculation about whether Starbucks, McDonald's, or even Monster Beverage might see Jamba as an increasingly attractive acquisition target.[32]

ENDNOTES

1. Q3 Earnings Press Release, November 4, 2014.
2. Dostal, E. 2013. Jamba Juice introduces kids' meals. *Nation's Restaurant News,* January 4, nrn.com/latest-headlines/jamba-juice-introduces-kids-meals.
3. Jamba Inc. 2010. Jamba Inc. Form 10K annual report, for period ending December 29, 2009. Available at ir.jambajuice.com/phoenix.zhtml?c=192409&p=irol-sec.
4. Jamba Inc. 2012. Jamba Inc. Form 10K annual report, for period ending January 3, 2012. Available at http://ir.jambajuice.com/phoenix.zhtml?c=192409&p=IROL-secToc&TOC=aHR0cDovL2Fw aS50ZW5rd2l6YXJkLmNvbS9vdXRsaW5lLnhtbD9yZXBvPXRlbmsma XBhZ2U9ODEyNzg4OQ%3d%3d&ListAll=1&sXBRL=1.
5. Ibid.
6. FundingUniverse.com. Undated. Jamba Juice Company (company history). *www.fundinguniverse.com/company-histories/Jamba-Juice-Company-Company-History.html.*
7. Jamba Juice Company. 2006. Jamba Juice Company and Services Acquisition Corp. International announce merger. March 13,

www.sec.gov/Archives/edgar/data/1316898/000110465906015960/a06-6826_1ex99d1.htm.
8. Jamba Inc. 2008. Jamba, Inc. announces changes to its senior management team. *Business Wire,* August 6, ir.jambajuice.com/phoenix.zhtml?c=192409&p=irol-newsArticle&ID=1189166.
9. Jamba company presentation at ICR Xchange Conference, January 2015.
10. Jamba Inc. 2013 Annual Report.
11. Jamba Inc. 2013. Jamba Inc. Form 10K annual report, for period ending March 3, 2013. *http://ir.jambajuice.com/phoenix.zhtml?c=192409&p=irol-sec.*
12. Jamba Inc. 2011. Jamba Juice oatmeal favorite pick on *Good Morning America* today. *ABC News,* February 8, ir.jambajuice.com/phoenix.zhtml?c=192409&p=irol-news&nyo=0; video clip available at *abcnews.go.com/GMA/video/fast-food-oatmeal-how-healthy-is-it-12865436.*
13. *QSR Magazine.* 2012. Jamba Juice acquires premium tea company, Talbott Teas. February 21, *www.qsrmagazine.com/news/jamba-juice-acquires-premium-tea-company-talbott-teas.*
14. Galvez, J. 2014. Jamba Juice releases six new energy bowl flavors. *Franchise Herald,* September 23.
15. Jamba Inc. 2011. Jamba Juice announces two new "Ambassadors of WOW." *PRNewswire,* May 9, ir.jambajuice.com/phoenix.zhtml?c=192409&p=irol-newsArticle&id=1561602.
16. Jamba Inc. 2012. Jamba Juice growth continues: New stores open in Washington D.C. with tennis-great Venus Williams. *Business Wire,* July 9, ir.jambajuice.com/phoenix.zhtml?c=192409&p=irol-newsArticle&ID=1712664.
17. Lee, L. 2007. A smoothie you can chew on: To appeal to diners as well as drinkers, Jamba Juice is adding heft to its concoctions. *BusinessWeek,* June 11: 64.
18. Zacks Investment Research. 2008. Zacks analyst blog highlights: Jamba Juice, Krispy Kreme, Starbucks and PeopleSupport. January 10, news.moneycentral.msn.com/ticker/article.aspx?symbol=US:JMBA&feed=BW&date=20080110&id=8018383.
19. Jamba Inc. 2008. Jamba announces organizational changes and store development reductions. *Business Wire,* May 15, ir.jambajuice.com/phoenix.zhtml?c=192409&p=irol-newsArticle&ID=1189172.
20. Jamba Inc. 2012. Jamba announces significant progress in international expansion. *Business Wire,* July 17, ir.jambajuice.com/phoenix.zhtml?c=192409&p=irol-newsArticle&ID=1715180.
21. Jennings, L. 2011. Jamba Juice on growth, JambaGO. *Nation's Restaurant News,* December 9, nrn.com/archive/jamba-juice-growth-jambago.
22. Jennings, L. 2012. Jamba Juice launches next phase of growth. *Nation's Restaurant News,* January 10, nrn.com/archive/jamba-juice-launches-next-phase-growth.
23. *Drinks Business Review.* 2011. Nestlé Jamba All-Natural Energy Drinks to land at 600 Jamba Juice stores in U.S. March 11, energysportsdrinks.drinks-business-review.com/news/nestl-jamba-all-natural-energy-drinks-to-land-at-600-jamba-juice-stores-in-us-110311.
24. *QSR Magazine.* 2012. Jamba Juice offers CPG energy drinks. April 23, www.qsrmagazine.com/news/jamba-juice-offers-cpg-energy-drinks.
25. *QSR Magazine.* 2012. Jamba Juice unveils summer hiring campaign results. October 9, www.qsrmagazine.com/news/jamba-juice-unveils-summer-hiring-campaign-results.
26. Jennings, L. 2012. Jamba Juice works to make smoothies more healthful. *Nation's Restaurant News,* June 19, nrn.com/latest-headlines/jamba-juice-works-make-smoothies-more-healthful.
27. Matteson, S. 2012. Google Wallet: Where it's been and where it's going. *TechRepublic,* November 30, www.techrepublic.com/blog/google-in-the-enterprise/google-wallet-where-its-been-and-where-its-going/1672.
28. QSRweb.com. 2011. Tim Hortons rolling out smoothies in Canada. March 4, www.qsrweb.com/article/179756/Tim-Hortons-rolling-out-smoothies-in-Canada.
29. Sher, R. 2012. Google can survive too much innovation. You can't. *Forbes,* May 15, www.forbes.com/sites/forbesleadershipforum/2012/05/15/google-can-survive-too-much-innovation-you-cant/.
30. Munarriz, R. A. 2012. Is a smoothie war breaking out? *Motley Fool,* September 4, www.fool.com/investing/general/2012/09/04/is-a-smoothie-war-breaking-out.aspx.
31. CNBC. 2013. Jamba Juice CEO on increasing competition. CNBC interview. *Video.CNBC.com,* January 4, video.cnbc.com/gallery/?video=3000139247.
32. Munarriz, R. A. 2012. Is Jamba the next Teavana? *Motley Fool,* November 15, www.fool.com/investing/general/2012/11/15/is-jamba-the-next-teavana.aspx.

CASES

CASE 10

ANN TAYLOR: SURVIVAL IN SPECIALTY RETAIL*

Rumors at the beginning of 2015 about ANN Inc., specialty retailer of women's apparel sold under its Ann Taylor or LOFT brands, were swirling around the possibility of a private equity buyout or acquisition. Third-quarter revenues for ANN were down over 4 percent from the previous year. ANN's problems were similar to those of other mall-based retailers that faced equally weak mall traffic in 2014. This, coupled with west coast shipment delays that forced retailers to spend more for distribution via air freight, had affected many specialty shops, but ANN had also seen poor product performance in its core Ann Taylor brand, forcing it to engage in widespread discounting in order to move product.[1] This, plus ANN's warning of missed earning projections, stagnant same-store sales, slow inventory turnover, and significant margin compression, had led to the involvement of two major activist investors—one advocating for a sale and the other looking for strategic changes. Multiple analysts were pointing out that ANN had "a host of problems" that needed to be addressed if it was to return to growth.[2]

Regarding the overall shopping environment, going into 2015, specialty retailers had pretty much recovered from over five years of dismal performance. The National Retail Federation and Kantar Retail were predicting a more than 3 percent increase in apparel and home-goods retail industry sales in 2015, the biggest annual growth since 2011.[3] The economic troubles of 2008 had lasted through 2009, producing one of the worst retail seasons in recent memory. The year 2010 had been an uphill battle, but at least some retailers had seen improvement, especially the luxury vendors such as Neiman Marcus and Nordstrom. The feeling during 2011 was that customers had shown "a clear preference for select high-end apparel brands such as Gucci" and were "willing to pay a premium on something that delivers on luxury." At the same time, shoppers had also been "hunting down designer brands at steep discounts" at stores such as T.J. Maxx or Target, causing one businessman to label this the "barbell effect": "High-end brands are holding ground among consumers, while spending at value-oriented stores has also been pretty stable. [But] it's a tough place for mid-tier right now," namely, those retailers such as Gap, Chico's, and Ann Taylor.[4]

By 2013, luxury fashion spending may have been up, but the midmarket specialty apparel retailers continued to struggle. Customers were looking for value but also fashion—if a store had the right product, with the right price-point, it could be a winner. Quality could beat quantity, but the quest for this "right" balance had many retailers resorting to discounting month after month in order to drive sales or recover from bad guesses and poor inventory management.[5] The firm with the right "mix" could stand out, and, in 2013, Ann Taylor looked good.

However, Ann Taylor had had its own set of problems, mainly with its two divisions: the legacy Ann Taylor store for upscale professional women versus the LOFT's more casual fashion. Analysts had long worried that LOFT stores would cannibalize sales "as traditional Ann Taylor shoppers sought more relaxed, lower-priced merchandise."[6] Ann Taylor would be 61 years old in 2015 and needed to make sure it wouldn't become a victim of a midlife crisis. One major question was whether the Ann Taylor refined professional look could stay relevant when "more and more offices are adopting casual dress codes."[7] Kay Krill, ANN's CEO, had been reflecting on these issues for some time.

Krill had been appointed president of Ann Taylor Stores Corporation (ANN) in late 2004, and she succeeded to president/CEO in late 2005 when J. Patrick Spainhour retired after eight years as CEO. Even back then, there was concern among commentators and customers that the Ann Taylor look was getting "stodgy," and the question was how to "reestablish Ann Taylor as the preeminent brand for beautiful, elegant, and sophisticated occasion dressing."[8]

Krill's challenge was based on the ANN legacy as a women's specialty clothing retailer. Since 1954, Ann Taylor had been the wardrobe source for busy, socially upscale women, and the classic basic black dress and woman's power suit with pearls were Ann Taylor staples. The Ann Taylor client base consisted of fashion-conscious women from ages 25 to 55. The overall Ann Taylor concept was designed to appeal to professional women who had limited time to shop and were attracted to Ann Taylor stores by their total wardrobing strategy, personalized client service, efficient store layouts, and continual flow of new merchandise.

---

* This case was prepared by Associate Professor Pauline Assenza of Western Connecticut State University, Professor Alan B. Eisner of Pace University, and Professor Jerome C. Kuperman of Minnesota State University–Moorhead. This case is solely based on library research and was developed for class discussion of strategies rather than to illustrate either effective or ineffective handling of the situation. An earlier version of this case was published in *The CASE Journal* 5, no. 2 (Spring 2009). Copyright © 2009 The CASE Association. Current copyright © 2015 Pauline Assenza and Alan B. Eisner.

ANN had two branded divisions focused on different segments of this customer base:

- Ann Taylor (AT), the company's original brand, provided sophisticated, versatile, and high-quality updated classics.
- Ann Taylor LOFT was a newer brand concept that appealed to women who had a more relaxed lifestyle and work environment and appreciated the more casual LOFT style and compelling value. Certain clients of Ann Taylor and LOFT cross-shopped both brands.

ANN also carried both brands in factory outlet stores. The merchandise in each branded division's store was specifically designed to carry the brand label. The stores featured the previous years' top fashions and were located in outlet malls, where customers expected to find Ann Taylor and other major-label bargains. Both brands were also retailed online, on their respective websites.

ANN had regularly appeared in the *Women's Wear Daily* Top 10 list of firms selling dresses, suits, and evening wear and the Top 20 list of publicly traded women's specialty retailers. These listings recognized the total company, that is, the combined results of both divisions. Since 2005, the LOFT division, with more square footage per store, had outsold the flagship Ann Taylor division stores.[9] Since its emergence as a distinctly competitive entity, LOFT had been such a success for the company that some analysts credited the division for "keeping the entire ANN corporation afloat."[10] Financial data from 2011 to 2014 show the performance of LOFT compared to AT. (See Exhibit 1.)

Krill acknowledged the ongoing challenge: "To be successful in meeting the changing needs of our clients, we must continually evolve and elevate our brands to ensure they remain compelling—from our product, to our marketing, to our in-store environment."[11] Although Krill believed that, overall, Ann Taylor still had its historic appeal, the question remained whether that appeal could be sustained indefinitely in the risky and uncertain specialty retail environment, where success depended on the "ability to predict accurately client fashion preferences."[12]

Ann Taylor Background

Ann Taylor was founded in 1954 as a wardrobe source for busy, socially upscale women. Starting out in New Haven, Connecticut, Ann Taylor founder Robert Liebeskind established a stand-alone clothing store. When Liebeskind's father, Richard Liebeskind Sr., a designer, as a good-luck gesture gave his son exclusive rights to one of his best-selling dresses, "Ann Taylor," the company name was established. Ann Taylor was never a real person, but her persona lived on in the profile of the consumer.

Ann Taylor went public on the New York Stock Exchange in 1991 under the symbol ANN. In 1994 the company added a mail-order catalog business, a fragrance line, and freestanding shoe stores positioned to supplement the AT stores. The mail-order catalog attempt ended in 1995, and the lower-priced apparel concept, Ann Taylor LOFT, was launched. LOFT was meant to appeal to a younger, more casual and cost-conscious, but still professional, consumer. CEO Sally Kasaks incorporated more casual clothing, petite sizes, and accessories in an attempt to create a one-stop shopping environment to "widen market appeal and fuel growth."[13] Following losses in fiscal 1996 that could be attributed to a fashion misstep—cropped T-shirts didn't fit in with the workplace attire—Kasaks left the company. New ANN CEO Patrick Spainhour, who had been chief financial officer at Donna Karan and also had previous experience at Gap, shelved the fragrance line and closed the shoe stores in 1997.

Originally, the LOFT stores were found only in outlet centers, but in 1998 the LOFT stores in the discount outlet malls were replaced by a third concept, Ann Taylor Factory. The Factory carried clothes from the AT line. This "outlet" concept offered customers direct access to the AT designer items "off the rack" without elaborate promotion and with prices regularly 25 to 30 percent less than those at the high-end Ann Taylor stores. The LOFT concept was revamped, and stores were opened in more prestigious regional malls and shopping centers. By 1999 LOFT clothes were a distinct line of "more casual, yet business-tailored, fun, and feminine" attire, and they were about 30 percent less expensive than the merchandise at the flagship Ann Taylor division's stores. At that time, the LOFT was under the direction of Kay Krill, who had been promoted to the position of executive vice president of the LOFT division.

Ann Taylor attempted a cosmetics line in 2000, which it discontinued in 2001. In 2000 the online store at www.anntaylor.com was launched, only to be cut back in late 2001 when projected cash flow goals were not met. In early 2001 Spainhour restructured management reporting relationships, creating new president positions for both the AT and LOFT divisions, and Kay Krill was promoted from executive vice president to president of LOFT. In 2004 Krill was made president of the entire ANN corporation, bringing both Ann Taylor and LOFT under her control. In the fall of 2005 chairman and CEO J. Patrick Spainhour retired, and President Kay Krill was elevated to the CEO position. In a conference call following her promotion, Krill stated her goals as "improving profitability while enhancing both brands . . . restoring performance at the Ann Taylor division and restoring the momentum at LOFT."[14]

Krill felt that the outlook for fiscal year 2006 was cautiously positive, and she announced continued plans for expansion and related capital expenditures. However, challenges in the macroeconomic climate prompted Krill to announce a restructuring plan in 2008.[15] After a posted loss of $333.9 million in 2008 and the continuing economic uncertainty going into 2009, ANN was reluctant to give any profit forecast for the coming quarters. At the end of 2009, net sales had reached the lowest point since

EXHIBIT 1 AT versus LOFT Financial Performance, FY 2011–2014 (net sales in $ millions)

Go to library tab in Connect to access Case Financials.

Fiscal Year Ending	Feb. 2015	Feb. 1, 2014	Feb. 2, 2013	Jan. 28, 2012
Ann Taylor stores	$ 658.7	$ 668.0	$ 644.5	$ 494.0
Ann Taylor e-commerce	Included in above	Included in above	Included in above	124.4
Ann Taylor Factory Outlet	294.1	291.8	300.7	289.4
Total Ann Taylor brand	952.8	959.8	945.2	907.9
LOFT stores	1,276.4	1,272.9	1,202.2	991.0
LOFT e-commerce	Included in above	Included in above	Included in above	123.9
LOFT Outlet	304.2	260.8	228.0	189.7
Total LOFT brand	1,580.7	1,533.7	1,430.3	1,304.6
Total company	$2,533.5	$2,493.5	$2,375.5	$2,212.5
Comparable-Stores Sales Percentage				
Ann Taylor	(2.2)	1.1	1.1	5.2
LOFT	(1.7)	3.0	4.8	8.0
Total company	(1.9)%	2.3%	3.3%	6.8%
Net sales	100.0%	100.0%	100.0%	100.0%
Cost of sales %	49.0	46.1	45.2	45.4
Gross margin %	51.0	53.9	54.8	54.6
Selling, general, and administrative expenses %	45.9	47.1	47.8	48
Restructuring, asset, goodwill impairment %	0.7	—	—	—
Operating income (loss) %	4.4	6.8	7.0	6.6
Interest income %	—	—	—	—
Interest expense %	—	—	—	(0.1)
Income before tax %	4.4	6.8	7.0	6.5
Income tax provision %	1.7	2.7	2.7	2.6
Net income %	2.7	4.1	4.3	3.9
Percentage change from prior period:				
Net sales	1.6%	5.0%	7.4%	11.7%
Operating income	(34.3)	2.0	14.6	21.5
Net income	(33.6)	(0.2)	18.5	17.9

2005, and in 2010 they had still not rebounded enough to surpass 2007 figures. (See Exhibit 2.) At the end of 2011, sales had jumped over 11 percent from 2010, and although gross margins fell to 54.6 percent from 55.8 percent a year earlier, earnings per share had gone from −$5.82 in 2008 to $1.66 in 2011. Signaling a more focused strategy moving forward, Krill announced a name change for the company:

I am pleased to announce today that, in order to better reflect the multi-channel focus we have on our

EXHIBIT 2 ANN Net Sales ($ billions)

Year	Sales
2005	2.1
2006	2.3
2007	2.4
2008	2.2
2009	1.8
2010	2.0
2011	2.2
2012	2.4
2013	2.5

business, we have decided to change our corporate name from Ann Taylor Stores Corporation to ANN INC. Today, our Company is far more than a traditional "store-based" retailer. We have two distinct brands—Ann Taylor and LOFT—each of which operates across three channels and enables us to reach our client whether she is making her purchases at our stores, online or at our factory outlet locations.[16]

Going into 2013, things had improved once again, with total company comparable sales for the full year of fiscal 2012 increasing 3.3 percent. However, 2014 was not a good year, with sales and gross margins down in all areas. (See Exhibits 3, 4, and 5.) The concern going forward was how to manage all aspects of the business and position the company for long-term growth. As CEO Krill said, the challenge was to "aggressively manage our cost structure and increase value to shareholders."[17]

The Apparel Retail Industry

Industry Sectors

To better appreciate Ann Taylor's issues, it's helpful to understand the apparel retail industry. Industry publications such as the *Daily News Record* (DNR—reporting on men's fashion news and business strategies) and *Women's Wear Daily* (WWD—reporting on women's fashions and the apparel business) as well as industry associations such as the National Retail Federation (NRF) report data within the clothing sector. Practically speaking, industry watchers tend to recognize three categories of clothing retailers:

- *Discount mass merchandisers:* chains such as Target, Walmart, TJX (T.J. Maxx, Marshall's, HomeGoods), and Costco.
- *Multitier department stores:* those offering a large variety of goods, including clothing (e.g., Macy's and JCPenney), and the more luxury-goods-focused stores (e.g., Nordstrom and Neiman Marcus).
- *Specialty store chains:* those catering to a certain type of customer or carrying a certain type of goods, for example, Abercrombie & Fitch for casual apparel.

EXHIBIT 3 Income Statements ($ thousands)

Go to library tab in Connect to access Case Financials.

Period Ending	Feb. 2015	Feb. 1, 2014	Feb. 2, 2013	Jan. 28, 2012
Total Revenue	**2,533,460**	**2,493,491**	**2,375,509**	**2,212,493**
Cost of Revenue	1,242,506	1,150,183	1,073,167	1,004,350
Gross Profit	**1,290,954**	**1,343,308**	**1,302,342**	**1,208,143**
OPERATING EXPENSES				
Selling, General, and Administrative	1,161,838	1,173,234	1,135,551	1,062,644
Nonrecurring	17,303	—	—	—
Operating Income or Loss	**111,813**	**170,074**	**166,791**	**145,499**
INCOME–CONTINUING OPERATIONS				
Total Other Income/Expenses Net	(835)	(17)	(189)	—
Interest Expense	(363)	(94)	1,051	(1,052)
Income before Tax	110,615	169,963	167,653	144,447
Income Tax Expense	42,635	67,533	65,068	57,881
Net Income	**67,980**	**102,430**	**102,585**	**86,566**

Source: ANN Inc. 10-K filings.

EXHIBIT 4
Balance Sheets ($ thousands)

Period Ending	Feb. 2015	Feb. 1, 2014	Feb. 2, 2013	Jan. 28, 2012
Current Assets:				
Cash and Cash Equivalents	207,711	201,707	167,011	150,208
Short-Term Investments	—	—	—	—
Net Receivables	20,360	22,448	17,856	62,555
Inventory	265,022	239,667	216,848	213.447
Refundable/Deferred Income Taxes	35,316	36,106	39,598	—
Other Current Assets	72,489	61,287	64,716	49,107
Total Current Assets	600,898	561,215	506,029	475,317
Property, Plant, and Equipment	426,729	443,086	409,703	360,890
Other Assets	21,760	22,060	18,632	12,340
Deferred Long-Term Asset Charges	—	6,599	7,841	39,134
Total Assets	**1,061,506**	**1,032,960**	**942,205**	**887,681**
Current Liabilities:				
Accounts Payable	134,031	101,276	105,691	235,147
Short/Current Long-Term Debt	—	—	—	—
Other Current Liabilities	197,457	228,467	231,063	50,750
Total Current Liabilities	**331,488**	**329,743**	**336,754**	**285,897**
Other Liabilities	58,081	54,456	31,125	35,030
Deferred Long-Term Liability Charges	161,259	180,195	189,216	202,877
Total Liabilities	**550,828**	**564,394**	**557,095**	**523,804**
Stockholders' Equity				
Common Stock	561	561	561	561
Retained Earnings	847,252	779,272	676,842	574,527
Treasury Stock	(1,081,141)	(1,060,268)	(1,056,011)	(1,017,330)
Additional Paid-In Capital	749,711	751,765	768,215	811,707
Other Stockholders' Equity	(5,705)	(2,874)	(4,497)	(5,318)
Total Stockholders' Equity	**510,678**	**468,456**	**385,110**	**363,877**
Total Liabilities & Stockholders' Equity	**$1,061,506**	**$1,032,960**	**$942,205**	**$887,681**

Source: ANN Inc. 10-K filings.

Go to library tab in Connect to access Case Financials.

More specifically in the case of specialty retail, many broadly recognized primary categories exist, such as women's, men's, and children's clothing stores (e.g., Victoria's Secret for women's undergarments,[18] Men's Wearhouse for men's suits, Abercrombie Kids for children ages 7 to 14[19]). Women's specialty stores are "establishments primarily engaged in retailing a specialized line of women's, juniors' and misses' clothing."[20]

Specialty Retailer Growth: Branding Challenges

Unlike department stores that sell many different types of products for many types of customers, specialty retailers focus on one type of product item and offer many varieties of that item. However, this single-product focus increases risk, as lost sales in one area cannot be recouped by a shift

EXHIBIT 5
Statement of Annual Cash Flows

Go to library tab in Connect to access Case Financials.

Period Ending	Feb. 2015	Feb. 1, 2014	Feb. 2, 2013	Jan. 28, 2012
Net Income	67,980	102,430	102,585	86,566
OPERATING ACTIVITIES				
Depreciation	111,131	106,588	97,829	94,187
Adjustments to Net Income	18,317	18,291	64,442	38,149
Changes in Accounts Receivables	2,061	(4,647)	1,324	(2,060)
Changes in Liabilities	(5,107)	8,390	(7,573)	(24,649)
Changes in Inventories	(25,846)	(23,107)	(3,401)	(19,822)
Changes in Other Operating Activities	(12,139)	7,802	3,703	35,457
Total Cash Flow from Operating Activities	**156,397**	**215,747**	**258,909**	**207,828**
INVESTING ACTIVITIES				
Capital Expenditures	(108,284)	(140,655)	(147,286)	(118,918)
Investments	(617)	(2,758)	(1,977)	(1,288)
Other Cash Flows from Investing Activities	(147)	813	(649)	(250)
Total Cash Flows from Investing Activities	**(109,048)**	**(142,600)**	**(149,912)**	**(120,456)**
FINANCING ACTIVITIES				
Sale/Purchase of Stock	(36,188)	(36,217)	(94,823)	(169,736)
Net Borrowings	(3,384)	2,071	(2,801)	(1,511)
Other Cash Flows from Financing Activities	(1,273)	(3,839)	5,449	(188)
Total Cash Flows from Financing Activities	**(40,845)**	**(37,985)**	**(92,175)**	**(163,808)**
Change in Cash and Cash Equivalents	**6,004**	**34,696**	**16,803**	**(76,436)**

Source: ANN Inc. 10-K filings.

of interest to another, entirely different product area. Therefore, many specialty retailers constantly seek new market segments (i.e., niches) that they can serve. However, this strategy creates potential problems for branding.[21]

Gap Inc. is an example of a specialty retailer that added several brand extensions to appeal to different customer segments. In addition to the original Gap line of casual clothing, the company offered the following: Old Navy with casual fashions at low prices, Banana Republic for more high-end casual items, Athleta performance apparel and gear for active women, and Piperlime, an online shoe store. In 2005 Gap spent $40 million to open a chain for upscale women's clothing called Forth & Towne, which closed after only 18 months. The store was supposed to appeal to upscale women over 35—the baby-boomer or "misses" segment—but, instead, the designers seemed "too focused on reproducing youthful fashions with a more generous cut" instead of finding an "interesting, affordable way" for middle-aged women to "dress like themselves."[22]

Chico's FAS Inc. was another specialty retailer that tried brand expansions. Chico's focused on private-label, casual-to-dressy clothing for women age 35 and older, with relaxed, figure-flattering styles constructed out of easy-care fabrics. An outgrowth of a Mexican folk art boutique, Chico's was originally a stand-alone brand. Starting in late 2003, Chico's FAS decided to promote two new brands: White House/Black Market (WH/BM) and Soma by Chico's. Chico's WH/BM brand was based on the acquisition of an existing store chain, and it focused on women age 25 and older, offering fashion and merchandise in black-and-white and related

EXHIBIT 6 Selected Retail Performers: Descriptions

Company and Ticker Symbol	Number of Stores	Locations Served	Merchandise Market Served	Comments
Ann Taylor: ANN	1,050	46 states plus Puerto Rico, Canada, and Mexico	Specialty women's—private-label "total wardrobing strategy" to achieve the "Ann Taylor look" in suits, separates, footwear, and accessories	Brands are Ann Taylor for updated professional classics; LOFT for lower-priced, more casual wear; and Ann Taylor Factory & LOFT Outlet for outlet-priced items.
Talbots (bought out by private equity in 2012)	516	46 states plus Canada	Specialty women's—apparel, shoes, and accessories via stores, catalog, and Internet	Brands are Talbots and Modern Classics for women. Brands target high-income, college-educated professionals over 35 years old.
Chico's FAS: CHS	1,470	48 states plus U.S. Virgin Islands and Puerto Rico	Specialty women's—privately branded clothing, intimate garments, and gifts for women with moderate to high income via stores, catalog, Internet	Brands are Chico's for women over 30, White House/Black Market for women over 25, Soma intimates, and Boston Proper online and catalog (modern style, sensual feel).
Coldwater Creek Inc.: (bought out by private equity in 2014)	365	48 states	Specialty women's—apparel, accessories, jewelry, and gifts via catalog, Internet	Brand is Coldwater Creek for clothing, jewelry, and personal care products; targets women over 35 with income in excess of $75,000.

Source: Mergent Online; company reports.

shades. Soma was a newly developed brand offering intimate apparel, sleepwear, and active wear. Each brand had its own storefront, mainly in shopping malls, and was augmented by both mail-order catalog and Internet sales. The idea was that the loyal Chico's customer would be drawn to shop at these other concept stores, expecting the same level of quality, service, and targeted offerings that had pleased her in the past. In 2011 Chico acquired Boston Proper, a brand that sold women's high-end apparel and accessories focused on women between 35 and 55 years old, with sales only through catalogs and online. Boston Proper's intention was to create "a daring, modern style with a sensual feel designed for today's independent, confident and active woman."[23]

Although Chico's had been a solid performer during the decade, surpassing most other women's clothing retailers in sales growth, a downturn in 2006 caused Chico's shares to fall more than 50 percent when the company reported sales and earnings below analysts' expectations. Chico's had seen increasing competition for its baby-boomer customers, and it said it had lost momentum, partly because of "fashion missteps" and lack of sufficiently new product designs. The company's response was to create brand presidents for the three divisions to hopefully create more "excitement and differentiation."[24]

In an attempt to better manage the proliferation of brands, many firms, similar to Chico's, created an organizational structure in which brands had their own dedicated managers, with titles such as executive vice president (EVP), general merchandise manager, chief merchandising officer, or outright "brand president."[25] With each brand supposedly unique, companies felt the person responsible for a brand's creative vision should be unique as well.

An alternative to brand extension was the divestiture of brands. In 1988 Limited Brands acquired Abercrombie & Fitch (A&F) and rebuilt it to represent the "preppy" lifestyle of teenagers and college students ages 18 to 22. In 1996 Limited Brands spun A&F off as a separate public company. Limited Brands continued divesting brands: teenage clothing and accessories brand The Limited TOO in 1999, plus-size women's clothing brand Lane Bryant in 2001, professional women's clothing brand Lerner New York in 2002, and in 2007 the casual women's clothing brands Express and The Limited. Paring down in order to focus mostly on its key brands, Victoria's Secret and Bath & Body Works, the corporation made it clear that it had made a strategic decision to limit its exposure to changing clothing trends.[26]

Women's Specialty Retail: Competitors and the "Misses" Segment

The National Retail Federation, a trade group based in Washington, D.C., reported in 2007 that the retail niches showing the greatest growth were department stores, stores catering to the teenage children of baby boomers, and apparel chains aimed at women over 35.[27] The four major women's specialty retailers that had tried to target older upscale shoppers were Ann Taylor, Chico's FAS, Coldwater Creek, and Talbots. Ann Taylor was the only one of these with a significant brand extension for the younger professional, but all four had pursued a shopping environment and merchandise that were clearly focused on women over 35. (See Exhibit 6.)

This group of "older" women was part of the baby-boomer demographic, born between 1946 and 1964, and the purchasing power of these women had not gone unnoticed.[28] Historically, this "misses" market had been challenging to define, and therefore the category had been slow to innovate. To respond to diversity in the marketplace, women's specialty retailer Talbots Inc. acquired catalog and mail-order company J. Jill Group in 2006. J. Jill was a women's clothing specialty retailer offering casual fashion through multichannel mail-order, Internet, and in-store venues. J. Jill targeted women ages 35 to 55, while Talbots focused on the 45 to 65 age group. Although the acquisition had supposedly positioned Talbots as a "leading apparel retailer for the highly coveted age 35 female population,"[29] Talbots subsequently decided to sell off this division in 2009, in the wake of retailing's "abysmal holiday season." Analysts were not surprised, because Talbots had never made an acquisition before and had encountered problems integrating the two businesses.[30] Going into 2011, Talbots was struggling with merchandise that was perceived as too "mature," with stores that looked old-fashioned, and with vacancies in key upper-management positions. CEO Trudy Sullivan had been named one of the "worst CEOs of 2012" for her inability to turn the company around,[31] and by 2013 Talbots had shut dozens of stores and been bought out by a private equity firm for less than $3 per share.[32]

Coldwater Creek, with its large jewelry, accessory, and gift assortment in addition to apparel, described itself as "the fashion informed advocate for the 50 year old woman."[33] The company began by appealing with a Northwest/Southwest lifestyle approach that included a group of spa locations. Coldwater Creek created a common brand identity for its three distribution channels—catalog, Internet, and in-store shopping—but it too was having trouble finding the right mix of merchandise and presenting items properly in the stores. It also experienced key gaps in upper management. The company had suffered since the economic downturn of 2008, with its stock crashing from over $100 in 2006 to less than $2 in 2012, and it decided to close stores and reconsider merchandise targeted directly at its core demographic, rather than trying to bring in the younger shopper. In 2014 Coldwater Creek filed for bankruptcy, and was subsequently purchased by the same private equity group that previously acquired Talbots.[34] Coldwater Creek was subsequently relaunched as a catalog and online-based business. The stories of Talbots and Coldwater Creek illustrate how hard it can be for retailers to refine their fashion message and try to appeal to new, often younger customers "without alienating shoppers who have long been loyal fans."[35]

Chico's FAS was one of the first to introduce the concept of apparel designed for the lifestyle of dynamic mature women who were at the higher-age end of the boomer demographic.[36] Chico's had always been aware of the need to focus its branding on the older women's segment. As a result of this focus, Chico's ended the difficult 2008 year with "strong brand equity," one of the few specialty retailers with "staying power."[37] In 2011, of the four retailers focused on the "mature-women" segment, Chico's was the only one focused on inventory control and supply chain management as well as on moving away from relying on China's manufacturing power. Analysts therefore saw Chico's as having good prospects for maintaining positive margins going forward. By 2013, Chico's not only had rediscovered what its customers wanted but also had cut back on margin-squeezing discounting practices, and therefore it was considered the winner of the group.[38] In 2014, in recognition of its long-term superior performance, Chico's FAS was being considered as a possible acquirer of ANN.

In August 2007 Kay Krill announced that ANN would be creating a new chain of stores, expected to launch sometime in 2008 or 2009, targeting the "older-women" segment. Some analysts wondered about this move into an overlooked but risky market that had "tripped up several competitors." They pointed out that although ANN's clothes were expected to be more fashionable, the company still faced stiff competition, made even tougher given the uneven performance of AT and LOFT.[39] In 2008, as a result of the overall economic conditions, Krill announced that this new concept offering would have to be delayed at least until 2009,[40] and by 2010 there was no more mention of this initiative. Instead, Krill announced that the "boomer" terminology was outdated: "We never called ourselves 'misses.' We're timeless, modern and ageless, and we had to adjust and become more relevant to what modern consumers want today. It's been an evolution. I feel like we are on the right track."[41] ANN's goal was to sell clothes to more affluent women in general, regardless of age range. However, at the end of 2014 ANN had over twice as many LOFT stores as Ann Taylor stores, and the LOFT customer was normally a younger woman. Further differentiating within the LOFT space, LOFT Lounge was created to highlight a more relaxed, casual style. This store-in-store venue allowed for the testing of a new brand concept under the Lou & Grey name. Lou & Grey was a move into the active-wear fashion space and included lace sweatpants, knit moto jackets, and linen T-shirts. According to Krill, the brand was "pulling in a younger clientele, while not alienating 40- and 50-year-olds."[42] In 2014 the first freestanding Lou & Grey store opened in Westport, Connecticut.

Krill was also moving toward what was being called an "omnichannel" sales approach: using full-price stores mixed with factory outlets and online options for each brand. ANN's e-commerce business had more than doubled since 2010, and between 2011 and 2012 e-commerce comparable sales grew over 37 percent for the Ann Taylor brand and 29 percent for LOFT. By 2014, ANN was fully committed to the integrated omnichannel structure. Testing the international market, ANN opened its first Ann Taylor "boutique" store in Toronto, Canada, during 2012, with two more added soon after.[43] A LOFT store opened in Mexico in 2014.

	FY2014	FY2013	FY2012	FY2011	FY2010
Employees, total	NA	19,800	19,600	19,900	19,400
Inventory turns*	5.0	5.0	5.0	4.9	4.8
Net sales (revenue) per employee	NA	$125,933	$121,199	$111,486	$102,352
Number of stores/square footage:†					
Ann Taylor stores	261/1,246	276/1,371	275/1,389	280/1,460	266/1,453
Ann Taylor Factory	115/772	106/721	101/696	99/700	92/668
LOFT stores	548/3,106	537/3,072	512/2,950	500/2,904	502/2,930
LOFT Outlet	126/824	108/719	96/650	74/520	36/233
Total company	1,050/5,948	1,027/5,884	984/5,685	953/5,584	896/5,284

EXHIBIT 7 Stores' Operational Data

*Inventory turns can be calculated differently, depending on whether yearly average or year-end inventory values are used.
†Square footage in thousands.

Source: ANN Inc. 10-K filings; Mergent Online.

ANN Operational Information

At the end of fiscal year 2014, ANN had 1,050 stores in 46 states, the District of Columbia, and Puerto Rico, with flagship locations in New York and Chicago, and an international presence with three stores in Canada and a LOFT presence in Mexico. (See Exhibit 7.) The company also had an online presence since 2000, transacting sales at www.anntaylor.com and www.LOFT.com. This "very profitable" Internet channel was considered "a meaningful and effective marketing vehicle for both brands" and was a way for ANN to reach out to the entire international market.[44]

Substantially all merchandise offered in ANN's stores was exclusively developed for the company by its in-house product design and development teams. ANN sourced merchandise from approximately 133 manufacturers and vendors, none of which accounted for more than 10 percent of the company's merchandise purchases in fiscal 2013. Merchandise was manufactured in over 17 countries, including China (37 percent of purchases, 40 percent of total merchandise cost, down from 43 percent in 2012), the Philippines, Indonesia, India, and Vietnam. North American distribution was handled through a primary warehouse in Louisville, Kentucky, and online orders were handled by a third-party fulfillment center in Bolingbrook, Illinois. Other merchandise handling facilities were located in Toronto, Ontario, for Canadian store distribution, and a backup facility was in Industry, California.

Ann Taylor's Historic Issues: Brand Identity and Management Turnover

As with other specialty retailers, ANN had struggled with erratic performance in one division or the other and had suffered from excessive turnover in top management ranks. When ANN went public in 1991, the Ann Taylor brand, with its historically loyal following, was a candidate for brand extension. At one point in its history, the company had five separate store concepts: Ann Taylor (AT), Ann Taylor's Studio Shoes, Ann Taylor LOFT, Ann Taylor Petites (clothing for women 5 feet 4 inches and under), and Ann Taylor Factory. In addition, ANN's management had experimented with a makeup line and with children's clothes. By 2005, the company had closed the shoe stores, reduced the accessories inventory that stores carried, and eliminated the makeup line.

Since 1999 analysts had warned that ANN needed to be wary of cannibalization within the brands. The analysts speculated that customers might turn away from AT in order to buy at LOFT. ANN had always tried to respond to the customer with "wardrobing," a philosophy of "outfitting from head to toe," combining relaxed everyday wear with more dressy pieces.[45] Because LOFT sold more relaxed but still tailored items at a lower price than AT did, the concern was that some of AT's customers might shop at LOFT for things that they previously would have bought at AT.

Therefore, in 2005 Krill asked her staff to spend time with ANN customers and develop "brand books," or profiles, of typical AT and LOFT clients.[46] The "Ann" (AT) marketing profile was of a married 36-year-old working mother with two children and a household income of $150,000. She would lead a busy, sophisticated life. When giving a presentation to a client, she'd wear a formal suit with a blouse, not a camisole, underneath, and her idea of dressing down at work might be a velvet jacket with jeans.

In contrast, the typical LOFT client was in her 30s and married, with children; worked in a laid-back, less corporate environment; and had a household income between $75,000 and $100,000. She would call her style "casual chic" and might wear pants and a floral top with ruffled sleeves to work, while on the weekend she would wear a printed shoulder-baring halter top with cropped jeans.

Also in 2005, Krill tried to reconfigure ANN's top management, creating three positions that reported directly to her—COO, executive vice president (EVP) of planning and allocation, and EVP/chief marketing officer. These three additional positions provided specific expertise while still allowing Krill to "lead both divisions [AT and LOFT] in a more hands-on-way." Krill could then focus on merchandising and marketing, especially brand differentiation.[47] AT and LOFT continued to have separate EVPs for merchandising and design and separate senior vice presidents for divisional marketing, design, sourcing, and store direction.

In 2006 Krill lost her recently hired COO, Laura Weil, who left abruptly after only a few months on the job. Weil's many responsibilities at ANN had included merchandise planning; information systems; all supply chain operations, including sourcing, logistics, and distribution; real estate; construction and facilities; and purchasing, as well as finance, accounting, and investor relations.[48] Krill decided not to replace Weil and eliminated the position on the organization chart. Krill also assumed leadership of LOFT again. Krill commented, "I believe that building a winning team is critical to fully realizing our company's full potential."[49] However, it appeared that creating the "winning team" was taking longer than anticipated. One source wondered about the pressure on Krill, especially because she didn't have a strong operating partner to help with merchandising and other creative decisions.[50]

Even though Krill had made differentiation between AT and LOFT a top priority, analysts continued to challenge Krill's efforts, noting that it had been hard to get both divisions moving forward simultaneously. As one analyst said, "It just seems like it's a struggle to get both of these divisions firing on all cylinders at the same time."[51] Krill responded to the comment that consistency had been a problem: "The notion that Ann Taylor got soft because I was supporting the LOFT team is really a completely inaccurate comment. As CEO of the company I have to spend my time on many things, and if one of our businesses is softening in any way I will focus extra time on it."[52] At the end of 2008, Krill finally filled the AT and LOFT divisional president positions, and the new executives remained in place, at least into 2011. However, the Ann Taylor division did see a change in brand president in 2012.

In 2014, a strategic restructuring slimmed down ANN's management, eliminating approximately 100 corporate positions and bringing both LOFT and AT under one president, Gary Muto. CEO Krill announced that Muto was now responsible for all ANN's brands and all channels. The restructuring was expected to expand ANN's omnichannel capabilities and, in Krill's words, "enhance the productivity of our store fleet, grow our international presence, and develop new categories of growth, including the launch of the Lou & Grey brand, while also furthering our objective to maximize the profitable growth of ANN INC."[53]

Future Initiatives?

Since 2008 Krill had been acknowledging that differentiating LOFT from Ann Taylor was a challenge. In 2010, Krill believed the transition to a "world-class multi-channel retailer" would allow ANN Inc. to serve "two distinct segments of the market with two differentiated brands" across three channels—in the full-price store, in the factory store, or online.[54] And in 2011 she stated, "We have evolved both brands to be highly differentiated and distinct. Absolutely, the number-one challenge is to sustain the momentum of both brands and all channels."[55] Going into 2015, that challenge still remained.

ENDNOTES

1. Zacks Equity Research. 2015. ANN Inc. (ANN) stands on the back foot as 2015 unveils. *Zacks,* January 6, *www.zacks.com/stock/news/159433/ann-inc-ann-stands-on-the-back-foot-as-2015-unveils?source=sa.*
2. Hargrave, M. 2015. Ann Inc.: Two activist investors square off. *Seeking Alpha,* January 29, *http://seekingalpha.com/article/2864126-ann-inc-two-activist-investors-square-off.*
3. Elejalde-Ruiz, A. 2015. Retailers expect even stronger growth in 2015. *Chicago Tribune,* January 14, *www.chicagotribune.com/business/ct-retail-outlook-0115-biz-biz-20150114-story.html#page=1;* and Grannis, K. 2015. NRF forecasts retail sales to increase 4.1% over last year. *National Retail Federation,* February 12, *https://nrf.com/media/press-releases/nrf-forecasts-retail-sales-increase-41-over-last-year.*
4. Dickler, J. 2011. Consumers: We want Gucci or Target. Forget the Gap. Shoppers are once again showing a preference for high-end brands. *CNN Money,* March 9, *money.cnn.com/2011/03/09/pf/consumers_prefer_luxury/.*
5. Mahashwari, S. 2012. Retailers respond as millennials seek quality: Public "exhausted" by fast fashion; well-priced apparel now more appealing. *Chicago Tribune,* November 16, *articles.chicagotribune.com/2012-11-16/business/ct-biz-1116-bf-fast-fashion-20121116_1_american-apparel-apparel-retailers-higher-prices;* Berk, C. C. 2013. Dour December may not spell retail disaster this year. *CNBC,* January 2, *www.cnbc.com/id/100349579;* and Steigrad, A. 2013. Holiday's aftermath: Squeeze on profits. *Women's Wear Daily,* 502, no. 3 (January 4): 1.
6. Jones, S. M. 2012. Ann Taylor tailors new Mag Mile store to fit modern shoppers, improve sales. *Chicago Tribune,* March 1, *articles.chicagotribune.com/2012-03-01/business/ct-biz-0302-ann-taylor-20120229_1_ann-taylor-kay-krill-modern-shoppers.*
7. Hargrave, op. cit.
8. Warner, B., director, corporate communications, Ann Taylor Stores Corporation. 2007. ANN representatives noted that there was no apparent cause-and-effect relationship between AT sales decline and the growth of LOFT. Personal communication, July.
9. Tucker, R. 2004. LOFT continues to pace Ann Taylor. *Women's Wear Daily,* August 12: 12.
10. Ann Taylor Stores Corporation. 2007. Letter to shareholders. Ann Taylor Stores Corporation 2007 annual report. *investor.anntaylor.com/phoenix.zhtml?c578167&p5irol-reportsAnnual.*
11. Ann Taylor Stores Corporation. 2008. Q1 2008 Ann Taylor Stores earnings conference call. *SeekingAlpha.com,* May 22, *seekingalpha.com/article/78473-ann-taylor-stores-corp-q1-2008-earnings-call-transcript.*
12. Wilson, M. 1995. Reinventing Ann Taylor. *Chain Store Age Executive with Shopping Center Age,* January: 26.
13. Summers, M. 1999. New outfit. *Forbes,* December 27: 88.
14. Krill, K. 2005. As quoted in Ann Taylor Stores Corporation. 2005. Q3 2005 Ann Taylor Stores earnings conference call.

15. Ann Taylor Stores Corporation. 2007. Letter to shareholders.
16. Ann Taylor Stores Corporation. 2011. Ann Taylor reports substantially higher sales and earnings for fourth quarter and fiscal 2010. *Investor.AnnTaylor.com,* March 11, investor.anntaylor.com/phoenix.zhtml?c578167&p5irol-newsArticle&ID51538446.
17. PRNewswire. 2014. ANN INC. reports third quarter 2014 results. *PRNewswire,* November 21.
18. Victoria's Secret is a division of L Brands (formerly Limited Brands), which also operates Pink (a subbrand of Victoria's Secret focused on sleepwear and intimate apparel for high school and college students), Bath & Body Works, C.O. Bigelow (personal beauty, body, and hair products), The White Barn Candle Co. (candles and home fragrances), Henri Bendel (high-fashion women's clothing), and La Senza (lingerie sold in Canada and worldwide).
19. Abercrombie & Fitch, as of 2015, had three brand divisions in addition to the flagship Abercrombie & Fitch stores: abercrombie (the brand name is purposely lowercase) for kids ages 7 to 14; Hollister Co. for southern California surf-lifestyle teens; and Gilly Hicks: Sydney, launched in 2008, specializing in women's intimate apparel. RUEHL No. 925, launched in 2004 with more sophisticated apparel for ages 22 to 35, closed in 2010.
20. U.S. Census Bureau. Monthly retail trade and food services NAICS codes, titles, and descriptions. *www.census.gov/svsd/www/artsnaics.html.*
21. According to the American Marketing Association (AMA), a brand is a "'name, term, sign, symbol or design, or a combination of them intended to identify the goods and services of one seller or group of sellers and to differentiate them from those of other sellers.' . . . Branding is not about getting your target market to choose you over the competition, but it is about getting your prospects to see you as the only one that provides a solution to their problem." A good brand will communicate this message clearly and with credibility, motivating the buyer by eliciting some emotion that inspires future loyalty. From *marketing.about.com/cs/brandmktg/a/whatisbranding.htm.*
22. Turner, J. 2007. Go forth and go out of business. *Slate,* February 26, www.slate.com/id/2160668.
23. Chico's FAS. Corporate profile. *www.chicosfas.com/phoenix.zhtml?c572638&p5irol-homeProfile.*
24. Lee, G. 2007. Chico's outlines plan to improve results. *Women's Wear Daily,* March 8: 5.
25. The responsibilities of these positions include "creative vision" for the brand: marketing materials, store design, and overall merchandising (developing product, ensuring production efficiency, monitoring store inventory turnover, and adjusting price points as needed).
26. *Columbus Business First.* 2007. Limited Brands cutting 530 jobs. June 22, columbus.bizjournals.com/columbus/stories/2007/06/18/daily26.html.
27. Jones, S. M. 2007. Sweetest spots in retail. *Knight Ridder Tribune Business News,* July 31: 1.
28. See, for instance, the website *www.aginghipsters.com,* a "source for trends, research, comment and discussion" about this group.
29. Talbots Inc. 2006. Talbots completes the acquisition of the J.Jill Group. *Business Wire,* May 3, phx.corporate-ir.net/phoenix.zhtml?c565681&p5irol-newsArticle&ID5851481.
30. Abelson, J. 2008. Talbots is seeking a buyer for J.Jill. *Boston Globe,* November 7, www.boston.com/business/articles/2008/11/07/talbots_is_seeking_a_buyer_for_j_jill.
31. Williams, S. 2012. Huge CEO gaffes: Talbots. *Motley Fool,* July 6, www.fool.com/investing/general/2012/07/06/huge-ceo-gaffes-talbots.aspx.
32. Protess, B. 2012. After rejecting higher offers, Talbots agrees to $369 million buyout. *New York Times Dealbook,* May 31, dealbook.nytimes.com/2012/05/31/after-rejecting-higher-offer-talbots-agrees-to-369-million-buyout/.
33. Lomax, A. 2013. Chilly post-holiday news from Coldwater Creek. *Motley Fool,* January 15, www.fool.com/investing/general/2013/01/15/chilly-post-holiday-news-from-coldwater-creek.aspx.
34. Palank, J. 2014. Coldwater Creek, creditors group settle payment plan dispute. *Wall Street Journal,* July 11, www.wsj.com/articles/coldwater-creek-creditors-group-settle-payment-plan-dispute-1405098894.
35. Lutz, A. 2011. How Talbots grew—and lost—its customers. *Bloomberg Businessweek,* June 16, www.businessweek.com/magazine/content/11_26/b4234025390837.htm.
36. Some marketers believe that the boomers are a bifurcated demographic. Although the boomer market encompasses those born from 1946 to 1964, boomers born between 1946 and 1954 have slightly different life experiences than those born between 1955 and 1964 have.
37. *Wall Street Transcript Online.* 2009. Investor interest in specialty apparel companies examined in Wall Street transcript specialty retail report. March 25, *finance.yahoo.com/news/Investor-Interest-in-twst-14741666.html.*
38. Caplinger, D. 2012. Was 2012 Coldwater Creek's turning point? *Motley Fool,* December 14, www.fool.com/investing/general/2012/12/24/was-coldwater-creeks-2012-turning-point.aspx; Caplinger, D. 2013. Can Coldwater Creek stay hot in 2013? *Motley Fool,* January 7, www.fool.com/investing/general/2013/01/07/can-coldwater-creek-stay-hot-in.aspx; and Lomax, A. 2013. Chilly post-holiday news from Coldwater Creek. *Motley Fool,* January 15, www.fool.com/investing/general/2013/01/15/chilly-post-holiday-news-from-coldwater-creek.aspx.
39. Kingsbury, K., & Moore, A. 2007. Ann Taylor tries for a better fit. *Wall Street Journal* (Eastern edition), August 25: B6.
40. Barbaro, M. 2007. Ann Taylor said to plan boomer unit. *New York Times,* August 13: C3.
41. Moin, D. 2010. Scoring some hits.
42. Moore, B. 2014. New Ann Taylor brand Lou & Grey taps into active-wear fashion trend. *LA Times,* April 29, www.latimes.com/fashion/alltherage/la-ar-new-ann-taylor-brand-lou-grey-taps-into-active-wear-fashion-trend-20140428-story.html#page=1.
43. Cariaga, V. 2012. Ann Taylor apparel sales up as new strategy pays off. *Investor's Business Daily,* January 8, news.investors.com/print/business-the-new-america/010813-639740-ann-taylor-clothing-retail-sales-fashion-gap.aspx.
44. Information in this section comes from Ann Taylor Stores Corporation 10-K filing as of FY2012.
45. Kennedy, K. 2000. This is not your momma's clothing store—not by a longshot. *Apparel Industry Magazine* (Altanta), December: 22–25.
46. Merrick, A. 2006. Boss talk: Asking "What would Ann do?" In turning around Ann Taylor, CEO Kay Krill got to know her customers, "Ann" and "Loft." *Wall Street Journal* (Eastern edition), September 15: B1.
47. Moin, D. 2005. Ann Taylor Stores taps two to fill out executive ranks. *Women's Wear Daily,* March 3.
48. Moin, D. 2006. Laura Weil exits Ann Taylor. *Women's Wear Daily,* May 5: 2.
49. Ann Taylor Stores Corporation. 2006. Ann Taylor Stores 2005 annual report. *investor.anntaylor.com/phoenix.zhtml?c578167&p5irol-reportsAnnual.*
50. Moin, D. 2006. Rebound at Ann Taylor: CEO Kay Krill fashions retailer's new career. *Women's Wear Daily,* June 26: 1.
51. Ann Taylor Stores Corporation. 2008. Q4 2007 Ann Taylor Stores earnings conference call. *SeekingAlpha.com,* March 14, seekingalpha.com/article/68606-ann-taylor-stores-corporation-q4-2007-earnings-call-transcript?page58.
52. Ann Taylor Stores Corporation. 2008. Q1 2008 Ann Taylor Stores earnings conference call.
53. PRNewswire. 2014. ANN INC. announces strategic realignment. *PRNewswire,* March 14.
54. Ann Taylor Stores Corporation. 2011. Ann Taylor Stores' CEO discusses Q4 2010 results—earnings call transcript. *SeekingAlpha.com,* March 11, seekingalpha.com/article/257806-anntaylor-stores-ceo-discusses-q4-2010-results-earnings-call-transcript.
55. Moin, D. 2011. Growing Ann Taylor gets a new moniker. *Women's Wear Daily,* March 14: 8.

CASE 11

GREENWOOD RESOURCES: A GLOBAL SUSTAINABLE VENTURE IN THE MAKING*

"Money still grows on trees."

—**Larry Light, Deputy Editor**
for Personal Finance, *Wall Street Journal*[1]

"The answer to some of the world's most pressing concerns (global warming, alternative energy, sustainable forestry) lies in one of the earth's most renewable resources—trees."

—**GreenWood Resources, Inc.**[2]

Jeff Nuss and other senior managers of GreenWood Resources, Inc., emerged after a long deliberation from the conference room in their headquarters in Portland, Oregon, in June 2010. On the one hand, they were inspired by their global vision to build "a resource that lasts forever" and their belief the company, with nearly 70 employees, was finally taking off after almost 10 years of persistent efforts in building the key elements (opportunity, people, resources, and business networks) for a successful tree plantation venture. On the other hand, they just finished a grueling meeting during which they found it hard to reach a consensus on how to proceed with two strategic investment alternatives in rural China.

Since 2000, Jeff and several other senior managers had traveled to China on numerous occasions. The process of making a deal in the Chinese forest industry had proven to be more time-consuming than anticipated. Complex ownership structures, underdeveloped farming systems, and emerging, sometimes equivocal and unpredictable, government policies characterized the forest industry in China. Chinese farmers who embraced business models and management styles far different than those in the United States posed additional complications.

By March 2009, GreenWood had assessed some 20 potential investment projects in China. The Luxi and Dongji projects passed the initial phase of screening and became the company's top priorities. The due diligence on these two projects had been extensive, lasting over a year, but both projects still faced considerable obstacles and even potential deadlock. In June 2010, Jeff and his senior management team were still weighing the pros and cons of the two projects, which had been the subject of their last management meeting. They felt that GreenWood needed to proceed carefully to ensure the company's sustainable business criteria (rather than its financial return per se) were met in China but also realized the company needed to show some progress to its major investor in China, Oriental Timber Fund Limited. Jeff needed to bring a recommendation from his senior management team to the investment committee comprising himself and two representatives from Oriental. The decision deadline was approaching. Jeff anticipated that the next senior management meeting would result in a recommendation. Should GreenWood choose one of the two projects?

GreenWood Resources, Inc.

Founding of the Venture

In 1998, after 12 years of experience with CH2M Hill[3] as a bioresources engineer, Jeff Nuss, a native Oregonian, decided to start his own venture, GreenWood Resources, Inc., specializing in the development and management of high-yield, fast-growing tree plantations. Having looked into other potential businesses such as a golf course and a winery, he was eventually convinced, based on his education and years of experience working with poplar tree farms, that investments in tree plantations held great promise for the future (see Appendix 1 for background industry information).

Jeff's plan was to help institutional investors (pension funds, endowments, insurance companies, etc.) and wealthy individuals invest in professionally managed high-yield, short-rotation tree farms (Exhibit 1 illustrates tree rotation length and yield of several representative tree species). He wanted to operate farms in accordance with Forest Stewardship Council (FSC) certification. FSC's objective was to conserve biological diversity and enhance the long-term social and economic well-being of forest workers and local communities (see Exhibit 2).

Firms with FSC certificates were rare because the standards were stringent, often leading to higher operating costs. For example, FSC required the use of less toxic pesticides and herbicides, which were more expensive. It prohibited the use of genetically modified trees. It also demanded that 10 percent of tree farms be reserved for

---

* Copyright © 2014 by the *Case Research Journal* and by Lei Li, Nottingham University Business School China; Howard Feldman, University of Portland; and Alan Eisner, Pace University. This case is developed solely as the basis for class discussion. It is not intended to serve as endorsements, sources of primary data, or illustrations of effective or ineffective management. The authors acknowledge the able assistance of Wendy Ye and Pratik Rachh in the process of developing the case.

EXHIBIT 1 Tree Rotation Length and Yield

[Chart: Cubic Meters per Hectare per Year (y-axis, 7 to 42) vs. Rotation Length, Years (x-axis, 0 to 50). Species plotted: Eucalyptus (~5 years, ~40), Hybrid poplar (~10 years, ~35), Radiata (~20 years, ~22), Loblolly pine (~28 years, ~25), Douglas fir (~45 years, ~10).]

The figure shows that eucalyptus and hybrid poplar ripen for harvest much faster than other species.

Source: GreenWood's brochure.

EXHIBIT 2 Forest Stewardship Council (FSC) Principles and Criteria for Forest Management

1. **Compliance with laws and FSC principles and criteria.** Forest management shall respect all applicable laws of the country in which they occur, and international treaties and agreements to which the country is a signatory, and comply with all FSC principles and criteria.

2. **Tenure and use rights and responsibilities.** Long-term tenure and use rights to the land and forest resources shall be clearly defined, documented, and legally established.

3. **Indigenous people's rights.** The legal and customary rights of indigenous people to own, use, and manage their lands, territories, and resources shall be recognized and respected.

4. **Community relations and workers' rights.** Forest management operations shall maintain or enhance the long-term social and economic well-being of forest workers and local communities.

5. **Benefits from the forest.** Forest management operations shall encourage the efficient use of the forest's multiple products and services to ensure economic viability and a wide range of environmental and social benefits.

6. **Environmental impact.** Forest management shall conserve biological diversity and its associated value, water resources, soil, and unique and fragile ecosystems and landscapes, and, by so doing, maintain the ecological functions and the integrity of the forest.

7. **Management plan.** A management plan—appropriate to the scale and intensity of the operations—shall be written, implemented, and kept up to date. The long-term objectives of management, and the means of achieving them, shall be clearly stated.

8. **Monitoring and assessment.** Monitoring shall be conducted—appropriate to the scale and intensity of forest management—to assess the condition of the forest, yields of forest products, chain of custody, management activities, and their social and environmental impact.

9. **Maintenance of high-conservation-value forests.** Management activities in high-conservation-value forests shall maintain or enhance the attributes which define such forests. Decisions regarding high-conservation-value forests shall always be considered in the context of a precautionary approach.

10. **Plantations.** Plantations shall be planned and managed in accordance with Principles and Criteria 1–9, and Principle 10 and its Criteria. While plantations can provide an array of social and economic benefits, and can contribute to satisfying the world's needs for forest products, they should complement the management of, reduce pressures on, and promote the restoration and conservation of natural forests.

Source: Austin and Reficco (2006).[4]

native habitats. At the same time, however, the economic benefits were uncertain because most end users of wood products were not necessarily willing to pay a premium price for FSC-certified products. Nevertheless, Jeff felt it was the right thing to do. "At the end of the day, we do what we believe (is right)."

Key Milestones: Building Research Expertise and the Management Team

Looking back, Jeff recalled several key milestones for GreenWood. Having founded GreenWood with his limited personal wealth, Jeff's first milestone occurred when he convinced a large Oregon family office[5] to acquire an existing poplar plantation. As a result of this acquisition, GreenWood not only earned a steady fee through managing the poplar plantation assets for the family office but also inherited a group of staff experienced in plantation management. The head of this group was Dr. Brian Stanton, a renowned expert in poplar hybridization and genetic improvement. Over the years, Dr. Stanton's research team had developed dozens of poplar varieties characterized by high growth rate, strong pest resistance, high wood density, and broad site adaptability.

The second milestone came in 2002. On behalf of the family office, GreenWood helped sell the poplar plantation to GMO Renewable Resources, a large timber investment management organization (TIMO). Despite the ownership change, GreenWood remained the management company, taking care of the plantation assets. This enhanced the company's credibility and stature and helped initiate a business model which integrated tree improvement, nurseries, tree farm operations, product (i.e., log, lumber, chips) sales, and trading and ecosystem services (i.e., monetizing carbon credits, biodiversity credits, water quality, and renewable energy credits and managing land for total ecosystem value).

Other milestones included the formation of a seasoned management team and the development of a series of strategic relationships. In the course of formulating a viable global business plan and raising capital, Jeff was able to successfully put together what he believed was a highly competent management team (see Exhibit 3 for management team biographies and Exhibit 4 for the organizational

EXHIBIT 3 Executive Management Team Biographies, 2010

Jeff Nuss is the founder, chairman, and CEO of GreenWood Resources, Inc., and its subsidiaries and is directly responsible for the leadership and strategic direction of the company. He is a leading industry spokesman and advocate for novel methods of sustainable timber production and serves on the boards of the World Forestry Center, Agribusiness Council, and Western Hardwood Council. He received a BS in bioresource engineering and an MS in resource management and policy within the Civil Engineering Department of Oregon State University.

Hunter Brown is chief operating officer of GreenWood Resources, Inc. Prior to joining GreenWood, he was executive vice president for PACCESS, a global supply chain services management firm. He has extensive business experience in Asia. Hunter received a BS in forestry from the University of the South and an MS in forestry from Duke University, and he completed the Executive Program at the Darden School of Business at the University of Virginia.

Lincoln Bach is corporate controller of GreenWood Resources, Inc. Prior to joining GreenWood, he was corporate controller for an international family-wealth-management firm. He had previously served as an audit manager at Deloitte & Touche. He received a BS in accounting from Linfield College and is a CPA and CFP professional.

Brian Stanton is managing director of Tree Improvement Group & Nurseries at GreenWood Resources, Inc. For 20 years, he has overseen the technological developments for poplar on commercial tree farms in the U.S. where he has produced over 40,000 varieties of hybrid poplar that have been tested throughout Chile, China, Europe, and the United States. Brian is the chair of the Poplar and Willow Working Party for the International Union of Forest Research Organizations. He received a BS in biology from West Chester State College, an MS in forestry from the University of Maine, and a PhD in forest resources from Pennsylvania State University.

Don Rice is managing director of Resource Management Group at GreenWood Resources, Inc. Previously, Don was the Oregon poplar resource and manufacturing manager for Potlatch Corporation. Don has a degree in agricultural engineering from Washington State University.

Jake Eaton is managing director of resource planning and acquisitions at GreenWood Resources. He worked for 21 years with Potlatch Corporation. Jake has extensive global experience in short-rotation tree farm silviculture. He holds a BS in forest management from Oregon State University and an MS in silviculture and genetics from University of Montana.

Brian Liu is vice president and general manager of GreenWood Resources, Inc.'s China Operations. Previously, as an international trade representative for the State of Oregon Department of Agriculture, he successfully led the U.S. negotiation teams in opening the Chinese market for Oregon agricultural products. Brian was born and raised in Guangdong, China, and moved to the U.S. at the age of 14. He holds a BS in finance and an MBA in international management from Portland State University. He is fluent in English, Mandarin, and Cantonese.

Source: GreenWood Resources, Inc.

EXHIBIT 4 GreenWood Resources, Inc., Topline Organization Chart, 2010*

```
                                    Board of Directors
                                    Jeff Nuss, Chairman
                                            |
                                       Shareholders
                                            |
                                       Jeff Nuss
                                    President and CEO
                                            |
           ┌────────────────────────────────┼────────────────────────────────┐
   Investment/Capital              Operations                          Finance &
     Management                    Management                        Administration
    Jeff Nuss                      Hunter Brown                         TBD
 Chief Investment                  COO and EVP                    CFO and Compliance
     Officer                                                            Officer
```

Investment/Capital Management			Operations Management				Finance & Administration
Jeff Nuss, acting Managing Director **Capital Management Group**	Jake Eaton Managing Director **Global Acquisitions and Resource Planning**	Dr. Brian Stanton Managing Director **Tree Improvement Group & Nurseries**	Don Rice Managing Director **Resource Management Group**	Hunter Brown acting Managing Director **Product Sales and Trading**	TBD Managing Director **Ecosystem Markets and Values**	Brian Liu General Manager **GreenWood China**	Other Regional Managers
Investment Product Development, Compliance and Reporting Oversight, Investor Communications	Acquisitions and Due Diligence, Global Tree Farming Technology Standards, Research Project Delivery, FSC, Global Environmental	Tree Improvement Global Oversight, Breeding Activities, Regional Nursery Operations, Greenhouse Operations, Plant Material Sales, IP Expansion	Tree Farm Operations, Silvicultural Management, Irrigation Operations and Management, Resource Information System	Domestic and International Sales Activities for Logs, Chips, Lumber, etc. Improve linkage to markets from tree farms, connect regional relationships	Carbon Markets, Wetland Markets, Wind Development, Water Quantity, Quality Markets		

	Lincoln Bach **Global Corp. Controller & Administration**
	Investment and Portfolio Accounting and Reporting, Corporate Accounting and Reporting, HR, Administration Corp IT

*If regional subsidiaries are considered, GreenWood adopted a matrix structure. For example, Zhang Weidong (director of Resource Planning and Acquisition) and Jessica Zhi (the Luxi project manager) at GreenWood China both reported to Brian Liu but also took professional advice from Jake Eaton, who was essentially the global functional manager of Resource Planning.

Source: GreenWood Resources, Inc.

structure). For example, Hunter Brown, a veteran operational manager with experience in Asia, joined GreenWood as the chief operating officer. Brian Liu, a Chinese American with years of experience working for the Oregon State Department of Agriculture (responsible for the forest industry), was recruited to lead the company's China operations. Brian had supported GreenWood's endeavors while visiting China as a state government official, and he had been convinced to leave his stable government position to join GreenWood in 2005. In reflecting on his success in recruiting people, Jeff said:

> I am good at connecting to people. In that process, I am getting people around an idea and a vision and motivating (them). . . . I tried to first understand what is really their passion. If that passion can be aligned with (the vision of the company), it makes it really easy to get people on the same page and aboard.

Thanks to the dedication of its people as well as its growing business network, GreenWood looked to expand its operations to China and South America and launched two investment fund-raising campaigns to support its initiatives (see Exhibit 5: A Chronicle of GreenWood).

Entering the Chinese Poplar Plantation Industry

Perhaps the most important entrepreneurial initiative for GreenWood was the decision to commit itself to the Chinese poplar plantation market. The poplar plantation industry in the United States was of limited scale. From the very beginning Jeff believed that GreenWood needed to consider opportunities in other regions of the world.

In China, the potential of high-yield, fast-growing plantations in general, and poplar tree farming in particular, was projected to be significant. Furthermore, the concept of "sustainably managing" tree farms was attractive to many people given that growing demand for wood products had resulted in years of excessive logging and, ultimately, significant desertification and deforestation. The country's loss of forestland was almost ignored until the 1990s. In response, China launched a project in 2000 to plant trees and grass in an effort to slow desertification in northern China, including the Beijing region. Nationwide, China set a goal of raising its afforestation (i.e., establishing forestland by planting seeds or trees in open land) rate to 26 percent of its land area by 2050, which would require an increase of forestland in excess of 65 million hectares.[6] To achieve this ambitious goal, high-yield, fast-growing plantations would have to play an important role.

GreenWood's Experience in China

In 2000, Jeff was invited to join a Mercy Corps task force visiting China. Mercy Corps was a Portland, Oregon–based charity whose mission was to alleviate suffering, poverty, and oppression by helping people worldwide to build just, secure, and productive communities. Its cofounder, Ells

EXHIBIT 5 A Chronicle of GreenWood Resources, Inc.

Year	Event
1998	Jeff Nuss founded GreenWood with dedication to the innovative development and management of sustainable tree farms and their products.
1999	GreenWood started to manage poplar plantation assets on behalf of a large Oregonian family office.
2000	Jeff Nuss made the initial visit to China.
2001	Dr. Brian Stanton joined GreenWood.
2002	GreenWood helped sell the poplar plantation assets to GMO Renewable Resources on behalf of the Oregonian family office and consequently became a specialized poplar assets manager for GMO Renewable Resources.
2005	Hunter Brown and Brian Liu joined GreenWood.
2005	GreenWood established its Beijing office in China.
2006	GreenWood established its representative office in Chile.
2007	GreenWood raised $175 million through GreenWood Tree Farm Fund and acquired Potlatch's poplar plantation assets in Oregon.
2008	Oriental Timber Fund Limited made a capital commitment of $200 million for GreenWood to invest in tree plantation assets in China.
2009	Preliminary assessment of 20 potential investment projects was completed by March; the Luxi and Dongji projects became priorities.
2010	GreenWood was due to make an investment decision in China together with Oriental Timber Fund Limited.

Source: Interviews.

Culver, had grown up in China as a missionary's son in the 1940s and firmly believed tree farming could help Chinese rural communities develop and flourish. He convinced Jeff, who had never thought about visiting China, to travel with him to explore the potential opportunities.

GreenWood's entry into China took part in two stages. The first took place in the five years following Jeff's initial trip, from 2000 to 2005. During this period, Jeff and his colleagues visited China three or four times every year with the express purpose of establishing relationships with academics, government agencies, and various businesses in the Chinese forest industry. Greenwood learned the market and local business practices. It also brought plant materials for site adaptability tests to one of the local tree-growing companies with which it planned to partner.

Establishing GreenWood Resources China, Ltd. (GreenWood China), a wholly owned subsidiary of GreenWood, based on greenfield investment,[7] and opening its Beijing office in 2005 highlighted the second stage of GreenWood's entry into China. Brian Liu, vice president and general manager in charge of GreenWood China, explained why it took the company five years before setting up its operating facility:

> Since the No. 9 state council decree was promulgated to encourage Chinese people to go out and grow trees in 2003, a lot of entrepreneurs jumped in. The market was overwhelmed. Some entrepreneurs were doing the wrong thing. For example, "Wanli Afforestation Group" and "Yilin Wood Industry Co., Ltd.," two large local private forestry companies, were involved in some sort of financial scheme. . . . I personally felt something was going wrong, but we didn't know what. It's not the correct way. It's not the Western way. It's just too chaotic for a Western company. In addition, we had financial and personnel constraints.

Jeff recalled the decision to enter China:

> We collectively looked at what we had been doing in China. We came to the conclusion that if we were going to do anything, we couldn't do it from afar . . . we knew that we wanted to go and put a nursery there. . . . China had two main hybrid varietals of poplar trees imported from Europe. We have many new hybrid varietals. We felt the best opportunity for us was that (China) needed more (plant) materials, better materials. . . . The (Chinese) government was issuing policies in the forestry sector that were all laser-driven to industry-based plantations, of which 45 percent were represented by poplar plantations.

Despite the potentially immense opportunities in the Chinese tree plantation market and Jeff's experience, passion, and business connections, raising institutional capital proved to be very challenging. Investors looked to historical performance and operating scale, which made it difficult for a relatively young venture like GreenWood to attract investment funds. GreenWood wanted to raise US$5 million (in the form of equity) to fund its entry but was able to raise only about US$1 million. Regardless, Jeff believed GreenWood's global vision, entrepreneurial spirit, and relationships with the right people at the right places would eventually lead the company to success.

Brian remembered the process involved in setting up GreenWood's subsidiary in China:

> Jeff got a vision. It's critical that a leader has that vision because a lot of times, people are uncertain when it's a good time to do that. At that time, the company was small with a very limited budget. But his vision was he could get more money. . . . We came to China pretty much with that US$1 million. We didn't know how long it would last. It was very scary. It was a classic example of entrepreneurship. Let's just do it and don't look back.

Fund-Raising Success!

While GreenWood was grappling with funding difficulties in China, an acquisition opportunity arose in the Pacific Northwest region in the United States. Potlatch, a large timber company, changed ownership and decided to sell its poplar plantation assets located in Oregon. Jeff had consulted with Potlatch while working with CH2M Hill. He knew that an acquisition of Potlatch's tree farms would expand GreenWood's scale to a point where the company would be really attractive to capital investors. With the help of his business connections, Jeff established GreenWood Tree Farm Fund L.P. (GTFF) and raised US$175 million of private equity funding. GTFF used the money to purchase 18,000 acres of poplar trees from Potlatch, Inc., as well as three other poplar tree farms totaling an additional 17,000 acres. According to Jeff, this was a breakthrough for the firm that was almost serendipitous in the way it happened.

The expanded scale and personnel resulting from the US$175 million investment in GTFF enabled GreenWood to become a much more visible player in the tree plantation industry. In February 2008, Oriental, a GTFF investor interested in emerging markets, made a commitment of US$200 million to GreenWood for use in the Chinese market.[8]

Brian relished the experience:

> We changed our strategy. A lesson we learned is that you should be able to change. You should have an entrepreneurial spirit. We wanted to raise US$5 million (of equity) but ended up raising US$200 million (of capital commitment.)[9]

Risks and Challenges

China was an exploding timber market. The tree plantation industry, still in its nascent stage, was fragmented and lacked serious competition. GreenWood believed that abundant opportunities were available to it. For example, the company could use its elite plant materials and its sophisticated silvicultural (i.e., forest cultivation) management approach to substantially increase the annual growth of trees (quantity) in China as well as their quality.

GreenWood, however, faced a range of risks and challenges unique to China. First, there was a serious concern with the relatively weak intellectual property protection in the Chinese institutional system. Since plant materials existed in both tree nurseries and farms, it was hard to prevent people from "stealing" them. Elite plant materials were one of GreenWood's most valuable resources and were critical for developing its competitive advantages in China. GreenWood was confident, however, that it could capitalize on its years of experience to create increasingly better plant materials faster than any imitators could possibly copy them.

Second, there were political and social risks everywhere they turned. Chinese forestlands were owned either by the state or collectively. In practice, all kinds of government entities at different administrative levels (including small towns and villages) owned the lands, resulting in a very complex ownership structure. Many farmers worked small, government-allocated plots based on a lease contract of typically 20 to 30 years. GreenWood could negotiate long-term leases only with the local government, which either owned the lands and/or could represent farmers in striking a deal with foreign companies. A thorny issue was that "China's weak contract laws carried a risk for leaseholders. . . . In several instances, unhappy farmers waged protests against foreign companies when they felt they didn't get a fair share on the lease."[10] Thus, there was still a concern of potential expropriation for foreign investors.

Third, GreenWood needed to know where to find the most cost-effective tree farms and learn with whom to partner in acquiring and managing tree assets. The lack of proper documentation of plantation assets complicated this effort.

GreenWood also dealt with several other unique challenges. For example, the Chinese approach to silviculture was rudimentary compared to Western standards. There was a lack of knowledge in tree farm investment, plant materials development, and efficient irrigation, according to Zhang Weidong, director of the Resource Planning and Acquisition Group at GreenWood China.

The differences in silvicultural approaches presented the biggest challenge to Brian. In Western countries, long-term internal rate of return (IRR) was a prevalent business concept. This was at odds, however, with the mind-set of Chinese farmers, who had a short-term focus and wanted to know only the "value" of their timber assets per *mu* (0.067 hectare),[11] which was either a historical price based on the booming market of previous years or a price determined by cumulative capital expenditures plus a desired surplus. Brian noted that his team often used both the Western method and the Chinese method to conduct side-by-side comparisons:

> I call myself a translator, translating Western concepts and applying them to China. . . . It's easier said than done. It took us two years to figure it out.

Another big challenge was cultural, especially the differences in business cultures. GreenWood followed a strict Western procedure when conducting environmental and tree asset evaluations (preliminary investigation, survey, inventory analysis, comprehensive due diligence, etc.), which its potential Chinese partners perceived as inefficient (because the procedure was time-consuming) or even inappropriate (because certain tree plantation data were not available in China). Hunter, the COO of GreenWood, pointed out the key difference:

> The Chinese approach is an informal management style (as opposed to) the much more structured and organized contract-driven style in the U.S.

Furthermore, during the global economic downturn of 2008–2009, there was a growing perception that Green-Wood's market-based assessment and pricing were unfair to local farmers and communities.[12] Jake Eaton, director of GreenWood's Global Acquisitions and Resource Planning, acknowledged the disagreement with the company's potential Chinese partners regarding the valuation of existing tree plantation assets. For GreenWood, the valuation was based on current market prices, whereas its Chinese counterparts believed the market would quickly rebound and therefore the valuation should take into account the prices that prevailed prior to the economic downturn.

Business challenges in China notwithstanding, Green-Wood grew its business steadily. In 2009, it had about 10 employees in China (out of 70 companywide) and operated five tree nurseries which were used to test GreenWood's elite plant materials for site adaptability.

Investment Opportunities in China

With the capital commitment of US$200 million for the Chinese market, GreenWood, in conjunction with Oriental, established Green China Forestry Company, Ltd. (GCFC). GCFC was essentially responsible for making investment decisions in China. An investment committee, comprising Jeff and two representatives from Oriental, made investment decisions while GreenWood China provided daily management services for a fee (see Exhibit 6 for an illustration of the management and investment relationship). The investment decision-making process consisted of two phases. First, GreenWood China conducted preliminary investigations to identify potential projects.[13] Some 20 potential investment projects had been reviewed by March 2009 (see Exhibit 7).

Marc Hiller, a specialist in Forest Stewardship Council (FSC) at GreenWood, commented on the phase one evaluation:

> In every project, we look at the quality of the (assets), the ability to sell the timber to the markets. . . . Can the tree farms (potentially) meet the FSC requirements? . . . Do the current owners have a lot of conflicts with the local communities? . . . Does the local company have problems with its employees? . . . Were the local farmers coerced to turn in their tree assets for the consolidation purpose?[14] . . . Can we

acquire the assets at an attractive rate? . . . What are the financial and legal risks in acquiring the land?

Jeff also stressed the dual significance of financial viability and social responsibility:

> (The process) addresses the environmental and social issues. . . . The model (of sustainability) we hold ourselves to is FSC certification. . . . Of course, we've got to figure out how to become profitable. . . . Sustainability is not achieved unless you are economically sustainable.

Among the 20 potential projects, Luxi and Dongji were the most desirable based on preliminary analyses and thus entered phase two, which consisted of a more comprehensive due diligence analysis including economic, social, and environmental elements. The economic element was mainly reflected in the estimation of internal rate of return (IRR), net present value (NPV), and initial cash outlay. According to GreenWood, the investor's expected IRR was approximately 15 percent. The discount rate for NPV calculation was 10 percent.[15] The social and environmental due diligence analysis largely followed the FSC principles and criteria for forest management such as indigenous people's rights, community relations and workers' rights, compliance with laws and FSC principles, environmental impact, and so on, as described in Exhibit 2.

Both the Luxi and Dongji investments, if executed successfully, could achieve the investor's expected IRR, which was much higher than the approximate average return of 6 percent generated by timber investment in the United States. Moreover, it was anticipated that the investments would help improve the ecological environment in China and contribute to economic and social development in their respective local communities.

However, the two projects differed vastly in terms of physical locations, natural conditions, and partnership opportunities. The difference, as highlighted in GreenWood's detailed due diligence review, led to considerable discussion of the various pros and cons of the two projects.

Luxi Project[16]

Luxi County was located in Shandong, in east China. The county had fertile soil, sophisticated river and water irrigation networks, and other highly favorable natural conditions (ample sunlight, rain, and gentle slopes) for fast-growth, high-yield poplar plantations. Luxi had been making tremendous efforts in afforestation and sustainable economic development since 2002. A plan was executed to build a forestry park where tree plantation, landscaping, and tourism would be integrated to create an ecological system.

GreenWood explored investment opportunities in Luxi starting in late 2005. Since then, company personnel had visited Luxi many times surveying and analyzing tree farms and building *guanxi* (personal connections for mutual benefits)[17] with local government officials. The county government's support and coordination were critical for going forward with an investment since various local government agencies owned large parcels of poplar tree farms.

GreenWood was negotiating with the Luxi Forestry Bureau, a government agency with a mandate to implement government policies, regulate environmental construction, protect forest resources, and organize forestry development within Luxi County. Mr. Jiao, director of Luxi Forestry Bureau, indicated that he hoped GreenWood would help local farmers improve forestry management and facilitate local economic development by contributing capital and tree plantation know-how.

It was not, however, until December 2008 that GreenWood signed a nonbinding letter of intent (LOI) with the Luxi County government specifying the scope of the project. While commending GreenWood's meticulous style in dealing with the project, Jiao speculated that GreenWood's Portland headquarters had limited knowledge of the local situation and was not willing to delegate its responsibilities to the Beijing office. Consequently, the responses from GreenWood tended to be slow during the negotiation.

EXHIBIT 6 Relationships between GreenWood's Management and Investment Organizations

Source: GreenWood internal documents.

EXHIBIT 7 China Potential Investment Projects

ID	Location	Province (area)
1	BSY	Hebei
2	**Luxi**	**Shandong**
3	Gengmin	Jiangxi
4	Zuheng	Jiangxi
5	**Dongji**	**Inner Mongolia**
6	Chaoyang	Liaoning
7	Dong Ying	Shandong
8	Kaifeng	Henan
9	Kashi	Xinjiang
10	Lanzhou	Gansu
11	Meili	NingXia
12	Nanyang	Henan
13	Yili	Xinjiang
14	Weifang	Shandong
15	Daxing	Beijing
16	AIC	Hunan
17	Jilin	Hebei
18	Nanning	Guangxi
19	Shaoguan	Guangdong
20	Zhongfu	Shaanxi

Source: GreenWood's internal documents.

Jake Eaton agreed the process could have been faster. He pointed out that a major factor slowing down the negotiations was that GreenWood was often not talking to the real decision makers. Jessica Zhi, the Luxi project manager at GreenWood China, also mentioned the complexity of the Luxi project, in part because many local government bureaus were involved and at times leadership changes occurred.

If this project were selected, GreenWood planned to establish a wholly owned foreign enterprise in Luxi for acquiring and developing approximately 100,000 mu (6,667 hectares) of poplar tree plantations. The Luxi Forestry Bureau had been managing these tree plantations since 2002. It was expected to be a primary contractor for GreenWood, providing crop care activities at low labor costs and helping maintain the local relationships. The lease documents for the land were held by several government bureaus and were transferable. The land lease price was 300 to 400 renminbi (RMB), or US$43.90–58.60, per mu per year.[18] Typical lease length was 20 to 30 years, with some leases up to 70 years. GreenWood estimated that an investment of US$30–40 million was required in the first five years.

The high up-front fixed costs required by the Luxi project were a serious concern for the main investor, Oriental, as Jeff noted:

> If you look at the land (lease) pricing in China today, it would make more sense (for the investors) to buy (or lease) the land in another country (such as Australia, New Zealand, Poland and Romania).

As part of the negotiation process, the Luxi Forestry Bureau asked GreenWood to help set up a small wood-processing mill with an estimated investment of US$750,000. The mill, associated with high value-added activities, would provide employment opportunities to local residents. GreenWood, however, gave only a lukewarm response as the mill was not its essential business.

GreenWood planned to adopt a seven-year rotation strategy in Luxi (i.e., trees would be harvested at the age of seven for veneer log and pulpwood). It believed the locally tested GreenWood elite plant materials, coupled with favorable natural conditions and intensive management (e.g., site preparation, planting, spacing and thinning, weed and pest control, and fertilization) could readily enhance tree growth rate by 50 percent from 1.2 cubic meters (m^3) to $1.8 m^3$ per mu per year.

According to the data provided by the Luxi Forestry Bureau, GreenWood estimated the annual local timber demand within 100 kilometers (62 miles) of the project site was about 2.2 million m^3, which greatly exceeded the existing annual supply of 1 million m^3. As a result, local buyers looked to supplement their supply with imported timber. However, buyers found it increasingly difficult to depend on large volumes of imported timber because of high tariffs (e.g., for Russian logs) and high transportation costs required to bring logs into the area.

In addition to meeting the substantial demand in Luxi and its neighboring county, GreenWood was aiming at Linyi, a timber-processing hub and wood market about 300 kilometers (186.4 miles) from Luxi. There were about 2,600 mills in Linyi, and the largest 200 mills each needed more than 15,000 m^3 of timber annually. However, many of these mills were closing because their export-oriented businesses were seriously affected by the global financial crisis.

GreenWood tried to make an offer to the Luxi County government based on the local market prices of logs and its estimate of standing inventory volume. However, the county government argued that the assessment and subsequent offer would take unfair advantage of local entities and farmers, given the current economic meltdown in China due to the global financial crisis. Moreover, some government officials complained about GreenWood's slow pace in negotiating an agreement, which had resulted in the loss of seasonal planting and harvesting opportunities.

Dongji Project[19]

Dongji was located in the eastern part of the Inner Mongolia Autonomous Region in northeast China. The area suffered not only from a severe timber shortage but also from continued desertification. Although the area was semiarid and subject to windy weather all year, it was suitable for poplar cultivation due to its appropriate soil texture and access to the local river systems. The Dongji land was marginally fertile. It was estimated that the annual tree growth rate would not be much beyond 0.7 m^3 per mu even with GreenWood's elite plant materials and silvicultural management practices. One GreenWood analyst suggested that an annual rate of 0.9 m^3 per mu would be optimistic. Still, Dr. Stanton felt excited about the project because of the challenges it would bring to his research.

To combat desertification, the government of Dongji set up an ambitious goal of raising forest coverage from 22 to 30 percent from 2006 to 2010, resulting in a net increase of forestland by 10 million mu, of which 1.5 million mu was targeted for planting poplar trees.

Unlike the case in Luxi, private firms were essential in developing poplar tree plantations in Dongji. For example, Dongji Lideng Forestry Development Co., Ltd. (Lideng), a potential partner of GreenWood, held a 30-year lease on land totaling 126,600 mu planted with hybrid poplar, whereas 55 state-owned forest farms together had approximately 60,000 mu.

Lideng was a private forestry development company with activities in poplar plantation establishment, poplar nurseries, poplar stumpage, timber harvest rights transfer, and so on. To take advantage of the extensive land resources with large contiguous blocks and low land lease rates ranging from RMB15 to RMB25 per mu per year, the company planned to establish an additional 300,000 mu of poplar plantation within 3 to 5 years. This plan had already been approved by the State Forestry Administration, the central government agency for the forestry industry.

Lideng had a trained professional poplar tree planting team equipped with a patented deep planting technique suited to the harsh environment of northern China. The planting technique and its accompanying machinery were the result of a 13-year forestry development research project, led by the United Nations Food and Agriculture Organization (FAO). The company had an annual planting capacity of 200,000 mu. Lideng also told GreenWood that it had the sole right to propagate commercially superior plant materials developed by the FAO project.

In response to GreenWood's interest in its poplar tree farm assets, Lideng offered 82,644 mu out of its existing total for GreenWood's purchase. The remaining 43,000-plus mu had already been bought by individual investors through a government-approved Dongji Stumpage Trading Center, in which Huang Jingbao, the CEO and president of Lideng, was a senior consultant.

GreenWood planned what it considered a prudent strategy for Dongji. First, it would focus on deploying local hybrid varietals while testing the suitability of its home-grown elite plant materials. Second, it would adopt a 10-year rotation scheme due to the low annual growth rate in Dongji. Third, it would capitalize on Lideng's expertise in planting and crop care activities.

In Dongji, timber was mainly consumed in the local market. A potential capacity of 2 million m³ of annual wood consumption existed across 698 wood-processing mills. Though the local market experienced a limited impact from the economic meltdown, there was a concern that Russian timber could potentially flood the market due to Dongji's proximity to the Russian border. Moreover, the export market appeared to be relatively inaccessible for Dongji-based companies due to their inland locations.[20] Jeff and his senior management team also wondered whether there would be any reputational risks if GreenWood collaborated with Lideng. The latter had provided extensive silvicultural management services for Wanli Afforestation Group and Yilin Wood Industry Co., Ltd., the two large private forestry companies noted earlier that were currently under litigation for illegal fund-raising and the use of a pyramid scheme.

Huang believed Lideng and GreenWood would make a great partnership given the potential synergy between his company's local expertise and cost efficiency and GreenWood's sophisticated silvicultural management and leading poplar hybridization technology. However, he also believed his tree plantation assets had been undervalued by at least 20 percent based on GreenWood's assessment. Moreover, he had serious grievances with GreenWood's lengthy decision-making process. He considered dropping the deal if the negotiations continued to drag on for much longer.

What to Do?

Jeff and his senior management team knew expansion in China would help them achieve their vision of maximizing long-term returns for their investors and fulfilling the company's social and environmental responsibilities. They were also aware of potential business challenges as well as economic and political risks in an institutionally unique environment. After reading the two comprehensive due diligence reports, Jeff turned his attention to the financial data (see Exhibit 8) and a summarized assessment of

EXHIBIT 8 Estimated Investment Costs and Yields: Luxi versus Dongji[a]

	Total Existing Area[b] (mu)	Current Standing Inventory Volume (m³)	Stumpage Price (2008) (weighted average, RMB/m³)	Investment in Existing Plantation Assets (RMB)
Luxi	92,073	530,529	559	296,548,734
Dongji	202,650	225,391	445	100,298,995

	Land Lease and Related Expenses[c] (RMB/mu/year)	Crop Care Expenses (RMB/mu/year)	Planting Expenses (RMB/mu, 1st year)	Stumpage Volume at End of Each Rotation (m³/mu)
Luxi	367	110	632	12.6 (year 7)
Dongji	87	45	255	7.0 (year 10)[d]

[a] 1 hectare = 15 mu; 1 U.S. dollar = 6.83 renminbi; the numbers are rounded.

[b] These total existing areas were used in GreenWood's investment feasibility reports.

[c] The related expenses include management fee, security fee, etc.

[d] The growth rate of 0.7 m³ per mu per year for Dongji was deemed to be realistic, whereas the rate of 0.9 m³ per mu per year was mentioned as an optimistic scenario.

Source: Adapted from GreenWood's investment feasibility reports.

economic, social, and environmental viability of the two projects prepared by GreenWood staff (see Exhibit 9). Over a year had passed since the announcement of Oriental's capital commitment. Jeff understood that GreenWood needed to proceed with the investment with some sense of urgency, but he wanted to make sure that his team provided the best recommendations possible to the investment committee.

EXHIBIT 9 Assessment of Economic, Social, and Environmental Viability[a]

	Manager 1 (Beijing Office)[b]		Manager 2 (Beijing Office)		One Executive (Portland HQ)	
	Luxi	Dongji	Luxi	Dongji	Luxi	Dongji
Economic value	5	3–4	5	3	5	3
Social value	5	3–4	4	4	5	3
Environmental stewardship	1	5	3	5	3	5

[a] The scale is 1–5. (1 = very low potential value; 5 = very high potential value.)

[b] The manager pointed out that the ecological system had been considerably improved in Luxi in recent years. Thus, the potential value creation of environmental stewardship by GreenWood had declined.

Source: Interviews.

ENDNOTES

1. Light, L. (2009, May 6). "For Some, Sound of Profit Is 'Timber.'" *Wall Street Journal*.
2. See the company's website: *www.greenwoodresources.com*.
3. CH2M HILL provided a wide range of engineering and land development services including consulting, design, construction, procurement, operations and maintenance, and project management to federal, state, municipal, and local government entities as well as private industries in the U.S. and internationally.
4. Austin, J. and Reficco, E. (2006). Forest Stewardship Council. *Harvard Business School Case* (9-303-047).
5. A family office is a private company that manages investments and trusts for a single wealthy family.
6. Reporter (2009, May). "China to Fully Open Its Forestry Industry." *People's Daily* Online, *http://english.peopledaily.com.cn/200111/23/eng20011123_85194.html*, accessed on May 14, 2009.
7. Greenfield investment is direct investment to build a new manufacturing, marketing, or administrative facility, as opposed to acquiring existing facilities.
8. The name of this investor was disguised as requested by GreenWood Resources, Inc.
9. GreenWood planned to recruit shareholders (i.e., equity owners) for its business expansion but ended up playing the role of investment (and assets) manager for large investors such as Oriental Timber Fund, Ltd.
10. Hsuan, A. (2009, Feb. 23). "See a Forest through the Trees." *The Oregonian*.
11. *Mu* is a common metric for land in China. 1 hectare = 15 mu, or 2.47 acres.
12. Interviews with GreenWood's two potential partners.
13. Although GreenWood China was responsible for the investigations, the parent company was supervising the relevant activities and controlling the process.
14. When business developers needed to lease a large piece of land for commercial purposes in China, they often tried to incentivize and/or at times coerce through the government agencies the current land users (e.g., farmers) to transfer their land lease contracts.
15. In the broadly defined forest industry, investors prefer long-term hold, good cash flows, and net value appreciation of tree assets resulting from biological growth. Tree plantation assets are also perceived as insurance against economic/financial crisis.
16. This section draws heavily upon Luxi Investment Feasibility Report by GreenWood Resources China, Ltd.
17. "Guanxi, as compared to social capital in the West, tends to be more personal and enduring, and involves more exchanges of favors. In general, relationships tend to precede business in China, whereas in the west it is usually the reverse, i.e., relationships follow as a result of the business." Tung, Worm, and Fang, 2008, *Organizational Dynamics*, 37(1): 69.
18. 1 U.S. dollar = 6.83 renminbi (the Chinese currency) in 2009; the land lease price does not include the price for the trees.
19. This section draws heavily upon Dongji Investment Feasibility Report by GreenWood Resources China, Ltd.
20. Interview with an industry expert on May 11, 2009.

APPENDIX 1

BACKGROUND—TIMBER INVESTMENTS AND TREE PLANTATION MANAGEMENT

Timber Investments

The U.S. had some of the most productive timberland (i.e., tree-growing land) in the world. Traditionally, timber investment was dominated by such large integrated forest product companies as Weyerhaeuser, International Paper Company, Plum Creek Timber Company, and James River Corporation, to name a few.

Since the mid-1990s, however, there had been a significant trend toward institutional ownership of timberlands. Institutional investors such as timber investment management organizations (TIMOs) and real estate investment trusts (REITs) purchased large tracts of land from the traditional forest product companies because of the potential to generate attractive long-term capital returns.[1] "Timber often is likened to high-grade bonds, meant to be held for ten years or more. The average annual timber appreciation for the past decade was 4.1 percent versus minus 3.8 percent for the S&P-500 stock index."[2] Moreover, timber was not closely correlated with other asset classes. "Trees keep growing 4 percent per year, no matter what happens to inflation, interest rates or market trends."[3] In addition, potential federal and state tax benefits could be accrued from timber acquisitions.

Unfortunately, the downside of a timber investment was significant. It required a substantial amount of capital to be invested in a very illiquid asset with no quick payoff. For example, a minimum of $100,000 was required to participate in a TIMO.

Tree Plantations

U.S. commercial timberland was concentrated in the Northwest, Southeast, and Northeast regions of the country. The Northwest and Southeast were managed like farms, with landowners planting trees, allowing them to grow for a number of years, clear cutting the stand, and then planting again. Each cycle was a rotation. The Pacific Northwest contained 90 percent Western hemlock and Douglas fir with normal rotations of 45 to 60 years. In contrast, the Southeast United States was dominated by the Southern yellow pine species, with a typical rotation of 20 to 40 years. The Northeast United States had a diverse mix of trees, which were managed differently.

Plantation forests (as opposed to natural forests) were assuming a rapidly increasing role in commercial timber production. By 2005, the share of global timber production sourced from plantations was estimated as "approaching 50 percent." The largest plantation areas were located in Asia (China, India, and Japan), Europe (Russia, Scandinavia, and Eastern Europe), and the United States.[4]

The increasing importance of tree plantations was attributed to the fact that "less than half of the world's original forests remain, and ongoing deforestation is potentially devastating to the environment. Yet population growth and the increasing standard of living in many countries continue to drive the demand for timber products."[5]

High-yield, fast-growing tree farms lessen the pressure of deforestation by providing the type of timber products demanded by world markets. At the same time, tree farms are a sustainable environmental solution that can improve air and water quality, reclaim deforested land, and produce renewable energy in the form of biomass.[6]

Two popular, high-yield, and fast-growing tree species grown in plantation farms were eucalyptus and poplar. Eucalyptus was concentrated in tropical and subtropical regions of the world, while poplar was grown mainly in more temperate regions.

Hybrid Poplar Plantation Development[7]

Poplar was an important fiber resource for the global pulp and paper industry. In the United States, a number of prominent North American paper companies managed poplar plantations. Hybrid varieties, formed by crossing poplars, cottonwoods, and aspens, were among the first trees domesticated in North America by the pulp and paper industry. Several of these hybrid varieties were used to expand plantation development in the Pacific Northwest in the 1980s and 1990s.

As of 2009, hybrid poplars remained the best choice for hardwood plantation management for the manufacture of premium grades of communication papers throughout all of North America. There was also a growing trend to use hybrid poplars as a source for biomass feedstock for the emerging biofuels and composite-products industries and for hardwood lumber markets.

Key success factors for hybrid poplar plantations included (1) favorable natural site conditions (e.g., flat plain, river bottom), (2) elite plant materials (with high growth rate and strong pest resistance), and (3) sound silvicultural (forest cultivation) management, among others.[8]

Hybrid poplar plantations were tended throughout North America using cultivation methods that included mechanical and chemical methods of weed control, integrated pest management techniques, fertilization, and, in some cases, irrigation. Under competent management, hybrid poplar was the fastest-growing tree in the temperate zone.

APPENDIX ENDNOTES

1. Draffan, G. (2006, April). Notes on Institutional Ownership of Timber. *www.endgame.org/timo.html*, accessed on May 6, 2009.
2. Light, L. (2009, May 6). "For Some, Sound of Profit Is 'Timber.'" *Wall Street Journal*.
3. Ibid.
4. The Campbell Group. (2009, May 14). Global Supply. *www.campbell-group.com/timberland/primer/global-supply.aspx*, accessed on May 14, 2009.
5. GreenWood Resources, Inc., brochure.
6. Ibid.
7. This section draws heavily on an internal document of GreenWood Resources titled "Hybrid Poplar and the Pulp and Paper Industry in North America: Implications for a Secured Supply of Quality Fiber for Papermakers Worldwide."
8. *Silvicultural management* refers to integrated management of forestry, which includes land preparation, spacing and thinning, pruning, weed control, pest and disease control, fertilization, irrigation, and harvesting, among others.

CASES

CASE 12

TATA STARBUCKS: HOW TO BREW A SUSTAINABLE BLEND FOR INDIA*

In early 2015, the financial press reported that the Tata Starbucks joint venture had incurred major losses in its first full year in the Indian market. However, the company remained committed to making this venture a success over the long term.[1] Starbucks had had its eye on the large Indian market for a while. An attempt to enter the market several years earlier had failed due to complications with the Indian government and foreign direct investment (FDI) restrictions.[a] The company had withdrawn its application then and was an eager responder when India's esteemed Tata Group knocked on its door with a partnership opportunity. A 50-50 joint venture was formed, and Starbucks coffee was introduced to the Indian market in October 2012 with a generous initial investment of $80 million.[2] The Tata Global Beverages board of directors expressed a lot of excitement about the potential of the newly formed joint venture between the company and Starbucks.[b] "Through Tata Starbucks, your company offers the legendary Starbucks coffee experience, backed by the trust of the Tata name, to the Indian consumer," announced Cyrus P. Mistry, chairman of Tata Global Beverages.[3]

The Indian café market offered a lot of potential for the new Tata Starbucks alliance. While India was a nation known for its tea drinkers, sipping coffee and socializing at coffee shops was becoming increasingly popular. Domestic consumption of coffee had risen 80 percent in the past decade. Given these encouraging trends, Starbucks CEO, Howard Schultz, believed that India could one day rival the company's successful venture in China.

With its store count exceeding 40, the Tata Starbucks joint venture had clearly come a long way since it was kicked off in January 2012, but it was too early to celebrate. Continuing to succeed in the Indian café market would not be an easy task due to two key challenges—competition and profitability.

The market was intensely competitive, with multiple domestic and foreign players. The most formidable competitor was domestic giant Café Coffee Day (CCD), which had already adopted a strategy of flooding the market with its cafés, closely mimicking what Starbucks had done in the United States.

Another critical challenge companies faced was the ability to break even. High real estate costs and rental rates, along with competitive pricing pressures and India-specific cultural preferences, made it extremely difficult for coffee companies to recover their initial investments.

Tata Starbucks CEO Avani Davda admitted the initial consumer experiences had been a humbling experience. Tata Starbucks had opened its first store with a lot of fanfare in the trendy Horniman Circle area of Mumbai. Despite having a high-profile local partner, Starbucks was unable to use its name to secure any discounted rates in renting real estate. The first store was located in a Tata Group–owned 4,000-square-foot site that had been vacant for a while.

By 2015, Tata Starbucks appeared to have expanded to over 50 locations across the country in major metropolises like Mumbai, Delhi, Pune, and Bengaluru.[4] Yet this was well short of the initial expectations—the target at launch had been set at 50 stores by the end of the 2012 launch year. Clearly, something had changed in management's expectations of the size or pace of growth from the venture. Quarterly earnings presentations since then had boasted of robust store profitability with no numbers provided, possibly pointing to a slower and more selective approach to expansion.[5] However, in its first full year in the Indian market (12 months ending March 2014), Tata Starbucks reported losses of Rs 51.87 crores,[c] more than half its total sales of 95.42 crores during the same period.[1]

The joint venture appeared to be at the crossroads of an important strategic decision. It could revert to a plan to grow its store count aggressively, much like Starbucks did in the U.S. It is possible that this was the original intent. After all, the initial launch pricing had been set to be competitive with CCD's pricing (coffee drinks available for as low as Rs 100). This approach would put it in direct price competition with CCD, the domestic café market leader.

However, gaining market share among the youth of the country would allow Tata Starbucks to tap into a large demographic segment. India's population showed a pronounced skew to younger age brackets (see Exhibit 1) and lower incomes when compared to countries like Japan and the United States. Building a presence within these segments as CCD had done could be critical for success in the long term.

Alternatively, the venture could choose to embrace a premium-priced, niche approach similar to the one Starbucks

---

* This case was developed by graduate student Dev Das, Pace University; Professor Alan B. Eisner, Pace University; and Professor Helaine J. Korn, Baruch College CUNY. Material has been drawn from published sources to be used for class discussion. Copyright © 2015 Alan B. Eisner.

[a] The Government of India at the time permitted foreign retailers a maximum ownership stake of only 51 percent.

[b] Tata Global Beverages is the Tata Group subsidiary that manages coffee and tea sales.

[c] At the time, 50 Rs = 1 U.S. dollar; 1 crore = $10 million.

EXHIBIT 1 Age Distribution by Country, 2014

Age group	India	China	Japan	US
0–14 years (children)	29%	17%	13%	19%
15–24 years (early working age)	18%	15%	10%	14%
25–54 years (prime working age)	41%	47%	38%	40%
55–64 years (mature working age)	7%	11%	13%	13%
65 years and over (elderly)	6%	10%	26%	15%

Source: CIA World Factbook.

had used successfully in other Asian countries, like Japan and China. The premium offering would then cater to an older, business elite with higher spending power. This would result in less rapid growth, with a cherry-picked list of high-profile, business-friendly locations, that could also allow the venture to build a premium brand with premium pricing.

Would Starbucks and Tata under Davda's leadership finally be able to crack the code for sustained success in the competitive and complex Indian market? While Davda appeared proud of what the alliance had achieved at the 2014 Starbucks annual shareholders meeting, some critical strategic choices would need to be made to ensure the long-term success of Starbucks in India.

Schultz & Starbucks—Cultivating a Company from an Idea

Starbucks started out in 1971 with a single coffee roaster and retailer store in the Pike Place Market in Seattle. Since then the company had expanded its global footprint considerably, with over 17,000 coffee stores in more than 50 countries.[6] The visionary behind this international success story was CEO Howard Schultz.

Schultz joined the company in 1981 and quickly assessed its growth potential after visiting coffeehouses in Italy. He envisioned his coffeehouses offering much more than just a cup of coffee. They were to become a third place, in addition to home and work, for people to meet and socialize. In addition to serving coffee, the coffeehouses would help people connect with other people and their local communities. Employees would be trained on coffee, company products, and customer service to deliver a positive "Starbucks Experience" to each and every customer.

Starbucks quickly acquired a reputation for being an employer of choice and a socially responsible player:

- When the company went public in 1992, all employees were made "partners" in the company and given a share of Starbucks equity (commonly known as "bean stock"). Comprehensive health care coverage was also provided to both full-time and part-time employees.
- Efforts were made to ethically source products and establish strong relationships with coffee-producing farmers all over the world. In later years, the company began to utilize reusable and recyclable cups in its stores. Its employee partners contributed many hours of volunteer work to help with community causes.
- After the 2008–2009 recession and the introduction of the Affordable Care Act in 2010, several companies began to cut employee benefits to manage costs. Schultz refused to reduce benefits for his partners, arguing that this was a short-term reaction and not in the interests of a company in the long term.

The company's mission was to inspire and nurture the human spirit one person, one cup, and one neighborhood at a time. The company planned on doing this not just in the U.S. but across the globe. The Starbucks name had been taken from a character in Herman Melville's classic adventure novel, *Moby Dick*. It was felt that the history of the coffee trade and Seattle had a strong association with the sea. In keeping with the sea theme, the image of a Norse twin-tailed siren was adopted as the company logo.[6]

The company under Schultz's leadership performed remarkably well financially over time. Performance in 2013 showed total revenues up 12 percent to $14.9 billion, same-store sales up 7 percent, and $2.9 billion in cash flow. Operating income, however, was hit due to a one-time litigation charge with Kraft Foods Global, which resulted in a pretax charge of $2.8 billion to fiscal 2013 operating results. Excluding this one-time charge, operating income would have grown 23 percent to $2.5 billion.[7]

Initial Expansion into Asia—Targeting the Westernized and the Wealthy

The first store outside North America opened in the fashionable Ginza district in Japan in 1996. Within the next

EXHIBIT 2 Annual per Capita Income ($)

Source: World Bank data files.

few years, Starbucks became a well-known brand name in Japan. Like Starbucks shops in the United States, those in Japan featured comfy sofas with American music playing in the background. Unlike most Japanese *kisaten,* or local coffee shops, Starbucks did not allow smoking. The policy proved popular with women, who didn't smoke as much as men in Japan. Men eventually followed the women to Starbucks locations, and business started humming. Given the strong performance, the stock of Starbucks Coffee Japan Ltd. made its debut on the NASDAQ Japan exchange and performed strongly ever since. "Any way you measure it, we've exceeded our wildest expectations," CEO Howard Schultz announced jubilantly at the initial public offering in Tokyo, October 2001.

Tea-drinking Japan was not a total stranger to coffee. Dutch traders first brought coffee to Japan in the 17th century, but the shogun prohibited them from traveling freely in Japan, so very few Japanese were exposed to coffee and those who were lived mainly in port cities like Nagasaki. Coffee penetrated Japan further in the 1850s with the arrival of American ships. Soon after, Japanese started to travel overseas and brought back elements of the European coffee culture.

The first coffee shop opened in 1880s in Tokyo's Ueno district, and drinking the brew became associated with the wealthy classes. Over the next few decades, coffee increased in popularity within Japan, and a number of coffee chains entered the market. As business flourished between the United States and Japan, many Japanese traveled to the United States. West Coast cities like Seattle were popular destinations. So when Starbucks finally entered Japan in 1996, many Japanese were already familiar with the brand. Starbucks soon cultivated a loyal clientele of wealthy Japanese who considered it to be the original gourmet coffee shop and aspired to emulate the Western lifestyle.

Starbucks Coffee Japan turned its first profit in 2000, nearly four years after its initial launch. Clearly Starbucks entered markets with a commitment to win them over the long haul. Starbucks grew to over 1,000 stores in the country. For a while, sales volume per store in Japan was twice as high as that in the United States.[8]

Between 1996 and 1999, Starbucks expanded to additional markets in countries that had a high number of international travelers and a growing segment of westernized and wealthy locals. These were countries with high or growing per capita incomes (see Exhibit 2).

- Starbucks Singapore opened its first store in December 1996 at Liat Towers, strategically located along the nation's renowned Orchard Road shopping belt.
- Starbucks then entered the Philippines (1997), Taiwan, Thailand, and Malaysia (1998), and South Korea (1999), once again selecting premium locations frequented by the country's growing westernized, affluent classes and international travelers.[6]

Happy with its initial successes, Starbucks began planning expansions into countries with more entrenched cultures and large, diverse populations.

Next Expansion Wave—Cracking the Cultural Codes

Unlike Japan, tea-drinking China had little prior experience with coffee. In addition, the emerging superpower had deeply entrenched cultural traditions with regard to food and drink. Succeeding in China would be a critical challenge and opportunity for Starbucks. Cracking the cultural code there could facilitate conquering other emerging markets like India.

Starbucks opened its first store in Beijing in 1999. The company recognized there was a universal need among individuals to be respected for their differences and to feel connected with others. Starbucks catered to this need by applying its culture and values in a way that was conducive to local values and tastes.

Within China, instant coffee accounted for upward of 80 percent of all coffee consumption. Given the average Chinese consumer's limited prior exposure to coffee, instant coffee had proved to be a highly effective and affordable way of expanding consumption. Starbucks took a different approach and targeted affluent Chinese consumers with beverages priced up to 50 percent higher than the prices at its U.S. stores. Most Starbucks beverages in China cost upward of 30 renminbi (RMB), or about US$5. In contrast, Nestlé's Nescafé instant coffee could cost as little as RMB1.5 (US$0.10) per packet.

Fueled by Starbucks, the wealthy commercial capital Shanghai quickly became the coffee culture capital of China. The owner of Shanghai-based Café del Volcán, one of Shanghai's popular coffee retail outlets, noticed an interesting phenomenon in the initial days after opening his café. The prices had not yet been displayed, yet most customers ordered their beverages without inquiring about prices. Clearly the Shanghai elite were not price-sensitive. Much like Starbucks, the café then began to focus primarily on achieving the highest level of quality and service.

In 2011, a Starbucks outlet in China averaged US$600,000 in annual revenues. The strategy proved to be successful, with Starbucks' Chinese outlets becoming more profitable than those in the U.S. market. China/Asia Pacific operating margins in the last quarter of 2012 were 33.7 percent in comparison to 20.8 percent in the United States. "It's no doubt that one day China will become our second largest market after the United States, and it's possible that, over many years, potentially the largest one," mused Starbucks CEO Howard Schultz in an interview with *China Daily*.

While Nestlé and Starbucks had radically different methods for getting the Chinese to drink coffee, both succeeded. This success in part can be attributed to segmenting the market and recognizing the Chinese as unique consumers with different tastes and habits than those of American consumers. For instance, Chinese consumers did not like the bitter taste associated with black coffee or espresso, so both players tailored their beverages accordingly. Nestlé's Nescafé packets included sugar and powdered milk, while Starbucks emphasized milk-based drinks like frappuccinos, lattes, and mochas in its stores. Starbucks' Chinese menus also added some local flavor, with customized choices like green tea tiramisu and Chinese moon cakes.

In addition, Starbucks localized its outlets by offering large seating areas, since Chinese tend to not like to take their drinks off-site. Local Chinese customers began to enjoy the "Starbucks Experience" while sitting with friends and having something to munch on along with their coffee. Further, "family forums" were introduced to explain to parents the merits of having their children work at Starbucks. Large lounges with couches were provided at stores to accommodate working customers' need to relax for a bit during afternoons. Menus were modified to include foods that were tailored to local tastes, for example, a Hainan Chicken sandwich and a Thai-style Prawn wrap.[9]

By the end of 2013, Starbucks had opened its 1,000th store in the country. It was this success in China that made Schultz particularly eager to venture into India. Like China, India was another large market with culturally entrenched tastes.[10]

In a press interview, CEO Howard Schultz later reminisced:

> Our stores, domestically and around the world, have become the third place for customers between home and work. The environment, the store design, the free Wi-Fi—everything we've been able to do has created this primary destination. That is the same in Honshu (China), in Beijing, in Shanghai, in Spain, in Tokyo or in New York City. We've cracked the code on universal relevance.[11]

Conquering Unfamiliar Markets—Seeking the Magic Formula

With Starbucks' stellar performance in its initial expansion into Asia, numerous industry analysts speculated on the best practices that could be used by the company to penetrate other markets or be emulated by other companies.[12] Three key themes emerged:

1. *Be tactful in marketing the brand:*
    - Once Starbucks decided to enter China, it implemented a smart market-entry strategy. It did not use any advertising and promotions that could be perceived by the Chinese as an American intrusion into the local tea-drinking culture. It just quietly focused on carefully selecting premium locations to build its brand image.
    - Starbucks capitalized on the tea-drinking culture of Chinese consumers by introducing beverages using popular local ingredients such as green tea. It also added more milk-based beverages, such as frappuccinos, since the Chinese did not like the taste of bitter coffee.

2. *Find a good local partner:*
    - Working with the right partners could be an effective way to reach local customers and expand quickly without going through a significant learning curve.
    - China was not one homogeneous market. There were many Chinas. The culture of northern China was very different from that of the east. Consumer spending power inland was not on par with that in coastal cities. To address this complexity of the Chinese market, Starbucks partnered with three regional partners as part of its expansion plans.
    - In the north, Starbucks entered a joint venture with Beijing Mei Da Coffee Company. In the east, Starbucks partnered with the Taiwan-based Uni-President. In the south, Starbucks worked with Hong Kong–based Maxim's Caterers. Each partner brought different strengths and local expertise that helped Starbucks gain insights into the tastes and preferences of local Chinese consumers.

3. *Make a long-term commitment:*
    - Long-term commitment required patience. It took Starbucks time to educate the market and gain

customer loyalty. Starbucks also did an excellent job in recruiting and training its employees. This turned out to be a win-win strategy because employees were, after all, the face of the Starbucks brand and were at the heart of delivering the "Starbucks Experience" to customers.

This knowledge armed Starbucks as it prepared to penetrate an even more complex and competitive market—India.

Passage to India—Tata Group a Worthy Partner

Founded by Jamsetji Tata in 1868, Tata's early years were inspired by the spirit of nationalism. It pioneered several industries of national importance in India: steel, power, hospitality, and airlines. In more recent times, its pioneering spirit was showcased by companies such as TCS, India's first software company, and Tata Motors, which made India's first indigenously developed car, the Tata Indica, and the world's most affordable car, the Tata Nano.

The Tata Group comprised over 100 operating companies in seven business sectors: communications and information technology, engineering, materials, services, energy, consumer products, and chemicals. The group had operations in more than 100 countries across six continents, and its companies exported products and services to 150 countries.

Along with the increasing global footprint of Tata companies, the Tata brand was also gaining international recognition. In 2010, *BusinessWeek* magazine ranked Tata 17th on its "50 Most Innovative Companies" list. Brand Finance, a U.K.-based consultancy firm, valued the Tata brand at $18 billion and ranked it 39th among the top 500 most valuable global brands in its BrandFinance Global 500 2013 report.

Like Starbucks, Tata had a strong belief in social responsibility. The company created national institutions for science and technology, medical research, social studies, and the performing arts. Its trusts provided aid and assistance to nongovernment organizations (NGOs) working in the areas of education, health care, and livelihoods. Individual Tata companies were known to extend social welfare activities to communities around their industrial units. The Tata name had been respected in India for more than 140 years because of the company's adherence to strong values and business ethics.

The total revenue of Tata companies was $97 billion in 2012–2013, with nearly two-thirds coming from business outside India. Tata companies employed over half a million people worldwide. Every Tata company or enterprise operated independently. Each of these companies had its own board of directors and shareholders. The major Tata companies were Tata Steel, Tata Motors, Tata Consultancy Services (TCS), Tata Power, Tata Chemicals, Tata Teleservices, Titan Watches, Tata Communications, Indian Hotels, and Tata Global Beverages.

Much like Starbucks, the Tata Global Beverages unit was looking for a retail partner to sell its coffee products. Its broad product portfolio also included tea and bottled water. As with its Tata Group parents and Starbucks, Tata Global Beverages was proud of having strong values and purpose as a company. Thus a promising partnership was formed, and Starbucks was ready to make a grand entry into the market.[5]

Coffee in India—An Existing but Lesser-Known Tradition

Unlike China, tea-drinking parts of South India did have some historical experience with coffee. The crop was first cultivated in Ethiopia, and by the 1600s it was hugely popular throughout the Ottoman Empire. According to coffee historian and author Mark Pendergrast, the Turks boiled or roasted coffee beans before they left the Yemeni port of Mocha to keep them from being grown elsewhere. That is why, according to legend, a 17th-century Muslim pilgrim named Baba Budan taped seven coffee beans to his stomach and smuggled them to India. The hills where he planted those beans are now known as the Bababudan Giris.

When the British arrived in the 1600s, intending to break a Dutch monopoly on the spice trade, tea and coffee were "backyard crops" in India. Over the centuries, the British installed plantations and established more organized production processes. Tea, which was a much larger crop than coffee, was grown mostly in the north, while coffee was grown mostly in the south.

For decades, the Coorg (also called Kodavu) region in south India had been home to coffee plantations. The British began planting coffee there in the 19th century. When India gained independence in 1947, the original British planters sold their estates to the locals (known as Kodavas) and other southern Indians. Since the mid-1990s, when the Indian government changed its policies and allowed farmers to take control of their own sales, India's coffee industry experienced a boost in quality and profits and took a seat in gourmet coffee circles.[13]

With the alliance, Starbucks gained access to locally produced premium-quality beans from Tata-owned plantations in the Coorg region. Tata Coffee, a unit of Tata Global Beverages, produced more than 10,000 metric tons of shade-grown arabica and robusta coffees at its 19 estates in south India.[14] This was a strategic asset for Starbucks as it prepared to do battle with the domestic giant, CCD.

Indian Café Market—Dominated by Café Coffee Day

By 2014, the Indian coffeehouse market was $300 million strong and growing at a robust 20 percent rate from year to year. While the market was crowded with international and domestic players, Starbucks' main competition came from a domestic giant, Café Coffee Day (CCD). The presence of international coffee chains was significant, but the combined number of their outlets was only about one-third of the 1,500 outlets operated by home-grown CCD.[15]

CCD had been the market leader since its beginnings as a "cyber café" in 1996. As the retailing arm of the nearly 150-year-old Amalgamated Bean Coffee Trading Company Limited (ABCTCL), it had the benefit of sourcing its coffee locally from a network of ABCTCL-owned coffee plantations and using ABCTCL-manufactured coffee-roasting machines. This allowed CCD to insulate itself from global price fluctuations and serve coffee at lower prices than the competition. Most of the foreign competitors relied on imported coffee and foreign roasting machines.[16]

ABCTCL's charismatic CEO, V. G. Siddhartha, rapidly expanded CCD stores across the country. The mission of the company was to provide a world-class coffeehouse experience at affordable prices. This made the stores ubiquitous, much like Starbucks stores in the U.S. It also made CCD the destination of choice for the youth in the country who had limited money to spend and were looking for socially acceptable places to socialize. The majority of India still disapproved of socializing at bars, and cafés offered a respectable alternative. A 2014 industry study showed that the CCD brand was synonymous with coffee for most coffee drinkers in India.[17]

After CCD, the next-biggest player was the Barista chain, which started in 2000. In 2001–2004, Tata Global Beverages explored the option of partnering with Barista to sell its coffees but eventually sold its stake. In keeping with Barista's premium positioning, most of the company's products were imports and its coffee was roasted in Venice, Italy. In 2007, Barista was acquired by Italian coffee company Lavazza. However, profits proved elusive despite several years on the market and heavy investments. In 2013, Lavazza announced it would sell the Barista business.

Industry watchers said that the coffee business in India was becoming a difficult one to turn profitable even after years of operations. High rental expenses and intense competition had left most foreign players struggling to achieve profitability despite years of trying. According to industry estimates, rentals could account for 15 to 25 percent of the cost of running a café chain. Typical monthly rental market rates were 200 to 300 rupees (Rs) per square foot of real estate.[18] Then, there was the investment in making the stores appealing to customers, finding people to run them, and building a food and beverage menu that was hip enough to keep 18- to 24-year-olds—the target market for many coffee chains—coming back for more. CCD had found a way around this problem by entering into a revenue-sharing deal, paying 10 to 20 percent of a unit's proceeds as a fee. Coffee bars were a sit-in concept in India, where consumers generally hung around such outlets for hours, unlike the global phenomenon of grabbing coffee on the go from generally tiny outlets and kiosks.[19]

Industry experts argued that coffee chains in India had to maintain elaborate and plush outlets—not kiosks—to give Indian consumers what they were looking for from a coffee chain even if the proposition turned out to be very expensive, and this concept made it difficult for many companies to stay in the business and made it hard to scale up. Unlike countries such as the United States, where purchasing coffee was often a quick transaction at a counter or kiosk for customers on the go, the culture in India was to sit down and socialize for hours over coffee or tea.[20] Some frustrated customers stopped frequenting stores because it was so hard to find a free table.[17] This made it much harder for coffee retailers to turn a profit. According to Manmeet Vohra, Tata Starbucks marketing and category chief, peak hours in India were 2 p.m. to 6 p.m. (compared to 5 a.m. to 11 a.m. in the U.S.) and takeout orders accounted for barely 20 percent of the business in India (compared to 80 percent in the U.S.).[19]

Other international entrants like the U.K.'s Costa Coffee, the U.S.-based Coffee Bean and Tea Leaf Company, and Australia's Gloria Jean's Coffee experienced similar profitability challenges.[20] Costa Coffee entered the market in 2005 and soon found its stores were too small to handle the peak-time crowds. The Coffee Bean and Tea Leaf Company started out in 2007 and tried to entice customers by offering new menu items each month. Gloria Jean's Coffee entered the market in 2008 hoping it could crack the profitability code by serving coffee in more kiosks, which required a lower capital investment. However, achieving profitability continued to remain elusive for most international players.

Starbucks appeared to be doing well in its initial stores. In quarterly investor presentations, Tata Global Beverages reported robust profitability in its stores. While no numbers were shared by the company, the information was corroborated by industry experts. The 4,000-square-foot Horniman Circle store was estimated to be generating 8.5 lakh rupees in daily sales, which compared to 1 lakh rupees generated by the 400-square-foot CCD store at the Mumbai airport. Top Indian store revenues in U.S. dollars were comparable to those generated by the stores in China (about $600,000 per year). Since the real estate for the first store was obtained from the Tata Group, certainly that store, at least, was brewing a healthy profit.

Quick-Service Restaurant Chains—A Looming Threat

In addition to traditional coffee chains, the Indian café market was being encroached upon by other quick-service restaurant (QSR) options like McDonald's and Dunkin' Donuts. These players threatened to steal market share with lower-priced options for drinking coffee at existing quick-service establishments.

One of the major advantages for these chains over Starbucks and other competitors was the already-existing network of locations in the country that allowed ready access and brought down establishment costs. Further, this ubiquity and lower pricing would enable these players to tap into the larger demographic segments that made up a large section of the Indian population.

Amit Jatia, vice chairman and CEO of Hardcastle Restaurants, which is the McDonald's franchise for South Indian operations, stated: "McDonald's has the advantage as their ability to expand is better, considering that they have a larger footprint now."

Price was another factor by which McDonald's McCafé expected to hold an edge over Starbucks. Getting a cappuccino for 90 rupees for a global brand like McCafé sounded more appealing than spending more than 110 rupees for the same drink at Starbucks. Much like Starbucks, McCafé was sourcing its coffee locally from Chikmagalur in Karnataka.[21]

Tata Starbucks—Challenging Decision Ahead

In the words of John Culver, president of Starbucks Coffee China and Asia Pacific:

> We have studied and evaluated the market carefully to ensure we are entering India the most respectful way. We believe the size of the economy, the rising spending power and the growth of café culture hold strong potential for our growth and we are thrilled to be here and extend our high-quality coffee, handcrafted beverages, locally relevant food, legendary service and the unique Starbucks Experience to customers here.[22]

The business looked simple—have a standardized decor, choose a suitable location, and offer good coffee and food—but ensuring that a customer's cappuccino tasted the same as it did yesterday and that the service did justice to the iconic Starbucks brand name every single day was far more complex. Doing so required carefully selected partners (store managers and stewards who went through intensive training) and an incredibly complex planning effort. For that reason, Starbucks had avoided the franchisee route, which could have seemed like the obvious choice for rapid expansion.

Also, Starbucks had to meet the expectations of its world-traveled customers, who were aware of the "Starbucks Experience." Many of these customers would check whether the coffee tasted the same as it did abroad and whether the store ambience was equally comfortable. If the experiences matched up, they would become regulars.

But for sustained success, Starbucks needed to penetrate the domestic young and middle-income markets. Starbucks laid out plans for different formats, such as "abbreviated stores" that would be smaller in size and stores at college and school campuses. The stores in India began experimenting with their food menu. While Starbucks globally offered blueberry and chocolate muffins, it wanted to serve local innovations at its Indian locations. Coinciding with its first anniversary in India, the company launched a new, local India Estates blend. This blend was Tata Starbucks' special country-specific coffee, developed thoughtfully with Tata for the Indian market, and it reflected the high-quality arabica coffee available in India. Additionally, the company launched the Indian Espresso Roast, which was sourced locally through a coffee sourcing and roasting agreement between Starbucks and Tata. It was felt that the coffees captured the essence and rich heritage of the Indian coffee history.

The challenge facing CEO Davda and Tata Starbucks was a difficult one. How could the company maximize the long-term success of the venture in India? Doing so would mean going beyond "the westernized and the wealthy" targeting that had worked so well in relatively older and more affluent Asian markets. While the partnership with Tata was occasionally helping in negotiating for good real estate, Starbucks still needed to figure out how to leverage the partnership to win over the larger young and middle-income demographic segments. Store financials needed to be managed to maintain profitability. These issues would need to be addressed quickly as the company prepared to expand into the next tier of Indian cities.

"As they move from high traffic and high spends location, revenues or productivity of the stores will come down. Hence, per store sales might come down over the years once they open stores in smaller locations," said Devangshu Dutta, chief executive at the Indian retail consultancy Third Eyesight.[23]

ENDNOTES

1. Vijayaraghavan, K. 2015. Growth for now, but profits still need to come in, says Starbucks CEO Avani Saglani Davda. *Economic Times*.
2. Bahree, M. 2012. Starbucks will open cafes in India. *Wall Street Journal*.
3. Tata. 2012. Annual report.
4. PTI. 2014. Starbucks says India operations fastest growing in its history. www.livemint.com.
5. Tata. 2014. Company website.
6. Starbucks. 2014. Company website.
7. Starbucks. 2013. Annual report.
8. Belson, K. 2001. As Starbucks grows, Japan too is awash. *New York Times*.
9. Burkitt, L. 2012. Starbucks plays to local Chinese tastes. *Wall Street Journal*.
10. Barlow, N. 2013. China's coffee industry is booming. *China Briefing*.
11. Bartiromo, M. 2013. Starbucks' Schultz eyes global growth. *USA Today*.
12. Wang, H. 2012. Five things Starbucks did to get China right. *Forbes*.
13. Allison, M. 2010. As India gains strength, so does its coffee. *Seattle Times*.
14. Badrinath, R. 2012. Tata coffee to close ranks with Starbucks. *Business Standard*.
15. Madonna, A. & Badrinath, R. 2013. If we find something attractive we will look at it. *Business Standard*.
16. CCD. 2014. Company website.
17. Kaushik, M. 2011. A stronger caffeine kick. *Business Today*.
18. Srivastava, S. 2012. Starbucks India isn't celebrating yet. *Forbes*.
19. Sachitanand, R. 2014. How Starbucks and Cafe Coffee Day are squaring up for control of India's coffee retailing market. *Economic Times*.
20. Bailay, R. 2014. Coffee chain Starbucks expanding aggressively in India. *Economic Times*.
21. Anonymous. 2013. Coffee war: McDonald's McCafe set to make its Indian debut, aims to "wipe out" Starbucks. *Daily Bhaskar*.
22. Bhattacharya, A. 2013. Pour out the coffee. *Financial Express*.
23. Malviya, S. 2014. Starbucks outshines coffee chain rivals in first full year in India. *Economic Times*.

CASES

CASE 13

AVON: A NEW ERA?

If we stop and look over the past and then into the future, we can see that the possibilities are growing greater and greater every day; that we have scarcely begun to reach the proper results from the field we have before us.

—David McConnell, Avon Founder, late 19th century[1]

A Challenging Time

Moving into 2015,[2] CEO Sheri McCoy admitted the promised turnaround had taken longer than originally expected. Brazil, Avon's biggest market, had shown sluggish performance. Another key market, Mexico, continued to show soft performance. Overall, the number of Active Representatives (Avon Ladies) was down 4 percent. This was an improvement from declines seen in previous years but still short of expectations.

Macroeconomic headwinds were surely at play due to the recent global economic slowdown, but CEO McCoy admitted there were other execution-related setbacks. She said that the company needed to build strong execution into its DNA and that this would take time. Further, the executions needed to be evolutionary and include the direct-selling representative perspective. In the past, radical changes to selling approaches had been unsuccessful (e.g., selling Avon products in retail locations) because they attempted to do too much too fast and did not involve the critical direct-selling representatives in the planning process.

In several emerging markets within the Latin America, EMEA,[3] and Asia-Pacific regions, intense competition and price discounting threatened to erode market share and profitability. The company's price increases in these markets had only hurt its cause further.

Last but not least, Avon agreed to a $135 million settlement to address the charges that it had violated the Foreign Corrupt Practices Act (FCPA) in China. This was nearly 10 times higher than its original settlement offer to the Securities and Exchange Commission (SEC).

Despite the company's many problems, competitors remained interested in acquiring Avon to gain access to its army of direct-selling representatives.[4] This access would allow them to quickly penetrate attractive emerging markets such as Brazil, which had underdeveloped retail infrastructures.

During the question-and-answer session at the end of the 2014 third-quarter earnings call, investor analysts wondered if Avon would ever be able to return to its past glory, whether Avon would need to begin to exit from key markets like the U.S. due to dismal performance and low potential, and how it would fund the larger-than-expected penalties from the SEC. If the company could not be turned around, selling it would create more shareholder value.

For the first time since David McConnell founded the company in 1886, his vision of endless possibilities and growth was beginning to seem unattainable. How could newbie McCoy prove the naysayers wrong and return the iconic, direct-selling company to profitable growth? Or was it time to wake up and sell the company to an interested bidder?

Avon Background—First 100 Years Marked by Opportunity and Growth

Unique Opportunity for Women[1]

In 1886, David H. McConnell, a book salesman from rural New York, created a novel opportunity for women— a chance to become financially independent by selling perfumes. This was at a time when only one-fifth of women in the United States were working outside the home and for wages that were a fraction of what men earned. Most of these working women were employed in agriculture, domestic service, and manufacturing jobs, which did not always provide safe environments.

As a book salesman, McConnell had noticed that his women customers were far more interested in free perfume samples than in the books he sold. He had started using these samples as "door openers" when visiting the homes of potential customers. But McConnell had also noticed one more need that, if effectively tapped, could provide tremendous growth potential for both him and his women customers. Women were looking for ways to supplement their household incomes, and many would make the perfect perfume salespersons for other women customers. McConnell could offer women the opportunity to create and manage their own perfume businesses using a unique direct-selling approach. Earning a commission for selling perfumes to other women like themselves could create an exciting and glamorous solution for an existing need.

McConnell's first recruit for Avon, or the California Perfume Company as it was known then, was Mrs. P. F. E.

---

* This case was developed by graduate student Dev Das and Professor Alan B. Eisner, Pace University. Material has been drawn from published sources to be used for class discussion. Copyright © 2015 Alan B. Eisner.

Albee of New Hampshire. He provided Albee and other early sales representatives with an earnings opportunity within a supportive, familylike environment. The attractiveness of the offering was tremendous, and the army of representatives rose to 5,000 within only 13 years. With the seed of an idea, McConnell had created a "company for women," which would eventually become the slogan for the company a century later.

Pioneering Direct-Selling Model[1]

The company had pioneered a new direct-selling approach. Company representatives sold products directly to the end users, thus bypassing the need for a go-between distribution channel. This model generated efficiencies by eliminating the need for a middleman, in addition to allowing direct and regular contact with consumers.

In the late 19th century, direct selling at Avon connected women, who were otherwise isolated and immersed in domestic life, through what the company called "the original social network." An intimate, personal selling approach allowed many women to bond over beauty products. Many women no longer had to travel to the closest department store or drugstore to purchase beauty products or seek beauty advice. The Avon Ladies (as the sales representatives came to be known) brought the store to them.

In the 1970s and 1980s, when the company's core customer base of stay-at-home women began to shrink, the company adapted its direct-selling approach to keep up with the times. Avon Ladies began to leave samples and call-back brochures on front doorknobs and even began offering the opportunity to buy products at work.

Direct selling continued to evolve over the years as needs and technologies evolved. With more women entering the workforce, the company adjusted by offering options to sell Avon products at the workplace. The advent of the Internet prompted the company to offer online promotion and selling options.

The Power of Partnerships[1]

Fragrances were the first products Avon (then known as the California Perfume Company) sold, and they later became an integral part of the company product line. Avon relied on partnerships to market its fragrance products. Celebrities from the movie and music industries were often used in advertising and created excitement for new fragrance launches. In addition, partnerships with fashion designers were established for enhanced image and efficiency.

Avon Background—Next Century Brings Many Changes

Evolution of the Direct-Selling Model[1]

Throughout the history of the company, representatives could earn commission money only by selling to customers. With the launch of Avon's Sales Leadership program in the 1990s, representatives could also earn money by recruiting and training others. This new earnings avenue exponentially increased the amount of money an individual representative could generate.

With the advent of the Internet, Avon created a collection of digital tools that enabled representatives to use the technology in their businesses. Online ordering, an e-brochure, and customized online communities also allowed Avon Ladies to contemporize their offerings and image.

"The relevance of direct selling has to do with what the consumer expects from service," said Angie Rossi, group vice president of North America Sales. "There will always be a space for relationship-based service to the consumer." So, while the media and tools may change with time, the company believed the relevance of direct selling as a strategy would never diminish.

In 2012, Avon was producing and selling its products worldwide through its direct-selling, boutique store, and online channels.

Launch of New Products and Partnerships[5]

The first product that Avon sold was the Little Dot Perfume Set to customers in the United States. Over time, Avon product sales expanded to a wide range of color cosmetics, as well as skin care, fragrance, fashion, and home products. Some of its more established brand names were Avon Color, ANEW, Skin-So-Soft, Advance Techniques, and Mark. 2014 revenues came from three main categories:

- *Beauty* (73 percent of net sales): cosmetics, fragrances, and personal care products.
- *Fashion* (17 percent of net sales): jewelry, watches, apparel and accessories.
- *Home* (10 percent of net sales): home products and decorative products.

The company continued to rely on celebrity partnerships to launch and market its new (mainly fragrance) products. These included Uninhibited by Cher (1988) and Undeniable by Billy Dee Williams (1990). Outspoken by Fergie (2010) was the most successful fragrance launch in the company's history. The company then teamed up with the popular singer to offer a follow-up fragrance, Outspoken Intense (2011).

Avon also established partnerships with international design houses Christian Lacroix, Hervé Léger, and Ungaro, which allowed the company to offer premium products at affordable prices for its mainstream customer base. On the fashion apparel front, it teamed up with designer Diane von Furstenberg to create a customized line for Avon called The Color Authority.

Expansion into Emerging Markets

The 20th century had seen expansion into neighboring markets like Canada and Latin America. As the 21st century approached, Avon was rapidly expanding into additional emerging markets.[5]

The company started selling its products in China in 1990. However, a direct-selling ban in China forced the company to open brick-and-mortar retail locations (Beauty Boutiques) within the Chinese market. The ban was lifted in 2006, and the company then started to sell via both direct-selling and retail routes in China. Avon also expanded into Russia in 1993 with retail stores, and it started direct selling its products there in 1995.

By 2015, Avon products were sold in over 100 countries (sold through subsidiaries in 63 and through distributors in an additional 41). Operations were managed over four regions: North America, Latin America, EMEA,[3] and Asia-Pacific. Latin America now accounted for nearly half of total company revenues, with Brazil being the largest market (see Exhibit 1).

Global and Regional Competition

On a broader level, Avon's beauty products faced competition from international cosmetics companies (e.g., Procter & Gamble, L'Oréal, Estée Lauder, Revlon, and Mary Kay) as well as regional players (e.g., Natura in Brazil).[5]

In the direct-selling space, the company primarily competed with Mary Kay, which had a similar product lineup. Mary Kay Inc. was created in 1963 by Mary Kay Ash, direct-selling sales director, who believed women needed more opportunities in business.[6] Mary Kay and Avon used slightly different approaches to reimbursing their representatives:

- Avon representatives (Avon Ladies) bought their products on credit without paying for anything up front. After completing product sales, they reimbursed the company for the products and pocketed a 20 percent margin.
- Mary Kay representatives considered themselves "skin care consultants" and were required to invest $85 up front to buy a demo kit to provide skin care and makeup training to customers. Subsequent product sales provided a 20 to 40 percent margin.

Avon was the biggest direct-selling enterprise globally, with over 6 million sales representatives. Between 2006 and 2011, this selling route grew by an impressive 30 percent into a $136 billion global market. Unlike traditional retailers, which used a pull strategy to get customers into the store, direct selling was a push business.[7]

Direct selling also presented a tremendous entrepreneurship opportunity in emerging markets like Brazil, Russia, China, and India. Avon faced intense competition from Mary Kay in recruiting representatives in these markets.[8] In Brazil, Avon also faced intense competition from a regional direct-selling player, Natura. Direct selling accounted for nearly one-third of the sales of beauty products in the country, due to an underdeveloped retail sector.

Avon's remaining beauty competitors distributed their products to retail resellers such as department stores, drugstores, or cosmetic stores. In recent years more of these competitors and channels had begun offering discounted products that encroached on Avon's traditional value-shopping customer base. Many international competitors like L'Oréal had also made major strides in growing the retail channel within emerging markets like Brazil.[4]

In the fashion and home categories, Avon had competitors in the jewelry, accessories, apparel, housewares, and gift and decorative products industries globally, including retail establishments (principally department stores, gift shops and specialty retailers, and mass merchandisers) and direct-sales companies specializing in these products.[5]

EXHIBIT 1 Business by Region

Years Ended December 31	2014		2013		2012	
	Total Revenue	Operating Profit (Loss)	Total Revenue	Operating Profit (Loss)	Total Revenue	Operating Profit (Loss)
Latin America	$4,239.5	$ 279.8	$4,840.5	$ 478.6	$ 4,993.7	$ 443.9
Europe, Middle East & Africa	2,705.8	300.9	2,898.4	406.7	2,914.2	312.8
North America	1,203.4	(72.5)	1,458.2	(60.1)	1,751.1	(4.7)
Asia Pacific	702.7	20.9	757.9	(12.1)	902.4	5.1
Total from operations	8,851.4	529.1	9,955.0	813.1	10,561.4	757.1
Global and other expenses	—	(129.0)	—	(385.9)	—	(232.1)
Total	$8,851.4	$ 400.1	$9,955.0	$ 427.2	$10,561.4	$ 525.0

Source: Avon 2014 annual report.

Management Changes[9]

The 1990s ushered in a period of management change and the first woman CEO in the company's history. Andrea Jung arrived at the company in 1993 with a background in high-end retail (i.e., Neiman Marcus, I. Magnin, and Bloomingdale's). She was appointed by then-CEO Jim Preston to look into the feasibility of selling Avon products in retail outlets. Jung quickly assessed that Avon didn't have the right packaging or positioning to compete in that arena. Impressed by her work, Preston invited her to join the company full-time in 1994 as president of the product marketing group for Avon U.S., a newly created position.

When Preston retired in 1998 after nine years with the company, Charles Perrin (Avon board member and former head of Duracell) became the new CEO. Jung rose to the prominent role of president and chief operating officer. Perrin had planned on staying for about five years but remained for less than two. Jung then took over in November 1999, becoming the first woman to ever lead the company.

Focus Shifts from Direct Selling to Retailing and Marketing[9]

In 1998, Avon opened the Avon Center, with a store, spa, and salon, in Trump Tower on Fifth Avenue. When Jung became CEO in 1999, Avon adopted the slogan "the company for women," moving away from its long-time ad campaign "Ding Dong, Avon Calling." The change was meant to modernize Avon, but it also paralleled a shift in focus within the company. The old tagline emphasized the direct-selling side of the business; now the priority was retail.

A year later, Jung launched the "Let's Talk" global advertising initiative, with Venus and Serena Williams as spokespersons. Advertising spending jumped from $63 million in 1999 to a high point of $400 million in 2010. "Mark," a hipper, trendier product line, was launched to attract a younger demographic and contemporize the company's image.

Avon started with mall kiosks and followed with a plan to go into Sears and JCPenney with a new line called beComing. The new sales outlets and product line had the dual objectives of going higher-end and of introducing Avon to women who possibly had not encountered its products before. The venture faltered due to unclear goals and expectations. Sears backed out before the launch, and Avon's foray into JCPenney ended two years later, in 2003.

Despite these setbacks, the company grew its revenue from $287 million in 1999 to $846 million in 2004. Investors were equally pleased with the performance of the company's stock, which tripled in value during the same period.

Business Slows Down Due to Competition and Execution Issues[9]

In 2005, earnings flattened for the first time due to competitive encroachments in key markets. Avon completed a major restructuring, cutting 30 percent of managers and chopping its 15 layers down to 8. Consultants were hired and acquisitions explored to achieve growth. Senior managers were brought in from top-tier companies that Avon wanted to emulate. Liz Smith, who joined as president of global brand marketing in 2005 after working for Kraft, tried to bring a new kind of discipline to Avon. New rigor was infused into the marketing evaluation and execution process. The changes created some friction with existing managers. "Avon's an iconic brand," said one former marketing executive in the U.S. business. "It's not the same as macaroni and cheese."

Another restructuring began in 2009 and left employees demoralized and uncertain about the leadership and future of the company. Rather than working toward a long-term vision, employees often felt as though they were patching up problems for the short term. "At Avon, when something doesn't go right, just put some concealer on it," said a former communications manager. A major gap appeared to exist between what the company wanted to accomplish and what it was capable of executing:

- Avon, unlike other direct sellers, published a product brochure of more than 150 pages every two weeks in the U.S. market. The flexibility to change the product lineup frequently could have been a competitive asset, but it was not effectively implemented. Despite corporate efforts to give Avon a more upscale image, heavy discounting in the catalog created a different image for the company's products. "On the one hand you had high-tech skin care, a lot of celebrities," said Ron Robinson, former global director of product innovation at Avon, who now runs an industry website. "And then you had the discounting going on."

- In 2010, the company acquired Silpada, a direct seller of silver jewelry, for $650 million. But silver prices spiked, and Avon had to take a $263 million write-down in 2011's fourth quarter. The increase in commodity costs was bad timing, but analysts believed the company may have also overpaid for the asset.

- Also in 2010, Avon announced an ambitious five-year plan called the "Road to $20 billion." Less than a year later, the company cut off funding for most of the initiatives in this plan. Executives then communicated a new directive that Avon would eventually hit $20 billion but not by 2015. Avon had revenues of only $8.6 billion in 2014 (see Exhibit 2).

Problems in Emerging Markets[5,9]

Emerging markets like Brazil had underdeveloped retail infrastructures, and direct selling presented an efficient alternative for reaching consumers. Direct selling also presented a lucrative entrepreneurial opportunity for the women in these markets, much as it did for women in the

EXHIBIT 2 Avon Products, Inc., Consolidated Income Statements ($ millions, except per-share data)

	Year Ended December 31:		
	2014	2013	2012
Net sales	$8,615.9	$9,764.4	$10,405.3
Other revenue	235.5	190.6	156.1
Total revenue	8,851.4	9,955.0	10,561.4
Costs, expenses and other:			
Cost of sales	3,499.3	3,772.5	4,103.1
Selling, general and administrative expenses	4,952.0	5,713.2	5,889.3
Impairment of goodwill and intangible assets	—	42.1	44.0
Operating profit	400.1	427.2	525.0
Interest expense	111.1	120.6	104.3
Loss on extinguishment of debt	—	86.0	—
Interest income	(14.8)	(25.9)	(15.1)
Other expense, net	139.6	83.9	7.1
Total other expenses	235.9	264.6	96.3
Income from continuing operations, before taxes	164.2	162.6	428.7
Income taxes	(549.1)	(163.6)	(335.4)
(Loss) income from continuing operations, net of tax	(384.9)	(1.0)	93.3
Loss from discontinued operations, net of tax	—	(50.9)	(131.5)
Net loss	(384.9)	(51.9)	(38.2)
Net income attributable to noncontrolling interests	(3.7)	(4.5)	(4.3)
Net loss attributable to Avon	$ (388.6)	$ (56.4)	$ (42.5)
(Loss) earnings per share:			
Basic from continuing operations	$ (0.88)	$ (0.01)	$ 0.20
Basic from discontinued operations	—	(0.12)	(0.30)
Basic attributable to Avon	(0.88)	(0.13)	(0.10)
Diluted from continuing operations	(0.88)	(0.01)	0.20
Diluted from discontinued operations	—	(0.12)	(0.30)
Diluted attributable to Avon	(0.88)	(0.13)	(0.10)
Weighted-average shares outstanding:			
Basic	434.5	433.4	431.9
Diluted	434.5	433.4	432.5

Source: Avon 2014 annual report.

United States several decades ago, where it resulted in rapid recruiting and healthy sales.

Avon pursued an ambitious global growth strategy by expanding its presence in Brazil and China. Unfortunately, there were several hiccups in this ambitious effort.

Brazil Brazil was the third-largest beauty market, behind the United States and Japan. Importantly, direct selling accounted for almost 30 percent of the booming market. Vivienne Rudd, head of beauty research at Mintel, explained: "The retail structure in Brazil isn't sufficiently developed yet for the beauty industry, so direct sales is a much more valuable model." Brazil surpassed the U.S. in 2010 to become the biggest market for Avon in terms of sales, but managing operations proved to be a major challenge.

When the government required electronic invoicing for tax purposes in June 2010, Avon's computer systems were not prepared to handle the additional load. The change created service issues for representatives, forecasting problems, and product shortages.

A year later the company went ahead with implementing a new information-management system in Brazil, one it had been planning for nearly two years. However, when the new system went live, there were additional execution problems. Orders were missed, and shipments to representatives got delayed. The service problems dragged down sales, with nearly half of the decrease coming from lost sales due to a problem with representatives. Unlike the case in the U.S. direct-sales market, representatives in Brazil often sold for multiple companies, and Avon lost many of them to its regional competitor, Natura.

China In China, Avon's problems were more pronounced. Avon opened for business there in 1990 amid press reports that the company had sold out six months' worth of inventory in just four weeks. However, a direct-selling ban by the Chinese government in 1998 forced Avon to seek alternate approaches to selling and eventually open brick-and-mortar locations called Beauty Boutiques. Avon received the first license to resume direct selling in China in 2006.

Despite these efforts, in 2008 Avon received a whistleblower letter with allegations of bribery and possible violations of the Foreign Corrupt Practices Act. Avon began an internal investigation, which subsequently led to the departure of six employees. The highest-level dismissal took place in January 2012, when Avon reported that Charles Cramb, the former CFO, was no longer with the company. In October 2012, Avon disclosed that the SEC had opened a formal investigation. (The company finally settled for a whopping $135 million with the agency.)[10]

New CEO Seeks New Solutions

Faced with Avon's soft performance and legal issues, the board decided the company needed a change of leadership. Jung resigned as CEO in 2011, and the search for a new CEO began.

In April 2012, Sheri McCoy was appointed CEO of the company. She came with a proven track record at the Johnson & Johnson (J&J) Company, where she was responsible for the global pharmaceutical and consumer businesses. The consumer business included well-known skin care brands like Neutrogena. She had a good pedigree, with a master's in chemical engineering from Princeton and broad experience in a number of roles of increasing responsibility at J&J. Despite the impressive background, McCoy had no prior experience in direct selling. In some ways, her profile matched that of Jung when Jung took the reins of the company over a decade ago.

Shortly after becoming Avon CEO in 2012, McCoy sought the input of current and former sales representatives to hear firsthand what the company could do better.[7] She then used the information to develop a plan for the future, and she laid out how this plan would be different from things the company had tried in the past.

As she prepared to lead the transformation of the company, she made some critical changes to her executive team:[11]

- In August 2012, McCoy made her first C-level appointment: PR expert Cheryl Heinonen was recruited as chief communications officer and senior vice president of Corporate Relations. The company could clearly benefit from an image makeover.
- Soon after, McCoy appointed Jeff Benjamin and Scott Crum to lead the Legal and Human Resource departments, signaling the importance of legal compliance and personnel development in the new company environment.
- In December 2012, she appointed P&G veteran Patricia Perez-Ayala as chief marketing officer. Perez-Ayala had started her career with P&G in Venezuela and was an expert on Latin America.
- In 2013, more critical additions were made to the leadership team. Experienced transformation guru David Powell joined as senior vice president of Business Transformation and Supply Chain. Tupperware executive Pablo Munoz, who had a successful track record of direct selling and turning around businesses, was brought in to lead the ailing North American business. Brian Salsberg, an Asia-Pacific market expert from McKinsey, was recruited to head up Strategy.
- In 2015, James Scully joined the firm as its new CFO after 9 years at J.Crew, a multichannel apparel retailer. He replaced company veteran Kimberly Ross, who had resigned to pursue an external opportunity.

McCoy believed the company needed to evolve by focusing on three critical areas: executing growth platforms, driving simplification and efficiency, and improving organizational effectiveness. She indicated that the company was making progress in these three areas but that the turnaround would take time:[2]

- In the area of growth platforms, the company had begun refining its consumer value proposition. This involved clearly defining product categories and developing fully integrated marketing plans. It also included a renewed organizational focus on improving all aspects of the representative experience and achieving geographic optimization.

- In the area of simplification and efficiency, the company was streamlining complex processes and trying to create a mind-set of cost management.
- In the area of organizational effectiveness, a new culture of discipline and accountability was being implemented.

Soon after taking charge, McCoy pushed the adoption of technology at all levels, including mobile applications and online brochures. The company invested nearly $200 million in expanding its information technology systems and in updating and repositioning brands.[7]

Unlike past changes, however, these changes were implemented with the direct-selling representative at the center of the planning effort. In the past, some of the changes that had been implemented without active involvement of the sales representatives had failed due to lack of relevance and to inconvenience.

McCoy also cut about 1,500 jobs and announced Avon's exit from unprofitable markets as part of a plan to save $400 million by the end of 2015. In July 2013, Avon announced the sale of its Silpada jewelry unit to Rhinestone Holdings (original owner of Silpada) for $85 million.

McCoy believed marketing had played a critical role during the transformation. "We have to continue to look at how we make direct selling more modern in some ways," including using technology to amplify the social connections forged by the reps, she said. "You see this blurring of the channels, and that's why the brand is so important because in the end, the consumer is going to buy on the brand."

Some Competitors Eager to Buy

Avon had received takeover offers from, or been speculated as a takeover target by, a number of competitors, including Coty[12] and L'Oréal.[13] These companies had been interested in using Avon's army of direct-selling representatives to sell their own beauty products in emerging markets.

If CEO McCoy was unable to turn the company around quickly, there would continue to be takeover bids that investors would expect the board to consider.

The Rocky Road Ahead

High Tab of Litigation[14]

According to company releases, an internal investigation was being conducted and covered a broad range of areas: travel, entertainment, gifts, use of third-party vendors and consultants, joint ventures and acquisitions, and payments to third-party agents and others. The legal fees and costs for the outside counsel conducting the internal investigation totaled $59 million in 2009 and $95 million in 2010. The final tally for the internal investigation was expected to approach $250 million.

The SEC was expected to review the results of the internal investigation before making its final resolution. Avon hoped that conducting a thorough inquiry would result in a more favorable resolution for the company, such as a deferred or nonprosecution agreement with no criminal conviction.

In December 2014, the company revealed it had settled with the SEC for $135 million.[10]

Women-Centric Philanthropic Efforts

The "company for women" had a rich history and mission of supporting women-centric causes (see Exhibit 3). Its 2014 balance sheet (see Exhibit 4) shows at total of $249 million in assets relating to goodwill. Would the company be able to continue to fund these causes in the future? Could these commitments eventually become a financial liability for the company?

Breast Cancer

- Avon's Breast Cancer Crusade was launched in the United Kingdom in 1992. Through Avon's sales channel, an army of Avon Ladies was mobilized to raise awareness and funds for the cause. In 1998, the Avon Foundation was named the beneficiary of the first long-distance walk series for breast cancer. Five years later, the foundation launched its current highly successful event model in the United States: the Avon Walk for Breast Cancer, a marathon-and-a-half walk (39.3 miles) over two days.
- In 2005, the company started the Avon Walk Around the World for Breast Cancer series, bringing grassroots activism to a global scale. Walk Around the World mobilized a quarter of a million people each year for the breast cancer cause. This "walk" sometimes included runs, concerts, and educational seminars. World walkers trekked past historic sites, including the Great Wall of China and the Kremlin, and through diverse locales such as Kuala Lumpur and Prague.
- In 2007, popular actress Reese Witherspoon was appointed as Avon's global ambassador and as honorary chairperson of the Avon Foundation for Women.
- By 2015, the Avon Breast Cancer Crusade had become a powerful global force, and Avon was the leading corporate supporter of the breast cancer cause worldwide. The crusade had donated more than $780 million to accelerate research progress and improve access to care.

Domestic Violence

- The Avon Foundation supported efforts to build awareness of domestic violence as a problem. Through 2012, it had contributed $33 million to the cause.

The Future—A Fix or Sell Proposition

Heading into 2015, CEO McCoy had a big challenge and opportunity ahead of her. An ambitious turnaround plan was in place. However, she would quickly need to prove to shareholders that the plan was working and that the company was returning to growth and profitability. Shareholders were getting increasingly impatient and wanted to see their stocks appreciate again. If a turnaround was not the answer, they would expect the CEO and board to seek value by selling the company.

EXHIBIT 3 Avon Values and Principles[1]

Avon's Vision

- To be the company that best understands and satisfies the product, service and self-fulfillment needs of women globally.

Avon's Mission

Avon's mission is focused on six core aspirations the company continually strives to achieve:

- **Leader in global beauty:** Build a unique portfolio of beauty and related brands, striving to surpass competitors in quality, innovation, and value, and elevating Avon's image to become the world's most trusted beauty company.
- **Women's choice for buying:** Become the shopping destination for women, providing a personal, high-touch experience that helps create lifelong customer relationships.
- **Premier direct-selling company:** Expand Avon's presence in direct selling, empowering women to achieve economic independence by offering a superior earnings opportunity as well as recognition, service and support, making it easy and rewarding to be affiliated with Avon.
- **Most admired company:** Deliver superior returns to shareholders by pursuing new growth opportunities while maintaining a commitment to be a responsible, ethical company and a global corporate citizen that is held as a model of success.
- **Best place to work:** Elevate the company's leadership, including its high standards, respect for diversity, and commitment to helping Associates achieve their highest potential in a positive work environment.
- **To have the largest foundation dedicated to women's causes:** Be a committed global champion for the health and well-being of women through philanthropic efforts, with a focus on breast cancer, domestic violence and women's empowerment.

The Avon Values

- **Trust** means we want to live and work in an environment where communications are open—where people feel free to take risks, to share their points of view and to speak the truth as they see it. Trust people to do the right thing—and help them to understand your underlying reasoning and philosophy—and they won't disappoint.
- **Respect** helps us to value differences, to appreciate each person for her or his unique qualities. Through respect, we help bring out the full potential of each person.
- **Belief** is the cornerstone of empowering Associates to assume responsibilities and be the very best they can be. Believe in someone—and show it—and that person will move mountains to prove you're right.
- **Humility** simply means we're not always right—we don't have all the answers—and we know it. We're no less human than the people who work for us, and we're not afraid to ask for help.
- **Integrity** should be the hallmark of every Avon Associate. In setting and observing the highest ethical standards and doing the right thing, we fulfill a duty of care, not only to our Representatives and customers in the communities we serve, but to our colleagues and ourselves.

Principles That Guide Avon

- To provide individuals an **opportunity to earn** in support of their well-being and happiness.
- To serve families throughout the world with **products of the highest quality** backed by a guarantee of satisfaction.
- To render a **service to customers** that is outstanding in its helpfulness and courtesy.
- To give full **recognition to employees and Representatives,** on whose contributions Avon depends.
- To **share with others** the rewards of growth and success.
- To meet fully the obligations of **corporate citizenship** by contributing to the well-being of society and the environment in which it functions.
- To maintain and cherish the **friendly spirit** of Avon.

Source: *www.avoncompany.com.*

EXHIBIT 4 Avon Products, Inc., Consolidated Balance Sheets ($ millions, except per-share data)

	December 31:	
	2014	2013
Assets		
Current Assets		
Cash, including cash equivalents of $440.3 and $576.2	$ 960.5	$ 1,107.9
Accounts receivable (less allowances of $118.0 and $147.2)	563.5	676.3
Inventories	822.2	967.7
Prepaid expenses and other	618.3	689.3
Total current assets	2,964.5	3,441.2
Property, plant and equipment, at cost		
Land	45.8	55.3
Buildings and improvements	1,011.1	1,085.3
Equipment	1,235.7	1,343.9
	2,292.6	2,484.5
Less accumulated depreciation	(1,061.6)	(1,091.2)
Property, plant and equipment, net	1,231.0	1,393.3
Goodwill	249.3	282.5
Other assets	1,052.0	1,375.3
Total assets	$5,496.8	$ 6,492.3
Liabilities and Shareholders' Equity		
Current Liabilities		
Debt maturing within one year	$ 137.1	$ 188.0
Accounts payable	895.4	896.5
Accrued compensation	210.5	271.2
Other accrued liabilities	598.8	652.6
Sales and taxes other than income	168.6	186.8
Income taxes	36.8	45.4
Total current liabilities	2,047.2	2,240.5
Long-term debt	2,463.9	2,532.7
Employee benefit plans	501.8	398.0
Long-term income taxes	77.8	53.3
Other liabilities	100.8	140.3
Total liabilities	5,191.5	5,364.8
Commitments and contingencies		
Shareholders' Equity		
Common stock, par value $.25—authorized 1,500 shares; issued 750.3 and 748.8 shares	187.6	189.4

continued

EXHIBIT 4 *Continued*

	December 31:	
	2014	2013
Additional paid-in capital	2,207.9	2,175.6
Retained earnings	3,702.9	4,196.7
Accumulated other comprehensive loss	(1,217.6)	(870.4)
Treasury stock, at cost (315.6 and 314.9 shares)	(4,591.0)	(4,581.2)
Total Avon shareholders' equity	289.8	1,110.1
Noncontrolling interests	15.5	17.4
Total shareholders' equity	305.3	1,127.5
Total liabilities and shareholders' equity	$ 5,496.8	$ 6,492.3

Source: Avon 2014 annual report.

ENDNOTES

1. Avon company website, *www.avoncompany.com.*
2. Avon Q3 earnings call transcript, October 30, 2014.
3. Europe, Middle East, and Africa.
4. Passariello, C., & Glazer, E. 2012. Coty knocks on Brazil's door. *www.online.wsj.com,* April 5.
5. Avon 2014 annual report
6. Mary Kay company website, *www.marykay.com.*
7. Coleman-Lochner, L. 2013. Avon CEO embraces technology to reverse profit slump. *Bloomberg News,* February 22.
8. Stanley, A. 1996. Avon and Mary Kay create opportunities for women. *www.nytimes.com,* August 14.
9. Kowitt, B. 2012. Avon: The rise and fall of a beauty icon. *Fortune,* April 30.
10. Areddy, James T., & Wang, F. 2014. Avon aims to wash off China mud with $135 million graft settlement. *Wall Street Journal,* December 18.
11. Company press releases in 2012 and 2013.
12. *www.theguardian.com/world/2012/apr/02/avon-coty-cosmetics-fragrance-takeover.*
13. *www.cosmeticsbusiness.com/news/article_page/LOreal_and_Avon__the_next_takeover/57269.*
14. Hennings, Peter J. 2011. The high price of internal inquiries. *New York Times,* May 6

CASES

CASE 14
THE BOSTON BEER COMPANY: POISED FOR GROWTH*

As the Boston Beer Company continued its growth momentum into 2015, Martin Roper, the company's president and CEO, stated, "Our depletions[a] growth remained strong and benefited from the growth of our Samuel Adams, Twisted Tea, Angry Orchard and Traveler brands. With the launch of several new beers and ciders in the first quarter of 2015, and our planned increased investment behind Samuel Adams, Twisted Tea, Angry Orchard and Traveler brands, we believe we are well-positioned to maintain our momentum."[1]

Roper admitted that while the supply chain had improved, there was still plenty of room for further optimization. The company had completed a number of significant capital and efficiency projects in 2014 to increase its capacity and capabilities.

The focus in 2015 was on taking full advantage of these increased capabilities through improved operator training and on making supply chain improvements for improved product quality and customer service. Capital expansion was expected to slow in 2015, as the company sought to optimize its big investments from prior years.[1]

The Boston Beer Company, known for its Samuel Adams brand, was the largest craft brewery in the United States, holding a 1 percent stake in the overall beer market.[2] It faced growing competitive threats from other breweries, both large and small. In the past several years, the beer industry as a whole had been on a decline, while sales of wines and spirits had increased. The Boston Beer Company competed within the premium-beer industry, which included craft beer and premium imported beers like Heineken and Corona. Although the beer industry had been on a decline, the premium-beer industry had seen a small amount of growth and the craft-beer industry had seen a surge in popularity. Because of the success of the craft breweries in particular, the major breweries had taken notice and many new craft breweries had sprung up.

Anheuser-Busch Inbev and MillerCoors, LLC, accounted for over 80 percent of the beer market in the United States.[3] They had caught on to the current trend in the beer industry toward higher-quality beers and started releasing their own higher-quality beers. For example, Anheuser-Busch Inbev released Bud Light Wheat and Bud Light Platinum in an effort to provide quality beers to its loyal customers. MillerCoors introduced Blue Moon beer, and Anheuser-Busch Inbev released ShockTop to combat the popularity of Blue Moon. These companies also began to purchase smaller craft breweries, whose products had been rising in popularity. Anheuser-Busch Inbev purchased Goose Island Brewing Company in March 2011. MillerCoors started a group within the Tenth and Blake Beer Company for the purpose of creating and purchasing craft breweries. According to MillerCoors CEO Tom Lang, the plan was to grow Tenth and Blake Beer Company considerably in the coming years.[4] The two major companies used their massive marketing budgets to tell people about their craft beers.

According to the Brewers Association, 1,940 craft breweries and 1,989 total breweries operated in the United States. While craft breweries accounted for over 97 percent of all the breweries in the United States, they produced only approximately 25 percent of all beer sold.[5] However, with the rise in popularity of premium beers, the craft breweries were expected to continue to grab more of the market. As the country's largest craft brewery, the Boston Beer Company had revenue of over $900 million in 2014 and sold over 2 million barrels of beer. Other large craft breweries included New Belgium Brewing Company and Sierra Nevada Brewing Company.[6] In addition, some smaller breweries had been merging to take advantage of economies of scale and enhance their competitive position.

According to the Boston Beer Company, there were approximately 770 craft breweries that shipped their product domestically, up from only 420 a decade earlier. There were also an estimated 800 craft breweries in the planning stage, expecting to be operational within the next two to three years. Boston Beer Company assumed that 300 of those 800 would be shipping breweries (i.e., breweries that sell their product beyond their local market). Thus, within the next few years, Samuel Adams beer would be competing with over 1,000 other craft breweries around the country.

The Boston Beer Company competed not only with domestic craft breweries but also with premium-beer imports, such as Heineken and Corona, which sold beer in a similar price range. Like Anheuser-Busch Inbev and MillerCoors, Heineken and Corona had large financial resources and could influence the market. It was projected

---

* This case was developed by graduate students Peter J. Courtney, Eric S. Engelson, Dev Das, and Professor Alan B. Eisner, Pace University. Material has been drawn from published sources to be used for class discussion. Copyright © 2015 Alan B. Eisner.

[a] Industry term for shipments from warehouses to consumer outlets; more reflective of actual consumption than shipments to warehouses, which could involve temporary inventory fluctuations.

that premium imported beers would grow by 6 percent over the next five years.

The Brewers Association defined a craft brewery as brewing less than 6 million barrels per year and being less than 25 percent owned or controlled by another economic interest. Maintaining status as a craft brewery could be important for image and, therefore, sales. Thus, MillerCoors purchased less than a 25 percent stake in Terrapin Beer, still allowing it to maintain its craft brewery status.[7] The size of the Boston Beer Company, however, was an issue. With continued growth, the brewery could potentially increase its volume output to more than 6 million barrels per year, thus losing its craft brewery status. Furthermore, with the size of the company and its ability to market nationwide, the company ran the risk of alienating itself from other craft breweries that could believe Samuel Adams no longer fit the profile. Many craft breweries already believed that the company, which had been public since 1995, was more concerned with making money than with providing quality beer and educating the public on craft beers.

Size did have advantages, of course, providing more money for marketing and, especially in the beer business, facilitating distribution. A heavy complaint among all craft breweries was the difficulty they had distributing their product in the current three-tier system (discussed in a later section). The large breweries had power over the independent distributors because they accounted for most of their business. Thus, they could influence the distributors and make it difficult for craft breweries to sell their product. Because of its size, the Boston Beer Company had fewer problems with distributors than its smaller competitors did. Consequently, the company had less in common with other craft breweries and more with the major breweries in regard to distribution. This was good for Boston Beer Company's distribution but might have been bad for its image. One brewer from the Defiant Brewing Company in Pearl River, New York, said that the Boston Beer Company was becoming too large to be considered a craft brewery and that its substantial connections with distributors contributed to this notion.[8]

Clearly, the Boston Beer Company was facing a difficult competitive environment. It faced direct competition from both larger and smaller breweries and from premium imported beers. Some of the smaller craft breweries were growing quickly and wanted to be larger than the Boston Beer Company. Other craft breweries felt that the Boston Beer Company was too large already. Thus, while further growth would be beneficial in terms of revenue, growing too large could negatively affect the company's status as a craft brewery and the perceptions of its customers. The company had to pay close attention to maintaining its image among the growing customer base of premium-beer drinkers.

Company Background

Jim Koch started the Boston Beer Company in 1984 along with fellow Harvard MBA graduates Harry Rubin and Lorenzo Lamadrid. The company began with the sale of the now popular Samuel Adams Boston Lager, named after the famous American patriot who was known to have been a brewer himself. The recipe for the lager was passed down from generation to generation in Koch's family, dating back to the 1860s. Koch began home brewing the beer in his own kitchen and soliciting local establishments in Boston to purchase and sell it. Just one year after its initial sales, Samuel Adams Boston Lager was voted "Best Beer in America" at the Great American Beer Festival in Denver, Colorado. In 1985 Samuel Adams grew immensely and sold 500 barrels of beer in Massachusetts, Connecticut, and West Germany.[9]

To avoid the high up-front capital costs of starting a brewery, Koch contracted with several existing breweries to make his beer. This allowed the production of the Boston Lager to grow quickly from the relatively small quantities Koch could brew himself. Growth continued after that, and in 1988 the Boston Beer Company opened a brewery in Boston. By 1989 the Boston Beer Company produced 63,000 barrels of Samuel Adams beer annually.

The company went public in 1995, selling Class A common stock to potential investors. The stock was sold at two different prices, $15 to loyal customers and $20 through an IPO run by Goldman Sachs. Koch decided to reward his loyal customers by advertising the stock offering on the packages of his six-packs, estimating that 30,000 buyers would be interested. He believed that those who enjoyed the beer and supported it should be the ones to have a stake in the company. After 100,000 potential investors sent checks in, Koch randomly chose 30,000.[10] Managers from Goldman Sachs were upset that they did not receive the lowest-price offering. Koch owns 100 percent of the Class B common stock, which confers the right to make all major decisions for the company. This was seen as a risk to potential investors because Koch could make important decisions on the strategy of the company without receiving approval from them.

Continued success for the business led to the purchase of a large brewery in Cincinnati in 1997. Since 2000, Samuel Adams had won more awards in international beer-tasting competitions than any other brewery in the world. In 2008 the Boston Beer Company purchased a world-class brewery in Lehigh, Pennsylvania, to support growth.

As of 2015, the Boston Beer Company was the largest craft brewery in the United States, brewing over 2 million barrels of Samuel Adams beer, but it still served only a fraction of the total U.S. beer market. The company had expanded its selections to over 50 beer flavors, including seasonal and other flavorful beers, such as Samuel Adams Summer Ale, Samuel Adams Cherry Wheat, and Samuel Adams Octoberfest, as well as the nonbeer brands Twisted Tea and HardCore Cider. The Boston Beer Company planned to use the profits gained from its nonbeer brands to invest in Samuel Adams and build a stronger portfolio. Revenue for the company grew from $628 million in 2012

EXHIBIT 1 Boston Beer Co., Inc., Income Statements ($ thousands, except per-share and net-revenue-per-barrel data)

	Year Ended:		
	Dec. 27, 2014	Dec. 28, 2013	Dec. 29, 2012
Income Statement Data:			
Revenue	$966,478	$793,705	$628,580
Less excise taxes	63,471	54,652	48,358
Net revenue	903,007	739,053	580,222
Cost of goods sold	437,996	354,131	265,012
Gross profit	465,011	384,922	315,210
Operating expenses:			
Advertising, promotional and selling expenses	250,696	207,930	169,306
General and administrative expenses	65,971	62,332	50,171
Impairment of long-lived assets	1,777	1,567	149
Total operating expenses	318,444	271,829	219,626
Operating income	146,567	113,093	95,584
Other (expense) income, net	(973)	(552)	(67)
Income before provision for income taxes	145,594	112,541	95,517
Provision for income taxes	54,851	42,149	36,050
Net income	$ 90,743	$ 70,392	$ 59,467
Net income per-share basic	$6.96	$5.47	$4.60
Net income per-share diluted	$6.69	$5.18	$4.39
Weighted-average shares outstanding basic	12,968	12,766	12,796
Weighted-average shares outstanding diluted	13,484	13,504	13,435
Balance Sheet Data:			
Working capital	$ 97,292	$ 59,901	$ 73,448
Total assets	$605,161	$444,075	$359,484
Total long-term obligations	$ 58,851	$ 37,613	$ 25,499
Total stockholders equity	$436,140	$302,085	$245,091
Statistical Data:			
Barrels sold	4,103	3,416	2,746
Net revenue per barrel	$ 220	$ 216	$ 211

Source: Boston Beer Company.

to over $966 million in 2014, while operating costs grew from $219 million to $318 million. Net income increased from $59 million to $90 million in the same period (see Exhibits 1 and 2). In January 2015, the company stock was selling at $301, nearly $200 over the initial public offering in 1995.

The goal of the Boston Beer Company was to become the leading brewer in the premium-beer market. As of

EXHIBIT 2 Boston Beer Co., Inc., Balance Sheets ($ thousands, except per-share and net-revenue-per-barrel data)

Year Ended	Dec. 27, 2014	Dec. 28, 2013
Assets		
Current Assets:		
Cash and cash equivalents	$ 76,402	$ 49,524
Accounts receivable, net of allowance for doubtful accounts of $144 and $160 as of Dec. 27, 2014, and Dec. 28, 2013, respectively	36,860	42,001
Inventories	51,307	56,397
Prepaid expenses and other current assets	12,887	9,606
Income tax receivable	21,321	1,038
Deferred income taxes	8,685	5,712
Total current assets	207,462	164,278
Property, plant and equipment, net	381,569	266,558
Other assets	12,447	9,556
Goodwill	3,683	3,683
Total assets	$605,161	$444,075
Liabilities and Stockholders Equity		
Current Liabilities:		
Accounts payable	$ 35,576	$ 34,424
Current portion of debt and capital lease obligations	55	53
Accrued expenses and other current liabilities	74,539	69,900
Total current liabilities	110,170	104,377
Deferred income taxes	50,717	32,394
Debt and capital lease obligations, less current portion	528	584
Other liabilities	7,606	4,635
Total liabilities	169,021	141,990
Commitments and Contingencies		
Stockholders Equity:		
Class A Common Stock, $.01 par value; 22,700,000 shares authorized; 9,452,375 and 8,785,343 issued and outstanding as of Dec. 27, 2014, and Dec. 28, 2013, respectively	95	88
Class B Common Stock, $.01 par value; 4,200,000 shares authorized; 3,617,355 and 3,962,355 issued and outstanding as of Dec. 27, 2014, and Dec. 28, 2013, respectively	36	40
Additional paid-in capital	224,909	173,025
Accumulated other comprehensive loss, net of tax	(1,133)	(417)
Retained earnings	212,233	129,349
Total stockholders equity	436,140	302,085
Total liabilities and stockholders equity	$605,161	$444,075

Source: Boston Beer Company.

2015, it was the largest craft brewery, but it trailed Crown Imports, LLC, and Heineken USA in the premium-beer market. The company planned to surpass the large importers by increasing brand availability and awareness through advertising, drinker education, and the support of its over 300-member sales force. The salespeople for the company had a high level of product knowledge about beer and the brewing process and used this to educate distributors and the public on the benefits of Samuel Adams. The Boston Beer Company formed a subsidiary called Alchemy & Science to seize new opportunities in the craft brewing industry. The purpose of this group was to identify better beer ingredients, methods for better brewing, and opportunities to purchase breweries that would help the business grow. One such opportunity, for instance, led to the group's purchase of Southern California Brewing.

Over the years, the company had continued to invest in efficiency initiatives to lower costs within its breweries and increase margins. One large program that the company was employing was its Freshest Beer Program. Typically, bottled and canned beer sat in a distributor's warehouse for three to five weeks, while kegs sat for three to four weeks. In an effort to reduce storage time in the distributor warehouses by approximately two weeks and consequently increase freshness of the beer at retailers, the company focused not only on better on-time service, forecasting, and production planning but also on great coordination and cooperation with distributors. The company soon had 50 percent of its beer in the Freshest Beer Program, with the goal of expanding that number to 75 percent within a year by investing $50 million in the program.

While expansion and growth were more commonly deemed positive attributes, the Boston Beer Company was aware of the many possible risks in the growth of its business. With the acquisition of the Lehigh brewery, the Boston Beer Company now brewed over 90 percent of its beer at its own breweries. With capital tied up in large investments, there was a potential for the business to falter if an unexpected event affected one of the breweries and halted production at that facility. The company had also put forth a sizable investment to increase product offerings and another to keep its beer fresh during distribution. However, with its reliance on independent distributors, a mishap in its relationship with major distributors could lead to complications within its supply chain. The Boston Beer Company also depended on foreign suppliers of raw material ingredients for its beer. An unexpected shortage of a crop might lead to a drop in production volume. In effect, the image of the company would diminish if its products were not available to loyal fans whose enjoyment of the brand relied on the wide accessibility of its craft beer. With the surge of an enormous number of other craft-beer choices, customers had many options to choose from.

Industry

Although Samuel Adams was sold in other countries, the United States was where the majority of the product was sold and where the brand held the most prominence in the beer market. Within the beer industry, Samuel Adams fell into the craft-beer category (see Exhibit 3). In terms of volume of beer sold, the Boston Beer Company was the largest craft brewery in the country. The beer market consisted mainly of standard and economy lagers, which

EXHIBIT 3 Top Craft Beers in the U.S., by Brand Family

	Dollar Sales	% Change vs. Prior Year	Case Sales	% Change vs. Prior Year
Samuel Adams	$ 329,422,200	12.2	10,453,300	11.4
Sierra Nevada	190,116,300	11.0	5,799,218	10.4
New Belgium	137,241,000	9.8	4,199,610	10.1
Shiner	116,655,600	13.4	3,820,370	10.7
Lagunitas	56,247,280	84.9	1,433,315	84.6
Deschutes	53,422,040	13.4	1,727,256	13.7
Redhook	40,980,740	9.0	1,434,310	10.6
Widmer	39,497,740	−5.2	1,286,111	−5.3
Kona	34,705,940	29.2	1,113,577	27.5
Stone	34,467,000	39.5	641,476	39.4
Category total*	$1,882,415,000	19.4	55,316,610	16.6

*Includes brands not listed.

Source: Information Resources Inc.

accounted for nearly 75 percent of all volume sold. Samuel Adams brand beers were more costly than standard lagers and were counted with the premium beers, which together account for the other 25 percent of all beer sold.

There were over 200 million barrels of beer sold in the United States. Anheuser-Busch Inbev dominated the domestic beer industry, totaling over 48 percent of the market. MillerCoors also had a large share of the market at just over 30 percent. Together these two companies sold approximately 8 out of every 10 beers purchased in the United States. (See Exhibit 4.)

The third-largest brewer in terms of volume of beer sold was Mexican-owned Crown Imports, LLC, which accounted for less than 6 percent of the market. (See Exhibit 5 for the top imported beers.) As the seventh-largest brewery in the country, the Boston Beer Company had a 1.1 percent share of the market.

Changes in Drinking Habits

The consumption habits of beer drinkers appear to have changed in recent years. The beer industry as a whole was declining gradually over the years.[11] This was mostly due to the decline in the consumption of standard lager and economy lager. Even though the volume of beer sold declined, the craft brew market had in fact exploded. Within the same period, dark ales and premium lagers grew considerably. Wheat beers (a segment of dark ales) experienced an especially large growth of over 150 percent. One of the Boston Beer Company's popular beers, Samuel Adams Cherry Wheat, was in this category. Hard ciders also increased in popularity, and the company's Angry Orchard line performed exceptionally well. (See Exhibit 6.)

The Three-Tier System

Seventy-five percent of the volume of beer sold was sold at off-trade value in supermarkets, beer distributors, and such, while the other 25 percent was sold in bars and restaurants. Despite the vast difference in the volumes sold, the values of beer sold at off-trade and on-trade sites were equal because of the premium charged for beer at a bar or a restaurant.

Breweries were not permitted to own either off-trade or on-trade establishments, so their beer had to be distributed. Before Prohibition, however, beer was sold in tavernlike establishments called "tied houses," which supplied and sold their own beer. There were no regulations regarding brewing companies owning all of the retail tied houses and selling only their own beer. After Prohibition, a system was put in place to discourage monopolies in the supply and sale of beer. This system was called the Three-Tier System, and it divided the beer industry into suppliers, distributors, and retailers, all independent of each other. Aside from the brewpub, breweries could not own retailers or distributors, thus ensuring a level of competition in the brewing industry.[12]

Although the three categories of the industry were separate, they each had a large influence on one another. For instance, Anheuser-Busch Inbev and MillerCoors sold 80 percent of the beers in the country. That meant that 80 percent of distributors' volume, and consequently revenue, was from these two companies. Hence, the distributors

EXHIBIT 4 Top Domestic Beers in the U.S., by Individual Brand

	Dollar Sales	% Change vs. Prior Year	Case Sales	% Change vs. Prior Year
Bud Light	$ 5,946,776,000	−0.5	294,749,300	−1.1
Coors Light	2,360,430,000	3.1	118,469,600	1.8
Budweiser	2,110,352,000	−2.5	104,390,500	−3.3
Miller Lite	1,868,866,000	−3.1	94,262,870	−4.3
Natural Light	1,122,770,000	−6.5	72,203,900	−7.5
Busch Light	844,276,000	2.0	56,008,580	1.3
Michelob Ultra Light	777,196,700	10.6	31,626,370	6.5
Busch	673,394,400	−4.6	43,374,170	−5.2
Keystone Light	493,993,600	−3.9	33,586,780	−4.4
Miller High Life	476,895,100	−8.5	30,260,060	−9.8
Category total*	$23,707,870,000	0.8	1,198,722,000	−1.3

*Includes brands not listed.

Source: Information Resources Inc.

EXHIBIT 5 Top Imported Beers in the U.S., by Individual Brand

	Dollar Sales	% Change vs. Prior Year	Case Sales	% Change vs. Prior Year
Corona Extra	$1,221,351,000	7.1	41,170,180	5.6
Heineken	669,337,000	−0.5	22,449,080	−1.3
Modelo Especial	574,636,300	24.5	21,648,650	19.9
Dos Equis XX Lager Especial	236,406,800	23.1	7,910,841	21.3
Corona Light	216,736,800	5.6	7,610,628	4.5
Stella Artois	194,844,500	17.7	5,591,031	15.7
Tecate	155,522,500	−4.1	8,017,746	−5.3
Labatt Blue	99,702,080	−2.3	5,220,015	0.1
Labatt Blue Light	97,494,690	−4.6	5,258,278	−2.0
Newcastle Brown Ale	77,033,940	−8.2	2,452,254	−8.1
Category total*	$4,454,768,000	6.0	159,583,500	4.5

*Includes brands not listed.

Source: Information Resources Inc.

EXHIBIT 6 Top Flavored Malts and Hard Ciders in the U.S., by Brand Family

	Flavored Malts			
	Dollar Sales	% Change vs. Prior Year	Case Sales	% Change vs. Prior Year
Bug Light Lime	$ 461,965,000	209.6	13,146,440	210.4
Mike's Hard	389,984,100	−1.4	11,855,950	−0.5
Smirnoff Ice	206,452,700	−5.9	6,072,160	−5.7
Redd's	151,928,000	56,777.3	4,630,883	56,090.8
Four Loko	138,494,400	−5.3	4,207,976	−6.6
Twisted Tea Hard Iced Tea	123,470,200	12.3	4,111,125	12.9
Smirnoff Premium Malt Mixed Drinks	44,264,050	−5.2	1,303,707	−5.5
Sparks	24,373,400	−21.0	1,076,292	−18.7
Bacardi Silver	16,716,480	−38.2	519,723	−39.6
Margaritaville	15,280,470	8.4	534,678	8.7
Category total*	$1,642,405,000	33.6	49,211,810	31.5
	Hard Ciders			
Angry Orchard	$107,737,800	334.7	3,229,955	341.0
Woodchuck	42,786,700	10.8	1,254,826	10.6
Hornsby's	9,924,088	−29.2	316,551	−30.1
Michelob	8,772,720	46.8	289,008	41.9
Strongbow	8,471,371	56.5	229,508	60.3
Category total*	$211,930,800	100.7	6,083,067	101.0

*Includes brands not listed.

Source: Information Resources Inc.

valued the business of Anheuser-Busch Inbev and MillerCoors to a higher degree, in fear of losing their business. In an effort to maintain its dominant position in the industry, Anheuser-Busch Inbev had contracted with several distributors on the condition that they would not work with any other breweries. Likewise, the other large breweries imposed restrictions on their distributors regarding which other breweries they could work with.

The distributors acted as the intermediary in the beer industry, providing the beer to retailers. The beer that was available from retailers was a result of the products that their distributors carried. The distributors were major decision makers for what beer taps would be available in bars, as well as the location of beer selections in supermarkets. Small breweries did not like the system because the distributors were heavily influenced by the major breweries. Since distributors had little incentive to treat them as equal business partners, small breweries found it difficult to compete and achieve growth. Consequently, it was a challenge for a small brewery to gain widespread recognition in the industry. Despite this challenge, the Boston Beer Company made a name for itself and sold its beer to a network of approximately 400 distributors.

Competition

The Boston Beer Company mainly competed with other beers sold in the United States. Samuel Adams belonged to the craft-beer category, which had been rapidly growing over the previous several years. The company faced competition from other craft brewers, premium import brewers, and the two major domestic breweries, Anheuser-Busch Inbev and MillerCoors.

The U.S. Open Beer Championship was a highly recognized nationwide beer competition that included professional breweries as well as home brewers. In 2014 more than 3,000 beers in 81 different categories were submitted. The top 10 brewers were chosen on the basis of receiving the highest overall grade in the most categories collectively. Exhibit 7 lists the top 10 brewers in 2014 according to the U.S. Open Beer Championship. The Boston Beer Company received the fourth-place ribbon, an impressive feat with so many breweries participating. For the first time in 2014, the U.S. Open also judged three styles of ciders. The Boston Beer Company took home three medals and was named "Cidery of the Year" for its Angry Orchard ciders.[13]

Home brewing had become an extremely popular hobby, and in many instances it led home brewers to pursue their passion in the form of an actual brewery. The Homebrewers Association was founded in 1978 and includes more than 30,000 beer-enthusiastic members. Its rankings of the top 10 beers, top 10 breweries, and top 10 most diverse breweries are shown in Exhibit 8.[14]

The Boston Beer Company also competes with the noncraft breweries that sell premium imports and standard and economy lagers. In regard to dollar sales, a list of the top 10 beers in the United States is shown in Exhibit 4, followed by a list of the top imports in Exhibit 5. Samuel Adams did not crack the top 20 list.[15]

Sierra Nevada Brewing Company

Ken Grossman and Paul Camusi started the Sierra Nevada Brewing Company in 1980. It was the largest private craft brewery behind the publicly traded Boston Beer Company. Sierra Nevada made the highest-selling pale ale in the

EXHIBIT 7 Top 10 Brewers, U.S. Open Beer Championship, 2014

The top 10 breweries based on the number of beers placing first (3 points), second (2 points), or third (1 point) are:

1. Wormtown Brewing—Massachusetts

2. Stone Brewing—California

2. Deschutes Brewery—Oregon

4. Blue Point Brewing—New York

4. Sprecher Brewing—Wisconsin

4. Black Tooth Brewing—Wyoming

4. Rahr & Sons Brewing—Texas

4. Reuben's Brews—Washington

4. Boston Beer Company—Massachusetts

9. Green Bench Brewing—Florida

9. Peticolas Brewing—Texas

9. Big Island Brewhaus—Hawaii

Source: U.S. Open Beer Championship.

EXHIBIT 8 Top 10 Home-Brewed Beers and Breweries, 2014

Top-Ranked Beers

For the sixth consecutive year, Russian River Brewing Company took the top-ranked beer title for its double IPA, Pliny the Elder.

1. Russian River Pliny the Elder
2. Bell's Two Hearted Ale
3. Ballast Point Sculpin IPA
4. Bell's Hopslam
5. The Alchemist Heady Topper
6. Lagunitas Sucks
7. Dogfish Head 90 Minute IPA
8. Stone Enjoy By IPA
9. Founders Breakfast Stout
10. Goose Island Bourbon County Stout

Brewery Rankings

1. Russian River Brewing Company, *Santa Rosa, Calif.*
2. Bell's Brewery, *Kalamazoo, Mich.*
3. Stone Brewing Co., *Escondido, Calif.*
4. Dogfish Head Craft Brewery, *Milton, Del.*
5. Sierra Nevada Brewing Co., *Chico, Calif.*
6. Founders Brewing Co., *Grand Rapids, Mich.*
7. Firestone Walker Brewing Co., *Paso Robles, Calif.*
8. Lagunitas Brewing Co., *Petaluma, Calif.*
9. Deschutes Brewery, *Bend, Ore.*
10. New Belgium Brewing Co., *Fort Collins, Colo.*

Best Portfolio

(T indicates tie)

1. New Belgium Brewing Co. | 60 beers
2. Boston Beer Co. (Samuel Adams) | 53
3. Sierra Nevada Brewing Co. | 49
4. Dogfish Head Craft Brewery | 48
5. Stone Brewing Co. | 46
T6. Bell's Brewery | 41
T6. Short's Brewing Co. | 41
8. Deschutes Brewery | 40
9. The Bruery | 38
T10. Avery Brewing Co. | 37
T10. Boulevard Brewing Co. | 37
T10. Goose Island Beer Co. | 37

Source: Homebrewers Association.

United States. The company sold approximately 1 million barrels of beer in 2014 and distributed its beers in all 50 states. Sierra Nevada was one of the earliest craft breweries, and its founders were consequently referred to as pioneers in the craft brewing industry. The company planned to open another brewing facility within the next few years to continue growth of the business. Sierra Nevada created goodwill by promoting the craft-beer industry and by striving to be environmentally friendly in its beer's production. One of Sierra Nevada Brewing's goals was to overtake the Boston Beer Company as the largest craft brewery in the country.[16]

New Belgium Brewing Company

Jeff Lebesch founded the New Belgium Brewing Company in Fort Collins, Colorado, in 1991. New Belgium Brewing was the third-largest craft brewery in the United States, behind the Boston Beer Company and Sierra Nevada. The company's flagship beer was an amber ale called Fat Tire, but it had over 25 different beers in production. In recent years the company had sold over 700,000 barrels of beer, which were distributed in 29 states. Over the last several years, the company had growth of approximately 15 percent. New Belgium had plans to build a $100 million brewery in North Carolina by 2015 to compete with the other major breweries. Like Sierra Nevada, New Belgium focused on energy-efficient practices. The company also hoped to become the largest craft brewery in the country.[17]

Crown Imports, LLC

Crown Imports, LLC, was a joint venture between Grupo Modelo and Constellation Brands. Crown Imports had a portfolio of beers that included Corona Extra, Corona Light, Modelo Especial, Pacifico, and others. Crown Imports controlled approximately 6 percent of the market and had the number-one import into the United States, Corona Extra, which brought in over $1 billion in revenue in 2014. It had the third-largest market share in the United States, behind Anheuser-Busch Inbev and MillerCoors. The beer brands were owned by the public company Constellation Brands. Constellation owned over 200 brands of beer, wine, and spirits and had sales of almost $4.8 billion in 2014. With such a large financial backing, Crown Imports wanted to remain the number-one import in the country and close the gap in market share between it and the top two breweries. Due to its large amount of capital, Crown Imports was able to advertise its brands nationally. Crown also hosted several charitable events.[18] Crown recently started a campaign to make Corona Extra the most liked beer in America.

Heineken

Heineken was the second-largest import brewing company and the fourth-largest brewing company in the United States. The company had approximately 4 percent of the market for the last several years. The company was founded in 1873, and its beers were sold in 71 countries worldwide. Heineken imported popular brands such as Heineken, Amstel Light, Sol, Dos Equis, and Newcastle. Company sales exceeded $26 billion in 2013.[19] With Heineken's large size and reputation, it had the ability to advertise its products nationally. The Dos Equis brand had grown by over 10 percent since the popular "Most Interesting Man in the World" commercials began airing. Most of the brands offered by Heineken were in the price range of Samuel Adams, making them a close competitor.[20]

Anheuser-Busch Inbev NV

Anheuser-Busch Inbev was one of the largest beer companies in the world, with roughly $43 billion in revenue in 2014. The brewing portion of the company remained the largest brewery in the United States and had an approximate 50 percent stake in the U.S. beer industry.[21] It had the two best-selling beers in the country, Bud Light and Budweiser, and the fifth-best-selling beer, Natural Light. However, the company saw the sale of its products decline over the last several years. In an effort to combat the lower volume of sales, it had raised the prices of its beer products.

Additionally, the company had witnessed the explosive growth of the craft-beer industry. Although it could never be considered a craft brewery because of its size, Anheuser-Busch planned to make more craftlike beers, as it had done with its brand Shock Top. The company also planned to invest in and purchase small craft breweries, like Goose Island, which made the popular beer 312. Anheuser-Busch was not opposed to merging with other large breweries. The company was reported to be in talks with the maker of Corona to purchase that company. The size and influence of Anheuser-Busch posed a threat to the Boston Beer Company because of its substantial lead in available capital.

MillerCoors, LLC

MillerCoors, LLC, was the second-largest brewing company in the country, a joint venture between the Miller and Coors brands, accounting for approximately 30 percent of the market. It had two of the top five most popular beers, Miller Lite and Coors Light, and wanted to catch up with Anheuser-Busch Inbev. The company traded publicly as Molson Coors Brewing Company and SABMiller, whose stock sold for over $75 and $3,389, respectively, in January 2015. MillerCoors wanted to push its craft beers after witnessing the growth in the market. It had a popular craftlike beer called Blue Moon Belgian White. The company had also started the group Tenth and Blake to focus on the craft-beer industry and premium imports, and it planned to expand the group by 60 percent over the next few years. Some of its premium beers were Leinenkugel's Honey Weiss, George Killian's Irish Red, Batch 19, Henry Weinhard's IPA, Colorado Native, Pilsner Urquell, Peroni Nastro Azzurro, and Grolsch.[22]

Thinking about the Future for Beer

The Boston Beer Company created high-quality craft beers and sold them at higher prices than standard and economy lagers. It was the largest craft brewery in the United States and the seventh-largest overall brewery. While Boston Beer was delighted to be the largest craft brewery, its goal was to become the third-largest overall brewery in the country. Brand recognition is key to any business, and it was especially obvious in the beer industry. Anheuser-Busch Inbev and MillerCoors spent enormous amounts of capital each year to advertise their products. Due in large part to Anheuser-Busch Inbev and MillerCoors, beer had become synonymous with sports, and nowhere was this more apparent than the Super Bowl. Anheuser-Busch Inbev was one of the main sponsors of the Super Bowl in 2015, and beer commercials were apparent throughout the game. The challenge for craft brewers was that they needed to gain the attention of potential customers while the large brewers were spending a great deal of money vying for the same consumers. One might have argued that the larger brewers' beers did not encompass the same amount of flavor or high-quality taste as the craft beers did, but it was hard to be heard in a crowded space.

Jim Koch and the Samuel Adams team emphasized the amount of hops and flavor that their products had, and they wanted to get "better beer" to potential customers. Boston Beer even tried to help the craft-beer movement as a whole, with the potential of hurting its own Samuel Adams line of business. For instance, the company sold excess hops to small brewers that were struggling to pay for the rising cost. Boston Beer also partnered with Accion to provide microloans to small businesses trying to start up breweries and to help small breweries in distress.[23]

Over the last several years, the craft brewing industry had grown at the expense of standard and economy lagers. The major breweries had taken notice, and they started to build up their craft-style beer portfolios. In the past, the Boston Beer Company had the advantage of being one of the only craft breweries that was nationally recognized. With other craft breweries on a steady rise, the Boston Beer Company has to position itself to remain in front. Exhibit 9 shows the pricing and alcohol by volume for popular U.S. beers.

EXHIBIT 9 Comparison of Domestic Beer Brands 2014

Domestic Beers	Alcohol by Volume (%)	Average Price (six-pack)	Market Share*
Bud Light	4.20	$4.99	0.198
Coors Light	4.20	4.99	0.097
Budweiser	5.00	4.99	0.074
Miller Lite	4.20	4.99	0.041
Corona Extra	4.60	7.99	0.035
Natural Light	4.20	3.49	0.035
Busch Light	4.10	3.99	0.032
Busch	4.60	4.49	0.029
Miller High Life	4.70	3.99	0.024
Keystone Light	4.13	3.49	0.022
Blue Moon Belgian White	5.36	8.49	0.015
Heineken	5.00	5.99	0.010
Samuel Adams Boston Lager	4.90	8.49	0.009
Shock Top Belgian White	5.20	8.49	0.008
Sierra Nevada Pale Ale	5.60	8.49	0.008
New Belgium Fat Tire	5.20	8.99	0.007
Yuengling Lager	4.40	6.49	0.005
Dogfish Head Pale Ale	5.00	8.99	0.004
Brooklyn Brewery Lager	5.20	7.99	0.004

*Some shares are estimated due to undisclosed information.

Source: Global Market Information Database.

The Boston Beer Company made an effort to move away from contract brewing and toward brewing its own beer with the purchase of the large brewery in Pennsylvania. The company had also put a focus on growing the brand in countries outside the United States. For example, Boston Beer established a relationship with Moosehead Breweries in Canada to expand the Samuel Adams brand presence there. In addition, with the increased popularity of alcoholic beverages besides beer, Boston Beer positioned its Twisted Teas and HardCore Cider products to be recognized nationwide.

Boston Beer Company was in a tough position, as both the smaller craft breweries and the larger breweries wanted to compete with it. Only time would tell whether Boston Beer would continue to brew flavorful beers that people enjoy, in order to maintain a loyal customer base and see continued growth in the future.

ENDNOTES

1. Boston Beer Company Q4 2014 earnings call transcripts.
2. Global Market Information Database. 2012. The Boston Beer Company, in alcoholic drinks (USA). February.
3. Global Market Information Database. 2012. Beer in the US. February.
4. *Los Angeles Times.* 2011. MillerCoors CEO Tom Long seeks growth with craft beers. August.
5. *www.brewersassociation.org.*
6. *Washington Times.* 2012. Top ten: Craft beers of 2011. January.
7. Rotunno, Tom. 2011. MillerCoors crafts small beer strategy. *CNBC.com*, October 31, *www.cnbc.com/id/45079554.*
8. Personal interview with Woody from Defiant Brewery in Pearl River, NY, June 2012.
9. *www.bostonbeer.com.*
10. *New York Times.* 2012. An IPO that is customer-friendly. February.
11. Euromonitor International and author estimates.
12. *www.abdi.org.*
13. *www.usopenbeer.com.*
14. The Homebrewers Association.
15. *Dayton Business Journal.* 2012. Top 20 selling beers of 2011. January.
16. *www.sierranevada.com;* and Solomon, B. 2014. King of craft beer: How Sierra Nevada rules the hops world. *Forbes,* March 3.
17. *www.newbelgium.com.*
18. *www.crownimportsllc.com.*
19. Van Daalen, R. 2014. Heineken sees profits fall on weaker beer sales. *Wall Street Journal,* February 12.
20. *www.heineken.com.*
21. *www.ab-inbev.com.*
22. *www.millercoors.com.*
23. Anonymous. 2008. Sharing beers: Largest craft brewer offers scarce hops to rivals. *Associated Press,* April 6, *www.pantagraph.com/business/article_3f06ff0a-44a8-53c2-bd18--52b5e6e25977.html.*

CASES

CASE 15

ZYNGA: ROOM FOR A FINAL ROUND OR IS THE GAME OVER?*

In 2015, Zynga had a tough task ahead. Its revenues had plunged double digits in the final months of 2014, resulting in a $226 million loss for the year (see Exhibits 1 and 2). The year-over-year decline in revenues was primarily attributable to the absence of a new and innovative product pipeline.

*This case was developed by graduate students Eric S. Engelson, Dev Das, and Professor Alan B. Eisner, Pace University. Material has been drawn from published sources to be used for class discussion. Copyright © 2015 Alan B. Eisner.

The company had launched a new version of *Zynga Poker*, which includes a sophisticated design and feature set that inspires more competition, authenticity, and social connections between players. Zynga also launched *NFL Showdown* at the beginning of the NFL season with the intention of adding new features based on customer feedback and play patterns. However, the new product–driven growth was not able to reverse declines in existing online games.[1]

Zynga, located in San Francisco, California, had become a dominant player in the online gaming field,

EXHIBIT 1 Zynga Consolidated Income Statements ($ thousands, except per-share, user, and ABPU data)

	Year Ended December 31:		
	2014	2013	2012
Revenue:			
Online game	$ 537,619	$759,572	$1,144,252
Advertising and other	152,791	113,694	137,015
Total revenue	690,410	873,266	1,281,267
Costs and expenses:			
Cost of revenue	213,570	248,358	352,169
Research and development	396,553	413,001	645,648
Sales and marketing	157,364	104,403	181,924
General and administrative	167,664	162,918	189,004
Impairment of intangible assets	—	10,217	95,493
Total costs and expenses	935,151	938,897	1,464,238
Income (loss) from operations	(244,741)	(65,631)	(182,971)
Interest income	3,266	4,148	4,749
Other income (expense), net	8,248	(3,386)	18,647
Income (loss) before income taxes	(233,227)	(64,869)	(159,575)
Provision for (benefit from) income taxes	(7,327)	(27,887)	49,873
Net income (loss)	$(225,900)	$(36,982)	$ (209,448)
Deemed dividend to a Series B-2 convertible preferred stockholder	—	—	—
Net income attributable to participating securities	—	—	—
Net income (loss) attributable to common stockholders	$(225,900)	$(36,982)	$ (209,448)

EXHIBIT 2 Zynga Balance Sheets ($ thousands, except par value)

Year Ended	Dec. 31, 2014	Dec. 31, 2013
Assets		
Current assets:		
Cash and cash equivalents	$ 131,303	$ 465,523
Marketable securities	785,221	659,973
Accounts receivable, net of allowance of $0 at Dec. 31, 2014, and Dec. 31, 2013	89,611	65,667
Income tax receivable	3,304	6,943
Deferred tax assets	2,765	16,293
Restricted cash	48,047	3,493
Other current assets	22,688	23,507
Total current assets	1,082,939	1,241,399
Long-term marketable securities	231,385	416,474
Goodwill	650,778	227,989
Other intangible assets, net	66,861	18,282
Property and equipment, net	297,919	348,793
Other long-term assets	18,911	26,148
Total assets	$2,348,793	$2,279,085
Liabilities and Stockholders' Equity		
Current liabilities:		
Accounts payable	$ 14,965	$ 20,973
Other current liabilities	164,150	68,866
Deferred revenue	189,923	186,663
Total current liabilities	369,038	276,502
Deferred revenue	3,882	3,252
Deferred tax liabilities	5,323	—
Other noncurrent liabilities	74,858	122,060
Total liabilities	453,101	401,814
Stockholders' equity:		
Common stock,	3,096,982	2,823,743
$.00000625 par value, and additional paid-in capital—authorized shares: 2,020,517; shares outstanding: 905,860 shares		
Accumulated other comprehensive income (loss)	(29,175)	(1,046)
Accumulated deficit	(1,172,115)	(945,426)
Total stockholders' equity	1,895,692	1,877,271
Total liabilities and stockholders' equity	$2,348,793	$2,279,085

almost entirely through the use of social media platforms. The company name was established by the CEO, Mark Pincus, to pay tribute to his deceased beloved pet bulldog named Zinga. Although this might have seemed whimsical, Zynga was actually quite a powerful company. To exemplify Zynga's prominence, Facebook was reported to have earned roughly 12 percent of its revenue from the operations of Zynga's virtual merchandise sales.[2]

No other direct competitor was close to this revenue lead. Zynga's collection of games continued to increase, with more and more success stories emerging. Being a relatively new company to the market, its quick success was astonishing, something that not many others had been able to mimic. However, Zynga's impressive financials were possibly at risk because of what might have been considered questionable decision making. Many of Zynga's competitors, and even some partners, were displeased with the company's actions and began to show it in the form of litigation. Agincourt, a plaintiff in a recent lawsuit brought against Zynga, stated, "Zynga's remarkable growth has not been driven by its own ingenuity. Rather it has been widely reported that Zynga's business model is to copy creative ideas and game designs from other game developers and then use its market power to bulldoze the games' originators."[3] If lawsuits and other ethical issues continued to arise for Zynga as often as they had in the past, Zynga's powerful bulldog could start looking more like a poodle.

The Product

With a newfound abundance of software developers, the ability to create and distribute online games was increasing by the day, and the demand to play them was equally high. However, while many people found these games fun and, better yet, therapeutic, others couldn't understand the hype. The best way to understand the sudden infatuation was to view online gaming as a relaxation method. In movies, large executive offices were often shown with putting greens, dartboards, or even a bar full of alcoholic beverages. These amenities were all meant to serve the same purpose: to relieve stress during a hard day's work. We've all been there and looked for a way to cope. However, few of us had the opportunity to use such things as putting greens to unwind at the workplace. And even if we did, how long could we have afforded to engage in such an activity before being pulled back to our desks? Stress reduction at work was one of the many purposes that virtual games fulfilled: no need to leave our desks; no need to make others around us aware of our relaxation periods; and, better yet, no need to separate the task of relaxation from sitting at our computers while we worked. The ability to play these games on office computers and "relax" now and then as the day went by made online gaming all the more enticing. This, of course, was just one of many uses for the games. Some people played them after work or at the end of a long day. With the takeover of smartphones, people of all ages played these games on the go throughout the day—sitting on the bus, in the waiting room of a doctor's office, or at the Department of Motor Vehicles. It had never been easier to interact than through game play that was readily available with the click of a button.

Market Size

Compared to other game developers with games present on the Facebook platform, Zynga had been a dominant force (see Exhibit 3). Now it failed to surface even in the top 5 virtual-gaming rankings (see Exhibit 4). The King Company appeared to rule with its numerous popular games, including the billion-dollar offering—*Candy Crush Saga.*

Zynga's virtual games provided the opportunity for constant buildup and improvements, offering users virtual goods and services to increase their gaming experience. These items could be purchased using a credit card and were often needed to accomplish fast progressions in the games. These goods were advertised throughout the games and enticed the user by offering price cuts for larger purchases.

Zynga's virtual games could be played both remotely and through social media platforms, most commonly Facebook. Five of Zynga's games, *FarmVille, CityVille, Empire and Allies, CastleVille,* and *Texas HoldEm Poker,* were among the most popular games on Facebook. *CityVille* had over 100 million active monthly users within months of its release in late 2010.[4] On July 1, 2011, Zynga filed with the Securities and Exchange Commission with intentions of raising up to $1 billion in its IPO, and its stock began trading on NASDAQ December 16, 2011.[5]

Of course, Zynga was not the only virtual-gaming company striving for this degree of success. In fact, there were many others, in what seemed to be one of the fastest-growing industries. The capability to create online games was widespread. Creativity and innovation were the grounds on which competing companies challenged each other. Consequently, when all competitors were after the same audience, the industry was prone to a significant amount of head-butting rivalry.

Background of Competitors

RockYou was founded by Lance Tokuda and Jia Shen. Their first product was a slide-show service, crafted to work as an application widget. RockYou was one of the companies invited by Facebook to participate in the F8 event, in which Facebook announced the start of an open platform that would allow third parties to develop and run their own applications on Facebook. RockYou then shifted toward producing more in-depth social application games, such as *Toyland, Zoo World, Hero World,* and *MyCasino.* Its most played game, *Zoo World,* was a free social media application whereby users tried to build the best zoo they could. The company underwent a phase of major layoffs but continued to work on new and improved games.[6]

GameHouse, based in Seattle, Washington, was a developer, publisher, and distributor of casual games. GameHouse

EXHIBIT 3 Monthly Users of Facebook Gaming, 2014

Game	Monthly active users in millions
Candy Crush Saga	149.29
Farm Heroes Saga	39.97
Pet Rescue Saga	31.21
Criminal Case	26.91
Dragon City	24.37
Bubble Witch 2 Saga	23.19
8 Ball Pool	19.03
Clash of Clans	18.11
Hay Day	17.24
Trivia Crack	16.4

Source: Statista 2015.

EXHIBIT 4 Virtual-Gaming Revenue

Rank	Company	2013 Revenue (millions)	Key Games
1	King	$1,900	Candy Crush, Pet Rescue, Farm Heroes
2	Gung Ho	1,000	Puzzle & Dragons
3	Supercell	892	Clash of Clans, Hay Day
4	Kabam	360	The Hobbit, Kingdoms of Camelot, Kingdoms of Middle Earth, Fast & Furious 6
5	EA Mobile	339	FIFA 14, Plants vs. Zombies 2, The Simpsons: Tapped Out, Real Racing 3

Source: www.pocketgamer.biz, 2014 top developers list.

was acquired by RealNetworks for $14.6 million cash and about 3.3 million shares of RNWK common stock, which had an estimated value of $21 million at the time.[7] Prior to its acquisition, GameHouse generated an impressive amount of revenue through the sale of games on its own website, www.gamehouse.com, and through third-party affiliates and other distributors. GameHouse and RealArcade merged their websites into one portal in an effort to create one massive distribution center. RealArcade delivered its games on a downloadable demo basis, with a 60-minute trial time for most games. When the trial expired, the user needed to purchase the full version to continue playing. Users also had the option of purchasing a membership package for a monthly fee. GameHouse later began offering the full version of many of its games, supported by the sale of in-game advertising.[8]

EA Playfish, a subsidiary of Electronic Arts, began as Playfish Ltd., a developer of social network games that were free to play. *Who Has the Biggest Brain?* was the first success of Playfish Ltd. and was the gateway into the company's ability to raise funding. The company, like many of its competitors, generated revenue by selling virtual goods inside its games. Electronic Arts later acquired Playfish for $400 million. Soon after, Playfish drew approximately 55 million users a month, with over 37 million of those users coming from Facebook.[9] Users could purchase "Playfish Cards" at Walmart, Walgreens, and Toys 'R' Us stores, at which point they could register on the Playfish website to begin earning "Playfish Cash" that could be used to purchase virtual goods within the games. Playfish announced the change from Playfish Cash to individual cash for all games (except *Crazy Planets* at that time) and allowed users to trade for the new cash.[10]

CrowdStar, based in Burlingame, California, was another developer of social games. Founded by Suren Markosian and Jeff Tseng, it ranked fourth for most monthly active users among Facebook applications.[11] Its most popular titles were *Happy Aquarium* and *Happy Pets*. CrowdStar turned down an offer from Microsoft to acquire the company for more than $200 million.[12] The company subsequently raised an additional $23 million and planned on using the money to double its workforce and increase expansion on a global scale. CrowdStar also planned to add about 100 employees, including game developers, server developers, artists, producers, business analysts, and content managers. Peter Relan, CrowdStar's CEO, said the company needed to raise money to exploit opportunities for global expansion in places such as Japan, China, Eastern Europe, and Brazil.[13]

Background of the CEO

Mark Jonathan Pincus was the entrepreneur behind Zynga. He was also the founder of Freeloader, Inc., Tribe Networks, and Support.com.[14] In prior years, Mark was named CEO of the Year in the Crunchies awards,[15] as well as Founder of the Year.[16] Prior to his entrepreneurial endeavors, Pincus worked in venture capital and financial services for several years. After graduating from Wharton, he went on to obtain his master's degree from Harvard Business School. Soon after graduating, Pincus launched his first start-up, Freeloader, Inc., a web-based push technology service. Individual, Inc., acquired the company only seven months later for $38 million.[17] Pincus later founded his third start-up, Tribe.net, one of the first social networks. Tribe.net focused on partnerships with major, yet local, newspapers and was supported by *The Washington Post*, Knight Ridder Digital, and Mayfield Fund.[18] Unfortunately for him, Pincus's impressive background held no merit with his irritated competitors, who made their feelings widely known through a laundry list of threats and lawsuits.

Intellectual Property and Ethical Issues

Zynga was threatened with a lawsuit in which Nissan claimed that its trademarks were used without consent in Zynga's game *Street Racing*. Zynga consequently changed the thumbnail images and renamed all the cars that were branded Nissan and Infiniti to "Sindats" and "Fujis."[19] Zynga was criticized on *Hacker News* as well as other social media sites for filing a patent application involving the ability to obtain virtual currency for cash on gambling and other gaming websites. Many said that the concept was not new and that in fact significant prior art for the concept already existed.[20] The unveiling of *Mafia Wars* generated a lawsuit from the creators of *Mob Wars*. An attorney of the parent company of *Mob Wars* said that by making *Mafia Wars*, Zynga "copied virtually every important aspect of the game."[21] The lawsuit was later settled out of court for an amount between $7 million and $9 million.[22]

California-based web developer SocialApps also brought Zynga to court, seeking damages for alleged "copyright infringement, violation of trade secrets, breach of written contract, breach of implied-in-fact contract, and breach of confidence." SocialApps claimed to have entered into an agreement with Zynga, allowing Zynga access to the source code for SocialApps' Facebook game *MyFarm* in exchange for an undisclosed form of compensation. According to the suit, Zynga was given the code, at which point Zynga failed to pay SocialApps. SocialApps claimed that *MyFarm*'s source code was the foundation of *FarmVille*, as well as many of Zynga's similar games.[23] Following Zynga's release of the game *Hidden Chronicles*, *Forbes*' Paul Tassi wrote that Zynga "refuses to innovate in any way, and is merely a follower when it comes to ideas and game design."[24]

Ethical issues, although less tangible and therefore less definable than intellectual property, were equally as troubling in assessments of Zynga's operations. A former employee of the company revealed quotes that he had heard firsthand from CEO Mark Pincus, such as: "You're not smarter than your competitor. Just copy what they do and do it until you get their numbers." One contractor said he was presented with freelance work from Zynga related to imitating a competitor's application and was given precise instructions to "copy that game."[25] Furthermore, other past employees spoke out, even those at the senior level, to give insight into the corrupt ways that Pincus decided to operate the business. One of these past employees revealed a saying, "Do Evil," that was commonly used by employees in the office as a playful twist on the Google motto, "Don't Be Evil."[26]

Unfortunately, Zynga's problems went beyond its lack of respect for other companies. The wrath of Zynga's business decisions had even been harshly felt internally. A former high-level Zynga employee related a situation he encountered in which a group of designers brought a new and innovative idea to the table, only to have it turned down by Pincus because of his wariness to attempt a new idea that didn't fit the "tried-and-true" mold of other successes.[27]

Zynga had also been accused of taking advantage of its end consumers, particularly pertaining to a lack of security and safekeeping of consumer information. At one point, the Norwegian Consumer Council filed a complaint against Zynga to the Data Inspectorate concerning breaches of the Data Protection Act. According to the Consumer Council, Zynga's terms of use "do not offer a clear description of what is being collected in terms of information or what this information is being used for. Nor do they state how long the information is stored for or how it is protected against unauthorized access." The Consumer Council went even further with its forewarning, saying, "Many of the gravest examples of unreasonable and one-sided terms of use can be found in games providers such as Zynga."[28]

Zynga Going Forward

Despite all the back-end controversy, Zynga's main concern had always been the end consumers and their satisfaction with the games that Zynga put forward. Although Zynga game users tended to be pleased with Zynga's games, many users also noted that there seemed to be recurring obstacles that limited that pleasure. For instance, a vast population of Zynga users complained of lag time while playing the games. Even more people complained that when problems arose, Zynga support staff was nowhere to be found. The company had no customer service initiative and forced users to resort to sending their claims through email—which many people believed was ignored or never read. Furthermore, many believed that the company had made it too difficult to make real strides in the games without spending ridiculous sums of money. Based on their experiences, many users had come to believe the claim that Zynga was all about revenue generation and that everything else came second.

As Zynga looked to the future, where would its next big hit come from? With all of the accusations surrounding Zynga's past games, would the company continue on the same path it had become so notoriously known for and reap further accusations of imitating its competitors' existing games? Or would Zynga change its approach, gain a reputation for intellectual integrity, and begin creating true one-of-a-kind games—showing its capabilities as a leader in the industry rather than a follower? With all eyes on the company as the market leader, it was certain that it would not be easy for Zynga to get away with some of its earlier stunts, especially now as a public company. The newly implemented board of directors had already announced their intention to ensure proper decision making going forward, particularly regarding corporate governance.[29] With all of the changes and concerns that had to be accounted for as a public company, Zynga needed to watch its step or prepare to feel the wrath of its shareholders.

ENDNOTES

1. Zynga Q4 2014 earnings call transcripts.
2. www.vanityfair.com/business/features/2011/06/mark-pincus-farmville-201106.
3. http://news.cnet.com/8301-31001_3-20093473-261/zynga-targeted-in-patent-infringement-lawsuit/.
4. www.appdata.com/apps/facebook/291549705119-cityville.
5. www.reuters.com/article/2011/11/30/us-zynga-ipo-idUSTRE7AT2FJ20111130.
6. http://techcrunch.com/2010/10/15/rockyou-rocked-by-layoffs-as-it-switches-focus-to-social-games/.
7. http://investor.realnetworks.com/faq.cfm?faqid=2.
8. www.gamehouse.com/.
9. www.gamasutra.com/view/news/32496/Playfish_Social_Games_Reaching_55_Million_Monthly_Players.php.
10. www.insidesocialgames.com/2011/04/19/exclusive-playfish-ending-playfish-cash-going-almost-all-in-on-facebook-credits/.
11. www.appdata.com/devs/30679-crowdstar.
12. www.businessweek.com/news/2010-03-31/crowdstar-said-to-break-off-talks-to-be-bought-by-microsoft.html.
13. http://venturebeat.com/2011/05/23/social-game-leader-crowdstar-raises-23m-from-intel-and-time-warner/.
14. http://company.zynga.com/about/leadership-team/zynga-management.
15. http://venturebeat.com/2010/01/11/crunchies-winners-facebook-bing/.
16. http://techcrunch.com/2011/01/21/congratulations-crunchies-winners-twitter-takes-best-startup-of-2010/.
17. http://startup2startup.com/2009/06/24/june29-markpincus-zynga/.
18. www.nytimes.com/2007/03/03/technology/03social.html?page-wanted=1&_r=1&ei=5088&en=f718f182170673a4&ex=1330578000.
19. http://mafiawars.wikia.com/wiki/Zynga.
20. http://allfacebook.com/zynga-patent-currency_b20985.
21. www.bizjournals.com/sanfrancisco/stories/2009/07/13/story7.html.
22. http://techcrunch.com/2009/09/13/zynga-settles-mob-wars-litigation-as-it-settles-in-to-playdom-war/.
23. www.joystiq.com/2011/07/18/lawsuit-filed-against-zynga-over-farmville-source-code/.
24. www.forbes.com/sites/insertcoin/2012/01/06/zynga-stock-falls-as-second-post-ipo-game-fails-to-impress/.
25. http://blog.games.com/2010/09/08/zynga-ceo-to-employees-i-dont-fing-want-innovation/.
26. http://blogs.sfweekly.com/thesnitch/2011/11/zynga_corporate_culture.php.
27. www.sfweekly.com/2010-09-08/news/farmvillains/4/.
28. http://forbrukerportalen.no/Artikler/2010/Facebook_and_Zynga_reported_to_the_Data_Inspectorate.
29. http://investor.zynga.com/governance.cfm.

CASES

CASE 16

APPLE INC.: STILL TAKING A BITE OUT OF THE COMPETITION?*

On February 11, 2015, Apple Inc. made history by becoming the first U.S. publicly traded company to close above $700 billion in market value. This put Apple's value nearly double that of the next three largest companies in the S&P 500 Index,[1] and it firmly established expectations for future performance. Apple's market value had grown more than 50,600 percent since its initial public offering in December 1980.[2] To satisfy investors, consumers, and company enthusiasts, Apple would have to continue to deliver, and doing so might not be easy. As Apple had grown, the pace of innovation had slowed. There were still opportunities, but would Apple be the company to see them through to fruition?

The year 2015 was not the first time Apple had wowed investors. In September 2012 Apple stock had hit a price high of $702.10, at that time making Apple the most valuable company in the world, but the company had not been able to sustain that lofty valuation. September 2012 had also marked Tim Cook's first full year as CEO and the first full year since the death of Apple's visionary founder, Steve Jobs. Although most Apple watchers had mourned Steve Jobs's death on October 5, 2011, most also realized that Jobs's appointed successor, Tim Cook, came to the position as CEO with an impressive track record. Cook had continued to grow the company, and the 2012 year-end numbers showed continued financial success across almost all product lines. However, expectations were still very high, and rumors of a reduction in Asian supplier component orders for the iPhone for 2013 led investors to worry about a drop-off in demand for the company's flagship product. This worry led to a subsequent drop in Apple's stock price of nearly 24 percent.[3]

CEO Cook subsequently defused concerns over supply chain issues, but that didn't stop analysts and media watchers from wondering whether Apple had lost its luster.[4] This posed yet again the unavoidable question that had loomed large over the then 35-year-old Apple: What happens to a modern company whose innovations and inspirations are so closely tied to the vision of one leader when that leader's influence is no longer present?[5] By 2015, that question appeared to have been definitively answered: Apple, under CEO Cook, was not only the most valuable company in the world but was poised to grow even more (see Exhibits 1 and 2).

Apple, *Fortune* magazine's "world's most admired company" since 2008,[6] had distinguished itself by excelling over the years not only in product innovation but also in revenue and margins (since 2006 Apple had consistently reported gross margins of over 30 percent). Founded as a computer company in 1976 and known early on for its intuitive adaptation of the graphical user interface, or GUI (via the first mouse and the first on-screen "windows"),[7] Apple dropped the word *computer* from its corporate name in 2007. Apple Inc. in 2015 was known for having top-selling products not only in desktop (iMac) and notebook (MacBook) personal computers but also in portable digital music players (iPod), online music and "app" services (iTunes and App Store), mobile communication devices (iPhone), digital consumer entertainment (Apple TV), handheld devices able to download third-party applications, including games (iPod Touch via the App Store), tablet computers (iPad), and online services (iCloud), and the company was poised to enter and dominate the market of wearable technology (Apple Watch) and mobile payment systems (Apple Pay) (see Exhibit 3).

Although most of those innovations occurred after 1998, when Apple was under Steve Jobs's leadership, there was a 12-year period in which Jobs was not in charge. The company's ongoing stated strategy had been to leverage "its unique ability to design and develop its own operations systems, hardware, application software, and services to provide its customers new products and solutions with superior ease-of-use, seamless integration and innovative industrial design."[8] This strategy required not only product design and marketing expertise but also scrupulous attention to operational details. Given Apple's global growth in multiple product categories, and the associated complexity in strategic execution, would CEO Tim Cook be able to sustain the level of innovation the company had been known for? In the coming years, would Apple *still* be able to take a bite out of all competition?

Company Background
Founder Steve Jobs

Apple Computer was founded in Mountain View, California, on April 1, 1976, by Steve Jobs and Steve Wozniak. Jobs was the visionary and marketer, Wozniak was the technical genius, and A. C. "Mike" Markkula Jr., who had joined the team several months earlier, was the businessman. Jobs set the mission of empowering individuals, one person–one computer, and doing so with elegance of design and fierce attention to detail. In 1977 the first

---

* This case was prepared by Professor Alan B. Eisner of Pace University and Associate Professor Pauline Assenza of Western Connecticut State University. This case was based solely on library research and was developed for class discussion rather than to illustrate either effective or ineffective handling of an administrative situation. Copyright © 2015 Alan B. Eisner.

EXHIBIT 1 Apple Sales

	2014 ($ millions)	% Change	2013 ($ millions)	% Change	2012 ($ millions)
Product Net Sales					
iPhone	$ 101,991	12	$ 91,279	16	$ 78,692
iPad	30,283	(5)	31,980	3	30,945
Mac	24,079	12	21,483	(7)	23,221
iPod	2,286	(48)	4,411	(21)	5,615
iTunes, Software & Services*	18,063	13	16,051	25	12,890
Accessories†	6,093	7	5,706	11	5,145
Total net sales	**$182,795**	**7**	**$170,910**	**9**	**$156,508**
Cost of sales	112,258		106,606		87,846
Gross margin	**$ 70,537**		**$ 64,304**		**$ 68,662**
Gross margin %	38.6%		37.6%		43.9%
Research and development	$ 6,041		$ 4,475		$ 3,381
Percent of net sales	3%		3%		2%
Selling, general, and administrative	$ 11,993		$ 10,830		$ 10,040
Percent of net sales	7%		6%		6%
Total operating expenses	$ 18,034		$ 15,305		$ 13,421
Percent of net sales	10%		9%		9%
Region Net Sales					
Americas	$ 65,232	4	$ 62,739	9	$ 57,512
Europe	40,929	8	37,883	4	36,323
Greater China	29,846	17	25,417	13	22,533
Japan	14,982	11	13,462	27	10,571
Rest of Asia-Pacific	10,344	(7)	11,181	4	10,741
Retail	21,462	6	20,228	7	18,828

*Includes revenue from the iTunes Store, the App Store, the Mac App Store, the iBooks Store, AppleCare, licensing, and other services.
†Includes sales of Apple-branded and third-party accessories for the iPhone, iPad, Mac, and iPod.

Source: Apple 10-K SEC filing, 2014.

version of the Apple II became the first computer ordinary people could use right out of the box, and its instant success in the home market caused a computing revolution, essentially creating the personal computer industry. By 1980 Apple was the industry leader, and the company went public in December of that year.

In 1983 Wozniak left the firm, and Jobs hired John Sculley away from PepsiCo to take the role of CEO at Apple, citing the need for someone to spearhead marketing and operations while Jobs worked on technology. The result of Jobs's creative focus on personal computing was the Macintosh. Introduced in 1984 through the now-famous Super Bowl television ad based on George Orwell's novel *Nineteen Eighty-Four*,[9] the Macintosh was a breakthrough in terms of elegant design and ease of use. Its ability to handle large graphic files quickly made it a favorite with graphic designers, but its performance was slow and available compatible software was limited. That meant the

EXHIBIT 2
Apple First Quarter 2015 Sales

Go to library tab in Connect to access Case Financials.

	1st Quarter 2015 ($ millions)	1st Quarter 2014 ($ millions)	Percentage Change
Product Net Sales			
iPhone*	$ 51,182	$ 32,498	57
iPad*	8,985	11,468	(22)
Mac*	6,944	6,395	9
Services†	4,799	4,397	9
Other products‡	2,689	2,836	(5)
Total net sales	**$74,599**	**$57,594**	**30**
Region Net Sales			
Americas	$ 30,566	$ 24,789	23
Europe	17,214	14,335	20
Greater China	16,144	9,496	70
Japan	5,448	5,045	8
Rest of Asia-Pacific	5,227	3,929	33

*Includes deferrals and amortization of related nonsoftware services and software upgrade rights.
†Includes revenue from iTunes, AppleCare, Apple Pay, licensing, and other services.
‡Includes sales of iPod, Apple TV, Beats Electronics, and Apple-branded and third-party accessories.

Source: Apple 10-K SEC filing, 2015.

EXHIBIT 3 Apple Innovation Timeline

Date	Product	Events
1976	Apple I	Steve Jobs, Steve Wozniak, and Ronald Wayne found Apple Computer.
1977	Apple II	Apple logo first used.
1979	Apple II1	Apple employs 250 people; the first personal computer spreadsheet software, VisiCalc, is written by Dan Bricklin on an Apple II.
1980	Apple III	Apple goes public with 4.6 million shares; IBM personal computer announced.
1983	Lisa	John Sculley becomes CEO.
1984	Mac 128K, Apple IIc	Super Bowl ad introduces the Mac desktop computer.
1985		**Jobs resigns** and forms NeXT Software; Windows 1.01 released.
1986	Mac Plus	Jobs establishes Pixar.
1987	Mac II, Mac SE	Apple sues Microsoft over GUI.
1989	Mac Portable	Apple sued by Xerox over GUI.
1990	Mac LC	Apple listed on Tokyo Stock Exchange.
1991	PowerBook 100, System 7	System 7 operating-system upgrade released, the first Mac OS to support PowerPC-based computers.
1993	Newton Message Pad (one of the first PDAs)	Sculley resigns; Spindler becomes CEO; PowerBook sales reach 1 million units.

continued

EXHIBIT 3 *Continued*

Date	Product	Events
1996		Spindler is out; Amelio becomes CEO; Apple acquires NeXT Software, with Jobs as adviser.
1997		Amelio is out; **Jobs returns** as interim CEO; online retail Apple Store opened.
1998	iMac	iMac colorful design introduced, including USB interface; Newton scrapped.
1999	iMovie, Final Cut Pro (video editing software)	iBook (part of PowerBook line) becomes best-selling retail notebook in October; Apple has 11% share of notebook market.
2000	G4Cube	**Jobs becomes permanent CEO.**
2001	iPod, OS X	First retail store opens, in Virginia.
2002	iMac G4	Apple releases iLife software suite.
2003	iTunes	Apple reaches 25 million iTunes downloads.
2004	iMac G5	**Jobs undergoes successful surgery for pancreatic cancer.**
2005	iPod Nano, iPod Shuffle, Mac Mini	First video iPod released; video downloads available from iTunes.
2006	MacBook Pro	Apple computers use Intel's Core Duo CPU and can run Windows software; iWork software competes with Microsoft Office.
2007	iPhone, Apple TV, iPod Touch	Apple Computer changes name to Apple Inc.; Microsoft Vista released.
2008	iPhone 3G, MacBook Air, App Store	App Store launched for third-party applications for iPhone and iPod Touch and brings in $1million in one day.
2009	17-inch MacBook Pro, iLife, iWork '09	iTunes Plus provides DRM-free music, with variable pricing; **Jobs takes medical leave.**
2010	iPad, iPhone 4, Mac App Store	iPhone 4 provides FaceTime feature; iTunes reaches 10 billion songs sold.
2011	iPad2, iPhone 4S, iCloud	iPhone available on Verizon Wireless; **Jobs resigns as CEO, dies on October 5th. Tim Cook becomes CEO.**
2012	iBook Author, iPhone5, iPad Mini	iBook supports textbook creation on iPad. Apple becomes world's most valuable company (market cap). Mac Retina displays and skinny Macs introduced.
2013	Mega Mac, iPad Air	Workstation in a small aluminum cylinder.
2014	iPhone 6 Plus, Apple Watch, Apple Pay	Biggest iPhone yet; Apple Watch—computer on your wrist— introduced in 2014, actual delivery in 2015; Apple Pay mobile payment service; acquisition of Beats Electronic for streaming digital content.

Source: http://en.wikipedia.org/wiki/Timeline_of_Apple_Inc._products.

product as designed at the time was unable to significantly help Apple's failing bottom line. In addition, Jobs had given Bill Gates at Microsoft some Macintosh prototypes to use to develop software, and in 1985 Microsoft subsequently came out with the Windows operating system, a version of GUI for use on IBM PCs.

Steve Jobs's famous volatility led to his resignation from Apple in 1985. Jobs then founded NeXT Computer. The NeXT Cube computer proved too costly for the business to become commercially profitable, but its technological contributions could not be ignored. In 1997 Apple CEO Gilbert Amelio bought out NeXT, hoping to use its Rhapsody, a version of the NeXTStep operating system, to jump-start the Mac OS development, and Jobs was brought back as a part-time adviser.

Under CEOs Sculley, Spindler, and Amelio

John Sculley tried to take advantage of Apple's unique capabilities. Because of this, Macintosh computers became easy to use, with seamless integration (the original plug-and-play) and reliable performance. This premium performance meant Apple could charge a premium price. However, with the price of IBM compatibles dropping and Apple's costs, especially R&D, way above industry averages (in 1990

Apple spent 9 percent of sales on R&D, compared to 5 percent at Compaq and 1 percent at many manufacturers of IBM clones),[10] this was not a sustainable scenario.

Sculley's innovative efforts were not enough to substantially improve Apple's bottom line, and he was replaced as CEO in 1993 by company president Michael Spindler. Spindler continued the focus on innovation, producing the PowerMac, based on the PowerPC microprocessor, in 1994. Even though this combination produced a significant price-performance edge over both previous Macs and Intel-based machines, the IBM clones continued to undercut Apple's prices. Spindler's response was to allow other companies to manufacture Mac clones, a strategy that ultimately led to clones stealing 20 percent of Macintosh unit sales.

Gilbert Amelio, an Apple director and former semiconductor turnaround expert, was asked to reverse the company's financial direction. Amelio intended to reposition Apple as a premium brand, but his extensive reorganizations and cost-cutting strategies couldn't prevent Apple's stock price from slipping to a new low. However, Amelio's decision to stop work on a brand-new operating system and jump-start development by using NeXTStep brought Steve Jobs back to Apple in 1997.

Steve Jobs's Return

One of Jobs's first strategies on his return was to strengthen Apple's relationships with third-party software developers, including Microsoft. In 1997 Jobs announced an alliance with Microsoft that would allow for the creation of a Mac version of the popular Microsoft Office software. He also made a concerted effort to woo other developers, such as Adobe, to continue to produce Mac-compatible programs.

In late October 2001, Apple released its first major noncomputer product, the iPod. This device was an MP3 music player that packed up to 1,000 CD-quality songs into an ultraportable, 6.5-ounce design: "With iPod, Apple has invented a whole new category of digital music player that lets you put your entire music collection in your pocket and listen to it wherever you go," said Steve Jobs. "With iPod, listening to music will never be the same again."[11] This prediction became even truer in 2002, when Apple introduced an iPod that would download from Windows—its first product that didn't require a Macintosh computer and thus opened up the Apple "magic" to everyone. In 2003 all iPod products were sold with a Windows version of iTunes, making it even easier to use the device regardless of computer platform.

In April 2003, Apple opened the online iTunes Music Store to everyone. This software, downloadable on any computer platform, sold individual songs through the iTunes application for 99 cents each. When announced, the iTunes Music Store already had the backing of five major record labels and a catalog of 200,000 songs. Later that year, the iTunes Music Store was selling roughly 500,000 songs a day. In 2003 the iPod was the only portable digital player that could play music purchased from iTunes, and this intended exclusivity helped both products become dominant.

After 30 years of carving a niche for itself as the premier provider of technology solutions for graphic artists, web designers, and educators, Apple appeared to be reinventing itself as a digital entertainment company, moving beyond the personal computer industry. The announcement in 2007 of the iPhone, a product incorporating a wireless phone, a music and video player, and a mobile Internet browsing device, meant Apple was also competing in the cell phone/smartphone industry.

Also introduced in 2007, the iPod Touch incorporated Wi-Fi connectivity, allowing users to purchase and download music directly from iTunes without a computer. Then, in 2008, Apple opened the App Store. Users could now purchase applications written by third-party developers specifically for the iPhone and iPod Touch. These applications included games, prompting analysts to wonder whether Apple was becoming a competitor in the gaming market.

In 2010 Apple launched the large-screen touch-based tablet called the iPad and sold over 2 million of these devices in the first two months.[12] That same year, Apple's stock value increased to the extent that the company's market cap exceeded Microsoft's, making it the biggest tech company in the world.[13] In 2011 Steve Jobs made his last product launch appearance to introduce iCloud, an online storage and syncing service. On October 4, 2011, Apple announced the iPhone 4S, which included "Siri," the "intelligent software assistant." The next day, on October 5, came the announcement that Steve Jobs had died.

Apple continued to innovate, however, and on September 21, 2012, Apple had its biggest iPhone launch ever, with the iPhone 5. Over 2 million preorders for this larger and more powerful phone pushed the delivery date back to late October.[14] Later in the fall, Apple released the iPad Mini with a smaller screen. On September 19, 2012, Apple stock reached $702.10, its highest level to date, which made Apple the most valuable company in the world. The year 2013 saw the iPhone5C and the high-range iPhone5S, which introduced the Touch ID fingerprint recognition system. The iPhone 6 and 6 Plus, with larger displays, faster processors, and support for mobile payments, were released in September 2014 and allowed Apple to extend its already-strong market position with a record-setting sales performance over the 2014 holiday season.[15] The prototype of the Apple Watch was unveiled in 2014, with production scheduled to begin in 2015. Also introduced in 2014 was Apple Pay, a mobile payment system meant to augment all Apple mobile products. February 2015 saw Apple reach the highest market cap of any U.S.-traded company, indicating investor support and confidence in the company's innovative output.

Apple had become a diversified digital entertainment corporation. All the way back in 2005, analysts had believed Apple had "changed the rules of the game for three industries—PCs, consumer electronics, and music . . . and appears to have nothing to fear from major rivals."[16] On top of steady sales increases on its computers, the iPod, and iTunes, the added categories of iPhone and iPad had shown substantial growth. Apple had taken bites out of the competition on all fronts (see Exhibit 4). However, by 2013, Samsung had outperformed Apple in worldwide smartphone sales,[17] and Google's Android had captured the largest market share of cell phone operating systems. At the same time, both the Amazon Kindle Fire HD tablet and Microsoft's Surface tablet were nipping at the iPad's heels. The year 2015 was marked by competition in the wearable-tech space, and some were wondering if Apple had gotten too big to be nimble. Could Apple continue to grow and, if so, in what categories?

Apple's Operations

Maintaining a competitive edge required more than innovative product design. Operational execution was also important. For instance, while trying to market its increasingly diverse product line, Apple believed that its own retail stores could serve customers better than could third-party retailers. By the end of 2014, Apple had 437 stores open, including 178 international locations, with average store revenue of about $50.6 million, and had received trademark protection for its retail stores' "distinctive design and layout."[18]

In further operational matters, regarding a head-to-head competition against Dell in the computer market, for instance, while Dell's perceived early dominance might have been partly the result of its efficient supply chain management, Apple had outperformed Dell in inventory and other metrics since 2001.[19] To solidify its own supply chain, Apple entered into multiyear agreements with suppliers of key components. In addition, Apple had historically had the best margins, partly because of its simpler product line, leading to lower manufacturing costs.[20] Also, Apple had been outsourcing manufacturing and final assembly to its Asian partners, paying close attention to scheduling and quality issues.

Outsourcing to Asian manufacturers was not without its problems, however. In 2012, headlines worldwide accompanied the exposure of China's Foxconn manufacturing facility for labor abuses that led to worker suicide threats. Apple, as well as most other technology companies, used Foxconn facilities to assemble products, including the iPad and iPhone. After the story broke, Apple CEO Tim Cook visited the Foxconn plant and reviewed an audit of working conditions that found violations in wages, overtime, and environmental standards. Apple stated that it remained "committed to the highest standards of social responsibility across our worldwide supply chain,"[21] and Cook announced that Apple might be bringing some of the production of Mac computers back to the U.S., starting in 2013. Apple could do this without affecting its profitability, because of automation cost savings. As one supply chain expert said, "Apple's product line is highly standardized, with a very small number of products and very few configurations, and that makes it much easier to do automation."[22]

Supply chain, product design, and manufacturing efficiencies were not the only measures of potential competitive superiority. Apple had also historically paid attention to research and development, increasing its R&D investment year after year. In the first quarter of 2015, Apple spent $1.9 billion on R&D, an increase of 42 percent

EXHIBIT 4 Apple's Product Lines and Major Competitors

Product Category	Apple Products	Major Competitors
Computers	iMac, Mac Pro, Mac Mini, MacBook, MacBook Pro, MacBook Air	HP, Dell, Toshiba, Lenovo in the laptop; Acer and ASUS in the netbook form factor
Portable music/media players	iPod Shuffle, iPod Nano, iPod Classic, iPod Touch	Samsung, SanDisk, Archos, Microsoft Zune
Smartphones	iPhone	Nokia, RIM, Samsung, ZTE, LG, Google/Motorola, HTC
Music/media downloads	iTunes, the App Store	Amazon, Google Android apps
Handheld gaming devices	iPod Touch, iPhone	Nintendo, Sony
Software*	Safari web browser, QuickTime, iCloud	Microsoft IE, Mozilla Firefox, Google Chrome, Windows Media Player, RealNetworks, Dropbox, Google Drive
Home theater downloads	Apple TV	Roku, possibly Tivo
Tablet computers	iPad	Samsung Galaxy Tab, Amazon Kindle Fire, Google Nexus, Windows Surface
Wearable technology	Apple Watch	Samsung Gear, Pebble, Sony SmartWatch, Motorola Moto 360

*Includes only the software that is sold separately to use on either Windows or Mac computers.

from the previous year. Among its current rivals, Apple's R&D investment had previously been beaten only by Microsoft (number one), Google, Hewlett-Packard, and Amazon.[23]

As one of Steve Jobs's legacies, Apple had traditionally kept the specifics of its research and development a closely guarded secret and fiercely protected its innovative patents. A well-publicized series of lawsuits in 2012 highlighted rifts between Apple and Samsung, both a rival and a supplier. Samsung smartphones had captured more market share than Apple's iPhones in the beginning of 2012, and Apple argued that Samsung had succeeded with both its phones and tablets only by copying Apple's designs. Samsung replied by claiming that Apple had infringed on Samsung's patents.[24] U.S. intellectual property courts found in favor of Apple, but Japanese courts found in favor of Samsung. The ongoing battle meant Apple needed to look for other suppliers of chips and displays. In November 2014, supply chain watchers pointed out that Apple still had a major challenge ahead finding reliable suppliers for increasingly scarce components and that the continued reliance on Foxconn as the sole manufacturer of the iPhone 6 Plus meant that any disruption there could have major consequences for delivery.[25]

Status of Apple's Business Units in 2015

The Apple Computer Business

In the computer market, Apple had always refused to compete on price, relying instead on its products' reliability, design elegance, ease of use, and integrated features to win customers. From the beginning, some analysts had believed Apple had the opportunity to steal PC market share as long as its system was compatible, no longer proprietary, and offered upgrades at a reasonable cost.[26] This opportunity for increased market share was realized when Apple began using Intel processors in the iMac desktop and the MacBook portables, which allowed them to run Microsoft Office and other business software.

Apple's worldwide Mac computer sales during the first quarter of 2015 increased 9 percent over the same quarter in the previous year. Although there had been fears that sales of desktop computers, especially, would slow worldwide as the tablet and smartphone markets grew, the introduction of the MacBook Air allowed Apple to compete favorably even in the face of overall contraction. Apple computers had been able to gain market share for 33 of the 34 quarters since 2007. Sales of Apple computers worldwide during the third quarter of 2014 did see an increase over the previous year, consistently outgrowing the market and allowing Apple to take over the number-five slot from ASUS (Exhibit 5). According to market analysis done by IDC, the Mac's domestic market share grew from 12.4 to 13 percent, putting the Mac in third place overall in IDC's survey of PC vendor units shipped in the third quarter of 2014.[27] This was up substantially from 2010, when Apple had only 7.4 percent of the U.S. market.[28]

Personal Digital Entertainment Devices: iPod

Although many analysts at the time felt that the MP3 player market was oversaturated, Apple introduced the iPod Touch in 2007, intending it to be "an iPhone without the phone," a portable media player and Wi-Fi Internet device without the AT&T phone bill.[29] The iPod Touch borrowed most of its features from the iPhone, including the finger-touch interface, but it remained mainly an iPod, with a larger viewing area for videos. Apple released the fifth-generation iPod Touch in September 2012, with upgraded features like support for recording 1080p video and panoramic still photos and support for Apple's "Siri." A new version, the sixth generation of this product, debuted in 2015.

Apple reported selling 6 million of the iPod MP3 players over the 2013 holiday season, down from over 12 million iPod units during the previous season, and in the 2014 year-end report iPod sales were not singled out as a separate

EXHIBIT 5 Worldwide PC Market Share, Third Quarter 2014 (units in thousands)

Company	3Q14 Shipments	3Q14 Market Share (%)	3Q13 Shipments	3Q13 Market Share (%)	3Q14–3Q13 Growth (%)
Lenovo	15,707	20.0	14,130	17.7	11.2
HP	14,729	18.8	14,016	17.5	5.1
Dell	10,442	13.3	9,517	11.9	9.7
Acer Group	6,632	8.4	5,952	7.4	11.4
Apple	4,982	6.3	4,577	5.7	8.9
Others	26,026	33.1	31,714	39.7	−17.9
Total	78,519	100.0	79,905	100.0	−1.7

Source: IDC, Worldwide Quarterly PC Tracker, October 8, 2014, www.idc.com/getdoc.jsp?containerId=prUS25187214.

category. As with desktop computer sales, the MP3 player market was contracting overall as smartphone and tablet devices took over many music-related tasks. Even with the decline in iPod sales, Apple was still leading well over its rivals. Traditionally, the iPod had had a 70 percent share of the MP3 player market in the United States, and it was the top-selling player in the world.[30] Microsoft's entry into this space, the Zune, was discontinued in October 2011. Its market share never exceeded 1 percent.[31]

Mobile Communication Devices: iPhone

In 2007 further competition for the iPod had come from the blurring of lines between digital music players and other consumer electronic devices. While others may have seen the computer as central to the future of digital music, telecom companies worked to make the mobile phone a center of the digital world. Apple's entry, the iPhone, combined an Internet-enabled smartphone and video iPod. The iPhone allowed users to access all iPod content and play music and video content purchased from iTunes. More recent smartphone models increased the quality of the photo and video components to make even the digital camera or camcorder appear obsolete. The smartphone market in 2007 had been estimated at 10 percent of all mobile phone sales, or 100 million devices a year. Steve Jobs had said he "would like to see the iPhone represent 1 percent of all mobile phone sales by the end of 2008."[32] This proved to be a conservative estimate, and by 2015 Apple had achieved almost 20 percent, in a close tie with Samsung (see Exhibit 6).

By 2015, smartphones had become the device of choice for most manufacturers. Smartphones were also often the electronic data consumers' device of choice, with multiple features, including cameras and the ability to surf the Internet while being held in the hand, rather than taking up the space of a tablet or ultra-thin computer. However, the smartphone market was increasingly turning into a battle between mobile operating systems (OSs).

Apple's iPhone, running on iOS, had had considerable competition from Samsung's Galaxy smartphones. This was partly due to Samsung's use of Google's Android operating system. Historical worldwide leader Nokia had stumbled badly with its outdated Symbian operating system and was trying to regain a foothold by partnering with Microsoft, using the Windows Phone operating system. Although Research In Motion (RIM) still had some long-term BlackBerry fans, RIM had had problems updating its BlackBerry line of phones. The market share by operating-system map was now worth watching, with Android devices expected to continue to capture the majority of market share through 2016 (see Exhibit 7).[33]

In recent years it appeared that some of the "cool" factor had disappeared from the iPhone. In Asian markets,

EXHIBIT 6 Worldwide Market Share—Cell Phones, Fourth Quarter 2014

Manufacturer	Market Share, 4Q 2014	Market Share, 4Q 2013
Samsung	20.0%	28.8%
Apple	19.9	17.4
Lenovo + Motorola	6.6	4.8
Huawei	6.3	5.7
Xiaomi	4.4	2.0
Others	42.9	41.3

Source: IDC, Worldwide Quarterly Mobile Phone Tracker, January 29, 2015, www.idc.com/getdoc.jsp?containerId=prUS25407215.

EXHIBIT 7 Smartphone Operating-System Market Share, Third Quarter 2014

Smartphone OS	Market Share, Q3 2014	Market Share, Q3 2013
Google Android	84.4%	81.2%
Apple iOS	11.7	12.8
Microsoft Windows Phone	2.9	3.6
RIM BlackBerry OS	0.5	1.7
Others	0.6	0.6

Source: IDC, Smartphone OS Market Share, Q3 2014, www.idc.com/prodserv/smartphone-os-market-share.jsp.

especially, Apple's shares of mobile devices had fallen sharply, losing considerable ground to Samsung and HTC smartphones. Younger users, the 20-something college students and recent graduates, were looking for the next new thing, and that was increasingly an Android-driven device. A social media expert in Singapore noted, "Apple is still viewed as a prestigious brand, but there are just so many other cool smartphones out there now that the competition is just much stiffer." This was a problem, because, starting in 2012, this Asian market was also where consumers were adopting very quickly.[34] In addition, CEO Tim Cook's visit to China in the fall of 2012, presumably to woo China Mobile's chief executive into subsidizing the iPhone, hadn't had the expected result. China Mobile's wireless network, the world's largest, wouldn't be adding the iPhone without better terms from Apple. Instead, it offered its subscribers the Nokia Lumia Windows 8 phone.[35] Given all these challenges, could Apple continue to ride the success of the iPhone to greater profits? Many were skeptical.

However, during 2014, Apple's new iPhone with its larger screen size, in the 6 and 6 Plus models, was able to capture the consumer's attention, allowing Apple to close the gap with Samsung. This was especially notable in China, where Apple's refusal to drop the price allowed it to achieve almost a luxury status with the growing middle class in that country. Sales in China had grown substantially—achieving $38 billion in 2014, up from only $1 billion in 2009.[36] Elsewhere in 2014, iPhone sales had grown by 44 percent in the United States and were up more than 96 percent in Brazil, Russia, India and China, but by 2015 the overall smartphone market was slowing down as mature markets were increasingly dependent on replacement purchases and emerging markets appeared more interested in low-cost devices.[37]

However, in 2015, Apple was poised to capture market share in two distinct areas: among those consumers who had previously been "inhibited" by the smaller screen size of older phones and therefore were unwilling to go completely mobile until the iPhone 6/6 Plus appeared; and within the enterprise market, as corporate users began to appreciate Apple's interactivity and the robustness of the iOS. Also, although a "staggering" 1.06 billion Android-based smartphones were shipped in 2014, while the iOS market share declined slightly (until the fourth quarter, when the iPhone 6 began shipping), according to data from industry watchers the difference in operating profit per phone was equally staggering: Android OS profit per phone was $2.26, while iOS phones yielded $97.50. In the Android/iOS war, "strangling" profits in the quest for increased market share might not have been the best long-term strategy. Apple had the resources to grow and win.[38]

Tablet Computer: iPad

In April 2010 Apple released the iPad, a tablet computer, as a platform for audiovisual media, including books, periodicals, movies, music, games, and web content. More than 300,000 iPads were scooped up by eager tech consumers during the device's first day on store shelves. Weighing only 1.5 pounds, this lightweight, portable touch-screen device was seen as a gigantic iPod Touch.[39]

Considering that previous tablet computers had failed to catch on in the mass market, Apple made a bold move by introducing the iPad. Upon its release, some users criticized the iPad for a lack of features, such as a physical keyboard, a webcam, USB ports, and Flash support, and for its inability to multitask, share files, and print. However, features like the sleek design, touch screen, multiple apps, and fast and easy-to-navigate software made the iPad popular in business, education, and the entertainment industry. The iPad was selected by *Time* magazine as one of the "50 Best Inventions of the Year 2010."[40]

Until September 2010, Apple iPads accounted for 95 percent of tablet computer sales, according to research firm Strategy Analytics.[41] But by the end of 2012, that figure had fallen to 78.9 percent. The loss of share was due to the arrival of new tablet devices, such as Samsung's Galaxy, based on Google's open-source Android system. Other platforms and devices had also begun to appear, including Google's Nexus, Amazon's Kindle Fire HD, and Microsoft's Windows 8 Surface tablet.[42] By 2015, devices running the Android operating system had achieved a market share of 66 percent of new tablet shipments.[43]

In October 2014 Apple released the iPad Air 2, the fifth-generation iPad. With similarities to the iPad Mini, the Air was thinner, with a smaller screen bezel, yet still used the same 9.7-inch Retina Display as the previous iPad model. In addition to the physical redesign, the Air had more powerful cameras and slightly increased processing speed, but it was otherwise only a slight improvement over previous iPad versions.[44] Going into 2015 there were signs that the iPad models' sales, as well as the entire tablet industry, were "going downhill," partly due to the "jumbo" phones coming from the likes of Samsung (and Apple) and the low-cost Google-based Chromebook laptops (Exhibit 8).[45]

In this category, Microsoft's Surface Pro 3 was the only tablet that appeared to be growing: 24 percent increase in sales, year over year, during the fourth quarter of 2014. This indicated that a performance-oriented tablet appealed to users.[46] Apple needed to consider an upgrade.

The Software Market

Although Apple had always created innovative hardware, software development was also an important goal. Software had increasingly become Apple's core strength, especially in its computers, due to its reliability and resistance to virus infections and resulting crashes.[47] The premier piece of Apple software was the operating system. The iOS allowed Apple to develop software applications such as Final Cut Pro, a video-editing program for professionals' digital camcorders, and the simplified version for regular consumers, called iMovie. The iLife software package provided five

EXHIBIT 8 Worldwide Quarterly Tablet Market Share, Fourth Quarter 2014

Smartphone OS	Market Share, Q4 2014	Market Share, Q4 2013	Year-Over-Year Growth
Apple	28.1%	33.1%	−17.8%
Samsung	14.5	17.2	−18.4
Lenovo	4.8	4.3	9.1
ASUS	4.0	5.1	−24.9
Amazon	2.3	7.4	−69.9
Others	46.2	32.8	36.2

Source: IDC, Worldwide Quarterly Tablet Tracker, February 2, 2015, http://seekingalpha.com/article/2944766-apple-ipad-sales-may-surprise-in-fy-2016.

integrated applications, allowing the computer to become a home studio: iMovie; iDVD, for recording photos, movies, and music onto DVDs; iPhoto, for touching up digital photos; GarageBand, for making and mixing personally created music; and the iTunes digital music jukebox. Also available was iWork, containing a PowerPoint-type program called Keynote and a word-processor/page-layout program called Pages. Both iLife and iWork underwent major upgrades in 2009, further increasing their respective abilities to compete with Microsoft applications.

Apple's web browser, Safari, was upgraded in 2009 to compete with Windows Internet Explorer, Mozilla Firefox, and the new entrant, Chrome from Google. Apple announced, "Safari 4 is the world's fastest and most innovative browser,"[48] but analysts were quick to point out that Google's Chrome, which debuted six months earlier, was perhaps the first to take the browser interface in a new direction. One commentator called Chrome "a wake-up call for the Safari UI guys."[49] Browser market share data at the end of 2014 showed Chrome in the top spot, with a 45 percent global market share. Internet Explorer held a slim second place with 20 percent, and Firefox was a close third with 18 percent. Safari had a 10 percent share.[50]

In 2011 iCloud was introduced during one of Steve Jobs's last public appearances. The web-based storage service initially struggled to get traction, but in 2014 it was upgraded to iCloud Drive, allowing users to interoperate with Windows and connect all iOS devices. As an alternative to Google Drive and Dropbox, iCloud Drive gave Apple an intro into the enterprise/corporate user space, a market CEO Tim Cook had begun to target.[51]

In other software development areas, Apple had not been that successful. In 2012 Apple stumbled badly with its Maps software. Released in iOS6, Apple Maps was meant to replace Google Maps on the iPhone but instead produced distorted images and gave very bad directions. CEO Tim Cook had to apologize that Apple had fallen short of its commitment to making "world-class products," and he suggested customers go back to using its competitor's mapping software.[52]

iTunes

Arguably, Apple's most innovative software product was iTunes, a free downloadable software program for consumers that ran on either Mac or Windows operating systems. It was bundled with all Mac computers and iPods and connected with the iTunes Music Store, enabling purchases of digital music and movie files that could be downloaded and played by iPods, iPads, and the iPhone and, on PCs, by iTunes.

Although the volume was there, iTunes had not necessarily been a profitable venture. Traditionally, out of the 99 cents Apple charged for a song, about 65 cents went to the music label; 25 cents went for distribution costs, including credit card charges, servers, and bandwidth; and the balance went to marketing, promotion, and the amortized cost of developing the iTunes software.[53] However, even if not wildly profitable, iTunes was still considered a media giant, especially with over 43 million DRM-free songs available in its database as of 2015.[54]

Several competitors had tried to compete with the iTunes service. RealNetworks' Rhapsody subscription service, Yahoo MusicMatch, and AOL music downloads had all competed for the remaining market share, using the potentially buggy Microsoft Windows Media format, and all subsequently failed.[55] Even though one commentator said in 2004 that "ultimately someone will build a piece of software that matches iTunes,"[56] as of 2015 the only serious competition was from Amazon.

At the start of 2013, iTunes accounted for over 60 percent of all digital music sales. In second place was Amazon's MP3 store, with 16 percent market share. Google Play, eMusic, Zune Music Pass, Rhapsody, and a few others each captured 5 percent or less of the remaining sales. Growth, however, was occurring in the streaming service market, especially with the rising popularity of online radio and Internet streaming providers Pandora and Spotify, and by 2015 music sales on iTunes had fallen by over 14 percent worldwide. This trend helped explain why Apple acquired the monthly subscription streaming service Beats Music in 2014. The $3 billion acquisition included headphone maker Beats Electronics.[57]

The App Store

In March 2008, Apple announced that it was releasing the iPhone software development kit (SDK), allowing developers to create applications for the iPhone and iPod Touch and sell these third-party applications via the Apple App Store. The App Store was made available on iTunes, and it was directly available from the iPhone, iPad, and iPod Touch products. This opened the window for another group of Apple customers, the application developers, to collaborate with Apple. Developers could purchase the iPhone Developer Program from Apple for $99, create either free or commercial applications for the iPhone and iPod Touch, and then submit the applications to be sold in the App Store. Developers received 70 percent of the download fee that iPhone or iPod Touch customers paid to the App Store, and Apple got 30 percent of the revenue.

As of January 2015, over 75 billion apps had been downloaded from Apple's App Store, but Google Play, the app store for Android users, was gaining ground, indicating that Google might be attracting more top-tier developers and quality titles to its marketplace. However, downloads for both platforms slowed in 2014, causing market watchers to wonder if a plateau was coming. This might mean diminishing returns and a less prosperous business model for all concerned.[58]

Apple Pay

Introduced in late 2014, Apple Pay allowed iPhone 6 and 6 Plus users in the U.S. to make secure payments for goods and services using their phones. With over 1 million credit and debit card activations within the first 72 hours of its release, Apple Pay was intended to replace the user's wallet and, according to CEO Tim Cook, would "forever change the way all of us buy things," primarily because the process was more secure than a traditional card-based transaction. As of 2015, major retailers such as Macy's, Walgreens, McDonald's, Whole Foods, and Disney had all agreed to accept Apple Pay. Apple reportedly received 0.15 percent of each purchase price, making the service a potentially lucrative venture. Major competition was coming from Google Wallet, especially given Google's 2015 acquisition of technology from Softcard.[59] Google Wallet had also seen an increase in usage as the Apple Pay system was launched, indicating that 2015 might become an interesting year for alternative types of transactions to occur.[60]

New Products: Apple Watch and Apple Car

Apple Watch was the first all-new product since the iPad, and therefore CEO Tim Cook's most ambitious gamble. Once again, Apple was not the first company to enter the wearable-tech space; it was following the lead of Samsung, Sony, and Motorola and competing against fitness trackers produced by Nike, FitBit, and others. However, Apple's preorders for the launch in 2015 indicated demand would run to a combined 5 to 6 million units of the three watch models.[61] This product category was a bit of a departure for Apple as the company positioned the Watch as a personalized device, with the market segmented between mass market and luxury. The features on all three models were the same, but status was indicated by differences in the precious metals and craftsmanship of the cases, therefore justifying the price range from $349 for the sports model to $20,000 for the Apple Watch Edition.[62]

Rumors surfaced in 2015 that Apple had acquired resources, primarily engineers and related technology, that would enable it to develop an automobile, ready for market by 2020. Speculation was that Apple would not do the actual assembly but, as with its other products, would use its sophisticated supply chain expertise to outsource manufacturing, focusing its considerable innovation skills on the design and sale of a product that incorporated Apple technology in multiple configurations. As one observer said, "In this strategy, Apple's current products would act as building blocks and core components of future, more important products. The ecosystem would become *much* larger," therefore enabling Apple to continue to grow and dominate the innovation landscape.[63]

The Future of Apple

In 2012, during Tim Cook's first year as CEO, he had to deal with a flat economy, supplier troubles, increasing competition, investor panic, and possibly unrealistic expectations in the wake of Steve Jobs's demise, and yet the company still grew by 60 percent. By 2015, Apple's value had more than doubled. Although many observers feared that Apple would have to yield to the "law of large numbers"—the concept that companies which grow rapidly cannot maintain that growth pace over time—CEO Cook rejected this view as being "dogma" and believed that Apple still had major opportunities ahead.[64] And many of those opportunities existed because of Steve Jobs's and now Tim Cook's single-minded emphasis on pursuing only those projects where Apple could be the best at making a "significant, lasting difference" (and never "cheapening" the product offering), where Apple could use this philosophy and vision to attract the best and brightest key personnel, and where it could leverage its considerable skill in managing its distribution and supply chain while simultaneously delivering a complete customer experience.[65]

As Cook explained, in each of the markets Apple had entered, it was not the first to market. It was not the first to produce MP3 players, smartphones, or tablets, and it was not the first with wearable technology or a mobile pay system. Apple's strategy had always been to carefully analyze each market and then design products that were more attractive to users than any competitor's products could be.[66] Under Cook, Apple had transitioned itself "from being a hypergrowth company to being a premium, branded consumer company."[67] Apple was becoming "a wildly profitable company that continues to be a major (or dominant) player in various product categories,"[68] and those categories appeared to be expanding beyond consumer electronics. Apple was becoming a truly vertically integrated designer and marketer of products that increasingly inhabited a world "dominated by the Internet of Things"—Apple just loved "designing great stuff," and it could use its current products as "building blocks and core components of future, more important products."[69] Some of those future products might include enterprise software, magnetic locks, automobiles, solar power systems, and anything else that could take advantage of the Apple ecosystem. As one commentator said, "Tim Cook has a dream. *Apple Everywhere.* Coming to a world near you. In time."[70] Why not?

ENDNOTES

1. Wakabayashi, D. 2015. Apple: $710 billion and counting. *Wall Street Journal,* February 10, www.wsj.com/articles/apple-the-700-billion-company-1423602877. The other companies include Exxon Mobil Corp. with a market cap of $382 billion, Berkshire Hathaway Inc. at $370 billion, and Google Inc. at $363 billion.
2. Ibid.
3. Allsopp, A. 2012. Apple shares drop 6.4% on worst trading day in four years, analysts speculate why. *MacWorld,* December 6, www.macworld.co.uk/digitallifestyle/news/?newsid=3415160.
4. Travlos, D. 2013. Is Apple losing its brand equity? *Forbes,* January 19, www.forbes.com/sites/darcytravlos/2013/01/19/is-apple-losing-its-brand-equity/.
5. Stone, B., & Burrows, P. 2011. The essence of Apple. *Bloomberg Businessweek,* January 24–30.
6. World's most admired companies. 2015. *Fortune,* http://fortune.com/worlds-most-admired-companies/.
7. Apple was the first firm to have commercial success selling GUI systems, but Xerox developed the first systems in 1973. Xerox PARC researchers built a single-user computer called the Alto that featured a bit-mapped display and a mouse and the world's first what-you-see-is-what-you-get (WYSIWYG) editor. From www.parc.xerox.com/about/history/default.html.
8. Apple Inc. 2012. 2012 annual report, 10-K filing. Available at www.apple.com/investor.
9. January 24, 2009, was the 25th anniversary of the Macintosh, unveiled by Apple in the "Big Brother" Super Bowl ad in 1984. Watch via YouTube: www.youtube.com/watch?v=OYecfV3ubP8. See also the 1983 Apple keynote speech by a young Steve Jobs, introducing this ad: www.youtube.com/watch?v=lSiQA6KKyJo.
10. See Mank, D. A., & Nystrom, H. E. 2000. The relationship between R&D spending and shareholder returns in the computer industry. Engineering Management Society, *Proceedings of the 2000 IEEE,* 501–504.
11. Apple Inc. 2001. Ultra-portable MP3 music player puts 1,000 songs in your pocket. October 23, www.apple.com/pr/library/2001/oct/23ipod.html.
12. Apple Inc. 2010. Apple sells two million iPads in less than 60 days. Press release. May 31, www.apple.com/pr/library/2010/05/31Apple-Sells-Two-Million-iPads-in-Less-Than-60-Days.html.
13. BBC News. 2010. Apple passes Microsoft to be biggest tech company. *BBC News,* May 27, www.bbc.co.uk/news/10168684.
14. Keizer, G. 2012. Apple drains iPhone5 pre-order supplies in an hour. *Computerworld,* September 14, www.computerworld.com/s/article/9231285/Apple_drains_iPhone_5_pre_order_supplies_in_an_hour.
15. IDC. 2015. In a near tie, Apple closes the gap on Samsung in the fourth quarter as worldwide smartphone shipments top 1.3 billion for 2014, according to IDC. *IDC,* January 29, www.idc.com/getdoc.jsp?containerId=prUS25407215.
16. Schlender, B. 2005. How big can Apple get? *Fortune,* February 21, money.cnn.com/magazines/fortune/-fortune_archive/2005/02/21/8251769/index.htm.
17. Tofel, K. C. 2012. Why only Samsung builds phones that outsell iPhones. *GigaOM,* November 9, www.businessweek.com/articles/2012-11-09/why-only-samsung-builds-phones-that-outsell-iphones.
18. Apple Inc. 2012. 2012 annual report; and Palladino, V. 2013. Apple Store receives trademark for "distinctive design and layout." *Wired,* January 30, www.wired.com/design/2013/01/apple-store-trademark/.
19. Burrows, P. 2004. The seed of Apple's innovation. *BusinessWeek Online,* October 12, www.businessweek.com/bwdaily/dnflash/oct2004/nf20041012_4018_db083.htm.
20. Fox, F. 2008. Mac Pro beats HP and Dell at their own game: Price. *LowEndMac.com,* May 16, lowendmac.com/ed/fox/08ff/mac-pro-vs-dell-hp.html.
21. Lowensohn, J. 2012. Lingering issues found at Foxconn's iPhone factory. *CNET,* December 14, news.cnet.com/8301-13579_3-57559327-37/lingering-issues-found-at-foxconns-iphone-factory/.
22. Bennett, D. 2012. Apple's Cook says more Macs will be born in the U.S.A. *Bloomberg Businessweek,* December 10, www.businessweek.com/articles/2012-12-10/apples-cook-says-more-macs-will-be-born-in-the-u-dot-s-dot-a-dot.
23. Oliver, S. 2015. Apple's R&D spending shoots up 42% year-over-year, hit new $1.9B record in Q1. *AppleInsider,* January 28, http://appleinsider.com/articles/15/01/28/apples-rd-spending-shoots-up-42-year-over-year-hit-new-19b-record-in-q1; and King, R. 2011. Inventing the future of computing. *Bloomberg Businessweek,* October 31, www.businessweek.com/technology/inventing-the-future-of-computing-10312011.html.
24. Jones, A., & Vascellaro, J. E. 2012. Apple v. Samsung: The patent trial of the century. *Wall Street Journal,* July 24, online.wsj.com/article/SB10000872396390443295404577543221814648592.html?mod5wsj_streaming_apple-v-samsung-trial-over-patents.
25. Noel, P. 2014. iProblems: Learning from Apple's strained supply chain. *MBTMag,* November 11, www.mbtmag.com/articles/2014/11/iproblems-learning-apple%E2%80%99s-strained-supply-chain.
26. StealingShare.com. 2006. Growing market share—branding in the computer industry 2006. www.stealingshare.com/content/1137644625875.htm.
27. IDC. 2014. Global PC shipments exceed forecast with mild improvement in consumer demand, while Apple moves to #5 spot, according to IDC. *IDC,* October 8, www.idc.com/getdoc.jsp?containerId=prUS25187214.
28. *MacWorld Middle East.* 2011. Apple shipments up in US: Market share boosted. January 14, www.macworldme.net/2011/01/14/apple-shipments-up-in-us-market-share-boosted/.
29. Elmer-DeWitt, P. 2008. Apple challenges Sony and Nintendo. *Apple 2.0—Blogs,* December 13, apple20.blogs.fortune.cnn.com/2008/12/13/apple-challenges-sony-and-nintendo.
30. Hollister, S. 2014. The age of the iPod is over. *The Verge,* January 27, www.theverge.com/2014/1/27/5351918/apples-ipod-rides-into-the-sunset.
31. Rehman, A. 2010. iPod gains 76 percent of MP3 player market in US while Zune is a failure with just 1 percent share after 4 years. *AbdulRehman.net,* July 14, www.abdulrehman.net/ipod-gains-76-percent-of-mp3-player-market-in-us-while-zune-is-a-failure-with-just-1-percent-share-after-4-years/.
32. Ogren, E. 2007. Ballmer says iPhone won't succeed. Has Windows Mobile? *InformationWeek,* May 1, www.informationweek.com/blog/main/archives/2007/05/ballmer_says_ip.html.
33. IDC. 2012. Worldwide mobile phone growth expected to drop to 1.4% in 2012 despite continued growth of smartphones, according to IDC. *IDC,* December 4, www.idc.com/getdoc.jsp?containerId5prUS23818212#.UQSn-_J5V8E.

34. Wagstaff, J. 2012. In Asia's trend-setting cities, iPhone fatigue sets in. *Reuters,* January 27, news.yahoo.com/asias-trend-setting-cities-iphone-fatigue-sets-212849658--finance.html.
35. Farzad, R. 2012. The autumn of Apple's discontent. *Bloomberg Businessweek,* December 6, www.businessweek.com/articles/2012-12-06/as-apples-stock-slides-a-lone-analyst-sounds-the-alarm.
36. Wakabayashi, op. cit.
37. IDC, 2015, op. cit.
38. Hibben, M. 2015. Apple iOS versus Android: Is this the turn of the tide? *SeekingAlpha,* February 26, http://seekingalpha.com/article/2954606-apple-ios-versus-android-is-this-the-turn-of-the-tide.
39. Pogue, D. 2010. Looking at the iPad from two angles. *New York Times,* March 31, www.nytimes.com/2010/04/01/technology/personaltech/01pogue.html?_r=1&pagewanted=all&partner=rss&emc=rss.
40. McCracken, H. 2010. iPad. *Time,* November 11, www.time.com/time/specials/packages/article/0,28804,2029497_2030652,00.html.
41. Cellan-Jones, R. 2011. iPad 2 tablet launched by Apple's Steve Jobs. *BBC News,* March 2, www.bbc.co.uk/news/technology-12620077.
42. Johnson, J. 2013. Kindle Fire, Android tablets chip away at iPad market share. *Inquisitr,* January 2, www.inquisitr.com/465784/kindle-fire-android-tablets-chip-away-at-ipad-marketshare/#Q2bAVTfXbEpu72tB.99.
43. Statista. 2014. Global market share held by tablet operating systems from 2010 to 2014, by quarter. *Statista.com,* www.statista.com/statistics/273840/global-market-share-of-tablet-operating-systems-since-2010/.
44. Smith, D. 2013. Apple iPad "5" Air review: 3 major disappointments in the new fifth-generation iPad. *International Business Times,* November 2, www.ibtimes.com/apple-ipad-5-air-review-3-major-disappointments-new-fifth-generation-ipad-1452788.
45. Inquisitr. 2015. Galaxy Tab S2 tries to kill Apple's "already dying" iPad Air. *Inquisitr,* February 18, www.inquisitr.com/1853887/samsung-galaxy-tab-s2-tries-to-kill-apples-already-dying-ipad-air/.
46. Cho, A. 2015. Apple iPad sales may surprise in FY 2016. *SeekingAlpha,* February 24, http://seekingalpha.com/article/2944766-apple-ipad-sales-may-surprise-in-fy-2016.
47. Schlender, op. cit.
48. Apple Inc. 2009. Apple announces Safari 4—the world's fastest and most innovative browser. Press release. February 24, www.apple.com/pr/library/2009/02/24safari.html.
49. Siracusa, J. 2008. Straight out of Compton: Google Chrome as a paragon of ambition, if not necessarily execution. *ars technica,* September 2, arstechnica.com/staff/fatbits/2008/09/straight-out-of-compton.ars.
50. Widder, B. 2014. Battle of the best browsers. *Digital Trends,* November 25, www.digitaltrends.com/computing/the-best-browser-internet-explorer-vs-chrome-vs-firefox-vs-safari/.
51. Sanders, J. 2014. iCloud Drive: Apple's appealing recipe for cloud storage. *TechRepublic,* June 5, www.techrepublic.com/article/icloud-drive-apples-appealing-recipe-for-cloud-storage/.
52. Cheng, R. 2012. Apple CEO: We are "extremely sorry" for Maps flap. *CNET,* September 28, news.cnet.com/8301-13579_3-57522196-37/apple-ceo-we-are-extremely-sorry-for-maps-flap/.
53. Cherry, S. 2004. Selling music for a song. *Spectrum Online,* December, www.spectrum.ieee.org/dec04/3857.
54. www.apple.com/itunes/music/.
55. Leonard, D. 2006. The player. *Fortune,* March 8, money.cnn.com/magazines/fortune/fortune_archive/2006/03/20/8371750/index.htm.
56. Salkever, A. 2004. It's time for an iPod IPO. *BusinessWeek,* May 5, www.businessweek.com/technology/content/may2004/tc2004055_8689_tc056.htm.
57. Karp, H. 2014. Apple iTunes sees big drop in music sales. *Wall Street Journal,* October 24, www.wsj.com/articles/itunes-music-sales-down-more-than-13-this-year-1414166672.
58. Forrest, C. 2014. Google Play v Apple App Store: The battle for the mobile app market. *TechRepublic,* September 3, www.techrepublic.com/article/google-play-v-apple-app-store-the-battle-for-the-mobile-app-market/.
59. Hibben, M. 2015. Apple Pay vs. Google Wallet: The rematch. *SeekingAlpha,* February 25, http://seekingalpha.com/article/2948836-apple-pay-vs-google-wallet-the-rematch?auth_param=70583:1aernv3:56a2cade662c710219a5a9ca9968ad60&uprof=14.
60. *MacRumors.* 2015. Apple Pay overview. www.macrumors.com/roundup/apple-pay/.
61. Luk, L., & Wakabayashi, D. 2015. Apple orders more than 5 million watches for initial run. *Wall Street Journal,* February 17, http://blogs.wsj.com/digits/2015/02/17/apple-orders-more-than-5-million-watches-for-initial-run/?mod=rss_Technology.
62. Cybart, N. 2015. Don't focus on Apple Watch edition pricing. *SeekingAlpha,* February 25, http://seekingalpha.com/article/2950519-dont-focus-on-apple-watch-edition-pricing.
63. DoctoRx. 2015. The real importance of the Apple car project. *SeekingAlpha,* February 20, http://seekingalpha.com/article/2935276-the-real-importance-of-the-apple-car-project?auth_param=70583:1aeel0c:036a6dfaf470ca644123bac661ffb276&uprof=14.
64. Wakabayashi, op. cit.
65. Anonymous. 2015. Apple entering the car sector? Why this could be its next "large numbers" move. *SeekingAlpha,* February 19, http://seekingalpha.com/article/2932216-apple-entering-the-car-sector-why-this-could-be-its-next-large-numbers-move?auth_param=70583:1aecem7:c9db1ed4a42260643e3494528dcf5b94&uprof=14.
66. Hibben, M. 2015. How Apple defies the law of large numbers. *SeekingAlpha,* February 16, http://seekingalpha.com/article/2920846-how-apple-defies-the-law-of-large-numbers.
67. Russolillo, S. 2013. Apple losing luster: Is it now a value stock? *Wall Street Journal,* January 14, blogs.wsj.com/marketbeat/2013/01/14/apple-growth-or-value-stock/.
68. Grobart, S. 2013. Apple and Google: Slouching toward steady profits. *Bloomberg Businessweek,* January 22, www.businessweek.com/articles/2013-01-22/apple-and-google-slouching-toward-steady-profits.
69. DoctoRx, op. cit.
70. Ibid.

CASES

CASE 17

CAMPBELL: HOW TO KEEP THE SOUP SIMMERING*

At the first-quarter earnings call for the 2015 fiscal year, Denise Morrison, Campbell's president and chief executive officer, said:

> We were encouraged by our organic sales growth across most of our portfolio, particularly in U.S. Simple Meals and Global Baking and Snacking. Our U.S. soup performance was driven by a stronger seasonal sell-in and the timing of our quarter end relative to the Thanksgiving holiday. Although our year is off to a solid start, we are facing some challenges. Our gross margin performance did not meet our expectations due largely to higher than anticipated commodity costs and supply chain costs. We have plans to offset gross margin pressure in the remainder of the year. We also are facing headwinds from currency. Despite these challenges, we continue to make progress strengthening our core business and expanding into faster-growing spaces.[1]

Denise Morrison, who formerly headed the company's North American soup division, had taken over as CEO nearly four years ago. The change at the top for the company received a lukewarm response from investors, who were watching to see what drastic changes Morrison might have in store. Analysts suggested that Campbell may have missed an opportunity by picking insider Denise Morrison to lead the world's largest soup maker instead of bringing in outside talent to revive sales.[2]

By 2015, with Morrison at the helm, the Campbell Soup Company had launched more than 50 new products, including 32 new soups. This number was way up from prior years. Morrison also shocked experts with the $1.55 billion buyout of California juice-and-carrot seller Bolthouse Farms, the largest acquisition in Campbell's history.[3] Despite the revitalization of its product line, however, the company still failed to accomplish an impressive comeback.

Company Background

Probably known best for its red-and-white soup cans, the Campbell Soup Company was founded in 1869 by Abram Anderson and Joseph Campbell as a canning and preserving business. Over 140 years later, Campbell offered a whole lot more than just soup in a can. In 2014 the company, headquartered in Camden, New Jersey, competitively operated in five segments: U.S. Simple Meals, Global Baking and Snacking, International Simple Meals and Beverages, U.S. Beverages, and Bolthouse and Foodservice (see Exhibit 1).

In 2015 Campbell's products were sold in over 100 countries around the world, and the company had operations in the United States, Canada, Mexico, Australia, Belgium, China, France, Germany, Indonesia, Malaysia, and Sweden (see Exhibit 2).[4]

The company was pursuing strategies designed to expand the availability of its products in existing markets and to capitalize on opportunities in emerging channels and

---

* This case study was prepared by Professors Alan B. Eisner and Dan Baugher of Pace University and Professor Helaine J. Korn of Baruch College, City University of New York. The purpose of the case is to stimulate class discussion rather than to illustrate effective or ineffective handling of a business situation. Copyright © 2013, 2015 Alan B. Eisner.

EXHIBIT 1
Sales by Segment ($ millions)

Go to library tab in Connect to access Case Financials.

	2014	2013	2012	% Change 2014/2013	% Change 2013/2012
U.S. Simple Meals	**$ 2,944**	$2,849	$2,726	3%	5%
Global Baking and Snacking	**2,440**	2,273	2,193	7	4
International Simple Meals and Beverages	**780**	869	872	(10)	—
U.S. Beverages	**723**	742	774	(3)	(4)
Bolthouse and Foodservice	**1,381**	1,319	610	5	116
	$ 8,268	$8,052	$7,175	3%	12%

Source: The Campbell Soup Company, annual report, 2014.

EXHIBIT 2 Campbell's Principal Manufacturing Facilities

Inside the U.S.		
California	**New Jersey**	**Texas**
Bakersfield (BFS)	East Brunswick (GBS)	Paris (USSM/USB/ISMB/BFS)
Dixon (USSM/USB)	**North Carolina**	**Utah**
Stockton (USSM/USB)	Maxton (USSM/ISMB)	Richmond (GBS)
Connecticut	**Ohio**	**Washington**
Bloomfield (GBS)	Napoleon (USSM/USB/BFS/ISMB)	Everett (BFS)
Florida	Willard (GBS)	Prosser (BFS)
Lakeland (GBS)	**Pennsylvania**	**Wisconsin**
Illinois	Denver (GBS)	Milwaukee (USSM)
Downers Grove (GBS)	Downingtown (GBS/BFS)	

Outside the U.S.		
Australia	**Canada**	**Indonesia**
Huntingwood (GBS)	Toronto (USSM/ISMB/BFS)	Jawa Barat (GBS)
Marleston (GBS)	**Denmark**	**Malaysia**
Shepparton (ISMB)	Nørre Snede (GBS)	Selangor Darul Ehsan (ISMB)
Virginia (GBS)	Ribe (GBS)	

USSM—U.S. Simple Meals
GBS—Global Baking and Snacking
ISMB—International Simple Meals and Beverages
USB—U.S. Beverages
BFS—Bolthouse and Foodservice

Source: Campbell Soup Company 2014 annual report.

markets around the globe. As a first step, Campbell Soup Company, synonymous with the all-American kitchen for 125 years, acquired in 1994 Pace Foods Ltd., the world's largest producer of Mexican sauces. Frank Weise, CFO at that time, said that a major motivation for the purchase was to diversify Campbell and to extend the Pace brand to other products. In addition, he said, the company saw a strong potential for Pace products internationally. Campbell also saw an overlap with its raw material purchasing operations, since peppers, onions, and tomatoes were already used in the company's soups, V8, barbecue sauce, and pasta sauces.[5] To help reduce some of the price volatility for ingredients, the company used various commodity risk management tools for a number of its ingredients and commodities, such as natural gas, heating oil, wheat, soybean oil, cocoa, aluminum, and corn.[6]

Campbell Soup, a leading food producer in the United States, had a presence in approximately 9 out of 10 U.S. households. However, in recent years, the company faced a slowdown in its soup sales, as consumers were seeking more convenient meal options, such as ready meals and dining out. To compete more effectively, especially against General Mills' Progresso brand, Campbell had undertaken various efforts to improve the quality and convenience of its products.

China and Russia

For the longest time, consumption of soup in Russia and China had far exceeded that in the United States, but in both countries nearly all of the soup was homemade. Within the past few years, however, with the launch of products tailored to local tastes, trends, and eating habits, Campbell presumed that it had the chance to lead the soup commercialization in Russia and China. "We have an unrivaled understanding of consumers' soup consumption behavior and innovative technology capabilities within the Simple Meals category. The products we developed are designed to serve as a base for the soups and other meals Russian and Chinese consumers prepare at home."[7] For about three years, in both Russia and China, Campbell sent its marketing teams to study the local markets. The main focus was on how Russians and Chinese ate soup and how

Campbell could offer something new. As a result, Campbell came up with a production line specifically created for the local Russian market. Called "Domashnaya Klassika," the line was a stock base for soups that contains pieces of mushrooms, beef, or chicken. Based on this broth, the main traditional Russian soup recipes could be prepared.

But after just four short years, Campbell pulled out of the Russian market that it had thought would be a simmering new location for its products. Campbell's chief operating officer and newly elected CEO Denise Morrison said results in Russia fell below what the company had expected. "We believe that opportunities currently under exploration in other emerging markets, notably China, offer stronger prospects for driving profitable growth within an acceptable time frame," Morrison said. When the company entered Russia, Campbell knew that it would be challenging to persuade a country of homemade-soup eaters to adopt ready-made soups. When Campbell initially researched the overseas markets, it learned that Russians eat soup more than five times a week, on average, compared with once a week among Americans.[8] This indicated that both the quality and sentiment of the soup meant a great deal to Russian consumers—something that Campbell may have underestimated.

As for China, a few years after Campbell infiltrated the market, CEO Denise Morrison was quoted by *Global Entrepreneur* as saying, "The Chinese market consumes roughly 300 billion servings of soup a year, compared with only 14 billion servings in the U.S."[9] When entering the Chinese market, Campbell had determined that if the company could capture at least 3 percent of the at-home consumption, the size of the business would equal that of its U.S. market share. "The numbers blow your hair back," said Larry S. McWilliams, president of Campbell's international group.[10] While the company did successfully enter the market, it remained to be seen whether Campbell had the right offerings in place to capture such a market share or whether China's homemade-soup culture would be as disinclined to change as Russia's was.

U.S. Soup Revitalization

In September 2010, Campbell launched its first-ever umbrella advertising campaign to support all of its U.S. soup brands with the slogan "It's Amazing What Soup Can Do," highlighting the convenience and health benefits of canned soup. The new campaign supported Campbell's condensed soups, Campbell's Chunky soups, Campbell's Healthy Request soups, and Campbell's Select Harvest soups, as well as soups sold in microwaveable bowls and cups under these brands.[11] Despite other departments flourishing, the soup division continued to struggle.

Campbell Soup Company had begun moving attention away from reducing salt in its products and focusing more on "taste adventure" as its U.S. soup business was turning cold. Campbell Soup was one of the first large U.S. packaged-food makers to focus heavily on decreasing sodium across its product line. The salt-reduction push was one of the company's biggest initiatives of the past decade. "The company had pursued reducing sodium levels and other nutritional health initiatives partly to prepare for expected nutritional labeling changes in the U.S. But amid the attention on salt-cutting, management focused less on other consumer needs, such as better tastes and exciting varieties," said former CEO Douglas Conant. "I think we've addressed the sodium issue in a very satisfactory way. The challenge for us now is to create some taste adventure."[12]

Yet with Campbell reinventing its product offerings and revitalizing its soup line, Conant decided that his work was done and it was time to retire. He stepped down as CEO in July 2011 at the age of 60. Denise Morrison, formerly president of the North America Soup division, took the reins as chief executive. At the time of her promotion, many were hesitant to accept her as the best candidate for the position. After all, the soup division, which had been her responsibility, had been losing steam and encountering declining sales under her tenure. Yet the company reinforced its confidence in her to do the job, and Morrison assured everyone that changes were on their way and a shift in focus was in the works. Morrison said that Campbell would bring both the "taste and adventure" back to its soups, with a new and expanded product line offering unique new flavors and "adding the taste back" by doing away with sodium reduction.

Firm Structure and Management

Campbell Soup was controlled by the descendants of John T. Dorrance, the chemist who had invented condensed soup more than a century ago. In struggling times, the Dorrance family faced agonizing decisions: Should they sell the Campbell Soup Company, which had been in the family's hands for three generations? Should they hire new management to revive flagging sales of its chicken noodle and tomato soups and Pepperidge Farm cookies? Or should Campbell perhaps become an acquirer itself? The company went public in 1954, when William Murphy was the president and CEO. Dorrance family members continued to hold a large portion of the shares. After CEO David Johnson left Campbell in 1998, the company started to weaken and lose customers,[13] until Douglas Conant became CEO and transformed Campbell into one of the food industry's best performers.

Conant became CEO and director of Campbell Soup Company in January 2001. He joined the Campbell's team with an extensive background in the processed- and packaged-food industry. He had spent 10 years with General Mills, filled top management positions in marketing and strategy at Kraft Foods, and served as president of Nabisco Foods. Conant worked toward the goal of implementing the Campbell's mission of "building the world's most extraordinary food company by nourishing people's lives everywhere, every day."[14] He was confident that the company had the people, the products, the capabilities, and the plans in place to actualize that mission.

Under Conant's direction, Campbell made many reforms through investments in improving product quality, packaging, and marketing. He worked to create a company characterized by innovation. During his tenure, the company improved its financial profile, upgraded its supply chain system, developed a more positive relationship with its customers, and enhanced employee engagement. Conant focused on winning in both the marketplace and the workplace. His efforts produced an increase in net sales from $7.1 billion in fiscal 2005 to $7.67 billion in fiscal 2010.[15]

For Conant, the main targets for investment, following the divestiture of many brands, included simple meals, baked snacks, and vegetable-based beverages. In 2010, the baking and snacking segments sales increased 7 percent, primarily due to currency. Pepperidge Farm sales were comparable to those a year earlier, as the additional sales from the acquisition of Ecce Panis, Inc., and volume gains were offset by increased promotional spending. Some of the reasons for this growth were the brand's positioning, advertising investments, and improvements and additions in the distribution system. Conant also secured an agreement with Coca-Cola North America and Coca-Cola Enterprises Inc. for distribution of Campbell's refrigerated single-serve beverages in the United States and Canada through the Coca-Cola bottler network.[16]

In fiscal 2010, the company continued its focus on delivering superior long-term total shareowner returns by executing the following seven key strategies:[17]

- Grow its icon brands within simple meals, baked snacks, and healthy beverages.
- Deliver higher levels of consumer satisfaction through superior innovation focused on wellness while providing good value, quality, and convenience.
- Make its products more broadly available and relevant in existing and new markets, consumer segments, and eating occasions.
- Strengthen its business through outside partnerships and acquisitions.
- Increase margins by improving price realization and companywide total cost management.
- Improve overall organizational excellence, diversity, and engagement.
- Advance a powerful commitment to sustainability and corporate social responsibility.

Another major focus for Conant and Campbell Soup was care for their customers' wellness needs, overall product quality, and product convenience. Some of the main considerations regarding wellness in the U.S. market were obesity and high blood pressure. For example, building on the success of the V8 V-Fusion juice offerings, the company planned to introduce a number of new V8 V-Fusion Plus Tea products. In the baked snacks category, the company planned to continue upgrading the health credentials of its cracker (or savory biscuit) offerings. Responding to consumers' value-oriented focus, Campbell's condensed soups were relaunched with a new contemporary packaging design and an upgrade to the company's gravity-fed shelving system.[18]

In 2011, after 10 years leading the company, Conant retired. His successor, Denise Morrison, had worked for Conant for quite some time, not just at Campbell but at Nabisco as well as earlier in their careers. In August 2011, on her first day as CEO, she was set on employing a new vision for the company: "Stabilize the soup and simple meals businesses, expand internationally, grow faster in healthy beverages and baked snacks—and add back the salt."[19] With the younger generation now making up an increasingly large percentage of the population, Morrison knew that the company had to change in order to increase the appeal of its products. At that time, the U.S. population included 80 million people between the ages of 18 and 34, approximately 25 percent of the population. Early on in her role as chief executive, Morrison dispatched Campbell's employees to hipster hubs—including Austin, Texas; Portland, Oregon; London; and Paris—to find out what these potential customers wanted.[20]

To build employee engagement, Campbell provided manager training across the organization. This training was just one part of the curriculum at Campbell University, the company's internal employee learning and development program. Exemplary managers built strong engagement among their teams through consistent action planning. The company emphasized employees' innovation capabilities, leadership behavior, workplace flexibility, and wellness.

Challenges Ahead

In her new role, Morrison said she planned to "accelerate the rate of innovation" at the company. Morrison planned to grow the company's brands through a combination of more healthy food and beverage offerings, global expansion, and the use of technology to woo younger consumers. While *innovation* isn't a term typically associated with the food-processing industry, Morrison said that innovation was a key to the company's future success. As an example, she cited Campbell's development of an iPhone application that provided consumers with Campbell's Kitchen recipes. The company's marketing team devised the plan as a way to appeal to technologically savvy, millennial-generation consumers, Morrison said.[21]

Yet more than a few years into her governance, analysts still had a lukewarm response about Morrison taking over. They still expressed their doubt about whether Morrison was the right choice, rather than some new blood as a CEO replacement.

Industry Overview

The U.S. packaged-food industry had recorded faster current-value growth in recent years mainly due to a rise in commodity prices. In retail volume, however, many categories saw slower growth rates because Americans began to eat out more often again. This dynamic changed for a couple of years when cooking at home became a more popular alternative in response to the recession and the sharp rise in commodity prices in 2008.[22]

After years of expansions and acquisitions, U.S. packaged-food companies were beginning to downsize. In August 2011, Kraft Foods announced that it would split into two companies: a globally focused biscuits and confectionery enterprise and a domestically focused cheese, chilled processed meats, and ready-meals firm. After purchasing Post cereals from Kraft in 2008, Ralcorp Holdings spun off its Post cereals business (Post Holdings Inc.) in February 2012.[23]

Though supermarkets were the main retail channel for buying packaged food, other competitors were gaining traction by offering lower prices or more convenience. The recession forced shoppers to consider alternative retail channels as they looked for ways to save money. A big beneficiary of this consumer trend was the discounters, which carried fewer items and national brands than supermarkets but offered lower prices in return. For example, dollar store chains Dollar General and Family Dollar expanded their food selections to increase their appeal. Drugstore chains CVS and Walgreens expanded their food selections as well, especially in urban areas, to leverage their locations as a factor of convenience. Mass merchandiser Target continued to expand its PFresh initiative, featuring fresh produce, frozen food, dairy products, and dry groceries.[24]

The increasing availability of refrigeration and other kinds of storage space in homes influenced the demand for packaged goods in emerging markets. However, for consumers who lacked the ability to preserve and keep larger quantities, U.S. companies began selling smaller packages, with portions that could be consumed more quickly (see Exhibit 3).[25]

EXHIBIT 3 Leading U.S. Agricultural Export Destinations, by Value ($US)

	Country	CY2013	Country	CY2012	Country	CY2011
	World Total	144,101,559,716	World Total	141,269,778,632	World Total	136,368,898,500
1	China	25,880,644,237	China	25,855,185,834	Canada	19,040,891,979
2	Canada	21,326,516,722	Canada	20,629,128,111	China	18,891,225,522
3	Mexico	18,098,808,744	Mexico	18,920,817,269	Mexico	18,345,140,240
4	Japan	12,138,761,149	Japan	13,498,893,467	Japan	14,056,032,738
5	European Union-28	11,857,780,593	European Union-28	10,067,646,850	European Union-28	9,677,429,121
6	South Korea	5,135,962,712	South Korea	6,030,721,670	South Korea	6,971,825,313
7	Hong Kong	3,852,064,120	Hong Kong	3,403,354,049	Taiwan	3,611,280,692
8	Taiwan	3,088,863,591	Taiwan	3,211,889,925	Hong Kong	3,312,790,293
9	Indonesia	2,823,768,279	Indonesia	2,492,797,710	Indonesia	2,812,888,426
10	Philippines	2,509,046,614	Philippines	2,350,403,529	Egypt	2,507,078,974
11	Turkey	2,148,734,476	Turkey	1,990,771,662	Turkey	2,448,404,540
12	Vietnam	2,128,330,507	Egypt	1,868,407,646	Philippines	2,111,737,546
13	Brazil	1,906,663,898	Venezuela	1,690,430,314	Vietnam	1,644,148,259
14	Egypt	1,651,981,562	Russia	1,654,697,610	Thailand	1,343,296,353
15	Venezuela	1,545,396,029	Vietnam	1,651,985,897	Saudi Arabia	1,306,768,821

Source: U.S. Economic Research Service, U.S. Department of Agriculture, 2014, www.ers.usda.gov/data-products/foreign-agricultural-trade-of-the-united-states-(fatus)/calendar-year.aspx.

Competition

Campbell operated in the highly competitive food industry and experienced worldwide competition for all of its principal products. The principal areas of competition were brand recognition, quality, price, advertising, promotion, convenience, and service. (See Exhibits 4 and 5.)

Nestlé

Nestlé was the world's number-one food company in terms of sales, the world leader in coffee (Nescafé), one of the world's largest bottled-water (Perrier) makers, and a top player in the pet food business (Ralston Purina). Its best-known global brands included Buitoni, Friskies, Maggi, Nescafé,

EXHIBIT 4 Campbell's Competitors, by Market Capitalization and Financials

	CPB	GIS	PVT1	MDLZ	Industry
Market cap	$ 14.62B	$32.25B	N/A	$ 62.06B	$ 1.63B
Employees	19,400	43,000	31,900[1]	107,000	3.10K
Qtrly rev growth (yoy)	0.04	−0.03	N/A	−0.02	0.08
Revenue (ttm)	$ 8.36B	$17.64B	$11.53B[1]	$ 34.90B	$ 1.82B
Gross margin (ttm)	0.35	0.34	N/A	0.37	0.34
EBITDA (ttm)	1.57B	3.23B	N/A	5.32B	192.46M
Operating margin (ttm)	0.15	0.15	N/A	0.12	0.08
Net income (ttm)	$790.00M	$ 1.51B	$ 1.01B[1]	$ 1.85B	N/A
EPS (ttm)	2.79	2.40	N/A	1.99	0.94
P/E (ttm)	16.71	22.27	N/A	18.57	22.27
PEG (5 yr expected)	5.20	3.06	N/A	1.92	2.10
P/S (ttm)	1.73	1.81	N/A	1.76	1.17

GIS—General Mills, Inc.
Pvt1—H. J. Heinz Company (privately held)
MDLZ—Mondelēz International Inc.
Industry—Processed & Packaged Goods
[1] As of 2013

Source: Yahoo Finance, *finance.yahoo.com*.

EXHIBIT 5 Campbell Soup Top Competitors' Stock Prices

Source: *finance.yahoo.com/*, retrieved on January 16, 2015.

Nestea, and Nestlé. The company owned Gerber Products, Jenny Craig, about 75 percent of Alcon Inc. (ophthalmic drugs, contact-lens solutions, and equipment for ocular surgery), and almost 28 percent of L'Oréal.[26] In July 2007 it purchased Novartis Medical Nutrition, and in August 2007 it purchased the Gerber business from Sandoz Ltd., with the goal of becoming a nutritional powerhouse. Furthermore, by adding Gerber baby foods to its baby formula business, Nestlé became a major player in the U.S. baby food sector.

General Mills

General Mills was the U.S. number-two cereal maker, behind Kellogg, fighting for the top spot on a consistent basis. Its brands included Cheerios, Chex, Total, Kix, and Wheaties. General Mills was also a brand leader in flour (Gold Medal), baking mixes (Betty Crocker, Bisquick), dinner mixes (Hamburger Helper), fruit snacks (Fruit Roll-Ups), grain snacks (Chex Mix, Pop Secret), and yogurt (Colombo, Go-Gurt, and Yoplait). In 2001 it acquired Pillsbury from Diageo and doubled the company's size, making General Mills one of the world's largest food companies. Although most of its sales came from the United States, General Mills was trying to grow the reach and position of its brands around the world.[27]

Kraft Foods

The newly independent Kraft Foods Group was spun off by Mondelēz International (formerly Kraft Foods Inc.), dividing the North American grocery from the global snacks business in 2012. Kraft Foods Group was the fourth-largest consumer packaged-food and beverage company in North America. Its most popular brands included Kraft cheeses, beverages (Maxwell House coffee, Kool-Aid drinks), convenient meals (Oscar Mayer meats and Kraft mac'n cheese), grocery fare (Cool Whip, Shake N' Bake), and nuts (Planters). While Mondelēz was focused on growth overseas, Kraft Foods Group was looking to resuscitate its business in North America.[28]

Heinz Company

H. J. Heinz had thousands of products. Heinz products enjoyed first or second place by market share in more than 50 countries. One of the world's largest food producers, Heinz produced ketchup, condiments, sauces, frozen foods, beans, pasta meals, infant food, and other processed-food products. Its flagship product was ketchup, and the company dominated the U.S. ketchup market. Its leading brands included Heinz ketchup, Lea & Perrins sauces, Ore-Ida frozen potatoes, Boston Market, T.G.I. Friday's, and Weight Watchers foods. In 2013 Heinz agreed to be acquired by Berkshire Hathaway and 3G Capital.[29]

Financials

In the 2014 fiscal year, Campbell's sales from continuing operations increased 3 percent to $8.3 billion, driven by acquisitions and an additional workweek in the year. Organic sales declined 1 percent, while adjusted earnings per share (EPS) from continuing operations increased 2 percent to $2.53.

In the U.S. Simple Meals segment, sales were up 3 percent versus sales a year earlier. This compared to a 5 percent increase in fiscal 2013. The growth came from higher sales of Prego pasta sauces and Campbell's dinner sauces. However, sales declined in U.S. Soups as growth in Swanson broth was more than offset by declines in ready-to-serve and condensed soups.

The Global Baking and Snacking segment grew 7 percent (versus 4 percent in fiscal 2013) driven by marginal growth at Pepperidge Farm and continued gains in Goldfish crackers, fresh bakery items, and the Indonesian market.

The U.S. Beverages business saw a continued decline in sales, and the company initiated turnaround plans to jumpstart the business.

(See Exhibits 1, 6, 7, and 8.)

EXHIBIT 6 Campbell Balance Sheet ($ thousands)

Go to library tab in Connect to access Case Financials.

Period Ending	Aug 3, 2014	Jul 28, 2013	Jul 29, 2012
Assets			
Current assets			
Cash and cash equivalents	232,000	333,000	335,000
Net receivables	670,000	635,000	553,000
Inventory	1,016,000	925,000	714,000
Other current assets	182,000	328,000	169,000
Total Current Assets	**2,100,000**	**2,221,000**	**1,771,000**

EXHIBIT 6 Continued

Period Ending	Aug 3, 2014	Jul 28, 2013	Jul 29, 2012
Property plant and equipment	2,318,000	2,260,000	2,127,000
Goodwill	2,433,000	2,297,000	2,013,000
Intangible assets	1,175,000	1,021,000	496,000
Other assets	87,000	524,000	123,000
Total assets	**8,113,000**	**8,323,000**	**8,530,000**
Liabilities			
Current liabilities			
Accounts payable	1,218,000	1,259,000	1,284,000
Short/Current long term debt	1,771,000	1,909,000	786,000
Other current liabilities	—	114,000	—
Total current liabilities	**2,989,000**	**3,282,000**	**2,070,000**
Long term debt	2,244,000	2,544,000	2,004,000
Other liabilities	729,000	798,000	1,260,000
Deferred long term liability charges	548,000	489,000	298,000
Minority interest	(12,000)	(7,000)	—
Total liabilities	**6,498,000**	**7,106,000**	**5,632,000**
Stockholders' equity			
Common stock	12,000	12,000	20,000
Retained earnings	2,198,000	1,772,000	9,584,000
Treasury stock	(356,000)	(364,000)	(8,259,000)
Capital surplus	330,000	362,000	329,000
Other stockholder equity	(569,000)	(565,000)	(776,000)
Total stockholder equity	**1,615,000**	**1,217,000**	**898,000**
Net tangible assets	**(1,993,000)**	**(2,101,000)**	**(1,611,000)**

Source: Yahoo Finance.

EXHIBIT 7 Campbell Income Statement ($ thousands)

Go to library tab in Connect to access Case Financials.

Period Ending	Aug 3, 2014	Jul 28, 2013	Jul 29, 2012
Total revenue	8,268,000	8,052,000	7,175,000
Cost of revenue	5,370,000	5,140,000	4,365,000
Gross profit	**2,898,000**	**2,912,000**	**2,810,000**
Operating expenses			

continued

EXHIBIT 7 Continued

Period Ending	Aug 3, 2014	Jul 28, 2013	Jul 29, 2012
Research development	121,000	128,000	116,000
Selling general and administrative	1,530,000	1,653,000	1,532,000
Non recurring	55,000	51,000	7,000
Operating income or loss	**1,192,000**	**1,080,000**	**1,155,000**
Income from continuing operations			
Total other income/expenses net	3,000	10,000	8,000
Earnings before interest and taxes	1,192,000	1,080,000	1,155,000
Interest expense	122,000	135,000	114,000
Income before tax	1,073,000	955,000	1,049,000
Income tax expense	347,000	275,000	325,000
Minority interest	11,000	9,000	10,000
Net income from continuing ops	726,000	680,000	724,000
Non-recurring events			
Discontinued operations	81,000	(231,000)	40,000
Net income	**818,000**	**458,000**	**774,000**
Preferred stock and other adjustments	—	—	—
Net income applicable to common shares	**818,000**	**458,000**	**774,000**

Source: Yahoo Finance.

EXHIBIT 8 Campbell's Key Ratios

Valuation Measures	
Market cap (intraday)	14.62B
Enterprise value (Jan 17, 2015)	18.42B
Trailing P/E (ttm, intraday)	16.71
Forward P/E (fye Aug 3, 2016)	17.97
PEG ratio (5 yr expected)	5.20
Price/Sales (ttm)	1.73
Price/Book (mrq)	9.01
Enterprise value/Revenue (ttm)	2.20
Enterprise value/EBITDA (ttm)	11.72
Financial highlights	
Fiscal year	
Fiscal year ends	Aug 3

EXHIBIT 8 *Continued*

Valuation Measures	
Most recent quarter (mrq)	Nov 2, 2014
Profitability	
Profit margin (ttm)	10.53%
Operating margin (ttm)	15.14%
Management effectiveness	
Return on assets (ttm)	9.11%
Return on equity (ttm)	52.86%
Income statement	
Revenue (ttm)	8.36B
Revenue per share (ttm)	26.62
Qtrly revenue growth (yoy)	4.20%
Gross profit (ttm)	2.90B
EBITDA (ttm)	1.57B
Net income Avl to common (ttm)	790.00M
Diluted EPS (ttm)	2.79
Qtrly earnings growth (yoy)	36.00%
Balance sheet	
Total cash (mrq)	242.00M
Total cash per share (mrq)	0.77
Total debt (mrq)	4.07B
Total debt/equity (mrq)	253.55
Current ratio (mrq)	0.74
Book value per share (mrq)	5.12
Cash flow statement	
Operating cash flow (ttm)	1.05B
Levered free cash flow (ttm)	682.50M
Trading information	
Stock price history	
Beta	1.00
52-week change	10.57%
S&P500 52-week change	9.52%
52-week high (Jun 19, 2014)	46.67
52-week low (Feb 5, 2014)	39,60

continued

EXHIBIT 8 *Continued*

Valuation Measures	
50-day moving average	44.45
200-day moving average	43.84
Share statistics	
Avg vol (3 month)	1,545,940
Avg vol (10 day)	2,075,020
Shares outstanding	314.00M
Float	198.52M
% held by insiders	43.55%
% held by institutions	42.60%
Shares short (as of Dec 31, 2014)	12.28M
Short ratio (as of Dec 31, 2014)	6.90
Short % of float (as of Dec 31, 2014)	7.00%
Shares short (prior month)	12.63M
Dividends & splits	
Forward annual dividend rate	1.25
Forward annual dividend yield	2.70%
Trailing annual dividend yield	1.25
Trailing annual dividend yield	2.70%
5 year average dividend yield	3.10%
Payout ratio	45.00%
Dividend date	Feb 2, 2015
Ex-dividend date	Jan 8, 2015
Last split factor (new per old)	2:1
Last split date	Mar 18, 1997

Source: http://finance.yahoo.com/q/ks?s=CPB+Key=Statistics.

With regard to financials, Morrison stated:

> Fiscal 2014 was a year of investment for Campbell. We stated at the outset that we would accept lower operating profits to fund investments in brand-building and accelerated innovation across our portfolio.

Similarly, in the Beverages business, Campbell's sales were steady, but increased costs were up, wearing away margins. Also, the bakery division, including Pepperidge Farm, faced aggressive competition, industry consolidation, and heavy price discounting.

Sustainability

Campbell Soup Company was named to the Dow Jones Sustainability Indexes (DJSI) repeatedly and to the DJSI World Index. This independent ranking recognized the company's strategic and management approach to delivering economic, environmental, and social performance. Launched in 1999, the DJSI tracked the financial performance of leading sustainability-driven companies worldwide. In selecting the top performers in each business sector, DJSI reviewed companies on several general and industry-specific topics related to economic, environmental, and social dimensions. These included corporate governance, environmental policy, climate strategy, human capital development, and labor practices. Campbell included sustainability and corporate social responsibility as one of its seven core business strategies.[30] Campbell's Napoleon, Ohio, plant implemented a new renewable energy initiative, anchored by 24,000 new solar panels. The 60-acre, 9.8-megawatt solar power system was expected to supply 15 percent of the plant's electricity while reducing CO_2 emissions by 250,000 metric tons over 20 years.[31]

Additionally, Campbell employees volunteered an average of 20,000 hours annually at more than 200 nonprofit organizations. Supported by local farmers and Campbell, the Food Bank of South Jersey was earning revenue for hunger relief from sales of *Just Peachy* salsa. The salsa was created from excess peaches from New Jersey and was manufactured and labeled by employee volunteers at Campbell's plant in Camden.[32]

What's Next?

A new food-rating system unveiled in 2009, the Affordable Nutrition Index (ANI), analyzed both nutrition and the cost value of food, making it easier for consumers to find budget-friendly, nutritious foods. Dark-colored vegetables, certain fruits, and vegetable soups were among the most affordable, nutritious foods. "In today's economy, more people are making food choices based solely on cost, so it's important to guide them on ways to get nutritious options without hurting their wallets," said Adam Drewnowski, PhD, a professor at the University of Washington. "It is important to identify a wide range of affordable, nutritious choices that can help people build a balanced diet that fits their lifestyle and budget."[33]

As for Campbell, its advertising campaign failed to assist the company in gaining the expected traction in the ready-to-serve soup business. Campbell planned to correct this by introducing new products into what many considered a rather ordinary product line. But if the economy continued to improve, would Campbell's name still resonate with American consumers or would consumers venture back to restaurants? Would Campbell's soup simmer to perfection, or would the company be in hot water?

ENDNOTES

1. Company earnings call transcript, November 25, 2014.
2. Boyle, M. 2010. Campbell CEO pick may be lost chance, analysts say. *BusinessWeek*, September 29, www.businessweek.com/news/2010-09-29/campbell-ceo-pick-may-be-lost-chance-analysts-say.html.
3. Goudreau, Jenna. 2012. Kicking the can: Campbell's CEO bets on soup-in-a-bag for 20-somethings. *Forbes.com*, December 6, www.forbes.com/sites/jennagoudreau/2012/12/06/kicking-the-can-campbells-ceo-bets-on-soup-in-a-bag-for-20-somethings.
4. Campbell's. 2013. Our company. www.campbellsoupcompany.com/around_the_world.asp.
5. Collins, G. 1994. Campbell Soup takes the big plunge into salsa. *New York Times*, November 29: D1.
6. Campbell Soup Co. 2010. 2009 annual report.
7. Campbell Soup Co. 2008. 2007 annual report.
8. *Wall Street Journal*. 2011. Campbell Soup to exit Russia. June 29, online.wsj.com/article/SB10001424052702304447804576414202460491210.html.
9. *Want China Times*. 2013. Campbell Soup aims to break into Chinese market through chef endorsements. March 6, www.wantchinatimes.com/news-subclass-cnt.aspx?id=20130306000016&cid=1102.
10. Boyle, M. 2009. Campbell's: Not about to let the soup cool. *BusinessWeek*, September 17.
11. News release. 2010. Campbell launches "It's Amazing What Soup Can Do" ad campaign to promote Campbell's U.S. soup brands. September 7, investor.campbellsoupcompany.com/phoenix.zhtml?c=88650&p=irol-newsArticle&ID=1467644.
12. Brat, I., & Ziobro, P. 2010. Campbell to put new focus on taste. *Wall Street Journal*, November 24, online.wsj.com/article/0,,SB10001424052748704369304575632342839464532,00.html.
13. Abelson, Reed. 2000. The first family of soup, feeling the squeeze; Should it sell or try to go it alone? *New York Times*, July 30, www.nytimes.com/2000/07/30/business/first-family-soup-feeling-squeeze-should-it-sell-try-go-it-alone.html?pagewanted=all&src=pm.
14. Campbell Soup Co. 2008. 2007 annual report.
15. Campbell Soup Co. 2011. 2010 annual report.
16. Press release. 2007. The Coca-Cola Company, Campbell Soup Company and Coca-Cola Enterprises sign agreement for distribution of Campbell's beverage portfolio. investor.shareholder.com/campbell/releasedetail.cfm?ReleaseID5247903.
17. Campbell Soup Co. 2011. 2010 annual report.
18. Ibid.
19. Goudreau, op. cit.
20. Ibid.
21. Katz, Jonathan. 2010. Campbell Soup cooking up a new recipe? *Industry Week*, December 15, www.industryweek.com/companies-amp-executives/iw-50-profile-campbell-soup-cooking-new-recipe.
22. PRNewswire. 2012. U.S. packaged food market—Consumers seek out ethnic & bold flavours—new industry report. *PRNewswire*, March 12, www.prnewswire.com/news-releases/us-packaged-food-market—consumers-seek-out-ethnic–bold-flavours—new-industry-report-142292805.html.
23. *ReportsnReports*. 2013. Packaged food in the US. April, www.reportsnreports.com/reports/150486-packaged-food-in-the-us.html.
24. Ibid.
25. Graves, T., & Kwon, E. Y. 2009. Standard and Poor's foods and nonalcoholic beverages industry report. July.
26. Hoovers. Undated. Company profiles: Nestlé. www.hoovers.com/company-information/cs/company-profile.Nestlé_SA.6a719827106be6ff.html, accessed April 2013.

27. Hoovers. Undated. Company profiles: General Mills. *www.hoovers.com/company-information/cs/company-profile.General_Mills_Inc.a90ba57dc8f51a65.html*, accessed April 2013.
28. Hoovers. Undated. Company profiles: Kraft Foods. *www.hoovers.com/company-information/cs/company-profile.Kraft_Foods_Group_Inc.43af8ed4b4ae51f2.html*, accessed April 2013.
29. Hoovers. Undated. Company profiles: H. J. Heinz Company. *www.hoovers.com/company-information/cs/company-profile.H_J_Heinz_Company.1696a42275f81d38.html*, accessed April 2013.
30. News release. 2010. Campbell Soup company named to Dow Jones Sustainability Indexes. *investor.campbellsoupcompany.com/phoenix.zhtml?c=88650&p=irol-newsArticle&ID=1471159*.
31. Campbell Soup Co. 2013. 2012 annual report.
32. Ibid.
33. *Supermarket News*. 2009. New affordable nutrition index is first measurement tool to evaluate affordable nutrition. October 19, *supermarketnews.com/company/campbell/archives/1009-nutrition-index/*.

CASES

CASE 18

UNITED WAY WORLDWIDE*

In early 2015, United Way Worldwide hoped the recently concluded holiday season would have generated more contributions and provided a much-needed boost to the nonprofit's sagging revenues.[1] Stacey D. Stewart, the organization's U.S. president, had earlier appealed to holiday shoppers to consider the true meaning of the holidays. "Black Friday and Cyber Monday mark the beginning of the holiday shopping season," she had said. "Over the next several weeks—as we navigate mall parking lots, fill our shopping carts and test our patience in check-out lines— let's not lose sight of what's behind this excitement. It all comes down to the simple act of giving."

The organization had been hit particularly hard during the economic downturn in prior years, and contributions had yet to pick up after economists announced a rebound. Charitable giving usually rose about one-third as fast as the stock market.[2] United Way Missouri chapter executive director Tim Rich mourned the fact that a perfect storm of factors was causing the surge in need. "We're seeing stagnated wages, jobs with fewer hours and less pay, church giving is down," Rich said. "It's just harder to write a check right now." This challenging dynamic was reflective of United Way chapters all around the country.[3] The continued trend—reduction in giving, increase in need—had earlier prompted United Way to change its strategy.[4] On July 1, 2009, United Way of America (UWA) changed its name to United Way Worldwide (UWW) and merged with United Way International (UWI). UWW initiated a 10-year program, "Live United," focused less on distribution of funds and more on advancing the common good by addressing underlying causes of problems in the core areas of education, financial stability, and health. Yet with positive financial results still seemingly nonexistent, would donors finally become reenergized and create real change in the communities United Way served, or had universal struggles weakened the ability and eagerness to donate of even those most able to do so?

UWW provided support for over 1,800 local United Way members or affiliates operating in 41 countries.[5] These local organizations relied on their respective parents for resources such as leadership education, public policy advocacy, marketing support, and standards for ethical governance and financial reporting. United Ways worldwide were part of a federation of nonprofits formed by caring people to serve the needs of their communities. According to UWW's website, "We advance the common good by focusing on improving education, helping people achieve financial stability, and promoting healthy lives, and by mobilizing millions of people to give, advocate, and volunteer to improve the conditions in which they live." United Way raised funds and distributed them to the most effective local service providers; built alliances and coordinated volunteer support among charities, businesses, and other entities; and acted as a best-practice model of management and financial accountability—but this last item had become a source of problems. With three high-profile ethical scandals since 1995 at both the national and local levels, the United Way brand had to combat an erosion of trust at the same time that it was dealing with an increasingly competitive and changing environment for charitable contributors.

Even after over 120 years of solid financial performance and steady growth, since the year 2000 United Way had seemingly reached a plateau of fund-raising in the United States (see Exhibit 1). Certainly, there were options for growth from international members and from the energy and direction of nationwide objectives stated by United Way of America (education about and implementation of the national 2-1-1 phone network; the early-childhood educational initiatives Success by 6 and Born Learning; encouragement of nationwide voluntarism through the Lend a Hand public service announcements funded by a donation from the NFL; and the Assets for Family Success economic self-sufficiency program for working families). Yet charitable donations still had not topped the inflation-adjusted peak-year campaign of the late 1980s.[6]

In addition, veteran fund-raisers on all fronts were citing challenges, such as competition for donations, difficulty recruiting and keeping qualified fund-raisers, difficulty raising money for general operating costs, and a growing focus on large gifts from very wealthy individuals, which, when publicized, could reduce the motivation for smaller donors to contribute. (Small donors might think, "If someone like Bill Gates is providing funds, why do they need my dollars?")[7] From the donors' perspective, the opportunities for both individuals and businesses to engage in charitable giving had expanded, with over 40 percent of new nonprofits appearing since 2000.[8] Many of these, especially those supporting disaster relief in the wake of 9/11, Hurricane Katrina, and Hurricane Sandy, had a single-issue focus that had the potential for creating a

---

* By Professor Alan B. Eisner of Pace University, Associate Professor Pauline Assenza of Western Connecticut State University, and graduate students Luz Barrera and Dev Das of Pace University. This case is based upon public documents and was developed for class discussion rather than to illustrate either effective or ineffective handling of the situation. This research was supported in part by the Wilson Center for Social Entrepreneurship, Pace University. Copyright © 2015 Alan B. Eisner.

close bond with the donor. This meant that some individuals might have bypassed organizations such as the United Way, believing that the United Way had support targets that were too broad and preferring, instead, to specify exactly where donations should go. (Such a donor might think, "If I'm giving, I want to make sure my money is going where I want it to go, to the cause I want to support.")

Even prior to 9/11, American donors had expressed concern about their ability to access information regarding how their donations were going to be used, what percentage of the charity's spending went toward actual current programs, how their privacy was going to be protected when giving via the Internet, and whether the charity met voluntary standards of conduct.[9] It didn't help that many nonprofits, including United Way of America, suffered widely publicized scandals over misappropriation of funds. Organizations that serve community or broader social needs must continually be perceived as legitimate, as acting in an appropriate and desirable way within "some socially constructed set of norms, values, beliefs and definitions" in order to receive needed donations.[10] It was especially difficult for nonprofits such as United Way to maintain trust, because their products and services did not easily lend themselves to traditional quality assessment and performance review; and once that trust was broken, it was difficult to get it back.

Responding to this, United Way Worldwide's CEO, Brian Gallagher, formally initiated a shift in strategy. Responding to the environment, Gallagher first established new membership standards to enhance the level of accountability and transparency in United Way affiliates' operations (see Exhibit 6). He also rebranded United Way as doing "what matters" in the communities it served. Finally, he updated the "standards of excellence," providing a description of benchmark standards and best practices to better reflect the organization's strategic shift from its traditional role as strictly a fund-raiser to a new mission focused on identifying and addressing the long-term needs of communities.

These initiatives required that United Way affiliates buy into the change effort, because the power of the parent organization was limited to removing the affiliate from United Way membership if it didn't comply. As a nonprofit organization, it was imperative for United Way Worldwide to get the necessary support at the local level in order to achieve its stated organizational goals. Would Gallagher's various strategies be successfully implemented? Was the shift in strategy sufficient to ensure the continued viability of the United Way, or was its very mission perhaps no longer relevant?

Overview and History of the United Way of America

United Way was founded in 1887 as the Charity Organizations Society of Denver, raising $21,700 for 22 local agencies in its second year of operation. In 1913 this model was expanded to become a "Community Chest" in Cleveland, and in 1918 a dozen fund-raising federations met in Chicago to form the American Association for Community Organizations. From 1919 to 1929, over 350 Community Chests were created, and by 1948 more than 1,000 communities had United Way Community Chests in operation. In 1973 the partnership between United Way and the National Football League began, with the goal to increase public awareness of social-service issues facing the country. Through the partnership, United Way public service announcements featured volunteer NFL players, coaches, and owners, and NFL players supported their local United Ways through personal appearances, special programs, and membership on United Way governing boards.

In 1974 United Ways in America and Canada raised $1,038,995,000, marking the first time in history that an annual campaign of a single organization raised more than $1 billion. In the same year, United Way International was formed to help nations around the world create United Way–type organizations. The 1981–1985 and 1997–1998 campaigns generated the greatest percentage increase in revenues, possibly driven by economic trends. Amounts raised since 2000 generally failed to keep up with the rate of inflation (see Exhibit 1).[11]

The United Way was essentially a financial intermediary, providing fund-raising activities, primarily through donor organizations' employee payroll deductions, and then distributing those funds to agencies that could actually deliver services to clients in the target community. The parent organization, United Way Worldwide, serviced the local United Way chapters, which performed the bulk of the fund-raising. Although there were other sources of revenue, including individual donations and government grants, around 70 percent of donations came from employees in local businesses; of the employee contributions, 75 percent were considered unrestricted dollars that the local United Ways could put to use to address critical needs in their respective communities.

The parent organization, United Way Worldwide (UWW), was supported primarily by local United Way member organizations that paid annual membership fees based on an agreed-on formula, 1 percent of their communitywide campaign contributions. Trademark members, United Way member organizations raising less than $100,000, paid a fee of 0.3 percent of their total contributions. In addition to membership support, individual and corporate sponsorship, and federal grants, other sources for funds for the national umbrella organization were conferences, program service fees, promotional material sales, investment income, rental income, and service income (see Exhibits 2 and 3).

United Way was a system that operated as a federation—a network of local affiliates that shared a mission, a brand, and a program model but were legally independent from one another and from the national office. Historically, United Way had been the loosest of federations, with almost all power residing at the local level. Each United Way chapter member was not only independent but also separately incorporated and governed by a local volunteer board.

EXHIBIT 1 United Way Campaign History

Year	Amount Raised ($ billions)	Change	%	CPI (1982–1984, 100)*	Inflation Rate (%)	Amount Raised in Constant Dollars	Change	%
2000	3.912	143	3.8	172.2	3.4	2.272	9.5	0.4
2001	3.949	37	0.9	177.1	2.8	2.230	−42.0	−1.8
2002	3.709	−240	−6.1	179.9	1.6	2.062	−168.1	−7.5
2003	3.591	−118	−3.2	184	2.3	1.952	−110.1	−5.3
2004	3.606	15	0.4	188.9	2.7	1.909	−42.7	−2.2
2005	4.048	442	12.3	195.3	3.4	2.054	145.1	7.6
2006	4.143	95	2.3	201.6	3.2	2.043	−11.0	−0.5
2007	4.236	93	2.2	207.3	2.8	2.007	−36.0	−1.8
2008	4.023	−213	−5.0	215.3	3.8	1.919	−88.0	−4.4
2009	3.84	−183	−4.5	214.5	−0.4	1.795	−124.0	−6.5
2010	3.912	72	1.9	218.1	1.6	1.794	−1.0	−0.1
2011	3.927	15	0.4	224.9	3.2	1.746	−48.0	−2.7
2012	3.97	43	1.1	229.6	2.1	1.729	−17.0	−1.0
2013	3.939	−31	−0.8	233.0	1.5	1.691	−38.0	−2.2

*CPI is the annualized rate for a calendar year.

Source: United Way of America, research services, and author estimates.

Through communitywide campaigns, each local United Way, utilizing a network of local volunteers, raised funds to support a great variety of health and human services organizations.

Over the years, as United Way's local chapters grew bigger and more prosperous, they began to consider themselves more autonomous—gatekeepers, allocators, and managers of the local public trust—and began to question whether the seal of approval bestowed by United Way affiliation was worth it in light of the declining financial rewards. Therefore, some United Way agencies considered forming their own member-oriented, self-governing federations.

Current Competition and Challenges

By 2015 the charitable-giving industry had fragmented into tiny, single-focus agencies (some of them probably fraudulent) that could be both competitors and recipients of United Way programs. In addition, because United Way's traditional function had been to parcel out the contributions it received to local charities, donors had begun to question the need for an organization that essentially just processed money. (A donor might ask, "Why not just give directly to the charity of my choice?") The perception was that the administrative function of United Way and other blanket charities just added another level of overhead to organizational costs, with a smaller portion of the original donation actually reaching the intended target.

In addition, donors were increasingly supporting specific causes and therefore were more attracted to alternative recipient organizations, those possibly more responsive to the idea of community based on gender, race, or sexual orientation, among other socially driven issues.[12] A spokesperson for the American Cancer Society remarked, "Today a person might have an interest in prostate cancer, because his father died of it, or breast cancer, because it is a social issue as well as a health issue. We have to remember that an organization's mission is at least as important to supporters as its integrity." This meant that "donor-advised funds, which allow people to create grant-making accounts and recommend which charities get the money," were becoming increasingly popular.[13] This did not mean that traditional and venerable organizations like United Way, the Red Cross, the Salvation Army, and the American Cancer Society were necessarily in trouble; it just meant that they were perhaps in need of some strategic adjustment (see Exhibit 4).

The partnership between United Way and the disaster relief organizations, such as the Red Cross, the Salvation

EXHIBIT 2 Give.org Charity Report for United Way America, 2014

Governance
Chief Executive: Brian A. Gallagher, President and CEO
Compensation: $1,097,543*
Chair of the Board: Barry Salzberg
Chair's Profession/Business Affiliation: Accounting & Consulting
Board Size: 10   Paid Staff Size: 220

Uses of Funds as Percentage of Total Expenses for Year Ended December 31, 2011
- Fund-raising: 2.0%
- Administrative: 8.0%
- Programs: 90.0%

* January 1, 2011, to December 31, 2011, compensation includes annual salary and, if applicable, benefit plans, expense accounts, and other allowances.

Source: BBB Wise Giving Alliance at Give.org.

EXHIBIT 3 United Way of America Consolidated Financial Statements ($ thousands)

	Dec. 31, 2013	Dec. 31, 2012	Dec. 31, 2011	Dec. 31, 2010	Dec. 31, 2009	Dec. 31, 2008
Source of Funds						
Contributions	$ 48,634	$ 49,932	$ 50,481	$ 47,075	$ 51,992	$ 38,017
Membership support (net)	28,869	28,608	28,379	28,222	29,202	29,900
Campaign efforts (net)	(4,625)	7,507	44,757	49,143	53,525	59,100
Promotional material sales	694	2,995	3,364	3,838	3,764	5,968
Transaction fees	—	—	—	—	—	—
Conferences	2,708	2,639	2,061	2,173	1,816	2,810
Program service fees	2,238	2,212	3,276	1,270	1,072	1,512
Investment income	1,099	745	161	303	342	1,851
Rental and service income	—	—	—	—	—	—
Miscellaneous and other	1,044	895	870	1,074	671	1,551
Total Revenue	**$80,661**	**$95,532**	**$ 96,808**	**$ 92,385**	**$102,358**	**$102,103**

	Dec. 31, 2013	Dec. 31, 2012	Dec. 31, 2011	Dec. 31, 2010	Dec. 31, 2009	Dec. 31, 2008
Program Expenses						
Brand leadership	6,929	8,499	9,701	8,008	8,195	8,478
Community impact leadership	8,757	14,840	23,331	27,447	20,794	19,867
Campaign and public relations	5,739	4,888	4,183	8,070	8,711	12,864
Other expenses, e.g., investor relations, international expenses	$ 60,312	$ 59,708	$ 46,553	$ 42,145	$ 42,946	$ 49,632
Total Program Expenses	**$81,737**	**$87,935**	**$ 83,768**	**$ 85,670**	**$ 80,646**	**$ 90,841**
Total Revenue	$ 80,661	$ 95,532	$ 96,808	$ 92,385	$ 102,358	$ 102,103
Program expenses	81,737	87,935	83,768	85,670	80,646	90,841
Fund-raising expenses	2,392	2,973	2,084	2,055	1,003	1,055
Administrative expenses	5,791	6,448	7,767	7,269	8,827	12,517
Total expenses	$ 89,919	$ 97,356	$ 93,619	$ 94,994	$ 90,476	$ 104,413
Income in excess of expenses	(9,258)	(1,824)	3,189	−2,609	11,882	−2,310
Beginning net assets	39,501	38,607	42,239	45,368	37,906	42,220
Changes in net assets	(2,656)	894	−3,631	−3,130	7,463	−4,534
Ending net assets	$ 36,845	$ 39,501	$ 38,607	$ 42,239	$ 45,369	$ 37,906
Total liabilities	$ 29,859	$ 42,076	$ 64,861	$ 58,905	$ 56,426	$ 89,440
Total liabilities and net assets	$ 66,704	$ 81,577	$103,468	$101,144	$ 101,795	$ 127,346

Army, Boys & Girls Clubs, and Catholic Charities, was still a strong and viable one, but increasingly all these national charities needed to understand the need for a diversified revenue stream. In a video interview with UWW's Brian Gallagher, *Forbes* asked about what had changed. Gallagher noted that 55 percent of donations still came from employees in the workplace and corporate contributions from companies such as UPS, Microsoft, and IBM and that the relationship with the NFL was still a powerful one, with 50 percent of volunteers being recruited through the NFL campaign. He mentioned that online participation was growing and that individual donations averaged $200 per year per individual. These donations included contributions coming increasingly from women and people of color, accounting for $75 million from all United Way chapters in 2005.[14]

Entering 2015 with the donor community becoming increasingly diverse and the societal problems increasingly challenging, charitable nonprofits needed to engage in ongoing assessment of the relevance of their respective missions. This was not a new problem. In 1999 Michael Porter and Mark Kramer considered the strategic challenges facing nonprofits. Noting that the number of charitable foundations in the United States had doubled in the two decades after the 1970s, they believed that these philanthropic organizations were not devoting enough effort to measuring their results and to figuring out how to create the most value for society with the resources they had at their disposal. This value could have been created by selecting the appropriate grantees, signaling other donors of appropriately chosen charities, improving the performance of grant recipients, and advancing the state of knowledge and practice. However, many philanthropic organizations lacked a strategic focus: Their resources were scattered across too many fields, and their staffs were spread too thin, servicing too many small grants. One suggestion was that they engage in more performance assessment and unique positioning, with unique activities aimed specifically at creating value. This would require most nonprofits to also assess the effectiveness of their governance systems.[15]

Scandals and Governance

Echoing the plateau in the charitable-giving community, the year 2002 was bad for corporate scandals: Enron, ImClone, WorldCom, and Tyco all hit the headlines with examples of corporate greed and misappropriation of both funds and public trust. Given these types of wrongdoing in publicly held organizations, the tolerance of the general population for similar activities in nonprofits was

EXHIBIT 4 Top 10 U.S. Charities, 2014

Rank	Name	Private Support ($ millions)	Total Revenue ($ millions)	Fund-Raising Efficiency (%)	Charitable Commitment (%)	Donor Dependency (%)
1	United Way	3,870	4,266	91	86	100
2	Salvation Army	2,080	4,316	90	82	56
3	Feeding America	1,855	1,894	99	98	100
4	Task Force for Global Health	1,575	1,609	100	100	100
5	American National Red Cross	1,079	3,504	82	90	86
6	Food for the Poor	1,023	1,030	97	96	100
7	Goodwill Industries International	975	5,178	97	88	67
8	YMCA of the USA	939	6,612	87	85	50
9	American Cancer Society	871	935	77	73	100
10	St. Jude Children's Research Hospital	869	1,287	83	74	59

Note: For Catholic Charities and AmeriCares, the contributions were mostly donated goods, food, and medicine, not money.

Source: *www.forbes.com/sites/williampbarrett/2014///12/17/the-largest-u-s-charities-for-2014/*.

increasingly eroded, especially given the nature of the relationship—one based on donor trust.

The first major scandal at United Way had occurred 10 years earlier, in 1992, when William Aramony, president and CEO of United Way of America, and two other UWA executives were convicted of fraud, conspiracy, and money laundering in a scheme that siphoned around $1 million from the organization. This event was perceived as a turning point in public perceptions of charitable organizations and was blamed for the first drop in United Way donations since World War II.[16]

In 2001 the United Way of the National Capital Area—the Washington, D.C., chapter and the second-largest local United Way member in the country in donations—was in the news, again because of fraud. CEO Oral Suer had taken more than $500,000 from the charity to pay for personal expenses, annual leave, and an early pension payout he was not entitled to. Other employees had taken additional money for personal use, with the total fraud amounting to $1.6 million. Then, in 2002, new United Way National Capital Area CEO Norman O. Taylor was asked to resign over misstated revenues and questionable overhead and credit card charges. In 2003 the CFO of the Michigan Capital Area United Way, Jacqueline Allen-MacGregor, was imprisoned for the theft of $1.9 million from the charity, which she had used to purchase racehorses for her personal farm. Also in 2003, Pipeline Inc., a spin-off from the California Bay Area United Way that was created to collect contributions, was investigated for losing $18 million when the financial records did not accurately reflect the amount owed by the charity.[17] In 2006 a former CEO of the United Way of New York City was investigated for diverting organizational assets valued at $227,000 for his own personal use.[18]

To be fair, United Way was not the only high-profile charity to experience these kinds of problems. After 9/11, Katrina, and, most recently, Hurricane Sandy, the American Red Cross came under scrutiny for misdirection of disaster funds. In addition, the bookkeeper at Easter Seals of Iowa stole $230,000, the former president and seven others at Goodwill Industries of California embezzled $26 million, the financial administrator of the American Heart Association of New Jersey was convicted of theft of $186,000, and an executive at Goodwill Industries of Michigan was found guilty of stealing $750,000 from the agency over a 23-year period.[19] What could be done to curtail this disturbing trend?

The United Way of America's board during the Aramony scandal consisted of many Fortune 500 CEOs who were, according to Aramony, fully informed about his compensation and perquisites.[20] Yet it appeared they still failed to exercise appropriate oversight, as did the boards at the D.C. and Michigan chapters. Finding committed and knowledgeable board members was critical to United

Way's continued success. Given the federation model, each local chapter had its own board, recruited from community members who had not only fund-raising skills but also relationships with local leaders, politicians, or even regulators. Many local United Ways wanted to distance themselves from the scandals at UWA and high-profile chapters, and therefore they tried to stress local leadership and board autonomy. Serving on such a board required a commitment to the community and to the goals of the local United Way.

However, regardless of the degree of well-intentioned communication and disclosure, sometimes the goals of board members could have conflicted. A 2004 survey by McKinsey & Company of executives and directors at 32 of *Worth* magazine's top 100 nonprofit performers found that many nonprofit boards had recurring problems, one of which was consensus over mission and goals: "Only 46 percent of the directors we surveyed thought that other directors on their boards could both summarize the mission of the organizations they serve and present a vision of where those organizations hope to be in five years' time." In addition, for an organization such as United Way, the goals of the diverse stakeholders, both donors and recipients, may have differed widely. This lack of consensus, coupled with the difficulty of measuring and evaluating performance, meant that nonprofit boards in general needed to practice serious self-scrutiny: "The time when nonprofit boards were populated by wealthy do-gooders who just raised money, hired CEOs, and reaffirmed board policy is over."[21]

Given the degree to which the public trust had been violated by nonprofits that were found to be acting irresponsibly, the Senate Finance Committee was considering "tax-exempt reform containing provisions similar to those found in the Sarbanes-Oxley Act."[22] The 2008 scandal surrounding the Association of Community Organizations for Reform Now (ACORN), although focused on voter registration fraud, brought attention in Washington once again to the question of nonprofit legitimacy.[23]

This demand for greater accountability was not new. Nonprofits had sometimes been notoriously ineffective at accomplishing their social missions, inefficient at getting maximum return on the money they raised due to high administration costs, and willing to take on too much risk, through either inexperience or ignorance. Sometimes because of lax oversight procedures, individuals in control of the nonprofits were willing to engage in outright fraud, acquiring excessive benefits for themselves. These problems were enhanced due to nonprofits' failure to provide extensive analysis, disclosure, and dissemination of relevant performance information and due to the lack of sanctions.[24] If nonprofit organizations would not police themselves, watchdog agencies would create external standards and provide public feedback, sometimes to the detriment of the organization under scrutiny (see Exhibit 5).[25]

Gallagher's Response

In 2006 United Way of America CEO Brian Gallagher was invited by the U.S. Senate Finance Committee to participate in a roundtable discussion on needed reforms in nonprofit boards and governance. He was prepared to provide specific commentary. Since accepting the CEO position in 2001, Gallagher had been working to promote a change in the United Way strategy, including a change in mission, the creation of standards of performance excellence, and a requirement that local members certify their adherence to the membership standards.

Regarding the mission of United Way, Gallagher had worked to change the focus from fund-raising to community

EXHIBIT 5 Watchdog Agencies—Information Resources for Nonprofits

- American Institute of Philanthropy
  www.charitywatch.org
- Better Business Bureau Wise Giving Alliance
  www.give.org
- Board Source
  www.boardsource.org
- Charity Navigator
  www.charitynavigator.org
- Governance Matters
  www.governancematters.com
- Guidestar
  www.guidestar.org
- Independent Sector
  www.independentsector.org
- Internet Nonprofit Center
  www.nonprofits.org
- IRS Exempt Organizations
  www.irs.gov/charities
- National Association of Attorneys General
  www.naag.org
- National Association of State Charity Officials
  www.nasconet.org
- National Council of Nonprofits
  www.councilofnonprofits.org
- Network for Good
  www1.networkforgood.org
- New York State Attorney General
  www.charitiesnys.com
- OMB Watch
  www.ombwatch.org
- Standards for Excellence Institute
  www.standardsforexcellenceinstitute.org

impact—from "How much money did we raise?" to "How much impact did we have on our community?" In his initial statement to the Senate committee, Gallagher said:

> The ultimate measure of success is whether family violence rates have gone down and whether there is more affordable housing. And fund-raising is [just] part of making that happen. When you are asking people to contribute, you're asking for an investment in your mission. And like a for-profit business, you are then accountable to your investors, not just for keeping good books, but for creating value and offering a concrete return. For those of us in human development, that means efforts that lead to measurable improvements in people's lives. In other words, the organizations that produce the greatest results should grow and be rewarded. Those that do not should be forced to change or go out of business. The American public doesn't give us money just because our operations are clean. Why they really give us money is because they want to make a difference.[26]

As a result of the new mission, UWW required local affiliates to provide the national headquarters with annual financial reports and to embrace the revised standards of excellence developed by more than 200 United Way employees, volunteers, and consultants. Of interest is the fact that these standards were not mandatory but were presented as guidelines, giving chapters suggestions for how they might revise their local strategies. The standards urged the affiliates to identify community problems, raise money to solve them, and demonstrate measurable progress toward their goals by adopting a code of ethics that included an annual independent financial audit. The hope was that by adopting these guidelines, the chapters would be able to provide tangible proof to donors, especially wealthy contributors, that the United Way chapters and the charities they support were making a difference (see Exhibit 6).[27]

Local United Ways faced a continual challenge, with inevitable tension between the diverse constituencies they served: Were their primary "customers" the donors who contributed needed funds or the agencies that received these charitable donations? Or should the local United Way act as a networking institution, providing mechanisms for discussion of local problems and community-service needs? Or, going even further, should it act as an activist organization, leading the way with comprehensive community planning, advocating major public policy, and redistributing resources as needed? Kirsten Gronbjerg, of the Center on Philanthropy, Indiana University, stated, "The activist role is very difficult for United Ways to play, because they need to satisfy diverse constituency groups and therefore avoid conflict. As they become more donor-driven institutions, they will be less able to take an activist approach just when such an approach is sorely needed."[28]

In addition, the local United Ways needed to maintain their internal consensus, providing a coherent and inspiring vision for their mainly volunteer workforce while managing potential conflicts and sharing resources with other United Way chapters in their geographic areas. The problem of potentially scarce resources and the fact that traditional donor organizations were either consolidating their physical operations or leaving an area meant that the traditional broad base of business and industry was shrinking. This and other factors prompted the consolidation of several United Ways into more regional organizations. This

EXHIBIT 6 United Way New Standards of Excellence

Standards of Excellence, a comprehensive description of benchmark standards and best practices: Developed in conjunction with United Way executives, staff, and volunteers throughout the country, the standards are designed to enhance the effectiveness of the 1,350 United Way affiliates.

- **Introduction to the Standards of Excellence.** Spanning more than 100 pages, the new standards provide highly detailed descriptions regarding five key areas of operation.

- **Community Engagement and Vision.** Working with formal and informal leaders to develop a shared vision and goals for a community, including the identification of priority issues affecting the overall well-being of its citizens.

- **Impact Strategies, Resources, and Results.** Creating "impact strategies" that address the root causes and barriers of a community's priority issues; mobilizing essential assets such as people, knowledge, relationships, technology, and money; effectively implementing impact strategies; and evaluating the effectiveness of impact strategies in fostering continuous improvement.

- **Relationship Building and Brand Management.** Developing, maintaining, and growing relationships with individuals and organizations in order to attract and sustain essential assets.

- **Organizational Leadership and Governance.** Garnering trust, legitimacy, and support of the United Way in local communities through leadership and overall management.

- **Operations.** Providing efficient and cost-effective systems, policies, and processes that enable the fulfillment of the United Way's mission, while ensuring the highest levels of transparency and accountability.

Source: United Way of America, *http://liveunited.org/*.

movement meant potential savings and operational efficiencies from sharing marketing, financial management, and information technology functions.[29] However, it also meant a possible diffusion of mission over a larger community, with a potential loss of focus, and more challenges in communicating this mission and marketing services to a more diverse donor and recipient base. In 2009, 21 nonprofit groups in the Washington, D.C., area suspended their memberships in United Way and joined a new organization, Community1st. These groups were lured away from United Way by a promise of "lower overhead costs, easily customized fund-raising campaigns, and fewer restrictions on where donors' money is directed."[30]

The ongoing issues faced by United Way in its more than 120-year history had remained constant. Consider this: During the holiday season, "when local United Way drives take place almost everywhere, likely as not questions will arise about what United Way is up to, how well it is doing what it claims to do, and for that matter, whether United Way is the best way for you to do your charitable giving."[31] This statement was written in 1977, yet it could still have applied in 2015. Concerns about United Way seemed timeless, and Brian Gallagher was only one in a long line of CEOs determined to answer the critics once and for all.

ENDNOTES

1. Stacey D. Stewart. 2014. *Huffington Post,* December 2.
2. National Philanthropic Trust. Undated. Charitable giving statistics. *www.nptrust.org/philanthropic-resources/charitable-giving-statistics/.*
3. Tim Rich. 2014. *Columbia Daily Tribune,* December 2.
4. Riley, C. 2011. America's wealthy turn less charitable. *CNN Money,* February 6, *money.cnn.com/2011/02/06/news/economy/charity_gifts/index.htm*; and Zongker, B. 2010. Top charities see decrease in donations. *Associated Press,* October 18, *www.tulsaworld.com.*
5. United Way. 2012 annual report.
6. Barrett, W. P. 2006. United Way's new way. *Forbes.com,* January 16, *www.forbes.com.*
7. Barton, N., & Hall, H. 2006. A year of big gains. *Chronicle of Philanthropy,* October 26, *philanthropy.com/article/A-Year-of-Big-Gains/54908/.*
8. Barrett, op. cit.
9. Princeton Survey Research Associates. 2001. Executive summary of the Donor Expectations Survey, conducted in the spring of 2001. As reported by Give.org BBB Wise Giving Alliance, *www.give.org.*
10. Suchman, M. 1995. Managing legitimacy: Strategic and institutional approaches. *Academy of Management Review,* 20: 571–610.
11. From the United Way website, *liveunited.org.*
12. Graddy-Gamel, A. 2007. Review of *Contesting Community: The Transformation of Workplace Charity,* by Emily Barman (2006: Stanford University Press). *Philanthropy News Digest,* February 27, *foundationcenter.org/pnd/offtheshelf/ots_print.jhtml?id=171600045.*
13. Barton & Hall, op. cit.
14. Charitable giving diversifies. 2006. *Forbes* (video report), December 13, *www.forbes.com.*
15. Porter, M. E., & Kramer, M. R. 1999. Philanthropy's new agenda: Creating value. *Harvard Business Review,* 77(6): 121–130.
16. United Way ex-head sentenced to 7 years in prison for fraud. 1995. *New York Times,* June 23: B2.
17. Gibelman, M., & Gelman, S. R. 2004. A loss of credibility: Patterns of wrongdoing among nongovernmental organizations. *International Journal of Voluntary and Nonprofit Organizations,* 15(4): 355–381. This article provides a content analysis of worldwide NGO scandals from 2001 to 2004. Although the United States is overrepresented, it is certainly not alone in the world for incidents of wrongdoing.
18. Investigation finds former United Way of NYC CEO improperly diverted funds. 2006. *Philanthropy News Digest,* April 17, *foundationcenter.org/pnd/news/story_print.jhtml?id=140000004.*
19. Gibelman & Gelman, op. cit.
20. Sinclair, M. 2002. William Aramony is back on the streets. *NonProfit Times,* March 1.
21. Jansen, P., & Kilpatrick, A. 2004. The dynamic nonprofit board. *McKinsey Quarterly,* 2: 72–81.
22. Kelley, C., & Anderson, S. 2006. Advising nonprofit organizations. *CPA Journal,* 76(8): 20–26.
23. McRay, G. 2009. Bad seeds—Why the ACORN scandal matters to other nonprofits. *Foundation Group,* September 16, *www.501c3.org/blog/acorn-scandel-matters-to-nonprofits/.*
24. Herzlinger, R. 1996. Can public trust in nonprofits and governments be restored? *Harvard Business Review,* March–April: 97–107.
25. Gibelman, & Gelman, op. cit.
26. Gallagher, B. 2005. Statement of Brian A. Gallagher, president and CEO United Way of America, before United States Senate Committee on Finance. *liveunited.org,* April 5: 1.
27. Blum, D. E. 2005. Held to a new standard. *Chronicle of Philanthropy,* 17(13).
28. The Aspen Institute. 2002. United Way system at the crossroads: Valuable lessons from the United Way of Chicago. *Snapshots: Research Highlights from the Nonprofit Sector Research Fund,* November/December, no. 26.
29. Gosier, C. 2007. 3 chapters of United Way to combine. *Knight Ridder Tribune Business News,* February 23.
30. Greenwell, M. 2009. 21 regional nonprofits withdraw from United Way. *Washington Post,* April 29, *www.washingtonpost.com/wp-dyn/content/article/2009/04/28/AR2009042803701.html.*
31. United Way: Are the criticisms fair? 1977. *Changing Times,* October: 29.

CASES

CASE 19

THE GLOBAL CASINO INDUSTRY*

For well over 50 years, the casino business had been on a roll, on its way to becoming a $160 billion–a-year global industry. For much of that period, the United States had been leading the charge, accounting for nearly half of the global gambling revenues as recently as 2010. Most of these revenues came from Las Vegas and Atlantic City, which had become magnets for gamblers from around the world. Over the last couple of decades, these two locations accounted for almost one-third of the total revenues generated by all forms of casinos throughout the U.S.

Over the past decade, Las Vegas and Atlantic City had to deal with increased competition from other locations, as casinos opened in a number of states that legalized gambling in order to generate more tax revenues and promote tourism. Over a dozen states now generate substantial revenue from their casinos, many of which have opened on waterfronts such as rivers and lakes. When combined with Native American casinos, gambling revenues in other parts of the U.S. now exceed the amount that is generated by casinos in Las Vegas and Atlantic City.

Nevertheless, casinos in Las Vegas and Atlantic City had been able to rely upon gamblers who came from all over the world, as far away as China. Although casinos had operated for a long time in various locations in Europe and the Caribbean, no single location was able to compete with Las Vegas or Atlantic City. Las Vegas, in particular, offered more than two-dozen large casinos on its strip that had spent lavishly to differentiate themselves from all others. Luxor's pyramids and columns evoke ancient Egypt, Mandalay Bay borrowed looks from the Pacific Rim, and the Venetian's plaza and canals re-created the Italian city.

However, the dominance of Las Vegas and Atlantic City in the global market was challenged by the development of several casinos along a strip in the former Portuguese colony of Macau. Casinos had existed in Macau for decades, but they had basically served a local population. After a monopoly on casinos by a single local tycoon was terminated in 2002, there was a proliferation of mega-sized high-end casinos, developed and managed by some of the world's largest casino operators, including those from Las Vegas. This allowed Macau to grow from a tiny backwater territory to a booming center of gambling, with casinos generating over $40 billion, more than six times the revenue of the Las Vegas strip (see Exhibit 1).

More recently, the growth of casinos spread to other locations across the Asia-Pacific region. Singapore managed to generate substantial revenues from its two new casinos; casinos were being developed in the Philippines on a large plot overlooking Manila Bay; and efforts were under way to legalize casinos in Japan and build them in bustling Tokyo. All of these new locations were hoping to grab a share of the gambling revenues that had been generated by casinos in places such as Las Vegas and Macau.

Riding an American Wave

Although some form of gambling existed in the U.S. since colonial times, the recent advent of casinos stemmed from the legalization of gaming in Nevada in 1931. For many years, this was the only state in which casinos were allowed. After New Jersey passed laws in 1976 to allow gambling in Atlantic City, the large population on the east coast had easier access to casinos. However, the further growth of casinos was possible only since 1988, as more and more states legalized the operation of casinos because of the tax revenues that they could generate.

As casinos spread across the U.S., there was a growing tendency to regard casino gambling as an acceptable form of entertainment for a night out. A large part of the growth in casino revenues came from the growing popularity of slot machines. Coin-operated slot machines typically accounted for almost two-thirds of all casino gaming revenues. A major reason for their popularity was that it was

EXHIBIT 1 Top Casino Revenue Locations, 2014 ($ billions)

Location	Revenue
Macau	$48.0
United States	35.0*
Singapore	6.0
Australia	4.2
South Korea	2.0
Malaysia	1.8
Philippines	1.8

*$6.5 billion comes from Las Vegas.

Source: Morgan Stanley.

---

* Case prepared by Jamal Shamsie, Michigan State University, with the assistance of Professor Alan B. Eisner, Pace University. Material has been drawn from published sources to be used for purposes of class discussion. Copyright © 2015 Jamal Shamsie and Alan B. Eisner.

easier for prospective gamblers to operate a slot machine than to understand the nuances of various table games.

For the most part, casinos in Las Vegas and Atlantic City had been trying to draw gamblers over the years by developing extravagant new properties. The most ambitious new development in Las Vegas was MGM Mirage's City Center, an $8.5 billion minicity spread over 67 acres that includes luxury hotels, condominium units, restaurants, and shops. Even some of the older properties underwent extensive renovation; for example, Caesars Palace added a new Colosseum and a new Roman Plaza. Atlantic City welcomed the much-ballyhooed opening of the $2.4 billion Revel Hotel built on 20 acres of beachfront. It followed the opening several years earlier of another lavish resort, the Borgata Hotel, which offered amenities such as penthouse spas and tropical indoor pools.

Aside from ramping up the appeal of their particular properties, most casinos offered incentives to keep their customers from moving to competing casinos. These incentives could be particularly helpful in retaining the "high rollers" who came often and spent large amounts of money. Casinos also tried to maintain their business by providing complimentary rooms, food, beverages, shows, and other perks that were worth billions of dollars each year. Gamblers also earned various types of rewards through the loyalty programs that were offered by the casinos, with the specific rewards tied to the amount that the gamblers bet on the slot machines and at the tables.

Some of the larger casinos in the U.S. tried to fend off competition by growing through mergers and acquisitions. In 2004, Harrah's announced that it was buying casino rival Caesars, thus becoming the nation's leading operator of casinos, with several properties in both Las Vegas and Atlantic City. This deal came just a month after MGM Mirage had stated that it was buying the Mandalay Resort Group, enabling MGM Mirage to double the number of casinos it held on the Las Vegas strip. Firms that owned several casinos could pitch each of their properties to a different market and allow all of their customers to earn rewards on the firm's loyalty program by gambling at any of its properties.

Exploiting the Chinese Market

Though gambling had been legal for over a century in Macau, which was a former Portuguese territory, its casinos were typically small and seedy. In part, this was due to the monopoly on gambling in the territory that was held by Stanley Ho, a local tycoon. However, this began to change in 2002, as the liberalization of casino licensing led to the development of new casinos by some of the world's largest casino operators, including many of the U.S. firms that wanted to find markets outside Las Vegas. "The Las Vegas of the Far East" is how Sheldon Adelson, head of Las Vegas Sands, described the recent development of Macau.

As more and more casinos began to open, Macau grew explosively, with a tripling of casinos from the dozen or so that existed before 2002. Many were situated on the Cotai Strip, land that was once a stretch of water between the islands of Coloane and Taipa. Las Vegas–based firms such as Sands and Wynn were plowing billions of dollars into new casinos there. Sands, which already had a super-sized version of the Las Vegas–based Venetian with a Grand Canal and a Rialto Bridge, was adding a complex called the Parisian with a version of the Eiffel Tower. Even locally based Sociedade de Jogos de Macau was opening a $3.9 billion complex that would feature three hotels, including one modeled on the Palace of Versailles.

Macau's dramatic rise in the casino business owed much to a collision of geography and history. Despite the Chinese love of gambling, the leaders in Beijing had long forbidden casinos on the mainland. The government did, however, let the casinos continue to operate in Macau after the Portuguese handed over sovereignty in 1999. Like Hong Kong, Macau retained a degree of legal autonomy and was only a few hours' flying time or less from a billion potential gamblers in China. "We sit next to the biggest market in the world," said Edward M. Tracy, chief executive of the Hong Kong–based subsidiary of Las Vegas Sands. "It's one billion more people than the U.S."[1]

In fact, Macau was attracting a growing number of visitors from mainland China. Nearly 20 million people, or one in five Chinese, who ventured outside mainland China in a recent year went to Macau to gamble. Many came from neighboring Guangdong province, usually on day trips. But bigger spenders who came from as far away as Beijing clearly played an important role in fueling Macau's growth. These high rollers would spend as much as $10 million on gambling in a single trip. They accounted for up to 65 percent of the revenues for Macau's larger casinos (see Exhibit 2).

Even as Macau had shown remarkable growth over the last decade, its prospects for the future remained quite bright. Analysts at securities firms forecast that gambling revenue from Macau casinos could easily reach $80 billion by 2018. In part, this rise would be driven by an increase in visitors from mainland China because of rising affluence and improved transportation. China had increased the capacity of roads and high-speed trains to the territory, providing access for more visitors. Visitors from all over the world would also have better access because of a series of bridges that would connect Macau with Hong Kong's huge international airport.

EXHIBIT 2 Financials of Macau Casinos, 2014

	Share of Revenues	Share of Profits
High rollers	63%	35%
Low rollers	31	52

Source: Deutsche Bank.

Spreading across Asia

The growth of gambling revenues in Macau led countries across the Asia-Pacific region to abandon their hostilities to gambling and encourage the development of casinos. Casinos were developing in several countries, including Singapore, Philippines, Malaysia, South Korea, and Australia, and were likely to take off soon in other places such as Japan, Vietnam, Taiwan, and Sri Lanka. A group of investors even made a deal to open a casino near Vladivostok in Russia's Far East. They claimed that it took less time for a high roller in Beijing to fly there than to steamy Macau.

Singapore, in particular, was extremely successful with its two new up-market casinos. In 2010, the island state had issued permits to two large casino operators: The Marina Bay Sands was part of the Las Vegas–based Sands casino operations, and Resorts World Sentosa was run by Malaysia's Genting group. Even though Singapore limited the size of its casinos and discouraged locals from visiting them, they earned more than $6 billion, almost as much as all of the casinos on the Las Vegas strip.

Among the other contenders, Philippines looked as if it was poised to claim a substantial share of global casino revenues. Malaysia-based casino giant Genting kick-started Manila's casino craze when it opened Resorts World Manila opposite the capital's main airport in 2009. The opening of the new casino represented a departure from the older smoke-filled gambling dens and lured other casinos. Four new casinos were developed on a large plot overlooking Manila Bay. The first of these, Solaire Resort and Casino, is a sleek, plate-glass building with a suitably flashy interior created by Paul Steelman, a casino designer from Las Vegas.

Efforts were also under way to boost gambling in Japan by getting the government to lift its ban on casinos. At the time, gambling was confined to seedy places such as Kabukicho, a 1-kilometer block in Tokyo. However, the prime minister, Sinzo Abe, was likely to approve legalization of casinos as a way to boost Japan's sluggish growth. Proponents of casinos argued that they would boost the country's earnings from foreign tourists and deliver a tax windfall to the heavily indebted government. A Japanese business magazine argued that the country was being left behind as neighboring countries rushed to build upscale casinos with luxury hotels, designer shops, and cultural attractions.

The casino operators that were developing casinos all over the region were hoping that they could lure Chinese high rollers away from Macau. A Chinese businessman who visited Macau's casinos stated that the new Chinese leadership's crackdown on official corruption and flaunting of wealth would drive clients to other locations. "Beijing has too many cameras watching us in Macau," he explained.[2] Solaire, which recently opened in Manila, was willing to send a private jet to pick up big spenders from all across China. "If we can get 7% of Macau business to come here," said the casino's chief operating officer, "then we all achieve our goals for the market."[3]

Moving beyond Gambling

Over the last couple of decades, Las Vegas managed to move beyond gambling and offer visitors many choices for fine dining, great shopping, and top-notch entertainment. This allowed most of its higher-end casinos to generate revenues from offering a wide selection of activities apart from gambling. At MGM Mirage, for example, revenue from nongaming activities typically accounted for almost 60 percent of net revenue in recent years. During the 1990s, Las Vegas had tried to become more receptive to families, with attractions such as circus performances, animal reserves, and pirate battles. But the city was very successful with its recent return to its sinful roots, with a stronger focus on topless shows, hot nightclubs, and other adult offerings that were highlighted by the new advertising slogan "What happens in Vegas, stays in Vegas."

By comparison, visitors were drawn to Atlantic City mostly because of gambling. Although it offered a beach and a boardwalk, along which its dozen large casino hotels were lined, the city was never able to develop itself as a beach resort. The opening of the much-ballyhooed Revel a few years ago was part of a drive to make Atlantic City much more competitive with Las Vegas. But it failed to replicate the success of the Borgota Hotel, the major resort that had opened there in 2003. The failure to develop other forms of entertainment led to the closing of several big casinos, including the Revel, as casinos that opened in several neighboring states drew gamblers away from Atlantic City.

Macau had also been trying to reduce its dependence on gaming. By 2014, gambling revenues at its casinos accounted for almost four-fifths of the territory's economy. But these revenues began to decline, in part because of China's economic slowdown. Another factor was the country's sweeping crackdown on corruption. Many of the high rollers from the mainland were gambling with the proceeds of shady deals, which were now subject to greater scrutiny. This was forcing the casinos to shift their focus away from the older, hard-core gamblers, who came primarily to gamble, and toward younger, passionate gamblers, who saw gambling as only one part of their Macau experience.

The newer casinos offered more nongambling activities by including restaurants, shops, cinemas, spas, and even concert arenas. The shops inside Sands casinos in Macau, for example, generated as much as $2 billion of revenues. Edward Tracy, the head of Sands China, also brought in shows ranging from boxing matches to Bollywood award ceremonies. One of the newly opened casinos even had an enormous "fortune diamond" that emerged from a fountain every half hour to the delight of photo-snapping onlookers. "There's an opportunity for Macau to attract a new breed of customer, one that is looking for a more holistic experience," said Aaron Fischer, a gambling analyst at a brokerage firm.[4]

Macau was trying to overcome one of the most serious limitations of its small land area—just under 30 square kilometers—by expanding onto the thinly populated island of Hengqin. The island, three times the size of Macau, had been declared a special economic zone by Chinese officials so that it could develop accommodation and entertainment that would support Macau's aspirations for mass-market tourism. "Hengqin is the game changer for Macau," insists Sands China head Tracy.[5]

Gambling on the Future

In spite of growing competition from many other locations, Las Vegas and Atlantic City were fighting for visitors to come for various forms of entertainment in addition to gambling. Casinos were offering attractive restaurants, clubs, stores, and concerts and shows. "I think we're seeing a shift away from Las Vegas as the only gaming destination," said Stephen P. A. Brown from UNLV. "But it is holding up as a tourist destination."[6] Genting, the Malaysian gaming group, recently took over the site of the Echelon, which was abandoned because of lack of funds during the recession. Genting intended to develop a stronger presence in the U.S. market by building one of the biggest new resorts in Las Vegas, with a 3,500-room hotel and 175,000 feet of gambling space.

Casino operators in Macau were similarly continuing to place their bets on gambling, even as competition grew in neighboring countries. Eight new casino complexes, all of which would also offer many forms of entertainment, were in the works, promising to almost double the supply of hotel rooms on the strip. Galaxy Entertainment, a local casino firm, claimed that when its $7.7 billion expansion was finished, its already-huge Macau casino would be bigger than the Pentagon. Another local operator, SJM, developed a huge new resort on the Cotai strip that included a hotel designed by Versace, an Italian luxury-fashion house.

As gambling spread outside the United States, particularly to countries in the Asia-Pacific region, casinos were targeting visitors to come for their many offerings, including gambling. Their emphasis was shifting away from older customers, who came mainly for high-stakes gambling, and to younger customers, who enjoyed gambling but were also interested in eating, drinking, shopping, and taking in shows. "Gambling won't go out of fashion. It will just become part of a wider offering," said Ian M. Coughlan, president of Wynn Macau. "We've not really tapped all the demand that exists—we're far from it."[7]

ENDNOTES

1. Bettina Wassener. A hot streak for Macau. *New York Times,* March 26, 2014, p. B7.
2. The rise of the low rollers. *The Economist,* September 7, 2013, p. 63.
3. Ibid., p. 64.
4. Chris Horton. All in on gambling? Not for Macau. *International New York Times,* December 20–21, 2014, p. 1.
5. The rise of the low rollers, op. cit., p. 64.
6. Adam Nagourney. Las Vegas bounces back, with caveats. *International New York Times,* August 2, 2013.
7. Wassener, op. cit.

CASE 20

EBAY*

eBay CEO John Donahoe admitted, "2015 will be another challenging year, and we expect eBay's performance to soften further before we see stabilization and improvement."[1]

The year 2015 was a difficult one for eBay's Marketplaces unit due to a number of factors. First, a security-related password reset and web search engine optimization (SEO) changes heavily impacted customer traffic. eBay's loyal customers returned following the password changes, but the more occasional customers did not return as quickly as expected. Further, the SEO changes significantly diminished eBay's presence in natural search results, which impacted new-user growth. Second, a stronger dollar impacted eBay's cross-border trade, depressing U.S. exports and affecting the financial results for North America. With traffic and sales slowing over the years, eBay had tried to reposition its well-known auction site from being an online yard sale to being a trendy e-retailer. But the company faced intense competition from online giants like Amazon and Google and relative newcomers like Etsy, as well as traditional brick-and-mortar retailers like Walmart, Staples, and Home Depot, which were now aggressively promoting their online retail sites. The year also brought in considerable pressure from Carl Icahn, an activist investor. Icahn had challenged the board by increasing his stake in the company and pressuring it to spin off its noncore businesses. The company finally relented and agreed to spin off its PayPal and Enterprise businesses. It invested much time and resources in repurchasing shares to counter Icahn's influence (see the 2014 tax burden and cash outflow in Exhibits 1 and 3, respectively). It finally settled for an agreement to allow one of Icahn's representatives to join the board of directors. Finally, as eBay prepared itself for the split with PayPal in the second half of 2015, it announced that it was laying off 7 percent of its workforce, with many of the cuts coming from its legacy Marketplaces business. Further, the upcoming split would provide PayPal with $5 billion in cash and no debt but would leave eBay with $7.6 billion in debt and only $2 billion in net cash.

The online auction business that had shaken up the world of e-commerce when it was first launched nearly two decades ago was now clearly struggling. At the 2014 year-end earnings call, eBay CFO Bob Swan admitted: "Things will get worse in the first half of 2015 before they get better."[2] Then, in early 2015, president and CEO John Donahoe disclosed a substantial deal with the Securities and Exchange Commission (SEC). He had exercised his option to purchase 129,446 shares of the firm, priced at $53 per share. The substantial liquidation added to speculation that even senior management was beginning to doubt the future of the company.

Clearly, 2015 was going to be a critical year for eBay. There were many cooks in the kitchen (senior management, board of directors, activist investors, and potential acquirers) with different views of what was right for the company. Only time would tell which option would prove right for the company and increase shareholder value over the long term. Or would eBay be better off offering itself for sale to a bidder?

A Successful Past

Since its inception in 1995, eBay had enjoyed strong revenue growth and been a dominant player in the online auction industry. Within two decades, the company had grown considerably, and it had a net income of $3.5 billion before taxes and a net revenue of $17.9 billion in 2014 (see Exhibits 1, 2, and 3).

eBay's founder, Pierre Omidyar, envisioned a community built on commerce, sustained by trust, and inspired by opportunity. The company's mission was to "enable individual self-empowerment on a global scale" and employ "business as a tool for social good." Omidyar cited "trust between strangers" as the social impact tied to eBay's ability to remain profitable.

The company's unique business model united buyers and sellers in an online marketplace. eBay enabled e-commerce at multiple levels (local, national, and international) through an array of websites, including eBay Marketplaces, PayPal, Rent.com, Shopping.com, and eBay Style. The company's range of products and services evolved from collectibles to household products, customer services, automobiles, and the mobile industry. The variety of products attracted a range of users that included students, small businesses, independent sellers, major corporations, and government agencies.

Despite eBay's outstanding growth performance, the company still faced a number of challenges in both domestic and international markets. The low entry barriers in the online

---

* This case was prepared by Professor Alan B. Eisner and graduate students Dev Das, David J. Morates, and Shruti Shrestha of Pace University. This case was solely based on library research and was developed for class discussion rather than to illustrate either effective or ineffective handling of an administrative situation. Copyright © 2015 Alan B. Eisner.

EXHIBIT 1 Income Statements ($ millions, except per-share amounts)

	Year Ended December 31		
	2014	2013	2012
Net revenues	$17,902	$16,047	$14,072
Cost of net revenues	5,732	5,036	4,216
Gross profit	12,170	11,011	9,856
Operating expenses:			
Sales and marketing	3,587	3,060	2,913
Product development	2,000	1,768	1,573
General and administrative	1,843	1,703	1,567
Provision for transaction and loan losses	958	791	580
Amortization of acquired intangible assets	268	318	335
Total operating expenses	8,656	7,640	6,968
Income from operations	3,514	3,371	2,888
Interest and other, net	17	95	196
Income before income taxes	3,531	3,466	3,084
Provision for income taxes	(3,485)	(610)	(475)
Net income	$ 46	$ 2,856	$ 2,609
Net income per share:			
Basic	$0.04	$2.20	$2.02
Diluted	$0.04	$2.18	$1.99
Weighted-average shares:			
Basic	1,251	1,295	1,292
Diluted	1,262	1,313	1,313

Source: eBay SEC filings.

marketplace attracted a number of large dot-com competitors, including Amazon, Yahoo/Taobao, Google/Overstock, and Etsy. Historically, eBay had acquired other online competitors, such as StubHub (tickets), but established players such as Yahoo, Google, and Amazon posed a major threat to eBay's market share and ability to sustain profitability. Still, eBay's top management felt that the company would end up as a specialty business, an idea suggesting that it would face little threat from these major competitors. The company had no plans for further big acquisitions but intended to expand and identify synergies within existing business lines.

eBay did, however, acknowledge its inability to grow and compete in certain international markets. The company had created localized sites in 24 countries and established a presence in Latin America through its investment in MercadoLibre.com. However, eBay's numerous attempts to penetrate the Asia-Pacific market, specifically China and Japan, ended in failure, with the company pulling out of Japan and buying out Chinese start-up Eachnet, essentially canceling years of invested work. According to many analysts, the company's recent interest in its South Korean rival Gmarket Inc. and its joint venture with Beijing-based Tom Online were further indications that eBay couldn't compete in Asia-Pacific countries. To remain successful and enjoy the same financial performance as it had in the past, eBay needed to develop an effective strategy to compete in major Asian markets and mitigate the risk of existing local competitors.

eBay's overall strategy had traditionally comprised three primary components: products, sense of community,

EXHIBIT 2 Balance Sheet ($ millions, except per-share amounts)

	Year End	
	December 31, 2014	December 31, 2013
Assets		
Current assets:		
Cash and cash equivalents	$ 6,328	$ 4,494
Short-term investments	3,770	4,531
Accounts receivable, net	797	899
Loans and interest receivable, net	3,600	2,789
Funds receivable and customer accounts	10,545	9,260
Other current assets	1,491	1,310
Total current assets	26,531	23,283
Long-term investments	5,777	4,971
Property and equipment, net	2,902	2,760
Goodwill	9,094	9,267
Intangible assets, net	564	941
Other assets	264	266
Total assets	$ 45,132	$41,488
Liabilities and Stockholders' Equity		
Current liabilities:		
Short-term debt	$ 850	$ 6
Accounts payable	401	309
Funds payable and amounts due to customers	10,545	9,260
Accrued expenses and other current liabilities	5,393	2,799
Deferred revenue	188	158
Income taxes payable	154	107
Total current liabilities	17,531	12,639
Deferred and other tax liabilities, net	792	841
Long-term debt	6,777	4,117
Other liabilities	126	244
Total liabilities	25,226	17,841
Commitments and contingencies		
Stockholders' equity:		
Common stock, $0.001 par value; 3,580 shares authorized; 1,224 and 1,294 shares outstanding	2	2
Additional paid-in capital	13,887	13,031
Treasury stock at cost, 384 and 296 shares	(14,054)	(9,396)
Retained earnings	18,900	18,854
Accumulated other comprehensive income	1,171	1,156
Total stockholders' equity	19,906	23,647
Total liabilities and stockholders' equity	$ 45,132	$41,488

Source: eBay SEC filings.

EXHIBIT 3 Cash Flow Statement ($ millions)

	Year Ended December 31		
	2014	2013	2012
Cash Flows from Operating Activities			
Net income	$ 46	$2,856	$2,609
Adjustments:			
Provision for transaction and loan losses	958	791	580
Depreciation and amortization	1,490	1,400	1,200
Stock-based compensation	675	609	488
Deferred income taxes	2,808	(31)	(35)
Excess tax benefits from stock-based compensation	(115)	(201)	(130)
Gain on sale of equity investments	—	(75)	—
Gain on divestiture of businesses	—	—	(118)
Accounts receivable	16	(123)	(207)
Other current assets	(183)	(378)	(310)
Other noncurrent assets	14	(108)	(96)
Accounts payable	87	7	(16)
Accrued expenses and other liabilities	(347)	(3)	(164)
Deferred revenue	30	20	28
Income taxes payable and other tax liabilities	198	231	9
Net cash provided by operating activities	5,677	4,995	3,838
Purchases of property and equipment	(1,271)	(1,250)	(1,257)
Changes in principal loans receivable, net	(1,020)	(794)	(727)
Purchases of investments	(8,834)	(7,505)	(3,128)
Maturities and sales of investments	8,524	3,943	1,421
Acquisitions, net of cash acquired	(59)	(869)	(143)
Repayment of note receivable and sale of related equity investments	—	485	—
Proceeds from divested business, net of cash disposed	—	—	144
Other	(13)	(22)	(73)
Net cash used in investing activities	(2,673)	(6,012)	(3,763)
Proceeds from issuance of common stock	300	437	483
Repurchases of common stock	(4,658)	(1,343)	(898)
Excess tax benefits from stock-based compensation	115	201	130
Tax withholdings related to net share settlements of restricted stock awards and units	(252)	(267)	(186)
Proceeds from issuance of long-term debt, net	3,482	—	2,976

continued

EXHIBIT 3 Continued

	Year Ended December 31		
	2014	2013	2012
Repayments under commercial paper program	—	—	(550)
Repayment of debt	—	(400)	—
Funds receivable and customer accounts, net	(1,285)	(1,149)	(4,126)
Funds payable and amounts due to customers, net	1,285	1,149	4,126
Other	(9)	18	(4)
Net cash (used in) provided by financing activities	(1,022)	(1,354)	1,951
Effect of exchange rate changes on cash and cash equivalents	(148)	48	100
Net increase (decrease) in cash and cash equivalents	1,834	(2,323)	2,126
Cash and cash equivalents at beginning of period	4,494	6,817	4,691
Cash and cash equivalents at end of period	$6,328	$4,494	$6,817
Cash paid for interest	$ 99	$ 99	$ 15
Cash paid for income taxes	$ 343	$ 466	$ 789

Source: eBay SEC filings.

and aggressive expansion. All three components evolved around the various geographic and specialty platforms the company introduced.

Product Categories

eBay had an array of product categories and trading platforms that offered a range of pricing formats, such as fixed pricing. Relatively new for the company, the fixed-price format allowed eBay to compete directly with major competitors such as Amazon.com and penetrate new market space. Before fixed pricing, selling prices were solely determined by the highest auction bid, and this took days or weeks, depending on the length of the auction. eBay's different trading platforms also offered distinct services and target-specific market niches, which allowed eBay to broaden its customer base. The platforms included:

- *PayPal:* Founded in 1998 and acquired by eBay in 2002, PayPal enabled individuals to securely send payments quickly and easily online. PayPal was considered the global leader in online payments, with tens of millions of registered users. In 2011 PayPal's president, Scott Thompson, expected revenue to double, reaching $6 billion to $7 billion, by 2013. He also predicted that 75 to 80 percent of eBay transactions would be done through PayPal by 2013, up from 69 percent in 2010.[3] However, in 2014, the company decided it was more prudent to spin off its PayPal business as a separate company. The spin-off was being contemplated for the end of 2015.[4]

- *Online classifieds:* By 2009, eBay had the world's leading portfolio of online classified sites, including Kijiji, Intoko, Gumtree, LoQUo.com, Marktplaats.nl, and mobile.de. CEO John Donahoe said, "We are the global leader in classifieds, with top positions in Canada, Australia, Germany, Japan and the United Kingdom, and sites in more than 1,000 cities across 20 countries."[5]

- *Shopping.com:* With thousands of merchants and millions of products and reviews, Shopping.com empowered consumers to make informed choices, which drove value for merchants. In 2013, it was rebranded as the eBay Commerce Network.

- *Stubhub.com:* StubHub was an online marketplace for selling and purchasing tickets for sports events, concerts, and other live entertainment events.

- *eBay Express:* eBay Express behaved like a standard Internet shopping site but gave sellers access to over 200 million buyers worldwide. Sellers could design product categories within minutes, and buyers could purchase from multiple sellers by using a single shopping cart.

- *eBay Motors:* This specialty site was considered the largest marketplace for automobile buyers and sellers.

Buyers could purchase anything from automobile parts to new or antique vehicles.

- *Skype:* Acquired by eBay in October 2005, Skype was the world's fastest-growing online communication solution, allowing free video and audio communication between users of Skype software. By November 2009, Skype connected more than 480 million registered users.[6] eBay's acquisition of Skype was expected to enhance the customer experience by improving communication between buyers and sellers. In November 2009, however, eBay sold Skype to a group led by Silver Lake Partners, a private equity firm in Silicon Valley, which eventually sold the entity to Microsoft.

Sense of Community

The underlying key to all eBay sites and trading platforms was creating trust between sellers and buyers. The company created "community values," and this was why eBay users were willing to send money to strangers across the country. The Feedback Forum was created in February 1996 and encouraged users to post comments about trading partners. Originally, Omidyar had handled disputes between buyers and sellers via email by putting the disputing parties in touch with each other to resolve the issue themselves. He soon realized that an open forum in which users could post opinions and feedback about one another would create the trust and sense of community the site required. Buyers and sellers were encouraged to post comments (positive, negative, or neutral) about each other at the completion of each transaction. The individual feedback was recorded and amended to a user profile, which ultimately established a rating and reputation for each buyer and seller. eBay users could view this information before engaging in a transaction. The company believed that the Feedback Forum was critical for creating initial user acceptance for purchasing and selling over the Internet and that it contributed more than anything else to eBay's success.

Aggressive Expansion

To compete effectively and create a global trading platform, eBay continued to develop in U.S. and international markets that utilized the Internet. With intense competition in the online auction industry, eBay aimed to increase its market share and revenue through acquisitions and partnerships in related and unrelated businesses. For example:

- In June 2000 eBay acquired Half.com for $318 million.
- In August 2001 eBay acquired MercadoLibre, Lokau, and iBazar, Latin American auction sites.
- On August 13, 2004, eBay took a 25 percent stake in Craigslist, an online network of urban communities.
- In September 2005 eBay invested $2 million in the Meetup social networking site.
- In August 2006 eBay announced international cooperation with Google.
- In January 2007 eBay acquired online ticket marketplace StubHub for $310 million.
- In June 2010 eBay acquired RedLaser, a mobile application that let customers scan bar codes to list items faster on its online auction site and to compare prices.[7]
- In December 2010 eBay acquired Milo, a leading local shopping engine that provided consumers access to accurate, real-time, local-store inventory and pricing, giving them even more choices and flexibility when shopping online.[8]
- In December 2010 eBay acquired Critical Path Software Inc., a developer of smartphone applications, to accelerate its lead in mobile commerce.[9]
- In 2014 eBay announced its agreement to acquire Shutl, a U.K.-based marketplace that used a network of couriers to deliver local goods the same day. The news followed the announcement of eBay's click-and-collect service trial with Argos and its intention to expand eBay Now (local e-commerce delivery) to London.

Evolution of the Auction Market

Traditional Auctions

According to Greek scribes, the first known auctions occurred in Babylon in 500 BC. At that time, women were sold on the condition of marriage, and it was considered illegal for daughters to be sold outside auctions. Auctions evolved during the French Revolution and throughout the American Civil War, where colonels auctioned goods that had been seized by armies.[10] Although there were various types of auctions, they all provided a forum at which sellers could find buyers. Auctions were considered one of the purest markets because buyers paid what they were willing to spend for an item, thereby determining the true market value of the item. Over time, auction formats evolved, and through technological advances and improved communication they found a new home—the Internet.

Online Auctions

The primary difference between traditional and online auctions was that the online auction process occurred over the Internet rather than at a specific location where both buyers and sellers were present. Online auctions offered strategic advantages to both parties that were not typically available in traditional auctions. Buyers could select from millions of products and engage in multiple auctions simultaneously. Given the massive inventory of an online auction market, items were usually available in multiple auctions, allowing buyers to compare starting-bid prices and search for better prices. Sellers were exposed to millions of buyers, since more buyers had access to the Internet and felt comfortable making purchases online. Thus, the Internet gave buyers and sellers access to a marketplace that spanned the world.

Online auctions also offered the following strategic advantages:

1. *No time constraints:* A bid could be placed at any time.
2. *No geographic constraints:* Sellers and buyers could participate from any location with Internet access.
3. *Network economies:* The large number of bidders attracted more sellers, which attracted more bidders, and so on. This created a large system that had more value for both parties. Online auctions also allowed businesses to easily sell off excess inventory or discontinued items. This was done through either business-to-business (B2B) or business-to-consumer (B2C) auctions. Offering products and services in an online auction helped small businesses build their brand and reputation by establishing a devoted customer base. Finally, some businesses used the online marketplace as an inexpensive yet effective way to test-market upcoming products.

World of E-Commerce

Although Vannevar Bush originally conceived the idea of the Internet in 1945, it wasn't until the 1990s that the Internet became overwhelmingly popular. According to Internet World Stats, in June 2014 there were over 3 billion Internet users in over 150 countries. Exhibit 4 shows world Internet usage and population as of June 30, 2014, and Internet usage growth between 2000 and 2014.

As of 2014, North America was the region most penetrated by the Internet, with approximately 88 percent of the population online. However, Internet usage growth between 2000 and 2014 was considerably less in North America than in other regions. Internet usage growth was highest in developing regions, such as Africa, the Middle East, Latin America, and Asia, where penetration was low. Considering that close to 80 percent of the world's population resides in these areas, it was inevitable that Internet usage growth would continue to increase dramatically in these regions.

Although Asia constituted approximately 56 percent of the world's population, its penetration rate was only 27.5 percent. Compared to other regions with high usage growth rates, such as Africa and the Middle East, Asia invested more in its technology infrastructure and contained by far the most current Internet users, making it a more attractive market.

As the usage growth of the Internet increased, so did the popularity of e-commerce. E-commerce, or electronic commerce, was the concept of conducting business transactions over the Internet. Like online auctions, e-commerce eliminated boundaries such as time and geography, allowing businesses and customers to interact with one another constantly. As more users were exposed to the Internet, they became comfortable with the idea of conducting transactions online. In correlation with Internet growth usage, revenue generated through e-commerce had increased dramatically since the 1990s.

EXHIBIT 4 World Internet Usage and Population Statistics, June 30, 2014

World Regions	Population (2014 Est.)	Internet Users Dec. 31, 2000	Internet Users Latest Data	Penetration (% Population)	Growth % 2000–2014	Users % of Table
Africa	1,125,721,038	4,514,400	297,885,898	26.5	6,498.6	9.8
Asia	3,996,408,007	114,304,000	1,386,188,112	34.7	1,112.7	45.7
Europe	825,824,883	105,096,093	582,441,059	70.5	454.2	19.2
Middle East	231,588,580	3,284,800	111,809,510	48.3	3,303.8	3.7
North America	353,860,227	108,096,800	310,322,257	87.7	187.1	10.2
Latin America/Caribbean	612,279,181	18,068,919	320,312,562	52.3	1,672.7	10.5
Oceania/Australia	36,724,649	7,620,480	26,789,942	72.9	251.6	0.9
WORLD TOTAL	7,182,406,565	360,985,492	3,035,749,340	42.3	741.0	100.0

Notes: (1) Internet usage and world population statistics are for June 30, 2014. (2) Demographic (population) numbers are based on data from the US Census Bureau and local census agencies. (3) Internet usage information comes from data published by Nielsen Online, by the International Telecommunications Union, by GfK, local ICT regulators, and other reliable sources.

Source: Internet World Stats. 2014. Usage and population statistics. *www.internetworldstats.com/*. Information in this site may be cited, giving the due credit to www.internetworldstats.com. Copyright © 2001–2014, Miniwatts Marketing Group. All rights reserved worldwide.

In Asia, e-commerce had grown rapidly since China's admission into the World Trade Organization (WTO) on December 11, 2001. Induction into the WTO allowed China to conduct business with other nations more freely by reducing tariffs and eliminating market and government impediments.

Track Record of Proven Leadership

Computer programmer Pierre Omidyar founded the online auction website in San Jose, California, on September 3, 1995. Omidyar was born in Paris, France, and moved to Maryland with his family when his father took on a residency at Johns Hopkins University Medical Center. Omidyar became fascinated with computers and later graduated from Tufts University with a degree in computer science. While living and working in the San Francisco Bay Area, he met his current wife, Pamela Wesley, a management consultant, who later became a driving force in launching the auction website. The couple's vision was to establish an online marketplace at which people could share the same passion and interest as Pamela had for her hobby of collecting and trading Pez candy dispensers.[11] Omidyar also envisioned an online auction format that would create a fair and open marketplace, where the market truly determined an item's value. To ensure trust in the open forum, Omidyar based the site on five main values:

1. People are basically good.
2. Everyone has something to contribute.
3. An honest, open environment can bring out the best in people.
4. Everyone deserves recognition and respect as a unique individual.
5. You should treat others the way you want to be treated.

On Labor Day weekend in 1995, Omidyar launched Auction Web, an online trading platform. After the business exploded, Omidyar decided to dedicate more attention to his new enterprise and work as a consultant under the name Echo Bay Technology Group. When he tried to register a website for his company, Omidyar discovered the name *Echo Bay* was unavailable, so he decided to use the abbreviated version *eBay*, which also stood for "electronic bay area." The company's name was also selected to attract San Francisco residents to the site and prompt them to buy and sell items.

Initially, the company did not charge fees to either buyers or sellers, but as traffic grew rapidly, Omidyar was forced to charge buyers a listing fee to cover Internet service provider costs. When Omidyar noticed that the fees had no effect on the level of bids, he realized the potential for profitability of his business. To handle and manage the company's day-to-day operations, Omidyar hired Jeffrey Skoll (BASc from University of Toronto and MBA from Stanford University). Skoll was hired as the company's first president, and he wrote the business plan that eBay later followed from its emergence as a start-up to its maturity as a financial success. The two worked out of Skoll's living room and various Silicon Valley facilities until they eventually settled in the company's current location in San Jose, California.

By the middle of 1997, after less than a year under the name *eBay,* the company was hosting nearly 800,000 auctions a day.[12] Although the rapid expansion of eBay's traffic caused the company to suffer a number of service interruptions, the site remained successful and continued to gain the confidence of its strong customer base. Skoll remained president until early 1998, when the company hired Meg Whitman as president and CEO. At the time, the company had only 30 employees and was solely located in the United States; in a decade the number of employees went up to over 15,000. In September 1998 eBay launched a successful public offering, making both Omidyar and Skoll instant billionaires. By the time eBay went public, less than three years after Omidyar had created the company, the site had more than 1 million registered users. The company grew exponentially in the late 1990s and, based on its 2013 performance, indicated no sign of stopping. Exhibit 5 highlights the company's recent growth performance.

Whitman stepped down as the president and CEO of the company on March 31, 2008, but remained on the board of directors. Omidyar, the chairman of the board, said this about Whitman: "With humor, smarts and unflappable determination, Meg took a small, barely known online auction site and helped it become an integral part of our lives."[13] Both Omidyar and Whitman were confident that the new CEO, John Donahoe, was a good choice to lead eBay. Donahoe had joined the company in 2005 as president of eBay's largest division, Marketplaces, and within three years managed to double the revenues and profits for this business unit. Before joining eBay, Donahoe served as the CEO of Bain & Company, an international consulting firm based in Boston.[14] "I'm extremely confident in John's skills and the abilities of John's veteran management team," Meg Whitman commented on the transition.[15]

EXHIBIT 5 eBay Growth ($ millions, year end December 31)

Year	Total gross merchandise volume excl. vehicles
2007	46.57
2008	48
2009	48.35
2010	53.53
2011	60.33
2012	67.76
2013	76.5

Source: Statistica, 2015.

Whitman's confidence appears to have been well founded. New CEO Donahoe helped eBay make impressive progress. Although eBay's financial outlook was not dreadful when Donahoe took over in March 2008, there was a growing perception that its growth was beginning to decline and that its run as the leader of the e-commerce industry was behind it, as Amazon began to make strides toward becoming the next best thing. During the global financial crisis, eBay's stock fell to almost $10 per share in February 2009, far below the optimistic price of $58 that it had reached in 2004. Since 2009, however, the stock had been on a stable uptrend, more than doubling in value during the 12-month period from 2012 to 2013 and closing at almost $54 in January 2015. "What John Donahoe has accomplished over the past few years is one of the most remarkable feats in the valley's history," said Gil Luria, an analyst at Wedbush Securities. So what had the new CEO done to spurt this turnaround? Luria noted that eBay began investing more in technology and was willing to take risks regarding altering the look and feel of the platform's shopping experience.[16]

eBay Now was implemented to offer same-day delivery of products from online and offline merchants in San Francisco. ThinkEquity analyst Ron Josey wrote, "We view eBay Now as one of the most innovative products eBay has launched in some time." The new service functioned as a mobile app—one representation of Donahoe's vision for eBay to begin embracing the increasing trend of mobile and offline shopping. "We've gone from competing in a $500 billion e-commerce market to now a $10 trillion retail market," Donahoe recently told analysts.[17]

When grilled about the short-lived Skype deal, Donahoe said eBay did not regret having bought Skype when company executives believed eBay was in a mortal struggle with Google, which was also pursuing the service. He said the spin-off would allow eBay to focus on its core e-commerce and online payment businesses and avoid extra distractions. "We don't regret having done this at all. We compete in a dynamic market, and you have to move quickly and take risks," Donahoe said. "When we bought Skype we thought it had synergies with our other two businesses, and it turns out it did not. But it also turned out that it's a great stand-alone business." In May 2011, Microsoft agreed to buy Skype for $8.5 billion from Silver Lake. eBay said it would earn more than a 50 percent return from its initial investment of $2.6 billion in Skype six years earlier. "With this sale, we have realized a total return of $1.4 billion on our original investment in Skype," said John Pluhowski, a spokesman for eBay. Considering that eBay had bought Skype in a heavily criticized deal in 2005 and that it was considered a failed acquisition, the Microsoft agreement turned out to be good news for eBay, making eBay one of the big winners in the Microsoft and Skype deal.

Company Business Model

eBay's business model was based on a person-to-person marketplace on the Internet, where sellers conveniently listed items for sale and interested buyers bid on those items. The objective was to create a forum that allowed buyers and sellers to come together in an efficient and effective manner. The business model overcame the inefficiencies of traditional fragmented marketplaces, which tended to offer a limited variety of goods. According to former CEO Meg Whitman, the company started with commerce and what grew out of that was a community, essentially creating a community-commerce model.[18] The company's success relied primarily on establishing a trustworthy environment that attracted a large number of buyers and sellers. As eBay's reputation grew, so did the number of buyers and sellers, keeping the company in line with Omidyar's original vision. However, as new competitors entered the online auction business and the popularity of the Internet increased, eBay tweaked its business model to accommodate changes in the fast-paced environment.

The company was aggressively expanding globally and looking for new products and services to offer to customers. It was also looking closely at the kind of merchants who sold on eBay. In the beginning, eBay focused on a consumer-to-consumer business model, but since some of the individuals became small dealers, the model changed to a mix of consumer-to-consumer and business-to-consumer. The sellers wanted to maintain their business on eBay, since it was their most profitable distribution channel. eBay wanted new ways to generate revenue as a result of more small dealers and businesses selling their products through the company's website.

In addition to the primary revenue sources, there were specific elements of eBay's business model that made the company a success (see Exhibit 6). eBay's dominance of the online auction market and the large number of buyers, sellers, and listed items were primary reasons for eBay's tremendous growth. The trust and safety programs, such as the Feedback Forum, continued to attract and retain new and current eBay users. The cost-effective and convenient trading, coupled with the strong sense of community, added further value to the company's business model. However, as the company continued to grow and new trends evolved, eBay had to continue to adjust its model to remain competitive.

International Expansion

As competition intensified in the online auction industry, eBay expanded its international presence in an effort to create an online global marketplace. Gradually, eBay localized sites in the following countries:

- *Asia Pacific:* Australia, China, Hong Kong, India, Malaysia, New Zealand, Philippines, Singapore, South Korea, and Taiwan.
- *Europe:* Austria, Belgium, Denmark, France, Germany, Ireland, Italy, Netherlands, Poland, Spain, Sweden, Switzerland, and United Kingdom.
- *North America:* Canada and United States.

EXHIBIT 6 Net Revenues by Type ($ millions, except percentage changes)

Net Revenue Type	Year Ended December 31		
	2014	2013	2012
Marketplaces	$1,695	$1,520	$1,273
As a percentage of total			
Marketplaces net revenues	19.20%	18.30%	17.20%
Payments	$3,112	$2,675	$2,209
As a percentage of total			
Payments net revenues	39.40%	40.40%	39.60%
Enterprise	$923	$834	$708
As a percentage of total			
Enterprise net revenues	74.60%	71.50%	63.20%
Corporate and other	$2	$7	$26
Total net revenues	$5,732	$5,036	$4,216
As a percentage of net revenues	32.00%	31.40%	30.00%

Source: eBay SEC filings.

Intense Competitive Environment

As eBay's product offerings and pricing formats evolved, so did its range of competitors. Originally, the company faced competition from alternative auctions or other venues for collectors, such as flea markets and garage sales. However, as the company grew and introduced fixed pricing, the range of competitors included large companies like Walmart and Kmart that also had retail websites. eBay faced the harshest competition from major online companies, including Yahoo and Amazon, which also had online auctions that rivaled eBay's.

Yahoo!

eBay's large online competitor was Yahoo, which had a strong global presence, particularly in Asian markets. Yahoo originally started as a search engine and quickly evolved to include additional products and services, such as Yahoo! Mail, Yahoo! Maps, and Yahoo! Messenger. The company also offered e-commerce services through Yahoo! Shopping, Yahoo! Autos, Yahoo! Auctions, and Yahoo! Travel. As with eBay, Yahoo's e-commerce sites allowed users to obtain relevant information and make transactions and purchases online. However, Yahoo's business model primarily focused on generating revenue through search advertising. In the United States, in response to potential threats from web giant Google, Yahoo and eBay formed an alliance in which Yahoo utilized eBay's payment system, PayPal, and eBay gained additional advertising through Yahoo searches. Still, Yahoo posed a major competitive threat in foreign markets, particularly the Asia-Pacific area, through its partnerships with Gmarket and Taobao.

Amazon

Despite not having a huge presence in the online auction industry, Amazon was still considered a fierce online global competitor. Amazon started as Earth's biggest bookstore and rapidly evolved to selling everything, including toys, electronics, home furnishings, apparel, health and beauty aids, groceries, and so on. Still, books, CDs, and DVDs accounted for more than 65 percent of the firm's sales. Although Amazon had a large international presence, the company's linkage to brick-and-mortar shops in the United States made it a greater threat in local markets than in foreign markets. Amazon's international sites were in Canada, the United Kingdom, Germany, Japan, France, and China. Despite its large online presence, Amazon scaled back its online auction business, cutting staff and shutting down Livebid, as part of an overall corporate restructuring.

Google

Google started out as a browser much like Yahoo but recently ventured into the e-commerce space by acquiring Overstock.com. While it did not compete directly with eBay in the online auction market, it did compete with eBay in online retailing.

Etsy

As eBay tried to position itself as a trendy e-retailer, it directly competed with the trendy Etsy.com retailing site. The site was managed from an office in Brooklyn and had a strong and growing user base. Much like the customers of eBay, Etsy's customers went to its site for quaint collectible items.

Traditional Retailers

Given the trend toward e-commerce, many traditional brick-and-mortar companies like Walmart, Staples, and Home Depot were investing heavily in developing their online retail sites.

Taobao

eBay faced unyielding competition in China from Alibaba Group's Taobao.com, the largest Chinese online retailer. Like eBay, Taobao strived to implement a more interactive and user-friendly customer service initiative. Taobao began using an instant communication tool called Aliwangwang to help buyers and sellers interact with one another. Alipay, an online payment system, was started soon after.

Interestingly, Taobao's parent company, Alibaba, seemed to be exploring expansion opportunities in the United States. It had a record-breaking IPO in the New York Stock Exchange in September 2014. U.S. retailers and industry analysts expected Alibaba would soon launch a service targeted at American consumers. Alibaba sold to American consumers through its global retail service AliExpress. But its core Taobao service, often likened to eBay's Marketplaces, was not yet available to U.S. customers in English.

Jack Ma, chairman of Alibaba, had apparently learned from the eBay playbook. At the IPO he repeatedly stressed the importance of trust in an ecommerce venture. "Today what we got is not money. What we got is the trust from the people," Ma said. This had also been the mantra of Pierre Omidyar, founder of eBay.

The Future of eBay

Board of Directors versus Activist Investor

In 2014, activist investor Carl Icahn had put together a 0.8 percent ownership stake in eBay and started pushing for strategy changes. The company refused to take his advice, so Icahn bought more shares and tried again. By October, eBay had already decided to spin out its PayPal online payments service, but Icahn owned 2.5 percent of the company and insisted that management think about selling that operation to a cash-rich tech giant instead. eBay management still preferred the PayPal spin-off idea, much to Icahn's chagrin. Since then, his eBay ownership expanded to 3.7 percent, and the company is pretty much doing what he wants, or close to it.

So, alongside the 2014 year-end earnings report, eBay announced that it had reached a standstill agreement with Carl Icahn. The activist investor would not buy any more eBay stock in return for some concessions from eBay's active leadership. The concessions included adding an Icahn-selected individual to eBay's board of directors and accepting "certain corporate governance provisions" to PayPal's starting papers.

Icahn picked Icahn Capital hedge fund manager Jonathan Christodoro, who was a merger analyst and already served on four boards under Icahn's influence. eBay also gave Icahn the option of placing his candidate on either eBay's or PayPal's board when the two companies split later in the year. Given Christodoro's field of expertise, industry circles expected him to move on with PayPal and continue looking for buyout-style exit strategies.

eBay also announced that it was contemplating a sale or spin-off of its Enterprise division as well. "Enterprise is a good business, but it has become clear that it has increasingly divergent opportunities and limited synergies with eBay," said eBay CEO John Donahoe in a prepared statement. With limited synergies at work between the divisions, it could be better to just do a clean break and reinvest the resulting cash inflow somewhere else.

Icahn, of course, was expected to use his large stock ownership and board representation to explore his favorite options for using surplus cash. He was known to like selling operations that no longer made sense, but he was not a big supporter of making acquisitions himself. Instead, he preferred enormous share buyback and dividend programs, like the ones he had apparently suggested for Apple in recent years. eBay's board of directors would likely counter Icahn's influence by diluting Christodoro's powers. The company was reportedly planning to add two new directors, thus expanding the boardroom ranks to 15 members. The two additional board members were not just any old seat-fillers, either. Perry Traquina recently retired from Wellington Management after leading that investment service for 34 years. Just before he left Wellington, the company had convinced Oracle to buy Wellington protégé and cloud computing upstart Datalogix. In other words, Traquina was no stranger to buyout plans. The second addition, Frank Yeary, was also not a newcomer to mergers. Before cofounding investor advisory firm CamberView and serving as vice chancellor of UC Berkeley, Yeary was known as Citigroup's—wait for it—head of mergers and acquisitions.

There was a chance that these high-powered merger experts would simply work with Christodoro to set up an extremely favorable PayPal buyout. But they were more likely selected for their ability to argue against Icahn's adviser, picking apart merger talks before they went too far.

Either way, eBay had become a high-stakes game of chess. Icahn and his team wanted to monetize PayPal to the hilt before the service peaked, while eBay would rather hold on a little tighter and see where this train was headed. Industry analysts concluded that the arguments on both sides had merit but that the uncertainty of squabbling over the long-term strategy would hurt the company overall.

Interested Bidders

As eBay prepared to spin off its Payments and Enterprise businesses, the industry was rife with rumors about potential acquisitions of the remaining online auction business.

"It would give a player like Alibaba a legitimate foothold into the American market," predicted Sean Udall, CIO of Quantum Trading Strategies and author of *The TechStrat Report*.

Who exactly might acquire any of eBay's units, or the company itself someday, remained the speculation of analysts and the media. Amazon, Google, and Alibaba were each occasionally mentioned by Wall Street analysts.

Unhappy Customers

eBay's handling of a recent hacking incident created a number of disgruntled customers. The company had reset all customer passwords and adversely affected Internet browser search results. Further, a revision to the fee structure displeased a number of small business owners. Fleur Filmer, a customer who ran a picnic gear business called Hanging Rock Picnics, was frustrated with the way changes were introduced at eBay:

> Any fee increases are buried deep within policy updates and the level of fine print is staggering. My store has fared quite well but I must admit that fee increases from three per cent to four per cent [of gross sales value] up to nine per cent are very hard to absorb.... A lot of investment and resources have gone to their promotion of the majors online. They have actively gone after the big brands to establish eBay stores and haven't offered any new resources or assistance to small store owners.

New Competitors

eBay was once the go-to site for selling unwanted secondhand goods, but Facebook was now entering the fray. Millions of people had already conveniently bought and sold items using "For Sale" groups, and the social network was rolling out tools to make the process even easier. The new features were designed to regulate the process so buyers knew exactly what was for sale, how much it cost, and where it was going to be sourced from. Users said they preferred to trade on Facebook because the accounts showed the names and details of the persons buying and selling. On sites such as eBay and Craigslist members had a certain level of anonymity, and this made resolving problems with transactions more difficult.

The year ahead was going to be a challenging one for eBay. Investors and shareholders would be watching keenly to see if the management and board could fix things and chart a new course for the future. With senior management, an expanded board of directors, an activist investor, and potential acquirers in the mix, gaining alignment on the path forward would not be an easy task. Only time would tell which option would prove right for the company and increase shareholder value over the long term. Or would eBay be better off offering itself for sale to a bidder?

ENDNOTES

1. eBay. Q4 2014 earnings call transcript.
2. Horn, Eli. 2015. eBay facing collapse from Icahn's PayPal spinoff, report says. *Jewish Business News,* January 24.
3. Galante, J. 2011. PayPal's revenue will double by 2013, Thompson says. *Bloomberg News,* February 10, www.businessweek.com/news/2011-02-10/paypal-s-revenue-will-double-by-2013-thompson-says.html.
4. Bensinger, G. 2014. eBay to split as Apple, others prepare to challenge PayPal. *Wall Street Journal,* September 30.
5. eBay Inc. 2008. eBay Inc. buys leading payments and classifieds businesses, streamlines existing organization to improve growth. Press release, October 6, www.ebayinc.com/content/press_release/20081006005605.
6. eBay Inc. 2009. Annual report.
7. MacMillan, D. 2010. eBay buys bar-code app. *Bloomberg Businessweek,* June 23, www.businessweek.com/technology/content/jun2010/tc20100623_901174.htm.
8. eBay Inc. 2010. eBay acquires Milo, a leading local shopping engine. Press release, December 2, www.ebayinc.com/content/press_release/20101202006358.
9. eBay Inc. 2010. eBay acquires industry leading mobile application developer. Press release, December 15, www.ebayinc.com/content/press_release/20101215006520.
10. Doyle, R. A. 2002. The history of auctions. *Auctioneer,* November 1, www.absoluteauctionrealty.com/history_detail.php?id=5094.
11. *Internet Based Moms.* 2007. Pierre Omidyar—the man behind eBay. April.
12. Academy of Achievement. 2005. Biography—Pierre Omidyar. www.achievement.org, November 9.
13. eBay Inc. 2008. Meg Whitman to step down.
14. eBay corporate website, ebayinc.com.
15. eBay Inc. 2008. Meg Whitman to step down.
16. O'Brien, Chris. 2012. Is eBay's John Donahoe the best CEO in Silicon Valley? *Mercurynews.com,* November 4, www.mercurynews.com/chris-obrien/ci_21908264/obrien-is-ebays-john-donahoe-best-ceo-silicon.
17. Ibid.
18. Himelstein, L., & Whitman, M. 1999. Q&A with eBay's Meg Whitman. *BusinessWeek Online,* May 31, www.businessweek.com/1999/99_22/b3631008.htm.

CASES

CASE 21

YAHOO!*

On January 25, 2015, Marissa Mayer, chief executive of Yahoo, announced that it would spin off its remaining 15.4 percent stake in Alibaba, China's leading e-commerce firm, into a separate company. Yahoo had already sold a hefty chunk of its Alibaba stake the previous September when the Chinese company sold shares in an initial public offering. Yahoo made a gain of $10.3 billion from the sale but nearly 40 percent of that was eaten by taxes. The spin-off would allow the firm to avoid any taxes on the transaction, but it would represent the final step in the loss of its most valuable asset. The Alibaba stake had accounted for as much as 85 percent of Yahoo's total market value.

As it disposed of its investment in Alibaba, Yahoo focused on turning around its core Internet advertising business, which was suffering as advertisers and Internet users were switching their money and attention to flashier, more innovative services from competitors like Google, Facebook, and Twitter. Among other things, the firm was late to recognize that people around the world were turning to social networks and using mobile devices for access to the Internet, placing it in the position of having to catch up. At a time when its rivals were beginning to make most of their money from apps on phones, Yahoo had just 100 engineers working on mobile products.

When Mayer became CEO of Yahoo in 2012, she realized she had to move quickly to build the firm's presence on mobile devices. She went on a shopping spree, spending almost $1.3 billion to acquire 36 companies, mostly start-ups that had developed offerings for smartphones and tablets. The biggest of these was Tumblr, a blogging platform, which Yahoo acquired in 2013 for $1.1 billion. Mayer became personally involved in these acquisitions, focusing particularly on mobile-minded engineers. Revenues from the businesses that Mayer created or acquired grew at an annual rate of 80 percent.

In building up the firm's presence in mobiles, Mayer oversaw the release by Yahoo of a string of apps, such as Yahoo Weather and Yahoo News Digest, that won critics' accolades. As the firm prepared to release its financial results for 2014 (see Exhibits 1 and 2), Mayer claimed that

* Case prepared by Jamal Shamsie, Michigan State University, with the assistance of Professor Alan B. Eisner, Pace University. Material has been drawn from published sources to be used for purposes of class discussion. Copyright © 2015 Jamal Shamsie and Alan B. Eisner.

EXHIBIT 1 Income Statement ($ millions)

	Year Ending				
	Dec. 2010	Dec. 2011	Dec. 2012	Dec. 2013	Dec. 2014
Revenue	6,325	4,984	4,987	4,680	4,618
Gross profit	3,697	3,482	3,366	3,331	3,320
Operating income	773	800	566	590	143

Source: Yahoo!

EXHIBIT 2 Balance Sheet ($ millions)

	Year Ending				
	Dec. 2010	Dec. 2011	Dec. 2012	Dec. 2013	Dec. 2014
Total current assets	4,346	3,453	5,653	5,026	9,699
Total assets	14,928	14,783	17,103	16,805	61,960
Total current liabilities	1,626	1,207	1,290	1,340	4,529
Total liabilities	2,370	2,242	2,543	3,730	23,219
Total stockholders' equity	12,558	12,541	14,560	13,075	38,742

Source: Yahoo!

mobile was beginning to make a meaningful contribution to Yahoo's revenues, with expectations that the firm would top $1.2 billion for the full year. Yahoo, along with its Tumblr unit, had 550 million monthly users on mobile devices by the end of the year, up 17 percent from a year earlier. Furthermore, Yahoo's growth in users was outpacing the industry average.

The research firm eMarketer stated that Yahoo was poised to surpass Twitter for third place in the U.S. mobile ad market, although it still remained far behind Facebook and Google. But Mayer's recent acquisition of BrightRoll, a video ad firm, was expected to help narrow the gap. "There are pieces of the puzzle coming into place," said Brian Weiser, an analyst who followed Yahoo and had long been skeptical of its prospects. "It's clear that lessons have been learned."[1]

Gambling on a Theme Park

After a period of strong growth in the late 1990s, Yahoo saw a steep fall in revenues and profits as advertisers cut back on their spending after the dot-com bust. Under Tim Koogle, Yahoo had developed as a web portal that relied heavily on advertising revenues for profits. He had been confident that advertisers would continue to pay in order to reach the younger and technologically savvy surfers who would use his portal. As advertising revenues dropped off sharply, leading to a steep decline in the firm's stock price, Koogle was replaced in April 2001 by Terry Semel, an experienced Hollywood media executive who had once controlled Warner Brothers.

Semel pushed to build Yahoo into a site that could offer surfers many different services, with several of them requiring the customer to pay a small fee. With the expansion of services, Semel envisioned building Yahoo into a digital Disneyland, a souped-up theme park for the Internet age. The idea was that web surfers logging on to Yahoo's site, like customers squeezing through the turnstiles in Anaheim, would find themselves in a self-contained world full of irresistible offerings. To ensure that the various sites would be seamlessly linked to each other more closely, he moved swiftly to replace Yahoo's freewheeling culture with a more deliberate sense of order. All ideas had to be formally presented to a group called the Product Council that consisted of nine managers from different parts of the firm.

In spite of Semel's efforts to tightly control the growth of Yahoo into new areas, the push to develop a digital theme park led some analysts to question whether the firm was spreading itself too thin. Even some people inside Yahoo began to question its goal of providing a broad range of services that could attract an audience that could be sold to advertisers. In a scathing internal memo written in the fall of 2006, Brad Garlinghouse, a Yahoo senior vice president, compared Yahoo's strategy to indiscriminately spreading peanut butter across the Internet. "We lack a focused, cohesive vision for our company," he stated in the memo. "We want to do everything and be everything—to everyone.

We've known this for years, talked about it incessantly, but done nothing to fundamentally address it."[2]

Shareholder dissatisfaction with Yahoo's financial performance finally led to the resignation of Semel in July 2007. The firm turned to Jerry Yang, one of its cofounders—who had been serving as "Chief Yahoo"—to improve earnings and profits. He initiated a 100-day review of every aspect of the firm's operations but could not find ways to define the specific strengths that could be used to narrow its focus. Rob Sanderson, a technology analyst, pointed out that Yahoo had to make some critical choices. "They're relevant, and hold their audience pretty well, but the investor and media perception is that Yahoo is another AOL—a once-great company in decline," he explained.[3]

One of the biggest challenges faced by Yang was the offer made by Microsoft in early 2008 to buy Yahoo for $33 a share, or approximately $47.5 billion. Yang refused to sell his company for less than $37 a share, although its shares had been trading for around $20. Shareholders were upset because they stood to lose about $20 billion by the rejection of Microsoft's offer. "I don't think anything Yahoo puts out there is going to be comparable with what Microsoft was offering," said Darren Chervitz, comanager of the Jacob Internet Fund, which owns about 150,000 shares of Yahoo.[4]

Scrambling for a Focus

Less than a year and a half after he had assumed control, Yang decided to give up his role as CEO and revert to being the Chief Yahoo, the strategy position that he had held before. After an extensive search, the board appointed Carol Bartz as the new head of the firm. Bartz had been in charge of Autodesk, a computer-aided software design firm, for 14 years before joining Yahoo. She was expected to develop a stronger focus for the firm, which many perceived had been drifting, especially during Yang's turbulent leadership. Analysts were generally positive about her appointment, although many suggested that she lacked online media experience.

Bartz was expected to move quickly to reassure investors, who were angry with Yahoo's board for refusing to accept Microsoft's bid for the firm. Shortly after she took over, Bartz moved to overhaul the company's top executive ranks, consolidating several positions and creating others in an attempt to make the firm more efficient. She combined Yahoo's technology and product groups into one unit and created a customer advocacy group to better incorporate customer feedback. The changes were intended to speed up decision making within the company by making it "a lot faster on its feet," Bartz wrote in a Yahoo public blog. But Ross Sandler, an analyst with RBC Capital Markets, said the restructuring was more promising because it clarified responsibilities. "There has been confusion at the top for so long," he said. "This should solve that problem."[5]

Bartz also managed to refocus Yahoo on areas such as news, sports, and finance, where it had considerable strengths. While she moved the firm away from other activities she considered to be peripheral, Bartz invested heavily in content during her first year, hiring dozens of editorial employees and buying Associated Content, a freelance news site, to enhance local news coverage. She made some progress with revamping the technology behind the web portal that would make it possible to introduce new services much more quickly in the future. At the same time, Bartz managed to achieve an improvement in Yahoo's profit margins due to her aggressive moves to cut costs wherever possible.

But Bartz's most questionable move was handing over its search operations to Microsoft, which had invested heavily in relaunching its search engine and renamed it Bing. The terms of the 10-year agreement gave Microsoft access to search technologies that Yahoo had helped to pioneer and develop. Yahoo agreed to transfer many of its talented engineers to Microsoft and lay off 400 employees who ran the search operations. In return, Yahoo would receive 88 percent of the search-related ad revenue for the first five years of the deal, much higher than was standard in the industry. Nevertheless, some Yahoo shareholders expressed concerns that the company would lose its valuable search experience, which would be a difficult loss to recover from.

Even more questions were being raised about Bartz's abrasive style and her frequent use of foul language in public. This might have contributed to continual turnover among executives, particularly among the top level (see Exhibit 3). Moreover, some investors were losing patience with the slow pace of improvements, and this led to demands for Bartz's replacement by the board. Salim Ismail, a former Yahoo executive, elaborated on the situation: "They're putting on a Band-Aid when what they really need is major surgery."[6] The news that some private equity firms were considering a bid to buy Yahoo created even more pressures for some form of drastic action, leading to Bartz's ouster in September 2011.

Facing Up to a Broken Model

In July 2012, after some churning of CEOs, including the resignation of Scott Thompson over alleged discrepancies in his prior record, Yahoo was finally able to entice Marissa Mayer to defect from long-standing rival Google. The appointment of Mayer, who in her 13 years at Google had been responsible for the look and feel of some of the firm's most popular products, represented a major coup for Yahoo. With her taking charge, there was hope that her extensive experience would provide some much-needed direction for what had been increasingly viewed as a rudderless ship. "Yahoo finally has someone who has both business acumen and geek cred at the helm," said Chris Sacca, a venture capitalist who had previously worked with Mayer at Google. "She stands for a product-and-engineering-driven culture, and Yahoo has been missing that for years."[7]

Upon taking over, Mayer realized that Yahoo's biggest problem was its steady decline in digital advertising, which had accounted for roughly four-fifths of its revenues. The firm's share was approaching 2 percent, which paled in comparison to Google's 31 percent and Facebook's 8 percent. Most of this decline could be attributed to the heavy reliance of the firm on traditional banner and search advertising, which had been losing ground to newer forms that were more geared to mobile devices. "The type of advertising that Yahoo relies on is fundamentally challenged," said Jon Miller, a former chief executive of AOL.[8]

Mayer also recognized that there was a general lack of energy among employees within Yahoo, which had led to the growth of its reputation as a place where everyone took it easy. In fact, few people came to work, resulting in deserted offices and few signs of activity. Yahoo had made many promising acquisitions over the years but had failed to exploit their talent or technology to help them grow. Because of this pervasive lack of initiative, most of Yahoo's technology, including that which could be used to draw advertisers, had become quite outdated.

Soon after she took over, Mayer took steps to try to make Yahoo a more engaging place to work. She offered free food in the cafeteria to all of the employees, made the gym more freely accessible to everyone, and simplified the firm's travel and expense policy. Borrowing from the playbook of Google, she gave employees the option to trade in their BlackBerry phones for new iPhones and Android-powered phones so that they would be able to start making products for them. Finally, she began updating Yahoo's employees on the business in weekly Friday "FYI" meetings.

Mayer offered employees these benefits so that she could place more demands on their time. She began to evaluate her workforce through a rigorous quarterly review system in which performers received generous bonuses and the underperformers were dismissed. But Mayer's most controversial move was abolishing Yahoo's work-at-home policy and ordering everyone to come back to work in the office. Drawing lessons from the success of

EXHIBIT 3 Leadership

Year	CEO
1995–2001	Tim Koogle
2001–2007	Terry Semel
2007–2008	Jerry Yang
2009–2011	Carol Bartz
2012	Tim Morse (interim)
2012	Scott Thompson
2012	Ross Levinsohn (interim)
2012–	Marissa Mayer

Google's approach to business, she explained that face-to-face interaction among employees fosters a more innovative culture. Recent studies had shown strong support for this link. "If you want innovation, then you need interaction," said John Sullivan, a professor of management at San Francisco State University.[9]

Searching for a Fix

Mayer recognized that her most critical task upon taking over Yahoo was to raise desperately needed revenues from digital advertising in order to not fall further behind rivals such as Google and Facebook. One of Mayer's first moves was to hire a former colleague from Google, Henrique de Castro, as Yahoo's chief operating officer. She had hoped that de Castro would reorganize the firm's sales force in order to bring in new clients, but he ended up clashing with employees and alienating advertisers. Mayer moved swiftly to take over these efforts herself, working closely with others such as Kathy Savitt, who had moved up within the firm, and Ned Brody, whom she brought in from AOL.

Mayer was hoping to reverse Yahoo's decline of advertising revenue by turning the firm into a modern media empire with a constellation of what it called digital magazines on topics like food, technology, entertainment, and travel. She hoped that these magazines would bring back some of Yahoo's old mojo, attracting readers who would stay on the site longer and offering new ways for advertisers to make an impact. Built using technology acquired as part of its recent purchase of Tumblr, these magazines combined original articles and material licensed from other sites, as well as videos, into an endless page of titles aimed at enticing people to linger. "We think that digital magazines can be a great advance, creating a different category of content consumption," explained Mayer.[10]

Although Yahoo had tried offering different types of content before, Mayer believed that the potential for these magazines lay in their ability to mix advertising into their content in a way that made it look almost exactly like all the articles and videos on the page. The use of such an approach could allow digital magazines to present stories in a continually flowing stream, embedding advertising as content. The artificial sweetener Splenda, for example, is dishing up daily ideas for cutting down on calories, such as eating oatmeal instead of granola and using Splenda instead of sugar to sweeten chicken wings.

Mayer spent millions of dollars on this push, much of it to recruit celebrity talent. She snatched Julia Bainbridge from *Bon Appétit* to help with *Yahoo Food*. The newest magazine, *Yahoo Beauty*, is edited by Bobbi Brown, founder of the cosmetics line that bears her name. Well-known television news personality Katie Couric was hired to act as host and to conduct video interviews that are shown in these magazines, including in *Yahoo News*. This effort soon began to show positive results. During 2014, *Yahoo Tech* was pulling in more than 10 million unique visitors on desktop and mobile devices in the United States, and *Yahoo Food* had managed to attract over 8 million visitors according to comScore, a research firm.

More significantly, Mayer claimed that Yahoo's push into native ads, which resemble the content around them, was starting to bear fruit. She expected these ads would generate as much as $80 million in the fourth quarter of 2014. On the whole, she told analysts that her firm was seeing strong growth in its mobile, video, social, and native advertising—a group that she calls "the mavens"—with growth of as much as 95 percent in the fourth quarter of 2014 compared with the same quarter a year earlier.

Signs of Revival?

Mayer remained convinced that she could transform Yahoo into a next-generation tech company focused on mobile experiences, video, and communications that would compete squarely with Google and Facebook. Toward this end, Mayer continued to pursue the strategy of buying small firms that help Yahoo to update its technology to compete in the mobile world. She recently acquired video ad company BrightRoll for $640 million. Its acquisition has made Yahoo's video ad platform the largest in the U.S. Around the same time, Yahoo also bought MessageMe, a small photo and text-messaging start-up, and Cooliris, which provided a 3-D-like immersive media viewing experience.

Mayer, who built her reputation overseeing Google's Internet search business, indicated that Yahoo remains committed to the search business. She was discussing changes to its 10-year search partnership with Microsoft, which was at the midway mark. In November 2014, Yahoo struck a deal to replace Google as the default search service on Mozilla's Firefox web browser, which accounts for 3 to 5 percent of all searches.

Although Mayer's efforts won some praise from analysts, they were not sure whether these efforts would be enough to revive Yahoo. Above all, she had not been able to provide a clear vision of what the firm would stand for at the end of her shuffling of the firm's products. Nevertheless, there were some strong signs that Mayer had been able to push Yahoo to become more competitive. "I used to be very bearish on the prospects of what they could possibly do," admitted Ben Schachter, a securities analyst, in reflecting on the firm's performance in 2014. "Today, while I am not fully convinced that the turnaround can succeed, I'm more impressed than I was even six months ago."[11]

ENDNOTES

1. Farhad Manjoo. Turnaround on track, Yahoo chief still battles. *New York Times*, January 22, 2015, p. B10.
2. Elise Ackerman. Can "Chief Yahoo" Yang make it work this time as CEO? *Knight Ridder Tribune Business News*, June 24, 2007, p. 1.

3. John Swartz. Yahoo encounters a fork in road toward its future. *USA Today,* January 28, 2008, p. 2B.
4. Miguel Helft. Yahoo celebrates (for now). *New York Times,* May 5, 2008, p. C1.
5. Jessica E. Vascellaro. Bartz remakes Yahoo's top ranks. *Wall Street Journal,* February 27, 2009, p. B3.
6. Verne G. Kopytoff. Even under new captain, Yahoo seems adrift. *New York Times,* October 18, 2010, p. B4.
7. Andrew Ross Sorkin & Evelyn M. Rusli. Silicon Valley pioneer steps onto bigger, if shakier, stage. *New York Times,* July 18, 2012, p. B1.
8. Michael J. de la Merced & D. Gelles. Yahoo faces a moment of decision, again. *New York Times,* September 26, 2014.
9. Claire Cain Miller & Catherine Rampell. Yahoo orders home workers back to office. *New York Times,* February 26, 2013, p. A1.
10. Vindu Goel. Hoping visitors will linger a while. *International New York Times,* June 23, 2014, p. 17.
11. Michael J. de la Merced. After Alibaba spinoff, Yahoo may become a takeover target. *New York Times,* January 29, 2015, p. B2.

CASES

CASE 22
WORLD WRESTLING ENTERTAINMENT*

World Wrestling Entertainment (WWE) announced on January 27, 2015, that its WWE Network, which had been launched just 11 months earlier, had surpassed 1 million subscribers, making it the fasting-growing digital subscription service. The new subscription-only streaming video service provided viewers with round-the-clock access to wrestling matches, including pay-per-view events that were once only available on cable and satellite channels. Viewer data continued to indicate that, on average, close to 90 percent of subscribers accessed the network at least once a week and 86 percent of subscribers were satisfied with it. "We're thrilled that we've surpassed the 1 million subscriber milestone in less than a year," stated CEO Vince McMahon.[1]

The success of the WWE Network, along with programming on YouTube, helped to further the firm's goal of coupling its live wrestling matches with programming on television, on the web, and on mobile devices, allowing it to become one of the world's most social brands. The firm added to its presence on the Internet with an exclusive, multiyear agreement to bring WWE programming to Hulu Plus, offering next-day access to its television programs and other exclusive shows. Its apps for smartphones and tablets had also taken off with the launch of *WWE Active* in 2012.

All of these achievements clearly indicated that WWE had moved out of a slump that it had endured between 2001 and 2005. During the 1990s, Vince McMahon had used a potent mix of shaved, pierced, and pumped-up muscled hunks; buxom, scantily-clad, and sometimes cosmetically enhanced beauties; and body-bashing clashes of good versus evil to build an empire that claimed over 35 million fans. Furthermore, the vast majority of these fans were males between the ages of 12 and 34, the demographic segment that makes most advertisers drool.

Just when it looked like everything was going well, WWE hit a rough patch. The firm's failure with a football league during 2001 that folded after just one season was followed by a drop in revenues from its core wrestling businesses. WWE was struggling with its efforts to build new wrestling stars and to introduce new characters into its shows. Some of its most valuable younger viewers were also turning to new reality-based shows on television, such as *Survivor, Fear Factor,* and *Jackass.*

Since 2005, however, WWE had been rebuilding its fan base through live shows, television programming, web and mobile content, and consumer products. The firm was turning pro wrestling into a perpetual road show that made millions of fans pass through turnstiles in a growing number of locations around the globe. Its flagship television programs, *Raw* and *Smackdown!* were broadcast in 30 languages in 145 countries, reaching 600 million homes around the world. WWE was also signing pacts with dozens of licensees, including one with toymaker Mattel, to sell DVDs, video games, toys, and trading cards. "We continue to see the distribution of our creative content through various emerging channels," stated Linda McMahon, who stepped down as president and CEO in 2009 to pursue a career in politics.[2]

Developing a Wrestling Empire

Most of the success of the WWE can be attributed to the persistent efforts of Vince McMahon. He was a self-described juvenile delinquent who went to military school as a teenager to avoid being sent to a reformatory institution. Around 1970, Vince joined his father's wrestling company, which operated in northeastern cities such as New York, Philadelphia, and Washington, D.C. He did on-air commentary, developed scripts, and otherwise promoted wrestling matches. Vince bought the wrestling firm from his father in 1982, eventually renaming it World Wrestling Federation (WWF). At that time, wrestling was managed by regional fiefdoms in which everyone avoided encroaching on anyone else's territory. Vince began to change all that by paying local television stations around the country to broadcast his matches. His aggressive pursuit of audiences across the country gradually squeezed out most of the other rivals. "I banked on the fact that they were behind the times, and they were," said Vince.[3]

Soon after, Vince broke another taboo by admitting to the public that wrestling matches were scripted. Although he had made this admission in order to avoid the scrutiny of state athletic commissions, wrestling fans appreciated the honesty. The WWF began to draw in more fans through the elaborate story lines and the captivating characters of its wrestling matches. The firm turned wrestlers such as Hulk Hogan and Andre the Giant into mainstream icons of pop culture. By the late 1980s, the WWF's *Raw is War* had become a top-rated show on cable, and the firm had also begun to offer pay-per-view shows.

Vince faced his most formidable competition after 1988, when Ted Turner bought out World Championship

---

* Case prepared by Jamal Shamsie, Michigan State University, with the assistance of Professor Alan B. Eisner, Pace University. Material has been drawn from published sources to be used for purposes of class discussion. Copyright © 2015 Jamal Shamsie and Alan B. Eisner.

Wrestling (WCW), one of the few major rivals that was still operating. Turner spent millions luring away WWF stars such as Hulk Hogan and Macho Man Randy Savage. He used these stars to launch a show on his own TNT channel to go up against WWF's major show, *Raw is War*. Although Turner's new show caused a temporary dip in the ratings for WWF's shows, Vince fought back with pumped-up scripts, mouthy musclemen, and lycra-clad women. "Ted Turner decided to come after me and all of my talent," growled Vince, "and now he's where he should be."[4]

In 2001, Vince was finally able to acquire WCW from Turner's parent firm, AOL Time Warner, for a bargain price of $5 million. Because of the manner in which he eliminated most of his rivals, Vince earned a reputation for being as aggressive and ambitious as any character in the ring. Paul MacArthur, publisher of *Wrestling Perspective,* an industry newsletter, praised his accomplishments: "McMahon understands the wrestling business better than anyone else. He's considered by most in the business to be brilliant."[5]

In 2002, WWF was hit by a ruling by a British court that its original acronym *WWF* belonged to the World Wildlife Fund. The firm had to undergo a major branding transition, changing its well-known name and triple logo from WWF to WWE, for "World Wresting Entertainment." Although the change in name was costly, it remained unclear whether it would hurt the firm in the long run. "Their product is really the entertainment. It's the stars. It's the bodies," said Larry McNaughton, managing director and principal of CoreBrand, a branding consultancy.[6] Vince's wife, Linda, stated that the new name might actually be beneficial for the firm. "Our new name puts the emphasis on the 'E' for entertainment," she commented.[7]

Creating a Script for Success

Since taking over the firm, Vince had been changing the entire focus of the wrestling shows. He looked to television soap operas for ways to enhance the entertainment value of his live events. Vince reduced the amount of actual wrestling and replaced it with wacky yet somewhat compelling story lines. He began to develop interesting characters and create compelling story lines by employing techniques that were quite similar to those being used by many successful television shows. There was a great deal of reliance on "good versus evil" or "settling the score" themes in the development of the plots for his wrestling matches. The plots and subplots ended up providing viewers with a mix of romance, sex, sports, comedy, and violence against a backdrop of pyrotechnics.

Over time, the scripts for the matches became tighter, with increasingly intricate story lines, plots, and dialogue. All the details of every match were worked out well in advance, leaving the wrestlers themselves to decide only the manner in which they would dispatch their opponents to the mat. Vince's use of characters was well thought out, and he began to refer to his wrestlers as "athletic performers" who were selected on the basis of their acting ability in addition to their physical stamina.

Vince also ensured that his firm owned the rights to the characters that were played by his wrestlers. This would allow him to continue to exploit the characters that he developed for his television shows, even after the wrestler that played a character had left his firm. By 2015, Vince held the rights to many characters that had become familiar to audiences around the world.

By the late 1990s Vince had two weekly shows on television. Besides the original flagship program on the USA cable channel, WWE had added the *Smackdown!* show on the UPN broadcast channel. He developed a continuous story line using the same characters so that his audience would be driven to both shows. But the acquisition of the WCW resulted in a significant increase in the number of wrestling stars under contract. Trying to incorporate almost 150 characters into the story lines for WWE's shows proved to be a challenging task. At the same time, the move of *Raw* to the Spike TV channel resulted in a loss of viewers.

In October 2005, WWE signed a new agreement with NBC that moved *Raw* back to its USA channel. Its other show, *Smackdown!* moved to the Syfy channel and was climbing in the charts. Its newest show, *Total Divas,* was recently launched on the E! network. All of these programs were doing well in ratings, particularly among male viewers, because of the growth in popularity of a new breed of characters such as John Cena, Chris Benoit, Ray Mysterio, and Triple H. The visibility of these characters was enhanced through profiles on the WWE website and mobile apps.

Managing a Road Show

A typical workweek for the WWE was often grueling for the McMahons, for the talent, and for the crew. In 2015 the organization was putting on almost 330 live shows a year, requiring everyone to be on the road most days of the week. The touring crew comprised over 200 crew members, including stagehands. All of WWE's live events, including those that were used for its two long-standing weekly shows *Raw* and *Smackdown!* as well as the newer ones, were held in different cities. Consequently, the crew was always packing up a dozen 18-wheelers and driving hundreds of miles to get from one performance to the other. Since there were no repeats of any WWE shows, the live performances had to be held year-round.

In fact, the live shows formed the core of all of WWE's businesses (see Exhibit 1). They gave the firm a big advantage in the entertainment world. Most of the crowd showed up wearing WWE merchandise and screamed throughout the show. Vince and his crew paid special attention to the response of the audience to different parts of the show. The script for each performance was not set until the day of the show, and sometimes changes were even made in the middle of a show. This allowed the crew some flexibility to respond to the emotions of the crowd members as they witnessed the unfolding action. Vince boasted: "We're in contact with the public more than any entertainment company in the world."[8]

EXHIBIT 1 WrestleMania's Classic Bouts

Andre the Giant vs. Hulk Hogan

WrestleMania III, March 29, 1987

- *The lowdown:* A record crowd of 93,173 witnessed Andre the Giant, undefeated for 15 years, versus Hulk Hogan, wrestling's golden boy.
- *The payoff:* Hogan body-slammed the 500-pound Giant, becoming the sport's biggest star and jump-starting wrestling's first big boom.

The Rock vs. Stone Cold Steve Austin

WrestleMania X-7, April 1, 2001

- *The lowdown:* The two biggest stars of wrestling's modern era went toe-to-toe in the culmination of a two-year-long feud.
- *The payoff:* Good-guy Austin aligned with "evil" WWE owner Vince McMahon and decimated the Rock to win the title in front of a shocked crowd.

Hulk Hogan vs. The Ultimate Warrior

WrestleMania VI, April 1, 1990

- *The lowdown:* The most divisive feud ever—fan favorite Hulk Hogan defended his title against up-and-coming phenom the Ultimate Warrior.
- *The payoff:* Half the crowd went into cardiac arrest (the other half were in tears) when Hogan missed his patented leg drop and the Warrior won.

Bret Hart vs. Shawn Michaels

WrestleMania XII, March 31, 1996

- *The lowdown:* Two men who didn't like each other outside the ring locked up in a 60-minute Iron Man match for the title.
- *The payoff:* After an hour, neither man had scored a pinfall. Finally, Michaels, aka the Heartbreak Kid, pinned Hart in overtime to win the belt.

Kurt Angle vs. Brock Lesnar

WrestleMania XIX, March 30, 2003

- *The lowdown:* Olympic medalist Angle squared off against former NCAA wrestling champ Lesnar in a punishing bout.
- *The payoff:* The 295-pound Lesnar landed on his head after attempting a high-flying attack. But he recovered to pin Angle and capture the championship.

Source: *TV Guide.*

The live shows usually filled up, and the tickets and the merchandise sold at the shows managed to cover the cost of the production. But these live performances became a source for all the other WWE revenue streams. To begin with, they provided content for six hours of original television programming as well as for the growing list of pay-per-view and video-on-demand programming. In addition, these performance shows also created strong demand for WWE merchandise, ranging from video games and toys to magazines and home videos. In fact, sales of merchandise represented a significant and growing portion of the revenues from each of the live shows.

Much of the footage from the live shows was also being used on the WWE website, which is the growth engine for its new digital media business (see Exhibits 2 and 3). The firm even produced a show, *WWE NXT,* exclusively for the website. WWE also offered content on the apps that it had launched for smartphones and tablets. Finally, fans could also follow programming on Hulu Plus, with which the firm signed an exclusive multiyear contract in 2012. All of these channels served to promote the various offerings of the firm and carried many segments from its various other television programs.

The entire operations of WWE were overseen by Vince, along with some help from other members of his family. While the slick and highly toned Vince could be regarded as the creative muscle behind the growing sports entertainment empire, his wife, Linda, had for many years been quietly managing its day-to-day operations. Throughout its existence, she had helped to balance the books, do the deals, and handle the details that were necessary for the growth and development of the WWE franchise.

EXHIBIT 2
Breakdown of Net Revenues ($ millions)

Net Revenues	2014	2013	Increase (decrease)
Media Division	$339.9	$302.7	12%
Live Events	110.7	113.1	(2)
Consumer Products Division	78.1	78.5	(1)
WWE Studios	10.9	10.8	1
Corporate & Other	3.0	2.9	3
Total	$542.6	$508.0	7

Source: WWE.

EXHIBIT 3
Breakdown of Income, EBIT ($ millions)

OIBDA			
Media Division	$98.4	$117.0	(16)%
Live Events	30.8	27.0	14
Consumer Products Division	41.2	41.1	—
WWE Studios	(12.7)	(5.5)	131
Corporate & Other	(127.3)	(116.4)	9
Total	30.4	63.2	(52)
OIBDA as a percentage of revenues	6%	13%	

Source: WWE.

Their son and daughter had also been involved with various activities of the growing enterprise, with Stephanie McMahon holding an executive position in charge of creative development.

Pursuing New Opportunities

In 1999, shortly after going public, WWE launched an eight-team football league called the XFL. Promising full competitive sport unlike the heavily-scripted wrestling matches, Vince tried to make the XFL a faster-paced, more fan-friendly form of football than the NFL's brand. Vince was able to partner with NBC, which was looking for a lower-priced alternative to the NFL televised games. The XFL kicked off with great fanfare in February 2001. Although the games drew good attendance, television ratings dropped steeply after the first week. The football venture folded after just one season, resulting in a $57 million loss for WWE. Both Vince and Linda insisted that the venture could have paid off if it had been given enough time. Vince commented: "I think our pals at the NFL went out of their way to make sure this was not a successful venture."[9]

Since then, the firm returned to seeking growth opportunities that were driven by its core wrestling business. With more characters at its disposal and different characters being used in each of its shows, WWE was ramping up the number of live shows, including more in overseas locations. By 2014, the firm was staging almost 70 shows in locations around the world. Over the past few years, WWE introduced live performances in six new countries, such as UAE and Egypt. These shows helped to boost the worldwide revenues that the firm was able to generate from its merchandise, videos, and DVDs. The company opened offices in six cities around the world to manage its overseas operations. "While it is based in America, the themes are worldwide: sibling rivalry, jealousy. We have had no pushback on the fact it was an American product," said Linda.[10]

Considerable excitement was generated by the launch of WWE 24/7, a subscriber video-on-demand service. The new service allowed the firm to distribute for a fee thousands of content-hours consisting of highlights from old shows as well as exclusive new programming. Much of the firm's programming, both old and new, was also offered on its website, which continued to show strong growth (see Exhibit 4). By allowing audiences to watch WWE programming whenever they may want to, these new forms of distribution enabled the firm to reach out to new audiences.

The new push on mobiles and through Hulu provided even more opportunities for WWE to expand into digital media. The firm believed that offering its programming on

EXHIBIT 4
Breakdown of Net Revenues ($ millions)

	Year Ended December 31		
	2014	2013	2012
Net revenues:			
Network	$114,975	$ 86,264	$ 87,690
Television	176,670	163,428	140,871
Home Entertainment	27,313	24,322	33,002
Digital Media	20,910	28,661	25,738
Live Events	110,659	113,168	106,514
Licensing	38,565	43,633	46,286
Venue Merchandise	19,336	19,397	18,774
WWEShop	20,238	15,598	14,780
WWE Studios	10,882	10,778	7,877
Corporate & Other	3,072	2,721	2,481
Total net revenues	$542,620	$507,970	$484,013

Source: WWE.

smartphones and tablets would lead to significant growth in revenues, in part from additional sales of WWE merchandise. "Our fans have proven that they want to consume WWE content day and night and now, through our new mobile app, they can stay completely connected to the action wherever they are," said Jason Hoch, WWE's recently appointed senior vice president of digital operations.[11]

Finally, WWE also became involved with producing movies featuring its wrestling stars, releasing a few films over the past decade. Recent releases included Steve Austin's *The Condemned* and John Cena's *Legendary*. In 2015, WWE was working with Warner Brothers on a Scooby-Doo animated feature that deals with a mystery at WrestleMania. WWE superstars and divas were to appear in animated form and lend their voices. Besides generating box office revenues, these movies provided revenues from home video markets, distribution on premium channels, and offerings on pay per view.

Reclaiming the Championship?

Although WWE might have found it challenging to keep building on its already formidable fan base, there was no question that it continued to generate a lot of excitement. Most of this excitement was driven by the live shows that filled up the arenas. "They have the most excited fans that have come through our doors," said the director of sales and marketing at one of the arenas that holds WWE matches. "They make signs, dress up and cheer constantly."[12] The interest in the live matches was most evident each year with the frenzy created by WrestleMania, the annual pop culture extravaganza that had become an almost weeklong celebration of everything wrestling. No wrestler became a true star until his or her performance was featured at WrestleMania, and all true fans had to make the pilgrimage at least once in their life.

WWE had begun to expand its audience by toning down its sex and violence in recent years to make its shows more family-friendly. It no longer used fake prop blood, and it toned down the use of abusive language in order to get a rating of PG for its television programming. The use of new media, such as the launch of shows through streaming video, was also expected to bring in younger viewers. "I think any good entertainment product has to change with the times," said Vince. "You have to have your fingers on the pulse of the marketplace."[13]

More recently, Vince's wrestling empire was facing a challenge from mixed martial arts (MMA), a growing form of combat sport that combined kickboxing and grappling. Because of its similarity to wrestling, this new sport was expected to pull away some of WWE's fans. Although MMA started in Japan and Brazil, the Ultimate Fighting Championship (UFC) and International Fight League were promoting it as a new type of spectator sport in the U.S. But Dana White, president of UFC, said: "People have been trying to count the W.W.E. out for years. They are a powerhouse."[14]

Beyond this, there are questions about the future of WWE after Vince McMahon. Now approaching 69, Vince had single-handedly built his wrestling empire from his father's small regional business. Although he involved his wife and children in the firm, he was always the brains behind all of the strategic moves over the years. The launch of the WWE Network, which represented a significant new step, could be his final act in charge, according to industry observers. "If he has changed how pro wrestling and sports entertainment will reach audiences in the future, I don't think there's a better way to go out," said Brandon Stroud, a wrestling commentator and editor at the sports site *With Leather*.[15]

Those who understand don't need an explanation. Those who need an explanation will never understand.

—**Marty , a 19-year-old wrestling addict, quoted in** *Fortune,* **October 6, 2000**

ENDNOTES

1. *Business Wire.* WWE Network hits 1 million subscribers. January 27, 2015.
2. WWE. World Wrestling Entertainment, Inc. reports Q3 results. Press release, February 23, 2005.
3. Bethany McLean. Inside the world's weirdest family business. *Fortune,* October 16, 2000, p. 298.
4. Diane Bradley. Wrestling's real grudge match. *Business Week,* January 24, 2000, p. 164.
5. Don Mooradian. WWF gets a grip after acquisition. *Amusement Business,* June 4, 2001, p. 20.
6. Dwight Oestricher & Brian Steinberg. WW . . . E it is, after fight for F nets new name. *Wall Street Journal,* May 7, 2002, p. B2.
7. David Finnigan. Down but not out, WWE is using a rebranding effort to gain strength. *Brandweek,* June 3, 2002, p. 12.
8. McLean, op. cit., p. 304.
9. Diane Bradley. Rousing itself off the mat? *Business Week,* February 2, 2004, p. 73.
10. Brooke Masters. Wrestling's bottom line is no soap opera. *Financial Times,* August 25, 2008, p. 15.
11. *Business Wire.* WWE launches free mobile second screen app. August 17, 2012.
12. Brandi Ball. The face of the WWE. *McClatchy-Tribune Business News,* January 13, 2011.
13. Seth Berkman. The body slam is buffering. *New York Times,* March 31, 2014, p. B7.
14. R. M. Schneiderman. Better days, and even the candidates, are coming to WWE. *New York Times,* April 28, 2008, p. B3.
15. Berkman, op. cit., p. B1.

CASES

CASE 23
QVC*

The world's largest home shopping firm announced that it would debut a new brand of handmade, all-natural and tradition-inspired fine prepared food on its QVC channel on January 21, 2015. Called Ever So Saucy Foods, the line of fine foods would be prepared by Chef Frank in his Yaphank, New York, state-of-the-art facility. The foods would be hand-packed and then fresh-frozen by a proprietary blast-freeze process at −25 degrees Fahrenheit that would seal in the natural flavors and nutrients, while preserving the just-out-of-the-oven taste. The food line would also become available on QVC's website.

Since it was launched in 1986, QVC had rapidly grown to become the largest television shopping network. Although it entered the market a couple of years after rival Home Shopping Network, QVC managed to build a leading position. By 2014, its reach extended to almost 300 million households all over the world. It regularly shipped over 170 million products annually to customers, resulting in almost $8.8 million in sales (see Exhibits 1 and 2). It attracted audiences to watch its shows across the United States, United Kingdom, Germany, Japan, and, since 2010, Italy (see Exhibit 3).

The success of QVC was largely driven by its popular television home shopping shows that featured a wide variety of eye-catching products, many of which were unique to the channel. It organized product searches in cities all over the U.S. in order to continuously find new offerings from entrepreneurs that could be pitched at customers. During these events, the firm screened hundreds of products to select those that it would offer. In one of its recent searches, QVC evaluated the appeal of products such as nail clippers that catch clippings, bicycle seats built for bigger bottoms, and novelty items shaped like coffins.

But QVC was also trying to entice new customers by battling the perception that direct-response TV retailers sold just hokey, flimsy, or kitschy goods. Its jewelry selection featured prestigious brands such as Tacori, which was worn by TV stars. It offered clothing from couture designers such as Marc Bouwer, who had made clothing for Angelina Jolie and Halle Berry. And it recently added exclusive products from reality stars such as Kim Kardashian and Rachel Zoe. Such vendors introduced thousands of customers to QVC, often through social media like Facebook and Twitter. "Rachel Zoe brings so many new customers it's staggering," said CEO Michael George.[1]

Furthermore, QVC expanded its shopping experience to the Internet, attracting more than 7 million unique monthly visitors by early 2015. It continued to attract customers from its television channel to its website, making it one of the leading multimedia retailers. Building on this, the firm was creating a family of mobile shopping applications for smartphones and tablets. Although QVC was still developing this segment, mobile applications were already accounting for almost one-third of its sales.

Pursuing a Leading Position

QVC was founded by Joseph Segel in June 1986 and began broadcasting by November of the same year. In early 1986, Segel had tuned in to the Home Shopping Network, which had been launched just two years earlier. He was not particularly impressed with the crude programming

EXHIBIT 1 Annual Sales ($ billions)

Year	Sales
2014	$8.8
2013	8.6
2012	8.5
2011	8.3
2010	7.8
2009	7.4
2008	7.3
2007	7.4
2006	7.1
2004	5.7
2001	3.8
1998	2.4
1995	1.6
1992	0.9
1989	0.2

Source: QVC, Liberty Media.

---

* Case prepared by Jamal Shamsie, Michigan State University, with the assistance of Professor Alan B. Eisner, Pace University. Material has been drawn from published sources to be used for purposes of class discussion. Copyright © 2015 Jamal Shamsie and Alan B. Eisner.

EXHIBIT 2
Consolidated Income Statements ($ millions)

	Year Ended December 31		
	2014	2013	2012
Net revenue	$8,801	$8,623	$8,516
Cost of goods sold	5,547	5,465	5,419
Gross profit	3,254	3,158	3,097
Operating expenses:*			
Operating	753	740	715
Selling, general and administrative, including stock-based compensation	635	615	588
Depreciation†	135	127	126
Amortization†	452	431	400
	1,975	1,913	1,829
Operating income	1,279	1,245	1,268
Other (expense) income:			
Equity in losses of investee	(8)	(4)	(4)
Gains on financial instruments	—	15	48
Interest expense, net	(239)	(214)	(233)
Foreign currency gain	3	1	2
Loss on extinguishment of debt	(48)	(57)	—
	(292)	(259)	(187)
Income before income taxes	987	986	1,081
Income tax expense	(354)	(353)	(394)
Net income	633	633	687
Less net income attributable to the noncontrolling interest	(39)	(45)	(63)
Net income attributable to QVC, Inc. stockholder	$ 594	$ 588	$ 624

*Operating expenses consist of commissions and license fees, order processing and customer service, credit card processing fees, and provision for doubtful accounts.

†Depreciation and amortization include amortization of intangible assets recorded in connection with the purchase of QVC by Liberty Media.

Source: Liberty Media, QVC.

and the down-market products of the firm. But Segel was convinced that another televised shopping network would have the potential to attract a large-enough client base. He also felt that such an enterprise should be able to produce significant profits, because the operating expenses for a shopping network could be kept relatively low.

Over the next few months, Segel raised $30 million in start-up capital, hired several seasoned television executives, and launched his own shopping network. Operating out of headquarters that were located in West Chester, Pennsylvania, QVC offered 24-hour-a-day, seven-day-a-week television home shopping to consumers at home. By the end of its first year of operation, QVC had managed to extend its reach to 13 million homes by satellite and cable systems. Among its viewers, 700,000 had already become customers, resulting in the shipping of 3 million orders. Its sales topped $100 million, and the firm was actually able to show a small profit.

EXHIBIT 3 Geographic Breakdown of Revenue ($ millions)

	Year Ended December 31		
	2014	2013	2012
QVC-U.S.	$6,055	$5,844	$5,585
QVC-Germany	970	971	956
QVC-Japan	908	1,024	1,247
QVC-U.K.	730	657	641
QVC-Italy	138	127	87
Total	$8,801	$8,623	$8,516

Source: Liberty Media, QVC.

Segel attributed the instant success of his company to the potential offered by television shopping. "Television's combination of sight, sound and motion is the best way to sell a product. It is more effective than presenting a product in print or just putting the product on a store shelf," he stated. "The cost-efficiency comes from the cable distribution system. It is far more economical than direct mail, print advertising, or traditional retail store distribution."[2]

In the fall of 1988, Segel acquired the manufacturing facilities, proprietary technology, and trademark rights of the Diamonique Corporation, which produced a wide range of simulated gemstones and jewelry that could be sold on QVC's shows. Over the next couple of years, Segel expanded QVC by acquiring its competitors such as the Cable Value Network shopping channel (see Exhibit 4).

By 1993, QVC had overtaken Home Shopping Network to become the leading televised shopping channel in terms of sales and profits. Its reach extended to over 80 percent of all cable homes and to 3 million satellite dishes. Segel retired during the same year, passing control of the company to Barry Diller. Since then, QVC's sales continued to grow at a substantial rate. As a result, it consistently widened the gap between its sales and those of Home Shopping Network, which remained its closest competitor.

Striving for Retailing Excellence

Over the years, QVC managed to establish itself as the world's preeminent virtual shopping mall that never closes. Its televised shopping channel became a place where customers around the world could, and did, shop at any hour at the rate of more than five customers per second. It sold a wide variety of products, using a combination of description and demonstration by live-program hosts. QVC was extremely selective in choosing its hosts, screening as many as 3,000 applicants annually in order to pick three. New hosts were trained for at least six months before they were allowed to be on a show. In addition, most of the products were offered on regularly scheduled shows, each of which focused on a particular type of product and a well-defined market. Each of these shows typically lasted for one hour and was based on a theme such as "Now You're Cooking" or "Cleaning Solutions."

QVC frequently enticed celebrities such as clothing designers or book authors to appear live on special program segments in order to sell their own products. To prepare them to succeed, celebrities were given training on how to best pitch their offerings. On some occasions, customers were able to call in and have on-air conversations with program hosts and visiting celebrities. Celebrities were therefore often schooled in QVC's "backyard-fence" style, which means conversing with viewers the way they would chat with a friendly neighbor. "They're just so down-home, so it's like they're right in your living room demonstrating," said a long-time QVC customer.[3]

In spite of the folksy presentation, the sales were minutely managed. Behind the scenes, a producer scanned nine television and computer screens to track sales of each featured item. "We track new orders per minute in increments of six seconds; we can look backward in time and see what it was that drove that spike," said Doug Rose, who oversaw programming and marketing.[4] Hosts and guests were prompted to make adjustments in their pitch that might increase sales. A beauty designer was recently asked to rub an eyeliner on her hand, which immediately led to a surge of new orders.

QVC's themed programs were telecast live 24 hours a day, seven days a week, to millions of households worldwide. The shopping channel transmitted its programming live from its central production facilities in Pennsylvania through uplinks to a satellite. The representatives who staffed QVC's four call centers, which handled more than 180 million calls in 2014, were well trained to take orders.

Of all the orders placed with QVC, more than 90 percent were shipped within 48 hours from one of its distribution centers. The distribution centers had a combined floor space equal to the size of over 100 football fields. Everyone at QVC worked hard to make sure that every item worked as it should before it was shipped and that its packaging would protect it during the shipping process. "Nothing ships unless it is quality-inspected first," said one of the logistics managers for QVC. "Since our product is going business-to-consumer, there's no way to fix or change a product-related problem."[5]

EXHIBIT 4
QVC Milestones

Year	Event
1986	Launched by Joseph Segel, broadcasting from studios in West Chester, PA.
1987	Expands programming to 24 hours a day.
1988	Acquires Diamonique, manufacturer of simulated gemstone jewelry.
1993	Segel retires and Barry Diller is named chairman & CEO. Launches channel in U.K.
1995	Acquired by Comcast; Doug Briggs takes over as president & CEO.
1996	Launches Internet site.
2001	Launches channel in Japan.
2003	Sold off to Liberty Media.
2005	Mike George is named president.
2006	George takes over as CEO with retirement of Briggs.
2007	Ships its billionth package in the U.S.
2008	Launches QVCHD, a high-definition simulcast in the U.S.
2009	Rolls out several mobile services.
2010	Launches channel in Italy.
2012	Acquires e-commerce shopping site Send the Trend. Launches joint venture in China.
2013	Launches QVC PLUS as a second channel in the U.S.
2014	Announces launching of channel in France next year.

Source: QVC.

Searching for Profitable Products

More than 100 experienced, informed buyers combed the world on a regular basis to search for new products to launch on QVC. The shopping channel concentrated on unique products that could be demonstrated on live television. Furthermore, the price of these products had to be high enough for viewers to justify the additional shipping and handling charge. Over the course of a typical year, QVC carried more than 60,000 products. As many as 1,000 items were typically offered in any given week, of which about 20 percent were new products for the network. QVC's suppliers ranged from some of the world's biggest companies to small entrepreneurial enterprises.

All new products had to, however, pass through stringent tests that were carried out by QVC's in-house Quality Assurance Lab. In many cases, this inspection process was carried out manually by the firm's employees. Only 15 percent of the products passed the firm's rigorous quality inspection on first try, and as many as one-third were never offered to the public because they failed altogether. In addition, Jeffrey Rayport, author of a book on customer service, stated that "QVC staff look for a product that is complex enough—or interesting enough—that the host can talk about it on air."[6]

About one-third of QVC's sales came from broadly available national brands. The firm was able to build trust among its customers in large part through the offering of these well-known brands. QVC also relied upon promotional campaigns with a variety of existing firms for another one-third of its sales. It made deals with firms such as Dell, Target, and Bath & Body Works for special limited-time promotional offerings. But QVC was most successful with products that were exclusively sold on QVC or were not readily available through other distribution channels. Although such products accounted for another one-third of its sales, the firm was able to earn higher margins with these proprietary products, many of which came from firms that were either start-ups or new entrants into the U.S. market.

Most vendors were attracted to QVC because they reaped higher profits by selling through its channel than they would by selling through physical stores. Stores typically required that vendors help to train or pay the sales force and participate in periodic sales during which prices were discounted. QVC rarely sold products at discount prices. Maureen Kelly, founder of Tarte Cosmetics, said she typically made more from an eight-minute segment on QVC than she used to make in a month at a high-end department store.

Apart from searching for exclusive products, QVC was also trying to move away from some product categories, such as home appliances and electronic gadgets, which offered lower margins. It was gradually expanding into many new product categories that had higher margins, such as cosmetics, apparel, food, and toys. Several of these new categories displayed the strongest rates of sales growth for the shopping channel over the past couple of years.

Expanding upon the Customer Base

Since its start-up, QVC's shopping channel had managed to gradually penetrate almost all of the cable television and broadcast satellite homes in the U.S. But only about 10 percent of the households that it reached actually bought anything from the network. However, QVC developed a large customer base, and many of its customers made as many as 10 purchases in a year. QVC devotees readily called in to the live segments to offer product testimonials, were up on the personal lives of their favorite program hosts, and generally viewed the channel as entertaining. "As weird as it may sound, for people who love the network, it's good company," said Rayport.[7]

QVC was hoping to attract new customers on the basis of the reasonably strong reputation that surveys indicated it had established among a large majority of its current buyers. By its initials alone, QVC had promised that it would deliver "Quality, Value and Convenience" to its viewers. More than three-quarters of the shopping channel's customers gave it a score of 7 out of 7 for trustworthiness. This led most of its customers to recommend QVC to their friends.

QVC also benefited from the growing percentage of women entering the workforce, resulting in a significant increase in dual-income families. Although the firm's customer base spanned several socioeconomic groups, it was led by young professional families who had above-average disposable income. These families enjoyed various forms of "thrill-seeking" activities and ranked shopping relatively higher as a leisure activity than did the typical consumer.

The firm was also trying to increase sales by making it easier for customers to buy its products. It added features such as an interactive service that allowed customers to purchase products offered on its shopping channel with the single click of a remote. QVC also provided a credit program that allowed customers to pay for goods over a period of several months. Everything it sold was backed by a 30-day unconditional money-back guarantee. Furthermore, QVC did not impose any hidden charges, such as a restocking fee, for any returned merchandise. These policies helped the home shopping channel to attract customers for products that they could view but could neither touch nor feel.

In 2012, QVC built on its existing customer base by acquiring Send the Trend, Inc., an e-commerce destination known for trendy fashion and beauty products. It used proprietary technology to deliver monthly personalized recommendations, which could easily be shared by customers over their social networks, on an assortment of prestigious brands of jewelry, beauty, and fashion accessories. "The teams at QVC and Share the Trend share a passion for bringing the customer what she wants, in the way she wants it," said Claire Watts, the U.S.-based CEO of QVC.[8]

Positioning for Future Growth

In spite of its success on television, QVC had not ignored opportunities that were emerging in online shopping. Since 1995, the firm had offered a website to complement its television channel, providing QVC with another means of access to customers. Initially, the site offered more detailed information about QVC offerings. Later, it branched out to develop its own customer base by featuring many products that had not been recently shown on QVC's television channel. Over the past few years, QVC fine-tuned its website by offering mobile phone, interactive-television, and iPad apps.

By 2012, QVC.com, a once-negligible part of the QVC empire, accounted for about one-third of the firm's domestic revenue. CEO Michael George recently stated that 60 percent of QVC's new customers in the United States were buying via the Internet or mobile devices. "The online business is becoming such a crucial part of the business for QVC," remarked Douglas Anmuth, an analyst at Barclay's Capital.[9] Furthermore, QVC.com was now more profitable than QVC's television operation. It needed fewer call-center workers, and while QVC had to share profits on TV orders with cable companies, it did not have to pay them on online orders for products that had not been featured on the air for 24 hours.

Its online efforts did not lead QVC to move its emphasis away from television home shopping. The recent launch of a channel in Italy proved to be very successful, generating 58 percent more sales than the overall average generated from all of its other markets. The firm just started a joint venture in China, providing access to a huge developing market. With plans to start operations in France during 2015, it was also expanding to more European countries.

For many of its loyal consumers, nothing would ever replace shopping on television. The website did not offer the hybrid of talk show and sales pitch that attracted audiences to the QVC shopping channel. Online shoppers also missed out on the interaction between hosts and shoppers and the continuous feedback on the time left to order before an item would be sold out. "You know, on Sundays I might find a program on Lifetime Movie Network, but whatever I'm watching, if it's not QVC, when the commercial comes on I'll flip it back to QVC," said one loyal QVC fan. "I'm just stuck on them."[10]

ENDNOTES

1. Stephanie Clifford. Can QVC translate its pitch online? *New York Times*, November 21, 2010, p. B7.
2. QVC annual report, 1987–1988.
3. *New York Times*, November 21, 2010, p. B7.
4. Ibid.
5. Eugene Gilligan. The show must go on. *Journal of Commerce*, April 12, 2004, p. 1.
6. *USA Today*, May 5, 2008, p. 2B.
7. Ibid.
8. Send the Trend relaunches with QVC to bring shoppers a more personalized e-commerce experience. *PR Newswire*, October 2, 2012.
9. *New York Times*, op. cit.
10. Ibid.

CASES

CASE 24

NINTENDO'S WII U*

Did Nintendo have the pieces in place to take control of the gaming market?

The Nintendo Wii U console had been on the market for only a short while, with the addition of innovative controls and new game titles. One of the key areas of discussion in the popular press was whether or not the console defined the "next generation" of gaming. There had been uncertainties among industry experts, such as Gabrielle Shrager of Ubisoft and Mikael Haveri of Frozenbyte, as to whether or not the improved power and new controller interface justified the system being considered a "new" generation.[1]

The Wii U initially launched with 50 available games and a new controller interface, termed the GamePad. While the GamePad offered a new take on the Wii's controls, the new console was still compatible with the same motion-sensing controllers of the original Wii. However, the Wii U console was not sold with these controllers included. Instead, it came with just one of the new GamePads. Incorporating traits from tablet devices, the GamePad integrated both traditional input methods—such as buttons, dual analog sticks, and a D-pad (directional pad)—and a touchscreen. The touchscreen could be used to supplement a game by providing alternative functionality or an alternative view of a scenario in a game. With the Off TV Play function, the screen could also be used to play a game strictly on the GamePad screen, without the use of a television display at all. With the Wii U console turned on, the GamePad could be used to display the same picture on its screen as would be seen using a TV display. There were also nongaming functions, such as the ability to use the GamePad as a television remote. While Nintendo was the first of the competitors to release its new gaming console, there was no doubt that both Sony's PlayStation and Microsoft's Xbox would be close behind in releasing their own upgraded systems.

While Nintendo had hopes of becoming the leader in its industry with the Wii U, its initial sales were not what the company had anticipated. Its best week was its first: 400,000 Wii U units were sold in the week following its November 18, 2012, launch date. In Japan 300,000 units were sold in the console's launch week (see Exhibit 1). Arvind Bhatia, an analyst from Sterne Agee, believed that Wii U sales at US mega-chain retailer GameStop were far below the company's initial expectations for the holiday season. According to Bhatia, there was no shortage of Wii U units at GameStop outlets, a telltale sign that demand for the console was lacking during the holiday season.[2] Sure enough, in January and February 2013 sales dropped dramatically, to roughly 57,000 and 64,000 units, respectively—significantly lower than the original Wii sales following its launch. This undoubtedly caused worry among the Nintendo team, who had experienced huge sales spikes at the introduction of the original Wii.

Since its release, the Wii had led video games' entrance to the cultural mainstream. Neither the Microsoft Xbox 360 nor the Sony PlayStation 3 offered the sorts of game controls that could truly appeal to a mass audience, and particularly to families that wanted to have fun together at home. Only the Wii had intuitive, motion-sensitive game controllers so gamers could sway the controller around and swing and twist it in space to bowl or evoke some other action on the screen. Nintendo was the only company of the group whose numbers were solely focused on the gaming industry. Both Microsoft and Sony had highly diversified operations, in which gaming played only a small role. Therefore, in comparing their revenues, Nintendo's numbers were much more impressive than they might have seemed at first glance.

However, by the fall of 2010 the playing field was level, with Sony and Microsoft offering competition for the Wii motion-sensitive controllers. Looking at Kinect from Microsoft for the Xbox 360 and the Move system from Sony for PlayStation 3, it was clear that the two leading competitors had finally caught up with the Wii's lead in engineering and its ingenious human interface. For almost four years, the Wii had reshaped the home-entertainment experience. But, by 2011, some observers feared that the Wii no longer did anything unique that the PS3 or Xbox 360 would not do even better.[3] PlayStation 3 and Xbox 360 already had superior graphics to the Wii, and now they had motion-sensing controllers as well. With the debut of Nintendo's new generation of consoles, one question remained uppermost: While Nintendo's Wii U might have brought some intriguing improvements to the table, was it substantial enough to be considered the "new generation of gaming" and would it encompass innovation that its competitors would not be able to match—or worse—surpass? While the original Wii was able to hold on to its lead for a sustained period of time, the initial outlook for the Wii U did not look so optimistic, with the release of competing consoles apparently not far behind.

---

* This case was prepared by Professor Alan B. Eisner and graduate students Eshai J. Gorshein, and Eric S. Engelson of Pace University. This case was based solely on library research and was developed for class discussion rather than to illustrate either effective or ineffective handling of an administrative situation. Copyright © 2015 Alan B. Eisner.

EXHIBIT 1
Wii U Launch-Week Sales

Region	Units Sold	Time Period Following Launch
United States	425,000	First month
United Kingdom	40,000	First weekend
Japan	638,000+	First month
Total	1,103,000+	Within first month

Source: Saito, Mari, and Murai, Reiji. 2013. Year-end Wii U sales steady. *www.reuters.com/article/2013/01/07/us-nintendo-console-sales-idUSBRE90605420130107*.

Not too long after the release of the Wii U, Sony announced the planned release of its next gaming console, the PS4, on February 20, 2013. While Sony did not show the PS4 at its two-hour event in New York City that evening, the console was made available in time for the 2013 holiday season.[4]

Nintendo's inability to leap ahead of its competition could be seen clearly in its financial figures. As of 2014, Nintendo's income was off from previous years (see Exhibits 2 and 3).

Background

Although Nintendo dated back to 1889 as a playing-card maker, Nintendo's first video-game systems were developed in 1979 and known as TV Game 15 and TV Game 6.[5] In 1980 Nintendo developed the first portable LCD video game with a microprocessor. In 1985 Nintendo created the Nintendo Entertainment System (NES), an 8-bit video game console. The original NES was very successful, as its graphics were superior to any home-based console available at the time. As a result, more than 60 million units were sold worldwide.[6] The NES set the bar for subsequent consoles in platform design, as well as for accepting games that were manufactured by third-party developers.

When competitors began developing 16-bit devices, such as Sega's Genesis system and NEC's PC Engine, Nintendo responded with its own 16-bit system, the Super Nintendo Entertainment System (SNES). The Super Nintendo was released in 1991 and, when purchased, came with one game, *Super Mario World*. In 1996 Nintendo released Nintendo 64. The Nintendo 64 was the company's third-generation video game console and was named after the 64-bit processor. During its product lifetime, more than 30 million Nintendo 64 units were sold worldwide.[7]

The Nintendo 64, like its predecessors, used cartridges to play its games, but at the time the competing Sony and Sega systems were using CDs for game storage. Cartridges could store 64 megabytes of data, while CDs could store around 700 megabytes. Also, CDs were much cheaper to manufacture, distribute, and create; the average cost of producing a Nintendo 64 cartridge was $25, compared to 10 cents to produce a CD. Therefore, game producers passed the higher expense to the consumer, which explained why Nintendo 64 games tended to sell for higher prices than Sony PlayStation games. While most Sony PlayStation games rarely exceeded $50, Nintendo 64 titles could reach $70. To increase profits and to take advantage of the programming possibilities of the larger storage space, many third-party game developers that had traditionally supported Nintendo platforms began creating games for systems that used a CD platform (such as the PlayStation).[8]

In 2001 Nintendo released its GameCube, which was part of the sixth-generation era of video game systems. These systems included Sony's PlayStation 2, Microsoft's Xbox, and Sega's Dreamcast. Although the GameCube did not use cartridges, Nintendo began producing its games using a proprietary optical-disk technology. This technology, while similar in appearance to CDs, was actually smaller in diameter and could not be played using a standard CD player.

Genyo Takeda, general manager of Integrated Research and Development for Nintendo, explained that innovation and creativity were fostered by giving several different development teams "free rein to couple a dedicated controller or peripheral with a GameCube title and then seeing whether or not the end result was marketable. This project gave rise not only to the Donkey Kong Bongos and the Dancing Stage Mario Mix Action Pad, but also to a number of ideas and designs that would find their way into the Wii Remote."[9]

When Nintendo released the Wii video game console in 2006, it was already in the midst of a very competitive market. The previous generation of video game consoles consisted of the Sega Dreamcast, Sony PlayStation 2, Nintendo GameCube, and Microsoft Xbox. These systems were all released between 1999 and 2001 in the United States, and although the GameCube sold more systems than the Sega Dreamcast, it fell into third place behind the PlayStation 2 and the Xbox. The PlayStation 2 sold more than 115 million units worldwide, more than twice the combined unit sales of the GameCube and Xbox (21 million and 24 million, respectively).

The Term *Wii*

In 2006 Nintendo released its direct successor to the GameCube, the Wii (pronounced "we"). There were many reasons cited as to why the name *Wii* was chosen, but perhaps the most compelling reason was that "'Wii' sounded like 'we,' which emphasized that the console was

EXHIBIT 2 Income Statement (Japanese yen in millions, except per-share items)

Go to library tab in Connect to access Case Financials.

	Year Ended March 31				
	2010	2011	2012	2013	2014
Revenue	1,434,365	1,014,345	647,652	635,422	571,726
Cost of revenue	859,131	626,379	493,997	495,068	408,506
Gross profit	575,234	387,966	153,655	140,354	163,220
Operating expenses					
Other operating expenses	218,666	216,889	190,975	176,764	209,645
Total operating expenses	218,666	216,889	190,975	176,764	209,645
Operating income	356,568	171,077	−37,320	−36,410	−46,425
Other income (expense)	10,874	−43,143	−23,557	46,607	57,354
Income before taxes	367,442	127,934	−608,77	10,197	10,929
Provision for income taxes	138,896	50,262	−17,659	3,029	34,132
Net income from continuing operations	228,546	77,672	−43,218	7,168	−23,203
Other	89	−1	1		1
Net income	228,635	77,671	−43,217	7,168	−23,202
Preferred dividend		50	−13	69	20
Net income available to common shareholders	228,635	77,621	−43,204	7,099	−23,222
Earnings per share					
Basic	223.48	75.87	−42.23	6.94	−22.95
Diluted	223.48	75.87	−42.23	6.94	−22.95
Weighted average shares outstanding					
Basic	1,023	1,023	1,023	1,023	1,012
Diluted	1,023	1,023	1,023	1,023	1,012
EBITDA	363,665	177,870	−24,797	−23,773	−36,507

Source: http://financials.morningstar.com/income-statement/.

for everyone. Wii could be remembered easily by people around the world, no matter what language they spoke. No confusion."[10] Initially the system was known by its code name, Revolution, but later the name was changed to Wii. Nintendo stated that it wanted to make the Wii a system that would make anyone who tried it talk to his or her friends and neighbors about it.[11]

The Making of the Remote

The original Wii was created to establish a new standard in game control, using an innovative and unprecedented interface, the Wii Remote.[12] The Wii Remote was what made the Wii unique. The remote acted as the primary controller for the Wii. Its motion-sensor capabilities allowed the user to interact with and manipulate objects on the screen by moving and pointing the remote in various directions. The Wii Remote was the size of a traditional remote control, and it was "limited only by the game designer's imagination."[13] For example, in a game of tennis it served as the racket when the user swung his or her arm, while in a shooting game it served as the user's gun. Not only did the remote serve as a controller, but it also had a built-in speaker and a rumble feature for even greater tactile feedback and game involvement. Exhibit 4 shows the Wii and Wii Remote.

EXHIBIT 3 Balance Sheet (Japanese yen in millions)

	Year Ended March 31				
	2010	2011	2012	2013	2014
Assets					
Current assets					
Cash and cash equivalents	886,995	812,870	462,021	478,761	474,297
Short-term investments	365,326	358,206	496,301	424,540	320,918
Total cash	1,252,321	1,171,076	958,322	903,301	795,215
Receivables	131,876	135,689	43,378	45,873	
Inventories	124,673	92,712	78,446	178,722	160,801
Deferred income taxes	35,193	27,620	16,744	31,693	17,637
Other current assets	47,325	41,609	43,896	32,661	50,483
Total current assets	1,591,388	1,468,706	1,140,786	1,192,250	1,024,136
Net property, plant and equipment	79,586	80,864	87,856	86,152	94,190
Intangible assets	4,111	5,539	7,706	10,862	12,467
Deferred income taxes	35,929	35,017	57,185	37,690	34,214
Other long-term assets	49,972	44,171	74,868	120,924	136,657
Total non-current assets	169,598	165,591	227,615	255,628	282,274
Total assets	1,760,986	1,634,297	1,368,401	1,447,878	1,306,410
Liabilities and stockholders' equity					
Liabilities					
Current liabilities					
Accounts payable	264,613	214,646	867,00	107,045	47,665
Taxes payable	55,666	32,301	1,008	3,563	14,803
Other current liabilities	87,258	86,354	67,730	83,867	93,184
Total current liabilities	407,537	333,301	155,438	194,475	155,652
Pensions and other benefits					18,558
Minority interest	174	224	81	131	157
Other long-term liabilities	16,864	19,134	21,938	25,885	13,762
Total non-current liabilities	17,038	19,358	22,019	26,016	32,477
Total liabilities	424,575	352,659	177,457	220,491	188,129
Stockholders' equity					
Additional paid-in capital	11,733	11,734	11,734	11,734	11,734
Retained earnings	1,527,315	1,502,631	1,419,784	1,414,095	1,378,085
Treasury stock	−156,585	−156,663	−156,682	−156,692	−270,958

continued

EXHIBIT 3 Continued

	Year Ended March 31				
	2010	2011	2012	2013	2014
Accumulated other comprehensive income	−45,878	−75,841	−83,811	−41,617	−423
Total stockholders' equity	1,336,585	1,281,861	1,191,025	1,227,520	1,118,438
Total liabilities and stockholders' equity	1,761,160	1,634,520	1,368,482	1,448,011	1,306,567

Source: http://financials.morningstar.com/balance-sheet/.

EXHIBIT 4 Wii Console and Remote

EXHIBIT 5 Wii U GamePad Controller

The second part of the Wii Remote innovation was the Wii Nunchuk. The Nunchuk was designed to perfectly fit the user's hand, and it connected to the remote at its expansion port. The Nunchuk had the same motion-sensing capabilities that the remote had, but it also had an analog stick to help the user move his or her characters. The ambidextrous nature of the Wii controllers was something seldom seen in other game controllers; the Wii controllers permitted the user to hold the remote and Nunchuk whichever way felt most comfortable.[14] In addition to the analog stick, the Nunchuk had two buttons that gave the user quick access to other game functions. Thus, the Nunchuk offered some of the benefits of a standard game controller coupled with the high-technology motion sensors of the remote. Users could hold a Nunchuk in one hand and the Wii Remote in the other while playing the *Wii Sports* boxing game and be transported into the boxing ring with on-screen opponents. The game controls were intuitive for jabs and punches; however, a missed block did not hurt as much as if one were really in the boxing ring.

While the Wii U was still compatible with the original Wii controllers, Nintendo revamped the controller usability when designing the Wii U. The new GamePad sold with the Wii U allowed the user to be more in touch with the game and provided more depth by offering multiperspective capabilities on the Pad's screen. While using the TV display, players could now multitask within a game by using a variety of functions on their controller and could even play using solely the GamePad, with no TV display necessary. With the game console turned on, players had the option of using the GamePad as their main viewing screen, without the need for a TV monitor display (see Exhibit 5).

Features

In addition to the Wii Remote, there were other features unique to the Wii. One was the Wii Menu, which was the first screen that appeared on the television when the Wii was turned on. According to Nintendo, the Wii Menu easily integrated itself into the everyday lives of its users.[15]

The menu displayed several different icons; one of them was the Mii Channel (pronounced "me"). This channel gave users the ability to create and personalize a 3-D caricature of themselves. Another icon was the Everybody Votes Channel, which permitted individuals to vote in national and worldwide polls on a variety of topics. There was also the New Channel, which gave the individual breaking news from around the world, organized into a variety of topics. The Forecast Channel allowed the individual to view weather reports from anywhere around the world. Users also had the ability to download older Nintendo games from the Wii Shopping Channel. The Wii Message Board allowed users to leave messages on the Wii for other users of the same console or leave reminders for themselves. The Internet Channel allowed individuals to surf the Internet from their Wii. The Photo Channel allowed the user to view photos stored on a standard SD memory card. And, lastly, there was the Disc Channel, which gave the user the ability to play Wii games or Nintendo GameCube discs.[16] The Wii was backward-compatible with the Nintendo GameCube's games, memory cards, and controllers.

Innovative Enhancements

In 2014, Nintendo introduced Amiibo figurines that depicted popular Nintendo characters and each contained a wireless antenna and flash memory. They allowed consumers to include digital versions of their favorite characters in compatible video games.

The "toys to life" segment had been created in 2011 when Activision Blizzard launched the hugely successful Skylanders line of games and figures. Disney subsequently jumped into the ring by launching a competing product, Disney Infinity, in August 2013.

Nintendo hoped to penetrate the segment and boost sales of its Wii U console and 3DS handheld in the process. In late 2014, the company released its first round of Amiibo characters: Mario, Peach, Yoshi, Donkey Kong, Link, Fox, Samus, Wii Fit Trainer, Villager, Pikachu, Kirby, and Marth. It also planned to launch a host of additional popular characters like Zelda, Luigi, Diddy Kong, Little Mac, Pit, and Captain Falcon in 2015.[17]

Demographics

According to Nintendo, one of the key differences between the Wii and competitors' systems was the broad audience that the Wii targeted.[18] Many of the Wii games could be played by people of all ages, and the Wii Remote and Nunchuk were easier to use than the complicated controllers of the Sony PlayStation 3 or Microsoft Xbox 360. Nintendo's TV commercials for the Wii showed people of different ages and social classes playing the Wii. According to Nintendo, the Wii Remote allowed people of all ages to enjoy its use. The Wii offered something for both the advanced gamer and the person who had never played a video game before. The advanced gamer would enjoy the remote's unique features, whereas the novice gamer could use the remote as his or her hand and wouldn't need elaborate instructions on how to play a new game straight out of the box.

Although the Nintendo games were easily played by a greater range of ages, the graphics were undoubtedly a relative weakness of the product.[19] Thus, while Nintendo hoped to target people of all ages, it had long been seen as a system that made video games for children, as evident from its *Mario, Zelda,* and *Donkey Kong* series. However, despite this limitation, the innovation and uniqueness of its game play was enough to lure the masses, and sales were excellent.

Success, of course, bred competition. Upon seeing the success of the movement-sensing Wii, Microsoft and Sony moved quickly to release competing systems. Microsoft released its Kinect for the Xbox 360, while Sony released the Move for the PS3. Both the Move and Kinect used camera systems for their motion detectors, but in different ways. Move's camera sensed the movement of the light-up Move controller, whereas Microsoft's Kinect sensor tracked skeletal motion, eliminating the need for a controller.[20] While it was inevitable that gamers would have their favorite of the bunch, the relevant point was that it didn't take long for Microsoft and Sony to catch up to Nintendo. They moved forward to the new generation(s) of gaming on an even playing field for gamer interaction and motion detection.

Gaining the Interest of Game Developers

As evident from the history of game consoles, game developers had tried to make games more and more complex with each new generation of systems. This meant that more money was invested in the production of each subsequent generation of games. Because game developers were spending more money on developing games, they were at great financial risk if games did not succeed. Thus, many developers felt more secure in simply creating sequels to existing games, which in turn restricted innovation. The Wii's innovative controller, the Wii Remote, required a rethinking and reengineering of the human interface by game developers and programmers. Another issue with developing games for the Wii was that its graphics were not quite as good as those of the PlayStation 3 and Xbox 360, and therefore game developers were required to be more creative and develop special Wii editions of their games.

Many game developers used virtual-machine software in developing new games. It was believed that game developers could develop games for the Wii and then make them for other platforms on the basis of the same programming, thereby reducing production costs. However, while the Wii Remote distinguished itself from its competitors, it created a hurdle for developers. When developers created a game for the PlayStation 3, they could create the same game for the Xbox 360 and vice versa. When developers created a game for the Wii, however, it required significant rework to deploy the title for the other platforms. Converting a title from the Xbox 360 or PlayStation 3 also required significant work to modify the game to incorporate code for the Wii Remote's special features.

The Wii U's GamePad also had special features that made it less easily compatible with the likes of Microsoft and Sony. While this had served Nintendo well in the past, it also limited the selection of games available to the Nintendo audience. The selection of games had to be fulfilling enough to keep Nintendo's audience happy, without leaving them feeling that they were missing out on games available only on the other platforms. This was already a going concern with the Wii U, as many of the currently available games were refurbished versions of Nintendo classic games, with more to come, such as *Super Mario, Mario Kart,* and *Zelda*.[21]

The Competition

The launch of the Wii U and the announcements of competing systems by Microsoft and Sony in late 2012 and early 2013 were the beginning of the battle for market share in the fierce competition of the eighth generation of video game consoles (see Exhibit 6).

The price of $299 for the basic Wii U included the console, the GamePad, and an HDMI cord. The deluxe edition priced at $349 included all of the above, plus stands for both the console and the GamePad, a charging dock for the GamePad, and the game *Nintendo Land*.[22] While the prices of both the PlayStation 4 and the new Xbox were unknown, at a base price of $299 the Wii U was intended to compete with the upper echelon of the next generation of gaming consoles, unlike the low-cost provider position that the original Wii possessed.

Xbox 360

The Xbox 360 by Microsoft was released in November 2005. While the configurations were changed several times, the Xbox 360 was available at two different prices: $299.99 for the 250-GB model and $199.99 for the 4-GB model as of 2011. However, although its higher-end model was pricier than the Wii, Microsoft was in fact losing money on every Xbox sale, due to costs of production and manufacturing.

One of the important features of the Xbox 360 was Xbox Live. This feature allowed individuals to play online against other users around the world. Thus, Microsoft had created a community of individuals who were able to communicate with one another by voice chats and play against each other in a video game. Another service offered by Xbox Live was the Xbox Live Marketplace, which enabled

EXHIBIT 6 Game Systems Comparison, 2013

	Nintendo	Sony	Microsoft
Console name	Wii U	PlayStation 4 (with Move and 4 Eye)	Xbox 360 (with Kinect)
Game format	Wii U discs	Blu-ray disc, DVD, CD	Game discs, DVD, CD
Hard drive	8 GB or 32 GB (supports external hard drives)	8 GB of GDDR5 memory	120 GB or 250 GB
Price	$299.99 (8GB) $349.99 (32GB)	Not yet specified	$199.99 (4GB) $299.99 (4GB with Kinect) $299.99 (250GB) $399.99 (250GB with Kinect)
Internet connection	Wi-Fi	Ethernet, Wi-Fi, Bluetooth	Wi-Fi
Online services	Online game play, WiiConnect24, Wii Channels, stream movies, Miiverse	Online game play, HD Blu-ray player, stream movies and TV, optical digital output	Online game play, stream HD movies or TV
Controller	Wii U GamePad, Wii U Pro Controller, Wii Remote/Wii Remote Plus, Nunchuk, Wii Balance Board	DualShock 4 pad: upgraded vibrations, enhanced motion sensors	Xbox 360 wireless controller, Kinect Sensor
Backward compatibility	Yes (Wii)	No. Eventually Sony will provide service offering server-side emulation and streaming of old games.	Yes (certain Xbox games)
Game count	Launched with 23 games, more were announced. (Backward-compatible with Wii games)	Not yet released	782 (including 23 Kinect games)

Source: Company reports; *Gamestop.com;* and author estimates.

users to download movies, game trailers, game demos, and arcade games. It was estimated that more than 70 percent of connected Xbox users were downloading content from the Xbox Live Marketplace, totaling more than 8 million members. According to Microsoft, there were more than 12 million downloads in less than a year and, due to this popularity, major publishers and other independent gamers had submitted more than 1,000 Xbox Live games.[23]

Kinect for Xbox 360

In November 2010 Microsoft introduced Kinect for Xbox 360, which was based around a webcam-style add-on peripheral for the Xbox 360 console. It enabled users to control and interact with the Xbox 360 using gestures and spoken commands, without the need to touch a game controller. Kinect allowed the Xbox 360 to "see" the user and act according to the user's motions and gestures. This took the concept of the Wii and pursued it to its natural culmination, making the user the game controller. Kinect used software technology that enabled advanced gesture recognition, facial recognition, and voice recognition. Some critics believed that the concept used by Kinect had potential far beyond games and might even become a new way of controlling computers of all kinds. It automatically identified who one player was and paused when the player left its vicinity, so it was not hard to imagine this ingenuity controlling all kinds of devices, such as a PC, smartphone, or tablet.[24]

Xbox Next Generation

While little information had been officially released about the next-generation Xbox, some assumptions could be made. Media outlets had been leading heavy discussion regarding the consoles' seemingly certain release in time for the 2013 holiday season, putting it in direct competition with Sony's PlayStation 4. With both Sony and Nintendo making headway in the motion-detecting department, Microsoft would certainly do the same, either improving upon its Kinect or investing in a new device, similar to Sony's approach. Microsoft recently filed a patent relating to projecting augmented reality 3-D images onto the walls of the room the user was gaming in, in an effort to more fully immerse the user in the experience. With the code name "Fortaleza," this project had the basis of the Kinect technology at its core. While still speculative, it was supposedly going to work with Wi-Fi–enabled glasses, similar to Google's Project Glass glasses.[25]

Sony PlayStation 4

While no pricing had been set, there was a lot that was known about the PlayStation 4. The PS4 would include 8 GB of GDDR5 memory, which would enable rapid performance. Also, Sony revealed that, using the loading power of this memory, the user would be able to power down the PS4 midgame and then later turn it back on and within seconds be playing again right where he or she left off.

The PS4 would support Blu-ray discs, DVDs, and HDMI output, as well as analog and optical digital output. The included controller was the DualShock 4 pad. Its design and function were similar to that of the PS3 controller, but it offered upgraded vibrations, enhanced motion sensors, and a Vita-like touchpad. Sony revealed that the PS4 would launch with the ability to stream games directly to the PS Vita, Sony's handheld gaming device. As with the Wii U, this would allow users to play on the tablet controller through a wireless connection, without the use of a TV display. As for games, a number of titles had already been revealed for the PS4 during prelaunch. These included *Diablo III* (Blizzard), *Driveclub* (Evolution Studios), *Final Fantasy* (Square Enix), and several others.[26] Part of the PlayStation Network's success was the ability to play games online. This allowed individuals to play with other players located in other parts of the world. The PlayStation Network allowed users to download games, view movie and game trailers, send text messages, and chat with friends, and these capabilities were sure to continue.

PlayStation Move

In September 2010, Sony released the PlayStation Move, which basically copied the Wii's wandlike controller but with more accuracy. As with the Wii, users could wave the Move's controller around and swing it like a bat and hit the ball on the screen. The PlayStation Move combined a video camera with a physical controller packed with motion-sensing electronics, making it a technological cross between the Kinect and the Nintendo Wii. The Move Motion Controller, or "wand," combined a gyroscope, accelerometer, and magnetic sensor to track the controller in three dimensions, while the glowing ball at the end gave the PlayStation Eye camera a visual reference for handling aiming, cursor movement, and other motion.[27] While Wii's graphics were of low resolution and inferior detail, PS3 was a high-definition powerhouse. As one user said, "On the Wii, golf looks like a video game. On the PS3, golf looks like a golf course." Moreover, the PS3 played Blu-ray movie discs and could display 3-D images, two things the Wii could not do. Also, the PS3 had a full lineup of great traditional games. Sony had shipped 4.1 million units of PlayStation Move worldwide in the first two months after its release. Although Sony was criticized for merely imitating Wii's technology, it turned out to be a successful imitation.[28] The only obvious difference from Wii was the cost. While the Wii cost $199 and came with both the *Wii Sports* and *Wii Sports Resort* compilations (most buyers also added a second controller for around $40), the PS3 with Move cost twice as much, $400, and came with only one game compilation, called *Sports Champions*. A second Move controller cost around $50. The least expensive version of the PlayStation 3, which did not include Move, cost $350. Thus, Nintendo and Sony offered comparable controllers rigged to machines with very different technical power and with quite different prices. Despite the significant difference in price, however, the Move was a successful product offering for Sony. While the 4 Eye was being introduced with the PS4, Sony still intended to include and utilize the Move as well, but to what degree was uncertain.

PlayStation 4 Eye

This device was a newly developed camera system that was introduced for the first time with the release of the PlayStation 4. It utilized two high-sensitivity cameras equipped with wide-angle lenses and 85-degree diagonal angle views. Sony claimed that the cameras could cut out the image of a player from the background or differentiate between players in the background and foreground, enhancing game play. If it worked flawlessly, this would be a significant advancement in the realm of motion-sensing game play, one that Microsoft and Nintendo might not have the technology to match. There was also speculation that this new technology would include logging in through facial recognition and using voice and body movements to play games "more intuitively."[29]

Mobile Gaming

Recently another form of competition in the gaming industry became widely available. Mobile devices such as smartphones and tablets allowed casual gamers to have the ability to download and play a wide variety of free or low-priced games. The games could be seamlessly downloaded to the handheld device. While the interactivity on these devices was limited by a lack of controls and features, the convenience and price factors that they represented were something that console makers were starting to notice.

The Future of Wii U

While Sony and Microsoft envisioned long-term profits on software sales of PlayStation 3 and Xbox 360, both companies experienced losses producing their seventh-generation consoles. Among the three rivals, Nintendo was the only one earning a significant profit margin on each Wii unit sold. According to David Gibson at Macquarie Securities, sales of the Nintendo Wii brought $6 of operating profit per console.[30] While Sony's and Microsoft's gaming consoles were commonly thought of as superior to Nintendo's, perhaps the Wii's simplicity and family-friendly appeal assisted in its ability to become profitable. These traits attracted not only end users but game developers as well, allowing the Wii to have the largest selection of games compared with its competitors. Initially there were 235 games for the Nintendo Wii by the end of its release year. By early 2011, however, the total number of games for the Wii was 860, exceeding the total number of games available for its main competitor, Xbox 360 (782 games), depending on whether one counted backward compatibility with previous-generation games. The number of games indicated that the Wii was obviously a successful system—one that had drawn a good amount of interest from game developers and gamers around the world.

However, with Microsoft shipping record number of Kinect units within the first few months of its release, some analysts started predicting that the Nintendo's dominance in video game consoles was over. Microsoft and Sony had started to invade the casual family-user market, a key market for Nintendo's Wii, expanding beyond their former customer base of mainly hard-core gamers. The Xbox and PS3 were becoming more like an entertainment hub for families. Now, with the Wii U on the market and the introduction of its eighth-generation competitors expected soon, the competition seemed to be better suited to combat Nintendo. As motion-sensing gaming—the undisputed "next best thing" to come out of the gaming industry—was a capability that all competitors now encompassed, it would be a matter of whose system was most desirable to the gaming population and whether or not this solely would determine which system came out on top. With this technology being widespread across the industry, it might prove to be that much more difficult for Nintendo to set itself apart and portray itself as the "family favorite," as it did in its early days with the Wii. To win over the gaming population, could Nintendo rely on its lower price or its quantity of games, or would it have to find a new leg to stand on? With both of its competitors yet to release their next-generation consoles, perhaps the Wii U could attain a lead by simply being the first to market. Or would the new Amiibo figurines be the key to Nintendo's regaining its position as the eminent player in the interactive gaming market?

ENDNOTES

1. Ba-Oh, Jorge. 2013. Industry folk comment on Nintendo Wii U potential—new or next generation? January 1, *www.cubed3.com/news/17809/1/industry-folk-comment-on-wii-u-potential.html*.
2. Deering, Mark. 2013. Nintendo Wii U sales lackluster at GameStop during holiday quarter, says analyst. *Gadget Insiders*, January 6, *gadgetinsiders.com/nintendo-wii-u-sales-lackluster-at-gamestop-during-holiday-quarter-says-analyst/1204653/*.
3. Schiesel, S. 2010. A real threat now faces the Nintendo Wii. *New York Times*, December 3: F7.
4. Albanesius, Chloe. 2013. Sony unveils next-gen PlayStation, PS4. February 20, *www.pcmag.com/article2/0,2817,2415671,00.asp;* and Gomer, Gregory. 2013. Major Nelson posts countdown clock for Xbox 720 release on Microsoft blog. *BostInno*, January 4, *bostinno.com/2013/01/04/xbox-720-release-date-major-nelson-posts-countdown-clock-for-xbox-720-release-on-microsoft-blog-photos/#ss__280214_271816_0__ss*.
5. Nintendo. 2008. Annual report, March 31.
6. Nintendo. *www.nintendo.com/systemsclassic?type5nes*.
7. Nintendo, 2008, op. cit.
8. Bacani, C., & Mutsuko, M. 1997. Nintendo's new 64-bit platform sets off a scramble for market share. *AsiaWeek*, April 18, *www.asiaweek.com/asiaweek/97/0418/cs1.html; GamePro*. 2005. Biggest blunders. May: 45.
9. Nintendo. *wii.nintendo.com/iwata_asks_vol2_p1.jsp*.
10. Morris, C. 2006. Nintendo goes "Wii"... *CNNMoney.com*, April 27, *money.cnn.com/2006/04/27/commentary/game_over/nintendo/index.htm*.

11. Surette, T. 2006. Nintendo exec talks Wii online, marketing. *GameSpot.com,* August 17, *www.cnet.com.au/games/wii/0,239036428,240091920,00.htm.*
12. Nintendo. 2006. Annual report.
13. Nintendo. *wii.nintendo.com/controller.jsp.*
14. Ibid.
15. See wii.Nintendo.com.
16. Ibid.
17. Ewalt, D. M. 2014. Mario comes to life in Nintendo's Amiibo. *Forbes,* November 24.
18. Nintendo. 2007. Annual report, March 31.
19. *PC Magazine.* 2006. Nintendo Wii. November 13, *www.pcmag.com/article2/0,1895,2058406,00.asp.*
20. PlayStation Move vs. Xbox 360 Kinect. *cnet, http://reviews.cnet.com/2722-9020_7-1079.html.*
21. Stuart, Keith. 2013. Wii U: New Zelda and Mario games announced. Is it enough? *The Guardian,* January 24, *www.guardian.co.uk/technology/gamesblog/2013/jan/24/nintendo-wii-u-zelda-mario-more.*
22. *Wii U News.* 2012. Wii U price and release date announced. September 13, *wiiu.dcemu.co.uk/wiiu-price-and-release-date-announced-491879.html.*
23. Microsoft. 2007. As Xbox LIVE turns five, Microsoft announces next wave of social fun. November 13, *www.microsoft.com/Presspass/press/2007/nov07/11-13XboxLIVEFivePR.mspx.*
24. Boehret, K. 2010. Xbox Kinect: Just how controlling can a body be? *Wall Street Journal,* November 24, *online.wsj.com/article/SB10001424052748704369304575632723525779384.html.*
25. Rivington, James. Xbox One release date, news and features. *techradar, www.techradar.com/us/news/gaming/consoles/xbox-720-release-date-news-and-rumours-937167.*
26. Rivington, James. PS4 release date, news and features. *techradar, www.techradar.com/us/news/gaming/consoles/ps4-release-date-news-and-features-937822.*
27. Greenwald, W. 2010. Kinect vs. PlayStation Move vs. Wii: Motion-control showdown. *PC Magazine,* November 6, *www.pcmag.com/article2/0,2817,2372244,00.asp.*
28. Schiesel, S. 2010. A real threat now faces the Nintendo Wii. *New York Times,* December 2, *www.nytimes.com/2010/12/03/technology/personaltech/03KINECT.html.*
29. Rivington, PS4 release date, op. cit.
30. Schoenberger, C. R. 2008. Wii's future in motion. *Forbes,* December 12, *www.forbes.com/2008/11/28/nintendo-wii-wii2-tech-personal-cz-cs-1201wii.html.*

photo credits

Page 188: © The McGraw-Hill Companies, Inc./Jill Braaten, photographer
Page 188: © Robin Van Lonkhuisen/epa/Corbis

CASES

CASE 25

MCDONALD'S*

McDonald's announced on January 28, 2015, that Don Thompson would retire as president and chief executive at the end of February. He would be replaced by Steve Easterbrook, the firm's chief branding officer. The abrupt exit came after the world's largest restaurant chain posted one of its worst financial performances in years (see Exhibits 1 and 2). Revenue in the last quarter, through December, fell 7 percent to $6.6 billion. Earnings, however, dropped by 21 percent to $1.1 billion from $1.4 billion in the same period a year earlier. "People have seen results go from the best in the industry to one of the worst in the course of three years," said Will Slabaugh, an analyst.[1]

Days before his retirement, Thompson acknowledged that McDonald's results had fallen short of expectations, but he noted that the firm had suffered partly because of events beyond his control. Sales in Asia and the Middle East had fallen sharply because of food safety concerns with a Chinese meat supplier. McDonald's also had to face shortages of French fries in several markets because of a slowdown at the port in Los Angeles. Finally, some Russian outlets were temporarily closed by food inspectors, apparently in retaliation for Western sanctions against Russia over its military intervention in Ukraine (see Exhibit 3).

However, McDonald's faced its biggest challenge in the United States, its largest market, where it had 14,200 of its 35,000 mostly franchised restaurants. It had lost a lot of ground with consumers, especially millennials, who were defecting to traditional competitors like Burger King and Wendy's as well as to new designer burger outlets such as Five Guys and Shake Shack. Changing tastes were responsible for the loss of customers who were lining up at fast-casual chains such as Chipotle Mexican

---

* Case prepared by Jamal Shamsie, Michigan State University, with the assistance of Professor Alan B. Eisner, Pace University. Material has been drawn from published sources to be used for purposes of class discussion. Copyright © 2015 Jamal Shamsie and Alan B. Eisner.

EXHIBIT 1
Income Statement
($ millions)

	Year Ending December				
	2010	2011	2012	2013	2014
Revenue	24,075	27,006	27,567	28,106	27,441
Gross profit	9,637	10,687	10,816	10,903	10,456
Operating income	7,473	8,530	8,605	8,764	7,949
Income before taxes	7,000	8,012	8,079	8,204	7,372
Net income	4,946	5,503	5,465	5,586	4,758

Source: McDonald's.

EXHIBIT 2
Balance Sheet
($ millions)

	Year Ending December				
	2010	2011	2012	2013	2014
Total current assets	4,368	4,403	4,922	5,050	4,186
Total assets	31,975	32,990	35,386	36,626	34,281
Total current liabilities	2,925	3,509	3,403	3,170	2,748
Total liabilities	17,341	18,600	20,093	20,617	21,428
Total stockholders' equity	14,634	14,390	15,294	16,010	12,853

Source: McDonald's.

Grill and Panera Bread, which offered customized ordering and fresh ingredients (see Exhibit 4).

McDonald's response to this growing competition was to expand its menu with snacks, salads, and new drinks. From 33 basic items that the chain offered in 1990, the menu grew to 121 items by 2014. The greatly expanded menu led to a significant increase in costs and longer preparation times. This forced the firm to increase the prices of many of its items and to take more time to serve customers, moving it away from the attributes that it had built its reputation on. "McDonald's stands for value, consistency and convenience," said Darren Tristano, a restaurant industry consultant.[2]

EXHIBIT 3 Breakdown of Revenues ($ millions)

	2014	2013	2012
Company-operated sales:			
U.S.	$ 4,351	$ 4,512	$ 4,530
Europe	7,808	8,138	7,850
APMEA	5,270	5,425	5,350
Other Countries & Corporate	740	800	873
Total	$18,169	$18,875	$18,603
Franchised revenues:			
U.S.	$ 4,300	$ 4,339	$ 4,284
Europe	3,270	3,162	2,977
APMEA	1,054	1,052	1,041
Other Countries & Corporate	648	678	662
Total	$ 9,272	$ 9,231	$ 8,964
Total revenues:			
U.S.	$ 8,651	$ 8,851	$ 8,814
Europe	11,078	11,300	10,827
APMEA	6,324	6,477	6,391
Other Countries & Corporate	1,388	1,478	1,535
Total	$27,441	$28,106	$27,567

Source: McDonald's.

EXHIBIT 4 U.S. Market Share of Fast-Food Burger Chains

	McDonald's	Wendy's	Burger King	SONIC Drive-ins	Jack in the Box	Whataburger	Hardee's	Carl's Jr.	Five Guys
2008	46.9%	13.5%	14.3%	6.0%	4.9%	1.8%	2.6%	2.2%	0.5%
2009	48.0	13.0	13.8	5.9	4.8	1.8	2.6	2.1	0.8
2010	49.2	12.7	13.2	5.5	4.5	1.9	2.6	2.0	1.1
2011	50.1	12.5	12.2	5.4	4.4	1.9	2.7	2.0	1.4
2012	50.0	12.2	12.1	5.4	4.4	2.1	2.7	2.0	1.5
2013	49.7	12.2	11.8	5.4	4.3	2.7	2.1	2.0	1.6
2014	49.6	12.3	11.9	5.4	4.3	2.8	2.1	2.0	1.7

Source: *USA Today*, December 8, 2014, and author esitmates.

The fast-food chain had gone through a similar crisis before. Back in 2002–2003, McDonald's had experienced a decline in performance because of quality problems as a result of rapid expansion. At that time, the firm brought James R. Cantalupo back out of retirement to turn things around. He formulated the "Plan to Win," which was the basis of McDonald's strategy over the next decade. The core of the plan was to increase sales at existing locations by improving the menu, refurbishing the outlets, and extending hours. This time, however, such incremental steps might not be enough.

Pulling Out of a Downward Spiral

Since it was founded more than 50 years ago, McDonald's had been defining the fast-food business. It provided millions of Americans their first jobs even as it changed their eating habits. It rose from a single outlet in a nondescript Chicago suburb to one of the largest chains of outlets spread around the globe. But it gradually began to run into various problems that began to slow down its sales growth (see Exhibit 5).

This decline could be attributed in large part to a drop in McDonald's once-vaunted service and quality since its expansion in the 1990s, when headquarters stopped grading franchises for cleanliness, speed, and service. By the end of the decade, the chain ran into more problems because of the tighter labor market. As it struggled hard to find new recruits, McDonald's began to cut back on training, leading to a dramatic falloff in the skills of its employees. According to a 2002 survey by market researcher Global Growth Group, McDonald's came in third in average service time, behind Wendy's and sandwich shop Chick-fil-A Inc.

EXHIBIT 5 McDonald's Milestones

Year	Event
1948	Brothers Richard and Maurice McDonald open the first restaurant in San Bernardino, California, that sells hamburgers, fries, and milk shakes.
1955	Ray A. Kroc, 52, opens his first McDonald's in Des Plaines, Illinois. Kroc, a distributor of milk shake mixers, figures he can sell a bundle of them if he franchises the McDonalds' business and installs his mixers in the new stores.
1961	Six years later, Kroc buys out the McDonald brothers for $2.7 million.
1963	Ronald McDonald makes his debut as corporate spokesclown, using future NBC-TV weatherman Willard Scott. During the year, the company also sells its 1-billionth burger.
1965	McDonald's stock goes public at $22.50 a share. It will split 12 times in the next 35 years.
1967	The first McDonald's restaurant outside the U.S. opens in Richmond, British Columbia. Today there are 31,108 McDonald's in 118 countries.
1968	The Big Mac, the first extension of McDonald's basic burger, makes its debut and is an immediate hit.
1972	McDonald's switches to the frozen variety for its successful French fries.
1974	Fred L. Turner succeeds Kroc as CEO. In the midst of a recession, the minimum wage rises to $2 per hour, a big cost increase for McDonald's, which is built around a model of young, low-wage workers.
1975	The first drive-through window is opened in Sierra Vista, Arizona.
1979	McDonald's responds to the needs of working women by introducing Happy Meals. A burger, some fries, a soda, and a toy give working moms a break.
1987	Michael R. Quinlan becomes chief executive.
1991	Responding to the public's desire for healthier foods, McDonald's introduces the low-fat McLean Deluxe burger. It flops and is withdrawn from the market. Over the next few years, the chain will stumble several times trying to spruce up its menu.
1992	The company sells its 90-billionth burger and stops counting.
1996	In order to attract more adult customers, the company launches its Arch Deluxe, a "grown-up" burger with an idiosyncratic taste. Like the low-fat burger, it falls flat.
1997	McDonald's launches Campaign 55, which cuts the cost of a Big Mac to $0.55. It is a response to discounting by Burger King and Taco Bell. The move, which prefigures similar price wars in 2002, is widely considered a failure.
1998	Jack M. Greenberg becomes McDonald's fourth chief executive. A 16-year company veteran, he vows to spruce up the restaurants and their menu.
1999	For the first time, sales from international operations outstrip domestic revenues. In search of other concepts, the company acquires Aroma Cafe, Chipotle, Donatos, and, later, Boston Market.

EXHIBIT 5 *Continued*

Year	Event
2000	McDonald's sales in the U.S. peak at an average of $1.6 million annually per restaurant, a figure that has not changed since. It is, however, still more than sales at any other fast-food chain.
2001	Subway surpasses McDonald's as the fast-food chain with the most U.S. outlets. At the end of the year it had 13,247 stores, 148 more than McDonald's.
2002	McDonald's posts its first-ever quarterly loss, of $343.8 million. The stock drops to around $13.50, down 40% from five years ago.
2003	James R. Cantalupo returns to McDonald's in January as CEO. He immediately pulls back from the company's 10%–15% forecast for per-share earnings growth.
2004	Charles H. Bell takes over the firm after the sudden death of Cantalupo. He states he will continue with the strategies that have been developed by his predecessor.
2005	Jim Skinner takes over as CEO after Bell announces retirement for health reasons.
2006	McDonald's launches specialty beverages, including coffee-based drinks.
2008	McDonald's plans to add McCafés to each of its outlets.
2012	Don Thompson succeeds Skinner as CEO of the chain.
2015	Thompson resigns because of declining performance and is replaced by Steve Easterbrook, the firm's chief branding officer.

Source: McDonald's.

By the beginning of 2003, consumer surveys were indicating that McDonald's was headed for serious trouble. Measures for the service and quality of the chain were continuing to fall, dropping far behind those of its rivals. To deal with its deteriorating performance, the firm decided to bring back retired vice chairman James R. Cantalupo, 59, who had overseen McDonald's successful international expansion in the 1980s and 1990s. Cantalupo, who had retired only a year earlier, was perceived to be the only candidate with the necessary qualifications, despite shareholder sentiment for an outsider. The board felt that it needed someone who knew the company well and could move quickly to turn things around.

Cantalupo realized that McDonald's often tended to miss the mark on delivering the critical aspects of consistent, fast, and friendly service and an all-around enjoyable experience for the whole family. He understood that its franchisees and employees alike needed to be inspired as well as retrained on their role in putting the smile back into the McDonald's experience. When Cantalupo and his team laid out their turnaround plan in 2003, they stressed getting the basics of service and quality right, in part by reinstituting a tough "up or out" grading system that would kick out underperforming franchisees. "We have to rebuild the foundation. It's fruitless to add growth if the foundation is weak," said Cantalupo.[3]

In his effort to focus on the firm's core business, Cantalupo sold off the nonburger chains that the firm had recently acquired. He also cut back on the opening of new outlets, focusing instead on generating more sales from its existing outlets. Cantalupo pushed McDonald's to try to draw more customers through the introduction of new products. The chain had a positive response to its increased emphasis on healthier foods, led by a revamped line of fancier salads. The revamped menu was promoted through a new worldwide ad slogan, "I'm loving it," which was delivered by pop idol Justin Timberlake through a set of MTV-style commercials.

Striving for a Healthier Image

When Jim Skinner took over from Cantalupo in 2004, he continued to push for McDonald's to change its image. Skinner felt that one of his top priorities was to deal with the growing concerns about the unhealthy image of McDonald's, given the rise of obesity in the U.S. These concerns were highlighted in the popular documentary *Super Size Me*, made by Morgan Spurlock. Spurlock vividly displayed the health risks that were posed by a steady diet of food from the fast-food chain. With a rise in awareness of the high fat content of most of the products offered by McDonald's, the firm was also beginning to face lawsuits from some of its loyal customers.

In response to the growing health concerns, one of the first steps taken by McDonald's was to phase out supersizing by the end of 2004. The supersizing option allowed customers to get a larger order of French fries and a bigger soft drink by paying a little extra. McDonald's also announced that it intended to start providing nutrition information on the packaging of its products. The information would be easy to read and would provide customers with details on the calories, fat, protein, carbohydrates, and sodium that were in each product. Finally, McDonald's began to remove the artery-clogging trans-fat acids from the oil that it used to make its French fries, and it recently announced plans to reduce the sodium content in all of its products by 15 percent.

But Skinner was also trying to push out more offerings that were likely to be perceived by customers as being healthier. McDonald's continued to build upon its chicken offerings using white meat with products such as Chicken Selects. It also placed a great deal of emphasis upon its new salad offerings. McDonald's carried out extensive experiments and tests on them and decided to use higher-quality ingredients, from a variety of lettuces and tasty cherry tomatoes to sharper cheeses and better cuts of meat. It offered a choice of Newman's Own dressings, a well-known higher-end brand. "Salads have changed the way people think of our brand," said Wade Thoma, vice president for menu development in the U.S. "It tells people that we are very serious about offering things people feel comfortable eating."[4]

McDonald's was trying to include more fruits and vegetables in its well-known and popular Happy Meals. It announced in 2011 that it would reduce the amount of French fries and phase out the caramel dipping sauce that accompanied the apple slices in these meals. The addition of fruits and vegetables raised the firm's operating costs, since they were more expensive to ship and store because of their more perishable nature. "We are doing what we can," said Danya Proud, a spokesperson for the firm. "We have to evolve with the times."[5]

The rollout of new beverages, highlighted by new coffee-based drinks, represented the chain's biggest menu expansion in almost three decades. Under a plan to add a McCafé section to all of its nearly 14,000 U.S. outlets, McDonald's was offering lattes, cappuccinos, ice-blended frappes, and fruit-based smoothies to its customers. "In many cases, they're now coming for the beverage, whereas before they were coming for the meal," said Lee Renz, an executive who was responsible for the rollout.[6]

Refurbishing the Outlets

As part of its turnaround strategy, McDonald's had been selling off the outlets that it owned. More than 75 percent of its outlets were now in the hands of franchisees and other affiliates. Skinner was working with the franchisees to address the look and feel of many of the chain's aging stores. Without any changes to their decor, the firm was likely to be left behind by more savvy fast-food and drink retailers. The firm was in the midst of pushing harder to refurbish—or reimage—all of its outlets around the world. "People eat with their eyes first," said Thompson. "If you have a restaurant that is appealing, contemporary, and relevant both from the street and interior, the food tastes better."[7]

The reimaging concept was first tried in France in 1996 by Dennis Hennequin, an executive in charge of the chain's European operations, who felt that the effort was essential to revive the firm's sagging sales. "We were hip 15 years ago, but I think we lost that," he said.[8] McDonald's was applying the reimaging concept to its outlets around the world, with a budget of more than half of its total annual capital expenditures. In the U.S., the changes cost an average of $150,000 per restaurant, a cost that was shared with the franchisee when the outlet was not company-owned.

One of the prototype interiors being tested out by McDonald's had curved counters with surfaces painted in bright colors. In one corner, a touch-activated screen allowed customers to punch in orders without queuing. The interiors could feature armchairs and sofas, modern lighting, large television screens, and even wireless Internet access. The firm was also developing new features for its drive-through customers, who account for 65 percent of all transactions in the U.S. These features included music aimed at queuing vehicles and a wall of windows on the drive-through side of the restaurant allowing customers to see meals being prepared from their cars.

The chain was even developing McCafés inside its outlets, next to the usual fast-food counter. The McCafé concept originated in Australia in 1993 and was rolled out in many restaurants around the world. McDonald's introduced the concept to the U.S. as part of the refurbishment of its outlets. In fact, part of the makeover focused on the installation of a specialty beverage platform in all U.S. outlets. The cost of installing this equipment was about $100,000 per outlet, with McDonald's subsidizing part of the expense.

The firm planned to have all McCafés offer espresso-based coffee, gourmet coffee blends, fresh-baked muffins, and high-end desserts. Customers would be able to consume them while relaxing in soft leather chairs and listening to jazz, big band, or blues music. Commenting on this significant expansion of offerings, Marty Brochstein, executive editor of *The Licensing Letter,* said: "McDonald's wants to be seen as a lifestyle brand, not just a place to go to have a burger."[9]

Rethinking the Business Model

In response to the decline in performance, McDonald's was testing a number of new concepts, including a kiosk feature in four stores in southern California that allowed customers to skip the counter and head to tablelike kiosks where they could customize everything about their burger, from the type of bun to the variety of cheese to the many glossy toppings and sauces that can go on it. The firm later decided to expand the concept to 30 locations in five more states and to 2,000, or about one in seven, of the 14,000 outlets in the U.S.

With its "Create Your Taste" kiosk platform, McDonald's was hoping to attract more younger customers who might have been moving away from frozen processed food that was loaded with preservatives. No one mentioned anything about the quality of meat that the chain used for its burgers. "Today's customers increasingly prefer customizable food options, dining in a contemporary, inviting atmosphere and using more convenient ways to order and pay for their meals," CEO Thompson stated last year when the test was launched.[10]

However, there were risks involved with making such a change. The burgers were priced higher, at $5.49; could take seven minutes to prepare; and could be ordered only from inside the store and eventually brought to your table. This ran counter to the image of inexpensive and fast food that McDonald's had worked hard to build over the years. Nevertheless, the firm hoped this change would bring more customers into its outlets, bringing the U.S. counter–drive-through customer ratio closer to 50-50, up from the current 40–70.

At the same time, McDonald's was working to simplify its menu, reducing the number of "value meal" promotions—groups of items that together cost less than ordering the items individually. It tweaked its "dollar menu," replacing it with "dollar value and more" and raising the prices of many items as part of a bid to get each customer to spend more. But McDonald's had introduced these bargain menus because its prices had risen over the years, driving away customers to cheaper outlets. Over the previous five years, about 15 percent of the chain's sales had come from its dollar menu, on which everything cost a dollar.

McDonald's was trying out all options. It even quietly opened a sandwich and salad shop in Australia, a bit of a hybrid of Panera and Starbucks, with no sign of a golden arch or Ronald McDonald anywhere. And it recently signed a deal to begin selling its coffee in grocery stores. "They are throwing a lot of spaghetti at the wall, but it's not clear that any of it is the right spaghetti," said Sara Senatore, an investment analyst. "They have all these things going on and it's not obvious that's what consumers want from McDonald's."[11]

More Gold in These Arches?

Even though McDonald's had appointed a new CEO and made some changes in its organization, it was not clear how the chain could pull out of its present situation. In 2014, a survey in *Consumer Reports* showed that McDonald's customers ranked its burgers significantly below those of 20 competitors. McDonald's also had the lowest rank in food quality of all rated hamburger chains in the *Nation's Restaurant News* Consumer Picks survey. "McDonald's has a huge image problem in America," said John Gordon, a restaurant consultant.[12]

As it tried to make changes, McDonald's announced that it planned to open fewer stores in 2015 and pare capital investment to $2 billion, the least in more than five years. The firm was already trying out a variety of strategies in order to move away from burgers and increase its appeal to different segments of the market. Through the adoption of a mix of outlet decor and menu items, McDonald's was trying to target young adults, teenagers, children, and families. In spite of these efforts, 30 percent of sales came from just five items: Big Macs, hamburgers, cheeseburgers, McNuggets, and fries.

Restaurant analyst Bryan Elliott commented: "They've tried to be all things to all people who walk in their door."[13] McDonald's recent marketing campaign, anchored around the catchy phrase "I'm loving it," took on different forms to target each of the groups that the firm was seeking. Larry Light, the head of global marketing at McDonald's who pushed for this campaign, insisted that the firm had to exploit its brand by pushing it in many different directions.

For the most part, McDonald's tried to reach out to different customer segments by offering different products at different times of the day. It targeted young adults for breakfast with its gourmet coffee, egg sandwiches, and fat-free muffins. It attracted working adults for lunch, particularly those who were squeezed for time, with its burgers and fries. And its introduction of wraps drew in teenagers late in the evening after they had been partying.

Nevertheless, the expansion of the menu beyond the staple of burgers and fries raised some fundamental questions. Most significantly, it was not clear just how far McDonald's could stretch its brand while keeping all of its outlets under the traditional symbol of its golden arches. In fact, industry experts believed that the long-term success of the firm might well depend on its ability to compete with rival burger chains. "The burger category has great strength," added David C. Novak, chairman and CEO of Yum! Brands, parent of KFC and Taco Bell. "That's America's food. People love hamburgers."[14]

ENDNOTES

1. Beth Kowitt. Fallen arches. *Fortune,* December 1, 2014, p. 108.
2. *The Economist.* When the chips are down. January 10, 2015, p. 53.
3. Pallavi Gogoi & Michael Arndt. Hamburger hell. *Business Week,* March 3, 2003, p. 105.
4. Melanie Warner. You want any fruit with that Big Mac? *New York Times,* February 20, 2005, p. 8.
5. Stephanie Strom. McDonald's trims its Happy Meal. *New York Times,* July 27, 2011, p. B7.
6. Janet Adamy. McDonald's coffee strategy is tough sell. *Wall Street Journal,* October 27, 2008, p. B3.
7. Ben Paynter. Super style me. *Fast Company,* October 2010, p. 107.
8. Jeremy Grant. McDonald's to revamp UK outlets. *Financial Times,* February 2, 2006, p. 14.
9. Bruce Horovitz. McDonald's ventures beyond burgers to duds, toys. *USA Today,* November 14, 2003, p. 6B.
10. Bruce Horovitz. McDonald's sales down, but better than expected. *USA Today,* November 11, 2014, p. 6B.
11. Stephanie Strom. McDonald's tests custom burgers and other new concepts as sales drop. *New York Times,* January 24, 2015, p. B3.
12. *The Economist,* op. cit., p. 54.
13. Kowitt, op. cit., p. 110.
14. Julie Jargon. McDonald's is feeling fried. *Wall Street Journal,* November 9, 2012, p. B2.

CASES

CASE 26

PROCTER & GAMBLE*

Procter & Gamble, a leading global consumer products firm, announced a major reshuffling of its top ranks on January 21, 2015. David S. Taylor was assigned to take over the company's global beauty unit, effectively giving him control of a business that was in desperate need of attention. The appointment moved Taylor to the top of the list of candidates who might take over the firm after Alan G. Lafley stepped down. But the next CEO of P&G would have to figure out how to resurrect a firm that had been enduring flat sales growth and losing market share to competitors like Unilever and Colgate-Palmolive.

Since its founding 175 years ago, P&G had risen to the status of an American icon with well-known consumer products such as Pampers, Tide, Downy, and Crest (see Exhibit 1). In fact, the firm had long been admired for its superior products, its marketing brilliance, and the intense loyalty of its employees, who had respectfully come to be known as "Proctoids." But a downward spiral in the 1990s led the firm to turn to Lafley to try to turn things around. He managed to electrify a then-demoralized organization by shaking it up and expanding its sales through acquisitions. With 25 brands that generated more than $1 billion in sales, P&G became the largest consumer products company in the world.

Under Lafley's chosen successor, Bob McDonald, however, P&G's growth stalled as recession-battered consumers abandoned the firm's premium-priced products for cheaper alternatives. More significantly, the firm's vaunted innovation machine stalled, with no major product success during his tenure. P&G's decline eroded morale among employees, with many managers taking early retirement or bolting to competitors. Ed Artzt, who was CEO from 1990 to 1995, said: "The most unfortunate aspect of this whole thing is the brain drain. The loss of good people is almost irreparable when you depend on promotion from within to continue building the company."[1]

Pressure from the board forced Lafley to come out of retirement in May 2013 to make another attempt to pull P&G out of its doldrums. Soon after he took back the helm of the firm, Lafley announced that he would get rid of more than half of its brands. He said that the company would narrow its focus to 70 or 80 of its biggest brands and shed as many as 100 others whose performance had been lagging. "Less will be more," Lafley told analysts. "The objective is growth and much more reliable generation of cash and profit."[2]

The decision to get rid of brands and move out of businesses represented a clear change in strategy for Lafley, who had, during his earlier reign from 2000 to 2009, managed to double P&G's sales through a string of acquisitions. This expansion had not only added well-known brands but also moved the firm into new areas. Lafley had acquired Gillette in order to provide the firm with a major presence in the

---

* Case prepared by Jamal Shamsie, Michigan State University, with the assistance of Professor Alan B. Eisner, Pace University. Material has been drawn from published sources to be used for purposes of class discussion. Copyright © 2015 Jamal Shamsie and Alan B. Eisner.

EXHIBIT 1
Significant Innovations

- Tide was the first heavy-duty laundry detergent.
- Crest was the first fluoride toothpaste clinically proven to prevent tooth decay.
- Downy was the first ultra-concentrated rinse-add fabric softener.
- Pert Plus was the first 2-in-1 shampoo and conditioner.
- Head & Shoulders was the first pleasant-to-use shampoo effective against dandruff.
- Pampers was the first affordable, mass-marketed disposable diaper.
- Bounty was the first three-dimensional paper towel.
- Always was the first feminine protection pad with an innovative dry-weave top sheet.
- Febreze was the first fabric and air care product that actually removed odors from fabrics and the air.
- Crest Whitestrips was the first patented in-home tooth-whitening technology.

Source: P&G.

men's market for the first time. Similarly, by acquiring Clairol and Wella, Lafley had pushed P&G to build on its high-margin beauty products.

Fighting Off a Decline

For most of its long history, P&G had been one of America's preeminent companies. The firm had developed several well-known brands such as Tide, one of the pioneers in laundry detergents, which was launched in 1946, and Pampers, the first disposable diaper, which was introduced in 1961. P&G had also built its brands through its innovative marketing techniques. But by the 1990s, P&G was in danger of becoming another Eastman Kodak or Xerox, a once-great company that lost its way. Sales on most of its 18 top brands were slowing as it was being outhustled by more focused rivals such as Kimberly-Clark and Colgate-Palmolive.

In 1999, P&G decided to bring in Durk I. Jaeger to try to make the big changes that were obviously needed to get P&G back on track. But the moves that he made generally misfired, sinking the firm into deeper trouble. He introduced expensive new products that never caught on while letting existing brands drift. He also put in place a companywide reorganization that left many employees perplexed and preoccupied. During the fiscal year when he was in charge, earnings per share showed an anemic rise of just 3.5 percent, much lower than in previous years. And during that time, the share price slid 52 percent, cutting P&G's total market capitalization by $85 billion.

In 2000, the board of P&G asked Lafley to take charge of the troubled firm. He began his tenure by breaking down the walls between management and employees. Since the 1950s, all of the senior executives at P&G had been located on the 11th floor at the firm's corporate headquarters. Lafley changed this setup, moving all five division presidents to the same floors as their staffs. He replaced more than half of the company's top 30 managers, more than any P&G boss in memory had replaced, and he trimmed its workforce by as many as 9,600 jobs. He also moved more women into senior positions. In fact, Lafley skipped over 78 general managers with more seniority to name 42-year-old Deborah A. Henretta to head P&G's then-troubled North American baby care division.

Lafley was simply acknowledging the importance of developing people, particularly those in managerial roles, at P&G. For years, the firm had been known to dispatch line managers rather than human resource staffers to do much of its recruiting. For the few individuals who were hired, their work life became a career-long development process. At every level, P&G had a different "college" to train individuals, and every department had its own "university." The general manager's college held a weeklong school term once a year when there were a handful of newly promoted managers.

Under Lafley, P&G continued with its efforts to maintain a comprehensive database of all of its more than 130,000 employees, each of which was tracked carefully through monthly and annual talent reviews. All managers were reviewed not only by their bosses but also by lateral managers who had worked with them, as well as by their own direct reports. Every February, one entire board meeting was devoted to reviewing the high-level executives, with the goal of coming up with at least three potential candidates for each of the 35 to 40 jobs at the top of the firm.

Gambling on Its Brands

Above all, however, Lafley was intent on shifting the focus of P&G back to its consumers. At every opportunity, he tried to drill his managers and employees to not lose sight of the consumer. He felt that P&G had often let technology dictate its new products, rather than consumer needs. He wanted the firm to work more closely with retailers, the places where consumers first saw the product on a shelf. And he placed a lot of emphasis on getting a better sense of consumers' experiences with P&G products when they actually used them at home.

Over the decade of Lafley's leadership, P&G managed to update all of its 200 brands by adding innovative new products. It began to offer devices that built on its core brands, such as Tide StainBrush, a battery-powered brush for removing stains, and Mr. Clean AutoDry, a water-pressure-powered car-cleaning system that dried without streaking. P&G also began to approach its brands more creatively. Crest, for example, which used to be marketed as a toothpaste brand, was redefined as an oral care brand. The firm later added Crest-branded toothbrushes and tooth whiteners.

To ensure that P&G continued to come up with innovative ideas, Lafley confronted head-on the stubbornly held notion that everything must be invented within P&G; he asserted that half of its new products should come from outside the firm. Under the new "Connect and Develop" model of innovation, the firm pushed to get almost 50 percent of its new product ideas from outside the firm. This could be compared to the 10 percent figure that existed at P&G when Lafley had taken charge.

A key element of P&G's strategy, however, was to move the firm away from basic consumer products such as laundry detergents, which could be knocked off by private labels, to higher-margin products. Under Lafley, P&G made costly acquisitions of Clairol and Wella to complement its Cover Girl and Oil of Olay brands. The firm even moved into prestige fragrances through licenses with Hugo Boss, Gucci, and Dolce & Gabbana. By the time Lafley stepped down, beauty products had risen to account for about one-quarter of the firm's total revenues.

P&G's riskiest move had been its expansion into services, starting with car washes and dry cleaning. The car washes built on Mr. Clean, P&G's popular cleaning product. In expanding the brand to car washes, the firm expected to distinguish its outlets from others by offering additional services such as Febreze odor eliminators, lounges with Wi-Fi and big-screen televisions, and spray guns that children could aim at cars passing through the wash. Similarly, P&G's dry-cleaning outlets were named after Tide, its best-selling laundry detergent. The stores included drive-through services, 24-hour pickup, and environmentally benign cleaning methods.

Losing the Momentum

On July 1, 2009, Lafley passed the leadership of P&G to McDonald, who had joined the firm in 1980 and worked his way up through posts in Canada, Japan, the Philippines, and Belgium to become chief operating officer. McDonald took over after the start of a calamitous recession and had to deal with various emerging problems. Consumers in the United States and Europe were not willing to pay premium prices, and the firm's push to expand in emerging markets was yielding few results in the face of stiff competition from Unilever and Colgate-Palmolive, each of which already had a strong presence. Furthermore, commodity prices were surging, even as P&G's products were already too expensive for the struggling middle class that it was targeting everywhere.

To deal with all of these challenges, McDonald replaced Lafley's clear motto of "The consumer is boss" with his own slogan of "purpose-inspired growth." In his own words, this meant that P&G was "touching and improving more consumers' lives, in more parts of the world, more completely." "Purpose" was an undeniably laudable ambition, but many employees simply could not fathom how to translate this rhetoric into action. Dick Antoine, P&G's head of human resources from 1998 to 2008, commented: "'Purpose-inspired growth' is a wonderful slogan, but it doesn't help allocate assets."[3]

The new focus seemed to fit well with McDonald, who seemed more comfortable with the details of P&G's operations. He began to institute various procedures throughout the firm that were designed to increase efficiency. For example, he authorized an efficiency study that assessed every act and function performed by every employee and then reduced the number of specific procedures to be used across the entire firm to 88. Sonsoles Gonzalez, a manager who recently left the firm, said, "There was a lot of concern for productivity, but little interest in winning the consumer."[4]

Even when McDonald tried to broaden his scope, he found it difficult to establish priorities for P&G. Given the wide range of problems that he faced, in terms of pushing for growth across several different businesses in many markets, he made an effort to try to address all of them at the same time. Ali Dibadj, a senior analyst at Sanford Bernstein, commented on this multipronged effort by P&G: "The strategic problem was that they decided to go after everything. But they ran out of ammo too quickly."[5]

By the middle of 2012, it was becoming obvious that P&G was struggling under McDonald's leadership. Known for its reliable performance, the firm was forced to lower its profit guidelines three times in six months, frustrating analysts and investors alike. Even within the firm, many executives realized that McDonald would not be able to take the bold moves that might allow the firm to recover from its slump. Activist investor Bill Ackerman commented: "We're delighted to see the company's made some progress. But P&G deserves to be led by one of the best CEO's in the world."[6]

Striving for Agility

Shareholder dissatisfaction with the lack of improvement in performance led P&G to push McDonald out and bring back Lafley in May 2013. As soon as he stepped back in, Lafley was under pressure to respond to investor concerns that P&G had become too large and bloated to respond quickly to changing consumer demands. In April 2014, he began the process of streamlining the firm by selling most of its pet food brands—including Iams and Eukanuba—to Mars for $2.9 billion. P&G had acquired these brands in 1999 for $2.3 billion, paying a rich multiple at the time. The business initially grew quickly, but then slowed because of competition from larger players.

A few months later, in August 2014, Lafley took a bolder step. He announced that the firm would unload as many as 100 of its brands to better focus on 70 to 80 of its biggest ones—such as Tide detergent and Pampers diapers—that generated about 90 percent of its $83 billion in annual sales and over 95 percent of its profit. Lafley did not specify which brands would be sold off or shut down, but the company owned scores of lesser brands, such as Cheer laundry detergent and Metamucil laxatives. Of the brands P&G was expected to retain, 23 had sales of $1 billion to $10 billion, 14 had sales between $500 million and $1 billion, and 30 to 40 had sales of $100 million to $500 million (see Exhibits 2 and 3).

Lafley insisted that sales would not be the only criterion for shedding brands. He stated that some large brands would be jettisoned if they didn't fit with the firm's core business: "If it's not a core brand—I don't care whether it's a $2 billion brand—it will be divested."[7] He demonstrated this with the decision to spin off its Duracell brand into a stand-alone company. Although batteries had been generating $2.2 billion annually in sales, their sluggish growth did not fit with Lafley's push for a more focused company.

Although analysts were receptive to the reduction of brands, they pointed out that P&G had already sold off more than 30 established brands over the past 15 years that were supposedly hindering growth. Many of the sold-off brands were performing well with other firms. J.M. Smucker, for example, which bought Crisco shortening, Folgers coffee, and Jif peanut butter, had 50 percent sales growth since 2009. Some critics charged that P&G, which once was most successful in building and managing brands, had lost its touch.

In large part, the focus was on the cumbersome centralized and bureaucratic structure that had developed at P&G.

EXHIBIT 2 Business Segments, 2014

Reportable Segment	% of Net Sales*	% of Net Earnings*	GBUs (Categories)	Billion-Dollar Brands
Beauty, Hair and Personal Care	24	23	Beauty Care (Antiperspirant and Deodorant, Cosmetics, Personal Cleansing, Skin Care); Hair Care and Color; Prestige; Salon Professional	Head & Shoulders, Olay, Pantene, SK-II, Wella
Grooming	10	17	Grooming (Electronic Hair Removal, Female Blades & Razors, Male Blades & Razors, Pre- and Post-Shave Products, Other Shave Care)	Fusion, Gillette, Mach3, Prestobarba
Health Care	9	9	Personal Health Care (Gastrointestinal, Rapid Diagnostics, Respiratory, Vitamins/Minerals/Supplements, Other Personal Health Care); Oral Care (Toothbrush, Toothpaste, Other Oral Care)	Crest, Oral-B, Vicks
Fabric Care and Home Care	32	26	Fabric Care (Laundry Additives, Fabric Enhancers, Laundry Detergents); Home Care (Air Care, Dish Care, P&G Professional, Surface Care); Personal Power (Batteries)	Ariel, Dawn, Downy, Duracell, Febreze, Gain, Tide
Baby, Feminine and Family Care	25	25	Baby Care (Baby Wipes, Diapers and Pants); Feminine Care (Adult Incontinence, Feminine Care); Family Care (Paper Towels, Tissues, Toilet Paper)	Always, Bounty, Charmin, Pampers

* Percent of net sales and net earnings from continuing operations for the year ended June 30, 2014 (excluding results held in Corporate).

Source: P&G.

EXHIBIT 3 Financial Breakdown

Global Segment Results		Net Sales	Earnings/(Loss) from Continuing Operations Before Income Taxes	Net Earnings/(Loss) from Continuing Operations	Depreciation and Amortization	Total Assets	Capital Expenditures
Beauty	2014	$19,507	$ 3,530	$ 2,739	$ 394	$ 8,576	$ 502
	2013	19,956	3,215	2,474	375	8,396	541
	2012	20,318	3,196	2,390	379	8,357	569
Grooming	2014	8,009	2,589	1,954	576	23,767	369
	2013	8,038	2,458	1,837	603	23,971	378
	2012	8,339	2,395	1,807	623	24,518	392
Health Care	2014	7,798	1,597	1,083	199	5,879	253
	2013	7,684	1,582	1,093	191	5,933	248
	2012	7,235	1,520	1,022	186	5,832	251
Fabric Care and Home Care	2014	26,060	4,678	3,039	625	11,384	1,154
	2013	25,862	4,757	3,089	639	11,231	1,064
	2012	25,580	4,485	2,816	627	10,647	965
Baby, Feminine and Family Care	2014	20,950	4,310	2,940	908	10,946	1,317
	2013	20,479	4,507	3,047	837	10,926	1,560
	2012	19,714	4,271	2,927	753	9,203	1,495

continued

EXHIBIT 3 Continued

Global Segment Results		Net Sales	Earnings/(Loss) from Continuing Operations Before Income Taxes	Net Earnings/(Loss) from Continuing Operations	Depreciation and Amortization	Total Assets	Capital Expenditures
CORPORATE[1]	2014	738	(1,819)	(48)	439	83,714	253
	2013	562	(1,827)	(239)	337	78,806	217
	2012	820	(3,339)	(1,812)	636	73,687	292
TOTAL COMPANY	2014	83,062	14,885	11,707	3,141	144,266	3,848
	2013	82,581	14,692	11,301	2,982	139,263	4,008
	2012	82,006	12,528	9,150	3,204	132,244	3,964

[1] The Corporate reportable segment includes depreciation and amortization, total assets and capital expenditures of the Snacks business prior to its divestiture effective May 31, 2012, and of the Pet Care business.

Source: P&G.

Although Lafley had declared during his earlier reign as CEO that he would transform P&G into a more agile and networked organization, there had been little movement in that direction. Unlike many of its newer competitors, the firm still tended to rely less on working with outside partners. The Connect and Develop program, which had been started by Lafley to bring in new ideas from outsiders, led to 50 percent of the firm's new technologies coming from outside, but they were then reworked or modified by P&G's internal R&D group. This stifled innovation, with most of the firm's growth coming from line extensions of existing brands or from costly acquisitions.

Fighting for Its Iconic Status

Financial results for 2014 showed that P&G continued to stagnate, with little improvement in results from most of its businesses (see Exhibits 4 and 5). The firm announced that its performance during 2015 was not likely to be much better. After keeping pace with overall economic growth for decades, unit sales of P&G's core products like laundry detergent and toothpaste had been largely flat for the previous four years in the U.S., the firm's biggest market. Efforts to compensate by pursuing more aggressive growth in emerging markets had failed to produce any significant results.

For years, P&G had spent heavily to build on its success with legacy soap and detergent brands by acquiring hundreds of additional brands in new businesses that it hoped could also become part of consumers' daily routines. The recent effort to jettison over half of its brands indicated that the strategy was not working anymore. In particular, P&G was struggling with its push to place more emphasis on products that carried higher margins in order to move the firm away from its dependence on household staples.

The firm's aggressive push into beauty, for example, struggled to show much growth. Lafley had tried to build the firm's presence in this business for years, regarding it as a high-margin, faster-growing complement to the firm's core household products. Yet this business was generating the lowest profit margins. Sales of Olay skin care products and Pantene hair care products mostly sagged in recent years. Although P&G managed to build a line of perfumes

EXHIBIT 4
Income Statement ($ millions)

	Year Ending June				
	2010	2011	2012	2013	2014
Revenue	78,938	82,559	83,680	84,167	83,062
Gross profit	41,019	41,791	41,289	41,739	40,602
Operating income	16,021	15,818	13,292	14,481	15,288
Income before taxes	15,047	15,189	12,785	14,843	14,885
Net income	12,736	11,797	10,756	11,312	11,643

Source: P&G.

EXHIBIT 5
Balance Sheet ($ millions)

	Year Ending June				
	2010	2011	2012	2013	2014
Total current assets	18,782	21,970	21,910	23,990	31,617
Total assets	128,172	138,354	132,244	139,263	144,266
Total current liabilities	24,282	27,293	24,907	30,037	33,726
Total liabilities	67,057	70,714	68,805	71,199	75,052
Total stockholders' equity	61,115	67,640	63,439	68,064	69,214

Source: P&G.

around licenses with Dolce & Gabbana, Gucci, and Hugo Boss, it was forced to cut back on some of its smaller labels. "Beauty continues to have really big challenges," Dibadj stated.[8]

Even as P&G continued to struggle to overcome its stagnant sales, Lafley remained convinced that discarding brands would allow the firm to be managed more effectively. His resolve to reduce the number of brands that the firm managed represented a return to his earlier objective of trying to make the firm more agile. He believed that scaling down the firm would allow it to respond more quickly to changes in the market. "These changes simplify the way we organize and manage the company," he recently remarked.[9]

ENDNOTES

1. Jennifer Reingold & Doris Burke. Can P&G's CEO hang on? *Fortune,* February 25, 2013, p. 69.
2. Alex Coolridge. P&G plans to unload more than its brands. *Cincinnati Enquirer,* August 2, 2014, p. 1.
3. Reingold & Burke, op. cit., p. 70.
4. Ibid., p. 71.
5. Ibid., p. 70.
6. Ibid., p. 75.
7. Coolridge, op. cit.
8. Rachel Abrams. Cleaning house. P&G plans Duracell spinoff. *New York Times,* October 25, 2014, p. B3.
9. Ellen Bryon. P&G shakes up executive ranks. *Wall Street Journal,* October 23, 2014, p. B1.

CASES

CASE 27

MICROFINANCE
Going Global . . . and Going Public?*

In the world of development, if one mixes the poor and nonpoor in a program, the nonpoor will always drive out the poor, and the less poor will drive out the more poor, unless protective measures are instituted right at the beginning.

—Dr. Muhammad Yunus, founder of Grameen Bank[1]

More than 2.5 billion people in the world earn less than $2.50 a day. None of the developmental economics theories have helped change this situation. Less than $2.50 a day means that these unfortunate people have been living without clean water, sanitation, sufficient food to eat, or a proper place to sleep. In Southeast Asia alone, more than 500 million people live under these circumstances. In the past, almost every effort to help the very poor has been either a complete failure or at best partially successful. As Dr. Yunus argues, in every one of these instances, the poor will push the very poor out!

In 1972 Dr. Muhammad Yunus, a young economics professor trained at Vanderbilt, returned home to Bangladesh to take a position at Chittagong University. Upon his arrival, he was struck by the stark contrast between the developmental economics he taught in the classroom and the abject poverty of the villages surrounding the university. Dr. Yunus witnessed more suffering of the poor when, in 1974, inclement weather wiped out food crops and resulted in a widespread and prolonged famine. The theories of developmental economics and the traditional banking institutions, he concluded, were completely ineffectual for lessening the hunger and homelessness among the very poor of that region.

In 1976 Dr. Yunus and his students were visiting the poorest people in the village of Jobra to see whether they could directly help them in any way. They met a group of craftswomen making simple bamboo stools. After paying for their raw materials and financing, the women were left with a profit of just two cents per day. From his own pocket, Dr. Yunus gave $27 to be distributed among 42 craftswomen and *rickshaw* (human-driven transport) drivers. Little did he know that this simple act of generosity was the beginning of a global revolution in microfinance that would eventually help millions of impoverished and poor begin a transition from destitution to economic self-sufficiency. Dr. Yunus was convinced that a nontraditional approach to financing is the only way to help the very poor to help themselves.

The Grameen Project would soon follow—it officially became a bank under the law in 1983. The poor borrowers own 95 percent of the bank, and the rest is owned by the Bangladeshi government. Loans are financed through deposits only, and there are 8.35 million borrowers, of which 97 percent are women. There are over 2,500 branches serving around 81,000 villages in Bangladesh with a staff of more than 22,000 people. Since its inception, the bank has dispersed more than $10 billion, with a cumulative loan recovery rate of 97.38 percent. The Grameen Bank has been profitable every year since 1976 except three years and pays returns on deposits up to 100 percent to its members.[2] In 2006 Dr. Yunus and the Grameen Bank shared the Nobel Peace Prize for the concept and methodology of microfinance, also known as microcredit or microloans.[3]

What Is Microfinance?

Microfinance involves a small loan (US$20–$750) with a high rate of interest (0 to 200 percent), typically provided to poor or destitute entrepreneurs without collateral.[4] A traditional loan has two basic components captured by interest rates: (1) risk of future payment, and (2) present value (given the time value of money). Risk of future payments is particularly high when dealing with the poor, who are unlikely to have familiarity with credit. To reduce this uncertainty, many microfinance banks refuse to lend to individuals and only lend to groups. Groups have proven to be an effective source of "social collateral" in the microloan process.

In addition to the risk and time value of money, the value of a loan must also include the transaction costs associated with administering the loan. A transaction cost is the cost associated with an economic exchange and is often considered the cost of doing business. For banks like the Grameen Bank, the cost of administering ($125) a small loan may exceed the amount of the small loan itself ($120). These transaction costs have been one of the major deterrents for traditional banks.

Consider a bank with $10,000 to lend. If broken into small loans ($120), the available $10,000 can provide about 83 transactions. If the cost to administer a small loan

---

* This case was developed by Brian C. Pinkham, LL.M., and Dr. Padmakumar Nair, both from the University of Texas at Dallas. Material has been drawn from published sources to be used for class discussion. Copyright © 2011 Brian C. Pinkham and Padmakumar Nair.

($120) is $125, its cost per unit is about 104 percent (!), while the cost of one $10,000 loan is only 1.25 percent. Because of the high cost per unit and the high risk of future payment, the rate of interest assigned to the smaller loan is much higher than the rate on the larger loan.

Finally, after these costs are accounted for, there must be some margin (or profit). In the case of microfinance banks, the margins are split between funding the growth of the bank (adding extra branches) and returns on deposits for bank members. This provides even the poorest bank member a feeling of "ownership."

Microfinance and Initial Public Offerings

With the global success of the microfinance concept, the number of private microfinance institutions exploded. Today there are more than 7,000 microfinance institutions, and their profitability has led many of the larger institutions to consider whether or not to "go public." Many microfinance banks redistribute profits to bank members (the poor) through returns on deposits. Once the bank goes public through an initial public offering (IPO), however, there is a transfer of control to public buyers (typically investors from developed economies). This transfer creates a fiduciary duty of the bank's management to maximize value for the shareholders.[5]

For example, Compartamos Banco (Banco) of Mexico raised $467 million in its IPO in 2007. The majority of buyers were leading investment companies from the United States and United Kingdom—the geographic breakdown of the investors was 52 percent U.S., 33 percent Europe, 5 percent Mexico, and 10 percent other Latin American countries. Similarly, Bank Rakyat Indonesia (BRI) raised $480 million in its IPO by listing on multiple stock exchanges in 2003; the majority of investors who purchased the available 30 percent interest in the bank were from the United States and United Kingdom. The Indonesian government controls the remaining 70 percent stake in BRI. In Kenya, Equity Bank raised $88 million in its IPO in late 2006. Because of the small scale of Equity Bank's initial listing on the Nairobi Stock Exchange, the majority of the investors were from eastern Africa.[6] About one-third of the investors were from the European Union and United States."[7]

Compartamos Banco[8]

Banco started in 1990 as a nongovernmental organization (NGO). At the time, population growth in Latin America and Mexico outpaced job growth. This left few job opportunities within the largest population group in Mexico—the low-income. Banco recognized that the payoffs for high-income opportunities were much larger (dollars a day), relative to low-income opportunities that may return only pennies a day. Over the next 10 years, Banco offered larger loans to groups and individuals to help bridge the gap between these low-income and high-income opportunities. However, its focus is to serve low-income individuals and groups, particularly the women who make up 98 percent of Banco's members.

The bank offers two microfinance options available to women only. The first is the *crédito mujer* (women's credit). This loan ranges from $115 to $2,075, available to groups (12–50) of women. Maturity is four months, and payments are weekly or biweekly.

If a group of women demonstrates the ability to manage credit through the *crédito mujer,* they have access to *crédito mejora tu casa* (home-improvement loans). This loan ranges from $230 to $2,300 with a 6- to 24-month maturity. Payments are either biweekly or monthly.

The average interest rate on these loans is 80 percent. Banco focuses on loans to *groups* of women and requires the guarantee of the group—*every* individual in the group is held liable for the payment of the loan. This provides a social reinforcement mechanism for loan payments typically absent in traditional loans. The bank also prefers groups because they are more likely to take larger loans. This has proven effective even in times of economic downturn, when banks typically expect higher demand for loans and lower recovery of loans.

In 2009, with Mexico still reeling from the economic recession of 2008, Banco provided financing to 1.5 million Mexican households. This represented a growth of 30 percent from 2008. The core of the financing was *crédito mujer*, emphasizing the bank's focus on providing services for the low-income groups. The average loan was 4.6 percent of GDP per capita ($440), compared with an average loan of 54 percent of GDP per capita ($347) at the Grameen Bank in Bangladesh.[9] With pressure from the economic downturn, Banco also reduced its cost per client by more than 5 percent, and it continues (in late 2010) to have a cost per client under $125.

Consider two examples of how these microloans are used. Julia González Cueto, who started selling candy door-to-door in 1983, used her first loan to purchase accessories to broaden the image of her business. This provided a stepping-stone for her decision to cultivate mushrooms and nopales (prickly pear leaves) to supplement her candy business. She now exports wild mushrooms to an Italian restaurant chain. Leocadia Cruz Gómez has had 16 loans, the first in April 2006. She invested in looms and thread to expand her textile business. Today, her workshop has grown, she is able to travel and give classes, and her work is widely recognized.

Beyond the Grameen Bank

These are just a few examples of how capitalistic free-market enterprises have helped the world to progress. It is generally accepted that charitable contributions and government programs alone cannot alleviate poverty. More resources and professional management are essential for microfinance institutions to grow further and sustain their mission. An IPO is one way to achieve this goal when deposits alone cannot sustain the demand for loans. At the same time, investors expect a decent return on their investment, and this expectation might work against the most important goal of microfinancing, namely, to help the very poor. Dr. Yunus has recently reemphasized his concern of the nonpoor driving out the poor, and he talks about microfinance institutions seeking investments from "social-objective-driven" investors with a need to create a separate "social stock market."[10]

The Grameen Bank story, and that of microfinancing, and the current enthusiasm in going public raise several concerns. Institutions like the Grameen Bank have to grow and sustain a long-run perspective. The Grameen Bank has not accepted donor money since 1998 and does not foresee a need for donor money or other sources of external capital. The Grameen Bank charges four interest rates, depending on who is borrowing and for what purpose the money is being used: 20 percent for income-generating loans, 8 percent for housing loans, 5 percent for student loans, and interest-free loans for struggling members (unsympathetically called beggars). (Although these rates would appear to be close to what U.S. banks charge, we must point out that the terms of these loans are typically three or four months. Thus, the annualized interest rates would be four or five times the aforementioned rates.)

The Grameen Bank's "Beggars-As-Members" program is a stark contrast to what has been theorized and practiced in contemporary financial markets—traditional banking would assign high-risk borrowers (like beggars) the highest interest rate compared to more reliable borrowers who are using the borrowed money for generating income. Interestingly, the loan recovery rate is 79 percent from the "Beggars-As-Members" program, and about 20,000 members (out of 110,000) have left begging completely.[11] However, it is difficult to predict the future, and it is possible that the Grameen Bank might consider expanding its capital base by going public just like its Mexican counterpart.

Most developmental economists question the wisdom of going public, because publicly traded enterprises are likely to struggle to find a balance between fiduciary responsibilities and social good.[12] The three large IPOs mentioned above (Banco, BRI, and Equity First) all resulted in improved transparency and reporting for stockholders. However, the profits, which were originally distributed to bank members as returns on deposits, are now split between bank members (poor) and stockholders (made up of mostly EU and U.S. investors). Many of these microfinance banks are feeling the pressure of NGOs and bank members requesting lower interest rates.[13] This trend could potentially erode the large profit margins these banks currently enjoy. When faced with falling profits, publicly traded microfinance institutions will have to decide how best to provide financial services for the very poor and struggling members of the society without undermining their fiduciary duties to stockholders.

ENDNOTES

1. Yunus, M. 2007. *Banker to the poor: Micro-lending and the battle against world poverty.* New York: PublicAffairs.
2. The Grameen Bank removes funding for administration and branch growth from the initial profits and redistributes the remaining profits to bank members. This means that a poor bank member who deposits $1 in January may receive up to $1 on December 31! Grameen Bank, *www.grameen-info.org.*
3. Grameen Bank, *www.grameen-info.org.*
4. Microfinance banks vary to the extent that the rates of interest are annualized or specified to the term. Grameen Bank, for instance, annualizes the interest on its microloans. However, many other banks set a periodic rate whereby, in extreme cases, interest may accrue daily. Grameen Bank, *www.grameen-info.org.*
5. Khavul, S. 2010. Microfinance: Creating opportunities for the poor? *Academy of Management Perspectives,* 24(3): 58–72.
6. Equity Bank, *www.equitybank.co.ke.*
7. Rhyne, E., & Guimon, A. 2007. The Banco Compartamos initial public offering. *Accion: InSight,* no. 23: 1–17, *resources.centerforfinancialinclusion.org/insight/IS23en.pdf.*
8. Unless otherwise noted, this section uses information from Banco Compartamos, *www.compartamos.com.*
9. We calculated all GDP per capita information as normalized to current (as of 2010) U.S. dollars using the International Monetary Fund (IMF) website, *www.imf.org.* The estimated percentages are from Banco Compartamos, *www.compartamos.com.*
10. Yunus. 2007. *Banker to the poor.*
11. Grameen Bank, *www.grameen-info.org.*
12. Khavul. 2010. Microfinance.
13. Rhyne & Guimon. 2007. The Banco Compartamos initial public offering.

CASES

CASE 28
SAMSUNG ELECTRONICS*

In January 2015, executives from Samsung Electronics, the South Korean electronics giant, declared that they were making a big bet on the so-called Internet of things. This represented a return to the firm's concept of a digital home, where all of the firm's gadgets and appliances would be connected to the Internet. Samsung was just one of many players vying to shape the connected home of the future, and it was far from clear whose vision would prevail or even if it would be profitable.

The bet seemed to be necessary for Samsung because it faced profit pressures and strong competition from price-cutting Chinese start-ups such as Xiaomi and Huawei in the smartphone business (see Exhibits 1 and 2). Samsung had been a leader in sales of mobile phones, but its position was being challenged in a growing number of markets by lower-priced smartphones. At the same time, Samsung was facing stiffer competition from Apple, which had been matching Galaxy phones, tablets, and phablets by introducing larger and cheaper versions of its own highly popular iPhones (see Exhibits 3 and 4).

Analysts claimed that the problem lay with Samsung's reliance on selling hardware while other competitors, ranging from Apple to Xiaomi, offered exclusive software and Internet services for their devices that set their products apart from all others. Some competitors were also beginning to generate revenues from offering these services through their own app stores. Although Samsung offered some customized versions of the Android system that it used, they did not help differentiate its offerings from those of others that also offered Android smartphones. "That's really the difficult part for them," said Ben Bajarin, a consumer technology analyst. "Their customers are actually Google's, they're not necessarily theirs."[1]

Executives at Samsung claimed that the firm's strength lay in the diverse line of its products, which included

* Case prepared by Jamal Shamsie, Michigan State University, with the assistance of Professor Alan B. Eisner, Pace University. Material has been drawn from published sources to be used for purposes of class discussion. Copyright © 2015 Jamal Shamsie and Alan B. Eisner.

EXHIBIT 1 Income Statement (in billions of KRW)

	Year Ending December 31				
	2009	2010	2011	2012	2013
Revenue	136,323,670	154,630,328	165,001,771	201,103,613	228,692,667
Gross profit	41,728,806	51,963,504	52,856,651	74,451,682	90,996,358
Operating income	10,309,038	16,352,670	15,861,224	29,049,338	36,785,013
Net income	9,571,598	15,799,035	13,734,067	23,185,375	29,821,215

Source: Samsung.

EXHIBIT 2 Balance Sheet (in billions of KRW)

	Year Ending December 31				
	2009	2010	2011	2012	2013
Total current assets	54,211,297	61,402,589	71,502,061	87,269,017	110,760,271
Total assets	112,179,788	134,288,743	155,631,251	181,071,570	214,075,018
Total current liabilities	34,204,424	39,944,721	44,319,014	46,933,052	51,315,409
Total liabilities	42,734,204	48,818,652	58,150,956	63,977,518	69,632,402
Total stockholders' equity	72,925,734	89,229,623	101,725,852	121,480,206	150,016,010

Source: Samsung.

EXHIBIT 3 Smartphone Sales Worldwide, 2014

Company	Market Share
Samsung	32%
Apple	15
Huawei	5
LG	5
Lenovo	4
Xiaomi	4

Source: *USA Today.*

EXHIBIT 4 Smartphone Sales in China, 2014

Company	Market Share
Xiaomi	14%
Samsung	12
Coolpad	12
Lenovo	12
Huawei	11

Source: Canalys, *Wall Street Journal.*

EXHIBIT 5 Global Market Ranking, 2014

Product Category	Market Rank
Memory chips	1
Digital televisions	1
Mobile phones	1
Side-by-side refrigerators	1
DVD players	2
Washing machines	2
Camcorders	3
Digital cameras	3

Source: Samsung.

televisions, cameras, laptops, and even washing machines (see Exhibit 5). Although smartphones accounted for as much as two-thirds of its profits, Samsung could have increased its revenues from its other offerings. Furthermore, unlike all of its rivals, Samsung made most of its own components, which could have allowed it to offer better products with lower costs. This would have enabled the firm to generate profits even if profit margins on some of these products continued to decline.

In spite of its emphasis on hardware, Samsung was aware of the clear shift in electronics away from hardware to software. In 2014, the firm introduced its first smartphone that ran on Tizen, an operating system that it had developed with Intel and other partners. Although the system was not likely to challenge existing mobile operating systems such as Google's Android, Samsung was hoping that it would provide it with a platform on which to build its own services. The firm was well positioned to bring Tizen to the mass market by installing the software on televisions, cameras, and watches. Eventually, it might also become the system that Samsung could use to connect all gadgets and appliances to create the Internet of things.

Discarding a Failing Strategy

Although Samsung chairman Lee Kun-hee had called for a shift in the firm's strategy, the transformation would not have been possible without the ceaseless efforts of Yun Jong Yong, who was appointed to the position of president and CEO in 1996. When Yun took charge, Samsung was still making most of its profits from lower-priced appliances that consumers were likely to pick up if they could not afford a higher-priced brand such as Sony or Mitsubishi. It had also become an established low-cost supplier of various components to larger and better-known manufacturers around the world.

Although the firm was making profits, Yun was concerned about the future prospects of a firm that was relying on a strategy of competing on price with products that were based on technologies developed by other firms. The success of this strategy was tied to the ability of Samsung to continually scout for locations that would allow it to keep its manufacturing costs down. At the same time, it would need to keep generating sufficient orders to maintain a high volume of production. In particular, Yun was concerned about the growing competition that the firm was likely to face from the many low-cost producers that were springing up in other countries, such as China.

Yun's concerns were well founded. Within a year of his takeover, Samsung was facing serious financial problems that threatened its survival. The company was left with huge debt as an economic crisis engulfed most of Asia in 1997, leading to a drop in demand and a crash in the prices of many electronic goods. In the face of such a deteriorating environment, Samsung continued to push for maintaining its production and sales records even as much of its output was ending up unsold in warehouses.

By July 1998, Samsung Electronics was losing millions of dollars each month. "If we continued, we would have gone belly-up within three or four years," Yun recalled.[2] He knew that he had to make some drastic moves in order to turn things around. Yun locked himself in a hotel room for a whole day with nine other senior managers to try to find a way to save the firm. They all wrote resignation letters and pledged to resign if they failed.

After much deliberation, Yun and his management team decided to take several steps to try to push Samsung out of its precarious financial position. To begin with, they decided to lay off about 30,000 employees, well over one-third of the firm's entire workforce. They also closed down many of Samsung's factories for two months so that they could eliminate its large inventory. Finally, they sold off about $2 billion worth of businesses like pagers and electric coffeemakers that were perceived to be of marginal significance for the firm's future.

Developing a Premium Brand

Having managed to stem the losses, Yun decided to move Samsung away from its strategy of competition based largely on the lower price of its offerings. Consequently, he began to push the firm to develop its own products rather than to copy those that other firms had developed. In particular, Yun placed considerable emphasis on the development of products that would impress consumers with their attractive designs and their advanced technology. By focusing on such products, Yun hoped that he could develop Samsung into a premium brand that would allow him to charge higher prices.

To achieve this, Yun had to reorient the firm and help it to develop new capabilities. He recruited new managers and engineers, many of whom had developed considerable experience in the U.S. Once they were recruited, Yun got them into shape by putting them through a four-week boot camp that consisted of martial drills at the crack of dawn and mountain hikes that lasted all day. To create incentives for this new talent, Yun discarded Samsung's rigid seniority-based system and replaced it with a merit-based system for advancement.

As a result of these efforts, Samsung started launching an array of products that were designed to make a big impression on consumers. They included the largest flat-panel televisions, cell phones with a variety of features such as cameras and PDAs, ever-thinner notebook computers, and speedier and richer semiconductors. The firm calls them "wow products," and they are designed to elevate Samsung in the same way the Trinitron television and the Walkman had helped to plant Sony in the minds of consumers.

Finally, to help Samsung change its image among consumers, Yun hired a marketing whiz, Eric Kim, who worked hard to create a more upscale image of the firm and its products. Kim moved Samsung's advertising away from 55 different advertising agencies around the world and placed it with one firm, Madison Avenue's Foote, Cone & Belding Worldwide, in order to create a consistent global brand image for Samsung's products. He also began to pull Samsung out of big discount chains like Walmart and Kmart and place more of its products into more upscale specialty stores such as Best Buy and Circuit City.

Yun initiated the practice of working closely with retailers to get more information about the specific needs of prospective consumers. Unlike Apple, Samsung focused heavily on studying existing markets and innovating inside them. "We get most of our ideas from the market," said Kim Hyun-suk, an executive vice president at Samsung.[3] The firm was able to develop strong relationships with retailers because of this practice. Over the years, Samsung also attracted many wireless carriers because of its willingness to work with them on figuring out what to offer in their smartphones and tablets.

Speeding Up New Product Development

Yun took many steps to speed up Samsung's new product development process. He was well aware that he would be able to maintain the higher margins only as long as his firm kept introducing new products into the market well ahead of its established rivals. Samsung managers who had worked for big competitors said they had to go through far fewer layers of bureaucracy than they had to in the past to win approval for new products, budgets, and marketing plans, speeding up their ability to seize opportunities.

Apart from reducing the bureaucratic obstacles, Yun took advantage of the emerging shift to digital technologies. He made heavy investments in key technologies, ranging from semiconductors to LCD displays, that could allow the firm to push out a wide variety of revolutionary digital products. Samsung continuously invested more than any of its rivals in research and development, with the investment rising to almost $12 billion by 2014. It had assembled a large force of designers and engineers who worked in several research centers that were spread around the world (see Exhibit 6).

Yun forced Samsung's own units to compete with outsiders in order to speed up the process for developing innovative new products. In the liquid-crystal-display business, for example, Samsung bought half of its color filters from Sumitomo Chemical Company of Japan and sourced the other half internally, pitting the two teams against each other. "They really press these departments to compete," said Sumitomo president Hiromasa Yonekura.[4] As a result of these steps, Samsung claimed that it had reduced the time required to go from new product concept to rollout to as little as five months, compared to over a year in 2000.

In large part, this resulted from the effort of the firm's top managers, engineers, and designers, who worked relentlessly in the five-story VIP center nestled amid the firm's industrial complex in Suwon. They worked day and night in the center, which included dormitories and showers for brief rests, to work out any problems that might hold back a product launch. The progress made by the teams that pursued new product designs in the VIP center enabled Samsung to reduce complexity in the early stages of the design cycle. This allowed the firm to move its

EXHIBIT 6 Designers Employed

Year	Designers
2014	900
2012	850
2010	750
2008	600
2006	550
2004	475
2002	300
2000	200
1998	175

Source: Samsung.

products quickly to manufacturing with minimal problems and at the lowest possible cost. Kyunghan Jung, a senior manager of the center, explained: "Seventy to eighty percent of quality, cost and delivery time is determined in the initial stages of product development."[5]

The speedier development process allowed Samsung to introduce the first voice-activated phones, handsets with MP3 players, and digital camera phones that sent photos over a global system for mobile communications networks. For an example of the firm's speed and agility, Charles Golvin of Forrester Research talked about Samsung's ability to create four different industrial designs of its Galaxy S smartphone for four varying wireless network types around the world and deliver the phones simultaneously. "They've had a long history of responding to market trends with a lot of alacrity," he remarked.[6]

Perfecting a Design Process

As Yun was building the Samsung brand, he was also trying to position the firm to compete with all others on the basis of the irresistible design of its wide range of products, from home appliances to handheld computers to flat-screen televisions that would all be eventually linked to each other. In fact, the firm seemed to be well placed to develop attractive gadgets that straddled traditional technology categories. "We have to combine computers, consumer electronics and communications as Koreans mix their rice with vegetables and meats," said Dae Je Chin, the head of Samsung's digital media division.[7]

Although Samsung tried to pack its products with various attractive features, it drew on the knowledge of about 900 designers with backgrounds in disciplines as diverse as psychology, sociology, economics, and engineering. These designers, in turn, drew on information that was collected by over 60,000 staff members working in 34 research centers across the globe, in cities such as San Francisco, London, Tokyo, Mumbai, and Shanghai. Inside these centers, designers observed the way that consumers actually used various products. The wide Galaxy Note phone, for example, resulted from the responses of focus groups who wanted a device that was good for handwriting, drawing, and sharing notes. Asian consumers said that they found it easier to write characters on a device by using a pen rather than typing on a keyboard (see Exhibit 7).

"The research process is unimaginable," said Chang Dong-hoon, an executive vice president of Samsung who had led the company's design efforts. "We go through all avenues to make sure we read the trends correctly."[8] Samsung had been sending its growing group of designers to various locations to spend a few months at fashion houses, furniture designers, and cosmetic specialists to stay current with trends in other industries. Designers of the latest Galaxy smartphone said they drew inspiration from trips to ruins in Cambodia, vistas in Helsinki, a Salvador Dalí art exhibit in London, and even a balloon ride in Africa.

Furthermore, Samsung appointed designers to executive positions in order to make sure that they could get their ideas to top managers. In 2015, the firm recruited Lee Dontae, who had been a top executive at a leading U.K. design agency. He joined Chang Dong-hoon, who was recently given charge of the firm's design strategy team, which had been overseeing the design of products across all of the product lines. In the fall of 2014, Samsung unveiled a slick design website to shore up its self-proclaimed status as a design powerhouse. As a result of these and earlier efforts, Samsung had earned 210 design awards since 2006 at contests in the United States, Europe, and Asia. After the firm won awards at a recent U.S. consumer electronics show, an executive said: "Samsung strives to consistently lead the consumer electronics industry in product design and engineering innovation."[9]

Samsung was relying on the attractiveness of its products to make them the centerpiece of a digital home. In a showroom in the lobby of its headquarters in Seoul, the firm showed off many of its latest offerings, ranging from tablet computers to digital cameras. Visitors could put on goggles to watch characters jump out on 3-D televisions or could shuffle their feet on an interactive LED floor. Roger Entner, a wireless industry analyst at Neilson, said about Samsung's efforts: "With its resources and experience, it's trying to capitalize on the emergence of smart connected devices. The question is, 'Can they be a cutting-edge trendsetter like Apple?'"[10]

Creating a Sustainable Model?

Samsung recently launched a 10-year Vision 2020 corporate goal for the firm to join the ranks of the top 10 global companies by achieving $400 billion in sales. Although it already ranked as the largest technology company in the world by revenue, Samsung was determined to continue to grab market share from competitors across a wide range of product categories. To reach its targeted sales

EXHIBIT 7 Samsung Milestones

Year	Event
1969	Samsung Electronics established as maker of televisions with technology borrowed from Sanyo.
1977	Samsung introduces its first color television.
1981	Samsung begins to focus on undercutting Japanese rivals with me-too products, with little emphasis on design.
1988	Samsung launches first mobile phone.
1993	Samsung begins to reinvent the firm through design.
1994	Samsung hires design consultancy IDEO to help develop computer monitors.
1995	Samsung sets up in-house design school, the Innovative Design Lab of Samsung.
1996	Yun Jong Yong takes over as CEO; he declares "Year of Design Revolution," stressing that designers should lead in product planning.
1998	Asian financial crisis dents Samsung's ambitions, forcing it to cut design staff by 28%.
2000	Samsung once again focuses on design, and CEO Yun Jong Yong calls for design-led management.
2001	Yun initiates quarterly design meetings for top executives and opens design labs in Los Angeles and London.
2002	Samsung's "usability laboratory" inaugurated in downtown Seoul.
2004	Market value of Samsung rises above $100 billion.
2008	Lee Yoon Woo takes over as CEO from Yun.
2009	Samsung is set to announce its first loss since 2000; the firm announces major reorganization.
2010	Gee Sung Choi takes over as CEO.
2013	New co-leader team is formed.

Source: Samsung.

goal, Samsung was reorganizing to focus more strongly on each of its businesses, encompassing several different businesses, that were allocated to three major divisions: consumer electronics, IT and mobile communications, and device solutions.

However, after Lee Kun-hee, the chairman of Samsung Electronics who had helped transform the company into a technology giant, suffered a heart attack in May 2014, analysts began to question how the firm would perform when he stepped down. The firm had already changed its CEO a couple of times since 2008, after Yun's departure, before settling in 2013 on a team of co-CEOs. Lee's health issues had led the firm to consider a major shake-up in its management ranks. Among other possible moves, Samsung was considering combining the smartphone and the appliance divisions under B. K. Yoon, moving away from the unusual arrangement of dividing different businesses among three co-CEOs. If Yoon was given this added responsibility, he would be well positioned to help Samsung compete in the so-called connected home referred to as the Internet of things. He had been one of the main proponents of the company's push in this direction and was responsible for Samsung's 2014 acquisition of U.S. connected-home start-up SmartThings.

In the meantime, Samsung continued to push on advances in hardware. It developed a foldable video display screen that could be used in smartphones or other devices. Kwon Oh-hyun, the firm's chief executive, said that it planned to start bringing devices with foldable display screens to the market. Late in 2014, Samsung released a smartphone with a display that curved around one side of the phone, along with a virtual reality headset, as the firm looked beyond the traditional model. The headset, called the Samsung Gear VR Innovator Edition, was a nylon strap that allowed users to mount the Galaxy Note in front of their eyes, enabling users to play games and watch movies.

But Samsung's biggest strength possibly lay in its leading position in memory chips. As chip technology improved more incrementally, Samsung was one of the few companies left that could make investments in new generations of semiconductors. As a result, it could become one of the biggest suppliers to other smartphone manufacturers. It was already one of the major suppliers of chips, among other components, for firms such as Apple, Sony, and Hewlett-Packard. "Then Samsung will have greater control over the whole ecosystem," said Sundeep Bajikar, a securities analyst. "The benefits of that can be enormous."[11]

Change everything except your wife and children.

—Address to employees from Samsung chairman Lee Kun-hee to push for its transformation to a leading electronics brand

ENDNOTES

1. Brian X. Chen. Samsung besieged by low-cost competition. *International New York Times,* July 14, 2014, p. 15.
2. Frank Gibney, Jr. Samsung moves upmarket. *Time,* March 25, 2002, p. 49.
3. Brian X. Chen. Samsung's strategy to brake Apple juggernaut. *New York Times,* February 11, 2013, p. B1.
4. Peter Lewis. A perpetual crisis machine. *Fortune,* September 19, 2005, p. 65.
5. Cliff Edwards, Moon Ihlwan, & Pete Engardio. The Samsung way. *Business Week,* June 16, 2003, p. 61.
6. Roger Yu. Samsung cranks up creativity. *USA Today,* November 16, 2010, p. 4B.
7. David Rocks & Moon Ihlwan. Samsung design. *Business Week,* December 6, 2004, p. 90.
8. Chen, op. cit.
9. Anonymous. Samsung electronics gets 46 CES innovations awards for 2009. *Wireless News,* November 24, 2008.
10. Yu, op. cit.
11. Eric Pfanner. Chip profits help soften other losses at Samsung. *New York Times,* January 25, 2014, p. B 2.

CASES

CASE 29
HEINEKEN*

Dutch brewer Heineken inaugurated a new state-of-the-art brewery on the outskirts of Addis Ababa, Ethiopia, on January 18, 2015, in a ceremony that was attended by Jean-François van Boxmeer, chairman and CEO of the firm, and His Excellency Hailemariam Desalegn, the prime minister of the country. The new facility allowed Heineken to expand its capacity for beer production in Ethiopia, where it already operated two other breweries that it had acquired from the Ethiopian government in 2011. Besides producing the flagship Heineken beer, the new brewery would produce Bedele, Harar, and the newly launched Walia beer. "Our inauguration marks the latest chapter in our Africa story which began over 100 years ago," van Boxmeer stated on the occasion.[1]

The move came on the heels of acquisitions and capacity investments that Heineken had been making in other developing markets. In 2013, the firm had strengthened its position as the world's third-largest brewer by taking full ownership of Asian Pacific Breweries, the owner of Tiger, Bintang, and other popular Asian beer brands. With this deal, Heineken added 30 breweries across several countries in the Asia-Pacific region. A few years earlier, the firm had acquired Mexican brewer FEMSA Cervesa, producer of Dos Equis, Sol, and Tecate beers, to become a stronger, more competitive player in Latin America.

At the same time, Heineken maintained its leading position across Europe. It had made a high-profile acquisition in 2008 of Scottish-based brewer Scottish & Newcastle, the brewer of well-known brands such as Newcastle Brown Ale and Kronenbourg 1664. Although the purchase had been made in partnership with Carlsberg, Heineken was able to gain control of Scottish & Newcastle's operations in several crucial European markets, such as the United Kingdom, Ireland, Portugal, Finland, and Belgium.

These decisions to acquire brewers that operated in different parts of the world were part of a series of changes that the Dutch brewer was making to raise its stature in the various markets and to respond to changes occurring in the global market for beer. Even as sales of beer stagnated in the United States and Europe, demand was growing in other developing countries. This led the largest brewers to expand across the globe through acquisitions of smaller regional and national players (see Exhibits 1 and 2).

The need for change was clearly reflected in the appointment in October 2005 of Jean-François van Boxmeer as Heineken's first non-Dutch CEO. He was brought in to replace Thorny Ruys, who had resigned because of his failure to show much improvement in performance. Prior to the appointment of Ruys in 2002, Heineken had been run by three generations of Heineken ancestors, whose portraits still adorned the dark-paneled office of the CEO in the firm's Amsterdam headquarters. Like Ruys, van Boxmeer faced the challenge of preserving the firm's family-driven traditions while dealing with threats that had never been faced before.

Confronting a Globalizing Industry

Heineken was one of the pioneers of an international strategy, using cross-border deals to expand its distribution of its Heineken, Amstel, and about 175 other beer brands in more than 100 countries around the globe. For years, it had been picking up small brewers in several countries to add more

---

* Case prepared by Jamal Shamsie, Michigan State University, with the assistance of Professor Alan B. Eisner, Pace University. Material has been drawn from published sources to be used for purposes of class discussion. Copyright © 2015 Jamal Shamsie and Alan B. Eisner.

	Year Ended December				
	2010	2011	2012	2013	2014
Revenue	16,133	17,123	18,383	19,203	19,257
Gross profit	5,842	6,157	6,534	7,017	7,204
Operating income	2,044	2,151	2,181	2,328	2,687
Income before taxes	1,967	2,025	3,634	2,107	2,440
Net income	1,436	717	2,949	1,364	1,516

EXHIBIT 1
Income Statement
(in millions of euros)

Source: Heineken.

EXHIBIT 2
Balance Sheet (in millions of euros)

	Year Ended December				
	2010	2011	2012	2013	2014
Total current assets	4,318	4,708	5,537	5,495	6,086
Total assets	26,549	27,127	35,979	33,337	34,830
Total current liabilities	5,623	6,159	7,800	8,003	8,532
Total liabilities	16,321	22,323	24,288	21,935	22,421
Total stockholders' equity	10,228	4,804	12,762	12,356	13,452

Source: Heineken.

brands and to get better access to new markets. From its roots on the outskirts of Amsterdam, the firm had evolved into one of the world's largest brewers, operating more than 190 breweries in over 70 countries, claiming about 10 percent of the global market for beer (see Exhibits 3 and 4).

In fact, the firm's flagship Heineken brand ranked second only to Budweiser in a global brand survey jointly undertaken by *BusinessWeek* and Interbrand a couple of years ago. The premier brand had achieved worldwide recognition, according to Kevin Baker, director of alcoholic beverages at British market researcher Canadean Ltd. A U.S. wholesaler recently asked a group of marketing students to identify an assortment of beer bottles that had been stripped of their labels. The stubby green Heineken container was the only one that incited instant recognition among the group.

But the beer industry was undergoing significant change due to a furious wave of consolidation. Most of the bigger brewers began to acquire or merge with their competitors in foreign markets in order to become global players. To begin with, this gave them ownership of local brands that propelled them into a dominant position in various markets around the world. Beyond this, acquisitions of foreign brewers could provide the firms with manufacturing and distribution capabilities they could use to develop a few global brands. "The era of global brands is coming," said Alan Clark, Budapest-based managing director of SABMiller Europe (see Exhibit 5).[2]

Over the past decade, South African Breweries Plc acquired U.S.-based Miller Brewing to become a major global brewer. The firm recently acquired Fosters, the largest Australian brewer. U.S.-based Coors linked with Canada-based Molson in 2005, with their combined operations allowing the firm to rise to a leading position among the world's biggest brewers. In 2008, Belgium's Interbrew, Brazil's AmBev, and U.S.-based Anheuser-Busch all merged to become the largest global brewer, with operations across most of the continents. Last year, SABMiller made an unsuccessful bid to acquire Heineken in order to reduce the threat of being bought by Anheuser-Busch InBev.

Since its acquisition of Anheuser-Busch, InBev was planning to include Budweiser in its existing efforts to develop Stella Artois, Brahma, and Beck's as global flagship brands. Each of these brands originated in different locations, with Budweiser coming from the U.S., Stella Artois from Belgium, Brahma from Brazil, and Beck's from Germany. Similarly, the newly formed SABMiller was attempting to develop the Czech brand Pilsner Urquell into a global brand. Exports of this pilsner doubled shortly after SAB acquired it in 1999, but sales afterward plateaued. John Brock, the CEO of InBev, commented: "Global brands sell at significantly higher prices, and the margins are much better than with local beers."[3]

Wrestling with Change

Although the management of Heineken moved away from the family for the first time, the managers were well aware that the long-standing and well-established family traditions would be difficult to change. Even with

EXHIBIT 3
Geographic Breakdown of Sales (in millions of euros)

	2014	2013	2012	2011	2010
Africa & Middle East	2,643	2,554	2,639	2,223	1,988
Americas	4,631	4,495	4,523	4,029	3,296
Asia Pacific	2,088	2,037	527	216	192
Central & Eastern Europe	2,868	3,097	328	3,229	3,143
Western Europe	7,478	7,456	7,785	7,752	7,894

Source: Heineken.

EXHIBIT 4 Heineken Brands

Market	Significant Brands
U.S.	Heineken, Amstel Light, Paulaner,[1] Moretti
Netherlands	Heineken, Amstel, Lingen's Blond, Murphy's Irish Red
France	Heineken, Amstel, Buckler,[2] Desperados[3]
Italy	Heineken, Amstel, Birra Moretti
Spain	Heineken, Amstel, Cruzcampo, Buckler
Poland	Heineken, Królewskie, Kujawiak, Zywiec
China	Heineken, Tiger, Reeb[4]
Singapore	Heineken, Tiger, Anchor, Baron's
India	Heineken, Arlem, Kingfisher
Indonesia	Heineken, Bintang, Guinness
Kazakhstan	Heineken, Amstel, Tian Shan
Egypt	Heineken, Birell, Meister, Fayrouz[2]
Israel	Heineken, Maccabee, Gold Star[4]
Nigeria	Heineken, Amstel Malta, Maltina, Gulder
South Africa	Heineken, Amstel, Windhoek, Strongbow
Panama	Heineken, Soberana, Crystal, Panama
Chile	Heineken, Cristal, Escudo, Royal

[1] Wheat beer.
[2] Nonalcoholic beer.
[3] Tequila-flavored beer.
[4] Minority interest.

EXHIBIT 5 Leading Brewers, 2014

Brewer	Market Share*
1. Anheuser-Busch InBev (Leuven, Belgium)	21%
2. SABMiller (London, U.K.)	11
3. Heineken (Amsterdam, Netherlands)	10
4. Carlsberg (Copenhagen, Denmark)	6
5. Molson Coors Brewing (Denver, U.S.)	4

*Based on annual sales, in millions of U.S. dollars.

Source: *Beverage World*.

the appointment of non-family members to manage the firm, a little over half of the shares of Heineken were still owned by a holding company that was controlled by the family. With the death of Freddy Heineken in 2002, the last family member to head the Dutch brewer, control passed to his only child and heir, Charlene de Carvalho, who insisted on having a say in all of the firm's major decisions.

The family members were behind some of the changes announced at the time of van Boxmeer's appointment that would support the firm's next phase of growth as a global organization. As part of the plan, dubbed "Fit 2 Fight," the executive board was cut down from five members to CEO van Boxmeer and Chief Financial Officer René Hooft Graafland. The change was expected to centralize control at the top so that the firm could formulate a strategy to win over younger customers across different markets whose tastes are still developing.

Heineken created management positions that would be responsible for five different operating regions and several different functional areas. These positions were created to more clearly define different spheres of responsibility. Van Boxmeer argued that the new structure provided incentives for people to be accountable for their performance: "There is more pressure for results, for achievement."[4] He claimed the new structure had already encouraged more risk taking and boosted the level of energy within the firm.

The Executive Committee of Heineken was cut down from 36 to 12 members in order to speed up the decision-making process. Besides including the two members of the executive board, this management group consisted of the managers who were responsible for the different operating regions and several of the key functional areas. Van Boxmeer hoped that the reduction in the size of the committee would allow the firm to combat the cumbersome consensus culture that had made it difficult for Heineken to respond swiftly to various challenges even as its industry had been experiencing considerable change.

Finally, all of the activities of Heineken were overseen by a supervisory board, which consisted of 10 members. Individuals on this board were drawn from different countries and had a wide range of expertise and experience. They set up policies for the firm to follow in making major decisions on its overall operations. Members of the supervisory board were rotated on a regular basis.

Developing a Global Presence

Van Boxmeer was well aware of the need for Heineken to use its brands to build upon its existing stature across global markets. In spite of its formidable presence in markets around the world with its flagship Heineken brand, the firm had been reluctant to match the recent moves of formidable competitors such as Belgium's InBev and the U.K.'s SABMiller, which had grown significantly through mega-acquisitions. It was assumed that, in large part, the firm had been reluctant to make such acquisitions because of the dilution of family control.

For many years, Heineken had limited itself to snapping up small national brewers such as Italy's Moretti and Spain's Cruzcampo, which provided it with small but profitable avenues for growth. In 1996, for example, Heineken acquired Fischer, a small French brewer, whose Desperados brand was quite successful in niche markets. Similarly, Paulaner, a wheat beer that Heineken had picked up in Germany a few years ago, was making inroads into the U.S. market.

However, as other brewers were reaching out to make acquisitions all over the globe, Heineken was running the risk of falling behind its more aggressive rivals. To deal with this growing challenge, the firm broke out of its play-it-safe corporate culture to make a few big deals. In 2003, Heineken spent $2.1 billion to acquire BBAG, a family-owned company based in Linz, Austria. Because of BBAG's extensive presence in Central Europe, Heineken became the biggest beer maker in seven countries across Eastern Europe. The acquisition of Scottish & Newcastle in 2008 similarly reinforced the firm's dominance in Western Europe.

At the same time, Heineken was making a string of acquisitions in other parts of the world. Its recent acquisitions in Ethiopia, Singapore, and Mexico allowed it to build its position in these growing markets. The firm also made an aggressive push into Russia with the acquisition of midsized brewing concerns. Through several acquisitions since 2002, Russia became one of Heineken's largest markets by volume. Heineken ranked as the third-largest brewer in Russia, behind Sweden's Baltic Beverages Holding and InBev.

René Hooft Graafland, the company's chief financial officer, stated that Heineken would continue to participate in the consolidation of the $460 billion global retail beer industry by targeting many different markets around the world. During the last decade, the firm added several labels to Heineken's shelf, pouncing on brewers in far-flung places like Belarus, Panama, Egypt, and Kazakhstan. In Egypt, Ruys bought a majority stake in Al Ahram Beverages Co. and was using the Cairo-based brewer's fruit-flavored, nonalcoholic malts as an avenue into other Muslim countries.

Maintaining a Premium Position

For decades, Heineken had been able to rely upon the success of its flagship Heineken brand, which enjoyed a leading position among premium beers in many markets around the world. The brand had been the best-selling imported beer in the U.S. for several decades, giving the firm a steady source of revenues and profits from the world's biggest market. But by the late 1990s, Heineken lost its 65-year-old leadership among imported beers in the U.S. to Group Modelo's Corona. The Mexican beer was able to reach out to Hispanic Americans, who represented one of the fastest-growing segments of beer drinkers.

Furthermore, the firm was concerned that its Heineken brand was perceived as obsolete by many young drinkers. John A. Quelch, a professor at Harvard Business School who studied the beer industry, said of the Heineken brand: "It's in danger of becoming a tired, reliable, but unexciting brand."[5] The firm was therefore working hard to increase awareness of its flagship brand among younger drinkers. Heineken also introduced a light beer, Heineken Premium Light, to target the growing market for such beers in the U.S. Through such efforts, the firm managed to reduce the average age of Heineken drinkers from about 40 years old to about 30 years old.

At the same time, Heineken was pushing on other brands that would reduce its reliance on its core Heineken brand. It had already achieved considerable success with Amstel Light, which became the leading imported light beer in the U.S. and was selling well in many other countries. But many of the other brands that the firm carried were strong local brands that it had added through its string of acquisitions of smaller breweries around the globe. It managed to develop a relatively small but loyal base of consumers by promoting some of these as specialty brands, such as Murphy's Irish Red and Moretti.

Finally, Heineken was stepping up its efforts to target Hispanics, who accounted for one-quarter of U.S. sales. Besides developing specific marketing campaigns for them, it added popular Mexican beers such as Tecate and Dos Equis to its line of offerings. For years, these beers had been marketed and distributed by Heineken in the U.S. under a license from FEMSA Cervesa. In 2010, Heineken decided to acquire FEMSA, giving it full control over all of FEMSA's brands. Benj Steinman, publisher and editor of the *Beer Marketer's Insight* newsletter, believed Heineken's relationship with FEMSA was quite beneficial: "This gives Heineken a commanding share of the U.S. import business and . . . gives them a bigger presence in the Southwest . . . and better access to Hispanic consumers," he stated.[6]

Above all, Heineken wanted to maintain its leadership in the premium-beer industry, which represented the most profitable segment of the beer business. In this category, the firm's brands faced competition in the U.S. from domestic beers such as Anheuser's Budweiser Select and imported beers such as InBev's Stella Artois. Although premium brews often had slightly higher alcohol content than standard beers, they were developed through a more exclusive positioning of the brand. This allowed the firm to charge a higher price for these brands. A six-pack of Heineken, for example, cost $9, versus about $6 for a six-pack of Budweiser. Furthermore, Just-drinks.com, a London-based online research service, estimated that the market for premium beer would continue to expand over the next decade.

Building on Its Past

The recent acquisitions in different parts of the world—Asia, Africa, Latin America, and Europe—represented an important step in Heineken's quest to build on its existing global stature. In fact, most analysts expected that van Boxmeer and his team would make efforts to continue to build Heineken into a powerful global competitor. Without providing any specific details, Graafland, the firm's CFO, made it clear that the firm's management would take initiatives that would drive long-term growth. In his own words: "We are positive that the momentum in the company and trends will continue."[7]

Upon taking over the helm of Heineken, van Boxmeer had announced that he would have to work on the company's culture in order to accelerate the speed of decision making. This led many people both inside and outside the firm to expect that the new management would try to break loose from the conservative style that had resulted from the family's tight control. Instead, the affable 46-year-old Belgian indicated that he was trying to focus on changes to the firm's decision-making process rather making any drastic shifts in its existing culture.

Van Boxmeer's devotion to the firm was quite evident. Heineken's first non-Dutch CEO had spent 20 years working his way up within the firm. Even his cufflinks were silver miniatures of a Heineken bottle top and opener. "We are in the logical flow of history," he recently explained. "Every time you have a new leader you have a new kind of vision. It is not radically different, because you are defined by what your company is and what your brands are."[8]

Furthermore, van Boxmeer seemed quite comfortable working within the family-controlled structure. "Since 1952 history has proved it is the right concept," he stated about the current ownership structure. "The whole business about family restraint on us is absolutely untrue. Without its spirit and guidance, the company would not have been able to build a world leader."[9]

ENDNOTES

1. Newstex Global Business Blogs. January 19, 2015.
2. Jack Ewing & Gerry Khermouch. Waking up Heineken. *Business Week,* September 8, 2003, p. 68.
3. Richard Tomlinson. The new king of beers. *Fortune,* October 18, 2004, p. 238.
4. Ian Bickerton & Jenny Wiggins. Change is brewing at Heineken. *Financial Times,* May 9, 2006, p. 12.
5. Ewing & Khermouch, op. cit., p. 69.
6. Andrew Kaplan. Border crossings. *Beverage World,* July 15, 2004, p. 6.
7. Christopher C. Williams. Heineken seeing green. *Barron's,* September 18, 2006, p. 19.
8. Bickerton & Wiggins, op. cit.
9. Ibid.

CASES

CASE 30

FRESHDIRECT: IS IT REALLY FRESH?*

With a bold promise on its website entry page, FreshDirect claimed, "Our food is fresh, our customers are spoiled. Order on the web today and get next-day delivery of the best food at the best price, exactly the way you want it, with 100 percent satisfaction guaranteed."[1] Recently, however, many consumers questioned the freshness of the food delivered by FreshDirect. Since online shopping did not give customers the chance to feel and choose the products themselves, they had to rely completely on FreshDirect to select the food for them. This notion did not appeal to some customers.

Operating out of its production center in Long Island City, Queens, FreshDirect offered online grocery shopping and delivery service in Manhattan, Queens, Brooklyn, Nassau County, Riverdale, Westchester, select areas of Staten Island, the Bronx, New Jersey, Philadelphia, and parts of Connecticut. FreshDirect also offered pickup service at its Long Island City facility, as well as corporate service to select delivery zones in Manhattan and summer delivery service to the Hamptons on Long Island.

In addition, the company received court clearances to move its facility to the Bronx. A petition by the community group South Bronx United had earlier challenged the move from Long Island City, Queens, arguing that the city failed to properly analyze the potential environmental impact (e.g., air and noise pollution) that would result from a "truck-intensive" business. However, the judge ruled in FreshDirect's favor.

FreshDirect had threatened to relocate its operational hub and headquarters to New Jersey. But New York City and the state of New York offered close to a $130 million subsidy package, including tax breaks and abatements, to keep the online grocer in New York City.

FreshDirect CEO Jason Ackerman was delighted with the court decision. "We are eager to move forward with our plans to bring thousands of jobs to the Bronx and make it easier for people to get fresh food," he declared.[2]

When it was launched in July 2001 by Joseph Fedele and Jason Ackerman, FreshDirect pronounced to the New York area that it was "the new way to shop for food." This was a bold statement given that the previous decade had witnessed the demise of numerous other online grocery ventures. However, the creators of FreshDirect were confident in the success of their business because their entire operation had been designed to deliver one simple promise to grocery shoppers: "higher quality at lower prices."

While this promise was an extremely common tagline used within and outside the grocery business, FreshDirect had integrated numerous components into its system to give real meaning to these words. Without a retail location, FreshDirect didn't have to pay expensive rent for a retail space. To offer the highest-quality products to its customers, FreshDirect had created a state-of-the-art production center and staffed it with expert personnel. The 300,000-square-foot production facility located in Long Island City was composed of 12 separate temperature zones, ensuring that each piece of food was kept at its optimal temperature for ripening or preservation—and was kept colder and cleaner than in any retail environment.

Further quality management was achieved by an SAP manufacturing software system that controlled every detail of the facility's operations. All of the thermometers, scales, and conveyor belts within the facility were connected to a central command center. Each specific setting was programmed into the system by an expert from the corresponding department, including everything from the ideal temperature for ripening a cantaloupe to the amount of flour that went into French bread. The system was also equipped with a monitoring alarm that alerted staff to any deviation from the programmed settings.

Another quality control element that had been made an integral part of the FreshDirect facility was an extremely high standard for cleanliness, health, and safety. The facility itself was kept immaculately clean, and all food-preparation areas and equipment were bathed in antiseptic foam at the end of each day. Incoming and outgoing food was tested in FreshDirect's in-house laboratory, which ensured that the facility adhered to USDA guidelines and the Hazard Analysis and Critical Control Point food safety system and that all food passing through FreshDirect met the company's high safety standards.[3]

System efficiency was the key to FreshDirect's ability to offer its high-quality products at such low prices. FreshDirect's biggest operational design component for reducing costs was the complete elimination of the middleman. Instead of going through an intermediary, both fresh and dry products were ordered from individual growers and producers and shipped directly to FreshDirect's production center, where FreshDirect's expert staff prepared them for purchase. In addition, FreshDirect did not accept any

---

* This case was prepared by Professor Alan B. Eisner of Pace University as a basis for class discussion rather than to illustrate either effective or ineffective handling of an administrative situation. Thanks to graduate students Dev Das, Rohit R. Phadtare, and Shruti Shrestha for research assistance. Copyright © 2015 Alan B. Eisner.

slotting allowances.[4] This unique relationship with growers and producers allowed FreshDirect to enjoy reduced purchase prices from its suppliers, enabling it to pass even greater savings on to its customers.

Each department of the facility, including the coffee roaster, butcher, and bakery, was staffed by carefully selected experts, enabling FreshDirect to offer premium fresh coffees (roasted on site), pastries and breads (baked on site), deli, cheese, meats (roast beef dry-aged on site), and seafood. Perishable produce was FreshDirect's specialty—by buying locally as much as possible and using the best sources of the season, it was able to bring food the shortest distance from farms, dairies, and fisheries to the customer's table.

FreshDirect catered to the tastes of its Manhattan clientele by offering a full line of heat-and-serve meals prepared in the FreshDirect kitchen by New York executive chef Michael Stark (formerly of Tribeca Grill) and his team. Partnering with Chef Terrance Brennan of New York's French-Mediterranean restaurant Picholine, FreshDirect also sold "restaurant-worthy" four-minute meals. Made from raw ingredients delivered in a "steam valve system" package, these complete meals were not frozen but were delivered ready to finish cooking in a microwave.

The proximity of FreshDirect's processing facility to its Manhattan customer base was also a critical factor in its cost-effective operational design. The processing center's location in Long Island City put approximately 4 million people within a 10-mile radius of the FreshDirect facility, allowing the firm to deliver a large number of orders in a short amount of time.[5] In 2012, the company looked to expand and relocate its operations to the South Bronx waterfront, a move that by early 2013 had not yet occurred, as Bronx citizens, local groups, and activists protested the move, mainly for environmental reasons.

Further, cost controls had been implemented through FreshDirect's order and delivery protocols. Products in each individual order were packed in boxes, separated by type of item (meat, seafood, and produce packed together; dairy, deli, cheese, coffee, and tea packed together; grocery, specialty, and nonrefrigerated products packed together), and placed on a computerized conveyor system to be sorted, assembled, and packed into a refrigerated truck for delivery.

Orders had to be a minimum of $30, with a delivery charge between $5.99 and $8.99 per order, depending on the order dollar amount and delivery location. Delivery was made by one of FreshDirect's own trucks and was available only during a prearranged two-hour window from 6:30 a.m. to 10 p.m. every day of the week.

Competing with other online grocers, specialty gourmet/gourmand stores in Manhattan, and high-end chain supermarkets like Whole Foods, Trader Joe's, and Fairway, FreshDirect was trying to woo the sophisticated grocery shopper with an offer of quality, delivered to the customer's door, at a price more attractive than others in the neighborhood. Operating in the black for the first time in 2005,[6] by choosing to remain a private company and expanding gradually, FreshDirect's owners hoped to turn a daily profit, steadily recovering the estimated $60 million start-up costs, silencing critics, and winning converts.[7]

More recently, FreshDirect teamed up with online recipe website Foodily and launched a new service called Popcart. The service allowed users to order deliveries of food ingredients directly from online recipes, and it would operate exclusively through FreshDirect for some time. The Internet was a popular recipe source for home cooks, but shopping for ingredients was widely seen as an unpleasant chore. The new Popcart technology alleviated this burden by linking with the FreshDirect portal and providing next-day deliveries. "This is really at the heart and soul of making food shopping easier for consumers. About 70% of New Yorkers cook from scratch multiple times a week, and 30% cook multiple times a day. Think about that opportunity," said Jodi Kahn, chief consumer officer for FreshDirect.

Foodily had released an iPhone app in 2011 and received additional funding in 2013. The company's partnership with FreshDirect, however, was its first major step in offering the popular Popcart service nationwide.[8]

Founding Partners

FreshDirect was launched in July 2001. Cofounder and former chief executive officer Joseph Fedele was able to bring a wealth of experience in New York City's food industry to FreshDirect. In 1993 he cofounded Fairway Uptown, a 35,000-square-foot supermarket located on West 133 Street in Harlem. Many critics originally questioned the success of a store in that location, but Fairway's low prices and quality selection of produce and meats made it a hit with neighborhood residents, as well as many downtown and suburban commuters.

Cofounder Jason Ackerman, FreshDirect's vice chairman and chief financial officer, had gained exposure to the grocery industry as an investment banker with Donaldson, Lufkin & Jenrette, where he specialized in supermarket mergers and acquisitions. Fedele and Ackerman first explored the idea of starting a large chain of fresh-food stores, but they realized maintaining a high degree of quality would be impossible with a large enterprise. As an alternative, they elected to pursue a business that incorporated online shopping with central distribution. Using the failure of Webvan, the dot-com delivery service that ran through $830 million in five years of rapid expansion, as their example of what not to do, Fedele and Ackerman planned to start slowly, use off-the-shelf software and an automated delivery system, and pay attention to details such as forming relationships with key suppliers and micromanaging quality control.[9]

FreshDirect acquired the bulk of its $100 million investment from several private sources, with a small contribution coming from the State of New York. By locating

FreshDirect's distribution center within the state border and promising to create at least 300 permanent, full-time, private-sector jobs in the state, FreshDirect became eligible for a $500,000 training grant from the Empire State Development Jobs Now Program. As its name implied, the purpose of the Jobs Now program was to create new, immediate job opportunities for New Yorkers.

CEO Successions

Although the press was mostly positive about FreshDirect's opportunities, growth and operational challenges remained. In the words of an ex-senior executive of FreshDirect, "The major problem seems to be constant change in Senior Management. I think they are now on their 4th CEO."[10] At the time, the company was actually on its fifth CEO, and it later named its sixth. FreshDirect cofounder Joseph Fedele had remained CEO until January 2004, when cofounder Jason Ackerman succeeded him in that position. Since then, FreshDirect experienced multiple CEO changes. Jason Ackerman served as CEO of FreshDirect for a little over seven months, until Dean Furbush succeeded him in September 2004. Ackerman remained vice chairman and chief financial officer. The tenure of Dean Furbush lasted a little over two years. Steve Michaelson, president since 2004, replaced Furbush as CEO of FreshDirect in early 2007.[11] In 2008 Michaelson left for another firm, and FreshDirect's chairman of the board, Richard Braddock, expanded his role in the firm and took over as CEO. Braddock said, "I chose to increase my involvement with the company because I love the business and I think it has great growth potential." Braddock had previously worked at private equity firm MidOcean Partners and travel services retailer Priceline.com, where he also served as chairman and CEO.[12] Braddock wound up leaving the company in March 2011, at which time cofounder Jason Ackerman returned to the role of CEO for a second time.

Business Plan

While business started out relatively slowly, FreshDirect hoped to capture around 5 percent of the New York City grocery market. The company was originally slated for availability citywide by the end of 2002. However, to maintain its superior service and product quality, FreshDirect chose to expand its service area slowly. With the success of its business model and its steady growth strategy, by the spring of 2011 FreshDirect had delivery available to select zip codes and neighborhoods throughout Manhattan and as far away as Westchester, Connecticut, New Jersey, and the Hamptons on Long Island (in the summer only). This business model seemed to be working well for FreshDirect, as the company continued to gradually expand successfully into new areas surrounding its Long Island City facility.

In late 2012 FreshDirect began serving the Philadelphia area, particularly in and around Center City, with plans to eventually expand the service region to the greater Philadelphia area suburbs depending on customer response.

The company had a crossdock on Richmond Street, where orders were sorted after arriving from New York. However, the company was not in talks with Mayor Nutter's office for a distribution hub to support its expansion, said its chief marketing officer, John Leeman. "We met with the Nutter administration a few times just to let them know what we're doing," Leeman said in an interview.[13] Of course, the region's proximity to FreshDirect's base of operations in Long Island City was a major factor, given that there were no plans for facility expansions into Philadelphia. Orders were to be compiled and delivered from that hub, as part of FreshDirect's next-day-delivery model.

Because of the enthusiastic response to its Philadelphia launch and the extensive preregistration from suburban Philadelphia residents, FreshDirect very quickly, and sooner than expected, began expanding its service from Philadelphia's Center City to the greater Philadelphia area suburbs. "Originally we had planned to begin our suburban launch in late January to early February. However, the demand for our offering and incredible customer base we've built in Philadelphia caused us to speed up our plans," said Jason Ackerman. "We already have thousands of residents from Suburban Philadelphia pre-registered to be future customers and we wanted to meet this demand as soon as possible."[14]

The company employed a relatively low-cost marketing approach, which originally consisted mainly of billboards, public relations, and word of mouth to promote its products and services. FreshDirect hired Trumpet, an ad agency that promoted FreshDirect as a better way to shop by emphasizing the problems associated with traditional grocery shopping. For example, one commercial stressed the unsanitary conditions in a supermarket by showing a shopper bending over a barrel of olives as she sneezed, getting an olive stuck in her nose, and then blowing it back into the barrel. The advertisement ended with the question "Where's your food been?" Another ad showed a checkout clerk morph into an armed robber, demand money from the customer, and then morph back into a friendly checkout clerk once the money was received. The ad urged viewers to "stop getting robbed at the grocery store."[15] As of 2013, FreshDirect enlisted celebrity endorsements from New York City personalities such as film director Spike Lee, actress Cynthia Nixon, former mayor Ed Koch, supermodel Paulina Porizkova, and chef Bobby Flay.[16] Recently the company planned to change its marketing strategy by launching a new testimonial-based campaign using actual customers, rather than celebrities. FreshDirect was number 70 in the Internet Retailer Top 500 Guide. In 2010 the company claimed revenue of more than $250 million, an increase of $20 million from the previous year, and it had grown its customer base by 20 to 25 percent.[17]

Operating Strategy

FreshDirect's operating strategy employed a make-to-order philosophy, eliminating the middleman in order to create an efficient supply chain.[18] By focusing its energy on providing produce, meat, seafood, baked goods, and coffees that were made to the customer's specific order, FreshDirect offered its customers an alternative to the standardized cuts and choices available at most brick-and-mortar grocery stores. This strategy created a business model that was unique within the grocery business community. A typical grocery store carried about 25,000 packaged goods, which accounted for approximately 50 percent of its sales, and about 2,200 perishable products, which accounted for the other 50 percent of sales. In contrast, FreshDirect offered about 5,000 perishable products, accounting for approximately 75 percent of its sales, but only about 3,000 packaged goods, which made up the remaining 25 percent of sales.[19]

While this stocking pattern enabled a greater array of fresh foods, it limited the number of brands and available sizes of packaged goods, such as cereals, crackers, and laundry detergents. However, FreshDirect believed that customers would accept a more limited packaged-good selection in order to get lower prices, as evidenced in the success of wholesale grocery stores, which offered bulk sales of limited items. Jason Ackerman identified the ideal FreshDirect customers as those who bought their bulk staples from Costco on a monthly basis and bought everything else from FreshDirect on a weekly basis.[20]

FreshDirect's Website

FreshDirect's website not only offered an abundance of products to choose from but also provided a broad spectrum of information on the food that was sold and the manner in which it was sold (see Exhibit 1). Web surfers could take a pictorial tour of the FreshDirect facility; get background information on the experts who managed each department; get nutritional information on food items; compare produce or cheese on the basis of taste, price, and usage; specify the thickness of meat or seafood orders and opt for one of several marinades or rubs (see Exhibit 2); search for the right kind of coffee according to taste preferences; and read nutritional information for a variety of fully prepared meals. A large selection of recipes was available depending on the items chosen.

For example, if you wanted to purchase chicken, you were first asked to choose from breasts and cutlets, cubes and strips, ground, legs and thighs, specialty parts, split and quartered, whole, or wings. Once your selection was made—let's say you chose breasts and cutlets—you were given further options based on your preference for skin, bone, and thickness. The final selection step offered you a choice of rubs and marinades, including teriyaki, sweet and sour, garlic rosemary, poultry seasoning, lemon herb rub, and salt-and-pepper rub. Throughout, the pages offered nutritional profiles of each cut of meat as well as tips for preparation and storage.

FreshDirect employed several different delivery models. Customers within the city were attracted to the FreshDirect service because it eliminated the need to carry groceries for possibly a substantial distance from the closest grocery store or to deal with trying to park a car near their apartments to unload their purchases. Orders made by customers within the city were delivered directly to their homes by a FreshDirect truck during a prearranged two-hour delivery window.

Suburban customers were served in a slightly different manner. Many suburban customers worked at corporations in the tristate area that could arrange for depot drop-off in the office parking lot, creating a central delivery station. FreshDirect would send a refrigerated truck, large enough to hold 500 orders, to these key spots during designated periods of time. Suburbanites could then exit their office building, go to their cars, swing by the FreshDirect truck, pick up their orders, and head home. FreshDirect could also provide delivery to the parking lot of football or concert events to provide for tailgate or picnic needs. In addition to providing delivery, FreshDirect allowed customers to pick up their orders directly from the processing center. Orders were ready at the pickup desk 5 to 10 minutes after they were called in.

EXHIBIT 1 FreshDirect Website

EXHIBIT 2 Example of FreshDirect Seafood Selection

Business customers in Manhattan could also order for delivery at the office. Chef-prepared breakfast and luncheon catering platters and restaurant-quality individual meals were available for business meetings and upscale events. FreshDirect provided dedicated corporate account managers and customer service representatives for corporate clients; however, FreshDirect provided only delivery, not setup and platter-arrangement services. The corporate delivery minimum order was $50, and delivery costs were $14.99 (see Exhibit 3).

EXHIBIT 3 FreshDirect at the Office

The Retail Grocery Industry

In the United States, supermarket chains made over $584 billion in sales in 2014. The typical supermarket store carried an average of 38,718 items, averaged just about 46,000 square feet in size, and averaged over $20 million in sales annually.[21] The top 10 supermarket chains in the United States commanded a large amount of the total grocery industry business (see Exhibit 4).

The supermarket business had traditionally been a low-margin business with net profits of only 1 to 2 percent of revenues. Store profits depended heavily on a high volume of customer traffic and rapid inventory turnover, especially for perishables such as produce and fresh meat. Competitors had to operate efficiently to make money, so tight control of labor costs and product spoilage was essential. Online grocery retailers, like FreshDirect—because of the flexibility of information control, automated order fulfillment, and reduced real estate costs—could potentially have operating margins of up to 10 percent, rather than the 3 to 4 percent of traditional supermarkets.[22] Because capital investment costs were modest—involving mainly the construction of distribution centers and stores—it was not unusual for supermarket chains to realize 15 to 20 percent returns on invested capital.

The Online Grocery Segment

Total online grocery shopping sales were estimated to be about $27 billion in 2014.[23] However, this number accounts for less than 2 percent of total grocery sales. Online grocery shopping had been slow to catch on, and industry newcomers had encountered high start-up and operating costs. Sales volumes and profit margins remained too small to cover the high costs. The problem, according to industry analysts, was that consumers had been largely disappointed in the service, selection, and prices they had gotten

EXHIBIT 4 Top 10 North American Food Retailers, 2015

Supermarket Chain	Stores	2014 Sales ($ billions)	Comments
Wal-Mart Stores	4,987	$221.8	Includes Sam's Clubs.
Kroger	3,694	108.8	Includes jewelry, 5% of total sales.
Costco Wholesale Corp.	664	91.5	Groceries were 72% of total sales.
Target Corp.	1,921	73.6	Headquartered in Minneapolis.
Safeway Company	1,326	37.1	Based in California.
Loblaw Companies	1,058	30.6	Stop & Shop, Giant Foods.
Publix Super Markets	1,090	30.4	Based in Florida.
Ahold USA	766	26.0	Based in the Netherlands.
7-Eleven	8,285	25.3	Headquartered in Dallas.
Albertsons	1,103	23.0	Headquartered in Boise, Idaho.

Source: *Supermarket News.* 2014. http://supermarketnews.com/2014-top-75-clickable-list.

from industry members. This, coupled with the extensive investment needed in warehousing, fulfillment, and inventory control, meant that the "pure play" e-grocery business models were risky. There was a belief that better success would come from traditional grocery retailers that chose to venture online.[24]

However, some analysts expected online grocery sales to grow at a rapid pace as companies improved their service and selection, personal computer penetration of households rose, and consumers became more accustomed to making purchases online.[25] An article in *Computer Bits* examined the customer base for online grocers, looking specifically at the types of consumers who would be likely to shop online and the kinds of home computer systems that were required for online shopping. An Andersen Consulting report identified six major types of online shoppers (see Exhibit 5), and FreshDirect's Richard Braddock predicted that online grocery sales could account for as much as 20 percent or more of total grocery sales within the next 10 years.[26] A MARC Group study concluded, "Consumers who buy groceries online are likely to be more loyal to their electronic supermarkets, spend more per store 'visit,' and take greater advantage of coupons and premiums than traditional customers."[27] By 2016, online grocery sales were estimated to reach a value of $13.5 billion.[28]

One of the problems with online grocery shopping was that consumers were extremely price-sensitive when it came to buying groceries, and the prices of many online grocers were above those at supermarkets. Shoppers, in many cases, were unwilling to pay extra to online grocers for the convenience of home delivery. Consumer price sensitivity meant that online grocers had to achieve a cost structure that would allow them to (1) price competitively, (2) cover the cost of selecting items in the store and delivering individual grocery orders, and (3) have sufficient margins to earn attractive returns on their investment. Some analysts estimated that to be successful, online grocers had to do 10 times the volume of a traditional grocer.[29]

Potential Competitors in the Online Grocery Segment

When online grocers started appearing within the industry, many established brick-and-mortar grocers began offering online shopping in an attempt to maintain and expand their customer base. Two basic models were used for online order fulfillment: (1) pick items from the shelves of existing stores within the grocer's chain, and (2) build special warehouses dedicated to online orders. The demand for home delivery of groceries had been increasing, but in many market areas the demand had not reached a level that would justify the high cost of warehouses dedicated to fulfilling online orders.[30]

Safeway began an ambitious online grocery venture by establishing GroceryWorks, an online shopping system that included a series of warehouses dedicated to filling online orders. Unfavorable returns forced Safeway to reevaluate its system, and it eventually chose to form a partnership with Tesco, a U.K.-based grocer. Tesco filled its online orders from the shelves of local stores in close proximity to the customer's home. Safeway and Tesco worked together on GroceryWorks in Portland, Oregon, where they received a positive initial response from customers.[31]

The craze over health food had created room in the grocery industry for organic-food suppliers to enter as an attractive substitute to traditional groceries. When asked what kept him up at night, FreshDirect's former CEO Dean Furbush said that Whole Foods or Trader Joe's moving into a FreshDirect neighborhood was his biggest threat, as that hurt FreshDirect the most.

Whole Foods, the Austin, Texas–based supermarket chain with the organic-health-food focus, had already threatened FreshDirect's sales in Manhattan. Trader Joe's, another specialty food retailer, was also opening a store in downtown Union Square, prime territory for FreshDirect.[32] Although commentators believed there was enough room for all, including the street farm markets, FreshDirect

EXHIBIT 5 Types of Online Shoppers and Their Propensity to Be Attracted to Online Grocery Shopping

Types of Online Shoppers	Comments
Traditional	Might be older technology-avoiders or simply shoppers who like to sniff-test their own produce and eyeball the meat selection.
Responsible	Feed off the satisfaction of accomplishing this persistent to-do item.
Time-starved	Find the extra costs associated with delivery fees or other markups a small price to pay for saving time.
New technologists	Use the latest technology for any and every activity they can, because they can.
Necessity users	Have physical or circumstantial challenges that make grocery shopping difficult; likely to be the most loyal group of shoppers.
Avoiders	Dislike the grocery shopping experience for a variety of reasons.

Source: Andersen Consulting.

focused on organic foods to respond to the threats of Whole Foods and other specialty food stores.[33] With the shift among some customers to paying attention to local, sometimes organic, suppliers, FreshDirect highlighted its support of and partnership with the local companies that provided produce, poultry, fish, cheese, milk, eggs, and specialties such as wine (see Exhibit 6). However, its efforts were inconsistent in that area. For example, to help shoppers and checkout operators to distinguish between organic and nonorganic produce, FreshDirect wrapped organics in plastic, which in itself is not organic. FreshDirect chairman Jeff Turner recognized that such an approach seemed incongruous.[34]

Rivals in the NYC Online Grocery Segment

YourGrocer.com

FreshDirect's most geographically significant competitor in the online grocery industry was YourGrocer.com (see Exhibits 7 to 10). YourGrocer was launched in New York City in 1998 with the goal of being the leading online grocery service for the New York metropolitan area. By November 2001 the company ran out of money and was forced to shut down. In the spring of 2002, new capital resources were found, and the company reopened for business. However, the second time around, YourGrocer's approach was a little different.

YourGrocer was created with a bulk-buying strategy, believing that customers would order large, economical quantities of goods from the website and the company would make home deliveries in company trucks. During YourGrocer's first life, the ambitious business plan covered a large service area and included the acquisition of another online grocery company, NYCGrocery.com.[35] But the business plan was modified in the second life. The company reduced the size of its staff, got rid of warehouses,

EXHIBIT 6 FreshDirect Local Market Offerings

EXHIBIT 7 Profiles of Select Online Grocers

Name	Minimum Area Covered	Delivery Order Minimum	Delivery Charge	Method	Specialization
FreshDirect	Manhattan, Queens, Brooklyn, Staten Island, the Bronx, Nassau County, Westchester County, Fairfield County, Hoboken, Philadelphia, Jersey City	$30	$5.99–$8.99, depending on order size and destination; tipping optional	Trucks; delivers every day 6:30 a.m.–10 p.m. depending on location	• Mostly perishables: fresh produce, meats, baked goods. • Low prices because there is no middleman.
YourGrocer	Manhattan, the Bronx, Westchester County, Greenwich, Brooklyn, Queens, Rockland	None	$9.95 for orders > $75; $14.95 for orders < $75	Rented vans; delivers 9 a.m.–9 p.m. depending on location	• Bulk orders of packaged goods.
Peapod	Chicago, Boston, D.C., Long Island, Connecticut, New Jersey, Rhode Island, Milwaukee, Wisconsin, Indiana, New Hampshire, Maryland, Virginia, Pennsylvania	$60	$6.95	Trucks; delivery available 6 a.m. to 1 p.m. on Saturday and 6 a.m.–10 p.m. every other day; *pickup available as well*	• Partner with Giant Foods and Stop & Shop; items picked from shelves of local warehouses near customer's home.
NetGrocer	All 50 states; special service to Alaska, Hawaii, APO/FPO; no P.O. boxes	None	$9.99–$624.99, depending on order size and destination	FedEx; order delivered within 3–7 business days	• Mostly nonperishables.

Source: Company websites.

EXHIBIT 8 Comparison of Prices for Select Online Grocers

	Prices			
Grocery Item	FreshDirect	YourGrocer	Peapod	NetGrocer
Tide laundry detergent	$19.99/100 oz.	$27.89/170 oz. ($16.39/100 oz.)	$16.29/100 oz.	$22.39/100 oz.
Wish-Bone Italian dressing	$2.29/8 oz.	$5.70/36 oz.	$2.00/16 oz.	$4.49/16 oz.
Cheerios	$4.79/14 oz.	$4.20/20.3 oz	$4.79/18 oz.	$5.49/14 oz.
Ragu spaghetti sauce	$2.99/24 oz.	$3.63/45 oz.	$2.50/24 oz.	$4.05/26 oz.
Granny Smith apples	$4.99/4 pack (no per-lb. price)	$9.89/5 lb. bag ($1.98/lb.)	$0.99/each	$0.45/oz

Source: Company websites.

decided to rent instead of owning its delivery vans, and scaled down its delivery routes.[36] Nassau County and New Jersey were eliminated from the service area, leaving only Manhattan, the Bronx, Brooklyn, Queens, Rockland, Westchester County, and Fairfield County (Connecticut).

YourGrocer offered a limited selection of items that could be purchased only in bulk. Deliveries were made in varied time slots, depending on the customer's location in the New York area. There was a $9.95 delivery charge for orders over $75, and $14.95 for orders below $75.

Peapod

Founded in 1989 by brothers Andrew and Thomas Parkinson, Peapod (see Exhibits 11 and 12) was an early pioneer in e-commerce, inventing an online home-shopping service for grocery items years ahead of the commercial emergence of the Internet. With its tagline "Smart Shopping for Busy People," the company began providing consumers with a home-shopping experience in the early 1990s, going so far as to install modems in customer homes to provide an online connection.

From its founding in 1989 until 1998, the company's business model involved filling customer orders by forming alliances with traditional grocery retailers. The company chose a retail partner in each geographic area where it operated and used the partner's local network of retail stores to pick and pack orders for delivery to customers. Peapod personnel would cruise the aisles of a partner's stores, selecting the items each customer ordered, pack and load them into Peapod vehicles, and then deliver them to customers at prearranged times. Peapod charged customers a fee for its service and collected fees from its retail supply partners for using their products in its online service. Over the next several years, Peapod built delivery capabilities

EXHIBIT 9 YourGrocer.com Website

EXHIBIT 10 YourGrocer's Service Focus

New YourGrocer focuses on providing *three benefits* that families in the area most value:

1. **Easy ordering** over the Internet or on the phone to save hours of thankless shopping. You can use your last order as a starting point to save even more time.

2. **Delivery** right to the home or office, which eliminates the burden of lifting and transporting heavy and bulky items each month.

3. **Significant savings** with everyday low prices—not short-duration specials—which reduce what you pay for stock-up groceries and household supplies on average by 25% to 30% below local supermarkets.

Source: *www.yourgrocer.com*.

EXHIBIT 11 Peapod Website

EXHIBIT 12 Peapod Product Selection

in eight market areas: Chicago; Columbus, Ohio; Boston; San Francisco/San Jose; Houston, Dallas, and Austin, Texas; and Long Island, New York.

In 1997, faced with mounting losses despite growing revenues, Peapod management shifted to a new order-fulfillment business model utilizing a local company-owned central distribution warehouse to store, pick, and pack customer orders for delivery. By mid-1999 the company had opened new distribution centers in three of the eight markets it served—Chicago, Long Island, and Boston—and a fourth distribution center was under construction in San Francisco.

In the late spring of 2000, Peapod created a partnership with Royal Ahold, an international food provider based in the Netherlands. At the time, Ahold operated five supermarket companies in the United States: Stop & Shop, Tops Market, Giant-Landover, Giant-Carlisle, and BI-LO. In September 2000 Peapod acquired Streamline.com Inc.'s operations in Chicago and the Washington, D.C., markets and announced that it planned to exit its markets in Columbus, Ohio, and in Houston, Dallas, and Austin, Texas. All of these moves were made as part of Peapod's strategic plan for growth and future profitability. Under Peapod's initial partnership agreement with Ahold, Peapod was to continue as a stand-alone company, with Ahold supplying Peapod's goods, services, and fast-pick fulfillment centers. However, in July 2001 Ahold acquired all the outstanding shares of Peapod and merged Peapod into one of Ahold's subsidiaries.

Peapod provided online shopping and delivery service in many metropolitan areas, including Chicago, Boston, Rhode Island, Connecticut, New Jersey, Long Island, and Washington, D.C. Peapod employed a centralized distribution model in each market. As of 2013, Peapod had extended its delivery services to Baltimore, Maryland, Virginia, Indiana, and southeastern Wisconsin. In large markets, orders were picked, packed, loaded, and delivered from a freestanding centralized fulfillment center; in smaller markets, Peapod established fast-pick centralized fulfillment centers adjacent to the facilities of retail partners.[37] Peapod's proprietary transportation routing system ensured on-time delivery and efficient truck and driver utilization.

NetGrocer

NetGrocer.com was founded in 1996 and advertised itself as the first online grocer to sell nonperishable items nationwide (see Exhibits 13 and 14). NetGrocer served all 48 continental U.S. states and the District of Columbia and had special service to Alaska, Hawaii, APO, and FPO destinations. All customer orders were filled in its single 120,000-square-foot warehouse in North Brunswick, New Jersey. Orders were shipped by Federal Express and were guaranteed to reach any part of NetGrocer's service area within three to seven business days.

NetGrocer offered its customers a large selection of brand-name and specialty nonperishable items that were difficult to find in a local supermarket. The key customer segment for NetGrocer's services was busy families, urban dwellers, special-needs groups (e.g., dieters, diabetics), and senior citizens. Customers purportedly enjoyed the benefits of convenient online shopping from home 24 hours a day, access to thousands of products, and delivery of their orders directly to their homes. Manufacturers also benefited from NetGrocer, as they were able to distribute their products nationwide, rapidly, and easily.

Most Recent Challenges

As the online grocery retailing business continued to mature, all players needed to pay attention to customer perception. Online retailing giant Amazon.com had entered the dry-goods grocery delivery business, posing a threat to other online retailers because of its existing loyal customer base and legendary customer service. Creating a grocery section, Amazon offered over 10,000 nonperishable items, including "long-time staples, from Kellogg's to Jiffy Pop."[38] The selection of dry goods rather than perishables meant that Amazon, unlike FreshDirect and Peapod, didn't have to worry about delivery costs on time- and climate-sensitive items. However, even Amazon suffered grocery delivery failures, from out-of-stock problems to delivery glitches and website technical outages. Online grocery retailers needed to "serve their online customers just like they would serve the customers who come into their physical stores."[39]

In late 2014, Amazon announced it would launch its new Amazon Fresh grocery delivery service in New York City, within one neighborhood in Brooklyn. By targeting Park Slope, Amazon was dabbling into the city's competitive grocery services market that also included the

EXHIBIT 13 NetGrocer.com Website

EXHIBIT 14 NetGrocer Shipping Charges

Order Total Brackets	Region 3 Rates	Region 2 Rates	Region 1 Rates	Region 4 Rates
$0–24.99	$9.99	$9.99	$9.99	
$25–49.99	$15.99	$14.99	$9.99	$9.99
$50–74.99	$23.99	$20.99	$14.99	
$75–99.99	$29.99	$27.99	$16.99	
$100–124.99	$35.99	$31.99	$20.99	
$125–149.99	$41.99	$39.99	$26.99	
$150–199.99	$63.99	$59.99	$31.99	
$200–299.99	$92.99	$83.99	$49.99	$29.99
$300–499.99	$116.99	$110.99	$59.99	$39.99
$500–749.99	$218.99	$211.99	$119.99	$49.99
$750–999.99	$319.99	$312.99	$179.99	$59.99
$1000+**	$624.99	$613.99	$401.99	$199.99

Alaska & Hawaii Shipping Charges are based on the weight of your order and are now $25.00 for up to the first 5lbs. and $2.00 for each additional pound.

Shipping Regions: Region 4, Region 3, Region 2, Region 1, Alaska/Hawaii

neighborhood's famous food co-op. However, Amazon Fresh had flourished in other crowded markets, including Seattle, San Francisco, and Los Angeles, using a model that it hoped would work in New York as well. The Amazon Fresh model was built on membership in the Amazon Prime subscription service, which provided free delivery and streaming video to customers who paid a $99 annual fee. Amazon Fresh promised same-day delivery for orders placed before 10 a.m. or delivery the next morning for orders made before 10 p.m.

Additionally, Internet giant Google signed on local supermarket chain Fairway, which established Google Express as its official delivery partner. It was clear that the competition was going to heat up considerably in 2015.[40]

Even though FreshDirect had been able to woo local New Yorkers, gaining a *Fast Company* "Local Hero" award, the company had to absorb "hundreds of thousands of dollars in parking tickets to get its customers its orders within the delivery window."[41] The rising cost of fuel was also a potential threat, even though FreshDirect included a fuel surcharge on orders, based on the average retail price of gasoline.[42] These expenses could put significant pressure on FreshDirect's ability to achieve its target profit levels.

Environmental concerns also started to creep in as a major issue for FreshDirect. First, because of the conveyor packing system at the processing facility, FreshDirect was forced to use lots of cardboard boxes to deliver the groceries: Produce came in one box, dry goods in another, and a single tube of toothpaste in its separate cardboard delivery container. Although FreshDirect had transitioned to the use of 100 percent postconsumer recycled paper,[43] the reusability of the cardboard boxes was limited and the general public was increasingly becoming aware that its tax dollars were used to "collect and dispose of the huge stacks of cardboards that FreshDirect's customers leave in the trash."[44] As one environmentally conscious consumer observed, "I was baffled by the number of boxes they used to pack things. Groceries worth $40 came in five boxes. And after I unpacked, I had to discard the boxes. There was no system of returning them to FreshDirect to be recycled."[45]

A second issue that environmentally conscious consumers became concerned about was the additional exhaust fumes that FreshDirect trucks contributed to the urban atmosphere.[46] Issues of this nature were at the forefront of citizens' concerns regarding the environmental impact that FreshDirect's potential move into the South Bronx would have on their neighborhood. Third, FreshDirect trucks double-parked in busy city streets only made the traffic congestion problems worse. As one commentator stated, "It's probably no exaggeration to say that FreshDirect has built its financial success on its ability to fob off its social and environmental costs on the city as a whole."[47] Last, some city dwellers even expressed concern about FreshDirect's adverse effect on the overall makeup of their neighborhoods: "It is not just the impact they have on congestion, pollution, space, etc., but their very adverse impact on the best of businesses in neighborhoods that they can undersell because of their externalized costs. It is these small businesses, farmers markets and local grocery stores, that FreshDirect undercuts, that are some of the best businesses for supporting and preserving our walkable, diverse and safe neighborhoods."[48]

But criticism also came from those who felt FreshDirect needed to expand its business. By 2015 FreshDirect served a large portion of New York City and its five boroughs, yet there were neighborhoods that FreshDirect did not serve, and people living in them had started to accuse the company of discrimination. As one customer put it, "FreshDirect is the most convenient way to shop for groceries in NYC unless you live in a Public Housing building—they won't deliver to you!"[49] Others echoed similar concerns in terms of FreshDirect's decision to not serve specific neighborhoods: "These are neighborhoods that FreshDirect deems underserved, or in plain terms, not worth the bother."[50]

Some of the recent challenges FreshDirect faced were union-related. FreshDirect's 500 truck drivers recently joined Local 348 of the United Food and Commercial Workers Union. One of the reasons cited by the workers for this move was that "they made us work 12 and 14 hours a day, then when some of us refused we were suspended for three days without pay." Also, the workers complained that the wages were pretty low compared to wages at other grocery chains in New York. According to the workers, the initial beginning wage at FreshDirect was just higher than $7 per hour, with the average pay being around $8.50. Workers also claimed that the health benefit premiums were high and not easily affordable. A firm spokesperson replied to these complaints by saying, "We have incredibly generous benefits that are more than competitive."[51]

FreshDirect asked its 900 plant workers to provide legal papers proving their immigration status.[52] As a result, many workers left immediately, some of whom had been associated with FreshDirect for five to six years.[53] Surprisingly, around 80 percent of the workforce rejected the proposal to unionize. However, the number of workers voting was only 530, not 900, because so many employees had left the company after the immigration-status audit was announced.[54] FreshDirect was successful in suppressing the union revolt, but the remaining workers were demoralized and the company's image was tainted among its customers.[55]

Aside from dealing with the labor challenges, Fresh-Direct was working hard to woo its customers. FreshDirect started a line of four-minute meals. These fresh meals were packed in microwavable containers, and, as the name implies, they could be ready to eat after four minutes in a microwave oven. FreshDirect teamed up with some well-known Manhattan restaurants and chefs to introduce the four-minute-meal concept. The lineup included Rosa Mexicano for Mexican cuisine, chef Floyd Cardoz's Tabla for Indian cuisine, chef Tina Bourbeau's Presto Italiano line of Italian cuisine, and several others.[56] Another promotion was FreshDirect's "Valentine's Dinner for Two," which allowed customers to "prepare an easy and romantic restaurant-quality meal for a special someone in the comfort of their own homes." The menu had a variety of options, including appetizers, desserts, entrées, wines, champagnes, and so on. This menu came in the price range of $69 to $99, and the meal needed less than 20 minutes of cooking time.[57]

FreshDirect expanded its delivery options with a fixed-price unlimited-delivery program in addition to the standard per-delivery fee program, which cost $5.99 to $6.79 depending on location. The unlimited-delivery program gave customers an unlimited number of deliveries for a set fee of $69 for six months or $119 per year.[58] FreshDirect also reduced its minimum order to $30 from $50. Another innovation was the company's online customer-created shopping list. Customers could create and save their own shopping lists, such as a weekly list, mother-in-law list, and party list. In addition, the company offered its own tailored lists, such as Simple Suppers, Pantry Basics, Top 20 Most Popular FreshDirect Items, Healthy Snacks, and Entertaining Essentials, to help customers create lists of their own.[59]

Neither labor strife nor economic downturn had stopped FreshDirect's growth. Looking into the future, there was speculation that FreshDirect might want to "seek public funding to underwrite growth possibilities."[60] Since Whole Foods Market's acquisition of Wild Oats Markets, analysts felt that some private players in the New York market, such as FreshDirect, might consider pursuing investment capital through an initial public offering.

Another major issue for FreshDirect was its customers' concerns about how fresh the produce and meats really were. One of the biggest obstacles to the growth of online ordering of groceries was the inability to view and touch food, particularly fresh produce and meat. Online customers couldn't pick up and thump a melon or peel back the leaves on a head of romaine lettuce to check for freshness the same way they could in the grocery store. FreshDirect received numerous comments from consumers which basically stated, "I can't see, touch, and smell the products. I have to rely on you." This lack of control over identifying the freshness of the food caused major concerns for customers. The company recognized the problem and spun this negative aspect of online shopping into a positive one by creating a food-quality rating system. Consumer feedback had jump-started a new way of doing business for FreshDirect.[61]

The company's Daily Produce Rating System ranked the quality of fruits and vegetables available for delivery the next day. The five-star rating system gave shoppers "a foolproof way to ensure that the ripest fruits and crunchiest veggies are consistently delivered to their doorsteps," as advertised at the company's website. The Daily Produce Rating System was based on a daily inspection of all produce in stock by a quality assurance team. Rating criteria included taste, color, firmness, and ripeness. Rankings were based on an easy ratings scale:[62]

- Five stars signified "never better, the best we've seen."
- Four stars indicated "great/delicious."
- Three stars meant "good/reliably decent."
- Two stars indicated "average/inconsistent quality/generally OK."
- One star signaled "below average/expect wide inconsistency in quality/probably out of season."

Results were updated each morning on FreshDirect's website to let customers know which fruits and veggies were the best bets for deliveries to be received on the following day. FreshDirect also offered the same five-star rating service for seafood, and in 2010 some 50 to 70 percent of its customers used the feature.[63] The system aimed to simulate the in-store shopping experience, allowing the grocers to showcase their best stuff and customers to decide what looked good. "Not everyone is an expert on the seasonality of a fruit or vegetable, so this system takes the guesswork out of choosing the best available items," said FreshDirect's former chief marketing officer Steve Druckman. "Each of the buyers and managers who rate the produce have years on the job, so they have great expertise. I am not aware of any other online or conventional grocer that's developing a system such as this."[64]

However, the strategy came with a big risk: To gain customers' trust, FreshDirect would have to acknowledge that not every item it stocked was picture-perfect every day. Not everyone at the company was enthusiastic about the idea. Many feared backlash from consumers about FreshDirect's products not always being top quality. "Was it scary? Yeah!" recalled Glenn Walsh, the produce manager. "I thought it was insane in the beginning."[65]

Despite the risk, the company claimed that the rating system changed consumer buying patterns. Around 70 percent of customers said they purchased something they wouldn't have if it weren't for the rating system. Druckman asserted, "One hundred percent of customers changed buying patterns. The rating system works. If we put something out like black seedless grapes or golden pineapples with four stars, we'll sell twice as many of those because of their rating than otherwise."[66]

FreshDirect also decided to upgrade the company's website, using an internal database to profile customers and serve a customized online experience. For example, the site's software could analyze order patterns, reminding customers of their favorite products and suggesting other items they might like, a marketing tool that had worked well for Netflix and Amazon. In addition, the database recognized whether a visiting customer was a new, infrequent, lapsed, or loyal customer—and provided appropriate messages and ads.

Despite all of these innovations, given that only 2 percent of all grocery purchases were made online, FreshDirect still had a long way to go.

ENDNOTES

1. www.freshdirect.com/site_access/site_access.jsp.
2. Karni, A. 2013. FreshDirect foes lose in court. *Crain's New York Business*, June 3.
3. Dubbs, D. 2003. Catch of the day. *Multichannel Merchant*, July 1, multichannelmerchant.com/opsandfulfillment/orders/fulfillment_catch_day.
4. A "slotting allowance" is defined by the American Marketing Association as "1. (retailing definition) A fee paid by a vendor for space in a retail store. 2. (sales promotion definition) The fee a manufacturer pays to a retailer in order to get distribution for a new product. It covers the costs of making room for the product in the warehouse and on the store shelf, reprogramming the computer system to recognize the product's UPC code, and including the product in the retailer's inventory system." www.marketingpower.com/mg-dictionary-view2910.php.
5. Laseter, T., et al. 2003. What FreshDirect learned from Dell. *Strategy Business*, 30 (Spring), www.strategy-business.com/article/8202.
6. Schoenberger, C. R. 2006. Will work with food. *Forbes*, September 18, members.forbes.com/global/2006/0918/041.html.
7. Smith, C. 2004. Splat: The supermarket battle between Fairway, FreshDirect and Whole Foods. *New York: The Magazine*, May 24, nymag.com/nymetro/food/industry/n_10421.
8. Fahey, M. 2014. Foodily, FreshDirect start recipe delivery service. *Crain's New York Business*, August 5.
9. Dignan, L. 2004. FreshDirect: Ready to deliver. *Baseline: The Project Management Center*, February 17, www.baselinemag.com/print_article2/0,1217,a5119342,00.asp.
10. *Chelsea-Wide Blogs.* 2006. chelsea.clickyourblock.com/bb/-archive/index.php?t-128.html.
11. *Supermarket News.* 2007. Michaelson named CEO at FreshDirect; Furbush resigns. January 9, supermarketnews.com/retail_financial/-michaelson_named_ceo_at_freshdirect_furbush_resigns_337/index.html.
12. *InternetRetailer.com.* 2008. FreshDirect's chairman hopes to deliver the goods in bigger role. July 14.
13. Panaritis, Maria. 2012. Internet-only grocer now making rounds in Philly. *Philly.com,* October 3, http://articles.philly.com/2012-10-03/business/34219078_1_freshdirect-giant-food-stores-food-lovers.
14. Mainline Media. 2013. FreshDirect announces Suburban Philadelphia expansion. (Press release). *Mainline Media News,* January 20. www.mainlinemedianews.com/articles/2013/01/20/main_line_suburban_life/news/doc50f5cc875ff5b846224062.txt.
15. Elliot, S. 2003. A "fresh" and "direct" approach. *New York Times,* February 11.
16. Bosman, J. 2006. FreshDirect emphasizes its New York flavor. *New York Times,* January 31, www.nytimes.com/2006/01/31/business/media/31adco.html.
17. Bruno, K. 2010. Inside FreshDirect's expansion. *Forbes,* June 29, www.forbes.com/2010/06/29/freshdirect-online-grocery-braddock-cmo-network-grocery.html.
18. Laseter et al., op. cit.
19. Ibid.
20. Ibid.
21. Food Market Institute. Undated. Supermarket facts: Industry overview. www.fmi.org/facts_figs/superfact.htm.
22. Leonhardt, D. 2006. Filling pantries without a middleman. *New York Times,* November 22, www.nytimes.com/2006/11/22/business/22leonhardt.html?pagewanted51&_r52&adxnnlx51164556801-6ScpsMek8edyTRh8S2BWyA.
23. Renfrow, J. 2014. Online grocery sales to quadruple by 2023. *Fierce Retail,* October 6.
24. Kempiak, M., & Fox, M. A. 2002. Online grocery shopping: Consumer motives, concerns and business models. *First Monday,* vol. 7, no. 9, www.firstmonday.org/issues/issue7_9/kempiak. and author estimates.
25. Machlis, S. 1998. Filling up grocery carts online. *Computerworld,* July 27: 4.
26. Hamstra, M. 2010. FreshDirect CEO predicts online gains in next decade. *Supermarket News,* March 1, supermarketnews.com/retail_financial/freshdirect-ceo-projects-online-gains-0301.
27. Woods, B. 1998. America Online goes grocery shopping for e-commerce bargains. *Computer News,* August 10: 42.
28. Brook-Carter, C. 2010. Focus: UK, US central to online grocery sales growth. *Just-food,* February 23, www.just-food.com/analysis/uk-us-central-to-online-grocery-sales-growth_id109940.aspx.
29. Fisher, L. M. 1999. Online grocer is setting up delivery system for $1 billion. *New York Times,* July 10: 1.

30. *Frontline Solutions.* 2002. Online supermarkets keep it simple. Vol. 3, no. 2: 46–49.
31. Ibid.
32. Smerd, J. 2005. Specialty foods stores will go head-to-head at Union Square. *New York Sun,* March 4, www.nysun.com/article/10058?page_no51.
33. *Progressive Grocer.* 2005. NYC's FreshDirect launches street fight against Whole Foods. March 3, www.allbusiness.com/retail-trade/food-stores/4258105-1.html.
34. *New Zealand Herald.* 2007. We don't have time to waste. February 3.
35. Joyce, E. 2002. YourGrocer.com wants to come back. *ECommerce,* May 15, ecommerce.internet.com/news/news/-article/0,10375_1122671,00.html.
36. Fickenscher, L. 2002. Bouncing back from cyber limbo: Resurgence of failed dot coms after downsizing. *Crain's New York Business,* June 24.
37. Peapod Inc. Undated. Corporate fact sheet. www.peapod.com/corpinfo/peapodFacts.pdf.
38. Regan, K. 2006. Amazon dips toe into online grocery business. *E-Commerce Times,* June 15, www.ecommercetimes.com/-story/51136.html.
39. Hamstra, M. 2007. Online stores may need to bone up on their execution. *Supermarket News,* January 29, supermarketnews.com/viewpoints/-online-stores-bone-up-execution/index.html.
40. Mcenery, T. 2014. Amazon to deliver groceries only to Park Slope. *Crain's New York Business,* October 17.
41. Danigelis, A. 2006. Customers' first local hero: FreshDirect. *Fast Company,* September, www.fastcompany.com/customer/-2006/articles/local-fresh-direct.html.
42. See www.freshdirect.com/about/index.jsp and click on FAQs.
43. *Supermarket News.* 2007. FreshDirect transitions to eco-friendly boxes. May 11, supermarketnews.com/fresh_market/-freshdirect_eco_friendly/index.html.
44. *StreetsBlog.* 2006. FreshDirect builds a grocery empire on free street space. November 22, www.streetsblog.org/2006/11/22/fresh-direct-builds-a-grocery-empire-on-free-street-space.
45. Wadia, A. S. 2007. Is FreshDirect good for you? *Metroblogging NYC,* January 30, http://nyc.metblogs.com/2007/01/30/is-freshdirect-good-for-you/.
46. *StreetsBlog,* op. cit.
47. Ibid.
48. Ibid.
49. Rodriguez, N. 2007. FreshDirect.com discriminates! *Metroblogging NYC,* February 7, nyc.metblogs.com/archives/-2007/01/is_freshdirect.phtml.
50. Wadia, op. cit.
51. *Daily News* (New York). 2007. FreshDirect takes heat, workers try to unionize. September 28, www.nydailynews.com/news/2007/09/28/2007-09-28_try_to_un.html.
52. Lauinger, J. 2007. Workers say FreshDirect bosses pressing them to reject union vote. *Daily News* (New York), December 21, www.nydailynews.com/ny_local/queens/2007/12/21/2007-12-21_workers_say_freshdirect_bosses_pressing_-4.html.
53. Lauinger, J. 2007. FreshDirect axes immigrant workers. *Daily News* (New York), December 12, www.nydailynews.com/news/2007/12/12/2007-12-12_freshdirect_axes_immigrant_workers.html.
54. Lee, T. 2007. In wake of recent manpower loss, FreshDirect workers vote "No Union." *New York Times,* December 24, www.nytimes.com/2007/12/24/nyregion/24fresh.html?scp512&sq5freshdirect&st5cse.
55. Fickenscher, L. 2008. *Crain's New York Business,* January 14.
56. Backs, Melanie. 2010. FreshDirect redesigns 4-minute meals department; launches Foodie Fantasy sweepstakes. *PR Newswire,* October 12, www.prnewswire.com/news-releases/freshdirect-redesigns-4-minute-meals-department-launches-foodie-fantasy-sweepstakes-104771164.html.
57. *PR Newswire.* 2011. FreshDirect makes romance easy with Valentine's Day tasting menu. January 9, www.prnewswire.com/news-releases/freshdirect-makes-romance-easy-with-valentines-day-tasting-menu-53353382.html.
58. FreshDirect website, www.freshdirect.com; and Heller, A. 2008. Online grocers adjust. *Supermarket News,* October 20, http://supermarketnews.com/retail-amp-financial/online-grocers-adjust.
59. *ProgressiveGrocer.com.* 2007. FreshDirect rolls out customer-created shopping lists, reduces minimum order. October 19, www.progressivegrocer.com/top-stories/headlines/pantry-staples/id28192/freshdirect-rolls-out-customer-created-shopping-lists-reduces-minimum-order/.
60. Merrefield, D. 2007. How different companies approach the growth challenge. *Supermarket News,* February 5, supermarketnews.com/viewpoints/how-different-companies-approach-growth-challenge/index.html.
61. McConnon, Aili. 2009. The issue: FreshDirect focuses on customer service. *Bloomberg Businessweek,* July 1, www.businessweek.com/managing/content/jun2009/ca20090630_154481.htm.
62. FreshDirect. Undated. About our daily produce rating system. www.freshdirect.com/brandpop.jsp?brandId5fd_ratings.
63. Cohan, P. 2010. Growth matters: FreshDirect nudges its way to profits. *Dailyfinance,* March 23, www.dailyfinance.com/story/company-news/growth-matters-freshdirect-nudges-its-way-to-profits/19372267/.
64. Briggs, Bill. 2009. FreshDirect takes a new approach to customer service. *Internetretailer.com,* January 7, www.internetretailer.com/mobile/2009/01/07/freshdirect-takes-a-new-approach-to-customer-service.
65. Bruder, J. 2010. At FreshDirect, reinvention after a crisis. *New York Times,* August 12: B9.
66. *Perishable Pundit.* 2009. New York's FreshDirect succeeds when most online grocers have failed. May 22, www.perishablepundit.com/index.php?date505/22/09&pundit52.

CASES

CASE 31

JOHNSON & JOHNSON*

On January 20, 2015, Johnson & Johnson CEO Alex Gorsky proudly announced that his firm had sales of $74.3 billion during the previous year, representing an increase of 4.2 percent over 2013. Most of this growth came from the firm's pharmaceutical division, which Gorsky pointed out was clearly generating the largest revenues and was the fastest-growing such division in the drug industry in the United States. The results of this division compensated the relatively modest increases in revenue from the firm's medical devices and consumer health divisions, both of which were recovering from lawsuits and recalls.

Several years earlier, Johnson & Johnson (J&J) had settled with an estimated 8,000 patients over problems with its flawed all-metal artificial hip. The device had a design flaw that caused it to shed large quantities of metallic debris after implantation. It was finally recalled by the firm in 2010, after Johnson & Johnson had covered up the problems for almost five years after they began to surface. The settlement cost the firm as much as $3 billion to compensate patients who had to have the artificial hip replaced. The problems with this device would classify it as one of the largest medical failures in recent history.

The problems with the medical devices unit were compounded by serious issues that arose with the consumer products unit, leading it to recall many of its products—including the biggest children's drug recall of all time—that were potentially contaminated with dark particles. The Food and Drug Administration also slapped a plant at one of its business units, McNeil Consumer Healthcare, with a scalding inspection report, causing the company to close down the factory to bring it up to federal standards. The publicity that arose from these problems tarnished the name of one of the nation's most trusted firms.

Much of the blame for Johnson & Johnson's stumbles fell on William C. Weldon, who stepped down as CEO in April 2012 after presiding over one of the most tumultuous decades in the firm's history (see Exhibits 1 and 2). Critics said the company's once-vaunted attention to quality had slipped under his watch. Weldon, who had started out as a sales representative at the firm, was believed to have been obsessed with meeting tough performance targets, even by cutting costs that might affect quality. Erik Gordon, who teaches business at the University of Michigan, elaborated on this philosophy: "We will make our numbers for the analysts, period."[1]

Weldon was replaced by Alex Gorsky, who had headed the medical devices and diagnostics unit. Like his predecessor, Gorsky had worked his way up by meeting tough performance targets as a sales representative, and his appointment as CEO continued the firm's 126-year tradition of hiring leaders from within. "The future of Johnson & Johnson is in very capable hands," said Weldon.[2] However, the decision to hire another insider raised concerns that the firm was not very serious about changing the corporate culture that had created so many of its recent problems. "As somebody steeped in J.&J. culture, I would be very surprised to see big changes," said Les Funtleyder, a portfolio manager at a firm that owned J&J stock.[3]

---

* Case prepared by Jamal Shamsie, Michigan State University, with the assistance of Professor Alan B. Eisner, Pace University. Material has been drawn from published sources to be used for purposes of class discussion. Copyright © 2015 Jamal Shamsie and Alan B. Eisner.

EXHIBIT 1 Income Statement ($ millions)

	Year Ending December				
	2010	2011	2012	2013	2014
Revenue	61,587	65,030	67,224	71,312	74,331
Gross profit	42,795	44,670	45,566	48,970	51,585
Operating income	16,527	16,153	15,869	18,377	20,959
Income before taxes	16,947	12,361	13,775	15,471	20,563
Net income	13,334	9,672	10,853	13,831	16,323

Source: Johnson & Johnson.

EXHIBIT 2 Balance Sheet ($ millions)

	Year Ending December				
	2010	2011	2012	2013	2014
Total current assets	47,307	54,316	46,116	56,407	59,311
Total assets	102,908	113,644	121,347	132,683	131,119
Total current liabilities	23,072	22,811	24,262	25,675	25,085
Total liabilities	46,329	56,564	56,521	58,630	61,367
Total stockholders' equity	56,579	57,080	64,826	74,053	69,752

Source: Johnson & Johnson.

Cultivating Entrepreneurship

Johnson & Johnson relied heavily upon acquisitions to enter into and expand into a wide range of businesses that fell broadly under the category of health care. It purchased more than 70 different firms over the past decade. Among Johnson & Johnson's recent moves was the $20 billion purchase of Synthes, a leading player in trauma surgery. In November 2014, J&J completed its $1.75 billion acquisition of Alios BioPharma, which produced therapeutics for viral infections.

As it grew, Johnson & Johnson developed into an astonishingly complex enterprise, made up of over 250 different subsidiaries that were divided among three different divisions. The most widely known of these was the division that made consumer products such as Johnson & Johnson baby care products, Band-Aid adhesive strips, and Visine eyedrops. The division grew substantially after J&J acquired the consumer health unit of Pfizer in 2006 for $16.6 billion, the biggest acquisition in its 120-year history. The acquisition allowed J&J to add well-known products to its lineup, such as Listerine mouthwash and Benadryl cough syrup.

But Johnson & Johnson reaped far more sales and profits from its other two divisions. Its pharmaceuticals division sold several blockbuster drugs, such as anemia drug Procrit and schizophrenia drug Risperdal. A new drug, named Zytiga, prescribed to treat prostate cancer, was selling well. The medical devices division was responsible for best-selling products such as DePuy orthopedic joint replacements and Cypher coronary stents. These two divisions generated operating profit margins of around 30 percent, almost double those generated by the consumer business.

To a large extent, however, Johnson & Johnson's success across its three divisions and many different businesses hinged on its unique structure and culture. Most of its far-flung subsidiaries were acquired because of the potential demonstrated by some promising new products in their pipelines. Each of these units was therefore granted near-total autonomy to develop and expand upon its best-selling products (see Exhibit 3). That independence fostered an entrepreneurial attitude that kept J&J intensely competitive as others around it faltered. The relative autonomy that was accorded to the business units also provided the firm with the ability to respond swiftly to emerging opportunities.

Johnson & Johnson was actually quite proud of the considerable freedom that it gave to its different subsidiaries to develop and execute their own strategies. Besides developing their strategies, these units were also allowed to work with their own resources. Many of them even had their own finance and human resources departments. While this degree of decentralization had led to relatively high overhead costs, none of the executives who ran J&J, Weldon included, had ever thought that this was too high a price to pay. "J&J is a huge company, but you didn't feel like you were in a big company," recalled a scientist who used to work there.[4]

Pushing for More Collaboration

The entrepreneurial culture that Johnson & Johnson developed over the years clearly allowed the firm to show a consistent level of high performance. Indeed, Johnson & Johnson had top-notch products in each of the areas in which it operated. It had been spending heavily on research and development for many years, taking its position among the world's top spenders (see Exhibit 4). In 2014, it spent about 12 percent of its sales on about 9,000 scientists working in research laboratories around the world. This allowed each of the three divisions to continually introduce promising new products.

In spite of the benefits that Johnson & Johnson derived from giving its various enterprises considerable autonomy, there were growing concerns that these units could no longer be allowed to operate in near isolation. Shortly after Weldon had taken charge of the firm, he realized that J&J was in a strong position to exploit new opportunities by drawing on the diverse skills of its various subsidiaries across the three divisions. In particular, he was aware that his firm might be able to derive more benefits from the combination of its knowledge in drugs, devices, and

EXHIBIT 3 Segment Information ($ millions)

Johnson & Johnson was made up of over 250 different companies, many of which it had acquired over the years. These individual companies were assigned to three different divisions.

	Segments of Business and Geographic Areas		
	Sales to Customers		
Dollars in Millions	2014	2013	2012
Consumer —			
United States	$ 5,096	5,162	5,046
International	9,400	9,535	9,401
Total	14,496	14,697	14,447
Pharmaceutical —			
United States	17,432	13,948	12,421
International	14,881	14,177	12,930
Total	32,313	28,125	25,351
Medical Devices —			
United States	12,254	12,800	12,363
International	15,268	15,690	15,063
Total	27,522	28,490	27,426
Worldwide total	$74,331	71,312	67,224

	Segment Pretax Profit			
			Percent of Segment Sales	
(Dollars in Millions)	2014	2013	2014	2013
Consumer	$ 1,941	1,973	13.4%	13.4
Pharmaceutical	11,696	9,178	36.2	32.6
Medical Devices	7,953	5,261	28.9	18.5
Total	21,590	16,412	29.0	23.0
Less: Expenses not allocated to segments	1,027	941		
Earnings before provision for taxes on income	$20,563	15,471	27.7%	21.7

Source: Johnson & Johnson.

diagnostics, since few companies were able to match its reach and strength in these basic areas.

This led Weldon to find ways to make J&J's fiercely independent units work together. In his own words: "There is a convergence that will allow us to do things we haven't done before."[5] Through pushing the various far-flung units of the firm to pool their resources, Weldon believed that the firm could become one of the few that was actually able to attain that often-promised, rarely delivered idea of synergy. To pursue this, he created a corporate office that would get business units to work together on promising new opportunities. "It's a recognition that there's a way to treat disease that's not in silos," Weldon stated, referring to the need for collaboration between J&J's largely independent businesses.[6]

For the most part, however, Weldon confined himself to taking steps to foster better communication and more frequent collaboration among Johnson & Johnson's disparate operations. He was convinced that such a push for communication and coordination would allow the firm to

EXHIBIT 4 Research Expenditures ($ millions)

Year	Expenditure
2014	$8,494
2013	8,183
2012	7,665
2011	7,548
2010	6,864
2009	6,986
2008	7,577
2007	7,680
2006	7,125
2005	6,462

Source: Johnson & Johnson.

EXHIBIT 5 Significant Innovations

Antiseptic Surgery (1888)
Three brothers start up a firm based on antiseptics designed for modern surgical practices.

Band-Aids (1921)
Debuts the first commercial bandages that can be applied at home without oversight by a professional.

No More Tears (1954)
Introduces a soap-free shampoo that was gentle enough to clean babies' hair without irritating their eyes.

Acuvue Contact Lenses (1987)
Offers the first-ever disposable lenses that can be worn for up to a week and then thrown away.

Sirturo (2012)
Gets approval to launch a much-needed treatment for drug-resistant tuberculosis, the first new medication to fight this disease in more than 40 years.

Source: *Fast Company,* March 2014.

develop the synergy that he was seeking. But Weldon was also aware that any effort to get the different business units to collaborate must not quash the entrepreneurial spirit that had spearheaded most of the growth of the firm to date. Jerry Cacciotti, managing director of consulting firm Strategic Decisions Group, emphasized that cultivating those alliances "would be challenging in any organization, but particularly in an organization that has been so successful because of its decentralized culture."[7]

These collaborative efforts did lead to the introduction of some highly successful products (see Exhibit 5). Even the company's fabled consumer brands started to show growth as a result of increased collaboration between the consumer products and pharmaceutical divisions. The firm's new liquid Band-Aid was based on a material used in a wound-closing product sold by one of J&J's hospital-supply businesses. And J&J used its prescription antifungal treatment, Nizoral, to develop a dandruff shampoo. In fact, products that were developed in large part out of such cross-fertilization allowed the firm's consumer business to experience considerable internal growth.

Confronting Quality Issues

Even as Johnson & Johnson was trying to get more involved with the efforts of its business units, it ran into quality control problems with several over-the-counter drugs made by McNeil Consumer Healthcare. Since 2008, FDA inspectors had found significant violations of manufacturing standards at two McNeil plants, leading to the temporary closure of one of them. These problems had forced the firm to make several recalls of some of its best-selling products. Weldon did admit that problems had surfaced, but he insisted that they were confined to McNeil. He responded to them in an interview: "This is one of the most difficult situations I've ever had to personally deal with. It hits at the core of who J&J is. Our first responsibility is to the people who use our products. We've let them down."[8]

Quality problems had arisen before, but they were usually fixed on a regular basis. Analysts suggested that the problems at McNeil might have been exacerbated in 2006 when J&J decided to combine McNeil with the newly acquired consumer health care unit from Pfizer. Johnson & Johnson believed that it could achieve $500 million to $600 million in annual savings by merging the two units. After the merger, McNeil was transferred from the heavily regulated pharmaceutical division to the marketing-driven consumer products division, headed by Colleen Goggins. Because the consumer executives lacked pharmaceutical experience, they began to demand several changes at McNeil that led to a reduced emphasis on quality control.

Weldon realized the significance of the threat faced by Johnson & Johnson as a result of its problems with quality. He was especially concerned about the FDA's allegation that the firm had initially tried to hide the problems that it found with Motrin in 2009, hiring a contractor to quietly go from store to store buying all of the packets on the shelves. McNeil's conduct surrounding the recalls led to an inquiry by both the House Committee on Oversight and Investigations and the FDA's Office of Criminal Investigations.

Various changes were subsequently made at McNeil to resolve these quality issues. Goggins was pushed out of her post as senior executive in charge of all consumer businesses. Weldon allocated more than $100 million to upgrade McNeil's plants and equipment, appoint new manufacturing executives, and hire a third-party consulting firm to improve procedures and systems. Bonnie Jacobs, a McNeil spokeswoman, wrote in a recent email: "We will invest the necessary resources and make whatever changes are needed to do so, and we will take the time to do it right."⁹

The problems at McNeil, coupled with growing problems with J&J's artificial hips and contact lenses, also led Johnson & Johnson to make changes to its corporate oversight of its supply chain and manufacturing. In August 2010, the firm appointed Ajit Shetty, a longtime executive, to oversee a new system of companywide quality control that involved a single framework for quality across all of the operating units and a new reporting system. The need for these changes was highlighted by Erik Gordon, a professor at the Ross School of Business at the University of Michigan: "Nothing is more valuable to Johnson & Johnson than the brand bond of trust with consumers."[10]

Passing the Baton

In April 2012, Johnson & Johnson appointed Gorsky to lead the health care conglomerate out of the difficulties that it had faced over the previous few years. He had been with the firm since 1988, holding positions in its pharmaceutical businesses across Europe, Africa, and the Middle East before leaving for a few years to work in Novartis. Shortly after his return to Johnson & Johnson in 2008, he took over its medical device and diagnostic group. Because of his extensive background with the firm, and with the division that was being investigated about its faulty hip replacements, Gorsky might have been regarded as the ideal person to take over the job.

When he took over, DePuy, the firm's orthopedic unit, was already running into trouble with its newest artificial hip. The firm finally recalled the artificial hip, amid growing concerns about its failure among those who had received the implant. Until then, however, executives from the firm had repeatedly insisted that the device was safe. Andrew Ekdahl, the current president of DePuy, recently reiterated that position. "This was purely a business decision," he said.[11] In the trial in Los Angeles Superior Court regarding the defective hip replacement, however, Michael A. Kelly, the lawyer making the case against Johnson & Johnson, suggested that company executives might have concealed information out of concern for firm profits.

In spite of all these issues, Johnson & Johnson did not attempt to clarify what information Gorsky might have had about the problems associated with the artificial hip. Under the circumstances, his promotion to lead the firm surprised Dr. Robert Hauser, a cardiologist and an advocate for improved safety of medical devices. "He's been overseeing one of the major J&J quality issues and the board of J&J sees fit to name him the new C.E.O.," he questioned.[12] These issues raised concerns about the ability of the firm to effectively deal with the quality concerns and to take steps to prevent them from recurring in the future.

Gorksy's first job as Johnson & Johnson's chief executive was, in fact, to reassure shareholders that the firm would move quickly to overcome its problems with manufacturing defects, product recalls, and lawsuits. "We've got to adapt faster than ever before, be more agile than ever before," he stated at the firm's annual meeting after taking over.[13] He acknowledged that some of the problems could partly be attributed to the firm's attempt to continue to meet Wall Street's increasingly short-term demands. Gorsky announced that moving forward, J&J was committed to managing for the long term, actively soliciting feedback from all quarters and adhering to the mission that made customers the first priority.

Gorsky's biggest challenge, however, came from a proposal that Johnson & Johnson might be better off if it was broken into smaller companies, perhaps along the lines of its different divisions. There were growing concerns about the ability of the conglomerate to provide sufficient supervision to all of its worldwide subsidiaries. Gorsky dismissed the proposal, claiming that J&J drew substantial benefits from the diversified nature of its businesses. He did concede, however, that the firm would have to be more selective, careful, and decisive about the products that it would pursue.

Is There a Cure Ahead?

Under Gorksy, Johnson & Johnson began to divest some of its lower-growth businesses and reduce annual costs by $1 billion. In 2014, the firm sold off its blood-testing unit, called Ortho-Clinical Diagnostics, for $4.15 billion to the private equity firm Carlyle Group. It was actively seeking a buyer for Cordis, which made medical devices such as stents and catheters. Johnson & Johnson, which had helped to develop the roughly $5 billion global market for cardiac stents, announced that it was shifting its focus to other medical technologies that showed more potential for growth.

To repair the damage to its reputation from the many recalls across two of its divisions, Johnson & Johnson recently announced that it would remove a host of potentially harmful chemicals, like formaldehyde, from its line of consumer products by the end of 2015. It was the first major consumer products company to make such a widespread commitment. "We've never really seen a major personal care product company take the kind of move that they are taking with this," said Kenneth A. Cook, president of the Environmental Working Group.[14]

As he tried to plot a course for the future of Johnson & Johnson, Gorsky realized that he had to deal with a variety of issues. He was aware that much of the firm's success to date resulted from the relative autonomy that it granted to each of its businesses. At the same time, he realized that he had to provide more direction for the businesses to collaborate with each other in order to pursue emerging opportunities. He also understood that it was critical for J&J to develop sufficient controls that could minimize future problems with quality control.

In overall terms, it was clear that the health care giant had to rethink the process by which it managed its diversified portfolio of companies in order to ensure that it could keep growing without creating issues that could pose further threats to its reputation. "This is a company that was purer than Caesar's wife, this was the gold standard, and all of a sudden it just seems like things are breaking down," said William Trombetta, a professor of pharmaceutical marketing at Saint Joseph's University in Philadephia.[15]

ENDNOTES

1. Katie Thomas. J.&J.'s next chief is steeped in sales culture. *New York Times,* February 24, 2012, p. B6.
2. Katie Thomas & Reed Abelson. J.&J. chief to resign one role. *New York Times,* February 22, 2012, p. B8.
3. Thomas, op.cit., p. B1.
4. Peter Loftus & Shirley S. Wang. J&J sales show health care feels the pinch. *Wall Street Journal,* January 21, 2009, p. B1.
5. Avery Johnson. J&J's consumer play paces growth. *Wall Street Journal,* January 24, 2007, p. A3.
6. Holly Hubbard Preston. Drug giant provides a model of consistency. *Herald Tribune,* March 12–13, 2005, p. 12.
7. Amy Barrett. Staying on top. *Business Week,* May 5, 2003, p. 62.
8. Ibid.
9. Natasha Singer & Reed Abelson. Can Johnson & Johnson get its act together? *New York Times,* January 16, 2011, p. B4.
10. Ibid., p. B4.
11. Thomas & Abelson, op. cit.
12. Michael L. Diamond. J&J's CEO calls for fast action. *Ashbury Park Press,* April 27, 2012, p. 13.
13. Thomas, op. cit.
14. Katie Thomas. Johnson & Johnson to remove questionable chemicals in products. *New York Times,* August 16, 2012, p. B1.
15. Natasha Singer. Hip implants are recalled by J&J unit. *New York Times,* August 27, 2010, p. B1.

CASES

CASE 32
GENERAL MOTORS*

Mary T. Barra, the CEO of General Motors, had not found it easy as the first woman to take over a large automobile company. The third-largest automaker was engulfed by the gravest safety crisis in the company's history. It issued a record 84 separate recalls in the United States in 2014 involving more than 30 million cars, 2.6 million of which had a problem with defective ignition switches that could shut down engine power and disable airbags. General Motors (GM) had to make compensation offers to the families of 42 people who had died in accidents in vehicles with a defective switch, as well as to more than 50 people who had been injured. "It was clearly a tragedy and it was deeply troubling," Barra acknowledged.[1]

Barra realized that GM would continue to deal with the repercussions of the safety problems that it had failed to address. The firm was facing several investigations, including a federal trial, set to begin in early 2016, that would deal with several lawsuits against the firm. The U.S. Department of Transportation hit GM with a $35 million penalty, the maximum allowed under law, and imposed oversight of the automaker's safety practices for neglecting to inform government officials of the ignition switch defect in a timely manner. These new requirements represented a return of sorts to the oversight that GM had thought it was finished with in December 2013, when the U.S. government sold off the final piece of the company that it had acquired four years earlier as part of its bailout.

The biggest concerns about GM's practices were raised by an internal report released in June 2014 that faulted a lack of responsibility and accountability at the firm for its failure to recall defective cars for years after it had learned about the faulty ignition switch. Barra had already acknowledged this issue in an internal video that was broadcast a few months earlier to all employees. "Something went very wrong in our processes . . . and terrible things happened," she stated.[2] In response to the report, she promised to ensure that such neglect of safety issues would not occur again. But the depth of the dysfunction within the firm, as detailed in the report, made several industry analysts question how Barra would be able to keep this pledge.

On January 8, 2015, Barra used a media roundtable to state her intention to try to finally put this crisis behind and move on with the commitment to build the best cars that GM ever offered. "It was a year of great disappointment, but also great progress," she reflected.[3] She noted with great relief that the safety issues had not caused consumers to avoid the firm's new models. The firm had, in fact, ended the year on a high note in the United States, where its sales rose about 5 percent for the full year, with seven of its vehicles setting records for annual sales (see Exhibits 1 to 3). Those vehicles included both GM's smaller cars, like the Chevrolet Sonic and Spark, and its sport utility vehicles, like the Buick Enclave and Encore (see Exhibit 4). While Barra did not lay out specific goals for 2015, she said that GM expected to expand sales in its two largest markets, the United States and China, and break even in its long-troubled European division (see Exhibit 5).

* Case prepared by Jamal Shamsie, Michigan State University, with the assistance of Professor Alan B. Eisner, Pace University. Material has been drawn from published sources to be used for purposes of class discussion. Copyright © 2015 Jamal Shamsie and Alan B. Eisner.

EXHIBIT 1 Income Statement ($ millions)

	Year Ending December				
	2010	2011	2012	2013	2014
Revenue	135,592	150,276	152,256	155,427	155,929
Gross profit	16,800	19,105	10,813	18,054	13,808
Operating income	5,084	5,656	−30,363	5,131	1,530
Income before taxes	5,737	5,985	−30,257	7,458	4,246
Net income	6,172	9,190	6,188	5,346	3,949

Source: General Motors.

EXHIBIT 2 Balance Sheet ($ millions)

	Year Ending December				
	2010	2011	2012	2013	2014
Total current assets	53,053	60,247	69,996	81,501	83,670
Total assets	138,898	144,603	149,422	166,344	177,677
Total current liabilities	47,157	48,932	53,992	62,412	65,701
Total liabilities	102,718	106,483	113,178	123,737	142,220
Total stockholders' equity	36,180	38,120	36,244	42,607	35,457

Source: General Motors.

Moving through Bankruptcy

General Motors had fallen from its dominant position in which it held almost 50 percent of the U.S. market for automobiles. A succession of CEOs over the years failed to halt its decline in spite of their resolve to turn things around. When Richard Wagoner took over in 2000, he carried out three major restructurings, eliminating dozens of plants, tens of thousands of jobs, and hundreds of dealers. In spite of these efforts, GM announced a loss of $30.9 billion for 2008, amounting to a staggering $50 a share. The firm had not managed to post a profit since 2004, running up cumulative losses of over $82 billion between 2005 and 2009. Wagoner eventually began to run short of funds and turned to the U.S. government for loans in order to survive, but the Obama administration demanded his resignation for its support.

Wagoner was replaced on an interim basis by Frederick A. Henderson, who had been president and chief operating officer of the firm since 2008. Under Henderson, the firm was asked to negotiate with bondholders and the union for further concessions to reduce its bloated cost structure. Unable to reach any agreement, the firm announced in late July 2009 that it had to seek chapter 11 bankruptcy protection. Under the terms of the bankruptcy agreement, GM was able to wipe out a big chunk of its debt, reducing it from over $46 billion before the filing to about $17 billion afterward, saving about $1 billion a year in interest payments. The U.S. government agreed to invest another $30 billion in the firm, in addition to the $20 billion it had already contributed, in exchange for 61 percent of the stock in the new GM

Shortly after the bankruptcy filing, changes were made to the board of directors and there was a shake-up of the ranks of GM's senior management. The new board was determined to address problems that had been laid bare by the task force assigned by the government to investigate GM in early 2009. The task force had been particularly astonished by the firm's emphasis on past glories and its commitment to the status quo, which the team found to be quite widespread among the firm's management ranks. "Those values were driven from the top on down," said Rob Kleinbaum, a former GM executive and consultant. "And anybody inside who protested that attitude was buried."[4]

Over the following year, GM was led by two different board members. Edward E. Whitacre, Jr., ran the firm for about a year before being replaced by Dan Akerson. Akerson had been appointed by the U.S. government as a board member during GM's bankruptcy. A no-nonsense former navy officer, Akerson began to address the various problems that continued to plague the firm. There was a strong consensus among the executives that the company was beginning to change its approach to its business. Shortly after he took over, Akerson wrote in an internal memo: "Our results show that we are changing the company so we never go down that path again."[5]

In January 2014, GM was finally able to move past the bankruptcy as government-appointed Akerson was replaced by Barra, who had worked her way up within the firm and became the first woman to ever run a big automobile company. She had been a rank-and-file engineer, a plant manager, the head of corporate human resources, and, most recently, the senior executive overseeing all of GM's global product development. Barra's appointment came on the heels of the sale of the last shares that the U.S. government had held of the firm, finally ending its bankruptcy obligations. "This is truly the next chapter in G.M.'s recovery and turnaround history," Barra told employees upon her appointment. "And I am proud to be a part of it."[6]

Focusing on Fewer Brands

One of the issues that GM had wrestled with for years was the number of brands of vehicles that it offered. For years, the firm had built its position of dominance by offering cars that were designed for different customers by separate divisions. Each of these divisions came to represent a distinct nameplate or brand. Its extensive brand lineup had long been GM's primary weapon in beating back both domestic and foreign rivals. But as the firm's market share began to decline, it became difficult to design and market

EXHIBIT 3 Market Shares

	Year Ended December 31					
	2014			2013		
	Industry	GM	GM as a % of Industry	Industry	GM	GM as a % of Industry
North America						
United States	16,858	2,935	17.40	15,894	2,786	17.50
Other	3,379	478	14.10	3,201	448	14.00
Total North America	20,237	3,413	16.90	19,095	3,234	16.90
Europe						
Germany	3,357	237	7.10	3,258	242	7.40
United Kingdom	2,845	305	10.70	2,597	301	11.60
Russia	2,541	189	7.40	2,834	258	9.10
Other	9,988	525	5.30	9,715	592	6.10
Total Europe	18,731	1,256	6.70	18,404	1,393	7.60
Asia/Pacific, Middle East and Africa						
China	23,861	3,540	14.80	22,202	3,160	14.20
Other	19,119	838	4.40	19,117	898	4.70
Total Asia/Pacific, Middle East and Africa	42,980	4,378	10.20	41,319	4,058	9.80
South America						
Brazil	3,498	579	16.60	3,767	650	17.30
Other	1,803	299	16.60	2,173	387	17.80
Total South America	5,301	878	16.60	5,940	1,037	17.50
Total Worldwide	87,249	9,925	11.40	84,758	9,722	11.50
United States						
Cars	7,688	1,085	14.10	7,556	1,067	14.10
Trucks	4,753	1,113	23.40	4,247	998	23.50
Crossovers	4,417	737	16.70	4,091	721	17.60
Total U.S.	16,858	2,935	17.40	15,894	2,786	17.50

Source: General Motors.

cars under several brands. To cut costs, GM began to share designs and parts across divisions, leading to some loss of distinctiveness between the different brands.

Analysts had been questioning for many years GM's decision to stick with as many as eight U.S. brands, with the recent addition of Hummer. The decision to carry so many brands placed considerable strain on GM's efforts to revamp its product line on a regular basis. However, the firm finally agreed to cut out four of its brands—Pontiac, Saturn, Saab, and Hummer—when it was forced to turn to the U.S. government for funding to stay afloat. A. Andrew Shapiro, an analyst, believed that GM should have started to think seriously about cutting back on its car divisions during the 1980s. "There are always short-term reasons for not doing something," explained Shapiro.[7]

EXHIBIT 4 Vehicle Sales (in thousands of units)

	Year Ending	
	Dec. 31, 2013	Dec. 31, 2014
United States		
Chevrolet	1,947	2,033
GMC	451	502
Buick	206	229
Cadillac	183	171
Canada/Mexico/Central America	448	478
Europe		
Opel/Vauxhall	1,041	1,076
Chevrolet	350	178
Other	2	2
Rest of world		
Chevrolet	1,313	1,344
Buick	810	920
Wuling	1,484	1,609
Holden	124	120
GMC	34	29
Cadillac	55	79
Other	229	278
South America	1,037	878
Worldwide	9,714	9,925

Source: General Motors.

EXHIBIT 5 Income by Operating Regions, EBIT ($ millions)

Region	Year Ending Dec. 31, 2014
North America	6,603
Europe	(1,369)
Asia & Australia	1,222
South America	(180)

Source: General Motors.

Since cutting down on its brands, GM was working on revamping its remaining lineup of cars. The firm successfully reinvented Chevrolet as a global mass-market brand, with 60 percent of its sales now coming from outside the U.S. Recent sales were driven by the new Cruze and the plug-in hybrid Volt. But one of the firm's most significant accomplishments was the introduction of small, fuel-efficient cars like the Chevrolet Sonic and Spark. The success of these new cars demonstrated that GM could compete in the small-car segment. A GM executive explained the motivation behind designing and producing the firm's smallest and most fuel-efficient conventionally powered vehicles: "We wanted to prove we could do it."[8]

General Motors was also focusing on strengthening its roster of higher-profit, luxury models for its Buick and Cadillac divisions. Buick, the oldest active automobile brand in the U.S., was catering to a shrinking population of people over 65. Over the last couple of years, the firm worked on updating the brand by sticking to its image of "refined luxury" but moving the brand away from being regarded as a living room on wheels. GM discontinued the full-size Lucerne in 2011 and drastically redesigned the smaller LaCrosse. Since then, seven new models were added, including the Encore and several aimed at younger, performance-oriented customers. The Encore, a compact crossover sport utility vehicle, was the top-rated small SUV in the J.D. Power initial quality survey for two consecutive years.

Finally, in September 2014, GM announced that it was separating its Cadillac luxury brand from its other brands and relocating Cadillac's headquarters to the trendy SoHo area of New York City. Johan de Nysschen, whom the firm had hired away from Audi to manage the brand, had pushed for the change, as he believed that the marketing and sales departments would be more in touch with their target customers in super-fashionable SoHo than in Detroit. GM was also moving forward with the development of a new flagship model for Cadillac that was meant to compete with the Mercedes-Benz S-Class. "The objective for this upcoming model is to lift the Cadillac range by entering the elite class of top-level luxury cars," said de Nysschen.[9]

Revamping Product Development

For several years, GM had been trying to get all of the functional areas to work together more closely throughout the product development process. In the past, even if a bold design made it off the drawing board, it had little chance of surviving as it was handed over to marketing, then passed to engineering, and finally sent to manufacturing. Since then, there had been a concentrated effort to wean the GM culture away from a focus on engineering processes. The firm pushed designers to get more involved with the development process and pushed engineers to find ways to stick with the original car design.

Another problem that had plagued GM's product development process was the lack of standardization of "platforms" on which the firm built its cars. A platform was the basic underpinnings of a vehicle, and building multiple vehicles on a single platform reduced development and production costs. In India, for example, GM was producing seven car models using as many as six different underlying platforms, resulting in considerable inefficiencies. Executives admitted that the firm was lagging behind its rivals, and GM only recently began trying to cut the number of platforms down to 14 by 2018, compared to 30 in 2010. It was also planning to cut down to the use of 12 engine families and eventually just 10, compared to 20 a few years ago.

After the bankruptcy, GM had also been trying to push harder to make cars that would appeal to customers in order to reduce their reliance on sales incentives. One of the initiatives taken by the firm was to assign engineers to work in car dealerships to learn more about what customers wanted and needed in their cars and trucks. At the same time, it encouraged everyone involved with the design of new vehicles to raise concerns during the development process and to take steps to hold back a new model in order to make any changes that could improve its chances of success.

Finally, GM was also attempting to roll out new models faster by making changes to its cumbersome decision-making process. Under the old system, any product decisions would be reviewed by as many as 70 executives, with a decision often taking months to wind its way through a series of committees. To replace this, the firm reduced the number of executives overseeing a vehicle program and instituted a new system in which all product decisions were made in a single weekly meeting that was run by the top management team. The new approach has led to much faster decisions.

Responding to Safety Concerns

Days after Barra took over as CEO, GM executives decided that a recall of the 619,000 Chevrolet Cobalts and Pontiac G5s was necessary. Questions were raised about the delay of several years in recalling these vehicles in spite of knowledge of a faulty ignition switch that would cause these cars to shut off and would disable their airbags. In 2004, engineers had suggested a fix, but executives decided against it because of potential delays and cost overruns in production. General Motors finally decided to act after the reports of accidents that had led to deaths and injuries could no longer be ignored. This was particularly embarrassing for the firm as GM had developed the Cobalt to show that it was no longer cutting corners and was capable of making competitive small cars.

In testimonies before a subcommittee of the House Committee on Energy and Commerce, Barra acknowledged that the safety problems had resulted from deep underlying problems with the GM culture. A report was released in June by Anton R. Valukas, a former U.S. attorney whom the firm had hired to conduct a three-month investigation of the decision to ignore the problems with the ignition switch. Its findings indicated that all issues that arose at GM were typically passed through a number of committees without being resolved. Furthermore, no minutes were taken of any of the meetings to indicate who was responsible or accountable for any decisions that were made.

Valukas concluded that shifting responsibility for problems to others was deep in the firm's DNA. He referred to a GM salute that involved crossing one's arms and pointing outward toward others, indicating that the responsibility belonged to someone else. In particular, Valukas found that employees at GM were given formal training about how to avoid accountability in documenting any safety issues. They were told to avoid using words such as *problem* or *defect* and to replace them with softer words such as *safety* or *condition*. "The story of the Cobalt is one of a series of individual and organizational failures that led to devastating consequences," Valukas stated to a committee hearing.[10]

Under Barra, GM executives moved quickly to respond to the safety problems. The firm dismissed 15 employees, including a vice president for regulatory affairs and several corporate lawyers, and disciplined others. It appointed a new global head of vehicle safety and named a new vice president in charge of global product integrity. It more than doubled, to 55 members, a team of safety investigators who would work within engineering. Finally, it hired a compensation expert to examine claims and make cash settlements for individuals who either died or were injured as a result of accidents caused by the defective ignition switch. "We are a good company," Barra insisted. "But we can and must be much better."[11]

Firing on All Cylinders?

Barra was optimistic about the prospects for GM over the next year or two because of expected growth in the demand for cars and trucks in the U.S. as a result of stronger economic conditions and lower fuel prices. She expected to see the return of younger consumers to the market because of an improvement in the job market. A stronger market for vehicles would give Barra the chance to shift attention back to the firm's products and away from the vehicle recalls that engulfed her first year as CEO.

In spite of the recalls, GM sold nearly 3 million vehicles in 2014, up 5 percent from the previous year. All of its brands, with the exception of Cadillac, had strong sales. Even GMC, which sold larger vehicles, had a 48 percent increase in sales for its Yukon, a full-size SUV. Barra acknowledged that the firm had more work to do to improve sales of Cadillac, which dropped 5 percent over the past year and was losing ground to other luxury brands. "We have a defined plan for Cadillac and we are going to stick to it," Barra said. "We realize that we have work ahead with the brand, but we will stay disciplined. There was a time when Cadillac stood for luxury."[12]

General Motors was also expecting to grow in overseas markets. It was counting on new models of Chevrolet Cruze and Buick Enclave to increase sales in China, which remained its largest market outside the U.S. In spite of some growth in sales, GM was losing ground to other foreign rivals such as Ford's Focus and Volkswagen's Jetta. In 2013, China was designated as one of GM's five global regions and was separated from the rest of its international operations, which had recently been relocated to Singapore. This Singapore-based office was expected to pursue growth in other international markets, such as India.

On the basis of its recent accomplishments, Barra felt that GM had opportunities to grow if it could continue to make good vehicles. She wanted to see her firm make some stronger gains in sales, particularly in its largest markets. Its share of the market in the U.S. had remained stagnant at around 18 percent over the last three years. Barra understood that the firm would have to work hard to continue to climb. "I told the team that there is no destination here, that this is a continuous improvement journey," Barra said in an interview soon after she had taken over GM.[13]

ENDNOTES

1. Bill Vlasic. G.M. chief vows to move beyond last year's recalls. *International New York Times,* January 10–11, 2015, p. 11.
2. Bill Vlasic & Christopher Jensen. Something went "very wrong" at G.M., chief says. *New York Times,* March 14, 2014, p. B1.
3. Vlasic, op. cit.
4. Bill Vlasic. Culture shock: G.M. struggles to shed a legendary bureaucracy. *New York Times,* November 13, 2009, p. B4.
5. Michael J. De La Merced & Bill Vlasic. U.S. to shed its stake in General Motors. *New York Times,* December 21, 2012, p. B3.
6. Bill Vlasic. Company woman becomes new G.M. chief. *International New York Times,* December 12, 2013, p. 1.
7. Micheline Maynard. A painful departure for some G.M. brands. *New York Times,* February 18, 2009, p. B4.
8. Bill Vlasic. To make tiny American car, G.M. also shrinks plant and wages. *New York Times,* July 13, 2011, p. A19.
9. Aaron M. Kessler. Cadillac makes big plan to woo luxury market. *New York Times,* September 20, 2014, p. B3.
10. Bill Vlasic & Danielle Ivory. G.M. vows to address "cultural problems" that led to deadly recall delays. *International New York Times,* June 19, 2014, p. 18.
11. Ibid.
12. Jeff Bennett. GM chief: U.S. market could grow 3% in 2015. *Wall Street Journal,* January 9–11, 2015, p. 18.
13. Bill Vlasic. Speeding up G.M.'s comeback. *New York Times,* January 24, 2014, p. B1.

CASES

CASE 33

IS ONE FORD REALLY WORKING?*

In January 2015 Ford Motor Company reported its best January sales performance since 2004. Retail sales were up for passenger cars and utility vehicles, with the Mustang, Lincoln MKC, Lincoln Navigator, Explorer, and Escape leading the way. The Transit van segment also had its best January sales results since 2001, but the real star, as always, was the Ford F-Series pickup, America's best-selling truck for the 38th straight year. The all-new F-150, which hit an all-time annual record of 54,370 vehicles sold in January, was named 2015 North American Truck of the Year.[1]

Ford was hoping for a big year in 2015, driven primarily by the F-150 popularity. New CEO Mark Fields was relying on North American sales in 2015 to offset increasing losses in Europe, as well as uncertainty in Asia as Ford continued its cautious introduction of Lincoln into the Chinese luxury-vehicle market. Ford needed all the good news it could get, having posted a 2014 year-end profit that saw a 56 percent drop from 2013. As CEO Fields remarked,

> [Last year] was a solid yet challenging year for Ford—with our investments and a record number of new products launched around the world positioning us for strong growth this year and beyond. . . . The entire Ford team remains focused on our three priorities of accelerating our ONE Ford plan, delivering product excellence, and driving innovation in every part of the business.[2]

Given the current lackluster performance and associated ambivalence of the investment community in the wake of Ford's disappointing year-end numbers, Mark Fields had some significant decisions to make in the coming year. Fields had been promoted to CEO in July 2014 upon the retirement of Alan Mulally, who was widely hailed as one of the "five most significant corporate leaders of the last decade" and was the architect of Ford's eight-year turnaround from the brink of bankruptcy in 2006.[3] It was Mulally who had created the vision that drove Ford's revitalization—"ONE Ford." The ONE Ford message was intended to communicate consistency across all departments and all segments of the company, requiring people to work together as one team, with one plan, and one goal: "an exciting viable Ford delivering profitable growth for all."[4] Mulally had wanted to leverage Ford's unique automotive knowledge and assets to build cars and trucks that people wanted and valued, and he had managed to arrange the financing necessary to pay for it all. The 2009 economic downturn that caused a financial catastrophe for U.S. automakers had trapped General Motors and Chrysler in emergency government loans, but Ford was able to avoid bankruptcy due to Mulally's actions.

Mulally had worked to create a culture of accountability and collaboration across the company, and he had groomed his successor, Mark Fields, since 2012, instilling confidence among the company's stakeholders that Ford would be able to continue to be profitable once Mulally stepped down. Even with this preparation, CEO Fields was facing an industry affected by general economic conditions over which he had little control and a changing technological and sociocultural environment in which consumer preferences were difficult to predict. Fields would have to anticipate and address numerous challenges as he positioned the company for continued success.

Attempts at repositioning Ford had been under way for many years. In the 1990s, former CEO Jacques Nasser had emphasized acquisitions to reshape Ford, but day-to-day business activities were ignored in the process. When Nasser left in October 2001, Bill Ford, great-grandson of company founder Henry Ford, took over and emphasized innovation as a core strategy to reshape Ford. In an attempt to stem the downward slide at Ford, and perhaps to jump-start a turnaround, Bill Ford recruited Alan Mulally, who was elected as president and chief executive officer of Ford on September 5, 2006. Mulally, former head of commercial airplanes at Boeing, was expected to steer the struggling automaker out of the problems of falling market share and serious financial losses. Mulally created his vision of "ONE Ford" to reshape the company, and in 2009 he finally achieved profitability, committing to remaining "on track for both [Ford's] overall and North American Automotive pre-tax results to be breakeven or profitable"[5] in the coming years. Mulally was able to sustain this success past the initial stages of his tenure and maintained profitability until his retirement in June 2014. Mark Fields would have to take over from there (see Exhibit 1).

History of the Ford Motor Company

In 2015, Ford Motor Company, based in Dearborn, Michigan, had about 187,000 employees and 62 plants worldwide. It manufactured or distributed the automotive brands

---

* This case study was prepared by Professor Helaine J. Korn of Baruch College, City University of New York; Professor Naga Lakshmi Damaraju of the Indian School of Business; Professor Alan B. Eisner of Pace University; and Associate Professor Pauline Assenza of Western Connecticut State University. The purpose of the case is to stimulate class discussion rather than to illustrate effective or ineffective handling of a business situation. Copyright © 2015 Alan B. Eisner.

EXHIBIT 1 Ford Motor Company and Subsidiaries: Income Statement ($ millions, except per-share amounts)

Go to library tab in Connect to access Case Financials.

	Year Ended December 31		
	2014	2013	2012
AUTOMOTIVE			
Revenues	$135,782	$139,369	$126,567
Costs and expenses			
Cost of sales	123,516	125,195	113,039
Selling, administrative, and other expenses	10,243	9,997	9,041
Total costs and expenses	133,759	135,192	122,080
Interest expense	797	829	713
Interest income and other income/(loss), net	76	974	1,599
Equity in net income of affiliated companies	1,246	1,046	555
Income before Income taxes — Automotive	2,548	5,368	5,928
FINANCIAL SERVICES			
Revenues	8,295	7,548	6,992
Costs and expenses			
Interest expense	2,699	2,860	3,115
Depreciation on vehicles subject to operating leases	3,098	2,411	1,795
Operating and other expenses	776	768	693
Provision for credit and insurance losses	305	208	77
Total costs and expenses	6,878	6,247	5,680
Other income/(loss), net	348	348	365
Equity in net income of affiliated companies	29	23	33
Income before income taxes — Financial Services	1,794	1,672	1,710
TOTAL COMPANY			
Income before income taxes	4,342	7,040	7,638
Provision for/(Benefit from) income taxes	1,156	(135)	2,026
Net income	3,186	7,175	5,612
Less: Income/(Loss) attributable to noncontrolling interests	(1)	(7)	(1)
Net income attributable to Ford Motor Company	$ 3,187	$ 7,182	$ 5,613

Source: Ford Motor Company 10-K filings.

Ford and Lincoln across six continents and provided financial services via Ford Motor Credit. It was also the only company in the industry whose company name still honored the vision and legacy of its founder, Henry Ford.

American engineer and industrial icon Henry Ford had been a true innovator. He didn't invent the automobile or the assembly line, but through his ability to recognize opportunities, articulate a vision, and inspire others to join him in fulfilling that vision, he was responsible for making significant changes in the trajectory of the automobile industry and even in the history of manufacturing in America. Starting with the invention of the self-propelled

Quadricycle in 1896, Ford developed other vehicles, primarily racing cars, that attracted a series of interested investors. In 1903, 12 investors backed him in the creation of a company to build and sell horseless carriages, and Ford Motor Company was born.

Starting with the Model A, the company produced a series of successful vehicles, but in 1908 Henry Ford wanted to create a better, cheaper "motorcar for the great multitude."[6] Working with a group of handpicked employees, he designed the Model T. The design was so successful, and demand so great, that Ford decided to investigate methods for increasing production and lowering costs. Borrowing concepts from other industries, by 1913 Ford had developed a moving assembly line for automobile manufacture. Although the work was so demanding that it created a high degree of employee turnover, the production process was significantly more efficient, reducing chassis assembly time from 12½ hours to 2 hours 40 minutes. In 1904, Ford expanded into Canada and by 1925 had assembly plants in Europe, Argentina, South Africa, and Australia. By the end of 1919, Ford was producing 50 percent of all the cars in the United States, and the assembly line disruption in the industry had led to the demise of most of Ford's rivals.[7]

The Automotive Industry and Ford Leadership

The automotive industry in the United States had always been a highly competitive, cyclical business. In 2015 there were "a wide and growing variety of product offerings from a growing number of manufacturers,"[8] including the electric-car lineup from Tesla Motors, self-styled as "not just an automaker, but also a technology and design company with a focus on energy innovation."[9] The total number of cars and trucks sold to retail buyers, or "industry demand," varied substantially from year to year depending on general economic conditions, the cost of purchasing and operating cars and trucks, and the availability of credit and fuel. Because cars and trucks were durable items, consumers could wait to replace them, and, starting in 2013, the average age of light vehicles on U.S. roads was over 11 years. Due to this, high replacement demand for cars and car parts was forecast to result in increased sales for 2015 and beyond. These sales would be aided by an improvement in the general economic situation, reduced gasoline prices, and lower interest rates for car loans, all contributing to the best results for U.S. auto sales since the 2008 recession.[10] However, sales in the U.S. markets no longer belonged just to U.S. manufacturers (Exhibit 2).

Originally dominated by the "big 3" Detroit-based car companies—Ford, General Motors, and Chrysler—competition in the United States had intensified since the 1980s, when Japanese carmakers began gaining a foothold in the market. To counter the problem of being viewed as foreign, Japanese companies Nissan, Toyota, and Honda had set up production facilities in the United States and thus gained acceptance from American consumers. Production quality and lean production were judged to be the major weapons that Japanese carmakers used to gain an advantage over American carmakers. Starting in 2003, because of innovative production processes that yielded better quality for American consumers, Toyota vehicles unquestionably became "a better value proposition" than Detroit's products.[11]

Back in 1999, Ford Motor Company had been in good shape, having attained a U.S. market share of 24.8 percent, and had seen profits reach a remarkable $7.2 billion ($5.86 per share), with pretax income of $11 billion. At that time people even speculated that Ford would soon overtake General Motors as the world's number-one automobile manufacturer.[12] But soon Toyota, through its innovative technology, management philosophy of continuous improvement, and cost arbitrage due to its presence in multiple geographic locations, was threatening to overtake GM and Ford. In addition, unfortunately, the profits at Ford in 1999 had come at the expense of investing in Ford's future. Jacques Nasser, the CEO at that time, had focused on corporate acquisition and diversification rather than new vehicle development. By the time Chairman Bill Ford stepped in and fired Nasser in 2001, Ford was seeing declines in both market share and profitability. By 2005, market share had dropped to 18.6 percent and Ford had skidded out of control, losing $1.6 billion, pretax, in North American profits. It was obvious that Ford needed a change in order to adapt and survive. Observers believed that the Ford family would take action to prevent further losses: "Ford may need a strongman . . . a Ford characteristic—the 'prime minister' who actually runs the company under the 'constitutional monarch,' a member of the Ford family." It was speculated that Mark Fields, named head of Ford's North American operations in 2005, might be tapped to take that job.[13] This became a legitimate observation about Ford's approach to succession planning.

The Ford empire had been around for over a century, and the company had not gone outside its ranks for a top executive since hiring Ernest Breech away from General Motors Corporation in 1946 (see Exhibit 3).[14] Since taking the CEO position in 2001, Bill Ford had tried several times to find a qualified successor, "going after such industry luminaries as Renault-Nissan CEO Carlos Ghosn and DaimlerChrysler Chairman Dieter Zetsche."[15]

Among large corporations, it had become fairly common to hire a CEO from outside the family or board. According to Joseph Bower from Harvard Business School, about one-third of the time at S&P 500 firms, and about 40 percent of the time at companies that were struggling with problems in operations or financial distress, an outsider was appointed as CEO. The reason might have been to get a fresh point of view or to get the support of the board. "Results suggest that forced turnover followed by outsider succession, on average, improves firm

EXHIBIT 2 Sales and Share of U.S. Total Market by Manufacturer, 2015

	Sales, YTD			Market Share, YTD	
	2015	2014	% Chg	2015	2014
General Motors Corp.	202,786	171,486	18.3	17.6	16.9
Ford Motor Company	177,441	153,494	15.6	15.4	15.2
Toyota Motor Sales	169,194	146,365	15.6	14.7	14.5
Chrysler LLC	145,007	127,183	14.0	12.6	12.6
Nissan North America	104,107	90,470	15.1	9.0	8.9
American Honda Motor	102,184	91,631	11.5	8.9	9.0
Hyundai Motor America	44,505	44,005	1.1	3.9	4.3
Subaru of America Inc.	40,812	33,000	23.7	3.5	3.3
Kia Motors America	38,299	37,011	3.5	3.3	3.7
Mercedes-Benz	26,124	23,892	9.3	2.3	2.4
Volkswagen of America	23,504	23,494	—	2.0	2.3
Mazda Motor of America	20,271	18,813	7.7	1.8	1.9
BMW of North America	18,981	18,253	4.0	1.6	1.8
Audi of America Inc.	11,541	10,101	14.3	1.0	1.0
Mitsubishi Motors NA	6,493	4,867	33.4	0.6	0.5
Land Rover **	5,281	4,674	13.0	0.5	0.5
Porsche Cars NA Inc.	3,937	3,096	27.2	0.3	0.3
Volvo	3,794	3,792	0.1	0.3	0.4
Mini *	3,228	2,543	26.9	0.3	0.3
Jaguar *	1,266	1,347	−6.0	0.1	0.1
Maserati *	452	567	−20.3	—	0.1
Ferrari *	174	186	−6.5	—	—
Bentley *	96	192	−50.0	—	—
Rolls-Royce *	67	56	19.6	—	—
Total car	529,696	491,724	7.7	46.0	48.6
Domestic car	160,761	152,319	5.5	14.0	15.0
Import car	368,935	339,405	8.7	32.1	33.5
Total truck	621,427	520,858	19.3	54.0	51.4
Domestic truck	362,121	298,122	21.5	31.5	29.4
Import truck	259,306	222,736	16.4	22.5	22.0
TOTAL VEHICLES	1,151,123	1,012,582	13.7	100.0	100.0
Selling Days	26	25	—	—	—

* Imported cars only.
** Imported trucks only.

Source: www.motorintelligence.com.

EXHIBIT 3 Ford Family Tree

- Isaac Ford (1749–?)
  - William Ford (1775–1818?) — Rebecca Jennings (1776–1851)
    - Samuel Ford (ca1792–1842)
    - John Ford (c1799–1864) — Thomasina Smith (1803–1847)
      - Rebecca Ford [Flaherty] (1825–1895)
      - William Ford (1826–1905) — Mary Litogot O'Hem (c1839–1876)
        - Henry Ford (1863–1947) — Clara Jane Bryant (1866–1950)
          - Infant 1861
          - Edsel Bryant Ford (1893–1943) — Eleanor Lowthian Clay (1896–1976)
            - Henry Ford II (1917–1987) — Anne McDonnell (1919–1996)
              - Charlotte M. Ford (b. 1941)
              - Anne Ford (b. 1943)
              - Edsel B. Ford II (b. 1948)
            - Benson Ford, Sr. (1919–1978) — Edith McNaughton (1920–1980)
              - Benson Ford, Jr. (1949)
              - Lynn Ford [Alandt] (b. 1951)
            - Josephine Clay Ford [Ford] (1923–2005) — Walter Buhl Ford II (1920–1991)
              - Walter Buhl Ford III (1943–2010)
              - Eleanor Clay Ford [Sullivan] (b. 1946)
              - Josephine Clay Ford [Ingle] (b. 1949)
              - Martha Parke "Mutty" Ford [Morse] (b. 1948)
            - William Clay Ford, Sr. (b. 1925) — Martha Parke Firestone (b. 1925)
              - Martha Parke Firestone (b. 1925)
              - Sheila Firestone Ford [Hamp] (b. 1951)
              - Alfred Brush Ford (b. 1950)
              - William Clay Ford, Jr. (b. 1957)
              - Elizabeth Hudson Ford [Kontuls] (b. 1961)
            - Elena Anne Ford (b. 1966)
          - (Harvey S. Firestone, Jr. (1898–1973) — Elizabeth Parke (1897–1990))
        - Henry Ford
        - Jane Ford [Smith] (1829–1851)
        - Mary Ford [Ford] (ca1832–1882)
        - Nancy Ford [Flaherty] (1834–1920)
        - Samuel Ford (1837–1884)
      - Robert Ford (1803–1877)
      - George Ford (ca1811–1863)
    - Henry Ford (ca1830–1901)
      - John Ford (ca1865–1927) — Margaret Ford [Ruddiman] (1867–1960)
        - Jane Ford (c1868–1906)
        - William Ford (1873–1934)
        - Robert Ford (1871–1875)
        - Infant (ca1876–1876)

Note: Family tree includes descendants of Henry Ford who worked at Ford Motor Co. and their children.

Source: *BusinessWeek*, www.businessweek.com/1998/39/b3597003.htm.

performance."[16] Bill Ford claimed that to undertake major changes in Ford's dysfunctional culture, an outsider might be more qualified than even the most proficient auto industry insider.[17]

An outsider CEO might also help restore faith in Ford management among investors, who were discontented with the Ford family's high dividends and extravagant lifestyle. The Ford family controlled about 40 percent of the company's voting shares through their ownership of all its class-B stock and holdings of common stock. The class-B family shares had almost the same market value as that of the common stock, but the voting rights of the family shares were exceptionally high by industry standards. The dividend stream was an annuity, which over the years had enabled various family members to own a football team, fund museums and philanthropic causes, and even promote the Hare Krishna movement. Given that the company was experiencing serious financial problems, these activities raised stockholder dissent, as the annual retained earnings in the past had been dissipated as dividends instead of reinvested in firm operations or acquisitions to increase the net value of the firm.

In 2006, Alan Mulally had been selected as the new CEO and was expected to accomplish "nothing less than undoing a strongly entrenched management system put into place by Henry Ford II almost 40 years ago"—a system of regional fiefdoms around the world that had sapped the company's ability to compete in a global industry, a system that Chairman Bill Ford couldn't or wouldn't unwind.[18]

Mulally's Vision

Alan Mulally understood that organizational culture was key to organizational change and that change could be aided by an appropriate organizational structure. However, that restructuring had to be supported and inspired by a clear vision. Prior to joining Ford, Mulally had served as executive vice president of the Boeing Company and as president and chief executive officer of Boeing Commercial Airplanes. In those roles, he was responsible for all the Boeing Company's commercial airplane programs and related services.[19] Under Mulally's visionary leadership, Boeing had regained the top position in its market from its major European competitor, Airbus. The appointment of Mulally at Ford was seen by the market as a move to utilize his experience and success in managing manufacturing and assembly lines to help shape the future of Ford.

Alan Mulally had come from a metal-bending business that, like auto making, was influenced by global competition, had a unionized workforce, and was subject to complex regulations and rapidly changing technologies.[20] Although he was not an auto guy, he had a proven record in an industry that faced issues similar to those faced by the automobile industry, and a lot of his expertise and management techniques were highly transferable. In his own words, "Everybody says, well, I'm not a car guy, so you couldn't make a contribution here. But I'm a product (guy) and I'm a designer."[21]

Bill Ford praised Mulally as "an outstanding leader and a man of great character." In his email to Ford employees announcing the appointment of Mulally, Bill Ford wrote, "Alan has deep experience in customer satisfaction, manufacturing, supplier relations and labor relations, all of which have applications to the challenges of Ford. He also has the personality and team-building skills that will help guide our Company in the right direction."[22]

Mulally set his own priorities for fixing Ford: "At the top of the list, I would put dealing with reality." The newly elected CEO signaled that "the bigger-is-better worldview that has defined Ford for decades was being replaced with a new approach: Less is More."[23] Ford needed to pay more attention to cutting costs and transforming the way it did business than to traditional measurements such as market share.[24] The vision was to have a smaller and more profitable Ford.

Mulally's cutback plan built on the 14 plant closures and 30,000-plus job cuts announced by Ford in January 2007. Ford's new plan added two more North American plants to the closure list and exceeded the targeted $5 billion in cost cuts by the end of 2008,[25] but it pushed back a target for North American profitability by one year to 2009 and then again to 2011.[26] The company targeted seven vehicle manufacturing sites for closure. At the same time, it also planned to increase the plant utilization and production levels in each production unit, while focusing more on smaller, more fuel-efficient vehicles. The overall strategy was to use restructuring as a tool to obtain operating profitability at lower volume and create a mix of products that better appealed to the market.

By 2011, Ford had closed or sold a quarter of its plants and cut its global workforce by more than one-third. It also slashed labor and health care costs, plowing the money back into the design of some well-received new products, like the Ford Fusion sedan and Ford Edge crossover. This put Ford in a better position to compete, especially taking into consideration that General Motors and Chrysler had filed for bankruptcy in 2009 and Toyota had recently announced a major recall of its vehicles for "unintended acceleration" problems.[27] Ford's sales grew at double the rate of the rest of the industry in 2010, but entering 2011 its rivals' problems seemed to be in the rearview mirror, and General Motors, especially, was on the rebound.

Mulally had set three priorities: first, to determine the brands Ford would offer; second, to be "best in class for all its vehicles"; and, third, to make sure that those vehicles would be accepted and adapted by consumers around the globe—"if a model was developed for the U.S. market, it needed to be adaptable to car buyers in other countries."[28] Mulally said that the "real opportunity going forward is to integrate and leverage our Ford assets around the world" and decide on the best mix of brands in the company's portfolio.[29] The "best mix of brands" appeared to have been established going into 2011, after brands such as Jaguar, Land Rover, Aston Martin, and Volvo were all sold off and the Mercury brand was discontinued. Ford also had had an equity interest in Mazda Motor Corporation, which it reduced substantially in 2010, retaining only a 3.5 percent share of ownership. This left the company with only the Ford and Lincoln brands, but the Lincoln offerings had struggled against Cadillac and other rivals for the luxury-car market. Mulally acknowledged that this needed fixing, and forecast a date of 2013 for real changes in the Lincoln lineup.[30]

Since his appointment, Mulally had also made some additional structural and procedural changes in the company. For instance, instead of discussing business plans monthly or semiannually as they used to do, executives now met with Mulally weekly. The in-depth sessions were a contrast to executives' previous efforts to explain away bad news, said Donat R. Leclair, Ford's chief financial officer. "The difference I see now is that we're actually committed to hitting the numbers. Before, it was a culture of trying to explain why we were off the plan. The more eloquently you could explain why you were off the plan, the [easier] it was to change the plan."[31]

Mulally also did some senior executive reorganization at Ford, and many of the newly appointed executives reported to him directly, including a global head of product development. In addition, the head of worldwide purchasing, the chief of quality and advanced manufacturing, the head of information technology, the chief technical officer, and the leaders of Ford's European division, its Asia, Pacific, and Africa units, and its Americas unit all reported directly to him.[32]

Mulally's fearlessness had been well suited to pushing through projects at Boeing, but its suitability to Ford's good-old-boy culture was a question. Like every new leader, he had to move with confidence in his early days, but as an industry outsider he also had to take care to avoid violating long-standing industry norms.[33] Regarding his approach to culture change, one observer noted, "Mulally's approach to management and communication hasn't been seen before in the halls of Ford, which have historically been the atmosphere of a kingdom with competing dukes."[34] Mulally encountered conflict between his management style and the old "Ford way," but this didn't deter him from making changes.

One significant thing Mulally did was to break down the global structure in which Ford Europe, Ford Asia, Ford North America, Ford Australia, and Ford South America had long created redundancies of efforts, products, engineering platforms, engines, and the like, as a way of perpetuating each division's independence.[35] The geographic segments were reconfigured into Ford North America, Latin America (including Mexico), Europe, and Asia/Pacific/Africa. Mulally further consolidated top leadership to cover the major operations—the Americas, Europe, Asia/Pacific/Africa—and appointed leaders for global manufacturing and labor and for global marketing, sales, and service.

However, these restructuring efforts also had their drawbacks. Unable to accept the Mulally management approach, some senior executives left Ford. The international chief of the company, Mark A. Schulz, was one of them. "He had decided to retire after working for more than three decades at the company. Schulz was just one of a string of senior executives to leave after Mulally took over. Ford's second-ranking North American executive, its North American manufacturing chief and its chief of staff also all announced their departures after Mulally's hiring."[36] Ford lost some of its most experienced leaders because of the outsider CEO. Yet Mulally remained confident that his restructuring decision was still the right one for the long term.

Going into 2013, Mulally appeared to have reached his goal. As he said,

> We achieved several important milestones, including restoring Ford's investment-grade status and reclaiming the Ford Blue Oval, resuming regular dividend payments to our shareholders and achieving 14 straight quarters of operating profit. . . . We launched 25 vehicles and 31 powertrains globally in 2012, a testament to our ongoing commitment to product development. We also announced plans to revitalize our Lincoln brand . . . which will introduce an exciting new lineup of great luxury vehicles.[37]

In 2014, thanks to Mulally's vision and perseverance, Ford maintained its position. Ford had introduced 24 vehicles around the world, including the new Mondeo in Europe, but although the firm was still profitable, net income was down $4 billion from 2013. Even though Ford maintained its number-two position in Europe, behind Volkswagen, major losses had occurred in that sector, primarily due to Russian economic instabilities, and South America had also seen losses due to currency devaluation and changing government rules. In addition, Ford's push into the Asia-Pacific region, specifically China, was behind schedule. North American sales, while still strong, had resulted in operating margin reductions due to recalls and costs associated with the relaunch of the F-150. The one real bright spot was in financial services. Ford Motor Credit, the financing company that lends people money to buy new cars, saw its best results since 2011.[38]

As Mark Fields took over as CEO, he pointed to the ONE Ford plan as essential to Ford's future: "Our ONE Ford plan is built on compelling vision, comprehensive strategy, and relentless implementation, all leading to profitable growth around the world."[39] The actions of Mulally and now Fields, in enacting the ONE Ford plan, had attracted many long-term investors who believed in the strategy. Going into 2015 the financials, especially the balance sheet, appeared strong, and because of this, the company was able to reinstate and subsequently boost the dividend to shareholders, rewarding those investors who had stayed the course. (See Exhibits 4 and 5.)

EXHIBIT 4 Ford Motor Company and Subsidiaries: Sector Balance Sheets ($ millions)

Go to library tab in Connect to access Case Financials.

	December 31, 2014	December 31, 2013
ASSETS		
Automotive		
Cash and cash equivalents	$ 4,567	$ 4,959
Marketable securities	17,135	20,157
Total cash and marketable securities	21,702	25,116
Receivables, less allowances of $455 and $132	5,789	5,641
Inventories	7,866	7,708
Deferred income taxes	2,039	1,574
Net investment in operating leases	1,699	1,384
Other current assets	1,347	1,034
Total current assets	40,442	42,457
Equity in net assets of affiliated companies	3,216	3,546
Net property	29,795	27,492
Deferred income taxes	13,331	13,436
Other assets	2,798	2,824
Non-current receivable from Financial Services	497	724
Total Automotive assets	90,079	90,479
Financial Services		
Cash and cash equivalents	6,190	9,509
Marketable securities	3,258	1,943
Finance receivables, net	86,141	80,816
Net investment in operating leases	21,518	18,600
Equity in net assets of affiliated companies	141	133
Other assets	3,613	3,149
Receivable from Automotive	527	907
Total Financial Services assets	121,388	115,057
Intersector elimination	(1,024)	(1,631)
Total assets	$210,443	$203,905
LIABILITIES		
Automotive		
Payables	$ 18,876	$ 18,035
Other liabilities and deferred revenue	17,934	16,537
Deferred income taxes	270	267
Debt payable within one year	2,501	1,257

continued

	December 31, 2014	December 31, 2013
Current payable to Financial Services	527	907
Total current liabilities	40,108	37,003
Long-term debt	11,323	14,426
Other liabilities and deferred revenue	23,793	22,089
Deferred income taxes	367	430
Total Automotive liabilities	75,591	73,948
Financial Services		
Payables	1,159	1,496
Debt	105,347	99,005
Deferred income taxes	1,849	1,627
Other liabilities and deferred revenue	1,850	2,260
Payable to Automotive	497	724
Total Financial Services liabilities	110,702	105,112
Intersector elimination	(1,024)	(1,631)
Total liabilities	185,269	177,429
Redeemable noncontrolling interest	342	331
EQUITY		
Capital stock		
Common Stock, par value $.01 per share (3,938 million shares issued of 6 billion authorized)	39	39
Class B Stock, par value $.01 per share (71 million shares issued of 530 million authorized)	1	1
Capital in excess of par value of stock	21,089	21,422
Retained earnings	24,556	23,386
Accumulated other comprehensive income/(loss)	(20,032)	(18,230)
Treasury stock	(848)	(506)
Total equity attributable to Ford Motor Company	24,805	26,112
Equity attributable to noncontrolling interests	27	33
Total equity	24,832	26,145
Total liabilities and equity	$210,443	$203,905

Source: Ford Motor Company 10-K filings.

Ford and the Automobile Industry Changing Product Mix

Going into 2015, the entire automobile industry was facing disruption. The 2009 global economic downturn and financial crisis had had a significant impact on global sales volumes in the auto industry. It was possible that the once-profitable business of manufacturing and selling trucks and SUVs had changed. Especially in the U.S., oil prices had been fluctuating, making it difficult to anticipate consumer demand. In 2010, this had caused a shift in consumers'

EXHIBIT 5 Ford Motor Company and Subsidiaries: Sector Statements of Cash Flows ($ millions)

Go to library tab in Connect to access Case Financials.

	Year Ended December 31					
	2014		2013		2012	
	Automotive	Financial	Automotive	Financial	Automotive	Financial
Cash flows from operating activities of continuing operations						
Net income	$ 1,489	$ 1,697	$ 5,775	$ 1,400	$ 4,413	$ 1,199
Depreciation and tooling amortization	4,252	3,133	4,064	2,440	3,655	1,831
Other amortization	216	(178)	198	(158)	139	(325)
Provision for credit and insurance losses	—	305	2	208	6	77
Pension and OPEB expense	1,249	—	2,543	—	1,557	—
Equity investment (earnings)/losses in excess of dividends received	216	(27)	(529)	(14)	20	3
Foreign currency adjustments	827	(2)	227	1	(121)	5
Net (gain)/loss on changes in investments in affiliates	798	—	113	—	(594)	—
Stock compensation	172	8	152	7	134	6
Provision for deferred income taxes	483	580	(481)	(367)	1,209	545
Decrease/(Increase) in intersector receivables/payables	(83)	83	(136)	136	899	(899)
Decrease/(Increase) in accounts receivable and other assets	(2,826)	(71)	(1,486)	(554)	(2,343)	(165)
Decrease/(Increase) in inventory	(875)	—	(572)	—	(1,401)	—
Increase/(Decrease) in accounts payable and accrued and other liabilities	6,229	(495)	494	737	633	(34)
Other	(242)	(223)	(228)	(484)	(26)	(200)
Interest supplements and residual value support to Financial Services	(3,141)	—	(2,398)	—	(1,914)	—
Net cash provided by/(used in) operating activities	8,764	4,810	7,738	3,352	6,266	2,043
Cash flows from investing activities of continuing operations						
Capital spending	(7,360)	(103)	(6,566)	(31)	(5,459)	(29)
Acquisitions of finance receivables and operating leases (excluding wholesale and other)	—	(51,673)	—	(45,822)	—	(38,445)
Collections of finance receivables and operating leases (excluding wholesale and other)	—	36,497	—	33,966	—	31,570

continued

	Year Ended December 31					
	2014		2013		2012	
	Automotive	Financial	Automotive	Financial	Automotive	Financial
Net change in wholesale and other receivables	—	(2,208)	—	(3,044)	—	(1,178)
Purchases of marketable securities	(35,096)	(13,598)	(89,676)	(30,317)	(73,100)	(22,035)
Sales and maturities of marketable securities	38,028	12,236	87,799	30,448	70,001	23,748
Change related to Venezuelan operations	(477)	—	—	—	—	—
Settlements of derivatives	247	34	(284)	67	(788)	51
Proceeds from sales of retail finance receivables	—	—	—	495	—	—
Other	77	64	171	19	196	—
Investing activity (to)/from Financial Services	322	—	445	—	925	—
Maturity of Financial Services debt held by Automotive	—	—	—	—	201	—
Interest supplements and residual value support from Automotive	—	3,141	—	2,398	—	1,914
Net cash provided by/(used in) investing activities	(4,259)	(15,610)	(8,111)	(11,821)	(8,024)	(4,404)
Cash flows from financing activities of continuing operations						
Cash dividends	(1,952)	—	(1,574)	—	(763)	—
Purchases of Common Stock	(1,964)	—	(213)	—	(125)	—
Net changes in short term debt	(126)	(3,744)	(133)	(2,794)	154	1,054
Proceeds from issuance of other debt	185	39,858	2,250	38,293	1,553	30,883
Principal payments on other debt	(1,010)	(27,849)	(1,439)	(26,514)	(810)	(28,400)
Other	134	(109)	287	(30)	31	128
Financing activity to/(from) Automotive	—	(322)	—	(445)	—	(925)
Maturity of Financial Services debt held by Automotive	—	—	—	—	—	(201)
Net cash provided by/(used in) financing activities	(4,733)	(7,834)	(822)	8,510	40	2,539
Effect of exchange rate changes on cash and cash equivalents	(164)	(353)	(93)	56	—	51
Net increase/(decrease) in cash and cash equivalents	$ 392	$ (3,319)	$ (1,288)	$ 97	$ (1,718)	$ 229

continued

EXHIBIT 5 Continued

	Year Ended December 31					
	2014		2013		2012	
	Automotive	Financial	Automotive	Financial	Automotive	Financial
Cash and cash equivalents at January 1	$ 4,959	$ 9,509	$ 6,247	$ 9,412	$ 7,965	$ 9,183
Net increase/(decrease) in cash and cash equivalents	(392)	(3,319)	(1,288)	97	(1,718)	229
Cash and cash equivalents at December 31	$ 4,567	$ 6,190	$ 4,959	$ 9,509	$ 6,247	$ 9,412

Source: Ford Motor Company 10-K filings.

car-buying habits, reducing the demand for large vehicles, but by late 2014 gas prices had lowered enough to spur interest in SUVs once again. (See Exhibit 6.)

This trend should have been good for Ford, given its branding emphasis on the F-150, Escape, and Explorer, but in 2013 Ford had shifted production to the small and midsized cars, as well as making a major push to promote the Lincoln luxury vehicle. Going into 2015 this positioning hurt Ford. See Exhibit 7 for vehicle sales figures in the U.S. market.

The core strategy at Ford starting in 2011 centered on a change in products, shifting to smaller and more fuel-efficient cars. Ford imported European-made small vehicles, the European Focus and Fiesta, into North America. It also converted three truck-manufacturing plants to small-car production.[40] The Ford and Lincoln lines were upgraded, emphasizing fuel-economy improvement and the introduction of hybrid cars. In 2012 Ford launched six new Ford hybrid cars in North America and sold more hybrids in the fourth quarter of 2012 than during any quarter in its history. In 2014 Ford began producing its first hybrid electric car in Europe, the Mondeo Hybrid. This car was well known to those in the U.S., being based on the North American Fusion model hybrid vehicle. By 2014, Ford was the world's second-largest manufacturer of hybrids, after Toyota.[41]

In 2014 Ford launched more new products than at any other time in its history—23 new models, including a redesigned Mustang, the Ford Edge and Lincoln MKC crossovers, and the Super Duty version of the F-Series pickup. This push was part of Ford's design to increase sales and volume while also building margins and overall profitability, but it came at a cost. Ford had opened three assembly plants and added 14,000 jobs since 2012.[42]

In the U.S., Ford's market share had dropped over time—from 25 percent in 1999 to 15.5 percent in 2011,[43] with major blows to market share in the light-vehicle segment. Going into 2015, although still losing ground at 14.9 percent, Ford claimed the second spot in the U.S. market, just behind GM and ahead of Toyota (see Exhibit 8).

Ford's most successful vehicles were still the F-Series pickup trucks (see Exhibit 9). In 2015, for the 38th consecutive year, the Ford F-Series was ranked as America's top-selling vehicle.[44] Ford's vehicles had proven dependable as well, overall. However, it appeared that consumer perceptions had not kept pace with actual performance—in 2012 J.D. Power and Associates found that the Ford and Lincoln brands still had large lags between actual dependability performance and consumer perception. "Producing vehicles with world-class quality is just part of the battle for automakers; convincing consumers to believe in their quality is equally as important," said David Sargent, vice president of global vehicle research at J.D. Power and Associates. "It takes considerable time to positively change consumer perceptions of quality and dependability—sometimes a decade or more—so it is vital for manufacturers to continually improve quality and also to convince consumers of these gains."[45] In 2014, the Lincoln MKZ came in at number

EXHIBIT 6 U.S. New Vehicle Sales by Segment, 2006–2014*

Total 12.4 million

46% Pickups, SUVs, crossovers

*Nine months ended September.

Source: www.wsj.com/articles/gm-outlines-financial-plans-1412173772.

EXHIBIT 7 Overall Vehicle Sales by Segment, January 2015

	Segment totals, ranked by Jan unit sales			
	Jan 2015	% Change from Jan 2014	YTD 2015	% Chg from YTD 2014
Cars	529,696	7.7	529,696	7.7
Midsize	233,167	5.7	233,167	5.7
Small	219,344	12.2	219,344	12.2
Luxuty	77,061	2.0	77,061	2.0
Large	124	−38.0	124	−38.0
Light-duty trucks	621,427	19.3	621,427	19.3
Pickup	166,326	21.9	166,326	21.9
Crossover	281,630	14.7	281,630	14.7
Minivan	55,445	9.9	55,445	9.9
Midsize SUV	66,388	32.2	66,388	32.2
Large SUV	19,744	74.3	19,744	74.3
Small SUV	15,281	6.0	15,281	6.0
Luxury SUV	16,613	33.4	16,613	33.4
Total SUV/Crossover	399,656	19.7	399,656	19.7
Total SUV	118,026	33.5	118,026	33.5
Total Crossover	281,630	14.7	281,630	14.7

Source: www.motorintelligence.com.

EXHIBIT 8 U.S. Market Share by Brand, 2014 Year End

- BMW-Mini: 2.4%
- Chrysler Group/FCA: 12.6%
- Ford Motor Company: 14.9%
- General Motors: 17.8%
- Honda Motor Company: 9.3%
- Hyundai-Kia: 7.9%
- Mazda: 1.8%
- Daimler: 2.2%
- Nissan Motor Company: 8.4%
- Subaru: 3.1%
- Toyota Motor Corporation: 14.4%
- Volkswagen Group: 3.6%
- Other: 1.5%

Source: www.goodcarbadcar.net/search/label/US%20Auto%20Sales%20By%20Brand?max-results=5.

EXHIBIT 9 Best-Selling Vehicles in America, 2014 (in units sold)

Vehicle	Units Sold
Ford F-Series	753,851
Chevrolet Silverado	529,755
Ram P/U	439,789
Toyota Camry	428,606
Honda Accord	388,374
Toyota Corolla/Matrix	339,498
Nissan Altima	335,644
Honda CR-V	335,019
Honda Civic	325,981
Ford Fusion	306,860

Source: www.forbes.com/sites/niallmccarthy/2015/01/07/americas-best-selling-vehicles-in-2014-infographic/.

15 out of 28 vehicles rated by *Consumer Reports* as most reliable in the world, while the Ford Fusion 1.5-liter EcoBoost was rated 23rd.[46]

Globalizing the Ford Brand

In the auto industry it was common practice that different regions cooperated, and companies basically sold the same cars around the world. This had not been the case at Ford. Since it set up its European operations, Ford Europe and Ford North America had gone separate ways, but, starting in 2007, Mulally was determined to change that.

Under the ONE Ford vision, Mulally globalized the Ford brand, meaning that all Ford vehicles competing in global segments were the same in North America, Europe, and Asia.[47] The company was looking for a reduction of complexity, and thus costs, in the purchasing and manufacturing processes. The idea was to deliver more vehicles worldwide from fewer platforms and to maximize the use of common parts and systems. By 2009, Mulally felt he had positioned Ford to take advantage of its scale, global products, and brand to respond to the changing marketplace.[48] However, each year seemed to pose new challenges.

Going into 2015, the global marketplace for automobiles was gaining strength overall, but each geographic segment had its issues: North American auto sales reached a post-recession high in 2014, in spite of an increasing number of recalls; the Chinese and larger Asian market was still growing, although starting to slow; European economic concerns, especially in Russia, made this a difficult area to manage; South American government regulations and currency fluctuations impacted growth there (see Exhibit 10). The need for a global strategy was driving all major auto manufacturers to reduce the number of vehicle platforms while simultaneously adding models in response to consumer preferences. Although the increased complexity did raise costs, this more flexible approach allowed for improved product commonality and increased volume. As components could be shared between cars and platforms, this also reduced the number of suppliers. Ford, for instance, anticipated it would reduce its supplier base from 1,150 to 750.[49] Although seemingly a positive, this could also prove costly if a major supplier had a problem, as occurred with Japanese airbag manufacturer Takata in 2014.[50] Ford, specifically, had recalled 850,000 vehicles for airbag problems in 2014, at a cost of $500 million.[51]

Regarding global growth, Ford had developed two car plants in India and planned to open two more in 2015, while also increasing its commitment in China, having invested $5 billion in factories there since 2012.[52] Although the Chinese market was slowing, it was still forecast to grow 7 percent in 2015, with the luxury, or premium, and SUV sectors seeing the most expansion. Ford was betting on this to spur its Lincoln sales, having introduced the Lincoln lineup to China in April 2014 with eight dealerships. Seventeen more dealerships were scheduled to open in 2015.[53] Sales growth in this region was critical, given that Ford was late to the China market, with a 2014 share of less than 5 percent, while General Motors controlled 15 percent. Although Ford had partnered with Chinese manufacturer Changan to produce light vehicles such as the Focus, the Lincoln would be imported from America, leaving Ford to "deal with the added cost of import duties that would leave their premium vehicles in a difficult position against rivals who are already well positioned in China."[54]

Fields Restructures

Given all the global challenges and the continuing need for innovation, Ford's new CEO Mark Fields was feeling the pressure to perform following Alan Mulally's departure. Although Fields was clear that he would continue to support Mulally's legacy, he would do this by "tailoring aspects of the company to his preferences."[55] Fields

EXHIBIT 10 Ford Performance by Region 2014

AUTOMOTIVE SECTOR
FULL-YEAR & PRETAX
Millions

	Total	North America	South America	Europe	Middle East & Africa	Asia Pacific	Other Automotive
	$4,488	$6,898	$(1,162)	$(1,062)	$(20)	$589	$(755)
Memo: B/(W) 2013	$(2,448)	$(1,911)	$(1,129)	$380	$49	$262	$(99)

Net Interest $(583)
Other $(172)

Source: Ford 10-K.

made eight changes in management since he became CEO, among them the appointment of investment banker John Casesa as group vice president, Global Strategy; the hiring of analytics expert Paul Ballew as executive director and chief data and analytics officer, driving development of research into data science; and the opening of the Research and Innovation Center in Palo Alto, California, under the direction of former Apple engineer Dragos Maciuca. These moves indicated Fields was focused on driving the ONE Ford strategy worldwide and accelerating innovation in connectivity, mobility, and autonomous vehicles, among other things.[56]

Looking Ahead

Going into 2015, Ford Motor Company was the fourth-largest automobile manufacturer in the world, but, like all others that produced a multivehicle lineup, it was facing considerable uncertainty. Global markets were hard to predict, countries were increasing regulatory requirements for safety and environmental impact, all vehicles were seeing an increase in the amount of onboard technology that required a shift in both engineering and manufacturing priorities, worldwide manufacturers were making design changes that allowed more lean production and consolidation of suppliers, and consumers were changing how they purchased vehicles and rethinking what they wanted from the transportation experience overall.[57] These fundamental changes in the industry required leadership that could anticipate trends and allocate resources wisely, all while crafting a vision for the future that could inspire all relevant stakeholders to support and promote the company's success.

Several other shifts in the overall landscape were occurring: the interest, worldwide, in electric or alternative-fueled vehicles, the development of autonomously controlled cars that were also personally connected to a user who might not be the driver, and the reduction in demand for actual automobile ownership in favor of rental or on-demand transportation options. These shifts would create additional challenges for entrenched car manufacturers. In 2015 news surfaced that Apple might be entering the personal transportation industry with an Apple-branded electric or partially self-driving car, ready for market by 2020.[58] Ford and other carmakers needed to be prepared for this type of potential disruption.

As Mark Fields took over from Alan Mulally, he inherited a legacy developed over eight years of visionary leadership. Mulally had created accountability and collaboration across the company's management structure that allowed him to drive innovation in product development as well as technology: Ford had gone from selling 97 different automotive products to just 20, and it had turned cars and trucks into "mobile centers of entertainment and communication that paralleled the fast growth of smartphones and social media."[59] Fields would need to further spur innovation into "an era when cars may no longer need drivers," and he realized that to do this he needed to continue the "culture of openness and collaboration cultivated under Mulally." As Ford Chairman Bill Ford said, in the coming years, "there will be different realities—some we can anticipate, like mobility and this notion of global gridlock . . . some we can't anticipate. The best thing Mark can do is to continue to make us a very adaptable, nimble company."[60]

Ford management was clear:

> Our first priority is to accelerate the pace of progress of our ONE Ford plan. The ONE Ford plan has been fundamental to the progress we have made in recent

years, and it is fundamental to our performance going forward. In many ways we are starting to see the full benefits and strength of the ONE Ford plan, and we see an opportunity to accelerate our pace of progress to drive operational excellence and profitable growth for all.[61]

Could CEO Mark Fields expand ONE Ford to accommodate these future challenges? Henry Ford had had the initial vision of disruption in personal transportation. Would the 21st-century version of Ford Motor Company be as successful?

ENDNOTES

1. Ford Media. 2015. Ford U.S. sales up 15 percent in January; company sees best U.S. January retail sales results since 2004. February 3, https://media.ford.com/content/fordmedia/fna/us/en/news/2015/02/03/january2015sales.html.
2. Bunkley, N. 2015. Ford's 2014 profit fell 56%; European outlook worsens. January 29, http://europe.autonews.com/article/20150129/COPY/301309980/fords-2014-profit-fell-56-european-outlook-worsens&cciid=internal-aneinside-mostright.
3. Caldicott, S. M. 2014. Why Ford's Alan Mulally is an innovation CEO for the record books. *Forbes,* June 25, www.forbes.com/sites/sarahcaldicott/2014/06/25/why-fords-alan-mulally-is-an-innovation-ceo-for-the-record-books/2/.
4. Ford Motor Company. 2014. 10-K filing.
5. Ford Motor Company. 2009. Ford reports 4th quarter 2008 net loss of $5.9 billion; gained market share in U.S., Europe, achieved cost target. January 29, media.ford.com/images/10031/4Qfinancials.pdf.
6. The Henry Ford Museum. Undated. The innovator and Ford Motor Company. www.thehenryford.org/exhibits/hf/The_Innovator_and_Ford_Motor_Company.asp.
7. http://en.wikipedia.org/wiki/History_of_Ford_Motor_Company.
8. Ford Motor Company. 2014. 10-K filing.
9. www.teslamotors.com/about.
10. Zacks.com. 2014. Should you buy auto industry stocks now? Industry outlook. *Zacks.com,* September 16, www.nasdaq.com/article/should-you-buy-auto-industry-stocks-now-industry-outlook-cm395899#ixzz3T5qvJ5Pm.
11. Maynard, M., & Fackler, M. 2006. Toyota is poised to supplant G.M. as world's largest carmaker. *New York Times,* December 23, www.nytimes.com/2006/12/23/business/worldbusiness/23toyota.html?_r=0.
12. Flint, J. 2006. Ford: Overhaul time—again. *Forbes,* January 23, www.forbes.com/2006/01/23/ford-restructuring-autos-cz_jf_0123flint.html.
13. Ibid.
14. Knowles, F. 2006. Boeing exec flies the coop: Ford hires Mulally to turn things. *Chicago Sun-Times,* September 6.
15. Welch, D., Kiley, D., & Holmes, S. 2006. Alan Mulally: A plan to make Ford fly. *BusinessWeek.*
16. Khurana, Rakesh. 2002. *Searching for the corporate savior: The irrational quest for charismatic CEOs.* Princeton, NJ: Princeton University Press.
17. Berfield, S. 2006. The best leaders. *BusinessWeek Online,* December 18.
18. Kiley, D. 2007. Mulally: Ford's most important new model. *BusinessWeek Online,* January 9, www.businessweek.com.
19. Ford Motor Company Newsroom. Undated. Biography: Alan Mulally. media.ford.com/article_display.cfm?article_id524203.
20. Levin, D. 2006. Mulally's hire by Ford may be too late. Bloomberg.com.
21. Crain, K. 2006. Mulally wants fewer platforms, fewer dealers. *New York Times,* November 20.
22. Ibid.
23. Ibid.
24. Maynard, M. 2006. Ford expects to fall soon to no. 3 spot. *New York Times,* December 21, www.nytimes.com.
25. Ford Motor Company, 2009, op. cit.
26. Stoll, J. 2006. Ford looks to reshape business model, executive says. *Dow Jones Newswires,* September 18.
27. Durbin, D.-A., & Krisher, T. 2011. Ford stock falls after company misses expectations. *Associated Press,* January 28, www.businessweek.com/ap/financialnews/archives/March2011/D9L1JHCO1.htm.
28. LaRocco, L. A. 2014. For Mulally, Ford's culture is job one. *The Street,* March 3, www.thestreet.com/story/1543980/1/for-mulally-fords-culture-is-job-one.html.
29. Bunkley, N., & Maynard, M. 2007. Ford breaks string of losing quarters, but says respite will be brief. *New York Times,* July 27: C3.
30. Durbin & Krisher, op. cit.
31. Maynard. 2007. Ford chief sees small as virtue and necessity. *New York Times,* January 26, www.nytimes.com/2007/01/26/automobiles/26ford.html.
32. Bloomberg News. 2006. Ford reorganizes executives. *New York Times,* December 15.
33. Ibid.
34. Kiley, op. cit.
35. Kiley, D. 2007. The record year Ford hopes to shake off. *BusinessWeek Online,* January 26.
36. Bloomberg News, op. cit.
37. Ford Motor Company. 2013. Annual report. http://corporate.ford.com/annual-report-2012/message-to-the-stockholders-alan-mulally.html.
38. Geier, B. 2015. Ford's profit beats estimates, but its European outlook dims. *Fortune,* January 29, http://fortune.com/2015/01/29/fords-profit-beats-estimates-but-its-european-outlook-dims/.
39. Salerno, C. 2015. What major changes in Ford's management mean. *Seeking Alpha,* January 16, http://seekingalpha.com/article/2825536-what-major-changes-in-fords-management-mean.
40. Praet, N. V. 2008. US$8.7B loss turns Ford. *Financial Post,* July 25.
41. Crowe, P. 2014. Ford Mondeo Hybrid now in EU production. *Hybridcars,* November 28, www.hybridcars.com/ford-mondeo-hybrid-now-in-eu-production/.
42. Eisenstein, P. A. 2013. Ford to launch 23 models, add 5,000 US jobs in 2014. *CNBC,* December 12, www.cnbc.com/id/101269453#.
43. www.motorintelligence.com.
44. Ford Media. 2015. Ford U.S. sales up 15 percent in January; company sees best U.S. January retail sales results since 2004. February 3, https://media.ford.com/content/fordmedia/fna/us/en/news/2015/02/03/january2015sales.html.
45. J.D. Power and Associates. 2010. 2010 U.S. vehicle dependability study. March 18, www.jdpower.com/news/pressrelease.aspx?ID52010034; and 2012. 2012 vehicle dependability study. February 14, www.jdpower.com/content/press-release-auto/Q5wPftR/2012-u-s-vehicle-dependability-study.htm.
46. Canter, A. 2015. The top 28 most reliable automakers in the world: Survey rankings 2014. *CEO WorldBiz,* February 28, http://ceoworld.biz/2014/11/03/top-28-reliable-automakers-world-survey-rankings-2014.
47. Ford Motor Company, op. cit.
48. Ford Motor Company. 2008. Ford accelerates transformation plan. media.ford.com/article_display.cfm?article_id528660.
49. Hirsh, E., Kakkar, A., Singh, A., & Wilk, R. 2015. 2015 auto industry trends. *Strategy+business,* January, www.strategyand.pwc.com/perspectives/2015-auto-trends.
50. Ma, J., & Trudell, C. 2014. Air-bag crisis seen spurring shift from Japan's Takata. *BloombergBusiness,* October 24, www.bloomberg.com/news/articles/2014-10-23/air-bag-crisis-seen-spurring-shift-from-japan-s-takata.

51. Shepardson, D. 2014. New Ford recall to cost $500M, stock falls 7.5%. *Detroit News,* September 29, *www.detroitnews.com/story/business/autos/ford/2014/09/29/ford-recall-will-cost-million/16441255/.*
52. Ramsey, M., & Stoll, J. D. 2014. Ford sharply cuts full-year forecast. *Wall Street Journal,* September 29, *www.wsj.com/articles/fords-next-super-duty-pickup-to-be-aluminum-1412015106.*
53. Bunkley, N. 2014. Ford sets goal of 9.4M global sales by 2020, cuts profit outlook for '14. *Automotive News,* September 29, *www.autonews.com/article/20140929/RETAIL01/140929873/ford-sets-goal-of-9.4m-global-sales-by-2020-cuts-profit-outlook-for-14.*
54. Zahid, M. 2014. Ford's future in the world's largest economy. *Seeking Alpha,* December 3, *http://seekingalpha.com/article/2727035-fords-future-in-the-worlds-largest-economy.*
55. Salerno, C. 2015. What major changes in Ford's management mean. *Seeking Alpha,* January 16, *http://seekingalpha.com/article/2825536-what-major-changes-in-fords-management-mean.*
56. Ford Media. 2015. Ford opens new Silicon Valley research center to drive innovation in connectivity, mobility, autonomous vehicles. January 22, *https://media.ford.com/content/fordmedia/fna/us/en/news/2015/01/22/research-and-innovation-center-palo-alto.html.*
57. Hirsh, Kakkar, Singh, & Wilk, op. cit.
58. Anonymous. 2015. Apple entering the car sector? Why this could be its next "large numbers" move. *Seeking Alpha,* February 19, *http://seekingalpha.com/article/2932216-apple-entering-the-car-sector-why-this-could-be-its-next-large-numbers-move?auth_param=70583:1aecem7:c9db1ed4a42260643e3494528dcf5b94&uprof=14.*
59. Caldicott, op. cit.
60. Naughton, K. 2014. Ford's new CEO Fields faces challenges at company on roll. *BloombergBusiness,* May 2, *www.bloomberg.com/news/articles/2014-05-01/ford-names-fields-ceo-effective-july-1-saying-mulally-to-retire.*
61. Ford Motor Company. 2014. 10-K filing.

CASES

CASE 34

EMIRATES AIRLINE*

Emirates Airline was one of the three Middle East carriers that were singled out by the largest U.S. airlines in a report that was released on March 5, 2015. The report charged that the flagship airline of Dubai, along with Etihad Airways and Qatar Airways, had received over $42 billion in government subsidies and tax breaks since 2004. Claiming that this gave an unfair advantage to these state-owned airlines, the U.S. airlines demanded that the "open skies" treaties that had allowed these three airlines—Emirates, Etihad, and Qatar—access to the United States should be renegotiated in order to curtail their further expansion into the country.

No airline had grown like Emirates, which in the three decades since its birth could be crowned as the freewheeling sultan of the skies. By assembling the largest fleet of Airbus A380 super jumbos and Boeing 777 long-range jets, the airline had already become one of the leading transporters of passengers on international routes around the world (see Exhibit 1). The U.S. carriers were worried that they would meet the fate of the European carriers, whose market share had declined by double digits on routes where they competed with Emirates.

In particular, Emirates, along with newer upstarts Qatar and Etihad Airways, had managed over the years to radically redraw the map of the world, transferring the hub of

---

* Case prepared by Jamal Shamsie, Michigan State University, with the assistance of Professor Alan B. Eisner, Pace University. Material has been drawn from published sources to be used for purposes of class discussion. Copyright © 2015 Jamal Shamsie and Alan B. Eisner.

EXHIBIT 1 Top Global Airlines

There are several rankings of the world's airlines, but a few carriers have consistently been rated highest in service over the past five years. These airlines are listed below in no particular order.

	Started	Main Hub	Fleet	Destinations
Singapore	1972	Singapore	108	63
Cathay Pacific	1946	Hong Kong	161	102
Emirates	1985	Dubai	221	142
Thai	1960	Bangkok	91	78
Asiana	1988	Seoul	85	108
Etihad	2003	Abu Dhabi	102	109
EVA	1989	Taipei	68	73
Air New Zealand	1940	Auckland	106	58
Garuda	1949	Jakarta	119	102
Qatar	1994	Doha	146	146
ANA	1952	Tokyo	211	73
South African	1934	Johannesburg	60	42
Virgin Atlantic	1984	London	40	30
Qantas	1920	Sydney	118	42
Lufthansa	1953	Frankfurt	273	190

Source: Wikipedia, Skytrax.

international travel from Europe to the Middle East. Dubai, the hub of Emirates, currently handling 75 million passengers each year, became the world's busiest airport for international passengers. A new terminal, the largest in the world, was recently built at a cost of $4.5 billion just to accommodate the 224 Emirates aircraft that flew out to 145 destinations around the world.

Emirates claimed that it had worked hard to achieve its leading position by offering onboard amenities, like bars and showers on its aircraft, which other carriers find frivolous (see Exhibit 2). Beyond this, it pointed to the high standards of service from its crew on its flights. Emirates had built an elite force of 18,000 flight attendants who represented 140 nationalities and spoke more than 50 languages. They were selected from thousands who regularly lined up at Open Days, held in more than 140 cities in 70 countries, just to have a shot at becoming part of an iconic brand that was uniting people and places around the world.

Sir Tim Clark, the president of Emirates Airline, responded to the charges in the report by insisting that his carrier had never received government subsidies or obtained free or cheap fuel. The airline had always disclosed its finances, used international auditors, and posted regular quarterly profits. In fact, according to its financial statements, Emirates had shown profits for the last 27 years. In 2014, the airline generated these profits by carrying over 45 million passengers, ranking it behind only five U.S. and European carriers (see Exhibits 3–5). "We are confident that any allegation that Emirates has been subsidized is totally without grounds," Clark declared.[1]

Launching a Dream

The roots of Emirates can be traced back to Gulf Air, which was a formidable airline owned by the governments of Bahrain, Abu Dhabi, Qatar, and Oman. In the early 1980s,

EXHIBIT 2 Service for Premium Passengers on Emirates A380

- Offer 1,600 channels of in-seat entertainment
- Serve Cuvee Dom Pérignon 2000 champagne
- Serve Iranian caviar
- Serve gourmet cuisine prepared by chefs of 47 nationalities
- Offer largest selection of premium wines
- Use bone china by Royal Doulton
- Use specially made cutlery by British design house Robert Welch
- Provide Bulgari-designed amenity kits
- Feature a stand-up bar
- Offer two on-board walnut and marble design showers*

* Only for first-class passengers.

Source: Emirates.

EXHIBIT 3 Income Statement (United Arab Emirates Dirham)

	Year Ended March 31	
	2015	2014
Revenue	86,728	80,717
Other operating income	2,091	1,919
Operating costs	(82,926)	(78,376)
Operating profit	**5,893**	**4,260**
Finance income	175	247
Finance costs	(1,449)	(1,179)
Share of results of investments accounted for using the equity method	152	136
Profit before income tax	**4,771**	**3,464**
Income tax expense	(43)	(47)
Profit for the year	**4,728**	**3,417**
Profit attributable to non-controlling interests	173	163
Profit attributable to Emirates' Owner	**4,555**	**3,254**

Source: Emirates.

EXHIBIT 4 Balance Sheet (United Arab Emirates Dirham)

	Year Ended March 31	
	2015	2014
ASSETS		
Non-current assets		
Property, plant and equipment	80,544	71,582
Intangible assets	975	928
Investments accounted for using the equity method	544	495
Advance lease rentals	920	812
Loans and other receivables	619	428
Derivative financial instruments	21	5
Deferred income tax asset	4	—
Current assets	**83,627**	**74,250**
Inventories	1,919	1,706
Trade and other receivables	8,589	9,086
Derivative financial instruments	342	1
Short term bank deposits	8,488	8,754
Cash and cash equivalents	8,397	7,807
	27,735	27,354
Total assets	**111,362**	**101,604**
EQUITY AND LIABILITIES		
Capital and reserves		
Capital	801	801
Other reserves	(168)	(634)
Retained earnings	27,253	25,009
Attributable to Emirates' Owner	**27,886**	**25,176**
Non-controlling interests	**400**	**295**
Total equity	**28,286**	**25,471**
Non-current liabilities		
Trade and other payables	202	287
Borrowings and lease liabilities	42,426	38,500
Deferred revenue	1,650	1,440
Deferred credits	207	234

| | Year Ended March 31 | |
	2015	2014
Derivative financial instruments	521	599
Provisions	3,589	2,643
Deferred income tax liability	—	2
Current liabilities	**48,595**	**43,705**
Trade and other payables	27,770	27,079
Income tax liabilities	34	30
Borrowings and lease liabilities	5,382	3,931
Deferred revenue	1,244	1,227
Deferred credits	49	66
Derivative financial instruments	2	95
	34,481	32,428
Total liabilities	**83,076**	**76,133**
Total equity and liabilities	**111,362**	**101,604**

Source: Emirates.

EXHIBIT 5 Cash Flow Statement (United Arab Emirates Dirham)

| | Year Ended March 31 | |
	2015	2014
Operating activities		
Profit before income tax	4,771	3,464
Adjustments for:		
Depreciation and amortisation	7,446	6,421
Finance costs - net	1,274	932
(Gain) / loss on sale of property, plant and equipment	(132)	26
Share of results of investments accounted for using the equity method	(152)	(136)
Net provision for impairment of trade receivables	32	5
Provision for employee benefits	669	616
Net movement on derivative financial instruments	(17)	9

continued

EXHIBIT 5 *Continued*

	Year Ended March 31	
	2015	2014
Employee benefit payments	(534)	(485)
Income tax paid	(68)	(49)
Change in inventories	(213)	(142)
Change in receivables and advance lease rentals	194	(314)
Change in provisions, payables, deferred credits and revenue	(5)	2,302
Net cash generated from operating activities	**13,265**	**12,649**
Investing activities		
Proceeds from sale of property, plant and equipment	3,478	78
Additions to intangible assets	(157)	(105)
Additions to property, plant and equipment	(10,269)	(13,958)
Investments in associates and joint ventures	(13)	(7)
Movement in short term bank deposits	266	9,294
Finance income	169	308
Dividends from investments accounted for using the equity method	115	133
Net cash used in investing activities	**(6,411)**	**(4,257)**
Financing activities		
Proceeds from loans	2,215	—
Repayment of bonds and loans	(622)	(2,530)
Aircraft financing costs	(951)	(790)
Other finance charges	(341)	(271)
Repayment of lease liabilities	(5,628)	(2,652)
Dividend paid to Emirates' Owner	(869)	(726)
Dividend paid to non-controlling interests	(68)	(138)
Net cash used in financing activities	**(6,264)**	**(7,107)**
Net change in cash and cash equivalents	**590**	**1,285**
Cash and cash equivalents at beginning of year	7,800	6,520
Effects of exchange rate changes	3	(5)
Cash and cash equivalents at end of year	**8,393**	**7,800**

Source: Emirates.

the young sheikh of Dubai, Sheikh Mohammed bin Rashid al Maktoum, was upset by the decision of Gulf Air to cut flights into and out of Dubai. He responded by resolving to start his own airline that would help build Dubai into a center of business and tourism, given the emirates' lack of significant oil resources.

The sheikh recruited British Airways veteran Sir Maurice Flanagan to lay the groundwork for the new airline, which he bankrolled with $10 million in royal funding. He placed a member of his royal family, Sheikh Ahmed bin Saeed al Maktoum, in the top post. Ahmed bin Saeed, just 26 years old, had just graduated from the University of Denver in the U.S. Since he had not held a job before, the young sheikh looked to Flanagan in order to figure out how to run the airline.

However, the spectacular growth of Emirates can be attributed to Sir Tim Clark, who was handed the critical task of route planning. He recognized that about two-thirds of the world's population was within eight hours of Dubai, but the firm lacked the aircraft to take advantage of its location. This began to change with the arrival of more advanced aircraft, beginning with the introduction of the Boeing 777 in 1996 and then the Airbus A380 in 2008. The long range of these aircraft allowed Emirates to develop routes that could link any two points in the world with one stop in Dubai.

From serving 12 destinations in 1988, Emirates expanded at an alarming rate, particularly after 1996, when it started adding Boeing 777s to its fleet. The carrier continued to grow even through the recession that began in 2008, taking possession of more new aircraft than any other competitor. "We operated normally. We put on more aircraft. We carried more passengers," said Mohammed H. Mattar, senior vice president of the carrier's airport services.[2]

Providing the Ultimate Experience

Emirates strived to provide the best possible experience to its passengers in all sections of its aircraft. It was the first airline to offer in-flight television viewing on the back of every seat. "That seems pretty normal for long haul airlines now, but it wasn't then," said Terry Daly, who was in charge of service at the carrier.[3] Flight attendants, who were fluent in a dozen languages, passed up and down the aisles, providing service with a smile. Daly, who maintained the highest standards for all in-flight services, was known for once having fired eight service supervisors on a single day when he discovered that the flight attendants they supervised had deviated from his precise instructions on how to respond to requests from passengers.

From its start, Emirates was known for the quality and selection of food that the airline provided, even to passengers in the back of the aircraft. The catering division was the world's biggest—a multifloor maze of monorails, cameras, vast stocks of wines and liquors, multinational chefs slaving over steaming pans, kettles, and grills stretching into eternity, and the latest in robotics. The division delivered 115,000 meal trays to Emirates planes each day. "It's about making sure the culinary offering is absolutely first class across the airplane," said Daly.[4]

But Emirates always tried to push further and further on the service and amenities that it provided to its premium-class passengers. Included with a business-class ticket were limousine rides to and from the airport, personal assistance with the check-in process, and use of one of the airline's 30 worldwide lounges. One of 600 multinational and multilingual members of a welcome team called *Marhaba*, Arabic for "welcome," helps all first- and business-class passengers clear all formalities upon departure and upon arrival.

Over the years, as Emirates moved to larger and larger aircraft, it found ways to enhance the experience of its premium passengers during flight. The airline had pioneered the concept of a suite in first class with its launch of A340 aircraft in 2003. With the addition of the A380, the world's biggest jetliner (it had 50—more than any other competitor), Emirates was able to offer 14 first-class suites, each with a vanity table, closet, 23-inch TV screen, and electronic doors that sealed shut for total seclusion.

First-class passengers also had access to two enormous spa showers, a first in the industry. An event planner who flew first class said, "To walk onto the A380, to have an average size bathroom, a seven minute shower, full size bath towels and your own attendant is pretty amazing."[5] All premium-class passengers—both in first and business class—had access to a big, circular lounge, with a horseshoe-shaped stand-up bar in the center, for which Emirates forfeited a number of business-class seats.

Grooming a Special Employee

Emirates created a state-of-the-art facility to train its employees, from those who check in passengers to those who serve them on its planes. The exterior of the training facility resembled the fuselage of a jetliner. Inside, everyone paid particular attention to the flight attendants, who had to make sure that everyone on the aircraft received the highest level of service on every single flight. This was particularly important for a carrier whose flights were of long duration because it served destinations across all continents.

Catherine Baird was in charge of training the airline's new recruits, who constituted only about 5 percent of the applications received by Emirates. The low acceptance rate pushes people with diverse backgrounds to compete in an *American Idol*–style brains-and-beauty contest for a chance to travel around the world as an Emirates cabin crew member. According to a recent report, the crew had an average age of 26 years, compared to over 40 at U.S. airlines, and was 75 percent women. Their weight was carefully monitored, their makeup was mandatorily reapplied regularly, and unwed pregnancy was not allowed.

The airline offered a vast, no-expenses-spared crew training program, in which, for seven weeks, each new recruit moved through different departments with specialists in different areas. By the end of their training, the newcomers had been instructed in aspects of posture, etiquette, safety, and evacuation. There were strict standards for the color of the lipstick, the shade of the hair, and even the style of the lingerie. Everything had to go well with the pinstripe khaki uniform, the color of sand, with white scarves billowing like exotic sails. Women had to adhere to certain hairstyles that the crowning blood-red hat would work with. "When walking through an airport terminal, it's usually a *Catch Me If You Can* movie moment, with passengers all turning their heads," said one of the new recruits.[6]

As with everything else, Emirates went over the top in what it called *Nujoum,* the Arabic word for "stars," by including motivational team-building exercises in its training program. Travel writer Christine Negroni, who participated in one of these exercises, described the experience that the new recruits typically went through: "It is a combination of a customer service experience and a come-to-Jesus rally, highly produced like a Hollywood spectacular. If you had told me that Disney produced it, I wouldn't doubt it. By the end of the day, they are whipped into a frenzy of feeling *'What can I do for Emirates?'*"[7]

Communicating to the Masses

In spite of the extra touches that Emirates provided to its passengers, the carrier discovered, from focus groups it conducted, that its name was not well known in many parts of the world that it was expanding to. Emirates realized it needed to create a message that it could use to develop its brand among consumers and inform them what to expect from Emirates. This message could also be used to inspire existing and potential employees to rally behind the airline and work to deliver on its promise.

In its usual style of pushing for the best, Emirates summoned the world's top 10 advertising agencies to Dubai to compete for a massive international advertising campaign. StrawberryFrog, an advertising agency that had recently started operations in New York City, was one of the firms vying for the contract with the rapidly growing carrier. Its founder, Scott Goodson, had read an interview with Sir Tim Clark, the president of Emirates, shortly before the gathering of advertising agencies. "And in that article, he was talking about his vision, that he wanted Emirates to be a global company and wanted to make the world a smaller place by bringing people together," said Goodson.[8]

These comments inspired Goodson to come up with the idea of "Hello Tomorrow," which allowed his firm to clinch the contract with Emirates. These words became not just the idea for an ad campaign but for a new way to think about an airline. Through the use of powerful storytelling, words, images, music, and film, this message portrayed Emirates not just as a carrier that delivered a superior experience but as a catalyst for connecting a new global culture of shared aspirations, values, enthusiasm, and dreams.

Immediately afterward, the StrawberryFrog team spent 18 months at Emirates headquarters educating employees, making them foot soldiers in this campaign. In the early spring of 2012, the "Hello Tomorrow" brand was launched, a universal message in myriad languages in 150 countries. In television ads, an Emirates flight attendant pushed his drink cart as a mammoth A380 airplane seemed to be literally built around him, its various parts and personnel coming from countries spanning the globe, providing proof that the airline was truly a global enterprise.

Chasing Tomorrow?

Even as Emirates was trying to set itself apart from other carriers by enhancing the customer experience, it was facing new challenges. Many of its competitors were also trying to improve on their offerings, particularly for the passengers who were willing to pay a little more. Airlines were fighting with each other to attract this more upscale segment as the higher fare allowed them to increase their profits without having to add capacity. A few carriers, for example, were adding nanny services to some of their flights by providing staff who would entertain and engage children, particularly on long-range flights, so that parents could get a much needed break.

Another trend was the addition of a premium economy section that gave passengers in the back of the plane a little more leg space. Singapore Airlines was planning to beat all other competitors by providing a truly enhanced premium economy section. It would feature wider seats that reclined more, a cocktail table, more storage space, and a sleek 13.3-inch high-definition screen, the largest in its class. Passengers would be offered state-of-the-art noise canceling headsets to watch hundreds of channels of entertainment. Finally, they would have more options on a menu that was to be designed specifically for the premium economy class.

However, Emirates recently faced its biggest challenge when its UAE-based rival, Etihad, announced an improvement to the first-class suite that Emirates had pioneered 12 years earlier. Etihad introduced, with grand bravado, a three-room, $21,000 one-way "Residence" and nine $16,000 one-way, one-room "First Apartments," complete with Savoy Academy–trained butlers and private chefs, on its A380 flights. First offered on flights between Dubai and London, the carrier planned to expand these options to its flights between Dubai and New York and Dubai and Sydney.

Some industry analysts questioned the ability of Emirates to deal with these growing challenges. Joe Brancatelli, a business travel writer, recently stated: "I could make the case that Emirates moment has passed. Emirates was the trendy airline three or four years ago."[9] In a recent meeting to announce the latest performance figures for the airline, Emirates chairman and CEO His Highness Sheikh Ahmed bin Saeed al Maktoum brushed away these concerns. "Over the years, we have always managed to come up with new products," he responded to any concerns that were raised.[10]

ENDNOTES

1. Susan Carey. U.S. carriers claim unfair practices. *Wall Street Journal*, March 6, 2015, p. B3.
2. Mark Seal. Fly me to the moon . . . with a stop in Dubai. *Departures.com.*, Summer 2014, p. 276.
3. Ibid., p. 277.
4. Ibid.
5. Ibid., p. 278.
6. Ibid., p. 277.
7. Ibid., p. 310.
8. Ibid., p. 278.
9. Ibid., p. 275.
10. Ibid.

CASE 35

CIRQUE DU SOLEIL*

The founder of Cirque du Soleil, Guy Laliberté, after seeing the firm's growth prospects wane in recent years, was thinking about expanding his firm in new directions. For three decades, the firm had reinvented and revolutionized the circus. From its beginning in 1984, Cirque de Soleil had thrilled over 150 million spectators with a novel show concept that was as original as it was nontraditional: an astonishing theatrical blend of circus acts and street entertainment, wrapped up in spectacular costumes and fairyland sets and staged to spellbinding music and magical lighting.

Cirque du Soleil's business triumphs mirrored its high-flying aerial stunts, and it became a case study for business school journal articles on carving out unique markets. But following a recent bleak outlook report from a consultant, a spate of poorly received shows over the last few years, and a decline in profits, executives at Cirque said they were now restructuring and refocusing the business—shifting some of the attention away from the firm's string of successful shows and toward several other potential business ventures.

Cirque du Soleil had also suffered other setbacks. Plans for a new show that would have been based in Dubai fell through after the city had financial problems that stemmed from the 2008 recession. Cirque also recently suffered its first death during a performance, when an acrobat tumbled 94 feet during a stunt in a Las Vegas performance of the show *Ka* in 2013. After a hiatus of more than a year, Cirque brought a revamped version of the stunt back to the show with more stringent safety measures. "The recent struggles," said Chief Executive Daniel Lamarre, "certainly brought a lot of humility to the organization."[1]

For the first time in recent history, Cirque du Soleil failed to generate a profit in 2013. Its market had dropped 20 percent from $2.7 billion in 2008. In recent interviews with *The Wall Street Journal* at Cirque du Soleil's sleek headquarters in Montreal, top executives, including founder and 90 percent owner Guy Laliberté, revealed rare details of the firm's financial status and new business plans. The company was seeking to position itself as an attractive bet as Laliberté began to look for investors to buy a significant portion.

Debate swirled over whether Cirque du Soleil should return to its roots or aim for constant reinvention. At the end of 2011, Bain & Co., contracted by Cirque, reported that Cirque's market had hit saturation and the company needed to be careful about how many new shows it should add. Bain suggested Cirque seek growth by moving its concept to movies, television, and nightclubs. "Guy Laliberté always said we are a rarity—but the rarity was gone," said Marc Gagnon, a former top executive in charge of operations for Cirque du Soleil, who left in 2012.[2]

Starting a New Concept

Cirque du Soleil developed out of early efforts of Guy Laliberté, who left his Montreal home at the age of 14 with little more than an accordion. He traveled around, trying out different acts such as fire-eating for spare change in front of Centre Pompidou in Paris. When he returned home, he hooked up with another visionary street performer from Quebec, a stilt-walker named Gilles Ste-Croix. In 1982, Laliberté and Ste-Croix organized a street performance festival in the sleepy town of Baie St. Paul along the St. Lawrence valley.

By 1984, Cirque du Soleil was formed with financial support from the government of Quebec as banks were reluctant to support the band of fire-eaters, stilt-walkers, and clowns. Its breakthrough 1987 show *We Reinvent the Circus* burst on the art scene in Montreal as an entirely new art form. No one had seen anything like it before. Laliberté and Ste-Croix had turned the whole concept of circus on its head. Using story lines, identifiable characters, and an emotional arc, Cirque du Soleil embodied more than a mere collection of disparate acts and feats.

Despite its early success, Cirque du Soleil was struggling financially. It took a gamble on making its debut in the United States as the opening act of the 1987 Los Angeles Festival. Cirque managed to sell out all of its performances, which were run in a tent on a lot adjacent to downtown's Little Tokyo. Its success in Los Angeles led the troupe to open shows across the U.S. in cities such as Washington, San Francisco, Miami, and Chicago. Soon afterward, Cirque du Soleil performed in Japan and Switzerland, introducing its concept to audiences outside North America.

In 1992, Cirque du Soleil took a show called *Nouvelle Experience* to Las Vegas for the first time. It was performed under the big top in the parking lot of the Mirage. The success of this show led to the building of a permanent theater at Treasure Island for a show called *Mystère*,

---

* Case prepared by Jamal Shamsie, Michigan State University, with the assistance of Professor Alan B. Eisner, Pace University. Material has been drawn from published sources to be used for purposes of class discussion. Copyright © 2015 Jamal Shamsie and Alan B. Eisner.

a nonstop perpetual-motion kaleidoscope of athleticism and raw emotion that thrilled audiences. It became the first of the troupe's permanent shows and led to several others that opened in other hotels along the Las Vegas strip. The most spectacular of these was *O,* which included acts that were performed in a 25-foot-deep, 1.5 million–gallon pool of crystal clear water in a custom-built theater at Bellagio.

By the end of 2011, Cirque du Soleil had 22 shows—seven of them in Las Vegas. It had become an international entertainment conglomerate with 4,000 employees working in offices around the world. It had established its headquarters in a $40 million building in Montreal, where all of Cirque's shows were created and produced. Much of the building was devoted to practice studios for various types of performers and to the costume department that outfitted performers in fantastical hand-painted clothes. Cirque du Soleil recruited many types of talent, among them acrobats, athletes, dancers, musicians, clowns, actors, and singers.

Growing with the Concept

Cirque du Soleil hired key people from the National Circus School in its formative years in order to develop its concept of the contemporary circus. Its first recruit was Guy Caron, the head of this school, as the Cirque's artistic director. Shortly afterward, the troupe recruited Franco Dragone, another instructor from the National Circus School, who had been working in Belgium. Dragone brought with him his experience in *commedia dell'arte* techniques, which he imparted to the Cirque performers.

Together, Caron and Dragone were behind the creation of all the Cirque du Soleil shows during the firm's formative years, including *Saltimbanco, Mystère, Alegría, Quidam,* and the extravagant *O.* Under the watchful eye of Laliberté, Cirque developed its unique formula that would define its shows. From the beginning, it promoted the whole show, rather than specific acts or performers. Cirque eliminated spoken dialogue so that its shows would not be culture-bound, using instead strong emotional music that was played from the beginning to the end by musicians. Performers, rather than a technical crew, moved equipment and props on and off the stage to avoid disrupting the momentum as the show transitioned from one act to the next. Most importantly, the idea was to create a circus without a ring or animals, as Laliberté believed that the lack of these two elements would draw the audience more into the performance.

Even though Laliberté and his creative team were clearly innovative in their approach, they were not reluctant to obtain inspiration from outside sources. They drew on the tradition of pantomime and masks from circuses in Europe. They learned about blending presentational, musical, and choreographic elements from the Chinese. Caron readily admitted that Cirque took everything that had existed in the past and pulled it into the present, so that it would strike a chord with present-day audiences.

All of the Cirque du Soleil shows were originally developed to be performed under a Grand Chapiteau, or Big Top, for an extended period of time, before they were modified, if necessary, for touring in arenas and other venues. The troupe's Grand Chapiteau were easily recognizable by their blue and yellow coloring. The facility could seat more than 2,600 spectators and was accompanied by smaller fixtures that were necessary to accommodate practice sessions, food preparation, and administrative services. However, after the contract to develop *Mystère* for Treasure Island in Las Vegas, Cirque began to develop shows that were to be performed on a more permanent basis in specially designed auditoriums.

Losing Its Touch

Cirque du Soleil continued to expand even as the recession cut into demand. It launched 20 shows in the 23 years from 1984 through 2006, none of which closed during that time other than a couple of early ones. Over the next six years, however, it opened 14 more shows, 5 of which flopped and closed early. The reasons for the failures differed. One show, *Zarkana,* couldn't make enough money to cover its production costs playing in New York City's 6,000-seat Radio City Music Hall. *Iris,* in Los Angeles, played in Hollywood, a seedy neighborhood that despite heavy tourist traffic was commercially marginal. *Zaia,* in Macau, simply didn't appeal to local audiences. Perhaps more troubling, the company's nearly perfect record of producing artistic successes began to waver. *Viva Elvis* and *Banana Shpeel* were among several Cirque shows that garnered terrible reviews. Both shows closed quickly. "Shows like that diluted the brand," said Patrick Leroux, a professor at Montreal's Concordia University who had closely studied Cirque du Soleil.[3]

One problem, said Cirque du Soleil executives, was that audiences didn't understand the differences among various shows carrying the Cirque brand. As a result, many people would dismiss the opportunity to see, for instance, the show *Totem* thinking they had already seen something similar in the older *Varekai.* On the other hand, Cirque tried to move in different directions with each of the new shows that it developed. "We're constantly challenging ourselves," Laliberté said.[4] Audiences, however, complained that some newer shows were not as focused on the acrobatic feats that they had come to expect and enjoy from Cirque.

By August 2012, Laliberté was concerned and convened a five-day summit for executives at his estate outside Montreal. There, he and others drew up plans to lay off hundreds of executives and performers and pare the number of big new touring circus shows Cirque produced. The cuts began soon after and continued through 2013 and amounted to around $100 million of savings, according to Laliberté. They included everything from giving out fewer suede anniversary jackets for employees to cutting out child performers and tutors.

Laliberté also reexamined core production costs. The payroll for Cirque's show *O*, in Las Vegas, for instance, had ballooned thanks to a surge in contortionists. "I said, 'Why do we need six contortionists?'" Laliberté, 55, recalled while chain smoking in his office.[5] In addition to the layoffs, Cirque also suffered a blow to morale when acrobat Sarah Guyard-Guillot was killed in 2013 during a performance. The company overhauled the show's finale, a "battle" staged on a vertical wall with performers suspended from motorized wire harnesses. After the performer's death, Cirque continued to stage the show, replacing the live finale with a videotape of the scene from a past performance.

A New Direction?

Cirque du Soleil managed to generate profits out of a business model that was quite challenging. Kenneth Feld, of Ringling Bros. and Barnum and Bailey circus, commented: "If you think about spending $165 million on a show that seats 1,900 people, the economics are just staggering."[6] But Laliberté's stroke of genius was realizing that no Cirque show ever had to close. The troupe could either keep touring or play in locations such as Las Vegas and Orlando that drew a lot of tourists. By keeping as many shows running as possible, the troupe managed to build a repertory of shows that could all be running at the same time (see Exhibit 1).

EXHIBIT 1
Cirque du Soleil Shows

Grand Chapiteau & Arena Shows		Resident Shows	
1990	Nouvelle Experience	1993	Mystère* Treasure Island, Las Vegas
1992	Saltimbanco	1998	O* Bellagio, Las Vegas
1994	Alegría	1998	La Nouba* Downtown Disney, Lake Buena Vista
1996	Quidam*	2003	Zumanity* New York New York, Las Vegas
1999	Dralion	2005	Ka* MGM Grand, Las Vegas
2002	Varekai*	2006	Love* The Mirage, Las Vegas
2005	Corteo*	2008	Zaia The Venetian Macao
2006	Delirium	2008	Zed Tokyo Disney Resort, Tokyo
2007	Kooza*	2008	Criss Angel Believe* Luxor, Las Vegas
2007	Wintuk	2009	Viva Elvis Aria Resort & Casino, Las Vegas
2009	Ovo*	2011	Iris Dolby Theatre, Los Angeles
2009	Banana Shpeel	2013	Michael Jackson: One* Mandalay Bay & Resort, Las Vegas
2010	Totem*	2014	JOYA* Riviera Maya, Mexico
2011	Michael Jackson: The Immortal World Tour		
2012	Amaluna*		
2014	Kurios: Cabinet of Curiosities*		

*Still in performance.

Source: Cirque du Soleil.

However, the rising costs of new shows and the increase in the number of early flops had cut into the firm's revenues and profits. Although revenues dropped to $850 million in 2013 from $1 billion in 2012, Cirque still managed to return to profitability because of stringent cost controls. Chief Executive Daniel Lamarre said the company expected to reduce its revenues from Cirque-branded shows to 60 percent in 5 to 10 years, down from 85 percent now. Already the special-events unit had increased revenue to $37 million from $15 million, said Laliberté.

Laliberté's executive team had come up with a business restructuring plan to manage this diversification through the creation of discrete business units under a central corporate entity to try to beef up the noncircus side of the business. New Cirque subsidiaries included a musical-theater production arm based in New York City and a special-events producer that was beginning to operate under the name 45Degrees Events. Other new areas that Cirque was venturing into included small cabaret shows at hotels, children's television programs, and theme parks. Executives said that currently the company's biggest growth area wasn't a show at all. It was an expanding deal to provide ticketing services to the arena company AEG.

Yet circus experts said Cirque du Soleil was walking a fine line as it sought to expand into new ventures without damaging its central brand as a creative entity. But Laliberté was convinced that Cirque could apply its unique talents to other businesses. "We'll be more about intelligent analysis of each project," he remarked to critics who questioned the new direction.[7] For Laliberté, the stakes were high. He was seeking to sell 20 to 30 percent of the company to outside investors by emphasizing the more disciplined company structure and growth plan. The additional funding would help Laliberté to keep taking on new and different challenges.

ENDNOTES

1. Alexandra Berzon. Cirque's next act: Rebalancing the business. *Wall Street Journal*, December 2, 2014, p. B1.
2. Ibid., p. B4.
3. Ibid.
4. Christopher Palmeri. The $600 million circus maximus. *Business Week*, December 13, 2004, p. 82.
5. Berzon, op. cit., p. B4.
6. Palmeri, op. cit.
7. Berzon, op. cit., p. B 4.

CASES

CASE 36

PIXAR*

After delaying the release of *The Good Dinosaur,* leaving Pixar without an offering during 2014, everyone at Pixar was looking forward to the release of two films during 2015. *Inside Out,* about the emotions that live inside the mind of a young girl, was due out in June. It was to be followed in November by *The Good Dinosaur,* about a world in which dinosaurs never became extinct. Assuming that both films would perform well, Pixar could have a memorable year. "We put our hearts into these films," said John Lasseter, the company's chief creative officer.[1]

Since Pixar launched *Toy Story* in 1995, it had released 14 films, each of which debuted at the top of the box office charts (see Exhibit 1). Its films also received critical acclaim, with nine nominations and seven wins for Best Animated Film. This was far more awards than any other studio had received since the category was added in 2001. However, despite the commercial success of *Cars 2* and *Monsters University,* these recent films did not generate the rave reviews that had been accorded to all of Pixar's earlier offerings. This led many industry observers to question whether Pixar had lost some of its creativity since it became part of the Walt Disney Company.

Disney had acquired Pixar in 2006 for the hefty sum of $7.4 billon. The deal was finalized by the late Steve Jobs, Apple Computer's chief executive, who also served as the head of the computer animation firm. Disney CEO Bob Iger had worked hard to eventually acquire Pixar, whose track record made it one of the world's most successful animation companies. Both Jobs and Iger were aware, however, that they

---

* Case prepared by Jamal Shamsie, Michigan State University, with the assistance of Professor Alan B. Eisner, Pace University. Material has been drawn from published sources to be used for purposes of class discussion. Copyright © 2015 Jamal Shamsie and Alan B. Eisner.

EXHIBIT 1
Pixar Films

All of Pixar's films released to date have ended up among the top animated films of all time based on worldwide box office revenues in millions of U.S. dollars.

Rank	Title	Year	Revenue
1	Toy Story 3	2010	$1,065
2	Finding Nemo	2003	940
3	Monsters University	2013	745
4	Up	2009	735
5	The Incredibles	2005	630
6	Ratatouille	2007	620
7	Monsters, Inc.	2002	575
8	Cars 2	2011	560
9	Brave	2012	555
10	Wall-E	2009	535
11	Toy Story 2	1999	515
12	Cars	2006	460
13	A Bug's Life	1998	365
14	Toy Story	1995	390

Source: IMDB, Variety.

had to try to protect Pixar's creative culture while they also tried to carry some of it over to Disney's animation efforts.

In fact, it was these pressures to maintain its past success that led Pixar to delay the release of *The Good Dinosaur.* The firm pulled the film away from its director as it began to search for new ways to rework the story. Pixar had done this before, and the firm insisted that rethinking an animated film was not uncommon, especially when working with fresh, untested ideas. Given that animated films could take up to three years to complete, story changes could occur in the middle of production. This could require that someone else take the lead in order to complete the film.

Ed Catmull, president of Pixar, reiterated his firm's commitment to take whatever steps might be necessary to put out the best possible film. "Nobody ever remembers the fact that you slipped a film, but they will remember a bad film," he said.[2] Catmull's remarks indicated that Pixar was dedicated to having its lengthy process of playfully crafting a film replace the standard production line approach that had been pursued by Disney. This contrast in culture was best reflected in the Oscars that the employees at Pixar displayed proudly but which had been painstakingly dressed in Barbie doll clothing.

Pushing for Computer Animated Films

The roots of Pixar stretched back to 1975 with the founding of a vocational school in Old Westbury, New York, called the New York Institute of Technology. It was there that Edwin E. Catmull, a straitlaced Mormon from Salt Lake City who loved animation but couldn't draw, teamed up with the people who would later form the core of Pixar. "It was artists and technologists from the very start," recalled Alvy Ray Smith, who worked with Catmull during those years. "It was like a fairy tale."[3]

By 1979, Catmull and his team decided to join forces with famous Hollywood director George W. Lucas, Jr. They were hopeful that doing so would allow them to pursue their dream of making animated films. As part of Lucas's filmmaking facility in San Rafael, California, Catmull's group of aspiring animators was able to make substantial progress in the art of computer animation. But the unit was not able to generate any profits, and Lucas was not willing to let it grow beyond using computer animation for special effects.

Catmull finally turned, in 1985, to Jobs, who had just been ousted from Apple. Jobs was reluctant to invest in a firm that wanted to make full-length feature films using computer animation. But a year later, Jobs did decide to buy Catmull's unit for just $10 million, which was one-third of Lucas's asking price. While the newly named Pixar Animation Studios tried to push the boundaries of computer animation over the next five years, Jobs ended up having to invest an additional $50 million—more than 25 percent of his total wealth at the time. "There were times that we all despaired, but fortunately not all at the same time," said Jobs.[4]

Still, Catmull's team continued to make substantial breakthroughs in the development of computer-generated full-length feature films (see Exhibit 2). In 1991, Disney ended up giving Pixar a three-film contract that started with *Toy Story.* When the movie was finally released in 1995, its success surprised everyone in the film industry. Rather than the nice little film Disney had expected, *Toy Story* became the sensation of 1995. It rose to the rank of third-highest-grossing animated film of all time, earning $362 million in worldwide box office revenues.

Within days, Jobs decided to take Pixar public. When the shares, priced at $22, shot past $33, Jobs called his best friend, Oracle CEO Lawrence J. Ellison, to tell him he had company in the billionaires' club. With Pixar's sudden success, Jobs returned to strike a new deal with Disney. Early in 1996, at a lunch with Walt Disney chief Michael D. Eisner, Jobs made his demands: an equal share of the profits, equal billing on merchandise and on-screen credits, and guarantees that Disney would market Pixar films as it did its own.

Boosting the Creative Component

With the success of *Toy Story,* Jobs realized that he had hit something big. He had obviously tapped into his Silicon Valley roots and turned to computers to forge a unique style of creative moviemaking. In each of its subsequent films, Pixar continued to develop computer animation that allowed for more lifelike backgrounds, texture, and movement than ever before. For example, since real leaves are translucent, Pixar's engineers developed special software algorithms that both reflected and absorbed light, creating luminous scenes among jungles of clover.

In spite of the significance of these advancements in computer animation, Jobs was well aware that successful feature films would require a strong creative spark. He understood that it would be the marriage of technology and creativity that would allow Pixar to rise above most of its competition. To achieve that, Jobs fostered a campus-like environment within the newly formed outfit similar to the freewheeling, charged atmosphere in the early days of his beloved Apple, to which he returned as acting CEO. "It's not simply the technology that makes Pixar," said Dick Cook, former president of Walt Disney studios.[5]

Even though Jobs played a crucial supportive role, it was Catmull who was mainly responsible for ensuring that the firm's technological achievements helped to pump up the firm's creative efforts. He was the keeper of the company's unique innovative culture, which blended Silicon Valley techies, Hollywood production honchos, and artsy animation experts. In the pursuit of Catmull's vision, this eclectic group transformed their office cubicles into tiki huts, circus tents, and cardboard castles with bookshelves stuffed with toys and desks adorned with colorful iMac computers.

One of Catmull's biggest achievements was the creation of what was called the Pixar Braintrust (see Exhibit 3). This creative group of employees, which included directors, met on a regular basis to assess each movie that the

EXHIBIT 2 Milestones

Year	Event
1986	Steve Jobs buys Lucas's computer group and christens it Pixar. The firm completes a short film, *Luxo Jr.*, which is nominated for an Oscar.
1988	Pixar adds computer-animated ads to its repertoire, making spots for Listerine, Lifesavers, and Tropicana. Another short, *Tin Toy*, wins an Oscar.
1991	Pixar signs a production agreement with Disney. Disney is to invest $26 million; Pixar is to deliver at least three full-length, computer-animated feature films.
1995	Pixar releases *Toy Story*, the first fully digital feature film, which becomes the top-grossing movie of the year and wins an Oscar. A week after release, the company goes public.
1997	Pixar and Disney negotiate a new agreement: a 50-50 split of the development costs and profits of five feature-length movies. Short *Geri's Game* wins an Oscar.
1998–99	*A Bug's Life* and *Toy Story 2* are released, together pulling in $1.3 billion through box office and video.
2001–04	A string of hits from Pixar: *Monsters, Inc., Finding Nemo,* and *The Incredibles.*
2006	Disney acquires Pixar and assigns responsibilities for its own animation unit to Pixar's creative brass. *Cars* is released and becomes another box office hit.
2009	*Wall-E* becomes the fourth film from Pixar to receive the Oscar for a feature-length animated film.
2011	*Toy Story 3* receives five Oscar nominations and wins two, including one for Best Animated Film.
2011	Steve Jobs dies, leaving Ed Catmull in charge.
2013	*Brave* becomes the sixth film from Pixar to receive an Oscar for Best Animated Film.

Source: Pixar.

EXHIBIT 3 Sample of Roles

Ed Catmull	President, producer
John Lasseter	Chief creative officer, producer, director, writer
Jim Morris	Business manager
Brad Bird	Director, writer
Pete Doctor	Director, writer
Harley Jessup	Production designer
Bill Cone	Production designer
Ricky Nierva	Production designer, art director, character designer
Ralph Eggleston	Art director
Randy Barrett	Character designer, set designer, matte painter
Tia Kratter	Shading art director, digital painter
Bob Pauley	Character designer, sketch artist
Jay Shuster	Character and environment designer

Source: Pixar.

firm was developing and offer their ideas for improvement. It was this emphasis on creativity that kept Pixar on the cutting edge. Each of its films was innovative in many respects and made the best possible use of computer animation. "They're absolute geniuses," gushed Jules Roman, cofounder and CEO of rival Tippett Studio. "They're the people who created computer animation really."[6]

Catmull was also working hard to build upon this pursuit of creative innovation by creating programs to develop the employees. Employees were encouraged to devote up to four hours a week, every week, to further their education at Pixar University. The in-house training program offered 110 different courses covering subjects such as live improvisation, creative writing, painting, drawing, sculpting, and cinematography. For many years, the school's dean was Randall E. Nelson, a former juggler, who had been known to perform his act using chain saws so students in animation classes had something compelling to draw.

Becoming Accomplished Storytellers

A considerable part of the creative energy went into story development. Jobs understood that a film would work only if its story could move the hearts and minds of families around the world. His goal was to develop Pixar into an animated movie studio that was known for the quality of its storytelling above everything else. "We want to create some great stories and characters that endure with each generation," Jobs stated.[7]

For story development, Pixar relied heavily on 43-year-old John Lasseter, who went by the title of vice president of the creative. Known for his collection of 358 Hawaiian shirts and his irrepressible playfulness with toys, Lasseter was the key to the appeal of all of Pixar's films. Lasseter was very passionate about developing great stories and then harnessing computers to tell these stories. Most of Pixar's employees believed it was this passion that allowed the studio to ensure that each of its films was a commercial hit. In fact, Lasseter was regarded as the Walt Disney of the 21st century.

When it was time to start a project, Lasseter would isolate a group of eight or so writers and direct them to forget about the constraints of technology. The group members would bounce ideas off each other, taking collective responsibility for developing a story. While many studios tried to rush from script to production, Lasseter took up to two years just to work out all the details. Once the script was developed, artists created storyboards that connected the various characters to the developing plot. "No amount of great animation is going to save a bad story," he said. "That's why we go so far to make it right."[8]

Only after the basic story had been set did Lasseter begin to think about what he would need from Pixar's technologists. And it was always more than the computer animators expected. Lasseter, for example, demanded that the crowds of ants in *A Bug's Life* not be a single mass of look-alike faces. To solve the problem, computer expert William T. Reeves developed software that randomly applied physical and emotional characteristics to each ant. In another instance, writers brought a model of a butterfly named Gypsy to researchers, asking them to write code so that when she rubs her antennae, viewers could see the hairs press down and pop back up.

At any stage during the process, Lasseter might go back to potential problems that he saw with the story. In *A Bug's Life,* for example, the story was totally revamped after more than a year of work had been completed. Originally, it was about a troupe of circus bugs run by P.T. Flea that tries to rescue a colony of ants from marauding grasshoppers. But because of a flaw in the story—why would the circus bugs risk their lives to save stranger ants?—codirector Andrew Stanton recast the story to be about Flik, the heroic ant who recruits Flea's troupe to fight the grasshoppers. "You have to rework and rework it," explained Lasseter. "It is not rare for a scene to be rewritten as much as 30 times."[9]

Pumping Out the Hits

In spite of its formidable string of hits, Pixar had difficulty in stepping up its pace of production. Although they may cost 30 percent less, computer-generated animated films still take considerable time to develop. Furthermore, because of the emphasis on every single detail, Pixar used to complete most of the work on a film before moving on to the next one. Catmull and Lasseter later decided to work on several projects at the same time, but the firm was not able to release more than one movie in a year.

To push for an increase in production, Pixar built up its workforce to well over 1,000 employees. It also turned to a stable of directors to oversee its movies. Lasseter, who had directed Pixar's first three films, supervised other directors who took the helm of various films that the studio chose to develop. *Monsters, Inc., Finding Nemo, The Incredibles, Ratatouille,* and *Brave* were directed by some of this new talent. But there were concerns about the number of directors that Pixar could rely upon to turn out high-quality animated films. Michael Savner of Banc of America Securities commented: "You can't simply double production. There is a finite amount of talent."[10]

To meet the faster production pace, Catmull added new divisions, including one to help with the development of new movies and one to oversee movie development shot by shot. The eight-person development team helped to generate more ideas for new films. "Once more ideas are percolating, we have more options to choose from so no one artist is feeling the weight of the world on their shoulders," said Sarah McArthur, who served as Pixar's vice president of production.[11]

Finally, Catmull kept pushing technology in order to improve the quality of animation, with no more than 100 animators working on each film. Toward this end, Catmull oversaw the development of new animation software, called Luxo, which allowed him to use fewer people, who could be pushed to address various challenges that had to be faced. During the production of *Brave,* for example, the animators had to make the curly hair of the main character appear natural. Claudia Chung, who worked on the film, talked about their reaction to various methods they kept trying: "We'd kind of roll our eyes and say, 'I guess we can do that,' but inside we were all excited, because it's one more stretch we can do."[12]

At the same time, Catmull understood that the high standards of the firm could not be compromised for the sake of a steady flow of films. This was evident in Pixar's decision to delay the launch of *The Good Dinosaur* because the firm felt that it had to rethink the film to ensure that it would work well. Everyone at Pixar remained committed to Jobs's philosophy that every one of Pixar's films should grow out of the best efforts of the firm's animators, storytellers, and technologists. "Quality is more important than quantity," he emphasized. "One home run is better than two doubles."[13]

To preserve the firm's high standards, Catmull worked hard to retain Pixar's commitment to quality even as the firm grew. He used Pixar University to encourage collaboration among all employees so that they could develop and retain the key values tied to their success. And he helped devise ways to avoid collective burnout. A masseuse and a doctor came by Pixar's campus each week, and animators had to get permission from their supervisors if they wanted to work more than 50 hours a week.

To Infinity and Beyond?

Despite the less than stellar performance of a couple of Pixar's recent films, expectations were high for *Inside Out* and *The Good Dinosaur,* both of which would be released in 2015. It was quite likely that Pixar had been experiencing some growing pains rather than compromising on its standards under Disney. In fact, Steve Jobs had been convinced that Pixar's links with Disney would be mutually beneficial for both firms. In his own words: "Disney is the only company with animation in their DNA."[14] Lasseter denied any negative effects from Disney's acquisition of his firm and insisted that Pixar's films were increasingly being subjected to higher standards because of its string of successes.

After it acquired Pixar, Disney actually placed Catmull and Lasseter in charge of the combined animation business of both Pixar and Disney. *Tangled, Frozen,* and *Big Hero6,* which were both commercial and critical successes, were made at Disney under the supervision of these Pixar heads. For Lasseter, the new responsibilities for Disney represented a return to his roots. He had been inspired by Disney films as a kid and started his career at Disney before being lured away to Pixar by Catmull. "For many of us at Pixar, it was the magic of Disney that influenced us to pursue our dreams of becoming animators, artists, storytellers and filmmakers," Lasseter stated.[15]

But Catmull and Lasseter continued to face a challenging task, and they were still adjusting to the loss of Jobs, who passed away in 2011. At the same time, everyone at Pixar understood that a large part of their success could be attributed to the talent that the firm was able to recruit and train to work together. This led to a continuous exchange of ideas and fostered a collective sense of responsibility on all their projects. "We created the studio we want to work in," Lasseter had remarked. "We have an environment that's wacky. It's a creative brain trust: It's not a place where I make my movies—it's a place where a group of people make movies."[16]

Pixar's string of successful films was particularly striking, given that there had been a considerable increase in the number of animated films being released each year. Over the past decade, there were a few years in which as many as 16 films were offered as more and more studios tried to grab a share of this lucrative market. Last year's biggest box office success was *The Lego Movie,* put out by Warner Brothers, a newcomer to the category. The growth in competition had led to a string of losses at Dreamworks Animation, Pixar's largest competitor. Lasseter welcomed the increased competition because it forced Pixar to stick to its commitment to quality. "I like healthy competition," he recently stated. "I'd rather be in a healthy industry than be the only player in a dead industry."[17]

Think about how off-putting a movie about rats preparing food could be, or how risky it must've seemed to start a movie about robots with 39 dialogue-free minutes. We dare to attempt these stories, but we don't get them right on the first pass. This is as it should be.

—Ed Catmull, from his book, *Creativity, Inc.,* **published in 2014**

ENDNOTES

1. *Business Wire.* Disney Consumer Products gears up for a powerful year from Pixar. January 13, 2015.
2. Daniel Miller. Pixar film delay leads to layoffs. *Los Angeles Times,* November 23, 2013, p. B3.
3. Peter Burrows & Ronald Grover. Steve Jobs: Movie mogul. *Business Week,* November 23, 1998, p. 150.
4. Ibid.
5. Ibid., p. 146.
6. Ibid.
7. Marc Graser. Pixar run by focused group. *Variety,* December 20, 1999, p. 74.
8. B. Barnes. It wasn't a wreck, not really. *New York Times,* October 18, 2011, p. C4.
9. Burrows & Grover, op. cit., p. 146.
10. Andrew Bary. Coy story. *Barron's,* October 13, 2003, p. 21.
11. Daniel Terdiman. Bravely going where Pixar Animation tech has never gone. *CNET News,* June 16, 2012.
12. Pui-Wing Tam. Will quantity hurt Pixar's quality? *Wall Street Journal,* February 15, 2001, p. B4.
13. Peter Burrows & Ronald Grover. Steve Jobs' magic kingdom. *Business Week,* February 6, 2006, p. 66.
14. Charles Solomon. Pixar creative chief to seek to restore the Disney magic. *New York Times,* January 25, 2006, p. C6.
15. Ibid.
16. Bary, op. cit.
17. Richard Verrier. Animation boom may become glut. *Los Angeles Times,* August 20, 2013, p. B3.

CASES

CASE 12
RHINO CAPTURE IN KRUGER NATIONAL PARK

A. J. Strickland
University of Alabama

William E. Mixon
University of Alabama
MBA Candidate

EXHIBIT 2 Rhino population in South Africa

	2007	2010
White rhinos	15 000	17 500
Black rhinos	1500	4200

Dr. Markus Hofmeyr, head of Veterinary Wildlife Services for South African National Parks (SANParks), returned from another rhino capture with his team. They had captured their 252nd rhino for the year before the rainy season set in, with heat and rain making it almost impossible to continue the capture program. As Hofmeyr and his team were winding down another successful year, given that each rhino was worth between $30 000 and $35 000,[1] he began to reflect on next year's game capture. Hofmeyr faced the daunting question of how to continue to supplement the funding for SANParks' Park Development Fund. Over the years, the budget for his unit had been reduced, and pressure for self-funding of SANParks was increasing.

Some of the funding for SANParks' operations had long been provided by the South African national government in the form of an annual grant. That began to change in 2010, however, when a budget shortfall forced the government to initiate the removal of the grant over three years. The South African government shifted its strategy toward building a new South Africa, focused on providing additional funds for education, job creation through infrastructure expansions, better health care for all South Africans, and economic prosperity. Funding cuts outside of these priority areas threatened the ability of SANParks' Veterinary Wildlife Services to continue delivering normal veterinary and operational services— services that were beneficial to all SANParks wildlife and the habitat in which the wildlife had roamed for centuries. SANParks' budget allocation is shown in Exhibit 1.

Kruger National Park

Kruger National Park was established in South Africa in 1898 to protect the nation's fast-dwindling wildlife areas. By the turn of that century, it was estimated that white rhinos were extinct in Kruger. The first translocation of white rhinos to Kruger National Park occurred in 1961, and a total of 345 white rhinos had been relocated from the parks in Kwa Zulu Natal by the mid-1970s. In 2007, an assessment by the African Rhino Specialist Group estimated that 15 000 white rhinos and 1500 black rhinos existed in South Africa. As of 2009, research indicated that 10 000 white rhinos and 500 black rhinos existed within Kruger National Park, making it home to the largest rhino population in the world. Population estimates for rhinos in South Africa are shown in Exhibit 2.[*]

Kruger National Park covered 7722 square miles (20 000 square kilometers) of conservation area, with eight gates that controlled the flow of unauthorized traffic into the park. Since its establishment, it had become known for its unrivaled wildlife diversity and easy viewing and for its world leadership in advanced environmental management techniques, research, and policies. Many viewed Kruger as the best national park in all of Africa in all aspects— management, infrastructure, and, of course, biodiversity. The flagship of South Africa's 22 national parks, Kruger held a variety of species: 336 trees, 49 fish, 34 amphibians, 114 reptiles, 507 birds, and 147 mammals. Over time, the park had developed into a tourist attraction because of the wildlife and the beautiful scenery, which was representative of South Africa's Lowveld region. (The Lowveld consisted of areas around the eastern part of the country where the altitude was about 1000 feet.)

Tourist operations at Kruger were quite large, with the park offering 21 rest camps, 7 private lodge concessions, and 11 private safari lodges. Lodges that previously had been private were operated in partnership between communities and private companies, which provided concessions for parcels of land. The concessions were placed on tender, and areas were allocated for 25- to 30-year leases, during which operational activities linked with tourism were allowed. At the end of the period, the fixed assets became the property of SANParks, which could decide to extend the lease or retender the concession. An integral part of Kruger National Park's conservation effort was game capture. Traditionally, capturing game allowed Kruger

EXHIBIT 1 SANParks budget allocation (in U.S. Dollars)

Kruger National Park Budget	$4 951 900
Poaching	$275 100
Infrastructure	$275 100

to reintroduce certain species to previously uninhabited areas of the park, as well as to introduce rhino to the other national parks in South Africa and neighboring countries.

Game capture also enabled the park to better manage rare species by placing them in breeding enclosures. In some instances, game capture was used to reduce populations where that goal was impeded by natural regulatory mechanisms. Traditional game capture evolved into an income-generating operation as the demand for rhinos increased.

Income Generation from Game Capture

The sale of wildlife for income generation was accepted and supported by South Africa's National Environmental Management Act (2004). SANParks maximized income from wildlife sales by concentrating on selling high-value species. The two species sold without clearly required ecological reasons for their sale were white rhinos from Kruger National Park and disease-free buffalos from other parks. The only condition required when an animal was sold was that its removal could not negatively impact the populations from which it came. In 2009, 500 rhinos were sold in South Africa. Kruger National Park claimed 252 of these transactions; the others were sold from provincial parks and the private sector. A flow chart of sales transactions is shown in Exhibit 3. The average selling price for a white rhino was $30 300. Many wildlife biologists and other experts feared that these rhinos would eventually fall into the hands of private game hunters. Rhino hunting and rhino breeding for future sales or hunting were driving up the price for a rhino. SANParks accepted hunting as a legal form of wildlife utilization but did not support unethical put-and-take hunting practices because it was very difficult to determine what happened to a rhino after leaving SANParks. SANParks was not responsible for enforcing hunting regulations on wildlife; instead, this responsibility was passed on to each respective South African province. However, many provinces were understaffed, which weakened the regulation of hunting activities.

The most common method for selling rhinos outside Kruger National Park was through provincial and private-sector auctions. In 2009, 45 auctions accounted for most rhino sales outside SANParks. During that year, 252 rhinos on a direct tender were captured in the bush and sold at three auctions held by SANParks. The revenue generated from rhino sales in 2009 totaled $7 033 400. These revenue sales supplemented the conservation budget for SANParks' Park Development Fund. The buyers of the live rhinos were dealers who specialized in wild game or private owners who bought directly from SANParks. Rhinos were typically sold to a private game reserve for either tourist viewing or hunting. Rhinos were also sold or donated by SANParks to neighboring countries. Rhinos purchased in the private sector were sometimes sold internationally to zoos or to buyers who dealt in wild game.

Typically, white rhinos were sold more often than black rhinos, since black rhinos were rarer and much more aggressive. SANParks had sold only two black rhino bulls; the other black rhinos moved from Kruger were donated as part of conservation efforts to reestablish them in countries where they had gone extinct. The private sector bought black rhinos from Kwa Zulu Natal Wildlife, where the remaining black rhinos survived with white rhinos at the turn of the twentieth century. Kwa Zulu Natal moved from completely selling black rhinos to retaining full ownership of the adults and partial ownership of the offspring. Offspring were placed into a custodianship program that split the rights between two or more parties. North West Province sold black rhinos, as did the private sector. Compared with white rhinos, black rhinos were more difficult to introduce and had a higher intraspecies mortality rate from fighting. The tendency to fight made black rhinos a riskier investment than white rhinos, which bred and coexisted much better than black rhinos. The majority of white rhinos were purchased in cow/calf combinations, which were not hunted. White rhino bulls were much more likely than white rhino cows to be purchased for hunting. However, most provinces had

EXHIBIT 3
Flow chart of sales transactions

regulations that limited the number of rhinos eligible to be hunted. Before a rhino was killed, it had to have lived on the current property for more than two years; however, this regulation was very difficult to enforce. Park Services was a critical component of conservation for rhinos and other animals within the park.

Park Services

Veterinary Wildlife Services (VWS) offered a variety of operational and veterinary services for Kruger National Park. Veterinarian operations were critical to the conservation of wildlife within and outside the park. The service's operations included wildlife capture, holding, and translocation; park development; species conservation management; wildlife sales; animal exchanges and contractual commitments; regional cooperation; and research. VWS's aims and objectives and responsibilities are shown in Exhibit 4. Game capture operations began in the 1980s for Kruger National Park; Kruger had also operated game capture in other parks. In the 1990s, a second unit was established for operations outside Kruger. Both units were combined to form VWS in 2002, ensuring that

EXHIBIT 4 Aims, objectives, and responsibilities of sanparks' Veterinary Wildlife Services

The SANParks Strategic Organizational Objectives Framework
Prioritizational of services according to resources, ethical and legal constraints
Optimal utilization of resources
Development and training of the wildlife profession
Recognition that SANParks concerns itself with populations rather than individuals
The leveraging of information and skills developed in SANParks to the benefit of the SADC region
The recognition of the importance of the wildlife and ecological socio-interfaces
Coordination of research on wildlife diseases and their impact on human livelihoods, wildlife itself, and livestock
Implementation of wildlife capture and translocation programs
Reintroducing populations into national parks
Enhancing the conservation status of rate and threatened species
Controlling over-abundant wildlife populations to avert the threats of habitat degradation and loss of biodiversity
Generating revenue for SNAParks through wildlife sales
Enhancing breeding projects involving valuable and rare species
Building capacity in the veterinary and wildlife capture fields, particularly in persons from historically disadvantaged population groups

the service was serving SANParks' objectives and not just those of Kruger. Kruger aimed for VWS to 'provide ethical and professional services relating to capture, holding, translocation and research pertaining to wildlife.'[2] Some of the values and functions associated with VWS are shown in Exhibit 5.

SANParks' Game Capture Unit

SANParks' game capture unit had branch offices in three locations in South Africa: Kruger, Kimberley, and Port Elizabeth. The capture, translocation and reestablishment functions of SANParks' Veterinary Wildlife Services are shown in Exhibit 6.

Population growth, sex and age structure, spatial use, natural dispersal, resource distribution, and population dynamics were considered when making the decision to sell an animal to a private buyer. According to SANParks' chief executive officer, Dr. David Mabunda, 'SANParks, by selling or donating rhino, is assisting in the process of recolonization of the range in the country and outside. It should be noted that it would be foolhardy if South Africa were to have its only rhino population residing in the Kruger, because we run the danger of losing them should there be a major outbreak of disease or rampant poaching. We would be sitting ducks.' Bovine tuberculosis and anthrax were two diseases being monitored by VWS in efforts to

EXHIBIT 5 Veterinary Wildlife Services' values and functions

Veterinary Wildlife Values

VWS is a service delivery department for SANParks, providing specialist veterinary and wildlife handling and translocation support

The SANParks strategic organizational objectives framework of biodiversity, balancing, people and enabling systems will guide these services

The resource, ethical, and legal constraints as well as other drivers will make it necessary to prioritize the services that can be delivered. (Guided by the Wildlife Management Commitee recommendations.)

Optimal utilitization of resources

The leveraging of information and skills developed in SANParks to the benefit of the SADEC region, particularly in SANParks TFC involment

Development and training of the wildlife profession

The recognition of the importance of wildlife and ecological and diagnostic test development

Veterinary Wildlife Functions

Service to scientific services and park managment with regard to implementing veterinary aspects of removals and introductions into our parks, collar fitting, sample taking and any other activities that require handling of wildlife

Disease monitoring, management and surveillance (including sample taking, storing and distribution aid research)

Development of current veterinary aspects of capture, translocation and animal husbandry techniques

Veterinary support to special species management related to approved plans (e.g., predator management plans)

Conservation medicine (implementing and integrating disease and ecological principles in our function)

Veterinary research relevant to the service delivery component of VWS

Liaison and education at the appropriate national and international level

EXHIBIT 6
The capture, translocation and reestablishment functions of SANParks' Veterinary Wildlife Services

Capture, Translocation and Reestablishment Functions

Operational capture, care and translocation of wildlife species aligned with SANParks requirements

Import species and disease-free breeding projects

Coordination of game sales

Transfrontier development

International translocations

Coordination of capture by external entities

EXHIBIT 7
Veterinary Wildlife Service's disease management services

Disease Management Services

BTB monitoring in Buffalo and Lion within Kruger

Monitoring in all parks when opportunities arise

Sarcoid research in Mountain Zebra in Bontebok NP

Disease prevention principles applied to animal movements and quarantine facilities both in Kruger and Kimberley

better understand how to contain them, which in turn would lead to better decisions about disease management where required. Intervention was not always needed in wildlife populations, but an understanding of how a disease influenced population dynamics was. VWS disease management services are shown in Exhibit 7. In addition to these issues, SANParks concerned itself with Kruger National Park's capability to assess and evaluate financial implications and the risks imposed to its white rhino population by intense localized removals and emerging diseases.[3]

Capturing a Rhino

The rhino capture process involved the use of state-of-the-art equipment accompanied by a team of experts. A game capture team included a helicopter pilot, a veterinarian, an operational coordinator, a veterinary technician, five capture staff personnel, and two drivers for the translocation and crane trucks. Selected operating expenses of a rhino capture are shown in Exhibit 8.

Once a rhino was located, the capture process consisted of darting it with a drug combination from a helicopter.

EXHIBIT 8 Selected operating expenses of rhino capture

Game capture operating expenses	Cost per rhino	Cost per hour	Cost per day	Cost per year	Unit cost
Helicopter	N/A	$800	N/A	N/A	N/A
Transportation of rhino	$300	N/A	N/A	$11 000	N/A
Truck	N/A	N/A	$300	N/A	N/A
Boom	N/A	N/A	$300	N/A	N/A
Capture team	N/A	$200	$1400	N/A	N/A
RFID microchip	$50	N/A	N/A	N/A	$17

The fast-acting drug combination made the whole capture process less dangerous to the capture unit by rendering the rhino unconscious for evaluation before relocation. Once the rhino was unconscious, a team from the game capture unit moved in to examine it. The game capture unit conducted a medical examination of the rhino by taking blood samples to test for any signs of disease. At this point in the game capture process, three radio-frequency identification (RFID) microchips were tagged on the rhino for identification purposes. Inserting an RFID microchip involved drilling into the horn, which is made of keratin, a material similar to that which human hair and fingernails are composed of. Photos of the game capture process are shown in Exhibit 9.

Park officials used tagging as a method to better understand the rhinos' movement within their landscape. South African law mandated the tagging of any rhino darted as well. Park services were also looking at ways to place tracking devices on rhinos to increase the capability of understanding rhino movements within their landscape. Prevention was the main emphasis of the rhino poaching counteroffensive in Kruger. It was thought that these potential tracking devices would help deter poaching, but the main deterrent was gaining information from informants on possible plans for rhino poaching.

After the evaluation and tagging process, a partial antidote was administered to partially wake up the rhino but keep it in a semi-anesthetized state. Partial antidotes were necessary to protect the game capture team while walking the rhino into the transportation crate. After the rhino was successfully loaded into a transportation crate, a boom truck lifted the crate onto the translocation truck. A boom truck was needed since an average rhino weighed 3300 pounds (1500 kilograms). Typically, the average distance traveled by a rhino captured from Kruger National Park was 50 miles (80 kilometers), at a cost of $300 per rhino per 16

EXHIBIT 9
The game capture process

The game capture unit follows the helicopter in pursuit of a rhino.

The dart shot from the helicopter is inspected by game capture personnel.

Game capture unit personnel inspect the sedated rhino.

Game capture personnel drill a hole in the rhino's horn to insert the RFID microchip.

Game capture personnel inspect the sedated rhino.

Boom trucks are needed to load the rhino.

After the antidote is given, the staff helps the rhino stand up.

EXHIBIT 10 Dr. Markus Hofmeyr standing above several *Bomas* (holding pens)

miles. The next translocation process was maintenance in holding facilities (see Exhibit 10). Rhinos were placed in *bomas* (holding pens). *Bomas* allowed a rhino to become accustomed to a new habitat by slowly facilitating a passive release. Once released, the rhino was typically still confined to a larger pen or fenced-in area, depending on the buyer's intentions. It was estimated that 50 percent of the bulls transferred to private hunting companies were killed within two years, at a price of $2800 per inch of rhino horn.

Rhino Hunting

A typical rhino hunt could cost $82 400 per hunter. In 2009, South Africa generated an estimated $6.9 billion in revenues from tourist attractions; of that amount, hunting accounted for about 70 percent, or about $4.8 billion.[4] The cost of booking a rhino hunt varied depending on the safari company, as detailed in Exhibit 11. Most safari companies required a deposit of 50 percent of the basic cost of a safari, which was fully refundable until within three months of the contracted safari date. Accommodations varied according to packages offered by each safari company and were considered comparable to those of any other tourist attraction in the world. Some safari companies offered photo safaris and wedding packages, in addition to hunting services, to further generate revenue for operations.

Typically, each safari company recommended certain equipment and clothing for hunters to bring along with

EXHIBIT 11 Selected company safari expenses and trip details

Africa Sport Hunting Safaris

Services offered
- First-class rifle and bow hunting
- Ethical, professional hunters
- Personal attention to all our clients
- Family and photographic tours
- Specialized, well-maintained vehicles
- Luxury accommodation
- Excellent cuisine
- Dedicated staff

Firearms and calibers
- Rhino legal minimum .375 caliber and 3–9 × 40 variable-power telescope
- Ammunition recommended minimum of 40 full metal jacket/solids in addition to soft point bullets

Travel information
- Valid passport required

Trophy handling
- All animals will be skinned by our very experienced skinners, as well as marked, salted, and dried prior to being sent to a taxidermist. All documentation will be handled by Africa Sport Hunting Safaris

Clothing and other requirements
- Three sets of hunting clothing: long pants (zip-offs), long-sleeve shirts, socks, and underwear
- Hunting boots/shoes— comfortable
- Casual/running shoes
- Sweater/warm jacket
- Flip flops/sweat suit
- Cap/wide-brimmed hat
- Casual clothes
- Adjust your clothing to the time of year your hunt takes place.
- Winter May–August (35–70°F)
- Summer September–April (50–90°F)

(continued)

EXHIBIT 11 Selected company safari expenses and trip details *(continued)*

Personal
- Personal medical kit
- Sunblock— minimum 30 SPF
- Mosquito repellent
- Pair of sunglasses
- Toiletries

Additional equipment
- Small day pack
- Flashlight with spare batteries
- Binoculars
- Camera with spare film and batteries
- Pocket knife

Accommodation: luxury thatched chalets with a true African ambience
- Private rooms with ensuite bathrooms
- Running hot and cold water
- Electricity with converters
- Flush toilets

Food and beverages
- Traditional South African cuisine. For dietary requirements such as diabetes and high cholesterol, please make arrangements on booking of the safari

Additional services
- Facials and full body massages
- Manicures and pedicures
- Day excursions

South African hunting areas price list Limpopo Province 2010
- White Rhino — $45 000
- White Rhino (Green-Hunt) — $13 000

Daily rate: South Africa
- Dangerous Game — $800
- Plains Game
- 1 Hunter × 1 Professional Hunter: — $400
- 2 Hunters × 1 Professional Hunter: — $300
- All non-hunters are welcome at: — $200

Included in daily rate
- Pick up and drop off at Polokwane International Airport
- Hunting licenses and fees
- Transportation to and from hunting concessions
- Field preparation of trophies
- Professional hunters, trackers, skinners, and camp staff
- Fully equipped hunting vehicles
- Luxury accommodation and meals
- Drinks and beverages in moderation
- Daily laundry services

Excluded from daily rates
- Flights: international and domestic
- Charter flights where applicable
- All animals shot and wounded will be charged per price list
- Dipping, packing, taxidermy cost
- Non-hunting, traveling days at $150 per day
- Accommodation before and after hunt
- Any additional tours or excursions

(continued)

EXHIBIT 11 Selected company safari expenses and trip details (*continued*)

Methods of payment accepted
- U.S. currency
- Traveler's checks
- Wire transfers
- Credit cards
- Personal checks with prior approval

Members of:
- Professional Hunters Association South Africa
- Accredited Tour Guides
- Safari Club International
- North American Hunters Association
- National Rifle Association

Chattaronga Safaris

Daily fees hunter

1	$400
2	$350
3	$300
4	$300
Observer	$200

Included tariffs
- Accommodation including full board
- Liquor and beverages served in camp
- Full-time service of experienced professional hunter.
- Trained staff
- Trackers
- Skinners
- Field preparation of trophies
- All transportation within hunting areas
- All hunting licenses
- Pickup and drop-off at international airport: Limpopo-Polokwane, Kwa-Zulu Natal-Johannesburg, Mpumalanga-Johannesburg

Excluded tariffs
- International and domestic flights
- Traveling day (non-hunting days) at $180 per day
- Trophy fees of animal shot or wounded
- Rifle hire (firearms may be rented at $80 per day)
- Ammunition is available at cost
- Dipping, packing, taxidermy, and shipping
- Air charters and accommodation before and after safari
- Tips for staff, telephone calls, and curio purchases

Rhino safari

7 Day 1 × 1	$60 000

Includes representative 20' fake horn (because it is not standard practice to cut off the horn of a rhino).

Dumukwa

Daily rates

1 hunter/1 professional hunter	$400
2 hunters/1 professional hunter	$300
Non-hunters/observers	$200
Rhino dart	$8500
5 day 1 × 1 Hunt	

(*continued*)

EXHIBIT 11 Selected company safari expenses and trip details (*continued*)

Included in daily rates
- Full accommodation, meals, and use of camp facilities
- All liquid refreshments including wine, beer, bottled water, and sodas
- Daily laundry
- Service of professional hunter with his team of skinners and trackers
- Field preparation of trophies
- Transport of raw trophies to local taxidermist for the area you in hunt in
- All transportation during the safari including from and to the airport
- 14 percent value added tax (VAT) on all packages

Excluded in daily rates
- Internet, faxes, and telephone calls
- Airfare
- Hotel accommodation before and after the contracted safari
- Dipping and packing or mounting of trophies
- Shipping of trophies back to your country
- Optional hire of firearms

Zingeli Safaris

Included in daily rates
- Full board and lodging with traditional catering
- South African wines and beer in moderation, and soft drinks
- Experienced professional hunter and trained staff
- Trackers and skinners
- Field preparation, salting and packing
- Transportation of trophies to reliable and qualified taxidermist who will follow your instructions and fulfill the necessary requirements
- Use of hunting vehicle
- Laundry services
- Transportation to the ranch and return to Johannesburg International Airport or charter plane

Excluded in daily rates
- Air travel before, during and after the contracted period of the safari
- Accommodation and travel charges incurred before and after the contracted period of the safari
- Trophy fees for animals taken or wounded
- Value added tax (VAT) 14 percent on daily rates
- Air charters
- Gratuities to professional hunters and staff
- Preparation, packing, documentation, and export of trophies from South Africa

---

them. This list varied by season, since temperatures could range between 30°F (low) in the winter and 90°F (high) in the wet summer season. Expenses also varied according to the specific details of a trip such as length of stay, trophy fees, number of hunters and observers, and the daily rate charged per hunter. Airfare to and from South Africa also varied depending on how far in advance travel arrangements were made and whether the flight was direct. Typically, coach seating ranged from $800 to $1100, whereas first-class price ranges easily approached $3000. Rifles, bows, and darting weapons were offered in some packages, but rifles could be imported into South Africa under strict guidelines and regulations. However, hunters were not allowed to import automatic or semiautomatic weapons.

Some companies charged high trophy fees and low daily rates, in contrast to low trophy fees and high daily rates. Trophy fees varied according to the specific animal wounded or killed and were typically not paid until the end of the safari. Daily rates depended on the services offered and could include or exclude a number of amenities necessary to hunt in South Africa. In general, some safari companies offered a lower daily rate as a marketing tool to increase their customer base; a large trophy fee reflected the fact that a safari company's profits depended on a successful hunt by the customer. As Zingeli Safaris stated in its brochure, 'If you don't get your animal we lose; this is your guarantee that we will do our best to find you your dream trophy!' Customers incurred taxidermist fees, in addition to trophy fees, if they desired to have something tangible to take home.

Poaching

Demand for rhino horn in emerging markets such as Asia and India made rhino poaching highly profitable. In 2009, rhino horn was sold on the black market at $3600 per pound, but by 2010 the price was reported to be $7200 per pound. An average rhino horn weighed six to eight pounds. Businesses with ties to political insiders were entering the market to supply and sell rhino horn as wealth creation resulted from the growth of Asia's and India's economies.

The market for raw rhino horn was mainly driven by demand in China and Vietnam. Cultural beliefs, combined with increasing wealth, were creating a strong foundation for the demand of rhino horn. Asians believed that rhino horn was a very beneficial aphrodisiac, and Indians desired rhino horn daggers. These beliefs and desires were strong enough to produce enough capital to entice the illegal killing of rhinos without regard to law enforcers such as the SANParks Environmental Crimes Unit, South African Police Service, and park rangers.

Poachers were well equipped with highly sophisticated transportation such as helicopters and the latest military weaponry available in the region. They were able to strike fast within even the most protected game conservation areas. Poaching was even a problem in Kruger National Park, home to what some considered the best antipoaching unit in South Africa. In 2006, two rhinos were even poached by staff members employed by SANParks. In 2009 alone, there were about 50 rhinos poached in Kruger and 100 poached in South Africa as a whole. As of January 22, 2010, poachers had killed 14 rhinos in Kruger National Park as well.

Poachers were ruthless in the slaughtering of rhinos. They typically cut off the rhino's horns after darting it with a deadly poison (see Exhibit 12). Poachers also darted rhinos with an immobilizing antidote that sometimes left the rhino helpless in the wild to be eaten by other game. SANParks' CEO, Dr. David Mabunda, described poachers as 'dangerous criminals.' Their exploits were not limited to killing rhinos, but also included human trafficking, arms smuggling, prostitution, and drug trafficking.

'Poachers must beware,' Mabunda said in a statement announcing a $250 000 funding boost, in addition to the $5.2 million allocated to train and prepare the SANParks Environmental Crimes Unit and South African Police Service. Fifty-seven rangers equipped with night vision goggles and high-powered motorbikes had been dispatched to guard highly poached areas of the park day and night. Said Mabunda, 'This war we plan on winning.' In addition to the funding boost, plans were considered to guard the porous border near Kruger National Park with military personnel. Elisabeth McLellan, a species expert with the World Wildlife Foundation (WWF), was quoted as saying, 'The situation is bad for rhino worldwide, in terms of poaching.' Conservationists were facing an environment that had evolved into an industry, as world trade had reached a 15-year high for illegal rhino horn trading.

Kenyan authorities at Jomo Kenyatta International Airport had seized a 662-pound load of elephant tusk and rhino horn believed to have come from South Africa. It was speculated that the load, valued at approximately $1 million, was destined for China. Industry experts suggested that the high value placed on elephant tusk and rhino horn by consumers was driving the demand for both substances.

Animal Supermarket

Kruger National Park was determined to win the war against poaching, but determination alone wasn't enough to protect the rhino. Primary-market transactions involved buyers that protected the rhino— such as other national parks, private game farms, game dealers, and photography safari business owners— but secondary markets from the sale of captured rhinos had also developed. Hunters had become the most numerous buyers in the secondary market, which wasn't aligned with Kruger National Park's mission. Animal rights activists dubbed the sale of animals at Kruger National Park an 'animal supermarket.' Many believed that the commercial trade posed a greater threat than poaching did. Many also felt it was fundamentally wrong to herd animals from a popular wildlife reserve and sell them in efforts at 'conservation.' Wildlife activists accused SANParks of misusing the park by serving as nothing more than a private game breeder, and experts feared that the vast majority of the rhinos sold by SANParks would fall into the hands of private hunters.

SANParks' Justification

SANParks was guided in its decision to sell wildlife by Clause 55(2)(b) of the Protected Areas Act No. 57 of 2003 (as amended), which stated that 'SANParks may, in managing national parks, sell, exchange or donate any animal, plant, or other organism occurring in a park, or purchase, exchange or otherwise acquire any indigenous species which it may consider desirable to reintroduce into a specific park.' SANParks believed that it was critical to its conservation efforts to maintain the sale of animals to private entities. For years, SANParks had sold animals to fund conservation efforts, and in many cases the park had traded animals to obtain other species. Also, SANParks screened animals and buyers to ensure that animals were released not arbitrarily, but to buyers with the proper permits and

EXHIBIT 12 Rhino left to die after poachers cut off horn

EXHIBIT 13 Responsibilities of conservation biologists

- Identify key research themes necessary for national parks to achieve their conservation objectives
- Conduct research on key themes
- Coordinating research projects conducted by external scientific institutions in national parks.
- Integrating best available biodiversity data into park management through interactions with external researchers and research institutions
- Maintaining inventories of biodiversity in national parks, including species checklists for vertebrates and higher plants and the mapping of landscape. Geology, soil and vegetation
- Identifying and averting threats to biodiversity in national parks, including overabundance of certain wildlife populations, invasive alien plant and animal species, pollutants, human development, excessive resource exploitation or other factors
- Ensuring that development within parks takes place in a manner that does not compromise biodiversity conservation
- Conservation for rare and threatened species
- Provide scientific inputs on the rehabilitation of degraded landscapes
- Providing scientific inputs on biodiversity aspects of park management plans and activities
- Building capacity in conservation biology and related sciences, particularly in persons from historically disadvantaged population groups

intentions. Decisions to sell or donate wildlife were scientifically determined according to population dynamics, sex and age structure, spatial use, natural dispersal, and resource distribution.

SANParks' strategy was informed by the following objectives: population control, broadening of the range for populations, spreading the risk of managing wildlife, making the populations more resilient and viable, and fund-raising for specific conservation and land-expansion programs. The responsibilities of SANParks' conservation biologists are shown in Exhibit 13. The challenge facing SANParks was how to effectively communicate that selling rhinos was for the greater good.

ENDNOTES

* © 2010 by A.J. Strickland. All rights reserved.
1. All monetary amounts in this case are in U.S. dollars.
2. *Wildlife Research Magazine*.
3. Sam Ferreira & Travis Smith Scientific Services, SANParks, Skukuza, South Africa.
4. *Wildlife Research Magazine*.

COMPANY INDEX

A

ABC, 304
ABC News, 81
ABC-TV, C49
Abercrombie & Fitch, C60, C63
Accenture, 116, 134, 218
Access Health, 134–135
Accountable Care Organizations, 7
Ace Hardware, 161
Acer Group, C122, C123
Activision Blizzard, 300
Adelphia Communications, 205, 368
Adidas, 430
ADP Corporation, 281
AEG, C273
Aer Lingus, C17
AES, 371
Age Wave Consulting, 45
Agincourt, C113
Ahold USA, C224
AIG; see American International Group
Airbnb, 352
Airbus, 268, C18, C250, C262, C267
Air China, C18
Air New Zealand, C262
AirTran Airways, C8, C9, C11
AirTran Holdings Inc., C11
Akamai Technologies, 125
Al Abram Beverages Co., C218
Alberto-Culver, 169
Albertsons, 29, 148, C224
Alcon Inc., C136
Aldi, 10, 148, 152, 279
Alexander Wang, 160
Alfred Karcher, 86
Alibaba, 202, C167, C168
  Lionsgate's alliance with, 203
Alico, 183
Alios BioPharma, C234
Allegheny International, 43
Allegiant Travel, C18
Allergan, C29
Alliant Energy of Iowa, 369
ALLtech Inc., C39, C40
Alpha Natural Resources, 307
Amalgamated Bean Coffee Trading Company Limited, C87
Amazon, 3, 6, 50, 60, 92, 94, 132, 151, 165, 185, 264, 268, 283, 387, 388, 396, 406, C122, C123, C126, C156, C157, C167, C231
  description, C165

Amazon Fresh, C228–C229
Amazon Kindle, C122, C125
Amazon Payments, 22
Amazon Prime, difficult to copy, 93
Amazon Web Services, 61
AM Best, 220
AmBev, C216
America Association for Community Organizations, C144
American Airlines, 197, C9
American Cancer Society, C14
American Heart Association, C148
American Honda Motor, C248
American Institute of Philanthropy, C149
American International Group, 183
American International Group, case
  bonus payments to employees, C4–C6
  business strategy problems, C4
  credit default swaps, C4
  Fed loan to, C4
  in financial crisis of 2008, C4
  government bailout, C4
  negative reaction to bailout, C4
America Online, 182, C126, C169, C170, C171
Amgen, 10
Amoco, 183
AMR, 227
ANA, C262
Andersen Consulting, 134, C225
Andersen Windows, 162
Andersen Worldwide, 204
Anheuser-Busch, 195, 349, C216, C219
Anheuser-Busch InBev, C99, C104, C109, C216, C217
  description, C108
ANN Inc.; see Ann Taylor
Ann Taylor, case
  balance sheet, C61
  brand identity, C65–C66
  brands, C58
  cannibalization problem, C65
  company background, C58–C60
  competitors, C60–C64
  customer segments, C58, C65
  divisional problems, C57
  earnings problems, C57
  financial performance, C59
  future initiatives, C66

  income statement, C60–C61
  initial public offering, C58
  international expansion, C64
  LOFT store concept, C58
  losses in 2008, C58
  mail-order business, C58
  management change, C57
  management turnover, C66
  manufacturing, C65
  name change, C59–C60
  net sales, C60
  new brand concept, C64
  number of locations, C65
  omnibrand sales approach, C64
  operations, C65
  operations data, C65
  restructuring in 2014, C66
  restructuring plan, C58–C60
  in retail apparel industry, C60–C64
  statement of cash flows, C62
  store concepts, C65
  target market, C57
Ann Taylor LOFT; see Ann Taylor
AOL; see America Online
AOL Time Warner, 209, C174
Apollo Group, 294
Apple Car, C127
Apple Inc., 3, 43, 90, 98, 120, 137, 138, 153, 173, 183, 185, 196, 197, 262, 267, 283, 288, 302, 387, C29, C209, C210, C211, C213, C274, C275
  financial data, 111
Apple Inc., case
  acquisition of Beats Music, C126
  Apple Car, C127
  Apple Watch, C127
  business strategy, C121, C127–C128
  business units
    Apple Pay, C127
    App Store, C127
    iPad, C125
    iPhone, C124–C125
    iPod, C123–C124
    iTunes, C126
    new products, C127
    personal computers, C123
    software market, C125–C126
  company background
    CEOs Sculley, Spindler, and Amelio, C120–121
    return of Steve Jobs, C121–C122
    Steve Jobs, C117–C120

  corporate strategy change, C117, C121
  as digital entertainment corporation, C121–C122
  financial data by product and region, C118
  innovations, C121
  innovation timeline, C119–C120
  major competitors, C122
  management change in 2011, C117
  market shares
    in cell phones, C124
    in computers, C123
    in operating systems, C124
    in tablets, C126
  market value in 2015, C117
  operations, C122–C123
  outsourcing problems, C122
  patent litigation, C123
  product innovation, C117, C118–C120
  product lines, C122
  research and development expenditures, C122–C123
  sales 2014–2015, C119
Apple iPad, 153
Apple iPhone, 153
Apple iPod, 63
  and complementors, 64
Apple Pay, C121
  description, C127
Apple's App Store, 58, C121
  description, C127
Apple Stores, 52
Apple Watch, C127
aQantive, 182
Archos, C122
Arco, 183
Argos, C161
Ariba, 430
Armani, 160
Aroma Cafe, C196
Arthur Andersen, 16
ArtistShare, C23
Asiana Airlines, C262
Asian Pacific Breweries, C215
Assets for Family Success, C143
Association of Community Organizations for Reform Now, C149
Aston Martin, 352, C251
AstraZeneca, 201
ASUS, C122, C126
Atkins Challenge, C36

I-1

Atlas Door, case
  creating competitive advantage, 165–166
  description, 165
  inimitable strategy, 166–167
  sustaining competitive advantage, 166
AT&T, 48, 187, 195
Au Bon Pain, C49
Auction Web, C163
Audi, 66
Audi of America Inc., C248
Autobytel.com, 408
Autodesk, C169
AutoNation, 28
Autonomy, 182
AutoVAZ, 222
Avention, Inc., 453, 455
Avery Brewing Company, C107
Avon, case
  acquisition of Sipada, C91
  advertising expenditures, C92
  balance sheets, C97–C98
  business strategy revision, C94–C95
  company history, C89–C90
  competition in emerging markets, C89
  core values, C96
  corporate strategy change, C92
  demoralized employees, C92
  direct-market sales, C89–C90
  emerging market problems, C92–C94
    Brazil, C93–C94
    China, C94
  expansion into emerging market, C90–C91
  financial data by region, C91
  global and regional competition, C91
  growth potential questionable, C8
  guiding principles, C96
  income statements, C93
  job cuts, C95
  litigation costs, C95
  management change, C94
  mission, C96
  new product launches, C90
  partnerships, C90
  philanthropic efforts, C95
  replacement of executives, C92
  restructurings, C92
  revenue sources, C90
  and Securities and Exchange Commission, C89, C95
  settlement over bribery charges, C89
  shift to retailing, C92
  strategy implementation problems, C92
  takeover target, C95
  turnaround setbacks, C89
  turnaround vs. takeover, C96
  vision, C96
Axe, 157

B

Bain & Company, 116, C163, C270
Baltic Beverages Holding, C218
Banana Republic, C62
Banc of America Securities, C277
Bank of America, 205, C4
  in financial crisis of 2007–2009, 109–110
Bank Rakyat Indonesia, C207, C208
Barista, C87
Barnes & Noble, 93, 165, 268
Barrons.com, 205
Baskin-Robbins, C44, C45
Bassett Furniture, 406
Bath & Body Works, C63, C182
Battelle Research Institute, 83
Baxter International, 21
Bay Tact Corporation, 452
BBAG, C218
Bear Stearns, C4
Beats Electronics, 197, C126
Beats Music, C126
Beauty Boutiques, C94
Beca Group, 88
Beecham Group, 198
Behind the Numbers, 16
Beijing Mei Da Coffee Company, C85
Bell's Brewery, C107
Ben & Jerry's, 157, C40, C41, C44, C45
Benchmark, 58
Beneficial, 198
Bentley, C248
Berkshire Hathaway, 77, 186, 191, 323, C136
Best Buy, 16, 189, 252, 267, C211
Best Practices LLC, 407
Betaworks, 249
Better Business Bureau Wise Giving Alliance, C149
Biggby Coffee, 354–355
Biggest Loser, C28, C29, C30
Big Island Brewhaus, C106
BI-LO, C228
Biocon, 203
BlackBerry, 165
Black Tooth Brewing, C106
Blockbuster Inc., 38, 90, C49
  versus Netflix, 94–95
Bloomingdale's, C92
Blue Bell, C40, C41
Blue Cross of California, 62
Blue Point Brewing, C106
BMW, 65, 66, 80, 153
BMW-Mini, C257
BMW of North America, C248
BNP Paribas, 5
Board Source, C149
Boeing Company, 82, 83, 219, 229, 268, C9, C10, C11, C250, C251, C262, C267
  organizational design problem, 315–316

Boise Cascade, 190
Bolstr, C23
Bolthouse Farms, C130
Bombay Company, 406
Bon Appétit, C171
Borders, 6, 38
Borgata Hotel, C153, C154
Boston Beer Company, case
  balance sheets, C102
  in beer industry, C103–C104
  brand recognition, C109
  business strategy, C103
  company history, C100–C103
  competitive environment, C100
  competitive position, C110
  competitors
    Anheuser-Busch, C108
    Crown Imports LLC, C108
    Heineken, C108
    MillerCoors, C108
    New Belgium Brewing Company, C108
    Sierra Nevada Brewing Company, C106–C108
  continuous growth, C99
  distribution channels, C100
  and drinking habit changes, C101
  early operations, C100
  income statements, C101
  initial public offering, C100
  major competitors, C99–C100
  and Moosehead Breweries, C110
  organizational goal, C101–C103
  rank in craft brewing, C99
  as start-up, C100
  subsidiary, C103
  supply chain improvements, C100–C101
  in U.S. Open Beer Championship, C106
Boston Consulting Group, 21, 149, 201, 267, 282
Boston Market, C136, C196
Boston Proper, C63
Boston Scientific, 195
Bottega Venetta, 160
Boulevard Brewing Company, C107
Boys & Girls Clubs, C147
BP, 6, 19
Brand Finance, C8
BRCK, global start-up, 327
Brewers Association, C99, C100
Breyer's, C41
BrightRoll, C169, C171
Brinker International, 26
Bristol-Myers-Squibb, divestments, 201
British Airways, 5
British Petroleum, 183
British Sky Broadcasting, 305
Brunello Cucinelli, 160
Brusters's Real Ice Cream, C45
BSkyB, 305
Buick, 320

Burger King, C48, C55, C194, C196
  market share, C195
BusinessMinded.com, 391
Business Roundtable, 295, 330
  on sustainability practices, 331
Buzz, 388
BYD, strategy problems, 75

C

Cable Value Network, C181
Cabot Corporation, 194
Cadbury-Schweppes, 433
Cadillac, 320; see also General Motors
Caesars Palace, C153
Café Coffee Day, C82
  market dominance, C86–C87
Café del Volcán, C85
California Perfume Company, C89–C90
CalPERS, 299
Calvin Klein, 171
CamberView, C166
Camille's Ice Cream Bars, C45
Campbell Soup Company, 79, 85
Campbell Soup Company, case
  acquisition of Pace Foods, C131
  advertising campaign, C132
  balance sheet, C136–C137
  business strategy revision, C132–C133
  challenges facing, C133
  company background, C130–C131
  competitors, C135–C136
  employee engagement, C133
  export destinations, C134
  income statement, C138
  key financial ratios, C138–C140
  key strategies in 2010, C133
  management change, C130
  management of, C132–C133
  manufacturing facilities, C131
  new food-rating system, C141
  new product launches, C130
  organizational structure, C132–C133
  in packaged-food industry, C133–C134
  product reinvention, C132
  in Russia and China, C131–C132
  sales 2012–2014, C130
  stock price performance, C135
  strategies, C130–C131
  sustainability factors, C141
Canadean Ltd., C216
Cannondale, 153
Canon, 25
Cape Air, C17
Cargill, 91
  strategic business unit structure, 322
Carlsberg, C215, C217
Carl's Jr., market share, C195

Carlyle Group, C237
CarMax, 252
Carrier Air Conditioning, 41
Carvel, C44, C45
Casio, 185
Caterpillar Inc., 153, 169
  sustainable competitive advantage, 105
  value-chain activities, 104
Cathay Pacific, C262
Catholic Charities, C147
Cedars-Sinai Hospital, 186, 202
Celanese Chemical Corporation, 225
Center for Work-Life Policy, 116
Cerberus Capital, 182
Cereality, 158
ChannelAdvisor, 93
Charity Navigator, C149
Charity Organizations Society of Denver, C144
Chartwell Investments, 353
Cheesecake Factory, 153
Chegg, 116
Chemical Bank, 373
Chery Automobile Company, 66
Chevrolet, 320; *see also* General Motors
Chevrolet Cobalt, 65
Chevrolet Corvette, 66
Chevrolet Cruz, 56
Chick-fil-A Inc., C196
Chico's, C57
Chico's FAS Inc., C62, C63, C64
Chili's, 26
China Central Television, 75
China Mobile, C125
ChinaVision Media Group, 203
Chipotle, 77, 341
  efficient operations, 79
Chipotle Mexican Grill, C194–C195, C196
Chrysler Corporation, 16, 34, 62, 66, 153, 182, 197, 271, C245, C247, C248, C250
Chrysler Group/FCA, C257
CH2M Hill, C58, C73
Cigna, 48
Circuit City, 38, C211
Cirque du Soleil, case
  arrival in U.S., C270
  audience perceptions, C271
  business strategy debate, C270
  business strategy restructuring, C272–C273
  corporate strategy development, C271
  cost reductions, C272
  decline of growth prospects, C270
  failures after 2006, C271
  growth, C271
  history, C270–C271
  job cuts, C271
  in Las Vegas, C270–C271
  profit decline, C270
  shows, C272
  as start-up, C270
Cisco Systems, 3, 48, 132, 134, 138, 196, 323, 396, 408
  corporate-level strategy problems, 181
Citibank, 362
Citicorp, 232, C4
Citigroup, 96, 302, 374, C166
Clairol, C201
Clayton, Dubilier & Rice, 191
Cleveland Clinic, 186, 202
Clif Bar and Company, 287
Clorox, 21, 254
CNBC, 4, 304
CNET, 61
CNN, 38
Coca Cola Company, 169, 219, 224, 229, 233, 301, 330, 388, 405
Coca-Cola Enterprises Inc., C133
Coca-Cola North America, C133
Cosi, C49
Coffee Bean and Tea Leaf Company, C87
Cold Stone Creamery, C41, C44, C45
Coldwater Creek Inc., C63, C64
Colgate-Palmolive, 272, C201, C202
Comcast, 90, C182
Commerce Bank, 171
Community Chest, C144
Compartamos Banco, C207, C208
ConAgra, 56, 91, 184, 322
Cone Communications, 19
Conseco, 182, 198
Construction Users Anti-Inflation Roundtable, 331
Continental Airlines, 10, 92, 197
Cooliris, C171
Coolpad, C210
Cooper Industries, 184
Coors Brewing, 152–153, C216
Cordis, C237
Corona, C99
Corporate Citizenship, 19
Costa Coffee, C87
Costco Home Stores, 406
Costco Wholesale Corporation, C60, C223, C224
Coty, C95
Countrywide Financial, 293, 303
Covidien, 242
Craigslist, 224, C161, C167
Credit Suisse, 291, 374
Crisco, C202
Critical Path Software Inc., C161
CrowdCube, C23
Crowdfunder, C23
Crown Imports, LLC, C103, C104
  description, C108
CrowStar, C115
Crumbs Bake Shop, business-level strategy problem, 147
Cruzcampo, C218
Culver Franchising System Inc., C45
CVS Pharmacies, 158, C34
Cypress Semiconductor, 24

D

Daily Deal Media, 92
Daimler Benz, 182, C257
Daimler-Chrysler, C247
Dairy Queen, C44, C45
Dangji Lideng Forestry Development Co., Ltd., C77
Danone, 207
Dart, 206
DASH Diet, C30
Datalogix, C166
Dayton Hudson Corporation, 206
Deere & Company, 221
Defiant Brewing Company, C100
DeGarmo Group Inc., 46
Dell IdeaStorm, 86
Dell Inc., 164, 405, C122, C123, C182
Deloitte, 303
Deloitte & Touche, C68
Deloitte Consulting, 404
Deloitte Touche Tohmatsu, 404
Delta Air Lines, 12, 197, C11, C14, C18
Delta Pride Catfish, 56
DePuy, C237
Deschutes Brewery, C106, C107
Deutsche Bank, 374
Diageo, C136
Diamonique Corporation, C181, C182
Diesel, 160
Digg, entrepreneurship problem, 249
Digital Equipment Company, 40–41, 131
Digital Reasoning, 290
  data analytics, 291
Dingji Stumpage Trading Center, C8
Dippin' Dots, case
  bankruptcy filing, C38
  company growth, C42–C44
  competitors, C44, C45–C46
  entrepreneurship, C39–C40
  franchise growth, C42–C44
  franchising, C42
  in frozen dairy industry, C40–C42
  funding, C42
  growth strategy, C39
  innovation, C39–C40
  low-cost franchising operations, C38
  management change, C44
  marketing efforts, C44
  and McDonald's, C44
  new franchise system, C44
  new product development, C44–C46
  new product launch, C38
  online venture, C46
  operations, C38–C39
  out of bankruptcy in 2012, C38
  patent infringement suit, C44
  product line extension, C39
  product specifics, C40
  target market, C44
  timeline of milestones, C43
  uncertain future, C38
Dippin' Dots Franchising Inc., C44
DirecTV, 195
Dish Network, 95
Disneyland, 25
Diversity, 22, 267
dMarc, 381
Dogfish Head Craft Brewery, C107
Dolce & Gabbana, C201, C205
Dollar General, 148, C34
Donaldson Lufkin & Jenrette, C221
Donatos, C196
Donna Karan, C58
Double Fine, C24
Dow Jones & Company, 455
Dreamworks, C278
Dreyer's Edy's Grand, C41
Dreyer's Edy's Slow Churned, C41
Dreyer's Grand/Edy's Ice Cream, C40
Dropbox, 61
Duke Energy, 117, 195
Duke Power, 369
Dun & Bradstreet, 128, 455
Dunkin' Donuts, C87
DuPont Corporation, 21, 388
Duracell, 158, C202
Dutch Boy, 382
  innovation, 383

E

Eachnet, C156
EA Mobile, C114
EA Playfish, C114
EarlyShares, C23
Easter Seals of Iowa, C148
Eastman Kodak, C201
eBay, 3, 48, 197, 367, 388
eBay, case
  aggressive expansion, C161
  balance sheets, C58
  board of directors vs. activist investor, C166
  business model, C156
  company history, C156–C160
  competitors
    Amazon, C165
    Etsy, C165–C166
    Google Inc., C165
    online giants, C156
    Taobao, C166
    traditional retailers, C166
    Yahoo!, C165

eBay, case—*Cont.*
  customer complaints, C167
  divestitures, C166–C167
  divestment of PayPal, C156
  evolution of auction markets, C161–C162
  failure in Asia, C157
  growth statistics, C163
  income statements, C157
  international expansion, C164
  leadership of, C163–C164
  low entry barriers, C156–C157
  new competitors, C167
  problems in 2015, C156
  product categories, C160–C161
  revenues, C165
  statement of cash flows, C159–C160
  strategy, C157–C160
  trust element, C61
eBay Commerce Network, C160
eBay Express, C160
eBay Marketplaces, C156
eBay Motors, C161
eBay Style, C156
EBSCO Publishing, 454
Ecce Panis, Inc., C133
Echo Bay Technology Group, C163
Ecolab, 267
Edatanetworks, 250
Edward Marshall Boehm, Inc., case
  entrepreneurship, C3
  functional-level strategy, C3
  manufacturing process, C3
  marketing and sales, C3
  mission, C3
Etihad Airways, C18, C262, C268
El Al, C18
Electronic Arts, C114
ElevationLab, C24
E-Loan, 375
eMarketer, C169
Embraer, C18
EMC, 365
Emilio Pucci, 160
Emirates Airline, 163, C18
Emirates Airline, case
  advertising, C268
  balance sheet, C264–C265
  business strategy, C267, C268–C269
  customer service, C267
  employee training, C267–C268
  government subsidies alleged, C262–C263
  growth, C262–C263
  income statement, C263
  main competitors, C268
  management, C267
  as start-up, C263–C267
  statement of cash flows, C265–C266
Encyclopaedia Britannica, 76
Energizer, 158

E! network, C174
Enron Corporation, 16, 204, 205, 303, 368, C147
Environmental Working Group, C237
Equity Bank, Kenya, C207, C208
Ernst & Young, 303
Estée Lauder, C91
eTools, C29
Etsy, C156, C157
  description, C165–C166
EVA, C262
Evolution Fresh, 206–207, C55
ExxonMobil, 183, 301
Eyez, C24

F

Facebook, 3, 113, 125, 132, 160, 161, 195, 249, C18, C113, C114, C115, C167, C168, C169, C171, C179
Fairmont Royal York, 21
Fairway, C229
Fairway Uptown, C221
Family Dollar, C34
F&M Schaefer, 349
Fannie Mae, 41
Farm Fresh, 56
Federal Express, 14, 26, 88–89, 283, 292, 331, C228
FEMSA Cervesa, C21
FEMSA Corona, C219
Ferrari, 66, C248
Ferrari California T, 65
Fiat, 197
Fiat Chrysler, 62
Fidelity Investments, 299
Firestone Walker Brewing Company, C107
Fischer brewery, C218
FitBit, C28, C127
Five Guys, C194
  market share, C195
Flickr, C22
Food Bank of New Jersey, C141
Food Network, C44
Food Panda, 261
Foote, Cone & Belding Worldwide, C211
Ford Asia, C251
Ford Australia, C251
Ford Europe, C251
Ford Motor Company, 23, 24, 66, 153, 187, 220, 232, 235, 271, 302, 351, 366, C244
  leadership at, 352
  new CEO, 296
Ford Motor Company, case
  in automotive industry, C247–C250
  balance sheet, C252–C253
  breakdown of global structure, C250
  business strategy success, C251
  company history, C245–C247

competition from Toyota, C247
corporate strategy restructure, C250–C260
divisions, C246
executive reorganization, C251
financial performance by region, C259
global brands, C258
income statement, C246
in India and China, C258
job cuts, C250
management changes, C245
market share, C248, C257
market share in 1999, C247
new product launches, C250
new vehicle sales 2006–2014, C256
organizational culture change, C251
organizational structure changes, C250–C251
plant closures, C250
product mix change, C253–C258
restructuring, C253–C259
sales, C248
sales by segment, C247
sales for Jan. 2015, C245
statement of cash flows, C254–C256
strategy priorities, C250–C251
uncertain future, C259–C260
Ford Motor Credit, C251
Ford North America, C251
Ford South America, C251
Forrester Research, 169, 409, C212
Forth & Towne, C62
Fortune Brands, 28
Fosters, C216
Founders Brewing Company, C107
Fox Business Network, 304
Foxconn, C122
FOXInflight, C16
Frankfurt Stock Exchange, 261
Freddie Mac, 41
Freddy's Frozen Custard LLC, C45
Freeloader, Inc, C115
FreeMarkets Online, 66
Freeport McMoRan, 183
FreshDirect, case
  Amazon challenge, C228–C229
  business model, C222
  business risk, C231
  customer online ordering problem, C230
  Daily Product Rating System, C230–C231
  early financing, C221–C222
  environmental concerns, C229
  expanded delivery options, C230
  expansion, C222
  functional strategy, C220–C221
  Google challenge, C229
  history and management, C221–C222

management changes, C222
neglected neighborhoods, C229
operating strategy, C222–C223
operations, C220–C221
potential online competitors, C225–C226
restaurant partnerships, C230
in retail grocery industry, C224–C225
rivals in New York segment
  NetGrocer, C228
  Peapod, C227–C228
  YourGrocer.com, C226–C227
as start-up, C221–C222
union and labor problems, C230
website, C223–C224
Frito-Lay, 80
  Super Bowl ads, 81
Frosty Bites, C44
Fro.Zen.Yo, C45
Fundly, C23

G

G. Heileman, 349
Galaxy Entertainment, C155
Gale CENGAGE Learning, 454
Gallup, 113
GameHouse, C113–C114
GameStop, C184
Gap Inc., C57, C58, C62
Garuda, C262
General Dynamics, 172, 371
General Electric, 5, 20, 21, 48, 82, 84, 117, 118, 195, 204, 205, 214, 220, 305, 328
  360-degree leadership chart, 119
General Electric Aerospace, 172
General Electric Healthcare, 221
General Electric Medical Systems, 115
General Mills, 240, 286, C132, C135
  description, C136
General Motors, 23, 62, 86, 119, 153, 213, 302, 304, 320, 356, C28, C245, C247, C248, C250, C256, C257
  management change, 357
General Motors, case
  auto safety crisis, C239–C244
  balance sheet, C240
  bankruptcy, C240
  in China, C244
  focus on fewer brands, C240–C243
  income by regions, C242
  income statement, C259
  management changes, C240
  market share, C241
  product development changes, C243
  response to safety concerns, C243–C244
  sales 2013–2014, C242
  sales in 2014, C244

Genting group, C154, C155
Genzyme, 230
Gerber Products Company, 92, C136
Giant-Carlisle, C228
Giant-Landover, C228
Gibson guitars, 158
Gigaom, 409
Gillette Company, 185, C200
GlaxoSmithKline, 118, C29
Global Crossing, 204
Global Growth Group, C196
Global Reporting Initiative, 114
Global Scan, 157
Gloria Jean's Coffee, C87
Gmarket Inc., 197, C156
GMO Renewable Resources, C70
Goldman Sachs, 48, 291, 301, 374, C100
Good Humor, C41
Good Humor–Breyers, C40, C41
Goodwill Industries of California, C148
Goodwill Industries of Michigan, C148
Goodyear Aerospace, 172
Google Inc., 3, 25, 48, 111, 113, 114, 115, 116, 121, 124, 137, 161, 173, 183, 262, 268, 283, 387, 388, 408, 456, C122, C123, C125, C156, C161, C167, C169, C170, C171, C209, C210, C229
 business model errors, 381
 description, C165
Google/Overstock, C157
Google Play, C127
Google Ventures, 61
Google Wallet, C54
Goose Island Brewing Company, C99, C107, C108
Governance Matters, C149
Grameen Bank, C206, C207, C208
Graphene Frontiers, 385
Graybeck Electric Company, 408
Green Bench Brewing, C106
Green China Forestry Company LTD., C73
Green Tree Financial, 182, 198
GreenWood Resources, Inc., case
 in China
  assessing investment projects, C68
  Dongji project, C68, C77–C78
  entry decision, C72–C73
  and financial crisis of 2008, C74
  and Forest Stewardship Council, C68–C70
  fund raising, C73
  intellectual property protection, C73–C74
  investment opportunities, C74–C75, C76
  Luxi project, C75–C77
  organizational goal, C68

 political risks, C74
 risks and challenges, C73–C74
 silvicultural differences, C74
 social risks, C74
 viability assessment, C68, C79
management team, C70–C72
research expertise, C70–C72
as start-up, C68–C70
timeline, C72
GreenWood Resources China Ltd., C73
GreenWood Tree Farm Fund L.P., C75
Greybeck Partners, 249
Group Modelo, C218
Groupon, 37, 91–92, 297
 management problems, 3–5
Grow VC, C23
GrubHub, 261
Gucci, 159, 223, C57, C201, C205
Guidant, 195
Guidestar, C149
Gulf Air, C267
Gung Ho, C114
Gustin, C24
GVO, 356

H

H. J. Heinz Company, C135
 description, C136
Häagen-Dazs, C40, C41, C44
Hagen-Dazs Shoppe Co. Inc., C45
Half.com, C161
Hallmark, 252
Hamilton, 171
Hanging Rock Picnics, C167
Hanover Insurance, 363
Happy Joe's, C45
Hardcastle Restaurants, C88
Hardee's, market share, C195
Hardtofindrx.com, 224
Harley-Davidson, 90
Harley-Davidson Café, 90
Harrah's, C153
Harry Winston, 171
Headline Entertainment, C54
HealthSouth, 368
Heineken, C99
 description, C108
Heineken, case
 acquisitions, C216–C219
 balance sheet, C216
 brands, C217
 building on global stature, C219
 corporate strategy, C216–C219
 in Ethiopia, C215
 in globalized industry, C215–C216
 income statement, C215
 international strategy, C218
 leadership goals, C219
 leadership in premium beer industry, C219
 loss of import beer leadership, C218

 management change, C215, C216–C218
 organizational structure, C219
 reduced reliance on core brand, C218–C219
 sales by region, C216
 target market
  Hispanics, C219
  younger drinkers, C218
Heineken USA, C103
Henkel, 272
Hewlett-Packard, 5, 114, 120, 131, 133, 182, 241, C123, C213
Hill & Knowlton/Harris Interactive poll, 19
Hindustan Unilever, 117
HMR Diets, C30
Homebrewers Association, C106
Home Depot, 47, 161, 252, 284, 290, C156
HomeGoods, C60
Home Shopping Network, 173–174, C179, C181
 turnaround strategy, 174
Honda Accord, 66
Honda Amaze, 67
Honda Motor Company, 6, 66, 77, 332, C247, C257
Honda motorcycles, 153
Honeywell Electro-Optics, 172
Honeywell International, 43, 49
 layoffs vs. furloughs, 138
Horniman Circle, C87
Hotel Monaco, 153
Household International, 198
HSN; see Home Shopping Network
HTC, 137, C125
Huawei, C124, C209, C210
Hugo Boss, C201, C205
Hulu Plus, C173, C175, C176
Hummer, C241
Hyundai, 65, 66
Hyundai Elantra, 56
Hyundai-Kia, C257
Hyundai Motor America, C248
Hyundai Xcent, 67

I

I. Magnin, C92
iBazar, C161
IBM, 21, 23, 82, 83, 96, 124, 185, 198, 199, 202, 218, 232, 252, 288, 301, 305, 330, 356, 393, 441, 452, 453, C120, C147
 and health care industry, 186
Icahn Capital, C166
ICI, 186
IdeaWorks, 163
IDEO, 23, 417
Ignition Corporation, 124
iGoDigital, 391
IKEA, 9, 22
ImClone Systems, 16, C147
InBev, 195, C216, C218, C219

Independent Sector, C149
Indian Hotels, C86
Indiegogo, C23
Infogroup Inc., 452
InfoSpace, Inc., 456
Infosys, 218, 353
ING SRI Index Fund, 21
Innosight, 367
In-N-Out Burger, 395
Intel Corporation, 3, 5, 16, 48, 84, 114, 117, 118, 183, 225, 241, 266, 292, 390, 396, 400, C210
 financial data, 111
 real options analysis, 401
Internal Ventures Group, 396
International Finance Corporation, 223
International Paper Company, 20, 49, C80
Internet Nonprofit Center, C149
Internet World Stats, C162
Intoko, C160
Intuit, 367, 388, 396
Iowa Beef Processors, 91
Iridium, 398
IRS Exempt Organizations, C149
Ispionage, 40
iTunes Mac Store, 64
iTunes Music Store, C121

J

J. Crew, C94
J. D. Power & Associates, 75, C243, C256
 Airline Satisfaction Study, C18
J. Jill Group, C64
J. M. Smucker, C202
Jack-in-the Box, market share, C195
Jacob Internet Fund, C169
Jaguar, 187, 352, C248, C251
Jamba Juice, case
 acquisition by Services Acquisition Corp., C49
 balance sheets, C50–C51
 brand marketing, C49–C52
 business-level strategy, C48
 company history, C49
 competitors, C55
 expense reduction plan, C54
 franchise strategy, C49
 franchising, C52–C53
 growth potential, C55
 growth strategy, C54
 Healthy Living format, C54
 hiring practices, C54
 income statements, C50
 initial public offering, C49
 innovation management, C55
 innovative tactics, C52
 international growth, C52–C53
 licensing agreements, C54
 management change, C49
 merger in 1999, C49
 and Nestlé, C54

Jamba Juice, case—*Cont.*
　new product launch, C48
　nontraditional locations, C53–C54
　organizational goals, C48
　product line, C49–C52
　product line extension, C48
　revenues, C49
　as start-up, C49
　stock repurchase plan, C48
　store types and locations, C53
　Summer Jobs Initiative, C54
　turnaround, C48
James Irvine Foundation mission, 27
James River Corporation, C80
JCPenney, 65, C60, C92
Jenny Craig, C28, C29, C30, C31
Jet Airways, C18
JetBlue Airways Corporation, 5, 82
　competitive position, 174–175
JetBlue Airways Corporation, case
　business-level strategy revision, C16–C17
　business model, C17–C18
　Customer Bill of Rights, C16
　customer-first attitude, C18
　early history and growth, C15–C16
　entrepreneurship, C14–C18
　financial statement, C17
　focus on shareholder value, C14
　initial public offering in 2002, C15
　innovations, C15, C18
　interline agreements, C17–C18
　low operating margins, C18
　management change, C14, C16
　mission, C15
　net losses 2005–2006, C16
　noncompete agreement, C15
　overall low-cost strategy, C14–C16
　pricing model, C18
　reputation loss, C16
　as start-up, C15–C16
　stock price performance, C14
　Valentine's Day disaster of 2007, C16
Jiffy Pop, C228
Jimmy John's, 155
Johnson & Johnson, 39, 306, 396–397, C94
Johnson & Johnson, case
　acquisitions, C234
　balance sheet, C234
　business strategy change, C237–C238
　collaboration effort, C234–C236
　confronting quality issues, C236–C237
　divisions, C234
　income statement, C233
　innovations, C236
　litigation settlement, C233
　management change, C233
　organizational structure, C234
　pressure for breakup, C237
　quality problems, C233
　research and development expenditures, C236
　sales in 2015, C236
　strategic business units, C235
　subsidiaries, C234
Johnson Controls, 400
Joseph Schlitz Brewing, 349
JPMorgan Chase, 16, 301, 373–374
Juice Club, C49
Juice It Up!, C55
Just-drinks.com, C219

K

Kabam, C114
Kaiser Permanente, 162
Kantar Retail, C57
Kauffman Foundation, 254–255
Kazaas, 64
Kellogg's, 231, C136, C228
Kenexa, 199–200
Kentucky Fried Chicken, 188
Kentucky One Health, 6, 7
Keppel Offshore and Marine Ltd., 287
Kia, 65, 66
Kia Motors America, C248
Kickstarter, 255, 256
Kickstarter, case
　backers' concerns about, C24–C25
　business-level strategy future, C25
　business model, C22
　company history, C22–C23
　competitors, C23
　crowdfunding concept, C21
　failures, C24
　and JOBS Act of 2012, C22, C25
　management, C22–C23
　operations, C21–C22
　rules and regulations, C24–C25
　successes, C23–C24
　success rate, C21
Kidder Peabody, 205
Kijiji, C160
Kimberly-Clark, 430–431, C201
King Company, C113, C114
Kismetic Enterprises East, 354
Kiva, 285
KKR, 191
KKR Capstone, 191
Klondike, C41
Kmart, 65, 169, C165, C211
Kodak, 272
Kohl's, 48
Kona Ice, C45
Korean Air, C18
Korn/Ferry International, 120
KPMG, 116
Kraft Foods, 48, 67, 233, C34, C54, C132
　description, C136
Kraft Foods Global, C83
Krispy Kreme Doughnuts, 156
Kroger, 148, 291, C44, C224

L

L. L. Bean, 383
Labor Law Study Committee, 331
La Boulangerie Bakery, 187, 206
Lagunitas Brewing Company, C107
Lamborghini, 66
Lamborghini Huracan, 65
Lammoda, 261
Land Rover, 352, C248, C251
Lands' End, 383
Lane Bryant, C63
Las Vegas Sands, C153
Lavazza, C87
LawPivot.com, 61
LegalZoom.com, 61
Lego, 50
　crowdsourcing by, 52
Lehman Brothers, 303
Lending Tree, 375
Lenovo, C122, C123, C126, C210
Lenovo + Motorola, C124
Levi Strauss, 367, 373
Lexis, 256
LexisNexis, 452, 453, 455
Lexus, 153, 283
LG, C210
Liberty Media, C182
Life is Good T-shirts, entrepreneurship, 252
Lifetime Movie Network, C182
Limited Brands, C63
LinkedIn, 130, 159–160, 366
Linksys, 181
Lionsgate, 202
　alliance with Alibaba, 203
Lipton, 157
Lisl, 279
Little Monster Productions, 256
Litton industries, 43
LiveTV, C16
Loblaw Companies, C224
Lockheed Martin, 116, 172, 190
Loews Corporation, 191–192, 323
Loews theaters, C41
Logitech International, 326
Lokau, C161
Longines, 171
LoQUo.com, C160
Loral Corporation, 190
L'Oréal, 220, C91, C95, C136
Lotus, 96
Lou & Grey, C64, C66
Lowe's, 47, 161
Lufthansa, C17, C262
LunaTik, C24
Lyft Inc., 57–58

M

Macquarie Securities, C192
Macy's Inc., C60
Maggie Moo's, C44
Mandalay Bay, C15
Mandalay Entertainment, 22
Mandalay Resort Group, C153
Maranz, 153
Marble Slab Creamery, C41, C44, C45
MARC Group, C225
March Group, 331
Marina Bay Sands, C154
MarketWatch, Inc., 454
Marktplaats.nl, C160
Marks and Spencer, 292
　sustainability goals, 289
Marlin Steel Wire Products, 160, 161
Marriott Corporation, 149
Mars Central Europe, 286
Marshall's, C60
Martin guitars, 153
Mary Kay Inc., C91
Maserati, C248
Mattel, C173
Maxim's Caterers, C85
Mayo Clinic, 8, 330, C29
Mayo Clinic Diet, C29, C30
Maytag, 228
Mazda Motor Corporation, C251, C257
Mazda Motor of America, C248
McDonald's Corporation, 25, 86, 188, 190, 231, 290, 341, C44, C48, C49, C55, C87, C88
McDonald's Corporation, case
　balance sheet, C194
　business model rethink, C198–C199
　business strategy revision, C197–C198
　income statement, C194
　main competitors, C194–C195
　management change, C194
　market share, C195
　milestones, C196–C197
　reimaging of outlets, C198
　response to competition, C195
　revenues, C195
　sales decline, C194–C196
　strategy options, C199
　turnaround attempt, C196–C197
McKinsey & Company, C94, C149
McKinsey Corporation, 20, 41, 45
McKinsey Global Institute, 121
McNeil Consumer Healthcare, C233, C236–C237
MD Anderson Cancer Center, 8
Medifast, C28, C29, C30
Mediterranean Diet, C30
Medtronic, 25, 153
　tax situation, 242–243
Meetup, C22, C161

Memorial Sloan Kettering, 202
Menchie's, C45
MercadoLibre.com, C156, C161
Mercedes-Benz, 65, 66, 158, C243, C248
Merck, 48, 67, 99, 110
Mercy Corps, C72
Mergent, Inc., 452, 453, 455
Merrill Lynch, 45, 109–110, 205, C4
MessageMe, C171
Method Products, 254
MetLife, 183
Metorex, 6
MGM Mirage, C153, C154
Michelin, 153
Microsoft Corporation, 3, 41, 80–82, 113, 115, 118, 124, 173, 182, 219, 223, 225, 291, 302, 395, 396, 406–407, 431, C120, C121, C122, C123, C125, C126, C147, C161, C164, C169, C170
   financial data, 111
Microsoft Encarta, 76
Microsoft Exchange, 407
Microsoft Xbox, C184–C185, C189, C190–C191, C192
MidOcean Partners, C222
Milani Gelateria, C45
Miller Brewing, 349, C216
MillerCoors LLC, C99, C100, C104, C109
   description, C108
Milo, C161
Mini, C248
Mini Melts, C44
Mint.com, adaptive new entrant, 262
Mintel, C93
Minton China, C3
Mitsubishi, 21, C210
Mitsubishi Motors N. A., C248
Mollie Stone's Market, 254
Molson, C216
Molson Coors Brewing Company, C108, C217
Mondelez International, 67, C135, C136
Monster Beverage, C55
MonsterTRAK.com, 114
Moody's Investors Service, 96
Moosehead Breweries, C109
Moretti, C218, C219
Morgan Stanley, 152, 374, C35
Morningstar, 21
Morris Air, C1
Motel 6, 39, 40
Motorola, 25, 398, 403, C122, C127
Mozilla Firefox, C122, C126, C171
Murphy's Irish Red, C219
MyFitnessPal, C28
mySimon, 61
Mystery Brewing Company, 255

N

Nairobi Stock Exchange, C207
Napster, 64, 137
Narayana Hrudayalaya Heart Hospital, 121
NASDAQ Stock Exchange, 3, 147
National Association of Attorneys General, C149
National Association of State Charity Officials, C149
National Circus School, C271
National Council of Nonprofits, C149
National Federation of Independent Businesses, 67, 257
National Football League, C143, C144, C147, C176
National Health Care Service (UK), 125
Natura, C91
NBC, C174, C176
NEC, 19, C185
Neiman Marcus, 65, C57, C60, C92
Nestlé Corporation, 187–188, 235, C40, C54, C85, C136
NetAge Inc., 335
Netflix, 93, C231
   versus Blockbuster, 94–95
NetGrocer
   description, C228
   profile, C226
Network for Good, C149
Neutrogena, C94
New Belgium Brewing Company, C99, C107
   description, C108
Newman's Own, C198
New York Times Company, 269
NeXT Computer, C120
Nextel, 182
Next Labs, 408–409
Nielsen, C212
Nike, Inc., 18, 19, 49, 174, 220, 227, 231, 270–271, 332, 333, 397, C127
Nintendo, 63
Nintendo's Wii U, case
   balance sheet, C187–C188
   company history, C185
   compared to competition, C184
   competitors
      Microsoft Xbox, C184, C190–C191
      mobile gaming, C192
      Sony Playstations, C184, C191–C192
   corporate strategy, C189–C190
   customers, C189
   description of business, C184
   early competitors, C185
   early video games, C185
   features, C188–C189
   future options, C193

   game developers, C189–C190
   game systems comparisons, C190
   income statement, C186
   innovation and creativity, C185
   innovative enhancements, C187
   low initial sales, C184
   new game control standard, C186–C188
   release of Wii in 2006, C185–C186
   sales by country, C185
Nissan Leaf, 56
Nissan Motor Company, 66, C115, C247, C257
Nissan North America, C248
Nokia, 124, C122
Nokia Lumia Windows 8 phone, C125
Nordstrom, 65, 80, 87, 153, 371, C57, C60
Norman Regional Health Systems, 7
North Face, 153
North Oaks Health System, 7
Northrup Grumman, 21
Northwest Airlines, 197
Novartis, 184, 301, 330, C237
Novartis Medical Nutrition, C136
Novell, 272
NPD Group, 181, C29
Nucor Corporation, 176, 283
   financial data, 111
Nutrisystem, C28, C29, C30
Nutriva, 188
   vertical integration, 189
NYCGrocery.com, C226

O

O. R. T. Technologies, 223–224
Old Navy, C62
Oldsmobile, 320
Olympus Corporation, 16, 293
OMB Watch, C149
Omega, 171
On the Border, 26
Opryland USA, C42, C43
Oracle Corporation, 3, 133, 206, 220, 232, 302, 431, 441, C166, C275
   financial data, 111
Oregon Ice Cream LLC, C54
Oriental Timber Fund Limited, C68, C75
Orkut, 388
Ornish Diet, C30
Orrick, Herrington & Sutcliffe, 121
Ortho-Clinical Diagnostics, C237
Otis Elevator, 41
   manufacturing problem, 228
Outboard Marine Corporation, 25
Outdoor Industry Association, 19
OUYA TV, C24
Overstock.com, 404
Oxford GlycoSciences, 230

P

Pabst Brewing, 349
Pace Foods, C131
Pacific Gas & Electric, 304
Paciugo Gelato CaffÃ", C46
Panasonic, 235
   in China, 236
Panera Bread, 341, C55, C195, C199
Park Slope, C228
Patagonia, 18, 19, 26
Paulaner, C218
Paychex, 62
PayPal, 262, C156, C160, C166
Peapod
   description, C227–C228
   profile, C226
Pebble, C122
Pebble Watch, C24
PeopleSoft, 206
Pepperidge Farm, C132, C133, C136, C141
Pepsi Beverage Company, C54
PepsiCo, 81, 116, 162, 188, 219, 221, 330, 331, 405
Peticolas Brewing, C106
Pez, 388
Pfizer, Inc., 48, 92, 99, 195, 223, 224, 288, 385, C236
Phelps Dodge, 183
Picholine, C221
Pier 1 Imports, 39
Pike Place Market, Seattle, C83
Pillsbury, C136
Pilsner Urquell, C216
Pipeline Inc., C148
Piperlime, C62
Pixar, 431
Pixar, case
   acquired by Disney, C274–C275
   creativity, C275–C277
   employee roles, C276
   films, C274
   functional strategy, C275–C278
   growth, C277
   initial public offering, C275
   main competitor, C278
   milestones, C276
   origin of, C275
   purchased by Steve Jobs, C275
   quality commitment, C278
   story development, C277
   success of, C274
   technology improvement, C277
Pizza Hut, 188
Planet Smoothie, C55
Planning Perspectives Inc., 62
Playfish Ltd., C114
Plum Creek Timber Company, C80
Plum Organics, adaptive new entrant, 262
Plunkett Research, Ltd., 456
Polaris, 184
Polaroid, 131
Pontiac, 320

Popbar, C46
Popsicle, C41
Porsche, 65, 66, 86, 153, 157, 405
Porsche Cars NA Inc., C248
Porsche Cayenne, 86
Post Holdings Inc., C34
Potlatch Corporation, C68, C73
PPG Industries, 28, 42
  scenario planning, 43
Presto Italiano, C230
Priceline.com, 204, C222
PricewaterhouseCoopers, 122, 279
Principled Solutions Enterprise, 7
Procter & Gamble, 18, 19, 28, 39, 48, 50, 67, 117, 170, 173, 183, 219, 233, 252, 272, 324, 409, 452, C91, C94
  innovation, 386
Procter & Gamble, case
  acquisitions, C200–C201
  balance sheet, C205
  brand updating, C201
  continued stagnation, C204–C205
  corporate turnaround strategy, C201
  customer focus, C201
  downward spiral in 1990s, C200
  expansion into services, C201–C202
  financial data, C203–C204
  human capital development, C201
  human resource practices, C201
  income statement, C204
  innovations, C200
  loss of good employees, C200
  management changes, C202
  new product development, C201
  organizational structure revision, C201
  sell-off of brands, C200–C201, C202
  strategic business units, C203
  succession plan, C200
  turnaround failure, C202
Progress Energy, 195
Project: WorldWide, 258, 259
Project Eternity, C24
ProQuest LLC, 454
Providence Equity Partners, 102
Pryor Cashman LLP, 256
Publix Super Markets, C224
Pure Digital Technologies, 181
Puritan-Bennett Corporation, 331

Q

Qantas, C262
Qatar Airways, C18, C262
Quaker Oats, 168
Qualcomm, 3, 48
Quantum Trading Strategies, C167
Quiznos, 154
  decline, 155
Quora, 40

QVC, case
  acquisition, C183
  acquisitions, C181
  business strategy, C181, C183
  celebrity endorsements, C179
  company history, C179–C181
  customer base, C183
  growth, C179
  growth strategies, C183
  income statement, C180
  main competitor, C179
  milestones, C182
  new product introductions, C179
  online access, C179
  products avoided by, C182
  promotions by other firms, C182
  revenues by region, C181
  sales 1989–2014, C179
  search for profitable products, C182
QVC.com, C182
QVCHD, C182
QVC Plus, C182
Qwest Communications, 361

R

Radio Shack, 38
Rahr & Sons, C106
Rainmaker Entertainment, 396
Ralcorp Holdings, C34
Ralph Lauren, 174
Ralphs, 29, 148
Raytheon, 127, 372–373
RBC Capital Markets, C169
RealArcade, C114
Real Mango-Yogurt Cafe & Juice Bar, C46
RealNetworks, C114, C126
Recreational Vehicle Dealer Association, 188
Red Cross, C145
Red Hat, Inc., 430
  integrative thinking, 431
RedLaser, C161
Reebok, 233, 332
Renault, 152, 222
  low-cost policy, 151
Renault-Nissan, C247
Rent.com, C156
Repicci's Italian Ice, C46
Research in Motion, 124, 388
Resorts World Manila, C154
Resorts World Sentosa, C154
Reuben's Brews, C106
Revel Hotel, C153
Revlon, C91
Rhapsody, C126
Rhinestone Holdings, C95
Ricoh Americas Corporation, 225, 226
RightNow Technologies Inc., 156
Ringling Brothers and Barnum and Bailey, C272
Rita's Italian Ice, C46
Ritter's Frozen Custard, C46

Rocket Internet, 261
Rockwell Collins, 363
RockYou, C113
Rosa Mexicano, C230
Royal Ahold, C228
Royal Dutch Shell, 300, 405
Running Press, 265
Russian River Brewing Company, C107
Ruth's Chris, 153
Ryanair, 163, 270

S

S. C. Johnson, 254
Saab, C241
SABMiller, C108, C217, C218
SABMiller Europe, C216
Safeway Company, 300, C49, C224, C225
SAIC, 214
  international strategy problem, 213
Salemi Industries, 37
Salesforce.com, 388
Salomon Smith Barney, 182
Salvation Army, C145–C147
Samsonite, C44
Samsung Electronics, 137, 267, C122, C123, C124, C125, C126
Samsung Electronics, case
  balance sheet, C209
  business strategy shift, C209–C210
  Chinese competitors, C209
  corporate strategy goal, C212–C213
  design process, C212
  discarding failed strategy, C210–C211
  global market ranking, C210
  income statement, C209
  layoffs, C211
  losses in 1998, C210–C211
  management change, C210–C211
  milestones, C213
  new product development, C211–C212
  number of designers employed, C212
  premium brand development, C211
  product line, C209–C210
  reimaging, C211
  research process, C212
  retail store changes, C211
  smartphone sales, C210
Samsung Group, 25
SanDisk, C122
Sandoz Ltd., C136
Sands China, C154
Sanford C. Bernstein, 109, C202
SAP, 50, 113, 441, C220
  accessing knowledge, 135

Sapient Health Network, decision making, 419
Saturn Corporation, C241
Schlumberger, 82
Schmitz Cargobull, 84
  information technology at, 85
Scottish & Newcastle, C215, C218
Sears, 3, 65, 101, 115, C92
Security Mortgage Group, 433
Sega Dreamcast, C185
Sega Genesis, C185
Send the Trend, C182
Sephora.com, 80
Services Acquisition Corp. International, C49
7-Eleven, C224
Seventh Generation, 29
Shake Shack, C194
Shanghai Automotive Industry Corporation, 213
Shaw Industries, 77, 184, 186
Shell Oil Company, 19, 120, 300
Shopping.com, C156
ShopRunner, 93
Short's Brewing Company, C107
Shutl, 197, C161
Siebel Systems, 232
Siemens, 358
  use of "soft" power, 359
Sierra Nevada Brewing Company, C99
  description, C106–C108
Sikorsky Helicopters, 41
Silpada, C95
Silver Lake Partners, C161, C164
Singapore Airlines, 290, C262, C268
Single Source Systems, 28
SJM, C155
Skybus Airlines, C17
Skype, 134, C161, C164
Sleep Health Centers, 40
Slideshare, 40
Slim-Fast, C29, C30
Sloan-Kettering, 186
Sloan's Ice Cream, C46
Smith Kline, 198
SmithKline Beecham, 198
Smoothie King, C55
Smucker's, 252
Social Apps, C115
Sociedad de Jogos de Macau, C153
Sodima, 240
SoftBank, 182, 195
Solaire Resort and Casino, C154
Solectron, 116
Sonic Drive-ins, market share, C195
Sony Corporation, 6, 20, 397, C122, C127, C210, C211, C213
Sony Playstations, C184–C185, C189, C191–C192
South African Airlines, C262
South African Breweries Plc, C216

I-8 Company Index

South Beach Diet, C36
Southern Alliance for Clean
    Energy, 369
Southern California
    Brewing, C103
Southwest Airlines, 3, 5, 9, 84,
    92, 111, 269–270, 284, 384,
    C15, C17
Southwest Airlines, case
  acquisition of AirTran, C11
  automation, C10
  business-level strategy, C7–C8
  cities served by, C11
  corporate-level strategy, C8–C12
  cost control, C10
  cost increases, C9–C10
  early history, C7–C8
  earnings in 2014, C7
  entrepreneurship, C7–C12
  financial data, C9
  fined $1.6 million, C7
  growth strategy, C11–C12
  intensifying competition, C10
  international expansion, C9, C11
  management change, C8–C12
  mission statement, C8
  net income in 2013, C7
  oil price hedging, C7, C11–C12
  operating data, C9–C10
  organizational culture, C7–C8
  overall cost leadership, C7–C12
  performance appraisal, C7
  stock price performance, C12
  and Wright amendment, C9, C12
Spanx, adaptive new entrant, 262
Spike TV, C174
Spirit Airlines, 163
Sports Authority, 93
Sprecher Brewing, C106
Sprint, 182, 195
Square, 262
SsangYong, 213
Standards for Excellence
    Institute, C149
Staples, 16, C156
Starbucks, 187, 206–207, 251,
    C48, C49, C54, C55, C82,
    C87, C88, C199
  best practices for new markets
    good local partner, C85
    long-term commitment,
      C85–C86
    tact in marketing, C85
  in China, C84–C85
  company history, C83
  expansion into China, C84
  expansion into Japan, C83–C84
  expansion into Philippines, C84
  expansion into Singapore, C84
  human resource practices, C83
  initial expansion into Asia,
    C83–C84
  mission, C83
  revenues, C83
  social responsibility, C83
  and Tata Group, C86

Starbucks Coffee China, C88
Starbucks Coffee Japan Ltd., C84
Starbucks Singapore, C84
Stern Agee, C184
Stone Brewing Company,
    C106, C107
Stop & Shop, C228
Strategic Decisions Group, C236
Strategy Analytics, C125
StrawberryFrog ad agency, C268
Streamline.com Inc., C228
Strickland's Frozen Custard, C46
Stroh's Brewing, leadership
    mistakes, 349–350
StubHub, 197, C156, C161
Subaru, C257
Subaru of America Inc., C248
Subsea Infrastructure, 82
Subway, 155, 341, C197
Sub Zero Ice Cream, C46
Sumitomo Chemical
    Company, C211
Sunbeam Corporation, 204, 434
Sun Microsystems, 133
SunPower, 114
Supercell, C114
Support.com, C115
Sustainability Consortium, 331
Sustainable Apparel Coalition, 18
  description, 19
Sustainable Living Lab, 157
Swatch Group, 171
Symantic, 296
Symbid, C23
Sync Power Systems, C24
Synthes, C234

T

T. Rowe Price, 299
Tabla, C230
Taco Bell, 188, 394, C196, C199
  new ideas, 395
Takata, C258
Talbots, C63
Talbott Teas, C49
Talenti, C41
Tandem Computers, 120
Taobao, C166
Target Corporation, 206, C224
Target stores, 169, 301, C34, C57,
    C60, C182
Tarte Cosmetics, C182
Tasti D-Lite, C46
Tata Chemicals, C86
Tata Coffee, C86
Tata Communications, C86
Tata Consultancy Services, C86
Tata Global Beverages, C82, C86
Tata Group, 202, C82, C86
  business units, C86
Tata Motors, 66, 67, C8
Tata Power, C86
Tata Starbucks, case
  achieving sustainable
    success, C88

  competitors, C82
    Barista chain, C87
    Café Coffee Day, C86–C87
    costs in India, C87
    price wars, C88
    quick-service restaurant
      chains, C87–C88
  expansion by 2015, C82
  Indian café market, C82
  India's experience with
    coffee, C86
  joint venture, C82
  strategic decisions, C82–C83
Tata Steel, C86
Tata Teleservices, C86
TCS, 218
Teach for America, 24
Teavana Teas, C55
Techniq, 82
Tenth and Blake Beer
    Company, C99
Terrapin Beer, C100
Tesco, 49, 150–151, 280, C225
  corporate governance
    problem, 279
Tesla Motors, C247
Texas Instruments, 370
TGI Friday's, 233–234, C136
Thai Airlines, C262
The Bruery, C107
The Limited TOO, C63
The Point, 3
ThinkEquity, C164
Third Eyesight, C88
Third Millennium
    Communications, 124
3M Corporation, 22, 28, 92, 138,
    184, 203, 283, 284, 366, 396
TIAA-CREF, 299
TikTok, C24
Time Inc., 453
Time Warner, 182, 209, 301
Tim Hortons, C55
Titan Watches, C86
T.J. Maxx, C57, C60
TJX, C60
TLC Diet, C30
T-Mobile, 187
Tokyo Electric Power Company, 6
Tommy Hilfiger, 174
Tom Online, C156
TOMS Shoes, 270–271
Tops Market, C228
Toro Company, 364
Toshiba Corporation, 6, C122
Toyota Camry, 66
Toyota Motor Corporation, 6, 76,
    153, 220, 266, C247, C248,
    C256, C257
  JIT inventory systems, 77–78
Toyota Prius, 56
Toys "R" Us, 93, C114
Trader Joe's, C225
Travel Channel, C43
Tree Farm Fund L.P., C73
Tribeca Grill, C221

Tribe Networks, C115
True Value, 161
Trumpet ad agency, C222
Tuft and Needle, low-cost
    strategy, 264
Tumblr, C169, C171
Turkey Hill, C41
Twitter, 86, 249, 366, C22, C168,
    C169, C179
Tyco International, 16, 205,
    368, C147

U

Uber Technologies., 57–58
UBS, 374
Ultimate Fighting Championship,
    C177
Under Armour, Inc., adaptive new
    entrant, 262
Unilever PLC, 50, 67, 170, 267,
    272, C40, C202
  sustainability initiatives, 157
United Airlines, 92, 197
United Continental Holdings, C18
United Parcel Service, 49,
    430, C147
United Technologies Corporation,
    40, 228
  and competitive intelligence, 41
United Way of America, C143
United Way Worldwide, case
  appeal for contributions, C143
  competing charities, C145–C147
  competition for donations, C143
  corporate scandals, C147–C149
  donor trust problem, C144
  effect of economic
    downturn, C143
  as financial intermediary, C144
  financial statements,
    C146–C147
  governance response to
    scandals, C149–C151
  growth options, C143
  history of, C144–C145
  new standards of excellence,
    C150
  operations, C144–C145
  organizations supported
    by, C143
  Senate Finance Committee
    hearings, C149–C150
  strategy shift, C144
  watchdog agencies, C149
Universal Pictures, 81
Urban Institute, 45
U.S. Airways, 197
USAA financial services, 153
USA channel, C174

V

ValueJet, C11
Values Technologies, 120
Varian Medical Systems, 28

Venetian Hotel, C153
Verizon, 331
Versace, C155
Victoria's Secret, C63
Viewpoint DataLabs International, 95
Vimeo, C22
Virgin America, C17, C18
Virgin Atlantic, C18, C262
Virgin Group, 23, 191
Vodafone, 323
Volkswagen, 213, 220, C244, C251, C257
Volkswagen of America, C248
Volvo, 352, C248, C251
Vons, 29
Vought Aircraft, 315
Voyager.net, 354

W

Wachovia Corporation, 156
Waldenbooks, 6
Walgreens, C34, C114
Wall Street Journal, 269
Walmart Stores, 9, 17, 18, 19, 20, 49, 65, 148, 152, 162–163, 169, 219, 221, 267, 282, 283, 284, 292, 330, 331, 384, C60, C114, C156, C165, C211, C224
Walnut Venture Associates, 256
Walt Disney Company, C276, C278
 acquisition of Pixar, C274–C275
Wanli Afforestation Group, C78
Warner Brothers, C169, C177, C278
Waste Management, 204
WBG Construction, 365
WD-40 Company, 264
Webvan, C221
Weight Watchers International, C136
Weight Watchers International, Inc. case
 acquisition of Wello, C28
 advertising goals, C31
 balance sheet, C32–C-33
 brand credibility, C31
 business-level strategy revision, C36
 business model, C30–C31
 business model change, C27
 competition for, C27–C28
 competitive environment, C29–C30
 cost factors of weight-loss plans, C29
 customers, C35–C36
 Hispanic customers, C35
 history and expansion, C28–C29
 income statements, C32
 innovation, C31
 international expansion, C28
 main competitors, C30
 management change, C27–C28
 market for, C28
 online access, C27, C29
 profit margins, C31
 program innovations, C31–C35
 ranking, C29
 rebranding effort, C27
 revenues 2011–2012, C27
 revenue sources, C31
 and rise in obesity, C29
 start-up business model, C28
 statement of cash flows, C33–C34
 Super Bowl advertising, C27
 target market, C28, C35–C36
 trend analysis, C28
 variable cost structure, C31
 website, C28
Wella, C201
Wellington Management, C166
Wello, C28
WellPoint Health Network, 26, 62
Wells Blue Bunny, C41
Wells Fargo, 14, 25, 28, 116
Wendy's, 241, C194, C196
 market share, C195
WestJet, C9
Westlaw, 256
Wetherill Associates, 372
Weyerhaeuser, C80
Whataburger, market share, C195
WhatsApp, 195
Whirlpool, 23, 331
Whole Foods Market, Inc., 41, 148, 163, 365, C225, C230
Wikipedia, 76
Wild Oats Markets, C230
Winnebago, 188
Wipro, 218
World Championship Wrestling, C173–C174
WorldCom, 204, 205, 303, 368, C147
World Triathlon Corporation brand extension, 102
World Wildlife Fund, C174
World Wrestling Entertainment, case
 business strategy, C174
 buyout of competitor, C173–C174
 cable network, C173
 classic bouts, C175
 competition from mixed martial arts, C177
 development of, C173–C174
 failed football league, C173, C176
 growth strategies, C176–C178
 income, C176
 name change in 2002, C174
 new programs and products, C173
 operations, C174–176
 revenues, C176, C177
 turnaround after 2005, C173
Wormtown Brewing, C106
WPP Group PLC, 132, 358
WWE Network, C173
Wyeth, 195
Wynn Macau, C155
Wynn Resorts, 294

X

Xerox Corporation, 25, C201
XFL football league, C176
Xiaomi, C124, C209, C210
XM Satellite Radio, C16

Y

Yahoo!, 257, 268, 454
 description, C165
Yahoo!, case
 acquisitions, C168
 advertising decline, C170–C171
 balance sheet, C168
 broken business model, C170–C171
 corporate strategy problems, C169
 corporate strategy refocus, C169–C170
 employee benefits, C170–C171
 employee problems, C170
 income statement, C168
 leadership 1995–2015, C170
 management change, C169
 rejection of Microsoft offer, C169
 spin-off of Alibaba stake, C168
 turnaround attempt, C171
 turnaround of advertising business, C168
Yahoo MusicMatch, C126
Yahoo/Taobao, C157
Yeh Group, 430
Yilin Wood Industry Co., Ltd., C78
Yogurtland Franchising Inc., C46
Yoplait, 240
Young & Rubicam, 358
Young Brands, 418
YourGrocer.com
 description, C226–C227
 profile, C226
YouTube, 40, 90, 156, C173
Yum! Brands, 9, 188, C199

Z

Zappos, 154–155, 157, 261, 330, 337
Zara, 202
Zhejiang Geely Holding Company, 66
Zimbra, 407
Zola and Sundia Corporation, C54
Zuka Juice Inc., C49
Zulily, 151, 152
Zurich Financial Services, 232
Zynga, 25, C23
Zynga, case
 balance sheets, C112
 CEO, C115
 competitors, C113–C115
 customer complaints, C116
 future strategy, C116
 income statements, C111
 initial public offering, C113
 intellectuial property ethical issues, C115
 litigation, C113, C115
 market size, C113
 product line, C111, C113
 revenue decline, C112

NAME INDEX

A

Aaker, David A., 177, 246
Abby, E., 311
Abelson, J., C67
Abelson, Reed, C141, C238
Abrams, Rachel, C205
Accavitti, Mike, 234
Ackerman, Bill, C202
Ackerman, Elise, C171
Ackerman, Jason, C220, C222, C223
Ackerson, Dan, C240
Adams, S., 141
Adamy, Janet, C199
Adelson, Sheldon, C153
Adler, Charles, C22, C23, C25
Adler, P. D., 143
Afuah, A., 71, 345
Agarwal, Parul, C14n
Ahlstrom, D., 305, 313
Aiman-Smith, L., 413
Aime, F., 143
Akasie, J., 163
Akerson, Dan, 357
Albanesius, Chloe, C192
Albaugh, Jim, 315
Albee, Mrs. P. F. E., C89–C90
Albrinck, J., 413
Alcott, K., 246
Aldag, R. J., 440
Aldrich, H. E., 276
Alessandri, T. M., 312
Alexander, Melvin, 6, 7, 210
Alexander the Great, C47
Allard, M. J., 143
Allen-MacGregor, Jacqueline, C148
Aller, R., 345
Allison, M., C88
Allsopp, A., C128
Alsever, J., 48
Alvarez, S. A., 70
Amabile, T. M., 142
Amburgey, T. L., 345
Amelio, Gilbert, C120, C121
Amit, R., 107
Amram, M., 413
An, J., C25
Anard, B. N., 211
Anders, G., 178
Andersen, M. M., 345
Anderson, Abram, C130
Anderson, E., 106
Anderson, G., C47
Anderson, J. C., 105
Anderson, M. M., 106
Anderson, Richard, 12
Anderson, S., C151
Andreesen, Marc, 249
Andres, Mike, 341
Andre the Giant, C173, C175
Angel, R., 107
Angle, Kurt, C175
Angwin, J. S., 211
Anmuth, Douglas, C183
Anslinger, P. A., 210
Ansoff, H. Igor, 70
Ante, S., 275
Anthony, Scott, 245, 367
Antoine, Dick, C202
Aramony, William, C148
Areddy, James T., C98
Argawal, A., 311
Argent, Ron, 16
Argyris, Chris, 280, 310
Arikan, A. M., 32, 106
Arino, A., 211
Armstrong, R. W., 178
Arndt, A., 210
Arndt, Michael, 210, C199
Arno, A., 211
Arnold, D., 247
Arnott, D. A., 310
Arregle, J.-L., 106, 143
Arrfelt, M., 210, 307
Arrow, Kenneth, 42
Artzt, Ed, C200
Ash, Mary Kay, C91
Ashkenas, R., 328
Assenza, Pauline, C21n, C27n, C48n, C57n, C117n, C143n, C245n
Aston, A., 71
Auerback, John, C26
Augustine, N. R., 179
Austin, J., C79
Austin, R. D., 32, 177
Austin, Steve, C175, C177

B

Bacani, C., C192
Bach, Lincoln, C70, C71
Bachman, J., 246
Backs, Melanie, C232
Badan, Baba, C86
Bader, P., 144
Badrinath, R., C88
Baer, D., 32
Bahrami, H., 336
Bahree, M., C88
Baier, J., 141
Bailay, R., C88
Bailey, J., C19
Bainbridge, Julia, C171
Baio, Andy, C23
Baird, Catherine, C267
Bajarin, Ben, C209
Bajikar, Sundeep, C213
Baker, Kevin, C216
Baker, S., 71
Baker, Stephen, 181
Bakke, Dennis, 371, 378
Ball, Brandi, C178
Ballew, Paul, C259
Ballmer, Steve, 41
Ballou, J, 254
Balzar, Harry, C40
Bamford, C. E., 70
Banjo, S., 174
Bansal, P., 141
Ba-Oh, Jorge, C192
Barbaro, M., C67
Barboza, D., 374
Barger, David, 5, 32, C14, C16
Barkema, H. G., 179, 211
Barkley, Charles, C36
Barlow, N., C88
Barman, Emily, C151
Barnebik, Percy, 33
Barnes, B., 245, C278
Barnes, L. A., 440
Barnett, M. L., 71
Barnevik, Percy, 142
Baron, R. A., 141, 275, 413
Barra, Mary T., 119, 356, 357, C239, C240, C243, C244
Barrera, Luz, C143n
Barrett, Amy, C238
Barrett, Colleen, C8
Barrett, Randy, C276
Barrett, W. P., C151
Barrette, Michael, C39
Barringer, B. R., 346
Barsaoux, J., 310
Bart, C. K., 34
Bartholomew, D., C19
Bartiromo, M., C88
Bartlett, C. A., 179, 245, 321, 345
Bartness, A., 346
Barton, Dominic, 45
Barton, N., C151
Bartz, Carol, C169, C170
Barwise, P., 142
Bary, Andrew, C278
Basinger, J., 70
Battilana, J., 143
Bauer, Jason, 147
Bauer, T. N., 156
Baugher, Dan, C21n
Baum, J. A. C., 211
Baumgarter, P., 71
Baxter, Audrey, 273
Bay, Willow, C19
Baysinger, B. D., 311
Beamish, P. W., 245, 276
Bearden, W. O., 178, 179
Beartini, M., 100
Beatty, D., 312
Becker, G. S., 141
Becker, Will, 16
Beckers, S. F. M., 106
Beckhard, R., 32, 328, 377
Begley, T. M., 32
Bell, Charles H., C197
Beller, P. C., 310
Belson, K., C88
Belton, C., 245
Bendel, Henri, C67
Benioff, Marc, 388
Benjamin, Jeff, C94
Benkle, Y., 310
Bennett, D., C128
Bennett, Jeff, C244
Bennett, N., 311
Bennett, Steve, 296–297
Benoit, Chris, C174
Benoit, D., 141
Bensaou, B. M., 106
Bensinger, G., C167
Benz, M., 33
Berardino, Joseph, 204
Berfield, S., C260
Bergen, M. A., 277
Bergen, M. E., 177
Berk, C. C., C66
Berkman, Seth, C178
Berkowitz, E. N., 179, 246
Berle, Adolph, 293
Berman, Todd, 353
Berner, R., 267
Bernerth, J. B., 156
Bernoff, J., 378
Berns, Gregory, 128
Bernstein, A., 313
Berr, J., C36
Berrard, Steven, C49
Berry, Halle, C179
Berry, J., 211
Berry, M. A., 33
Bertini, M., 178
Bertrand, O., 246
Berzon, Alexander, C273
Besley, S., 211
Bethune, Gordon, 150

Bezos, Jeff, 93, 264
Bhagat, C., 311
Bhagat, R. S., 246
Bhambhu, Arun, C7n
Bhatia, Arvind, C184
Bhattacharya, A. K., 246, C88
Bhattacharya, C. B., 33
Bhide, A. V., 276, 312, 412
Bickerton, Ian, C219
Bierce, Ambrose, 293
Bierman, L., 312
Bigelow, C. O., C67
Bigley, G. A., 32
Billman, E., 19
Binder-LePape, Jennifer, 261
Bindley, K., C25
Bird, A., 142
Bird, Brad, C276
Birkinshaw, J., 11, 32, 247, 310, 346, 412
Blake, S., 143
Blank, Arthur, 24
Blank, D., C19
Blanton, Buddy, 363
Block, Z., 413
Bloom, M., 312
Bloomberg, Georgina, 4
Bloomberg, Michael, 4, C54
Blum, D. E., C151
Blyler, M., 107
Bodick, N., 178
Bodwell, C., 33
Boehm, Edward Marshall, C3
Boehret, K., C193
Bogner, W. C., 141
Boh, W. F., 143
Bolland, Marc, 289
Bonamici, K., C18
Bonnabeau, E., 178
Boris, C., C26
Bosman, J., C231
Bosse, D. A., 33
Bothe, Marie, 372
Boudette, N., 352
Bouquet, C., 310
Bouwer, Marc, C179
Bowen, D. E., 378
Bowen, H. P., 209
Bower, J. L., 11
Bower, Joseph, C247
Bowie, N. E., 206
Boyd, D. P., 32
Boyle, M., 71, C141
Brabeck, Peter, 235, 247
Bradberry, T., 377
Braddock, Richard, C222, C225
Brader, J., C232
Bradley, Diane, C178
Bradshaw, Adam, 46
Brancatelli, Joe, C268–C269
Brandenberger, A., 62, 71
Brandes, P., 312
Branson, Richard, 23, 33, 142
Brat, I., C141
Bray, C., 311
Breech, Ernest, C247

Breen, B., 405
Brennan, Terrance, C220
Brenneman, K., 419
Bresser, R. F., 107
Briggs, Bill, C232
Briggs, Doug, C182
Brigham, B., 211
Brigham, E. F., 211
Brin, Sergey, 388
Broache, A., 70
Brochstein, Marty, C198
Brock, John, C216
Brock, Ruthie, 451n
Brockner, J., 377
Brockovich, Erin, 304
Brody, Ned, C171
Brook-Carter, C., C231
Brooker, K., 179
Brouthers, L. E., 246
Brown, Bobbi, C171
Brown, C., 132
Brown, E., 345
Brown, Hunter, C70, C71, C72, C74
Brown, J. S., 135
Brown, R. H., 246
Brown, R. L., 70
Brown, S. L., 412
Brown, Stephen P. A., C155
Brown, T., 178
Brown, Tim, 23, 417
Brownell, M., 5
Bruno, K., C231
Brush, C., 412, 413
Brusman, M., 377
Bruton, G. D., 305, 313
Bryan, M., 262
Bryant, A., 32, 33, 34, 142, 275, 346, 378, 412, 440
Bryant, Clara Jane, C249
Bryce, D. J., 406
Bryon, Ellen, 70, C205
Buchanan, L., 252, 277
Buckingham, M., 378
Buckley, M. R., 246
Buckman, R. C., 143
Buffett, Warren, 38, 75, 279
Bunderson, J. S., 345
Bungay, S., 33
Bunkley, N., C260, C261
Burgelman, R. A., 277, 345, 413
Burke, A., 256
Burke, Doris, C205
Burkin, L., C88
Burnham, Dan, 373
Burnison, Gary, 120
Burrill, Greg, 365
Burrows, Peter, 32, C128, C278
Burrus, D., 177, 178
Burt, Ronald S., 127, 143
Burton, R. M., 413
Bush, J., 72
Bush, Vannevar, C162
Buss, D., 262
Bussey, J., 246, 386
Butz, H. E., 178
Bygrave, W. D., 251, 275, 276

Bynum, A., 211
Byrne, Carol, 451n
Byrne, J., 70, 412

C

Cacciotti, Jerry, C236
Calagione, Sam, 253
Caldicott, S., 352
Caldicott, S. M., C260, C261
Calia, M., 201
Callahan, Brian R., C38n
Callanan, J., 377
Camillus, J. C., 33, 43
Camp, B., 414
Campbell, A., 209, 210
Campbell, J. T., 106
Campbell, Joseph, C130
Campbell, Terrie, 224, 226
Camusi, Paul, C106
Cannella, A. A., Jr., 311, 312
Cantalupo, James R., C196, C197
Canter, A., C260
Caplan, J., 178
Caplinger, D., C67
Cappelli, P., 141, 143
Capron, L., 246
Cardin, R., 142
Cardinal, L. B., 412, 413
Carey, J., 71, 262
Carey, Susan, 32, 175, C18, C269
Carey, Dennis, 296
Cariaga, V., C67
Carley, W. M., 142
Carlson, D. S., 378
Carlson, Jeff, 352
Carmeli, A., 309
Carnegie, Andrew, 112
Caron, Guy, C271
Carpenter, M., 311
Carr, N. G., 71
Carrott, G. T., 33
Carter, Dennis, 118
Carter, N. M., 310
Casciaro, T., 143
Casesa, John, C259
Cash, J. I., Jr., 106
Casico, W. F., 210
Cassar, H., 276
Cassidy, J. C., 178
Catmull, Ed, 431, C275–C278
Cattani, K., 178
Cava, M., 261
Cehn, S.-F. S., 346
Cellan-Jones, R., C129
Cena, John, C174, C177
Cerny, K., 346
Chahine, S., 312
Chakrabarti, A., 246
Challenger, J., 70
Chamberlain, M., 33
Chambers, Jim, C28
Chambers, John, 181
Champion, David, 158
Champoux, J. E., 377
Champy, James, 337, 346

Chan, C., 247
Chan, P., 178
Chandler, Alfred D., Jr., 344, 345
Chang, A., 203
Chang, M., 143
Chang, V., 142
Charan, Ram, 32, 38, 296, 350, 377
Charitou, C. D., 70
Charnovita, S., 33
Chasan, F., 300
Chatman, J., 142
Chatterjee, S., 34, 311
Chen, Brian X., 209, C214
Chen, I., 203
Chen, M. J., 266, 270, 277
Chen, Perry, C22, C23, C25, C26
Chen, Winston, 116
Chen, X.-P., 276
Cheng, R., C129
Cher, C90
Cherry, S., C129
Chervitz, Darren, C169
Chesbrough, H., 209, 412
Chesky, Brian, 352–353, 377
Chick, S. E., 85, 106
Cho, A., C129
Cho, H. J., 414
Choi, T. Y., 345
Choo, C. W., 413
Chouinard, Yves, 19
Chrisman, J. J., 276
Christakis, N. A., 143
Christensen, C. R., 440
Christensen, Clayton M., 383–384, 387, 388, 411, 412
Christodoro, Jonathan, C166
Chuanfu, Wang, 75
Chuang, C. M., 247
Chung, Claudia, C277
Ciampa, K., 377
Cieply, M., 245
Clark, Alan, C216
Clark, D., 409
Clark, N., 160
Clark, Tim, C263, C267, C268
Clay, Eleanor Lowthan, C249
Clayton, Paul E., C52
Cleary, Kevin, 287
Clifford, Stephanie, C183
Cochran, P. S., 310, 378
Coff, R. W., 107, 312, 413
Cohan, P., C232
Cohen, D., 143
Cohen, David, 251
Cohen, T. 5
Cohen-Dumani, Michael, 409
Colarelli, G., 411
Colby, S. J., 27
Colchester, M., 272
Cole, M. S., 156
Coleman, D. R., 440
Coleman, J. S., 143
Coleman-Lochner, L., 386, C36, C98
Collins, G., C141
Collins, J. C., 310, 406

Collins, Jim, 258, 276, 283, 310, 352, 377
Collis, D. J., 33, 106, 107
Colvin, Geoff R., 31, 32, 54, 70, 71, 119, 178, 210, 350, 377, 412
Colvin, J. G., 246, 413
Compart, A., C19
Conant, Douglas, C132, C133
Cone, Bill, C276
Conley, J. G., 144
Conley, J. H., 378
Conlin, M., 404
Conyon, M. J., 312
Cook, Dick, C275
Cook, Kenneth A., C237
Cook, Scott, 367, 388
Cook, Tim, 137, C117, C122, C125, C126, C127, C128
Coolridge, Alex, C205
Cooper, Alan, 115
Cooper, S., 276
Copeland, M. V., 276
Copeland, T. E., 210
Corcoran, Barbara, C49
Coronado, Julia, 195
Corsi, C., 312
Corstjens, M., 177
Cote, David, 137
Cotte, J., 33
Coucke, K., 346
Coughlan, Ian M., C155
Coulter, C., 157
Couric, Katie, C171
Courtney, H., 70
Courtney, Peter J., C99n
Covey, S. R., 377, 378
Covin, J. G., 403
Cox, J., 378
Cox, T. L., 143
Coy, P., 70, 210
Coyne, E. J., Sr., 179
Coyne, K. P., 179
Coyne, S. T., 179
Craig, J., 414
Craig, S., 141
Crain, K., C260
Cramb, Charles, C94
Creed, Greg, 395
Crockett, R. O., 413
Crook, J., 262
Cross, R., 70, 142, 143
Crowe, Dan, C28–C29
Crowe, P., C260
Cruise, Tom, 80
Crum, Scott, C94
Csere, C., 72
Cueto, Julia Gonzalez, C207
Culver, Ells, C72–C73
Culver, John, C88
Cuomo, Andrew, C5, C6
Cybart, N., C129

D

Dacin, M. T., 211
Dacin, T., 345

Daft, R., 377
Dagnino, G. B., 178
Dahan, E., 178
Dahlvig, Anders, 310
Daily, M., C18
Dale, G., 312
Daley, J., 264
Dalí, Salvador, C212
Dalton, C., 298
Dalton, D., 298
Daly, Terry, C267
Damanpour, F., 411
Damaraju, Naga Lakshmi, C7n, C14n, C245n
Daniels, J. D., 345
Danigelis, A., C232
Danna, D., 106
Danneels, E., 144, 414
Das, Dev, C48n, C82n, C89n, C99n, C111n, C143n, C156n, C220n
Das, T. K., 346
Daum, J., 312
Davda, Avani Saglani, C82, C83, C88
D'Aveni, Richard A., 178, 350
Davenport, Craig, 419
Davenport, T. H., 142, 178, 346, 365, 412
Davey, J., 309
David, P., 312
Davidson, P., 277
Davies, A., 70
Davies, M., 270
Davis, I., 377
Davis, P. S., 178, 414
Davis, S., 177
Davison, L., 135
Dawn, K., 345
Day, G. S., 70, 106, 178
Day, J. C., 143
Day, J. D., 413
Deal, T. E., 310
Dean, B. V., 178
Dean, T. J., 70
De Carvalho, Charlene, C217
De Castro, Henrique, C171
Deeds, D. L., 276
Deephouse, D. L., 106
Deering, Mark, C192
DeGeneres, Ellen, C21
Dekas, K. H., 141
DeKluyver, C. A., 421
De La Merced, Michael J., C172, C244
Delgrosso, P., 177
Dell, Michael, 405
Delmas, M. A., 33
DeLong, T. J., 32
De Meuse, K. P., 179
Dennis, W. J., 276
De Nysschen, Johan, C243
Deogun, N., 209, 210
DePillis, L., C36
Desalegn, Hailemariam, C215
DeSanctis, G., 346

De Santis, Jake, C5, C6
DesRoches, D., 254
Dess, Gregory G., 32, 76, 106, 136, 141, 143, 177, 178, 209, 210, 211, 247, 309, 310, 344, 345, 346, 377, 403, 413, C4n, C7n, C14n
De Tienne, D. R., 276
Deutsch, T., 311
Devers, C., 307
Dewhurst, M., 142, 310
Dharwadkar, R., 312
Dholakia, U. M., 177
Diamond, Michael L., C238
Dias, Fiona, 93
Dibadj, Ali, C20, C202
Dibrell, C., 414
DiChiara, Jennifer M., C27n
Dickey, M., 210
Dickler, J., C66
Dickson, P., 276
Dickson, P. R., 178, 179
DiFucci, John, 206
Dignan, L., C231
Dill, K., 312
Diller, Barry, C181, C182
Dillow, C., 291
Dimon, James, 16, 373–374
Disney, Walt, C277
Distelzweig, H., 344
Ditkoff, S., 27
Dixon, M., 178
Dobson, C., 32
Doctor, Pete, C276
Doh, J. P., 33
Dolan, B., C36
Dolan, K., 377
Dolida, Roger J., 331
Domoto, H., 247
Donahoe, John, 3, 31, 367, C156, C160, C163, C164, C166, C167
Donghoon, Chang, C212
Donnelly, Brian, 224
Dontae, Lee, C212
Dorrance, John T., C132
Dorsey, Jack, C22
Dostal, E., C55
Dougherty, D., 412
Douglas, C. A., 142
Douglas, S. P., 246
Douma, B., 378
Doval, P., 72
Doving, E., 144
Dowell, G., 276
Dowling, G. R., 141, 178
Dowling, N., 377
Downes, L., 31, 64, 70, 107
Downing, L., 177
Doyle, R. A., C167
Doz, Yves L., 247, 344, 346
Dr. Dre, 19
Draffan, G., C81
Dragone, Franco, C271
Dranove, D., 72
Dressner, H., 412

Drewnowski, Adam, C141
Drews, David, 258, 259
Droege, Scott, 178
Droge, C., 413
Drucker, Peter F., 37, 40, 70, 276, 384, 408, 412, 414, 440
Druckman, Steve, C231
Drum, B., C19
Dubbs, D., C231
Dubini, P., 276
Duke, Mike, 331
Duncan, Robert E., 344, 346
Dunkelberg, Bill, 67
Dunlap, S., 143
Dunlap-Hinkler, D., 211, 277
Dunne, D. D., 412
Durbin, D.-A., C260
Durnan, K., C36
Dutta, Devangshu, C88
Dutta, S., 106
Duvall, M., C19
Dyer, Jeff H., 37, 105, 141, 247, 388, 406, 412
Dykes, B., 199

E

Eaglesham, J., 374
Earl, M. J., 106
Earley, K, 114
Easterbrook, Steve, C194, C197
Easterby-Smith, M., 378
Eaton, Jake, C70, C71, C74, C77
Ebbers, Bernie, 205
Ebner, D, 189
Eddy, N., 411
Edelstein, S., 71
Eden, L., 246
Edge, A. G., 440
Edvinsson, Leif, 141
Edwards, Cliff, C214
Efrati, A., 311
Eggers, J. P., 392, 412
Eggleston, Ralph, C276
Ehrenfeld, J. R., 33
Eickhoff, Gerald, 124
Einhorn, B., 247
Einstein, Albert, 427
Eisenberg, Melvin Aron, 293
Eisenhardt, K. M., 144, 209, 276, 311, 344, 412
Eisenstein, P. A., C260
Eisner, Alan B., C7n, C14n, C21n, C27n, C38n, C48n, C57n, C68n, C82n, C89n, C99n, C111n, C117n, C130n, C143n, C152n, C156n, C168n, C173n, C179n, C184n, C194n, C200n, C209n, C215n, C220n, C233n, C239n, C245n, C262n, C270n, C274n
Eisner, Michael D., C275
Ejelade-Ruiz, A., C66
Ekdahl, Andrew, C237
Elenkov, D. S., 70
Elfenbein, H. A., 33

Elgin, B., 369
Ellinghaus, Uwe, 80
Elliot, S., C231
Elliott, Bryan, C199
Ellis, B., 311
Ellison, J., 19
Ellison, Lawrence J., C275
Ells, Steve, 79
Ellsworth, D., 142
Elmer-DeWitt, P., C128
Elson, Charles, 434
Elstrom, 210
Emerson, Ralph Waldo, 41
Eng, D., 177, 254
Engardio, Pete, 245, 345, C214
Engelson, Eric S., C21n, C99n, C111n, C184n
Ensing, I. M., 346
Entner, Roger, C212
Enz, C., 440
Erhun, F., 401
Erickson, T. J., 141, 142
Erickson, Tamara, 46
Espinoza, J., 276
Estes, Tim, 291
Esty, D. C., 21, 33
Ethiraj, S. K., 106
Evans, B., 312
Evans, P., 309
Evans, R., 440
Ewalt, D. M., C193
Ewing, Jack, 32, C219
Eyring, M. J., 32, 245

F

Fackler, M., C260
Faems, D., 247
Fahey, E., 178
Fahey, J., 210
Fahey, L., 70
Fahey, M., C231
Fahlander, A., 141
Fairbanks, B., C47
Fairchild, D., 160
Fake, Caterina, C22
Falconi, M., 345
Fama, Eugene, 311
Farrell, J., 70, C25, C26
Farzad, R., C129
Fatone, Joey, C44
Faughnder, R., 203
Fedele, Joseph, C220, C221, C222
Feeny, D., 106
Feintzweig, R., 311
Feld, Kenneth, C272
Feldman, D. C., 47
Feldman, Howard, C68n
Felps, W., 32
Felsted, A., 289
Felton, N., 141
Fenner, L., 277
Ferdman, R. A., 79
Ferguson, G., 70
Ferguson, I., 246
Ferguson, S., 419

Fern, M. J., 412, 413
Ferrier, W. J., 266, 270, 277, 413
Fey, C. F., 312
Fickenscher, L., C232
Field, H. S., 156
Field, J, M., 106
Fields, Mark, 352, C245, C247, C258–C259, C260
Filatotchev, I., 311
Filmer, Fleur, C167
Finegold, D., 33
Finkelstein, Ben, 90
Finkelstein, S., 440
Finnigan, David, C178
Fiorina, Carly, 5
Firestone, Harvey S., Jr., C249
Firestone, Martha Parke, C249
Fischer, Aaron, C155
Fischer, Scott, C38, C39, C43, C46
Fish, Robert, 355
Fisher, A., 142, 209
Fisher, L. M., C231
Fisher, M. L., 105
Fisman, R., 246
Fitzgerald, F. Scott, 429
Fitzpatrick, D., 374
Fitzsimmons, J., 277
Fjeldstad, O. D., 105
Flanagan, Maurice, C267
Flay, Bobby, C222
Fleisher, L., 309
Fleming, John, 19
Fletcher, Ian, 234
Flint, J., 178, C260
Florian, E., C36
Folta, T. B., 413
Fontana, Dominic, C44
Fontrodona, J., 378
Forbath, T., 32, 247
Forbush, Dean, C222, C225
Ford, Alfred Brush, C249
Ford, Anne, C249
Ford, Benson, Sr., C249
Ford, Benson, Jr., C249
Ford, Bill, 296
Ford, Charlotte M., C249
Ford, Edsel B., Jr., C249
Ford, Edsel Bryant, C249
Ford, Eleanor Clay (Sullivan), C249
Ford, Elena Anne, C249
Ford, Elizabeth Hudson, C249
Ford, George, C249
Ford, Henry, C249
Ford, Henry (1863–1947), 23, 293, 362, C245, C246, C249
Ford, Henry, II, C249, C250
Ford, Isaac, C249
Ford, Jane, C249
Ford, Jane (Smith), C249
Ford, John (1799–1864), C249
Ford, John (1865–1927), C249
Ford, Josephine Clay, C249
Ford, Josephine Clay (Ingle), C249

Ford, Lynn (Alandt), C249
Ford, Margaret, C249
Ford, Martha Parke "Mutty" (Morse), C249
Ford, Mary, C249
Ford, Nancy, C249
Ford, Rebecca, C249
Ford, Robert (1803–1877), C249
Ford, Robert (1871–75), C249
Ford, Samuel (1792–1842), C249
Ford, Samuel (1837–1884), C249
Ford, Sheila Firestone, C249
Ford, Walter Buhl, II, C249
Ford, Walter Buhl, III, C249
Ford, William (1775–1818), C249
Ford, William (1826–1905), C249
Ford, William (1873–1934), C249
Ford, William Clay, Jr., C245, C247, C249, C250, C259
Ford, William Clay, Sr., C249
Forrest, C., C129
Foster, A. C., 29
Foust, D., 71
Fowler, G. A., 93
Fowler, S. W., 106
Fox, F., C128
Fox, M. A., C231
Frank, Barney, 41
Frank, R., 311
Fredrickson, J. W., 345
Freeman, Carrie, 114
Freeman, K., 178
Freeman, R. E., 32, 33, 143, 277, 292, 311, 344
Freiberg, J., C12
Freiberg, K., C12
Frey, B. S., 33
Friend, Elizabeth, 155
Frier, S., 186
Friesen, P. H., 345
Frita, B., 277
Fritz, M., 71
Froholdt, M., 345
Fromartz, S., 275
Fruk, M., 210
Fry, E., 201
Fryer, B., 246, 310
Fulmer, I. S., 311
Fulmer, R. M., 378
Funtleyder, Les, C233
Furu, P., 312

G

Gaal, Stephen, 256
Gaba, V., 276
Gabarro, J. J., 32
Gadiesh, O., 178
Gagliardi, N., C47
Gaglio, C. M., 276
Gagnon, Marc, C270
Gaines-Ross, L., 106
Gajilan, A. T., C19
Galagher, Brian A., C151
Galante, J., C167
Galbraith, J. R., 317, 344

Gallagher, Brian A., C14, C144, C147, C149, C150, C151
Galvez, J., C56
Galvin, Chris, 403, 413
Gao, Y., 246
Garcia-Morales, V. J., 377
Garda, R. A., 270
Garg, V., 142
Garnier, J-P., 106
Garten, J. E., 246
Garvin, D. A., 32, 344, 377
Gasparro, A., 177
Garlinghouse, Brad, C169
Gates, Bill, C120, C143
Gates, D., 344
Gates, Dominic, C12
Gaudet, Tracy, 328, 329
Gee, P., 277
Gee Sung Choi, C213
Geier, B., C260
Geithner, Timothy, C5
Gelles, D., C172
Gellman, L., 5
Gelman, S. R., C151
George, B., 301, 312
George, Michael, C179, C182, C183
Georgescu, Peter, 358
Gerdes, L., 142
Gerhart, B., 311
Germano, S., 262
Gerstner, Lou, 355–356, 377
Geschke, Jim, 400
Ghemawat, P., 71, 218, 245, 247
Ghoshal, Sumantra, 70, 141, 179, 245, 246, 321, 345
Ghosn, Carlos, 151, C247
Gianforte, Greg, 156
Gibbert, M., 412
Gibelman, M., C151
Gibney, Frank, Jr., C214
Gibson, C. B., 144, 346
Gibson, David, C192
Gikkas, N. S., 246
Gilad, Benjamin, 451
Gilbert, J. L., 178
Gillette, F., 224
Gilley, Matthew, 47, 156
Gilligan, Eugene, C183
Gilmore, J. H., 178
Gimbel, B., 210, 246, C12
Gimbel, S., 177
Ginsberg, A., 412
Gladwell, Malcolm, 124
Glass, J. T., 346
Glazer, E., 245, 374, C98
Glazer, G., 155
Glickman, Jodi, 130
Goddard, J., 32
Goel, Vindu, C172
Goffee, R., 141
Goggins, Colleen, C236
Gogoi, Pallavi, C199
Goldsmith, Marshall, 32, 131, 144, 328, 377
Goldstein, N. J., 310

Goleman, Daniel, 360, 377
Golisano, Tom, 62
Goll, I., 71
Golvin, Charles, C212
Gomez, Leocadia Cruz, C207
Gompers, P. A., 413
Gonzalez, Sonsoles, C202
Gooderham, P. N., 144
Goodman, Stephen, 255–256
Goodson, Scott, C268
Goodstein, L. D., 178
Goold, James, C48n
Goold, M., 209, 210, 310
Goranova, M., 312
Gordon, Erik, C233, C237
Gordon, John, C199
Gorshein, Eshai J., C184n
Gorsky, Alex, C233
Gosier, C., C151
Goteman, I., 310
Gottfredeson, M., 346
Goudreau, Jenna, C141
Gough, 374
Gourville, J. T., 100
Govindarajan, V. G., 211, 245, 246, 247, 345
Graafland, René Hooft, C217, C218, C219
Graddy-Gamel, A., C151
Graebner, M. E., 209, 296, 377
Graen, G. B., 310
Grannis, K., C66
Grant, A., 285
Grant, Jeremy, C199
Grant, R. M., 89, 107
Graser, Marc, 107, C278
Gratton, L., 142, 344
Graves, T., C142
Graybow, M., 311
Green, J., 307
Green, S., 106
Greenberg, Herb, 4
Greenberg, Jack M., C196
Greenblatt, Drew, 160
Greene, P., 412, 413
Greenwald, B., 71
Greenwald, W., C193
Greenwell, M., C151
Greenwood, R., 33
Gregersen, Hal B., 387, 388, 412
Gregg, F. M., 245
Greve, H. R., 211
Grimm, C. M., 266, 270, 277
Grobart, S., 209, C129
Groenfeldt, T., 186
Gronbjerg, Kirsten, C150
Gross, D., 311
Grossman, Ken, C106
Grossman, Mindy, 114, 173, 174
Grossman, S., 142
Grossman, W., 312
Groth, A., 345
Grove, Andrew, 5, 84, 117, 118, 142, 266, 277, 292
Grover, Ronald, C278
Grow, B., 70, 210

Gruber, Peter, 22
Guenther, C., 157
Guerin, D., 19
Guimon, A., C208
Guinan, P. J., 144
Gulati, R., 277
Gumbel, P., 246
Gunther, M., 19, 31, 412
Gupta, A. K., 245, 246, 247, 346
Gurdjian, P., 378
Gurley, Bill, 58
Gustafsson, K., 52
Gustin, S., 5
Guterman, J., 70
Guth, R. A., 407
Guth, W. D., 178, 210, 412, 440
Guthridge, M., 310

H

Haas, M. R., 141, 345
Habib, M. M., 345
Hagel, J., III, 135, 246, 411
Halbeisen, T., 378
Haleblian, J., 199
Halkias, M., 93
Hall, B. J., 310
Hall, Brian, 120
Hall, D. J., 345
Hall, H., C151
Hall, J., 70
Hall, R. H., 311, 344
Hall, S., 210, 312
Hall, W. K., 178
Hambrick, D. C., 179, 210, 270, 277, 311, 312
Hamel, Gary, 33, 37, 70, 209, 346, 412, 413
Hammer, Michael M., 337, 346, 363, 378
Hammonds, K. H., 32, 405
Hamstra, M., C231, C232
Hancock, B., 142
Handy, Charles, 33, 331, 345
Hannah, S. T., 378
Hansegard, J., 300
Hansen, M. T., 141, 143, 144, 412
Hardy, Jeffrey, 223
Hardy, Q., 34
Hargrave, M., C66
Hargreaves, S., 246
Harnish, V., 34
Harrar, G., 346
Harrigan, K., 210
Harris, E., 311
Harris, J., 142
Harrison, D. A., 378
Harrison, J. S., 21, 32, 33, 143, 277, 311, 344, 346
Hart, Bret, C175
Hart, M., 412, 413
Hart, Stuart L., 20, 33
Harveston, P. D., 246
Harvey, C. P., 143
Harvey, M., 246
Hasan, F., 106

Haslam, S. A., 310
Haspeslagh, P., 210
Hastings, Reed, 95
Hatch, N. W., 141
Haughton, K., 72
Haugland, S. A., 211
Hauser, Robert, C237
Haveri, Mikael, C184
Hawkins, Asher, 55
Hax, A. C., 210
Hayashi, A. M., 128
Hayek, Nicolas, 171
Hayes, R., 411
Hayes, Robin, 5, C14, C18
Haynes, K. T., 296, 311
Hayward, Tony, 19
Heathfield, S., 285
Heavey, S., 276
Hedin, Hans, 451
Heiferman, Scott, C22
Heifetz, R., 378
Heine, K., 71
Heineken, Freddy, C217
Heinonen, Cheryl, C94
Helft, Miguel, 264, 277, C172
Helgesen, S., 378
Heller, A., C232
Hellmich, N., C37
Helms, M. M., 33, 178, 245, 344, 378
Helper, S., 71
Hemp, P., 32
Henderson, Frederick A., C240
Henderson, Larry, 224
Henkoff, R., 106, 142
Hennequin, Dennis, C198
Hennings, Peter J., C98
Henretta, Deborah A., C201
Henriques, D. B., 311
Heracleous, L., 178
Hertzler, E., 401
Herzlinger, R., C151
Hessel, E., 32
Hesselbein, S., 32, 328, 377, 378
Hesseldahl, A., 64
Hewlett, S. A., 123, 143
Hibben, M., C129
Higginbotham, Stacey, 409
Hill, A. D., 143, 210
Hill, C., C36
Hill, K., 70
Hiller, Marc, C74
Hillman, A., 296, 311, 312
Hills, G. E., 276
Hilmer, F. C., 346
Hiltzik, M., 344
Himelstein, L., C167
Hindo, B., 209
Hintz, Brad, 109
Hirsh, E., C260, C261
Hirst, G., 391
Hirvensalo, Irmeli, 451
Hitt, M. A., 32, 33, 89, 106, 107, 141, 143, 179, 199, 209, 210, 211, 246, 247, 277, 311, 312, 344, 345

Ho, Stanley, C153
Ho, V. T., 287
Hoch, J. E., 335
Hoetker, G., 105
Hogan, Hulk, C173, C175
Holcomb, T. R., 179
Holden, B., 369
Hollender, J., 33
Hollister, S., C128
Holme, C., 157
Holmes, S., C260
Holt, J. W., 378
Holt, John, 367
Hoover, V. L., 266, 277
Hopkins, M. S., 71, 331
Horn, Eli, C167
Hornery, J., 413
Hornigan, J., 70
Horovitz, Bruce, C199
Horton, Chris, C155
Hoskin, R. E., 413
Hoskisson, R. E., 89, 209, 247, 311, 312, 344, 345
Hotard, D., 178
Hout, T. M., 71, 218, 245, 246
Howe, J., 71
Howe, Jeff, 50
Howell, J. M., 412
Howell, Robert A., 111
Hrebiniak, L. G., 32, 210, 344
Hsieh, Tony, 154, 337, 339, 377
Hsuan, A., C79
Huang Jingbao, C78
Huchzermeier, A., 85, 106
Hudson, Linda, 371
Hughes, J., C12
Hult, T. M., 72, 210
Humer, Franz, 433
Hurd, Mark, 5, 24
Hutt, M. D., 211
Huy, Q. H., 33
Hwang, I., C36
Hymowitz, C., 386

I

Ibarra, H., 34, 143
Icahn, Carl, C156, C166
Iger, Bob, C274
Ignatius, A., 210
Ihlwan, Moon, C214
Immelt, Jeffrey, 20, 82, 106, 214
Imperato, G., 106
Ingram, S., C36
Ingram, T. N., 178
Inkpen, A. C., 247, 346
Iosebashvili, I., 246
Iovine, Jimmy, 19
Ireland, R. D., 89, 106, 107, 141, 209, 210, 211, 246, 247, 345, 412
Isaacson, W., 310
Isobe, T., 247
Ivory, Danielle, C244
Ivy, Lance, C23
Iyer, B., 178, 346

J

Jackson, E. M., 312
Jackson, M., 105
Jackson, S. E., 33
Jacobs, A., 177
Jacobs, Bert, 252
Jacobs, Bonnie, C236
Jacobs, D. L., 61
Jacobs, John, 252
Jaeger, Durk I., C201
James, Raymond, 4
Janis, Irving L., 432, 434, 440
Jannesson, Erik, 451
Janney, J. J., 413
Jansen, P., C151
Janssens, M., 247
Jap, S. D., 106
Jargon, J., 155, 342
Jargon, Julie, C199
Jarvis, J., 345
Jatia, Amit, C88
Jean, S., 246
Jeffries, A., C26
Jenks, John, 27
Jenner, Hartmut, 85
Jennings, L., C56
Jennings, Rebecca, C249
Jensen, Christopher, C244
Jensen, Michael C., 311, 312
Jessup, Harley, C276
Jia Jiang, 156
Jiang, Y., 305, 313
Jin, B., 247
Jindra, B., 311
Joachimsthaler, E., 246
Jobs, Steven, 5, 43, 64, 120, 137, 141, 185, 288, 310, C117, C120, C121, C127, C128, C274, C275, C276, C277, C278
Joch, Jason, C177
Johannessen, J. A., 411
John, Daymond, C49
John, Prince of England, C2
Johnson, Avery, C238
Johnson, David, C132
Johnson, J., C129
Johnson, M. W., 32, 245
Johnson, R. A., 312
Johnson, S., 71, 143
Joire, Myriam, C26
Jolie, Angelina, C179
Jones, A., C6, C128
Jones, Archie, 198, 199
Jones, Charisse, C12
Jones, Curt, C38, C39, C40, C42, C43, C44, C46
Jones, G., 141
Jones, L., C47
Jones, S. M., C66, C67
Jones, T. J., 32
Jordan, B. D., 441n
Joseph, D., 377
Josey, Ron, C164
Joshi, S., 210
Joyce, E., C232
Joyce, W. F., 32, 210, 344
Jung, Andrea, C92, C94
Jung, Kyunghan, C212

K

Ka, G., 209
Kafka, P., C26
Kahn, J., 71
Kahn, Jodi, C220
Kaiser, R. B., 142
Kakkar, A., C260, C261
Kale, P., 106, 247
Kampur, D., 217
Kang, E., 311
Kanter, Rosabeth Moss, 412
Kao, J., 412
Kaplan, Andrew, C219
Kaplan, M., 93
Kaplan, R. E., 142
Kaplan, Robert S., 32, 97, 100, 107, 142
Kaplan, Steven, 300, 412
Kapur, D., 218
Kardashian, Kim, C179
Karlgaard, Rich, 31, 32, 107, 123
Karni, A., C231
Karp, H., C129
Karri, R., 177
Kasaks, Sally, C58
Kashwarski, T., 33
Kasten, Tom, 367
Katz, J. A., 276
Katz, J. H., 143
Katz, Jonathan, C141
Katzenbach, J. R., 346
Kaushik, M., C88
Kazanjian, R. K., 317, 344
Kean, Jim, 419
Kearney, A. T., C18
Keats, B., 344
Kedia, B. L., 246
Keegan, R. A., 81
Keenan, F., 408
Kehoe, C., 311
Keil, Thomas, 210, 311, 389, 412
Keizer, G., C128
Kelleher, Herb, 4, 5, 84, 92, C7, C8, C12, C15
Kelleher, J. B., 71
Kelley, C., C151
Kellmurray, B., 107
Kelly, Bill, 419
Kelly, Celeste, 273
Kelly, Gary C., C7, C8–C12
Kelly, Maureen, C182
Kelly, Michael A., C237
Kempf, Karl, 401
Kempiak, M., C231
Kengelbach, J., 211
Kennedy, A. A., 310
Kennedy, K., C67
Kenny, David, 125
Kenworthy, T. P., 344
Kerin, Roger A., 179
Kerr, J., 310
Kerwin, K. R., 72
Kessler, Aaron M., C244
Ketchen, D. J., Jr., 72, 266, 277, 412
Kets de Vries, M. F. R., 33, 142, 345
Keynes, John Maynard, 28
Khanna, T., 211, 277, 311, 313
Khavul, S., C208
Khermouch, Gerry, C219
Khosla, S., 247
Khurana, Rakesh, C260
Kichen, S., 141
Kidd, J. B., 247
Kidwell, R. E., Jr., 311
Kiley, D., C260
Killick, A., 132
Kilmann, R. H., 346
Kilpatrick, A., C151
Kim, Eric, C211
Kim, H. E., 412
Kim, J., 312
Kim, L., 178
Kim, P. H., 276
Kim, W. C., 277
Kim Hyun-suk, C211
King, A. A., 71
King, I., 401
King, R., C128
King, Rollin, C7
Kingsbury, K., C67
Kirchhoff, David, C27
Kirkland, J., 70
Kirkman, B. L., 144
Kirn, S. P., 107
Kiron, D., 178
Klein, Zach, C22
Kleinbaum, Rob, C240
Kleiner, Morris, 273
Kleinfeld, Klaus, 359
Klemmer, D., 211
Klemp, G., 378
Kletter, D., 413
Kline, D., 247
Kling, K., 310
Knowles, F., C260
Koch, Ed, C222
Koch, Jim, C100, C109
Koetsler, J., C26
Koogle, Tim, 257, C169, C170
Kopp, Wendy, 24
Koppel, B., 345
Kopytoff, Verne G., C172
Kor, Y. Y., 32
Korn, Helaine J., C27n, C130n, C245n
Kosner, A. W., C36
Kosnik, R. D., 312
Kotabe, M., 211, 247, 277
Kotha, S., 276
Kotik, Robert, 300
Kotter, J. P., 377
Kouzes, J. M., 363, 378
Kowitt, B., 70, 207, 329, C98
Kowitt, Beth, C199
Kozlowski, Dennis, 205
Kozlowski, S. W., 335
Kramer, M. R., C151
Kramer, Mark, C147
Krantz, M., C26
Kratter, Tia, C276
Krause, R., 312
Krill, Kay, C57, C58, C59, C60, C64, C66, C67
Kripalani, M., 218
Kris, Mark, 186
Krisher, T., C260
Krishnan, H., 210
Krishnan, M. S., 106, 178
Krishnan, R. A., 210
Kroc, Ray A., C196
Kroll, M., 178, 276, 311
Krueger, Alan, 273
Kuehn, K., 33
Kuemmerle, W., 345
Kulatikala, N., 413
Kumar, M. V. S., 209
Kumat, N., 71
Kun-Hee Lee, 25
Kuperman, Jerome C., C48n, C57n
Kurti, N., C47
Kutaragi, Ken, 397
Kwak, M., 64, 72
Kwon, E. Y., C142
Kwon, S. W., 143
Kwon Oh-hyun, C213
Kyriazis, D., 209

L

Laamanen, T., 210, 311
Labianca, G., 143
Labianca, Joe, 143, 144
Lachenauer, Rob, 267, 277
Lacity, M., 106
Lady Gaga, C21
Lafley, A. G., 117, 252
Lafley, Alan G., C200, C201, C202, C204, C205
LaForge, R. W., 178
Lal, R., 177
Laliberté, Guy, C270, C271, C272, C273
Lam, K., 106
Lam, Y., 267
Lamadrid, Lorenzo, C100
Lamarre, Daniel, C270, C272
Lambkin, M., 414
La Monica, P. R., 206
Lampel, Joseph, C2n
Landes, D. S., 245
Lane, C., C36
Lane, P. J., 209
Lanese, Lory, 117
Lang, Tom, C99
Laplume, A. O., 33
Largay, J. A., III, 378
LaRocco, L. A., C260
Laseter, T., C231
Lash, J., 33

Lashinsky, A., 141
Lasseter, John, C276, C278
Latham, G. P., 142, 310, 413
Lau, Jeanie, 385
Lauinger, J., C232
Lavelle, M., 32
Laverty, K. J., 413
Lawler, E. E., III, 33, 378
Lawrence, Joanne, 198
Lawrence, T. B., 106
Lazaridis, Michael, 388
Leana, C. R., 144, 378
Leclair, Donat R., C251
Lederman, G., 114
Lee, C. H., 287
Lee, D., 144
Lee, G., C67
Lee, G. K., 144
Lee, J., C36
Lee, K., 310
Lee, L., C56
Lee, Spike, C222
Lee, T., C232
Lee Kun-hee, C210, C213, C214
Leeman, John, C222
Lees, R. J., 32
Lee Yoon Woo, C213
Lefkofsky, Eric, 3
Lei, D., 178, 246
Leifer, R., 411, 412
Lemer, J., C12
Lemonis, Marcus, 147
Lenzner, R., 142, 210
Leonard, D., C129
Leonard, Dorothy, 131, 144
Leonard, Tom, C43, C44
Leonhardt, D., C231
Lepore, J., 412
Lerner, J., 413
Leroux, Patrick, C271
Lesnar, Brock, C175
Lester, P. B., 378
Lester, R. H., 311
Leu, C., 211
Levesque, L. C., 32, 344
Levin, D., 357, C260
Levin, D. Z., 130
Levine, D., 311
Levine-Weinberg, A., 207, 209
Levinsohn, Ross, C170
Levit, A., 282
Levitt, Theodore, 229, 246
Lewin, A. Y., 246
Lewis, Catherine, C35
Lewis, Dave, 279
Lewis, Ken, 205
Lewis, Peter, C214
Li, J. J., 106, 143, 211
Li, J. T., 247
Li, Lei, C68n
Libert, B., 71
Lichthental, John, 225
Liddy, Edward M., C5–C6
Lieberman, David, 356
Lieberman, M. B., 414
Liebeskind, Richard, Sr., C58

Liebeskind, Robert, C58
Light, D. A., 70, 143
Light, Larry, C68, C79, C81, C199
Lim, O. J., 31
Lim, Y., 178
Lin, H. C., 277
Lin, John, 144
Linblad, C., 311
Ling, Y., 412
Lipin, S., 209, 210
Lipnack, Jessica, 335
Lipparini, A., 106
Lipton, M., 34
Litogot, Mary, C249
Little, Arthur D., 210
Litz, R. A., 33
Liu, Brian, C70, C71, C72, C73, C74
Liu, S. X. Y., 106
Llóréns-Montes, F. J., 377
Lobel, Orly, 113, 141
Locke, Edwin A., 310
Loeb, M., 32
Loftus, Peter, C238
Lohr, S., 179
Loikkanen, V., C26
Lomax, A., C67
London, T., 32
Long, W., 276
Lopez, José Ignacio, 142
Lorange, P., 70, 346, 377
Lorenzetti, L., 342
Lorenzoni, G., 106
Lorsch, J. W., 312, 377
Löscher, Peter, 359
Lowensohn, J., C128
Lowry, Adam, 254
Lu, J. W., 245, 276
Lubatkin, M. H., 412
Lublin, J., 352
Lucas, George W., Jr., C275
Lucchetti, A., 311
Luchs, K., 210
Luehrman, T. A., 107
Luk, L., C129
Lumpkin, G. T., 143, 276, 403, 411, 413
Lundberg, C. C., 440
Lunnan, R., 211
Luria, Gloria, C164
Lutz, A., C67
Lutz, Robert, 16–17, 119
Lyons, D., 414

M

Ma, H., 177
Ma, Jack, C166, C260
Mabey, C., 142
MacArthur, Paul, C174
MacCormack, A., 32, 247
Machlis, S., C231
MacMillan, A., C36
MacMillan, D., 71, C167
MacMillan, I. C., 178, 179, 246, 413

Madhok, A., 247
Madoff, Bernie, 368
Madonna, A. B., C88
Mahashwari, S., C66
Mahmood, I., 246
Maiello, M., 277, 312
Main, J., 378
Majluf, N. S., 210
Makino, S., 245, 247
Makri, M., 209
Maktoum, Ahmed bin Saeed al, C267, C269
Maktoum, Mohammed bin Rashid al, C267
Malhotra, D., 209
Mallas, S., 414
Mallik, O., C26
Malone, Michael S., 48, 141
Malone, Tom, 124
Malviya, S., C88
Mandel, M., 71
Mandelker, G., 311
Mang, P. Y., 413
Manjoo, Farhad, C171
Mank, D. A., C128
Mankins, M., 142, 434
Mann, J., 178
Mann, T., 228
Manning, S., 246
Manville B., 365
March, J. G., 346, 413
Marcial, G. G., C37
Marcus, Bernard, 24
Margolis, J. D., 33
Marino, J. T., 264
Markham, S. K., 413
Markides, C. C., 70
Markkula, A. C. "Mike," Jr., C117
Markman, G. D., 309
Markovich, S., 321
Marks, M. S., 106, 179
Marriott, J. W., Jr., 149, 177
Marshall, M., 123, 143
Martin, A., 211
Martin, J., 141, 142, 247
Martin, J. A., 344
Martin, J. E., 144
Martin, K. L., 32, 344
Martin, R., 377
Martin, Roger L., 428–430, 431, 440
Martin, T., 177
Martin, X., 247
Martinez, Arthur, 3
Mason, Andrew, 3–4, 297
Mass, N. J., 107
Massini, S., 246
Masters, Brooke, C178
Mathur, S. K., 70, 218
Matlack, C., 72
Mattar, Mohammed H., C267
Matteson, S., C56
Matthews, C., 32
Matthews, C. H., 276
Matthews, Elizabeth, 395
Mattioli, D., 114

Mauborgnee, R., 277
Maurer, H., 311
Maxon, Terry, C12
May, R. C., 70
Mayer, Marissa, C168, C169, C170, C171
Maynard, Micheline, 105, C244, C260
Mazumdar-Shaw, Kiran, 203
McAfee, A., 106
McArthur, Sarah, C277
McCarthy, Barry, 95
McCarthy, D. J., 311
McConnell, David H., C89, C90
McConnon, Aili, C232
McCoy, Sheri, C89, C94, C96
McCracken, H., C129
McDermott, C. M., 411
McDonald, Bob, C200
McDonald, M. L., 209, 296, 311
McDonald, Maurice, C196
McDonald, Richard, C196
McDonnell, Anne, C249
McDonough, Robert, 228
McDougall, P. P., 318n, 345
Mcenery, T., C232
McFall, Michael, 355
McGahan, Anita M., 72, 106
McGee, J., 291
McGrath, C., 143
McGrath, J., 312
McGrath, Rita Gunther, 178, 179, 246, 389, 411, 412, 413
McGregor, J., 378
McIlwee, Laurie, 279
McIntire, L., 33
McKay, G., C151
McKinnon, J. D., C6
McKnight, William, 366
McLain, S., 72
McLaughlin, K. J., 345
McLaughlin, R., 211
McLean, Bethany, 304, 313, C178
McMahon, Linda, C173, C174, C175, C176
McMahon, Stephanie, C176
McMahon, Vince, C173–C175, C177
McMillan, G., C26
McMullan, W. E., 276
McNamara, G., 178, 199, 210, 307
McNary, D., 203
McNaughton, Edith, C249
McNaughton, Larry, C174
McNerney, Jim, 315–316
McNicol, J. P., 246
McVae, J., 33
McVey, Henry, 152
McWilliams, Larry S., C132
Means, Gardiner C., 293
Meckling, W. H., 311, 312
Meehan, Sean, 142
Mees, Charles, C16
Mehta, S. N., 178, 310
Meier, D., 209
Meiland, D., 106

Meindl, J. R., 31
Meiners, Roger, 228
Melrose, K., 378
Melrose, Ken, 364
Melville, Herman, C83
Melzer, I., 310
Mendelow, A. L., 413
Merchant, H., 247
Merino, M., 70
Merrefield, D., C232
Merrick, A., C67
Meyer, A. D., 276
Meyer, K. E., 247
Meyer, P., 378
Meyer, Peter, 366
Michael, D. C., 246
Michaeli, Rainer, 451
Michaels, Jillian, C29
Michaels, Shawn, C175
Michaelson, Steve, C222
Michel, J. G., 277
Michelangelo, 205
Michelle, S., C47
Mider, Z., 307
Miles, R. E., 336
Miller, A., 32, 177, 310, 344, 377, 378, 414
Miller, Claire Cain, C172
Miller, D., 32, 203, 310, 345, 403
Miller, D. J., 209, 412
Miller, Daniel, C278
Miller, F. A., 143
Miller, J., 321
Miller, Jon, C170
Miller, K. D., 414
Miller-Kovach, Karen, C35
Millick, Ethan R., C25
Milner, Alex, 224
Minow, Neil, 15, 32, 311, 312
Mintzberg, Henry, 10–11, 12, 31, 32, 280, 310, 440, C3n
Misangyi, V. F., 32
Mischkind, L., 310
Mistry, Cyrus P., C82
Mitchell, Margaret, 41
Mitchell, R., 310
Mitsuhashi, H., 211
Mittal, D., 210
Mochari, I., 407
Mohammed, R., 177
Mohr, E., 310
Moin, D., C67
Mol, M. J., 412
Moliterno, T. P., 142
Mollick, Ethan R., C21
Monahan, J., 276
Monahan, Tom, 262
Monk, N., 107
Monks, Robert, 15, 32, 311, 312
Montes-Sancho, M. J., 33
Montgomery, C. A., 106, 107
Montgomery, D. B., 414
Moon, Y., 171, 179
Mooney, A. C., 440
Mooradian, Don, C178
Moore, A., C67

Moore, B., C67
Moore, Geoffrey A., 405, 414
Moore, J. F., 346
Moran, P., 143
Morates, David J., C156n
Morison, R., 106
Morita, Akio, 20
Morris, B., 310
Morris, C., C193
Morris, E., 440
Morris, Jim, C276
Morris, June, C15
Morrison, Denise, C130, C132, C133, C191
Morrissey, C. A., 412
Morrow, J. S., 179
Mors, M. L., 143
Morse, E. A., 106
Morse, G., 210
Morse, Tim, C170
Mosey, Tom, C44
Moskin, J., C47
Moss, S. A., 377
Mottershaw, Heather, 395
Mouio, A., 210
Mowery, D. C., 346
Moynihan, Brian, 109
Moza, M. P., 247
Mozilo, Angelo, 293
Mudambi, R., 71, 211, 247, 277
Muir, Max, 267
Mulally, Alan, 24, 296, 351, 352, C245, C250, C251, C258
Mullaney, T. J., 408
Mulligan, J., C19
Mumm, J., 312
Munarriz, R. A., C56
Munoz, Pablo, C94
Murdoch, James, 305
Murdoch, Rupert, 305
Murnigham, J. K., 130, 209
Muro, Gary, C66
Murphy, D., 377
Murphy, K., C47
Murphy, K. J., 312
Murphy, P., 246
Murphy, William, C132
Murray, Bill, 52
Murray, Lance, C12
Murthy, N. R. Narayana, 353
Mussberg, W., 345
Mutsuko, M., C192
Mutzabaugh, A., C12
Mysterio, Ray, C174

N

Nader, Ralph, 304–305
Nagarajan, G., 221
Nagarju, B., 218
Nagourney, Adam, C155
Nahapiet, J., 141
Nair, H., 32, 245
Nair, Padmakumar, C206n
Nalebuff, B. J., 62, 71
Narasimhan, O., 106

Narayan, A., 211
Narayanan, V. K., 70
Nasser, Jacques, C245, C247
Naughton, K., 71, C261
Ndofor, H., 277
Needham, Charles, 6
Neeleman, David, C14, C15, C16, C19
Negroni, Christine, C268
Neilson, G. L., 32, 322, 344, 413
Nelson, A. J., 440
Nelson, B., 41, 310
Nelson, Randall E., C277
Nero, C47
Netessine, S., 85, 106, 310
Neuborne, E., 179
Newbert, S. L., 32, 106
Newman, A. A., C37
Newman, D., 377
Nexon, M., 142
Ng, S., 177
Ng, T. W. H., 47
Niblack, R. M., 412
Nicas, J., C18
Nick, D., C26
Nidetch, Jean T., C27, C28, C36
Nidumolu, R., 19
Nierve, Ricky, C276
Nilsson, Fredrik, 451
Nipper, Mads, 52
Niven, P., 107
Nixon, Cynthia, C222
Nmarus, J. A., 105
Nobel, Carmen, 372
Nobel, R., 247
Noel, P., C128
Nohria, N., 144, 277, 412
Nonaka, I., 141
Noorda, Raymond, 272
Noot, Walter, 95
Nordstrom, Dan, 80
Norton, David P., 32, 97, 100, 107
Novak, David C., 9, 418, C199
Noyes, K., 276, 385
'N Sync, C44
Nunes, P., 31, 64, 70, 107
Nuss, Jeff, C68, C70, C71, C72, C73, C75, C77, C78
Nutt, P. C., 32
Nyberg, A. J., 311
Nystrom, H. E., C128

O

Obama, Barack, C5, C25
O'Brien, Bob, 205
O'Brien, Chris, C167
O'Brien, J. M., 142
O'Brien, J. P., 413
O'Brien, William, 363
O'Connor, G. C., 411
O'Connor, M., 224
Odlyzko, A., 70
Ododaru, O., 34
O'Donnell, J., 177
O'Donnell, S. W., 247

Oestricher, Dwight, C178
Ogden, E., C128
Oh, H., 143
Ohmae, Kenichi, 245, 346
Okie, Francis G., 24
O'Leary, Kevin, C49
O'Leary-Kelly, A. M., 310
Oliff, Michael, C14n
Oliver, C., 211
Oliver, S., C128
Olsen, B., 411
Olsen, Kenneth H., 40–41
Omidyar, Pierre, 388, C156, C161, C163, C164, C166, C167
O'Neal, Shaquille, C44
O'Neill, H. M., 344
Ordonez, L., 378
O'Reilly, B., 377
O'Reilly, C. A., 142, 346
O'Reilly, Charles, 340
Orey, M., 70
Orwell, George, C118
Osawa, J., 23
Oster, S. M., 210
Ostrower, J., 344
Ouchi, William, 310
Ousik, V., 414
Oviatt, B. M., 318n, 345
Ovide, S., 412
Oxley, J. E., 346
Ozzie, Raymond, 96

P

Page, Greg, 322
Page, Larry, 388
Paine, Lynn S., 369–370, 378
Palanjian, A., 262
Palank, J., C67
Palazzo, A., 203
Palazzo, G., 311
Palladino, V., C128
Palmer, Amanda, C24
Palmer, T. B., 72
Palmeri, Christopher, 177, C273
Palmisano, Sam, 252
Panaritis, Maria, C231
Pandit, Vikram, 96
Paranjpe, Nitin, 117
Parda, L. D., 71
Pare, T. P., 209
Parise, S., 142, 144
Park, Daehee, 264
Parke, Elizabeth, C249
Parker, James F., C8
Parkinson, Andrew, C227
Parkinson, Thomas, C227
Passariello, C., C98
Patscot, Stephen, 115
Patterson, Michael, 385
Patton, Paul, 80
Pauleen, D. J., 246
Pauley, Bob, C276
Pauling, Linus, 128
Paulson, Henry, C4
Pawlowski, Janina, 256–257

Paynter, Ben, C199
Pearce, J. A., II, 33, 179
Pearson, A. E., 377
Pearson, D., 151
Pech, R., 267
Peck, S. I., 312
Pedroza, G. M., 277
Peluso, M., 157
Pendergast, Mark, C86
Peng, C., 401
Peng, M. W., 305, 313
Pennings, J. M., 412
Pentland, A., 143
Pepitone, J., 275
Perera, J., 163
Perez-Ayala, Patricia, C94
Peridis, Theo, 144
Perkins, A. B., 141
Perman, S., 405
Perna, G., C47
Perrenot, G., C36
Perrewe, P. L., 378
Perrin, Charles, C92
Perron, Kirk, C49
Perry, S., 27
Pestana, Miguel, 157
Peteraf, M., 72, 143, 277
Peters, L. S., 411
Peters, S., 211, 247
Peters, Tom J., 310
Peterson, K., 344, C18
Petrucciani, Tony, 28
Pfanner, Eric, C214
Pfeffer, Jeffrey, 31, 113, 141, 142, 329, 345, 377
Phadtare, Rohit R., C220n
Phelan, Dan, 118
Phelps, C., 211
Phillips, C., 346
Phillips, R. A., 33
Picasso, Pablo, 128
Picken, J. C., 76, 106, 136, 141, 178, 209, 210, 309, 310, 346
Pil, F. K., 378
Pinchot, G., 412
Pinchot, Gifford, 393
Pincus, Mark Jonathan, C113, C115
Pine, B. J. H., 178
Pinkham, Brian C., C206n
Pinto, J., 378
Pitts, R. A., 144, 345
Ployhart, R. E., 142
Pluhowski, John, C164
Pogue, D., 277, C129
Polek, D., 211
Polyani, M., 141
Pondy, L. R., 346
Poppo, L., 143
Porizkova, Paulina, C222
Porras, J. I., 283, 310, 406
Porter, F., 254
Porter, Michael E., 32, 52, 53, 58, 62–63, 70, 71, 72, 76–77, 78, 81, 105, 148, 150, 154, 177, 204, 209, 210, 211, 215, 217, 218, 245, 246, C147
Posner, B. Z., 363, 378
Poulfelt, F., 345
Pound, J., 311
Poundstone, W., 311
Powell, David, C94
Powell, T. C., 177
Powers, E., 32, 344
Praet, N. V., C260
Prahalad, C. K., 37, 70, 178, 209, 247
Pressman, A., 70
Preston, Holly Hubbard, C238
Preston, Jim, C92
Price, A., 342
Priem, R. L., 70, 345
Prieto, I. M., 378
Prior, V., 70
Pritchard, David, 291
Protess, B., C67
Proud, Danya, C198
Prusak, L., 143, 412
Puffer, S. M., 311
Pui-Wing Tam, C278
Puryear, R., 346
Putin, Vladimir, 222
Pylas, P., 32

Q

Quelch, John A., C218
Quick, Becky, 67
Quigley, J. V., 34
Quinlan, Michael R., C196
Quinn, James Brian, 280, 310, 346, C3n, C19
Quinn, R. T., 107

R

Rachh, Pratik, C68n
Raisingham, D., 440
Rajiv, S., 106
Ramamurti, R., 217
Raman, A., 245
Raman, A. P., 353
Ramirez, J., 27
Rampell, Catherine, C172
Rampersad, H., 107
Ramsey, M., C261
Ramstead, E., 345
Randall, D., 312
Randazzo, S., 177
Rao, A. R., 177
Rao, R., 344
Rapp, Birger, 451
Rappaport, A., 210, C12
Rasheed, A. M. A., 345
Rasheed, Abdul A., C4n
Rasheed, M. A., 71
Rashid, R., 143
Raths, D., 419
Rattner, J., C36
Raum, T., C6
Ray, S., C19
Raynor, M. E., 411
Rayport, Jeffrey F., 105, C182, C183
Rechner, P. I., 440
Reed, J., 234
Reed, S., 210
Reed, T., 32
Reedy, E. J., 254
Reeves, Terry, C44
Reeves, William T., C277
Reficco, E., C79
Regan, K., C232
Rehman, A., C128
Reinartz, W., 178
Reinert, U., 246
Reingen, P. H., 211
Reingold, Jennifer, C205
Reisinger, D., 64
Reiter, C., 105
Reitzig, M., 346
Relan, Peter, C115
Renaud, K., 132
Renfrow, J., C231
Renneboog, L. D. R., 310
Reuer, J. J., 211, 247
Reutzel, C. R., 312
Rhodes, D., 177
Rhyne, E., C208
Rice, Don, C70, C71
Rice, M. P., 411
Rich, Tim, C143, C151
Richard the Lionheart, C2
Richter, A., 413
Ricks, D., 247
Ridge, Garry, 264
Ridge, J. W., 143
Rigas family, 205
Rigby, D. K., 210
Riley, C., C151
Ring, P. S., 211
Ritzman, L. P., 106
Rivera, J., 245
Rivington, James, C193
Rivkin, J., 246, 313
Robb, A., 254
Roberto, M. A., 377
Roberts, D., 72
Roberts, E. B., 411
Roberts, J., 413
Roberts, P., 178
Roberts, P. W., 141
Robin Hood, case, C2
Robins, J. A., 107
Robinson, D., 406
Robinson, Mark, 50
Robinson, Ron, C92
Robinson, S. L., 310
Robinson-Jacobs, K., 81
Rock, The (Dwayne Johnson), C175
Rocks, David, C214
Rodriguez, N., C232
Rodriguez, P., 246
Rogers, C., 352
Rogers, James, 117
Rogers, T. J., 24
Rollag, K., 142
Roman, Jules, C276
Romanelli, E., 277
Romo, Tammy, C7, C12
Rondinelli, D. A., 32, 33
Ronstadt, R., 440
Roos, A., 211
Roos, J., 346
Root, Alan, 22
Root, J., 142
Roper, Martin, C99
Rose, Charlie, 209
Rose, Doug, C181
Rose, Kevin, 249
Rosen, B., 144
Rosenberg, T., 401
Rosenblum, D., 71
Rosenblum, P., 309
Rosenfeld, E., 395
Rosenzweig, Dan, 116
Rosli, Evelyn M., C172
Ross, Kimberly, C94
Rossetti, C., 345
Rossi, Angie, C90
Roth, David, 158
Roth, K., 107
Rothaermel, F. T., 276
Rothenbuecher, J., 209
Rothenstein, Steve, C38
Rotunno, Tom, C110
Roulse, T., 246
Roundy, P. T., 209
Rowley, I., 72
Rowley, T. J., 211
Rows, S. A., 441n
Roy, J. P., 211
Royer, I., 413
Rubin, Harry, C100
Rubin, Jami, 201
Rubin, Slava, C23
Rucci, A. J., 107
Rudd, Vivienne, C93
Rudden, E., 246
Rugman, Alan M., 237, 247
Ruisel, I., 377
Rukstad, M. G., 33
Rumelt, R. P., 345
Runyan, R., 413
Rupp, L., C36
Rush, Patrick, 109
Rusli, E., 209
Russo, M. V., 29
Russolillo, S., C129
Rutherford, Linda, C12
Ruys, Thorny, C215
Ryan, Eric, 254
Ryan, L., 312
Ryan, M. K., 310
Ryschkewitsch, Mike, 365

S

Saari, Lise M., 82–84, 85
Sacca, Chris, C170
Sachitanand, R., 218, C88
Safferstone, T., 32
Saffo, P., 141

Safizadeh, M. H., 106
Sahlman, William A., 71, 421
Saias, M. A., 345
St. John, W., 277
Sakaibara, M., 346
Salahi, L., C36
Salancik, G. R., 31
Salerno, C., C260, C261
Salkever, A., C129
Salsberg, Brian, C94
Salzberg, Barry, C14
Sambol, David, 293
Sampson, R. C., 412
Sanchez, Raymond, 433
Sandberg, W. R., 440
Sanders, J., C129
Sanderson, Rob, C169
Sandler, N., 246
Sandler, Ross, C169
Sant, Roger, 378
Sargent, David, C256
Sasseen, J., 312
Sasso, M., C18
Sauer, P. J., 434
Savage, Macho Man Randy, C174
Savitt, Kathy, C171
Savner, Michael, C277
Schaal, D., C19
Schaeffer, Leonard, 62
Schafer, S., 378
Schaffer, R. H., 377
Schandler, T., 378
Schawlow, Arthur, 120
Scheck, J., 311
Schecter, S. M., 179
Schein, Edgar H., 319, 344
Schendel, D., 247
Schenkel, M. T., 276
Scherer, A. G., 311
Scherzer, L., 106
Schiesel, D., C193
Schiesel, S., C192
Schijven, M., 179, 199
Schindler, Pamela, 433
Schiro, Jim, 122
Schlangenstein, M., C12, C18, C19
Schlender, B., C128, C129
Schmidt, C., 141
Schmidt, G., 178
Schneider, Ben, 83
Schneider, J., 70
Schneider, M., 312
Schneiderman, R. M., C178
Schoemaker, J. R., 107
Schoemaker, P. J. H., 70
Schoenberger, C. R., C193, C231
Schoettler, Steve, C23
Schol, M., 33
Schoonhoven, C. B., 276
Schoppen, W., 312
Schreyogg, G., 70
Schrottke, J., 209
Schultz, Howard, 207, 251, C82, C83–C85
Schulz, Mark A., C251

Schwartz, N. D., 246
Schweiger, D. M., 440
Schweitzer, M. E., 378
Schwert, G. William, 209
Scott, B. R., 344
Scott, F. S., 70
Scott, L., 71
Sculley, John, C118, C120–C121
Scully, James, C94
Seal, Mark, C269
Sedgwick, D., 378
Segalla, M., 141
Segel, Joseph, C179–C180, C181, C182
Seglin, J. L., 276
Seibert, S., 276
Seijts, G. H., 142, 413
Sellers, P., 211, 245, 310
Selznick, David O., 41
Semadeni, M., 312
Semel, Terry, C169, C170
Sen, S., 33
Senatroe, Sara, C199
Senge, Peter M., 9, 23, 32, 33, 362, 378
Serwer, A., C12, C18
Sesterfield, R. W., 441n
Sethi, R., 414
Sexton, D. A., 34
Shah, B., 70
Shah, R. H., 211
Shamsie, Jamal, C152n, C168n, C173n, C179n, C194n, C200n, C209n, C215n, C233n, C239n, C262n, C270n, C274n
Shane, S., 413
Shanley, M., 72
Shapira, Z., 413
Shapiro, A. Andrew, C241
Shapiro, C., 76
Shapiro, J., 142
Sharer, Kevin, 10, 32
Sharma, A., 247, 412
Sharp, Richard, 252
Shaw, Peter, 186
Shchetko, N., 276
Shechner, S., 409
Sheehan, M., 105
Sheff, D., 378
Shen, Jia, C113
Shepardson, D., C261
Shepherd, D. A., 276
Sher, R., C56
Sher, Robert, C55
Sherbin, L., 123, 143
Shetty, Ajit, C237
Shintaku, J., 23
Shipton, H., 391
Shook, C., 142
Short, J. C., 72, 156
Shrader, R. C., 276
Shrager, Gabrielle, C184
Shrestha, Shruti, C156n, C220n
Shriver, J. M., 277
Shuster, Jay, C276
Siddhartha, V. G., C87

Sidhu, I., 33
Siebel, Tom, 232, 246, 310
Sieracki, Eric, 293
Silva, C., 310
Silverberg, Brad, 124
Silver-Greenberg, J., 141
Silverman, B. S., 346
Silverman, R. E., 5
Silvestri, L., 345
Simmons, Cal, 254
Simmons, P. J., 21
Simon, B., 234
Simons, R., 310
Sims, H. P., Jr., 378
Simsek, Z., 276, 412
Sinclair, M., C151
Singer, Natasha, C238
Singh, Ayush, 4, 5, C260
Singh, H., 210, 247
Singh, J. V., 106
Singh, K., 246
Singh, S., 221
Siracusa, J., C129
Sirkin, Harold L., 21
Sirmon, D. G., 106, 143, 179, 211, 312
Sirota, D., 310
Sirower, M. L., 210
Sisario, B., 210
Skinner, Jim, C196, C197
Skoll, Jeffrey, C163
Slater, R., 142
Sleuwaegen, L., 346
Slevin, D. P., 346, 403, 413
Sloan, Alfred, 23, 362
Slocum, J. W., Jr., 144, 178, 310
Slowinski, G., 346
Slywotsky, A., 413
Smerd, J., C232
Smith, Alvy Ray, C275
Smith, B. R., 276
Smith, Brad, 396, 412
Smith, C., C231
Smith, D., 142, C129
Smith, Douglas K., 336, 346
Smith, Fred, 14
Smith, G., 246
Smith, J., 32
Smith, K. G., 178, 266, 270, 277
Smith, Liz, C92
Smith, R., 272
Smith, Stephen, 369
Smith, Thomasina, C249
Snow, C. C., 179, 266, 277, 336, 412
Snyder, B., 174
Snyder, Nancy, 23
Snyder, S. J., C26
Sole, Kenneth, 433
Solomon, B., C110
Solomon, Charles, C278
Solomon, King of Israel, C47
Solomon, R., 247
Sonpar, K., 33
Sorensen, Jay, 163
Sorkin, Andrew Ross, C172

Sorrell, Martin, 132
Souder, D., 277
Soule, E., 378
Spainhour, J. Patrick, C57, C58
Spector, J., 71
Spencer, J. W., 144
Sperling, John, 294
Spindler, Michael, C121
Spinelli, S., 251, 275
Spurlock, Morgan, C197
Srivastava, S., C88
Stabell, C. B., 105
Stadter, G., 107
Stafford, E. R., 211
Staley, O., 71
Stalk, George, Jr., 165, 178, 267, 277
Stamboulidis, G., 267
Stanley, A., C98
Stanton, Andrew, C277
Stanton, Brian, C70, C71, C72, C77
Stanton, S. A., 378
Stanton, Steven, 363
Stark, Michael, C220
Staw, B. M., 377
Stead, D., 177
Stearns, T. M., 440
Stecklow, S., 311
Ste-Croix, Giles, C270
Steelman, Paul, C154
Steensma, H. K., 378
Steere, W. C., Jr., 412
Steere, William, 385
Stefanova, Katina, C12
Steffens, P., 277
Steigrad, A., C66
Stein, Art, 147
Steinberg, Brian, C178
Steinmann, Benj, C219
Steinmann, H., 70
Stelter, D., 177
Stephan, J., 311
Stetler, B., 106
Steuerle, Eugene, 45
Stevens, D., 71
Stevens, J. M., 378
Stevens, Paul, C12
Stewart, Stacey D., C143, C151
Stewart, Thomas A., 112, 141, 142, 210, 276
Stewart, W. H., 70
Stibel, J. M., 177
Stieglitz, N., 71
Stoll, J. D., C260, C261
Stone, B., 93, C128
Stone, R., 119
Strack, R., 141
Straus, S., 144
Strickland, A. J., III, 310
Strickler, Yancey, C22, C23, C25, C26
Stringer, R., 413
Stroh, Bernard, 349
Stroh, Bernard, Jr., 349
Stroh, Greg, 349

I-20 Name Index

Stroh, Julius, 349
Stroh, Peter, 349–350, 377
Strom, Stephanie, 207, C199
Stross, R. E., 245
Stroud, Brandon, C178
Stuart, Keith, C193
Stuckey, J., 346
Studzinski, J., 300
Stumpf, John, 14
Su, K. H., 277
Suchman, M., C151
Suer, Oral, C148
Sull, D. N., 34, 144, 412
Sullivan, John, C171
Sullivan, Trudy, C64
Summers, M., C66
Sun, J. J. M., 106
Sunoo, B. P., C37
Surette, T., C193
Sutcliffe, K. M., 70, 345
Swaminathan, A., 276
Swaminathan, V., 211
Swan, Bob, C156
Swartz, J., 313
Swartz, John, C172
Sweeney, J., 404
Sweo, R., 70
Swinney, J., 413
Symonds, W. C., 178

T

Takeda, Genyo, C185
Takeuchi, I., 141
Tallman, Joseph, 134
Tang, J., 70
Tang, Y., 211
Tanner, J., 178
Task, A., 32, 211
Tassi, Paul, C115
Tate, B., 377
Taylor, A., C6
Taylor, A., III, 72, 178
Taylor, B., 234
Taylor, C., C26
Taylor, Norman O., C148
Taylor, Teresa, 361
Taylor, W. C., 144
Teece, David J., 137, 144
Tekleab, A. G., 378
Teng, B. S., 346
Teramoto, Y., 247
Terdimann, Daniel, C278
Tervino, L. K., 310
Tesluk, P. E., 144, 378
Thain, John, 205, 211
Theoret, A., 440
This-Benckhard, N, C47
Thoma, Wade, C198
Thomas, J. G., 33
Thomas, Katie, C238
Thomas, R., 143
Thomas, R. J., 70
Thomas, Ryan, 81
Thompson, Arthur A., Jr., 310

Thompson, Don, 341, C194, C197, C198
Thompson, Ken, 156
Thompson, Scott, C170
Thorndike, E. L., 377
Thornton, E., 177, 210
Thurm, S., 71
Tichy, Noel M., 377
Tierney, T. J., 144, 377
Tietzen, Terry, 250
Timmons, J. A., 251, 275, 276
Tiwana, A., 211
Tofel, K. C., C128
Tohme, N. S., 312
Tokuda, Lance, C113
Toman, N., 178
Tomé, Carol B., 290
Tomlinson, D., 71
Tomlinson, Richard, C219
Torres, N. L., 276
Torvalds, Linus, 431
Touryalai, H., 141
Tracy, Edward M., C153, C154, C155
Traquina, Perry, C166
Travlos, D., C128
Tretter, M. J., 345
Triandis, H. C., 246
Trimble, C., 211, 345
Triple H., C174
Tristano, Darren, C195
Trombetta, William, C238
Trudel, R., 33
Trudell, C., C260
Trumo, Donald, C43
Tsai, W., 277
Tsao, A., 70
Tu, H., 178
Tucker, R., C66
Tuggle, C. S., 312
Tukiainen, T., 413
Tully, S., 310, 345
Turk, T. A., 312
Turner, Fred L., C196
Turner, J., C67
Turner, Jeff, C226
Turner, S. F., 413
Turner, Ted, 38, C173–C174
Tushman, Michael L., 340, 346
Tuttle, B., C18, C19
Twain, Mark, 356
Tylor, David S., C200
Tyrangiel, J., 144
Tyson, L. D., 71

U

Udall, Sean, C167
Uhl-Bien, M., 310
Uhlenbruck, K., 246
Ulaga, W., 178
Ultimate Warrior, C175
Unnikrishnan, M., C19
Useem, Michael, 296
Uzzi, B., 143

V

Vaaler, P. M., 178
Vaarnas, Markko, 451
Vagelos, P. Roy, 110
Valeant-Yemichek, Julie, 47
Valikangas, L., 412
Valukas, Anton R., C243
Van Aukun, P. M., 34
Van Boxmeer, Jean-François, C215, C217, C218, C219
Van Buren, H. J., 144
Van Buren, M. E., 32
Van Daalen, R., C110
Van de Kamp, P., 345
Vanderkol, Bill, 189
Van Doorn, J., 106
Van Gogh, Vincent, 128
Van Looy, B., 247
Van Putten, A. B., 246
Varian, H. R., 76
Vascellaro, Jessica E., 267, 411, C128, C172
Veiga, J. F., 276, 412
Veloso, F. M., 412
Verbeke, Alain, 237, 247, 344
Verdú-Jover, A. J., 377
Verhoef, P. C., 106
Vermeulen, F., 211
Verne, Jules, 52
Verrier, Richard, C278
Very, P., 143
Veryzer, R. W., 411
Vesper, K. H., 275, 276
Vestring, T., 246
Victor, B., 345
Viehbacher, Christopher, 297
Viguerie, P., 70
Vijayaraghavan, K., C88
Vinh, K., C26
Vlasic, Bill, C244
Vogel, C., 276
Vogel, D. J., 33
Vogt, H., 327
Vohra, Manmeet, C87
Von Furstenberg, Diane, C90
Von Hippel, Eric, 71

W

Waddock, S., 33
Wadia, A. S., C232
Wagh, Girish, 67
Wagner, M., 404
Wagner, S., 346
Wagoner, Richard, C240
Wagstaff, J., C129
Wakabayashi, D., C128, C129
Wakayama, T., 23
Walker, B. A., 211
Walker, H. J., 156
Walker, J., 275
Walker, Jay, 211
Wall, S. J., 378
Wallace, B., 277
Wallace, J., 344

Waller, Brent, 52
Walsh, Glenn, C231
Walsh, J. P., 312
Walsh, Jack, 84
Walter, J., 130
Walters, B. A., 70, 211, 247, 276, 311
Walton, Sam, 17, 24
Wan, W. P., 247
Wang, F., C98
Wang, H., C88
Wang, L., 413
Wang, Shirley S., C238
Ward, Elizabeth, C54
Warner, B., C66
Warner, F., 142
Warner, Melanie, C199
Wasik, J., 256, 276
Wassener, Bettina, C155
Wasserman, E., 421
Waterman, Robert H., 310
Waters, J. A., 12
Wathieu, L., 178
Watkins, M. D., 70
Watson, R., 405
Watson, Thomas, 362
Watson, Thomas J., 186
Watson, Tom, 23
Wattercutter, A., C26
Watts, Claire, C183
Watts, Colin, C36
Weaver, G. R., 310
Weaver, K. M., 276
Webber, A. M., 141
Weber, J., 310
Weber, K., 70
Weber, L., 142
Weil, Laura, C64
Weilart, M., 345
Weinberg, D., 144
Weinberg, N., 312
Weiner, H., 345
Weintraub, A., 408
Weise, Frank, C131
Weise, K., 70
Weiser, Brian, C169
Welch, D., 71, C260
Welch, Jack, 5, 204–205, 211, 328
Weldon, William C., C233, C234, C235, C236
Wellington, F., 33
Wells, R. M. J., 412
Welsch, H. L., 276
Wen, S. H., 247
Werder, A. V., 311
Werhane, F. H., 206
Wernerfelt, B., Jr., 143
Wesley, Pamela, C163
Weston, J. F., 211
Weston, J. S., 310
Weston, John, 281
Westphal, J. D., 209, 296, 311, 377
Wetlaufer, S., 247, 310, 378
Whalen, J., 19
Wheelwright, S., 411

Whelan, D., 71
Whitacre, Edward E., Jr., C240
White, A., 272
White, D., 346
White, Dana, C177
White, James D., C48, C49, C52, C54, C55
Whited, R., 329
Whitman, Meg, C23, C163, C164, C167
Whitwam, R., 385
Wiersema, F., 412
Wiersema, M. F., 107, 209
Wiggins, Jenny, C219
Wilder, B., C129
Wilk, R., C260
Willcocks, L. P., 106
Williams, Billy Dee, C90
Williams, Christopher C., C219
Williams, G., 277, C36
Williams, M. A., 143
Williams, Michael, 353–355
Williams, R., 378
Williams, S., C67
Williams, Venus, C52
Williams-Grut, O., 261
Williamsom, Oliver E., 210
Williamson, P., 245
Wilson, D., 177
Wilson, H. J., 71, 144

Wilson, K., 344
Wilson, M., C66
Wilson, Mackenzie, C21
Wilson, R. J., 412
Wilson, Susan, C21
Wind, Yoram, 246
Winder, Catherine, 396
Wingfield, N., 144, 211
Wingo, Scott, 93
Winston, Andrew S., 10, 32, 33, 106, 141, 430, 440
Winter, C., 247
Wirtz, J., 178
Wise, R., 71, 413
Wiseman, R., 210, 307
Witherspoon, Reese, C96
Wolfenson, J., 70
Wolter, C., 412
Wong, C., 246
Wong, Chris, C26
Wong, S.-S., 143, 287
Wong, V., 395
Woo, E., 377
Wood, J., 106
Woods, B., C231
Woolley, S., 32
Worrell, D., 262
Worthan, J., C26
Wozniak, Steve, C114, C117
Wright, P., 178, 276, 311

Wriston, A., 345
Wriston, Walter, 205, 362
Wulf, J., 322
Wynn, Steve, 294
Wysocki, Bernard, 124

X

Xiang Junbo, 373–374

Y

Yakubovich, V., 310
Yang, Jerry, C169, C170
Yang, Q., 247
Yao, X., 276
Ye, Wendy, C68n
Yeary, Frank, C166
Yeoh, P. L., 107
Yew, Jack, 242
Yoffie, D. B., 64, 72
Yolton, Mark, 135
Yonekura, Hiromasa, C211
Yoon, B. K., C213
Yosano, Kaora, 245
Young, Andrew, 19
Young, Bob, 430, 431
Young, M. N., 305, 306, 313, 345
Yu, Roger, C214
Yukl, G., 377
Yun, S., 378

Yun Jong Yong, C210, C211, C213
Yunus, Muhammad, C206, C208

Z

Zaccaro, S. J., 144
Zacharakis, A. L., 276
Zahid, M., C261
Zahra, S. A., 247, 412
Zajac, E. J., 311
Zardkoohi, A., 311, 413
Zell, D., 143
Zelleke, A., 312
Zellner, W., C18
Zelman, K. M., C36
Zhang, R., 378
Zhang Weidong, C71, C74
Zhao, A., 254
Zhao, H., 276
Zhi, Jessica, C71, C77
Zhou, K. Z., 143
Zhou, Q., 391
Zhu, D. H., 106
Zillman, C., 79, 155
Ziobro, P., C141
Zoe, Rachel, C179
Zollo, M., 209
Zongker, B., C151
Zrike, Stephen, 169
Zweig, Jason, 42, 70

SUBJECT INDEX

A

Ability barriers, 127
Academy of Management Journal, 156
Accountability, 354
Accounting, 87–88
  irregularities at Tesco, 279
Achievable opportunity, 253
Acid-test ratio, 423, 445
Acquired diversity, 123
Acquisitions; *see also* Mergers and acquisitions
  by Apple Inc., C126
  by Avon, C92
  by Boeing, 315
  by Campbell Soup Co., C131
  by Cisco Systems, 181
  definition, 195
  failure for Stroh's Brewing, 349–350
  by Heineken, C215–C219
  hostile takeovers, 205
  by Jamba Juice, C49
  by Johnson & Johnson, C234
  Pixar by Disney, C274–C275
  by Procter & Gamble, C200–C201
  by QVC, C181, C183
  resulting in divestiture, 183
  by Southwest Airlines, C10–C11
  studies of failures, 182
  value distribution, 182
  by Weight Watchers, C28
  by World Wrestling Entertainment, C173–C174
  by Yahoo!, C168
Action plans, 28
Actions, 8
Activist investor, and eBay, C166
Actor's reputation, 271
Adaptability, 339
Adaptation; *see also* Local adaptation
  versus cost reduction, 229–230
  in transnational strategy, 235
Adaptive new entry
  definition, 262
  differentiation in, 264
  examples, 262
  pitfalls, 262–263
Administrative costs, 190
Advertising
  Campbell Soup Co., C132
  decline at Yahoo!!, C170
  decline for Yahoo!, C168
  Emirates Airline, C268

  goals for Weight Watchers, C31
  mistakes by Coca Cola Company, 224
  problem for Google, 381
  Super Bowl ads, 81
  on Super Bowl by Weight Watchers, C27
Advertising battles, 57
Advertising expenditures, Avon, C92
Affordable Care Act, 6
  health care industry response, 7
Affordable Care Act of 2010, C83
Africa
  GDP per person growth 2001–2011, 215
  population and Internet usage, C162
Age distribution, China, India, and Japan, C83
Agency costs, 338
Agency theory
  and back-solver dilemma, 400–401
  and CEO duality, 301–302
  definition, 294
  principal-agent conflicts, 294
  risk-sharing problem, 294
Age of Unreason (Handy), 331
Aggregate demand, 169
Aging of populations, 45
Agreeableness, 258
Agricultural export destinations, C134
Airline industry
  Emirates Airline, C262–C269
  glossary of terms, C13, C20
  interline agreements, C17–C18
  JetBlue Airways, 173–174, C14–C18
  profit pool, 163
  Southwest Airlines, C7–C12
  top global airlines, C262
  in United States
    bases of competition, C15
    deregulation in 1978, C15
    segments, C15
    and Wright amendment, C9, C12
Air Transport World, C!6
Alignment, 339
Alternative solutions in case analysis, 424
Ambidexterity, 10, 339
Ambidextrous behavior, 11
Ambidextrous organizational design

  adaptability, 339–340
  alignment, 339–340
  breakthrough innovations, 340
  definition, 340
  effectiveness, 340
  key attributes, 340
  performance results, 340
American Business Ethics Award, 370
American Heritage Dictionary, 283
Americans with Disabilities Act, 47
Analysis, 8
Analysis-decision-action cycle
  business-level strategy formulation, 437
  corporate entrepreneurship, 439–440
  corporate-level strategy formulation, 438
  entrepreneurial strategy formulation, 438
  ethical organization creation, 439
  external environment analysis, 436–437
  intellectual assets, 437
  internal environment analysis, 437
  international strategy formulation, 438
  learning organization creation, 439
  organizational design creation, 439
  organizational goals and objectives, 436
  strategic control, 439
Angel investors, 255
  definition, 254
Antitakeover tactics
  benefits for multiple stakeholders, 206
  definition, 205
  golden parachute, 205
  greenmail, 205
  poison pills, 205
Antitrust enforcement
  in France, 272
  weak in U.S., 272
Apparel retail industry
  branding challenges, C61–C63
  comparative performance, C63
  competitors, C62–C64
  recovery from financial crisis, C57
  sectors, C60

Appreciation of currencies, 223
Appropriate objectives, 28
Arbitrage opportunities, 219
Arizona State Veterinary Medical Examining Board, 272
Asia
  casino industry, C154
  eBay's failure in, C157
  population and Internet usage, C162
Asset restructuring, 192
Asset sales, 200n
Asset surgery, 173
Asset utilization ratios
  capital intensity ratio, 97, 423, 448
  days' sales in inventory, 97, 423, 447
  days' sales in receivables, 97, 423, 447–448
  inventory turnover, 97, 423, 447
  receivables turnover, 97, 423, 447–448
  total asset turnover, 97, 423, 448
Associating, by innovators, 388
Association of Southeast Asian Nations, 238
Atlantic City casinos, C152–C153
Attractive opportunity, 253
Auction market
  eBay, C156–C167
  online auctions, C161–C162
  traditional auctions, C161
Auditors, 303, 304
Australia, population and Internet usage, C162
Automated manufacturing systems, 161–162
Automobile industry
  best-selling vehicles in U.S., C258
  in China, 213
  Ford Motor Company, C245–C260
  General Motors, C239–C244
  hybrid cars, 56
  market shares and sales, C248
  market shares by brand, C257
  strategic groups, 65–67
  in United States, C247
Autonomous teams, 403
Autonomy
  definition, 403
  measuring and monitoring, 403
  pitfalls of teams, 403
  techniques, 404
Autorité de la Concurrance, France, 272

I-23

Auto safety problem, General Motors, C239–C244
Average collection period, 448
Aviation Consumer Action Project, 304

B

Baby boomers, replaced by Millennials, 116
Back-solver dilemma, 400–401
Backward integration, threat of, 54
Bailout
 of AIG, C4
 of banks in 2008, C4
Balanced scorecard
 benefits
  customer perspective, 100
  financial perspective, 101
  innovation and learning perspective, 100
  internal business perspective, 100
 definition, 100
 versus financial ratio analysis, 99–100
 limitations and downsides, 101
Balance sheet, 441
 Ann Taylor, C61
 Avon, C97–C98
 Boston Beer Company, C102
 Campbell Soup Co., C136–C137
 eBay, C158
 Emirates Airline, C264–C265
 Ford Motor Company, C252–C253
 General Motors, C240
 Heineken, C216
 Jamba Juice, C50–C51
 Johnson & Johnson, C234
 McDonald's, C194
 Nintendo, C187–C188
 Procter & Gamble, C205
 Samsung, C209
 Weight Watchers, C32–C33
 Yahoo!, C168
 Zynga, C112
Bangalore, India, 227
Bank financing, 255
Bankruptcy
 Blockbuster Inc., 94–95
 Dippin' Dots emergence from, C38
 filing by Dippin' Dots, C38
 General Motors, C240
Banks
 and corporate governance, 303
 government bailout, C4
Bargaining power of buyers
 conditions for, 54–55
 definition, 54
 effect of Internet, 58–60
 for legal services, 61
 potential backward integration, 55
 third-party services, 55

Bargaining power of employees, 96
Bargaining power of managers, 96
Bargaining power of suppliers
 conditions for, 55–56
 definition, 55
 effect of Internet, 60
Barrier-free organization
 versus boundary mind-set, 328–329
 brainstorming in, 329–330
 definition, 329
 environmental sustainability practices, 331
 external constituencies, 330
 holocracy, 330
 permeable internal boundaries, 329–330
 pros and cons, 331
 risks, challenges, and potential downsides, 331
 teams in, 329–330
 Veterans Administration, 329
Barriers to change
 behavioral, 356
 definition, 355
 at General Motors, 357
 personal time constraints, 356
 political, 356
 systemic, 355–356
 vested interest in status quo, 355
Barriers to collaboration; *see* Collaboration
Barriers to entry
 government red tape, 272
 low for online auctions, C156–C157
 low in focus strategy, 161
 for new ventures, 260
Batman, 52
Beer industry, 349–350
 changing drinking habits, C104
 comparison of domestic brands, C109
 globalization, C215–C216
 Heineken, C215–C219
 leading brewers in 2014, C217
 major competitors, C99–C100, C106–C108
 three-tier system, C104–C106
 top craft beers, C103
 top domestic beers, C104
 top flavored malts and hard ciders, C105
 top home-brewed beers, C107
 top imported beers, C105
 top 10 U.S. brewers, C106
Beer Marketer's Insight, C217
Behavioral barriers to change, 356
Behavioral control, 439
 aspect of strategic control, 280
 boundaries and constraints, 288–290
 definition, 281
 evolving from boundaries and constraints, 291–292

focus on implementation, 282–283
and organizational culture, 283–284
rewards and incentives, 284–288
situational factors, 290, 291
Benchmarking
 for best practices, 366
 competitive, 366
 definition, 366
 functional, 366
 internal, 365
Bentley College Center for Business Ethics Award, 370
Best practices
 to attract Millennials, 116
 from benchmarking, 366
 for entering new markets
  good local partner, C85
  long-term commitment, C85–C86
  tact in marketing, C85
Better Business Bureaus, 256
Better Homes and Gardens, 383
Big data, 162
Big Pivot (Winston), 10, 430
Bloomberg Businessweek, 5, 39, 75, 200, 304, 383, C216
Board of directors
 versus activist investor at eBay, C166
 assuming role of, 420
 auditors *vs.* advisers, 296
 avoiding cronyism, 16
 broad view of firm, 298
 changing face of, 1987–2011, 298
 criticisms of, 16
 definition, 295
 director independence, 297
 duties, 295
 effective *vs.* ineffective, 295–296
 executive compensation issue, 16
 expertise, 297
 focus on past, present, and future, 297
 full participation, 297
 functions, 15–16
 Heineken, C218
 impact on CEOs, 296–297
 independent members, 16
 interlocking directorships, 297
 manageable size, 297
 management talent development, 297–298
 norms of transparency and trust, 298
 and principal-agent conflicts, 294
 of Tesco, 279
Boards That Lead (Carrey & Useem), 296
Bonus payments, AIG employees, C4–C6

Book value *vs.* market value, 110–111
Bots, 61
Bottom of the pyramid populations, 214
Boundaries, types of, 328
Boundaries and constraints
 definition, 288
 evolving to reward systems, 291–292
 focus on strategic priorities, 288
 minimizing improper conduct, 289
 in nonprofits, 288
 operational efficiency, 289–290
 purposes, 288
 short-term objectives, 288–289
Boundaryless, 328
Boundaryless organizational design, 316
 barrier-free organization, 328–331
 definition, 328
 internally focused, 336
 made to work
  common culture, 337
  communication, 337
  cooperation and integration, 336–337
  horizontal structure, 337
  horizontal system processes, 337
  human resource practices, 337–338
  information technology, 337
  internal and external relationships, 338–339
  shared values, 337
 modular organizations, 331–333
 types, 328
 virtual organizations, 333–336
Boundary mind-set, 328–329
Bozo Filter, 115
Brand(s)
 Ann Taylor, C58
 building preferences for, 169
 cutback by General Motors, C240–C243
 development at Samsung, C211
 global, 229
 globalization by Ford, C259
 Heineken, C217
 luxury brands, 160
 sell-off by Procter & Gamble, C200–C201, C202
 updating at Procter & Gamble, C201
 Weight Watchers, C31
Brand extension, 102
Brand Finance Global 500 2013 report, C86
Brand identification dilution, 158–159
Brand identity, Ann Taylor, C65–C66

Branding, challenge in retail apparel, C61–C64
Brand marketing, Jamba Juice, C49–C52
Brand recognition, Boston Beer Company, C104
Brand reputation, 86
Brand value, 75
Brazil, problems for Avon in, C93–C94
Breakaway positioning
 definition, 170
 operation of, 170
 Swatch Group, 171
Breakthrough technology products, 54
Breast Cancer Crusade, C95
Bribery, alleged against Avon, C94
Bridging relationships, 126–127
Built to Last (Collins & Porras), 283
Bureau of Labor Statistics
 on Millennials, 116
 on older workers, 45, 46
Business cycles, 64
Business environment, 436–437
Business groups
 definition, 306
 functions, 306–307
 in Japan and South Korea, 306
Business incubators, 439
 definition, 394
 function, 395
Business-level strategy, 14
 Apple Inc., C121, C123–C128
 Boston Beer Company, C103–C104
 Campbell Soup Co., C130–C131, C132–C133
 in case analysis, 437
 change at Johnson & Johnson, C237–C238
 competitive advantage, 148–164
 debate at Cirque du Soleil, C270
 definition, 147
 Dippin' Dots, C38–C39
 discarding failure at Samsung, C210–C211
 Emirates Airline, C267, C268–C269
 failure at Kickstarter, C25
 FreshDirect, C222–C223
 generic strategies
  combination strategies, 161–164
  differentiation strategy, 153–159
  focus strategy, 159–161
  overall cost leadership, 148–153
 industry life-cycle changes, 167–173
 Jamba Juice, C48, C54, C55
 JetBlue Airways, 174–175
 McDonald's, C197–C199

 options for Nintendo, C192
 problem at Crumbs Bake Shop, 147
 QVC, C181, C183
 reinvention at Weight Watchers, C36
 revision at JetBlue, C16–C18
 revision by Avon, C94–C95
 shift at Samsung, C209–C210
 strategic management concepts, 164–167
 success for Ford, C251
 sustainability, 148–164
 Tata Starbucks, C82–C83
 for turnaround at Procter & Gamble, C201–C202
 turnaround strategies, 173–174
 World Wrestling Entertainment, C174
Business model
 broken at Yahoo!, C170–C171
 change at Weight Watchers, C27
 early, for Stroh's Brewing, 349
 eBay, C156, C164
 FreshDirect, C222
 JetBlue Airways, C17–C18
 Kickstarter, C22
 problem for Google, 381
 rethinking at McDonald's, C198–C199
 Weight Watchers, C28, C30–C31
Business plan framework for case analysis, 421
Business risk, FreshDirect, C231
Business risk taking, 407
Business services, 395
Business-to-business auctions, C162
Business-to-business sales, 60
Business-to-customer auctions, C162
Business-to-customer sales, 59
Buyer channel intermediaries, 60
Buyers; *see also* Bargaining power of buyers
 buyer channel intermediaries, 60
 end users, 59
 switching costs faced by, 54

C

Cannibalization problem for Ann Taylor, C65
Capabilities, collaboration *vs.* building, 386
Capacity augmentation, 57
Capital intensity ratio, 97
Capital requirements, as barrier to entry, 54
Capital restructuring, 192
Careers
 and environmentally aware organizations, 68
 and five-forces analysis, 68
 and general environment, 68

 implications of social networks, 128
 and SWOT analysis, 68
Caribbean, population and Internet usage, C162
Case analysis
 analysis-decision-action cycle, 436–440
 benefiting from
  being concise, 426–427
  insights from other analyses, 427
  learning from others, 427
  open mind, 426
  outside research, 427
  participate and persuade, 426
  performance appraisal, 427
  personal experience, 426
  taking a stand, 426
  thinking out of the box, 427
 conduct of, 419–425
  alternative solutions, 424
  business plan framework, 421
  familiarity with material, 421–422
  financial ratio analysis, 423
  oral presentation, 425
  preparation for discussion, 420
  problem identification, 422
  recommendations, 424–425
  role playing, 420
  strategic analysis, 422–424
  thinking like a participant, 420
  written presentation, 428
 cycle of activity in, 419–420
 decision-making techniques
  conflict-inducing techniques, 431–435
  heretical questions, 430–431
  integrative thinking, 428–430
 definition, 417
 effective teams
  attention to strategy, 433
  focused agenda, 433
  real decisions, 433–434
  time factor, 433
 functions, 417
 Sapient Health Network, 419
 skills enhanced by, 418
Case analysis teams, 433–434
Cash coverage ratio, 97, 423, 446–447
Cash cows, 193
Cash ratio, 97, 423, 445
Casino industry; *see* Global casino industry
Causal ambiguity, 92
CE; *see* Corporate entrepreneurship
Celebrate Your Mistakes (Holt), 367
Celebrity endorsements
 Avon, C90
 FreshDirect, C229
 QVC, C79
Center for Auto Safety, 305

Center for Study of Responsive Law, 305
Central Europe, GDP per person growth 2001–2011, 215
CEO compensation, 96, 299–300, 367
CEO duality
 agency theory supporters, 301–302
 meaning of, 300
 unity of command opponents, 301
CEOs
 Apple Inc., C117–C122
 and board of directors, 296–297
 contrasting fortunes of, 5
 effective, 84
 erosion of value creation by, 204–205
 with high emotional intelligence, 359
 public view of, 16
 and Sarbanes-Oxley Act, 304–305
 Zynga, C115
Chaebols, 306
Change, barriers to, 355–356
Change management
 from corporate entrepreneurship, 393–399
 entrepreneurial orientation, 402–408
 from innovation, 382–393
 Nest Labs, 408–409
 real options analysis, 399–402
Chapter 11 bankruptcy, C38
Charities
 accountability problem, C149
 fragmented giving, C145–C147
 top ten in United States, C148
 United Way, C143–C151
 watchdog agencies, C149
Cheaper by the Dozen, C44
Chief financial officers, 290
 and Sarbanes-Oxley Act, 304–305
China
 age distribution, C83
 Campbell Soup Co. in, C132
 casino industry, C153
 Ford Motor Company in, C258
 General Motors in, C244
 GreenWood Resources in, C72–C79
 GDP per person growth 2001–2011, 215
 minimum wage, 228
 per capita income, C84
 problems for Avon in, C94
 Starbucks in, C84
China Daily, C85
Chinese market, 203
Claremont McKenna College, 372
Clients, loyalty to professionals, 96
Closure relationships, 126
Cluster of dissent, 367

CNBC/Burton-Marsteller Corporation Perception Index, 16
CNN Money, C38
Codes of ethics, 290, 372
Codifying knowledge, 134–135
Coercive power, 357
Cognitive abilities, 358
Cold War, end of, 172
Collaboration
  barriers to
    hoarding barrier, 127
    not-invented-here barrier, 127
    search barrier, 127
    transfer barrier, 127
  effort at Johnson & Johnson, C234–C236
  electronic teams, 132–134
  with innovation partners, 390–392
Collusion among soap makers, 272
Combination strategies
  automated and flexible manufacturing, 161–162
  coordinating extended value chain, 162–163
  definition, 161
  and five-forces model, 163
  goal, 161
  mass customization, 161–162
  for new entrants, 265
  pitfalls
    miscalculation of revenue sources, 164
    stuck in the middle position, 163
    underestimating value-chain challenges, 164
  profit pool concept, 163
  using data analytics, 163
Commitment to excellence, 258
Common-size balance sheet, 441
Common-size income statement, 441
Communication in boundaryless organizations, 337
Companies; *see also* Corporations; Organizations
  ambidextrous organizational design, 339–340
  attracting human capital, 114–116
  average life of, 3
  burden of doing business, 223
  developing human capital, 116–118
  enhancing human capital, 114
  financial position
    comparison with industry norms, 98–99
    comparison with key competitors, 99
    historical comparisons, 98
  generation and distribution of profits, 95–96

information sources
  company rankings, 453–454
  competitive intelligence, 451
  guides and tutorials for researching, 452–453
  public company information, 452
  public or private, 451
  research analysis, 455–456
  search engines, 456
  SEC/Edgar-disclosure reports, 453
  strategic and competitive analysis, 454–455
  subsidiary or division, 451–452
  U.S. or foreign, 451–452
  websites, 44
market *vs.* book value, 110–111
meeting needs of poor, 214
motivations for international expansion, 219–221
performance evaluation
  balanced scorecard, 99–101
  financial ratio analysis, 97–99
preventing information transfer, 119
questions about innovation efforts, 389
resources and sustainable competitive advantage, 90–95
retaining human capital, 118–121
risks in international expansion
  Country Risk Rating, 221–222
  currency risk, 223–224
  economic risk, 223
  management risk, 224–225
  political risk, 222–223
total performance indicators, 101
types of resources
  intangible, 89–90
  organizational capabilities, 90
  tangible, 88–89
  using data analytics, 162
Competing for the Future (Hamel & Prahalad), 37
Competition
  among teams, 365
  for Avon in emerging markets, C89
  for Ford by Toyota, C257
  global and regional for Avon, C91
  from new entrants, 161
  for Pixar, C278
  underpinnings of, 64
Competitive actions
  defensive actions, 271
  guerrilla offensives, 270–271
  strategic actions, 269–270
  tactical actions, 269–270

Competitive advantage; *see also* Generic strategies; Sustainable competitive advantage
  Atlas Door, 165–167
  and business performance, 149
  codifying knowledge for, 134–135
  from core competencies, 185
  definition, 8
  from demand conditions, 216
  dynamic capabilities to protect, 137
  from general administration, 84
  in global markets
    cost reduction *vs.* adaptation, 229–230
    global strategy, 231–232
    international strategy, 23–231
    multidomestic strategy, 233–234
    regionalization *vs.* globalization, 237–238
    response to local pressures, 230
    trading blocs, 238
    transnational strategy, 235–237
  in industry life cycle
    decline stage, 171–173
    growth stage, 169
    introduction stage, 169
    maturity stage, 169–171
    turnaround strategy, 173–174
  innovation essential for, 384
  from knowledge workers, 113
  not achieved
    by competitive aggressiveness, 406–407
    by proactiveness, 405
  from organizational values, 283
  profit pool concept, 162
  response to new entrants, 269
  from social networks, 259
  timing as source of, 389
Competitive Advantage (Porter), 76
Competitive aggressiveness
  defensive uses, 406
  definition, 406
  not leading to competitive advantage, 406–407
  pronouncements, 406
  and SWOT analysis, 406
  techniques, 407
Competitive analysis checklist, 59
Competitive benchmarking, 366
Competitive dynamics, 14, 265–272
  choosing not to react
    co-opetition, 272
    forbearance, 271–272
  definition, 266
  hardball strategies, 267
  likelihood of reaction
    actor's reputation, 271
    competitor's resources, 271

  market dependence, 271
  model of, 266
  motivation and capability to respond, 268–269
  new competitive action, 266
  threat analysis, 268
  types of actions
    defensive actions, 271
    frontal assault, 269–270
    guerrilla offensives, 270–271
    strategic actions, 269–270
    tactical actions, 269–270
Competitive environment, 283, 354–355
  Boston Beer Company, C100
  for coffee chains in India, C82, C86–C88
  definition, 52
  effect of Internet on five forces, 58–61
  factors in, 52
  five-forces model of competition, 52–58
  for Weight Watchers, C29–C30
Competitive intelligence
  caution on, 41
  definition, 39
  examples, 39
  guidelines, 41
  websites for, 40
Competitiveness; *see* Diamond of national advantage
Competitive parity, 149
Competitive position
  Boston Beer Company, C110
  enhanced by diversification, 201
  and five-forces model, 163
  stuck in the middle, 148
Competitive reaction, factors affecting likelihood
  actor's reputation, 271
  competitor's resources, 271
  market dependence, 271
Competitive strategy, 437
  combination strategies, 161–164
  differentiation strategy, 153–159
  focus strategy, 159–161
  overall cost leadership, 148–153
  short-lived competitive advantage, 164–165
  Southwest Airlines, C8
  strategic management concepts for, 165–167
Competitive success, difficulty in maintaining, 3
Competitors
  in airline industry, 163
  for Ann Taylor, C60–C64
  for Apple Inc., C122
  for Avon in emerging markets, C91
  for Boston Beer Company, C99–C100
  for Campbell Soup Co.
    General Mills, C136
    H. J. Heinz Company, C136

I-26 Subject Index

Kraft Foods, C136
Nestlé, C136–C137
comparison of financial performance, 99
for Dippin' Dots, C44, C45–C46
for eBay, C156
  Amazon, C165
  Etsy, C165–C166
  Google Inc., C165
  new, C167
  Taobao, C166
  traditional retailers, C166
  Yahoo!, C165
for Emirates Airline, C268
for FreshDirect, C225–C228
for Heineken, C217
inimitability problem, 91–93
intensity of rivalry among, 56–58
for Jamba Juice, C55
for Kickstarter, C23
for Nintendo
  Microsoft, C190–C191
  mobile games, C192
  Sony, C191–C192
numerous or equally balanced, 57
reacting to proactiveness, 405
resources of, 271
in retail apparel, C62–C64
for Samsung, C209
for Southwest Airlines, C10
for United Way, C145–C147
for Weight Watchers, C27–C28, C30
for World Wrestling Entertainment
  buyout of World Championship Wrestling, C173–C174
  mixed martial arts, C177
for Zynga, C113–C115
Complementors
and Apple iPod, 64
concept of, 63
conflicts among, 63
Complements, 63
Compliance-based ethics programs
definition, 370
versus integrity-based programs, 369–371
Condé Nast Travelers, C16
Conflict-inducing techniques
devil's advocacy, 434–435
dialectical inquiry, 434, 435
groupthink and its prevention, 432–434
to improve decision making, 432–435
Conflict resolution, 339
Conglomerate, 323
Connectors, 124–125
Conscientiousness, 258
Consolidation strategy, 172
Consumer pressure, 216

Consumer Price Index, 39
Consumer Reports, C199
Consumers
in Asian markets, 218–219
building preferences for brands, 169
in China, C85
drinking habit changes, C104
information from Internet, 59
Contemporary approach to strategic control
behavioral control, 281
and environmental changes, 281
informational control, 281
necessary characteristics, 281–282
Continuous replenishment program, 79
Contracts, 190
Control
alternative approaches, 291
in bureaucratic organizations, 290
data analytics to enhance, 291
fundamental types, 290
mechanisms for, 280
rules-based, 289–290
Control systems
characteristics, 281–282
employee views, 282
managerial views, 282
Cooperation by co-opetition, 272
Co-opetition, 272
Coordination
in boundaryless organizations, 336–337
costs in offshoring, 228
Core competencies
definition, 185
difficult to imitate, 185
to enhance competitive advantage, 185
leveraging, 184
and value chain, 185
Core values, 354
Avon, C96
Corporate citizenship, 19
Corporate counsel, 370
Corporate credos, 372
Corporate Culture (Deal & Kennedy), 283
Corporate entrepreneurship, 15, 195
in case analysis, 439–440
in change management, 382
definition, 393
dispersed approaches, 395–397
advantages, 395–396
disadvantages, 396
entrepreneurial culture, 396
and exit champions, 398–399
product champions, 397
project definition, 397
project impetus, 397
resource allotments, 396–397

factors determining projects, 393–394
focused approaches, 394–395
business incubators, 394–395
new venture groups, 394
goals, 393
intrapreneuring, 393
measuring success of
exit champions, 398–399
financial *vs.* strategic goals, 398
need for entrepreneurial orientation, 402
pursuit of opportunities, 394
use of innovation, 393
Corporate ethical performance, 368
Corporate governance
aspect of strategic control, 280
board of directors, 15–16
CEO compensation, 307
and CEO duality, 300–302
definition, 15, 292
executive compensation issue, 16
external control mechanisms
auditors, 303
banks and stock analysts, 303
market for corporate control, 302–303
media, 304–305
public activists, 304–305
regulatory bodies, 304
and financial performance, 292
internal control mechanisms, 294–300
board of directors, 295–298
management rewards, 299–300
for monitoring behavior of managers, 295
shareholder activism, 298–299
international perspective
business groups, 306–307
expropriation of minority shareholders, 306
principal-principal conflicts, 305–306
need for improvement, 16
primary participants, 15, 292
problems for United Way, C147–C151
role in investment decisions, 292
role in strategic management, 15–16
scandal at Tesco, 279
and strategy implementation, 14
Corporate lawyers and Sarbanes-Oxley Act, 304–305
Corporate-level strategy, 14; *see also* Acquisitions; Mergers and acquisitions
acquisition by Southwest Airlines, C11
acquisition by Weight Watchers, C28

Anheuser-Busch, C108
antitakeover measures, 206
Apple Inc., C117, C121
in case analysis, 438
casino industry, C152–C155
change at Southwest Airlines, C8–C12
Cirque du Soleil, C271
diversification, 183–184
diversification at Starbucks, 206–207
divestiture of acquisitions, 183
divestments, 200–202
erosion of value by managers, 204–205
failure at McDonald's, C199
goals for Samsung, C212–C213
GreenWood Resources in China, C72–C79
Heineken, C215–C219
interline agreements at JetBlue, C17–C18
internal development, 203–204
Jamba Juice, C49
franchising, C50–C53
nontraditional locations, C53–C54
joint ventures, 202–203
means of achieving diversification, 195
merger and acquisition blunders, 183
problem at Cisco Systems, 181
problems at Yahoo!, C169
refocus at Yahoo!, C170–C171
related diversification, 184, 185–192
revision at Ford, C250–C260
revision at McDonald's, C196–C198
strategic alliances, 202–203
for turnaround at Procter & Gamble, C204
unrelated diversification, 184, 191–195
value destruction from acquisitions, 183
value of acquisitions to investors, 195
Corporate parenting, 184
definition, 191
Corporate restructuring, 184
Corporate scandals, 16, 205, 279, 303, 353, 368, C147–C149
Corporate venturing, internal, 404
Corporation Perception Index, 16
Corporations; *see also* Companies; Corporate governance
agency theory, 294
aligning interest of owners and managers, 294–300
CEO compensation, 307
CEO duality, 300–302
definitions, 293
dominant growth patterns, 317

Corporations—*Cont.*
  international perspective, 305–307
  managerial self-interest, 294
  public view of, 16
  separation of owners and managers, 293–294
  strategy-structure relationship, 316–318
Cost advantage
  erosion of, 61
  relative to rivals, 151
Cost argument for diversity management, 122
Cost control, Southwest Airlines, C10
Cost disadvantages independent of scale, 54
Cost focus strategy
  definition, 159
  erosion of cost advantage, 161
Cost increases, for Southwest Airlines, C9–C10
Cost reduction
  versus adaptation, 229–230
  Cirque du Soleil, C271–C272
  from diversification, 201
  by Jamba Juice, C54
  JetBlue Airways, C18
  pressure in global strategy, 232
  for value-chain activities, 220
Costs
  of developing intellectual property, 137
  of going green, 21
  hidden in offshoring, 227–228
  legal battles over, 137
  from vertical integration, 190
  Weight Watchers, C29
Cost savings, 186–187
Cost structure, Weight Watchers, C31
Cost surgery, 173
Counterfeit drugs, 224
Counterfeiting, 223
Country Risk Rating, 221–222
Craft beer
  major competitors, C99–C100, C106–C108
  number of breweries, C99
  top sellers in U.S., C103
Creative intelligence, 387
Creativity, 89
  enabling, 366–367
  at Pixar, C275–C277
  stimulating, 391
Creativity argument for diversity management, 122
Credit default swaps, C4
Credit rating, lowered at AIG, C4
Cross-functional skills, 333
Cross-functional teams, 337, 340
Crossing the Chasm (Moore), 405
Cross selling strategy, 109
Cross-training, 337

Crowdfunding
  competitors, C22, C23
  concept, C21
  definition, 255
  evaluation of opportunities, 256
  and JOBS Act of 2012, C22, C25
  Kickstarter, C21–C25
  loose rules for, 255–256
  market size, 255
  potential downsides, 255
Crowdsourcing
  compared to crowdfunding, C22
  definition, 50
  for differentiation ideas, 157
  effects on general environment, 50
  examples of, 50
  at Frito-Lay, 80, 81
  by Lego, 52
  leveraging power of, 86
  perils of
    high demand uncertainty, 86
    hijacking by customers, 86
    strong brand reputation, 86
    too many initiatives, 86–87
  successes, 50
Cultural differences
  advertising mistakes, 224
  challenge for managers, 224–225
  and mergers, 198
  Starbucks and China, C84–C85
Currency fluctuations, 196, 223
Currency risk
  definition, 223
  hedging strategies, 223
  and Israel's shekel, 223–224
  managing, 220
Current ratio, 97, 423, 444–445
Customer Bill of Rights, C16
Customer complaints
  eBay, C167
  Zynga, C116
Customer focus, updating at Procter & Gamble, C201
Customers
  Ann Taylor, C58, C65
  and balanced scorecard, 100
  and corporate social responsibility, 19
  focus on, for information, 366
  integrated into value chain, 85–87
  for Nintendo, C189
  and perils of crowdsourcing, 86–87
  prosumer concept, 85–86
  of QVC, C183
  of Weight Watchers, C35–C36
Customer service, 80
  Emirates Airline, C267
  JetBlue Airways, C16, C18
Customer service organizations, 155–156
Customer value, from core competencies, 185

D

Daily News Record, C60
Data analytics, 162
  to enhance control, 291
Data Protection Act, Norway, C115
David C. Lincoln Award for Ethics and Excellence in Business, 370
Days' sales in inventory, 97, 423, 447
Days' sales in receivables, 97, 423, 447–448
Debt-equity ratio, 97
Decision making
  failure for Stroh's Brewing, 349–350
  intended *vs.* realized strategy, 10–12
  in multidomestic strategy, 233
  with multiple stakeholders, 9
  using conflict to improve
    devil's advocacy, 434–435
    dialectical inquiry, 434, 435
  with wisdom of employees, 365
Decisions, 8
Decline stage
  definition, 171
  examples, 172
  and new technology, 172
  strategic options
    consolidation, 172
    exiting the market, 172
    harvesting strategy, 172
    improving price-performance trade-off, 173
    maintaining, 172
    retreating to defensible ground, 173
    using new to improve the old, 173
Dedication, of entrepreneurial leaders, 258
Defensible ground, retreating to, 173
Defensive actions, 271
Demand conditions
  consumer pressure, 216
  high uncertainty, 86
  in India, 218
Demographics, 45
  age distribution in Asia, C83
  Millennials, 116
Demographic segment of the general environment
  definition, 45
  impact on industries, 51
  key trends and events, 44
Department of Agriculture, C220
Department of Defense, 172
Department of Justice, 353
Department of Transportation, C7
Department stores
  branding challenges, C61–C64
  characteristics, C60

Designing the organization, 351–352, 354
Design process at Samsung, C121
Developing countries
  meeting needs of poor in, 214
  reverse engineering for, 221
Developing human capital; *see also* Human capital
  encouraging widespread involvement, 117
  evaluation, 118
  mentoring, 117–118
  monitoring progress, 118
  training, 116
Development teams, 367
Devil's advocacy, 434–435
Devil's Dictionary (Bierce), 283
Dialectical inquiry, 434, 435
Diamond of national advantage
  conclusions on, 218
  definition, 215
  demand conditions, 216
  factor endowments, 215–216
  firm strategy, structure, and rivalry, 216–217
  in India, 27–218
  related and supporting industries, 216
Differentiate, ability to, 418
Differentiation
  competitive parity on basis of, 149
  lack of, 57
  lack of parity in, 152
  too much, 158
Differentiation focus strategy, 159
Differentiation strategy; *see also* Combination strategies
  crowdsourcing for ideas, 157
  definition, 153
  easily imitated, 158
  enhanced by sharing activities, 187
  examples, 153–155
  failure at Quiznos, 155
  and five-forces model, 157
  forms of, 153
  for new entrants, 264
  pitfalls
    brand dilution, 158–159
    easily imitated, 158
    to high price premium, 158
    too much differentiation, 158
    uniqueness not valuable, 158
    varying perspectives between buyers and sellers, 159
  requirements, 148
  value-chain activities, 154
  varying perspectives, 159
Digital technologies; *see* Internet
Direct-market selling, by Avon, C90–C95
Director independence, 297
Disclosure requirements, 303
Disclosures, and crowdfunding, 256

I-28 Subject Index

Discount mass merchandisers, C60
Discovery skills, 387
Disintermediation, 60
Dispersed approaches to CE
 advantages, 395–396
 definition, 395–396
 disadvantages, 396
 and entrepreneurial culture, 396
 product champions, 397
 resource allotments, 396–397
Dispersed approach to CE, and autonomy, 403
Disruptive innovation, 383, 384
Dissolution, 200n
Distribution channels
 access as barrier to entry, 54
 access by web-based businesses, 58
 access to, 54
 Boston Beer Company, C100
Diversification; *see also* Related diversification; Unrelated diversification
 achieving
  by internal development, 203–204
  by joint ventures, 202–203
  by mergers and acquisitions, 195–202
  by strategic alliances, 202–203
 and antitakeover tactics, 205–206
 definition, 183
 effects of managerial motives, 204–205
 examples, 183
 hierarchical relationships, 183
 horizontal relationships, 183
 managers *vs.* shareholders on, 294
 for risk reduction, 194–195
 and shareholder value, 183
 by Starbucks, 206–207
 types of, 183–184
Diversity
 acquired, 123
 inherent, 123
Diversity management
 and demographic trends, 122
 to improve effectiveness, 122
Divestments/Divestiture
 acquisitions resulting in, 183
 Bristol-Myers Squibb, 201
 definition, 200
 by eBay, C156, C166–C167
 enhancing competitive position, 200
 means of, 200n
 objectives, 200–201
 principles for success, 201–202
Divisional organizational structure
 advantages, 320, 325
 breaking down boundaries, 321
 conflicting goals, 321
 costs, 321

decision making in, 320
definition, 320
disadvantages, 320, 325
Ford Motor Company, C246
functional organizational structure, 319
General Motors, 320
holding company structure, 323
Johnson & Johnson, C234
options, 317
problem at Ann Taylor, C57
strategic business unit structure, 322–323
Dogs, 193
Doing the right thing, 350
Doing things right, 350
Domestic violence, C95
Dow Jones Industrial Average, 49
Downsizing by Avon, C95
Drive, of entrepreneurial leaders, 258
Dual-reporting structures, 324, 325
Durable opportunity, 253
Dynamic capabilities
 definition, 137
 examples, 138
 to protect competitive advantage, 137

E

Earnings
 decline at Ann Taylor, C57
 losses by Ann Taylor, C58
 Southwest Airlines, C7
Earnings before depreciation, interest, and taxes, 447
Earnings before interest and taxes, 447
Eastern Europe, GDP per person growth 2001–2011, 215
E-commerce, C162–C163
Economic indicators, 49
Economic risk
 counterfeit products, 223
 Country Risk Rating, 222
 definition, 223
 piracy, 223
Economic segment of the general environment, 49
Economies of scale
 advantages independent of, 54
 as barrier to entry, 53
 and capacity augmentation, 57
 in global strategy, 231–232
Economies of scope
 definition, 184
 in related diversification, 184–187
Economist, 48
Economy, central role of knowledge in
 explicit knowledge, 112
 human capital, 112
 intellectual capital, 110–112

knowledge development, 110
knowledge management, 112
social capital, 112
tacit knowledge, 112
Edelman Trust Barometer, 93
Educational history, and crowdfunding, 256
Effectiveness, 10
Effectiveness-efficiency trade-off, 10
Efficient, 10
Egotism
 definition, 204
 examples, 205
Electronic network, 79
Electronic storage, 60–61
Electronic teams
 advantages, 133
 challenges associated with, 133–134
 definition, 132
 to enhance collaboration, 132–134
 generating social capital, 133
 no geographic constraints, 133
 potential process losses with, 135
 versus traditional teams, 133
Email, 131–132, 337
Emerging markets
 Avon in, C90–C91
 problems for Avon in Brazil, C93–C94
 China, C94
Emotional intelligence
 benefits, 359
 definition, 358
 empathy, 361
 key management attribute, 355
 motivation, 350
 potential drawbacks, 361–362
 self-awareness, 359–360
 self-regulation, 350
 social skill, 361
Emotional stability, 258
Empathy, 361
Employee development, value creation through, 136
Employee empowerment
 for decision making, 365
 from effective leadership, 364
 soliciting inputs, 364–365
Employee engagement, 284
 Campbell Soup Co., C133
Employee exit costs, 96
Employee replacement cost, 96
Employee retention, 118–120
 value creation through, 136
Employees
 bargaining power, 96
 benefits at Yahoo!, C170–C171
 benefits of ethical orientation, 369
 demoralized at Avon, C92
 demoralized at Yahoo!, C170
 diversity management, 122–123

in holocracy, 330
inspiring passion in, 287
layoffs *vs.* furloughs, 138
older workers, 45–47
orientation programs, 117
prevention focus, 391
promotion focus, 391
roles at Pixar, C276
view of control systems, 282
Employee training; *see* Training
Employment contracts, 119
Employment history, and crowdfunding, 256
End users, 59
Enforcement costs, 190
Engaged: Outbehave Your Competition to Create Customers for Life, 114
Engineering, primary activities, 87–88
Entrepreneurial culture, 396
Entrepreneurial leadership
 definition, 257
 distinguished from managers, 258
 insights on, 259
 personality traits, 258
 team approaches, 258–260
Entrepreneurial opportunities
 deliberate search, 251–253
 discovery phase, 251
 evaluation phase, 253
 and external environment, 250–251
 insights on, 259
 leadership for, 257–260
 qualities for viability, 253
 recognition, 251
 resources for
  financial resources, 253–256
  from government, 257
  human capital, 256
  social capital, 256–257
 sources of, 250
Entrepreneurial orientation
 autonomy, 403–404
 competitive aggressiveness, 406–407
 definition, 402
 dimensions of, 402–403
 innovativeness, 404, 405
 proactiveness, 404–406
 risk taking, 407–408
Entrepreneurial resources
 financial, 253–256
 from government, 257
 human capital, 256
 social capital, 256–257
Entrepreneurial strategy, 14
 in case analysis, 438
 and competitive dynamics, 265–272
 definition, 260
 entry strategies
  adaptive new entry, 262–263
  decision factors, 260

Entrepreneurial strategy—Cont.
  imitative new entry, 261–262
  pioneering new entry, 260–261
  examine barriers to entry, 260
  generic
    combination strategies, 265
    differentiation strategy, 264
    focus strategy, 264–265
    overall cost leadership, 263–264
  industry analysis, 260
  necessary factors, 260
  problems at Digg, 249
  and threat of retaliation, 260
Entrepreneur magazine, C41, C42, C43
Entrepreneurship
  decline in U.S., 273
  definition, 250
  Dippin' Dots, C39–C40
  Edward Marshall Boehm, Inc., C3
  GreenWood Resources in China, C72
  insights on opportunities, 259
  Internet devices, 408–409
  JetBlue Airways, C14–C18
  Kickstarter, C21–C25
  Southwest Airlines, C7–C8
  top-down approach, 396
Entry modes, international
  exporting, 239
  franchising, 239–240
  joint ventures, 240–241
  licensing, 239–240
  options, 238
  strategic alliances, 240–241
  wholly owned subsidiaries, 241
Environmental analysis
  anticipating and adapting to change, 281
  requirements, 37
Environmental forecasting
  caution on, 42
  danger of, 40–41
  definition, 40–42
  firm-specific, 40
  inputs to, 38
  poor predictions, 41
Environmental issues, 19–20
  for FreshDirect, C229
Environmentally friendly manufacturing, 78
Environmental monitoring, 39
Environmental scanning, 39
Environmental sustainability, 20, 157
Environmental sustainability practices, 331
Environmental trends
  impact on industries, 51
  key trends and events, 44
Equity carve-outs, 200n
Equity markets, 49
Equity multiplier, 97, 423, 446
Era of Lego innovation, 54

Escalation of commitment, 402
Ethical behavior, commitment to, 352–353, 354
Ethical organizations, 15
  in case analysis, 439
  codes of ethics, 372
  corporate credos, 372
  and corporate scandals, 368
  green marketing problem, 369
  individual *vs.* organizational ethics, 368–369
  integrity-based *vs.* compliance-based ethics, 369–371
  JPMorgan Chase problem, 373–374
  key elements, 371
  leaders as role models, 371
  management approaches, 370
  policies and procedures in, 373
  potential benefits, 368–369
  reward and evaluation systems, 372–373
Ethical orientation
  benefit for employees, 369
  of leaders, 368
Ethical values, 368
Ethics
  compliance-based, 369–371
  definition, 368
  individual *vs.* organizational, 368–369
  integrity-based, 369–371
  at Zynga, C115
Ethics awards, 370
Ethics management approaches, 370
Ethiopia, Heineken in, C215
Europe, population and Internet usage, C162
European Union, 49, 238
  GDP per person growth 2001–2011, 215
Every Business Needs an Angel, 254
Excellence
  commitment to, 258, 352–353, 354
Excessive product-market diversification, 302
Executive compensation, 16, 96
  bonuses at AIG, C4–C6
Executive leaders, 23
Executives, insight from Melvin Alexander, 7–8
Exit barriers, 57
Exit champions, 398–399
Exiting the market, 172
Expansion by eBay, C161
Expediters, 79
Experience
  versus initiative, 385
  value of, 22
Experience curve, 149
Experimenting, by innovators, 388
Expertise, of directors, 297
Explicit knowledge, 134
  definition, 112

Exporting
  beachhead strategy, 239
  benefits, 239
  definition, 239
  risks and limitations, 239
Exports, agricultural destinations, C134
Expropriation of minority shareholders, 306
Extended value chain, 162–163
  underestimating expenses, 164
External boundaries, 328
External constituencies, 330
External control view of leadership, 6
External environment, narrow focus on, 76
External environment
  analysis, 12
  in case analysis, 436–437
  checklist, 59
  competitive environment
    five-forces model, 52–58
    strategic groups, 64–67
  competitive intelligence, 39–40
  environmental forecasting, 40–42
  environmental monitoring, 39
  environmental scanning, 39
  general environment
    and crowdsourcing, 50, 52
    demographic segment, 45
    economic segment, 49
    global segment, 49
    impact of trends on industries, 51
    key trends and events, 44
    political/legal segment, 47–48
    relationship among segments, 49–50
    sociocultural segment, 45–47
    technological segment, 48–49
  and informational control, 281
  perceptual acuity, 38
  recognizing opportunities or threats, 37
  scenario analysis, 42
  SWOT analysis, 42–43
  in turnaround strategy, 173
External governance control mechanisms
  auditors, 302–303
  banks, 303
  definition, 302
  market for corporate control, 302–303
  media, 304–305
  public activists, 304–305
  regulatory bodies, 304
  stock analysts, 303
External information, gathering and integrating, 366
External relationships
  costs, 338–339
  costs and benefits to develop, 338
External staffing, 385–386

F

Factor endowments
  creation of factors of production, 215
  definition, 215, 216
  firm-specific factors, 216
  in India, 217
  industry-specific factors, 216
  resource deployment, 216
Factors of production, 215–216
Failures
  Cirque du Soleil, C271
  formalize forums for, 367
  at Kickstarter, C24
  and professional development, 367
Fast Company, C229
Fast-food burger chains
  competitors, C194–C195
  market shares, C195
  McDonald's, C194–C198
Federal Aviation Administration, C18
Federal Reserve System, loan to AIG, C4
Filmmaking industry; *see* Movie industry
Financial crisis of 2007–2009
  bailouts of 2008, C4
  Bank of America and Merrill Lynch, 109
  effect on General Motors, 357
  and GreenWood Resources, C74
  Honeywell International in, 138
  impact on AIG, C4
  impact on banks, C4
  impact on United Way, C143
Financial data
  Ann Taylor, C59
  Apple Inc., C118
  for Avon by region, C91
  Campbell Soup Co., C135, C136–C138
  Ford Motor Company, C259
  Procter & Gamble, C203–C204
  Southwest Airlines, C9
Financial goals, 101
Financial leverage ratios; *see* Long-term solvency ratios
Financial performance, and corporate governance, 292
Financial perspective, in balanced scorecard, 101
Financial ratio analysis
  asset management ratios, 447–448
  changes over time, 98
  common-size balance sheet, 441
  common-size income statement, 441
  comparison of financial ratios, 442
  comparison with industry norms, 98–99
  comparison with key competitors, 99

I-30 Subject Index

definition, 423
historical comparisons, 98
long-term solvency measures, 445–447
market value measures, 449–450
profitability measures, 448–449
short-term solvency measures, 444–445
standard financial statements, 441
summary of ratios, 423, 450
types of ratios, 97
Financial ratios
asset utilization/turnover ratios, 97
Campbell Soup Co., C138–C140
differences across industries, 99
long-term solvency/financial leverage ratios, 97
market value ratios, 97
problems with, 99–100
profitability ratios, 97
short-term solvency/liquidity ratios, 97
Financial Reporting Council (U.K.), 279
Financial resources, 89
accessing sources of, 259
angel investors, 254
bank financing, 255
from crowdfunding, 255–256
venture capitalists, 254–255
Financial rewards, 120–121
Financial risk taking, 407
Financial statements, 441
and crowdfunding, 256
JetBlue Airways, C17
United Way, C146–C147
Financial strategic objectives, 28
Financial system risk, Country Risk Rating, 222
Financial *vs.* strategic CE goals, 39
Financing
Dippin' Dots, C42
FreshDirect, C221–C222
GreenWood Resources in China, C73
Firm infrastructure
in differentiation strategy, 154
in overall cost leadership, 150
Firms; *see* Companies; Corporations; Organizations
Firm strategy, structure, and rivalry
definition, 216
in India, 218
intensity of rivalry, 216
search for new markets, 217
First-mover advantage, 405, 406
First-mover strategy, 169
Five-forces model
bargaining power of buyers, 54–55
bargaining power of suppliers, 55–56

definition and function, 52–53
and differentiation strategy, 157
effect of Internet
on bargaining power of buyers, 58–60
on bargaining power of suppliers, 60
on intensity of rivalry, 61
on threat of new entrants, 58
on threat of substitutes, 60–61
and focus strategy, 160–161
improving competitive position, 163
intensity of rivalry among competitors, 56–58
and overall cost leadership, 151–152
problems with
static analysis, 62–63
zero-sum game assumption, 62
threat of new entrants, 53–54
threat of substitute products and services, 56
Fixed costs, high, 57
Fixed strategic goals, 280
Flexibility, reduced in overall cost leadership, 152–153
Flexible manufacturing systems, 161–162
Focused approach to CE
and autonomy, 403
business incubators, 394–395
definition, 394
new venture groups, 394
Focus strategy
cost focus, 159
definition, 159
differentiation focus, 159
examples, 159–160
and five-forces model, 160–161
luxury brands, 161
for new entrants, 264–265
pitfalls
ease of imitation, 161
erosion of cost advantage, 161
new entrants, 161
too focused, 161
target market, 148
Forbearance, 271–272
Forbes, 5
Forecasting
environmental, 40–42
scenario analysis, 42
Foreign Corrupt Practices Act, and Avon, C89, C94
Forest management criteria, C69
Forest Stewardship Council, C68–C70, C74
Fortune, 5, 39, 54, 110, 115, 164, 200, 304, 386
Forward integration, threat of, 56
France, collusion case, 272
Franchising
benefits, 240
definition, 239
by Dippin' Dots, C38, C42–C44

ice cream companies, C45–C46
Jamba Juice, C52–C53
by Jamba Juice, C49
number of franchisers in U.S., 239
reimaging by McDonald's, C198
risks and limitations, 240
Frozen dairy industry
consumer spending, C40
franchises in 2014, C45–C46
international competitors, C40
overview, C40
segmentation, C41–C42
top ten brands, C41
Fuel prices for airlines, C11–C12, C16
Functional benchmarking, 366
Functional-level strategy
Dippin' Dots, C39–C40
Edward Marshall Boehm, Inc., C3
Emirates Airline, C263, C267
at Kickstarter, C21–C22, C24–C25
Pixar, C275–C278
Robin Hood, C2
Southwest Airlines, C8
Functional organizational structure, 316–318, 340
advantages and disadvantages, 319, 325
definition, 318
short-term thinking, 319
stove pipes or silos, 319
types of activity in, 318–319
worldwide, 326
Funding, for Corporate entrepreneurship, 395
Furloughs, 138
Future of Work (Malone), 124

G

Game developers, C189–C190
General administration, 84
General Agreement on Tariffs and Trade, 49
General environment
choice-restricting developments, 6
crowdsourcing, 50, 52
definition, 43
demographic segment, 45
economic segment, 49
global segment, 49
impact of trends on industries, 51
key trends and events, 44
political/legal segment, 47–48
relationships among segments, 49–50
sociocultural segment, 45–47
technological segment, 48–49
Generation Y, 115–116
Generic strategies
and business performance, 149

combination strategies, 161–164
definition, 148
differentiation strategy, 148, 153–159
focus strategy, 148, 159–161
for new ventures
combination strategies, 265
differentiation strategy, 264
focus strategy, 264–265
overall cost leadership, 263–264
overall cost leadership, 148–153
Geographic-area division structure, 317, 326
Geographic boundaries, 328
Ghostbusters, 52
Glass-Steagall Act, repeal of, 47
Global brands and products, 229
Ford Motor Company, C259
Global casino industry, case
in Asian market, C154
in Chinese market, C153
corporate strategy, C152–C155
financial data for Macau, C153
Las Vegas and Atlantic City, C152–C153
moving beyond gambling, C154–C155
operations, C152–C153
spread in United States, C152–C153
top revenue locations, C152
Global competition, global and regional for Avon, C91
Global economy
convergence of living standards, 214–215
General Electric's operations, 214
opportunities and risks, 214
rise of globalization, 214
Global Entrepreneur, C132
Global integration, 214
Globalization
beer industry, C215–C216
definition, 214
emerging markets, 214
and empathy, 361
of Ford brand, C258
by Heineken, C218
and income differences, 214
and industry analysis, 61–62
opportunities and risks, 49
versus regionalization, 237–238
and trading blocs, 238
Global markets
achieving competitive advantage
cost reduction *vs.* adaptation, 229–230
global strategy, 231–232
international strategy, 230–231
multidomestic strategy, 233–234
regionalization *vs.* globalization, 237
and trading blocs, 238

Global markets—Cont.
 transnational strategy, 235–237
 challenges in, 5
 responsiveness to local pressures, 230
Global segment of the general environment
 definition, 49
 impact on industries, 51
 key elements in, 49
 key trends and events, 44
 middle class in emerging countries, 49
Global start-ups
 BRCK, 327
 definition, 326
 management of, 327
 requirements, 326
Global strategy; see also International strategy
 cost reduction pressure, 232
 definition, 231
 economies of scale, 231–232
 risks and challenges, 232
 standard level of quality, 232
 strengths and limitations, 232
Going green, 21
Golden parachute, 205
Good Morning America, 383, C52
Good to Great (Collins), 258, 283
Government
 AIG bailout, C4
 bank bailouts, C4
 requests for proposals, 390
Government contracting, 257
Government legislation/policy
 complexity of regulations, 48
 and corporate governance, 47
 effect on high-tech industries, 47
 and mergers and acquisitions, 196
Government red tape, 272
Government resources, for new ventures, 257
Great Law of the Haudenosaunee, 29
Great Recession, 272
Green Berets, 291
Green initiatives, 21
Greenmail, 205
Green strategies
 to attract and retain talent, 113
 as marketing ploy, 369
Greenwashing, 369
Gresham's law of planning, 356
Gross domestic product, 39
Gross domestic product per person growth 2001–2011 by region, 215
Groupthink, 129–131
 definition, 432
 poor decisions from, 432–434
 preventing, 434
 symptoms, 432

Growth
 Boston Beer Company, C99
 Cirque du Soleil, C271
 decline in prospects for Cirque du Soleil, C270
 Dippin' Dots, C42–C44
 of eBay, C163
 Emirates Airline, C262–C263
 limited for Avon, C89
 options for United Way, C143
 Pixar, C277
 potential for Jamba Juice, C55
 of QVC, C79
 Tata Starbucks in 2015, C82
Growth for growth's sake, 204
Growth rate of products, 219
Growth/share matrix, 293
Growth stage
 definition, 169
 strategies for, 169
Growth strategy
 Dippin' Dots, C39
 by Jamba Juice, C48
 QVC, C183
 Southwest Airlines, C9–C11
 World Wrestling Entertainment, C176–C178
Guerrilla offensives, 270–271
Guiding principles, Avon, C96
Guinness World Records, C38, C43
Gulf of Mexico oil spill, 19

H

Hacker News, C115
Hardball (Stalk & Lachenauer), 267
Hardball strategies
 deceive the competition, 267
 devastate profit sanctuaries, 267
 massive and overwhelming force, 267
 plagiarize, 267
 raise competitor's costs, 267
Harvard Business Review, 11, 20, 112, 130, 138
Harvard Business School, 223
Harvesting strategy, 172
Hazard Analysis and Critical Control Point food safety system, C220
Health care industry, 7–8
 and Watson computer, 186
Health Living Council, C54
Hedging strategies, 223
Heretical questions, 430–431
Hierarchical leaders, 335
Hierarchical relationships, 183, 191
Hierarchy of goals, 24
High-tech computerized training, 88–89
High-tech industry
 and H-1B visas, 47

short-lived competitive advantage, 164–165
 uncontrolled growth, 204
Hiring, 113
 for attitude, train for skill, 115
 Bozo Filter, 115
 by Jamba Juice, C54
 matching approach, 114–115
 Robin Hood, C2
 at Southwest Airlines, 115
Hispanic population, C35
Hoarding barrier, 127
Holding company structure, 318
 advantages and disadvantages, 323
 definition, 323
Holocracy, 330
H-1B visas, 47
Hong Kong
 cultural tips for doing business, 224–225
 per capita income, C84
Horizontal boundaries, 328
Horizontal organizational structure, 337
Horizontal relationships, 183
Horizontal system processes, 337
Hostile takeovers, 205
Human capital, 89, 437
 attracting talent
  hire for attitude, train for skill, 115
  matching approach, 114–115
  Millennials, 115–116
  networking, 115
  recruiting approaches, 115
 characteristics of, 112–113
 definition, 112
 developing, 116–118
  evaluating, 118
  in India, 217
  mentoring, 117–118
  monitoring progress, 118
  at Procter & Gamble, C201
  widespread involvement, 117
 enhancing
  diversity management, 122–123
  redefining jobs, 121
 foundation of intellectual capital, 112–123
 hiring and developing, 113–114
 mismanagement of, 109
 for new ventures, 256
 obtained by acquisition, 197
 protecting, 112
 retaining, 118–121
  challenging work, 120
  financial and nonfinancial rewards, 120–121
  identifying with firm mission and values, 120
  stimulating environment, 120
 technology for leveraging
  codifying knowledge, 134–135

 electronic teams, 132–134
 networks for information sharing, 131–132
 value creation through, 136
Human Equation (Pfeffer), 329
Human resource management
 definition, 82
 in differentiation strategy, 154
 examples, 82–84
 in overall cost leadership, 150
Human resource practices
 at Bank of America, 109
 in boundaryless organizations, 337–338
 at Procter & Gamble, C201
 Southwest Airlines, C8
 Starbucks, C83
Human resource professionals, lock and key mentality, 114
Hybrid cars, 56
Hypercompetition (D'Aveni), 350

I

Illusion of control, 401–402
Illusion of invulnerability, 432
Illusion of unanimity, 432
Imitation
 difficult for competitors, 91–93
 easy in differentiation strategy, 158
 of focus strategy, 161
 strategy easy for, 152
 of synergies, 198
Imitative new entry
 definition, 261
 imitation of, 262
 Rocket Internet, 261
Immigration
 H-1B visas, 47
 and job creation, 48
Improper conduct, minimizing, 290
Inbound logistics
 definition, 77–78
 in differentiation strategy, 154
 just-in-time systems, 77–78
 in overall cost leadership, 150
Inc. magazine, 147, C42, C44
Incentives
 creating effective programs, 286–288
 financial and nonfinancial, 120–121
 for managers, 299–300
 motivating with, 284–285
 other than money, 286
 potential downsides, 285–286
 for talent referrals, 115
Income
 of General Motors by region, C242
 Southwest Airlines, C7
 World Wrestling Entertainment, C176

Income statement, 441
 Ann Taylor, C60
 Avon, C93
 Boston Beer Company, C101
 Campbell Soup Co., C138
 eBay, C157
 Emirates Airline, C262
 Ford Motor Company, C246
 General Motors, C240
 Heineken, C216
 Jamba Juice, C50
 Johnson & Johnson, C233
 McDonald's, C194
 Nintendo, C186
 Procter & Gamble, C204
 QVC, C180
 Samsung, C209
 Weight Watchers, C32
 Yahoo!, C168
 Zynga, C111
Incremental innovation, 383
 time line, 389
Incremental launch, 386
Incremental management, 8
Incubator, 394
India
 age distribution, C83
 Barista chain, C87
 Café Coffee Day, C85–C87
 diamond of national advantage, 217–218
 Ford Motor Company in, C258
 GDP per person growth 2001–2011, 215
 nation of tea drinkers, C82
 offshoring to, 227
 per capita income, C84
 quick-service restaurant chains, C87–C88
 software industry, 217–218
 Tata Starbucks, C82–C83
Indirect costs, hidden in offshoring, 227
Indonesia, per capita income, C84
Industries
 beer industry, C214–C219
 business cycles, 64
 consolidation from mergers, 197
 frozen dairy products, C40–C42, C45–C46
 intensity of rivalry among competitors, 56–58, 61
 packaged-food industry, C133–C134
 reasons for threat of new entrants, 58
 retail grocers, C224–C228
 slow growth, 57
 strategic business units, 193
 timber industry, C68–C81
 video games, C111–C116, C184–C192
 women's apparel, C60–C64
Industry analysis
 assumptions, 64

caveats on using, 61–64
 complementors concept, 63
 effect of Internet on five forces, 58–61
 five-forces model, 52–58
 and globalization, 61–62
 for new ventures, 260
 not avoiding low-profit industries, 62
 quantification of five forces, 64
 static analysis problem, 62–63
 strategic groups, 64–67
 time horizon, 64
 value net concept, 63
 zero-sum game assumption, 62
Industry information sources; see Companies
Industry life cycle, 437
 caveat on, 168
 decline stage, 171–173
 definition, 167
 growth stage, 169
 illustration, 168
 importance of, 167
 introduction stage, 169
 maturity stage, 169–171
 and process innovation, 383
 and product innovation, 382
 and turnaround strategies, 173–174
Industry norms, financial performance, 98–99
Industry-specific standards, 366
Infomediary services, 61
Information
 focus on customers for, 366
 networks for sharing, 131–132
 private, 128
 redistributing, 365
Informational control, 439
 aspect of strategic control, 280
 in contemporary approach to strategic control, 281–282
 definition, 281
 and internal-external environments, 281
 key issues, 281
 and organizational learning, 281
 in traditional approach to strategic control, 280
Information power, 357
Information technology
 in boundaryless organizations, 337
 for extended value chain, 162–163
 role in enhancing value, 84–85
Inherent diversity, 123
Inherent morality of group, 432
Inimitability
 Amazon Prime, 93
 of core competencies, 185
 of intangible resources, 89–90
Inimitability of resources
 causal ambiguity, 92

Groupon's problem, 91–92
 implications, 91
 path dependency, 92
 physical uniqueness, 92
 social complexity, 92–93
Initial public offering
 Ann Taylor, C58
 Boston Beer Company, C100
 Google Inc., 3
 Groupon, 3
 Jamba Juice, C49
 JetBlue Airways, C15
 and microfinance, C207
 Pixar, C275
 Zynga, C113
Initiative vs. experience, 385
Innovation, 89
 in change management, 382
 collaboration with partners, 390–392
 competing in a dynamic market, 392–393
 from creative intelligence, 387
 cultivating skills for, 387
 defining scope of
  focus on common technology, 388
  questions about results, 389
  strategic envelope, 387–388
 definition, 382
 Dippin' Dots, C39–C40
 disruptive, 384
 and diversity, 123
 at Dutch Boy, 383
 essential for competitive advantage, 384
 flexibility for, 367
 incremental, 383–384
 Internet devices, 408–409
 Jamba Juice, C52
 Johnson & Johnson, C236
 Kickstarter, C21–C25
 management challenges, 384–387
  building capabilities vs. collaboration, 386
  experience vs. initiative, 385
  incremental vs. preemptive launch, 386
  internal vs. external staffing, 385–386
  seeds vs. weeds, 385
 management of, at Jamba Juice, C55
 nanotechnology, 48
 at National Aeronautics and Space Administration, 392
 at Nintendo, C189
 physiolectics, 48–49
 problems for Apple Inc., C121
 process, 382–383
 at Procter & Gamble, 386, C200
 product, 382
 radical, 383–384
 research insights, 391

staffing to capture value of, 389–390
 sustaining, 383
 timeline for Apple Inc., C119–C120
 time pacing, 389
 value of unsuccessful, 392–393
 Weight Watchers, C31–C33
Innovation and Entrepreneurship (Drucker), 408
Innovation and learning perspective, in balanced scorecard, 100
Innovation partners, 390–392
Innovation teams, 389
Innovativeness
 definition, 404
 pitfalls
  competitive climate, 404
  economic downturns, 404
  wasted expenditures, 404
 requirements, 404
 techniques, 405
Innovator's DNA, 388
Input control, to attract talent, 114
Inputs
 effective management of, 216
 increased cost of, 152
 procurement, 80–82
 in transnational strategy, 235–236
In Search of Excellence (Peters & Waterman), 283
Institutional investors
 as activists, 299
 social concerns, 300
Intangible resources
 definition, 89
 types, 89–90
Integrate, ability to, 418
Integrated Workforce Experience, 132
Integration in boundaryless organizations, 336–337
Integrative thinking
 applied to business, 436
 characteristics
  architecture, 429–430
  causality, 428–430
  resolution, 430
  salience, 428–430
 definition, 428
 at Red Hat, Inc., 431
Integrity-based programs
 versus compliance-based programs, 369–370
 definition, 370
Intellectual assets
 analysis of, 13
 in case analysis, 437
Intellectual capital
 definition, 111
 explicit knowledge, 112
 human capital, 112

Intellectual capital—*Cont.*
  human capital as foundation of, 112–123
  and market *vs.* book value, 110–111
  protecting intellectual assets, 135–138
  role of social capital, 123–131
  social capital, 112
  tacit knowledge, 112
  using technology to leverage, 131–135
Intellectual property
  development costs, 137
  legal battles over, 137
  protecting, 135–137
  protection in China, C73–C74
  software piracy, 223
  at Zynga, C115
Intellectual property rights
  definition, 136–137
  economic risk, 223
  protection in offshoring, 228
Intended strategy, 10–12
Intensity of rivalry among competitors
  definition, 56
  effect of Internet, 61
  factors leading to
    augmented capacity, 57
    high exit barriers, 57
    high fixed or storage costs, 57
    lack of differentiation, 57
    lack of switching costs, 57
    numerous equally balanced competitors, 57
    slow industry growth, 57
  and price competition, 57
  Uber Technologies *vs.* Lyft Inc., 57–58
Interest coverage ratio, 446
Interest rate increases, 49
Interline agreements, C17–C18
Interlocking directorships, 297
Internal benchmarking, 365
Internal business perspective in balanced scorecard, 100
Internal constituencies, 330
Internal corporate venturing, 404
Internal development, 195
  benefits, 203–204
  definition, 203
  example, 203
  potential disadvantages, 204
Internal environment analysis, 12–13
  in case analysis, 437
  and informational control, 281
  for new business creation, 250–251
  performance evaluation
    balanced scorecard, 99–101
    financial ratio analysis, 97–99
    resource-based view of the firm, 88–96

in turnaround strategy, 173
  value-chain analysis, 76–88
Internal networkers, 23
Internal relationships
  costs, 338–339
  costs and benefits to develop, 338
Internal staffing, 385–386
International Chamber of Commerce, 223
International Dairy Foods Association, C43
International division structure, 317, 326
International expansion
  Ann Taylor, C64
  by Avon, C90–C91
  Campbell Soup Co.
    failure in Russia, C131–C132
    success in China, C132
  casino industry, C153–C154
  eBay, C164
  ethics of relocation for tax purposes, 242
  insights for
    adaptation challenges, 226
    human resource management challenges, 226–227
    knowledge transmission, 226
    opportunities and threats, 226
  Jamba Juice, C52–C53
  motivations
    arbitrage opportunities, 219
    enhancing product growth, 219
    increase market size, 218–219
    learning opportunities, 220
    optimize value-chain location, 219–220
    reverse innovation, 220–221
  and organizational structure, 324–327
    geographic-area division, 326
    global start-ups, 326–327
    international divisions, 326
    and multidomestic strategy, 325–326
    primary types, 325
    worldwide functional division, 326
    worldwide product division, 326
  potential risks, 221–225
    currency risks, 223–224
    economic risk, 223
    management risk, 224–225
    political risk, 222–223
  by Starbucks, C83–C84
  by Weight Watchers, C28
International Public Relations Association, 81
International strategy, 14
  achieving competitive advantage
    cost reduction *vs.* adaptation, 229–230

global strategy, 231–232
  global *vs.* regional, 237–238
  international strategy, 230–231
  multidomestic strategy, 233–234
  transnational strategy, 235–237
in case analysis, 438
casino industry, C153–C154
definition, 231
diamond of national advantage, 215–218
entry modes, 238–241
  exporting, 239
  franchising, 238–240
  joint ventures, 240–241
  strategic alliances, 240–241
  wholly owned subsidiaries, 241
global dispersion of value chains, 225–228
and global economy, 214–215
GreenWood Resources, C73
Heineken, C218
motivations for expansion, 218–221
multinational companies in, 231
in orphan drug industry, 230–231
problem for SAIC in China, 213
risks and challenges, 231
risks of expansion, 221–225
Southwest Airlines, C9
strengths and limitations, 231
International trade
  agricultural export destinations, C134
  increases in, 49
Internet
  bots, 61
  effects on five-forces model
    bargaining power of buyers, 58–60
    bargaining power of suppliers, 60
    intensity of rivalry, 61
    threat of new entrants, 58
    threat of substitutes, 60–61
  legal services on, 61
  sales by Avon, C90
  usage by region, C162
Internet devices, 408–409
Internet technologies, 337
Interpersonal networks, 127
Interrelationships, 85
Intrapreneuring, 393
Introduction stage
  definition, 169
  first-mover advantage, 169
  late-mover advantage, 169
  strategies for, 169
Inventory costs, hidden in offshoring, 227

Inventory management
  continuous replenishment program, 79
  just-in-time systems, 77–78, 216
Inventory turnover ratio, 97, 423, 447
Investment decisions
  and agency theory, 401
  and corporate governance, 292
Investments
  opportunities in China, C74–C75, C76
  transaction-specific, 190
Investors
  activist, C166
  and crowdfunding, 255
  and value of acquisitions, 199–200
Investor's Business Daily, 304
Ironman brand name, 102
Israel, currency strategy, 223–224

J

Japan
  age distribution, C83
  GDP per person growth 2001–2011, 215
  just-in-time systems, 216
  keiretsus, 306
  per capita income, C84
  Starbucks in, C83–C84
Jeopardy, 186
Job creation, and immigrants, 48
Job cuts
  Cirque du Soleil, C271–C272
  Ford Motor Company, C250
  by Samsung, C211
Job rotation, 337
Jobs, redefining, 121
JOBS Act; *see* Jumpstart Our Business Startups Act of 2012
Jobs Corps Culinary Arts Center, C54
Joint ventures, 195
  definition, 202
  to develop and diffuse new technologies, 202
  to enter new markets, 202, 203
  for international expansion
    alliance management knowledge, 241
    benefits, 240
    clearly defined strategies, 240
    cultural differences, 241
    partnership clarification, 240
    trust element, 240
  potential downsides, 203
  to reduce costs, 202
  Starbucks and Tata Group, C82, C88
Journal of Applied Psychology, 335
Journal of Organizational Behavior, 391

Jumpstart Our Business Startups
    Act of 2012, C22, C25
Just-in-time systems, 77–78, 216

K

Keiretsus, 306
Key economic indicators, 49
Knowledge
    creation of, 112
    explicit, 112, 134
    internal, 365–366
    redistributing, 365
    role in economy, 111–112
    source of new ideas, 382
    tacit, 112, 134
Knowledge economy, 437
    definition, 110
Knowledge flows, 135
Knowledge management, 112
Knowledge transfer, 220, 393
    not automatic, 236
Knowledge workers, 13
    loyalty to colleagues, 123
    segment of the economy, 110
    source of competitive
        advantage, 113

L

Labor costs, hidden in
    offshoring, 227
Labor problems at FreshDirect,
    C230
Las Vegas casinos, C152–C153
Late-mover strategy, 169
Latin America
    GDP per person growth
        2001–2011, 215
    population and Internet
        usage, C162
Layoffs, 138
Leaders
    ambidextrous, 11
    bases of power
        diagram, 358
        organizational, 357–358
        personal, 357–358
    as communicators, 354
    detrimental effects, 353
    ethical orientation, 368
    hierarchical, 335
    and organizational design, 354
    organizational types, 23
    as role models, 371
    stimulating creativity, 391
    traits for success, 358
Leadership
    change at General Motors, 357
    characteristics, 350
    to create ethical organizations,
        368–374
    to create learning organizations,
        362–367
    definition, 350
    at eBay, C163–C164

effective, 84
effective uses of power, 356–358
emotional intelligence, 358–362
entrepreneurial, 257–260
external control view of, 6
at Ford Motor Company, 352
FreshDirect, C221–C222
independent activities
    culture of excellence and
        ethics, 352–353
    designing the organization,
        351–352
    setting a direction, 351
insights on, 354–355
overcoming barriers to change,
    355–356
problem for Stroh's Brewing,
    349–350
romantic view of, 5
at Siemens, 359
at Starbucks, C83
in strategy implementation, 14
in virtual organizations, 335
at Yahoo! 1995–2014, C170
Leadership Assessment
    Instrument, 372–373
Leadership Challenge (Kouzes &
    Posner), 363
Leadership development
    programs, 363–364
Leadership roles, 439
Learning from mistakes
    Bank of America, 109
    Boeing Company, 315–316
    Cisco Systems, 181
    Crumbs Bake Shop, 147
    Digg social network, 249
    Google Inc. and advertising, 381
    Groupon, 3–5
    SAIC in China, 213
    Salemi Industries, 37
    Stroh's Brewing failure,
        349–350
    Tesco, 279
    vision problem at BYD, 75
Learning opportunities from
    international expansion, 220
Learning organizations, 15,
    362–367
    accumulating and sharing
        internal knowledge,
        365–366
    in case analysis, 439
    challenging status quo, 366
    definition, 363
    empowering employees,
        364–365
    enabling creativity, 366
    gathering and integrating
        external knowledge, 366
    inspiring and motivating, 363
    leadership development,
        363–364
Legal services, on Internet, 61
Legitimate power, 357

Licenses, and crowdfunding, 256
Licensing
    benefits, 240
    definition, 239
    by Jamba Juice, C54
    number of workers
        requiring, 272
    risks and limitations, 240
Licensing Letter, C198
Linebackers, 79
Linux operating system, 50
Liquidity measures; *see* Short-
    term solvency measures
Litigation
    costs for Avon, C95
    and crowdfunding, 256
    settlement by Johnson &
        Johnson, C233
    against Zynga, C113, C115
Local adaptation, 214; *see also*
    Adaptation
    Honda Motors, 234
    for local markets, 229–230
    McDonald's, 341
    in multidomestic strategy,
        233–234
    weak in global strategy, 232
Local line leaders, 23
Location strategy
    Ann Taylor, C65
    dependence on one, 232
    Jamba Juice, C53–C54
    of value-chain activities,
        218–220
Lock-in effect, 338–339
Logistics
    inbound, 77–78
    outbound, 78–79
Long-term perspective, 9–10
Long-term solvency measures,
    445–447
    cash coverage ratio, 97, 423,
        446–447
    debt-equity ratio, 97, 423, 446
    equity multiplier, 97, 423, 446
    times interest earned ratio, 97,
        423, 446
    total debt ratio, 97, 423, 446
Losses by Samsung in 1998,
    C210–C211
Low-fare airlines
    in airlines industry, C15
    JetBlue Airways, C14–C18
    Southwest Airlines, C7–C12
Luxury brands, 160

M

Macau casinos, C152, C153, C155
Maintaining, 172
Major airlines, C15
*Making the Grass Greener on
    Your Side* (Melrose), 364
Malaysia, per capita
    income, C84

Management
    Campbell Soup Co., C132–C133
    Emirates Airline, C267
    FreshDirect, C221–C222
    of global start-ups, 327
    GreenWood Resources,
        C70–C72
    incremental, 8
    T-shaped, 127
Management assumptions, 37–38
Management change
    Ann Taylor, C57, C66
    Apple Inc. in 2011, C117
    by Avon, C92, C94
    Campbell Soup Co., C130
    Dippin' Dots, C44
    Ford Motor Company, C245
    FreshDirect, C222
    General Motors, C240
    Heineken, C215, C216–C218
    Jamba Juice, C49
    JetBlue Airways, C14, C16
    Johnson & Johnson, C233
    at Procter & Gamble,
        C200, C202
    at Samsung, C210–C211
    Southwest Airlines, C8
    Weight Watchers, C27–C28
    at Yahoo!, C167
Management risk
    and cultural differences,
        224–225
    definition, 224
Management talent development,
    297–298
Managerial conceit
    definition, 401
    escalation of commitment, 402
    illusion of control, 401–402
    overconfidence, 401–402
Managerial motives
    definition, 204
    erosion of value creation
        by egotism, 204–205
    growth for growth's sake, 204
Managerial restructuring, 192
Managerial role models, 292
Managers
    agency theory and back-solver
        dilemma, 400–401
    ambidexterity, 10, 11
    attracting talent, 110
    bargaining power, 96
    credibility and ego, 198
    distinguished from
        entrepreneurial leaders, 258
    effecting transformational
        change, 23
    excessive product-market
        diversification, 302
    golden parachutes, 205
    maintaining adaptability,
        339–340
    mindsets, 37
    monitoring behavior of, 295

Managers—Cont.
  necessary trade-offs, 10
  need for alignment, 339–340
  on-the-job consumption, 302
  power of, 129
  private information, 128
  proactive, 8
  self-interested actions, 294
  shirking by, 302
  view of control systems, 282
Managing innovation; see Innovation
Manufacturing
  Ann Taylor, C65
  automated and flexible systems, 161–162
  Campbell Soup Co., C131
  Edward Marshall Boehm, Inc., C3
  environmentally friendly, 78
  offshoring, 225–227
  outsourcing, 225–227
  process innovation, 382–383
Manufacturing alliances, 257
Market commonality, 268
Market dependence, 271
Market for corporate control
  antitakeover tactics, 303
  conditions leading to, 302
  definition, 302–303
  and takeover constraints, 303
Market for Weight Watchers, C27–C28
Marketing and sales
  definition and components, 79–80
  in differentiation strategy, 154
  Edward Marshall Boehm, Inc., C3
  in overall cost leadership, 150
Marketing argument for diversity management, 122
Marketing strategy
  by Avon, C92
  crowdsourcing, 80, 81
  Dippin' Dots, C44
  Jamba Juice, C49–C52
  product placement, 79–80
Market potential evaluation, 253
Market power, 183
  definition, 187
  from related diversification
    pooled negotiating power, 187–188
    vertical integration, 188–190
Market pruning, 173
Market responsiveness, reduced, 228
Market segments
  Ann Taylor, C58, C65
  entered by acquisitions, 197
  women's apparel, C62–C64
Market share
  Apple Inc.
    cell phones, C124

  operating systems, C124
  personal computers, C123
  tablets, C126
  auto industry by brand, C257
  Ford Motor Company, C247, C248, C257
  General Motors, C241
  loss of, 161
  McDonald's, C195
  Samsung, C210
Market size
  for crowdfunding, 255
  motive for international expansion, 218–219
  for Zynga, C113
Market-to-book ratio, 40, 97, 423
Market value
  Apple Inc., C117
  versus book value, 110–111
Market value measures
  market-to-book ratio, 97, 423, 450
  price-earnings ratio, 97, 423, 449–450
Massachusetts Institute of Technology Media Lab, 54
Mass customization
  definition, 161
  example, 162
Matching approach in hiring, 114–115
Matrix organizational structure
  advantages, 323–324, 325
  definition, 323
  diagram, 324
  disadvantages, 324, 325
  multinational companies, 323
  worldwide, 326
Maturity stage
  breakaway positioning, 170–171
  definition, 169–170
  intensity of rivalry, 170
  reverse positioning, 170–171
  strategies for, 169–171
Measurable objectives, 28
Media, and corporate governance, 304–305
Medicare, problems with, 48
Mentoring
  benefits, 117
  for CE, 395
  at Intel, 117–118
MERCOSUR, 238
Mergers, 195
  Jamba Juice, C49
Mergers and acquisitions; see also Acquisitions
  to acquire human capital, 197
  advice on, 199–200
  to attain bases of synergy, 197
  diversification through, 195–198
  versus divestments, 200–202
  to enter new markets, 197
  examples of blunders, 182
  global value, 196

  and government policies, 196
  leading to industry consolidation, 197
  limitations
    cultural issues, 198
    high takeover premium, 198
    imitation by competitors, 198
    managerial ego, 198
  motives and benefits, 196–197
  to obtain resources, 196
  recent examples, 195
M-Form structure, 326
Microfinance, case
  Banco Compartamos, C207
  Grameen Bank, C206, C207–C208
  in Indonesia, C207
  and initial public offerings, C207
  in Kenya, C207
  nature of, C206–C207
  origin of, C206
  and worldwide poverty, C206
Middle class, in emerging countries, 49
Middle East
  GDP per person growth 2001–2011, 215
  political risk, 222
  population and Internet usage, C162
Millennials
  attracting, 115–116
  best practices to attract, 116
Mindguards, 432
Mind-sets, 131
Minimum wage, in China, 228
Mission, 436
  Avon, C96
  Edward Marshall Boehm, Inc., C3
  identifying with, 120
  at James Irvine Foundation, 27
  Starbucks, C83
  at WellPoint, 26
Mission Impossible: Ghost Protocol, 80
Mission statement
  compared to vision statement, 27
  and corporate values, 27
  definition, 26
  effective, 26
  examples, 26
  Southwest Airlines, C8
  and strategic objectives, 27–28
MIT; see Massachusetts Institute of Technology
Moby Dick (Melville), C83
Modular organizations, 328, 331–333
  advantages of outsourcing, 332
  apparel industry, 332
  compared to virtual organizations, 334

  definition, 332
  in-house competencies, 332
  preconditions, 332
  pros and cons, 333
  strategic risk in outsourcing, 333
  value-chain activities, 332
Monitoring progress, 118
Mortgage-backed securities, 109, C4
Motivation
  to inspire passion, 287
  of leaders, 360
  from reward systems, 284–288
  and social skill, 361
Motivational barriers, 127
Movie industry, 219
  Pixar, C274–C278
  product placement, 80
Multidomestic strategy
  decentralized decisions, 233
  definition, 233
  Honda Motors, 234
  Kraft Foods, 233
  and organizational structure, 325–326
  product names, 233
  risks and challenges
    adaptation not received, 233–234
    cost structure and adaptation, 233
    evolution of local adaptation, 234
  strengths and limitations, 234
Multinational companies
  definition, 218
  failure to integrate acquisitions, 182
  international strategy, 231
  jobs in foreign operations, 49
  local adaptation *vs.* global integration, 214
Multitaskers, 11
Multivisional structure, 326

N

Nanotechnology, 48
NASDAQ, 3
National Aeronautics and Space Administration, 172
  and Innocentive, 392
  size of staff, 392
National Retail Federation, C60, C63
Nations
  bottom of the pyramid populations, 214
  developing countries, 214
  factors affecting competitiveness
    demand conditions, 216
    factor endowments, 215–216
    firm strategy, structure, and rivalry, 216–217
  India, 217–218
  related and supporting industries, 216

Nation's Restaurant News, C199
Navy SEALS, 291
Net disposable income, 39
Net sales, Ann Taylor, C60
Networking
   to attract talent, 115
   for CE, 395
   by innovators, 388
Network lever, 127
Network traps, 129
Neuroscience research, 387
New entrants, competition for focus strategy, 161
Newness, 382
New product development
   changes at General Motors, C243
   Dippin' Dots, C45–C46
   Edward Marshall Boehm, Inc., C3
   at Procter & Gamble, C201
   at Samsung, C211
   World Wrestling Entertainment, C173
New product launch
   by Avon, C90
   by Campbell Soup Co., C130
   by Dippin' Dots, C38
   Ford Motor Company, C256
   incremental or preemptive, 386
   Jamba Juice, C48
New venture groups, 439
   definition, 394
   Taco Bell, 395
New ventures, 438; *see also* Entrepreneurial orientation; Start-up(s)
   assessing effectiveness of, 39
   entrepreneurial opportunities, 250–253
   examine barriers to entry, 260
   generic strategies, 263–265
   industry analysis, 260
   leadership, 257–260
   necessary factors, 260
   project definition, 397
   project impetus, 397
   reasons for failure, 259
   resources for, 253–257
   social networks for competitive advantage, 259
   threat of retaliation, 260
New York State Common Retirement Fund, 300
New York Times, C52
Niche market, 159
Nickelodeon, C44
Nineteen Eighty-Four (Orwell), C48
Noncompete agreement, JetBlue Airways, C15
Noncompete clauses, 119
Nonfinancial rewards, 120–121
Nonfinancial strategic objectives, 28

Nongovernment organizations, Tata assistance to, C86
Nonprofit organizations, boundaries in, 288
North America, population and Internet usage, C162
North American Free Trade Agreement, 49, 238
Norwegian Consumer Council, C115
Not-invented-here barrier, 127

O

Obama administration, C54
Obamacare, 6
Obesity, worldwide increase in, C29
Observing, by innovators, 388
Obsolescence of cost advantage, 153
Oceania, population and Internet usage, C162
Offshoring
   from decline in transportation costs, 227
   definition, 225
   elusive benefits and greater costs, 227–228
   recent explosion of, 225–227
   versus reshoring, 228
Oil-price hedging, C11–C12
Oil production, C12
Older workers
   Bureau of Labor Statistics on, 46
   research about, 45, 46–47
   stereotypes, 46
Omnichannel sales approach, C64
One-click purchasing, 60
Online access
   Dippin' Dots, C46
   QVC, C79
   Weight Watchers, C27, C29
Online auctions, C161–C162
Online grocery shopping
   competitors, C225–C228
   customer perceptions, C230
   FreshDirect, C220–C231
   price comparisons, C227
   profiles of grocers, C226
   sales in 2014, C224
   shopper behavior, C225
On-the-job consumption, 302
Openness to experience, 258
Open-sourcing model for talent, 120
Operational effectiveness, 8–9
Operational efficiency and effectiveness, 289–290
Operations
   Ann Taylor, C65
   Apple Inc., C122–C123
   casino industry, C152–C153
   at Chipotle, 79
   cultural differences, 225
   definition, 78

   in differentiation strategy, 154
   early, at Boston Beer Company, C100
   FreshDirect, C220–C221
   increased from global presence, 218–219
   Kickstarter, C21–C22
   in overall cost leadership, 150
   in service sector, 87
   United Way, C144–C145
   World Wrestling Entertainment, C174–C176
Operations data
   Ann Taylor, C65
   Southwest Airlines, C9–C10
Opportunities; *see also* SWOT analysis
   entrepreneurial, 250–260
   in external environment, 37
   misses, 25
Opportunity analysis framework, 251
Opportunity evaluation, 253
Opportunity recognition
   definition, 251
   deliberate search, 251–253
   discovery phase, 251
   evaluation phase, 253
   qualities for viability, 253
Opposable Mind (Martin), 428
Options, 399
Oral case presentation, 425
Organizational barriers to change, 355–356
Organizational bases of power, 356–357
   coercive power, 357
   information power, 357
   legitimate power, 357
   reward power, 357
Organizational boundaries, 15
Organizational capabilities
   causal ambiguity, 92
   definition, 89
Organizational control, 352–353
Organizational culture
   change at Ford, C251
   commitment to excellence and ethics, 352–353, 354
   consumer-oriented, 285
   definition, 283
   entrepreneurial, 396
   examples, 283
   at Ford Motor Company, 352
   Heineken, C218
   managerial role models, 292
   publications on, 283
   role of, 283–284
   role of training, 291–292
   shared in boundaryless organizations, 337
   sustaining
      by culture committee, 284
      with rallies and pep talks, 284
      with storytelling, 284

Organizational design, 15; *see also* Ambidextrous Organizational design; Boundaryless Organizational design
   in case analysis, 439
Organizational flexibility argument
   for diversity management, 122
Organizational goals and objectives, 9
   analysis of, 12
   Boston Beer Company, C101–C103
   in case analysis, 436
   common, 23–24
   financial, 101
   GreenWood Resources, C68
   Heineken, C218
   hierarchy of, 24
   Jamba Juice, C48
   rewards aligned with, 292
Organizational integrity, 369
Organizational learning, and informational control, 281
Organizational resources, 89
Organizational structure; *see also* Ambidextrous Organizational design; Boundaryless Organizational design
   benefits, 316
   Campbell Soup Co., C132–C133
   change at Ford, C250–C251
   definition, 316
   divisional structures, 320–325
   dominant growth patterns, 317
   functional structure, 318–319
   horizontal, 337
   international implications
      geographic-area division, 326
      global start-ups, 326–327
      international division, 326
      primary types of structure, 325
      worldwide functional structure, 326
      worldwide product division, 326
   Johnson & Johnson, C234
   and leadership, 351–352
   McDonald's, 341
   problem at Boeing, 315–316
   revision at Procter & Gamble, C201
   Robin Hood, C2
   simple structure, 318
   and strategy formulation, 327
   strategy-structure relationship, 316–318
   types, 316–318
   United Way, C144–C145
Organizational vision; *see* Vision
Organizational *vs.* individual rationality, 9

Organization for Economic Cooperation and Development, 218
Organizations; *see also* Companies; Corporations; Ethical organizations; Learning organizations
 attracting talent, 110
 barrier-free, 328–331
 bureaucratic *vs.* decentralized, 124
 case for sustainability initiatives, 21–22
 changes from social networks, 125
 core competencies, 185
 egotism and greed in, 205
 environmental issues, 19–21
 environmentally aware
  competitive intelligence, 39–40
  environmental forecasting, 40–41
  environmental monitoring, 39
  environmental scanning, 39
  perceptual acuity, 38
  scenario analysis, 42
  SWOT analysis, 41–42
 flatter, 129
 gathering and integrating external information, 366
 key stakeholders, 17
 linking employees to, 120
 modular, 331–333
 protecting dynamic capabilities, 137–138
 protecting intellectual assets, 136–137
 redistributing knowledge, 365
 setting a direction, 351
 social responsibility, 18–19
 stakeholders, 17–18
 strategic management perspective throughout, 22–23
 structural hole, 127
 transformational change, 23
 triple bottom line, 19–21
 types of boundaries, 328
 types of control in, 290
 types of leaders, 23
 value-chain activities, 85
 virtual, 333–336
Organization Science, 130
Orientation programs, 117
Orphan drug industry, 230–231
Outbound logistics
 definition, 78–79
 in differentiation strategy, 154
 in overall cost leadership, 150
Outside consultant, assuming role of, 420
Outsiders, 367
Outsourcing
 by Boeing, 315–316

by boundaryless organizations, 316
from decline in transportation costs, 227
definition, 225
by modular organizations, 332
problems for Apple Inc., C122
recent explosion of, 225–227
in service sector, 227
strategic risks, 333
Overall cost leadership; *see also* Combination strategies
 basis of, 148
 and competitive parity, 149
 definition, 148
 examples, 150–151
 experience curve, 149
 and five-forces model, 151–152
 JetBlue Airways, C14–C18
 for new entrants, 263–264
 pitfalls, 159
  easily imitated, 152
  increased cost of inputs, 152
  lack of parity and differentiation, 152
  obsolescence, 153
  reduced flexibility, 152–153
  too much focus on too few value-chain activities, 152
 Southwest Airlines, C7–C12
 tactics required, 148–149
 value-chain activities, 150
Overconfidence, 401–402

P

Packaged-food industry, C133–C134
Parenting advantage, 191
Partnerships
 with Avon, C90
 with FreshDirect, C230
Patent litigation, 137
 Apple *vs.* Samsung, C123
 by Dippin' Dots, C44
Path dependency, 92
Pension Rights Center, 305
Pentagon attack of 2001, C15
People lever, 127
Pep talks, motivating with, 284
Per capita income, selected nations, C84
Perceptual acuity
 definition, 38
 improving, 38
Performance bonuses, 16
Performance enhancement, value chain, 219
Performance evaluation
 balanced scorecard, 99–101
 in ethical organizations, 372–373
 financial ratio analysis, 97–99
 at General Motors, 119
 for human capital, 118

versus team success, 118
 360-degree evaluation and feedback systems, 118, 119
 in traditional approach to strategic control, 280
Permeable internal boundaries, 329–330
Personal bases of power
 definition, 357
 expert power, 358
 referent power, 357–358
Personal risk taking, 407
Personal time constraints, 356
Personnel Psychology, 46
Pharmaceutical companies
 counterfeit drug problem, 224
 orphan drug industry, 230–231
Philanthropy, by Avon, C95
Philippines
 per capita income, C84
 Starbucks in, C84
Physical resources, 89
Physical space, 395
Physical uniqueness, 92
Physiolectics, 48–49
Pictures, to build organizational culture, 285
Piecemeal productivity improvements, 173
Pied Piper effect, 124
Pioneering new entry, 260–261
 definition, 261
 differentiation in, 264
 disruptive of status quo, 261
 pitfalls, 261
Piracy, 223
Planning, Gresham's law, 356
Plant closings, Ford Motor Company, C250
Poison pills, 205
Policies, in ethical organizations, 373
Political barriers to change, 356
Political/legal segment of the general environment
 complexity of regulations, 48
 definition, 47
 elements of, 47
 H-1B visa issue, 47
 immigration, 47–48
 impact of legislation, 47
 impact on industries, 51
 key trends and events, 44
Political risk
 absence of rule of law, 222
 Country Risk Rating, 222
 definition, 222
 doing business in China, C74
 Middle East, 222
 U.S. ranking, 222–223
Ponzi scheme, 368
Pooled negotiating power, 184
 definition, 187
 examples, 187–188
Population, worldwide, C162

Portfolio management, 184, 438
 definition, 192
 description and potential benefits, 192–194
 growth/share matrix, 193
 limitations, 194
 research on, 192
 and shareholder value, 194
Poverty
 bottom of the pyramid populations, 214
 and microfinance, C206–C208
Power
 definition, 356
 of managers, 129
 organizational bases, 356–357
 personal bases, 357–358
 and political barriers to change, 356
 use at Siemens, 359
Preannouncements, 406
Preemptive launch, 386
Pressure to conform, 432
Prevention focus, 391
Price(s)
 McDonald's *vs.* Starbucks, C88
 rivalry based on, 57
Price competition, 57
Price-earnings ratio, 97, 423, 449–450
Price-performance trade-off, 173
Price premium, too high, 158
Pricing model, JetBlue Airways, C18
Primary activities
 Caterpillar Inc., 104
 definition, 77
 in differentiation strategy, 154
 illustration, 78
 inbound logistics, 77–78
 marketing and sales, 79–80
 operations, 78
 outbound logistics, 78–79
 in overall cost leadership, 150
 service, 80
 in service organizations, 87–88
Prime Time Live, 304
Principal-agent conflicts, 294, 305
 versus principal-principal conflicts, 306
Principal-principal conflicts, 305–306
Private information, 128
Proactiveness
 competitor reactions, 406
 definition, 405–406
 examples of failure, 405
 first-mover advantage, 405
 not leading to competitive advantage, 405
 requirements, 407
 techniques, 407
Problem identification, 422
Problem-solving argument for diversity management, 122

Procedures, in ethical
   organizations, 373
Process innovation, 382–383
Procurement
   definition, 80
   in differentiation strategy, 154
   at Microsoft, 80–82
   in overall cost leadership, 150
Product champions, 397, 439–440
   compared to exit champions, 399
   definition, 397
Product differentiation, as barrier
   to entry, 53
Product division structure,
   worldwide, 326
Product expatriates, 333
Product innovation, 382
   Apple Inc., C117, C119–C120
Production, multinational
   effort, 225
Productivity, piecemeal
   improvements, 173
Product line
   Apple Inc., C122
   eBay, C160–C161
   Jamba Juice, C49–C52
   Samsung, C209–C210
   for Zynga, C111
Product-line extension
   brand identification dilution,
      158–159
   Dippin' Dots, C39
Product-line extension, Jamba
   Juice, C48
Product-market diversification,
   excessive, 302
Product mix, changed at Ford,
   C253–C258
Product names, in multidomestic
   strategy, 233
Product placement, 79–80
Product pruning, 173
Product reinvention, Campbell
   Soup Co., C132
Products
   avoided by QVC, C182
   from breakthrough technology, 54
   complements, 63
   counterfeit, 223
   enhancing growth rate, 219
   global, 229
   luxury brands, 160
   nature of, at Dippin' Dots, C40
   search by QVC, C182
   substitutes, 56, 60–61
Profit
   decline at Cirque du Soleil,
      C270
   and employee bargaining
      power, 96
   and employee exit costs, 96
   and employee replacement
      cost, 96
   and executive compensation, 96
   flawed pursuit of, 102

generation and distribution of,
   95–96
low, 54
and manager bargaining
   power, 96
and shareholders, 96
and stakeholders, 96
Profitability
   difficult for coffee business in
      India, C87
   root causes of, 64
Profitability measures
   profit margin, 97, 423, 448
   return on assets, 97, 423, 449
   return on equity, 97, 423, 449
Profit margin, Weight
   Watchers, C31
Profit margin ratio, 97, 423, 448
Profit pool
   for airlines, 163
   definition, 162
   miscalculation, 164
Project definition, 397
Project impetus, 397
Promotion focus, 391
Promotions, and QVC, C182
Property rights, 136–137
Prosumer concept, 85–86
Public activists, and corporate
   governance, 304–305
Public Company Accounting
   Oversight Board, 303
Purchasing power of poorest
   people, 214

Q

Quality
   commitment at Pixar, C278
   in global strategy, 232
   problems for Johnson &
      Johnson, C233, C236–C237
Questioning, by innovators, 388
Question marks, 193
Quick ratio, 97, 423, 445
Quick-service restaurants, In
   India, C87–C88

R

Radical innovations
   definition, 383
   time line, 389
Radio advertising, 381
Radio frequency identification
   tags, 224
Rallies, motivating with, 284
Rare resources, 91
Real estate investment trusts, C80
Realistic objectives, 28
Realized strategy, 10–12
Real options, 399
Real options analysis
   application to strategic
      decisions, 399–400

characteristics, 399
definition, 399
at Intel, 401
potential pitfalls
   agency theory and back-solver
      dilemma, 400–401
   managerial conceit, 401–402
Rebranding, Weight
   Watchers, C27
Receivables turnover, 97, 423,
   447–448
Recommendations, in case
   analysis, 424–425
Recruiting
   Pied Piper effect, 124
   sound approaches, 115
Redefining jobs, 121
Reengineering the Corporation
   (Hammer & Champy), 337
Regional airlines, C15
Regional competitors, for
   Avon, C91
Regionalization
   definition, 237
   versus globalization, 237
   McDonald's, 341
   trading blocs, 238
Registration, and crowdfunding,
   256
Regulatory bodies, 304–305
Reimaging, by Samsung,
   C211–C212
Reintermediation, 60
Related and supporting
   industries
   definition, 216
   in India, 218
   joint efforts among firms, 216
   to manage inputs, 216
Related diversification, 438
   definition, 184
   for economies of scope
      leveraging core competencies,
         184–186
      sharing activities, 186–187
   enhancing revenue and
      differentiation, 187
   for market power
      pooled negotiating power, 184,
         187–188
      vertical integration, 184,
         188–190
Reputation, 89
   of competitors, 271
Requests for proposals, 390
Research and development, 167
   at Samsung, C212
Research and development
   expenditures
   Johnson & Johnson, C236
   problems for Apple Inc.,
      C122–C123
   wasted, 404
Research expertise, GreenWood
   Resources, C70–C72

Reshoring, 228
Resource acquisition argument for
   diversity management, 122
Resource allotments, 396–397
Resource-based view of the firm
   Blockbuster bankruptcy,
      94–95
   definition, 88
   generation and distribution of
      profits, 95–96
   perspectives, 88
   resources and competitive
      advantage
      availability of substitutes,
         93–94
      inimitability, 91–93
      rarity, 91
      value, 90–91
   types of resources
      intangible, 89–90
      organizational capabilities, 90
      tangible, 88–89
   uses, 88
Resources
   availability of substitutes,
      93–94
   available substitutes, 93–94
   of competitors, 271
   inimitability of, 91–93
   intangible, 89–90
   obtained by acquisition, 196
   organizational capabilities, 90
   rarity of, 91
   for start-ups, 253–257
   and sustainable competitive
      advantage
      availability of substitutes,
         93–94
      and Blockbuster bankruptcy,
         94–95
      inimitability, 91–93
      rarity of resource, 91
      value of resource, 90–91
      tangible, 88–89
      value of, 90–91
Resource similarity, 268
Restructuring, 184
   Ann Taylor, C58–C60, C66
   by Avon, C92
   definition, 191
   example, 191–192
   Ford Motor Company,
      C258–C259
   types of, 192
Retail alliances, 257
Retailers
   customer service, 80
   primary activities, 87
   store changes by Samsung, C211
Retail grocery industry
   online segment, C224–C228
   supermarket chains, C224
   top ten U.S. retailers, C224
   types of online shoppers, C225
Retailing by Avon, C92

Retention bonuses, C4
Retention cash awards, 16
Return on assets ratio, 97, 423, 449
Return on book assets, 449
Return on book equity, 449
Return on equity ratio, 97, 423, 449
Return on investment, 39
 for sustainability initiatives, 21
Return on sales
 historical trends, 98
Revenue enhancement, 187
Revenues
 Apple Inc., C122
 Boston Beer Co., C99
 decline at Zynga, C111
 eBay, C165
 from going green, 21
 in growth stage, 169
 McDonald's, C195
 for QVC by region, C181
 sources for Weight Watchers, C31
 Starbucks, C83
 Starbucks in China, C85
 top casino locations, C152
 Weight Watchers, C27
 World Wrestling Entertainment, C176, C177
Revenue sources
 in airline industry, 163
 for Avon, C90
 miscalculation, 164
Reverse innovation
 definition, 220
 in developing countries, 221
 from international expansion, 220
 process for emerging markets, 221
Reverse mentoring, 117–118
Reverse positioning
 Commerce Bank, 171
 definition, 170
 operation of, 170
Reward power, 357
Rewards
 financial and nonfinancial, 120–121
 redistributing, 365
Reward systems, 291–292
 creating effective programs, 286–288
 definition, 284
 in ethical organizations, 372–373
 for managers, 299–300
 motivating with, 284–285
 other than money, 286
 potential downsides, 285–286
Risk reduction
 currency risks, 220
 goal of diversification, 194–195

Risks
 of doing business in China, C73–C74
 exporting, 239
 franchising, 240
 in global strategy, 232
 in international expansion, 221–225
 international strategy, 231
 joint ventures, 240–241
 licensing, 240
 strategic alliances, 240–241
 transnational strategy, 235–236
 wholly owned subsidiaries, 241
Risk-sharing problem, 294
Risk taking
 definition, 407
 managing risks, 407–408
 pitfalls, 408
 techniques, 408
 types, 407
Rivalry
 and low switching costs, 61
 occasions for, 56–57
Rivals, cost advantage relative to, 151
Role models, 371
Romantic view of leadership, 5
Rule of law
 absent in Russia, 222
 definition, 222
 United States ranking, 222–223
Rules-based control, 289–290
Russia
 absence of rule of law, 222
 Campbell Soup Co. failure in, C131–C132
 GDP per person growth 2001–2011, 215

S

Sales
 Apple Inc. 2014–2015, C119
 Campbell Soup Co., C130
 decline at McDonald's, C194–C196
 of Ford by segment, C257
 by Ford in Jan. 2015, C245
 General Motors, C242, C244
 Heineken by region, C216
 Johnson & Johnson, C233
 new vehicles by Ford 2006–2014, C256
 Nintendo, C184
 by QVC 1989–2014, C179
 by segment for Ford, C257
Sarbanes-Oxley Act, 47, 290, 298
 and corporate governance, 304–305
 on whistleblowers, 373
Saudi Arabia, oil production, C12
Scenario analysis
 definition, 42
 at PPG Industries, 43

Scent of a Mystery, 261
Search barriers, 127
Securities and Exchange Commission, C113
 and Avon, C89, C94, C95
 and crowdfunding, 256
 filings with, 304–305
 and Groupon, 4
 and Merrill Lynch, 109
Seeds *vs.* weeds, 385
Self-awareness, 359–360
Self-censorship, 432
Self-interest, problem for social capital, 131
Self-regulation, 360
Sell-offs, 200n
Separation of owners and managers, 293–294
Service representatives, 155–156
Services
 complements, 63
 definition, 80
 in differentiation strategy, 154
 in overall cost leadership, 150
 substitutes, 56, 60–61
Service sector
 outsourcing, 227
 value-chain activities, 87–88
Setting a direction, 351, 354
Seventeen, C44
Shale oil production, C11–C12
Shared value, 18, 337
Shareholder activism
 and corporate governance, 298–299
 at eBay, C166
 social concerns, 300
Shareholders
 and balanced scorecard, 101
 expropriation of minority, 306
 versus stakeholders, 16–17
Shareholder value
 and activist investor, C166
 as corporate goal, 16–17
 from portfolio management, 194
 short-term perspective, 9–10
 versus stakeholders, 17
Sharing activities, 184–186
 costs and benefits, 187
 definition, 186
 deriving cost savings, 186–187
 enhancing differentiation, 187
 revenue enhancement, 187
Shark Tank, C49
Shirking, 302
Shopping infomediaries, 61
Shopping robots, 61
Short-term objectives, 28, 288–289
Short-term perspective, 9–10
Short-term solvency measures
 cash ratio, 97, 423, 445
 current ratio, 97, 423, 444–445
 quick ratio, 97, 423, 445

Simple organizational structure, 316, 318
Singapore
 per capita income, C84
 Starbucks in, C84
Skill sets
 access to, 128–129
Skills for innovation, 387
Skunkworks, 404
Small Business Administration, 257, C42
Small Business Development Centers, 257
Smartphones, 381
 legal battles over, 137
 sales in China, C210
 sales worldwide, C210
Social capital
 to attract and retain talent, 124
 bridging relationships, 126–127
 closure relationships, 126
 definition, 112
 development of, 123
 driving opportunities, 339
 from electronic teams, 133
 example, 123–124
 for new ventures, 256–257
 overcoming barriers to collaboration, 127
 potential downsides
  deep-rooted mind-sets, 131
  expense of socialization process, 131
  groupthink, 129–131
  self-interest, 131
 rekindling connections, 130
 research on, 130
 and social networks, 124–129
 value creation through, 136
Social complexity
 definition, 92
 examples, 92–93
Socialization process expense, 131
Socially complex processes, 112
Socially responsible investing, 20
Social network analysis, 125–126
Social networks
 benefits for firms
  access to diverse skill sets, 128–129
  managerial power, 129
  private information, 128
 bridging relationships, 126–127
 closure relationships, 126
 connectors, 124–125
 implications for careers, 128
 network traps
  wrong behavior, 129
  wrong relationships, 129
  wrong structure, 129
 organizational change from, 125
 overcoming barriers to collaboration, 127
 to share information, 131–132
 structural holes, 127

Social responsibility
  Avon, C95
  definition, 18
  demands for, 18–19
  and Seventh Generation, 29
  Starbucks, C83
  Tata Group, C86
Social risk, doing business in China, C74
Social skill, 361
Sociocultural segment of the general environment
  definition, 45
  educational attainment of women, 45–47
  impact on industries, 51
  key trends and events, 44
Software industry in India, 217–218
Software piracy, 223
South Korea
  chaebols, 306
  per capita income, C84
Special Required Navigation Performance Authorization Required, C18
Specialty store chains
  branding challenges, C61–C64
  characteristics, C60
Specific objectives, 28
Speculate, ability to, 418
Spin-off, 200n
  of Alibaba stake by Yahoo!, C168
Split-offs, 200n
Staffing
  to capture value of innovation, 389–390
  internal *vs.* external, 385–386
Stakeholder management
  versus shareholder value, 16–17
  symbiosis view, 17–18
  zero-sum game thinking, 17
Stakeholders
  and balanced scorecard, 101
  benefited by antitakeover tactics, 206
  definition, 9
  key, for firms, 17
  at Procter & Gamble, 18
  and profits, 96
  types of, 17
Standard & Poor's 500 Index, 3, 16, 20, 298, C80
Stars, 193
Start-up(s); *see also* New ventures
  Boston Beer Company, C100
  Cirque du Soleil, C270
  decline in number of, 273
  Emirates Airline, C263–C267
  financial resources, 253–256
  FreshDirect, C221–C222
  global, 326–327
  government resources, 257

GreenWood Resources, C68–C70
  human capital, 256
  by Jamba Juice, C49
  JetBlue Airways, C15
  Kickstarter, C22–C23
  social capital, 256–257
  sources of opportunities, 250
  Southwest Airlines, C7–C8
Start-up costs, ice cream franchises, C45–C46
Statement of cash flows
  Ann Taylor, C62
  eBay, C159–C160
  Emirates Airline, C265–C266
  Ford Motor Company, C254–C256
  Weight Watchers, C33–C34
Static analysis, 62–63
Static assessment, 76
Status quo
  challenging, 366–367
  dissatisfaction with, 350
  vested interest in, 365
Stereotyped view of opponents, 432
Stock analysts, 303
Stock-keeping units, 150
Stock market indexes, 49
Stock options, 399
Stock price performance
  Campbell Soup Co., C135
  change at Southwest Airlines, C12
  decline 2008–2011, 16
  Google Inc., 381
  of Groupon, 3, 4
  JetBlue Airways, C14
Stock repurchase plan, Jamba Juice, C48
Storage costs, high, 57
Storytelling, 284
  to build organizational culture, 285
Strategic actions
  definition, 269
  examples, 270
Strategic alliances, 195
  definition, 202
  to develop and diffuse new technologies, 202
  to enter new markets, 202, 203
  for international expansion
    alliance management knowledge, 241
    benefits, 240
    clearly defined strategies, 240
    cultural issues, 241
    partnership clarification, 240
    trust element, 240
  potential downsides, 203
  to reduce costs, 202
  as social capital for new ventures, 257
Strategic analysis, 422–424

Strategic business units
  Apple Inc., C123–C127
  Campbell Soup Co., C130
  cash cows, 193
  dogs, 193
  Johnson & Johnson, C235
  limitations of growth/share matrix, 194
  Procter & Gamble, C203
  question marks, 193
  stars, 193
Strategic business unit structure, 318
  advantages and disadvantages, 322
  definition, 322
  synergies, 322
Strategic control
  aspects of, 280
  behavioral control, 282–292
  in case analysis, 438
  contemporary approach, 281–282
  corporate governance, 292–307
  definition, 280
  informational control, 280–282
  problem at Tesco, 279
  and strategy implementation, 14
  traditional approach, 280
Strategic decision maker, assuming role of, 420
Strategic decisions
  real options analysis, 399–400
  Tata Starbucks, C82–C83, C88
Strategic direction, coherence in common goals and objectives, 23–24
  hierarchy of goals, 24
  mission statement, 26–27
  strategic objectives, 27–28
  vision, 24–26
Strategic envelope, 387–388
Strategic groups
  as analytical tool
    chart direction of strategy, 65
    identify barriers to mobility, 65
    identify competitive position, 65
    trend analysis, 65
  comparison of financial performance, 99
  definition, 64
  dimensions of, 65
  identifying, 64–65
  worldwide auto industry, 65–67
Strategic leadership, 350; *see also* Leadership
Strategic management; *see also* Learning from mistakes
  abilities
    differentiate, 418
    integrate, 418
    speculate, 418
  attributes

effectiveness-efficiency trade-off, 10
  goals and objectives, 9
  multiple stakeholders, 9
  short- *vs.* long-term perspectives, 9–10
in changing global environment, 23
and competitive advantage, 8
definition, 8
integrative view of organization, 22–23
questions raised by, 417
types of leaders, 23
Strategic management process, 8
  and corporate governance, 15–16
  environmental sustainability, 19–22
  intended *vs.* realized strategy, 10–12
  social responsibility, 18–19
  stakeholder management, 16–18
  strategy analysis, 12–13
  strategy formulation, 14
  strategy implementation, 14–15
Strategic objectives
  avoiding too many, 28
  benefits, 28
  criteria for, 28
  definition, 27
  financial, 28
  mission statement, 27
  nonfinancial, 28
  short-term, 28
  types of, 28
Strategic priorities, 288
Strategic substitutes, 94
Strategic *vs.* financial CE goals, 39
Strategy analysis
  definition, 12
  elements of, 12–13
Strategy formulation
  and contemporary approach to strategic control, 281
  definition, 14
  elements of, 14
  and organizational structure, 327
  in traditional approach to strategic control, 280
Strategy implementation
  with action plans, 28
  and contemporary approach to strategic control, 281
  definition, 14
  elements of, 14–15
  focus of behavioral control, 282–283
  problem for Avon, C92
  in traditional approach to strategic control, 280
Strategy/Strategies
  business-level, 14
  Campbell Soup Co., C130–C131
  corporate-level, 14

Strategy/Strategies—Cont.
definition, 8
eBay, C157–C160
entrepreneurial, 14
in health care industry, 7–8
incremental changes, 280
indicators for monitoring, 39
intended *vs.* realized, 10–12
international, 14
priorities at Ford, C250–C251
Robin Hood, C2
shift at Southwest Airlines, C11–C12
shift at United Way, C144
source of implementation problems, 351
and value of experience, 22
Strengths; *see also* SWOT analysis
not leading to advantage, 76
Strike, and Seventh Generation, 29
Structural equation modeling, 335
Structural hole, 127
Structure of Corporation Law (Aron & Eisenberg), 283
Stuck in the middle, 148
for combination strategies, 163
JetBlue Airways, 173–174
Subsidiaries
of Boston Beer Company, C103
Johnson & Johnson, C234
Subsidies, alleged for Emirates Airline, C262, C263
Substitutes
definition, 56
identifying, 56
readily available, 93–94
Summer Foods, C44
Summer Jobs Initiative, C54
Super Bowl
ads on, 81
advertising by Weight Watchers, C27
Supermarkets
problems for, 148
in retail grocery industry, C224
Supplier base in India, 218
Suppliers
delayed payments to, 67
differentiated products, 56
disintermediation by, 60
dominated by few companies, 55
industry unimportant to, 55
not contending with substitutes, 55
products as important inputs, 55
and reintermediation, 60
role of, 60
switching costs for buyers, 56
threat of forward integration, 56
Supply chain, Boston Beer, C99
Support activities
Caterpillar Inc., 104
definition, 77
in differentiation strategy, 154
general administration, 84

human resource management, 82–84
illustration, 81
in overall cost leadership, 150
procurement, 80–82
technology development, 82
Sustainability; *see also* Generic strategies
factors for Campbell Soup Co., C135
measurable goals, 289
Sustainability initiatives
intangible benefits, 22
return on investment on, 21
Sustainability report, 114
Sustainable competitive advantage, 8–9
and Blockbuster bankruptcy, 94–95
Caterpillar Inc., 105
firm resources
availability of substitutes, 93–94
inimitability, 91–93
rarity, 91
value, 90–91
Sustainable global economy, 20
Sustaining innovation, 383
Switching costs
as barrier to entry, 54
effect of Internet, 57–60
faced by buyers, 54
lack of, 57
SWOT analysis, 90, 91
and competitive aggressiveness, 406
definition, 42
functions, 42–43
versus intuition and judgment, 43
limitations, 76
Symbiosis view of stakeholders, 17–18
Synergos, 183
Synergy/Synergies, 183, 438
bases of, attained by acquisition, 197
imitated by competitors, 198
from market power, 187
from sharing activities, 186
Systemic barriers to change, 355–356

T

Tacit knowledge, 134
definition, 112
Tactical actions
definition, 269
examples, 270
Takeover
Avon as target, C95
resisted by Yahoo!, C170–C171
by World Wrestling Entertainment, C173–C174

Takeover premium, 198
Talent
attracting, 110
emigration to form start-ups, 124
Google policies for attracting, 121
and green strategies, 113
open-sourcing model, 120
worldwide shortage, 121
Talent retention
and empathy, 361
by social capital, 124
Tangible resources
computerized training, 88–89
definition, 88
types, 88–89
Target market
Ann Taylor, C58
Dippin' Dots, C44
of focus strategy, 148
for Heineken
Hispanics, C219
younger drinkers, C218
isolation from, 232
Weight Watchers, C28, C35–C36
Taxes, relocation to lower, 242
Taxi industry, 57–58
Teams
autonomous, 403
in barrier-free organizations, 329–330
in boundaryless organizations, 336–337
for case analysis, 433–434
competition among, 365
cross-functional, 337, 340
for development, 367
leadership exercised by, 258–259
in virtual organizations, 335
Technical assistants, 117–118
Technical skills, 358
Technological developments and trends, 48–49
Technological resources, 89
Technological segment of the general environment
definition, 48
impact on industries, 51
key trends and events, 44
new developments and trends, 48–49
Technology
improvement by Pixar, C277
to leverage human capital
codifying knowledge, 134–135
electronic teams, 132–134
networks for information sharing, 131–132
for mass customization, 161–162
source of new ideas, 382
used in hiring, 115
value creation through, 136
Technology alliances, 257

Technology development
definition, 82
in differentiation strategy, 154
in overall cost leadership, 150
Teenage Mutant Turtles, 52
Television commercials
Super Bowl ads, 81, C27
Tender offer, 205
10-K reports, 452
Terrorist attack of 2001, 18, C15
Thailand, per capita income, C84
Theory Z (Ouchi), 283
Third-party services, 55
Threat analysis
definition, 268
and market commonality, 268
resource similarity, 268
Threat of new entrants, 250
barriers to entry, 53–54
definition, 53
effect of Internet, 58
Threat of retaliation, for new ventures, 260
Threat of substitute products and services
definition, 56
effect of Internet, 60–61
identifying substitutes, 56
Threats; *see also* SWOT analysis
in external environment, 37
360-degree evaluation and feedback systems
definition, 118
at General Electric, 119
Timber industry
forest management criteria, C69
Forest Stewardship Council, C68–C69, C74
hybrid poplar plantation development, C80–C81
investments, C80
tree plantations, C80
Time, C125
Time horizon in industry analysis, 64
Timely objectives, 28
Time pacing of innovation, 389
Times interest earned ratio, 97, 423, 446
Tipping Point (Gladwell), 124
Top-down approach to entrepreneurship, 396
Top executives, replaced at Avon, C94
Top 50 Global Green Brand ranking, 114
Top-level executives; *see also* CEOs; Managers
erosion of value creation by, 204–205
role of, 23
and Sarbanes-Oxley Act, 304–305
Tort reform, 47

Total asset turnover ratio, 97, 423, 448
Total debt ratio, 97, 423, 446
Total equity, 446n
Total performance indicators, 101
Tracking development, 118
Trade-offs, 10
Trading blocs, 238
Traditional approach to strategic control
 based on feedback loop, 280
 crafting strategy, 280
 definition, 280
Training, 116
 cross-training, 337
 Emirates Airline, C267–C268
 in organizational culture, 291–292
Transaction cost perspective, 190
Transaction costs, 338
Transaction-specific investments, 190
Transfer barrier, 127
Transformational change, 23
Transformation process, 87
Transformers: Age of Extinction, 219
Transnational strategy
 definition, 235
 enhanced adaptation, 235
 Nestlé Company, 235
 Panasonic, 236
 risks and challenges
  knowledge transfer not automatic, 236
  location and cost of inputs, 235–236
 strengths and limitations, 237
 value-chain activities, 235
Transparency, 93, 354
Travel and Leisure, C!6
Trend analysis, 39, 44
 by Weight Watchers, C28
Tribal loyalty, 120
Triple bottom line
 definition, 19
 and environmental revolution, 19–20
Triple bottom line approach, 18
Trust, 93
T-shaped management, 127
Turnaround
 attempt at McDonald's, C196–C198
 attempt by Yahoo!, C171
 failed effort at Procter & Gamble, C200–C205
 by Jamba Juice, C48
 setbacks for Avon, C89
 versus takeover for Avon, C96
 World Wrestling Entertainment, C173
Turnaround strategy
 asset and cost surgery, 173
 definition, 173

at Home Shopping Network, 174
internal and external analysis for, 173
piecemeal productivity improvements, 173
selective market/product pruning, 173
Turnover ratios; *see* Asset utilization ratios
20-F reports, 451–452

U

Unanimity, illusion of, 432
Unethical behavior, 372
Unethical conduct, minimizing, 290
Unification lever, 127
Unions, and FreshDirect, C230
Uniqueness not valuable, 158
Unit costs, 230
United Food and Commercial Workers strike, 29
United States
 counterfeit drug problem, 224
 decline in entrepreneurship, 273
 failure of Tesco in, 279
 government red tape, 272
 GDP per person growth 2001–2011, 215
 licensing of workers, 272
 number of franchisers, 239
 Open Beer Championship, C106
 per capita income, C84
 retail grocery industry, C224–C228
 rule of law ranking, 222–223
 timberland, C80
 weakened antitrust, 272
United Way, C54
Unity of command, 301
University of South Carolina, 54
Unrelated diversification, 438
 corporate parenting, 184, 191
 definition, 191
 holding company structure, 323
 portfolio management, 184, 192–194
 restructuring, 184, 191–192
 risk reduction as viable goal, 194–195
U.S. News & World Report, 372
USA Today, 81, 383, C52

V

Valentine's Day disaster for JetBlue Airways, C16
Value
 of counterfeit goods, 223
 definition, 77
 of mergers and acquisitions 2000–2014, 196
 of resources, 90–91

of unsuccessful innovation, 392–393
Value chain
 and core competencies, 185
 extended, 162–163
 global dispersion
  Bangalore, India, 227
  from decline in transportation costs, 227
  increase in total costs, 227–228
  offshoring, 225–227
  outsourcing, 225–227
  in service sector, 227
  World Trade Organization report, 225
 integration of customers, 85–87
 and reintermediation, 60
Value-chain activities
 Caterpillar Inc., 104
 in differentiation strategy, 154
 focus on one or few, 152
 in harvesting strategy, 172
 in international strategy, 231
 interrelationships
  across organizations, 85
  within organizations, 85
 optimizing location of
  cost reduction, 220
  performance enhancement, 219
  risk reduction, 220
 in overall cost leadership, 150
 primary
  definition, 77
  inbound logistics, 77–78
  marketing and sales, 79–80
  operations, 78
  outbound logistics, 78–79
  service, 80
 in service organizations, 87
 support
  definition, 77
  general administration, 84
  human resource management, 82–84
  procurement, 80–82
  technology development, 82
 transnational strategy, 235
Value-chain analysis, 437
 definition, 76
 uses, 76–77
Value-chain concept, 75
Value-creating activities, 75
 underestimating expenses, 164
Value-creating opportunity, 253
Value creation, 77
 contexts of, 250
 from employee development, 136
 from employee retention, 136
 from human capital, 136
 necessary factors, 250
 from social capital, 136
 from technology, 136

Value net concept, 63
Values, shared in boundaryless organizations, 337
Vanity Fair, 4
Venture capital, 255
Venture capitalists, 254–255, C49
Vertical boundaries, 328
Vertical integration, 184, 187
 administrative costs, 190
 benefits and risks, 188–190
 definition, 188
 issues to consider, 188–190
 at Nutriva, 189
 transaction cost perspective, 190
Vertical relationships, 191
Vested interest in status quo, 365
Videoconferencing, 337
Video game industry, C111–C116
 demographics, C189
 game developers, C189–C190
 Microsoft Xbox, C190–C191
 mobile gaming, C192
 Nintendo Wii U, C184–C190, C192
 Sega, C185
 Sony Playstations, C191–C192
Vietnam, per capita income, C84
Virtual, 333
Virtual organizations, 328
 challenges and risks
  building relationships, 334
  clarity of objectives, 334
  strategic plan, 334–335
  temporary alliances, 334–335
 characteristics, 334
 compared to modular type, 334
 core competencies, 334
 definition, 333
 internal, 334
 pros and cons, 336
 teams in, 335
Virtual teams, 335
Vision, 436
 Avon, C96
 definition, 24
 of entrepreneurial leaders, 258
 examples, 25
 Ford Motor Company, C250
 identifying with, 120
 at James Irvine Foundation, 27
 of leaders, 350
 leadership trait, 24
 not rooted in reality, 75
 reasons for failure
  elusive, 25
  inconsistent management, 25
  irrelevance, 25
  not anchored in reality, 26
  too much focus, 25
 source of implementation problems, 351
 at WellPoint, 26
Vision statement, 25
 compared to mission statement, 27

W

Wage costs, hidden in offshoring, 227
Wage inflation, in developing countries, 228
Wall Street Journal, 3, 39, 124, 200, 268, 269, 304, C52
Watson computer, 186
Way to the Top (Trump), C43
Weaknesses; *see* SWOT analysis
Web-based storage, 61
Websites, for competitive intelligence, 40
Weeds, 385
Whistleblowers, 373
Wholly owned subsidiaries
  benefits, 241
  definition, 241
  GreenWood Resources, C73
  risks and limitations, 241
Wikipedia, 50
Win-win solutions, 338
Wisdom of Teams (Smith), 336
Women
  Avon customers, C89–C90
  Avon salesforce, C90
  educational attainment, 45–47
  in workforce, 45
Women's Wear Daily, C60
Work, challenging, 120
Workforce
  diversity management, 122–123
  electronic teams, 132–134
  layoffs *vs.* furloughs, 138
  percent in manufacturing, 110
  percent in service sector, 110
Working Knowledge, 372
Workplace, stimulating environment, 120
World Economic Forum Global Report, 222
World Health Organization, C29
World Trade Center attack of 2001, C15
World Trade Organization report on production, 225
Worldwide functional division, 317
Worldwide functional structure, 326
Worldwide matrix structure, 317, 326
Worldwide product division structure, 317, 326
Wright amendment, C9
  elimination of, C12
Written case analysis, 428

Z

Zero-sum game, 62
Zero-sum thinking of stakeholders, 17

Clear and Rigorous Concepts Deserve Fresh & Excellent Cases

Dear Instructor,

Thank you for requesting this complimentary copy of *Strategic Management: Text and Cases!* Whether you are already familiar with this text or this is your first time reviewing it, I believe this strategy textbook will provide you with both great concepts and cases! Instructors who use this textbook tell us that the discussion of the key theories and concepts, combined with current and interesting examples, enables their students to grasp the difficult, yet crucial, information that they need in order to prepare themselves to succeed in business. A key component of most strategic management courses, however, is going beyond the discussion of concepts and theories. Case studies provide students with an important opportunity to read about companies and realistic situations and then use critical-thinking skills to suggest answers for the problems they have studied. I've created this guide to assist you with your course planning. This document not only includes a grid that identifies the primary and secondary cases that relate to the chapters of this book but also includes some of my personal teaching suggestions. My coauthors and I have also added a large selection of corresponding videos, PowerPoint presentations, Excel spreadsheets for financial tables, and web links for more information on the case companies. For those of you who have used previous editions of the book, you will see many of the same companies in the cases. However, we have carefully updated the case stories to present cases that are fresh enough for students and rigorous enough for instructors. We hope that this also reduces instructor preparation time in choosing familiar companies. Additionally, as you evaluate and use the cases in our 8th edition, I welcome your feedback and suggestions, which can be sent to aeisner@pace.edu. I look forward to your insightful comments.

Sincerely,
Alan B. Eisner
Pace University

ROBIN HOOD (CASE 1)

I love to start the first session of the semester with a short case. One of my all-time favorites is "Robin Hood" by Joseph Lampel. This classic case is an excellent introduction to strategic management using a nonbusiness situation. Since it is only one page, I ask students to read it during class and discuss it. In the case, Robin Hood and his Merrymen are in trouble, as wealthy travelers are avoiding Sherwood Forest. I weave a discussion of problem identification and potential solution analysis that helps to set the tone for case discussions for the rest of the semester. This case brings up mission issues that go with Chapter 1 ("Strategic Management"). The United Way Worldwide (Case 18) and QVC (Case 23) cases also link well with Chapter 1 if you are looking for alternatives.

THE GLOBAL CASINO INDUSTRY (CASE 19)

In this edition we have totally revamped this case to match Chapter 2 ("Analyzing the External Environment of the Firm") because it offers a great platform for exploring environmental analysis in the global casino industry. The dominance of Las Vegas and Atlantic City in the global market has been challenged by the development of several casinos along a strip in the former Portuguese colony of Macau. More recently, this growth of casinos has spread to other locations across the Asia-Pacific region. All of these new locations are hoping to grab a share of the gambling revenues. Additionally, the expansion of Native American casinos and the emergence of online gaming have put pressure on revenues. This case has a wealth of information for industry analysis and makes for a great in-class discussion or written assignment case. We also have a great revised case on Weight Watchers International Inc. (Case 7) for those looking for lighter fare.

UNITED WAY WORLDWIDE (CASE 18)

Our United Way Worldwide case works well with Chapters 1 and 2 ("Strategic Management" and "Analyzing the External Environment of the Firm") as well as Chapters 3 and 4 ("Assessing the Internal Environment of the Firm" and "Recognizing a Firm's Intellectual Assets"). The case also can be used with Chapter 5 ("Business-Level Strategy"), giving it a lot of flexibility. In the case, CEO Brian Gallagher establishes new membership standards for United Way affiliates' operations, rebrands United Way as doing "what matters" in the communities it serves, and addresses the long-term needs of communities. Gallagher needed to convince the United Way affiliates to buy into the change effort but did not have much leverage over them.

AVON: A NEW ERA? (CASE 13)

In this brand-new case, Avon Company has a new CEO, Sheri McCoy, who faces the problem of how to stimulate the faltering direct-selling model the company was built on. Can she repair the Avon model, or should she sell off the firm? This case works best with Chapters 5 and 6 ("Business-Level Strategy" and "Corporate-Level Strategy"). The rich detail in this case also allows it to work with Chapter 2 ("Analyzing the External Environment of the Firm") as well as Chapter 3 ("Assessing the Internal Environment of the Firm").

ANN TAYLOR: SURVIVAL IN SPECIALTY RETAIL (CASE 10)

The founding brand, the Ann Taylor division, struggled to maintain focus and present basic, professional clothing to its iconic customers after being upstaged by its younger sister, Ann Taylor Loft. This case has been revised with new information and is quite versatile in the classroom. This case works with Chapter 1 ("Strategic Management") and Chapter 2 ("Analyzing the External Environment of the Firm"). It also fits well with a discussion of resources, complementing Chapters 3 and 4 ("Assessing the Internal Environment of the Firm" and "Recognizing a Firm's Intellectual Assets"), corporate diversification (Chapter 6, "Corporate-Level Strategy"), or the topics of Chapters 9 through 11 ("Strategic Control and Corporate Governance," "Creating Effective Organizational Designs," and "Strategic Leadership").

CAMPBELL SOUP: HOW TO KEEP THE SOUP SIMMERING (CASE 17)

In this revamped Campbell Soup case, CEO Denise Morrison has brought the company from slow simmer to boil with the launch of more than 50 new products, yet profit slipped by 5 percent. Will Campbell's soup simmer to perfection, or will the company be in hot water? Who hasn't had soup before? Everyone in the class has product experience. This case works well with Chapter 5 ("Business-Level Strategy") as well as Chapters 2 and 3 ("Analyzing the External Environment of the Firm" and "Assessing the Internal Environment of the Firm").

JETBLUE AIRLINES: GETTING OVER THE "BLUES"? (CASE 5)

The revised JetBlue Airlines case is great with Chapter 5 ("Business-Level Strategy"). JetBlue's airline start-up success story was facing new challenges as operational problems surfaced and pilot unionization occurred as its third CEO entered the cockpit. The question that always gets asked with this case is how the firm can maintain a cost leadership position with a customer-centric focus. Students in my classroom seem very engaged with this company's success story, yet they are also challenged to create recommendations for JetBlue moving forward. This case can be paired with our Southwest Airlines case (Case 4).

APPLE INC.: STILL TAKING A BITE OUT OF THE COMPETITION? (CASE 16)

I like to use our revised Apple case with Chapters 3 and 4 ("Assessing the Internal Environment of the Firm" and "Recognizing a Firm's Intellectual Assets"). Apple, under CEO Tim Cook, appeared to be reinventing itself as a dominant player in multiple categories beyond consumer electronics, including wearable technology, a mobile pay system, and even, perhaps, automobiles. This case also works with Chapter 2 ("Analyzing the External Environment of the Firm") to encourage discussion of how consumer tastes have continued to shift the overall competitive landscape for technology devices. Instructors can also use the case with Chapters 5 and 6 ("Business-Level Strategy" and "Corporate-Level Strategy") to look at business- and corporate-level strategic solutions. Apple resonates with almost every student because almost all of them have an iPod, iPad, or iPhone.

TATA STARBUCKS: HOW TO BREW A SUSTAINABLE BLEND FOR INDIA (CASE 12)

Despite perky initial performance, this joint venture will need to work hard to brew up profits as it expands further. Will the Starbucks and Tata joint venture under CEO Avani Davda's leadership be able to crack the code for success in the competitive and complex Indian café market? This case works best with Chapter 7 ("International Strategy"). Great alternative cases for "International Strategy" include the newcomer case "Emirates Airline" (Case 34), completely revamped case "eBay" (Case 20), and stalwart case "Heineken" (Case 29).

FRESHDIRECT: IS IT REALLY FRESH? (CASE 30)

This revised FreshDirect case is quite flexible and comprehensive because it fits with a discussion of Chapter 2 ("Analyzing the External Environment of the Firm"), Chapter 3 ("Assessing the Internal Environment of the Firm"), Chapter 5 ("Business-Level Strategy"), Chapter 8 ("Entrepreneurial Strategy and Competitive Dynamics"), Chapter 11 ("Strategic Leadership"), and Chapter 12 ("Managing Innovation and Fostering Corporate Entrepreneurship"). FreshDirect is a New York City–based online grocery store with a state-of-the-art production center; top-notch personnel; leading-edge manufacturing software; the highest standards of cleanliness, health, and safety; and an informative and user-friendly website. Despite a large potential target audience, the online segment has been slow to catch on. For FreshDirect, maintaining high product quality while keeping prices low led to razor-thin margins and abundant competition from both online and traditional grocers.

AMERICAN INTERNATIONAL GROUP AND THE BONUS FIASCO (CASE 3)

This short case is terrific with Chapter 9 ("Strategic Control and Corporate Governance") and Chapter 11 ("Strategic Leadership"). The U.S. government pumped an astounding $85 billion into AIG alone to prevent it from going bankrupt at the end of 2008. Insurance companies are generally supposed to be risk-averse and prudent. How should AIG deal with the aftermath of such a big mess?

JOHNSON & JOHNSON (CASE 31)

I love to use this revised Johnson & Johnson case with Chapter 10 ("Creating Effective Organizational Designs"), and it has a strong tie-in to Chapters 6 and 11 ("Corporate-Level Strategy" and "Strategic Leadership"). Executives from health care conglomerate Johnson & Johnson had known about a critical design flaw with an artificial hip but decided to conceal this information from physicians and patients; the company also had quality control problems with several over-the-counter drugs made by J&J's McNeil Consumer Healthcare. Could more centralized control improve quality? Johnson & Johnson's CEO, Alex Gorsky, hoped to strike a balance between direction and freedom for the firms' more than 250 business units as he pushed to get the firm to grow again.

CIRQUE DU SOLEIL (CASE 35)

The new Cirque du Soleil case is a high-flying account of this innovative circus entertainment business. Poorly received shows over the past few years and a decline in profits caused executives at Cirque to announce restructuring and refocusing efforts—shifting some of the attention away from its string of successful shows and toward several other potential business ventures. This case is excellent with Chapter 12 ("Managing Innovation and Fostering Corporate Entrepreneurship") as well as Chapter 11 ("Strategic Leadership") and Chapter 8 ("Entrepreneurial Strategy and Competitive Dynamics").

YAHOO! (CASE 21)

We have revised one of my favorite end-of-semester cases, "Yahoo!," to account for the new competitive environment. It fits with Chapters 11 ("Strategic Leadership") and 12 ("Managing Innovation and Fostering Corporate Entrepreneurship"). Yahoo's CEO, Marissa Mayer, was determined to make the company a stronger force on smartphones and tablets. Will Mayer be able to lure back advertisers, reinvigorate a muddled brand, and improve morale at a company that has been marred by executive churn, constant cost cutting, and mass layoffs? The Samsung Electronics case (Case 28) is a great alternative as well.

Case Number	CASE TITLE	INDUSTRY	# of pages	1 Strategic Management	2 External Environment	3 Internal Analysis	4 Intellectual Assets	5 Business-Level Strategy	6 Corporate-Level Strategy	7 International Strategy	8 Entrepreneurial Strategy	9 Strategy & Competitive Dynamics	10 Strategic Control & Corporate Governance	11 Organizational Design	12 Strategic Leadership / Managing Innovation	PowerPoint	Excel
1	Robin Hood	Hypothetical/Classic	1	P												✓	
2	Edward Marshall Boehm, Inc.	Housewares & Accessories, Porcelain Collectibles- Classic	1	P	P	P	s	P	P							✓	
3	American International Group and the Bonus Fiasco	Insurance	3									P	s	P		✓	
4	Southwest Airlines: Is LUV Soaring?+	Airline	7		s	s	s	P	P		s	s		s	s	✓	✓
5	JetBlue Airlines: Getting Over the "Blues"?+	Airline	7		s	s	s	P	s				P	P	P	✓	
6	Backers Beware: KickStarter Is Not a Store+	Crowdfunding	6	s	s						P					✓	
7	Weight Watchers International Inc.+	Weight Loss	11	s	P	s	s	P	s		P	s		s	s	✓	✓
8	Dippin' Dots: Is the Future Frozen?+	Ice Cream	10	s	s	s	s	P	s		P	s		s	P	✓	✓
9	Jamba Juice: Feeling the Squeeze or Juicing Up?+	Smoothies/QSR	9		P	P	s	P	P		s	s	s	s		✓	✓
10	Ann Taylor: Survival in Specialty Retail+	Retail, Women's Fashion	11	s	s	s	s	s	P							✓	✓
11	Greenwood Resources: A Global Sustainable Venture in the Making*	Natural Resources	14	s	P	P	s	s	s	P						✓	
12	Tata Starbucks: How to Brew a Sustainable Blend for India*	Coffee	7	s	s	s	s	s	s	P						✓	
13	Avon: A New Era?*	Cosmetics	10	s	P	P	s	P								✓	✓
14	The Boston Beer Company: Poised for Growth+	Beer	12		s	s		P								✓	✓

#	Case Title	Industry	Chapters
15	Zynga: Room for a Final Round or Is the Game Over?+	Multimedia & Online Games	6
16	Apple Inc.: Still Taking a Bite Out of the Competition?+	Computers, Consumer Electronics	13
17	Campbell: How to Keep the Soup Simmering*	Processed & Packaged Goods	13
18	United Way Worldwide+	Nonprofit	9
19	The Global Casino Industry*	Casino Industry	4
20	eBay+	Internet	12
21	Yahoo!+	Internet	5
22	World Wrestling Entertainment+	Entertainment	6
23	QVC+	Retail	5
24	Nintendo's Wii U+	Video Games	10
25	McDonald's+	Restaurant	6
26	Procter & Gamble+	Consumer Products	6
27	Microfinance: Going Global . . . and Going Public?	Finance	3
28	Samsung Electronics+	Consumer Electronics	6
29	Heineken+	Beer	5
30	FreshDirect: Is It Really Fresh?+	Grocery	13
31	Johnson & Johnson+	Pharmaceuticals, Personal Care Products, Medical Devices	6
32	General Motors*	Automotive	6
33	Is One Ford Really Working?*	Automotive	17
34	Emirates Airline*	Airline	8
35	Cirque du Soleil*	Entertainment	4
36	Pixar+	Movies	5

KEY

P = **Primary**
s = **Secondary**
* = **New**
+ = **Revised**

Summary of Financial Ratio Analysis Techniques

Ratio	What It Measures
Short-term solvency, or liquidity, ratios:	
Current ratio	Ability to use assets to pay off liabilities.
Quick ratio	Ability to use liquid assets to pay off liabilities quickly.
Cash ratio	Ability to pay off liabilities with cash on hand.
Long-term solvency, or financial leverage, ratios:	
Total debt ratio	How much of a company's total assets is financed by debt.
Debt-equity ratio	Compares how much a company is financed by debt with how much it is financed by equity.
Equity multiplier	How much debt is being used to finance assets.
Times interest earned ratio	How well a company has its interest obligations covered.
Cash coverage ratio	A company's ability to generate cash from operations.
Asset utilization, or turnover, ratios:	
Inventory turnover	How many times each year a company sells its entire inventory.
Days' sales in inventory	How many days on average inventory is on hand before it is sold.
Receivables turnover	How frequently each year a company collects on its credit sales.
Days' sales in receivables	How many days on average it takes to collect on credit sales (average collection period).
Total asset turnover	How much of sales is generated for every dollar in assets.
Capital intensity	The dollar investment in assets needed to generate $1 in sales.
Profitability ratios:	
Profit margin	How much profit is generated by every dollar of sales.
Return on assets (ROA)	How effectively assets are being used to generate a return.
Return on equity (ROE)	How effectively amounts invested in the business by its owners are being used to generate a return.
Market value ratios:	
Price-earnings ratio	How much investors are willing to pay per dollar of current earnings.
Market-to-book ratio	Compares market value of the company's investments to the cost of those investments.

A Summary of Five Types of Financial Ratios

I. Short-term solvency, or liquidity, ratios

$$\text{Current ratio} = \frac{\text{Current assets}}{\text{Current liabilities}}$$

$$\text{Quick ratio} = \frac{\text{Current assets} - \text{Inventory}}{\text{Current liabilities}}$$

$$\text{Cash ratio} = \frac{\text{Cash}}{\text{Current liabilities}}$$

II. Long-term solvency, or financial leverage, ratios

$$\text{Total debt ratio} = \frac{\text{Total assets} - \text{Total equity}}{\text{Total assets}}$$

Debt-equity ratio = Total debt/Total equity
Equity multiplier = Total assets/Total equity

$$\text{Times interest earned ratio} = \frac{\text{EBIT}}{\text{Interest}}$$

$$\text{Cash coverage ratio} = \frac{\text{EBIT} + \text{Depreciation}}{\text{Interest}}$$

III. Asset utilization, or turnover, ratios

$$\text{Inventory turnover} = \frac{\text{Cost of goods sold}}{\text{Inventory}}$$

$$\text{Days' sales in inventory} = \frac{365 \text{ days}}{\text{Inventory turnover}}$$

$$\text{Receivables turnover} = \frac{\text{Sales}}{\text{Accounts receivable}}$$

$$\text{Days' sales in receivables} = \frac{365 \text{ days}}{\text{Receivables turnover}}$$

$$\text{Total asset turnover} = \frac{\text{Sales}}{\text{Total assets}}$$

$$\text{Capital intensity} = \frac{\text{Total assets}}{\text{Sales}}$$

IV. Profitability ratios

$$\text{Profit margin} = \frac{\text{Net income}}{\text{Sales}}$$

$$\text{Return on assets (ROA)} = \frac{\text{Net income}}{\text{Total assets}}$$

$$\text{Return on equity (ROE)} = \frac{\text{Net income}}{\text{Total equity}}$$

$$\text{ROE} = \frac{\text{Net income}}{\text{Sales}} \times \frac{\text{Sales}}{\text{Assets}} \times \frac{\text{Assets}}{\text{Equity}}$$

V. Market value ratios

$$\text{Price-earnings ratio} = \frac{\text{Price per share}}{\text{Earnings per share}}$$

$$\text{Market-to-book ratio} = \frac{\text{Market value per share}}{\text{Book value per share}}$$